Ordeal of the Union

Byrd's History of Senate

"Contrabands" Building Stockade at Alexandria, 1861

Ordeal of the Union

VOLUME 3

The War for the Union:

THE IMPROVISED WAR
1861–1862

WAR BECOMES REVOLUTION
1862–1863

by ALLAN NEVINS

With a new Introduction by
James M. McPherson

Collier Books
MACMILLAN PUBLISHING COMPANY
NEW YORK

MAXWELL MACMILLAN CANADA
TORONTO

MAXWELL MACMILLAN INTERNATIONAL
NEW YORK   OXFORD   SINGAPORE   SYDNEY

Collier Books   Maxwell Macmillan Canada, Inc.
Macmillan Publishing Company   1200 Eglinton Avenue East
866 Third Avenue   Suite 200
New York, NY 10022   Don Mills, Ontario M3C 3N1

Macmillan Publishing Company is part of the Maxwell Communication Group of Companies.

Library of Congress Cataloging-in-Publication Data
Nevins, Allan, 1890–1971.
    Ordeal of the union / by Allan Nevins; with a new introduction by James M. McPherson.—1st Collier Books ed.
        p.   cm.
    Vol. 1 originally published: Ordeal of the Union. New York: Scribner, 1947; v. 2 originally published: The emergence of Lincoln. New York: Scribner, c1978; v. 3–4 originally published: The war for the Union. New York: Scribner, 1959–1971.
    Includes bibliographical references and indexes.
    ISBN 0-02-035441-X (v. 1).—ISBN 0-02-035442-8 (v. 2).—ISBN 0-02-035443-6 (v. 3).—ISBN 0-02-035445-2 (v. 4)
    1. United States—History.   I. Title.
    E468.N428   1992   92–3522   CIP
    973—dc20

Macmillan books are available at special discounts for bulk purchases for sales promotions, premiums, fund-raising, or educational use. For details contact:

                    Special Sales Director
                    Macmillan Publishing Company
                    866 Third Avenue
                    New York, NY 10022

First Collier Books Edition 1992

10 9 8 7 6 5 4 3 2 1

Printed in the United States of America

GENERAL INTRODUCTION

ALLAN NEVINS's life illustrated the American dream of upward mobility that he wrote about in many of his books. Born on an Illinois farm, Nevins became America's foremost historian and the recipient of the top honors of his profession, including two Pulitzer prizes, a National Book award, and the presidency of both the American Historical Association and the American Academy of Arts and Letters. In an active career that spanned sixty years, he wrote at least fifty books, edited seventy-five others, and authored uncounted hundreds of articles and reviews. At the time of his death in 1971, fourteen different publishers had books written by Nevins in print.

This prodigious output was achieved not only by inspiration but also by the ninety-nine percent perspiration that Thomas A. Edison defined as genius. Nevins did not have armies of research assistants and collaborators to do his work. The twelve-to-fourteen-hour days he had put in on the farm as a youth trained him for even longer hours as a journalist and historian. Stories abound of missed appointments, skipped lunches, and disappearances into his study during dinner parties at his home where bemused guests would soon hear his typewriter clacking away. Nevins learned how to write under the pressure of deadlines during nearly two decades as a journalist before he joined the faculty of Columbia University as DeWitt Clinton Professor of American History in 1931. But it would be far from accurate to characterize his historical writings as "journalism." The prose flows lucidly and pulses with energy—and, admittedly, with an occasional tinge of purple. But Nevins's books were the product of exhaustive research, thorough mastery of sources, and a professional command of the historiography of his subject.

The subject was most often biography, of the life-and-times genre, which won him Pulitzer prizes in 1932 and 1937 for biographies of Grover Cleveland and Hamilton Fish. But Nevins's crowning achievement was his eight-volume series on the era of the Civil War, published from 1947 to 1971. The final two volumes won Nevins a posthumous National Book award in 1972. The title originally intended for the whole series, *Ordeal of the Union*, became the title for the first two volumes, covering the period from the Mexican War to the Inauguration of James Buchanan in 1857. The next two, with the title *The Emergence of Lincoln*, carry the story down to Lincoln's Inauguration in 1861. The final four volumes, one for each year of the Civil War, bear the general title of *The War for the Union*. The grandeur and sweep of these eight volumes—four thousand pages, one million, seven hundred thousand words—are worthy of the great theme they treat, the drama and trauma of internecine conflict, the *ordeal* of American nationality in which the United States was preserved and purged of its great anomaly, slavery, in a war that cost nearly as many American lives as all the rest of the nation's wars combined. The Civil War was America's *Iliad* and Allan Nevins was its Homer. Befitting Nevins's skill at biography as well as the Homeric model, the narrative and interpretation are carried forward by the story of the dominant individuals of the age, chiefly Abraham Lincoln who makes brief appearances in the first two volumes and "emerges" in the next two, becoming in the final four the Agamemnon of this American *Iliad*.

Each of the two pairs of volumes in the original series has been combined into one volume for this edition, and the whole given the main title originally intended, *Ordeal of the Union*.

INTRODUCTION TO THIS VOLUME

In the present volume the theme of deomcratic nationalism that suffuses the whole series comes into full flower. Nevins shared with Lincoln the conviction that the military conflict launched by the Confederate attack on Fort Sumter was the great test of American nationhood. The republic founded by the generation of 1776 was a fragile experiment in a world of monarchies, empires, dictatorships, and theories of aristocracy. Americans were painfully aware of the dismal fate of most republics through history. Many people alive in 1861 had seen two French republics succumb to emperors. Latin American republics rose and fell with bewildering rapidity. Would the United States also collapse into anarchy or tyranny? If secession were permitted to succeed, Lincoln believed, it would set a fatal precedent whereby a minority could secede whenever it did not like what the majority stood for, until the United States fragmented into a dozen petty, squabbling countries, the laughingstock of European conservatives who had known all along that this absurd democratic republic could never survive.

The successful establishment of a slaveholding Confederacy would also enshrine the ideal of slavery and inequality, a contradiction of the ideal of equal natural rights on which the United States was founded. "This issue embraces more than the fate of these United States," said Lincoln on several occasions during the two years covered by this volume. "On the side of the Union it is a struggle for maintaining in the world that form and substance of government whose leading object is to elevate the condition of men . . . to afford to all an unfettered start in the race of life." Lincoln insisted that "the central idea pervading this struggle" was the necessity "of proving that popular government is not an absurdity." If in a free government based on majority rule "the minority have the right to break up the government whenever they choose," it would "go far to prove the incapability of the people to govern themselves."

Nevins reiterates these sentiments. Preservation of the Union, he writes, was "of decisive import to half the world." Its breakup "would feed the confidence of every despot from the Hermitage on the Neva to Francia's palace in Paraguay," while its triumph would give hope to "the Sheffield foundryman, the Lyons silk weaver, and the Bavarian peasant." Nevins recognizes and sympathizes with the painful choice facing many southerners who found themselves pulled in opposite directions by the conflicting allegiances of nation and section. He honors the choice made by Kentuckian Cassius M. Clay, who confessed "great repugnance in drawing the sword against my own kindred, but now when I see that a dissolution would be regarded all over Europe as a condemnation of republicanism, I feel there are no ties sacred enough to withhold me from the battlefield." Robert E. Lee's choice to go with his state, by contrast, leads Nevins to question "whether the man who thus preferred State to nation did not lack a certain largeness of view, did not respond to a parochial type of patriotism, and did not reveal an inadequate comprehension of the American destiny." That destiny would surely be grim if the Confederacy triumphed, writes Nevins, for "Farewell [then] to all ideas of American greatness, and of American leadership of the liberal forces of the globe! Instead, the emergence of two jagged, unhappy, mutually resentful fragments, one a slave-mongering nation of oppressor and oppressed."

The triumphant destiny of nationalism in 1865 is foreshadowed in this volume, which covers the first two years of the war to the eve of the Gettysburg campaign in 1863. The focus is mainly on the North; less than 20 percent of the text is devoted to the Confederacy. If these volumes were simply a history of the Civil War, Nevins states, this disproportion would be unwarrantable. "This history, however, has been planned to cover a much longer period, and its emphasis therefore falls on what is permanent in the life of the nation. From this standpoint much of the Confederate effort appears too transitory to require detailed treatment." The victorious North laid the foundations for "the emergence of modern America"; thus its war effort is the one most worth studying.

In 1861 the economy and government of the United States were ill prepared for a war. Mobilization of men and resources was a haphazard, mainly local process with little firm direction or coordination at the national level. Confusion, corruption, and waste abounded. It was "an improvised war." But order gradually emerged from chaos. By the time Edwin M. Stanton replaced the hapless Simon Cameron as secreary of war in January 1862, the decentralized, inchoate American economic, financial, and transport network had become an efficient infrastructure that enabled the Union armes forces to become the best equipped, best fed, and most mobile in the history of the world to that time. The national government took over from states the responsibility for organizing and sustaining this unprecedented war effort. "In short, pressures of war were compelling the amorphous nation of 1860 to acquire form and structure," writes Nevins. "The necessity of rallying and concentrating its forces was converting the limp, sprawling North into a coordinated and directed society which set a new value on efficiency. A modern America was being born."

By 1863 this transformation had taken on revolutionary proportions. The revolution went beyond the conversion of "an inchoate nation, individualistic in temper and wedded to improvisation, into a shaped and disciplined nation." Equally important was the Lincoln administration's radical expansion of its war aims. At first Lincoln's goal was restoration of the Union of 1860. But the dominant institution in half of that Union had been slavery. This institution had not only riven the nation and plunged it into war; it also sustained the Confederate war effort, for the slaves constituted most of the southern labor force without which the Confederacy's capacity to sustain the war would be disabled. Gradually, haltingly, not without bitter opposition, the Lincoln administration moved to strike against slavery as a military measure to cripple the Confederate war economy, as a political stroke to do away with the chief cause of contention, and as a moral *coup de plume* to end the great anomaly that mocked the cause of liberty for which the North professed to fight. In the final two chapters of this volume, Nevins eloquently sets forth the lineaments of the dual revolution: "Anvil, Loom, and Piston" and "Chattels No More."

The military campaigns occupy a subordinate part of Nevins's treatment of these sweeping changes. The first battle of Bull Run gets only five pages, the second scarcely more, and even the fighting at Antietam, the bloodiest single day in American history, is described in fewer than seven pages. Civil War military buffs must go elsewhere for a traditional narrative of drum and trumpet and clashing arms. But that is the point; there are many other places for them to find such narratives, but nowhere else for such incisive and magisterial accounts of mobilization, logistics, transportation, industry, political leadership, and military strategy in the context of war aims as they will find here. These are the things that made the battles possible and give them meaning. This volume is a good place for the novice in Civil War history to start; it is an essential place to go for the reader who supposes himself an expert in military history, to enable him to understand how the battles fit into the big picture.

JAMES M. MCPHERSON

CONTENTS

ILLUSTRATIONS

PREFACE

THE CIVIL WAR, fought by every element in the Northern and Southern population, was a people's war, a *Volkskrieg*, in a fuller sense than any earlier conflict of modern time. On both sides the resourcefulness, stubborn courage, and devotion to high aims, the disorderliness, theatricality, and impatience, were alike popular traits. Behind the uprising after Sumter lay the demagogy, selfishness, and blindness of the period since Winfield Scott had occupied Mexico City; years of yeasty growth, leavened by little political honesty or wisdom, which the author has described in four previous volumes, *Ordeal of the Union* and *The Emergence of Lincoln*. They reflected little credit on the people. Now suddenly the storm changed the atmosphere. The people, both Confederates and Unionists, rose to the most desperate effort of their history. The tenacity with which the North fought on to total victory and the South to almost total ruin vindicated their claim to heroic strength of character, and left the country memories which partially redeem the record of a needless war.

. This volume and those which follow, treating the plain people as the real heroes and heroines of the war, have as a primary theme the impact of the war on national character. Their thesis, insofar as a single idea can be applied to a struggle so manysided, is that the war measurably transformed an inchoate nation, individualistic in temper and wedded to improvisation, into a shaped and disciplined nation, increasingly aware of the importance of plan and control. The improvised war of 1861–62 became the organized war of 1863–64. The invertebrate country of Bull Run days, goaded by necessity, gathered its energies together, submitted to system, and became the partially-structured country which heard the news of Five Forks. Northern manufacturing enterprises that had been unicellular became complex and organic; primitive transportation lines became parts of a fast-growing network; mercantile undertakings, professional groups, and cultural enterprises, gelatinous in 1861, became muscular enough to bear their share of the burden. To organize armies, to organize the production of arms, munitions, clothing, and food, to organize medical services and finance, to organize public sentiment—all this required unprecedented attention to plan, and an unprecedented amount of cooperative effort. The resultant alteration in the national character was one of the central results of the gigantic struggle.

No writer treating the Civil War as a detached unit could fail to give equal emphasis to the Southern and the Northern story. This history, however, has been planned to cover a much longer period, and its emphasis therefore falls on what is permanent in the life of the nation. From this standpoint much of the Confederate effort appears too transitory to require detailed treatment. The interesting Confederate Constitution, for example, never came into full operation, died in 1865, and had practically no influence on national polity. My regret over the abbreviation of the Confederate story is diminished by the fact that Southern historians have provided several admirable records. In the same way, my regret that tactical military operations are crowded out of a work devoted primarily to political, administrative, economic, and social history, is diminished by the fact that the long list of books of military history is daily swelled by useful additions.

While the people are Hero in the Civil War, they could have accomplished nothing without leadership. A full treatment of Lincoln and his Cabinet, as of the civil leaders of the South, as they responded to growing war demands, is reserved to the next volume. But by the close of 1861 it was becoming clear that Lincoln also was hero of the conflict in a very special sense. For historical reasons the country depended on its professional politicians for guidance. In the first year only a few important figures were drawn from business and industry to hold important executive posts in Washington: notably Anson Stager and Thomas A. Scott in the War Department, and Gustavus V. Fox in the Navy Department. The politicians controlled. And with some merits, what faults the politicians disclosed! Seward performed great services; but his proposal that the North provoke a war with Spain and France to extricate itself from its difficulties, as criminal as it was stupid, must make Americans blush that they had a foreign minister capable of such an act. Chase also did important service; but his uncontrollable vanity and ambition tempted him to mean courses. The ablest man would have failed in Cameron's place, but Cameron was both erratic and incompetent. Montgomery Blair was the most contriving member of an incredibly contriving, self-interested family. Well it was for the republic that out of such a political milieu rose a Chief Executive who combined the noblest qualities of the heart with a singularly lucid intellect and a piercing vision.

The author gratefully acknowledges the help of the Carnegie Corporation and its head, Mr. John Gardner; of Mrs. David Levy; of Mr. Lessing Rosenwald; of Mrs. Jean Conti; of Dr. Abraham Flexner; of Mr. Frank E. Hill; of Professors David Donald and Louis Starr; of Mr. Bruce Catton and Mr. E. B. Long; of Miss Marian McKenna and Mrs. Mira Wilkins; of Dr. Wayne Andrews; of Dr. John Pomfret and the staff of the Huntington Library; of Drs. Carl White, Richard Logsdon, and Roland Baughman of the Columbia University Library; of Dr. Joseph Rappaport, Dr. Saul Benison, and of a host of others generous in aid as in sympathy.

Allan Nevins
The Huntington Library,
May 1, 1959

PART I

The War for the Union

THE IMPROVISED WAR

1861–1862

Winds of Doctrine

IT IS LATE afternoon of the first day of March, 1861; early spring in the South, but still winter in the North. The sun, sloping westward, shines brightly on the whole eastern half of the United States, filling the Atlantic bays with light, gilding the Appalachian crests, and giving the Mississippi valley a promise of vernal warmth. It finds the people busy with their wonted occupations. Ships crowded with immigrants are gliding into Boston and New York. Factory smoke curls over all southern New England, the Philadelphia area, and the Pittsburgh gateway. Railroad lines, glistening toward the West, hum with traffic; the rivers are dotted with steamboats from St. Paul to New Orleans. While the Gulf plains are already green, in the Carolinas and Tennessee farmers begin to follow the receding frost with black furrows.

To the spiritual ear, a medley of voices rises to the skies. From a minister: "Peace! Let us have peace." A brisk merchant: "Our city board of trade calculated ten years ago that we might have thirty million people by this census. I scoffed at them. But now the government figures our population at 31,375,000. What a market!" A promoter breaks in: "And see where the growth lies! Pennsylvania's up 600,000, New York's up 800,000, but Illinois is up by nigh on to a million. The Northwest—that's the coming country." A blander voice succeeds: "But don't forget Georgia. Ten years ago she was lagging. Now she has more than a million people. And don't forget that cotton calls the tune, either." Peace, industry, growth, hope, seem for a moment universal.

Then harsher voices break in. From several quarters: "War!—we must prepare for war." Discussion grows heated. A Yankee speaks: "Nobody blames the South for having slavery; the whole world is to blame. But I do blame them for wanting to spread it over the whole West." A Virginian replies: "All over the West nothing! Hasn't Kansas just come in as a free State? Aren't Minnesota, Oregon, California all in the Union as free States? When do *we* gain anything?" "Gentlemen, gentlemen!" interposes a New Yorker. "Haven't you read Seward's latest speech? He says we have more than a

1

million square miles of territory left, enough for twenty-four new States. And though much of this area lies far south and has been under a slave code for years, how many slaves live in it? Seward says just twenty-four; one for each new State. Climate and soil govern the issue. We are quarreling about nothing."

At this a Kansan sharply interrupts. "*Who* makes the quarrel? You Southerners do. James Harlan of Iowa told Congress: 'You offensively thrust slavery on us as a great good to be desired and extended and perpetuated by all the powers of the national government.'" An Illinoisan applauds: "And we stand with Lyman Trumbull, who says, 'A Union which can be destroyed at the will of any one State is hardly worth preserving.'" But a Southerner responds with deep feeling: "No, it is *you* who make the quarrel. Jefferson Davis spoke the exact truth when he said, 'The temper of the Black Republicans is not to give us our rights *in* the Union, or to allow us to go peacably *out* of it.'"

Three cities on which that March sun shines warmest are centers of special tension: Montgomery, Charleston, Washington. The outer streets of Montgomery, with fine houses, churches, lawns, and trees, are lovely, but the center of town is untidy. The neo-classical State capitol is not yet worthy of its noble site above the Alabama. A brick building close by, topped by a Confederate flag, houses the new government. Its broad whitewashed hall is full of chatting politicians. Their voices compete with the noises drifting in from outside: a company at drill, a band, hucksters, and, at the fountain near the principal hotel, an auctioneer selling a few slaves.

A Mississippian: "Ten days yesterday since we swore in Davis as provisional President. We're making progress. You Georgians should be satisfied. You have Alec Stephens as Vice-President and Robert Toombs as Secretary of State."

A Georgian: "Poor consolation for losing the Presidency. Except for his one weakness"—he crooks his elbow significantly—"Bob Toombs would have made a better chief than Davis. But I grant you Porcher Miles may be right when he says, 'Mr. Davis was the choice of the whole people of the South.'"

An Alabamian, soothingly: "Nobody should complain. Each of the seven States has a member of government. Alabama has Leroy P. Walker as Secretary of War. Louisiana has Judah P. Benjamin as Attorney-General. South Carolina has Christopher G. Memminger in the Treasury. Texas has John H. Reagan as Postmaster-General—a smart man even if he did begin life as a plantation overseer. And Florida has Stephen R. Mallory, raised down Key West way, to head our navy if we ever get one."

A South Carolinian: "We're making a nation, and at record speed too.

They tell me the permanent Constitution will be ready in another week. We'll adopt it unanimously, just as we've taken all important steps unanimously. If we only had more States!"

The Georgian again: "Don't worry; the seven today may be twice that many soon. Here is a letter Herschel V. Johnson has just written: 'I look with intense anxiety to the action of the border States. If they join us, we will constitute a respectable power among nations and shall be able to maintain an advancing career. If they adhere to the old Union, I shall regard it as a precursor of their emancipating at an early day. That will be a calamity on us. Without expansion, slavery must be limited in duration. But with a Southern Confederacy of fourteen States, we can maintain the Monroe Doctrine and acquire, when necessary, other lands suited to slave labor.' "

The South Carolinian: "If fighting begins, Tennessee and North Carolina and Virginia will come soon enough; maybe Maryland, maybe Kentucky and Missouri. Commissioners have gone to Washington to demand Sumter again. That's where the first blow may come."

Sumter! On this first day of March, the name is on everybody's lips. In Charleston the atmosphere is feverish. Every square contains soldiers camping or drilling; many of them in gray trousers and jackets, with yellow facings and palmetto buttons. Some ships in the harbor carry palmetto flags; so do the massive storehouses fronting the wharves. Three miles out the famous fort frowns over the harbor entrance. To South Carolinians it looks formidable, though actually it is small by European standards, is mainly of brick, not stone, and shows errors of construction—the inflammable barracks are within the walls. All the promenaders on the Battery are talking of it:

Cautious Speaker: "Heaven knows what answer the commissioners will get. This is what the Buchanan Administration wrote Governor Pickens when we demanded Sumter just after we fired on the *Star of the West* last January. 'If, with all the multiplied proofs which exist of the President's anxiety for peace . . . . the authorities of South Carolina shall assault Fort Sumter and peril the handful of brave and loyal men shut up within its walls, and thus plunge the country into the horrors of civil war, then upon them and those they represent must rest the responsibility.' If weak Buchanan won't give Sumter up, how can Lincoln do it? We are on the brink of what Buchanan calls a horrid civil war."

Fiery Speaker: "Maybe—maybe not. Buchanan didn't resent the firing on the *Star of the West*, though New York and Pennsylvania voted him men to fight with. When Lincoln sees that he must give Sumter up to avoid fighting, he'll do it meekly enough. Why, the South has already seized a long list of national forts and arsenals."

Conservative Speaker: "Lincoln won't give Sumter up for two reasons. First, the eyes of the country are on Sumter as a test case; the eyes of every Republican governor, every Republican Senator. Second, he has no power to give it up. Joseph Holt put that in a nutshell for Buchanan. The President can no more cede Sumter back to South Carolina constitutionally than he can cede the District of Columbia back to Maryland."

Fiery Speaker: "I differ. R. M. T. Hunter of Virginia was correct when he told the Senate that Washington has no right to hold the Southern forts. The legislatures ceded these places to the government, not for pecuniary considerations, but for the defense of the States. Now they cannot possibly be used for defense, and *may* be used for offense."

Conservative Speaker: "I repeat, we were within an inch of war last January. The Sumter garrison was on the very point of firing on Fort Moultrie when the *Star of the West* retreated. Major Anderson then threatened to use his guns to close the harbor. Fort Sumter is a bomb—with a time fuse attached. When her provisions run low six weeks hence, we shall see what stuff Lincoln is made of."

Washington, three days before the inauguration, is agitated by precisely that question: What stuff is Lincoln made of? General Winfield Scott has brought a thousand regular troops into the city, who are supported by volunteer companies. Batteries are being strategically placed. Leading Republicans are besieging the President-elect in Parlor No. 6 of Willard's Hotel. The streets are thronged with a heterogeneous mass: office-seekers, newspapermen, Baltimore plug-uglies, mere tourists, jubilant free-soilers.

Office-seeker: "Did you see what the Washington correspondent of the New York *Herald* said about Lincoln ten days ago? He wrote: 'He is unequal to the crisis, and will feel it so sensibly when he arrives here that it is inferred he will rush for safety into the arms of some man of strong will, who will keep his conscience and manage the government.' The *Herald* says this will be either Seward, with Wall Street, the Cotton Whigs, and the conservative Republicans behind him, or Salmon P. Chase, supported by Horace Greeley, William Cullen Bryant, Ben Wade, Lyman Trumbull, and other hotheads."

Newspaperman: "The New York *Tribune* takes a more judicious view. It thinks pretty well of Mr. Lincoln. Its correspondent, James S. Pike, says that as soon as Lincoln takes office, he will be under such pressure as no man in the country ever suffered before. Will he make heavy concessions to the South? Pike doesn't know, but he says Seward will advise him to do so. And he concludes that the Lincoln Administration will try to preserve peace. 'My conjecture,' he writes, 'is that its stature will about come up to the old compromise standard.' "

Republican: "I have just seen a letter by George W. Julian of Indiana after he talked with the next President. Julian assured a friend: 'Lincoln is *right*. His backbone is pronounced good by the best judges.'"

Second Republican: "And I have just talked with Senator Charles Sumner, who manages to keep in touch with everything. He quoted to me a telling remark by Old Abe. Lincoln said that the Administration and the party must not become 'a mere sucked egg, all shell and no meat—the principle all sucked out.'"[1]

Thus began the uneasiest and most momentous March in American history; the last peaceful March for four agonizing years. The sun went down on a Confederate President who in his recent inaugural, after praying for peace, had said: "if . . . the integrity of our territory and jurisdiction be assailed, it will but remain for us with firm resolve to appeal to arms and invoke the blessing of Providence on a just cause. . . ." It went down on a President-elect in Washington whose inaugural address, after pleading for peace, contained an unequivocal pledge: "The power confided to me will be used to hold, occupy, and possess the property and places belonging to the government, and to collect the duties and imposts." If the words of the two leaders stated anything, they stated a frontal collision.

[1] Julian's letter about Lincoln's backbone, undated but by internal evidence written about March 1, is in Julian Papers, Indiana State Library.

The Crisis

IT WAS in a somber mood that Americans read Lincoln's inaugural plea to the seceded states, March 4, 1861. Men still living could recall the nation as it took shape in Washington's Presidency—and already it was rent into discordant halves! Harrowing as the hour was to those who thought only of the domestic future of America, it was yet more distressing to those who recalled what the Founders had often said about her world mission. Not many years earlier Tocqueville had written: "From the eighteenth century and the [French] Revolution, as if from a common source, two streams flowed forth; the first led mankind toward free institutions, the other led mankind toward absolute power." The young nation which, as Lincoln had said in Independence Hall on his way to Washington, once offered the world such hope of liberty and equality, might now become an object of derision and reproach. As Columbia faltered, the European champions of absolutism gained in arrogance.

For while America stood convulsed and divided, never had her living example of freedom, democracy, and humanitarianism been more needed by other peoples. Of Tocqueville's two streams, the grimmer seemed triumphing. In France, the glowing dreams of 1789 forgotten, a pinchbeck Napoleon exercised swaggering powers. He commanded the army and navy; he decided on alliances and wars; he dominated the discordant European concert. He appointed the ministers, the council of state, the senate, and the high court; he laid before the legislative assembly its principal bills; and he convened and adjourned that body at will. Subject only to mass opinion, he strove to cow even that monster into subjection. He chained the press, exiled enemies, prohibited political meetings, and turned universal suffrage into a farce. Nor was the situation better in most other lands of the Continent.

Across the Rhine in Prussia, government lay in the hands of a reactionary king and a hidebound group of Junkers intent on perpetuating the principles of feudalism. Since 1848 constant efforts had been made to turn back the hands of the clock. The people had been abused by an unscrupulous police,

6

a postal espionage that spied upon the letters of men high and low, von Roon's strict enforcement of three-year conscription, and a ministry which interpreted the constitution by nullifying its more liberal provisions. In the background, like a shark circling a shattered boat, waited Bismarck, a fierce believer in the Prussian crown, Prussian absolutism, and Prussian power; eager to bring parliamentary institutions to the kill.

Elsewhere men could speak of Tocqueville's free impulses in the language of the Psalmist: "Oh how suddenly do they consume away, perish, and come to a fearful end!" The circling sun looked down on camps and cannon, gendarmes and prisons, provocateurs and plotters. From the convict settlements of Siberia to the garrisons of Polish towns, Russia was a terrorized land. In the Orient, despotism ruled unchecked from the Levant to Mongolia. Throughout the Austrian domains, Hapsburg absolutism had restored all the tyrannies existing before the tempest of 1848: among the Italians of Venetia and Lombardy, the Hungarians, the Bohemians, and the volatile Austrians themselves. The old stagnant order had momentarily quivered when in 1859 Vienna had been compelled to cede Lombardy to Piedmont, and would quiver again when a new imperial constitution was written this very year; but the constitution would remain mere paper. Spain lay in her accustomed torpor. The whims of Isabella II, swayed by religious fanaticism and ideas of divine right, the intrigues of a court camarilla, the feeble conservatism of weak, short-lived ministries, the obscurantism of a church which hated literacy and freedom of thought—all these forces kept the Spanish people enchained.

The Old World power where freedom broadened slowly down was Britain; the Britain of that middle-class devotion to social progress typified by John Bright and Richard Cobden, of the strong moral impulses represented by Gladstone, and of the increasing domination of thought by Manchester Liberalism and its ideas of peace, free trade, industrial energy, and governmental *laissez faire*. But, always a land of compromise, Britain at the moment was ruled by the aristocratic Whigs under the jovial, clearheaded, imperious Palmerston—"old Pam," a great believer in freedom abroad, and a strong brake on its progress at home—and the cautious Lord John Russell, once active in reform but now warily immobile. Under their government the ruling principle of Lord Melbourne, "Why can't they leave it alone?" had full sway. If the abuses which the Chartist movement had tried to extirpate no longer flourished unchecked, change came in but slowly. The cardinal points of the People's Charter, universal male suffrage, the secret ballot, abolition of property qualifications for the House, and salaries for members, were still to be gained. The poor were voteless, gross inequalities among constituencies persisted, and education lay beyond the reach of half the children of the land.

The social structure of Britain was still stratified by harsh class lines and honeycombed by ancient abuses. Westminster still held Ireland under an oppressive yoke. Power and privilege rested with the nobility, gentry, and upper-middle classes, and so long as Palmerston and Russell kept office, change would be gradual.

Had the prospects of freedom abroad been hopeless, the paralysis of America might have seemed less deplorable. It would not have mattered that the spirits of Washington, Adams, and Jefferson could no longer be invoked to fight alongside those of Burke, Fox, and Condorcet. But under the superficial ice of reaction the liberal currents ran with tremendous force. In England the orderly popular agitation of the masses was too stubborn to be stayed. The voices of reform—Dickens, Kingsley, Harriet Martineau, John Stuart Mill, and even Tennyson with his denunciation of "Timour-Mammon grinning on a pile of children's bones"—were loud and eloquent; a bolder Whiggism was coming gradually to birth. Bright and Cobden, the *Daily News* and the *Spectator*, the great social ameliorists like Shaftesbury, and such battlers against orthodoxy as Buckle, Lyell, and Darwin, were stirring the pool of opinion. In France, despite the bitter humiliations of 1848–49, the battlers for freedom—Victor Hugo, Gambetta, Chevalier—never lost heart. The victories of Garibaldi, Victor Emmanuel, and Cavour in Italy heartened the friends of liberty all over Europe. Clough and the Brownings sang of the Italian cause. Exiles like the German Forty-eighters rejoiced when Italy in 1859 emerged as a European power, and in Hungary and Poland patriots plucked up heart.

Never might the example and encouragement of a free, united, progressive America have been more effective. For three generations, in a world of fitful political progress and frequent relapse, the Western republic had represented to uncounted millions a sober, steady hope. It was the brightest governmental and social experiment ever made. The young nation had no monarch, no aristocratic institutions, and almost no vestiges of feudalism. It was without fixed class lines, without official prejudice as to religion, and without bars to the refugees from European lands. "Power, at thy bounds," Bryant wrote, "calls back his baffled hounds." That suffrage should be the right of every adult male, that the highest authority should repeatedly be given to men of the poorest origins, that public moneys should be spent on schools and not armies, that social equality should be enforced by opinion as vigorously as it was protected by law, all seemed to European liberals a kind of miracle. The experiment was new and its scale was unprecedented. Would the republic endure? Or would its failure, like that of some democracies of the past, prove that only a centralized autocracy could govern wide areas and large populations with efficiency?

The situation in which the United States stood on March 4, 1861, was thus of decisive import to half the world. The disruption of the republic would feed the confidence of every despot from the Hermitage on the Neva to Francia's palace in Paraguay, and strike dismay to the Sheffield foundry-man, the Lyons silk weaver, and the Bavarian peasant. The circumstances in which disruption was threatened, moreover, were peculiarly painful.

The nation had endured part slave, part free, for seventy years under the Constitution. During that period the opinion of the civilized world respecting slavery had radically altered. The institution was arraigned by the conscience of enlightened men in older lands, condemned by most people of the Northern States, and deplored by a considerable body of Southerners. It stood indicted not only as profoundly immoral, but as a grievous economic, social, and political handicap to the nation. All progress at the South was clogged by the necessity of restraining and disciplining a helot population, of keeping it in ignorance, and of fettering agriculture and industry by its low capacities. The governing whites could not escape from the unhappy influence, intellectual and moral, of the retarded blacks. In the long run the situation was intolerable. The honor, moral integrity, and international influence of the nation all demanded that it be brought to an end. Yet during these seventy years America had done singularly little for the slaves. It had not attached them to the soil, protected their family life, or provided for their schooling. Many vocal Southerners had departed so far from the Jeffersonian abhorrence of slavery that they now declared it a permanent institution. Since its vitality depended on expansion, most Southerners demanded the right to enlarge its bounds.

A powerful party had arisen in the North, determined to end the expansion. Lincoln as its leader had also proclaimed a much larger and more radical idea: the idea that the nation must accept the principle that slavery was a temporary institution, and at once take thought on the grim questions of when, and how, and under what safeguards it would be abolished.

It had always been clear that acceptance of this principle by a majority of Americans would precipitate a sectional crisis. Since slavery interpenetrated and conditioned all Southern life, the main body of Southerners, proud, sensitive, apprehensive of racial amalgamation even while permitting a great deal of miscegenation, regarded the principle with doubt or horror. To talk about ending slavery in a distant, indefinite age was hard enough; to think about ending it in 1870 or 1890 was terrifying. The Republican party wished the

South to face realities. Lincoln said bluntly that the crisis must be reached and passed; that is, the South must honestly face the great principle, and agree to its soundness. Then, patiently, cooperatively, South and North could agree on ways, means, and times for extinguishing the anachronistic system. Lincoln knew that, as Jefferson had said, the South had the wolf by the ears. He knew that both sections shared responsibility for the origins and growth of the institution, and both should bear the burden of getting rid of it. But on this one point he was firm: it must be put in the path of ultimate extinction.

The election of 1860 had proved two facts. It showed that a majority of Americans were now in favor of halting the expansion of slavery, and so setting a period to its existence; for most Douglas Democrats wished to put bounds to it by popular sovereignty just as the Lincoln Republicans wished to fence it in by Federal restriction. It also showed that the South could not be brought to meet and *pass* the crisis; that it balked at accepting the principle of the transiency of slavery. A dominant body of Southerners stubbornly insisted on dealing with slavery and race relations only in their own way and at their own leisure. Thus alone, said some, can we keep it as a positive good. Thus alone, said others, can we feel safe from the agonies of a precipitate social and economic revolution. Robert Toombs gave the Senate the conditions on which the South would remain in the Union. They were that its people should have equal rights to migrate to the Territories with *all* their property; that property in slaves should be protected like any other, leaving control over slavery to the States; that persons committing crimes against slave property should not be permitted to take refuge in other States; that fugitive slaves should be surrendered; and that Congress should pass laws to punish all who, like John Brown, aided invasion or insurrection in any State.

A group of leaders, in a carefully planned conspiracy, took steps which first split the Democratic party and so ensured Lincoln's election, and which then used his election to inspire Southern secession. As they did so, Southerners emphasized their own interpretation of the Constitution. The nation, they said, was a confederation of sovereign independent States. Already the South had suffered heavily from the North in taxation, tariffs, and an unequal distribution of national benefits; and they would not tolerate the erection of a consolidated democracy, for this, as Calhoun had predicted, would end in control, proscription, and political disfranchisement.

The whole future of the American nation, as the chief exponent and shield of liberal democracy, was thus placed in doubt by a struggle concerning an institution which the moral impulses of the age pronounced a blot on the national shield, and concerning the constitutional ideas involved in this contest. Sensitive leaders felt keenly the tragic bearing of the convulsion on world affairs. Many Southerners winced at the renunciation of Jeffersonian principles by their hotheads.[1] Many Union men saw that the meaning of the American dream to mankind was being put to the test. "I felt great repugnance in drawing the sword against my own kindred," wrote a Kentuckian, "but now when I see that a dissolution would be regarded all over Europe as a condemnation of republicanism, I feel there are no ties sacred enough to withhold me from the battlefield."[2] Charles Sumner had returned from Europe in 1860 after an observation of affairs in France, Italy, and Britain which convinced him that liberalism was slowly moving forward, always alert to the American scene. "I need not say to you," he wrote a British friend, "that I find much to disappoint me in the tone of persons and things. I long to see my country beautiful, great, and good, and am unhappy."[3]

Would the country recapture the international ideal held aloft by Washington in his Farewell Address? "It will be worthy of a free, enlightened, and at no distant period a great nation to give to mankind the magnanimous and too novel example of a people always guided by an exalted justice and benevolence." Now the vision of the founder, like a torch dashed to earth, seemed quenched by darkness.

[1] T. S. Gourdin of Florida, editor of the *Southern Confederacy*, wrote that with the formation of the Confederacy, "we must abandon the old idea of our forefathers that 'all men were born free and equal,' and teach the doctrine of the diversity of the races, and of the supremacy of the Anglo-Saxon race over all others. We must take the ground never dreamed of by the men of '76, that African Slavery is right in itself, and therefore should be preserved." Quoted in N. Y. *Tribune*, March 12, 1861.

[2] Cassius M. Clay, St. Petersburg Legation, June 30, 1861, to Francis Lieber; Lieber Papers, H.L.

[3] Sumner to the Duchess of Argyll, Washington, May 22, 1860; H.L.

2

Peace or War?

"GOD GRANT that the Constitution and the Union shall be perpetual," exclaimed Buchanan to the crowd when he reached his Lancaster home just after Lincoln's inauguration. Most Americans still believed a sectional adjustment possible without bloodshed. They were naturally optimists; they had discounted radical threats for so many years that they could not now take them at face value, and the idea of a brothers' war was too monstrous to seem credible. A reporter of the New York *Tribune* speculated on the use to be made of the extra troops in Washington when the capital "resumes its wonted quiet." Rebellion had asserted itself, but civil war had not begun.

As yet, only seven States had left the Union. In at least three, Georgia, Alabama, and Louisiana, strong evidence existed that a really fair plebiscite might have shown a majority for the national tie, while in the four others, Mississippi, Texas, South Carolina, and Florida, vigorous minorities had opposed secession. Southerners could not point to a single right except that of the prompt return of fugitive slaves which was being abridged or directly threatened, and some of the Northern States with personal liberty laws were repealing or amending them. While half a dozen Republican governors, led by E. D. Morgan of New York, Richard Yates of Illinois, and N. P. Banks of Massachusetts, recommended that such laws be wiped from the books, Rhode Island, Massachusetts, and Vermont took appropriate action.[1] If the South had no concrete grievances of importance, many asked, why should it revolt? Had not Congress just submitted, by two-thirds vote in each chamber, a constitutional amendment forbidding any change in the organic law which

---

1 On this subject see Appleton's *Annual Cyclopaedia, 1861,* pp. 436, 452, 556, 576 ff., 634; McPherson, *Pol. Hist. of the Rebellion,* 44; Rhodes, *Hist. U. S. from the Compromise of 1850,* III, 253; Randall, *Civil War and Reconstruction,* 229. Ohio had no law, but Governor Dennison urged conditional repeal in other States. The governors of Maine and Michigan opposed repeal. The total number of cases arising under personal liberty laws was probably small; see W. B. Hesseltine, *Lincoln and the War Governors,* 103 ff., 124 ff. Lincoln said that if the laws were as bad as Southerners asserted (he had never read one), they should be repealed.

would enable the government to interfere with slavery inside a State? [2] Was it not certain that this amendment, if needed to save the Union, would be quickly ratified?

In the wide border area, when Lincoln entered the White House, the situation appeared hopeful. The Delaware legislature, after hearing a secessionist agent from Mississippi, had voted down his proposals—the house unanimously. Governor Thomas H. Hicks of Maryland, though asserting that the State sympathized with the South and hoped to see it given new guarantees, had stubbornly refused to call an extra legislative session as a first step toward rebellion, and had been overwhelmingly supported by the people. In Kentucky the senate, appealing to the South to recede, voted more than two to one against a State convention. Arkansas chose a convention with a decidedly conservative majority, and Missouri elected one which did not include a single advocate of immediate secession. In Virginia, the house in January had voted down a secessionist resolution. The Unionists had carried the elections for a convention, and from the moment that this body met in mid-February, it had been under the sway of astute conservatives. North Carolina, in a popular election, defeated the call for a convention, and at the same time chose eighty-two conservatives as against thirty-eight secessionists to sit in that body if it ever met. The people of Tennessee likewise voted decisively against a convention, and still more decisively for a Unionist majority of delegates.

"Here are eight of the fifteen States," rejoiced the New York *Tribune,* "declaring that they wish and mean to stay in the Union, and not follow the defeated and bankrupt officeholders into the abyss of secession, treason, and civil war." The borderland, lamented the Charleston *Mercury,* was ready to accept much less than the proposed Crittenden compromise, which would have restored the Missouri Compromise line across the Federal Territories and protected slavery south of it.[3] Many Union men, believing that the cotton States had been thrown into revolt by a temporary emotional reaction following Lincoln's election, thought that a counter-reaction might soon hurl the fire-eaters into oblivion.

Lincoln shared this hope. Three days after the inauguration, Representative T. A. R. Nelson of Tennessee, a strong unionist of the American Party, obtained an interview at the White House. Lincoln said that he was anxious to maintain peace, and believed that the Federal revenues should not be col-

---

2 This passed the House Feb. 28 by 133 to 65; the Senate March 2 by 24 to 12; *Cong. Globe,* 36th Cong., 2d Sess., 1285, 1403.

3 N. Y. *Tribune* March 7, 1861; Charleston *Mercury* Feb. 14, 1861. For action of the border States see *Ann. Cyc.* 1861, pp. 256, 257; 395; 442–444; 677–679; 729–731.

lected in the seceded States until men had time for reflection. As he still regarded Southerners as members of the national family, he was not inclined to deny them mail facilities. Congress was equally hopeful and still more anxious for peace. Up to the end of its session on March 3, it had been careful not to give the South needless offense. No Republican Senator made any effort to press the bill outlawing slavery in the old Territories which the House had passed in the first session of the 36th Congress. It was not necessary (New Mexico after ten years of slavery protection had only twenty-two slaves, ten of them transients), and not politic.[4]

Nor did the Republican majority, passing bills to organize the new Territories of Dakota, Colorado, and Nevada, include any formal prohibition of slavery. It was a basic Republican doctrine that the natural state of any Territory was one of freedom, and that action was hence unnecessary; but the party leaders also wished to avoid any provocative act. Nor did Congress pass any measure giving the President military weapons to meet the crisis. Two bills for this purpose—"force bills," in Southern parlance—were introduced in the House, but not carried.

All but a few extremists hoped for peace, but on what terms? The answer was clear. To men of the North and the borderland, with a restoration of the Union; to men of the cotton kingdom, with a peaceable separation. All efforts at an arrangement had thus far proved abortive. The Crittenden compromise, which Lincoln opposed, had been defeated by a substitute resolution affirming that no need existed for amendment of the Constitution. Though this resolution passed, 25 to 23, only when six senators from the lower South refused to vote, the Republicans were mainly responsible for it. They had three main reasons for defeating Crittenden's plan. The first was that, protecting slavery south of 36° 30', it might stimulate Southern annexationist schemes in Mexico, Central America, and Cuba. The second was that it nominally handed over to slavery a region nearly as large as the original thirteen States, which had come to the United States as free soil, without a single slave when annexed; and it did this at a time when the party, declaring its solemn conviction that the government had no power to plant slavery on soil previously free, had just elected Lincoln on a platform forbidding slavery extension. The third reason, comprehending the other two, lay in Lincoln's moral imperative: the South must agree that slavery was temporary.

Meanwhile, the Peace Convention, with its eminent delegates from twenty-one States, had foundered in floods of oratory. The shrewd Adams-Seward

4 Representative Nelson describes his interesting interview with Lincoln in the Knoxville *Whig*, March 19, 1861. For slavery in New Mexico see the speech by C. F. Adams in *Cong. Globe*, 36th Cong., 2d Sess., Appendix, 124–127.

plan for putting an end to quarrels over slavery in the Territories by immediately admitting the whole Southwest (the present area of New Mexico, Arizona, Nevada, and Utah) as one State had been rejected by Southerners, for that State would obviously come in free.[5]

Yet most men still believed that peace would be preserved. They calculated, on the basis of the vote for Lincoln, Douglas, and the Bell-Everett ticket, that a decisive majority of Americans wished for peace, moderation, and compromise. Those who, like Zachariah Chandler of Michigan and Barnwell Rhett of South Carolina, wanted "a little bloodletting," were a small minority.[6]

[I]

Southern expectation of peace was based on the idea that the North would yield. Secessionist leaders hoped that the Lincoln Administration would let the new cotton republic go its way without hindrance. Many in the deep South cherished an illusion that Yankees were interested only in money-grubbing. Utterly materialistic, secessionists told themselves, Northerners lacked the fine sense of honor and fighting spirit which characterized the best "Southrons." Moreover, according to the Dixie view, these New Englanders or Ohioans, aware that they would soon be worsted, shrank from conflict. Had not all the great American generals, Washington, Andrew Jackson, Winfield Scott, Zachary Taylor, been Southerners? Had not the Mexican War been won mainly by Southern troops? Did not military schools, military parades, and military adventures appeal to the South, while Northerners kept their noses in ledgers? This confidence was buttressed by Northern talk of peace, the anti-war fulminations of Northern Democrats, a faith in border State protection, and a feeling that the South was irresistible.

Secessionist leaders had taken note of Franklin Pierce's irresponsible assertion that before any Northern army reached the South it would have to fight organized forces in its own section. Unfortunately, they heard many similar Northern voices.

Douglas, telling the Senate on January 3 that peace was the only sane course, declared that if war began, reunion would be impossible. The alternatives were subjugation and extermination on one hand, and separation on the other; and since extermination was unthinkable, he felt convinced that war would mean "final, irrevocable, eternal separation." His follower Senator

5 Nevins, *Emergence of Lincoln*, II, 397 ff., details measures and efforts in Congress and elsewhere for peace; see also Randall, *Civil War and Reconstruction*, 200 ff. The Adams-Seward plan is best followed in the manuscript diary of C. F. Adams.
6 The phrase is Zack Chandler's; Nevins, *Emergence of Lincoln*, II, 411, 412.

George Pugh of Ohio found the idea of coercing the South "utterly revolting." John A. Logan of Illinois echoed them, saying that war would not only fill the land with widows and orphans, but result in "disunion forever." Henry M. Rice of Minnesota assured the Senate that it must never expect the Northwestern States to vote a man or a dollar for war. Numerous journals spoke in like terms. The Detroit *Free Press* had the effrontery to predict that if a conflict came, *"that war will be fought at the North,"* and to threaten that in Michigan 65,000 men would interpose between any Union army and the Southern people. The Cincinnati *Enquirer* warned coercionists that if Ohio troops were called out, they might march against the government, not for it.[7]

Southerners could not believe that the North was capable of war when they read that citizens in southern Ohio, Indiana, and Illinois, assuming that disunion would be permanent, proposed taking the lower part of these States into the Confederacy. This was a very real movement. "I believe, upon my soul," the editor of the Chicago *Tribune* had written Senator Lyman Trumbull in January, "that if the Union is divided on the line of the Ohio, we shall be compelled to struggle to maintain the territorial integrity of this State." Samuel Medary, former territorial governor of Kansas and Minnesota, had just established a journal in Columbus, Ohio, which pledged obstruction to the use of force. Similar fulminations came from the Chicago *Times and Herald*, controlled by Cyrus H. McCormick, the New York *Day Book*, and the Boston *Courier*. No paper was blunter than the New York *Express*:

If the people of one section madly proposes to itself the task of trying to whip the other, the hope of reconciliation is extinguished forever. . . . There is a chance that fraternal relations, though temporarily ruptured, may one day be restored, if peace is preserved.

When the municipal elections this spring, from Cleveland to Chicago, revealed a shift in favor of the Democrats, hope that this party might prevent coercive action increased in the South. Buchanan later denounced the politicians and editors who assured the Confederacy it would have powerful allies. "This, with the persistent inaction of Congress and General Scott's 'views,' induced the leaders of the Cotton States to believe there was but little danger of Civil War."[8]

7 Pierce fruitlessly wrote the other ex-Presidents (Tyler, Fillmore, Van Buren, Buchanan, a singularly uninspiring lot) proposing a meeting to suggest remedial measures. Douglas' speech is in *Cong. Globe*, 36th Cong., 2d Sess., Appendix, 35–42; Pugh's *Ib.* 29–35; Logan's *Ib.* 178–181. Pugh spoke Dec. 20, 1860; Logan, Feb. 5, 1861. Vallandigham called coercion "atrocious and fruitless"; O. C. Hooper, *The Crisis and the Man*, 7. Rice's speech is in *Cong. Globe*, 36th Cong., 2d Sess., 1373. Cf. Wood Gray, *The Hidden Civil War*, 45 ff.

8 C. H. Ray quoted in Wood Gray, *op. cit.*, 45; O. C. Hooper, *op. cit.*, 1–35; A. C. Cole, *Era of the Civil War*, 253–257; N. Y. *Express* (controlled by Benjamin and Fernando Wood), Jan. 16, 1861; Buchanan, July 1, 1863, to Royal Phelps, in Miscellaneous Presidents'

Still greater was the Southern faith in a protective borderland shield. If this area was against secession, it was equally adamant against coercion.

Hicks of Maryland declared that his State would make common cause with its sisters in resistance to tyranny if need arose. Even Unionists in Kentucky asserted that they would desert the government if it used force. The Virginia house with but five dissenting votes denounced any thought of coercive action. In Nashville the legislature served notice that if any Union force were sent south, Tennesseeans would join as one man in repelling the invaders. These declarations had fervent conviction behind them. The great majority in the border region, Southern in origin, tastes, and sympathies, would feel a blow against Southern culture as one which smote themselves. Devoted as they were to the Union, they shrank from the idea of saving it by blood. And behind their antagonism to force lay a hope that if time were allowed for reflection, the two sections would find reason overcoming passion, and agree on a reasonable compromise.

The feeling of the cotton States that war was impossible because they were unconquerable was partly braggadocio, for the region was rich in Captain Bobadils. It sprang more rationally, however, from the military preparations they were making, and the deep hold taken by the doctrine that King Cotton ruled Britain and France.

The new republic, against countless handicaps, was trying to establish forces able to face the Northern regulars and militia. Its Congress had passed legislation creating a provisional regular army of 10,500 officers and men, including 4 brigadier generals and 9 colonels. P. G. T. Beauregard, resigning from the Union army, had been appointed brigadier and hurried to the command at Charleston. An act of February 28 authorized the President to receive State forces if tendered, or volunteers with State consent. Southerners hoped that their troops, under the new flag of 3 stripes, red, white, and blue, with a union of 7 stars, would soon number 50,000. Meanwhile, the States were filling their ranks. Mississippi in January had authorized the formation of a division of infantry and was sending a force to Pensacola. Its volunteers came in more rapidly than they could be equipped, officered, and drilled. In Louisiana the secession convention established 2 standing regiments, 1 infantry and 1 artillery, while by mid-February the State had issued arms to 28 volunteer companies with a strength of 1765. A similar story could be told of the other cotton States. On March 9, under a law passed

---

File, NYPL. Buchanan laid the blame for "go in peace" utterances on certain Republicans, but Democratic leaders were of course much the more numerous and flagrant offenders. "My voice was unheeded," he wrote, "though I often warned them [the secessionists] that the first gun fired at Charleston would unite all parties."

three days earlier authorizing the President to ask for any number of volunteers up to 100,000, Secretary of War L. P. Walker called on all the seceded States to furnish quotas, chiefly for garrisoning forts; and he stood ready to issue a further call at any time.[9]

Meanwhile, the Montgomery government was blithely taking over a great part of the arms and munitions lodged in old Federal repositories. It deeply galled the North to read of large stores thus "stolen" from the United States. New Orleans on March 6 gave an imposing ovation to General David E. Twiggs, fresh from his surrender (still in national uniform, and before passage of the State ordinance of secession) of nineteen army posts in Texas. Bands pounded along Canal Street, which was dressed in pelican bunting and palmetto flags; oratory resounded, cheers echoed; and Twiggs, his large bald head uncovered, bowed right and left from his barouche with General Braxton Bragg, heading files of troops. Early in the year Southern forces had taken over Fort Pulaski at Savannah, Fort Morgan at Mobile, and Fort Barrancas at Pensacola, with their contents. The head of the navy department, S. R. Mallory, was busy recruiting sailors.[10]

Even if peace reigned, it seemed probable that the Confederacy might be more of a military nation than the United States. At first it would use its armed power to deter the North from attack. Then its ardors might turn elsewhere. Vice-President Alexander H. Stephens, after predicting to an Atlanta audience that Sumter would be surrendered, the North would accept the situation, and the border States would eventually join their sisters, spoke in Columbus, Georgia, of martial conquests. The Confederacy, acting on the principle that slavery must be extended and perpetuated, might in time acquire Cuba and parts of Mexico and Central America.[11]

Altogether, the cotton kingdom flexed its muscles with a sense of exuberant strength. Its leaders had cherished the forecast of Langdon Cheves at the Nashville Convention: "Unite and you shall form one of the most splendid empires on which the sun ever shone." And never for a moment did the Deep South forget what Senator James H. Hammond and others said of its power to rally European support. A threat to the cotton kingdom would be a stroke at the jugular vein of the greatest naval powers of the globe.

"The first demonstration of blockade of the southern ports," prophesied Major W. H. Chase of Florida in the January issue of *De Bow's Review*,

9 J. D. Bragg, *Louisiana in the Confederacy*, 53–55; *Statutes at Large. Provisional Govt. CSA*, 43–52; O. R. I, iv, pt. 1, 135; N. Y. *Tribune*, March 19, 1861.
10 Moore, *Rebellion Record*, I, 7 ff.; Twiggs, a Georgian by birth, was soon made a major general in the Confederate army, but was too old for active service.
11 Columbus *Sun*, quoted in N. Y. *Tribune*, March 19, 1861; Johnston and Browne, *Alexander H. Stephens*, 356, 363, 396. Slavery was the cornerstone, said Stephens.

William H. Seward

General Winfield Scott

"would be swept away by English fleets of observation hovering on the Southern coasts, to protect English commerce and especially the free flow of cotton to English and French factories. The flow of cotton must not cease for a day, because the enormous sum of £150,000,000 is annually devoted to the elaboration of raw cotton; and because five millions of people annually derive their daily and immediate support therefrom in England alone, and every interest in the kingdom is connected therewith. Nor must the cotton states be invaded by land, for it would interrupt the cultivation of the great staple." Even the Northwest, he continued, would act to protect the free ports and markets of the South.[12]

Cotton would maintain peace, for cotton ruled the world.

[II]

Most Northerners expected peace to prevail for a quite different set of reasons. They thought that the seven cotton States had no vital grievances and would soon come to their senses, that the new republic was too weak to be viable, and that the border area would offer persuasive arguments for a return. They had seen so many other crises—1820, 1833, 1850—disappear that they gave rein to cheering hopes. "I guess we'll keep house," said Lincoln. They had heard so much gasconade that they lumped most secessionists with the fire-eaters. "I incline to believe," wrote Charles Eliot Norton on March 5, "that they will not try violence, and that their course as an independent Confederacy is nearly at an end." In a let-them-cool-down mood the *Atlantic* published a resigned quatrain:

> Go then, our rash sister! afar and aloof—
> Run wild in the sunshine away from our roof;
> But when your heart aches and your feet have grown sore,
> Remember the pathway that leads to our door!

On the absence of substantial Southern hurts, Douglas was emphatic. He argued that the South had gained more than if the line of 36° 30′ had been revived by the Crittenden amendment. "There stands your slave code in New Mexico protecting slavery up to the thirty-seventh degree as effectually as laws can be made to protect it. . . . The South has all below the thirty-seventh parallel, while Congress has not prohibited slavery even north of it." It was true that slavery had a legal right to spread farther than for climatic and economic reasons it might actually go. What a Southern historian was later to call the natural limits of slavery had perhaps been reached. Charles Francis

---

12 *De Bow's Review*, vol. 30, January, 1861; Chase, an ardent secessionist, argued that the potency of cotton made Southern armies and fleets superfluous.

Adams was equally derisive as to Southern grievances. To complain of personal liberty laws which had never freed a single slave, of exclusion from territory which slavery could never hope to occupy, and of fear of Federal interference with slavery in the States, against which the North was now willing to erect a solemn bar—this was puerile. Adams called upon the Southerners to recover from what he called "panic, pure panic." [13]

Adams, like Seward and many others, was certain the Confederacy must soon collapse from inner weakness. It could never be more than a secondary power, he declared; never a maritime state. It labored under the necessity of keeping eight millions of its population to watch four millions. If independent, it would have to guard several thousand miles of frontier against the flight of slaves to territory where they could never be reclaimed. "The experiment will ignominiously fail." So thought John W. Forney, writing his Philadelphia *Press* from Washington that anybody who talked with secessionists could see that they lacked heart in their enterprise, and looked forward to the speedy collapse of their whole conspiracy. Douglas, who never faltered in his hope that inner weakness would undo the new nation, announced late in March: "Division and discontent are beginning to appear in the revolting Southern Confederacy." [14]

Always bold and imaginative, Douglas was revolving a plan of which he spoke to William H. Russell of the London *Times* and others; a plan for a North American customs union embracing Canada, Mexico, and the United States, which he hoped would pave the way to reunion. Like others, he believed in the healing power of delay. He wished to fix a conciliatory character upon Administration policy, and, as he told friends, to "tomahawk" the Administration if it took a belligerent line. On March 6 he therefore gave the Senate an elaborate misinterpretation of Lincoln's inaugural as a pacific manifesto. He was delighted, he said, to find Lincoln so conservative in temper, for the Union could never be cemented by blood. The President had promised to abstain from any offensive acts, had let clear Federal rights lie dormant, had suggested that the Constitution be amended, and had promised to allow the people to devise such changes as they desired. Furthermore, he had declared that in every exigency he would lean to friendly solutions. [15] Douglas went on, in a pernicious warping of Lincoln's words:

---

13 Sandburg, *Lincoln: The War Years*, I, 120 ff.; C. E. Norton, *Letters*, I, 219; Adams in *Cong. Globe*, 36th Cong., 2d Sess., *Appendix*, 127 (Jan. 31, 1861); Douglas, *Cong. Globe*, 36th Cong., 2d Sess. (March 25, 1861), p. 1504; *Atlantic*, May, 1861.

14 Adams, *ut sup.*; Forney is quoted in Springfield *Republican*, March 19, 1861, Douglas in Chicago *Morning Post*, March 27, 1861.

15 Russell, *My Diary North and South*, April 4, 1861, for Douglas' plan; *Cong. Globe*, 36th Cong., 2d Sess. (March 6, 1861), pp. 1436–1439. But Douglas frankly told Welles that he had no influence. The Democratic party had broken up; the Republican party had no use for him; nobody would follow him. *Diary*, I, 34, 35.

In other words, if the collection of the revenue leads to a peaceful solution, it is to be collected; if the recapture of Fort Moultrie would tend to a peaceful solution, he stands pledged to recapture it; if the recapture would tend to violence and war, he is pledged not to recapture it; if the enforcement of the laws in the seceding States would tend to facilitate a peaceful solution, he is pledged to their enforcement; if the omission to enforce these laws would best facilitate peace, he is pledged to omit to enforce them; if maintaining possession of Fort Sumter would facilitate peace, he stands pledged to retain its possession; if, on the contrary, the abandonment of Fort Sumter and the withdrawal of the troops would facilitate a peaceful solution, he is pledged to abandon the fort and withdraw the troops.

Of far greater importance, in this crisis, was Seward's belief in peace. The veteran New York politician, who for a dozen stormy years in the Senate had closely observed Southern friends and enemies, and who as a man of tortuous expedients believed that expediency ruled human conduct, was certain that war could be avoided. As Gideon Welles put it later, Seward had no doubt that he could set to work immediately the new Administration came in, reconcile the main differences, and within ninety days restore harmony to the nation. *He* was head of the Republican party, and *he* would be the real power behind the weak railsplitter. During the brief month of William Henry Harrison's Administration he had dominated that President; during Zachary Taylor's sixteen months he had again swayed the scepter; now he would be Grand Vizier once more. Thrusting Lincoln aside, he would rely on time, forbearance, and patience to bring the cotton States back.

"I learned early from Jefferson," Seward had told the Senate, "that in political affairs we cannot always do what seems to us absolutely best." He would like to see all the Territories organized at once into two States, one Southwestern, one Northwestern, reserving the right later to subdivide them into several convenient new States; but such a reservation was constitutionally impossible, and he believed that the embarrassments resulting from the hasty incorporation of two areas of such vast extent and various characteristics and interests would outweigh the immediate advantages of halting the slavery quarrel. To admit one great Southwestern State was as far as he would go. Meanwhile, he would trust to cool second thoughts:

When the eccentric movements of secession and disunion shall have ended, in whatever form that end may come, and the angry excitements of the hour shall have subsided, then, and not until then,—one, two, or three years hence—I should cheerfully advise a convention of the people, to be assembled in pursuance of the Constitution, to consider and decide whether any and what amendments of the organizational law ought to be made.[16]

16 Welles, Nov. 27, 1872, to I. N. Arnold, Arnold Papers, Chicago Hist. Soc.; *Cong. Globe*, 36th Cong., 2d Sess., Jan. 12, 1861.

Seward, thin and worn, said just before Lincoln came in: "The majority of those around me are determined to pull the house down, and I am determined not to let them." [17] He had written Lincoln on February 24 that he knew the real peril much better than his Republican colleagues in Washington, and that only the soothing words which he had spoken "have saved us and carried us along thus far." A man of ripe political experience, he could show impressive astuteness, and had a fine capacity for persuasive public speech. Yet he revealed at times superficial thinking, erratic judgment, and a devious, impetuous temper, which were the more dangerous because he was cockily self-confident. He had immense vanity; in fact, remarked the British minister, so much more vanity, personal and national, than tact, that he seldom made a favorable impression at first.[18] Now he was sure that he could restore the Union with one great if—if Lincoln would let him take the helm.

Justice John A. Campbell of the Supreme Court, a mild, sagacious Alabama unionist, attended a dinner party which Douglas gave shortly before the inauguration and which Seward dominated as the great power-to-be. When asked for a toast, Seward proposed: "Away with all parties, all platforms, all persons committed to whatever else will stand in the way of the American Union." After dinner, Campbell told the company that slavery was a transitory institution, which though yet strong in the deep South was steadily dying in the border area. Once the Constitution was amended to protect slavery in the States from any national interference, the only question would be that of New Mexico, which was unsuited to slavery anyhow. "How, Mr. Seward," he asked, "can you fail to effect an adjustment?" The Senator replied: "I have a telegram from Springfield today in which I am told that Senator Cameron will not be Secretary of the Treasury, and that Salmon P. Chase will be; that it is not certain that Cameron will have a place in the Cabinet; and that my own position is not fully assured. What can I do?" He had hoped that Simon Cameron might abet his conservative labors for peace.

What he did was to make a last-minute movement to keep Chase, whom he feared as a radical, out of the Cabinet. When this failed, he nevertheless took the State Department, confident that he could manipulate Lincoln and so save national peace.[19]

Horace Greeley likewise believed a rapid readjustment possible. His suggestion that the erring sisters go in peace was qualified by his insistence that they should first prove that a majority of their people wished to go, for he was

17 C. F. Adams to R. H. Dana, Jr., Feb. 28, 1861; Dana Papers, MHS.
18 Newton, *Lord Lyons*, I, 117; Nicolay and Hay, *Abraham Lincoln: A History*, III, 319, 320.
19 Campbell, undated memorandum "Relative to the Secession Movement," Confederate Museum; Nevins, *Emergence of Lincoln*, II, 452–455; N. Y. *Weekly Tribune*, April 30, 1861.

confident that in Florida, Alabama, and Louisiana no such majority existed. Even late in the spring he told a Cooper Union audience that the Southern people were at heart for the old ties. "I believe that the tide makes for the Union, and not against it; that secession is exhausting itself as a fever; and if it can be judiciously handled for a few months, it will burn out." S. F. B. Morse proposed an amicable temporary separation pending negotiations for a new and better Union. The two peoples should conclude an immediate alliance, divide the national property, and sever the flag (the blue union diagonally, the stripes horizontally) until such date as their junction should again make the banner one.[20]

This faith that if Lincoln's Administration accepted the status quo, vigorously waving a palm branch, the cotton domain would come back, was shared by that old Jacksonian Democrat George Bancroft. He assured an English historian that Southern leaders had seceded only with a view to reconstructing the Union on their own terms, possibly with New England (as Bennett's *Herald* suggested) left outside. John Bell of Tennessee, lingering in Washington after March 4 and repeatedly seeing Lincoln, entreated the President not to molest the Confederacy, for any attempt to reinforce the forts or collect the revenues would result in bloodshed and Border State secession. He advised an indefinite truce. The more the cotton States armed and the heavier the taxation they imposed, the sooner would a wave of popular discontent rise, resulting at last in a friendly reconstruction. Bell might have quoted such voices of discontent as the New Orleans *True Delta*:

The odds and ends of every faction which have combined themselves together to precipitate the cotton states into revolution have shown an audacity which Marat, Danton, or Robespierre might have envied. Special privilege, a rag money aristocracy, and favored classes, will now be fastened upon unfortunate Louisiana; and in return the people will have the consolation derivable from the reflection that one of her greatest domestic interests is destroyed and her importance as a state of the Union dwarfed into a pigmy association with decaying, retrograding, and penniless confederates. The depth of our own degradation for the time distracts the attention of the people from the progress of oligarchical usurpation and tyranny in our sister States, which are made participators with us in a humiliating calamity.[21]

If worst came to worst, in the opinion of some Northern observers, unity could be restored on the basis of Manifest Destiny; that is, on the common ambition of powerful groups North and South to take possession of the whole continent and its islands.

20 Morse manifesto, undated, S. F. B. Morse Papers, LC.
21 M. A. DeWolfe Howe, *Bancroft*, II, 135–136; *True Delta*, April 10, 1861. Bell's views are summarized by M. J. Crawford, writing March 3, 1861, to Toombs; Toombs Letterbooks, South Caroliniana Library.

[III]

The realities of the crisis were grimly different from these dreams. Peace, as time proved, was impossible. It was impossible because neither North nor South could now yield. Both were prisoners of the situation created by long years of paltering and evasion.

The Confederacy must stand fast because its goal was not readjustment, but independence. The successful secessionist conspiracy had been a drive, we repeat, to give the people of the Deep South full power to settle their own problems in their own way. Retreat would mean a sacrifice of their constitutional principles, a humiliating blow to their pride, and a definite subordination to the North and Northwest. The heads of the Confederacy were not bluffing, but in deadly earnest. They were determined to maintain their new nation at all hazards and whatever cost.

Certainly every public and private utterance emphasized the permanency of their government. Mrs. Jefferson Davis, who like her husband would have preferred to see the Union kept intact on Southern terms, wrote Buchanan on March 18 that she had found the opposition in Montgomery to reconstruction quite violent. "I fear me greatly, my dear old friend, that you are really the last of an illustrious line." This was the conviction of John Slidell of Louisiana. He wrote S. L. M. Barlow, one of the first great corporation attorneys of New York and an ardent Democrat of conservative views, that reconstruction was a hopeless idea at any time or under any conditions. "At this point there is unanimity of feeling of which you can form no idea without passing some time amongst and mixing freely with our people." We could quote other men at tiresome length. Louis T. Wigfall of Texas in the Senate on March 7 repeated Robert Toombs' statement that the seceded States would never come back under any circumstances. Treat them as independent and the nation could have peace, he vociferated; treat them as part of the Union and it would have war. Wlliam M. Browne, former editor of the Washington *Constitution*, now in the Confederate State Department, was amazed by Northern talk of reconciliation. "Knowing, as we do here," he wrote from Montgomery March 6, "the temper of the people, not the politicians—their hopes, aspirations, resolution, and resources—we look upon union as impossible as the annexation of the Confederate States to Great Britain in their old colonial condition."

The roots of this Southern determination ran deep indeed. Secession, as old Barnwell Rhett said, was not the work of a day, but had been preparing for twenty years.[22]

---

[22] Slidell to Barlow, New Orleans, March 24, 1861, Barlow Papers; Browne to Barlow, March 6, 18, 1861, *Ibid*. Still only in his middle thirties, handsome, wealthy, and cultivated,

Sectional pride, and sensitiveness to sectional honor, had played a large part in crystallizing Confederate resolution. The South was denied equality in the Union, men argued, when it was debarred from taking its slave property into the common Territories. This feeling of sectional jealousy and patriotism more than any other explains the surge of rejoicing that swept across the cotton kingdom as the secession ordinances were adopted. How humiliating now to fall back! But material motives played their part. Convinced that the South was systematically exploited by Northern merchants, brokers, shippers, and bankers, estimating that Yankee harpies bled it of a hundred and fifty millions a year, and resentful of Northern tariffs, coastal trade monopoly, and fishing subsidies, Southern leaders believed they had issued a declaration of economic freedom. They would build a richer agriculture; they would have their own flourishing ports and fleets; they would make New Orleans, Mobile, Charleston, and Savannah opulent seats of finance and industry.

But above all, Southern determination rested on a sense of fear which had grown more acute ever since John Brown's raid; a foreboding that they could never entrust the intertwined problems of slavery and race adjustment (they feared that emancipation would mean eventual amalgamation, a negroid South) to a Northern majority. "A crisis must be met and passed"; but they refused to *pass* it—to take the decision to put slavery on the road to ultimate extinction. They feared Northern clumsiness, precipitancy, and ruthlessness. Henry W. Hilliard of Alabama stated this frankly in a letter to a New England friend. "It is supposed," he wrote, "very generally, that we apprehend some immediate mischief from Mr. Lincoln's administration; some direct and plain interference with our rights; and we are appealed to by our northern friends to await some hostile demonstration on his part; we are reminded that his character is conservative. . . . Now all this may be conceded, and yet if the whole southern mind could be brought to yield implicit faith in these assurances, still the attitude of the southern states would remain unchanged. It is not any apprehension of aggressive action on the part of the incoming administration which rouses the incoming administration to resistance, but it is the demonstration which Mr. Lincoln's election by such overwhelming majorities affords, of the supremacy of a sentiment hostile to slavery in the nonslaveholding states of the union." [23]

The South contained many who felt a repugnance to slavery. Hilliard

Barlow belonged to the Buchanan wing of the party. Keitt of South Carolina said, "I have been engaged in this movement ever since I entered political life"; Springfield *Republican*, Jan. 19, 1861. A Northerner interviewed Davis, Toombs, and R. M. T. Hunter in Washington in December and January of the secession winter, and presented his report, "Conversational Opinions of the Leaders of Secession," in the *Atlantic*, Nov., 1862, pp. 613–623. All three regarded secession as final; Toombs and Davis spoke of using force to sustain it.
23 Quoted in Springfield *Republican*, Jan. 1, 1861.

knew that world sentiment was hostile to it. What he meant was that the
Lower South could not commit its fate, in its position of delicacy and peril, to
a sectional majority which might prove heedless and dogmatic. This was the
Hobbesian ultimate of fear, the chief cause of war; the fear of a people that
its way of life would be overthrown by a rival power and creed. The South
could not turn back.

[IV]

Still less could the North yield on the mighty issue of disunion. How
long had its leaders been explicit on that point! "Liberty and Union, now and
forever, one and inseparable"—every schoolboy knew the reply to Hayne.
"Our Federal Union: it must be preserved!"—every Northern youth thrilled to
Jackson's sentiment. Webster had said in his Seventh of March speech that the
idea of peaceable secession was an absurdity. Henry Clay that same year had
declared that if any State put itself in military array against the Union, he was
for trying the strength of the nation. "I am for ascertaining whether we have
a Government or not—practical, efficient, capable of maintaining its authority. . . . Nor, sir, am I to be alarmed or dissuaded from any such course by
intimations of the spilling of blood. If blood is to be spilt, by whose fault is it?"
Thomas Hart Benton had fiercely asserted that the Union must be upheld, if
need be, by arms, and President Taylor had promised cold shot and hempen
rope to traitors. Lincoln but echoed these leaders when he placed in his
inaugural his single veiled threat to Southerners: "In your hands, my dissatisfied fellow-countrymen, and not in mine, is the momentous issue of civil war."

Beyond a sentimental attachment to the idea of Union, beyond old fealties,
loomed irreducible material considerations. Divorce usually means a partition
of property. Men might pause but briefly over the question whether they could
divide the Fourth of July, Yorktown, Lundy's Lane, and Buena Vista; but the
government held title to vast physical possessions. Said the Chicago *Tribune:*
"No party in the North will ever consent to a division of the national territory,
the national armaments, the national archives, or the national treasury." A
President consenting to it would have courted instant impeachment. What
of the Southwest? If peaceable secession were permitted, the Confederacy
would lay claim to part of New Mexico and Arizona, with hope of a frontage
on the Pacific. Confederate sympathizers in Texas, Arkansas, and Missouri
would almost certainly attempt to seize the Indian Territory, a key to the
Southwestern domain. Where would the international border be drawn, and
how would it be policed? Once demarcated, that boundary would certainly
be crossed by numberless runaway slaves—and streams of free Negroes; it

would be invaded by Northern agitators; and new John Browns would raid more Harpers Ferries.[24]

How, asked John Minor Botts of Virginia in a letter to disunionists, are you going to dispose of the Mississippi River? That question stung Northwestern emotion like a poisoned barb. Let the South try to sever the stream, said Douglas, and the men of Illinois would follow its waters inch by inch with the bayonet to the Gulf. The lower part of the great river had been paid for out of the common purse for the common national good. When Northerners read that Mississippi had placed a battery at the Vicksburg bluffs which was halting steamboats bound downstream, their blood boiled. Congressmen and editors spoke in no modulated tones. "We would like to see them help themselves," retorted the Memphis *Evening Argus*. Later the Confederate Congress conceded the full and free navigation of the river, but it made no provision for the landing or transshipment of cargoes. As river boats could not go to Europe nor ocean ships ascend to St. Louis, import and export shipments were thrown under Confederate power. Amos Kendall, the veteran Jacksonian, told an Illinois friend that if he were an editor he would make the nation ring with his protests. He would declare that the West should never submit to such a situation; that its industrial and commercial interests were hanging over an abyss; and that when Southern complaints touching slavery had been removed, the seceding States must reënter the Union—under compulsion if necessary.[25] He knew that compulsion was war.

It was obvious, moreover, that the precedent of Southern secession might be fatal to the entire national future. Winfield Scott in the "Views" he had sent Buchanan had babbled of a land of four capitals, at Albany, Washington, Columbia, S. C., and Alton or Quincy, Illinois. Each of these four new countries would have ports on navigable waters. But what if some interior States were shut out of the new confederations and left landlocked? What if Michigan could at any time join Canada, closing the Soo? For that matter, what if the Confederacy found Texas becoming opposed to slavery, withdrawing from the new bond, and making herself independent again? American stability, credit, prestige, and power would be dealt shattering blows by a principle of withdrawal which held the potentialities of unlimited dissolution—of national suicide. A once great nation might be Balkanized. The idea, abhorrent to all thoughtful Northerners and many Southerners, was abhorrent most of all to those who saw the nation as a beacon-light of stability, moderation, and freedom in a disorderly world.

24 Clay's speech (a reply to Dawson of Georgia) is in *Cong. Globe*. For Benton see *Thirty Years*, II, 200; for Douglas' views, Milton, *Eve of Conflict*, 396; the editorial in the Chicago *Tribune*, Dec. 12, 1860, was repeated more emphatically Dec. 22.
25 Kendall to J. D. Caton, March 14, 1861; Caton Papers, LC.

[V]

The Confederacy in March faced a vital issue: Should it wait or strike? If it waited, it might gain by finding time to install its government, organize its resources, and import foreign materials. It might also lose by giving Union sentiment in large areas, such as northern Alabama, time to reassert itself once the first fine rapture of independence began to decline. But above all, its attention was centered on border States. If it waited, would they gravitate to the Confederacy, or fix their allegiance yet more firmly in the Union? If it struck, would the shock make them embrace secession or recoil from it?

The best opportunity for a stroke presented itself at Fort Pickens on Pensacola Bay and Fort Sumter in Charleston Harbor, two thorns in Confederate flesh. Pensacola was much the less sensitive spot. Florida was not South Carolina. Here a Yankee lieutenant occupied Pickens, which could be easily reinforced from the sea, with a tiny body of troops under a workable arrangement that he should hold his island fort unharmed while Florida forces occupied the neighboring mainland positions without disturbance.[30] Danger of an explosion was slight, and he had provisions for five months.

Sumter held a different status. Recent events had made it to Northerners a symbol of the maintenance of the Union, and to Confederates a symbol of foreign intrusion. Radical Northerners believed that it must be held, radical Southerners that it must be taken. Under Robert Anderson, a veteran of the Mexican War, it symbolized the choice between acquiescence in secession, or stern resistance to it.

Confederate leaders had forcibly indicated their determination to attack Sumter if it were not quickly evacuated. Judah P. Benjamin wrote S. L. M. Barlow in New York as early as January 17, 1861, that an act of war impended at Sumter or Pickens. "At neither can it be long delayed." When Jefferson Davis was elected President, William Porcher Miles of South Carolina was at hand in Montgomery. He favored an early assault, but urged his State government not to permit it until the Confederate authorities gave the word. Our attack, he wrote, would necessarily plunge the new nation into war with the United States, and that before the six other States were prepared. Davis on March 1 appointed Beauregard to command at Charleston. As he did so he informed the Governor, Francis W. Pickens of South Carolina, that he was anxious to vindicate Southern rights territorial and jurisdictional, and that he

his predecessor to inaugurate a civil war." Dunbar Rowland, ed., *Jefferson Davis, Letters, Papers, and Speeches*, V, 36–38. Potter's statement is in *Lincoln and his Party in the Secession Crisis*, 375.

30 On Lieutenant Slemmer and his opponents see O. R., I, i, 333–342.

had discussed with Beauregard the works needful to reduce Sumter most speedily. Confederate authorities hurried a colonel to New Orleans to buy fifteen tons of cannon powder for immediate shipment to Charleston. The moment the governor of Florida read a synopsis of Lincoln's message he telegraphed Pickens in South Carolina: "Will you open at once upon Fort Sumter?" [31]

Yet before Lincoln took office, the Buchanan Administration, fortified by the addition of Edwin M. Stanton, Joseph Holt, and John A. Dix to the Cabinet, repeatedly warned the Confederate leaders that an attack on the fort would mean war. Buchanan not only refused to withdraw the troops from Sumter, but declined to promise not to reinforce them. Indeed, as he wrote later, he uniformly declared he would send reinforcements whenever Major Anderson requested them or the safety of the post demanded them. Joseph Holt, as Secretary of War, met South Carolina's demands for evacuation with the stiffest denials. The United States held absolute sovereignty over the fort, he declared; the government possessed no more authority to surrender it than to cede the District of Columbia to Maryland; the small garrison was not a menace, but was maintained to protect South Carolina from foreign foes. If rash leaders assaulted Sumter "and thus plunge our country into civil war, then upon them and those they represent must rest the responsibility." [32]

Charleston throughout March resounded with martial activities, for Beauregard put new energy into preparations for war. He found the harbor already bristling with guns, every point of access from the sea fortified, the channel obstructed, and watch maintained to make sure that not even a small boat reached Fort Sumter. Charlestonians, their State troops drilling day and night, thought they had done everything possible. But Beauregard mobilized a large body of Negro laborers to strengthen the harbor defenses, improved the position of the guns, enlisted more artillerists, and hastened the arming of small vessels to operate in coastal waters. Secretary of War Walker urged him on: "Give but little credit to rumors of an amicable adjustment," he wrote March 15. During battery practice a heavy ball struck the Sumter walls; and though an officer was sent at once to explain that it was a chance shot, Charlestonians guessed that their gunners were fixing the range of the fort. A floating battery was heavily armed to be anchored near Sumter.[33]

31 Barlow Papers; Miles Porcher to F. W. Porcher Feb. 9, 1861, Amer. Art. Assn. Catalogue Feb. 5, 1929, p. 39; Davis to Governor Pickens, A. S. W. Rosenbach Collection; Memminger, Feb. 16, 1861, to Col. M. A. Moore, Memminger Papers South Caroliniana Lib. Gov. W. O. Perry to Gov. Pickens, March 5, 1861, Pickens-Bonham Papers LC.
32 Curtis, *Buchanan*, II, 541 ff.; Holt, Feb. 6, 1861, to Attorney-General J. W. Hayne of S. C., N. Y. *Tribune*, Feb. 9, 1861.
33 O. R. I, i, 275, 276; Charleston correspondence, March 9, 10, in N. Y. *Tribune*, March 13, 16, 1861.

CHARLESTON
HARBOR

Many officers were spoiling for a fight. Beauregard, reporting March 22 that all his batteries would be in full trim in a few days, was able to add that Sumter was nearly out of fuel and provisions. Five days later he expressed hope that the fort would soon surrender, for the uncertainty ought not to last beyond the period when he had completed all his preparations to compel Anderson to surrender.[34]

[VI]

Meanwhile, in Washington, Abraham Lincoln, new to high office, totally untrained in administrative duties, inexperienced in the leadership of Congress and public sentiment, and quite unacquainted with his Cabinet, had to face a multiplicity of problems with scanty assistance and amid constant distractions. For secretarial aid he had only two men, John Hay and John G. Nicolay, both able, but very young, very green, and very provincially Western. The country would have gained had Lincoln brought some capable Republican of more experience, like Horace White of the Chicago *Tribune* staff, who had reported the Lincoln-Douglas debates, to reinforce them. The first week Lincoln had to receive callers in droves, meet the diplomatic corps as it paid its respects, address delegations from six States, handle a swollen mail, and hold his first formal Cabinet meeting (March 9). That week Seward, on whose friendly if contriving advice he could best lean, was ill with lumbago.

In his first days Lincoln had to fill the principal existing vacancies before the Senate adjourned its short special session; to consult with General Scott on the bad position of the army, whose two principal administrative officers, Samuel Cooper as adjutant-general and Joseph E. Johnston as quartermaster-

34 O. R., I, i. 280, 283; Beauregard to Walker, March 22, 27.

general, leaned to the South; and to study the possibility of keeping Maryland, Virginia, Kentucky, and Missouri in the Union. Washington was speculating on antagonisms within the Cabinet, with Seward, Cameron, and Bates understood to be moderate, while Chase, Montgomery Blair, and Welles supposedly held more extreme views.[35] Martin J. Crawford, one of three Confederate commissioners whom Jefferson Davis had just sent to Washington to explore the chances of a treaty of amity, was busily inquiring as to the intentions of the new regime, and reporting to Montgomery on March 6 that Seward and Cameron could be relied on to maintain a peace policy. Another commissioner, John Forsyth, arrived on his heels, and both men began using ex-Senator Gwin of California and Senator R. M. T. Hunter of Virginia in an effort to establish unofficial relations with Seward.

When did Lincoln have time to ponder the one question that mattered: the question what course could best serve the cause of peace and reunion? Not during his first levee, which so jammed the White House that for an hour those who wished to leave had to get out through the windows. And not while he was incessantly besieged by office-hunters and Congressional patronage-dispensers. At first he refused to limit his hours for seeing people. But when he found that he had no time to take a drink of water, he fixed them at ten o'clock till three, and later at ten till one.[36]

Lincoln thought it appalling that while the national house was on fire at one end, he had to be letting out rooms at the other. Sane observers were equally aghast. We have no national policy, no administration plan, one of Greeley's friends lamented near the end of March; while the government crumbles underfoot, the only problem considered is whether some supplicant should be a tide-waiter, a village postmaster, or an Indian agent. But the system existed; the President had no escape.

He was in fact the focal point of pressures which reached out to every town and county with a sizable Republican vote. After filling his Cabinet, he had but one important personal appointment to make—that of Hiram Barney, a capable attorney, to be collector of the port of New York. Barney, a friend of William Cullen Bryant, had extended Lincoln some valued courtesies at the time of the Cooper Union address, and had supported him in the Chicago convention. The President took a certain interest also in sending Charles Francis Adams to London, W. L. Dayton to Paris, Norman Judd to Berlin, and that eccentric egotist Cassius M. Clay to St. Petersburg. In the main, however, his appointments had to be parceled out to clamorously selfish men and groups.[37]

35 Blaine, *Twenty Years*, I, 285, 286.
36 N. Y. *Herald*, March 9, 1861; Helen Nicolay, *Lincoln's Secretary*, 82, 83.
37 The Barney appointment is discussed in Alexander, *Political Hist. N. Y.*, II, 390–396; cf. Wm. Allen Butler (a law partner), *A Retrospect of Forty Years*, 349, 350.

Every Republican in Congress wished to strengthen his political organization; every editor coveted a post-office connection to swell his subscription list; every jobless politician wanted a salary. The Illinois members, for example, met in conclave to draw up a slate of appointments to be requested of Lincoln. After dividing marshalships, district attorneyships, and territorial posts, they demanded a slice of foreign-service pie. Senator Lyman Trumbull wanted two consulships, Representative Elihu Washburne one, and Representative W. P. Kellogg one. Joseph Medill of the Chicago *Tribune*, meanwhile, wished one of his staff made the new Chicago postmaster. "If Mr. Scripps has it," he explained, "the country postmasters of the Northwest would work to extend our circulation." And Illinois was but one State! Three-quarters of the March correspondence of the typical Senator, Representative, or Cabinet member in this hour of crisis pertained to jobs. A clamor of greed and grumbling filled the capital.[38]

In this matter Lincoln was the victim not merely of the national system, but of the special necessities of the Republicans. They did not as yet have a coherent, well-organized party. It had been born some half dozen years earlier as a patchwork of local organizations; it had fought the campaign of 1856 under a hastily-chosen nominee as a coalition of new, uncertain State organizations, and had lost; in the three years after 1856 it had largely disappeared from view as a national entity. Its enthusiastic rally in 1860, a marvel of improvisation, might have failed again but for the Democratic schism. Its members included former Whigs, former Know-Nothings, former Freesoil Democrats, and young men who were simon-pure Republicans. Now it needed the cement of national office to make it a unified, well-knit party on a truly national basis. Its chieftains— governors, Senators, Representatives, editors, State and local committeemen— were resolved that it should obtain this cement, and anxious to determine its quality. Lincoln was well aware that parties are essential to democratic government, and that his Administration could not possibly succeed without strong party support. In the hours he gave to applicants he was not merely dividing spoils; he was building a foundation.

Throughout March the hotels were jammed. In one, three hundred unbathed men slept in the dining room. Anybody could get into the White House, and nearly everybody did. The physical and psychological pressure on

38 Medill's letter, March 4, 1861, is in the Lyman Trumbull Papers, LC; see also the Washburne Papers. Among the dissatisfied elements the Constitutional Unionists were prominent. Edward Everett resentfully noted that in Maryland, Kentucky, and Missouri, where the Republican vote had been trifling and the Constitutional Union vote tremendous, Lincoln had bestowed the three great plums on Republicans—Montgomery Blair, Cassius M. Clay, and Edward Bates. Everett, March 31, 1861, to Sir Henry Holland; Everett Papers, MHS.

Lincoln was crushing. On March 14 one correspondent shouldered his way through the fragrant throng. "I saw the President this morning, and his whole air was that of not only a worried but an ill man. He would require a fortnight's rest, it seemed to me, to enable him to let off a joke or a jolly backwoods reminiscence." Not until hundreds of appointees had been confirmed, and the special Senate session had ended on March 28, could the Administration give wholehearted attention to the grave national issues.

To add to Lincoln's difficulties, Douglas as the chief Democratic leader spent March indicating that he would harass the Administration mercilessly unless it sacrificed almost everything for peace. He seemed a very different Douglas from the man who had recently talked of hanging traitors. For one reason, he was trying to pull the defeated Democratic party together, and to rally Union forces in the South. For another, he was drinking heavily again, a fact which explained some excesses of language and one bout of fisticuffs on the Senate floor. But when all allowances are made, his attacks were outrageously sharp. He introduced a resolution calling on the Administration to tell the Senate how many forts, arsenals, and navy yards it held inside the seceded States, with what forces, and with what intentions. His object, he stated, was to press the government into a definite avowal of policy. In his opinion, it had but three courses open: It could amend the Constitution to preserve the Union, it could assent to a peaceable division, or it could make war to subjugate the lost States. "The first proposition is the best and the last is the worst," he declared.

If Douglas wished assurances that Lincoln would not wantonly provoke war, he got them. Senator Fessenden, assuring him that the President would use no questionable powers and violate no law in an effort to collect the revenues, obviously spoke for Lincoln. It was not clear that the government had any right to collect customs dues aboard a warship, and it would certainly not do so without explicit mandate from Congress. Yet day by day Douglas kept up his scoriac outbursts, often using bitter personalities. His manner was satanically provoking. Sometimes he exhibited a heavy-handed malignity, sometimes he was patronizingly sarcastic. You state that you mean peace, he said tauntingly, and yet pass laws that cannot be enforced without war. You talk of maintaining the Federal authority, yet you have not a Federal officer, acting by your authority, in the whole secession area. However affronted, his opponents thought it best to bite their lips in silence.[39]

One eloquent foreign voice, in these dark days, was raised to hearten Amer-

39 *Cong. Globe,* 36th Cong., 2d Sess., 1436 ff. "I expect to oppose his [Lincoln's] administration with all my energy on those great principles which have separated parties in former times," Douglas said March 6; but on a Constitutional amendment to settle the slavery issue, he would support Lincoln.

ican friends of freedom. Elizabeth Barrett Browning wrote an American acquaintance that some evils were worse than civil conflict. "My serious fear," she declared, "has been, and is, not for the dissolution of the body but the death of the soul—not of a rupture of states and civil war, but of reconciliation and peace at the expense of a deadly compromise of principle. Nothing will destroy the republic but what corrupts its conscience and disturbs its frame—for the stain upon the honor must come off upon the flag. If, on the other hand, the North stands fast on the moral ground no glory will be like your glory." [40] These were the sentiments of millions of lovers of the Union.

Most men on both sides in the sectional struggle felt that they stood upon sound moral ground. It was all-important that the leaders on each side, and especially on the Union side, should act on high principle and not expediency. Would Lincoln, so untried in great responsibilities, yield to the heavy pressures for peace at any price—for delay beyond the point of no return? Or would he stand by his declaration that evasion must stop? Before the answer was given, a quietly desperate struggle between him and Seward had to be decided.

40 N. Y. *Independent*, March 10, 1861.

3

Contest for Power: Seward and Lincoln

LINCOLN headed what was essentially a coalition government. His Cabinet represented groups of diverse origins and principles—conservative Whigs, freesoil Whigs, Union Democrats of Jacksonian cast, and radical adherents of new Republican ideas. Of its members a majority—Secretary of State Seward, Secretary of the Treasury Chase, Secretary of War Cameron, and Attorney-General Bates—had aspired to the Presidency, and Chase and perhaps Seward hoped for that prize in the future. The Cabinet had not even the semblance of unity, and its level of responsibility was low. As the diaries of Chase, Bates, and Secretary of the Navy Gideon Welles show, they had no trust in each other. Several were at critical moments to prove disloyal to the President; and at least two were so undependable that part of their duties had to be taken over by others, Cameron ceding certain military responsibilities to Chase, and Bates certain responsibilities over civil justice to Seward. Lincoln, like other leaders of coalitions which included headstrong men (Lloyd George in the First World War, for example), had to fight for his tenure of power. His first battle was to be for the control of his Administration, his second for the control of military strategy—and others were to follow.

From the moment South Carolina seceded, Seward had been actuated by the idea of compromise; from the moment he took the State Department, he had cherished a belief that he could dominate Lincoln. Having led rough Zack Taylor when he was only Senator, now as the ablest Cabinet member he would lead the rustic neophyte from the Sangamon. Recent events strengthened his confidence. He had revised the inaugural address, put his friend Cameron into the Cabinet even if he had failed to keep Chase out, and easily established himself as Lincoln's chief adviser.[1]

To comprehend Seward's attitude, we should glance at a few comparative

---

[1] The exact extent of Seward's influence over Lincoln is hard to gauge. But we may agree with Douglas that it was much greater than it should have been. Lincoln often sat listening to his breezy, genial, cynical talk and drew profit from his experience. It was temporarily an Eisenhower-Taft situation, rather than a Wilson-Underwood situation. Welles, I, *Diary*, 34, 35.

facts. He was almost eight years older than the President. When little Abe
Lincoln was a ragged backwoods lad trudging to log schools in Indiana for
brief intervals of ciphering, Seward was studying at Union College. While
Lincoln was keeping store, splitting rails, and surveying at New Salem,
Seward was leader of the New York Senate. The year 1842 found Lincoln
a struggling Springfield lawyer; it found Seward completing four busy years
as governor of the Empire State. When Lincoln left the House in defeat
after one term, Seward sat in the Senate as almost the peer of Clay or Webster.
Throughout the 1850's Seward seemed the chief embodiment of the freesoil
cause; no other Republican leader gained so much experience or renown;
and wearing the laurels of twelve years of versatile Senate service, he
entered the party convention of 1860 the leading candidate and to most
citizens unquestionably the strongest man—to be beaten by a raw Western
attorney.

Just before the inauguration he inspired a friend to publish in the New
York *Evening Post* a letter presenting him as a paladin of peace, who would
effect an early restoration of the Union if only New York enemies, fanatic
abolitionists, and (it was hinted) an inexperienced President did not prevent
him. The letter writer lamented that never before had so many members of
Congress been open applicants for Presidential favors. "This, and the impression which exists that Mr. Lincoln is opposed to any form of compromise,
makes members firm who ne'er were firm before, and creates obstacles to
the settlement of our difficulties which ten words from the lips of Mr. Lincoln
would dispel in a moment." [2] Let Seward be the *deus ex machina!* A Southern
commissioner reported what was doubtless an accurate transcript of Seward's
loose, fluent talk just after the inauguration. "I have built up the Republican
party, I have brought it to triumph, but its advent to power is accompanied
by great difficulties and perils. I must save the party, and save the government in its hands. To do this, war must be averted, the negro question must
be dropped, the irrepressible conflict ignored, and a Union Party to embrace
the border slave States inaugurated. . . . [Then] the people of the cotton
States, unwillingly led into secession, will rebel." [3]

It is certain that the three main ideas in this passage were really held by
Seward. First, he believed that *he* must take the leadership; he had so written

2 This letter in the *Evening Post* was acridly dissected by the N. Y. *Tribune* of Feb. 27.
We are credibly informed, said the *Tribune*, "that the very language of this letter is the same
as has been repeatedly used by Mr. Seward in private conversation." Greeley very wrathfully accused Seward of trying to take charge of the Administration and reduce Lincoln to
a cipher.

3 Forsyth, March 8, 1861, to Robert Toombs; Toombs Letterbook, South Caroliniana
Library, Univ. of S. C.

his wife. Second, he believed that the Republican Party must be broadened into a Union Party, powerful in the border States, and quiet on the slavery issue. Third, he assumed that if the seven cotton States were isolated, their people would soon beg for readmittance. Winfield Scott wrote Seward on March 3 outlining various alternatives before the government, and ending with alternative number four—let the seceded States depart in peace. This implied that the head of the army regarded Seward, not Lincoln, as general manager of the new regime, and Seward showed the letter widely around Washington to confirm that belief and strengthen the peace party.

Back of Seward's policy lay a profound moral defect. He could not take the great issue of Southern intransigence, so all-important to the future of the nation, with due seriousness. He thought that any storm, even this, could be controlled by cunning management, party bargains, and dexterous maneuvering; he did not realize that he was facing men in deadly earnest, whose determination was fixed, and was dealing with a movement far too powerful for mere shrewd manipulation. Douglas, among others, saw through his shallow conceit. Douglas knew that he had been hand-in-glove with various Southern Senators all winter, playing a dangerous game with them. The time for games had now passed.

[I]

On inauguration day Sam Ward, son of a rich New York banker, skilled lobbyist, and friend of many leaders in both parties, launched an effort to encourage Seward's peacemaking. He wrote the Secretary that he had talked with several Confederate leaders; that he had learned that Robert Toombs was the master spirit of the new government (an illusion Toombs liked to create); and that the Southern Congress was adamant for independence. He warned Seward that if the Southern commissioners who had come to open negotiations in Washington were sent back unrecognized, President Davis could not restrain the incensed South Carolinians from attacking Sumter. His informants, ex-Senator W. M. Gwin of California and Senator R. M. T. Hunter of Virginia, thought that the question of treating with the commissioners ought to be submitted to the Senate, where twenty-two favorable Democratic votes could be counted on.

It is clear that Ward, Gwin, and Hunter assumed that Lincoln was a nullity, and hoped that Seward would so manage affairs as to preserve peace.[4]

4 Ward's letters are in Bancroft, *Seward*. II, 542–545; see also Crawford, *Genesis*, 322; Rhodes, *History*, III, 328: Bancroft. *Seward*, II, 111.

In Montgomery, meanwhile, Judah P. Benjamin was voicing the indignation of the Confederate Government over the way in which Washington let matters drift, and its determination shortly to seize the forts.

Seward was perfectly willing to hold indirect parleys with the Confederate commissioners. He allowed Gwin, a warm sympathizer with the South, to run back and forth between him and the three agents, Martin J. Crawford, A. B. Roman, and John Forsyth, who regarded themselves as envoys of a foreign power. While the trio threatened immediate blows against Forts Sumter and Pickens, Seward pleaded for delay and peace. Finally, the commissioners sent the Secretary a memorandum agreement (March 8) offering a wait of twenty days in return for a promise that the existing military position would be preserved in every respect. Seward meanwhile assured Sam Ward that the Administration would take no warlike steps; and Ward delightedly urged his New York friends to buy stocks and keep on buying.[5] Momentarily, the commissioners hoped they had entrapped Seward. If he signed their memorandum, he in effect recognized the Confederacy![6] When the paper arrived, however, the wily Secretary was abed with lumbago and declared that his physician had forbidden him to transact any business whatever. Gwin at this point dropped his dubious and doubtless distasteful activities as a go-between.[7]

Seward was certainly too shrewd a fox to be ensnared. However anxious he was to take a conciliatory line, evacuate Fort Sumter, and charm the Confederate States back into the Union, he could not possibly recognize the commissioners as agents of an independent government. Undiscouraged, the three emissaries persuaded Senator Hunter to accept the role of intermediary. When on March 11 the convalescent Seward returned to the State Department, he found that conservative slaveholder on his doorstep. The Secretary was embarrassed and uneasy, and when Hunter pressed him, merely said that he would ask the President about the propriety of an informal interview. Next day he wrote Hunter that he could not see the commissioners. Nevertheless, Crawford and Forsyth remained of good heart, informing Toombs cheerfully on March 12:

> While . . . a refusal to treat with us . . . in the absence of the evacuation of the Charleston and Pensacola forts is, from our point of view, certain war, the Administration still talks of peace. A gentleman from Tennessee had a half hour's private conversation with Mr. Lincoln this morning, and he assured him there would be no war and he was determined to keep the peace. . . . Mr. Crittenden of Kentucky told Mr. Crawford this morning that General Scott was also for peace, and would sustain Mr. Seward's policy, and if

5 Ward, March 9, 1861, Barlow Papers.
6 The commissioners to Toombs, March 8, 1861, Toombs Letterbook, South Caroliniana.
7 W. M. Gwin, MS Memoirs, Bancroft Library, Univ. of California, 190–200.

Sumter should be evacuated we think it will be the influence of General Scott upon the President which will produce that result. . . .

We are still of the opinion that Fort Sumter will be evacuated.[8]

Lincoln at this point, in fact, almost made up his mind that the evacuation of Sumter was a military necessity. Major Robert Anderson, commanding there, had suddenly reported on February 28 that he did not think an attempt to reinforce the post could succeed without 20,000 disciplined men. This had astonished the outgoing Secretary of War, Joseph Holt. Anderson had been told to report frequently on the condition of his garrison and on any warlike preparations around him; he had not suggested that the preparations were threatening or that reinforcements were needed; nevertheless, since an exigency might arise at any moment, Holt had quietly prepared a small expedition which was ready to sail from New York on a few hours' notice with troops and provisions. Now Anderson estimated that a relief attempt would be hopeless without forces far beyond the nation's immediate means—large naval units to break past the defenses into Charleston Harbor, and a powerful army to overwhelm the hostile fortifications from the rear. Where were the warships and the troops? Only eight companies were stationed in Washington, and only seven at Fort Monroe—all required where they were.[9]

It was all too true that Anderson's position was increasingly precarious. The South Carolina authorities permitted him to buy meat and vegetables in Charleston only from one market day to another, and forbade him to lay in a stock of nonperishables like flour.[10] In Washington, A. D. Bache of the Coast Survey and Col. J. G. Totten, chief engineer of the army, agreed that the strengthening of Fort Moultrie, the erection of land batteries, and the obstruction of channels had put Sumter in grave danger. Army officers talked of Charleston as "a new Sebastopol." Nearly the entire available force of South Carolina was in the field, and squads of recruits were arriving in an unsteady stream from other Southern States—even Maryland. Special trains were leaving Richmond with mortars, shot, shells, and ammunition. Even as Lincoln took his oath Governor Pickens telegraphed the Tredegar Iron Works: "Please send 400 shells for Dahlgren guns in addition to those already ordered." [11] The floating battery was anchored within range of Sumter, and Beauregard expressed confidence that he could blow Anderson out of the place at a moment's notice.

But various Union leaders refused to believe that a huge fleet and army

8 Toombs Letterbook, South Caroliniana Library.
9 Secretary Holt to Lincoln, March 3, 1861; Robert Todd Lincoln Papers, LC. It would take weeks to bring back the small forces garrisoning the Southwest.
10 N. Y. *Tribune*, March 11, 1861.
11 See telegrams of L. P. Walker, Pickens, and others in Pickens-Bonham Papers, LC.

would be needed to save Sumter, and declared it outrageous to talk of giving up the fort. Gideon Welles shook his beard with the exclamation, "Astounding!" Attorney-General Bates was resentfully perplexed. Above all, Postmaster-General Montgomery Blair, determined that the Union must be maintained at any cost, was profoundly stirred.[12] His brother-in-law Gustavus V. Fox, a man of determined chin and bald, domelike brow, systematic and energetic, and an Annapolis graduate who had overseen the transport of troops to Vera Cruz during the Mexican War, felt the same way. Blair had just brought him to Washington from his business in Massachusetts to advise General Winfield Scott, head of the Army, and he was ready to play his part. When Lincoln on Saturday, March 9, held his first Cabinet meeting, everyone agreed that more information was needed.

That same day Lincoln asked Scott to answer three questions in writing: How long could Sumter hold out? Could it be reinforced or supplied during that period with existing means? If not, what additional forces would be needed? On the following Monday, March 11, Scott laid his depressing answers before Lincoln. Sumter had hard bread, flour, and rice for only 26 days, with salt meat for 48; and to relieve the fort with existing resources was impossible, for he would need a strong fleet, 5000 additional regulars, and 20,000 volunteers.

These responses shocked Lincoln. He held Scott in high respect, for the old general had always been deeply attached to the Union, and there was of course no question of his impressive military achievements. Lincoln had supported him when he was the Whig Presidential candidate in 1852. He trusted Scott sufficiently to be appalled by his report. What he did not realize was that Scott in this matter was largely an echo of Seward, who adroitly manipulated him, and that the commander at times showed evidences of senility, although, as we shall see, he could if aroused plan ably and boldly. When the President on March 5 had requested Scott to be vigilant in maintaining all Federal forts and posts, the General had done almost nothing.[13] But this Lincoln did not yet know.

It is not strange that on these three days, March 9–11, Lincoln almost

12 O. R., I, i, 196–198; Bates, *Diary*, 177, 178; Welles, *Diary* (retrospective), I, 4.
13 Lincoln, worried over Fort Pickens at Pensacola, on March 11 repeated in writing his order to Scott to maintain Federal positions. Next day Scott started orders to the commander of some troops on the warship *Brooklyn* off Pensacola to land his company to reinforce Pickens. But this order was not obeyed! The naval commander refused to let the men land. He wrote Secretary Welles April 1 that such a movement "would most certainly be viewed as a hostile act, and would be resisted to the utmost." He would not begin the war under Scott as head of the Army, though he would willingly obey any order from Welles as head of the Navy. "Omitted Letters" in G. V. Fox Correspondence, N. Y. Hist. Soc.

gave way. In Washington the *National Intelligencer,* long the nation's principal Whig newspaper, appeared with an earnest editorial plea for withdrawal. The *National Republican,* a newspaper close to some Administration leaders, the same day explicitly announced that the Cabinet had decided to evacuate both Sumter and Pickens. It is possible that Seward nudged the elbows of both editors. Certainly he helped spread word of an imminent evacuation, and told J. C. Welling of the *National Intelligencer* to convey the news to a Union leader in the convention which Virginia was then holding. On the 12th the Charleston *Courier* and *Mercury* announced that Sumter would soon be in Confederate hands without a fight.

This news, in fact, rapidly spread through the country. The New York *Herald* carried a dispatch on the 12th denouncing the reports as a stockjobbing scheme, and a cloak for secret Administration efforts to strengthen the fort. But next day it ate its words. "I am able to state positively," wrote the Washington correspondent, "that the abandonment of Fort Sumter has been determined upon by the President and his Cabinet."

Fierce and swift was the wrath of all radical Republicans. The lobbies of hotels rang with denunciation. Ben Wade's profanity was fearful to hear. Greeley's *Tribune* uttered an angry wail. To give up the fort in the first fortnight of power! To abandon what Buchanan in spite of all his imbecility and cowardice had held! This would be an acknowledgment that the Union was dissolved forever unless it was saved later by the most abject concessions. Perhaps, wrote Greeley, the North really was too demoralized to act with vigor, or perhaps circumstances necessitated the step; but he could not help thinking that if the Administration were to accept disunion, it might begin with a step less humiliating. John A. Dix commented that the grief and anger of the North would almost ruin the Administration. Western Congressmen were particularly indignant.[14]

[II]

Yet Lincoln had not fully made up his mind, and Lincoln still gripped the reins.

The anxious Cabinet held two sessions on March 14, the first from ten to one, the second from four till seven. The members now divided sharply on Scott's report that evacuation was practically unavoidable. Montgomery Blair, a tall, ministerial-looking attorney who as a boy had often listened to the talk of his father and Andrew Jackson, and who believed that his West

14 N. Y. *Times, Tribune, Herald,* March 12–15, 1861; note especially J. S. Pike's Washington correspondence in the *Tribune.*

Point training enabled him to speak on military topics, led the opposition to surrender. Since nullification days his family had made the word "Union" a shibboleth. He had represented Dred Scott before the Supreme Court. Now he felt certain that Winfield Scott was growing imbecile, and that neither Seward nor Cameron understood the kind of action that the crisis demanded. Violence was not to be met by temporizing. "It is my deliberate opinion," he had recently written, "that if such a policy is acted on we shall have a long and bloody war and permanent disunion"; on the other hand, if a strong Northern blow were struck, the Southern masses would rise against the Confederate Government.[15] One root of the difficulty, in Blair's opinion, was the widespread Southern conviction that all Yankees lacked courage. Appeasement by the surrender of Sumter would convince them of this, and simply make a collision more probable. The Southern Gascons needed a lesson, nor should it be costly. And Montgomery Blair was only one of many who believed that a firm attitude would mean a shorter war.

Blair came to the Cabinet armed with a plan for the naval relief of Sumter prepared by his brother-in-law. Gustavus V. Fox proposed sending to Charleston, under convoy of the seven-gun vessel *Pawnee* and the revenue cutter *Harriet Lane*, a steamship laden with stores and two tugboats. If on reaching Charleston they found Confederate gunboats opposing their entry, the two warships must destroy or drive ashore the Southern craft, Major Anderson assisting with his guns. Then, at nightfall, the tugboats would run past the shore batteries and relieve the fort. Even if one tug was lost, the other could deliver the stores and a limited number of troops, after which the tugs would be abandoned while their crews joined the garrison. The scheme was endorsed by experienced sailors. At Kinnburn on the Black Sea eight British gunboats one night had safely passed Russian forts mounting eighty guns. What Fox was now proposing was something like the running of Vicksburg and Mobile during subsequent naval operations. However, two naval men who at first leaned to the plan, Commodore S. H. Stringham and Commander J. H. Ward, shortly became convinced that it was impracticable.[16]

Seward protested violently. He was adamant in his opposition to any attempt at relief. It was the duty of the Administration, he argued, to defer to the opinion of General Scott, Major Anderson, and other high military officers that any such effort would be abortive and costly. A relief expedition would precipitate hostilities, and if war was to begin, the North should not strike the first blow. Alongside Seward stood his old friend Cameron, the conservative Indiana wirepuller Caleb B. Smith whom Lincoln had reluctantly

15 Blair, Jan. 23, 1861, to John A. Andrew; Andrew Papers, MHS.
16 Fox's plan is in *Confidential Correspondence of G. V. Fox*, I, 8 ff.

appointed to the Interior Department, and, with some reservations, Attorney-General Bates.[17]

The two Cabinet meetings reached no conclusion. Thereupon Lincoln, desiring a more considered statement of views, on the 15th sent every Cabinet member a letter asking whether, as a political measure, it was wise to try to provision Sumter. To this query Blair alone gave an unqualified yes. He declared once more that firm action would do more than weak appeasement to avoid prolonged bloodshed and end the rebellion. Chase took a stand which, had it been widely known, would have astonished the nation. He had gone into the Cabinet with the reputation of an unflinching radical, the doughtiest champion of those whom C. F. Adams called the ramwells—that is, the die-hards. But at the moment it was actually true that, as Greeley's Washington correspondent wrote, he was no extremist, but "moderate, conciliatory, deliberate, and conservative." [18] One important factor in his hesitation was his fear that a war would be very difficult, and perhaps impossible, to finance. He was under pressure from Eastern bankers who had warned him that they would not take his pending eight-million-dollar loan unless the government pursued a peace policy. Now he wrote Lincoln that if relieving the fort meant enlisting huge armies and spending millions, he would not advise it. It was only because he believed that the South might be cajoled by full explana-tions and other conciliatory gestures into accepting the relief effort without war that he supported it. That is, he was for relief only with careful ex-planations.

The other replies said no. Wordy letters of Caleb B. Smith and Gideon Welles boiled down to a simple statement that relief would be politically un-wise. Cameron stressed the weight of adverse military opinion. Bates, like Seward, emphasized the argument that the North ought not to provoke hos-tilities. Our right is unquestionable, he wrote, and we have the means to act. But "I am willing to evacuate Fort Sumter, rather than be an active party in the beginning of civil war." Seward's position hardly needed restatement. While he declared that the nation must be kept intact even if this ultimately meant war, he argued that Sumter was useless, and conciliation would give the Unionists of the South an opportunity to rally and undo the work of the fire-eaters. He would try to collect the national revenues, but only at sea. "I would defer military action on land until a case should arise when we would hold the defense. In that case, we should have the spirit of the country and the approval of mankind on our side." Essentially true is the statement which Montgomery Blair later made: "Alone in the Cabinet, I resisted the surrender

17 Welles, *Diary*, I, 8 ff.
18 N. Y. *Tribune*, March 6, 1861.

of Forts Sumter and Pickens and the dissolution of the Union which that surrender signified, and put my resignation on the issue." [19]

Lincoln yet hesitated. That he inclined toward an early evacuation is indicated by three pieces of evidence. The first is that on March 18 he placed a memorandum in his office papers summarizing the arguments for and against it, with the weight heavily against any effort at relief. The second is that on the same day he sent inquiries to Welles (about naval force), Bates (about legal right), and Chase (about general practicability) respecting the offshore collection of tariff duties, an indication that he leaned toward the plan suggested by Seward. The Secretary of State, according to Welles, was spending much of each day at the White House, vigilantly informing himself of every act, word, and idea of Lincoln and the other Cabinet members. The third bit of evidence is that Montgomery Blair in desperation wrote out his resignation, determined to quit if no effort were made to relieve Major Anderson.

The President was keeping an uneasy eye on Virginia, where on February 4 a convention had been elected to deal with the problems of the hour. The Union men had won a decisive victory, which Seward had hailed as a gleam of sunshine in a storm. Only 30 unconditional secessionists had been elected among 152 members, and by a vote of more than two to one the people required that any findings of the convention must be submitted to a plebiscite. Disunion had met "a Waterloo defeat," declared the Richmond *Whig*. But the Unionists represented various shades of opinion, and if the North attempted coercion, a majority would at once become disunionists. Through confidential channels, both Lincoln and Seward tried to keep in touch with the convention.

In fact, Lincoln immediately after his arrival in Washington had talked one evening for several hours with a border group which included the venerable William C. Rives of Virginia, Judge George W. Summers of that State, and James B. Guthrie of Kentucky, head of the Treasury under Franklin Pierce. All had gathered in a semicircle about the President-elect, who sat awkwardly in a chair, his feet on the rungs, his elbows on his angular knees, and his large hands cupped under his cheeks. After telling a story drawn

19 To Cassius M. Clay, Dec. 31, 1881; Henry B. Joy Collection. Chase was actually willing to let the cotton States go. He later wrote Alphonso Taft that he had taken the view that the government had two feasible alternatives: to enforce the laws of the Union everywhere, or to recognize the Confederacy of seven States as an accomplished fact, let it try its experiment of separate nationality, and forbid any further dismemberment of the nation, enforcing its authority vigorously. April 28, 1861; Chase Collection, Univ. of Pa. It is an equally striking fact that Charles Sumner also had been conditionally ready to let the cotton States depart in peace. He had written the Duchess of Argyll, Dec. 14, 1860, that he approached the question with the greatest caution, and that if secession could be restricted to the seven States, "I shall be willing to let them go." Sumner Papers, HL.

from his frontier law experiences, and one from Aesop, both of which made good points, Lincoln laid down the principles on which he said he would stand firmly: slavery must not be extended into any Territory, and the laws must be faithfully executed. Various men spoke. At last Rives, a dignified and impressive figure, made with trembling voice an eloquent plea. He referred to the potential horrors concealed in the lowering clouds, and to his own profound love of the Union. But if Lincoln resorted to force, he said, Virginia would secede, and old as he was he would fight for Virginia.

At this Lincoln uncoiled his huge frame from the chair, advanced a step, and according to one account said: "Mr. Rives, Mr. Rives! If Virginia will stay in I will withdraw the troops from Fort Sumter." The story has a plausible ring. It is certain that Lincoln was intensely concerned lest Virginia go out, and hopeful that the convention would adjourn without action. He later told John Hay about the call of these border leaders. "He promised," Hay records in his diary for October 22, 1861, "to evacuate Sumter if they would break up their convention, without any row or nonsense. They demurred. Subsequently he renewed [the] proposition to Summers, but without any result. The President was most anxious to avoid bloodshed." Lincoln remarked that it would be sound policy to trade a fort for a State. But the Virginia convention kept on sitting, obviously in order to vote secession if the government took any step that could be construed as coercion.[20]

[III]

In this duel of Montgomery Blair with Seward, it momentarily seemed that Seward was winning. But the situation was suddenly changed by a dramatic intervention.

Blair apprised his father, the venerable Francis P. Blair, living at Silver Springs near Washington, of his probable resignation. The stalwart Jacksonian, one of the elder statesmen of the nation, a founder of the Republican Party, and a great power throughout the border area, was fiercely aroused. At the next session of the Cabinet (apparently Monday, March 18) he followed

---

20 Charles S. Morehead of Kentucky, who was a member of the Peace Convention in Washington, later described this meeting in a speech reported in the Liverpool, O., *Mercury*, Oct. 13, 1861. He had served a term with Lincoln in Congress, and Lincoln sent word through a friend asking him to call. It was Morehead who then arranged to bring in Rives, Guthrie, General Donovan of Missouri, and Judge George W. Summers of Virginia. The conversation began at nine in the evening in Lincoln's quarters in his hotel. Morehead told also of meeting with Seward, who pledged his honor that no collision would take place between North and South. "'Nay,' said he, 'Governor Morehead,' laying his hand on my shoulder to make it more emphatic, 'let me once hold the reins of power firmly in my hands, and if I don't settle this matter to the entire satisfaction of the South in sixty days, I will give you my head for a football!'" For editorial comment see N. Y. *Tribune*, Nov. 6, 1862.

Montgomery to the White House, ensconcing himself in Nicolay's office. As soon as the meeting broke up, he sought Lincoln. He found the President in the Cabinet room reading the written statements of the members. "Will you give up the fort?" Blair demanded. Lincoln did not say. He merely replied that nearly all the Cabinet favored it.

"It would be treason to surrender Sumter, sir," trumpeted the old man. He told Lincoln that the step would "irrevocably lose the Administration the public confidence." Acquiescence in secession would be a recognition of its constitutionality. Scott was timid and senile; as for Seward, the man had never known what principle and firmness meant. "If you abandon Sumter," Blair declared, in effect, "you will be impeached!" And returning to Silver Springs, he wrote the President that while he did not question Scott's patriotism, he regarded Seward as a thoroughly dangerous counselor.

Lincoln's secretaries tell us that he was at heart for holding Sumter, and that only the bulk of adverse opinion had shaken his resolve. The aged Blair produced a telling effect. "His earnestness and indignation aroused and electrified the President," recalls Gideon Welles; "and when, in his zeal, Blair warned the President that the abandonment of Sumter would justly be considered by the people, by the world, by history, as treason to the country, he touched a chord that responded to his invocation. The President decided from that moment that an attempt should be made to convey supplies to Major Anderson, and that he would reinforce Sumter." This is a gross overstatement. Lincoln did not yet fully make up his mind. When he did decide, it was on the basis of complex factors, not Blair's plea alone, and this final resolve was to provision Sumter, not reinforce it. But the plea was nevertheless potent.[21]

Lincoln, still hesitant, determined to send personal agents to Charleston as investigators. Montgomery Blair proposed that Gustavus V. Fox make a quick visit to look into the position of Sumter, and Lincoln consented subject to the approval of Cameron and Scott. Immediately afterwards the President arranged an inquiry into the political situation. Stephen A. Hurlbut of Illinois, an old associate, a Charlestonian by birth and a whilom law student under the famous South Carolina jurist James Louis Petigru, was in Washington. He would command the confidence of prominent Charlestonians. On March 21 Lincoln asked him to hurry down and test Seward's supposition that South Carolina harbored many crypto-Unionists. Hurlbut, telegraphing his sister that he was making her a visit, at once departed. Lincoln's friend Ward Hill

21 Rhodes make no mention of Blair's call on Lincoln; neither do Nicolay and Hay. It was briefly noted in Crawford's *Genesis*, p. 368. Welles, *Diary*, I, 13, 14, gives a fuller account, and Smith, *Blair*, II, 9-13, fuller still.

Lamon, who had come from Springfield to seek the Federal marshalship in Washington—a big, loquacious bumbler of more self-assurance than discretion—also went down. In fact, he and Hurlbut traveled together, each supposing that *he* was the principal emissary.

Fox should be back on March 25th, Hurlbut and Lamon on the 27th. A final decision would have to be made immediately afterward. The Virginia convention still marked time. Public opinion North and South still waited in rising anxiety.

[IV]

The intentions of Confederate leaders, meanwhile, were in no doubt whatever. They meant to establish their independent republic forever. William M. Browne spoke for nearly everyone at Montgomery when on March 22 he warned a New York friend that they would attack Sumter if Federal troops were not soon removed. "I am still very confident we shall have a collision," Judah P. Benjamin informed S. L. M. Barlow on April 3. "We have almost certain intelligence of an intention to reinforce Pickens, and that is of course war, and must be so treated by us at all hazards." [22]

The Confederate commissioners were later to accuse Seward of flagrant deception in leading them to believe throughout March that the evacuation of Sumter was imminent. But that the commissioners themselves attempted to delude and deceive Seward by tacitly encouraging his belief in eventual Southern return there is no doubt! Crawford admitted as much when early in March he notified Toombs that he had acquiesced in Seward's plea for delay, on condition that the existing status be rigidly preserved. "His reasons, and my own, it is proper to say, are as wide apart as the poles; he is fully persuaded that peace will bring about a reconstruction of the Union, whilst I feel confident that it will build up and cement our Confederacy, and put us beyond the reach either of his arms or diplomacy." He did not tell Seward that! [23]

The same point was made with yet greater vigor by Crawford and A. B. Roman in a letter of March 26. Poor Seward still thought that peace would lead to a reunion. Very well, they would fool him to the top of his bent. "We believe the peace party is strengthening every day in the North, and we further believe that every day's peace lessens the chance of war. . . . We know that we are independent of this government, living under our own Constitution, and enforcing our own laws, levying tribute upon the North,

22 Barlow Papers.
23 March 6, 1861; Toombs Letterbook.

and doing all things which a free people may of right do. These things aid us at home in solidifying our Government and preparing our people for any emergency; abroad it gives us power, character, and influence. We should do nothing therefore lightly to disturb our rapid growth, and show us less prepared for war than this Government supposes us to be." [24]

As intermediary the commissioners were now employing John A. Campbell of the Supreme Court, a lover of the Union, and a man of fine integrity, cultivation, and tact. He and Seward were old friends who could talk frankly. To some interviews Campbell took Supreme Court Justice Samuel Nelson, a New York Democrat of nearly seventy. Just what promises did Seward give? Just what deceptions did he practice? [25]

Campbell on March 15, after seeing Seward, told Crawford he felt confident that the Administration contemplated no change prejudicial to the Confederacy, and that Sumter would be evacuated in five days. This of course reflected his conversation with Seward. The five days having expired, the commissioners asked Campbell to inquire into the delay. Three times on March 21-22 the judge again saw Seward. Once more Campbell on returning from these talks expressed unabated confidence that Sumter would shortly be evacuated, and that no change would be made in the status of Pickens.

At one point Seward most improperly let his expectations of imminent evacuation carry him away. Judge Campbell remarked that he was going to write a letter to Jefferson Davis. "What shall I say to him on the subject of Fort Sumter?" he inquired. "You may say to him," replied Seward, "that before that letter reaches him—how far is it to Montgomery?" "Three days," rejoined Campbell. And Seward completed his sentence: "You may say to him that before that letter reaches him, the telegraph will have informed him that Sumter will have been evacuated."

Nevertheless, the commissioners well understood that all this represented no pledge by Seward, but simply expressed his confidence that he could manipulate Lincoln and control events. They well knew that inside the Cabinet and party a terrific struggle was taking place. They realized that, as Crawford and Roman ungenerously put it on March 26, "The *courage* and *pertinacity* of Mr. Chase [they should have written Blair] may prevail over the craftiness and timidity of Mr. Seward." "We believe," they reported, "that he [Seward] will impress the President so strongly with his wisdom that he will ultimately control him, but this may be a mistake, and he [Lincoln] may at last fall upon

24 March 26; *Ibid.*
25 Campbell was hotly denounced in Alabama for his unwavering adherence to the Union. He and Judge Nelson shared a conviction that they could combine loyalty to the Union with opposition to coercion. It was Judge Nelson who, after talking with Seward, arranged for Campbell to serve as intermediary.

the other side." Clearly, they were under no deception. They possessed a correct view of realities.

Playing for high stakes, the commissioners used every possible tool, every expedient, every device. Not satisfied with two Supreme Court justices as go-betweens, they soon utilized the Russian minister, Stoeckl. Roman conversed with Stoeckl in fluent Louisiana French, and made a tentative plan for a meeting, seemingly accidental, between himself and Seward at Stoeckl's residence. This fell through. Meanwhile, the commissioners still used threats. Crawford, for example, had Campbell tell Seward on March 14 that Sumter was a point of the greatest possible danger, as hostilities might commence at any moment. At all times the commissioners, speaking scornfully of Seward behind his back, hoped to use him as a cat's-paw. "It is well that he should indulge in dreams that we know are not to be realized," they had exultantly commented to Toombs.[26]

The Confederate Government was coolly determined to parley so long as negotiations seemed profitable, and to begin shooting when violence became expedient. Toombs on April 2 wrote the commissioners in derision of Seward's hopes: "It is a matter of no importance to us what motives may induce the adoption of Mr. Seward's policy by his government. We are satisfied that it will redound to our advantage, and therefore, care little for Mr. Seward's calculations as to its future effects upon the Confederate States." [27] Dr. Gwin returned in April from a trip to Mississippi, full of confidence in the future of the Confederacy.[28] We know that Northern acts of apparent acquiescence in separation were not strengthening the Unionists in the South, but weakening them.[29] That combative young Virginia orator Roger A. Pryor, who had just resigned from Congress, was traveling through the Carolinas assuring hearers that one resolute Confederate blow would bring the upper South into the new republic.

26 Letters of Crawford and later Crawford, Forsyth, and Roman in Toombs Letterbook, March 8, 22, 25, 1861. It is fair to say that Seward at first seemed as willing as Roman for the meeting at Baron Stoeckl's, and withdrew from the arrangement only because he feared unfavorable publicity.
27 Bancroft, Seward, II, 119. James G. Randall in Lincoln the President, I, 324, speaks of Seward's "definite pledge of evacuation," as do other writers. This is a misuse of words. No pledge was given because (1) Seward obviously had no power to give one, and (2) Campbell's reports clearly state a prediction—a belief in strong probability—but not a categorical promise. It is plain from the commissioners' reports that they at first accepted Seward's belief, but that by March 22 they were doubtful, and that on March 26 they knew that he would probably lose his game. If the Commissioners did not know that Seward was characteristically loose of speech, anybody in Washington could have told them.
28 Curtis, Buchanan, II, 539.
29 William Watson, a young Scottish engineer of Baton Rouge, and F. A. P. Barnard of the Univ. of Mississippi, are among a number who so declare; Watson, Life in the Confederate Army; John Fulton, Memoirs of F. A. P. Barnard, 276, 277.

Seward had gradually evolved a definite program. He hoped that the Virginia convention, after rejecting secession, would call a meeting of delegates from the border States, as some leaders talked of doing; that this body would formulate a plan of reunion; and that a national convention would follow. Actually, he was playing with a dangerous idea.[30] The proposed border gathering might easily result in a new wave of secession and a Border Confederacy, which would first try to dictate to both North and South a set of terms for reunion; then if the North balked, as well it might, the border area would have grounds for joining the cotton States. By April, however, sentiment in Virginia was plainly shifting toward abandonment of the Union, and secessionist managers in the convention were inclined to drop the idea of a Border Confederacy.[31]

Suppose that Seward's idea of a national convention to hammer out terms of reunion had ultimately prevailed. Would the seven Confederate States have responded? On the contrary, the probability was that the gap would have steadily widened. Each side would accommodate its institutions, usages, and requirements to the new order. Under shelter of the Confederacy a large body of special interests would spring up—mercantile groups fostered by its low tariffs; shipping groups nourished by the direct trade between New Orleans, Mobile, and Charleston on one hand, and Liverpool, London, and Havre on the other; planting groups able to buy more cheaply in Europe than in the North; thousands of officeholders and contractors paid in Confederate money; publishers, writers, editors, lecturers, and politicians capitalizing on Confederate nationalism; and manufacturers exploiting the cry, "Buy Confederate wares." Erstwhile doubters would find that the cotton kingdom could really do without the North and West. Meanwhile, many Northerners would lose their sense of shock over the rending of the national fabric. Peace feeling in many Northern communities would grow. Tokens of this trend were already appearing. Wendell Phillips was silenced by a mob when he tried to speak in Cincinnati late in March. Elections early in April resulted in the defeat of two Republican Congressmen in Connecticut and two more in Rhode Island, and in Democratic victories in St. Louis and other important cities; a reaction attributed to confusion and discouragement among Union men.[32]

---

30 George W. Summers of the Virginia Convention indirectly let Montgomery Blair know that he and his associates hoped to call a border convention in Nashville or Frankfort, submit a plan of compromise to both sides, and adjourn until fall. Meanwhile they would begin the spring canvass to defeat secessionism in Virginia. Summers to J. C. Welling, March 19, 1861, Blair Papers, LC.

31 Wash. correspondence dated April 1, 1861, in N. Y. *Tribune.*

32 For election results see N. Y. *Herald,* April 6, 7, 10.

Sam Ward, who not only talked with Southern leaders in Washington but traveled in the South, formed a more astute judgment of the situation than Seward. Later, in the spring of 1862, he heard Seward say that if the South had been allowed to go in peace, within two years it would have come back. "I differ from you," he declared. "I found among the leaders a malignant bitterness and contemptuous hatred of the North which rendered this lesson necessary. Within two years they would have formed entangling free trade and free navigation treaties with Europe, and have become a military power hostile to us." [33]

[V]

What of the investigators sent to Charleston? Gustavus V. Fox posted back with encouraging word that a relief expedition was quite practicable. The vital requirement, in his opinion, was a naval force strong enough to drive off the petty warships in the harbor if they offered resistance. "All else is easy." He told the President that Scott's adverse judgment was worthless, for the question of sending a squadron past the forts at night was naval, not military. He compiled for Lincoln a list of various operations in which ships had passed land batteries with impunity. At Blair's instance he appeared at several Cabinet meetings to advise the President, and in one had the satisfaction of hearing the eminent engineer Colonel G. M. Totten declare his plan feasible.

On Fox's heels returned Stephen A. Hurlbut, who had seen a number of prominent Charlestonians. "From these sources," he wrote, "I have no hesitation in reporting as unquestionable—that separate nationality is a fixed fact—that there is an unanimity of sentiment which is to my mind astonishing —that there is no attachment to the Union." It would be useless, he reported, to appeal to the laboring masses. Power in South Carolina and the Confederacy was swayed by men who, while they desired to avoid war, intended and expected a peaceable separation, after which they believed that the two sections would be friendlier than before. "But it is equally true that there exists a large minority indefatigably active and reckless who desire to precipitate collision, inaugurate war, and unite the Southern Confederacy by that means."

The Confederacy would never turn back, warned Hurlbut; unless the United States resisted, at least five States (he had no information on Louisiana and Texas) were irrevocably gone. As yet, he believed that the garrison at Sumter could be withdrawn without insult, but in another week even that

33 March 27, 1862; Barlow Papers.

would probably be impossible. "I have no doubt that a ship known to contain only provisions for Sumter would be stopped and refused admittance." He closed with a note of warning. This was a time to expect the worst, and to be prepared for it; to yield only from strength, not from weakness; and if not to yield, to be yet more amply prepared.

The bumbling Lamon likewise returned with an oral report that no real Union party existed in South Carolina, that the people of the cotton States were infuriated, and that the masses were being hurried into open rebellion. He had talked with Governor Pickens, former Representative Lawrence Keitt, Postmaster Huger, and the Unionist James Louis Petigru; and Petigru himself had declared that the only alternatives now were peaceable secession or war. Lamon was in close touch with Seward. It was under Seward's influence that he actually told Governor Pickens that he had come to arrange for the withdrawal of the garrison, and that after his return he wrote the governor that he would be back in a few days to assist in the evacuation! He also gave Major Anderson the impression that no relief would be attempted. All this was outrageous, and when Lincoln heard of Lamon's letter to Pickens, he indignantly denied that the man possessed any authority to make such a statement.[34]

The critical hour had now struck. Congress, the people of the country, the merchants and manufacturers suffering from a grave interruption of business, the Virginia convention, all were in anxious suspense. The uncertainty as to Administration policy must be ended. On March 28 a series of events brought matters to a head.

First, the press that morning published dispatches revealing that General Scott a fortnight earlier had ordered the *Brooklyn*, lying off Pensacola, to reinforce Fort Pickens. Actually, as we have seen, it had *not* been reinforced because its commander would not obey Scott's orders, but the press did not know this. Much more importantly, Lyman Trumbull that day introduced an ominous resolution. Expressing the impatience of the unyielding Republicans, it breathed a hint of impeachment. "Resolved," it ran, "That in the opinion of the Senate, the true way to preserve the Union is to enforce the laws of the Union; that resistance to their enforcement, whether under the name of anti-coercion or any other name, is encouragement to disunion; and that it is the duty of the President of the United States to use all the means in his

34 G. V. Fox, Confidential Correspondence, I, 12. Hurlbut's long and well written report is in the R. T. Lincoln Papers; see also Nicolay and Hay, III, 391, 392. For Lamon's report see his *Recollections of Abraham Lincoln, 1847–65*, 70–79; Lamon's communications with Pickens and Anderson are in O. R., I, i, 221, 222, 281, 282. See also Crawford, *Genesis*, 337. Lamon's papers in the Huntington Library throw no light on the subject except to confirm his general ineptness.

power to hold and protect the public property of the United States, and enforce the laws thereof. . . ." This was a shot aimed straight at Seward.[35]

And in the third place, Lincoln's first state dinner, held that evening, was followed by a dramatic scene. Just as the party at the White House broke up, he called his Cabinet into a separate room, shut the door, and with evident emotion told them that Scott that day had advised evacuating Fort Pickens at Pensacola as well as Sumter. Montgomery Blair tells us that a silence of amazement followed. Everyone knew that Seward had prompted Scott. The hush was broken by Blair's impassioned denunciation of the old general—in effect a denunciation of Seward. As it was common knowledge that Pickens could be held indefinitely, Scott's advice was obviously given on political, not military, grounds.[36]

Blair knew that Seward had overshot his mark. Lincoln's emotion proved it. To give up Sumter under military necessity would be bad enough, but to give up Pickens as well would be ignominious surrender. The Cabinet without dissent (Cameron was absent in Harrisburg) condemned Scott's recommendation. Its members knew that Trumbull's resolution was supported by a large majority of Senate Republicans, and a vociferous body of Northern opinion. In a recent caucus of Republican Senators, only three had dared to advocate the abandonment of Sumter, while the others had angrily denounced any such act as national dishonor.[37]

Lincoln unquestionably felt a sense of betrayal when he told his Cabinet of Scott's stand. That night, knowing that he must meet the crisis, he did no sleep. He rose greatly depressed. To a friend he remarked that he was "in the dumps"—for he knew that he must try to relieve Sumter, and relief mean war.

When the Cabinet met again at noon on March 29, a desultory discussion showed that Seward was now on the defensive. He hardly dared lift his voic Nobody but the feeble Caleb B. Smith concurred in the proposal to give t both forts, and he only if military necessity should dictate it. Bates finall cut through the talk with a suggestion that Lincoln should state his question and all should give their written replies on the spot. These replies, some c them headed "In Cabinet," revealed a marked crystallization of opinion.

35 Wash. *National Intelligencer*, N. Y. *Herald*, *Times*, *Phila. Press*, etc.; *Cong. Globe* 36th Cong., 2d Sess., p. 1519.

36 Nicolay and Hay, III, 394; Welles, *Lincoln and Seward*, 64–69, with Montgomery Blair's letter to Welles, May 17, 1873. Scott had earlier, March 17, sent Secretary Cameron a memorandum which is given in O. R., I, i, 200, 201. The state dinner is graphically described by W. H. Russell, *My Diary North and South*.

37 The Confederate commissioners, writing Toombs on March 22, reported that the Senate caucus was "violently and bitterly opposed" to evacuation, and that "their influence and power has been brought to bear on the Govt. to prevent it." Toombs Letterbook.

Chase had now firmly made up his mind. "I am clearly in favor of maintaining Fort Pickens and just as clearly in favor of provisioning Fort Sumter," he wrote. "If the attempt be resisted by military force Fort Sumter should, in my judgment, be reinforced." Welles was equally emphatic. "I concur," he stated, "in the proposition to send an armed force off Charleston with supplies of provisions and reinforcement for the garrison at Fort Sumter, and of communicating, at the proper time, the intentions of the government to provision the fort, peaceably if unmolested." He thought resistance highly probable, and held that this would justify the government in using all the force at its command. He concluded: "The time has arrived, when it is the duty of the government to assert and maintain its authority." Bates declared that Pickens should be supplied and reinforced at all hazards, and a naval force should be kept on the Southern coast sufficient to blockade any port. As for Sumter, the time had come either to evacuate or relieve it.[38]

Caleb Smith in his written opinion proposed evacuating Sumter as a necessity, but defending Pickens, blockading the Southern ports, and enforcing the collection of revenues. Seward was of course for abandoning Sumter immediately. But even he declared that he would at once, and at every cost, prepare for war at Fort Pickens and in Texas, to be waged, however, only to maintain the possessions and authority of the United States. It is certain that at heart he really wished to give up Pickens. It is also certain that he yielded ground only because he saw that the opposition to his ideas was so overwhelming that he would lose all chance of maintaining his leadership unless he shifted his stand.[39]

Blair, anxious for the immediate relief of Sumter, stood triumphant. A fortnight earlier a majority of the Cabinet had been against that step; now three out of six were for making the attempt, and the other three were for militant action at other points—action that would mean war. Seward remarked to Montgomery C. Meigs that all men of sense saw that war must come.[40] This, however, may have been either adroit dissimulation or a passing mood of discouragement, for he still clung to the hope that, by hook or crook, he could maintain peace.

Opinion among the sterner Republican leaders was hardening, for they perceived that if mere drift prevailed much longer, pacifism in the North would infect many people. Henry J. Raymond's *Times* had declared ten days earlier that it saw "a growing sentiment throughout the North in favor of

38 Bates, *Diary*, 180. It was Sam Ward who reported Lincoln's depression; letter to Barlow, March 31, 1861, Barlow Papers. Text of Bates's paper in Robert Todd Lincoln Papers; essential excerpts in Nicolay and Hay, III, 429–432.
39 Seward's biographer Bancroft believes that his statement that he now wished to hold Pickens was just a pretense; C. W. Elliott in his *Winfield Scott*, 703 ff., takes the same view.
40 Meigs, MS Diary.

letting the Gulf States go." Thurlow Weed's Albany *Evening Journal* agreed with the *Times* that Lincoln should never adopt a coercive policy without the sanction of a special session of Congress. Even that influential New England organ, the Springfield *Republican,* was reluctant to hold the cotton States by force.[41] Impressed by both the rising intransigence of the Lower South and the vigor of the Northern peace party, and feeling that national salvation or ruin must be put to the test at once, most Republican chieftains were becoming insistent that Lincoln take a resolute stand.

Ben Wade shared the views expressed in Lyman Trumbull's militant resolution. In seven States, he told the Senate, the people were dominated by usurpers. "A military despotism tramples their rights under foot," and they should be rescued at once. Zack Chandler of Michigan spoke with characteristic vehemence. If the Administration did not act to maintain the Union, he would quit the disgraced soil of the United States and join the Comanche Indians. Wigfall of Texas retorted that the Comanches had already suffered too much from contact with the whites, but Chandler was in deadly earnest.[42] Owen Lovejoy was too warmly devoted to Lincoln to use harsh language, but he wrote the President in blunt terms that he must relieve the fort, or—an unconstitutional act—recognize the Confederacy. Greeley was declaring that if Sumter had of necessity to be given up, the nation would be heartsick; but that if the Administration surrendered Pickens as well, it would sink lower than Buchanan's, and America would become a second-rate power. Carl Schurz was writing Lincoln to predict general disheartenment and loss of the fall elections if he did not send reinforcements forward. Bryant of the New York *Evening Post,* Forney of the Philadelphia *Press,* and Medill of the Chicago *Tribune* were demanding a firm stand.[43]

From some quarter a call went out to the stanchest Republican governors to assemble in Washington if they could, and Curtin of Pennsylvania and several others prepared to hurry to the capital.

[VI]

Thus it was that the last act of the drama began; an act which reached its climax in Seward's final desperate effort to seize the rod of authority from Lincoln.

Lincoln was now ready to use Gustavus V. Fox's plan for sending pro-

41 N. Y. *Times,* March 31, April 3; Albany *Evening Journal,* March 23; Springfield *Republican,* March 20–26, 1861.
42 *Congressional Globe,* 36th Cong., 2d Sess., p. 1514 (March 27, 1861); Halsey Wigfall, Washington, March 30, to Louise T. Wigfall, Wigfall Family Papers, Univ. of Texas.
43 N. Y. *Tribune,* March 27, and see the editorial "Come to the Point," April 4, 1861; Springfield *Republican,* April 11, 1861. Lovejoy's and Schurz's letters in the Robert T. Lincoln Papers are typical of a number there.

vision ships to Sumter, with warships behind them in readiness for use. He
asked Fox to write a memorandum on the requirements of the expedition.
In a dozen lines, Fox suggested that the *Pawnee, Pocahontas,* and *Harriet Lane*
be prepared for sea, that a large steamer and three tugs be hired, that three
hundred sailors and two hundred soldiers be ordered ready for service, and
that provisions be collected sufficient for a hundred men during one year.[44]
Approving this scheme, Lincoln on March 29 directed the War and Navy Departments to get the expedition ready to sail by April 6; and although he later
explained to Congress that it was to be withheld or sent forward as circumstances dictated, only some strong evidence that retention would save Virginia
and pave the way to reunion could now alter his decision. That decision
made war almost inevitable. Lincoln gave his order in the deepest agony of
spirit. On March 30 he had a bad sick-headache, and "keeled over," as Mrs.
Lincoln put it, for the first time in years.[45]

Seward also was in profound agony of spirit. Would he have to confess
that Montgomery Blair and the Congressional iron men had worsted him,
that Lincoln had rejected his guidance, and that his dream of replacing the
Republican Party by a Union Party, saving the country, and emerging as the
greatest statesman of the century, had dissolved? He still had faith in appeasement. Was that faith to be quenched in torrents of blood?

The policy Lincoln had thus far pursued needs little explanation. His
inaugural address had been one long plea for patience, forbearance, and the
avoidance of rash action. He had called for "patient confidence in the ultimate
justice of the people," had asked the nation to "remain patient," and had reminded everyone that "nothing valuable can be lost by taking time." He had
given Southerners a solemn pledge: "The government will not assail you, unless you first assail it." He had announced that he would avoid provocative
acts to allow the people "that sense of perfect security which is most favorable to calm thought and reflection." After this, he had to strain patience even
to the point of seeming infirm. But he had made two facts entirely clear. He
would not tolerate secession, "the essence of anarchy," and he would use
the power confided to him to hold the property and places belonging to
the government, and to collect its revenues. He could not fail to provision
Sumter once that was shown possible, or to hold Pickens.

A different judgment must be delivered on Seward's policy. It had one
fine aspect in its humanitarian and idealistic quality. Growing up with the
republic, he had talked with Jefferson, had sat at the feet of John Quincy
Adams, and had labored side by side with Webster, Benton, and Clay. He

44 Nicolay and Hay, III, 433; O. R., I, iv, 227.
45 Message of July 4, 1861; Nicolay and Hay, III, 434. Sam Ward, writing S. L. M. Barlow
March 31, quoted Mrs. Lincoln on the President's prostration; Barlow Papers. All witnesses
testify that the double strain of the crisis and the office-seekers had worn him to exhaustion.

cherished the lofty vision of a Union of fraternal concord, and had written that image into the single eloquent passage of Lincoln's inaugural. But his course had a base aspect in its devious duplicity. Ever since March 4 he had been partially deceiving Lincoln on one side, and the Southern commissioners (themselves brazen deceivers) on the other. He had been using the aged Scott as a tool; Scott's memoranda on the heavy forces needed to coerce the South, on the impossibility of reinforcing Sumter, and on the desperate plight of Pickens, precisely fitted Seward's policy. He continued to stand in a most equivocal position in relation to the Southern commissioners, and as late as April 7 sent Judge Campbell a message: "Faith as to Sumter fully kept. Wait and see." [46]

Once Lincoln determined to send a relief expedition to Sumter, Seward saw that he must change his strategy. To maintain an ascendancy over the President, he would have to move boldly and fast. On April 1, Greeley's *Tribune* blazed with headlines: "Fort Sumter to be Reinforced. Views in Favor of It. A Peaceful Movement. The Attack Left to the South." The dispatch below, dated from Washington March 31, stated that heavy pressure had been brought to bear for holding Sumter at all hazards; that Northwestern members of Congress (this meant Trumbull, Lovejoy, Elihu Washburne, Zack Chandler, Ben Wade, and others) were specially urgent; that feeling in the Cabinet had changed; and that several naval officers were now confident that steamships could run the Charleston batteries. This was so correct that the correspondent obviously had some inside informant. Next day the Confederate commissioners telegraphed Toombs in Montgomery: "The war wing presses on the President; he vibrates to that side." Secretary of War Walker at once telegraphed Beauregard in Charleston to treat the Sumter garrison as a force with which he might at any moment be in conflict.[47] In Virginia secession feeling had hardened; the cord with the Union was ready to snap at any moment.[48]

46 See Bancroft, *Seward*, II, 123 ff.; Gideon Welles, *Lincoln and Seward*, 59, 60; Elliott, *Scott*, 70 ff. Seward on April 1 talked with Campbell, and wrote out for him an explicit assurance: "I am satisfied that the Government will not undertake to supply Fort Sumter without giving notice to Governor Pickens." This of course alarmed Campbell, who asked if Lincoln had undertaken to supply Sumter—as he had. "No, I think not," replied Seward. "It is a very irksome thing for him to surrender it. His ears are open to everyone, and they fill his head with schemes for supply. I do not think he will adopt any of them. There is no design to reinforce it." So Campbell some years after the event remembered Seward's words. If his report is accurate, Seward was counting on Lincoln's retreat, or was self-deceived, or to cloak his own defeat was deceiving Campbell. See Campbell's MS "Facts of History," Crawford Papers, LC. Blair believed that Seward was capable of any trickery. "Nobody," he wrote, "has ever long associated with him who had not heard him recount by the hour his successful political strategy." Welles, *Lincoln and Seward*, 68.

47 O. R., I, i, 284–286.

48 On April 6 the Richmond correspondent of the N. Y. *Herald* wrote: "The revolution is daily gathering strength." He added that Unionists in the State convention were anxious to adjourn before the tide swept it into disunion.

Sumter, according to Fox, could hold out only till mid-April. Seward had but a few days in which to retrieve the situation. His acts bore the stamp of almost insane desperation.

First, he attempted to substitute for the relief of Sumter, which meant war, a diversionary expedition to Fort Pickens. On the afternoon of March 29 he took to the White House his friend Montgomery C. Meigs, widely known as the West Point engineer who had built the Rock Creek aqueduct and was in charge of the Capitol wings and dome. On the way he explained that he wished to hold Pickens and the Texas ports, letting the conflict begin there if the Confederates chose. Lincoln asked if the Pensacola fort could be held. "Certainly," replied Meigs, "if the navy does its duty." The upshot, after Meigs had prepared and submitted a detailed plan, was that Lincoln told him to take it to Scott at once: "Tell him that I wish this thing done, and not to let it fail unless he can show that I have refused him something he asked for as necessary." And Scott, stiffening his tall frame, quoted Frederick the Great: " 'When the king commands, all things are possible.' " [49]

Thus was authorized a movement that Seward hoped might become a substitute for the Sumter effort, and so gain delay. He and Meigs drove rapidly ahead with their plan. They fitted out vessels laden with troops and stores. They put Lieutenant David D. Porter and Colonel Harvey Brown in naval and military command respectively. Needing a warship powerful enough to beat off possible assailants, they fastened upon the one strong ship readily available, the *Powhatan;* and they prepared for Lincoln's signature orders commandeering that vessel, which in the pressure of business he signed without proper inspection.

Seward saw to it that the closest secrecy surrounded the expedition. To nobody on the ships but the commanders, and to nobody in Washington but the President and Seward's close group, was the destination known until the squadron was within sight of the sand dunes of Pensacola. Secretary Welles of the navy was not consulted, and the *Powhatan* was taken from him without his knowledge just as he and Fox were planning to send it to accompany the Sumter relief expedition!

In the second place, Seward made a direct plunge for the powers of the Presidency. That Lincoln was suffering terribly from his multitudinous anxieties, from the unending harassment of patronage hunters, from the conflict between his hatred of bloodshed and his determination to do his duty, was

49 Meigs, MS Diary, LC; Nicolay and Hay, III, 436, 437; Meigs in the *National Intelligencer,* Sept. 16, 1865, replying to G. V. Fox. Scott in January had renewed earlier pleas to Buchanan to be allowed to reinforce Pickens, but nothing effective was done; *Memoirs,* II, 622–624. Lincoln assented because he thought all along that whatever happened at Sumter, reinforcement of Pickens would help assure the country of Administration staunchness. *Collected Works,* IV, 424.

plain to everyone. His prostration by migraine was immediately followed by a most unusual flare of temper. On March 31 a California delegation called to protest against the influence of Senator Edward D. Baker over appointments, and presented a paper severely reflecting on Baker's motives. For a quarter century Lincoln had counted Baker one of his dearest friends; he had named a son for him; he respected his oaken character. Tearing the paper into shreds and flinging it into the fireplace, he dismissed the group with stinging words.[50] The next day Seward chose to hand the overburdened executive what he hoped would be a decisive document, his paper entitled "Some Thoughts for the President's Consideration." He proposed that he should take the helm; what was more, that he should provoke a war with Spain and France.

This memorandum has usually been treated as an inexplicable piece of folly. Seward remonstrated with Lincoln for his supposed lack of policy, domestic or foreign; declared that the central question must be changed from slavery to union versus disunion; stated that he would let Sumter go because it was generally associated with the slavery question; and asserted that he would simultaneously reinforce all the Gulf forts, and put the scattered navy in readiness to blockade the South, for this would bring the issue of union to the front. This part of the memorandum was erratic enough. But the really startling section was Seward's plan for healing national division by precipitating a great foreign conflict:

I would demand explanations from *Spain* and *France*, categorically, at once.
I would seek explanations from Great Britain and Russia, and send agents into ,*Canada*, *Mexico*, and *Central America*, to rouse a vigorous continental *spirit of independence* on this continent against European intervention.
And if satisfactory explanations are not received from Spain and France, Would convene Congress and declare war against them.
But whatever policy we adopt, there must be an energetic prosecution of it.[51]

Seward calmly offered to assume all responsibility, and pursue and direct the new policy incessantly.

The fact was that the Administration possessed a domestic policy, which Lincoln had outlined in his inaugural. It had also a foreign policy, embodied in Seward's own instructions, approved by Lincoln, to our envoys. Moderate but firm, these instructions directed our ministers to assert that the government would never consent to a dissolution of the Union; that the United States was determined and able to maintain its integrity; that it wanted no help, and would brook no interference. Our envoys were told never to discuss

50 This scene is described by the Washington correspondent of the N. Y. *Tribune*, April 1, 1861.
51 Text in Nicolay and Hay, IV, Ch. I.

the merits of the quarrel between North and South as if they admitted of argument. They were to emphasize the commercial advantages of a preservation of the Union. They were also to use language of generous forbearance in speaking of the South; and they were to declare that if war came, it would be by the act not of Washington, but of its armed, open, and irreconcilable enemies.[52]

Seward's plan was foolish indeed, but it was not such incomprehensible folly as has always been supposed. The usual explanation is that he thought merely of the unifying effect of a foreign war. He did, of course, think partly of this. He knew that chauvinism is always latent in every nation, that American editors and politicians always got a ready response to anti-Spanish, anti-French, and anti-British utterances, and that Douglas, Cass, and others had often given reckless vent to xenophobia. In a speech at the New England Society dinner in New York the previous December, Seward himself had been cheered for boasting that if a foreign foe attacked the metropolis, "all the hills of South Carolina would pour forth their populations to the rescue." [53] But Seward's plan was more subtle in nature than a mere effort to merge the sectional conflict in intercontinental conflict.[54]

The key to his scheme is found in reports by the British minister, Lord Lyons, of various conversations with the Secretary; and its essence lay not in the idea that South Carolinians would leap to defend New York, but in the idea that they would strongly object to seeing New York conquer Cuba without their help. It was war with Spain that Seward had primarily in mind, and this because he knew that powerful Southern forces had long desired just such a war. He never thought of embroiling America with Great Britain. That would be far too doubtful a contest. But he did believe that the United States could easily defeat Spain, which had just invaded Santo Domingo, and that in defeating her could swiftly overrun Cuba and Puerto Rico.

The moment Washington opened war on Spain, Seward believed, the cotton States would tremble lest Cuba become free soil—either as an independent republic, or a State of the Union. That, indeed, had long been a bugbear of the Lower South. To avert such a calamity, he hoped that Southerners would join the attack. If the Confederacy did not forego its independence to share in the new conquest, then the United States would at least gain a great island base for operating against the Confederates, and for closing the Gulf. It would also

52   See instructions to C. F. Adams, *Diplomatic Correspondence, 1861*, p. 59.
53   Seward, *Works*, IV, 649.
54   This is the view of Seward's motivation stated, for example, by Nicolay and Hay, by Rhodes, and by Bancroft in his *Seward*, II, 134–137. But these writers had not studied Lyons' dispatches in the British Foreign Office. Seward was far too much of a Talleyrand to be actuated by simple motives.

gain other advantages: The ending of the slave trade to Cuba, a closer relationship with Great Britain, which had long tried to destroy that monstrous traffic, and the enhanced respect of other nations. If France entered the war, the United States would also seize the French islands.

Seward disclosed these views in a number of confidential talks with Lord Lyons this spring. In one conversation he suggested that America and Britain should sign a convention for suppressing the Cuban slave trade and guaranteeing the independence of Santo Domingo. He expatiated at the same time upon the readiness of the United States to defy Spain, and upon the fruits she might win from a Spanish war. "For his own part," he said, "he should have no objection to make an anti-African-Slave Trade demonstration against Spain; if she were rash enough to provoke it. Such a demonstration might have a good effect upon the Southern States. These States had always held that the maintenance of slavery in Cuba was essential to their own safety. It might not be a bad lesson to them to see how much they had put at hazard by attempting to withdraw from the protection of the United States." [55]

That Lincoln was thunderstruck by Seward's cool proposal that he should divest himself of his constitutional functions, delegate the Presidential authority to another, bury in oblivion the great freesoil victory, and arbitrarily thrust the nation into war with a European power—perhaps two powers—need not be said. His management of the situation offered a signal proof of his statesmanship. That same day he wrote a short reply characterized by tact, common sense, and firmness, which annihilated Seward's proposals, but left Seward unharmed. He knew, of course, that not a word of the matter must reach the public. This reply remained in Lincoln's papers. Perhaps it was shown to Seward; perhaps Lincoln, with characteristic magnanimity, decided that it would be kindlier to transmit its substance orally. Not until a quarter century had elapsed did Lincoln's secretaries give the world its first knowledge of the incident. [56]

The President pointed out that in his inaugural address he had defined his domestic policy—he would "hold, occupy, and possess the property and places belonging to the government" and would collect the duties and imposts—and that he still maintained that policy. Seward had approved it, but Seward now proposed to abandon Sumter. As for external affairs, he and Seward had been preparing circulars and instructions to ministers in perfect harmony "without even a suggestion that we had no foreign policy." Upon Seward's closing proposition that whatever policy was adopted must be energetically prosecuted,

55 British Foreign Office Papers (hereafter cited F. O.), 4/1137, Lyons, May 11, 1861, to Lord John Russell.
56 See Roy P. Basler, ed., Collected Works of Abraham Lincoln, IV, 316–318.

and either the President must do this himself or devolve the responsibility on some member of his Cabinet, Lincoln commented: "I remark that if this must be done, I must do it. When a general line of policy is adopted, I apprehend there is no danger of its being changed without good reason, or continuing to be a subject of unnecessary debate; still, upon points arising in its progress, I wish, and suppose I am entitled to have the advice of all the cabinet."

From that hour the question who should lead the nation was decisively answered.

Seward, still hoping that the Sumter expedition might be held back while the Pickens relief squadron went forward, had a third card to play—a weak and dubious card. On April 2 or 3 he asked Allan B. Magruder, a Virginia Whig practicing law in Washington, to accompany him to the White House, where Lincoln was expecting their call. The President requested Magruder to hurry to Richmond, and bring G. W. Summers, a Union leader in the Virginia Convention, to Washington. It was common knowledge that Virginia now teetered on the edge of secession, and some believed that public sentiment might force the convention to declare for it at any moment. As Virginia acted, so would North Carolina, Tennessee, and perhaps Kentucky. If they all seceded, the Confederacy would become highly formidable. Seward hoped that using an influential intermediary, the Administration might arrange a last-minute bargain, agreeing to let Sumter go if Virginia would stay in the Union. On the way back from the White House, the Secretary still expressed confidence that the troubles would blow over without war, and the Union be saved! Magruder hurried off, and on April 4 he returned, not with Summers, but with another Virginia Unionist, Colonel John B. Baldwin.

Of the ensuing conference between Lincoln and Baldwin we have no first-hand account. We possess only Magruder's confused statement of what Baldwin told him, published fourteen years later. From this narrative it appears that Lincoln was in great agony of spirit, but that at no point did he offer to evacuate Sumter, and that he regarded the die as cast in favor of its relief. His first words were, "Mr. Baldwin, I am afraid you have come too late." And when Baldwin begged him to issue a proclamation waiving the right to hold Sumter and Pickens, and calling a national convention, Lincoln looked at him with manifest disapproval. "Sir," he said, "that is impossible." [57]

57 No episode of the time is murkier than this interview arranged by Seward. Magruder's "A Piece of Secret History," *Atlantic*, vol. 35 (April, 1875), 438–445, is hazy and obviously inaccurate. The subject is again hazily treated in several letters by George Plummer Smith to John Hay, Jan. 7, 9, 20, 1863, in the Robert Todd Lincoln Papers. John Minor Botts in *The Great Rebellion* briefly mentions it. Baldwin made no proposal to the convention. In 1866 he published a pamphlet on the interview (Staunton, Va.) which categorically asserts that Lincoln made no offer, and said repeatedly, "I am afraid you have come too late." Cf. W. L. Hall, "Lincoln's Interview with John B. Baldwin," *South Atlantic Quarterly* (1914), XIII, 260–269.

[VII]

It was indeed too late. Both sections by this date believed that war was at hand. On April 4 Lincoln received a letter written by Major Anderson on the first saying that by sharp economy he could make his rations last about a week longer. Startled, the President bade Secretary Cameron order Anderson to hold out until the 11th or 12th, and tell him that the relief expedition would go forward. On the 6th the *Powhatan* sailed from New York for Fort Pickens, precipitating an acrid quarrel between Seward and Welles. The Secretary of the Navy, justly incensed that Seward should have taken his most effective warship and crippled the Sumter expedition without even notifying him, never ceased to believe that his colleague was a double-dealer—particularly as Seward so bungled Lincoln's order transferring the *Powhatan* to the Sumter force that it went to Pensacola after all! [58] On the 6th, Lincoln started a State Department clerk to Charleston to notify the governor of South Carolina, in very placatory terms, that the government would attempt to supply Fort Sumter with provisions only. He also sent an army lieutenant with word that if South Carolina did not resist the provisioning, the United States would not attempt to throw in unannounced arms or ammunition.

And at last the Sumter expedition got off. The little *Harriet Lane* sailed April 8; the transport *Baltic*, with Captain Gustavus V. Fox, troops, and stores, went off with two tugs on the 9th; and the *Pocahontas* on the 10th. This limping, scattered exit was appropriate to an expedition which had been tardily planned, weakly organized, poorly equipped, and belatedly dispatched. But at any rate, it was on its way. [59]

The country waited tensely. A number of Northern governors who had

58 He signed the order "Seward" instead of "Lincoln," and Captain Mercer could not obey it. Welles tells the story in his *Lincoln and Seward*, 54 ff., with graphic detail and strong feeling. He also penned a sixteen page narrative, undated, which is partially quoted in *The Collector* (Walter R. Benjamin), LXIX, No. 4 (April, 1956). Orders and letters concerning the Sumter and Pickens expeditions will be found in O. R., I, i, where Meigs's statements are particularly useful.

An interesting adventure story is connected with the Pickens expedition. When Welles on April 6 received word that Captain Adams had not obeyed orders to reinforce Pickens, a piece of news which took him and Lincoln aback, he summoned Lieutenant John L. Worden. It was just before midnight. Welles gave the young man secret dispatches to be carried to Adams. Donning civilian garb, Worden set off at once. On the way to Atlanta he found his car filled with Southern troops, and fearing he might be searched, memorized the dispatch and destroyed it. It was nearly midnight on April 10 when he reached Pensacola. He had to obtain a pass to reach Captain Adams from General Braxton Bragg. Later Bragg said he got the pass only by asserting that he had an oral message of a peaceful nature; Worden denied making any such statement. At noon on the 12th the young man reached Adams. That night Pickens was reinforced by 470 soldiers, marines, and a few days later, a further reinforcement of about 600 men was added. With a garrison of 1100 and provisions for six months, Pickens was safe. See the Worden Papers, Lincoln Memorial University. Harrogate, Tenn.

59 O. R., I, i, 230–236, 245, 291.

met in Washington to reinforce the Senators and Representatives demanding action, and to counteract Seward, waited. The stock market waited. Thurlow Weed and Samuel Blatchford, on what they thought inside information, sold out their shares and waited. A fog of secrecy closed in upon government offices. All the departments, by strict Presidential order, debarred reporters. Seward directed that any clerk who admitted a stranger to his room without express permission should be dismissed. New York correspondents told Sam Ward that the Cabinet was as impenetrable as the Venetian Council of Ten: "The oldest rats and foxes can glean nothing." [60]

By the 12th the little fleet should be off the Charleston bar. Lincoln knew that any moment thereafter the telegraph might bring news of war.

60 S. W. Crawford, *Genesis,* 416, 417; Sam Ward to S. L. M. Barlow, April 6, 10, Barlow Papers.

4

The North Lurches to Arms

NEWS THAT an expedition had started for Sumter fell upon Charleston like a tensely awaited tocsin. The first word came by irregular channels. Seward, who had kept the expedition to Pickens secret even from Welles and Cameron, the two Secretaries most concerned, divulged the Sumter plans to a newspaper correspondent and friend, James E. Harvey, whom he had just nominated as Minister to Portugal. Harvey, a native of South Carolina, at once telegraphed Charleston: "Positively determined not to withdraw Anderson. Supplies go immediately, supported by naval force if their landing be resisted. A Friend." [1] Then on Monday night, April 8, Lincoln's two messengers reached the city with their official notification. One of them, learning that the Confederacy would allow no provisioning of Sumter, at eleven in the evening started back for Washington. An hour later, amid a heavy rainstorm, seven guns from Citadel Square gave the signal for an immediate muster of all reserves. Hundreds of men sprang to arms; the home guard clattered through the wet streets arousing laggards; and all night the long roll kept citizens awake. By dawn 3,000 men had been called to the colors, and telegrams were summoning 4,000 more from the interior.

It was now necessary for Montgomery to make *its* momentous decision. What Davis would do could hardly be doubted. To be sure, no military reason whatever existed for an attack on Sumter. The victualing of the fort might reasonably be regarded as a mere maintenance of the status quo. But as dominant Northern sentiment made it necessary for Lincoln to try to maintain the post, so dominant Confederate sentiment necessitated its reduction. Any retreat might dangerously encourage Southern Unionism.

---

1 Seward's act was susceptible of being read either as impulsive folly or double-dealing. Why tell a South Carolinian? Montgomery Blair always believed this was another move to wreck the Sumter expedition. The dispatch, he pointed out, was sent the very day that Lincoln ordered the expedition; it was sent by Seward's intimate friend; and when Senators tried to have Harvey removed from his diplomatic post, Seward prevented them. Letter to S. L. M. Barlow, 1865, no day, Barlow Papers. See O. R., I, i, 187, for the telegrams; Nicolay and Hay, IV, 32, for Seward's lame explanation.

When Beauregard telegraphed the message from Lincoln, Secretary of War Walker at once notified President Davis. The Cabinet, hastily summoned the morning of the 9th, realized the gravity of the issue. They deliberated long and earnestly. Walker, the Secretary of War, an Alabamian who was well aware of his section's unreadiness for conflict, was reluctant to move.[2] Toombs was still more averse, for he predicted that an attack would open a bloody civil war, and he could not take the responsibility of advising it. As they talked he grew more decided. "Mr. President," he pleaded, "at this time it is suicide, murder, and will lose us every friend at the North. You will wantonly strike a hornet's nest which extends from mountain to ocean, and legions now quiet will swarm out and sting us to death. It is unnecessary; it puts us in the wrong; it is fatal."[3] But others took a different view. Judah P. Benjamin had committed himself to an assault. So had C. G. Memminger, the head of the Treasury. Senator Jere Clemens of Alabama said later that he heard J. G. Gilchrist, an Alabama leader, address Walker in impassioned terms: "Sir, unless you sprinkle blood in the face of the people of Alabama, they will be back in the old Union in less than ten days!"[4]

The strong current of radical Southern feeling carried Davis along with it. A host of men in the cotton States were impatient for a blow. From Austin to Beaufort, they were angered by the failure of the Confederate commissioners to obtain any Northern concessions. "These men," stormed the Savannah *Republican*, "should require to know within five days whether the forts on our soil, and justly belonging to us, are to be given up, or whether we shall be compelled to take them by force of arms." Already Georgia troops had left for Pensacola in readiness to attack Fort Pickens. South Carolina could hardly be restrained any longer. Davis feared that the peppery little State would act for itself, with resultant confusion, and he knew that most people of the Lower South would regard further delay as cowardice. Representative David Clopton of Alabama had expressed their view weeks before: "The argument is exhausted, further remonstrance is dishonorable, hesitation is dangerous, delay is submission, 'to your tents, O Israel!' and let the God of battles decide the issue."[5]

The Cabinet decided to strike for a multiplicity of reasons: A desire to bring the hesitant borderland, Virginia at its head, into the Confederacy without more ado; a hope that the North would offer more bluster than fight;

2 So L. P. Walker wrote S. W. Crawford, *Genesis*, 421.
3 Stovall, *Toombs*, 226; U. B. Phillips in his life of Toombs accepts this statement.
4 Jeremiah Clemens in a speech at Huntsville, Alabama, March 13, 1864, reported in N. Y. *Tribune*, March 24.
5 Savannah *Republican* quoted in Charleston correspondence, April 2, N. Y. *Tribune*, April 5, 1861; Clopton to C. C. Clay, Jr., Dec. 13, 1860, Clay Papers, Duke Univ.

a conviction that Britain and France must soon recognize the nation on which they depended for cotton. But above all, Southern nationalism impelled the government. The idea that a Federal fort should be maintained in one of the principal ports of the Confederacy seemed intolerable, while the desire to display Southern prowess in arms had grown irrepressible. On the 10th, Secretary Walker notified Beauregard that he should at once demand the evacuation of Sumter, and if it were refused, proceed to compel its surrender.

A bare chance of prolonging peace yet remained. The following afternoon, Beauregard sent three aides to demand Anderson's surrender. The major, in handing them a written refusal, remarked: "Gentlemen, if you do not batter the fort to pieces about us, we shall be starved out in a few days." [6] Actually, with stern belt-tightening, he could have subsisted on his dry stores longer.

This statement Beauregard naturally deemed so important that he telegraphed it to Montgomery. President Davis and Secretary Walker conferred. Walker then replied that the government did not wish to bombard Sumter needlessly. If Anderson would state a time for his evacuation, and would promise meanwhile to fire no gun without provocation, "you are authorized thus to avoid the effusion of blood. If this or its equivalent be refused, reduce the fort as your judgment decides to be most practicable."

Four men—James Chesnut, a former South Carolina Senator and wealthy plantation owner who had said that commerce, culture, and Christianity derived their "chief earthly impulse" from slavery, Roger A. Pryor, the fiery Virginia lawyer, duelist, and secessionist, and two aides—took the proposal to Anderson just after midnight on the night of April 11–12. After a long conference with his officers, he offered to evacuate Sumter by noon of the 15th, engaging meanwhile not to open fire unless he received orders from his government or additional supplies.[7] He thus went as far as he could to meet Walker's demands. Actually, Anderson, a Kentuckian, believed that Sumter ought to be given up for both political and military reasons. He did not wish to be relieved or reinforced, and he disapproved of the relief expedition.[8]

But Chesnut, Pryor, and the two aides, reading his answer on the spot, decided that his proviso, which left him free to use his guns to cooperate with a relief force trying to enter the harbor, was unacceptable. Rejecting the terms, they informed Anderson that their batteries would open in an hour. In this

6 O. R. I, i, 301.
7 O. R. I, i, 14; Crawford *Genesis*, 422-426.
8 See his letter of April 8, 1861, O. R. I, i, 284. Anderson was married to a Georgian, and though by conviction he was a Unionist, he had a natural sympathy with the South. His disapproval was partly founded on his belief that the expedition must fail disastrously. Then, too, he felt very bitter about being left sitting on so exposed a limb. Among his many letters, published and unpublished, that of April 8, 1861, to Lorenzo Thomas, O. R. I, i, is specially interesting

they took upon themselves a tremendous responsibility. They might have telegraphed Walker again, and could have had Davis' reply in a few hours. A wait would have cost nothing. The victualing expedition would in any event have been a failure, for without the *Powhatan* it lacked sufficient strength to provision the fort against Confederate opposition.[9] But the four had color of authority to act, and were impatient. Pryor two days earlier had told a crowd that he knew the way to put Virginia into the Confederacy in less than an hour by Shrewsbury clock: "Strike a blow!"

On the day just ended, April 11, both North and South seemed to know that war was but a few hours away. In Montgomery the War Department was swamped with applications from regiments, battalions, and companies for active service. In Washington the swearing in of volunteer militiamen, begun the previous day, was continued, and sentries were stationed on all roads leading into the city. By nightfall the capital was garrisoned by about 500 regulars and 700 militia. The Confederate commissioners departed, first sending Seward a letter in which they charged that the Administration had grossly deceived them.[10]

Charleston that day had been full of rumors—a false report that the Federal fleet was just off the bar; a true report that the *Harriet Lane* had been sighted; reports that Anderson would and would not surrender. With business suspended, thousands flocked to the waterfront. Occasional armed patrols swirled up and down the streets. At nightfall a bombardment was reported imminent. Some people congregated before the two newspaper offices, while others climbed to the housetops. Trains poured new spectators into the city, who hurried to the Battery. Signal lights burned and flashed in the harbor, where the sea was calm under bright stars. Soon after midnight a speck-like boat moved toward Sumter; men waited while St. Michael's intoned two, then three; four came, and the speck moved away from the fort.

Then, at four-thirty, as the east began to pale, the dull boom of a mortar came from Fort Johnson, and a moment later a shell burst just over Sumter. It was a signal shot. A brief pause ensued. Then other guns announced that war had begun; among them, the columbiad of the iron battery on Morris Island was fired by that exultant secessionist, Edmund Ruffin of Virginia.

9 Admiral Porter later asserted that as the Charleston bar had only thirteen feet of water and the *Powhatan* drew twenty-one, she could not have crossed it, or have gotten within five miles of the Confederate guns. "Statement" in Crawford Papers, LC.

10 One of the gloomiest Washington observers was E. M. Stanton, lately of Buchanan's Cabinet. On April 10 he commented caustically that the Administration was "panic-stricken." On the 11th he reported a general distrust of the sincerity of Lincoln and the Cabinet, and a sharp diminution of loyalty within the city. But Stanton was always morose and censorious. Curtis, *Buchanan*, II, 538–542.

[I]

Looking backward, we can now see that a conflict between North and South had been certain when Lincoln was inaugurated. Nothing the government might legitimately have done could have averted it. The seven States of the cotton kingdom were determined to erect a separate republic; the United States was determined to maintain the Union. At some point and some moment battle was certain. It would have taken place at Pickens if not at Sumter, in Texas if not at Pickens, or on the banks of the Mississippi if not in Texas. The powerful groups which had carried secession through would never turn back; no government in Washington worthy of the name could assent to the disruption of the nation.

The point at which the Civil War could possibly have been averted lay much further back. If the plan of Yancey, Rhett, and others to divide the Democratic Party at Charleston had been defeated, as with more Southern wisdom it could have been, Union men might well have controlled the situation in that party and the South. If the timid, irresolute Buchanan had acted at once after South Carolina's secession to call a national convention, a remedy for Southern disaffection might have been devised. But by March 4 war could no more be prevented than the Niagara River could be halted on the brink.[11]

Nevertheless, the conduct of affairs both North and South between March 4 and April 14 furnished a spectacle as painful as it was confusing.

In Washington, what situation could have been more anomalous than that of a President moving in one direction, and his chief Cabinet officer moving in another, while Congress and subordinate leaders groped in the dark? It is impossible to acquit Lincoln of great clumsiness. His central policy was sound: he would hold all the national forts and places he *could* hold, and let the South make war if it attacked them. But he groped his way, failing to act incisively. He should have ascertained more rapidly the exact length of time Sumter could hold out, the precise temper of Montgomery, and the true possibilities of

---

11 A careful sociologist studying the origins of war in general states that the pattern rarely shows a spiral movement of public opinion that gets out of control and ends in a stampede. Instead, it shows that groups representing some special or political interest lay their plans for war well in advance. These men coolly weigh their chances—their ability to arouse sectional or national sentiment in favor of some "cause," their economic potential, their relative military strength. The decision to make war is in most instances reached months or even years before the first shots. Thus the Samuel Adams-James Otis group long planned the Revolution; the European coalition began in 1792; the Austrian ultimatum to Serbia was planned in March, 1909; Mussolini set the dateline for the Ethiopian war a good two years in advance; Hitler long planned the attack on Poland. The Civil War conforms to this pattern. Yancey and others planned to sunder the Democracy, "fire the Southern heart," and precipitate secession. *Cf.* Theodore Abel, "The Element of Decision in the Pattern of War," *American Sociological Review*, Vol. 6 (December, 1941), 853-9.

victualing Sumter. Instead, showing too little personal initiative, he left it to Seward and Scott to tell him how long Sumter could stand without reinforcement. He left it to Montgomery Blair and Gustavus V. Fox to find out that a possibility of reinforcing it did exist. He left the real intentions of the Southern leaders and people to guesswork.

Moreover, Lincoln as yet gave his associates no sense of authentic and alert leadership. Most Cabinet members thought that he was concerting measures with Seward. Yet on April 1, Seward was convinced that no policy existed and that Lincoln was incapable of formulating one. Montgomery Blair in the opposite faction decided that Lincoln had no backbone, no principle, no policy but a mistaken readiness to yield, and he called in his father to turn the balance. Winfield Scott thought Lincoln weak, or he would never have proposed to abandon Pickens. Judge Campbell believed leadership totally wanting. "The tone of the [inaugural] message will be followed," he wrote, "and its recommendations will be allowed to slide, as are the expressions common to that class of thieves known as politicians." [12] Charles Francis Adams, visiting Washington March 28, got from Seward an alarming picture of the President: "No system, no relative ideas, no conception of his situation—much absorption in the details of office dispensation, but little application to great ideas. The Cabinet without unity, and without confidence in the head or each other." Adams' call on Lincoln confirmed this image: ". . . the course of the President is drifting the country into war, by its want of decision. . . . The man is not equal to the hour." [13]

As for Seward, his conduct was highly exasperating. He could not shake off the delusion that he was to be prime minister and show the rough railsplitter how to act. Worse still, he totally miscalculated the national situation. He thought that if peace were kept at any price, the South would drift back. Instead, every day these seven States, with a domain stretching from Charleston to Corpus Christi and from New Orleans to Atlanta, with important economic groups anxious for all the low-tariff gains they could seize, with politicians hungry for Confederate office, with poets, editors, lawyers, ministers, physicians, and others ardently nursing the idea of Southern independence, with a rising generation proud of Dixie virtues and scornful of Yankee vices, would drift further away. Once fully established, such political separations—like those of Southern Ireland from Britain, Norway from Sweden, Pakistan from

12 Campbell's first notes on Lincoln are severe. The inaugural he called a mere stump speech. "It is wanting in statesmanship—of which he has none—and dignity and decorum. I should call it an incendiary message, one calculated to set the country in a blaze. He is a conceited man—evidently he has been a great man in Springfield, Illinois." To his mother, March 6, 1861, Campbell Papers, Alabama State Archives.

13 Adams, MS Diary, March 28, March 31, 1861.

India—have a way of making themselves permanent. Too much pride, too many selfish interests, too fervent a loyalty, crystallize within the new boundaries.[14] Montgomery Blair was more straightforward than Seward, but he equally miscalculated the situation. He thought that a few hard blows at the the Confederate oligarchs would move the Southern people to overthrow their government and come back into the fold. He totally misconceived the inevitable Southern response to blows.

The Confederacy showed an equal lack of wisdom. Still more unfortunately, its leaders showed little indeed of the tormented shrinking from war that was to be found in Washington.

The firing on Sumter was an act of rash emotionalism. What would it really matter if it remained for months in Northern hands? It offered neither impediment nor threat to the Confederacy. Let it alone, and although at some point the North could certainly have fought to maintain the Union, a period of Northern inaction was not only possible but probable. Given Seward's belief in waiting, and Lincoln's vast patience and forbearance, a protracted pause might have ensued, during which the Confederacy could have exported cotton, imported arms and munitions, stocked defense plants with machinery, and drilled troops. The astute Alexander H. Stephens, counseling delay, showed more statesmanship than Jefferson Davis. Indeed, Davis might well have recalled that in January he had written Governor Pickens to leave Sumter alone: "The little garrison in its present position presses on nothing but a point of pride."

But the callousness evinced in Montgomery's rush into battle is especially discreditable. In Washington the debating, the hesitations, and the agony of the leaders, at least point to an underlying sense of the awful responsibilities of the hour. In the end the government gave Charleston courteous notice that it was sending supplies to a famished garrison, protested its pacific temper, and declared that it would not fire until fired on. In Montgomery, however, the debate was brief and hasty; neither Davis, great gentleman though he was, nor any associate showed real agony of spirit; and the final decision put it in the power of Beauregard, living in "an ecstasy of glory and rhetoric," [15] and two impetuous aides to start the bloodiest war of the century.

The one bright element in the history of these six dark weeks is the complete integrity of purpose exhibited by Lincoln. Adhering to his oath, he never wavered in his determination to hold Pickens. He wavered on Sumter only

14 Even restricted to seven States, the Confederacy would have had an area of 560,000 square miles, a population of 5,000,000, and resources far excelling those of most nations of the globe. Arkansas seemed likely to join in any event, adding some 53,000 square miles and 435,000 people.
15 T. Harry Williams, *Beauregard*, 50.

when the highest military authority told him it could not be held, and reverted to his determination when other authorities reassured him. He did not for a moment share Seward's delusion that appeasement would solve the problem, or Montgomery Blair's delusion that the Southern people were not really behind their leaders; he saw the realities. That he lacked vigor, foresight, and organizing capacity is all too clear. He did not clearly understand the currents of opinion in the South. But his honesty of intention was plain. A humane, kindly man, he felt the greatest distress over the impending bloodshed. A patriot who had devoted his best thought to the Constitution, laws, writings, and traditions handed down by the architects of the republic, he grieved over the demolition of the harmonious structure they had built. He wrestled with himself in the sleepless hours recorded by his secretaries. But his purposes were always elevated, and when war came he could feel that he had but performed his sworn duty.

In your hands, not mine, he had told Southerners, lies the issue of peace or war. The shells that burst over a Federal fort, awaiting a victualing expedition which had orders not to fire unless it was fired upon, gave the answer to that statement.[16]

[II]

The thunderclap of Sumter produced a startling crystallization of Northern sentiment. Apathy had seemed in the air. The timidities of Buchanan, the futilities of the Peace Convention, the later alternations of hope and fear, had given rise to a sense of helplessness. But Sumter disclosed the irrevocable determination of the Lower South to divide the nation; Anderson's hoisting of the white flag on the 13th, followed by his evacuation of the fort next day, was a stain upon Northern honor. Anger swept the land. From every side came news of mass meetings, speeches, resolutions, tenders of business support, the

16 The efforts of some Southern historians (C. W. Ramsdell, "Lincoln and Fort Sumter," *Journal of Southern History*, III, 259 ff.; Clement Eaton, *A History of the Southern Confederacy*, Ch. 21) to suggest that Lincoln needlessly brought on the war by trying to provision Sumter may be left to fulfill their presumed purpose of comforting sensitive Southerners. Ramsdell did not explore the question whether Davis needed to attack the Federal fort! Lincoln was required by the Constitution to protect the properties of the United States; he could have been impeached had he failed to do so; he had explicitly pledged himself in his inaugural to do so; and dominant Northern sentiment demanded that he do so. He warned the South in direct terms that he would do so. The proposition that he should have let Sumter go in the hope of ultimate reunion is really a proposition that he should have broken his oath and defied the public will just to take a fearful risk—the risk of division into two and perhaps several jangling, inferior republics. Confederate leaders meanwhile yielded nothing, and promised nothing but defiance. See James G. Randall's decisive refutation of the Ramsdell thesis in *Lincoln the Liberal Statesman*, and in *Lincoln the President*, II, 342–350.

muster of companies and regiments, the determined action of governors and legislatures.

In this eruption of emotion most Northerners took unthinking pride. It seemed a purifying hurricane which swept away all sordid aims. Idealists had been disheartened by the trickeries, bargains, and compromises of the past ten years; by the Ostend Manifesto, the Nebraska Act, the Lecompton swindle, the filibustering, the corruption, and the absorption in moneymaking. Now, they said, the flame of devotion to the principles of Washington, Hamilton, and Marshall was burning brightly again. Even the most timid took courage, even the most partisan became firm nationalists. As mass meetings cheered the Union and Constitution, as churches followed Trinity by flinging the Stars and Stripes from their steeples, and as armories resounded with the tramp and clash of drilling troops, many felt that they had emerged into an effulgent new era. They forgot that excitement was not patriotism. They forgot that an ounce of planning, forethought, and coordination was worth many pounds of passionate demonstration.

The very basis of organization was endangered by the delusion that victory would be quick and cheap. The New York *Commercial Advertiser* spoke of the rebels as a "small minority." Greeley's *Tribune* exulted in the notion that the first week would see 10,000 men in Washington, the second 20,000, the third 40,000. Raymond's *Times* believed the "local commotion" could be quelled "effectually in thirty days." The Philadelphia *Press* also deemed a month sufficient, while the *Public Ledger* seemed to think that a mere proclamation would suffice.[17] In Chicago the *Tribune* declared that the west alone could end the conflict in two or three months. Soldiers, politicians, and ministers all had the optimism that Lowell's Hosea Biglow later ruefully recalled:

> I hoped, las' Spring, jest arter Sumter's shame
> When every flagstaff flapped its tethered flame,
> An' all the people, startled from their doubt,
> Come musterin' to the flag with sech a shout,—
> I hoped to see things settled 'fore this fall,
> The Rebbles licked, Jeff Davis hanged, an' all . . .

One of the few immediate attempts to analyze the uprising was made by the historian Bancroft. While the politicians had been wavering, he believed,

17 *Commercial Advertiser*, April 15; N. Y. *Tribune*, April 17; *Public Ledger*, April 15, etc. *Harper's Weekly* observed (May 4) that men might as well fight as try to do business. "The war has begun and the trade of the year is as thoroughly ruined as it can be. We shall do no mischief by prosecuting the war vigorously. By prosecuting it vigorously we shall secure peace and fair trade next year." An astounding somersault was performed by the *Independent*, which had shared W. L. Garrison's pacifism. Now it praised war as a vital defense of the Constitution, a restorer of national life, and a divine retribution for slavery; but it too expected a short war. May 4, 11, etc.

the people had pondered the situation and had reached four basic conclusions. One was that the populous Northwest could never let the lower course of its great central waterway pass into foreign hands. The second was that dwellers on the upper Chesapeake, its headwaters flowing from New York and Pennsylvania and its principal railroad clasping the West, felt the same jealous anxiety over their communications. As a third consideration, people feared the expansive temper of the Confederacy. It claimed Maryland, Virginia, Washington and the States below, it claimed Missouri, it claimed the best avenues to California, and it claimed the boundary with Mexico—which it would soon invade. So, wrote Bancroft, "I witnessed the sublimest spectacle I ever knew," an irresistible rush to the defense of law, order, and liberty.[18] It is strange that Bancroft said nothing about the passionate attachment of millions to the idea of Union, inculcated by every national leader from Franklin to Webster, and nothing about the fact that the success of the great American experiment in democratic self-government, as an example to the world, depended on maintenance of the Union.

Major Anderson, his officers and men, reached New York April 18 to meet a wild demonstration. Joseph Holt soon reported a talk with him. "He was satisfied," wrote Holt, "that the course pursued had been the means of fixing the eyes of the nation on Sumter, and of awakening to the last degree its anxieties for its fate; so that . . . its fall proved the instrument of arousing the national enthusiasm and loyalty. . . ."[19] This was just what Lincoln meant when he shortly told Orville H. Browning of Illinois that the plan of supplying Sumter had in a sense succeeded: "They attacked Sumter—it fell, and thus, did more service than it otherwise could."[20]

18 M. A. DeWolfe Howe, *Bancroft*, II, 137–138.
19 Anderson came in on the steamer *Baltic;* Holt to Buchanan, May 24, 1861, Curtis, *Buchanan*, II, 550, 551.
20 Browning's report of Lincoln's words, not written down on the spot but recorded later, cannot be regarded as literally accurate. Lincoln said something like this statement; it was a gloss on his careful explanation of his course in his first message to Congress in July; and he meant that although the North failed to hold Sumter, the sudden and unnecessary Southern seizure of it aroused Northern determination. Browning, *Diary*, July 3, 1861. He meant just this when he wrote Gustavus V. Fox on May 1 in similar terms. A really trustworthy report of Lincoln, closer to the event than Browning's, can be found in the letter of Senator Garrett Davis of Kentucky, April 28, 1861, detailing an interview in the White House "early last week." Lincoln was "frank and calm, but decided and firm." He said that he had decided not to try to reinforce the Sumter garrison, "but merely, and only, to supply its handful of famishing men with food," a purpose he had distinctly communicated to the Southern authorities. "The President further said, that events had now reached a point where it must be decided whether our system of federal government was only a league of sovereign and independent States, from which any State could withdraw at pleasure, or whether the Constitution formed a government with strength and powers sufficient to uphold its own authority, and to enforce the execution of the laws of Congress." Frankfort, Ky., *Commonwealth*, May 3, 1861.

[III]

Clear-sighted Americans saw that the whole issue of the war, and with it the position of the United States in the world, depended on the border States. If all of them went out, the Union could not be saved. If even Kentucky and Missouri went out, along with Virginia and Tennessee, Northern victory would be almost impossible. The next few weeks, deciding this question, would decide almost the whole game. Could they be held?

The next six weeks, April 14–June 1, were a period of touch and go. It was touch and go whether Maryland and Baltimore would not fall under the control of secessionists; whether Washington would not be captured and Lincoln and his Cabinet put to flight; whether the Virginia forces which seized Harpers Ferry and Norfolk would not close in on some other important point; whether Kentucky and Missouri would not slip away; whether so many army officers would not resign as to cripple the nation. In facing these contingencies, the Administration paid in dire anxiety for its failure to take some elementary precautions for war. While the South armed itself, Washington had done nothing. True, Seward and Lincoln wished to avoid provocative steps. But would it have been provocative to get a few more regulars into Washington from the West, or to suggest to Governor Curtin that two strong militia regiments be ready at Harrisburg? Fortunate it was that Curtin *had* taken a few simple steps, and that the recently elected governor of Massachusetts, John A. Andrew, had done more. Fortunate it also was that Virginia did not possess a governor as impetuously earnest as Curtin, and as farsightedly efficient as Andrew.

For although Virginia moved, she moved slowly. Her convention on April 17 passed an ordinance of secession subject to popular ratification in May. Word of this "resumption of sovereignty," telegraphed over the North, ended the fatuous predictions that Arkansas alone of the hesitant States would secede. However, declared Greeley's *Tribune*, the rebels might gain little, for Richmond would have to give close attention to the angry Unionists of western Virginia and the restive slaves. Some support was lent this view by the heavy vote against the secession ordinance, 55 to 88, by Governor Letcher's previous unwillingness to leave the Union, and by the convention's tardiness in placing the State in full cooperation with the Confederacy—no alliance being effected until April 25. Vice-President A. H. Stephens, hurrying to Richmond, complained that Virginians were far behind the times and preferred talk to war.[21]

Nevertheless, the position of Washington was serious. Lincoln's proclamation of April 15 asking for 75,000 militia was indignantly rejected by the

21 *Tribune*, April 19, 1861; Johnston and Browne, *Stephens*, 399 (April 25).

governors of Virginia, North Carolina, Kentucky, Tennessee, and Missouri, and given only a conditional response by Maryland and Delaware.[22] It was of course heartily accepted by all the others, and the War Department fixed the State quotas, asking New York for 17 regiments, Pennsylvania 16, Ohio 13, Illinois 6, Massachusetts 2, and so on—each regiment to consist, as nearly as possible, of 780 officers and men. But the militia system at once showed its characteristic state of decay. In some cities it consisted only of amateurish bandbox forces, which had served to hold balls, grace public parades with showy uniforms, and attend inaugurations; in smaller places it mustered an array of rural bumpkins. One of the familiar gems of Congressional humor was a speech by Tom Corwin ridiculing the Kentucky militia "generals" who restored their men after their drill by a treat of watermelons and whiskey at a country store. Now it was necessary to call out volunteers to create new militia regiments. The want of depots of proper arms, clothing, and other equipment was distressing. And how get them to Washington? Could that city be properly garrisoned in time?

While the Charleston batteries still pounded Sumter, the Confederate Secretary of War boasted in a Montgomery speech: "The flag which now flaunts the breeze here will float over the dome of the old Capitol at Washington before the first of May." [23] Various Southern journals predicted that a column from the Lower South, reinforced in North Carolina and Virginia, would seize the Federal District before the North could defend it. Which nation would first mass its troops on the Potomac? Tidewater Virginia seemed to spring to arms overnight. The day of Sumter a New Orleans businessman sent a Yankee friend a threat: Davis had 60,000 troops ready to march, "and all say here that Baltimore, Philadelphia, and New York will be taken within thirty days. . . ." [24] While W. H. Russell reported to the London *Times* from Montgomery that the Confederacy intended to attack and hold Washington, the British minister, Lord Lyons, wrote that the principal fear of the Lincoln Administration was for the city.[25]

When Virginia seceded, the tiny detachments scattered through Washington were strengthened, more troops and cannon were placed at the Long

22   O. R. Series III, i, 67 ff. deals with this militia call. The governors sent their first contingents to the field, under Lincoln's call, organized as brigades and divisions. They therefore took the generals of militia, like Ben Butler, who had more idea of military organization than anyone else at hand.

23   N. Y. *Evening Post*, April 23, 1861.

24   For the brag by Secretary Walker, a fire-eating protege of Yancey, see N. Y. *Evening Post*, April 23, 1861. This paper erroneously reported that Jefferson Davis had reached Richmond to lead an immediate attack on Washington. For the New Orleans letter dated April 11, see N. Y. *Tribune*, April 24.

25   Frederick W. Seward, *Seward 1846–1861*, p. 545; Russell, *My Diary* (London ed., 1863), I, 259, 260.

Bridge, and batteries were posted on strategic hills. New volunteer companies were set to drilling. Two irrepressible gentlemen dangerous chiefly to their own side, Senator James H. Lane of Kansas and Cassius M. Clay of Kentucky, organized companies of their own, Lane bivouacking his men in the East Room of the White House. Veterans of 1812 shakily stumped into line. A home guard of elderly men, fitly called the Silver Grays, was whipped together. All told, the national capital in the first anxious days after Sumter had for its protection one dilapidated fort twelve miles down the Potomac, six companies of regulars, about two hundred marines at the navy yard, two companies of dismounted cavalry, and the flatfooted, flatchested, untrustworthy militia or uniformed volunteers of the District, numbering fifteen companies on April 13 and about twice as many a week later.[26]

Winfield Scott's plan, if the city were attacked by overwhelming force, was to make a citadel of the Treasury Building, with the President and Cabinet in the basement, and all the troops concentrated about Lafayette Square.

The general hoped for the best; when the news of Sumter came, he expected the early arrival of a war steamer to cruise the Potomac, and some artillery from the regular forces in the Northwest. Lincoln imperturbably continued his accustomed round of conferences and other duties, only now and then revealing his deep anxiety—as in an impulsive walk to the arsenal, whose doors stood open unguarded. The general alarm nevertheless continued great. When on April 18 the first little force arrived from the North, five tough-looking companies of Pennsylvania militia whom Curtin, with the aid of a regular officer, Fitz-John Porter, had hurried off, only slight relief was felt. Unfortunately, these men had only thirty-four muskets and no ammunition! But they could be equipped, and they were marched to the Capitol. Word also came that a stronger body of Pennsylvania volunteers was on the Susquehanna opposite Havre de Grace.[27]

[IV]

This was improvisation, but one governor, Andrew of Massachusetts, had really planned. Early in January he had begun to equip all the volunteer com-

---

26 Scott's daily reports to Lincoln, R. T. Lincoln Papers; Margaret Leech, *Reveille*, Ch. 4. John G. Nicolay, sitting in the White House, thought that the District Militia were politically unreliable, and might turn against the government, so that they would all find themselves looking down the muzzles of their own guns. "We were not only surrounded by the enemy, but in the midst of traitors." To his wife, April 26, Nicolay Papers, LC. Winfield Scott had told a Cabinet meeting that he thought Fort Washington could be taken by a bottle of whiskey.

27 Leech, *Reveille*, 65; Nicolay and Hay, IV, 70, 71; W. B. Wilson, *Acts and Actors in the Civil War*, 24 ff.

panies and set them drilling nightly. Before darkness fell on the day of Lincoln's call for troops, colonels of regiments at New Bedford, Quincy, Lowell, and Lynn had orders to muster on Boston Common. April 16th found them parading under the elms, drums beating, flags flying. Next day the governor commissioned Ben Butler as commander of the brigade, and before night all four regiments had departed for the front.[28] The Sixth Massachusetts, 800 strong, went first by rail. Breakfasting next morning at New York hotels, they marched down Broadway, beflagged, crowded, and throbbing, to the Hudson ferry. The band played but a single bar of "Yankee Doodle" before it was drowned out. The roar of cheers, the thrashing handerchiefs and banners, the hot emotion of the densely jammed spectators, made the scene the most impressive that men could remember. But at that moment secessionists in Baltimore were busy arousing mob passion.

Baltimore, the third city of the nation, had half the population of Maryland. More than a third of her great trade was with the South and Southwest. For weeks the Baltimore *Sun* and *Examiner* had been stirring the bitter waters of anti-Northern feeling. "If we are to grow, thrive, and prosper as a manufacturing city," the *Sun* had declared, "our sources of prosperity must be in the South." Ross Winans, who had introduced the eight-wheeled railroad-car system and established in Baltimore the largest railroad machine shops in the country, a man sometimes rated hardly second in wealth to William B. Astor, was helping to finance the secessionist cause. Such merchants as Johns Hopkins and William T. Walters did a huge Southern business. Slave property in the State was valued at sixty to seventy million dollars. The tidewater arm had immemorial ties of blood and sentiment with Virginia. Louis M. McLane, just back from diplomatic service in Mexico, had told a secessionist meeting that he favored confronting any Northern force on the Susquehanna with arms. Most officers of the city government, the mayor excepted, were on the secessionist side, and so were a majority of the legislature, which the loyal but wabbling Governor Thomas H. Hicks refused to call into session. The city was a powder tub ready for a match.[29]

28 Lossing, *Civil War*, I, 401, 402; Schouler, *Massachusetts in the Civil War*, I, 49 ff.
29 Senator Anthony Kennedy told the chamber in 1863 that "in 1860 the trade of the city of Baltimore, according to the report of her chartered Board of Trade, amounted to $168,000,000; $26,000,000 over her great railroad lines to the West, and $100,000,000 directly to the South and Southwest." *Cong. Globe*, 37th Cong., 3d Sess., pp. 1374, 1375. This was an exaggeration. According to the Baltimore correspondent of the N. Y. *Tribune*, March 12, 1861, Pennsylvania, Ohio, and Indiana bought almost two-thirds of the general merchandise sold in Baltimore, the Upper South the other third, and the Lower South but a small amount. But Baltimore, struggling amain with New York and Philadelphia, greatly valued her Southern connections. The influential Severn Teackle Wallis, who had studied law with William Wirt, leaned to the secessionist side and wrote many editorials for the *Examiner*. By the census of 1860 New York and Brooklyn had 1,072,300 people, Philadelphia had 562,500, and Baltimore 212,400.

As the cars of the Sixth Massachusetts rumbled across upper Maryland, Southern sympathizers poured into Monument Square; not a ragged, disorderly rabble, but a well-dressed crowd numbering merchants and lawyers of note. Shortly before noon on the 19th the troop train drew into the President Street station. The men had to be moved across town to the Camden Street station— and the mob was gathering fast. By quick, determined action, the troops might have kept control of the situation, but a series of disastrous errors was made.

One error was that of the mayor, who had sent police to the Camden Street station, a mile from the true danger point. Another was that of the colonel, who should have unloaded his men, formed them in solid column with bayonets fixed, and marched them across town at the double-quick, but who instead kept them in the cars, to be drawn slowly by horses along tracks in Pratt Street. When the mob obstructed the cars, attacked them with paving stones, and tore up the tracks, most of the regiment had to climb down amid a rain of missiles. Somebody fired, and before the melee ended, four infantrymen and a larger number of the mob had been killed and many injured. The city police finally did most to restore order. Although the Sixth reached Washington at five in the afternoon, seven companies of unarmed Pennsylvania volunteers remained at the President Street station until they were sent back to the Susquehanna.[30]

Anti-Northern feeling rose higher than ever in Baltimore. "The excitement and rage of everyone, of all classes, of all shades of opinion," reported the British consul, "was intense. Strong Union men harangued the crowd, declaring they were no longer such, and demanding immediate action."

That day brought news that the little Union garrison at Harpers Ferry had destroyed arms, armory, and arsenal, and retreated across the Potomac to Hagerstown, Maryland. At Norfolk the commandant of the Navy Yard was about to scuttle all but one of the warships there afloat. Baltimore, raging like a hornet's nest, would ambuscade any fresh Federal troops who attempted a passage. Thus hostile forces ringed Washington. When a body of Ohio militia reached Pittsburgh on April 19 on their way to the capital they were suddenly halted by orders from Governor Dennison, who had heard that Cincinnati was about to be attacked. The burning question was whether Maryland and Virginia secessionists, while the entire border rose, would cut off all access to Washington.

During four days, April 19–22, bellicose Marylanders swept both city and State government before them like straw upon a flood. Cowed by the violent

30 For the riot, see G. W. Brown, *Baltimore and the Nineteenth of April, 1861;* Marshal George Kane's report to the police board, *Cong. Globe,* 37th Cong., 1st Sess., 200, 201; Mayor Brown's report, O. R. I, ii, 15–20; N. Y. *Tribune,* May 9, 1861.

ROUTES OF APPROACH
TO WASHINGTON

Southern demonstrations of the 18th and 19th, Governor Hicks gave way. He had thus far stood by the Union, refusing a special session of the legislature, and pledging Lincoln four regiments if they were used only in Maryland and the District of Columbia. But now he told a seething crowd in Monument Square that he would suffer his right arm to be torn from his body before he would raise it to strike a sister State; he telegraphed Lincoln, "Send no more troops here"; and he announced that his main object was to save the State from civil war. Mayor George W. Brown made a concurring declaration that no Maryland boys would fight the sons of other States. The two wrote President John W. Garrett of the Baltimore & Ohio advising him to take all Northern soldiers back into Pennsylvania. Worse still, Hicks, Brown, and Police Marshal George P. Kane agreed in midnight conclave that the best way to avoid a renewal of the fighting between rioters and Union troops would be to destroy the railroad bridges connecting Baltimore with the North. Kane, thinking he had an authorization to do this, sent out gangs which demolished the short Canton bridge just outside the city, the long bridges over Gunpowder and Bush Creeks (arms of the Chesapeake), and two wooden bridges at Cockeysville fifteen miles north of Baltimore.

No step could have done more to isolate Washington. The seat of government was cut off from the loyal States by rail through Baltimore from the night of April 19. Meanwhile, the mob remained dominant in Baltimore throughout April 20–21. It shut the President Street station, forced Unionists to haul down their flags, and patrolled the streets trying to seize Union soldiers.

Kane, espousing the secessionist side, was ready to go to any length. He telegraphed a Maryland Congressman to send out messengers to arouse Virginia and Maryland riflemen and hurry them to Baltimore: "Fresh hordes will be down upon us tomorrow. We will fight them and whip them, or die." On the 21st the wires were cut, and Washington thereafter could send telegrams north only by the precarious Harpers Ferry route.[31]

The reign of terror continued until April 24th. Hundreds of Unionists were driven from Baltimore, and thousands more fled. When Ben Butler arrived in Philadelphia on the 20th with 800 Massachusetts militia, he found the direct route to Washington closed. With instant resourcefulness he took his troops by rail to Chesapeake Bay, put them on a boat, and steamed down to Annapolis. Governor Hicks having the effrontery to protest against this landing on sacred Maryland soil, Butler delivered a spirited rebuke. If necessary, he said, he was ready to treat Maryland as enemy territory; and taking possession of the frigate *Constitution*, so dear to Yankee hearts, he announced that this partially consoled Massachusetts for the loss of her sons.

Meanwhile, Governor Hicks surrendered to the demand for a special session of the secessionist controlled legislature;[32] and hard on Ben Butler's heels the New York Seventh, a crack parade regiment, also had to take the bay route to Annapolis. One of its officers was the gifted Major Theodore Winthrop, who wrote a graphic account of its southward journey. Some 1700 Pennsylvania militia, partly unarmed, had revolted against their detention on the Maryland boundary, and were marching down the empty railroad line toward Cockeysville north of Baltimore. In Washington, Lincoln himself uttered the anguished cry: "Why don't they come? Why don't they come?" Speaking to the Massachusetts soldiers, he said that he didn't believe there was any North; the Seventh Regiment was a myth—"You are the only realities."

In his alarm and indignation, the President immediately after the Baltimore riot summoned Mayor Brown and Governor Hicks. On Sunday morning, April 21st, Brown and three prominent Baltimoreans (Hicks was ill) were ushered into the President's office, where General Scott and the Cabinet joined them. Though Lincoln was anxious to avoid fresh collisions, he made clear the absolute necessity of safe transit for Federal troops. No forces would be used against Maryland, he said, and none for aggression upon the South. But Wash-

31 Kane's story as given in the *Congressional Globe, ut sup.*, is scathingly interpreted there by Representative Francis Thomas, who had no doubt of his disloyalty. He was arrested and long held in confinement. Governor Hicks and Mayor Brown both denied later that they had really intended the destruction of the bridges, and it seems they had given only a limited and partial assent. G. L. P. Radcliffe, *Governor T. H. Hicks and the Civil War,* 54 ff.

32 For Hicks' explanation see the speech he later made as Maryland Senator, *Cong. Globe,* 37th Cong., 3d Sess., 1376, 1377; an enlightening statement on the whole situation.

ington *must* be protected, and since troops could no longer be safely brought up the Potomac, they *must* cross Maryland. General Scott underlined this warning. It was not a question of using Baltimore streets, he said. Regiments might by-pass the city by taking the water route to Annapolis or wagon roads to the Relay House just southwest of Baltimore.[33]

Mayor Brown assured Lincoln that the city authorities would do their utmost to prevent mob interference with the roundabout routes. Lincoln then directed that the Pennsylvania militia at Cockeysville either march around Baltimore to the Relay House, or go back to York and Harrisburg.

It was an extraordinary spectacle, this of the President of the United States and the general of its armies parleying with a mayor and suspending the right of national troops to march through his city to save Washington. When later it became known, it aroused intense indignation in the North.[34] But it reflected the disorganization of the hour: the lack of efficient action to forward troops from New York and Philadelphia; the poor information facilities of the government, which remained ignorant of the fervid Northern rising; above all, the want of antecedent military preparation in Washington. Under the circumstances, Lincoln acted sagaciously. He did not have sufficient military power to risk enforcing a right of transit, and provocative orders might have stirred tens of thousands of wavering Marylanders to join Virginia in attacking the capital.

[V]

Then by April 25 the skies cleared. In Maryland the Unionists rallied. It is true that in Baltimore the secessionists and neutralists remained dominant; the city council appropriated half a million for defending the place, Mayor Brown asked citizens to lend their arms and ammunition, and Southern sympathizers organized companies to repel the Northern "myrmidons."[35] But many eastern Marylanders realized that if Baltimore continued obstructive it would be stormed and perhaps laid in ashes, while western Marylanders were mainly loyal. News arrived that troops were concentrating in Pittsburgh,

---

33 Actually the Overland line from the Northern Central R. R. to the Relay House, the point eight miles southwest of Baltimore where one branch of the Baltimore & Ohio led to Washington, was more difficult than Scott believed. No good common road of less than thirty miles connected the two railroads. President J. Edgar Thomson of the Pennsylvania Central wrote from Philadelphia April 23 that more vigor should be shown in organizing troop movements, that Baltimore should be put under martial law, and that Maryland should be made to feel the weight of national power. O. R., I, ii, 587, 596-597.

34 See N. Y. *Tribune* editorial, May 3, 1861.

35 Radcliffe, *Hicks and the Civil War*, 67.

Head of the Foreign Relations Committee:

SENATOR CHARLES SUMNER

Robert E. Lee

York, Philadelphia, and other cities.[36] Federal units took possession of the railroad from Philadelphia to Perryville on Chesapeake Bay, strengthened the track, brought down new locomotives, arranged for three trains a day, and got three steamboats plying to Annapolis.

"If the route from Annapolis to Washington City is open," J. Edgar Thomson wrote Secretary Cameron April 23, "we have transportation facilities on the Chesapeake equal to the movement of fifteen thousand troops a day to your city, together with any amount of provisions, etc." And the Annapolis–Washington railway *was* open. Ben Butler had found in an Annapolis railroad shed a rusty half-dismantled locomotive, and had asked his men if anybody could repair it. A private stepped forward to reply: "That engine was made in our shop; I guess I can fit her up and run her." Cameron had Vice-President Thomas A. Scott of the Pennsylvania Central take a body of picked railroadmen, including young Andrew Carnegie, to Annapolis to help put the line in order. Annapolis was suddenly full of troops, waiting for the first train.[37]

When Thursday the 25th dawned in Washington the spirits of loyal men had sunk to a low ebb. The city still seemed hemmed in by rebel elements, and Southern sympathizers were exultantly circulating rumors of a Virginia drive. General Scott was getting ready to issue General Orders No. 4, which went out next day: "From the known assemblage near this city of numerous hostile bodies of troops it is evident that an attack upon it may be expected at any moment." The North was trembling for the capital. In Albany, Governor Morgan heard the "most painful reports" of its peril. In Philadelphia all city regiments were detained by a woeful deficiency of guns and ammunition.[38]

Then, at noon, a mighty shout came from the Sixth Massachusetts encamped on Capitol Hill. They had seen a troop train drawing into the station. Citizens began running pell-mell to the scene. As the train stopped a wild burst of cheering was heard even at the Treasury. Under a bright sun, the trim ranks of the Seventh were soon marching up Pennsylvania Avenue, whose sidewalks filled magically. The men kept soldierly step under their unstained banners, and when their band struck up onlookers danced with delight. On they came, past Willard's, past the Treasury, through the White House grounds, and under the very eaves of the mansion. Lincoln emerged to wave

36 When Ben Butler in Philadelphia heard of the attack on the Sixth Massachusetts, he not only hurried Col. Munroe's regiment to Annapolis, but telegraphed to Governor Andrew for artillery; and Andrew leaped to throw new bodies of troops aboard trains. They reached New York the night of Sunday the 21st, clattered aboard two waiting transports on Monday, and sailed with all possible speed to join Munroe at Annapolis.

37 O. R. I, ii, 596; *Butler's Book*, 202.

38 O. R. I, ii, 600–602.

them a greeting, the happiest-looking man in town. As an Illinois man remarked, "He smiled all over." [39] Then the footsore, sunburnt privates, turning back to the marble-paved courtyard of Willard's, half-stripped to splash
in the fountain. That evening they too went into bivouac on Capitol Hill,
enlivening the soft spring night by selections from their band.

Troops now poured steadily into Washington. Colonel Elmer Ellsworth's
Zouaves, recruited largely from the New York Fire Department, left for the
capital. The Seventy-first New York arrived and found quarters in the temporary hall erected for the inauguration ball. The first Rhode Island came
in, commanded by a West Pointer recently with the Illinois Central, the burly,
bewhiskered Ambrose E. Burnside, and accompanied by the slender "boy governor," William Sprague of the rich cotton-textile family. The Twelfth and
Sixty-ninth New York, the First and Second Connecticut, the New Jersey
Brigade, and other units were soon being disposed about town. A scurrying,
squealing covey of transports, ferries, and small boats kept Annapolis harbor
busy. Even Westerners arrived; Secretary Chase on the 24th had besought
the Ohio authorities to add 50 per cent to their contingents, and hurry them
forward by the Pennsylvania Central—"Delays and mistakes are dangerous."

The soldiers represented American life in all its colorful contrasts. Some
of the First Zouaves were dangerous criminals, some of the Seventh the fashionable elite of Gramercy Square, many of the Yankee boys mill-hands,
many of the Westerners fresh from the plow. Ben Butler made merry over one
fearful hardship suffered by the Seventh New York. They left behind at
Annapolis a thousand velvet-carpet campstools which never caught up!

For the moment the fast-arriving soldiers found their experience entrancing.
It was nearly all gaiety, movement, color, and adventure. [40]

Three units were soon quartered in the Capitol, the Sixth Massachusetts in
the Senate, the Eighth Massachusetts under the dome, the Seventh New
York in the House. Odors of lilac and horse-chestnut blooms drifted in at the
windows. At daybreak reveille blared through the dim interior. Chaffing,
shouting, and singing, the soldiers marched for their meals to the hotels, where
they scuffled with squads of waiters for food. The regiments competed hotly
with each other in drills. The Rhode Islanders attracted particular attention
by their natty uniforms, shining arms, and long baggage trains, with vivandières
(a short-lived feature) adding a romantic touch. Dress parades, band concerts,
and "universal promenading" made Washington livelier than ever before.
With trees leafing out, shoals of ambitious men arriving to seek military com-

39 N. Y. *Tribune*, April 26, 1861, Wash. correspondence.
40 See Theodore Winthrop's delightful essay, "Washington as a Camp," *Atlantic,* vol. 8
(July, 1861), 105–118.

missions, and shops busy, the city was too prosperous to listen to secessionist sympathizers. As the May sunshine grew hotter and the streets livelier with uniforms, most units moved under canvas. They specially liked the large Sibley tent; a wrinkle, wrote Theodore Winthrop, taken from savage life, for it was the Sioux tepee made more compact, handsome, and, if the flaps were kept open, healthy.

The rapid increase of Federal strength completely changed the situation in Maryland. Some men had been for rough action; Governor Morgan of New York had telegraphed Cameron to open a way through Baltimore "cost what it may," and the First Zouaves had boasted that they could go through the city "like a dose of salts." [41] But a refluent wave of Union sentiment soon surged across the State. General Scott late in April created the Department of Annapolis, a belt twenty miles wide on each side of the Annapolis–Washington railway, with the iron-fisted Ben Butler in command, and placed all eastern Maryland, outside this belt, in the Department of Pennsylvania under Major General Robert Patterson. Baltimore began a grand-jury investigation of the riot. [42] When Hicks met the legislature in Frederick its members were overawed by the massing of Union forces and the strength of loyal sentiment in the central and western counties.

Baltimore was soon in an especially chastened mood, for the mob outbreak and flight of citizens caused a collapse of rents, realty prices, tax receipts, and trade. When businessmen asked the government to restore railway service, telegraphs, and mails, Secretary Cameron refused until Federal forces controlled the city and his own agents the railroad offices. Before the end of April, Fort McHenry had been heavily reinforced, Fort Morris garrisoned, and gangs of men put to work restoring the railway bridges. On May 5, Ben Butler's troops occupied the Relay House. Next day the Northern Central Railroad was in full running order, and a Union recruiting office was opened on Baltimore Street. Finally, on the night of May 12, Butler used a thousand men and a battery to occupy Federal Hill commanding the city, and seize some arms about to be shipped south. The movement was dramatically executed in thick darkness, amid a violent thunderstorm, the lightning gleaming on the fixed bayonets. [43]

Increasing numbers of troops poured into Washington. Throughout large parts of the North men had volunteered in throngs, anxious to serve before

41 Morgan's letter, April 25, 1861, is in O. R. I, ii, 600.
42 O. R. I, ii, 607, 611.
43 N. Y. *Tribune*, May 16, 1861, on Baltimore business troubles; *Butler's Book*, 227–230. The British consul, reporting to his government April 27 that many of the laboring classes were in a state of starvation, feared rioting and revolt, and sent his family to Philadelphia for safety; FO 5/778.

the short war ended. In Indiana, Governor Morton announced the day of Lincoln's call that he could forward 30,000 men instead of the six regiments requested. When a Massachusetts volunteer was asked in New York how many were coming, he replied: "How *many?* We're *all* a-coming." New York authorized the enlistment of 30,000 two-year men. Money, too, was poured out generously. Congress, in its anxiety to avoid provocative action, had made no special appropriation available before it adjourned. All loyal States, all large cities, and many towns, however, were ready to appropriate funds. What occurred in the Empire State was typical. While the common council of New York City on April 22 voted a million to equip regiments and half a million for the families of soldiers, a tumultuous city mass meeting appointed a Union Defense Committee which immediately raised large sums. The Brooklyn common council set aside $100,000 for the Thirteenth Regiment and its dependents. Rochester made available $130,500; Buffalo $50,000; Troy $10,000. All this was in addition to a State appropriation of three millions signed by Governor Morgan a few days after Sumter.[44]

Men (untrained) and money were momentarily plentiful. But where were the arms, uniforms, tents, blankets, and camp kitchens? Where was the barest organization for feeding troops, drilling them, and nursing them when ill? What, above all, was to be the method of coordinating national, state, and local efforts, a vast jumble?

Coordination moved like a rusty oxcart. The fate of Major-General John E. Wool, commander of the Department of the East, offers an example. He arrived in New York on April 22, and from quarters in the St. Nicholas Hotel threw himself into the work of providing arms and forwarding troops.[45] He ordered the Federal quartermaster and commissary offices in New York to give transportation and thirty days' rations to each soldier bound for Washington; he conferred with the Union Defense Committee on plans for relieving the capital; he chartered transports and armed steamers for troops; he sent ammunition, gun carriages, and provisions to Fortress Monroe; he directed Governor Richard Yates in Illinois to send a force to seize possession of the arsenal in St. Louis (for his jurisdiction extended to the Mississippi); he telegraphed Frank P. Blair to aid the movement; he ordered heavy cannon and other war materials to Cairo; and when Ellsworth's Zouaves were held up by stupid State orders he sent them forward. He had efficient co-workers in

44 O. R. I, iii, *passim,* for a wealth of material; N. Y. *Tribune,* April 23, 1861, for interviews with volunteers; J. A. Stevens, ed., *Minutes, Correspondence, and Reports of the Union Defense Committee* (1885). Connecticut showed an equally militant temper. While the legislature voted two millions and guaranteed every soldier ten dollars a month in addition to Federal pay, Hartford raised $64,000, New Haven $30,000, and other places similar sums.
45 Wool Papers, N. Y. State Library.

Chester A. Arthur, the State's assistant quartermaster-general, who from a downtown office arranged for feeding, clothing, and to some extent arming the soldiers, and John A. Dix, chairman of the Union Defense Committee. The Committee on April 31 adopted resolutions praising Wool's energy and ability, and the value of his long experience and military skill.

But at that very moment Wool was ordered back to Troy; and when he asked why, Cameron replied that his emergency activities, while Washington was cut off and could not be consulted, had seriously embarrassed the War Department! [46]

Shortages, confusion, and delays reigned paramount. Of small arms an apparently adequate supply existed on paper in public repositories, but for three reasons troops often went without them. Many were too poor to use, facilities existing for their distribution were weak, and Scott wished most of the best pieces kept for long-term troops, not issued to three months' militia to be abused and lost. The government had no cannon foundry. Uniforms, blankets, tents, and medical equipment were all in very short supply. Food was abundant, but its preparation and distribution were so poor that units detained in populous cities—for example, Pennsylvania troops in Harrisburg and Philadephia—were literally half-starved. The press soon reported that some companies in the capital itself had but two meals a day, and those of bread, fat salt pork, and water. Governors and adjutant-generals found it easy to write orders and sign contracts, but the arms and goods were slow to arrive.

Even barracks and proper camps were wanting. Early in May the diarist George Templeton Strong found several hundred men stuffed into a building at Broadway and Fourth Street, the air mephitic and ammoniacal—"I never knew before what rankness of stench could be emitted by unwashed humanity." [47] The installation of Washington troops in public buildings was eloquent of the slapdash improvisation of the time. Amid the general indiscipline, it was no wonder that a private whose regiment was visited at the Capitol by Lincoln remarked saucily to the President: "Now, sir, stand by us, for we mean to stand by you."

All over the country, the ninety-day regiments departed with the most rudimentary equipment. New York had better resources than some other States. Yet a large part of the Eighth New York went southward in citizens' dress and without arms. When the Thirteenth New York, the pride of Brooklyn, marched to its transport, about 200 of its 650 men were left be-

46 Dix, *Dix*, II, 1–16; George F. Howe, *Arthur*, 24; Stevens, *Union Defense Committee, passim*; O. R. I, ii, 160.
47 Strong, *Diary*, III, 148. For difficulties of Mobilization see K. P. Williams, *Lincoln Finds a General*, II, 796–800.

hind because they had no muskets. The others had received them, with knapsacks and blankets, at the last hour. As for the Sixty-ninth New York, it embarked only after scenes of indescribable confusion. Men accepted and men still clamoring for acceptance had crowded early that morning into Prince Street. Here, in front of Colonel Corcoran's house, a large truck was stationed. "The rush at this point," wrote a reporter, "was perfectly tremendous, so eager were the men to obtain their equipment. The captain of each company was stationed on the vehicle, and here the acceptance or rejection of the recruits occurred." As each man was enrolled a blanket was thrown over him. He was passed to another man, who snatched off his hat and put a regimental cap on his head. Still another man thrust a musket into his hands, while others gave him a tin plate, knife, fork, and tin cup.[48]

The War Department was a scene of hurry, endless intensive work, uncertainty, and chaos. Cameron hired all the clerks and copyists his rooms could hold. He, the commissary-general, and the quartermaster-general kept their forces busy without reference to clocks. Some men stayed in the building twenty-four hours a day, gobbled food brought from a restaurant, and caught a few hours' sleep on a settee. Yet from troops everywhere still came reports of hunger, discomfort, and general mismanagement.

Most serious of all was a conflict of views in high circles. General Scott thought that troops should be brought to Washington even if ill equipped; Secretary Cameron maintained that no large number should come until they had a full outfit for camp and field. Lincoln, deferential to Scott's military experience, inclined to take his side.[49]

[VI]

It is in the light of these difficulties that we must weigh the question whether Lincoln erred in not calling at once for more than 75,000 ninety-day men. Douglas said that *he* would have called for 200,000. Greeley clamored for a large force. "Assuming that the crushing out of the rebellion is a question of time and cost only," the *Tribune* commented, "we hold it cheaper to employ 400,000 men in six months than 200,000 to close it up in a year." Lincoln might have been wiser to call for 100,000 or 150,000 men, and assuredly should have made the term longer. But if a larger number had been demanded, the confusion, the hardships of ill-fed, ill-clothed, ill-housed troops, and the public irritation over duplication, waste, and shortages, would have been multiplied. Moreover, the problem of costs was serious. As matters

48　N. Y. *Tribune*, May 9, 1861; G. T. Strong, *Diary*, III, 132; N. Y. *Tribune*, April 24.
49　Meneely, *War Department in 1861*, 159 ff.

stood, Chase was despondent and harassed, uncertain whether money could be raised for exigent needs. The President underrated the formidability of the Confederacy, the determination and talent of its leaders; he hoped, with Seward, that the flame of revolt would still die down, and he feared that too threatening a military effort might affect border State sentiment adversely.[50]

In one decision, that not to call Congress into special session, Lincoln made no error. For several reasons it was wise to defer the session for ten weeks, and public opinion approved his course.

It was necessary, first of all, to make sure that Washington was a safe place in which to sit. In the second place, he could do everything essential without Congressional action; in fact, during the emergency Congress would be rather an encumbrance than help. As a third consideration, key men of Congress would be summoned as wanted. Thus before the end of May, Senator William Pitt Fessenden of Maine got a letter from Chase saying that Lincoln wished him and other important members of the Senate Finance Committee to come to Washington at once to help prepare financial measures. Finally, so long as Lincoln and Seward cherished even faint hopes of a peaceable conclusion and a restoration of the Union, they feared the loud hostility of radical-minded members of Congress to compromise measures.

But action in Washington depended in great measure on action by the States in revolt. What, in these weeks, was the Confederacy doing?

50 For discussion of this subject see Ropes, *Story of the Civil War*, I, 111, 112; Comte de Paris, *Civil War*, I, Book II, Ch. IV; and such later writers as Fred A. Shannon, *Organization and Administration of the Union Army*, I, 31 ff. Ropes points out that Lincoln's call for 75,000 was followed on May 3 by a call for 42,034 three-year volunteers, 22,714 men for the regular army, and 18,000 men for the navy. Altogether, this raised the available army to 156,861 men, and the navy to 15,600 men, "certainly a very respectable force." Kenneth P. Williams has a judicious treatment of call for troops in *Lincoln Finds a General*, II, 796–800.

5

The Confederacy at War

THE ARDOR of the South after Sumter was as impressive as that of the North—and the lack of hardheaded planning just as remarkable. Feeling was even more vehement, indeed, than above the Potomac. Since the South had no great cities, scenes of mass enthusiasm were impossible. But its young men had been even quicker to enlist, and its women more eager to applaud them. Its clergy were as ready to consecrate stands of colors, its propertied men as generous in subscribing to loans, as in New England. In all the towns bands played, military companies paraded, bonfires blazed, and orators harangued the crowds.[1] Rural districts were equally exuberant. John B. Gordon, leading some North Georgia volunteers in coonskin caps from Atlanta to Montgomery, found the line of travel in unbroken uproar. Troops gathered at the stations under banners of strange device; fires lighted the hilltops; fife-and-drum corps shrilled and thumped; cannon exploded their salutes; and girls rushed aboard the cars to pin blue cockades on the men.[2] A war of resistance to tyranny, a struggle for freedom like that of 1776—so everybody believed. Sang ardent Henry Timrod: "Hath not the morning dawned with added light?"

For the moment an astonishing unanimity seemed to possess most of the South. A Northern journalist traveling through the Gulf States found the Unionists "completely crushed out for the time." [3] In countless breasts, of course, affection for the old nation contended with loyalty to the new. In South Carolina the aged Alfred Huger melted into tears when he thought of the past; in Virginia the youthful John S. Wise watched the Stars and Stripes hauled down with indescribable emotions. Many dissenters were prudently silent.[4] But so convinced were most Southerners of the right of secession and so sternly did they condemn coercion that Lincoln's call for troops brought

1 A. H. Bill, *The Beleaguered City*, 38, 39, pictures the excitement in Richmond.
2 Gordon, *Reminiscences*, 10.
3 Albert D. Richardson, letter in N. Y. *Tribune*, May 18 (dated May 10), 1861.
4 Russell, *My Diary*, Chs. 13–17 deal with feeling in S. C.; Wise, *The End of an Era*, 160.
The real extent of the Union feeling in the South will be considered later.

a wave of anger that overthrew all differences. In an instant, the editor of the *Southern Literary Messenger* told the novelist John P. Kennedy, the proclamation transformed 75,000 Virginia Unionists into bitter enemies of the United States. Conservative leaders of the Virginia convention turned about face.[5]

Instantly the center of Southern interest moved from Charleston to the Potomac. Jefferson Davis on hearing of Sumter telegraphed his congratulations: "All honor to the gallant sons of Carolina, and thanks to God for their preservation." But at once he sent further messages: the governor of Virginia was asking for troops, and the regiment at Columbia and a regiment from Charleston were needed on the James, for the defense of the northern boundary of the Confederacy had suddenly become a matter of extreme urgency.

It was certain that Virginia would leave the Union, the only question being whether she would go at once or wait for the border States. Her convention went into secret session. Not only most delegates from the western counties, but some others, contended for delay. While they debated, mob excitement in Richmond rose until Union members feared violence; but the pause was brief. On April 17 the convention by the before-noted vote of 88 to 55, with 10 members absent, passed an ordinance of secession, to be submitted to the people May 23. Meanwhile the convention assumed supreme authority, and Governor Letcher ordered all military units to hold themselves alert. A fresh wave of enthusiasm rolled over Richmond. John Tyler joined in addressing a "spontaneous people's convention" sitting in town; Letcher had the Confederate flag, with an eighth star for Virginia, hoisted over the capitol; and a nocturnal procession flowed through the streets, cheering an orator who predicted the capture of Washington within sixty days.[6]

The alliance of Virginia and the Confederacy was quickly cemented by formal compact. When State leaders appealed to Montgomery for succor, Davis and the Cabinet prevailed on Vice-President Alexander H. Stephens to leave Georgia for Richmond on April 19. On his way north he spoke at station after station, insisting that Washington be taken as soon as possible. Though the South mingled aggressiveness with apprehension, the cry "On to Washington!" was fervently raised. Reaching Richmond on April 22, Stephens conferred with John Tyler and six other commissioners on a treaty of alliance with the Confederacy, and addressed the convention, outlining Southern

---

5 John R. Thompson to Kennedy, May 16, 1861; Kennedy Papers, Peabody Institute.
6 Letcher had behaved with cool moderation; to an early mob in Richmond he said that their banners meant nothing to him, for Virginia was still one of the United States, and that the cannon they dragged was State property which they must restore at once. Hill, *Beleaguered City*, 39; *Ann. Cyc.* 1861, p. 735.

policy. Already Richmond was so full of soldiers, with more pouring in by every train, that Governor Letcher soon had to stop the flow.

On April 24 the alliance of Virginia and the Confederacy was signed. Next day the convention ratified it. This step, momentous in itself, was potent in its influence on North Carolina and Tennessee, still delaying action.[7] The old Dominion lent the cause a dignity it had not before possessed, and promised to bring new and valuable leaders to the government and army.

That the South had spiritual qualities of its own which in several respects were superior to those of the North few impartial observers denied; and these qualities Virginia had once shown at their best. When Southerners asserted that they were maintaining a special way of life which independence alone could safeguard, they meant not only the social system based on slavery, but a dignity, repose, jealousy of personal honor, and courtesy that the hurried Yankee world could not match. They might be leisurely to the point of indolence, but their best circles stood closer to the Renaissance ideal of humanism; they might possess less social conscience than the Puritanic reformers of the North, but they had a mellower urbanity, and a keener sense of the romantic. Versatile Virginians like William Byrd and Thomas Jefferson had established the humanistic tradition of the South, and the Virginian John Esten Cooke had come nearest the spirit of Walter Scott. The slave-selling State of 1861 had slipped downward, but it was still a proud State.

[I]

Like the North, the Confederacy underestimated the magnitude of the struggle before it. Until autumn, most people anticipated a short contest. When the Confederate Congress met on April 29 in Montgomery to deal with what Davis called a declaration of war by Lincoln, it showed a confident optimism. Davis in his message dwelt with pride on the response of the South to the crisis. Transportation companies had freely offered the use of their lines; a convention of Southern railway presidents in Montgomery had not only reduced the rates for men and munitions, but had offered to accept compensation in Confederate bonds; farmers, mechanics, and professional men had all been eager to make sacrifices. Age and youth alike had rushed to the colors, and men of high civil rank had been willing to enlist as privates. We shall never be subjugated by arms, proclaimed Davis. He told Congress that he had 19,000 men under arms in various places, that 16,000 more were being assembled in Virginia, and that under existing legislation he planned to organize forces of 100,000, to be ready for instant action. He

7 Davis, *Rise and Fall*, I, 328 ff.

asked for a new grade of command, that of general, to outrank the major-generals of various States.[8]

"You count without your host," a brother-in-law of Jefferson Davis had told Charles Sumner the previous winter; "when the fighting begins it will all be north of the Susquehanna." [9] This idea that the resistance of Northern Democrats to all Yankee war measures would defeat coercion quickly died. But the Southern muster of force was so prompt and exuberant that multitudes believed in a quick victory. Many Southerners were persuaded that inasmuch as the North had grown rich at their expense, collecting fat brokerages and shipping charges, making fortunes by buying raw cotton cheap and selling cotton textiles high, and levying tariffs on Southern consumption, the Yankee economy would collapse after secession. "Look at the four hundred millions in Northern losses," exclaimed Alexander H. Stephens in May; "the leeches are now realizing whose wealth sustained them!" As news of the Northern business depression floated down, Southern editors gloated over the prospect of grassy New York streets. The South was one of the richest lands in the world, exulted the Richmond *Examiner*, and the North one of the poorest—sixty-eight Boston bankruptcies in a week proved it. Many who did not go so far as this nevertheless held that much of the Northern strength was artificial, and that of the slave States basic and impregnable. While the Yankee world depended on manufactures for which the demand might wither overnight, the South relied upon farm commodities for which the market exceeded the supply. The Northern economy was topheavy, the Southern stable.

We have already noted the allied concept, related to Napoleon's sneer at the nation of shopkeepers, that the commercial-minded Yankee lacked fighting spirit. To some the war lay between gentlemen and yeomen on one side, and "vulgar, fanatical, cheating counter-jumpers" on the other. Beauregard was convinced that the average Southerner was physically stronger than the average Northerner. "Yankee trash" was a familiar phrase, varied by suggestions that most New York soldiers were thugs and jailbirds.[10] Southern newspapers and letters of the spring of 1861 are full of vaunts that one Confederate equaled five of Lincoln's "myrmidons," that a Southron (another favorite term) could whip a Yankee with one hand tied behind his back, and that Northerners could be defeated with children's popguns. Unfortunately, John B. Gordon later ruefully remarked, they wouldn't fight that way! Such gasconade is common in all wars, but in this one many Southerners believed it.

8 *Messages and Papers of the Confederacy*, I.
9 Sumner to Duchess of Argyll, Boston, June 4, 1861, HL.
10 W. H. Russell quotes both the counter-jumper phrase and Beauregard; *My Diary*, Chs. 18, 19. He notes also the thug-and-jailbird characterization, Ch. 30.

"Just throw three or four shells among those blue-bellied Yankees," a Northern newspaper correspondent heard a young man tell a crowded car in North Carolina, "and they'll scatter like sheep." This correspondent was so pained by the oft-repeated declaration that Yankees were cowards that he almost rejoiced in the brilliant prospect the South enjoyed for learning the truth.[11]

Even if the North fought well, averred many Southerners, it could never subjugate a freedom-loving people who battled on the defensive for their homes and institutions. As Great Britain had failed in the Revolution, so Federal power must fail now. What did it cost the government to get fifteen hundred Seminole warriors out of the Everglades? demanded a Tennessee Congressman. Thirty millions! "When you talk of conquering States, the whole arithmetic fails of figures to count the cost." [12] Distance was a defense. Above all, a population of eight millions determined to die rather than yield could no more be beaten down than the Swiss had been by the Austrians, the English by the Armada, or the Dutch by Philip II. This belief had a poignant intensity. When John Tyler traced the Anglo-Saxon struggle for liberty and self-determination from Magna Charta down through Naseby and Saratoga to Sumter, he touched a vibrant chord. But all the defenses named might prove treacherous.[13] River and railroad could conquer distances; the "inside lines" of the South lost meaning when a Union army moved up the Tennessee into the heart of the Confederacy; and the North too could state principles which steeled the arm and exalted the spirit.

When rugged John H. Reagan of Texas declared that if war came the South would show how brave men could die, Emory B. Pottle of New York uttered a rejoinder of ringing truth. "I do not doubt it," he told the House, "and I tell the gentleman that he knows little of the North if he thinks the example will be thrown away upon us. Sirs, you do injustice to our common ancestry if you doubt that we can meet the shock of battle upon equal terms with you. Who doubts the courage of either section?" While the Southerners had a greater taste for military pursuits, no statement was more fallacious than the frequent remark that they displayed a superior fighting ability.[14]

11 Gordon, *Reminiscences*, 7; Albert D. Richardson in N. Y. *Weekly Tribune*, May 18, 1861.
12 James H. Thomas in *Cong. Globe*, 36th Cong., 2d Sess., p. 437.
13 Richmond *Examiner*, April 20, 21.
14 *Cong. Globe*, 36th Cong., 2d Sess. (Jan. 25, 1861), 570. Perhaps the Southerners did have a greater aptitude for war, for it is true they rode and shot better—at first. But Northerners and Southerners were the same people, with essentially the same characteristics. If the Southerners possibly had a little more ardor, the Northerners possibly had a little more endurance; but both statements are dubious. The best brief statement of the differences between Northern and Southern troops is in Comte de Paris, I. He thinks the Northerner somewhat superior, as being better educated, and therefore more resourceful and quicker-minded, but he was a prejudiced witness.

The Southerners' faith in a short war derived much, finally, from their before-mentioned confidence in the power of cotton. From Jefferson Davis to the humblest farmer, countless men accepted the doctrine so often preached by James H. Hammond and others that cotton was king. A child can break a thread of cotton, wrote Benjamin H. Hill of Georgia, but on that thread hangs the world.[15] W. H. Russell, dining in Charleston, heard a Carolinian tell the British consul that England was a helpless subject of this potentate. "Why, sir, we have only to shut off your supply of cotton for a few weeks, and we can create a revolution in Great Britain." Even a steward on a Mississippi River steamboat assured Russell that all the world could not beat the South, for King Cotton was autocrat of Europe.[16] If the Upper South doubted his potency, in the Lower South few questioned the weight of his scepter. It was a dangerous theory, for it encouraged a policy which played into the hands of the Northern blockade.

The wilder Southern utterances on this subject had long amazed Britons. "There is something truly astonishing," the London *Economist* had said in 1851, "in the infatuations which seem to possess the Southern States of America." If civil war took place, "no bribes, however enormous, would induce the English people—or any class among them, however interested in the result—to lend its aid to a revolt which they believe to be utterly unprovoked, the result of the worst political passions, and likely to end in the degradation of the Southern States."

The London *Spectator* had spoken in similar terms. Lord Derby, head of the Conservative Party, quoting the Charleston *Mercury* on the power of cotton to make Britain recognize and even ally herself with a Southern republic, termed such statements the fruit of a distempered fancy. He warned Southerners that Britain would not intervene, that any reduction of the Southern cotton supply would merely stimulate its cultivation from Brazil to India, and that they would find themselves hoist by their own petard. In the five years 1845–49, the South had supplied Britain with 84 per cent of her cotton requirements, and the rest of the globe had given her 16 per cent. In the five years 1855–59, the South had furnished but 76 per cent, and other countries 24.[17]

The cotton kingdom cherished its dream because it knew so little of European realities. Few Southerners were students of the economy of other nations; fewer still traveled attentively abroad or talked with foreign businessmen. The fact that the South was provincial enabled the ignorant Governor R. K. Call of Florida to gain wide credence for his statement that Britain

15 Quoted by Coulter, *The Confederate States*, 184, 185.
16 Russell, *My Diary*, Chs. 14, 51.
17 Full material on this subject may be found in a pamphlet, "Disunion and Its Results to the South," dated Washington, Feb. 18, 1861, of anonymous authorship; HL. It warned the South that King Wheat, King Corn, and other kings were more powerful than cotton.

completely depended on the South. "A failure of our cotton crop for three years would be a far greater calamity to England than three years' war with the greatest power on earth." [18]

[II]

The second session of the Provisional Confederate Congress, a unicameral body whose members were appointed by the State secession conventions, sat in hot, humid, mosquito-ridden Montgomery from April 29, and dealt with problems of the utmost magnitude. It was a mediocre body, indebted to the secrecy of its sessions for its short-lived reputation for sense and courage. As one member remarked, it had few if any superior minds, and seldom held a debate marked by noteworthy wisdom. Its informality was reminiscent of Washington: the same want of dignity and earnestness, the same spectacle of feet on desks, dark-circled spittoons, buzzing gossipers, and lobby vultures sharpening their beaks. Most of the ability of the South was drained into the Army, Cabinet, and diplomatic service. In Howell Cobb as president it had an urbane leader until he left to pursue martial glory. Thomas S. Bocock of Virginia, who had once barely missed election to the national speakership, entered early in May. Others of repute included William Porcher Miles of South Carolina, Benjamin H. Hill of Georgia, and Louis T. Wigfall of Texas; in general, however, observers wondered why so many hacks had been chosen.[19]

Congress not only gave Davis the large force for which he asked, but permitted him to accept volunteers without State consent. It authorized an issue of $50,000,000 of 20-year 8 per cent bonds, or, alternatively, an issue of $30,000,000 in such bonds and $20,000,000 in treasury notes, not bearing interest. It debated an embargo on the export of cotton by sea, and prohibited the payment of debts beyond the confines of the border States. Obviously, these enactments all possessed cardinal importance.[20]

The first gave the Confederacy the partial—but only partial—basis of an army bound to serve for three years unless it won an earlier peace. This was something the Union did not have for long months to come. Down to Sumter

---

18 Letter of Governor R. K. Call of Florida to John S. Littell, pamphlet dated Feb. 12, 1861; HL.

19 See the sketch in T. C. DeLeon, *Four Years in Rebel Capitals*, 31, 32, and the full account in E. M. Coulter, *The Confederate States of America*, Ch. VII. The United States later published the *Journals* of the Confederate Congress in seven volumes, and the Southern Historical Society has published press reports of proceedings.

20 Coulter, the *Confederate States*, 134 ff.; Eaton, *History of the Southern Confederacy*, 54 ff.; Johnston and Browne, *Stephens*, 401–404. The Provisional Congress lasted from Feb. 4, 1861, to Feb. 17, 1862, holding five sessions. The first Congress, which was the first body elected by the people, met Feb. 18, 1862. W. C. Rives, a member, wrote scathingly of the Provisional Congress to A. L. Rives, Aug. 14, 1861; Rives Papers, Univ. of Virginia Library.

the Confederacy had been receiving militia and volunteers for six months or a year, and only by consent of their States. Now that the situation had radically changed, the President was authorized (May 8, 13) to receive up to 400,000 men, without delaying for State permission, who would serve for three years or the duration. Recruits wishing to enlist for only six or twelve months might still come in as members of a State unit. An array of short-term, intermediate-term, and long-term troops therefore soon appeared at the front, some of them State volunteers, some militiamen, and some national volunteers. The resulting confusion and jealousy were serious.

It would have been far better for the Southern cause could a uniform enlistment of three years have been prescribed. But Secretary Walker, whom Alexander H. Stephens called "rash in counsel, irresolute in action," and who haggled over prices when the Confederacy needed every gun it could obtain, furnished poor leadership; while Congress and the people could not believe in three years of battle and bloodshed. President Davis almost alone had publicly and constantly predicted a long and costly war.[21] For these prophecies, ardent advocates of secession had berated him as slow and conservative; now hotheaded patriots abused him as pessimistic and feeble-hearted. Vice-President Stephens, at this stage in sympathetic rapport with Davis, also told everybody that the conflict would be prolonged and sanguinary, would require the severest sacrifices, and would fail if the people did not show endurance. He was similarly attacked. As the troops gathered, all exuberance and thirst for the clash of arms, many feared only that victory would be won before they could share it. Their elders anticipated a few fierce combats, and then a negotiated peace of independence.

In passing its first financial measures, Congress again took shortsighted views. The new head of the Treasury, Christopher G. Memminger, a Charleston attorney who had long been chairman of the finance committee of the South Carolina House, had methodical industry, but no particular expertness, vision, or force of personality, and he also thought in terms of a short war. He had begun work in a bare room in Montgomery, unswept, uncarpeted, unfurnished, and without a cent of public money, so that even his desk and chair were paid for from his own pocket. His whole official term was to be a career of expedients, and the first emergency measures were typical of those to come. He made it plain that he expected no great immediate revenue from import or export duties, and not more than $15,000,000 the first year from direct taxes, which most of the States assumed anyway and paid

21 Davis insists on this in his *Rise and Fall of the Confederate Government*, with ample evidence; and his final speeches in the United States Senate show that he had a clear expectation of a long, savage conflict. For Walker see C. A. Evans, *Confederate Military History*, I. This fastidious Alabamian, disliking contractors, groaned: "No *gentleman* can be fit for office."

in their own notes. The seeds of a lusty inflation were sown in the marketing of $50,000,000 of treasury notes.

Happily for his power to meet the most immediate needs, he obtained some $560,000 in Federal cash and bullion from the mint and custom house in New Orleans, while various States, towns, and individuals—Alabama in the van with $5,000,000—made loans or gifts. But it was clear even in the spring of 1861 that the Confederacy would float to victory or defeat on a sea of paper.[22] Not until the spring of 1863 did Congress pass a comprehensive tax law—too little and too late.

The bill for an embargo on cotton was of course simply an application of the Confederate doctrine that King Cotton, by judicious squeezes on the British windpipe, could compel foreign assistance. We hold the aces, rejoiced the Charleston *Mercury*, and we shall bankrupt every cotton factory in Britain and France if those nations do not acknowledge our independence. Other newspapers advised the planters to keep the cotton on their plantations; thus it could neither fall into Union hands nor relieve that desperate European stringency which would soon force foreign intervention. The cotton merchants, the warehouse owners, the insurance writers, and the factors doing a brokerage business all united in urging retention of the great staple. Before long the principal British consuls in the South reported to the foreign office that planters and government were alike determined to carry through a plan of economic coercion: no cotton except in return for recognition and the breaking of the Northern blockade! The first bill for an embargo, with such popular feeling behind it, seemed certain to pass; so did later bills.

But not quite. When embargo came to the point of enactment, an unseen but easily identifiable influence halted it. Jefferson Davis saw clearly that while the threat of such a law might effectively influence foreign opinion, actual passage would carry pressure too far. So unfriendly a measure would anger the British and French governments. The proper pose of the Confederacy was that of an anxious friend of free commercial intercourse, only too ready to ship its staple abroad once the North permitted. The President therefore let Congress pass bills cutting off trade with the United States, and forbidding exports of Southern crops to Europe except through Southern ports, but he went no further.[23]

22 J. C. Schwab, *The Confederate States*, 10 ff. Some Federal money and bullion were obtained at the Dahlonega (Ga.) mint, and the Charlotte (N. C.) assay office. The Confederacy provided for a million dollars in interest-bearing notes in March, 1861. The total of specie on which it was able to lay hands during its whole existence amounted only to $27,000,000. Schwab, 43.
23 See Frank L. Owsley, *King Cotton Diplomacy*, Ch. I. Congress did levy a duty of one-eighth of one per cent a pound on cotton exports, to pay the interest on early loans (Feb. 28). Davis, *Rise and Fall*, I, 486; Schwab, 239, 240.

The first civil policies of the government had thus been fairly well fixed when a convention in Raleigh unanimously passed a secession ordinance for North Carolina on May 20, and Virginia by overwhelming popular vote on May 23 decided in favor of leaving the Union. The way was now open for a transfer of the capital of the Confederacy to Richmond. When Vice-President Stephens visited Virginia, he had all but promised that this step would be taken. The Virginia convention issued a formal invitation which filled most members of Congress with enthusiasm. They were heartily tired of Montgomery, with its wilting temperatures, pestiferous insects, and still hungrier lobbyists and office-seekers. The city's hotels were overcrowded, dirty, and ill served; the flies were fearful; the streets lifeless and uninteresting. Richmond by comparison was a metropolis. President Davis vetoed the bill for the transfer, but Congress at once repassed it.[24]

Some Southerners believed that strategic considerations pointed to the choice of a railway center less exposed to Federal attack: Lynchburg, Chattanooga, or Nashville. The arguments for Richmond, however, were overwhelming. The importance of the city as a rail and iron-manufacturing center, its Tredegar Works holding a national reputation, and the value of northern Virginia and the Shenandoah Valley as storehouses of grain, meat, and other supplies, made their defense absolutely vital. As it was certain that the most formidable army of the Confederacy would soon hold positions between the James and the Potomac, command could best be exercised from Richmond.

Sentimental factors were also potent. Here on the historic James stood a handsome capitol building; here was Crawford's statue of Washington, with its attendant cluster of Virginia celebrities; here were spots hallowed by Jefferson, Patrick Henry, George Mason, Madison, and John Marshall. And finally, certain political arguments had great weight. Since part of the border area was still hesitant, since the Lower South had launched secession and many feared that the cotton kingdom would dominate the Confederacy, and since the primacy of Virginia in the Southern sisterhood could not be denied, Richmond was to be preferred above all other cities of the new nation.[25]

Howell Cobb predicted that Virginia soil would soon become a vast battle-ground, dyed with the blood of the bravest Southern heroes. Even those who derided his suggestion that at critical moments members of Congress might doff their togas and buckle on their armor, felt that the government could well gain from proximity to its forces.[26] Communications both north and south would be easier, and to plant the capital so far toward the front

24 Bill, *Beleaguered City*, gives an interesting sketch of the transfer.
25 Coulter, *Confederate States*, 100, 101.
26 Speech at Atlanta May 22, 1861, *Ann. Cyc.*, 140.

would show a sense of strength. At this date Stephens and others expected President Davis to take command of the Army of Virginia in person, and some believed that the brief, sharp conflict would be mainly confined to the Old Dominion.[27] It took time to reveal the disadvantages of an exposed position not quite 110 miles from Washington and close to tidewater. It also took time to show that the choice of Richmond had some unfortunate effects on the broad lines of Confederate strategy, for it reduced the scale of army movements, and it strengthened the natural tendency to favor Eastern as against Western demands.

With a distinguished entourage, Davis left Montgomery on Sunday evening, May 26, for Virginia. All along the way, at Atlanta, Augusta, Wilmington, Goldsboro, and other towns, crowds assembled which, despite announcements that the President was ill and wished privacy, demanded speeches. Shouts of "The old hero!" and "We want Jeff Davis!" brought him out for a few fervent sentences. Having reached Richmond, he drove behind four white horses, between cheering banks of people, to the Spotswood Hotel. The sound of saw and hammer vibrated from Capitol Hill, where buildings were being altered for the new government. Davis, with Toombs and the State Department and Memminger and the Treasury, took up offices in the former custom house. The War Department under Walker, with other departments and bureaus, found rooms in the ugly brick Mechanics' Institute, where the headquarters for Virginia troops occupied the top floor.

[III]

Alexander H. Stephens, fierily addressing a crowd at Atlanta, told it that however long the struggle, triumph was certain. "We have now Maryland and Virginia and all the Border States with us. We have ten millions of people with us, heart and hand, to defend us to the death. We can call out a million people, if need be; and when they are cut down we can call out another, and still another . . . a triumphant victory and independence, with an unparalleled career of glory, prosperity, and independence, await us." [28] But did the Confederacy really have the Border States?

Once Lincoln called for troops, the secession of Virginia, North Carolina, Tennessee, and Arkansas was so certain that the Confederacy immediately treated all four as quasi-members. Although all had been fundamentally Unionist in sentiment, the hostility of all to coercion was overwhelming. What the ablest Southern religious editor, George McNeil of the *North*

27   Johnston and Browne, *Stephens*, 403.
28   N. Y. *Tribune*, May 9, 1861.

Carolina Presbyterian, had said of his State was essentially true of the others. After taking pains to ascertain popular feeling, McNeil had written an article addressed to the nation declaring that although three-fourths of the North Carolinians were anxious to preserve the Federal tie, while only one-fourth stood for secession, practically all of them would resist coercive action. "We have yet to see an individual who would tolerate an invasion of the South." In other States the secessionists had been a distinct minority. Tennessee had voted decisively against a convention to debate separation, and East Tennessee had voted four to one. In Arkansas the *State Gazette* had declared March 30 that all informed men put the Union majority at fully 20,000.[29] History, wrote an agonized Virginian, would record that a majority in the Old Dominion carried their struggle for national unity to the point of pusillanimity and dishonor.[30] But a great majority were against coercion.

Why? If they believed in the Union and the Union was attacked, why join the assailants and not the defenders? Theoretically, because they did not believe in the indissoluble Union of which Washington repeatedly spoke, but in the dissoluble Union of John Taylor of Caroline. They held the compact theory of the Federal tie. Emotionally, because they felt themselves identified with the Lower South. Pragmatically, because they saw that slavery and other special economic interests which they shared with the cotton kingdom would be endangered by its defeat. But if they ever thought of themselves as true Unionists they had a twisted logic and a confused set of loyalties; they should have called themselves tepid, conditional, and halfway Unionists. Andrew Jackson would have applied more scorching adjectives. They had none of Jefferson's conviction, as expressed in a letter to Washington in 1792, that the rending of the Union into two or more parts would be an evil of incalculable proportions.

In Virginia the result of the referendum at once became foregone. The most prominent "Union" men in Richmond, including several who had been emphatic in their assertions of attachment to the nation in recent public meetings, took their stand with Governor Letcher. John Baldwin of Augusta County, who had spoken powerfully for the Union in the convention, wrote the Staunton *Spectator* that their only hope now was in "making ready for the biggest fight that is in us." Only one Unionist leader of high rank remained unyielding: John Carlile, after resisting secession on the convention floor until adjournment, returned to western Virginia to lead the struggle against it there. Throughout the tidewater area a spirit of intimidation reigned:

29 *North Carolina Presbyterian*, Nov. 24, 1860; *Ann. Cyc.* 1861, p. 678, for Tennessee; *Arkansas State Gazette*, March 30, 1861.
30 Wm. Frazier, Rockbridge, Va., May 20, 1861, to Horatio King; H. King Papers, LC.

No Union man dared vote his convictions, and opposition to secession was measured only by absenteeism from the polls. Vigorous use was made of Senator James Mason's letter stigmatizing antagonists as traitors, and of a judicial charge to a grand jury declaring that any citizen who adhered to the Federal government might be indicted for treason.[31]

Under these circumstances, the referendum was a farce; the State had really been out of the Union since April 17 and the plebiscite simply ratified a *fait accompli*. The soldiers voting in their camps, where any opposition voice would have been drastically silenced, were practically unanimous. The piedmont counties were almost as solidly for the ordinance as the tidewater area. Most localities in western Virginia were against it, but they stood alone. Had a fair, calm election been possible, Norfolk County, which sold much produce to Northern cities, and the counties around Washington, connected with the free States by commercial and social ties, would have polled a large Union vote, but prudence dictated abstention. "At Alexandria," wrote a Falls Church man who successfully stood for Congress this spring, "where there were really some four hundred Union men, only some forty votes were given for the nation"; the others were sullenly silent.[32] Many who voted for secession did so with long, sad thoughts.

North Carolina seceded with a greater outward show of unanimity, but a deeper inner division. Even among the Democrats, few had tolerated a spirit of fire-eating radicalism. Non-slaveholding groups had long and energetically opposed the efforts of slaveholders to pass tax measures favorable to their own interests. W. W. Holden, the erstwhile secessionist editor of the *North Carolina Standard*, so changeable that he was called the Talleyrand of the State, had come over to the Union position. The proportion of slaveowners in the commonwealth was smaller than in its neighbors, and most of them held comparatively few hands. Among the Quakers and the small upcountry farmers abolitionist sentiment possessed great vigor. No State had more genuine reluctance before Lincoln's call for troops, just as none after joining the Confederacy contributed more valorously to the cause.[33]

When Lincoln issued his call, Governor John W. Ellis not only denounced him for warring upon popular liberties, but seized the arsenal at Fayetteville, with 37,000 small arms and 3,000 kegs of powder, the mint at Charlotte, and three forts on the coast; asked for the enrollment of 30,000 men; and promised

31 Beverley B. Munford, *Virginia's Attitude Toward Slavery and Secession;* C. H. Ambler, *History of West Virginia.* Files of the *National Intelligencer* throw special light on the Virginia struggle.
32 Letter of Charles H. Upton in N. Y. *Tribune,* May 28, 1861.
33 C. C. Norton, *The Democratic Party in Ante-Bellum N. C.* (1931), *passim;* Elizabeth Y. Webb, "Cotton Manufacturing in North Carolina 1861–65," *N. C. Hist. Rev.,* (April, 1932), 117–137.

the Confederacy a regiment. Holden swung back to secession in an editorial, "We Must Fight." A special legislative session arranged the election of a convention on May 13, which eight days later unanimously passed a secession ordinance. For the moment most opposition was overborne, although some old Whigs, like George Badger, grumbled over the methods used, and would have preferred a declaration of independence to one of secession. Here, as in Virginia, true Unionists held their tongues. Jonathan Worth, a leader of special elevation who had lately written that nineteen-twentieths of the people he saw were for the old national tie, now sadly recorded: "The voice of reason is silenced. Furious passion and thirst for blood consume the air." He still believed that no separate government could ever be as good as the united nation men were pulling down.[34]

Tennessee in the last Presidential election had given John Bell, champion of the Constitution and the Union, a decisive majority over Breckinridge. At a Nashville meeting shortly before Lincoln's inauguration, Bell had expressed the hope that all would yet be well with the nation. Large parts of the State were as much opposed to a rupture of the national bond as Ohio or Pennsylvania. The Nashville *Democrat*, defending the Union to the last, declared that leaders of the Deep South had plotted to betray the border. "We must expect that the cottonocracy will attempt to precipitate a war with the General Government, with the express purpose of dragging Tennessee into their meshes."[35] The popular vote taken to elect a convention had indicated that approximately 92,000 of those who voted were in favor of the Union, and only 25,000 for abandoning it.

It therefore required determined effort by the secessionist governor, Isham G. Harris, a radical proslavery attorney of force and ability, and by the secessionist majority in the legislature, to carry Tennessee rapidly into the Confederacy. When Harris informed Lincoln that the State would raise 50,000 men, if necessary, to defend Southern rights, influential citizens published an address urging a neutral stand. Harris convoked the legislature only to confront a hostile minority. An ordinance for submitting independence to popular vote passed the Senate 20 to 4, but the House only 46 to 21, and another ordinance for an alliance with the Confederacy met similar dissent. Actually Harris was staging a *coup d'état*, for the legislature had no authority to vote an alliance. This measure (May 1) committed Tennessee to the Confederate cause, just as a law to raise an immediate force of 25,000, with a reserve of 30,000, and to issue bonds for $5,000,000, committed it to military

34 J. G. de Roulhac Hamilton, *Correspondence of Jonathan Worth*, I, 99, 149. Holden in the *Standard* on Feb. 15, 1861, predicted that secession and war would end in abolition of slavery, repudiation of debts, general beggary, and military government.
35 Quoted in Havana, Ill., *Squatter Sovereign*, Feb. 28, 1861.

action. When the referendum was taken on June 8, the people went to the polls without real power to decide the result. As in Virginia, they could only ratify a *fait accompli*. Nevertheless, 47,238 voted no, as against 104,913 voting yes, and in East Tennessee the result was 32,923 for the Union, 14,780 against it.[36]

Like Virginia and North Carolina, Tennessee had such strong bonds of blood, social similarity, and economic interest with the Lower South that she was certain to join it. But East Tennessee, had Northern forces been within reach, might well have done what West Virginia did to remain in the Union.

The situation in Arkansas presented some unusual features. There, as in other border States, many slaveholders had been conservative Unionists. It was the slaveholding districts that had voted most strongly for Bell or Douglas, while northern and northwestern Arkansas, an area of small farmers with few slaves, had given Breckinridge his small majority. Among the well-to-do the old Whig tradition remained strong, while many believed that secession would jeopardize slavery. After Lincoln's election, however, the slaveholding counties caught fire from the revolt of the cotton kingdom, while the hillier sections showed a strong attachment to the nation. Doubtless the small farmers had voted for Breckinridge as an expression of Southern sentiment, but now realized that they would fare much worse in a divided than a united country; doubtless also the slaveholders, while actuated largely by sectional emotion, were now inclined to believe that their human property would be safer in the Confederacy than in Lincoln's Union. At any rate, the voting on the Presidency and then on secession showed that in the two distinct geographical areas of Arkansas an abrupt change of alignment took place in the winter and spring of 1860–61. The planters who had so largely stood for Bell or Douglas now ardently espoused the Confederate cause, while the farmers of northwestern Arkansas in particular turned to a staunch Federal allegiance.

The governor of Arkansas bade Lincoln expect no troops, and prepared to lead the people in resisting Northern "usurpations." The State convention which had recently adjourned was hastily reassembled (May 6). As it passed an ordinance of secession with a shout, one former Union delegate after another rose to declare his entire loyalty to the South. The convention authorized the governor to call out 60,000 men (an inflated figure, for the white population was under 325,000!), and to issue $2,000,000 in bonds. State troops seized Fort Smith. No referendum now being deemed necessary, on May 18 Arkansas formally joined the Confederacy. But as in Tennessee, a stubborn opposition simmered under the surface—an opposition that was to make the

36   J. W. Fertig, *The Secession and Reconstruction of Tennessee*; J. W. Patton, *Unionism and Reconstruction in Tennessee*; *Ann. Cyc.*, 1861, pp. 679–683.

area adjoining Kansas a Union stronghold, and that was eventually to rally behind the one brave delegate who risked his life by voting no on secession, Isaac Murphy, and lift him to the governorship of the reconstructed State.[37]

Altogether, the secession of the Upper South, adding four new stars to the Confederate flag, was a very different process from that of the cotton kingdom. Instead of a reckless surge of emotion we meet anxious deliberation, anguish of heart, a bitter clash of opinion, and dark forebodings of the future. We meet men who flung sternly reproachful cries at the North: "We struggled so long, we sacrificed so much!—and now your measures leave us no choice." We meet other men who addressed the Confederate leaders with yet more passionate rebukes: "We fought so hard for your rights, we gained so much and held such firm expectations of gaining more!—and now you drag us into a needless war, where we must stand the brunt of invasion, and our sons must die for your desperate policies." We meet States almost or quite torn physically asunder by the uncontrollable forces of the time. We meet the finest spirits and ablest generals of the South, thrust, they believed, into decisions which were at once disastrous and unavoidable. Here in the wide borderland lay the most poignant tragedy of a tragic period.

[IV]

One of the finest spirits who felt constrained to an unhappy choice, Robert E. Lee, sent on May 5 a letter to a Northern girl who had requested his photograph. "It is painful," he wrote, "to think how many friends will be separated and estranged by our unhappy disunion. May God reunite our severed bonds of friendship, and turn our hearts to peace! I can say in sincerity that I bear animosity against no one. Wherever the blame may be, the fact is that we are in the midst of a fratricidal war. I must side either with or against my section or country. I cannot raise my hand against my birthplace, my home, my children. I should like, above all things, that our difficulties might be peaceably arranged, and still trust that a merciful God, who I know will not unnecessarily afflict us, may yet allay the fury for war. Whatever may be the result of the contest, I foresee that the country will have to pass through a terrible ordeal, a necessary expiation perhaps for our national sins. May God direct all for our good, and shield and preserve you and yours!"[38]

The tide of secession, running with such fresh force after Sumter, gave

---

37 L. L. Harvin, "Arkansas and the Crisis of 1860–61" (MS Master's Essay, Univ. of Texas) covers the subject in detail. See also David Y. Thomas, *Arkansas in War and Reconstruction*. The secessionists in Arkansas had been watching events, ready to seize any opportunity.

38 Private source; not "my section *of* country," as Freeman, *Lee*, I, 475, has it.

the South many of the ablest officers of the army and navy. In all, nearly
a third of the nation's commissioned military men, 313 in number, resigned.
The War Department offices were also partly stripped. Of ninety regular
employees there in 1860, thirty-four were gone by midsummer of 1861.
Three had died, and some had perhaps been displaced for age, ill health,
or political reasons, but most of them had left to join the South.[39]

Among the resignations those of Robert E. Lee, Joseph E. Johnston, E.
Kirby-Smith, Franklin Buchanan, and Matthew Fontaine Maury were longest
remembered. Those of lesser stature included Colonel Samuel E. Cooper, the
adjutant-general, and Major John Withers, assistant adjutant-general. Cooper's
course awakened the keenest censure in the North, for he had been born in
New Jersey; his mother was a New Yorker, his father a Massachusetts man;
he had entered West Point from New York, had played an efficient part in
the Seminole and Mexican wars, and had spent nearly ten years in his important post. But the influence of his Virginia wife, sprung from the George
Mason family, his Virginia home, and his close friendship with Jefferson Davis,
proved paramount. He became adjutant- and inspector-general of the Confederacy, to serve throughout the war. Colonel Lorenzo Thomas, who took his
place, was nearly sixty, more experienced, and more energetic, but vain, un-
stable, and of poor judgment.

Highly creditable to Joseph E. Johnston was the mental anguish he suffered
in deciding to resign. This gallant soldier, shrewd, cautious, systematic, was a
Virginian through and through, his father a soldier under "Light-Horse Harry"
Lee, his mother a niece of Patrick Henry. But since graduation from West
Point his whole life had been given to the Union. He had been wounded five
times in the Mexican War; he had been first to plant a regimental flag on
the walls of Chapultepec; he had been a staff officer with the Utah expedition, and in 1860 had become quartermaster-general of the army. Officers who
consulted him in the spring of 1861 found him pacing up and down his
Washington office in deep thought, his fine head bent forward, his absorption
so complete that he had to be addressed several times before he awoke. One
visitor heard him muttering to himself in painful perplexity. Overwrought,
he exploded at the slightest interruption. Finally, on April 22, when Virginia's
departure was certain, he closeted himself with Secretary Cameron.

"I must go with the South," he said, in effect, "though the action is in the
last degree ungrateful. I owe all that I am to the government of the United
States. It has educated me and clothed me with honor. To leave the service
is a hard necessity, but I must go. Though I am resigning my position, I

---

39 A. Howard Meneely, *The War Department, 1861,* 106–109. The Cameron Papers and
Gideon Welles Papers, LC and NYPL, contain much on the resignations.

trust I may never draw my sword against the old flag." He wept, and tears stained his cheeks as he hurriedly left the room.

Major E. Kirby-Smith, a son of Florida whose army experience and connections were chiefly in the South and Southwest, had resigned early, but with only less travail. He wrote his mother that he had broken all the ties that bound him to the army "not suddenly, impulsively, but conscientiously and after due deliberation." He was the youngest man in the force to be senior major of his regiment, twenty years in advance of his contemporaries. "I sacrifice more to my principles than any other officer in the Army can do." But he would rather carry a musket in the cause of the South than be commander-in-chief under Mr. Lincoln. He departed with a State that the Union had bought with national funds.[40]

Robert E. Lee reached his critical decision much more easily, for as his principal biographer writes, it was the product of instinct, not deep reflection. He was too clearsighted not to recognize the true character of the movement in the cotton kingdom. Writing his wife in January, 1861, he had said that if the upper tier of States trusted the Gulf secessionists, they would be "dragged into the gulf of revolution." The word "dragged" was deliberately chosen. The same month he wrote his son Fitzhugh that secession was naught but revolution. "The framers of our Constitution never exhausted so much labor, wisdom, and forbearance in its formation and surrounded it with so many guards and securities, if it was intended to be broken up by every member of the Confederacy at will. It is intended for 'perpetual union,' so expressed in the preamble, and for the establishment of a government, not a compact, which can only be dissolved by revolution or the consent of all the people in convention assembled. It is idle to talk of secession." He had recently been made colonel of the First Cavalry, and brought to Washington to be near headquarters. To friends he said that he had a profound contempt for the business of secession.[41]

40 On Johnston see Cobb's MS Reminiscences of Washington in 1861, Cameron Papers, LC. Johnston wrote in resigning that he hoped some thirty years' service, "with as much labor, hardship, danger, and loss of blood as the duties of the military service in this country often imposed, may be thought to entitle me to early consideration of this communication." Letter of April 22, 1861; extra-illustrated set of *Battles and Leaders*, HL. Johnston was the only general officer who went to the South from Federal services; Lee was a colonel. But Johnston was a staff, not a field officer, a fact which entered into the subsequent disputation about rank. Gov. Letcher made him a major-general of Virginia troops two days after Lee got a similar appointment. Kirby-Smith's letters to his mother, written from Texas March 3, March 25, 1861, in the Kirby-Smith Papers, Univ. of N. C., are illuminating. While the family name appears to have been Smith, I follow the DAB form of Kirby-Smith.
41 On the events leading up to Lee's resignation the letters in Fitzhugh Lee's life are illuminating, but Fitzhugh's comment is misleading, and Long's life is a better guide. Douglas Freeman states that Lee decided by instinct, without thought; see both his life and his DAB article. Lee's own story is given in his letter to Reverdy Johnson, Feb. 25, 1868, in

After this, why did he act (as he measurably did) against his own convictions? Unquestionably, because of State and local loyalties, family affections and interests, and personal ties too strong to be sundered. Winfield Scott, who not only thought Lee the ablest officer in the army, but had a warm personal fondness for him, openly avowed his desire to have him made the principal Union field commander. Lincoln and Cameron were ready to accept this judgment, but so uncertain of Lee's fidelity to the Union that they asked old Francis P. Blair to talk with him. The two met at Blair's house on April 18. Lee's answer was unhesitating. He declined Lincoln's quasi-offer, stating frankly that although opposed to secession and deprecating war, he could take no part in an invasion of the South. He did consent to discuss the subject with Scott, and went directly to his headquarters, but again said no firmly.⁴²

Meanwhile, Virginia had left the Union, and the president of the Virginia convention informed Lee that, at the instance of Governor Letcher, it wished to make him commander-in-chief of the Commonwealth forces. On April 20 he presented his resignation, writing that it would have been offered earlier but for the struggle it had cost him to separate himself from—what? Not from the Union, of which Virginia had been the strongest pillar in Washington's day, but "from a service to which I have devoted the best years of my life and all the ability I possessed." Hurrying to Richmond, he received an ovation in which all the State leaders joined, and took up his command April 23.

How tremendous a loss the North incurred in Lee's departure it took time to reveal, although many men partly divined it at once. His decision naturally aroused intense Northern bitterness. Erstwhile friends renounced him, the press compared him with Benedict Arnold, and admirers of his father-in-law, the late George Washington Parke Custis, speculated on the grief that his choice would have given to that adopted son of Washington. We can easily understand and sympathize with his course. But it was no allegiance to the Confederacy that he felt, no sympathy with basic Confederate principles; it was

J. W. Jones, *Life and Letters of Robert E. Lee*, 131, 132. John Hay heard a friend of Lee's say in 1863 that he had expressed utter contempt for secession right up to his departure; *Diaries and Letters*, 70. Other sources of prime value are Nicolay and Hay, IV, 97 ff.; Smith, *The Blair Family*, II; Simon Cameron in *Cong. Globe*, Feb. 19, 1868; and Montgomery Blair's letter to William Cullen Bryant, *National Intelligencer*, Aug. 9, 1866. Most lives of Lee are less than candid on his deep aversion to secession and to the intrigues of the cotton kingdom leaders.

42 Lee inherited his State loyalty. His father, "Light-Horse Harry," had exclaimed: "Virginia is my country. Her I will obey." S. F. Horn, *The Robert E. Lee Reader*, 15. But that George Washington would have been horrified by his exaltation of State above nation we may feel morally certain. It was perfectly true also that, as Edward Everett wrote, officers of the army and navy were servants of the government in a peculiar sense. Unlike civil officers, they were engaged and maintained for life, and a State government had no more right than the British government to discharge them from the service. Everett to Charlotte Wise, April 26, 1861; Everett Papers, MHS.

simply loyalty to the proud Old Dominion with which the Lees had for nearly two and a half centuries been associated. Nobody today dreams of questioning Lee's sincerity, devotion to duty, or nobility of mind. Winfield Scott had said, "He is true as steel, sir! true as steel!" But we may well question whether the man who thus preferred State to nation did not lack a certain largeness of view, did not respond to a parochial type of patriotism, and did not reveal an inadequate comprehension of the American destiny.[43]

Maury was actuated by the same motives that swayed Lee. Loving the Union, detesting secession, and hoping to the last for compromise, he believed that his primary allegiance lay with his birth State Virginia and his home State Tennessee. The line of duty, he had written on March 4, was clear: "Each one to follow his own State, if his State goes to war; if not, he may remain to help on the work of reunion."[44] Three days after Virginia seceded he left for Richmond to be commissioned, at fifty-five, commander in the Confederate navy.

Franklin Buchanan showed decidedly less principle. He too loved the Union, rejected the doctrine of secession, and condemned the course of the cotton kingdom. But he loved his native Maryland, where he had relatives and property, felt a horror of abolitionists, freesoilers, and coercionists, and as Gideon Welles observes, was much courted and caressed by Southern sympathizers. As head of the Washington navy yard he had moved in a society predominantly slaveholding. The day after the Baltimore riot he handed Welles his resignation, saying that he could never stand idly by while Maryland blood flowed in the streets of his native city; and he offered his services to Governor Hicks. When it became clear that Maryland was not going out, after all, he tried to withdraw his resignation, but Welles curtly informed him that it was too late. September found him a captain in the Confederate navy.[45]

These accessions greatly strengthened the Confederacy. Lee was worth an army in himself. Not all the officers from the Upper South, however, valued State above nation. In the most anxious April days a Virginia committee headed by the venerable Judge John Robertson called on Winfield Scott at his headquarters. The two men had been fellow students at William and Mary in 1806! But Scott instantly stopped his old college mate: "Friend Robertson, go no further! It is best that we part here, before you compel me to resent a mortal insult."[46] David Glasgow Farragut, a Tennessean by birth and for forty years

43 See Lossing's caustic personal comment in his *Civil War*, I, 421, 422; Washington correspondence in N. Y. *Tribune*, May 9, 1861.
44 D. F. M. Corbin, *Matthew Fontaine Maury*, 186.
45 Charles Lee Lewis, *Admiral Franklin Buchanan*, Ch. 12 ff.
46 Townsend, *Anecdotes of the Civil War*, 4, 5.

a Virginian by residence, kept his uniform, broke with his friends, and sent his family North.

So too, at Carlisle Barracks another Virginian, George H. Thomas, colonel of the Second Cavalry, maintained his allegiance. His sisters never forgave him. Philip St. George Cooke, colonel of the Second Dragoons, stayed in the Union Army with a vitriolic denunciation of the Catilines of the Deep South. The oligarchs of South Carolina, he wrote, had made themselves leaders in revolution and ruin; aided by demagogues and rebellious spirits, they had dragged or dragooned the reluctant voiceless people of six other States into line; and now they were lighting the torch of war for the whole South. "I owe Virginia little; my country much." [47] John Newton and John W. Davidson, both Virginians and both destined to be major-generals, stood fast by the Union.

For its navy the Confederacy gained less than for its army. Southern youth, prizing an army career, had displayed much less taste for the sea. Of all grades and branches, 322 naval officers resigned, some of them men of high ability. At the Annapolis Academy an assistant professor wrote Welles that he was sure of the loyalty of but five men out of forty officers and other gentlemen employed there. A great majority stuck with the flag, however, while the merchant marine offered a reservoir of experienced captains and mates on which the North, but not the South, could draw. [48]

[V]

Virginia had hardly seceded when military action began on its borders. Washington by late April was too strongly held to be attacked. But State troops, under Letcher's orders, at once moved against the valuable Harpers Ferry armory and arsenal, and the Gosport Navy Yard near Norfolk, with its dock, storehouses, and nine warships. As we have noted, the tiny force guarding Harpers Ferry fired the buildings and made a hurried retreat. At Gosport the *Cumberland*, the only ship in commission, was hastily towed to safety. All other property—the vessels *New York, Pennsylvania, Merrimac,* and others, with provisions, cordage, and machinery—was consigned to flames on the 20th in a spectacular conflagration. The most valuable vessel, the *Merrimac,* would have been extricated, for she had steam up ready to move, but that the cowardly commandant of the navy yard suddenly revoked his permission. While the North felt deep humiliation over these losses, Virginia disunionists thrilled with exultation.

The eight weeks following Sumter witnessed a defiant convergence of

47 See the long letter by Philip St. George Cooke dated June 6, 1861, in the *National In-telligencer,* June 22, 1861.
48 J. R. Soley, *The Blockade and the Cruisers,* 8.

Southern troops upon Virginia. When Jefferson Davis installed himself in Richmond, armies were assembling at Harpers Ferry, covering the Shenandoah Valley, under Joseph E. Johnston; at Manassas, covering the direct approach from Washington, under P. G. T. Beauregard; and at Norfolk, covering the peninsula between the James and York Rivers, under Benjamin Huger and John Magruder. The whole South hummed like a hive of angry bees. Government officers traveling to the new capital wrote that the country seemed one vast camp. The main distributing points were Richmond and Lynchburg, where troops arrived at the rate of 4000 a week. Every train came laden with soldiers and supplies. What was most needed was one directing mind, for until June the Virginia army and the Confederate forces had separate heads.[49]

Like the first Northern recruits, the Confederate levies were a motley host. Most of them were young, and many mere boys; all but a sprinkling of veterans of the Mexican and Indian wars were completely raw; and they were generally ill clad, ill armed, and ill disciplined. The gentlemanlike militia companies of Charleston, Richmond, and other cities presented the best appearance, and volunteers from the backwoods and poor-white areas made the worst. "To see from a distance a mass of these dirty, tobacco-chewing, drinking, swearing, smoking, fetid troops," wrote one observer, "almost leads one to think that the swamps of the Carolinas have become locomotive swamps, as it were, made flesh." The rush to arms had carried into the ranks a good many professional and businessmen who would tarry there but a short time. One company at Harpers Ferry had for captain a Mexican War officer, for first lieutenant a former member of Congress, for sergeant a judge, and for corporal a former United States consul, while the rank and file included lawyers, physicians, and planters.

Camp Lee on the outskirts of Richmond gathered regiments of weird variety, all in exuberant spirits and athirst for battle. The First Texas, flying the Lone Star flag, a unit later to grow into Hood's renowned Texas Brigade; the New Orleans Tigers under the pelican banner; a Zouave unit from Louisiana in scarlet trousers, blue shirts, and richly embroidered jackets; the Third Alabama, smartly uniformed, with a hundred body servants and a mountain of baggage; Georgia troops in green-trimmed butternut, and Mississippians under the magnolia ensign—all fraternized with Virginia lads. One regiment aroused special enthusiasm: the Maryland Guard, its members straggling in by various routes, but all in blue-and-orange Zouave uniforms. Richmond was soon alive with lank North Carolinians, longhaired Arkansans, Tennessee mountain-

49 Files of the Richmond *Whig* and the Baltimore *South;* Kirby-Smith Papers, Univ. of N. C. (he was stationed first at Lynchburg and then at Harpers Ferry); Richmond correspondence, N. Y. *Daily Tribune,* May 27.

eers with fringed leggings, and citified young men from St. Louis and Nashville. Many carried bowie knives or pistols, nearly all drank, and they made fatal duels and affrays commonplace.

While most officers were of superior character, the coarseness, ignorance. and rowdiness of many privates disheartened onlookers. Richmond citizens soon grew disillusioned. Ruffians as well as gallants had leaped to the flag. The New Orleans Tigers included brass-knuckled, dagger-carrying desperadoes, the scourings of the New Orleans levee; the Maryland Guard had some Baltimore plug-uglies; tough frontiersmen and drunken young planters swelled the host. As in Washington, so in Richmond saloons, brothels, and gambling dens began to flourish as never before. Robberies and assaults swamped the police. It was necessary to confine the Tigers to a separate camp. Richmond began to realize that if she was the heroine of a rich historical pageant, her house was no longer her own, and for better or worse all Virginia was tied to the Lower South.[50]

Officers in the Mississippi Valley, refusing to concede that Virginia would be the main seat of war, prepared to fight on a broad front. New Orleans built a breastwork of cotton bales along the levee, armed and manned 12 river steamboats, and by May 15 enlisted 2,000 men. The personnel of a Baton Rouge company indicated the popular character of the first response: 25 mechanics, 24 merchants and clerks, 11 farmers, 9 planters, 4 engineers, 1 lawyer, and 11 miscellaneous. More than a third of this company had been born abroad, and more than a seventh in the North. Gideon J. Pillow, hero of the Mexican War, was expected soon to lead an irresistible army of Valley boys to the rescue of Kentucky and the conquest of southern Illinois. By mid-May the Confederate forces, moving northward from Memphis to New Madrid and Belmont on the Missouri side of the Mississippi, were confronting some 5,000 Union troops at Cairo.

But the South, even more than the North, was fearfully lacking in equipment. Men cried "To arms!"—but there were no arms, no cannon, no uniforms, no medical supplies, beyond those hastily and scantily scraped together. Josiah Gorgas, a man of quiet resourcefulness amounting to genius, reported on May 7 that not quite 160,000 small arms of all kinds were available in the various public repositories within the seceded or seceding States. This included about 15,000 rifles and 120,000 muskets stored in various arsenals east of the Mississippi, a few thousand more in arsenals west of the Mississippi, and a small body of arms belonging to States and military organizations.[51] But many of

50 Bill, *Beleaguered City*, 149–152; Richmond correspondence in N. Y. *Tribune*, May 27, 1861; Bell I. Wiley, *Johnny Reb*.
51 William Watson, *Life in the Confederate Army*; Report to Chairman F. S. Bartow of the Cong. Committee on Military Affairs; Jefferson Davis, *North American Review*, vol. 149 (Oct., 1889), p. 476.

the arms were defective, many so antiquated that they were more dangerous to the holder than the foe, and many out of reach. At Harpers Ferry the Virginia troops seized some 5,000 muskets, and what was far more valuable, part of the machinery for making more. At the Norfolk navy yard about 500 cannon, good, poor, or totally unusable, were captured. Of ammunition the South was desperately short.

From every post rose the same complaints. "Words cannot express to you our deplorable condition here," wrote Kirby-Smith from Harpers Ferry May 29, "unprovided, unequipped, unsupplied with ammunition and provisions. . . . The utter confusion and ignorance presiding in the councils of the authorities that were is without a parallel." At Pensacola, W. H. Russell found ammunition on hand for only one day's firing, and poor stuff at that. From Corinth, Mississippi, Julian Alcorn addressed his wife in pathetic terms. "My position is most difficult and perplexing, chief in command of five thousand men, fresh volunteers, poorly clad, rather poorly fed; without a sufficient supply of anything." [52] Governor Letcher later extenuated his blunders in trying to supply the Virginia troops by pointing out that until the arrival of Lee in Richmond he had nobody of military capacity to advise him.

Soldiers from Norfolk to Galveston drilled with every variety of musket, shotgun, rifle, carbine, or fowling piece. They drilled in frock coats, swallow-tails, jackets, and shirtsleeves. They guarded their powder, for it was too scarce for target practice. They sweetened their fare of corncake, fat bacon, and peas with molasses fetched in a jug from home. They lightened their evening hours with fiddle and accordion. [53] As the first fever for combat subsided, the impression grew that the great battle to which all looked, and which many believed would be final, was several months distant, for it would take that long to organize the armies South and North. Throughout June the general expectation was still for a short war. Even the perspicacious Judah P. Benjamin, changing his mind, now thought it would last only three or four months. [54] Of the coming horrors of battlefield mutilation, hospital agonies, and home-front exhaustion, few had the slightest premonition.

The wonder was that under these circumstances, amid hurry, guesswork, and reckless expedients, in an atmosphere of shortsighted optimism, so much

52 Kirby-Smith Papers, Univ. of N. C.; Julian Alcorn, June 6, 1861; Alcorn Papers, Univ. of N. C.

53 See, for example, F. G. DeFontaine's "Personal Reminiscences" in the magazine *Blue and Gray*, June, 1893. The drunkenness and rowdyism of many men and some officers mortified their fellows. "I cannot and will not stand such association," wrote W. C. Carrington, July 4, 1861, from Centreville; Brock Collection, HL.

54 An account of Benjamin's change of opinion is given by John Slidell in a letter of July 20, 1861, to S. L. M. Barlow; Barlow Papers. But Slidell, originally confident of a brief conflict, now anticipated a stubborn contest. The fact probably is that many men felt alternations of hope and despondency regarding the duration of the conflict.

was accomplished. Many local leaders showed appalling incapacity. "The imbecility and inaction of some of our State governments," Kirby-Smith wrote, "is and will be almost as disastrous as treachery." [55] Others, however, revealed astonishing resourcefulness.

Virginia was foremost in effective preparation. For this the energy of Letcher and quick organizing capacity of Lee were chiefly responsible. An estimate of the number of troops required for defense of the important points, 51,000 men, had been swiftly made. Quotas had been assigned various parts of the commonwealth, points of rendezvous established, and mustering officers appointed. By mid-June about 40,000 Virginians were in the field. Arms had been distributed: about 2,000 rifles and carbines and 41,650 muskets from eastern and central Virginia, with 13,000 pieces from Lexington, making 56,650 in all. Staff officers, including heads of the commissary, quartermaster, medical, and engineering departments, were acting with fair efficiency. Lee, pleased by the alacrity of the volunteering (except in western counties) was equally gratified by the promptness with which arrangements were made for instructing, equipping, and provisioning the forces. The State arsenal at Richmond had been rapidly expanded and the work of preparing munitions expedited. It had been found necessary to make carriages, caissons, battery wagons, and other items for the artillery, but Lee was able to report on June 15 that 115 guns for field service had already been provided, from which 20 light batteries of 4 guns each, with the requisite horses and harness, had been organized.

In addition, a Navy Department, theretofore unknown in Virginia, had been created. Defensive works had been built on the Elizabeth, James, York, and Rappahannock Rivers, naval batteries numbering some 320 pieces of heavy ordnance had been planted, and ammunition prepared—while some 120 pieces of heavy ordnance had been sent to other parts of the Confederacy. Between April 31 and June 14, Virginia expended for war $1,839,000, a sum which outstanding bills would bring to nearly $2,000,000. The stores and other property purchased, Letcher boasted, had been paid for as bought, and the credit of the State thus fully maintained. [56]

But other States, with weaker executives than Letcher, less gifted military leaders than Lee, and populations less ready for mobilization, lagged in the rear. Organization for war was much more difficult in Alabama, Mississippi, and Arkansas, while the threat of battle seemed less exigent. Nor was Virginia

---

55 J. H. Parks, *Kirby-Smith*, 127.
56 These facts are drawn from Letcher's message of June 17, 1861; Lee's long report to Letcher June 15; the letter of Captain S. Barron, of the Office of Naval Detail, June 10, 1861, to Letcher; the report of a committee of the Virginia Council June 3, 1861, on a conference with President Davis, and other documents in the Letcher Papers, Va. State Library.

Horace Greeley of *The Tribune*

Henry J. Raymond of *The Times*

herself without vital deficiencies. J. B. Jones in the War Department wrote June 18: "We have not enough ammunition to fight a battle. There are not percussion caps enough in our army for a serious skirmish." [57]

[VI]

Somewhat belatedly and reluctantly, Virginia transferred her forces to the Confederacy on June 8, 1861. Lee, who would have liked to retire to private life but who never failed to heed the voice of duty, became in some degree an acting assistant Secretary of War, and in part a deputy chief of what would later have been termed a general staff.[58] Beauregard, at Manassas, had an army of perhaps 20,000, which was steadily being reinforced. Joseph E. Johnston, under War Department orders, had taken command at Harpers Ferry, whence he was presently to fall back near Winchester to cover the Shenandoah Valley. "The want of ammunition," he explained in retreating, "has rendered me very timid." [59] Of the 8,000 rough-looking men he found at Harpers Ferry, 1,000 had not been armed, and he lacked artillery horses. Far across the commonwealth, where the hard-cropped tidewater plantations fronted the Atlantic, two experienced soldiers, Huger and Magruder, occupied positions on both sides of Hampton Roads. Huger had been brevetted thrice in the Mexican War for gallantry; in the same conflict T. J. Jackson, the future "Stonewall," had sought command under Magruder because he knew that if hard fighting was to be done, Magruder would be there. Other forces stood at Aquia Creek.

Most of Virginia, save for the western counties beyond the Allegheny wall, was ready to resist a Union onslaught. Along the Mississippi, at Memphis, at Island No. 10, at points just below the Kentucky-Tennessee line, at New Madrid and other Missouri points, forces of the Confederacy were gathering in formidable numbers. Hope rose high in Southern breasts that Missouri and Kentucky might soon be detached to strengthen them. Thus June of 1861 might be called the honeymoon month of the Confederacy. Eleven States seemed solidly inside it. It now held an imperial domain stretching from the Chesapeake to the Rio Grande, from the Georgia sea islands to the Indian Territory and even the far Southwest, from the frontier settlements of Arkansas to the oldest of American buildings in St. Augustine. Everywhere parade grounds echoed to the grounding of muskets and the bark of drill sergeants.

57 *Diary of a Rebel War Clerk,* I.
58 Freeman, *Lee,* I, 515 ff.
59 O. R. I, ii, 934. Johnston reached Harpers Ferry as a brigadier-general in the Confederate service, a post he accepted in preference to that of major-general in the army of Virginia. He found T. J. Jackson there, and Jackson, after insisting on seeing documentary proof of Johnston's seniority in rank, gave him cordial support. Freeman, *Lee,* I, 515, 516.

Troop trains still moved forward past cheering towns, where women thrust knapsacks, flowers, and dainties upon the soldiers. As bands blared, ardent youths remembered that theirs was the race of Agincourt, Yorktown, and Waterloo, and pulses leaped at the thought of new victories. Swords were bright, uniforms were fresh, limbs were unwearied. Despite all the confusion, the inadequacies, the clash of rival ambitions, the future looked roseate; beyond immediate sacrifice lay independence, and beyond that a resplendent national future.

Yet amid the bugles and roses, the pomp and parade, thousands watched what was happening with perturbation and anguish. For every Southerner who cheered, another was torn by regret and anxiety.

The provost-marshal at Cairo arrested a youth of seventeen, obviously guileless and of gentle breeding, as a spy. It turned out that the lad was from Pittsburgh, had served three months with the Twelfth Pennsylvania Volunteers, and had been honorably discharged. On the entreaty of his heartbroken mother he was trying to slip south, braving death to find a brother just wounded in Jeff Thompson's Confederate band.[60] A brothers' war indeed!—as a thousand instances proved; a war sometimes of father against son. It is no wonder that a citizen of Memphis wrote across the hostile lines to Horatio King in Washington to express his grief at what was going on. "It is a magnificent day, the sky is without a cloud, the air perfectly charming it is so bland, and indeed the city is as quiet as a sabbath in the country; but my God, what a contrast does the physical aspect of things present to the state of the country. I never have seen any excitement that approached the present in intensity. Men's passions seem to be surging and rolling like the billows of a storm-lashed ocean. It is terrible, terrible! Where is it to end?" [61] And a million women felt, at least intermittently, like John Esten Cooke's niece Nancie, who poured out her heart to that cultivated Virginia author:

"When will this frightful time be over? Sometimes I think I have gotten used to it, and then again when I am by myself, the thought that all I love best are in such constant danger almost drives me wild." [62]

60 This episode is related in a communication of the provost-marshal at Cairo to Lincoln's friend Gen. John A. McClernand, Oct. 26, 1861; McClernand Papers, Ill. State Hist. Lib. The boy's name was Charles Shaler.
61 J. W. Merriam of Memphis, April 21, 1861, to King; King Papers, LC.
62 Nancie Cooke, June 8, 1861, Cooke Papers, Duke Univ.

balance in Missouri and perhaps to help the secessionists in Kentucky.
in Buchanan's term the national government had taken some steps to
the arsenal, increasing the garrison to more than 400, with the able,
te, and unquestionably loyal Major Peter V. Hagner in command. Most
l officers thought the position safe. Not so Captain Nathaniel S. Lyon,
t Pointer of Connecticut origin and Mexican War experience who was
ed to the arsenal early in February. This thin, sandy-haired, red-bearded
man, his blue eyes full of fire, had learned on the Kansas border to hate
avery men, and was determined to take every precaution against loss of
post. He had wanted the command himself. Impetuous and explosive, he
essed highly fanatical traits.[2] He assailed the appointment of Hagner as
did favoritism on the part of General W. S. Harney, head of the Depart-
nt, declared that Hagner's deliberation in strengthening the arsenal showed
mbecility or damned villainy," and indicted Lincoln himself as lacking resolu-
on to deal with treason. Backed by Frank P. Blair, Jr., he obtained command
f the arsenal troops in the middle of March, while Hagner kept control of the
rdnance stores; and he gave notice that if Hagner in an emergency opposed
he marshaling of home-guard troops to defend the place, he would pitch him
into the river.

The taking of Sumter gave the expected impulse to the secessionist movement. Governor Jackson met the President's call for troops with an insulting
rebuff. Missourians in general, declared the St. Louis *Republican*, "denounce
and defy the action of Mr. Lincoln." The recent election of D. G. Taylor, a
wobbly anti-coercionist, as mayor, seemed to enhance the opportunities of
the pro-Southern elements for seizing the city and State.

Hungry for the 60,000 muskets, the 90,000 pounds of powder, the 1,500,000
ball cartridges, and the field guns lying in the arsenal, the secessionist legislators
bethought themselves of a plan for paralyzing their opponents and making
the most of their own strength. They passed a law placing the entire St. Louis
police force, the local militia, and the sheriff under four commissioners, to
named by the governor and to sit with the mayor. This meant that Cl
Jackson could manipulate the police, control the disloyal comp
perhaps paralyze the loyal home guard. As police commissio
promptly appointed three virulent secessionists and one anti-
countenanced the dressing of the city with Confederate fl
sympathizers might do in St. Louis had just been illus
Kansas City, where a small arsenal had been seized
in seditious Clay County.

2 The eulogistic tone of Ashbel Woodward, *Ge*
estimate in L. U. Reavis, *Gen. William Selby Harn.*

6

Struggle for the Western Border

IT WOULD BE erroneous to suppose that in the tense days after mid-April
all eyes were bent on Washington, Montgomery, and Richmond. Events in
the Mississippi Valley crowded as thickly on each other, and were of equal
import to the nation. The Northwest had a body of determined governors—
among others Richard Yates of Illinois, who promptly called out 6000 volunteers, took military possession of Cairo, and inspired the legislature to appropriate $3,500,000 for war; Oliver P. Morton of Indiana, who believed that the
conflict should be made "instant and terrible"; and Samuel J. Kirkwood of
Iowa, who borrowed from his friends to help equip the first levies. They
looked southward to a closely balanced border.

Nobody had ever accused the Kentuckians and Missourians of a want of
fighting temper. The men who had built palisades against the Shawnees with
Harrod, hewed farms from the forest with Boone, and marched to Chihuahua
with Doniphan, had bequeathed their children a readiness to face any foe. In
the convulsion of 1861, however, the overwhelming desire of the borderland
was to remain neutral. Their attitude suggested the nervousness of the bystander who sees that he may suffer more from a quarrel than either participant; but the paramount fact was that they preferred moderation, for in the
main they detested as equally repugnant the idea of secession and the idea of
abolition. The Bell-Everett platform of the Union, Constitution, and compromise had precisely expressed majority sentiment. Here, as in Maryland,
the spring wrote a record of their all but frantic effort to stay out of a conflict which they thought insane.

It is also the record of strenuous rival efforts by the Union and the Confederacy to win them to active collaboration. Their assistance might turn the
scale. In this contest, which side would blunder least? If Lincoln emphasized
freesoil too much and Union too little, he would certainly fail. If Jefferson
Davis pressed too hard and stressed ties of blood and institutions too arrogantly,
he would fail. The struggle for the border, with its general solidarity of outlook, its mingled devotion to State Rights and to the nation, and its mixed

economic interests, demanded patience, diplomacy, and psychological understanding as much as the exertion of force.

[I]

Of cardinal importance to the salvation of the Union was Missouri, by far the richest and strongest trans-Mississippi State. Its population was that of Massachusetts—each had about 1,200,000. It held one of the principal cities of the nation, St. Louis, with perhaps 175,000 people, and with factories, warehouses, mercantile establishments, influential newspapers, river shipping, and a well-stocked arsenal. If the secessionists could carry Missouri into the Confederacy, they might cut off Kansas, fan smoldering disloyalty in southern Illinois, and double the danger of the North's losing precariously-poised Kentucky.

When Sumter fell, the position of Missouri was doubtful. In the recent Presidential election Douglas and Bell had run neck and neck, Douglas leading by fewer than 500 votes. Both had far outstripped Breckinridge. If most of the aggregate Douglas, Bell, and Lincoln vote were considered a vote for the Union, the people stood about four to one against secession. Everyone knew the ardent attachment of the large German population in and near St. Louis to the Union; everyone knew, too, how much the prestige of the Blair family and the memory of the firm nationalism of Thomas Hart Benton counted.

But Union men who hoped that no attempt would be made to lead the State astray soon learned their error. The Missouri *Republican*, the oldest and long the ablest journal in the area, closely connected with the strongest men and richest interests of St. Louis, throughout the campaign had exerted its influence in favor of the Union. Nobody had supposed it would waver in its adherence to the principles of Webster and Clay. Suddenly, however, on December 31, 1860, it had carried an editorial addressed to the legislature then just assembling which fell upon Union men like a thunderclap. Northern wrongs to the South, it declared, demanded redress. The legislature should call a convention of all the slave States in Baltimore, and meanwhile assemble a State convention to consider such constitutional amendments as Congress might submit. If no remedy for the Southern grievances was attained before March 4, Missouri should then secede.

Union men had rubbed their eyes as they read. Their standard bearer had deserted to the enemy. "From that hour," writes one of the leaders, Charles D. Drake, "the secession conflict raged in Missouri as I believe it never would have raged if that paper had kept on the track it trod before." This is an overstatement, for the conflict was irrepressible. Nevertheless, the stand taken by

the journal did encourage the proslavery and pro-S... discouraged the Yankee freesoilers, liberty-loving G... who had organized as Wide-Awakes for Lincoln. proslavery politician who had helped overthrow Ben... elected governor as a Douglas Democrat, now rallied his... a secessionist standard.

"Probably not one member of either house had, bef... an avowed disunionist," adds Drake; "but when that bod... appeared that a majority of men in each house was made... stripe, who were ready to follow Claiborne Jackson's traito... waters had begun to boil like the Mississippi in flood.[1]

The legislature had given disunionists their cry, "No coerc... on February 21 a reply to the coercionist resolutions of Ohio a... "It is the opinion of the General Assembly that the people of... instantly rally on the side of their Southern brethren, to resist t... all hazards and to the last extremity." Throughout February a gr... ness of feeling was manifest on both sides, which Lincoln's inau... tensified. Claiborne Jackson, more and more ardent in the secessio... had established a confidential correspondence with Confederate le... and his friends had been hopeful that the State convention which, by l... decree, was elected on February 18 to consider Federal relations, wou... a secessionist character. But by a majority of about 80,000 the State pron... against disunion, choosing not a single secessionist delegate to the conve... After a committee had made a moderate, well reasoned report, the conve... voted 89 to 1 that Missouri had no adequate cause for dissolving her con... tion with the Union. Before March closed, both the legislature and convent... adjourned, leaving the State apparently committed to the Union and to peac... Only the extremists who rallied about Claiborne Jackson at one pole an... Nathaniel Lyon and Frank Blair at the other demanded belligerent policies.

Impromptu military units long before the inauguration had been drilling on... both sides. Along the Missouri River secessionists organized companies; in St. Louis, Unionists formed a strong home guard from the Wide-Awakes. In this situation, the Federal arsenal was the natural object of plots and counterplots. The secessionists hoped that when Washington took decisive action and war ...gan, they could seize the arms and equip their forces to carry Missouri into ... Confederacy. Had not the convention voted 89 to 6 in favor of evacuating ...nal troops from Southern forts? The arsenal held enough war materials to

...ake's MS autobiography, Mo. State Hist. Soc., is an enlightening document. See ...ene M. Violette, *A History of Missouri*; Lucy L. Tasher, "The Mo. Democrat and ...War," *Mo. Hist. Review*, XXXI, 1937, pp. 402-419

To Union men—to the incandescent Lyon, to the tall, lithe, hard-hitting, hard-drinking Frank Blair, at forty-one the youngest of the Blair clan and the idol of Missouri Republicans, to James O. Broadhead, a prominent lawyer, it seemed time to strike. To lose the arsenal, standing on low ground near the river and open to attack by water and land, would be to lose everything. Lyon by secret messengers induced Governor Yates of Illinois to put militia, under Presidential orders, on the steamboat *City of Alton*. On the night of April 25 the boat swiftly crossed the river, the militia swarmed ashore, and the arsenal gates were thrown open. Lyon had everything in readiness; 21,000 muskets, 500 rifle carbines, artillery, and large quantities of cartridges were hurried on board. Taken by the steamboat to Alton, where citizens joyously unloaded them, they at once went by rail to Springfield. "The secessionists are euchred," proclaimed the Union men.[3]

[II]

Even yet the situation seemed precarious. Lyon, fortifying the arsenal grounds, urged the enlistment of loyal men and formation of more home guards. Blair was elected colonel of a regiment which occupied Jefferson Barracks, about ten miles from the city. But most of the aristocratic older families of St. Louis sympathized with the South, a turbulent riverfront element might at any moment get out of hand, and much of the interior passionately hoped for Confederate success. In Lexington on the Missouri River, secessionists broke up a Union meeting. Business in Kansas City and St. Louis was half prostrate, thousands were out of work, and many prudent citizens were moving away. Claiborne Jackson actually had little power, but that little he used to make trouble. He called a special session of the legislature for May 3 to consider measures for enabling Missouri to defend herself, and he opened it with a message in which he threw himself squarely behind the Confederacy. He also gave orders, as was his legal right, for the regular annual brief militia encampments. "Our interests and sympathies are identical with those of the slaveholding States," he proclaimed, "and necessarily unite our destinies with theirs." [4] Such sentiments angered the loyal half of the State, which feared that the legislature might really take some provocative step.

3 Carr, *Missouri*, 293 ff., Galusha Anderson, *Border City*, 68 ff., Drake, MS Autobiography, and R. J. Rombauer, *The Union Cause in St. Louis, 1861*, cover the subject in detail. St. Louis contained a subtreasury with Federal money. Blair had led in converting the Wide-Awakes into a home guard military organization under a Committee of Safety; James Peckham, *Lyon and Missouri in 1861*.
4 John McElroy, *The Struggle for Missouri*; Galusha Anderson, *Border City*; T. L. Sneed, *The Fight for Missouri*; W. B. Stevens, *Centennial History of Missouri*, I; Drake, MS Autobiography.

And fanaticism evoked counter-fanaticism. General D. M. Frost, commander of the State militia, at the beginning of May formed a camp of about 700 men in Lindell's Grove on the western margin of St. Louis. He and many of his soldiers stood for armed neutrality. They were too weak, too divided in sentiment, too open in their movements, to menace the city or the now depleted arsenal. Frost, a West Point graduate and responsible man, had in fact offered to assist the Federal commanders in making certain of full national control of government property; an offer perhaps insincere, but worth receiving tolerantly. The governor, who nevertheless hoped that Camp Jackson, as it was called, might eventually be used to take the arsenal, saw to it that the men got arms and ammunition, partly smuggled from Federal sources. On May 8 a steamer from New Orleans brought in cannon and munitions, seized at the Baton Rouge arsenal, labeled "marble" and "ale." The governor had just written Confederate friends that he was confident the State would secede along with Kentucky and Tennessee. "They are all bound to go out and should go out together if possible," he declared, stating that this might be within a month. "Missouri can put in the field today 20,000 men, better armed than our fathers were, who won our independence." [5]

Camp Jackson certainly needed watching, and could not safely be allowed to grow. But its situation, commanded by surrounding hills, was weak; its force was puny compared with the 10,000 well-armed Union troops and loyal volunteers hard by; and all its drills were open to the public. General Harney, a loyal veteran of the Seminole and Mexican Wars, and a man who knew Missouri well, believed that peace could safely be preserved. Yet Lyon, who was new to the State, for he had arrived in February, let his hatred of slavery and puritanical zealotry overmaster him; he rushed into inflammatory action just when calmness was needed.

In his eyes, according to his biographer, Camp Jackson was a fearful menace. Announcements that it would break up on or about May 10 might be only a dark stratagem; and if it did break up, the men might go home to enlist in secessionist units. Moreover, reading of the Baltimore riot, Ben Butler's seizure of the Annapolis railroad, and the Northern mobilization, Lyon decided that it was time to strike a hard blow at secession in Missouri and thus teach traitors their place. The applause which the Northwest had given his raid on the arsenal encouraged him. According to a dramatic but dubious story, he had toured the camp disguised as the venerable mother-in-law of Frank Blair, peering at the militiamen and their piled arms through a black veil as his wheelchair was pushed down the alleyways, and noting indignantly that one

5 Full text of letter in *Loyal Legion Papers, Missouri Commandery*, I, 23–25. Cf. Smith, *Borderland*, 230 ff.

company street was called "Davis," and another "Beauregard." Enlisting the support of Blair and three other members of the committee of safety—though two members objected that a Federal marshal might easily replevin the Baton Rouge arms—Lyon prepared to attack the camp. He would demolish this nest of rebels—he would show hesitant neutrals which side to choose! On the 10th he moved several thousand troops about the camp, summoned its officers to surrender, and made the militia prisoners.[6]

This was reckless enough. Still more injudicious was Lyon's decision not to parole the disarmed militia, but to march them into St. Louis as a spectacle. Southern sympathizers had poured into the streets, excited and resentful. As they saw the dejected prisoners file past under guard of Yankee and German volunteers, passions broke loose; they hurled first gibes, then stones; and at a point where a unit called Die Schwarze Guard by friends and Dutch Blackguards by enemies had halted, a collision occurred. Lyon's forces began firing indiscriminately, twenty-eight persons were killed or mortally wounded, scores were injured, and the city was thrown into an uproar.

This was the blackest day in all St. Louis' history. Fear and anger rose on both sides to the fever point. Next day a new affray cost six lives. The secessionists raged against Lyon, German newspapers, and the home guard; loyal citizens kept a sullen silence. Inevitably, some Union men in Missouri and many readers of brief and distorted accounts of the affair in the Northern press hailed Lyon as a hero whose resolute action had saved the State. That legend, popularized in history and fiction, has survived.[7] But the truth is that Lyon and Frank Blair, Jr., both rash, headstrong, and excitable, had dealt an unnecessary stroke, aroused emotions better left quiescent, and in one day done far more harm to the Union cause and the best interests of Missouri than Frost and Claiborne Jackson, left alone, could have accomplished in a month. Their action, under the excitement of the time, is understandable, but it was unwise.

From this moment Missouri was given over to four years of violence and a cruel intestine war. As rumors spread that German volunteers were threatening to burn the city, a thousand people fled town in a single afternoon. Some streets were left entirely deserted. Not until General Harney, returning to headquarters, published a reassuring proclamation, was calm partly restored. While disloyal elements were only partly cowed in the city, the Missouri River

6 General Harney, who as departmental commander would certainly have restrained Lyon, was temporarily absent from the area; in fact, Lyon deliberately took advantage of his absence. Frost, apprised of the coming attack, wrote Lyon declaring he had no disloyal designs, and again offering to help preserve peace and order in the area. O. R. I, iii, 7–8.

7 See the accounts in the *Annual Cyclopaedia*, 1861, pp. 660, 661; in John Fiske, *The Mississippi Valley in the Civil War* (highly misleading); in Winston Churchill, *The Crisis*; and in Nicolay and Hay, IV, 198 ff.

belt was vibrant with Southern feeling. Reports reached many towns that German troops and antislavery fanatics were butchering men, women, and children. Some communities rose en masse, determined to arm themselves with pitchforks and scythes, if nothing better, march on St. Louis, and stamp out the violence. Only later reports and the news of Harney's judicious measures partially allayed the anger. That sagacious commander ordered all the German volunteers out of the city, replacing them by United States regulars; kept riotous groups off the streets; closed political meetings; punished crime; and searched the town for arms, confiscating more than a thousand rifled muskets and two small cannon. Most of the citizens who had fled soon returned.[8]

However, Harney could not undo the harm wrought by Lyon and Blair; for the moment the news of the St. Louis bloodshed reached Jefferson City, full civil war in the State lay just ahead. A scene of angry pandemonium in the legislature gave way to determined action. The governor's bill to arm the State on the Confederate side had till then slept; now it was revived, passed with instant speed, and sent to Claiborne Jackson to be signed. Cooperation with the Indians was authorized. The members had hardly gone to their lodgings to sleep when a telegram that Lyon and 2,000 men were marching to seize the governor and legislature roused the town. Bells were rung, the legislature was convened in midnight session, and new measures were passed to arm the State.[9] In the next five days the legislature paid every cent in the treasury into the military fund, authorized Jackson to borrow another million to equip troops, and empowered him to organize the military forces, seize the railroads and telegraphs, lease a foundry at Boonville to manufacture arms, and do anything else needful.

The governor acted with energy to throw Missouri on the Confederate side. Secessionists poured into Jefferson City and other mustering points. As major-general in command Jackson appointed Sterling Price, a highminded man of Virginia birth who had been colonel in the Mexican War, Congressman, a courageous Democratic governor, and president of the recent convention. He was a conditional Unionist until the aggressive acts of Lyon and Blair converted him to secession. Another former governor, J. S. Marmaduke, who had also been a conditional Unionist, went into the State forces. Secessionist forces seemed about to dominate most of the State outside St. Louis. Some of them, collecting in irregular bands which drove Union men from their homes, inaugurated the guerrilla activities which in time seemed likely to make half of

8 St. Louis correspondence dated May 13 in N. Y. *Tribune*, May 14, 1861. The Columbia (Mo.) *Statesman*, April–June 1861, throws valuable light on events from the Union standpoint. On March 28, 1862, the *Statesman* published revealing letters by Claiborne Jackson written during the crisis.
9 Peckham, *op. cit.;* W. F. Switzler, *Illustrated History of Missouri*, 315.

Missouri a desert.[10] On the Confederate side all was unity and determination.

One result of the reckless Blair-Lyon policy, on the other hand, was to divide the Union supporters. General Harney did his utmost to restore confidence in moderate policies. He of course never wavered in his allegiance to the Union cause. Missouri must remain loyal, he declared; he would maintain the national authority wherever his arm could reach; and he would never tolerate the recent legislative enactments, the fruit of needless excitement. Though he endorsed Lyon's coup (a necessary act, despite his private doubts), he spoke in what he called "tranquillizing" terms, and asked authority to enlist an Irish regiment to mollify the general feeling against Federal forces which were composed almost entirely of Germans. Had it been possible, he would have dismissed the home guards. Blair and Lyon watched this policy with hostility.[11]

What was more serious, Blair and Harney soon clashed on the question of a truce. In his sagacious way, the veteran general began negotiations with Price, asking him to suspend the recent military act. A meeting followed, at which the two agreed on a pacific manifesto (May 21). Both, they said, were intent on "restoring peace and good order," and relied on the Federal and State governments to effect this. Price would use all his State forces to maintain order; Harney would make no military movements likely to create excitement or jealousy. Thus was proclaimed an armed truce like that which Lincoln was countenancing in Kentucky, a sensible procedure. On May 29, Harney reported that the State was gradually being pacified, and this was true.[12]

Lyon and Blair, however, outraged by Harney's course, did their utmost to bring it into discredit. During May, Blair began pulling wires in Washington for Harney's removal and the appointment of Lyon in his stead. The peppery soldier from Connecticut reported to Washington on June 3 his belief that a Confederate movement into northwestern Arkansas was being coordinated with mysterious and industrious shifts of Price's forces toward southwestern Missouri. The two collected and made the most of stories of secessionist outrages on Unionist farmers and villagers, some true, some untrue.

Inevitably, conservative Union men aligned themselves behind Harney, while radicals took the side of Blair. Among the moderates was Ethan Allen Hitchcock, another veteran soldier of honorable record, who later declared that he had drafted the Price-Harney agreement. Among the radicals was the editor of the Missouri *Democrat*, the most influential Republican journal in the

10 Smith, *Borderland*, 241, states: "Much of the later bitterness with which guerrilla warfare was carried on in Missouri was probably due to the feelings engendered by the occurrences at Camp Jackson."
11 Harney's course may be followed in his letters to the War Department, O. R. I, iii, 373 ff.
12 O. R. I, iii, 375–382.

[handwritten: The Democrat, most influential Rep journal in the state]

State. As Blair made it clear that he must have Harney's head on a platter, the schism extended to the Cabinet in Washington. Montgomery Blair exerted himself fiercely on the side of the brother he hoped one day to see in the White House. Attorney-General Bates took Harney's side, but without energy. It became plain, though Lincoln hesitated, that the general's tenure was coming to a close.[13]

The Blairs had a motto of rule or ruin—of fighting to a finish. With clan spirit, they fought always for each other. It is evident that Frank Blair intended to be the Missouri Warwick, dominating the State politically and militarily. Lincoln was unwilling to give Lyon the command, declaring that he seemed too rash. Finally, however, he yielded to the pressure and sent Frank Blair an order for Harney's removal, to be used only if an emergency arose which justified such extreme action. The day after sending it, overcome by doubts of its propriety, he followed it with another letter, in which he impressed upon Blair that it was to be delivered only if Blair thought this "indispensable." Of course Blair did think so. In characteristically ruthless fashion, on May 31 he gave the humiliated Harney the order for dismissal.

Now the path was open for disrupting the truce. On June 11, at a long-famous conference in the Planters' House in St. Louis, Blair and Lyon faced Price across a table. The Covenanter and the Ironside met the Cavalier. They grimly laid down demands that Price, who had long detested Blair, could not meet. In fact, they declared they would yield not one inch for the sake of State concord. Price strode out to rally his forces, and to begin open war.

In thus carrying Missouri into full civil war before mid-June, Blair and Lyon acted according to their honest conviction and best lights, but with rash arrogance. In great part, the horrors and losses from which this unhappiest of States was to suffer were traceable to their precipitate, intolerant course. Born fighters both, they preferred mortal conflict to a patient reliance on compromise and delay. Although the situation was full of danger, the preponderant evidence indicates that Harney was right in believing that the loyal Missourians needed only time and tranquillity to consolidate their position in the Union. As he said, Union men outnumbered secession men in the interior of the State two to one; in St. Louis, which had nearly one-sixth the population of the State, Union sentiment was not only ascendant, but was bulwarked by strong Federal forces; and Missouri was half surrounded by Kansas, Iowa, and Illinois, all belligerently devoted to the Union. The truce which Harney had made with Price offered more advantages to the North than the

13 Smith, *Blair Family in Politics*, II, Ch. 29; Snead, *Fight for Missouri*, 100 ff.; E. A. Hitchcock, *Fifty Years in Camp and Field*, 431. Nicolay and Hay, IV, 217 ff., take the side of the Blairs, for Lincoln accepted that side; but Lincoln did not yet know how selfishly contriving the Blairs often were.

South, for every day of peace fortified loyal sentiment. It is clear that Price, an honorable conditional-Union man anxious to see difficulties composed, was doing all that he could to restore order. He had kept his promise of dismissing his force.

Blair, however, insisted on having his way. He had exceeded the authority which Lincoln entrusted to him in giving Harney his dismissal, for that act was by no means indispensable to meet an emergency, as Lincoln had stipulated. Lyon was still more insistent on taking his own course. This Yankee captain was as intemperate in speech as in action. "Rather than concede to the State of Missouri for one single instant the right to dictate to my Government in any matter however unimportant," he had told Price, "I would see you . . . and every man, woman, and child in the State dead and buried. This means war." [14]

Four days after the conference in the Planters' Hotel, fighting commenced at Lexington. It was certain that the Union forces could in time conquer the State. But it was also certain that their conquest would leave it seething with hatreds, divided county by county, even farm by farm, by the bitterest antagonisms, and racked with internecine war. Of all border States, we repeat, Missouri was destined to suffer most, and her suffering was to a great extent the work of three men: the fire-eating Claiborne Jackson, the fanatical Lyon, and the ambitious Frank Blair. Her strength was to fall mainly on the Union side, but it was nothing like the strength she might have exerted.

[III]

In Kentucky, Union feeling up to the time of Lincoln's inauguration had been strong. The lifelong teachings of Henry Clay still swayed many hearts. Kentucky had been the first-born child of the Union, her sons had been nationalists since the War of 1812, and most of her river counties looked to Cincinnati and Pittsburgh as their natural gateways. Just before the Presidential election the Kentucky and Ohio legislators had held a fraternal gathering at Columbus, Ohio. John Bell's Constitutional Union Party had carried the State. Many slaveholders believed that the only safety for the peculiar institution, which must wither if exposed to the chill blasts of world opinion, lay in the Union. Even Paducah, closely connected by trade with the Gulf States and the center of a populous slaveholding district, kept a Unionist majority.

To be sure, Kentuckians were so intimately bound by blood, culture, and institutions with Virginia and North Carolina, which had mainly peopled the State, that the thought of war with the South was abhorrent. If majority

14 Quoted by Snead, 199, 200; he was present. See also Smith, *Borderland*, 253. Lyon's aide quotes him in only a slightly less bloody-tongued utterance; Peckham, 248.

sentiment was firmly against secession, it was just as strongly against coercion of the secessionists.[15] But in the recent election the vote for Bell, Douglas, and Lincoln had totaled 93,073 as against 53,143 for Breckinridge. Kentuckians had enthusiastically supported Crittenden's proposals for compromise, as an alternative; many looked favorably on Governor Beriah Magoffin's plan for guaranteeing slavery within the States, enforcing the return of fugitives, and drawing a new territorial line along the 37th parallel.

The State had its share of able men. Leslie Combs, a veteran of the War of 1812, a Whig leader who had once been Clay's ablest lieutenant at the State capital, and an inspiring speaker, was as stanch in his devotion to the nation as the conscientious, universally respected John J. Crittenden. James Guthrie, first citizen of Louisville and the ablest banker and railroad executive of the region, was destined to bring both his influence and his invaluable Louisville & Nashville Railroad to the Union cause. Kentucky, in contrast with her slave neighbor up the river, was happy in having such a trio to battle the Southern sympathizers Breckinridge and Magoffin.

It was an agonizing hour for the fair land of bluegrass and rhododendron. Foreseeing that war might soon roll along the Ohio and Cumberland, that family might fight against family, that armies from the northern and eastern counties might battle against armies from the southern and western, the best leaders had looked to compromise, and, if that failed, to neutrality.[16] Combs had denounced the "Destructionists"—the men North and South who used every device to create bitterness. By shrewd action, the moderates had managed to keep control of the situation. Early in January the Bell-Everett chieftains, meeting in Louisville, had established a Union State Central Committee to organize their followers behind a moderate Unionist program, and thus had done much to keep in hand the special legislative session which met January 17.[17] Possibly Breckinridge hoped that this body would "precipitate"

15 The Frankfort *Commonwealth* and Lexington *Observer and Reporter*, both Union Journals, steadily inveighed in March and April, 1861, against secession. The former attacked (April 12) the "trickery and cunning of the conspirators" of the Deep South ever since they had disrupted the Democratic convention in Charleston.

16 Many Kentuckians were worried about navigation rights on the Mississippi. C. F. Burnham, a member of the legislature, wrote James S. Rollins of Missouri March 15, 1861: "We will denounce the piratical laws of the Southern Congress on the obstruction of the navigation of the Mississippi and the imposing of tariff duties on shipping on that stream. We will take nothing from them as a concession, we *demand* its free navigation as a *right* which must never be interfered with." Rollins Papers, Mo. Hist. Soc.

17 An unsigned memorandum to Lincoln, dated April 1, 1861, written probably by Green Adams, is in the R. T. L. Papers. "In Kentucky the Union party has a majority of about 40,000," it states. "They are faithful and loyal to the general government and the Constitution, anxious for its supremacy being maintained and above all are anxious for Peace. But the minority, and it is a dangerous minority, are open or disguised disunionists according to locality."

the State into secession. If so, he was foiled. "Thank God," Combs wrote later, "there were found loyal and patriotic Democrats who preferred principle to party—their country to a selfish and arrogant faction—and they united with us to save the Union." [18]

The moderates had no difficulty in defeating Governor Magoffin's scheme for a convention to consider the secession issue. Instead, the legislators demanded that the South halt its secession movement, and that the North give up all idea of coercion. They also invited the other States to join in a national convention. To Breckinridge, who delivered a speech declaring that the Union could not be restored, and that Kentucky should mediate for continued peace between the two independent confederacies, they listened coldly.

When Sumter fell, the passionate anxiety of the people to keep their State from becoming a battleground for contending armies found immediate expression. Governor Magoffin telegraphed Lincoln that Kentucky would furnish no troops "for the wicked purpose of subduing her sister Southern States," but a week later refused a similar call for men from Jefferson Davis. The State Union Committee declared that Kentucky could tie herself neither to the chariot wheels of the Lincoln Administration nor the Gulf State wagon, and should repel any invasion of her sacred soil. Guthrie told a Louisville meeting that it would be equally wrong to supply militia for the national government or to raise volunteers for the Confederacy. To be sure, plenty of excited and bellicose partisans could be found, those for the Union chiefly in the cities and eastern Kentucky, those for the cotton kingdom in the wealthier agricultural districts. The great majority, however, with a fervor which in retrospect appears pathetically sincere, hoped to avoid setting brother against brother. They had a premonition of the terrible moment when at Missionary Ridge the Fourth Kentucky, U.S.A., lined up in full view of the Fourth Kentucky, C.S.A., and kinsmen stared down each others' muzzles.

Let the war, wrote one editor, the brilliant George D. Prentice of the Louisville *Journal*, find the Transylvania land calm in armed neutrality, an asylum for victims of the carnage, "a sublime example to her erring sisters." Let her, wrote a poet, rise serene above strife:

Orbed in order, crowned with olives, there invoking peace, she stands. . . .

Magoffin by proclamation warned both the Federal and Confederate governments not to encroach on Kentucky soil, and forbade citizens to make any hostile demonstrations against either side. While he leaned strongly to the secessionist position and continued to urge a State convention, Union strength

18 Combs in N. Y. *Tribune*, May 9, 1861; letter dated Lexington, Ky., April 29. For an excellent general account of events see E. M. Coulter, *The Civil War and Readjustment in Kentucky*.

easily sufficed to hold him in check. The governor momentarily believed that he might persuade Ohio, Tennessee, Indiana, and Missouri to join Kentucky in a movement for mediation. Leaders of Tennessee and Missouri, when he opened negotiations, seemed responsive, but Governors Morton and Dennison north of the Ohio returned emphatic negatives.[19]

Inevitably, Magoffin seemed to the leaders both in Washington and Richmond to be playing a double part. For a time after Sumter, he secretly let Confederate recruiting agents operate in Kentucky; then, conscious of the danger of provoking stern Federal action, he drew back. By April 24, General Gideon J. Pillow was warning the Confederate War Office that the governor, surrounded by Black Republicans, was undependable. "I condemn and utterly abhor his neutral policy, or rather his alliance with Lincoln; but yet I am satisfied that he will ultimately break the shackles with which he is now manacled." [20] Lincoln's informants were equally certain that Magoffin was allied with black secessionists and Jefferson Davis. In reality, he was honestly torn between his Southern sympathies and his love of the Union. He was author of the plan by which six arbiters, chosen by party caucuses, drew up a neutrality agreement that had been given approval in advance by the legislature. Despite his temporary sanction of some secret Confederate recruiting, he was substantially loyal to this agreement.

And secession received a crushing moral blow in Kentucky when on May 4 voters went to the polls to elect a Border State convention which the legislature had called to meet later that month in Frankfort. At the last moment the Southern Rights party, foreseeing defeat, withdrew its ticket, so that a full Union slate was chosen. But it was the size of the vote which counted. Two-thirds as many ballots were cast as in the recent Presidential election, and the Union vote in Louisville was substantially larger than the Presidential vote.[21] Clearly, Kentucky would stand firm—unless rash Federal leaders, by gratuitous violence, thrust the southern and eastern sections into the arms of the Confederacy. The legislature which Magoffin called into a new session May 6 found the election results a clear verdict for the Union; and this verdict

19 *National Intelligencer*, April 18, 1861. Former Senator Archibald Dixon also stood for neutrality; see Coulter, 41 ff. Senator Garrett Davis was wholeheartedly for neutrality. "Let Kentucky look for herself. . . . Let her stand immovable as a rock peering above the tempest-tossed ocean." Frankfort *Commonwealth*, May 3, 1861. But the lion-hearted Joseph Holt had no use for neutralists. This Kentuckian, now living in Washington, wrote a long letter May 31 to J. F. Speed, published in the Louisville *Journal*, saying the ship *Union* must be saved: "The man who, in such an hour, will not work at the pumps, is either a maniac or a monster."

20 O. R. I, xlii, pt. 2, 68–70.

21 Louisville *Journal*, May 6, 1861; *Ann. Cyc.*, 1861, pp. 396, 397. The border convention proved abortive, only Missouri and Kentucky sending delegates.

was presently underwritten by a special election to fill Congressional seats, nine of the ten districts selecting stanch Union men.[22]

In this critical hour Lincoln displayed masterly comprehension and alertness. He believed, as he wrote later, that to lose Kentucky with her 1,200,000 people and her strategic position on the Ohio and Mississippi would almost be losing "the whole game." Avoiding threats, showing a warm feeling for his and his wife's birth State, offering promises of kindly treatment, he kept the velvet glove over the iron gauntlet. To Garrett Davis he gave the friendliest assurances, saying:

That he intended to make no attack, direct or indirect, upon the institutions or property of any State; but on the contrary, would defend them. . . . And that he did not intend to invade with an armed force, or to make any military or naval movements against any State, unless she or her people should make it necessary by a formidable resistance of the authority and laws of the United States. . . . That he contemplated no military operations that would make it necessary to move any troops over her territory—though he had an unquestioned right at all times. . . . That if Kentucky made no demonstration of force against the United States he would not molest her. That he regretted the necessity of marching troops across Maryland, but forces to protect the seat of the United States Government could not be concentrated there without doing so; and he intended to keep open a line of communication through that State to Washington City, at any risk, but in a manner less calculated to irritate and inflame her people.[23]

At once, in mid-May, Kentucky assumed a formal status of neutrality. The House voted 69 to 26 that the Commonwealth should take no part in the war except as mediators and friends to the belligerents. Governor Magoffin announced a strict neutrality in terms that might have been used by Brazil or Norway. Good Kentuckians, he declared, should refrain from words or deeds likely to "engender hot blood."

Many Kentucky merchants, busy with invoices and ledgers, continued to trade profitably with both North and South. Louisville remained such a great collecting center for goods shipped into the Confederacy that she aroused the jealous wrath of Cincinnati. Although early in May Union troops blockaded the Mississippi at Cairo, trains continued to puff southward on the Louisville & Nashville, bulging with provisions, clothing, shoes, and hardware. Even munitions leaked through. Groaning wagons swelled the flow, for corn that sold

22 The Congressional elections were held June 30; the vote was Union, 92,460; State Rights, 37,700.
23 Garrett Davis' letter describing his interview with Lincoln, written to George D. Prentice from Baltimore April 28, was published in the Frankfort *Commonwealth*, May 3, 1861, and reprinted in *Cong. Globe*, 37th Cong., 2d Sess., Pt. 4, pp. 82, 83.

at twenty cents a bushel north of the Ohio fetched fifty cents farther south. This trade had the tacit consent of Lincoln, anxious to keep Kentucky's good will, and bitterly did Northwestern governors and editors upbraid him. Not until August 16, nearly a month after Bull Run, did he bow to recent Congressional legislation by proclaiming a stoppage of commercial intercourse with the South. And even after that, under a liberal permit system instituted by Chase in the Treasury, trade with the South continued in Kentucky on a reduced scale.

[IV]

It was certain that Kentucky, barring some revulsion of sentiment, was safe for the Union. It was also certain that neutrality could not permanently endure. A sense of tension and imminent conflict pervaded the State. "We will remain in the Union," wrote Garrett Davis, "by voting if we can, by fighting if we must, and if we cannot hold our own, we will call on the General Government to aid us." [24]

The State, everyone agreed, had to be armed. But who would control its forces? Magoffin asked the legislature to appropriate $3,000,000 to be used by himself and Adjutant-General Simon Buckner in augmenting and arming the State Guard, already a strong body. Buckner was in secret correspondence with the Confederate leaders. When the governor proclaimed himself commander-in-chief of all State forces, the legislators took alarm. They placed the military under a board of four trusty Union men, created a home guard to counteract the State Guard, and required privates and officers of both organizations to swear allegiance to the Union. The military board were directed to take charge of the State arsenal at Frankfort, and of every gun, bullet, and pound of powder in State possession anywhere. Thus was Samson shorn of his locks. Many communities had been mustering local units. Those which stood for the Union now found themselves strongly supported by the board, the legislature, and Union leaders who had direct communication with Lincoln and Stanton.[25]

By the end of May the Unionists had thus gained decided advantages. Lincoln's friend Joshua F. Speed, a wealthy businessman in Louisville, and his older brother James Speed, an influential jurist there, threw their energies into support of the national government. The President quietly sent out Major Robert Anderson and Naval Lieutenant William Nelson, both Kentuckians.

24 May 16, 1861, to McClellan; O. R., III, i, 236.
25 See the letter of "Union" in Frankfort *Commonwealth*, May 29, 1861, describing how the legislature "in the name of an outraged people have taken from the hands of the Governor all his military power."

Anderson was directed to establish an office in Cincinnati to recruit Kentucky and West Virginia volunteers, while Nelson was to distribute 5000 government muskets and bayonets among loyal men. Senator Garrett Davis and various associates visited Cincinnati for arms and distributed them to companies far and wide. Anderson decided, on the advice of Guthrie, the Speeds, and others, that it would be impolitic to try to raise any Kentucky regiments for the Union army, for this would break the nominal "neutrality." Organization and arming of home-guard units, however, proceeded rapidly.[26] Meanwhile, the loyalty oath compelled Simon Buckner to carry a large body of the State Guard into Confederate service farther south—the Louisville *Journal* shrieking after him: "You are the Benedict Arnold of the day! You are the Catiline of Kentucky! Go, thou miscreant!"[27]

As these advantages were gained, however, a sharp difference of opinion developed in the North. Lincoln, certain that Kentucky was the very pivot of the war, remained willing for the time being to accept her "conditional Unionism." That neutral status, he believed, would save the State intact while sentiment for full participation developed. The government posted large Union forces at Cairo, but did not attempt to enter Kentucky. Early in May, Colonel B. M. Prentiss at Cairo felt some fear that Confederate troops might suddenly be concentrated at Columbus, the Kentucky terminus of the railroad from New Orleans, and attack him. An officer of Kentucky militia therefore called to say that he would equally resist a Northern invasion from Illinois, and a Southern invasion from Tennessee. Although Lincoln accepted this attitude, much Northern sentiment found it intolerable. Who is not for us, many said, is against us!

Lincoln's tolerance of wavering elements, his insistence on a cautious, placatory policy, struck aggressive Northerners as both impolitic and irresolute. To them no Halfway House was permissible; better an open traitor than a hypocrite. Governors Morton, Yates, and Dennison asserted that they were ready to move forward sufficient troops to support a vigorous Union regime in Kentucky. Northern editors began contrasting the decided action by which Blair and Lyon had discomfited Claiborne Jackson in Missouri with Lincoln's kid-glove handling of Magoffin. A little boldness, they said, will bring numerous Kentucky regiments to our colors and shorten the war. When Major Anderson, under Administration orders, rejected a regiment raised among Kentucky Unionists, and its heads appealed to leading members of Congress, their response was emphatic: If Kentucky chooses to leave the

26 Nicolay and Hay, IV, 234 ff.; Coulter, *passim*. The Frankfort *Commonwealth*, June 7, 1861, carries Garrett Davis' long statement to a legislative committee on the work he had done to aid Anderson and Nelson in distributing arms from Cincinnati and Louisville.
27 September 27, 1861.

Union because the nation accepts the voluntary service of her sons, let her try! Old Tom Ewing, born the year the Constitution went into effect, who had read Virgil in the Ohio wilderness, opposed Jackson's financial measures, and served in Zachary Taylor's Cabinet, wrote Crittenden: "There can be no truce or compromise until the opposites have met in force and measured strength—and the sooner the better." [28]

Unquestionably, however, Lincoln showed the greater wisdom. While the slowly gathering Northern armies were still largely unequipped, Virginia had joined the Confederacy, formidable forces had gathered at Richmond, Manassas, and Harpers Ferry, and fighting had begun in western Virginia and central Missouri. Lincoln did not want the flames to spread—as yet—to Kentucky. He knew how easily a few echoing shots could loose an avalanche of passion. One Kentucky Unionist, reporting late in April that every town and precinct was organizing military companies, added: "If the war is general between the two sections I presume more havoc will be made in this State than anywhere else." [29] Men might sneer at what James Russell Lowell termed Lincoln's "Little Bo-Peep policy," but he intended to stay that havoc. He wanted to see the State kept an integer until its position in the Union column was fairly secure.

The President did allow himself one jest on the subject. A Kentucky State senator wrote him a bombastic protest against the stationing of troops in Cairo. Lincoln replied, in a letter unfortunately lost, that if he had only known that Cairo, Illinois, was in this Kentuckian's senatorial district, he would not have sent any soldiers within a hundred miles of the point.[30] But his conviction was clear and firm.

Time proved his sagacity. To the last year of the war Missouri, where Blair's rough policy had prevailed, was a source of deep anxiety and a potential liability; but Kentucky, though much more exposed, soon became one of the bastions of the North. She gave in all perhaps 75,000 men to the Union armies as against a third that number to the Confederacy, and under the shock of invasion, as we shall see, stood firm.[31]

28 Cf. Lossing, Civil War, I, 460 ff.; Anderson to J. J. Crittenden, June 25, Thomas Ewing July 8, 1861, Crittenden Papers, Duke Univ.
29 C. F. Burnham of Richmond, Ky., April 22, 1861, to James S. Rollins; Rollins Papers, Mo. State Hist. Soc.
30 Frankfort Commonwealth, May 29, 1861.
31 J. S. Johnston gives this estimate in Confederate Military History, IX, 201.

7

Struggle for the Eastern Border

THROUGHOUT the early weeks of the war the Stars and Stripes over the national capitol were challenged by a Confederate banner in plain view on the Virginia hills, a symbol of the proximity of danger not lost upon the troops who were fast turning the sleepy town into a busy garrison city. The unfinished white obelisk of Washington Monument, a litter of stone blocks, sheds, and derricks about its base, and the skeleton Capitol dome, its iron ribs stark against the sky, were symbolic too; they seemed eloquent of the incomplete national edifice. Washington was full of new sights and sounds; the tramp and clatter of regiments drilling; parades with drum and fife; whitish-brown camps springing up all along the slopes of the northern outskirts; guns practicing at the navy yard. As May and June brought hot, dry days, mule-drawn trains of army wagons churned dust into the air—"Real estate is high," jested the citizens—and stenches increased.

The first strategic necessity, from the Union point of view, was to make Maryland secure, seize western Virginia, and fortify the south bank of the Potomac. Only when Washington felt that it was safe, could it turn to larger tasks. For a time the area within a half-arc drawn fifty miles north and a hundred and fifty west of the city was of burning concern.

Maryland, whose half-million white people could not long ignore the facts of geography, was undergoing a rapid change of sentiment. It was more fortunate than Kentucky in that a great river was its southern, not northern, boundary. Temporarily the confused Governor Hicks talked of neutrality. He not only told the legislature when it met April 26th that the State's only safety lay in a neutral position, but actually proposed to Lincoln that Lord Lyons, the British minister, be asked to mediate between the "contending factions"! This chimera of neutrality beguiled the legislators into a denunciation of both Southern secession and Northern coercion. The House sent deputies to Lincoln to protest against seizure of the Maryland railroads and treatment of the State as a conquered province. James M. Mason, recently senator from Virginia, had hurried to Baltimore to talk with the speaker, other officers, and many members, whom he reported so "earnest and zealous in the cause of the South" that he felt sure they would take steps "to place the authority of the State in hands ready and competent to act with Virginia." But beyond a few protests, and an academic declaration in favor of Southern independence, the Southern sympathizers in the legislature dared not go.

Dominant sentiment was swinging to the Union side. "A large majority of the inhabitants," reported the British consul, "including the wealthy and intelligent portion, are only waiting for sufficient encouragement and protection to avow their loyalty"; and a little later Reverdy Johnson, head of the Maryland bar, who was denouncing secession as treason and bringing his influence as former senator and attorney-general to the support of the Union, noted that national sentiment was fast increasing. Confederate destruction of property of the Chesapeake & Ohio Canal and Baltimore & Ohio Railroad assisted in the revulsion. When Maryland elected members of Congress early in June the Union won the entire slate.[1]

From their fortified position on Federal Hill overlooking Baltimore, the Union forces brooked neither open opposition nor covert treachery. Ben Butler, arresting the gray-haired ironmaster Ross Winans on the charge that he had made 5000 pikes for rebels and committed other offenses, declared that hanging a man worth fifteen millions would teach traitors a lesson. Winans was released in chastened mood. Governor Hicks also rapidly saw a new light. On May 15, to meet the President's request of a month earlier, he called out four regiments; and although they were not accepted, the time for ninety-day troops having passed, recruiting stations steadily sent forward Union volunteers. Indeed, throughout the war Maryland nearly filled its quotas. Before long the governor was collecting arms to keep them out of the hands of Southern sympathizers and taking other steps in aid of the Union. The adherence of West Virginia to the North naturally strengthened the national cause in the State. Replying to secessionist demands that Maryland follow her sister Virginia, the novelist John P. Kennedy demanded, "*Which Virginia?*" [2]

Like other border areas, eastern Maryland remained hotly divided in sentiment. Many women flaunted secessionist rosettes; haughty citizens ostentatiously brushed their coats as they passed Union soldiers; heads of the City Club shut its doors against Northern officers; newsboys sold Confederate songs and caricatures; shop windows carried pictures of Davis and Lee; crowded theaters applauded Southern sentiments. On the other side, women

1 House Document A, 1861; E. M. Archibald (British consul), April 27, 1861, FO/5 778; G. L. P. Radcliffe, *Hicks and the Civil War*, 78 ff.; James M. Mason, April 25, 1861, to the governor of Virginia, Mason Papers, Va. State Library.
2 Radcliffe, 97–104; *Butler's Book*, Ch. V; O. R. II, i, 563 ff.

who sympathized with the North presented flags to Union regiments; men cheered the national banner; appreciative crowds watched Yankee parades. Some families saw brother aligned against brother. But the division and peril never approached that in Missouri; like little Delaware with *her* obstreperous slaveholders, Maryland was entirely safe.[3]

[I]

On the morning of May 7, 1861, a group representing a recent convention of governors in Cleveland called at the White House. Morton of Indiana, Yates of Illinois, Dennison of Ohio, Curtin of Pennsylvania, and others had met to concert their plans. The deputation told Lincoln that they would furnish any number of men required to smash the rebellion if he would only press a determined and spirited policy. While they did not defend the impatience expressed in some quarters, they declared that their states required some assurance that the government was in earnest and would go forward energetically, without compromises. These governors feared Seward's influence over Lincoln.

"A question had arisen," wrote young Nicolay in his diary, "as to how these States should protect their borders. If for instance Kentucky should secede, as was feared, Cincinnati would be insecure without the possession of Covington Heights across the river. Yet if they took them, the whole State would be in arms at the pretended invasion. The General Government had not indicated what it would do in this case. Ohio desired to know. . . ."[4]

Ohio would have to wait before invading Kentucky, but along another broad front Ohio could act at once. Obviously, western Virginia, like Maryland, could never be surrendered to the Confederacy. Its strategic value was altogether too vital to the nation. This mountainous district offered a buffer zone protecting eastern Ohio, western Pennsylvania (including Pittsburgh), and the flank of any Federal army which marched into the Shenandoah Valley. It covered a long stretch of the Ohio River. It fairly secured the Baltimore & Ohio Railroad, the one line which with its direct links joined Washington with Louisville, Indianapolis, and St. Louis; a line enabling the United States to transfer troops between the eastern and western theaters much more readily than the South could move them. The protection which West Virginia gave eastern Kentucky would presently make the invasion of eastern Tennessee, toward Knoxville, much easier; while it was not actually valuable as a base for striking into the Confederacy, it did help protect some of the points

3 For Delaware see Harold Hancock, "Civil War Comes to Delaware," *Civil War History*, II (Dec., 1956), No. 4.
4 Nicolay Papers, LC. Nicolay does not give us Lincoln's reply.

of debouchment for energetic invasion of the South. Finally, retention of these western counties, with more than 350,000 population, kept fully 30,000 men out of the Confederate army, and at times tied up sizable Confederate forces.

The action taken by western Virginia after Sumter showed how irresistibly, in a crisis, popular feeling can burst through all artificial barriers. The people beyond the Alleghenies, bound by natural economic ties more closely to their northern neighbors than to eastern Virginia, had cared little about the so-called wrongs of the South, but very keenly about the maltreatment they suffered from the Tidewater and Piedmont. They complained that they were grossly underrepresented in the legislature, that the three-fifths rule in counting slaves deprived them of their share of seats in Congress, that they were outrageously overtaxed, and that while very poor in communications they got nothing like their share of public improvements. By no means least, they felt aggrieved by the disdainful attitude of proud eastern planters and merchants toward the "mountaineers." [5]

For each of their complaints they could offer substantial evidence. Trans-Allegheny Virginia in 1860 had 135,000 more white people than eastern Virginia, yet under the constitution the eastern counties held control of the Senate. Despite its larger white population, the west had only five Congressional seats, the east eight. Inasmuch as slaves under twelve years of age were exempt from taxation and older slaves were assessed much below their true value, the east, according to Francis H. Pierpont, the principal western leader, each year escaped paying $900,000 in taxes justly its due; and inasmuch as the State had built no railways nor canals west of the Alleghenies, practically all of the $30,000,000 by which the State debt had been augmented since 1851 had gone for internal improvements in the east.[6]

Small wonder that the Morgantown *Star* declared that the grievances of the western folk against Richmond were tenfold greater than those of the slaveholders against the Yankees! If Virginia were now to float the cotton kingdom kite aloft, the westerners did not mean to be hitched to the extreme tail. They knew how vulnerable they were to attack. Cannon on the Ohio shore could demolish Wheeling, converging forces could crush the panhandle in an iron vise, and troops could sweep up the Monongahela for a hundred miles. It is evidence of the astonishing blindness of the leading Virginia secessionists that they paid no heed to monitions that the westerners would no longer be mere hewers of wood and drawers of water.

5 James C. McGregor, *Disruption of Virginia*, 73–75; and see his maps.
6 McGregor, 76; E. C. Smith, *Borderland*, 105. It was one of the weaknesses of slavery that it helped breed sectionalism in some States, and encouraged the older and richer sections, in general, to discriminate against the newer and poorer.

When the Virginia convention voted its ordinance, the trans-Allegheny unionists had already determined to form an independent State. Some of their delegates in Richmond, evading arrest, hurried home by way of Washington. Others held a hasty consultation in the Powhatan Hotel, decided that as soon as they were safe beyond the mountains they would call a convention and carve out their new commonwealth, obtained passes from Governor Letcher, and took the most direct road back, braving threats of violence. A few days later they were inciting their fellow citizens to resolute action. In eloquent speeches they explained how the barons of the lowland had swept the State into war, expatiated on the insults they had received, and assured the people that their only safety lay in separation. In Wheeling, a delegate fresh from Richmond exhorted men to enlist so effectively that a week later a regiment was ready. The Wheeling *Intelligencer* argued uncompromisingly for the Union and a new mountain star in the flag. In Wellsburg, the citizens, after hearing another fiery speaker, hurried a committee to Washington, obtained 2000 small arms from the War Department, returned to the panhandle, and distributed them to eager recruits.[7]

The movement, spontaneous, full of extralegal irregularities, and varying from place to place in public support, spread like the wind. Community after community held mass meetings. One gathering of special note at Clarksburg, the birthplace of Stonewall Jackson, called a convention in Wheeling for May 13, each county to elect at least five delegates.[8] But this somewhat premature summons, carried to every hamlet, met an uneven response, for it stated no clear object, and did not intimate that the convention would have any special authority. When on the appointed day more than four hundred men met in Wheeling, they represented only twenty-five counties, and included few persons of note. John S. Carlile, a self-educated, forceful man whose oratorical gifts had carried him into Congress, and whose aggressive championship of the Union had made some Richmond secessionists thirst for his blood, emerged as the leader, but he was overruled when he suggested immediate steps to create a new State.

Northern observers who believed that western Virginia was aflame for the nation were only partly right. It was not only love for the Union but resentment over their special grievances which actuated the majority. Like most border people from the Patapsco to the Missouri, West Virginians were ready to cry: "A pox upon your warring houses!" This May convention in Wheeling

7 W. P. Willey, *An Inside View of the Formation of the State of West Virginia,* 51–53; Smith, *Borderland,* 189.

8 Virgil A. Lewis, *How West Virginia Was Made, passim.* All the 150 counties of Virginia were free to send delegates; the only question was how many counties would respond. West Virginia later incorporated a half hundred.

voted almost unanimously that secession was intolerable; but, pausing, it then took a moderate and prudent course. To plunge forward immediately and create a new State, as Carlile suggested, would estrange many conditional Union men and drive some into the arms of the rebellion. Western Virginia as a whole was unready for so bold a step. Under the shrewd guidance of Francis H. Pierpont, an attorney and coal dealer of Wheeling, the delegates agreed that if the secession ordinance was approved in the pending referendum, a special election should be held for a second convention in Wheeling.[9]

This course was sagacious, for probably a majority of the people were then equally against a disruption of the Union and a disruption of Virginia. A delayed State of fifty counties was certainly better than an immediate State of twenty-five. Western leaders did their best to roll up a heavy negative vote in the referendum on secession. They succeeded, for although the returns have disappeared, it is known that in twelve typical counties of the northwest, the vote was nearly ten to one for the Union.[10] They had candidates for Congress named in three districts. They appealed to Lincoln and the governors of Ohio and Pennsylvania for assistance, and Dennison of Ohio ordered George B. McClellan, just appointed the State commander, to concentrate his troops on the Ohio ready to cross as soon as Virginia's secession was officially declared. Some Northerners were disappointed by the delay; the Philadelphia *Press*, New York *Tribune*, Cincinnati *Gazette*, and other journals which had been eagerly hailing a new mountain commonwealth dedicated to liberty and nationality wrung their hands. But caution afforded time for sentiment to harden.

Hardly was news of Virginia's final decision received before the western hills and valleys began to witness stirring scenes. McClellan's glittering columns swung across the Ohio and pushed on, without him, in a converging movement from Marietta and Wheeling. On June 3, in the first real field action of the war, a little Confederate command which had been putting the torch to railroad bridges was surprised and routed at Philippi. Virginia troops had begun moving up from the southern borders of the region. Officers on both sides, however, reported that the people were overwhelmingly for the North, and as McClellan soon drove the Confederates back, Pierpont and his associates could proceed unchecked with the work of political reorganization. They had a new plan—a better plan.[11]

9   Lewis, *op. cit.*, 34 ff.; Smith, *Borderland*, 194 ff.
10   J. M. Callahan, *History of West Virginia*, I, 352.
11   Pierpont in an autobiographical sketch in the Brock Papers, HL, gives himself entire credit for the plan to be adopted. He first explained it to the Committee of Safety which had been organized, he states, saying: "When our State is organized and recognized at Washington, then we can divide." The Committee and leading men of Wheeling endorsed

Our business, they announced when the second Wheeling convention opened—a gathering in which thirty-four counties and four-fifths of the trans-Allegheny population were represented—is not to create a State, but to preserve one. "Let us save Virginia, and then save the Union." In other words, establishment of a new State was postponed in favor of the creation of a government which purported to speak for all Virginia, and expected to receive recognition as such from Lincoln. Under this plan, Union men were to be elected to all State offices, and Washington was to treat their regime as constitutionally sovereign all the way from Norfolk to Wheeling. A precedent for Lincoln's action had been found in President Tyler's decision in 1844, later upheld by the Supreme Court, recognizing one of two rival State governments in Rhode Island as valid.[12]

Thus "the Restored Government of Virginia," using the regular seal of the Commonwealth with the words "Liberty and Union" added, rose in June in opposition to the Virginia of the Confederate sisterhood. The convention unanimously elected Pierpont, apparently principal author of the plan, as governor. Showing exuberant energy, he helped organize a loyal legislature, collected $40,000 from the national government as Virginia's share of public land sales since 1841, and within fifty days raised ten regiments of troops, nine of them composed of Virginians. The legislature elected two Senators, who were at once admitted to Congress along with three Representatives against the strenuous protests of James A. Bayard of Delaware.[13] Lincoln, in his message opening the new Congress in July, emphatically declared the legitimacy of the Wheeling regime: "These loyal citizens this government is bound to recognize and protect as being Virginia." It is clear that the President, as Attorney-General Bates suggests, had helped devise the scheme.[14] Bates wrote in his diary:

I have good relations with all the leading men of that region who come here. At first, we had some difficulty in weaning them from their long-conceived thought of a new State, stretching from the Blue Ridge to the Ohio. That done, they assumed to be Virginia, and are now represented in both Houses and fully recognized. This is "at once an example and fit instrument"

the plan. When the second Wheeling convention met, the delegates were told of the plan, and they "went to work with a will." See also W. P. Willey, *Inside View.* But he seems to have had powerful collaborators in Washington.

12 Lewis, *How West Virginia Was Made*, 369–372; O. R. III, i, 378. This second Wheeling convention began June 11, 1861.

13 John S. Carlile and Waitman T. Willey were elected Senators. Bayard was a crypto-traitor in thought if not act. He wrote S. L. M. Barlow as late as June 27 arguing for an agreed division of the nation on the line of the Potomac and Ohio Rivers, predicting a despotic military regime in the North, and declaring that the country was much too large anyway for a representative government; Barlow Papers.

14 Bates, July 14, 1861, to J. O. Broadhead; Broadhead Papers, Mo. Hist. Soc.

for bringing back all the States, and restoring the integrity of the Union. It needs but a slight change of circumstances to induce East Tennessee, West North Carolina, North Alabama and perhaps North Georgia, to follow the example. There is another inducement to this course, of a coarser nature, which will have a greater effect in fact than will be openly avowed. By treating the proceedings of the Rebel Governments within the States as unauthorized and simply void, they will get rid of enormous debt liabilities without incurring the odium of downright repudiation.

This example of Virginia, and its recognition by the General Government, has already struck terror into half the insurgent States. Its moral influence in settling the contest will be equal to at least 50,000 of our best troops.

The new plan, which turned out to possess no such political potency as Bates hoped, was destined shortly to dissolve into the simple original project for a separate State. Creation of the "restored" government thus became a roundabout, awkward, perplexing mode of effecting the inevitable partition. What was important was the fact that as early as June, 1861, this important area was detached from Virginia; detached to make an effective shield for southeastern Ohio, southwestern Pennsylvania, the Baltimore & Ohio, and the armies west of Washington; and detached to be also an effective corridor for threatening the Confederacy.

[II]

Suddenly the military border moved south; the secession of Virginia met a sharp counter-stroke. On May 24, ten thousand Union troops breakfasted on the soil of the Old Dominion. Richmond's adherence to the Confederacy having become effective the day before, it was now constitutional for Lincoln to use force to repossess the national property in the State.

The troops found this march a poetic experience. Before officers of the New York Seventh dismissed parade on May 23, the privates saw their colonel parleying with others. Something was in the wind! Soon irrepressible cheers from the company streets greeted orders that the men be ready to march at a moment's notice. "Alexandria!" "Harpers Ferry!" "Richmond!" they exulted. It was a clear night of full moon, refulgent, mild, and dewy. At an hour past midnight the drums beat; the men fell into column, tramped through the shadowy trees to the highroad, and soon swung through outer Washington. A pause ensued while a Jersey brigade, 3000 strong, passed them, the troops chaffing each other gaily. Then they resumed the march, till they saw a broad pathway of reflected moonlight shining on the Potomac, and opening their files, rumbled out on the Long Bridge. As they reached the Virginia shore, dawn was breaking. Directly in front of them stood the sinking moon, bright and handsome as a new twenty-dollar gold piece, a splendid oriflamme. On they went past a racecourse to a ridge, where the Jersey boys, their picks and spades ringing amid abundant profanity, were constructing a tête-du-pont to protect the bridgehead. As the sun rose some New Yorkers took a hand. Others curiously inspected Lee's Arlington House, its paint fading, its yard weedy, its propylaeum of stuccoed columns crumbling a little, and its interior presenting to Theodore Winthrop "a certain careless, romantic, decayed-gentleman effect, wholly Virginian." [15]

General Scott had planned to have the 75,000 three-months men, once Washington was safe, entrench themselves on Arlington Heights, and then move against Harpers Ferry, while nine or ten regiments meanwhile made a thrust against Fort Monroe. He acted none too soon. Confederate pickets had been seen on the Heights, and engineers were surveying positions for batteries. At Alexandria, Lieutenant-Colonel A. S. Taylor of the Virginia forces had orders to defend the town unless overwhelmingly outnumbered.[16] Cannon planted at Alexandria could close the river and batter the public buildings of Washington. But now, as strong forces of Union infantry, artillery, and cavalry crossed the Long Bridge and the Aqueduct Bridge at Georgetown, only a few shots were fired. Staking out lines, throwing up earthworks, posting cannon, the Union troops immediately built Fort Corcoran on the Arlington estate and Fort Runyon not far away, the first strong points in a system of Virginia fortifications which ultimately became ten miles long. The North was elated. It applauded Irvin McDowell, whom Secretary Cameron—much to the irritation of Winfield Scott, who had other plans —had ordered to head the movement.[17]

Yet the blundering confusion inseparable from hasty Federal improvisation was at once evident. Five days later McDowell reported that Alexandria remained almost totally unfortified because the men had no transportation to the hills, no tools, and worst of all, no plans; that horses were starving; and that many of the scattered troop units were getting insufficient food because they lacked wagons, established lines of communication, and officers with enough experience to look after them.

One incident of the occupation had a poignant meaning to both North and South. Of the young Northern officers none was better known than

15 Theodore Winthrop, "Washington As a Camp," *Atlantic Monthly*, Vol. 8 (July, 1861), 105–118.
16 O. R. III, i, 233; O. R. I, ii, 24.
17 Scott had opposed the rapid promotion of McDowell because he thought it injured General J. K. F. Mansfield, who, distinguished as chief engineer under Zachary Taylor in the Mexican War, had been appointed to command the Department of Washington, and had been foremost in urging the seizure and fortification of Arlington. See *Committee on the Conduct of the War*, II, 37.

Colonel Elmer Ellsworth of Illinois, head of a Zouave regiment which he had drilled into remarkable efficiency. Lincoln and others knew that his life had been a heavy struggle against poverty, a model of stainless virtue, and an example of burning ambition channeled into public service. He had long since dedicated himself to an important cause, the complete reorganization of the militia system of the United States. He had studied every branch of military science; and to illustrate his principles, he had organized in May, 1859, a company which he drilled to such discipline, endurance, skill, and energy that when taken on an eastern tour, it aroused the admiration of all beholders. Nominally a law student in the Lincoln-Herndon office, he had traveled to Washington with the President-elect's party. Then, working night and day, he had gone to New York to enlist his model regiment.

Springing up the stairs of the Marshall House in Alexandria to haul down the Confederate flag, he was shot on his descent by the proprietor. This Virginian, James W. Jackson, knew that his action meant instant death, but—as devoted as the youthful Illinoisan—he never hesitated. Flags South and North went to half-mast. Jackson's body was carried to an obscure grave, while Elsworth's was taken to lie in state in the East Room of the White House and to become the center of a memorable funeral demonstration in New York.[18]

Scott's blow heartened the North, which a month earlier had seen Washington threatened and now could claim a small corner of Confederate soil. Nevertheless, to carry Southern outposts on the fringe of the capital was no great feat. The really important point before Washington was Manassas Junction, twenty-five miles southwest of Alexandria, which Ben Butler had already urged Scott to take by storm.[19] Here, where the railroad running south from Alexandria to Richmond joined a line from the Blue Ridge, Confederate forces had collected in such strength that a heavy price would have to be paid for gains.

[III]

On the whole, the North had achieved a great deal in holding most of the debatable borderland. To protect Washington, it had to use military force to keep the whole upper Chesapeake region safe; to protect Ohio, it had to gain the strategic prize of West Virginia. Although the Western borderland was too new to have reared many true statesmen, Kentucky had produced

18 Ellsworth's death probably inspired John Hay's poem written long after, "Thanatos Athanatos" (Deathless Death) on "Soldier boys who snatched death's starry prize":
"Their memories hold in death's unyielding fee
The youth that thrilled them to the fingertips."
19 Parton, *Butler in New Orleans*, 105.

in Henry Clay an illustrious apostle of nationalism and moderation, and had raised up lesser men who shared his pride in the republic and faith in compromise. These successors, whose spirit harmonized with Lincoln's, now kept the commonwealth in the Union, and prevented angry factions from flying at each other's throats. Missouri alone represented a partial failure. Its one eminent leader, Benton, had left no inheritors; rather, the angry partisans, the David Atchisons, Trusten Polks, and Henry T. Blows, had found equally intemperate successors. The State had been saved to the Union, which had every geographical advantage in taking it, but saved only in a feverishly diseased condition which was certain to grow worse. A Southern historian remarks that the Confederacy lost Kentucky because it was too impatient to be tolerant, and too impetuous to be tactful. The North had lost the best possibilities in the Missouri situation by the same errors.

Strategically, the North held the entrances to the Shenandoah Valley, the Cumberland and Tennessee Rivers, and the Lower Mississippi. In population it had much the greater part of some thirty-four million people; in resources, it had grain, meat, minerals, factories, and shipping in abundance. Many vital parts of the Confederacy lay in a comparatively narrow strip along the Atlantic and Gulf, from Norfolk at one extremity to the Rio Grande at the other—exposed everywhere to attack by sea. Of the remainder, the interior States of Tennessee and Arkansas were vulnerable by river invasions, Far different would have been the situation had the Confederacy rounded out its domains by seizing Kentucky, Missouri, and western Virginia. The balance then would have swayed against the Union.

8

Grandiose Plans and Blundering Leaders

WHEN SENATOR HENRY WILSON and Judge Rockwood Hoar spent May 1 paying calls on Lincoln and every Cabinet member to urge aggressive fighting, they spoke for millions of fellow citizens. In a war of the people, the masses always chafe for headlong action. Like a sluggish river which a thunderstorm has made swift and angry with rising water, the feeling of the North since Sumter had become fierce and impatient. Wait until Jefferson Davis' legions rolled over the Potomac to tweak the noses of the Northern garrison? Never! In the East the cry was for an early seizure of Richmond, in the Northwest for a rapid march down the Mississippi Valley, and everywhere for the resolute suppression of rebellion and punishment of traitors. It would cost something, but even editors who dilated on practical difficulties believed with Greeley that when Lincoln had 30,000 brave men in Washington, 45,000 more ready for the field, and 500,000 at home biting their nails for service, Virginia might as well surrender.[1]

In this hour of indignant emotion the voice of dissent was largely drowned. Fervent supporters of the Union were cheered by the emergence of a strong party of war Democrats under Stephen A Douglas. The moment he heard of Sumter, the Illinois Senator abandoned his attacks on the Administration and began urging it to grimmer effort. "What would I do with the traitors left in Washington?" he said to an inquirer. "If I were President, I'd convert or hang them all within forty-eight hours."

He was quick to call at the White House. Lincoln later said that he was the first to warn him of impending trouble in Maryland, to point out the advantages of the Chesapeake–Annapolis route, and to emphasize the importance of holding Fort Monroe. The Associated Press at once announced that he had pledged the fullest support to the Union. Hastening west, he

---

1 N. Y. *Tribune*, May 2, 1861.

spoke in Cleveland, Columbus, Indianapolis, Chicago, and above all, in the Springfield so familiar with his voice.

An audience tense with anticipation jammed the State capitol as the Speaker, young Shelby M. Cullom, introduced Douglas. He rose magnificently to the occasion, presenting himself as no mere baiter of the South, but an earnest patriot determined to fortify his people. That experienced political reporter, Horace White, wrote later that he could not imagine any orator, ancient or modern, exhibiting greater power.[2] The idol of Midwestern Democrats clearly thought the nation in terrible peril. He addressed a vast unseen audience as he appealed for unity, disclaimed any personal ends—"There is no path of ambition open to me in a divided country"—and urged a mighty effort. "The shortest way to peace," he said, "is the most stupendous and unanimous preparation for war. The greater the unanimity the less blood will be shed. The more prompt and energetic the movement, and the more important it is in numbers, the shorter will be the struggle."

Though the Illinois legislature had already proved its determination, Douglas' influence was much needed to win over one section of the Democratic press and politicians. Newspapers like the Cincinnati *Enquirer*, Indianapolis *State Sentinel*, and Chicago *Times and Herald*, along with some hesitant members of Congress, awoke to a new sense of duty under his prodding. The *National Intelligencer* shortly published a letter by Douglas, dated May 10, recalling the wholehearted backing that Clay and Webster had given Jackson in the nullification crisis.

When Douglas penned this letter he was prostrated in his Chicago home by inflammatory rheumatism and other ailments. He had long overworked, drunk too much, and generally neglected his health. His death on June 3 was mourned as nothing short of a national calamity even by journals that had opposed him for years. Had he lived he would doubtless have resumed his partisanship on many questions of policy, but his scorn for copperheadism would have been bitingly expressed. He would have been a constant advocate of energetic war measures, would have cooperated warmly with such old-time Democrats as Gideon Welles, whose appointment to the Cabinet he had applauded, and would have lifted his voice across the battle lines to assure former followers in the South that peace might be had on the basis of a restored Union, but with nothing less. He had already told Lincoln that Seward was too moderate, and was exerting too much influence on the Administration.

2 White, *Lyman Trumbull*, 153. Cullom wrote later that he had never been so impressed by oratorical genius; March 19, 1883, to I. N. Arnold, Arnold Papers, Chicago Hist. Soc. See also the *Atlantic*, "Reminiscences of Stephen A. Douglas," vol 8 (August, 1861), 205-213.

"Who can take his place?" lamented Representative S. S. Cox of Ohio. Had he continued to lead the War Democrats, then men like Fernando Wood, Vallandigham, and Bayard would have played a lesser role, and the party would have exercised a healthier influence in national affairs. One lack which Lincoln felt sorely was a cooperative yet critical Democracy.[3]

[I]

The question of the grand strategy to be pursued by the growing Federal armies had to be determined at least roughly before Henry Wilson's aggressive war could be begun. The atmosphere of haste, ignorance, and makeshift fostered a variety of conflicting plans. Not only did the country have nothing remotely resembling a general staff, but its military leaders had never given the slightest attention to problems of an intersectional war. Cameron, however expert in political intrigue, had neither the technical knowledge nor imagination to devise broad war plans. From the outset, divisions on strategy were evident in the Cabinet, the army, and the public. Three main proposals soon emerged: Blair's, Scott's, and McClellan's.

Montgomery Blair's proposal was for quick hard blows in Virginia, based on the theory that the Southern masses were not behind the Confederate government and would soon forsake it. Thus the conflict, waged also with psychological weapons, might be short. He wrote Governor Andrew of Massachusetts on May 11:

I have great difficulty in impressing my policy upon the Administration in the condition of things here. The great obstruction in the way in the past and in the present is Gen. Scott. He does not appreciate as I do the condition of things at the South. He regards the whole Southern people as consolidated in hostility to the North and thinks of making war upon them as if making war upon a foreign government whereas the truth is that the conspirators who have got arms in their hands under color of state authority are scarcely more obnoxious to the North than they are to the great masses of people at the South, but they have armed themselves under color of one pretext or another, so that even the armed men who would desert from their policy have no longer any election, and the unarmed masses—the Union men of the South— are overawed by the armed marauders that Jeff Davis has sent throughout the country.

3   The fullest inheritor of Douglas' mantle was James W. Sheahan, editor of the Chicago *Morning Post*, an able, intelligent, and patriotic Democratic organ. It is a misfortune that Douglas' letters to Sheahan, a hundred or more, seem to have perished. In his obituary editorial in the *Post*, Sheahan wrote, "He poured forth his opinions respecting men and measures with the utmost freedom." I. W. Morris, of the Democratic House delegation, declared that Douglas had no confidence in Vallandigham, "as I know from frequent conversations with him," either as a man or a politician. Chicago *Morning Post*, July 12, 1862. The *Post* of July 22, 1862, has the best text of the Chicago and Springfield speeches.

It would require but a very inconsiderable part of the forces at our command to put down this band of plunderers, if used vigorously, and as soon as they are put down, the deliverers will be welcomed in Virginia, as they now are in Maryland. . . .

It would be hard to say which was the more fatuous, Blair's belief that the South would at once turn against Davis' government, or his illusion that Union forces could strike a powerful blow before May 22. He went on:

My suggestion has been that we should at once organize a Southern Army. To do this we should select a leader for the Southern Army, give him his staff, select the best, the most accomplished of our officers to surround him, detail troops, procure transports, and organize a great army that should rendezvous at Hampton Roads and menace Norfolk and Richmond. The band of marauders that now pervade the State of Virginia would then rush to meet the threatened invasion, the people of Virginia would speak their real sentiments at the approaching election, and their votes if not our ballots would drive the marauders out of the State on the 22d instant.[4]

More realism underlay Scott's famous anaconda plan for crushing Southern resistance by combining a naval blockade with concentric military pressures.[5] In outlining this scheme for enveloping the Confederacy by tight cordons on its northern frontier, the Mississippi, and the Gulf and Atlantic coasts, Scott emphasized his conviction that it would bring the secessionists to terms with minimal losses. He even thought that an invading army of 60,000 volunteers and 25,000 new regulars could take possession of the Mississippi. He proposed, while sealing up the Atlantic and Gulf ports, and using one large force to hold the rebels in Virginia, to organize this striking army of perhaps 85,000 on the Ohio River, give them four or five months' hard drill, and then, when frost had killed "the virus of malignant fevers below Memphis," to move them and a flotilla of gunboats rapidly down the Mississippi to New Orleans, garrisoning towns and posts at proper points.

Scott assumed that the great majority of Southerners supported the Confederate government, and would fight hard. He believed that they could muster a main army of 100,000 to 150,000 men to defend Richmond. Rather than attack this array, he thought it good policy by cordon and blockade to starve the South into submission. He told August Belmont that he was confident of achieving a peace by the spring of 1862.[6]

Scott's plan was radically defective in concentrating attention on the ter-

---

4 Andrew Papers, MHS. Blair's knowledge of Southern sentiment was pure divination or guesswork; he thought the Blair family necessarily understood Southerners.

5 For Scott's plan see O. R. I, li, pt. 1, pp. 338, 339, 369, 370, 387.

6 Scott's correspondence with McClellan's O. R. I, li, pt. 1, 338, 339, 369, 370, 387, is supplemented by material in Elliott, *Scott*, 720 ff., and Swinton, *Army of the Potomac*, 41, 42. For the statement to Belmont see Belmont's letter of June 7, 1861, to the Rothchilds in *A Few Letters and Speeches*, 47.

ritory of the Confederacy and the weakening of its people, when the Confederate armies were the true objects of attack. An amateur could point out objections. How could Scott keep the large Confederate army in Virginia immobile? What if Southerners took the offensive in the Ohio and Mississippi valleys before Union forces moved? What if 80,000 men were totally inadequate, if the fortresses on the Mississippi held out, and if the blockade proved leaky? These objections all stemmed from Scott's inattention to Southern armies as the true centers of operations. An antogonist is not knocked out by blows on his extremities.

Nevertheless, Scott's plan had great merits. He precisely identified a number of cardinal factors in the war: the importance of blockade, the need for careful labor in drilling and equipping armies, the value of cool weather for Southern operations, and the priority to be given recovery of the Mississippi. In the end, the South was actually to be largely paralyzed by a combination of pressures. He showed insight, too, in warning everybody against the impatience of Northern politicians and public, when hasty action might mean disaster. When on May 3 he formed the Department of the Ohio and appointed McClellan its commander and the leader of the projected invading force, he urged the young general to emphasize preparation: "Lose no time, while necessary preparations for the great expedition is in progress, in organizing, drilling, and disciplining your three months' men, many of whom, it is hoped, will ultimately be found enrolled under the call for three years' volunteers. Should an urgent and immediate occasion arise meantime for their services, they will be the more effective." The slow, inexorable strangulation of the Confederacy by the coils of an anaconda represented by the blockade, the capture of coastal strips and ports, the conquest of the Mississippi, and the advance of encircling armies, was indeed—when joined with field victories—to be the main road to victory.

Scott's plan also evinced a grasp of the strategic fact that large armies invading the South would have to get their supplies by river or rail, and be tied to these facilities. Until Sherman marched to the sea through one of the few areas which produced a rich food surplus, the river and railway map was to be pretty much the map of war.[7] It is curious to note, however, that Scott's proposals for seizing the Mississippi rested entirely on a campaign downriver; the naval conquest of New Orleans from the Gulf was not proposed until much later.

McClellan himself, only a fortnight after the war began, had prepared an all too impetuous plan. When promoted from his State position in Ohio to be department head and major-general in the regular army, he learned con-

7 On this fact see Spenser Wilkinson, *War and Policy*, 37.

fidentially of Scott's plan for marching "an iron band" of 60,000–85,000 troops along the Mississippi River, supplied by boats. He did not like it; indeed, when he wrote his memoirs long after, he remained convinced that occupation of the Appalachian chain early in the war would have yielded more rapid and decisive results than any thrust down the Mississippi. He at once laid before Scott two other proposals for using an army of 80,000 Northwestern troops as soon as it could be mustered and disciplined. One plan was for throwing it across the Ohio River at Gallipolis, marching it up the Great Kanawha Valley, and deploying it to capture Richmond. Promptly executed, wrote McClellan, this movement would not fail to relieve Washington, and if aided by a decided advance in the east, "secure the destruction of the southern army." A cooperating column could occupy Louisville and prevent any interference by Southern troops operating from Kentucky. McClellan's alternative proposal was to move the 80,000 men across the Ohio at Cincinnati or Louisville, march straight to Nashville, "and thence act according to circumstances." [8]

Scott demurred, and found no difficulty in explaining to Lincoln the weakness of the two schemes. What about enlisting and equipping the men McClellan wanted in such a hurry? What about the difficulty of overland transport across such great distances and rough terrain? What about angering western Virginia and Kentucky by thus invading them? Scott contrasted McClellan's strategy of dagger blows with his own over-all strategy of encircling pressures. "For the cordon a number of men equal to one of the general's columns would probably suffice, and the transportation of men and all supplies by water is about a fifth of the land cost, besides an immense saving in time." [9]

That Lincoln at first leaned toward Scott's faith in deliberate anaconda pressures is evident from a number of facts: His continued deference to Scott's military experience and wisdom, his restriction of the May call for troops to some 42,000 volunteers and some 22,700 regulars, his statement to Congress when it met in July that he hoped for a speedy termination of the war, and his letter to Simon Buckner declaring that he wished to suppress the insurrection with the least possible annoyance to well-disposed people

8 O. R. III, li, pt. 1, pp. 338, 339. A Swiss observer later propounded the curious theory that it was an error to make Washington, which could be amply covered by gunboats on the Potomac and by forts, the main Eastern base. Instead, a great fortified camp should have been created at Harpers Ferry, giving Washington flank protection, and offering opportunity to advance on Richmond, the Shenandoah, and western Virginia. Lieut.-Col. Ferdinand Lecomte, *The War in the U. S., A Report to The Swiss Military Dept., Aug., 1862* (N. Y., 1863).

9 May 2, 1861; O. R. III, li, pt. 1, p. 339 (Scott's endorsement on McClellan's letter of April 27, 1861).

everywhere. Seward of course continued to shrink from bloody battle and hold to his faith in reconciliation. Even Chase, dismayed by his financial problems, was in no mood to press for large-scale aggressive war. Attorney-General Bates assured a Missouri friend that he would rather save the nation by over-awing all opposition than by fighting, and would as far as possible avoid bloodshed. The Administration, he explained, was convinced that the Chesapeake and the central Mississippi were the two controlling areas that must be held with massive grip. The first would dominate the Maryland–Virginia region, and the second with the ocean blockade would shut the South in an iron prison.

Thus the whole Cabinet, except Montgomery Blair, down to midsummer of 1861 accepted Scott's belief that a systematic tightening pressure all round the South would swiftly bring its people to terms. A happy dream! [10]

Indeed, the central defect of all Northern thought in these months was a gross underestimation of difficulties and dangers. Scott underestimated the power of the South to strike while his "cordon" was being knotted. McClellan —who actually asserted that his columns, after taking Richmond and Nashville, could rapidly converge on Pensacola, Mobile, and New Orleans—underestimated the Confederate ability to halt his march. Blair underestimated Southern devotion and tenacity. Impatient editors and politicians forgot Daniel Webster's dictum that, in war, if there are blows to be given there are also blows to be taken. The few who foresaw a protracted conflict founded their ideas on wrong premises, though Scott showed more wisdom than most men in saying the struggle might take two or three years because its weapons would be as much economic as military. [11]

[II]

Scott, as the architect of grand strategy, maintained a firm grip on the military helm. He labored under various maladies of age. After dinner he would call his body servant to wheel his roomy armchair around and put his feet up for a nap; sometimes he fell asleep in the midst of a conference. He was

10 Scott wished to divide his 85,000 troops into two bodies. The smaller would board river transports, headed and flanked by powerful gunboats; the larger would march by land as nearly abreast as practicable, supplied by heavy freighters. They would begin somewhere on the Ohio and proceed "on the first autumnal swell in the rivers." O. R. III, i, 177 ff.; Elliott, *Scott*, 722. General John A. Dix had a somewhat similar plan. He would make no offensive move until November; use the summer to train troops in camps of instruction; garrison Washington with 50,000 men; and in autumn launch two invading columns of 100,000 men each, one in Virginia, the other in the West. Morgan Dix, *Memoir of John A. Dix*, II, 28, 29.

11 Scott predicted to Seward, Chase, and Cameron a three-year war: "For a long time thereafter it will require the exercise of the full powers of the Federal Government to restrain the fury of the non-combatants!" Marcus J. Wright, *General Scott*, 330.

nevertheless capable, if some crisis arose, of twelve or fourteen hours' work a day. His headquarters in a shabby brick building on Seventeenth Street were crowded with officers, politicians, contractors, newpapermen, and railway officials. An unending stream of mail and telegrams poured in on him.[12] Experienced, systematic, and conscientious, he had a much better grasp of business than Secretary Cameron. An Ohioan who brought McClellan's special scheme for ending the war to Scott learned that many radical politicians were impatient of the general's anaconda plan. But he found Scott's headquarters a busy place where decisions were quick and clear, and the atmosphere electric; when he called on Cameron he found an aimless, cluttered, evasive office.[13]

Scott had to sustain the first Southern strokes, the loss of Norfolk and Harpers Ferry—blows that more vigilance on the part of the Administration might have blocked.

The navy yard opposite Norfolk, three-quarters of a mile long and a quarter-mile wide, contained riches at which we have already glanced: Machine shops, foundries, an ordnance building, a sawmill, sail lofts, and at least 2000 cannon, 300 of them new Dahlgren guns. Among the warships were the huge three-decker *Pennsylvania* of 120 guns, and the steam-frigate *Merrimac*, its engines in need of repairs. Nothing had ever been done to fortify the navy yard, and the nearest troops were at Fort Monroe, separated by many miles and much water. The failure of the Lincoln Administration to garrison the place of course arose from its unwillingness to give offense to Virginia or provoke the Confederacy. Not until more than a month after the inauguration was the commodore in charge of the yard ordered to get the ships and other movables ready to be taken beyond danger, and even then he was warned to take no steps that would give needless alarm.[14]

A single regiment at Norfolk, supported by the warships anchored at the yard, could have held both places until reinforcements arrived; and with Fort Monroe at their backs, the Union forces could have dominated that whole corner of Virginia. But as matters stood, when a Virginia officer arrived on the scene April 18, he was able to take rapid action for the seizure of invaluable materials. Bringing up the Richmond Grays and six hundred men

12 E. D. Keyes, *Fifty Years' Observation*; Elliott, *Scott*, 724. The general fell asleep while talking to an Iowa delegation under Senator Grimes.

13 A. F. Perry, *A Chapter in Interstate Diplomacy*, Papers, Ohio Commandery Loyal Legion, III, 333–363.

14 Gideon Welles treats the question of the capture of Norfolk at length in his *Diary*, I, 41–54. He admits that the local commander showed feebleness and incapacity, while some associates were treacherous. But Welles says in his own defense: "In repeated verbal applications to General Scott in the months of March and April, as a precautionary measure, I met a refusal, on the ground of military necessity and inability to comply. He had not, he said, troops to defend Harper's Ferry. . . ."

from Petersburg, he called out the military companies of Portsmouth and Norfolk. The Northern commodore had delayed until too late in getting the *Merrimac* into the safety of Hampton Roads. An engineer from Washington had repaired the machinery and gotten up steam, and explicit orders had come to put all the more valuable ships in safety. But the fatuous commodore listened to junior officers who told him that no danger existed. "How could I expect treachery on their part?" he asked later. "The mere fact of their being Southern men was not surely a sufficient reason for suspecting their fidelity!" [15]

Too late Washington awoke to the situation, and replaced the commodore by the vigorous Captain Hiram Paulding, who made a frenzied attempt on the night of April 20–21 to destroy everything at the yards. Much of the property, however, survived his torch and dynamite. Taking possession of the smoking premises at dawn on the 21st, the Confederates were able to salvage the drydock, foundry, ordnance building, and other structures, much of the machinery, and hundreds of good cannon. [16] They soon began shipping ordnance to other places. Before long, heavy guns with fixed ammunition had been placed at almost every exposed point on the entire Southern coast, and at numerous entrenched camps inland. The Confederates simultaneously seized Fort Norfolk near the city, with about 150 tons of powder and many loaded shells. Of the warships, the *Merrimac* and the *Plymouth* were raised, and the former was converted into an ironclad of formidable strength. Besides gaining all this, the Southerners were able to intrench themselves in a position that would cripple any future Union movements in the region of the lower York and James. Warships issuing from Norfolk could attack along a wide coastline. [17]

Harpers Ferry lay within a short march of Washington and southern Pennsylvania, and by prompt action it also might have been held. The capture of the armory and arsenal was later described by one of the principal Confederate officers engaged as a purely impromptu affair. From the begin-

15   This officer, Charles S. McCauley, had received his orders April 10. See also Lossing, *Civil War*, I, 393, for details.
16   See report of a Virginia officer sent to inventory the place; Richmond *Enquirer*, Feb. 4, 1862, quoted in Lossing, I, 397, 398.
17   John A. Dahlgren, an inventive officer who had given the country an efficient ordnance workshop, and who took command of the Washington navy yard when Franklin Buchanan joined the Confederacy, wrote in his diary, Feb. 3, 1862: "It is now evident that the pivot of affairs lay in the period beginning at the time when the attack on Sumter was decided, and the abandonment of Norfolk. The loss of Norfolk was almost fatal; could that have been held, the fate of Virginia might have been otherwise. The Department had one month to send there a suitable Commandant and officers, which was not done. So the latter deserted and the former was helpless. How much it has cost, only to ward off the consequences of this mistake. . . ," M. V. Dahlgren, *Memoirs of John A. Dahlgren*, 355.

ning of the year the superintendent had warned the Ordnance Bureau that an attack might be imminent. Yet only a tiny force was sent to guard the machinery, the ammunition, and the 20,000 rifles, and by April 18 it was reduced to forty-five men. Though at that moment 20,000 rifles were absolutely priceless to the Union, the War Department had half a company to watch them!

This rash exposure invited attack. Ex-Governor Henry A. Wise laid the plans; volunteer officers at a night meeting April 16 at the Exchange Hotel in Richmond worked out the details; the railroads of northern Virginia promised transport; and volunteer companies were alerted for orders from Governor Letcher. Troop units from Staunton, Charlottesville, Culpeper, and other points gathered in Winchester, and on the night of the 17th marched to the Ferry. Expecting a sharp battle, they were astonished when they found the arsenal blazing but deserted, for the little Union guard, warned that the enemy were at hand, had destroyed the munitions and stolen away. The novelist Hawthorne later described the ruins as dismal piles of broken bricks and smashed pillars, amid which lay gunbarrels in heaps of hundreds, twisted by the flames and rusted by weather.[18]

Had only a fighting regiment been there! During the first week the Confederates kept but 1300 raw recruits at the place. This force stopped a train which was carrying General William S. Harney, just humiliated by Frank Blair, from St. Louis to Washington. As sympathetic Confederate officers escorted the captured officers to a Richmond train, Harney gazed at the few hundred soldiers in sight, and with a twinkle inquired of the commander: "Where is your army encamped, general?"[19] Three batteries that the Southerners brought up had no caissons and no horses.

Within the next month, however, the Confederates raised their detachments at or near Harpers Ferry, commanding the confluence of the Shenandoah and Potomac, to the 8,000 men already noted. Still more important, they sent a Mexican War veteran to take command—the first appearance of Thomas J. Jackson on the stage where he was to become immortal. In the worn, dingy blue uniform of a professor at the Virginia Military Institute, Jackson instituted a rigid discipline and brought system into all the camp arrangements. With his six feet of height, powerful limbs, and strongly marked features set off by a heavy beard, he was an impressive figure. The troops quickly learned that he was gentle with the ignorant but unsparing with shirkers. Alert, energetic, a master of quick military movement, he merited his future sobriquet only in that his large frame and determined air gave him a rocklike firmness. "The

18 Statement by Col. Roger Jones, *Battles and Leaders*, I, 125; Hawthorne, "Chiefly About War Matters," *Atlantic*, vol. 10 (July, 1862), 43–61.
19 *Battles and Leaders*, I, 119, 120.

presence of a master mind," writes a subordinate, "was visible in the changed condition of the camp"; and this influence persisted after the command was transferred on May 23 to Joseph E. Johnston.

And who faced Johnston? A soldier near seventy, who after fighting in the War of 1812 and Mexican War, and spending decades in business, had been mustered into service as a ninety-day major-general of volunteers—Robert Patterson of Pennsylvania. On June 3 he took command at Chambersburg, Pennsylvania, of a little army consisting chiefly of Keystone militia. He at once proposed an advance against the Confederates on Maryland Heights, a sound strategic move. Scott approved the undertaking and sent him reinforcements, merely enjoining him to attempt nothing without a clear prospect of success, for the enemy would profit from even a drawn battle. When Patterson advanced with about 15,000 men, Johnston not only abandoned the Heights, destroyed the railroad bridge, and retreated south of the Potomac, but fell back to a point near Charlestown, Virginia. On June 16, Patterson repossessed Harpers Ferry—after the Confederates had carried off all the valuable arsenal machinery.[20]

But what then? He telegraphed Scott, saying that he wished to make the Ferry his base and march on Winchester. Scott quite properly asked the reason, writing him: "The enemy is concentrating upon Arlington and Alexandria, and this is the line first to be looked to." He was right, for the Confederates were gathering their forces at Manassas, hoping to advance on Alexandria; and Jefferson Davis had written Beauregard on June 13 that he planned soon to unite Johnston's troops with Beauregard's to give the advance impressive strength. Patterson remained where he was.

Although Scott had lost important pawns in the Norfolk naval base and Harpers Ferry arsenal, he had high hopes of the larger game.

[III]

On May 28, four days after troops moved across the Potomac to seize Alexandria, Brigadier-General Irvin McDowell was appointed head of the Department of Northeastern Virginia. This alert, capable officer, tall, deep-chested, and strong-limbed, had a reputation for efficiency, but in singularly limited fields. An Ohioan of Scotch-Irish family, a West Pointer in the class of 1838, a man of cultivation and foreign travel, he had served almost exclusively in staff positions. Duty at the Military Academy, in Mexico as adjutant-general

20 See Robert Patterson, *A Narrative of the Campaign in the Valley of the Shenandoah.* Scott's letter of instruction to Patterson was dated June 8, 1861; O. R. I, ii, 694. John Sherman served briefly on Patterson's staff.

to Wool, on various departmental staffs and at army headquarters—such was his record. He was liked by Scott, who had known him since he entered the army, and by Secretary Chase, influenced by the fact that McDowell came from his own town of Columbus. But McDowell was a man of distinct faults. He talked unguardedly, and was given to sharp sayings which helped make him one of the most unpopular officers of the army. He was a gargantuan feeder, who would soon show a portly figure and puffy face. And even Chase, while lauding him as brave, truthful, able, and intensely earnest, criticized his brusque aloofness. "He is too indifferent in manner," commented Chase. "His officers are sometimes alienated by it. He is too purely military in his intercourse with his soldiers." [21]

McDowell, as he later testified, never believed in Scott's march down the Mississippi. But he did agree with Scott that they must drill a large army, work which would take four or five months at least, and he contemplated no early battle.

Unit after unit was sent across the Potomac, until on June 24 McDowell was able to report that he had twenty infantry regiments, "good, bad, and indifferent," of nearly 14,000 men, with 250 cavalry and one serviceable field battery of 6 rifled guns. As more troops were steadily arriving, he hoped soon to have a field army of 25,000 men, leaving 10,000 in the Washington fortifications. McDowell held the sound conviction that long wagon trains groaning with impedimenta were unsoldierly.

It is difficult to describe the levies assembled under McDowell except in terms of a rabble. The peasants who milled about Wat Tyler with clubs and pitchforks were little inferior in equipment and training. To be sure, a few regulars theoretically seasoned the mass with some discipline and experience—one infantry battalion, a few cavalry and the single battery [22]—but actually they had no effect upon it; for the army was really made up of ninety-day militia, eager for discharge in July, and the first of the green three-year men who had responded to Lincoln's call in early May. Many Johnny Raws did not know how to fold their blankets properly, handle firearms safely (Senator Wilson, appalled by the accidents, urged that they be deprived of revolvers),

---

21 James Harrison Wilson, dining with McDowell, was impressed by his vigor. But noting that he gobbled up every dish within reach, finishing with an entire watermelon, he agreed with Gen. J. B. McPherson that he was too greedy a gourmand to be a good general. *Under the Old Flag*, I, 66. Carl Schurz writes that his censorious temper made him by the fall of 1862 the most hated officer in the entire army. But Chase, while granting his faults, attributed his unpopularity partly to the fact that he turned a harsh face toward all marauding and looting, and that he worked his troops down to Spartan fighting trim. Schurz, *Reminiscences*, II, 382, 383; Chase, Sept. 4, 1862, in Chase Papers, Pa. Hist. Soc.

22 This on June 24; three additional companies of regular artillery were in the Washington intrenchments. O. R. I, ii, 718 ff.

dig intrenchments, or otherwise take cover under fire.[23] The two inveterate camp enemies mentioned by Defoe in *Memoirs of a Cavalier*, idling and sotting, stalked through the Union lines. Later one commander explained a disaster by saying that although the men had not marched enough to tire them, "They had been loafing around a great deal; had been out a great deal of nights, and had been broken of their rest, and had not had full rations."

Reluctance to drill, an insubordinate temper, and a tendency to shirk hardship were general. W. H. Russell saw camps which stank abominably because the men had dug no latrines. He saw a soldier, diving into an earth-pit, halted by a sergeant's yell: "Dempsey, is that you going into the magazine wid yer pipe lighted?" On the march the recruits stopped to pick blackberries, refill their canteens, and lounge. Many officers, petty politicians or local dignitaries, were so incompetent that the story of captains ordering their companies to "Swing around like a barn door" were not wholly apocryphal.[24] The Massachusetts businessman, J. M. Forbes, transacting military business in Washington early in June for Governor Andrew, was alarmed by what he saw. One stupid officer infuriated him: "Of *such materials* is the U. S. Quartermaster's Department now composed!" He wrote prophetically: "I shall be surprised if they don't get a *big scare* at Washington one of these days, and should be glad to see our [Massachusetts] preparations of all *essentials* so complete that we could on a pinch hurry off our six Regiments at short notice. Tents and wagons in such a case might follow later." [25]

Nor was this amateur army given proper headquarters organization. McDowell, who had been partly educated in France and had spent 1859 traveling and studying there, knew the paper requirements of an army. His motley force was grouped in five divisions of 2,000 to 3,600 men each, but the five brigadiers, Samuel P. Heintzelman, Theodore Runyon, D. S. Miles, Daniel Tyler, and David Hunter, were poorly acquainted with their duties, with their subordinates, and with their own capacities. Nobody, not even McDowell, had ever handled a division before; Hunter and Heintzelman, both West Pointers, had been majors before the war, but Hunter only as paymaster in Mexico. For staff work McDowell assembled the proper number of quartermasters, commissary officers, and medical officers, and assigned men to ordnance, signal service, inspection, and engineering, but regulars were so few that he had to employ many novices.

McDowell's own headquarters was lamentably under-officered. He had no chief of staff to help him take comprehensive views and to catch up his work if

23   Henry Wilson, June 27, 1861, to Governor Andrew; Andrew Papers, MHS.
24   George W. Bicknell, *Hist. 5th Maine;* Samuel Merrill, *The 70th Indiana,* etc.; *Committee on the Conduct of the War,* II, 182.
25   Forbes to Andrew, June 9, 1861; Andrew Papers, MHS.

he were disabled; nor did he have any group to help him make plans, move forces, and see that his orders were executed. W. H. Russell, breakfasting with him on July 6, found him unaccompanied by any aide. When they walked later through the Washington streets, not one of the many soldiers they passed saluted. No military police or provost guard was available to keep order among the troops, who bought liquor at will and at night became drunkenly riotous. Some days later, Russell on reaching Washington from Annapolis found McDowell alone on the station platform, peering anxiously into the cars for two batteries that had gone astray. Russell expressed astonishment to find an army commander running such errands. "I am obliged to look after them myself," sheepishly explained McDowell, "as I have so small a staff, and they are all engaged out at my headquarters." But he had no real staff at all, observed Russell; just some plodding pedants to write memoranda and ignorant young fellows to strut about.[26]

His intelligence service was practically nonexistent. Telling Russell that a decent map of Virginia was unprocurable, he admitted that he knew little or nothing of the country in front, and had no cavalry officer capable of making a reconnaissance.

For these defects McDowell was far from being solely responsible. Winfield Scott, irritated when Cameron ordered McDowell across the river, had vainly urged the general to protest. In his displeasure he treated McDowell coldly, impeded the flow of troops to his camps, and denied him expert assistance. Clinging to his Mississippi plan, Scott wanted nothing but a holding operation in Virginia. "No additions were made to the force at all," testified McDowell later. "With difficulty could I get any officers." In vain did McDowell tell Secretaries Cameron and Chase that his burden was too great for one man, and that he could not organize, discipline, and lead his army without trained aides.

Scott's irritation increased when McDowell felt it necessary to argue before a Cabinet meeting against the Mississippi expedition on the ground that it would encounter excessive obstacles and perils. To capture New Orleans, said the general, the North should take Pakenham's short route. The head of the new Department of Washington, General J. K. F. Mansfield, also showed jealous chilliness toward McDowell.[27]

It could not justly be said that McDowell and his five division commanders

26 Russell, *My Diary*, July 16. Gurowski, *Diary 1861–62*, p. 61, says he saw McDowell do detail work which even in a half-organized army belonged to the chief of staff. Russell's opinions, corroborated by testimony before the Committee on the Conduct of the War, are expert, for he had seen much of armies and campaigns, and edited in London the best military periodical in the world.

27 *Committee on the Conduct of the War*, II, 37 ff.

gave their troops insufficient drill; the difficulty rather was in the wrong kind of drill. Numerous parades in June found the troops marching with increased precision. When on the 17th Cameron and McDowell reviewed eight infantry regiments, with some cavalry and artillery, in the most imposing military display yet made, spectators voiced a lively admiration. But of long route marches, charges, scaling exercises, and target practice there was almost none. Had the war been a contest in drill-ground evolutions, the army would have done well. As it was, McDowell shortly had to explain that his men were so unused even to light marching-order loads that a force which should have covered a six-mile road in four hours without strain actually took eleven hours and arrived in exhaustion. Though by June 20 his lines extended twenty miles along the Potomac and at some points reached ten miles into Virginia, offering room for businesslike maneuvers, his idea was to break in his troops gradually.

By that date three armies had taken shape in Virginia: Patterson's at ruined Harpers Ferry, Ben Butler's at Fort Monroe, and McDowell's. McClellan had largely completed his successful West Virginia campaign.[28] Lyon commanded a small force in Missouri with which he hoped to purge the State. But what armies! The authors of over-all strategic plans talked of sweeping marches to New Orleans, to Nashville, to Richmond, to Mobile and Pensacola; and here were crude, poorly armed cohorts that for the most part could not be trusted to march twenty miles in hostile territory. Any dream can be indulged by men who plan in the supramundane spirit of Simon the Magician. It is now time to turn to an examination of realities, and measure the discipline, equipment, morale, and cohesion of the legions that had been assembled to vindicate the unity of the republic.

28 One of McClellan's subordinates on June 3, with a small Indiana brigade, routed a Confederate force with such hot pursuit that the event was termed "the Philippi races." Then on July 11, W. S. Rosecrans, second in command, defeated the Confederate forces on Rich Mountain led by John Pegram and W. S. Garnett. Credit for the West Virginia campaign lay as much with the subordinate officers, including the able Jacob D. Cox, as with McClellan.

The Greenhorn Armies

THE TRADITIONAL DISTRUST of Anglo-Americans for military establishments had long been reflected in their treatment of regular troops. In America as in Britain the army had been starved. Captain Jenks of the Horse Marines had been as much a figure of fun as Tommy Atkins. The American regular force, absurdly small for its severe duties on the Indian frontier, and totally inadequate as a nucleus in the event of foreign collision, nevertheless satisfied the nation. After the Mexican War its strength had been fixed at 10,120. Later its numbers were enlarged, especially when in 1855 four regiments were added; but just before the Civil War it barely exceeded 16,000. This, as one administrator after another pointed out, was insufficient to keep the western tribes in order.

The flames of Indian hostilities had flickered up at many points in the West during the 'fifties, falling and rising again, but never quite being extinguished. One reason for adding the four new regiments in the middle of the decade was that a detachment of troops had just been murdered by the Sioux. In Texas and New Mexico punitive expeditions were needed to suppress Indians guilty of outrages on the settlers and the emigrant trains. A considerable force under Harney had to invade the Sioux country, partly to protect western Kansas and Nebraska, and partly to keep the Oregon Trail clear. In the Territories of Washington and Oregon sharp fighting took place. The line of the Indian frontier in the Far West grew more perilous as emigration and settlement thickened. In 1857 the Secretary of War, reckoning that an aggregate of 6700 miles of emigrant roads had to be watched, declared that his forces found adequate protection impossible. The country had sixty-eight forts of a large and permanent character and seventy less substantial posts where garrisons were needed. They were scattered over three million square miles, so that a visit even to a dozen of the most important required a long, arduous journey. Down to 1861 the War Department constantly besought Congress for more men, and a better system of strongholds.

[I]

The organization of the army was manifestly defective. Its basis was in part the British army system as it had existed in the colonies, and it retained many defects which the British army had pruned away. The several grades of generals were appointed by the President, but below this rank, promotion by seniority was the inflexible rule, so that no matter how incompetent the officer, he was steadily pushed up the ladder. As Secretary of War Floyd remarked, "The *worst* officer of any army *must*, if he lives, come to be one of the most important and responsible officers under the government," a regimental head. An almost insurmountable wall separated line officers from the staff (that is, medical, quartermaster, commissariat officers), who constituted an independent corps. Seldom serving in the field, the staff could not gain an adequate fund of observation and experience, while their independent status deprived them of proper opportunities as aides to the commanders. The system also begot an unhappy accumulation of red tape and prerogative—of general stuffiness.[1]

When we add that the pennypinching national economy kept the army ill paid, so that a major-general received only $3480 a year, a brigadier $2112, and colonels from $1332 in the infantry to $1512 in the cavalry, we can understand why so many able men left the service. (The Chief Justice was paid $8500; Cabinet members and Associate Justices got $8000, Senators and Representatives $5000.) Lower officers were worse off still. After long, arduous waiting, a captain of infantry had to rear his family on $768 a year, and a major on $888, with small contingent allowances. Although no prudent British father would allow his son to enter the army without private means, in general the British pay was fully double the American scale.[2]

One branch, the engineers' corps, an exception to the general rule, did offer scope to energetic and ambitious young men. For one reason, its activities lay mainly outside the tribal country. "Service in the Indian campaigns," Secretary Jefferson Davis remarked, "though little calculated to excite the military ardor of the soldier, is attended by equal hazard and even by greater privation than belongs to warfare with a civilized foe." It was dirty, exhausting, risky work; icy blizzards, burning heat, raging streams, blinding dust storms, were commonplace incidents of duty; long periods of loneliness and monotony, demoralizing in the extreme, were followed by fierce spasms of hardship and peril.

1 See the annual Reports of the Secretaries of War, 1850–60, particularly those of Jefferson Davis and John B. Floyd.
2 *Harper's Magazine*, Vol. 11 (Sept., 1855), 552–555. It was generally agreed that a captain ought for the good of the service to get at least $1800, a colonel $3000. The pay schedule adopted early in the century had been continued without regard to rising costs. The base pay of $7 a month for privates explained in part the general American contempt for "sogers."

In the engineering service, however, officers might distinguish themselves by road building, dam construction, harbor work, exploration, or erection of public buildings, becoming as famous as Lee or Montgomery C. Meigs.

Throughout the 1850's the army engineers were busy making military roads in the West. They surveyed the Great Lakes, gathering materials for accurate charts and marking reefs and shoals with buoys. Military parties were sent to survey unknown areas and explore the most practicable railroad routes between the Mississippi and Pacific. This was suitable work, for the defense of the Pacific Coast in war would require a railroad, and it was also work which army engineers could best perform. Robert E. Lee found no satisfaction in routine garrison duty, but when assigned to the problem of removing some bars in the Mississippi opposite St. Louis which threatened to destroy the usefulness of the port, he delighted in a task worthy of his best efforts. From beginning to end, Lee's labors had carried him over much of the nation. He improved the channel of the upper Mississippi at Keokuk rapids. He performed engineering work at Cockspur Island near Savannah. In New York Harbor he saw to the making of elaborate changes in Fort Lafayette and Fort Hamilton. Other engineers dealt with assignments just as complex; for example, Captain Randolph B. Marcy, who by 1861 was a veteran of western exploration, skilled in road-marking, fort-placing, and guidebook-writing.

That the regular army was on the whole well officered its severest critics seldom denied. Its leaders had received their training in three schools: West Point, the Mexican War, and various branches of civil life. Many of the best officers of the conflict now beginning had enjoyed a combination of all three.

West Point, as founded in the Jefferson Administration, was originally a school for training military engineers, with a plan based largely upon that of the Royal Military Academy of Woolwich. But under the farsighted, meticulously careful, and progressive administration of Sylvanus Thayer, who in 1817 began re-creating the institution, its course was broadened while its discipline became more severe. "Sylvanus Thayer is a tyrant," Andrew Jackson ejaculated in 1832. "The autocrat of all the Russias couldn't exercise more power!" But he was a wise, benevolent autocrat, and when he left in 1833 the academy had a growing reputation.

Some capable teachers came; Dennis Hart Mahan, for example, whose book on strategy and military history, *Outpost* (1847), proved that he was the best military scientist of his time in America.[3] In 1854 Colonel William J. Hardee, asked by the government to prepare a system of drill which would permit of quicker evolutions, compiled a handbook of tactics based primarily on

3 R. E. Dupuy, *Where They Have Trod,* and Schaff, *The Spirit of Old West Point,* *passim.*

French practice.[4] Immediately introduced at West Point, his tactics became standard in the army. Under Lee, who was superintendent 1853–55, the course was lengthened to five years to make room for English, military law, and more of practical training.

The active service of the Mexican War gave many young officers useful lessons not only in handling troops, but in resourcefulness and persistence. Robert E. Lee was only a captain when, during the march on Mexico City, he made a perilous night journey to headquarters with news of an enemy concentration which Scott called "the greatest feat of moral and physical courage performed by any individual during the campaign." Grant was but a lieutenant when at Cerro Gordo he helped lead the advance over chasms so steep that his men could barely climb the precipices. Robert Anderson was a captain of artillery when, accompanying Scott, he penned the letters to his wife which furnish the most charming and graphic account of the campaign. At Buena Vista, Captain Braxton Bragg fought gallantly to convert defeat into victory, and at the most desperate moment Jefferson Davis did turn the balance with his regiment of Mississippi Rifles. The 900-mile march of John E. Wool from San Antonio to Saltillo, the yet longer march of A. W. Doniphan to Chihuahua, the surprise attack of Persifor F. Smith which destroyed a Mexican army at Contreras, the assault of Joseph E. Johnston on Chapultepec, and the varied service seen by T. J. Jackson and McClellan, all counted as tuition for an infinitely more grueling contest.

Both before and after the Mexican War, West Point men who would later play large parts in the conflict of North and South steadily left the regular army for civil employ. In a country so rich in opportunity, the wonder is that so many—Thomas, Ewell, Lee, Pope, Sheridan, Buell—stayed. Meade, who graduated from West Point in 1835, resigned the next year, but came back to the army in 1842. Hooker, who graduated in 1837, left in 1853 to seek his fortune in California. Sherman, of the class of 1840, forsook the army in 1853 to give restless trials to banking, law, and the management of a military college. Grant, taking his West Point degree in 1843, was out of the army eleven years later, drifting from occupation to occupation. William S. Rosecrans, of the class of 1842, stayed in military life but a dozen years before engineering, coal mining, and oil refining engaged his talents. McClellan thirteen years after he quit West Point was chief engineer of the Illinois Central. All these men learned much from their wide experience of both civil and military affairs.[5]

4 The Washington *National Intelligencer*, Nov. 2, 1854, states that Hardee's text was taken from the system of the Chasseurs de Vincennes in France.

5 Nearly 300 West Point graduates became Northern generals in the war, and about 150 became Southern generals; E. C. Boynton, *History of West Point*. Sixty-five Southern cadets resigned from West Point to take Confederate commissions.

But the fact remains that the regular army was a poor nucleus for a rapidly expanding force in a great conflict. The limited scale upon which its various branches operated made for inertia, narrowness, and slackness. The medical department, for example, had been organized by Secretary John C. Calhoun in 1818 under an excellent plan. The first surgeon-general, a capable, energetic man, had required every post surgeon to keep full and accurate records upon everything pertaining to climate, disease, and "medical topography" and to forward them to the Medical Bureau in Washington. The next incumbent utilized these records to publish two useful volumes in 1856, one on medical statistics, the other an army meteorological register. But beyond collecting some illuminating if limited information, the Medical Bureau thereafter achieved almost nothing.

Its officers were mere post doctors, who, with one brilliant exception later to be noted, lacked not only experience in the problems of a large medical establishment, but capacity to organize a service to meet these problems. Nobody had really studied camp sanitation; nobody, despite the ghastly lessons taught the British and French in the Crimea, really understood hospital requirements. The same stagnation, hidebound worship of routine, and pettiness of outlook obtained among the rank and file of the quartermaster and commissary departments.

All the principal army services, in short, would have to be rebuilt on a new basis. The regulars were only a trickling little stream which would soon be merged with the plunging waters of a river of volunteers.

[II]

What were the principles and methods by which the construction of a great volunteer army in the North began? We have seen how Eastern governors hurriedly sent the first militia regiments to Washington. But the 75,000 ninety-day men constituted the merest stopgap.[6]

In the initial emergency Lincoln, incessantly busy with other matters, had to depend on the Cabinet. So far as Cameron went, this meant depending on a reed, for that fumbling Secretary let delays, confusion, and blundering overmaster him. Salmon P. Chase provided the first clear guidance.

On May 3, as we have noted, Lincoln issued a proclamation calling for 42,034 volunteers to serve three years or the duration, and next day Cameron in General Order No. 15 specified that they should be organized in forty regiments. Lincoln simultaneously directed a small augmentation of the regular

6 The three-month men on July 1 actually numbered 77,875; *Ann. Cyc.* The 16,000 regulars were partly needed in the West to hold the Indians in check.

army. It was Chase who inspired these steps. That energetic, ambitious leader while governor of Ohio had carried through a reorganization of the military establishment of the State, lifting it to a new plane of efficiency; he had many military friends; and once war began, he was anxious to see it waged with implacable resolution. If he had had his way, the government would have called for 65,000 more men instead of 42,000. And it was Chase who, by Lincoln's express direction and with Cameron's consent, took up the problem of organizing the new levies.

Just how this astonishing delegation of powers of the War Department to the head of the Treasury took place we do not know. Perhaps at some Cabinet meeting Chase pointed to his experience with military administration in Ohio. Everyone knew that Scott specially respected him, and that McDowell was a protégé; the overworked Cameron was ready to agree; and Lincoln, who had a low opinion of Cameron and was impressed by Chase's masterful, dynamic ways, gladly assented. The moment Chase entered a room energy, system, rapidity (and grasping ambition) entered with him. He asked McDowell, who in the beginning was assistant adjutant-general, and W. B. Franklin, a West Point graduate who was superintending architect of the Treasury, to draw up a basic plan which he revised.[7]

The first question before these men was vital. Should they make a bold new plan for a consolidated national army, or should they accept the traditional reliance on State regiments, State officered and largely State-equipped, to be slowly and imperfectly welded into a national force? In short, should purely military considerations rule, or political and popular pressures be dominant? From the standpoint of professional military men, a dazzling opportunity presented itself. The Administration might use the crisis to demand a unitary national army, its officers to be appointed by Washington; its men to be recruited not by States but by regions or departments; and each regiment to be divided into three battalions, one regularly posted to a home base to enlist and drill recruits so that the command would always be kept full.[8] If Chase and his advisers had asked for this and for a general conscription act, they would have offered the country a military plan which French or Prussian officers could applaud—a plan not unlike that which later enabled the country to fight two world wars with signal efficiency.

But even McDowell and Franklin dared not go so far. They recommended that the three-year regiments be made part of the regular army, with national

7 Schuckers, *Chase*, 183–186; Meneely, *War Department, 1861*, 137 ff.; Upton, *Military Policy of the U. S.*, 234. Franklin had graduated at the head of his class (1843) and fought at Buena Vista; the fact that his father was long clerk of the House of Representatives helped him take national views.
8 Upton, 234.

numerals, and with officers commissioned by the President on nomination by the governors. They suggested that the regiments be apportioned among the States according to their representation in Congress, that the three-battalion system be adopted, and that each Congressional district be required to keep its regiment full. This was a hybrid national-State system. And Chase rejected even this mild advance. He knew that to put boys from Connecticut, New York, or Wisconsin into units designated simply by regular-army numbers, not by State names, would kindle a mighty popular revolt. For himself, he said, he would "rather have no regiments raised in Ohio than that they should not be known as Ohio regiments." He was against the three-battalion plan for volunteers (though not for the regulars), arguing that it would be unwise to abandon a regimental organization with which all State militia were familiar; and he thought that to avoid too great a centralization of authority in the Federal Government, the States should appoint the regimental officers.

In thus sticking to the old-fashioned system, Chase gauged public sentiment well. However great a price that system had cost the nation in the Revolution and the War of 1812, the people would not abandon it. Congress had to ratify his plan, which we shall consider in detail later, and Congress would have balked at a consolidated army. All Illinoisans wanted to speak of "The Fifty-fifth Illinois"; all New Yorkers of "The Eighty-eighth New York."

The next two problems were interrelated: How should the forty volunteer regiments be apportioned among the States, and how rapidly should they be sent to the front? These questions were bound to bring the State and Federal authorities into collision. Aflame with patriotic zeal, a number of governors had encouraged the enlistment of troops beyond reasonable limits, and were under pressure to put them on a firing line. Legislatures had created camps of instruction; State executives had hurried troops to these camps and were feeding and drilling them at great expense; the men were eager to fight, and other groups at home were eager to take their places.

In his general order for the forty regiments, Cameron did not specify State quotas, so that a vast deal of confusion and uncertainty ensued all over the North. The companies drilling in a thousand communities and coalescing into regiments hoped for prompt acceptance by Washington. Their officers besieged the governors, who in turn bombarded Washington for instructions and concessions. Representatives and Senators hurled themselves upon the War Department. As day after day no orders came, the companies continued to drill, parade, and swear, and to write angry letters to political friends.

When the Union Defense Committee of New York found that conflicting laws and orders interfered with the prompt use of fourteen regiments it was equipping, a committee hurried to the capital and held an impatient interview of several hours with Lincoln on May 15. The President agreed that the four-teen regiments might forthwith be moved to Washington.[9] At once jealous Pennsylvanians expressed great indignation. Chiefly from units already drilling, Governor Curtin formed a reserve of fifteen regiments under a new military bill which he pushed through the legislature. These reserve regiments, destined to honorable fame in a dire national crisis, demanded that they get just as fair treatment as the New Yorkers.

Belatedly, Cameron on May 15 did write a letter, not received by some governors for a week, announcing to each State its quota. The one sent to John A. Andrew in Boston was typical of all. Cameron informed the impatient Andrew, who knew that more than ten thousand men were drilling and fuming in the Bay State, that he could send forward only six new regiments. "It is im-portant," wrote the Secretary, "to reduce rather than to enlarge this number, and in no event to exceed it. Let me earnestly recommend to you, therefore, to call for no more than eight regiments, of which six only are to serve for three years, or during the war, and, if more are already called for, to reduce the number by discharge." [10] In State after State, Cameron's strict limitations, and his admonitions to keep recruiting and mobilization down, fell on the public zeal like a chilling fogbank.

Nearly all the principal governors continued to strain at the leash, eager to move further and faster than the War Department thought feasible. Bucking-ham of Connecticut, for example, had made an agreement in Washington with General Scott (sanctioned, he thought, by Cameron) for acceptance of some extra regiments which were imploring active duty. Returning to Connecticut, he was outraged to find this agreement canceled by Cameron's new action on State quotas. Curtin was similarly incensed when Cameron notified him that the government would accept only ten three-year regiments from Pennsyl-vania, for this meant sending large bodies of enthusiastic Keystone volunteers home. Curtin exploded in an angry letter to Cameron: "It would be well for me to understand how authority is divided, so we can move with certainty, and the ardor of the people of this State should not be again cooled by changes." Yates thought that Lincoln's own State was very shabbily treated.[11]

Austin Blair of Michigan, too, a man of radical temper who favored prompt, sweeping, and aggressive policies, condemned the Administration policy of limiting the troops to be accepted. He predicted that the nation would soon rue it. After putting the First Michigan early on the scene in Washington, he

9 N. Y. Tribune, May 16, 1861.
10 Schouler, Mass. in the Civil War, I, 167.
11 Meneely, 146, 147. Governor Buckingham's troops were to include a regiment armed free of charge by Colonel Colt with Colt's revolving breech-loading rifles (an arm by no means perfected); Buckingham, Buckingham, 163, 164.

had pressed forward the preparation of three additional regiments. When the War Department sent him word that it would be better to reduce than increase that number, numerous additional companies drilling throughout Michigan either broke up or found service under the banners of other States. Governor Blair indignantly kept on with his program of training, and had the satisfaction of seeing the Fifth Michigan leave Detroit for Virginia late in the summer. He wished to see overwhelming Union forces hurled upon the enemy like Caesar's legions—"pay them out of his property, feed them from his granaries, mount them upon his horses, and . . . let him feel the full force of the storm of war." [12]

[III]

The fact was that the War Department wished to avoid explaining publicly the chief reason for limiting the armies. This was that to hurry masses of men to Washington before uniforms, arms, camps, and hospitals were ready would be a calamity. Arsenals and armories were half-empty; few depots of military stores existed; tents and uniforms could not be made overnight, or good drill-masters supplied. Of the 30,000 volunteers in Washington, wrote a well-informed journalist on May 15, not more than 2000 would be called soldiers by a British or French general.

When the emergency first developed, Scott thought that troops need be given only a gun and ammunition before going to Washington for full equipment; Chase and Cameron wished to see the States furnish them a full outfit for field and camp before they came. Lincoln at first tended to take Scott's side, but as the dispute persisted saw that his Cabinet officers had the greater reason. The shortage of equipment could be far better understood in Washington than in Indianapolis or Boston, where many imagined that the government had vast storehouses full of everything. Actually, the supply of arms alone was partially adequate, and difficulties of distribution hindered their use. The government had no foundry for cannon. Uniforms, blankets, tents, medicines, all were grossly deficient. Hence it was that Cameron wrote Lincoln as late as July 1 that one of the main difficulties was to keep down the size of the army; hence Lincoln finally informed Congress on July 4: "One of the greatest perplexities of the government is to avoid receiving troops faster than it can provide for them." [13]

The commissary officers in Washington, purchasing large quantities of food

---

12 Message to the legislature, Jan. 2, 1862.
13 O. R. III, i, 303. Chase was of course partly actuated by his dread of unnecessary expense while the Treasury was still ill served. On this see W. P. Fessenden, Aug. 27, 1861; Fessenden MSS, Columbia Univ.

for the incoming troops, found themselves without organization to distribute it properly. They had insufficient horses and wagons; they had no cooking facilities in many of the buildings where thousands of men were housed. Not only stoves and utensils, but blankets, cots, mattresses, and tents were urgently needed. Forehanded commanders tried to provide for their troops before arrival at the capital. For example, Colonel H. W. Slocum, the popular head of the New York Twenty-seventh, had sent his lieutenant-colonel in advance to see that victuals were ready; but the officer could do nothing, and the men found only two barrels of salt pork. They went to bed supperless and angry. The First Massachusetts, miraculously reaching Washington some two hours ahead of schedule, also found no provisions ready. Those who had no money went hungry the first night. Next morning they rustled up some boxes of salt red herring, soda crackers, and a quantity of wormy, sour ship-bread, and with coffee made in two rusty caldrons found in a hardware store, got the semblance of a meal.[14] In a day when most families breakfasted on stewed fruit, oatmeal, meat or eggs, potatoes, and bread and butter, this was sorry fare.

Such shortages were virtually nation-wide. The governors, so creditably anxious to raise heavy armies and deal stout blows, learned this as soon as they went into the national market for necessaries.

Buckingham of Connecticut, for example, at once found a shortage of arms. His State had a thousand muskets of Mexican War age, and two thousand smoothbore percussion muskets that were practically useless. It owned thirty pieces of artillery, but no caissons or harness. He had money aplenty, but to find good arms to buy was another matter. The difficulties of transport were highly irritating. The First Connecticut left New Haven by sea May 9, a thousand men jammed on a little steamer that could scarcely accommodate two hundred in comfort; no food, little water, and practically no plumbing. He met another shortage in uniforms. The quartermaster-general, paying $7.50 each for a supply, had to take many made of blue satinet, this being a euphonious term for shoddy, a cotton warp filled with reclaimed wool. A New Haven Congressman later charged that many of the uniforms were not worth eighty cents, but shortages had driven the price high. No attention was paid to the size and measurements of the volunteers; and men in uniforms too short or too long, falling into shreds before a month expired, were as ludicrously pathetic as circus clowns.[15]

Yet the governors still insisted on drilling troops, doing their best to equip them, and if possible getting them sent off to some front. Well it was that they

14 Leech, *Reveille in Washington*, Ch. V; C. B. Fairchild, *Hist. of the 27th Regt. N. Y. Volunteers;* W. H. Cudworth, *Hist. of the First Regt. Mass. Infantry.*
15 See Buckingham's Annual Message to the Leg. (May Session), 1861; New Haven *Register, Journal,* and *Courier,* June 13-15, 1861; Hartford *Courant,* June 17, 1861.

did so! Anxious to fight a hard war, they were wiser than those who like Montgomery Blair expected a short, easy conflict; wiser by far than Seward, who on April 28 told a New Yorker that the Administration wished to preserve the Union by winning the disloyal to loyalty, not by waging aggressive warfare. Curtin's fourteen reserve regiments were to do some of the best fighting of the war. Buckingham's extra regiments battled on bloody fields, and Connecticut flags were the first planted on the soil of South Carolina and Mississippi.[16]

Even more impatient and aggressive than these men was the redoubtable John A. Andrew of Massachusetts, a host in himself when the war began. "We wish to go *onward*, not to *stand still*," he exhorted a Cabinet member, adding that in defense of the Union, "We relent at no sacrifice." When Cameron on May 15, informing him of the Massachusetts quota of three-year volunteers, earnestly recommended that he furnish no more than eight regiments in all, of whom only six would be three-year men, Andrew was bitterly disappointed. Six regiments! Three had already gone to the camps, leaving only three more to be supplied. Yet at that time more than ten thousand men in Massachusetts were organized into companies, hot for service.[17] How could he select fifty companies from two hundred demanding action? He would not! The legislature had created camps for five volunteer regiments, and, defying Cameron's instructions, Andrew filled them, making these five commands a reserve. However, about three thousand ardent Massachusetts men at once enlisted elsewhere —six companies in New York alone—and others went back to their homes. The general feeling was of chagrin and bitterness, and Andrew shared it.

He continued to press on the Administration the importance of using more men and making war more aggressively, thus shortening the conflict. Visiting Washington, the short, stout, bustling governor, his curling hair disordered, his eyes gleaming behind his spectacles, began to snap at Cameron like a pertinacious airedale. "I shall give you ten regiments fully equipped within forty days!" he exclaimed. Horace Greeley helped to publicize his demands in the press. General Hiram Walbridge of New York, busy to the same end, spoke to Lincoln in Andrew's behalf. At last, in mid-June, Cameron consented to receive ten additional regiments from Massachusetts. By the middle of July the six regiments originally bargained for had all marched off to the front; Fletcher Webster's regiment, which in honor of an illustrious name had been given independent acceptance by the Department, followed on June 24; and before

16 George L. Clark, *Hist. of Conn.*, 391. On Friday, May 10, Governors Dennison (Ohio), Curtin, Blair, and Randall (Wisconsin) spoke from a hotel balcony in Cleveland. Austin Blair said they were daily telegraphing the President, "Call on us for more troops." Cleveland *Leader*, N. Y. *Tribune*, May 9.

17 Pearson, *Andrew*, I, 233; Schouler, *Mass. in the Civil War*, I, 165.

the close of the first week in August three more regiments had gone. This left seven still recruiting.

Thus the little Bay State, with a population of a million and a quarter, was assigned seventeen regiments in all, far more than her due proportion. Despite the governor's forty-day pledge, September arrived before the last regiment was moved forward. But Andrew's radical aggressiveness was unabated. Speaking to this last regiment at a dinner given it on its passage through New York, he demanded relentless military action and hailed the coming day when Southerners would find slavery falling beneath their own parricidal stroke.[18]

The geographical situation of Ohio gave special importance to the zeal of Governor William Dennison, a former Cincinnati attorney who displayed unexpected grasp and energy. It was he who, hearing from friends of the high capacity of McClellan, sent for him, talked with him, and had him made major-general commanding all the State militia. He also sent James A. Garfield to Illinois for 5000 arms, and hurried another agent to New York who got about an equal quantity there and ordered more from England. Dennison took practical control of the railways, telegraphs, and express lines for war purposes; he besought the governors of Indiana and Illinois to join him in invading Kentucky, a proposal vetoed by Lincoln; he argued the thesis that the proper line of defense was not the Ohio River but the mountains below it; and he persuaded the War Department to extend the boundaries of the department assigned to McClellan so that they covered that area. It was Dennison who on May 11 telegraphed Secretary Chase asking him to see that McClellan got a three-year commission, so that he would outrank all others in that theater. "Ohio must lead throughout the war." And it was mainly because of Dennison's preparations that before June two Northern columns were marching into Virginia beyond Parkersburg. Ohio had gone far toward justifying Dennison's insistence on a preëminent role in the war, and her military sons—Hayes, Garfield, McKinley—were to make her a new Mother of Presidents.[19]

New York, too, refused to accept the limits that Cameron tried to place on her efforts. Here the problem of troop supply gave rise to a three-cornered quarrel, sustained with acrid intensity and *opéra bouffe* drama by Governor E. D. Morgan, the Union Defense Committee of the metropolis, and Secretary Cameron. We need sketch only its outlines.

The legislature, thinking Lincoln's call for seventy-five thousand militia inadequate, not only hastened their dispatch, but under a hurried law of April

18 Pearson, *Andrew*, I, 250.
19 Whitelaw Reid, *Ohio in the War*, I, 53–57. By the end of 1861 the attorney-general of Ohio was able to report that the State had furnished, beyond its 22,380 three-month men, no fewer than 77,844 men enlisted for three years. If Dennison had been given his way, he would have raised more, and have sent them more rapidly to the front.

18 authorized the raising of thirty-eight volunteer regiments for two years' service. One two-year regiment had left for the front, and companies of the other thirty-seven were moving to the rendezvous points when Lincoln issued his call on May 3 for three-year troops! Cameron then fixed the New York quota at only ten regiments. He and Morgan forthwith began exchanging angry epistles over the questions whether ten or more should be accepted, and whether for two or three years. The dispute was complicated by a confusing series of War Department dispatches May 13–15 to Morgan, speaking of ten, eleven, and fourteen regiments, and of terms of two years, three years, and "two or three years." Cameron and his chief clerk were themselves confused.

Meanwhile, Cameron wrote the Union Defense Committee that, needing nine regiments "to serve during the war," he hoped the Committee would supply them if Morgan refused to do so. This accentuated a conflict which had rapidly developed between Morgan, who insisted that he and his State military board should keep firm control of military affairs, and the Committee, which after busily organizing regiments wished to get them off its hands and off the expense accounts of the metropolis.[20]

Lincoln himself had to intervene to help arrange a workable compromise. In mid-May, after talking with anxious members of the Defense Committee, he gave them a decision supported by General Scott: he would take fourteen regiments from them if the men would serve three years. In this decision Lincoln was moved by the praiseworthy energy the Committee had displayed when Washington stood in peril, by its subsequent enterprise, and by his realization that its influential members would be most useful to the government in the flotation of loans.[21] Both he and Seward, however, were anxious not to offend Morgan, or to create a situation in which the governor and committee would give more time to fighting each other than to defeating the Confederacy. They hastily assured Morgan that the fourteen city regiments were not to be deducted from the thirty-eight State regiments that Albany was offering, but were to be added.

Seward wrote Thurlow Weed in Albany to this effect. "Tell the Governor in God's name to send on the whole quota," he enjoined Weed. "I will take care of it." Lincoln had General Scott convey the same message to Morgan. Simultaneously, the President warned the Defense Committee that he felt real concern "lest a seesawing commence, by which neither your troops nor the governor's will get along in any reasonable time."[22]

Unfortunately, friction between Governor Morgan, an earnest, businesslike

20 Meneely, 157–160; E. D. Morgan to Cameron, May 10, 1861, Morgan Papers, N. Y. State Library. See James Rawley, *Edwin D. Morgan, 1811–1883: Merchant in Politics.*
21 Chase to Dennison, May 16, 1861, cited in Meneely, 160.
22 Weed, *Life of Thurlow Weed*, II, 333; *Hist. Union Defense Committee*, 185, 186.

man with a rigid sense of the dignities of his office, and the Defense Committee, which was determined to extend its proud record, persisted and grew. While the President and Seward wished fourteen Committee regiments added to the thirty-eight State regiments, Chase and Cameron wished them subtracted. "It is the P——, General S——, and I against the two C's," Seward had written Weed. When the Committee pressed for assurances that it might act independently of Morgan, Cameron on May 18 telegraphed a pointed refusal. He and the President were at partial cross-purposes in the matter. It appears that they were not even well informed of each other's views and actions. While Lincoln on May 22 asked Morgan to come to Washington for a face-to-face discussion, with Committee members present, Cameron the same day dispatched an aide northward to talk with the governor and Committee, and give them a fresh summary of the War Department's position. It turned out that Morgan could not take time to visit Washington.

It also turned out that the Defense Committee, so clamorous for furnishing fourteen regiments, actually had fit recruits for only eight! [23] And Cameron's assistant found that it was by no means certain Morgan could furnish his thirty-eight. It is no wonder that this assistant reported that he had become suspicious of all promises and believed that a high Federal officer should take charge of the whole New York situation.[24]

Ultimately, all the New York agencies that were pressing regiments upon the reluctant War Department won at least a partial victory. That of Morgan might be termed complete. Cameron, after fresh protestations that he would take none but three-year men, finally capitulated and accepted the full thirty-eight regiments of two-year men. The last regiment left the State July 12. But still, in this era of improvisation, confusion waved its scepter. Several of the thirty-eight, unfortunately, had been recruited for three months of Federal service, and two years of State service, so that the men naturally supposed that at the end of ninety days they would be returned to their New York homes. When the War Department ruled that they must complete two full years and held them for the national army, mutinies developed in four regiments, and were not suppressed without great vexation.[25] These thirty-eight volunteer regiments aggregated some 37,000 men. The Defense Committee stuck to its insistence on fourteen regiments. And the noisy, unprincipled Daniel Sickles, who had received special Administration permission to raise a brigade, filled up three regiments by mid-July and soon afterward partially recruited two more.

23 O. R. III, i, 226; four regiments had already gone forward and 4500 men were ready to make up four more.
24 Meneely, 163, 164.
25 Special Orders 322, Aug. 2, 1861; *Report*, Bureau of Military Record 1865, pp. 54 ff.

Altogether, New York during 1861 led the nation by raising more than 120,000 men, distributed among 125 regiments, battalions, and batteries. Of these, not far from half were ready before Bull Run produced a new situation and an urgent new call for troops.[26]

[IV]

Altogether, it was a remarkable chapter of headlong action which the Northern governors wrote in the three months following Sumter. As yet, the republic had more vigor in its State governments than in its still unorganized national departments, headed by inexperienced, overworked, and sometimes weak men. The determined war spirit of the North was far better exemplified by the ablest State executives—Morton, Dennison, and Austin Blair in the Middle West, Buckingham, Andrew, Morgan, and Curtin in the East—than by the uncertain Cameron, the cautious Bates, the conservative Caleb B. Smith, or even Montgomery Blair with his bemused trust in Southern Unionism. To be sure, the governors often moved all too heedlessly and hastily, but they moved with unflinching resolution.

The story in other States was in general outline much like that in Ohio, Massachusetts, and New York. Nearly everywhere, enthusiastic agencies or ambitious men were pressing military units on the governors, sometimes real companies and battalions, sometimes mere paper plans for companies. Nearly all the governors, beset by a thousand local pressures, urged on by newspapers and politicians vocal for aggressive war, and coping with legislatures which were much more ready to provide camps of instruction than to appropriate money for keeping bodies of troops in them for any period, pressed the nation to take troops off their hands—more troops—yet more troops. They were impatient of delays. As Andrew wrote of his own action, they moved "as if there was not an inch of red tape in the world." The governors believed that the Administration was underestimating the task ahead, and the people would have pressed them on from behind even if they had not so believed.

Inevitably, the Administration, with Cameron wringing his hands over chronic deficiencies in supplies, and Chase tormented by financial exigencies, tried first to stem the torrent of proffered troops, then in May and early June partially yielded, and soon thereafter tried again to build cofferdams. As the special Congressional session called for July 4 drew near, Cameron's reluctance to accept troops increased. He already had in national camps a far larger aggregate of ninety-day militia and long-term volunteers than he had ever expected. He, Chase, and several Congressional leaders had been toiling long

26 *Report*, Bur. Mil. Record, 39 ff.; O. R. III, i, 344, 345, 483, 494.

hours on a comprehensive plan to meet the situation. He wanted to accept no more responsibility until Congress had given its approval.

With all real fighting still ahead, the soldiers could take their shortages and privations with summer insouciance. The war was yet in its gala period of cheers, music, exciting new scenes, and exalted patriotism, and a happy release from humdrum toil.

We may take the First New Hampshire as an example. When it struck its tents near Concord at the end of May it rolled southward through green fields, burgeoning woods, and a continuous ovation. Crowds assembled at every station to cheer the special train. At Norwich, Connecticut, the columns, smart in dark gray with red-cord facings, marched aboard two Sound steamers. At dawn next morning they found waiting on the Hudson River pier a Granite State committee with a presentation flag, a bevy of ladies, and a speech. Headed by their band, they marched across Manhattan, impressing spectators with their four women nurses for each company, shining arms, and seventeen four-horse wagons carrying camp equipment, provisions, and ammunition. They dined at the large New York hotels, and as the sun sloped westward marched through more cheering crowds to take their twenty-car train to Washington.[27] Many a farm lad and mechanic in that regiment had never before been twenty miles from home, never ridden on train or steamboat, never seen a city or glittering hotel. The war was romance, the muskets and bayonets were for parade, and the nurses were proof of home solicitude, not a portent of wounds and disease.

In short, confusion, improvisation, and deficiencies that under a grimmer war test would have been intolerable could be grimacingly endured, while excitement and exaltation fixed the mood of the day. On May 26 a frothy wave of emotion surged through Washington. Three guns suddenly boomed from the War Department, the signal that fighting had begun across the Potomac and that all troops must move across the bridge to participate. Dragoons clattered past the Treasury; batteries tore down the Avenue; the Fifth Massachusetts double-quicked toward the Potomac, followed by a Connecticut regiment and District volunteers. Soldiers yelled, civilians cheered, women screamed, and a general uproar followed the yellow coil of dust that marked the onrush. For half an hour Washington was bedlam. Congressmen, buckling pistols to their waists, shook hands and offered jubilant bets on victory. Then, as troops reached the Long Bridge, came word that it was a false alarm growing out of some target practice.

Still the Administration clung to the theory that the Confederacy could best be crushed by anaconda pressures from every side. Lincoln during April

27 N. Y. *Tribune*, May 27, 1861.

had proclaimed the blockade of all Confederate ports, and Scott had written that the government relied greatly on its "sure operation." [28] As rapidly as possible, vessels had been posted outside the chief southern ports. The wife of Senator James Chesnut, living in Richmond and seeing Jefferson Davis frequently, noted on his authority July 16: "We begin to cry out for more ammunition and already the blockade is beginning to shut it all out."

But as news came of the fortification of the Mississippi, and the mustering of formidable Confederate forces in Tennessee and southeastern Missouri, it became plain that Scott's dream of a great amphibian expedition proceeding relentlessly down the Father of Waters would have to be qualified. Seizure of the Mississippi was sound, but it would take time. It also became evident that the large Confederate army gathering under Beauregard at Manassas might have to be attacked shortly lest it attack Washington; that, in short, Confederate movements would do much to determine the grand strategy of the war. On July 1, 1861, the total strength of the Union forces was placed at 186,000. Of these, McDowell had about 30,000 facing Beauregard.

The nation waited. North and South, a sense that the ominous pause of late June and early July preluded fateful scenes of action grew deeper. The armies, excited by small clashes in West Virginia and Missouri, waited. Business, depressed from Maine to Texas by the innumerable derangements of the crisis, waited. Anxious wives and mothers, torn between pride and grief, waited. Throughout the wide South four million Negroes, feeling emotions of wonderment and hope they had never before known, waited. Not since Naseby and Sedgmoor, Camden and King's Mountain, had an English-speaking people, a people above all others used to compromise and hostile to fanaticism, been called upon to understand the tragedy of a civil conflict.

The leaders of the now divided peoples waited too, each resigned, but each apprehensive and sorrowful. When Mrs. James Chesnut talked to Davis, she was impressed by his melancholy outlook, and recorded that throughout all he said ran "a sad refrain." A sculptor friend of Lincoln has written that about two weeks before he left Springfield for Washington "a deepseated melancholy seemed to take possession of his soul." Lincoln had felt a pang of personal grief in the death of Elmer Ellsworth, to whose parents he had written a sorrow-sharing letter. His secretaries were growing used to his smile, "in which there was so much of sadness." [29] Nevertheless, each leader in his own way faced the terrible situation with fortitude.

28 O. R. III, i, 122.
29 Mrs. Chesnut, *Diary*, 1905 edition, 71; John Hay, "Life in the White House," *Century Magazine*, Vol. 41, Old Series (Nov., 1890), 33–37. T. D. Jones, Cincinnati *Commercial*, Oct. 18, 1871.

10

The Union Leaders

BECAUSE THE national organization for waging a great war was wretchedly rudimentary, Congress, though half deluded by the idea of a short conflict, now had to follow Lincoln's first steps by beginning to construct a system to meet the task which lay before the North. The brunt of the labor fell on Republican veterans whom seniority gave important committee positions.

At high noon on July 4, 1861, portly Hannibal Hamlin let his gavel fall in the Senate, while the brisk, wiry John W. Forney as clerk rapped for order in the House. Both men gazed on sadly depleted chambers. In the Senate, even after Orville H. Browning had taken the vacant seat of Douglas, and two members had been sworn in from newly admitted Kansas, the roster reached only forty-four. For all eleven States of the Confederacy a solitary man, Andrew Johnson of Tennessee, answered the roll. In the House, after the chaplain had instructed God on the realities of the crisis, 159 responded, but two from western Virginia were at once challenged. Everybody anticipated a brief session, and many predicted that it would last only a fortnight, for little beyond initial measures to carry on the war would be discussed.

The organization of the House at this opening of the Thirty-seventh Congress was quickly completed. After one ballot Galusha A. Grow was chosen Speaker over Frank Blair, his nearest competitor, while Emerson Etheridge was elected clerk. Grow, a tall Pennsylvanian of dynamic aspect, with a dome-like forehead and intense steely eyes, was not yet thirty-eight. His rapid rise was attributable partly to talent, partly to the assistance of his law partner David Wilmot, and partly to his zealous championship of homestead legislation. A man of homespun simplicity, a working and not a talking leader, and a former Democrat who had been quick to join the new Republican Party, he was popular both at home and in the House. This former bark spudder of the Tunkhannock frontier, in fact, represented the best type of self-made American. Etheridge, an uncompromising Unionist, had been one of the nine slave-State members of Congress who had fought the Kansas-Nebraska Act. Himself from western Tennessee, he had come to Washington a few weeks earlier to plead for aid to the terrorized Unionists of East Tennessee. His election was a tribute to a courageous man who, his friends said, would be murdered if he returned home.

Frank Blair's appointment as chairman of the House Military Affairs Committee, a post in which he would collaborate with Henry Wilson of the Senate Committee, gave promise of energetic action. Thaddeus Stevens of Pennsylvania, beginning his fourth term, took the powerful and thankless chairmanship of Ways and Means. His senatorial counterpart was William Pitt Fessenden of Maine, equally shrewd but far milder in temper. The wise, equable old John J. Crittenden of the House Committee on Foreign Affairs had the task of working with the strong-willed Charles Sumner of the similar Senate body. These chairmanships would carry throughout the war, except that Blair, entering the army, would give way to William A. Richardson of Illinois, and Crittenden, dying in 1863, to Daniel W. Gooch of Massachusetts. It will be noted that Crittenden, the Nestor of Congress, whose national service had begun as Jefferson left the White House, had gladly taken a House seat at the end of his Senatorial term.[1]

In the Senate, New England was now clearly dominant. The departure of Seward and Chase for Cabinet posts had given Sumner, Fessenden, Henry Wilson, and John P. Hale of New Hampshire greater prestige than ever. Hale was head of the naval affairs committee. Westerners grumbled over the fact that Yankees also held the chairmanships of the committees on postoffice, claims, patents, printing, and public buildings.[2] Sumner, by virtue of his real if stilted oratorical power, literary talent, pedantic learning, friendships among the principal intellectual luminaries of England and America, and record as an implacable warrior against slavery, loomed highest among the members. Even on the Republican side many distrusted his fanaticism, egotism, and harshness of language, and all were irritated by his pomposity, which led Lincoln to remark that although he had seen little of bishops, "Sumner, you know, is my idea of a bishop." To border members his puritanical intolerance often seemed edged with malice, as if in assailing Southern institutions he was as much interested in injuring white men as in helping blacks. But nobody of sense ever questioned his ability, integrity, or elevation of purpose. His critical attitude toward Seward, though their disagreements impeded the conduct of foreign affairs, was well warranted.[3]

1 Crittenden had accepted a Federal post in Illinois as early as 1809.
2 The only New England Senator who did not have a chairmanship was the newcomer Lot M. Morrill of Maine. One House observer later wrote that New England's quasi-monopoly of posts "created no small degree of jealousy and ill-feeling in other sections"; Blaine, *Twenty Years*, I, 323.
3 C. F. Adams, *R. H. Dana*, II, 253, 258. Dana believed that Sumner in his large and influential correspondence with Britons denounced Seward freely, but this was untrue.

Most of the prominent Midwesterners in the Senate were of New England derivation. Lyman Trumbull of Illinois, Lincoln's friend, came of the famous Connecticut family. Ben Wade of Ohio had been reared in western Massachusetts on a poverty-stricken hill farm, never outgrowing its rough vocabulary. Zack Chandler of Michigan, a man of unbounded self-confidence, aggressiveness, and radicalism, sprang from a rural New Hampshire township; and so did James W. Grimes of Iowa, a leader of iron independence and shrewd judgment. Timothy O. Howe of Wisconsin, who had courageously insisted that the Fugitive Slave Act ought to be obeyed, could speak of his Maine origins. On sectional questions all these descendants of New England tended toward a certain uniformity of view. Trumbull, for example, for all his general moderation, often voted with his radical colleagues.

The House, far more than the Senate, had an acknowledged chieftain. When James G. Blaine in 1881 undertook to name three parliamentary leaders in America who had taken positions comparable with that of Chatham in the British legislature, he listed Clay, Douglas, and Thaddeus Stevens of Pennsylvania. Here again was a son of New England, for Stevens came from Vermont, and had graduated from Dartmouth. Close thought, wide reading, and grim conviction, with long practice at the bar, gave him an unrivaled power in debate. His broad shoulders, pushed up in a perpetual shrug, bore a tremendous head of peculiar shape—broad at the back and high in front, with a heavy ridge above the deep-set, lustrous eyes. His strongly-marked features were formidable, for the stubborn chin and projecting lower lip, beetling eyebrows, and ready frown gave him a pugnacious appearance. His large frame was ungainly, and his walk, since he had a clubfoot, lumbering. When he spoke, his high-keyed voice flung out his crisp, sententious, neatly turned sentences with belligerent decision. Humor, picturesqueness of language, and literary eloquence he seldom employed, but he possessed a dry wit of Damascene sharpness with which, his face solemnly impassive, he would sometimes take off an opponent's head so dexterously that he convulsed the House.

Above all, however, his lucidity, force, and grasp of fact and principle made him feared. He remembered dates, figures, and precedents with invariable exactness. Those who were stung by his brusque manner and savage sallies to grapple with him were usually swiftly downed by his battering-ram mind and devastating use of his tenacious memory. In conducting House business, he detested technicalities, tricks, and trifles; by a few whip-crack sentences he would bring members back to the main point. He had an overmastering sense of the magnitude of the issues confronting the republic, which made him scornful of defenders of slavery or palterers with treason. He demanded that the war be fought with unrelenting vigor, he insisted on extirpating the taproot of secession, and just now he meant to keep the House hard at work until an effective Administration program had been enacted. In this determination he had efficient aides. One was Elihu B. Washburne of Illinois, the most vigilant and conscientious of the western members, whose eight years' experience made him an expert in the rules of the House; another was Owen Lovejoy of the same State, fierily eloquent for the emancipation cause for which his brother had died; and a third was the hardworking Justin S. Morrill of Vermont.[4]

Both House and Senate leaders were anxious to work with Lincoln in prosecuting the war effort, but both were already determined to move further and faster than he thought wise. Between Sumner and Lincoln useful friendship was destined in time to develop, founded on a mutual esteem which overrode their immense incompatibility of temperament. Sumner, who had enough of an uncertain, flickering greatness of his own to divine the far deeper, more stable greatness of Lincoln, had quickly made himself a familiar of the White House. He was learning to admire Lincoln's patient sagacity, his passion for justice, and the Euclidean precision of his intellectual processes, even though the President's magnanimity seemed weakness to him, and the President's humor (a quality of which Sumner had none) quite incomprehensible.

Thaddeus Stevens kept away from the White House and the departmental offices. Stubbornly, even belligerently, independent, he would have regarded friendly calls on the President as a fawning on power. He wished to be free to attack Cabinet officers with incisive criticism.[5] He had bitterly resented the appointment of Cameron to the War Department, regarding himself as better Cabinet material and coveting the Treasury. He thought Lincoln too tardy, too ready to temporize and compromise, too anxious to consult public sentiment. As yet, however, he was willing to restrain his impatience and cooperate energetically with Administration leaders.[6]

For the time being the Republicans, so new to power, had real unity. For

4 Here are more Yankees of rural origin; Washburne, like the Lovejoys (both Owen and the martyred Elijah) came from Maine.

5 Because Stevens made many enemies, cared little for appearances or public opinion, and drew a saturnine mask over his private life, dubious gossip and legend clustered about him. But beyond a propensity to gambling, no important dereliction was ever proved by real evidence. He had many kindly traits, including a warm liking for young men, a passionate sympathy for the handicapped and abused (to whom he gave freely), and great devotion to his mother. He visited her annually, and said that it was the greatest joy of his life that he was able to present her "a well-stocked farm and an occasional bright gold-piece which she loved to deposit in the contribution of the Baptist church which she attended." Josiah Bushnell Grinnell, who knew him well, credited him with a character of great sensibility. "On a reverse in business partial friends proposed a gift of one hundred thousand dollars—a gift delicately declined in further proof of a sensitive rather than of a sordid nature." *Men and Events of Forty Years*, 189.

6 A. K. McClure, *Lincoln and Men of War-Times*, includes a discerning chapter, pp. 277-295, on Lincoln and Stevens.

that matter, there was temporarily much truth in what one member said, that Congress had only two parties, Union and anti-Union. Most of the true War Democrats aligned themselves with War Republicans. Lincoln was urging formation of a Union Party, which duly appeared this summer in New York and other States. No trouble would be encountered in carrying the needed measures.

Among Lincoln's many worries, however, one was the question of the real extent of Democratic support. He eagerly questioned members and scanned the early debates. In the Senate the worst Border dissenters, notably James A. Bayard of Delaware, James A. Pearce of Maryland, Trusten Polk of Missouri, and most hostile of all, John C. Breckinridge, he thrust outside serious consideration. Representing the hard-shell slaveholders, they held ideas that had been antiquated in Monroe's day. Polk, Breckinridge, and Jesse D. Bright of Indiana were later to be expelled for disloyalty, and Breckinridge was to command Confederate troops.

It was the Douglas Democrats who counted, and happily for the Administration, they showed the right mettle. Had their leader been present he would have differed from the Republicans on important issues, but he would have been a very Hampden in national patriotism. The brilliant E. D. Baker of Oregon, Lincoln's beloved friend, evinced the same militant spirit that had made him colonel of a regiment in the Mexican War. James A. McDougall of California, another old friend, John R. Thompson of New Jersey, and that stanch Jacksonian Unionist, Andrew Johnson, who had risked his life in opposing the Tennessee secessionists, were all dependable. Determined to crush the Confederacy, these Valiants-for-Truth despised any Faint-Heart. They would fight to the last against what McDougall called "the mad assault of misguided men on the integrity of the Union."

In the House some Douglasites threatened to show a more lukewarm spirit. The rhetorical S. S. Cox of Ohio, from the Cincinnati district, who touched a hornet's nest by accusing the Western Reserve of being slow to answer the war trumpet, declared that he would fight to restore the Union, but for nothing beyond that goal. "I will vote for what is required to enable the Executive to sustain the Government—not to subjugate the South, but to vindicate the honor, peace, and power of the Government." His whole attitude was wittily equivocal; but then Cox, a graduate of Brown and a former editor of the *Ohio Statesman*, might be trusted not to go too far in defending the South. His worst offense was a resolution suggesting that Lincoln should appoint seven conservative Northerners, including Van Buren, Filmore, and Pierce, to confer with seven Southern commissioners on peace and Union; an effort to muddy the waters, but not so bad as Clement L. Vallandigham's resolution forbid-

est alike; heavy
what would be
He quoted Cal-
n."
volunteers now
lonel's uniform,
As a boy he had
ied to his grave,
adopted citizen.
uestions. But his
war, he said; its
the commanders
operty. Breckin-
t, the*n,* were the
Northern weapons
brilliant, *p*olished
applause, b*ut* he

another Republic,
quent or dignified
rple flowing over
the illustrations of
as just, and that
would have been
risen in his place,
expenditure of its
t is a grand com-
these words to be

about the Roman
Rock." The speech,
ce on the scene in
ted throughout the
materials and money
f peaceful progress,
hey would have the
overnment, unvexed

until h
more th
inois, anoth
ith a Jackson
replied to Va

upon the overthrow
me to us and ask terms
o say to them that we
down your arms and ab
The offenses have been too se
nd of subjugation about which
at patriots may live, and in order
ll prevail. If the gentleman from
n favor of such subjugation.[8]

, which throughout the session
were certainly present when
y took place on August 1. From
iridge, had flown one poisoned
had charged the Republicans
of hasty, arbitrary passion in
iemisphere, and had predicted
ional liberty. The feeling that
nd felicitous diction, was as
ivis, had grown until an ex-
to use martial law to suppress

ained the floor. "The drama,
ed, "and we begin to catch
for the regulation of mili-
the confiscation of Southern
Every day, the Constitu-
Public and personal liberties

r soon sealed his fealty
it. See the accounts in
Men, I, 42 ff.; Henry L.

gall); 96 (Cox).

e, the College of New Jersey,
n bar. He had held that after
sion of Kentucky, but tempo-
now expected him to act as
le July 16 assailing Republicans
treasonable sophistry" by the

awaited th*e* *s*outh, North, and V
...lesolate th*e* *w*hole continent, and
...led and i*mp*lacably hostile nations.
...r is disu*nion*, eternal and final disunio
...de Baker, *w*ho had raised a regiment of
...Vashingto*n*, entered the chamber in his c
...atigue cap a*nd* riding whip. He gained the floor.
...lliant Lon*d*o*n* pageant with which Nelson was car
...was the mo*re* fervently American because he was ar
...egan calm*ly*, putting Breckinridge some searching q
...dings quick*ly* carried him away. The nation was waging
armies mus*t* *a*dvance beyond the jurisdiction of civil courts
must th*ere*fore exercise authority over life, liberty, and p
ridge *w*ished to halt the armies and yield to rebellion. Wh
pleas *he* was making? Were they not intended to blunt the I
and animate Southern fighters? "Sir, are they not words of
treason, even in the very Capitol?" The galleries broke int
continued:

What would have been thought if, in another Capitol, in
in a yet more martial age, a senator as grave, not more el
than the Senator from Kentucky, yet with the Roman p
his shoulders, had risen in his place, surrounded with all
Roman glory, and declared that advancing Hannibal v
Carthage ought to be dealt with in terms of peace? Wha
thought if, after the battle of Cannae, a senator there had
and denounced every levy of the Roman people, every
treasure, and every appeal to its old recollections? . . .
mentary upon the American Constitution that we permit
uttered.

Fessenden replied in a stage whisper to the question
traitor: "He would have been hurled from the Tarpeian
made so impressive by Baker's sudden striking appearan
military uniform, so filled with fire and logic, reverbera
country. What does it matter, asked Baker, if we expend
without measure? "In a year's peace, in ten years at most
we can restore them all"—and as guerdon of their toils, t
reunited nation, the Union, the Constitution, and a free g
by the treason which Breckinridge was preaching.[10]

10 This scene, rendered more memorable by the fact that Bake
to the flag with his death, was later described by many who saw
Blaine, *Twenty Years*, I, 344, 345; Forney, *Anecdotes of Public*

[I]

The atmosphere of Washington as Congress sat was hardly conducive to thoughtful debate. Regiments steadily streamed into the capital. Through the open windows members heard the blare of bands and stentorian commands of officers, and caught the gleam of gun barrels and gay colors, as troops marched from the trains. With a hundred thousand soldiers in the Washington area, the city seemed an ever vaster camp. Pennsylvania Avenue had been so cut up by Army wagons that riding over it was like traversing a corduroy road. The streets were thronged every afternoon and night by tipsy, quarrelsome troops, who crowded the saloons, brawled on corners, or stood lonesomely in doorways. Bloody altercations were frequent, for drunken men flourished bayonets and revolvers without rebuke. The Washington police consisted of a day force of only sixteen men and an auxiliary night guard of fifty paid by the national government. Though the mayor had fixed 9:30 P.M. as closing hour for saloons, the rule was widely disregarded. On July 4 most proprietors shut their drinking places because they feared the soldiers would get out of hand, as many did. Among the troops swarmed undesirables of many kinds. The city, wrote one private, "is lousy with secessionists, and is the den, the very lair, of swindlers."

Washington shops were filled with martial trappings—swords, epaulets, dirks, pistols, and spurs. Bookstores displayed volumes on infantry tactics, artillery drill, and camp management, along with titles like Count Gasparin's *Uprising of a Great People*, and patriotic sheet music. One officer bought for twenty-seven dollars books whose titles he loosely recorded:

Callan's *Military Laws*	Mahan's *Out Posts*
Halleck's *Military Art*	*Standing Orders Seventh Regiment*
Nolan's *Cavalry Horse*	*School of the Guides*
Maxims, etc., on the Art of War	Benet's *Court Martial*
The Art of War	*Ordnance Manual*
Casey's *Tactics*	Field Manual Battalion Drill

Field Manual on the Evolutions of the Line [11]

All the hotels and boardinghouses were now jammed, with rooms renting at premium prices. "Soldiers are cheated here most unmercifully," wrote one. Lobbies were crowded with generals (Lincoln told of a boy who threw a stick

---

Dawes, "Two Vice-Presidents, John C. Breckinridge and Hannibal Hamlin," *Century Magazine*, July, 1895. Breckinridge, thinking that Sumner had uttered the remark on the Tarpeian Rock, at once scathingly denounced him; *Cong. Globe*, 37th Cong., 1st Sess., 376 ff.

11 See the statement by the Commissioner of Public Building in the Report of the Secretary of the Interior, Nov. 30, 1861; Washington newspapers; and the MS Diary of Colonel J. A. Mulligan in the Chicago Hist. Soc. Mulligan bought the books listed.

at a dog and hit five brigadiers), colonels, and majors in every variety of uniform; with Zouaves in red, blue, and gray; with men of crack militia regiments, sailors in bell-bottom trousers, and cavalrymen in boots. Among the epaulets moved women flaunting their finery. "Hoops and buttons have the highways and byways, ogling each other," wrote a disgusted Western officer. "Beauty and sin done up in silk, with the accompaniment of lustrous eyes and luxurious hair, on every thoroughfare offer themselves for Treasury notes."

Of all the hotels, Willard's stood preëminent. It was more clearly the center of the Union, observed Hawthorne a little later, than the Capitol or White House. "You are mixed up with office-seekers, wire-pullers, inventors, artists, poets, prosers (including editors, army correspondents, attachés of foreign journals, and long-winded talkers), clerks, diplomatists, mail contractors, railway directors, until your own identity is lost among them." Political mendicants were irrepressible once more, for the business depression had augmented their numbers. They swarmed into departmental offices, pursued Congressmen to their rooms, and thrust letters of application into reluctant hands on the streets. The hot, dingy city gave the general impression of a vast miscellaneous disorder. It was little wonder that visitors took refuge from its stench and struggle in juleps, gin slings, whiskey-skins, and brandy smashes.[12]

As the place grew more crowded, its sanitary condition became worse. The medical authorities had good reason to fear an outbreak of typhoid among civilians and troops. Even yet the Washington aqueduct to bring water from Great Falls was unfinished, for much grading and facing with masonry remained to be done on the tunnels, while work on the distributing basin had been interrupted when laborers were hurried off to erect intrenchments on the Virginia shore. The Washington canal in the heart of town, constructed at great cost and regarded at first as a valuable improvement, had become an intolerable nuisance. It was a grand open receptacle for nearly all the filth of the city. The sewage from public buildings, hotels, and many private residences drained into it, and had filled it in many places with accumulations of offensive soil and rank vegetation above the water level. This sewer stretched within almost a stone's throw of the Capitol, Treasury, and White House. As an official report declared:

The accumulated filth and excrement of the city is constantly held in a state of semi-solution in this hotbed of putrefaction, by means of the ebb and flow of the tides, over a surface of more than a million square feet. And whatever portion of it ultimately finds its way into the Potomac River is spread

12 Mulligan, MS Diary; Hawthorne, "Chiefly About War Matters," vol. 10, *Atlantic* (July 1862), 43–61.

out in thinner proportions over several hundred acres of flats immediately in front of the city, the surface of which is exposed to the action of the sun at intervals during the day, and the miasma from which contaminates every breath of air which passes, from that direction, through or over the city.[13]

The unfinished state of the Capitol pained many of its occupants. Though government provision for work on the dome had stopped a fortnight after Sumter, the contractors had decided to go ahead at their own risk. The porticoes and steps of the Capitol wings had still to be completed; part of the interior of the wings was unfinished; and the bronze statute of Freedom to rise over the whole was still in progress. It was painful, also, to have the entire basement of the Capitol devoted to a huge army bakery. Fat bakers in white aprons and paper caps busied themselves in rooms once sacred to clerks and committees. The crypt under the rotunda was used for storing flour. Army wagons clattered over the lawns and walks, and smoke from the ovens drifted into the rooms where Congress sat. When flues were installed, they discharged the smoke into the hot air pipes for warming the Congressional Library, so that it was impossible to make winter use of the books until the bakery was removed.

Happily, however, most Capitol rooms had been so thoroughly renovated that few traces remained of its brief use as a barracks. Buchanan's portrait had been removed from the rotunda, and the names of secessionist Senators erased from their desks. The shrubbery had been renewed, the walls repainted or whitewashed, the floors polished, and the chambers carpeted with a cool matting. The White House, too, had been refurnished—though Lincoln rather liked the battered furniture which remained in various rooms. To a fashionable New Yorker who condoled with him for dwelling in so dilapidated a mansion, he dryly replied: "All I know is that it is much the nicest house I have ever lived in." [14]

It was well for everyone in the government to realize that the nation's business was now war. The day Congress met, a parade of New York troops swept along Pennsylvania Avenue. Lincoln, the Cabinet, and other dignitaries watched it from a pavilion near the White House, and later he, Scott, and others spoke briefly to the throng.

---

13 Commissioner of Public Buildings in Interior Dept. Report, Nov. 30, 1861; Report of R. Seymour, Senate Misc. Doc. 83, Thirty-eighth Cong., 1st Sess., 20.

14 See Senate Exec. Docs. Nos. 1 and 2, 37th Cong., 2d Sess., on the state of the public buildings, and the Washington aqueduct. The Treasury had also been entirely renovated after troop occupancy, the soldiers at one time having used every room from basement to attic.

[II]

If Republican feeling was adamant for the Union, it had not yet hardened into a demand for action against slavery. The venerable Crittenden offered on July 19 a long-famous resolution on the objects of the war. It declared:

. . . that this war is not waged, upon our part, in any spirit of oppression, nor for any purpose of conquest or subjugation, nor purpose of overthrowing or interfering with the rights or established institutions of these States, but to defend and maintain the supremacy of the Constitution and to preserve the Union, with all the dignity, equality, and rights of the several States unimpaired; that as soon as these objects are accomplished, the war ought to cease.

This Crittenden resolution carried in the House 117 to 2, the dissenters being Charles J. Biddle of Philadelphia, Democrat, and A. G. Riddle of Ohio, Republican. In the Senate the resolution passed 30 to 5. Southern leaders, who had frequently accused the Republican Party of intending to destroy their institutions, might have found in it a proof of forbearance, and it unquestionably helped placate border sentiment.[15]

Lincoln's message to Congress was calm and mild, addressed to reason and not passion. Its most caustic passages related to Virginia, whose leaders, he believed, had tricked him by pretending adherence to the Union at the very time that they were concerting aid to the Confederacy. Now war would sweep over them: "The people of Virginia have thus allowed this giant insurrection to make its nest within her borders, and this government has no choice left but to deal with it where it finds it." Much of the message was devoted to a justification of his course in the Sumter crisis. If he had yielded, he wrote, the Union would have gone to pieces, and republican government would have tottered. He could not betray so vast and sacred a trust. He and those supporting him had chosen their course "without guile, and with pure purpose," and they must press forward with manly hearts to victory. But he uttered not a single harsh word upon the Southern people.

The President's request that Congress give the government at least 400,000 men and $400,000,000 precipitated a debate as hot as the July sun that swung over Washington. Not that anybody doubted that the great new volunteer army must and would be created without delay. The three-month men would be returning home immediately; the forces under McDowell, McClellan, and Lyon were obviously insufficient to sweep through the South; and the country was eager for decisive action. Congress was actually determined to give Lincoln not less that 500,000 men. But the mode of organizing this force, the system of choosing, measuring, and replacing its officers, the standards of pay and

15 *Cong. Globe*, 37th Cong., 1st Sess., 222, 223. Passage took place in the House July 22, in the Senate July 25. It was by no means a firm commitment.

subsistence, and several lesser questions, excited grave differences. The War Department, too, would have to be strengthened, and members differed about the means.

Every effort was made by Administration leaders to expedite action. The very first bill introduced in the Senate was Henry Wilson's measure for the new volunteer army. Reported out of committee within a week, on July 10, it was passed after rapid discussion before the day closed, 34 to 4. It provided the 500,000 troops that Senate leaders thought necessary. Unfortunately, the Senate's action had been *too* hasty; a day later Wilson called the measure back from the House for changes, some of them important. On the 12th he presented it again, and it at once passed in amended form, 35 to 4. The House that same day took up a measure of its own, whipped into shape by Frank Blair and his committee, which it passed without delay. A conference committee ironed out the differences, and on July 18, only a fortnight after Congress met, an act was ready for Lincoln's signature. He signed it July 22.[16]

Quick work!—but in this brief period some interesting questions had been discussed. One was the length of service. An Ohio Democrat in the House, objecting to the three-year term fixed by Republican leaders, which he said proved that the government had no faith in its ability to quell the rebellion promptly, argued for one year on the ground that volunteers would be much more easily found for a short term. The majority insisted on three years or the duration of the war. A minority also opposed the figure of 500,000 fixed by the two military committees. Surely, declared McClernand of Illinois, Lincoln and Scott had known the number actually needed when they proposed 400,000. Various border members, notably Senator Saulsbury of Delaware and Representative Burnett of Kentucky, went further. Half a million men smelled to them of a war of subjugation, and Saulsbury proposed 200,000, which he thought enough to defend Washington and the North while a peaceful solution was being arranged. The angry majority voted him and four other border Senators down.[17]

[III]

Sitting until August 6—and its pace was soon accelerated by Bull Run—Congress in twenty-nine working days passed seventy-six public acts, ranging from the volunteer army bill to the creation of a better police force for Wash-

16 *Cong. Globe,* 37th Cong., 1st Sess., 50–54, 64, 147, 194, 205. The nation now stood at much the point in this war which it had reached in the Revolution when Congress, under date of September, 1776, provided for the enlistment of 88 battalions of 750 men each to serve for the duration.
17 The men who voted with Saulsbury were Trusten Polk (Mo.), W. P. Johnson (Mo.), Anthony Kennedy (Md.), and Lazarus Powell (Ky.).

ington. A great increase in the navy was authorized, and eleven regiments were added to the regular army.

The augmentation of the regular army provoked much opposition, for as we have said, most Americans regarded the regular establishment with contempt. Many of the soldiers were misfits, who had enlisted more often from love of adventure, idleness, drunken impulse, or fear of civil punishment than from patriotism. A majority of them lived the sullen, stupid lives of men without wives or family, and without ambition. They usually served in lonely, uncomfortable frontier posts, spending most days in monotonous drill and evenings in dull vacuity. Bad officers tyrannized over them, and good officers gave them no comradeship. Naturally, they turned to drink, gambling, and horseplay, their privations proving less hurtful than their degradations. Although the army held a better position than in Europe, parallels for Thackeray's picture in *Barry Lyndon* were easily found, and many American captains would have echoed Lord Melbourne's statement that the worst men make the best soldiers. The Anglo-Saxon distrust of standing armies in time of peace was reinforced by the special American feeling that in a land so full of opportunity, something was wrong with a man who found refuge in the military.

The Administration proposal to add 24,000 men to the regulars therefore elicited a variety of adverse arguments. Some in both houses, including Lovejoy, Trumbull, and E. D. Baker, thought that in view of the great new volunteer army, more regulars were unnecessary, and that once added, it would be hard to reduce their numbers. Senator Grimes believed that good men had too great a prejudice against the regulars to enlist, that a large standing army was unrepublican, and that after the war it would be an intolerable expense. In the House, Blair's Military Affairs Committee took the position that the volunteer army would be adequate to win the war, and that if the regulars were to be strengthened, it should be at the end of the conflict. Bluff Henry Wilson supported the expansion that Scott and the War Department asked.[18] However, he blurted out that if he had his own way, he would disband the regulars entirely and distribute their officers among the incoming volunteers:

The truth is, that this army of ours is paralyzed toward the head. Your ablest officers are young captains and lieutenants; and if I wished today to organize a heavy military force, such as we are calling into the field . . . I would abolish the [regular] army as the first act, and I would then take officers

18 *Cong. Globe*, 37th Cong., 1st Sess., 40–49, 124, 125, 148–154. Much of the account of the British regular army in Dr. John Brown's paper on Dr. Henry Marshall in *Horae Subsecivae* might be applied to its American counterpart. For a later phase of the bad situation see R. de Trobriand's *Army Life in Dakota*, Lakeside Press ed., xxii, xxiii.

from the Army, and place them where their talents fit them to go, without reference to the ranks they occupied in the old regiments.

The augmentation passed only with a proviso that when the war ended the regular army should be reduced to 25,000 men. Another amendment, potentially important, authorized the high command to assign regular officers to the volunteers to heighten their efficiency, guaranteeing them their old army positions when peace came. Thus a halting step was taken toward merging some of the experienced officers into the raw army.

Despite this new legislation, the standing army really gained little in strength. By the end of the year, when hundreds of thousands had entered the volunteer forces, only about 7,000 had joined the regulars. They preferred the citizen army partly for its more genial, tolerant discipline, and partly for its better name, but most of all because of State loyalty. Lincoln, signing the bill July 29, thought it in the main good; but actually it had both good and bad sides. The new regiments of regulars proved, on the whole, better officered and disciplined than the volunteers, and when scattered among the Eastern and Western armies, set an example of cleanliness in camp and steadiness in battle. But they absorbed a body of regular captains and lieutenants who, distributed through the volunteers, might have done much to improve their fighting quality.[19]

Already a new star, dimming the luster of Scott's name, was rising fast and influencing Congress. McClellan, against the opposition of the old general, swiftly wrote into law his demand for adequate staffs. On July 30 he penned the measure; next day Henry Wilson introduced it; and McClellan took pains to lobby for it—showered, as he moved through the Capitol halls, with congratulations on his West Virginia feats. Scott's opposition to large staffs was grounded largely on the fact that he had managed affairs in Mexico with only two aides! The new law, signed by Lincoln on August 5, authorized the President to appoint such a number of aides as might be requested by all major-generals and commanders of higher rank (Scott being a brevet lieutenant-general). The immediate object was to give McClellan, previously restricted to three aides, as large a staff as he wanted, but other general officers also profited. Later on Cameron, troubled by a thousand politicians, journalists, and excitement hunters who wanted to get on somebody's staff, thought

19 The regulars by the end of 1861 had a strength of only 22,425; *Report of the Provost-Marshal General*, I, 102; cf. Upton. McClellan thought that either the regular army should have been broken up temporarily, and its members sprinkled among the regiments and staffs of the volunteer army to instruct and discipline that body, or it should have been built up to real strength, and used as a select reserve for critical junctures. *Own Story*, 97. Part of the regulars had to be kept in the West. Thus the Ninth Infantry remained in California to control Indians during the war, and the Fifth Infantry was busy with Indians in New Mexico.

that the law should be amended to fix some limitation. By and large, how-ever, the Act was a necessity.[20]

One additional measure, the enlargement of the War Department, had the greatest urgency. The personnel with which Cameron was trying to manage the greatest war effort of the century was hardly strong enough to deal with a sizable Indian outbreak.

The department occupied a drab little two-story brick structure adjoining the White House grounds, its gaunt homeliness slightly relieved by a colon-nade of white Corinthian pillars occupying about one-third of the elevation. Here in a narrow office the intellectual-looking Cameron, his forehead wide and high, his eyes gleaming under his frosted brow, moved nervously about, seeing the endless stream of army men, commission hunters, and contractors, jotting down memoranda which he instantly lost, and jerking out directions to assistants. Crowded into the same building were the adjutant-general, quarter-master-general, commissary-general, chief engineer, and chief of ordnance. The offices of the surgeon general and paymaster-general had been placed in another small building at E and Fifteenth. The whole War Department per-sonnel had numbered but ninety when Lincoln was elected, and so many ex-perienced men were lost during the secession upheaval that only fifty-six were still serving in the late summer of 1861, the harassed bureaus being com-pelled to take on assistants without legal authority. In passing judgment on Cameron, we must bear in mind that for nearly four months after Sumter he had to struggle along with a creaky, antiquated administrative mechanism, operated by a mere handful of men.

Under the new legislation a War Department of decent strength became possible. Cameron had been helped from the start by his tireless friend Thomas A. Scott of the Pennsylvania Railroad; and Scott was now made Assistant Secretary in charge of all government transportation lines. The adjutant-general, Lorenzo Thomas, promoted to be brigadier-general, was given an assistant adjutant-general with a colonel's rank, and eighteen other assistants with ratings from captain to lieutenant-colonel. The office of commissary-general had been in particularly bad shape, for its two aged heads had been quite unequal to their mounting duties, and it was of the first importance to strengthen them with capable helpers. The overburdened quartermaster-gen-eral, Montgomery C. Meigs, who would eventually prove one of the principal architects of Northern victory, received twenty-seven new staff officers, all soon as busy as beavers. And so it went down the line. The surgeon-general's office, headed by the feeble, stubborn Clement A. Finley, an ill-educated army

20 McClellan, *Own Story*, 82, 114, 136; *Cong. Globe*, 37th Cong., 1st Sess., 361, 385, 441; O. R. III, i, 705.

surgeon who had risen to his place by seniority, was beyond rescue by any effort that Congress could yet make, but it was somewhat improved by the provision of new medical personnel.

One striking provision of the new legislation permitted the use of women nurses in the general permanent army hospitals. Another gave each regiment a chaplain, who must be an ordained clergyman of some regular Christian denomination—for an effort by Vallandigham of Ohio to obtain recognition for the Jews unhappily failed.

[IV]

To wage the war, greater financial resources were an urgent necessity. Chase had estimated that not less than $320,000,000 would be needed in the next year; but because he thought the conflict would be short, and wished to find out how much the tariff law of March would yield, he proposed raising only $80,000,000 by taxation. Congress therefore passed an act authorizing him to borrow a quarter of a billion dollars during the year by the sale of treasury notes, in denominations of not less than $50, bearing interest at the rate of 7.3 per cent, a $5,000-dollar note thus returning its holder a dollar a day; or by the sale of coupon bonds at 7 per cent, not redeemable for 20 years. A direct tax of $20,000,000 a year was levied in fixed proportions on the States and territories, ranging from $2,604,000 for New York to $3,240 for Dakota Territory. Congress also imposed a few new tariff duties for revenue, notably on sugar, tea, and coffee; and voted an income tax which was not to be effective for ten months. On its final day it enacted a confiscation law, declaring that all property used in supporting the Confederate cause was a lawful subject of prize and capture.

In debating the direct tax, sectional feeling naturally flared high. Middle Western members vigorously denounced the basis of assessment, which was real estate alone, asserting that while their farms would be heavily burdened, the mortgages, bank and corporation stock, and manufacturing property of the East would be taxed lightly if at all. Representative Isaac N. Arnold of Illinois computed that his State would pay practically 7 mills on its property, while Massachusetts would escape with 2.6 mills. To these complaints Thaddeus Stevens answered that while the direct tax would indeed fall most heavily on the New States, any internal revenue taxes on horses, carriages, watches, liquors, and so on, would be paid chiefly by the large cities and older States. The new income tax, which on British experience Stevens thought might be the most equitable of all, would also eventually rest hard on the East. The bill passed the House 77 to 60, with prominent Westerners of both parties—Arnold, Frank Blair, William S. Holman, S. S. Cox, George Pendleton—opposing it. The vote in the Senate was 34 to 8, and of the 8 no fewer than 6 were openly or covertly hostile to the whole war effort.[21]

The creation of a large public debt at the high interest rate of 7 per cent or more a year provoked astonishingly little debate for so portentous a measure. The sum authorized exceeded any previous total of national indebtedness. But Congress agreed with Chase that for a short war borrowing was a sound principle; and it accepted the view of financial leaders that the loan could not be floated with a lower interest return. Banks of New York, Boston, and Philadelphia, rallying at once to the task of distributing treasury notes to the public, found it far from easy.

Debate raged fiercely, however, around the confiscation bill. John J. Crittenden threw his great prestige against it. Since Congress had no power to touch slavery within the States, he argued, when it undertook to confiscate slave property used in aid of the rebellion it performed an unconstitutional act. Thaddeus Stevens retorted that this constitutional argument would come ill from rebels who were seeking to overthrow the Constitution. A better rejoinder was made by William Kellogg of Illinois. True, we have no power to legislate on slavery, he declared. But we do have power to punish treason by confiscation, taking a man's house, land, and furniture; and we can similarly take his right to service in another, for the penalty operates on the individual, not the institution.

In the course of debate Lyman Trumbull added an amendment under which any slave who was permitted by his owner to work on any Confederate fort, navy yard, dock, ship, or intrenchment, or to give any military or naval service whatever to the rebellion, was set free. Breckinridge raged against this amendment.[22] Although the bill was fought to the end by most Democrats and Border members, it passed the House 60 to 48, and the Senate 24 to 11.

The slavery question in one form or another, in fact, kept cropping up throughout the session. The general feeling of Republicans was expressed by Senator Henry S. Lane of Indiana, who stood by the Crittenden resolution. "But let me tell you gentlemen, that although the abolition of slavery is not an object of the war, they may, in their madness and folly and treason, make the abolition of slavery one of the *results* of this war."

Another dramatic scene took place in the Senate when Andrew Johnson rose to plead for the rescue of his people of eastern Tennessee. This stout

21 John A. Bingham of Ohio clashed with Roscoe Conkling of New York, and Schuyler Colfax of Indiana with Justin S. Morrill of Vermont, on this sectional issue. *Cong. Globe*, 37th Cong., 1st Sess., 325 ff.

22 "I tell you, sir," declared Breckinridge, "that amendment is a general act of emancipation." *Cong. Globe*, 37th Cong., 1st Sess., 261.

champion of the common man, self-taught or rather wife-taught but a powerful debater, had escaped the Confederacy through the Cumberland Gap, leaving his people enduring an Iliad of wrongs: houses broken open, property pillaged, leaders arrested, and unoffending citizens murdered. He did not beg help as a suppliant, he said; "I demand it as a constitutional right." Had his rugged mountain folk been given 10,000 stand of arms when the contest began, they would have asked no further assistance.

Drama also attended the vehement clash between John C. Ten Eyck of New Jersey, demanding that Congress appropriate a million and a half for one or more armored ships or floating batteries, and various opponents who talked of naval "jobs." The debate showed that French and British experiments with armored ships had attracted wide attention, and that the French ironclad *La Gloire* and British ironclad *Warrior* were regarded as potential threats to American ports. Out of this debate was to come the means of building—in the very nick of time—the armored *Monitor*.[23]

Inevitably, and healthfully, the short session mustered a thin battle line of defenders of civil liberty. Congress just before adjourning passed an act punishing with fine and imprisonment those who conspired to overthrow the government or resist its authority. This was mild enough, and far more alarm justly sprang from Lincoln's suspension of the writ of habeas corpus within definite geographical limits. He had begun with a proclamation covering the Washington-Philadelphia lines of communication (April 27). Senator James A. Pearce of Maryland condemned not the suspension, but the unguarded nature of the step and the arbitrary acts committed under its shelter.

In Great Britain, as he and others pointed out, martial law had been very sparingly used—not in the Gordon riots, nor in the Chartist disturbances, nor in grave Irish troubles. When used, it had carried a careful limitation of the period during which persons arrested might be held without bail or mainprize. But in Maryland, a State predominantly loyal and now perfectly quiet, troops had marched into various towns to search for arms, had forcibly entered houses, had seized men without any decent ground for suspicion, and had imprisoned them without orders from superior authority. The police commissioners of Baltimore, said Pearce, had been jailed without any grand-jury indictment or specification of illegal conduct by any other agency, simply

23 Ten Eyck was specially interested in the ironclad vessel called the *Stevens Battery* lying incomplete at Hoboken, with $812,000 necessary to finish it. The eminent Robert L. Stevens had modeled and constructed it without a dollar of compensation, and his brother Edwin Augustus Stevens, his executor and heir, had now offered to give his skill and services free to make the ship available. Most naval experts, while uncertain of the value of such craft as cruisers, agreed on their importance for harbor defense. *Cong. Globe*, 37th Cong., 1st Sess., 345–347. The Senate passed the measure Ten Eyck desired by the close vote of 18 to 16.

because General N. P. Banks had accused them of "some purpose not known to the Government"—and they were still imprisoned!

When the Senate Judiciary Committee under Lyman Trumbull brought in a bill to authorize, define, and regulate the use of martial law, a chorus of dissent broke forth. It would be tiresome to trace the debate, and it suffices to say that both advocates and antagonists realized that the subject was extremely delicate. Everyone agreed that in suppressing rebellion the military authorities needed large powers and would certainly take them; but nearly everyone agreed that to define these powers was a dangerous matter—too much might be granted, or too much withheld. Loyal and disloyal men were intermingled in many communities; suspicion often fell on the wrong person; oaths meant little to scoundrels; and in some areas patriots had less trust in the regular courts than in military tribunals. "There is difficulty environing us everywhere," said Senator Edgar Cowan of Pennsylvania. Trumbull regarded his bill as the most important of the session. "I think that the idea that the rights of the citizen are to be trampled upon and that he is to be arrested by military authority, without any regulation by law whatever, is monstrous in a free government." Yet he admitted that the measure might not accomplish its object.[24]

Thus it was that the bill, opposed by some because it limited existing powers too much, and by others because it extended them too far, was postponed from day to day until it failed. On the final Senate vote for postponement, radical Republicans like Fessenden, Collamer, and Wade stood alongside balky conservatives like Bayard and Saulsbury. The sphere of military control remained undefined.[25]

[V]

Congress adjourned on August 6 in a very different mood from that in which it had first met, for military disasters soon to be described had chastened it. It had accomplished the legislation generally expected of it; now the executive branch had to make the most of the new laws. The President and Cabinet probably drew a breath of relief when it rose, for they felt freer. Power was steadily passing from the legislative to the executive, and the country looked to Lincoln for action.

Though generally cooperative, Congress had shown a natural jealousy of its functions. One of the first measures wanted by the Administration was

24   This subject is fully covered in *Cong. Globe*, 37th Cong., 1st Sess., 332–343. McDougall of California, for the Douglasite wing of the Democracy, advocated throwing out almost the whole bill.
25   *Cong. Globe*, 37th Cong., 1st Sess., 374 ff.

a resolution validating all Lincoln's acts, orders, and proclamations, including his suspension of the writ of habeas corpus. Because Congress believed that it alone had power to suspend the writ, this ran into heavy opposition. All efforts to carry it failed until the end of the session, when the validation, shorn of any mention of habeas corpus, was tacked to a bill increasing the pay of army privates, and thus smuggled through.[26]

For three reasons the President had not attempted to exert much direct influence on the activities of Congress. The first was that he had full confidence in such leaders as Henry Wilson and Frank Blair in military affairs, and Thaddeus Stevens in finance; the second that he was preoccupied with the army movements in front of Washington; and the third that he was also engrossed in the politico-military affairs of Kentucky and Missouri. So long as this short session gave him the men and money he needed, and did not move too harshly in confiscating Southern property, he was content to let it alone. He disliked even the mild confiscation act passed, and doubtless grimaced over Thaddeus Stevens' vituperation in the debate: "If their whole country must be laid waste and made a desert, in order to save this Union from destruction, so let it be." [27] But he signed the act without protest. Lincoln was never a leader of Congress in the sense in which Woodrow Wilson, Theodore Roosevelt, and Franklin D. Roosevelt later often led it, and now, as a novice in the Presidential chair, he was specially hesitant. Later on, the bungling military and financial legislation might have been improved had he played a prime minister's part; but that time had not yet come, and nobody was disturbed because his message contained not a single proposal for legislation beyond the curt request for troops and money.

Lincoln did not yet loom up the colossal central figure in Washington which he was subsequently to become. Intimates saw him in various lights, but not yet as a great man. All Presidents grow in office, but he was to grow far more than most of them.

The glimpses that soldiers and public got of him were of a pleasant, honest-minded, awkward man. Troops saw him at parades, looking kindly and a bit absent; once holding his two little boys by the hand; taking off his hat clumsily at the salute to the flag and putting it on again country-fashion, gripped by the rear rim; stooping as a boy came by with a pail of water to take a great swig. When Francis Lieber, the German-American expert on international law, was taken by Seward to call, he decided that Lincoln was better than people thought him, "but oh, so funny!" Seward in departing said, "I shall immediately return with Lord Lyons; you had better put on your black

---

26 N. Y. *Tribune*, Aug. 7–10, 1861.
27 *Cong. Globe*, 37th Cong., 1st Sess., 415.

coat—you ought to have put it on for Dr. Lieber." To this jocular remark Lincoln replied: "I intended to do so, but the doctor will excuse me; I was not aware it was so late." It was easy for prejudiced men to make cutting remarks. "That sand-hill crane in the Presidential chair," wrote one correspondent; "the joking machine men call Abraham Lincoln." [28] Himself unassuming, he was no respecter of persons. One reason why Charles Francis Adams, Sr., carried from the White House so unfavorable an impression was perhaps that Lincoln showed no awe of Adamses, and half-ignored the Quincy man to talk about political appointments with Seward. Robert Gould Shaw, calling in all the hurly-burly a fortnight after Sumter, formed a truer impression:

We were shown into a room where Mr. Lincoln was sitting at a desk, perfectly covered with papers of every description. He got up and shook hands with us in the most cordial way, asked us to be seated, and seemed quite glad to have us come. It is really too bad to call him one of the ugliest men in the country, for I have seldom seen a pleasanter or more kind-hearted looking one, and he has certainly a very striking face. His voice is very pleasant; and though, to be sure, we were there only a few minutes, I didn't hear anything like Western slang or twang in him. He gives you the impression, too, of being a gentleman. [29]

His sense of the tremendous responsibility on his shoulders deepened his natural melancholy. Above all, it deepened his thoughtfulness. What casual callers could not see beyond the kindness, honesty, and sadness that shone from his angular, furrowed countenance was this ingrained thoughtfulness. They would depart impressed by the wonderful mobility of his face, which could be grimly uncompromising, touchingly careworn, or infectiously mirthful. They could not see, when the door shut, the quick change to intense earnestness as he studied papers, or to concentration as, in the words of Nicolay, "he would sometimes sit for an hour in complete silence, his eyes almost shut, the inner man apparently as far from him as if the form in his chair were a petrified image." [30] Habituated to meditation from his lonely frontier boyhood, trained to precise logical processes by the law, he brought to the Presidency a capacity for intense lucid thinking matched by no other executive. His mind was slow and cautious, but in clarity it excelled Hamilton's, in penetration Madison's, and in weight Webster's. One of his greatest

28 The N. Y. *Tribune* correspondent Samuel Wilkinson so called Lincoln in letters to S. H. Gay; Gay Papers, Columbia University.
29 C. F. Adams, Sir., MS Diary, MHS; MS Diary of Robert Gould Shaw, May 2, 1861.
30 Helen Nicolay, "Characteristic Anecdotes of Lincoln," *Century Magazine*, vol. 84 (August, 1912), 699.

gifts as President, to be revealed in due time, was his ability to think problems through to irresistible conclusions.

His other great qualification was his intuitive understanding of the popular mind, and of political necessities and possibilities. He knew that to be a great statesman he had to be a great politician, like Jefferson and Jackson before him. More than these men, he believed in the goodness and wisdom of the whole people; they could not be fooled long, and he was the last man to wish to fool them. The aggressive Thaddeus Stevens thought that he ought to have led opinion more trenchantly, even recklessly; but Stevens closed his career saying, "My life has been a failure." [31] The patient, watchful Lincoln knew that it was better to be accused of tardiness than to be rash in policy or impracticable in method. He, not Stevens, was the true Commoner. He had no excessive regard for Congressmen, among whom he had once sat, and not only usually resisted any Congressional encroachment on his sphere of action, but was ready at need to invade what Congress deemed its sphere. But his regard for the people never failed.

The Whig tradition, which so many Republicans inherited, regarded Congress as the prime seat of national power, and Clay, Webster, and Seward had labored to make it just that. Lincoln, however, shared the Democratic view— the Jackson-Polk view—that the President as the direct representative of the people should be the vital source of governmental energy. Serving in Congress and later watching affairs closely, he had seen how efficiently Polk acted as commander-in-chief, and how he managed the Mexican War in all its details, administrative, fiscal, and military. He saw Polk, even more effectively than Jackson, tell Congress what to do; he was unquestionably aware that Polk drove his Cabinet with tighter rein than any former President, and the lesson was not lost on him—only he substituted tact for dictation.

He was always ready to manage Congress by giving its members jobs, letting them romp a little with contracts and appropriations, and lending them a hand at logrolling. He specially valued his Congressional spokesmen, like faithful William Kellogg of Illinois and headlong Frank Blair. Nobody showed more consummate skill in dealing with politicians of varied types, often crass, selfish, vain, or corrupt. In time he was to exercise this skill masterfully in handling the ambitious Chase, the unscrupulous Ben Butler, the self-centered Sumner, and the dictatorial, tempestuous Stanton. His magnanimity never failed—he gave even his sleepless rival and frequent detractor, Chase, the

31 Quoted by A. K. McClure, *Lincoln and Men of War-Times*, 286. McClure writes that Lincoln "never cherished resentment even when Stevens indulged in his bitterest sallies of wit or sarcasm at Lincoln's expense."

Chief Justiceship—but neither did his skill. When he turned from the politicians to the people, however, his attitude was one of deference to a higher power. While he knew that he must take the responsibility for decisive enunciations of policy, and did so, he also knew that he did not manage the people: in the last analysis, they managed him.

During this spring and summer of 1861, people poured through the White House in a steady stream. They numbered old Illinois intimates laden with advice, politicians bearing opinions and demands, contractors, youths seeking commissions, inventors, adventurers anxious to raise irregular commands, officers after promotion, governors, Congressmen. "It would be hard to imagine a state of things less conducive to serious and effective work," writes John Hay, "yet in one way or another the work was done. In the midst of a crowd of visitors who began to arrive early in the morning and who were put out, grumbling, by the servants who closed the doors at midnight, the President pursued those labors which will carry his name to distant ages. There was little order or system about it; those around him strove from beginning to end to erect barriers to defend him against constant interruption, but the President himself was always the first to break them down. He disliked anything that kept people from him who wanted to see him, and . . . he would never take the necessary measures to defend himself." And his time was not all wasted. He gained much information, some ideas, a good deal of cheer, and above all steady inspiration, from the thronging callers.[32]

Ideally, the Northern war effort should have been run with consistent system, energy, and flair for organization; but this was quite outside Lincoln's nature. Nor was the country ready for this. It needed a half-century of national growth to enable Wilson to organize his Cabinet, the War Industries Board, the War Labor Board, the General Staff, and other agencies for efficient centralized control of a great war.

Lincoln's principal failure in the first half of 1861 was his neglect to create some group or agency to collect facts and analyze opinions bearing upon national war resources, on men, munitions, and manufacturing capacity, on enemy strength, and on the best fields of military action. With a fumbling, nerveless Secretary of War, no General Staff, no office in Washington acquainted with industry, commerce, and labor, and no intelligence bureau, such an advisory agency would quickly have become invaluable. Sir William Robertson, when made Chief of the Imperial General Staff in 1915, outlined

32 See James G. Randall, *Lincoln the President*, Vols. I and II, *passim*; John Hay, "Life in the White House in the Time of Lincoln," *ut supra*; Charles A. Dana's dictated notes on Lincoln in Ida M. Tarbell Papers, Allegheny College; William O. Stoddard, *Inside the White House in War Times*; Tyler Dennett, *Lincoln and the Civil War in the Diary and Letters of John Hay*; David Donald, *The Enduring Lincoln.*

to the War Office under Kitchener what he thought was the nation's cardinal need. It was "a supreme directing authority whose function is to formulate policy, to decide on the theatres in which military operations are to be conducted, and to determine the relative importance of these theatres." This authority, civilian in personnel, was to gather information through many channels, chiefly military. It was to suggest the men to carry out policy, and under the Prime Minister "exercises a general supervision over the conduct of the war." [33] The United States needed something of the kind in 1861.

[VI]

Nobody could expect Lincoln's relationship with his constitutional advisers, the Cabinet, to be systematic, nor to find him making the Cabinet an effective, coherent body. He expected each Cabinet member to "run his own machine," as he put it. But in the summer of 1861 it was already clear that his relations with the Cabinet would never be satisfactory. The executive group showed nothing of the unselfish cooperation, the earnest association and consultation for the public good, the cordial unity in dealing with Congress, that have marked many Cabinets; and the nation thereby lost heavily.

In part the difficulty lay with the peculiar constitution of the Cabinet. Made up largely of men who had been eager rivals for the Presidency, and who headed special factions in the Republican Party, it lacked basic harmony. Deep personal antagonisms marred relations between Montgomery Blair and Chase, between Welles and Seward.[34] But beyond this, the President was too careless, independent, and busy, after the first weeks, to attempt to create executive unity. "Why do you talk about a Cabinet?" presently burst out Chase to a friend. "There is no Cabinet to be member of." This was precisely the complaint of Greeley's *Tribune*. Lincoln had so withdrawn himself from those to whom he should be closest, grumbled Greeley, and had formed such a set habit of acting or not acting just as his own judgment dictated, that "the impression has become almost universal in the popular mind . . . *that he has no Cabinet,* in the true sense of that term." Attorney-General Bates felt himself an outsider; I am merely a Law Officer, he declared. Secretary Welles, too, was outspoken in censuring the lack of any system:

I have administered the Navy Department almost entirely independent of Cabinet consultations, and I may say almost without direction of the President, who not only gives me his confidence but intrusts all naval matters to

33 Sir Frederick Maurice, *Atlantic Monthly*, vol. 137 (June, 1936), 772 ff.
34 Welles writes: "Between Seward and Chase there was perpetual rivalry and mutual but courtly distrust. Each was ambitious. Both had capacity. Seward was supple and dexterous; Chase was clumsy and strong." *Diary*, I, 139.

me. This has not been my wish. Though glad to have his confidence, I should prefer that every important naval movement should pass a Cabinet review. . . . So in regard to each and all the Departments; if I have known of their regulations and instructions, much of it has not been in Cabinet consultations.[35]

Welles' statement was quite valid for the first part of the war. Governor Dennison of Ohio returned from a trip to Washington reporting that the departments were little governments in themselves. Lincoln had said to him: "Now, Dennison, if Jeff Davis was to get me and I told him all I know, I couldn't give him much information that would be useful to him." [36]

In the absence of general Cabinet consultation, Welles specially resented the opportunity thus given the wily, experienced Seward to push himself forward as chief adviser to the President. Lincoln, he thought early in the war, lacked self-reliance. Perplexed by events, the President relied too much on the far wider knowledge of Seward, whose self-confidence, talkativeness, and easygoing geniality had a ready appeal. No one else, Welles jealously noted, attempted to obtrude himself, or even to suggest that other Cabinet members should be consulted on some of the important measures of the government. Chase alone, greatly irritated by Seward's presumptions, made an occasional effort to talk intimately with Lincoln, learn what was going on in other departments, and offer counsel. Later in the war Welles and Chase were to transfer their antagonism for a time from Seward to Edwin M. Stanton, for the Secretary of War then seemed nearest the seat of power. Wrote Chase:

The President decides all questions concerning the war either by himself or with the advice of the Secretary of War and Commander in Chief [Stanton and Halleck]. The Heads of other Departments, unless perhaps that of the State, are so rarely consulted that they might as well not be consulted at all. Of course being intensely interested in what goes on I can't help saying what I think occasionally; but I do not see good enough come of it to make me vain of my influence.[37]

As this statement suggests, Lincoln was determined to manage the war effort himself, and the determination grew as he increased in wisdom and power. He was not going to let the Cabinet direct any considerable part of it. He had emphatically put Seward in his place on April 1, although retaining him as a close friend and adviser. He overruled Cameron in the matter of the Massachusetts and Pennsylvania regiments. He got General Scott to support him in overruling Cameron again in the critical step of making the able

35 Chase to E. D. Mansfield, Oct. 27, 1863, Chase Papers, Pa. Hist. Soc.; N. Y. *Tribune*, Jan. 27, 1865 (editorial); Bates, Aug. 13, 1864, to J. O. Broadhead; Broadhead Papers, Mo. State Hist. Soc.
36 MS Diary of Wm. T. Coggeshall, Military Secretary to Dennison, Foreman Lebold Coll.
37 Welles, *Diary*, I, 131–139 (Sept. 16, 1862); Chase to Hiram Barney, July 21, 1863. Chase Papers, Hist. Soc. of Pa.

Montgomery C. Meigs quartermaster-general.[38] Generals were soon to be as great a problem to him as politicians. At first he deferred too much to Scott, as he did to Seward, but he was sufficiently vigilant to refuse to let the hot-headed Nathaniel Lyon take command in Missouri. The self-distrust of which Welles speaks was partly a mask. He had a way of drawing out interlocutors with questions, as if still undecided, when his mind was quite made up.

"Mr. Lincoln was always the master," said Charles A. Dana later, "and he did not put on the appearance of it at all. He never gave a hair's breadth, never gave way—he always had his own way. The relations between him and all the Secretaries were perfectly cordial always and unaffected, and without any appearance of his thinking himself the boss, but it was always his will, his order, that determined a decision." This is an overstatement, especially for Lincoln's first year, but it has essential truth. Edward Everett Hale shortly described Lincoln's combination of firmness and tact in different terms. "Nothing shows the power of the President more at the present moment," he wrote after visiting the White House early in 1862, "than the way in which every person you meet thinks and gives you to think that he and the President are hand in glove, and indeed, quite agree." [39]

The inadequacies of the White House secretarial staff were numerous. One observer remarked caustically of John Hay: "As he looks like seventeen, he is under the necessity of acting like seventy." Its main defect, however, was that it was too small. Time quickly developed one specially grievous need: A fact-finding agency responsive to the President's special demands. A single efficient man with reference books and filing cabinets might have done much. Lincoln could not depend on his Cabinet members for many facts about their spheres of concern; on Stanton for exact figures of army strength, for example. He could not depend on anybody for good material on geography and topography; when the main Eastern army went to Harrison's Landing, nobody could tell him what the Landing was like. He could never depend on generals for reliable data on enemy strength. Most of all, he needed more information on the men he appointed to military and civil office. Often he groped in the dark. Somebody to sift official reports, run through newspapers, and approach politicians for critical and confidential judgments would have been invaluable. Of course Lincoln would still have made mistakes. But he would not so readily have appointed John Pope to a command in which he almost ruined the Union cause, or have sent the feeble Dayton as minister to France.

In the summer of 1861, however, both President and Cabinet were yet un-

38 Lincoln, *Collected Works*, IV, 394, 395.
39 Dana's Memoranda, Ida M. Tarbell Papers, Allegheny College; Hale's Memorandum April 26, 1862, in E. E. Hale, *Memories of a Hundred Years*, II, 189, 190.

tried. The quality of the statesmanship possessed by Lincoln, Chase, Seward, and their associates remained to be tested. The sculptor L. W. Volk had made a life mask of Lincoln in Chicago in the spring of 1860; the sculptor Clark Milles was to make another in the spring of 1865. The contrast between the two faces would measure the ordeal through which the President was to pass, and the growth he would attain, in four of the most harrowing years of our history.

11

The First Test of Strength

BY THE TIME Davis reached Richmond and Beauregard partly organized his command at Manassas, the grand strategy of the Confederacy had taken shape. On land, a generally defensive policy was to be pursued while the new nation awaited aid from cotton-starved Europe. The Confederate Congress declared a defensive attitude by resolution just after Sumter, Jefferson Davis proclaimed it in his message to Congress, and Robert E. Lee as head of the Virginia forces asserted it in special orders: "The policy of the State, at present, is strictly defensive." Since the Confederacy as yet lacked strength to invade the North, the defensive policy, despite Beauregard's protests, was inescapable. It imposed on the South a manifest disadvantage in the loss of the initiative. While the North could choose its point of attack, the Confederacy was like a wary duelist, waiting to parry a lunge or a slash. One countervailing advantage was the ability to use distance for defense, transferring troops by inside lines, so far as transport facilities permitted—for inside lines are useless without traffic arteries—while the Union was making long outside marches. Another advantage was the power of awaiting attack behind entrenchments.

The defensive military policy of the South would have had far greater effectiveness if the section had been buttressed by natural physical barriers. Unhappily for its generals, the Confederacy had no Pyrenees, no Vosges, no Carpathians, while the South found it utterly impossible to gain and hold the Ohio, which might have been a real rampart. West and northwest the section was pierced by great rivers: the Mississippi, the Red, the Tennessee, the Cumberland. From Ohio, the Monongahela led southward; from Pennsylvania the Shenandoah Valley opened a corridor. Eastern Virginia was singularly exposed. The Potomac tributaries and the York, Rappahannock, and James, all admitted hostile armies well within the Old Dominion. From the sea, Wilmington, Charleston, Mobile, and above all New Orleans seemed readily assailable. The Confederates lay in a besieged fortress with many entry-ports open. Nevertheless, the principal Southern leaders believed they could withstand all

Union attacks until the Yankees grew tired of the butchery, or Europe intervened.[1]

The energy that the South might have put into a rapid exchange of cotton for arms while the seas remained fairly open went instead into a brisk but essentially futile campaign of privateering.[2] Davis' proclamation (April 17) that all who wished to use privately armed ships to resist Northern aggression might apply for letters of marque sent a spasm of activity through Southern ports. Two days later Lincoln proclaimed that any Southerner molesting American commerce under such authority would be subject to the penalties for piracy; but of course the North could not hang captured privateersmen, for instant retaliation would have followed. Southern leaders being eager to get the "militia of the sea" into action, the rebel Congress passed comprehensive legislation, signed by Davis early in May, which secured to holders of letters of marque and reprisal practically the whole proceeds of their captures. The same law gave Northern merchantmen in Southern ports thirty days to get home, a privilege which the North did not extend to Southern ships. Bounties were offered for the destruction of enemy warships of superior force, and for every naval rating taken prisoner.[3]

The enthusiasm in Southern seaports for the combined opportunity of striking the Yankees and pocketing a neat profit was feverish. Wharves, counting-rooms, and hotel lobbies responded with talk of Drakes to sweep the ocean. The New Orleans *Daily Crescent* dreamed that within 4 months at least 750 swift vessels averaging 4 mighty guns apiece would be crippling the Northern strength. Unhappily for the Confederacy, some of the best Southern ships were seized in Northern harbors. Three fine vessels of the Charleston line, the *South Carolina, Massachusetts,* and *James Adger,* with the *Bienville* of the New Orleans line, were soon Northern cruisers. What they might have done for the South is suggested by the feats of the *Nashville,* also of the Charleston line, which served the Confederacy as transport, privateer, and warship. However, despite the Southern lack of good shipyards and mechanics, some busy hornets were soon sent out.

1 On Confederate strategic policy see Davis, *Rise and Fall,* I, Ch. VI; Clifford Dowdey, *The Land They Fought For,* 126; Eaton, *Southern Confederacy,* 124, 125. John M. Daniel in the Richmond *Examiner* inveighed against the "policy of retreat"; see editorials June 12, June 15, July 2, etc., and F. S. Daniel, *The Richmond Examiner During the War.*
2 The exchange of cotton for arms at this date could not have been large, nearly all the 1860 crop having been exported or sent to New England, but it might have been useful. See Owsley, *King Cotton Diplomacy,* 25 ff.; Coulter, *Confederate States,* Ch. X; J. H. Reagan, *Memoirs,* 113; Schwab, *Confederate States,* 13–16, 233, 234.
3 Statutes, Provisional Govt. CSA, 2d Sess., Ch. III; Richardson, *Messages and Papers of the Confederacy,* I, 60–62; Robinson, *The Confederate Privateers,* 17–20, 30 ff.; and on Washington's belated offer to adhere unconditionally to the Declaration of Paris outlawing privateers, 64th Cong., 1st Sess., Senate Doc. 332. For fundamental material on the Confederate privateers see *O. R. Union and Conf. Navies,* Series II, i, 247–249.

New Orleans on May 16 dispatched the little steamer *Calhoun*, which that same evening captured a Maine bark with 3,000 barrels of lime. She was immediately joined by two other New Orleans privateers which began cruising the Gulf. Beauregard had urged Louisiana to fortify the Mississippi below the city, arming Forts Jackson and St. Philip with the heaviest guns to be found, and constructing heavy booms, one of timber and one of barges, across the river. This was delayed, but the privateers delighted Creole hearts. Charleston, meanwhile, had her first privateer active June 2, when the schooner *Savannah*, armed with one 1812-style eighteen-pounder, put to sea on a brief and unfortunate cruise. After capturing a Maine brig laden with Cuban sugar, she was seized by a Union warship. Landed in New York, the small crew were ironed, confined in the Tombs, and tried for piracy, with the death penalty staring them in the face until the jury happily disagreed.[4] Another Charleston privateer named for Jefferson Davis, a brig armed with five English guns of 1801 vintage, went to sea in June, and soon captured a Philadelphia freighter and a Massachusetts schooner. A third, the *Dixie*, sailed in July and within four days placed a prize crew aboard a Yankee bark full of coal.

By this time merchants and shipowners in all North Atlantic ports were clamorous for an immediate intensification of the blockade. Even if the Confederacy could place only a few dozen privateers on the ocean, unless its ports were quickly sealed it would deal Northern commerce a staggering blow. Steamship companies, shippers, and insurance interests demanded that the government put guns and gunners on important steamers like those which brought forty millions in gold from San Francisco to New York every year, furnish convoys on dangerous routes, and station warships in such busy sea lanes as Vineyard Sound.[5]

Even during May, blockading vessels trailed their smoke across the skies outside Charleston, Savannah, Mobile, and New Orleans. But no Yankee ever uttered a frostier understatement than Secretary Welles's remark that the navy was "not as powerful or in numbers as extensive as I wished." When Sumter fell, only forty-two ships, including tenders and storeships, were in commission. Six were in Northern ports, four at Pensacola, one on the Great Lakes, and the others dotted over the globe from the Mediterranean to the East Indies. With authority from Lincoln, Welles instantly ordered the buying or leasing of twenty vessels.[6] He assigned an Atlantic force the task of closing

4 Four of the twelve jurors stood for acquittal; see Robinson, *Privateers,* 135–147, for details.
5 Nineteen New York insurance companies demanded that the navy give immediate protection to commerce; O. R. I, i, 9.
6 Welles established in New York an advisory board of five, including Governor E. D. Morgan, William M. Evarts, and Moses Grinnell, to assist in forwarding men and supplies. His MS diary contains some matter not in the published version.

Confederate ports from the Chesapeake to Key West, and shortly divided it into North Atlantic and South Atlantic squadrons under Louis M. Goldsborough and Samuel F. Du Pont respectively. A Gulf squadron was instructed to shut every port in that area. Blockade runners were soon being captured. The seizure of three British ships off Charleston on May 22 posed a difficult diplomatic question, which was settled when the government, after Seward appealed to Welles, released them.[7]

It was soon evident that no exterior patrol would suffice to shut the Southern ports. Along such an extended coast, with so many inlets, harbors, and bays, it was easy for blockade runners and privateers to slip in and out. Only when some of the major ports had been captured could the movement of ships be brought under control. By July conversations were under way between the army and navy upon an amphibious expedition against Wilmington. Meanwhile, the navy had let contracts for the hurried construction of warships. The sloop *Tuscarora* was launched at Philadelphia on August 22. "Her keel was growing in the forest three months ago," boasted Welles. Vessels of every size and shape were also bought for refitting and arming. "Alas! It is like altering a vest into a shirt to convert a trading steamer into a man of war," lamented Du Pont, but the work went on. Although summer found the blockade still highly ineffective, naval officers could reflect that the war was young.

The South, indeed, by midsummer had a premonition of the days when imports would cease, and shortages become crippling. Northern commercial interests equally felt a foreboding of grave damage to the American merchant marine. Long so proud, it might be swept from the seas or compelled to take refuge under foreign flags.

[I]

On land, meanwhile, the time had come for harder blows. North and South, the clamor for fighting grew ever more strident. In Richmond the rebel war clerk Jones wrote in his diary for June 12: "The vast majority of our people are for 'carrying the war into Africa' without a moment's delay."[8] From Washington a gallant New York soldier, Francis Barlow, destined to become known as the boy general and to have his monument reared at Gettysburg, wrote that the demand for crushing the enemy made a campaign so imperative that if Lincoln objected, he might be replaced by a military dictatorship.[9] "Already the murmurs of discontent are ocean-loud against the slow and cau-

---

7 West, *Welles*, 117; J. R. Soley, *The Blockade and the Cruisers*, 8, 9.
8 Jones, *Rebel War Clerk's Diary*, I, 51.
9 Francis Barlow had enlisted as a private April 19, married the next day, and left his bride at the church to go to the front. His letter of May 27, 1861, is in the S. L. M. Barlow Papers.

tious courses of the war. I see this in the files of responsible and pervading correspondence which crowd the Secretaries' mails, and I know it from the President himself."

The sight of troops pouring to the front gave people on each side a false impression of strength. When Beauregard left Montgomery for the Virginia front on May 29 his train, according to a Boston-born physician aboard, counted 148 cars, all filled with troops bound for Augusta and points north, and drawn by two locomotives.[10] This may be an exaggeration, but it is true that Southerners who cheered massive troop trains expected a prompt advance. Jefferson Davis explained to Joseph E. Johnston on July 13 that a North Carolinian who accused the government of wantonly holding back 17,000 eager men from his State was writing nonsense. Volunteers swarmed everywhere, but Davis had to tell these eager units: "I have not arms to supply you." [11] In Washington, it was assuredly a mistake to show members of Congress on July 4 an imposing military pageant, some 25,000 troops filling Pennsylvania Avenue like a blue river, while their tread sounded like dull thunder, for the spectacle made many members recklessly impatient. "This was war," wrote one. "We should bring on the battle." [12]

Each side underrated the need for preparation, and undervalued the fighting quality of its opponents. "It was a favorite notion," wrote General Barnard later, "with a large class of Northern politicians (and the people too) that nothing but an imposing display of force was necessary to crush the rebellion." [13] Surely, since pioneers had fought under Andrew Jackson at the wave of a hat, a regiment hardly needed three months' drill! Why wait, when only a thirty-mile march was needed to overwhelm the enemy?

Both the Confederate camp at Manassas and the Union camps before Washington were slovenly. Neither army had properly assembled and organized its baggage trains, tents, food arrangements, or medical supplies. Beauregard could have said precisely what McDowell did say later: "I had no opportunity to test my machinery, to move it around and see whether it would work smoothly or not." Yet each section waved aside reasons for delay. "True enough, you are green," men admitted. "But the enemy is green too—you are all green alike." [14]

The North had a taste of the bloody realities of war on June 10. Ben Butler —urged on by Montgomery Blair, who denounced the "miserable do-nothings" in Washington and expressed confidence that a march to Richmond would be easy—moved that day to capture two Confederate posts, Big and Little Bethel,

10 Dr. Martin McQueen in Syracuse *Journal*, May 27, 1861.
11 O. R. I, ii, 976–977.
12 A. G. Riddle, *Recs. of War Times*, 29.
13 Barnard, *The C. S. A. and the Battle of Bull Run*, 42.
14 Hurlburt, *McClellan and the Conduct of the War*, 103.

a few miles from Fort Monroe. The command was given to an incompetent. He used faulty old maps, sent out two columns on a night march which, instead of joining hands and cooperating, actually fired into each other, and by this tragic mishap gave the alarm to the Confederates at Little Bethel, who fell back on Big Bethel. He then completely botched an attempt to flank this well-chosen position, where the enemy was protected by a swampy creek and a battery of guns. As Butler later wrote, "Everything was mismanaged." The Union forces withdrew just as the Confederate leader, fearing reinforcements from Fort Monroe, himself retreated! The reason which the Northern commander later offered for retiring was that his troops were hungry from long marching. Actually they had covered about eleven miles, and if they had halted to eat lunch from their haversacks, they could have kept the position the enemy was abandoning! [15]

It was evident, meanwhile, that the Northern forces were loose, clumsy, and inharmonious. The aged Scott reigned without actually ruling. He had three armies, Patterson's in the Harpers Ferry area, McDowell's at Alexandria, and Ben Butler's at Fort Monroe, which he failed to coordinate, and whose commanders all distrusted him.[16]

Patterson, who on June 28 had 14,350 men facing Joe Johnston's 10,700, made a series of erratic movements. Elated by his success in driving Johnston from Harpers Ferry, he thought that with Scott's support he could win a brilliant victory; but Scott, with superior insight, disapproved of his plans, and withdrew some of his troops. The result was that the Pennsylvania general believed that he had been checked just as he was on the point of seizing a bright advantage. Had he held Charlestown just south of the Potomac, he would have been in a position to strike at Winchester, intercept Johnston if that general suddenly moved to join Beauregard at Manassas, or himself march rapidly to reinforce McDowell. Instead, he put himself in a remoter position at Martinsburg.[17] Relations between Scott and McDowell continued bad, with Scott petulant and McDowell resentful. By July 16-17, returns for the McDowell-Mansfield command in the Washington-Alexandria area showed

15 On the two Bethels, see *Butler's Book*, 266-270; Swinton, *Army of the Potomac*, 31. The saddest loss at Big Bethel was that of Theodore Winthrop, a more than promising American man of letters.

16 Lossing, *Civil War*, I, 525, 526; Swinton, 33, 34; O. R. I, ii.

17 For Patterson's Shenandoah operations see O. R. I, ii, 156-187, 607, 694; his own *Narrative* is best read in the light of T. L. Livermore's careful paper on the campaign in Military Hist. Soc. of Mass., I, *Campaigns in Virginia 1861-62*. Alonzo H. Quint's *The Second Mass. Infantry* gives an interesting view. Patterson when forced to retreat had to endure silently a great deal of public criticism. "Great injustice is done you and your command here," John Sherman, who had been on his staff, wrote from Washington June 30, "and by persons in the highest military position." When Patterson placed his forces at Martinsburg they were behind Johnston, who was thus free to move to Manassas at any time with Patterson trailing in his rear.

Burnside's Rhode Island Brigade at Bull Run

John Charles Frémont

37,321 officers and men present for duty, but McDowell felt that Scott had denied him the staff, equipment, and latitude in training which he needed.

If Patterson and McDowell distrusted the head of the armies, Butler's opinion was scorching. The day he was appointed major-general, May 16, he called on Scott to exchange angry accusations. Scott accused him of running terrible risks in Baltimore, thwarting the government's pacific plans, and showing general highhandedness. Butler retorted that Scott knew nothing of the situation, had made dangerous concessions to the disloyal mayor, and should have helped him suppress the murderous plug-uglies. Though Cameron and Chase urged the indigant Butler to stay in the service, and Montgomery Blair assured him he was entirely right, his irritation grew when he found Fort Monroe shockingly ill equipped. It had no horses, no proper water supply, no provisions but hardtack and meat; the seven or eight thousand men he commanded were insufficient to do more than keep Magruder at bay. The sympathetic Blair, who had hoped to see Butler march direct on Richmond, wrote Cameron on June 22 in high dudgeon. Instead of 20,000 men with proper artillery, cavalry, and wagon trains, Butler had less than half that force, no transport, no cavalry, and few guns. Blair added:

> My want of confidence in the enterprise of the General-in-Chief grows. Besides, he does not approve our policy and is not heartily with us. He means to play Pacificator. I counsel you to take these matters into your own charge, seeing that you have the responsibility.[18]

The West Virginia campaign furnished new evidence of want of plan and liaison in Washington. McClellan exaggerates the facts when he declares that from first to last he had no "advice, orders, or instructions from Washington or elsewhere," and acted on his own initiative; for actually he got some helpful information from Scott. But he was left altogether too much to his own resources. He issued a proclamation to the people of West Virginia of strong political tinge, and an equally political address to his soldiers. When he sent Lincoln copies, with a letter explaining his reasons for the invasion, he got no comment from President, Secretary of War, or General Scott. It was unfortunate that Cameron and Scott did not fully and promptly inform McClellan of their plan of action in front of Washington. Had they done so, the troops flushed with victory at Rich Mountain might have marched, as McClellan suggested, toward the Shenandoah to help Patterson pin down Joseph E. Johnston.[19]

18 See *Butler's Book*. Blair in the rough draft of his letter to Cameron included a sentence later deleted: "As our friend Chase even has fallen out with the Genl I hope we will pluck up courage to take our affairs into our own hands." Blair Papers, LC.

19 See McClellan's published *Report*, 15–17, 51, 52; for Scott's advice see O. R. I, ii, 648, 743, etc.

[II]

Like two wrestlers glowering at each other across the ring, McDowell and Beauregard early in July faced each other across twenty miles of broken Virginia countryside. The Union commander, after detaching about 6,000 men to protect his communications, had 30,000 troops with 49 guns; the Confederate general had some 22,000 men with 29 guns. Both might be rapidly reinforced—the Southern army by Johnston's Shenandoah force, which at the beginning of July comprised about 11,000 men with 20 guns, and the army of McDowell by Patterson's larger force.[20] In this matter of reinforcing Beauregard and McDowell the Confederacy held the advantage, partly because Johnston could use the railroad from Winchester to Manassas, while Patterson had no ready means of reaching the area.

The Administration had good reasons for wishing to see McDowell offer battle. One was that the ninety-day men were soon to quit, they hoped to see action before they left, and obviously they ought to be used. Another was that European governments might be impressed by Northern vigor. The most important, however, was that Northern morale must be sustained.

Impatient Congressmen varied their debates by grumbling loudly about procrastination. Wagons and horses were needed? Well, buy them! Regiments had to be organized into brigades and divisions? Well, shove them in! Zack Chandler, who came to the Senate full of plans for seizing rebel property, thought that Scott could avoid hard fighting just by showing a little energy: he could simply surround the scoundrels, make their case hopeless, and compel them to retreat to Richmond. Chandler and others were talking about hanging the worst traitors as soon as they were caught.[21] Half of the press was ringing with demands for hard blows. As an echo of Horace Greeley's suggestions, Fitz-Henry Warren, a Washington correspondent of the *Tribune*, wrote his famous "Forward to Richmond" article; Greeley allowed Charles A. Dana to repeat and reinforce it in subsequent issues; and other newspapers caught it up. "Forward to Richmond! Forward to Richmond! The Rebel Congress must not be allowed to meet there on the 20th of July!"—so from June 26 onward ran the *Tribune*'s daily iteration of "The Nation's Battle-Cry." [22]

20 On numbers see Ropes, I, 127, 128; *Battles and Leaders*, I, 175; O. R. I, ii, 309, 487. A few ninety-day men did quit just before the battle, and the position of the whole body affected Union morale.
21 Chandler to his wife, Washington, June 27, 1861, Chandler Papers, LC; F. W. Banks, Washington, July 9, 1861, to S. L. M. Barlow, Barlow Papers; Washington correspondence dated July 11, 12, in N. Y. *Tribune*, July 13, 1861.
22 Cf. Charles A. Dana, "Greeley as a Journalist," N. Y. *Sun*, Dec. 5, 1872; and Dana's dictated statement to Ida M. Tarbell in Tarbell Papers, Allegheny College. Dana had been with the *Tribune* since 1847 and in some of Greeley's absences had taken full charge.

ich nobody made any comment except Mansfield, commanding in Wash-
, who said that he had not thought about the matter, knew nothing about
was unprepared to speak! The relation of Patterson's army to the move-
was discussed, and one participant states that Scott explicitly promised
e it keep the Confederates in the Shenandoah engaged: "I assume the
sibility for having Johnston kept off McDowell's flank." Finally, Mc-
ll submitted his plan to the army engineers, who made no constructive
tion. In short, no real debate on the wisdom or mode of the attack took

ce the plan was accepted, McDowell had great difficulty in implement-
Some regiments crossed the Potomac late, and a few not till the very
e was to start his army. He set out with no baggage trains, and though
ssessed ammunition wagons and ambulances, had no facilities to carry
or tents. The men carried three days' rations in their haversacks. Said
alous Mansfield, in effect, "I have no transportation to give you." Said
, head of the quartermaster arrangements: "I have transportation, but
ield does not want me to supply it until the troops move." Said the
urdened McDowell: "I agree to that, but between you two I get noth-
So he set off, telling Scott he was not really ready to go: "So far as
ortation is concerned, I must look to you behind me to send it forward."
egregiously bad marching of his troops McDowell explained by saying
Americans were unused to foot travel. Starting on Tuesday morning,
6, the army did not reach Centerville until Thursday afternoon, when it
ed until the battle advance began Sunday morning the 21st. Why?—
because its provisions had not come up.[24]
ctually, McDowell's plan was well conceived and well drafted. By de-
g Beauregard at Manassas, he would not only dispel the threat to Wash-
n, but seize the important junction between the Orange & Alexandria
oad and its lateral branch to the Shenandoah. He had the advantage of
ior numbers, better ordnance, about 1600 regular soldiers, and the pros-
of a timely reinforcement by Patterson. But a sharp check at Blackburn's
on the Bull Run July 18 discouraged his men, who wondered whether
Confederate line could really be penetrated. He and the army engineers
the next two days trying to discover the best place for attack. Meanwhile
rson, whose duty was to hold Joseph E. Johnston, marched in precisely
rong direction. He had been alarmed by vague reports that he had 30,000
,000 troops before him. In a half-hearted demonstration, he moved toward

McDowell dates the East Room conference June 29; Montgomery C. Meigs says the
ning of July. See McDowell's testimony, *Comm. on Conduct of the War*, II, 35 ff.;
Papers, Box IV, LC; and O. R. I, ii, *passim*, full of material on the campaign.

FIELD OF OPERATIONS
IN VIRGINIA

on wh
ingto
it, and
ment
to ha
respo
Dowe
sugge
place.

O
ing it
day h
he po
food
the je
Meig
Mans
overt
ing."
trans
The
that
July
camp
partly

A
featil
ingto
Rail
supe
pect
Ford
the (
used
Patte
the v
to 4(

On the Confederate side various prodders, including t
iner, had made Jefferson Davis nearly as anxious to hazard
Davis wrote Johnston July 13 that the one great object w
ern columns capacity to take the offensive and prevent
enemy's forces.[23]

Nothing could have been more haphazard than the
Dowell's forward thrust was determined upon. First, Scott
submit a plan of operations against Manassas, with an e
needed. Second, McDowell sent his plan to Scott, who re
Third, a council was held June 29 in the East Room of th
tended by Cabinet members and leading officers. McDo

23 O. R. I, ii, 976, 977.

Winchester and Johnston on July 16, but then next day retreated to Charlestown, and a little later pulled still farther back to Harpers Ferry. Johnston no sooner learned that Patterson had fallen back than he exultantly set his troops in motion, hurrying them on as fast as he could to join Beauregard.

The result was that on July 20 the main body of Johnston's force joined Beauregard. His intelligence service, for he had Major J. E. B. Stuart's cavalry to scout for him, was as superb as Patterson's was worthless. While Patterson was asking Scott for aid at Harpers Ferry, Johnston's command was fraternizing with the defenders of Manassas. This, said McDowell later, was "the fatal thing" that decided Bull Run.

Yet it was not the only fatal element. At first the Union advance on the 21st seemed victorious. Pressing against the Confederate left, McDowell's raw volunteers threw the Southerners back in some disorder. The main fighting began about ten; at noon the battle was raging heavily beyond Bull Run, around and on the hill capped by the Henry farmhouse; reports of a disaster swept Richmond. The gallant James S. Wadsworth of New York thought at two o'clock that the Union army had won the field. But command liaison on the Union side was very poor, so that troops moved in piecemeal and raggedly. Then, soon after three, a new part of Johnston's army, fresh from the trains, arrived on the scene—the brigade of E. Kirby-Smith. That force, delivering a severe discharge of musketry, followed it with a hot charge. Some Union elements stampeded, and as Beauregard ordered an attack along the whole line, the Union troops were swept back. By five they were in full retreat.

Beauregard had possessed complete warning of the Federal advance, for at 8:00 P.M. on July 16 a sealed letter, brought him by relays from the Confederate spy Mrs. Greenhow in Washington, had announced in cipher that McDowell had been ordered to move. Early next morning he telegraphed the news to Jefferson Davis. On the 17th the Richmond authorities had been able to order Johnston's Army of the Shenandoah to join Beauregard, and T. J. Jackson's brigade had forthwith led the van in the march to the nearest railroad station. Scott, meanwhile, had failed to give Patterson positive orders.[25]

Not only were the Southern forces better coordinated, but they had better officers and showed superior morale. During the battle the Confederate generals kept close under fire. Johnston and Beauregard were in the front lines at critical moments, Brigadier-General B. E. Bee was mortally wounded, Colonel

25 See Col. Alfred Roman's *Beauregard*, I, 71 ff. (practically an autobiography); Johnston's *Narrative*, 50 ff.; Gen. James Wadsworth's testimony in Committee on the Conduct of the War, II; Swinton, *Army of the Potomac*, 58, 59; Ropes, I, 131 ff. Swinton and Ropes emphasize the defective leadership and uneven fighting on both sides. *Comm. on Conduct of the War*, II, 103. By Patterson's own statement, he could have held Johnston with 8,000 men; *op. cit.*, 107. A mass of military dispatches may be found in O. R. I., li, pt. 2.

J. F. Thomas, chief ordnance officer, fell while leading broken troops back into battle, and Jubal Early was equally intrepid. It was while Bee was appealing to his South Carolinians to sustain the honor of their State that he pointed to a brigade of the Army of the Shenandoah standing on the Henry house hilltop awaiting the Northern onslaught: "Look, there is Jackson with his Virginians standing like a stone wall against the enemy." [26] The men responded by a spirited charge. Young Jeb Stuart, leading two companies of cavalry, made his first appearance on a battlefield by a timely onslaught against the Union right flank, sweeping through the supports of two Federal batteries and leaving the guns an easy prey to an advancing regiment of Virginians. Throughout the hottest part of the battle the Confederate morale rose.

The Union troops had the disadvantage of advancing over unknown terrain against a foe of unknown strength. Raw troops fight more steadily when stationary, as most of the Confederate units were; in attacking they become confused and disorganized. Many Northerners entered the fight hot, tired, and thirsty from previous marching. Sights of wounds and agony frightened the green men. General William B. Franklin went forward with the Fifth and Eleventh Massachusetts to try to extricate an exposed battery. The infantrymen could not be brought up to the mark: they would rush forward, deliver a volley, and then, instead of taking hold of the guns, fall back to a safe place to reload. The Union artillery was badly served, and Griffin's expert West Point Battery showed the usual contempt of regulars for volunteers. Early in the combat it tore through the New York Seventy-first at top speed for a front-line position, cutting the regiment in two. Later, it ran out of ammunition. The caissons tore recklessly back for a fresh supply, scattering the units in their path, and men who saw the horses and gunners madly ripping out for the rear, thought all was lost—and ran too.

The Union retreat, at first orderly, quickly became a disgraceful rout. As Beauregard's lines swept forward, the panic grew, and soon men were in headlong flight, amid heat, dust, anguish, and terrific profanity. W. H. Russell, riding forward on horseback, found himself among the first fugitives. "What does this mean?" he demanded, and an exhausted officer gasped: "Why, it means that we are pretty badly whipped." [27]

The scene between Manassas and Alexandria that evening was never to be forgotten. The fields were dotted with fugitives, mounted officers outstripping

26 *Century*, XLVIII, vol. 48 (May, 1894), 155, 156.
27 Russell's vivid description, *My Diary*, Ch. 50, is corroborated by the photographer Mathew Brady, caught in the flight; Representative A. O. Riddle, quoted in S. S. Cox, *Three Decades*, 158; Horace White, *Lyman Trumbull*, 165–168. Trumbull, who had gone to the battle with Senator Grimes and others, wrote: "Literally, three could have chased ten thousand."

BULL RUN

DISPOSITION OF

CONFEDERATE FORCES

privates afoot. Down the Centreville highway poured a river of wagons, ambulances, soldiers belaboring mules, and dirty, disheveled troops. Every vehicle was jammed with men, who threw out even ammunition to make room. The ground was covered with provisions, overcoats, knapsacks, blankets, muskets, canteens, and cartridge boxes. Drivers whipped their teams; reeling soldiers clung to stirrups and wagon gates; and at every interruption of traffic masses of troops yelled frantically with rage: "The cavalry is on us! Get along, get along!" Over the crossroads rose columns of dust, for here, too, masses of troops were fleeing as from some unknown terror. As the flight roared northward, its noise like that of a great river, more and more men fell out from exhaustion. At Centreville some fresh reserve regiments formed line on a good defensive slope, and the fleeing forces might well have considered themselves safe.[28] But when a neighboring battery opened fire, the thud and flash precipitated a fresh panic.

It was the familiar story whose moral Kipling later compressed into three lines:

Ye pushed them raw to the battle as ye plucked them raw from the street,
And what did ye look they should compass? War-craft learned in a breath
Knowledge unto occasion at the first far view of Death?

In Washington that Sunday intense suspense had gripped everyone. Scott, anxious to allay men's anxiety, talked confidently of success and went to

28 A reserve brigade under Miles and a brigade under Richardson, in and just beyond Centerville, had taken no part in the fighting, maintained good order, and served as a dependable rear guard; Ropes, I, 153.

church at eleven. Early in the afternoon the President began receiving telegrams every quarter hour from Fairfax Court House, three or four miles from the battlefront. They at first gave the impression that the Union forces were retiring, and Lincoln, alarmed, went to see Scott, whom he found asleep. The General explained that the noise of battle was often misleading, for the wind made the firing seem first near, then far. Lincoln, returning to the White House, found news that the battle still raged, but that McDowell now seemed to be winning. Pleased by word that the Confederates had been driven back, he went for a ride. His secretary Nicolay records:

At six o'clock . . . Mr. Seward came into the President's room with a terribly excited and frightened look, and said to John [Hay] and I, who were sitting there, "Where is the President?" "Gone to ride," we replied.

"Have you any late news?" said he.

I began reading Hanscom's dispatch to him.

Said he: "Tell no one. That is not so. The battle is lost. The telegraph says that McDowell is in full retreat, and calls on General Scott to save the capital, etc. Find the President and tell him immediately to come to General Scott's." [29]

[III]

The Confederates made no real pursuit. By a determined thrust from either the east or west, they might have turned the small reserve force at Centreville. Some regiments on the Confederate left did ford Bull Run and set out to follow the fleeing troops, but were recalled by a staff command given in error. That night President Davis and the principal Confederate generals held a battlefield conference.[30] Davis was at first willing to send the freshest units, the brigades of Ewell, D. R. Jones, and Longstreet, in pursuit, but because doubts were thrown upon a major's report that he had seen a wild flight, with abandoned wagons and choked roads, he finally decided against the step. Johnston believed that his raw troops, poorly supplied with food and ammunition, could not execute forced marches and attack the fortified lines before Washington. He thought his troops more disorganized by victory, indeed, than the Union forces by defeat. Beauregard also opposed an attempt at pursuit. Previously hot to take the offensive and advance on Washington, he now declared that the prostration of the men, the shortage of supplies—the Manassas army had never possessed food for more than two days, and sometimes no rations at all, while it now held only enough ammunition for half a battle—and the general confusion, forbade a forward thrust.

29 Nicolay to his wife, July 27, 1861; Nicolay Papers, LC.
30 Davis had reached the battlefield just in time to witness the rout of the Union forces, and at once exultantly telegraphed his War Department that 15,000 Confederates had defeated 35,000 Federal troops. Roman, *Beauregard*, I, 111.

This decision deeply disappointed both Richmond and the many Southern sympathizers in Washington. Mrs. Greenhow, who had repeatedly assured Beauregard that the Union works south of the Potomac had been barely commenced and mounted few guns, and that a Confederate advance was greatly dreaded in the capital, ended more than one dispatch after Manassas: "Come on! Why do you not come?" But Johnston and Beauregard made a correct decision. By an implacable pursuit, flogging on their tired soldiers, the Confederates could have taken more prisoners and stores, making the defeat still more humiliating. But as they approached Washington they would have met the reserves from Centreville, the divisions of Mansfield and Runyon, some 11,000 Pennsylvania troops who arrived on Monday, and perhaps Patterson's force. Beyond the fortifications lay the Potomac. The night after the battle a dull, drenching rain began which continued all next day, turning the roads into mud. The railroad bridge across Bull Run had been destroyed. And the Confederates were hungry. Their commissary service, in the hands of the ill-tempered, inept Colonel Lucius B. Northrop, who had refused to let Beauregard sweep the area south of Washington clean of provisions, was distressingly inefficient.[31]

Even without pursuit, the Confederates claimed fully 1200 prisoners; 28 fieldpieces of good quality, 8 of them rifled, with more than 100 rounds for each gun; some 500 muskets and 500,000 rounds of ammunition; and horses, wagons, caissons, and ambulances. Losses on both sides have been variously computed, but the best source places the Union killed at 481, the Confederate at 387.[32]

The exultation of part of the Southern press and public was not only unrestrained, but tinged with an arrogant tone. "The breakdown of the Yankee race, their unfitness for empire," declared the Richmond *Whig*, "forces dominion on the South. We are compelled to take the sceptre of power. We must adapt ourselves to our new destiny. We must elevate our race, every man of it, breed them up to arms, to command, to empire." [33] The Louisville *Courier-Journal* was equally insolent. The South, remarked the editor, had until a few

31 "The want of food and transportation has made us lose all the fruits of our victory," wrote Beauregard, July 29. "We ought at this moment to be in or about Washington, but we are perfectly anchored here, and God only knows when we will be able to advance; without these means we can neither advance nor retreat." Roman, *op. cit.*, 121, 122. George Cary Eggleston in *A Rebel's Recollections* emphatically states the view of those who thought the army should have pursued. Jubal Early in his reminiscences emphatically agrees that advance was impracticable and impolitic; *Narrative*, 43–46.

32 O. R. I, ii, 327, gives Union killed 481, wounded 1011, and missing 1216; the Confederate killed at 387, wounded at 1582.

33 July 23, 1861. One able Southerner, the engineer R. H. Lucas, said he would not give ten cents on the dollar for New York property; Manigault, MS Recollections, Univ. of N. C., 326, 327.

weeks since governed the North as its Norman ancestors had governed the Saxon churls. The Yankee revolt would not last long, for, "dastards in fight and incapable of self-government, they will inevitably fall under the control of a superior race. A few more Bull Run thrashings will bring most of them once more under the yoke, as docile as the most loyal of our Ethiopian chattels." [34] *DeBow's Review*, picturing the North as divided and half-prostrated, predicted that the battle would confirm the independence of the South.[35]

Needless to say, responsible men like Davis and Lee knew that the test had only begun.

34 Quoted in Rossiter Johnson, *War of Secession*, 70.
35 September, 1861.

12

A Resurgent North

THE EFFECT of Bull Run at the North, as its meaning sank in, was as stimulating as a whiplash. It blew away illusions like rags of fog in a northwest gale. Andrew D. White, a young upstate New Yorker already winning prominence as an educator, heard of the battle as he was entertaining Charles Sumner's younger brother, fresh from Washington. White was angry over a recent statement by Seward that the Administration had determined to end the rebellion even if it took 50,000 men to capture Richmond and dictate terms that summer. In what kind of dreams was Seward indulging? White and George Sumner agreed that defeat was healthy if it stopped such fatuous misconceptions.[1]

The defeat brought Northern dissidents to better support of the war, and stimulated every State to intensified effort. Illinois telegraphed the War Department offering seventeen regiments. Indiana telegraphed offering ten. As regiments of ninety-day men were mustered out in New York, the rank and file showed a strong desire to reënlist—but with the stipulation that they must have officers of real capacity. The first shock in Washington had been appalling. To see McDowell's rabble, a host of dirty, ragged, hungry men, come pouring in to beg food from door to door and sink to sleep on pavements and doorsteps; to see the hotels crowded with road-stained officers, some brazen, some ashamed—this disheartened loyal citizens. But the *National Intelligencer*, indignant over reports North and South that the city was frightened, published a front-page editorial August 3 to declare that the capital remained undaunted, undiscouraged, and confident of ultimate success.

A second Northern uprising was at once evident. Governor Curtin, now justified in his insistence on a State reserve of fifteen regiments fully armed and ready for an emergency, could claim first place in the movement. The arrival of his troops in Washington just after the battle heartened the North. Volunteers thronged forward. Seward five days after the battle wrote Charles Francis Adams in London that military and civil panic had quickly ceased, and the

[1] White, *Autobiography*, I, 87–88.

true result was already seen in a vigorous reconstruction of the war effort on an expanded scale.[2] Within a fortnight a strong new army of more than 75,000 men, enlisted for three years or the duration, was in the training camps.

A complete reorganization of command was clearly necessary. At the very moment that public confidence in McDowell fell to zero, the press was spreading broadcast a Napoleonic proclamation from McClellan:

Soldiers of the Army of the West!
I am more than satisfied with you.
You have annihilated two armies, commanded by educated and experienced soldiers, intrenched in mountain fastnesses fortified at their leisure. You have taken five guns, twelve colors, fifteen hundred stand of arms, one thousand prisoners, including more than forty officers—one of the two commanders of the rebels is a prisoner, the other lost his life on the field of battle. You have killed more than two hundred and fifty of the enemy, who has lost all his baggage and camp equipage. All this has been accomplished with the loss of twenty brave men killed and sixty wounded on your part.[3]

These statements were the more impressive because their author had served with distinction in Mexico, had been an official observer of the Crimean War, and combined a West Point education with managerial experience in business. McClellan was careful to point out that *he* had inspired his men: "I have not hesitated to demand this of you, feeling that I could rely on your endurance, patriotism, and courage." The New York *Herald* led the press in extolling him. "The name of General McClellan is upon every lip," it declared July 15. Cabinet members, military men, and the universal populace joined in his praise; "Hurrah for McClellan!" men even shouted in the streets. His energy, skill, and organizing efficiency delighted everybody.

His one-month campaign to conquer northwestern Virginia indeed appeared to be brilliant. Nobody could deny his high administrative capacity. A critical scrutiny, however, would have demolished some of his eloquent pretensions. He had possessed a heavy preponderance in numbers, and one still heavier in firepower, for the Confederates were poorly equipped. He had marked advantages of transport in the use of the Baltimore & Ohio on the north and the Great Kanawha on the south. He operated in a friendly country. At Parkersburg, for example, his troops had met a general ovation, "gray-headed old men and women, mothers holding up their children to take my hand, girls, boys, all sorts, cheering and crying, 'God bless you!'" The campaign hardships of which he spoke feelingly ("long and arduous marches," "insufficient food," "inclemency of the weather") did not bother a young Ohio officer named

2 *Diplomatic Correspondence*, 1861.
3 This pronunciamento was dated July 16; O. R. I, ii, 205–208. All the younger generals then fancied themselves embryo Napoleons, and cultivated Napoleonic rescripts; except a few who thought themselves Wellingtons.

Rutherford B. Hayes serving with him. On the contrary, Hayes exulted in the fine mountain scenery, clear streams, wooded slopes, and generally warm, clear weather.

McClellan's handsome, soldierly presence, kind, modest manners, and evident care for his troops, made a happy impression. The obverse of the medal was his readiness to lay claim to credit belonging to others, to depreciate and rebuke subordinates publicly, and to exaggerate the enemy strength. A colonel had won Philippi while McClellan sat at his office desk in Cincinnati. At Corrick's Ford, General T. D. Morris, with 1800 men, had routed the enemy and killed Robert S. Garnett, the Southern leader (July 13). Two days earlier Union forces had been aided in the most important battle, Rich Mountain, by a lucky accident. General W. S. Rosecrans was to attempt to turn the Confederate flank and attack the heights from the rear while McClellan assaulted in front. As Rosecrans advanced, his pickets seized a farm youth who led them by a secret way directly behind Colonel John Pegram's entrenchments on the mountain, where they won an overwhelming success. McClellan, by contrast, did badly; he failed to attack at the proper time, scaled the mountain late, and lost the chance of completely crushing the enemy.

While understating the forces opposed to subordinate officers like Jacob D. Cox and Rosecrans, McClellan constantly overstated those facing himself. Cox complained later that the general had systematically depreciated him. He had similarly written General Morris a series of insulting reprimands, culminating in the statement that if Morris asked for any more reinforcements, "I shall take it as a request to be relieved from your command and return to Indiana." When McClellan publicly castigated Rosecrans, that general sent him a reasoned justification closing with a spirited rebuke: "Review, if you please, that letter which you have put on record, and say whether, after you receive this, both private feelings and public interest are likely to be the better for it." [4]

McClellan's official Rich Mountain report seemed to give all the credit to himself. Yet J. D. Cox could truthfully assert that Rich Mountain disclosed some characteristics of McClellan that were destined later to come out more fully. "There was the same overestimate of the enemy, the same tendency to interpret unfavorably the sights and sounds in front, the same hesitancy to throw in his whole force when he knew that his subordinate was engaged." [5]

On the very Sunday night of Bull Run Lincoln began to draft new plans.

4 For this West Virginia campaign see O. R. I, ii, 194 ff.; McClellan's *Report*, and his *Own Story*; Ambler, *History of West Virginia*, 335 ff.; J. M. Callahan, *Semi-Centennial History of West Virginia*, 154 ff.; Festus P. Summers, *The Baltimore & Ohio in the Civil War*, 69–89; J. W. Thomas, "Campaigns of McClellan and Rosecrans in West Virginia, 1861–62," *West Virginia History*, vol. 5 (July, 1944), 245–308; and Jacob D. Cox, *Reminiscences*, I, 64 ff. Cox was one of the first (but far from the last) of talented officers from civil life to feel the enmity of West Point leaders.
5 Cox, *Reminiscences*, I, 58.

When two days later he finished this private memorandum of nine points of military policy, he said nothing about a changed military leadership; this was not necessary. His program embraced the strengthening of the blockade, of Butler's force, and of the Shenandoah army; it called for reorganizing McDowell's army, and pushing operations in the West; and it demanded the rapid dispatch of the new volunteer recruits to the Washington camps. A few days later Lincoln added that Manassas Junction and Strasburg should be seized and permanently held, with an open line from Washington to Manassas.[6] He was planning a fresh advance on that route. Nobody now talked of an easy march down the Mississippi, or from Cincinnati across country to Mobile, or even, as Montgomery Blair had done, from Fort Monroe to Richmond. The main object was to strike the formidable Southern armies, and in Washington, one voice chose the leader: McClellan.

Hot July days; hot contentions wherever Congressmen gathered; hot letters passing back and forth, like E. M. Stanton's denunciation of Administration "imbecility" to Buchanan; mint juleps and gin slings pouring down hot throats. On July 26, McClellan reached the city. Ambition burned in his brain as, calling on Scott, he heard that he was now where Napoleon had stood after Arcola: "Soldiers, like a torrent you have rushed down from the heights of the Apennines!" Next morning brought a call on Lincoln—their first meeting. He met the President coolly and confidently, and was invited to attend the Cabinet meeting at one. Scott was jealous of that invitation, declaring, "You shall not go when *I* am not asked," and he detained McClellan. The general had to explain this later to Lincoln, who was wryly amused.[7]

Within ten days after Bull Run, nearly the whole high command under Scott was changed. Patterson, his term of service expiring, gave way to N. P. Banks on July 27. In West Virginia, Rosecrans took McClellan's place. Frémont was just settling himself in Missouri. McClellan at once set about reorganizing his forces. He found on arrival at his Washington headquarters that he had about 50,000 infantry, less than 1000 cavalry, 650 artillerymen, and 30 cannon. He also found that the streets, hotels, and barrooms were full of drunken officers and men absent without leave from their units, "a perfect pandemonium"; that not a single regiment was properly encamped; that no preparations had been made for defense, not even to the placing of troops in military positions; and that the forts on the Virginia side lay detached, with no real defensive line.[8] McClellan further discovered that Scott was not the

6 Lincoln, *Collected Works*, IV, 457, 458; Nicolay and Hay, IV, 368.
7 McClellan, *Own Story*, 66, 67.
8 McClellan's dark picture in his *Own Story*, 66, 67, which enhances the magnitude of his achievement in reorganization, is to be taken with some reserve. Progress *had* been made in manning the fortifications; O. R. I, ii, 755, 756.

only officer with an excessive jealousy of his own position; neither McDowell nor Mansfield was cordial to the young officer now placed over them.

At any rate, the holiday was over. Grim war had begun.

[I]

The North was now busy raising its great new volunteer army of 500,000. The spirit needed was that of Tom Paine in an earlier crisis: "I call not upon a few, but upon all; not on this State or that State, but on every State; up and help us; lay your shoulder to the wheel; better have too much force than too little, when so great an object is at stake. Say not that thousands are gone, turn out your tens of thousands." But more than a determined spirit was required.

This really tremendous Union task of the summer and fall, the raising, equipping, and organizing of some 500 regiments, the greatest citizen army in history, demanded a careful Federal plan. This plan should have comprehended five desiderata which were not met: a close Federal control of the work, with due regard for State pride; an accurate determination of the State quotas; full use of regular army officers and men, widely distributed, to help train and command the new army; careful selection among both civilians and regulars for officers; and an end to the use of independent private recruiters in raising companies and regiments.

Congress was partly at fault for the lack of realistic plan, but the larger blame falls on Secretary Cameron, of whom a wrong view has been taken. He was not dishonest, for no proof exists that as Secretary he took a penny not his own. This veteran spoilsman was not a whit more inclined to play politics with his high office than Chase or Blair. But he was an incompetent administrator; flustered, inexact, forgetful, he had no ability to organize an efficient War Office as Chase and George Harrington organized an efficient Treasury, and Welles and Gustavus V. Fox organized an efficient Navy Department. He lacked vigilance in guarding against contract abuses; and worst of all, he was totally unable to plan.

The Military Act which became law on the morrow of Bull Run was a curious mixture of merits and defects. It did provide for a three-year army, the President to call forth the men as needed and apportion them among the States on the basis of population. It did provide that the President might appoint major-generals and brigadier-generals from the regular army. It did take a few precautions to ensure greater efficiency among subordinate officers than they had shown at Big Bethel and Bull Run. From colonels down, they were to be chosen as before under State laws, the higher officers in the main to be appointed by the governors, and the lower elected by the men; but every general commanding a separate department or army was authorized to create a board to examine the qualifications and conduct of any officer. If the board's report was unfavorable, the officer's commission would be canceled. The mere existence of this provision did something to improve the character of the army.

The faults of the Act, however, were glaring. It would have been wise to scatter officers and carefully picked men of the regular army widely among the incoming volunteers to leaven the whole lump with their sound ideas of discipline. General Scott, however, insisted on maintaining the regular army practically intact, and Cameron supported him. Nor was Congress inclined to differ from them. Most members at this stage of the war distrusted West Point as a school of Southern, aristocratic, snobbish flavor, and believed that gifted amateurs could quickly become efficient generals; that men like Ormsby Mitchel, Lew Wallace, Frémont, Jacob D. Cox, and Carl Schurz were quite as good as the McDowells, Mansfields, Lyons, and McClellans. Senators John Sherman and Ben Wade merely expressed a general prejudice this summer in assailing West Point. "I know," said Fessenden in replying to Sherman, "that the Senator from Ohio has peculiar views about this institution. He thinks commanders are born, not made. I do not. I think they are made. I think education is necessary." [9] Greater seminal use of the best regulars, say one to every twenty-five volunteers, would not only have promoted efficiency, but would have had a nationalizing tendency; yet it was never tried.

Under the new law, as under the old, recruiting was by States and localities, with provision for reimbursing them for the costs of raising, arming, paying, and transporting troops to the point where they entered Federal service. This was an irresponsible, extravagant, and confused method.[10] Regimental officers were commissioned by the governors, not the President. Naturally privates thought of themselves as Vermont men, Wisconsin men, and Pennsylvania men, not as national troops; and colonels and majors looked to Yates, Morgan, and Andrew for control and support, not to Washington. The provision that regimental vacancies should be filled by letting the men elect lieutenants and captains while officers chose majors and colonels added to the decentralizing tendencies of the system. Congress, in this plan, seized on what Emory B. Upton later termed the worst vice in State practice; fortunately, it was short-lived.

A few farsighted men perceived that ideally the North needed a national army. Early in the summer of 1861, ex-Governor Rodman Price of New Jersey, James L. Curtis of New York, and John C. Frémont held a conference at the Astor House in New York, where they drew up a plan for the free interchange of Eastern and Western troops. Curtis went to Washington, and

9 *Cong. Globe,* 37th Cong., 1st Sess.
10 Emory B. Upton, *Military Policy of the U. S.,* 260.

persuaded Frank Blair to lay the proposal before Cameron. The Secretary approved of it, as Curtis wrote Frémont, "and advised my proceeding forthwith to raise regiments and send them forward to St. Louis. Mr. Blair, Sr., suggested that he (Frank) should see President Lincoln and ask his approval. The President said, after reading the paper, that it was a grave and important suggestion, that he would submit it to the Cabinet." Though Attorney-General Bates termed it the best idea of the day, the Cabinet failed to approve it. Curtis remained hopeful, believing that if Cameron assented, Frémont might take ten thousand Pennsylvania troops west.[11] However, the plan came to nothing, for it conflicted with State pride and the regional prejudices of many people. To the end of the war the Western forces remained largely of Western origin, the Eastern forces of Eastern antecedents. John Pope actually wanted a complete Illinois army, kept intact, moved as a body, and officered by Illinoisans from corporals to major-general.[12] And as a second consideration, the War Department was totally unequipped to raise a national army. State adjutant-generals and other officers had to shoulder the task of preparing forces.

When the Comte de Paris after service on McClellan's staff came to explain the organization of the huge volunteer army to Frenchmen, he found much to censure. To him the fundamental weakness of the system so hurriedly devised this summer was the want of any means by which the national government could enforce discipline. Having no power to appoint or demote officers below the rank of brigadier-general, the Federal authorities possessed but a nerveless grasp of the army. From colonels down, the great host of officers looked to the State capitals; all arrangements were temporary, and nearly all were tinged with politics; the troops never felt the insistence on efficiency which a firmly constituted hierarchy of command, exempt from party pull and push, could offer. Many politically favored officers shot rapidly to a colonelcy, brigadiership, or, like Ben Butler, still higher, simply for lending their influence and bringing forward a body of troops. More than one subaltern of the regular army, made a colonel, grew disgusted with volunteers and politics, and returned to minor rank in his old regiment. When regiments disbanded, officers lost their places. A sense of uncertainty pervaded the whole officer corps.[13]

The Comte also specially censured the failure to provide a vigorous system of recruitment to fill vacancies caused by battle, sickness, and desertion. Once a regiment left its State, no more men applied to its recruiting office—if it had any. The influential leaders who had formed it were far away in camp; the choice places had all been filled; and public sentiment was interested in raising

11 Curtis, N. Y., Aug. 6, 1861, to Frémont; Blair-Lee Papers.
12 Pope to Yates, Yates Papers, Ill. State Lib.
13 Upton, 258; Comte de Paris, *Civil War*, I, 266, 267, 273, 274.

new units, not in strengthening old ones. A sharp battle, or a week in a malarial area, might cut an outfit in half, but the new regiments coming in furnished it no reinforcement. These fresh regiments brought all the inexperience that had cost their predecessors so dear, while the example and tuition of the veterans, which might have been so useful under a process of consolidation, were left unused. Meanwhile, the old skeleton regiments were often too weak to be effective in battle. Some army commanders tried to repair this defect. McClellan, for example, shortly issued General Order No. 105 requiring that volunteer regiments should immediately report deficiencies in strength to the Adjutant-General, and that incoming men should be requisitioned to fill the gaps. In practice, however, these orders were but partially executed.[14]

The volunteer army, as the war proceeded, thus became filled with regiments of three-quarters, half, or quarter strength, sometimes given good replacements, sometimes weak ones, and sometimes none at all. They were officered by men selected sometimes for capacity, but frequently for family influence, militia experience, or personal or political reasons; more often than not, by aggressive men whose organizing enterprise or community popularity brought them to the front. Promotions and replacements of officers were often arbitrary, and sometimes the morale of a regiment was ruined for months by a single wretched choice; the Tenth Massachusetts Volunteers from the Berkshire area, for example, almost went to pieces when it got an incompetent major.[15] The first Massachusetts three-year men marched off under a colonel whom Charles Francis Adams, Jr., termed "a notorious incompetent"; and Adams assured his father that all the Bay State regiments but one were so wretchedly officered this summer that it would be a miracle if they did not disgrace themselves. At Big Bethel, indeed, a brigadier did disgrace Massachusetts.

In the West, Joseph Medill begged Senator Trumbull to see that Brigadier-General S. A. Hurlbut was denied confirmation. He had been drunk in Chicago every day for a week; he led his Zouave regiment off for Missouri still so drunk he could hardly walk; and the city, with 1500 sons under his command, felt outraged by his appointment. Nevertheless, he stayed. Half the good volunteer colonels could have echoed the plaint of the head of the Eighteenth Illinois: "I have some 4 or 5 officers in my regt who are utterly worthless." [16]

14 Cf. Shannon, *Organization*, I, 190. A typical regiment reduced to a shadow of its old strength was the Twentieth Massachusetts Volunteers, whose historian, George A. Bruce, states that after Mine Run late in 1863 it mustered but 150 officers and men present for duty, having suffered to that date 745 war casualties.
15 J. K. Newell, *The Tenth Mass. Volunteers, passim.*
16 W. C. Ford, ed., *Cycle of Adams Letters*, I, 12, 13; Medill, July 13, 1861, Trumbull

Privates could be punished summarily for any misdemeanor. But officers, as the Comte de Paris noted, had to be brought before a court-martial for even small offenses, and could not be given as much as two days' confinement without formal sentence. The trial process, borrowed from the little regular army with its high sense of officers' prerogatives, thus became a shield to protect officers guilty of neglect, misconduct, or even gross insubordination.

Fortunately, the legislation for the new army did contain provisions which made it possible to strengthen the higher command. Representative A. S. Diven of New York wished to write into it a requirement that the President must select the six new major-generals and eighteen new brigadiers from West Point graduates, or officers who had spent at least five years in the regular army, or men whose war service had proved their ability to command.[17] Since this was felt to be too restrictive, it failed. But Senator James W. Nesmith of Oregon, who held enlightened views upon military management, fared better with a permissive amendment, allowing the President to select general officers from the line or staff of the regular army.

Saying that he knew major-generals and brigadiers who could not pass an examination as first lieutenant in any militarily advanced country, Nesmith spoke feelingly of the murderous results of appointing politicians and other upstarts, totally ignorant of the art of war, as ranking commanders. It was not true, he declared, that men would be happier under amateurs of popular repute from their own States; when shells burst and bullets hissed, they preferred an officer who knew his profession. Henry Wilson warmly seconded him, and the amendment passed.[18]

[II]

Just how was the new army of half a million raised? On the morrow of Bull Run no spur was necessary, for the people felt a grim determination to get the war fought and won. The governors, telegraphing offers of fresh troops, asked how many would be accepted. The War Department's invariable answer was, "Send them all"; and thus by noon of July 24, fully 75,000 had been taken, with more coming.[19]

Lincoln thought it unnecessary to issue a new proclamation calling for volunteers, and unwise for the moment to apportion quotas among the States. The policy of the War Department was to accept, under blanket authority of

Papers, LC; Col. H. R. Lewis, Mound City, Ill., Sept. 7, 1861, to McClernand, McClernand Papers, Ill. State Hist. Lib.
17 *Cong. Globe,* 37th Cong., 1st Sess., 95–100.
18 *Cong. Globe,* 37th Cong., 1st Sess., 52.
19 O. R. III, i, 140 ff.; N. Y. *Herald,* July 25, 1861.

the half-million bill of July 22, all the troops the governors believed they could raise, just as fast as they could muster them. Throughout the late summer and fall Cameron periodically besought the governors to send on all the regiments they had organized. Sometimes he engaged to supply arms and other equipment, but more frequently he suggested that the States provide their own muskets, uniforms, and the like, sending the bills to the Treasury.

Lincoln made requests on the same basis. He asked Governor Morgan to provide 25,000 three-year men, for example, but in such informal fashion that the request does not appear in the records; and it was not until nearly a year later, when it became necessary to determine what New York's quota *should* have been in order to reach a basis for determining the size of a fresh demand, that the proper share of the Empire State was fixed.[20] Morgan was quick to comply with Lincoln's request and to do more. Four days after Bull Run he issued his own proclamation for the 25,000 men, and almost immediately added an extra four regiments.

Other governors showed equal alacrity in meeting the nation's demands. It soon became clear that the half-million men, and more, would be obtained without difficulty. The real question was whether the troops would be raised efficiently, equitably, and under the best organization permitted by the new law. As we might expect, hurry and improvisation answered this query with an emphatic No.

While the States were raising their fresh regiments, the ninety-day men were returning home. The governors, heartily abetted by the War Department, hoped to induce many to reënlist. In numerous instances, however, these short-term veterans set something like an adverse backfire blazing. They brought home shocking stories of weak officers, bad camps, and uncoordinated army movements. Thousands, too, became rebellious over the delay—and sometimes the total failure—to pay them for their services. Several Pennsylvania regiments which reached camp near Harrisburg and found no provision whatever made for their shelter, subsistence, or compensation, grew mutinous. They filled the city with men searching for quarters and means of cooking rations, threatened to seize the money in the Adams Express office, and frightened citizens with angry talk of breaking open the shops. Governor Curtin had to detail a regiment of three-year troops to protect the capital, while young Don Cameron begged his father to send the troops at once to camps nearer their homes. In the end they were moved to encampments scattered over the State, where paymasters pacified them.

20 Phisterer, *N. Y. in the War of the Rebellion*, I, 22, 23. An Act signed by Lincoln July 31 gave him power to accept volunteers without previous proclamation and in whatever numbers he thought desirable; O. R. III, i, 372.

Similar episodes took place in Ohio, though Governor Dennison had gone to Washington especially to make sure that the troops would be promptly paid and mustered out. In New York, too, Governor Morgan complained to the War Department that failure to recompense the old regiments discouraged new enlistments.[21]

Much worse were the confusions and jealousies created everywhere by the readiness of the War Department to permit and even encourage recruiting by individuals and irregular groups. For this practice, which angered the governors, burdened the army with many deplorable officers, and produced widespread confusion, Lincoln as well as Cameron was to blame.

A chorus of protest came from the State capitals. "I hope," Morton of Indiana telegraphed Cameron July 25, "the War Department will accept of regiments only through me." The same day Governor Kirkwood of Iowa informed the Department that he would countenance no more regiments raised by individuals. A Pennsylvania official who indignantly inquired whether it was not now illegal to accept troops otherwise than through the governors could hardly have been calmed by the assurance that it was entirely legal, and that the Department had accepted twice as many from ambitious colonels as from State executives. Yates of Illinois was particularly exasperated. Telegraphing the Department repeatedly for exclusive authority to handle all State recruits, he got no answer until on August 14 he burst out to Cameron: "I could have had troops today sufficient to have opposed any force but for the interference from Washington in accepting independent regiments without notice to me, breaking up our organization." The Secretary at once gave him the desired authority. But five days later Austin Blair was making the same indignant protest. "I will furnish all the troops you call for," wrote Blair, "much sooner and in better order than these independent regiments can." [22]

The intentions of Lincoln and Cameron were good. They wished to expedite recruiting, fan the war spirit, and strengthen the impression of government eagerness to accept all the men who crowded forward. The Secretary seems to have surmised that all objection would be removed if the regimental officers were required to apply to their governors for commissions, and then ordered to report in Washington as soon as possible.[23]

This, of course, was far from the fact. Industrious village Hampdens, and budding Harrisons and Houstons, donning their sashes, duplicated State re-

---

21 O. R. III, i, 358–366 for Pennsylvania; *Ibid.*, 357, for Ohio, and Reid, *Ohio in the War*, I, 56; O. R. III, i, 415, for New York. The Paymaster-General himself went to Harrisburg late in July to iron out the difficulties.
22 O. R. III, i, 350, 390, 409 ff., 410, 428.
23 Cameron to O. P. Morton and Edwin Morgan, Aug. 29, 1861, O. R. III, i, 465; Austin Blair to Cameron, August 19, 1861, Austin Blair Papers.

cruiting efforts. They drained more troops from one area than another, with resultant ill feeling. They demanded colonelcies and captaincies. Meanwhile, they created an apparent competition between State and Federal recruiting. In New York, for example, Dan Sickles, the murderer of Philip Barton Key, used his characteristic swagger and impudence to organize his own brigade. He and his officers were contemptous of State authority, holding themselves quite above it. It required a general order from Cameron, placing all independent regiments in New York under Morgan, and emphasizing the governor's authority to reorganize, officer, and equip such regiments in the way he thought best, to bring Sickles down to earth. This order ended a highly embarrassing situation; and as it placed no fewer than sixteen independent regiments under clear State authority, Albany greeted it with profound relief.[24]

Other States, however, continued to suffer. The much-harassed Dennison of Ohio telegraphed Cameron on August 25 asking whether he had empowered a certain man to raise an artillery regiment. "If so, for God's sake withdraw the authority. Such a commission will make a farce of the public service." It was impossible to pursue any system in organizing Ohio troops, he added, so long as these irregular units raised their heads from Ashtabula to Hamilton. Ohio was actually raided from outside, two regiments being offered to Oliver P. Morton in Indiana. When Morton hesitated to accept them, the War Department wired him: "Lay aside etiquette. Organize soldiers as rapidly as you can. Get them, no matter where from, so they are good, loyal men." Not until September 10 did the outraged Dennison obtain authority to reorganize and equip all regiments.[25]

But even he had less to endure than Governor Curtin of Pennsylvania, a party rival of Cameron's. Stung beyond endurance, Curtin finally made a fervent plea to Lincoln. After pointing out that the new military law permitted the President to accept independent units only when the States failed to respond, he went on:

On the 26th day of July last a requisition was made on the Executive of this State for ten regiments of infantry in addition to the forty-four already furnished. . . . Active measures were immediately taken to comply with the requisition, but unfortunately the Government of the United States went on to authorize individuals to raise regiments of volunteers in this State. Fifty-eight individuals received authority for this purpose in Pennsylvania. The direct authority of the Government of the United States having been thus set in competition with that of the State, acting under its requisition, the

24 S. W. Burt, *Memoirs*, 46, 47; O. R. III, i, 483, 484.
25 Frémont had empowered John A. Gurley to send him volunteers from Ohio, and some recruits were actually sent to Missouri from the State; O. R. III, i, 466, 473 (Indiana), 519, 520 (Missouri). The authority on Sept. 10 was Special Order No. 243; O. R. III, i, 495, 496.

consequence has been much embarrassment, delay, and confusion. . . . The result is what might have been expected—that after a lapse of twenty-six days not one entire regiment has been raised in Pennsylvania since the last requisition. There are fragments of some seventy regiments, but not one complete; yet men enough have been raised to form near thirty complete regiments.[26]

Yet a week after Curtin's appeal, the War Department was authorizing James S. Negley of Pittsburgh to finish organizing an independent brigade of three or more regiments, thus piling confusion on confusion. When Cameron finally acted on Curtin's protest, he rebuked the governor for having written directly to the President. He also explained that Lincoln had never received the letter, for it had been filed in the War Department without having been read by anybody—which under Cameron seems to have been standard departmental practice for countless papers; and Cameron himself had not seen it until a messenger from Curtin brought him a copy! Cameron forthwith issued another special order placing all independent units in Pennsylvania under full authority of the governor; and the department took steps to chase out of the State some zealous recruiters from New York, Illinois, and California—complete outsiders and interlopers.[27]

Much more might be said on this strange tolerance of independent recruiting. Ben Butler and John A. Andrew became combatants in the most complex, protracted, and celebrated case of individual interference with State recruiting, which shook all New England, and supplied enough tragi-comic episodes for an *opéra bouffe*.[28] A President more exact, systematic, and vigilant than Lincoln, a Secretary more alert and clearheaded than Cameron, would have prevented these difficulties. It was bad enough, though unavoidable, to put recruiting under twenty-odd States, not the nation; it was far worse to let hundreds of ambitious men, some patriotic, some selfish, and most of them unfit, romp about the field.

However, despite all vexations, the recruits, from farm, forge, factory, store counter, and professional desk, rolled in. The initiative was taken by communities, local leaders, or both interacting. Village or town authorities would hold a mass meeting; politicians would deliver stump speeches, ministers would pray, the local editor would read the peroration of Webster's Reply to Hayne, the crowd would sing "America"—and young men would enroll their names. Or the local militia company would form a nucleus, or some burning patriot would raise an oriflamme.

A typical piece of New England recruiting is described by Thomas W. Hyde, a Maine lad who was soon brevetted a brigadier in his middle twenties.

26 *Ibid.*, 439, 440.
27 O. R. III, i, 491–534.
28 Meneely, 213–221; Schouler, *Mass. in the Rebellion*, I, 275–281; O. R. III, i, 810–866.

He heard the news of Bull Run in the shipbuilding town of Bath. Together with Senator Fessenden's son, he got State authority to raise men, opened an office, and advertised that soldiers would receive $22 bounty, $15 a month with full equipment, and $100 with lifelong glory when mustered out. Before long squads of eager young men were housed in Sibley tents dotting the beautiful green slopes between the State House at Augusta and the Kennebec. The officers of the various companies, summoned to ballot for regimental leaders, chose a regular-army captain for colonel, a three-month sergeant for lieutenant-colonel, and the reluctant Hyde for major. "I did not know then," he writes, "that the principal duties of a major were to ride on the flank of a rear division, say nothing, look as well as possible, and long for promotion." Off they went—the band playing them to the train, handkerchiefs waving from every farmhouse, cheers at every station, and lunch in Faneuil Hall.

Meanwhile, a typical piece of big-city, large-scale recruiting was furnished by the Fifty-fifth Illinois in Chicago. The attorney David Stuart, a friend of Douglas, obtained Cameron's direct authority to raise the 2,000 men of the Douglas brigade, put his own money and best energy into the effort, secured the aid of Democratic politicians and several Methodist ministers, and with the magic name of Douglas to assist him, had the brigade ready for service before October ended.[29]

The now rampant war spirit overcame every impediment: the high cost of getting and initially maintaining the recruits, for the nation reimbursed the States and the individuals concerned for only a part of their expenses; the want of a proper allotment system to provide for soldiers' families; the lack of arms; the irritations of dealing with hidebound, narrow-minded, arrogant fossils in the national quartermaster and commissary establishments, and endless departmental red tape. Senator Grimes wrote Cameron in mid-September that if the government would adopt the allotment-ticket system used in the navy, Iowa would soon send him 4,000 men even better than those already accepted; and before the close of the month, the War Department did belatedly set up home-allotment procedures. State complaints, fervent and long-continued, also got rid of an asinine War Department rule that no fewer than a company minimum, sixty-four men, could be mustered into service at one time. Recruits sometimes had been kept waiting six or eight weeks, without uniforms, blankets, or rations, and with not even a lieutenant sworn in to command them, until they reached the magic total of sixty-four. But after Cameron, responding to the protests of Morgan and Dennison, abolished

29 See Thomas W. Hyde, *Following the Greek Cross;* A Committee of the Regiment, *The Story of the Fifty-fifth Illinois.* Stuart, who was under a cloud because he had been involved in a notorious divorce case, proved a good officer; Hyde became one of great distinction. Fessenden's son was slain at Second Bull Run.

the rule, volunteers were sent, as fast as their names could be signed on muster rolls, to convenient camps, and set to drilling. A first lieutenant would take charge of half a company, and a captain and second lieutenant were added when full strength was reached. This new plan worked well.[30]

Still the men came in: a rush in late July, a new flood in August, and fresh hosts in early fall. They came in spite of a fundamental change in the economic situation. Business all summer had been depressed, but the harvest season and the letting of innumerable contracts created an autumn boom. Farms, shops, and war industries drained away the surplus labor supply. Skilled hands in particular thought twice before taking army pay, even after it had been lifted to what some foreign observers deemed an exorbitant figure. As the cost of living rose, men with family responsibilities could not be happy about a wage of $11 a month, even with a bounty of $100, as authorized by the military act, superadded.[31] Inevitably, such social and economic pressures made for an army of youths and young men. Veterans later used to say, "The war was fought by boys," and although this was not true, a little more than 13 per cent of the enlistments were 18 and almost 30 per cent were under 21. Officers, too, were generally young; in the volunteer army the mean age at entrance into service was found to be 30.44.

[III]

The gathering of the huge volunteer forces in and about Washington was an inspiring sight, which gave many who witnessed it an exultant confidence. The new volunteers, though even by fall far from being well-taught soldiers, were much superior to the ninety-day men. "Finer material could not be found in physique," wrote W. H. Russell after seeing a review held by McClellan and McDowell, marred by only one tatterdemalion unit sent from New York City. He thought no division of the regular army line in any country of the globe could show a greater number of tall, robust men in fine physical trim. The big, hearty, outdoor recruits who composed so great a part of the popular host—the lumberjacks, fishermen, hardfisted young farmers, stevedores,

30 New York State by November had main recruiting depots in the metropolis, Albany, and Elmira, and not fewer than twenty regimental camps in the interior of the State. These tent camps had been created to make it more convenient for recruits to assemble for drill, and to gain the active aid of prominent citizens. Morgan to Cameron, Nov. 4, 1861; Morgan Papers, N. Y. State Lib.

31 Governor Morgan was so much impressed by these high costs that he tried to give a premium of $2 a recruit to anyone who brought in not less than 32 acceptable men to one of the main depots. This special bounty he thought would not cost more than $25,000 for the State's 25 new regiments, and would do much to stimulate enlistments. But Cameron refused to foot the bill, and the governor revoked his order in mid-October. O. R. III, i, 452, 453, 465; Burt, *Memoirs*, 54.

WASHINGTON AND
ITS ULTIMATE
DEFENSES

and draymen—stood hardship well; but it was soon noted that the clerks, bookkeepers, schoolmasters, and mechanics from the towns, even the men most delicately nurtured, stood it rather better. As greater precautions were taken, and as crisp autumn weather came on, the health of the army, in the East more rapidly than in the West, improved.[32]

While Washington had still all the confusion of a great armed camp, the military elements had become more orderly. The surrounding hills were whiter than ever with tents, for the reinforcements had spread over them, but the camps showed system and cleanliness. One observer, standing on an eminence at sunset, saw with his spyglass the evening parades of 34 regiments. On another occasion he counted 150 army wagons in line on Pennsylvania Avenue, and an hour later saw a drove of 700 fine cavalry horses clattering over the Long Bridge. But the barrooms were empty of army blue, roistering soldiers had disappeared from the streets, and officers in hotel lobbies were few. Their places had been taken by hundreds of sad-eyed citizens come to look for

32 Russell, *My Diary*, Aug. 26, 1861; *Following the Greek Cross*, 21, 22; Adams, *Doctors in Blue*, chapters 3, 10. The Sanitary Commission with incomplete data found that in the first year Western troops had a much higher sick rate than Eastern, and enlisted men one much higher than officers. For age of the troops, see the Sanitary Commission pamphlet, "Ages of U. S. Volunteer Soldier" (1866), which abounds in interesting facts. It gives the average age of 1,012,273 volunteers at date of enlistment as 25.8.

relatives lost since the battle or lying in hospitals. The new provost guard was so efficient that it stopped Ben Butler as he was getting into his carriage at the National Hotel, and held him until he was identified.

The numbers, energy, and determined spirit of the host seemed to promise great victorious movements to come, perhaps ending in the lightning flash of a new Solferino. Captain J. R. Hawley of Connecticut, later to become editor, governor, and Senator, reached the capital late in September. He breakfasted at the Soldiers' Retreat, a large rough new building for feeding troops, washed in another big structure hard by fitted with tanks and troughs, and, marching with his regiment two miles up Fourteenth Street, encamped in an open field.

"Oh, but this is grand!" he wrote his wife. "Troops, troops, tents, the frequent thunder of guns practising, lines of heavy baggage wagons, at reveille and tattoo the air filled with the near and distant roll of drums and the notes of innumerable bugles—all the indications of an immense army, and yet no crowding, no rabble. Nobody knows how many there are, but I guess from certain facts that there must be over 200,000 in all—including those across the river and in General Banks's division. Indeed, I have good evidence that there are about 275,000, *not* including Gen. Dix's command at Baltimore." [33] Although this was an overestimate, already many believed that the new army was a formidable human machine that should soon roll inexorably and victoriously southward.

[33] Hawley, Sept. 25, 1861; Hawley Papers, LC.

13

Giant in Swaddling Clothes

ANXIOUS though the people were to get on with the war, the late summer lull had at least this important effect: It gave North and South a pause to assess their situation. They began to comprehend that they were locked in a life-and-death grapple. Ex-Senator John Slidell of Louisiana wrote S. L. M. Barlow just before Bull Run that in all the South he did not know a solitary man who would reëstablish the Union on any terms. "You can scarcely hope to subjugate us. We *know* that you cannot, and if your views prevail, there can be no other termination of the war than by the mutual exhaustion of both parties." [1] The idea bit deep that the war must be fought to a devastating conclusion. Assistant-Secretary of War P. H. Watson told McClellan that the rebels would persist to the death gasp.[2] Though great numbers on both sides still looked forward to 1862 as the year of victory, most men of sense knew that the contest might be protracted, that it would test the people to the utmost, and that it would produce a new America.

Lincoln sat daily for long hours in his office on the south side of the White House; the kind of office that a county judge or prosperous doctor might be expected to have. Its furnishings were a large cloth-covered table for Cabinet meetings, a smaller table where the President usually wrote, a high wall desk with pigeonholes for papers, two horsehair sofas, an armchair, and some straight-backed chairs. Over the marble mantel of the brass-fendered fireplace hung a faded steel engraving of Jackson. Elsewhere on the wall were a photograph of John Bright, and a number of framed military maps. His secretaries, Nicolay and Hay, gave him efficient help, and a young Illinois newspaperman, W. O. Stoddard, went through the mail to sort out trivial or offensive letters. Other assistants he had none except an occasional clerk lent from some department. The offices of Cabinet members were equally primitive. They had changed little since 1800. The same wooden tables, desks, pigeonholes, and ledger-size copybooks as in John Adams' day, the same quill pens and scuffed carpets,

1 July 20, 1861, Barlow Papers.
2 Chase, *Diary and Corr.*, 50, 51; this talk was Nov. 11, 1861.

and the same anemic staffs docketing papers, surrounded Chase, Welles, Cameron as they struggled with visitors.[3]

These executives looked out on a nation which seemed as vertebrate as a jellyfish. They could ask for aid from individuals, but not from capable associations or societies, which hardly existed. The war necessarily had to be a vast social and economic as well as military effort. But where were the leaders trained in social and economic organization? The nation had only small managerial groups and little skill in cooperative effort. Of the 8,200,000 people whose occupations were noted by the recent census, 3,300,000 were farmers, planters, and farm laborers, and many more were indirectly connected with agriculture. A shrewd observer, Sir Morton Peto, shortly estimated that seven-eighths of the population was engaged in tillage or the callings materially dependent thereon; an understandable exaggeration.

This agricultural country, just passing through a transportation revolution, was fairly well organized for farming and for all kinds of communication— by railways, canals, telegraphs, and express systems. The manufacture of farm machinery, the handling of farm products, the milling of grain, the packing of meats, the sending of a new host of settlers westward every year, and the supply of this host with consumption goods, were all competently done. As yet, however, they did not carry the country far from the old order of small enterprises, local outlooks, and unrestricted individualism.

A war machine can be built quickly and efficiently only if many components already exist. The Department in 1861 had no difficulty in making decisions. It soon found that the half-million volunteers embodied under the July legislation would wear out shoes in two months and uniforms in four; they therefore needed 3,000,000 pairs of shoes and 1,500,000 uniforms a year. It was easy to decide that they must have mountains of arms, a hundred miles of wagons, great base hospitals, and incredible miscellaneous supplies. The difficulty lay in implementing the decisions.

Problems of selection became acute; which firm could really fill the orders? Problems of scheduling were even more perplexing; how could everybody down the line of supply be told just what was needed, and when, and where? Industrial discipline was as important as military discipline; factories, contractors, and agents had to be held to rigid performance. And nobody knew the indispensable facts! Figures of industrial capacity, lists of companies, data on car supply, information on the ability of heads of firms—all this was beyond the reach of the tiny Washington departments. Such terms as "co-ordination," "priorities," "allocation of materials," and "flow of supplies" lay far in the future; the idea of "production management" was beyond human

3 Leonard D. White, *The Jacksonians*, 548.

ken. The realities which such words represented could no more exist in America of 1861 than the roof of an unbuilt house could float in mid-air, for no supporting structure existed.

The government which was now girding itself for war labored under the sharpest limitations. It had always been a government of noninterference, made for the freedom of the individual; of calculated inaction, to give State and local agencies the fullest scope; of economy, passivity, and short views.

No national banking system existed. Washington paid no real attention to agriculture; a weakly supported, feebly administered bureau in the new Interior Department represented the only Federal provision for the fundamental industry of the land. So important a subject as public health had never engaged the attention of any national bureau, or for that matter, of any State. In Europe the English sanitarian Edwin Chadwick, the French pathologists, and the new school of medical statisticians had spurred the leading governments into at least elementary attention to public sanitation. But Americans were stone deaf to their one eminent figure in the field, Lemuel Shattuck, whose report on conditions in Massachusetts (1850) had met blank indifference.[4] So, too, the transportation revolution which was remolding America proceeded without any attention in Washington save for land-grant legislation and a few Far Western surveys. Any proposal that government guidance should accompany government subsidies would have met a hostile wall.

One significant index of the weakness of the central government was the deficiency of trustworthy statistical data. The national censuses were ample in numerical facts, decently accurate, and issued with really useful interpretation. A few cities and one State, Massachusetts, had systems of vital registration; New York took an efficient census of its own in 1855. As yet, however, the country was without the great mass of trustworthy data later to be gathered continuously by numerous Federal agencies.[5]

Statistics are a function of complexity in government as of society, for whenever new problems demand new solutions it becomes necessary to probe into exact conditions and measure precise results. For want of an apparatus of consistent fact-finding, Americans groped in the dark in meeting the crisis of 1861. When armies had to be raised, for example, it was important to know the ages of the male population. The census merely furnished facts on the population, male and female, in each five-year bracket to the age of twenty, and each ten-year bracket thereafter; all this set down by counties.

4 John Koren, *History of Statistics;* and see the article on statistical needs by ABC in *National Intelligencer,* May 29, 1856.

5 Such as the Bureau of Agricultural Economics, Interstate Commerce Commission, Bureau of Foreign and Domestic Commerce, Bureau of Labor Statistics, and Bureau of Internal Revenue, to name but a few.

Hence in the fifteen–nineteen age bracket, the government did not know how many were boys of fifteen, and how many young men of nineteen. In the succeeding age bracket, it did not know how many were twenty, and how many were twenty-nine. Yet by the date of the Civil War, all important European nations but Switzerland had permanent statistical bureaus under proficient management. The proposals for such a bureau in Washington, made by S. B. Ruggles and others, had met stubborn opposition from state-rights quarters.

In short, Lincoln presided over a weak government which suddenly had to be made strong. And behind the government lay a largely inchoate society; a society which believed in accomplishing the impossible, but whose libertarian bent made accomplishment terribly difficult. A tremendous gulf separated the unformed nation of the Civil War from the nation that in the next great conflict was to mobilize its energies so massively under the Council of National Defense. Where were the technicians in 1861? Where were the efficient business administrators? Where were the thousand organizations, industrial, commercial, financial, professional, to lend them support? Where were the principles and precedents?

If we briefly examine this society, we shall see that Great Britain in the first throes of the Napoleonic struggle had been better adapted to wage war than the shambling, uncertain American giant of 1861. "Organization" is a key word, and from one point of view the transformation of an unorganized land into an organized nation was the key process of the Civil War.

[I]

The country we have called invertebrate, and this invertebracy reflected a deeply ingrained spirit. "In the United States," wrote August Laugel during the conflict, "there is a horror of all trammels, systems, and uniformity." [6] Americans were hostile to discipline and jealous of every encroachment on personal freedom. As autumn leaves fell on drilling soldiers and thickening lines of factory hands, some observers saw that old ways were falling too. "The Great Rebellion a Great Revolution"—so ran the title of a *Herald* editorial on November 24, 1861. Our manufactories have been revolutionized, said the paper, our mode of living has been changed, and "everything the finger of war touches is revolutionized." A few discerning men saw the essence of this revolution. It was the conversion of a loose, inchoate, uncrystallized society into one organized for a mighty and many-sided effort.

6 Laugel, *The United States During the War*. The roots of individualism ran deep into frontier experience, and deep also into the Protestant emphasis on individual interpretation of truth and the individual will; deep too into Nonconformist tradition, Lockean and Jeffersonian ideas of the right of revolution, and egalitarian principles.

Crèvecœur in delineating the American had emphasized his love of in-dependence and impatience of control. Cooper and Melville depicted a popu-lation of unfettered, self-assertive character. "Call me Ishmael!"—even that was better than repression. Emerson's chapter on "Solidarity" in *English Traits* contrasted British unity—"marching in phalanx, lock-step, foot after foot, file after file of heroes, ten thousand deep"—with American separatism. Thoreau, living on a patch of ground, experimenting with civil disobedience, and giving up his little pencil factory to preach an ideal society of noble vil-lagers, and Cooper crying, "God protect the country that has nothing but commercial towns for capitals," [7] appealed in different ways to deep American instincts.

Most people instinctively veered away from strong social and economic combinations just as they veered away from strong government. John Taylor of Caroline, sharing Jefferson's idealism, inveighed against "monopoly and incorporation," and argued that capitalist combinations went arm-in-arm with a powerful centralized government, both fostering caste rule, the exploitation of farmers and laborers, and social injustice. Such doctrine, like the appeals of William Leggett and George Henry Evans to radical workmen, harmonized with the natural attitude of millions. Horace Greeley, anxious to better both the farmers and city wage earners, and striving to democratize the land system, was too wise to attack industry. Like a good Whig, he wished to see it grow. But he never lost his suspicion of the larger forms of business organization. In the midst of war the *Tribune* published long indictments of corporations: their profiteering, mismanagement, nepotism, and the tyrannies of their agents and officers. They were "heartless," wrote Greeley.[8]

Reared in an ungirt, unplanned society, Americans since the seventeenth century had been busy improvising. The first demand of the frontier, farm, and small shop was for such improvisations as the log cabin, the long rifle, the hand-hewn chest, the Conestoga wagon, and the overshot water wheel. The term "homemade" had a wider application in America than elsewhere. An in-genious people not only respected the amateur but belittled the expert. Peter Cooper building his engine *Tom Thumb*, Lincoln patenting his device for lifting boats over shoals, Goodyear spilling his rubber on a stove, Ezra Cornell wrecking his pipe-laying machine so that he could string his telegraph on poles, all believed that an amateur could do anything, and many concluded that organization would inhibit the gifted amateur. Generations later, Henry Ford reflected this attitude by shunning organizational charts, destroying business forms, and refusing to assign fixed duties to officers of the huge Rouge plant.

7 Cooper, *Correspondence*, II, 404.
8 See, for example, the long editorial April 3, 1863, entitled "Manufacturing Mismanage-ment."

Making Gun Carriages at the Richmond Armory

The Springfield Armory

ent rate on letters, for in all large cities private carriers profitably dis-
ed mail at that rate, and in New York about ten million letters were
tely carried as against a million sent by post. The committees asked for
ulsory prepayment by stamps, and free letter delivery in all large towns.
urope dead letters were returned to senders; in the United States they
e simply burned—four to five millions yearly. Though some reforms
re adopted, the situation continued wretched. Although in 1860 the Ameri-
population materially exceeded the British, the number of letters posted
the United States was only 184,000,000, one-third the 564,000,000 posted
Britain. The post office had three regular rates on letters, five surcharges,
d forty-nine rates on papers and periodicals. Drop letters in New York
umbered 1,500,000 in 1860; in London, 63,200,000.[12] "We are now enduring
a postal system," remarked *Putnam's Magazine*, "which worries government,
vexes and injures the public, demoralizes the officials, and pleases nobody."
Bryant's *Evening Post* asserted that a barrel of flour could be sent by an express company from New York to New Orleans more quickly than the government could transport a letter over the same ground.[13]

The horror of all trammels, system, and uniformity, to use Laugel's phrase,
prevented farmers from associating in production or marketing. Rural cooperation had taken firm root on the European continent immediately after
the Napoleonic wars, and by 1860 was gaining maturity in Denmark, Germany, Switzerland, and other lands. New Zealand was soon to show how
strong it could become in a pioneer community. The large size of American
farms, mobility of the population, and individualistic temper of rural areas
prevented any similar growth in the United States; nor did the government
offer the slightest encouragement. Similarly, national labor unions as yet
counted for almost nothing. In 1857 nine or ten such unions had been gaining
vigorous stature when the panic felled all but three, the typographers', the hat
finishers', and the journeymen stonecutters'. Before Sumter a few others, including the iron-molders' union under the indomitable William H. Sylvi-
emerged. None had much vigor, for a half-dozen environing forces
unfavorable: the steady immigration of unskilled labor, lingering pub
tility toward "conspiracy" in the labor market, the adolescent c'
the factory system, the ruthlessness or paternalism of emplo*
the strong individualism of native Americans.[14]

12 Representative Hutchins of Ohio in 1862 vigorously attac
gress; see editorial, N. Y. *Tribune*, June 25, 1862.
13 Dec. 13, 1855; and still true in 1860. The governmen
14 Commons, *et al.*, I, 335-453, gives the history of
and of the revival down to the war; see also George
tion, 252 ff., 283 ff.

Even in old Eastern cities, experts commanded little
B. Angell, entering the office of the Chief Engineer of Bost
the staff had worked their way up from rodmen's jobs by rul
Work was under way on the Cochituate water system.
Angell was the only man in the whole office who had stu
could deal with the involved formulae for water problem
prove the force of Francis Wayland's argument that it was h
can colleges dealt less in theology, and more in science and te

The nation was full of good craftsmen and husbandmen,
alone or in small groups. Company B of the Tenth Massachusett
regiment, contained a typical array: 23 farmers, 3 merchants, 2
shoemakers, 2 hostlers, 2 carpenters, a seaman, laborer, clerk, b
painter, peddler, blacksmith, calico printer, cloth manufacturer, an
factory superintendent.[10] Such men, facing ordinary problems, could
with happy dexterity. But war presents innumerable large-scale p
which demand experts supported by large-scale organizations. In tim
the experts and the organizations were to appear—and with them would e
a new nation.

As they appeared, the country lost a certain freshness and bucolic ch
and the strength which it gained was a coarser strength; but the gain
greater than the loss. The dynamism of national life, with population movi
westward, new towns shooting up, and immigration combining with a high birt
rate to stimulate growth, had kept life plastic and full of picturesque novelty.
Successive frontiers had meant successive rerootings, seldom deep or strong.
American life was to remain dynamic, but it would soon be dynamic in a different way, with larger elements of a disciplined, hardened kind. Its roots
were to go deeper, and the plastic freshness was to be exchanged for well-
planted power.

Much of the lack of organization was basically immaturity. The nation had
no standard time, so that New York, Philadelphia, Washington, and Pittsburgh kept what time each city or its railroads liked. Only two American
cities in 1860 had paid fire departments; all the others—New York until 1865,
Philadelphia until 1870—depended on volunteers. All New England in 1860
had only three hospitals; the entire South had one in Charleston, one in Savannah, one in Mobile, "perhaps one" in Richmond, and one in New Orleans
nowned for its wretchedness.[11]

Only an immature country would have endured the wretched postal fa-
es against which New York and Boston committees had protested in
James Harper, Peter Cooper, and others that year pleaded for a uniform

ell, *Reminiscences*, 78; Wayland, *Thoughts on the Present Collegiate System* (1842).
Newell, *The Tenth Mass. Volunteers*.
Martin, *The Standard of Living in 1860*, 233–236.

Thus neither agriculture nor labor when the war began was able to speak with united voice, furnish the government trained administrative talent, or lend any organized assistance to the war effort. Business and finance of course offered more resources, for they could not exist without some degree of organization. Nevertheless, it was a rudimentary degree, with short-comings more conspicuous than strength; as we shall see if we examine even the best-developed field, that of transportation.

[II]

Transportation could be expected to make comparatively rapid progress in systematization, for it was nurtured by the vast American distances, the irresistible westward movement, and the general American restlessness. The development of the West had seemed the nation's great primary task. The building of turnpikes, canals, and railroads to carry people across mountains, prairies, and plains, the shipment of crops eastward and a thousand varieties of commodities westward, and the necessity for extending the commercial and cultural interchanges of new and old states, had required careful planning and administration of communications.

The east-west railroads, particularly north of the Ohio, were in 1860 the country's most imposing business creations, their securities the very core of the investment market. National expansion had required an increasing con-solidation of railway controls. The Pennsylvania, for example, had attained a more extensive dominion than most people realized. Its main Philadelphia-Pittsburgh line, with branches and leased strips, covered 423 miles, of which 250 were double-tracked. This, however, was but the beginning. In 1856, three lines westward, in Ohio, Indiana, and northern Illinois, had merged as the Pittsburgh, Fort Wayne and Chicago. The Pennsylvania, which had in-vested substantial sums in building the three lines, received nearly $770,000 in stock. Thomas A. Scott, the Pennsylvania's vice-president and general super-intendent, was appointed to the board of the new company; George W. Cass, a director of the Pennsylvania, was made president. For all practical purposes the Pennsylvania thereafter controlled an additional 465 miles of railroad in the Middle West. Before 1860, the Pennsylvania had come to dominate about 165 miles of railroad reaching to the Ohio River and through southern Ohio, and about 200 miles running northwest from Pittsburgh to Cleveland. Thomas A. Scott again appeared on the boards of the tributary roads.[15]

The same process which gave the Pennsylvania an imperial system could

15 H. V. Poor, *History of the Railroads and Canals of the U. S.*, I, 470 ff.; H. W. Schotter, *Pennsylvania Railroad Company, 1846–1926.*

be traced in the development of the New York Central. At the outbreak of the war, this line from Albany to Buffalo, and the connecting Lake Shore and Michigan Southern, gave a group headed by Erastus Corning control over 650 miles of continuous rail into Chicago. The Erie, a hill-and-valley line from New York (Piermont) to Dunkirk on the lakes, was as yet still seeking a westward extension. But the Baltimore and Ohio, which ran to Parkersburg, made connections there to Cincinnati, and thence extended to St. Louis by a controlling arrangement with the Ohio and Mississippi, was very powerful indeed, and thirty-eight year-old John W. Garrett, its recently elected head, was a man of wide influence. Paralleling the early boundary between the Union and Confederacy, the B. & O. was to play an important role in the conflict. It was a source of great strength to the North by 1861 that three strong trunk lines, obviously soon to be joined by a fourth, connected the northern seaboard with the midwest.[16]

Other remarkable achievements in organization were the anthracite railroads, with their docks, freight yards, and coal trestles. Of the north-south lines the Illinois Central, as yet terminating at Cairo, and the Louisville & Nashville, a 185-mile road completed on the eve of conflict, had great importance. In the South the Memphis & Charleston, finished in 1857 on a line through Atlanta, cherished dreams of a grandeur it was never to attain.[17] Since every isolated community longed for the scream of a locomotive, ideas of growth animated the whole railroad world. Superintendent J. G. Kennedy of the Census, announcing that the railways of the nation had hauled 26,000,000 tons on their 30,800 miles of track in 1860, declared that three-quarters of this bulk had been created in the previous decade.

Yet from the standpoints of management and equipment, the railroads had a rudimentary aspect. The British expert S. F. Van Oss, writing much later, remarked on their adolescent traits. "Englishmen live in a country which has arrived at maturity; America still is in its teens." [18] Slow wood-burning locomotives ran all too often over rickety tracks on erratic schedules. The existence of at least eight different gauges required frequent loading and unloading. Most railway heads were less interested in methodical organization and progress than in slapdash policies and quick returns. Management tended to be autocratic, one man or a small clique controlling lines large or small. Speculation exulted in almost unchecked license. Few large roads had arrived at a scientific allocation of functions among their officers; the B. & O. was in fact conspicuous

16   Festus P. Summers, *The Baltimore and Ohio in the Civil War.*
17   A Confederate quartermaster officer testified that Southern railroad managers showed "the best business talent" in the South; O. R. IV, ii, 882.
18   Van Oss, *American Railroads as Investments*, 10.

for its well-planned departmentalization.[19] Still fewer lines had heads of pre-eminent ability. The two strongest executives were Garrett, trained in his father's commission house, and J. Edgar Thomson of the Pennsylvania, a proficient engineer who had studied railroad practice in Europe. The mere promoter was much more common.

The rule of small business salaries applied to railroads as to other establishments. In 1856 the Illinois Central cast about for a chief engineer. As its officers had seen George Brinton McClellan's report on his survey of a railway route across the Cascade Mountains, they selected him. His captain's pay had totaled $1,326 a year. President W. H. Osborn offered him $3,000 a year for three years. He showed marked administrative enterprise. Before long he was in general charge of railroad operation in Illinois, and by the end of 1857 was vice-president. He helped meet the depression that winter by harvesting Lake Michigan ice to be sold by the carload all the way to Cairo when summer became torrid. Early in 1858 he contracted with a group of steamboat owners to establish an Illinois Central line of packets to New Orleans, thus for the first time linking Chicago and the Gulf by scheduled year-round transportation. Yet his salary remained $3,000,—a proof of the low esteem for managerial talent.[20]

The fact was that the transportation revolution presented some remarkable feats in organization alongside glaring gaps and failures. No pageantry of the time excelled that of the western rivers. The mile-long line of boats smoking and throbbing at the St. Louis levee, surpassed by a still longer line at New Orleans; the floods of pork, tobacco, corn and cotton that the Ohio, the Cumberland, the Arkansas, and the Red poured into the central Mississippi stream; the motley passengers—fur traders, immigrants, Indians, soldiers, cotton planters, land speculators, gamblers, politicians, British tourists; the inter-city rivalries, the desperate races—these made the steamboat world a tremendous spectacle. The 1600 steamboats which plied the Mississippi before the war had cost perhaps $60,000,000; the 900 steamboats, barges, and flatboats which

19 As early as 1848 it had a master of transportation, a master of the road, a master of machinery, and a general superintendent, along with division superintendents; Hungerford, *The Baltimore & Ohio*. Centralized purchasing by large roads, even the B. & O., was unknown; each large department purchased for itself.

20 33rd Cong., 1st Sess., House Exec. Doc. 129; C. J. Corliss, *Main Line of America*, 90, 91. It need not be said that the broad foundation of all transport in the republic was the ox, mule, and horse, the cart and wagon. Between 1850 and 1860 the number of horses rose from 4,337,000 to 6,249,000, giving an average of one horse to each family of five. The number of asses and mules rose from 559,000 to 1,151,000, predominating in the South; a panegyric of the mule may be found in the census volume on Agriculture, p. cxiii. It is significant of the survival of primitive rural conditions that the number of working oxen rose from 1,701,000 to 2,255,000, the South having 858,500 and the Middle West 820,000. *Ibid.*, cviii–cxv.

plied the Ohio carried an annual Cincinnati-Louisville commerce valued at
$35,000,000. This traffic on the great water highways, creating cities wealthier
than Venice or Shanghai, represented no inconsiderable planning and organizing. Packet owners made various attempts at combination, but they were loose
and abortive. During the war, the immense flotillas were to prove invaluable
to the Northern armies. But the railroads already threatened them, the conflict strengthened the railroad lines, and before long the gaudy steamboat
commerce was to prove as evanescent as the caravel.

In maritime commerce, meanwhile, defects of American planning and
enterprise cost shipowners dear. The beautiful clipper ships, the transatlantic packets flying the Black Ball flag, and the coastal vessels had written proud
pages in the American record. But on the Atlantic, the British-owned Cunarders
showed better organization and safer management than their Yankee rivals
operated by Edward Knight Collins, naval architect and shipping merchant.
In twenty-six transoceanic passages in 1852 the Collins ships made much the
faster time; but a strain of American recklessness appeared in the exclamation of Captain Asa Eldridge of the *Pacific*, "If I don't beat the *Persia*, I will
send the *Pacific* to the bottom." Successive misfortunes, including the loss
of the *Arctic* in 1854 with more than 300 dead, the foundering of the *Pacific*,
and the withdrawal of the government subsidy, were too disastrous to be
survived. Meanwhile, American shipbuilders clung tenaciously to wooden
vessels propelled by sails or paddle-wheels, though British builders were turning to iron ships and screw propellers. Even the boasted *Vanderbilt* was a
wooden ship with two walking-beam engines and two great paddle-wheels
forty-two feet in diameter. The emigrant business began passing to British vessels. In the summer of 1857 the *National Intelligencer* carried a significant article, "Losing Our Carrying Trade." It pointed to reports that the better
organized British yards were building 300 oceangoing steamboats: [21]

What are to become of sailing vessels when these 300 ocean steamers, or
even one-half of them, shall be navigating the Atlantic Ocean? Already sailing
vessels have to content themselves with the most bulky and least profitable
freight; passengers, specie, light and costly goods, and so on being carried almost exclusively by steamers. The mode of travel and transportation upon the
ocean is undergoing the same change that has already taken place on land;
the old slow coach or vessel is being cast aside for the rapid rail-car and the
storm-defying steamer. England, seeing this inevitable change, has, with the
sagacity, prescience, and bold energy which characterize her, thrown her-

[21] Louis C. Hunter's admirable *Steamboats on the Western Rivers*, 237-240, 308-357,
covers organization and disorganization in the river steamboat business in careful detail.
On Atlantic shipping see R. G. Albion, *The Rise of New York Port, 1815-60;* George W.
Sheldon, "Old Shipping Merchants of New York," *Harper's Monthly*, vol. 84 (Feb., 1892),
457-471; *National Intelligencer*, July 25, 1857.

self forward in this revolution, and has covered, and is covering, the great highways of commerce with her steamers, and taking from all other nations, and especially from us, the most profitable portion of the carrying trade of the world.

New England might have been expected to organize large-scale transportation with special acumen. Instead, the section conspicuously failed in farsighted organization. The Boston & Worcester was completed in 1835, and the Western, from Worcester to the Hudson opposite Albany, in 1842. But down to the war the two railroads had not been united, though of course through trains were run over them. Moreover, Boston had no connecting railroad across upper New York to the lakes. The Boston-Albany line was fifty miles longer then the rival New York-Albany line, and had to traverse the rough Berkshires, while New York City offered a much better port and a far more magnetic shipping center. Hence, as C. F. Adams, Jr., pointed out, New York railroads, merely by intersecting any line that Boston tried to build across New York State, could draw down its traffic to the metropolis.

Meanwhile, in southern New England unification proved equally unattainable. The Hartford & New Haven was completed during Van Buren's Presidency, and the New York & New Haven was finished in Taylor's, but it was not until a decade after Sumter that they were consolidated. Thus the regime of small affairs continued dominant on the New England railroad scene even while J. M. Forbes was mobilizing Boston capital to help build the Michigan Central, the future Chicago, Burlington & Quincy, and the Hannibal & St. Joseph.[22]

Unevenness—ragged, sporadic action in a desert of individualism—was the keynote of the country's organizational activity. That handmaiden of transport, the telegraph system, was in its way astonishing. From a swarm of small companies a number of large concerns was presently born; and then by a program of consolidation carried out in the fall of 1857, the American Telegraph Company became dominant in the East, while the Western Union held a similar primacy in the West. The American, when Lincoln was elected, had nearly 300 offices and 13,500 miles of wire, controlling the business from Halifax to New Orleans. Over it and all the remaining companies the North American Telegraph Association held a loose control.

The country, which had long suffered from a jumble of little precarious companies, hoped for a reign of order. That might indeed have been the result but for the covert mutual enmity between the American and the Western Union. While the former wished to support Cyrus W. Field's Atlantic cable

22 C. E. Kirkland, *Men, Cities, and Transportation*, I, 127 ff., II, 72 ff.; Van Oss, *American Railroads*.

project, the latter was much more interested in a telegraph line to California. They were rivals in absorbing the surviving independents, and they quarreled violently over relations with the Associated Press, which the Western Union befriended and the American attacked as a dangerous news-gathering monopoly. The telegraph war which loomed up in 1860 showed that organization had gone far, but not far enough.[23]

That other handmaiden of transport, the express system, a uniquely American growth, had been somewhat more completely organized. So efficient were the various express companies that a Boston gentleman who wished to give a dinner party with Western buffalo hump, Ozark wild turkey, New Orleans shrimp, Minnesota wild rice, Georgia scuppernongs, and Shenandoah apples could command them all. The large sums the government used throughout the country were safely handled by express; all the long-distance financial exchanges of the country were conducted in the same way. Consolidation had been nearly as important in this industry as in the telegraph business. A union of two older companies had given birth in 1850 to the American Express, guided by Henry Wells and William G. Fargo, and this in turn soon organized Wells, Fargo to carry on the Western business, and the United States Express Company as an Eastern subsidiary. Various smaller concerns survived. In monetary terms the business was small; but the speed, economy, safety, and responsibility with which the agencies delivered letters, money, and parcels all over the continent made them invaluable to the country, and illustrated organizational enterprise at its best.[24]

The trunk-line railroads, steamboat interests, and telegraph and express companies were well enough organized to serve the Northern war effort effectively. But could as much be said of the equally important manufacturing industries?

[III]

Any reader of the massive report on manufactures in the census of 1860 is struck by the smallness of the units listed. Generally speaking, production rested on a multiplicity of petty establishments. The nation's pig iron came from 286 furnaces, with an average invested capital of about $14,000 each, and an average annual product much below that figure. Pennsylvania, the most

23 Robert L. Thompson, *Wiring a Continent*, 310–342.
24 Alvin S. Harlow, *Old Wayvills, passim.* Henry Wells published in the N. Y. *Tribune,* Feb. 20, 1864, a complete account of his and his companies' achievements. The earliest important line had been W. F. Harnden's Boston-New York package express; Wells had been the first to suggest and execute an express business to Buffalo, then Chicago, and ultimately the Far West. Total operating costs of the three corporations in 1864 were only about ten millions.

important iron State, had an industry of small furnaces widely scattered. In the Lehigh Valley gangs of smoke-grimed, hard-muscled men operated about twenty anthracite furnaces, in the Schuylkill Valley as many more, and in the Susquehanna Valley twenty-five. A westward drift had spawned iron-making centers in the Juniata, Johnstown, and Lewisburg districts, but they too were small; the four furnaces of the noted Cambria works could not average 10,000 tons apiece.

And the manufactories which took the iron? The firearms of the country came in 1860 from 239 establishments, with an average invested capital of less than $11,000. Connecticut, thanks to the Colt, Winchester, and other plants, was the main seat of fabrication, yet the 9 factories at work there employed fewer than 900 people in 1860, and the value of their product fell below $1,200,000. Smallness was equally characteristic of the sewing-machine industry, based upon American ingenuity and readily adapted to war work. Isaac M. Singer had founded his company only in 1851, and was still working hard to effect a pooling of patents and a union of enterprises. The census reported sewing machines made by 74 companies in a dozen States; and the 5 factories of Connecticut, which held the lead, divided an output of some 24,000 machines valued at just over a million.

Some industries of wide fame worked on a surprisingly modest scale. Though John A. Roebling was already well known for his wire-rope and suspension bridges, his Trenton factory had a capital of only $100,000, and its 70 hands made rope worth only $70,000 annually. And though Richard M. Hoe had revolutionized the printing of large newspapers by his rotary presses, the country had 14 press manufacturers, all small, with an aggregate yearly product of less than a million dollars.[25]

Surely, it would be said, the manufacturers who supplied agriculture and transportation had organized large enterprises; and it was true that important foundations had been laid. The largest manufacturer of locomotives, at Paterson, N. J., however, employed only 720 men in 1860 to build 90 engines. The largest car-wheel factory in the country, at Wilmington, Delaware, employed only 200 hands to cast 30,000 car wheels annually. One of the best-known industries in the land was the shovel factory of Oliver Ames & Sons in Massachusetts; running 26 tilt-hammers in 4 plants, it made 250 dozen spades and shovels a day, still rather a small-scale operation. Yet more famous was Cyrus H. McCormick's factory in Chicago, which produced 4,131 reapers and mowers in 1860. To meet varying regional needs, farm-implement manufacturing was widely distributed. In this field several corporations were achieving an impressive capital and a fairly complex organization. Nevertheless, the

25 Census of 1860, *Manufactures;* see the long introduction.

rule of smallness still had general validity. In the single county of which Canton, Ohio, was seat, the aggregate product of fifteen firms or individuals was worth more than twice as much as McCormick's whole output.[26]

New York City and its vicinity had a variety of machine shops which had sprung up principally to furnish iron forgings and castings, together with marine engines, to shipbuilders. They included the Fulton, the Allaire, the Neptune, the Morgan, the Delamater, and the Novelty iron works, with several more in Brooklyn. The works of the Stevens family in Hoboken and the Continental Iron Works at Greenpoint, Long Island, fell into the same category. Nearly all were destined to become important during the war. The Allaire establishment, successor to Robert Fulton's Jersey City shop, dated back to 1816, the Novelty Works to 1830, and the Morgan Works to 1838. At Cold Springs on the Hudson the West Point Foundry also had vigorous engineering facilities, and later planted branch machine shops in New York City. Other sturdy engine-building plants were found on Western waters, at Pittsburgh, Steubenville, Cincinnati, and Louisville. Undertakings of considerable size did not daunt the major shops. The Novelty Works had cast a sixty-ton bedplate for the engine of Collins's ship *Arctic,* the Corliss Engine Works at Providence turned out flywheels 25 feet in diameter, and a Philadelphia machine shop bored castings 18 feet long and 16 feet in diameter.

Yet these machine shops, however ambitious some of their undertakings, were small compared with British works and primitive in organization. They were obviously expansible, but when war demands came nobody knew how fast or effectively they could expand. Although they were becoming more specialized, they offered no products comparable with the finer parts of the reaper or sewing machine.[27]

Of all American manufactures, none had grown so strikingly during the previous half-century as textiles. The first complete textile factory, the Boston Manufacturing Company at Waltham, had been born of war in Madison's day. It had paved the way for the larger factories in the Merrimac Valley, and demand had grown so heavily that the country now had 1,091 cotton factories alone, more than half of them in New England. Massachusetts alone

---

26 The manufacture of labor-saving farm machinery, naturally one of the greatest branches of American endeavor, had given some men and firms nation-wide renown. S. M. Osborne & Co. in Auburn, N. Y., Adrian Platt & Co. in Poughkeepsie, R. L. Howard in Buffalo, and C. Aultman & Co. in Canton had a general fame. H. & C. Studebaker had begun their wagon business at South Bend in 1852. Already in 1860 a machine bound grain by wire. The census report stated that four-horse harvesters with two men to bind and two to shock could harvest twenty acres of grain a day; "we shall soon have machines that will cut, gather, and bind up the grain in one operation." *Manufactures,* cciv *et seq.*

27 For the machine shops see N. Y. *Tribune,* Feb. 7, 1863, an informative article; Clark, *History of Manufactures,* 107 ff.; Bishop, *History of American Manufactures,* III, 112.

counted 217 cotton factories; New England employed nearly three-fourths of the capital and made two-thirds of the product in the cotton industry. Some mills, like those of the Sprague family in Rhode Island, were imposing. It was in woolens, however, that the highest degree of concentration had been effected. Worsted manufacture was conducted mainly by three establishments, the Pacific Mills at Lawrence, Massachusetts, the Manchester Print Works at Manchester, New Hampshire, and the Hamilton Woolen Company works at Southbridge, Massachusetts. These three organizations loomed up as giants on the flat American scene with their total of 3,400 hands. The largest, the Manchester mill owned by the Merrimac Mills Corporation, which also made cotton prints in large quantities, was one of the few industrial wonders of the land. At Lawrence a fourth enterprise, the Bay State Mills, had become the world's leading makers of cashmeres, shawls, and other fine woolens. The census commented on the completeness and order of the large New England woolen factories.

A nation needing mountains of uniforms could take encouragement from the vigor of the ready-made clothing industry. It had grown up with democratic mass demand, cheap cloth, and the sewing machine until 3,800 firms with a capital of nearly $25,000,000 were engaged in it. A silent revolution was merging many small shops into large wholesale establishments. The average product was largest in the Middle Atlantic and Yankee shops, approaching $25,000 a year. East of the Alleghenies female hands were giving way to men. The principal cutters and salesmen in the bigger shops were often former merchant tailors, glad to invest their capital and influence in the large units. Thus, "with all the advantages of large capital and machinery," remarked the census, they could "supply every town and village with ready-made clothing at the lowest prices." [28]

Though in a hundred areas industry was forming larger units, even the biggest were still usually ill organized and amateurishly administered. One-man supervision predominated, and managerial problems were solved by trial and error. The McCormick factory was managed by Leander McCormick, Cyrus's brother, and four foremen. The Cooper & Hewitt iron works at Trenton were directed by Abram S. Hewitt, with advice from Peter Cooper and assistance from Edward Cooper. Erastus B. Bigelow, founder of a thriving carpet business, a determined enemy of corporate as distinguished from individual management in manufactures, published in 1858 a testy pamphlet on

28 Census, *Manufactures*, xxxii, lx, etc. The making of boots and shoes had grown into a large industry in Massachusetts, which by the State census of 1855 turned out nearly 12,000,000 pairs of boots and some 17,000,000 pairs of shoes. The whole number of shops in the country making boots and shoes in 1860 was 2,439. But as yet the industry was poised between the domestic and factory systems.

the subject.[29] Businesses should not be controlled from commercial and financial centers, he argued, but on the spot; for unity of purpose, one head was worth far more than the divided responsibilities of a large corporate organization. Isaac Singer, Samuel Colt, and Oakes Ames would have agreed. So long as the controlling brain was as keen as McCormick's, Hewitt's, or Bigelow's, it might well be superior to group management. Some industries were specially adapted to one-man control, and some business geniuses had to rule alone.

The most typical American manufactory in 1860 was the property of a man or family who had founded it, ownership passing from father to sons. This was true even of the older houses. The varied enterprises of Phelps, Dodge & Company, for example, were carried on by a close-knit group, members of the Dodge, Phelps, Stokes, and James families. Five men in 1860, of whom "the Christian merchant" William E. Dodge was the best-known, held total ownership and direction. From their Cliff Street offices in New York they managed the largest metals business in the country, a New Jersey bank, railroad interests, wide tracts of timber, iron, and coal lands about Scranton, and other undertakings with quiet efficiency.[30] But incompetents could wreck a business as easily as talented creators could make it. No New England textile mill was more noted than that of the Middlesex Company in Lowell, but its heads lost the entire capital by appalling "mistakes and irregularities."[31] And the trend of the times was toward multiple ownership and management.

As concentration gave birth to larger units, control by individuals and families declined. To reduce costs by standardization of product and improvement of methods; to stimulate or seize upon changes in market demand; to hold orders by prompt delivery of excellent goods—this, no less than growth in size and capital, required a more elaborate managerial organization. Larger buildings, larger stocks of materials, larger working forces, and more complex machinery meant expert planning and supervision. This fact was being illustrated by the shoe industry on the eve of the war. Amid a multitude of domestic producers and tiny cobbler shops, factories of real size had emerged primarily because customers had to be sought, materials purchased cheaply, labor supervised vigilantly, and innovations rapidly adopted. By 1860 steam power was being introduced into the larger manufactories, making the hand power of small shops seem pitifully slow.[32] Lyman Blake's machine for stitching uppers to soles had been invented, and would at once accelerate the tendency toward big and complex shops, with more and more elaborate staffs.

29 Entitled "Depressed Condition of Manufactures in Massachusetts."
30 R. G. Cleland, *Phelps-Dodge 1834–1950*, Ch. III. The Connecticut shops of the Ansonia Brass and Copper Company made a wide variety of products.
31 Crowley, *History of Lowell.*
32 Blanche E. Hazard, *Origin of the Boot and Shoe Industry in Mass.*, 123 ff.

This change in corporate administration, however, was in 1860 still slow and gradual. After all, in most areas the shift from small to large units had to wait on the progress of railroad facilities, and the consequent rise of regional or national markets. State impediments to large-scale organization were formidable. Without notable exception, State laws forbade corporations to hold property in other States, or stock in other companies, except under special charter. It was with great difficulty that legislators grasped the fact that it might serve the general good to encourage companies to undertake broad interstate activities. General incorporation laws were themselves recent, the Connecticut statute of 1837 being the first of broad character. Chief Justice Lemuel Shaw of Massachusetts did an important work 1830–60 in adapting the law of partnerships to corporations, and sheer economic necessity widened the influence of his decisions.

Until after the war, however, joint stock corporations were restricted mainly to railroads, banks, and insurance companies; State and railroad securities remained the staple of the stock exchanges. Manufacturing was not to adopt the corporate form on a broad scale until after Appomattox, and not to own interstate properties until still later. One reason for the formation of the Standard Oil trust as late as 1881 was that State laws blocked such interstate ownership.[33]

[IV]

Of the great range of organized activity among the churches, the educational bodies, the professional groups, the publishers, the writers, the social service societies, and lesser participants in voluntarism, how much was likely to aid a government at war? How much of this activity encouraged the principle of cooperative effort? Very little.

All the powerful church organizations, with two exceptions, had split in two on the sectional issue. The Catholics, an ecumenical body under foreign governance, remained ostensibly united. So, formally, did the Episcopalians, for even after communicants in the Confederacy established a separate church, the General Convention called the roll of the Southern dioceses. The other denominations rallied with fervor to the conflict. Quoting "The Lord thy God is a God of war," Southern Presbyterians, Baptists, and Methodists, as sects, as earnestly aligned themselves with their chosen cause as Northerners of the same churches supported the Union. Probably most Americans gained their

33 F. H. Chase, *Lemuel Shaw;* Arthur H. Dean, *William Nelson Cromwell,* 18. New York by an act of 1811 had permitted incorporation by general law rather than by special enactment, but the authority had strict limits.

first lessons in organization and cooperation from their church bodies. These great agencies enrolled millions who knew no society, club, or company, they enlisted men in active continuous work to an extent never equalled even by the political parties, and they touched life at more points than any other body. For women they furnished the one great means of organized expression.

But although the churches were in fact multifariously useful for the war, they were dismayingly limited in their usefulness. North and South, they undertook a great variety of labors. They supplied chaplains for the armies; they distributed Bibles, devotional books, and tracts; they supported revivals in camp; they helped meet problems of poverty and home relief behind the lines. Northern church leaders formed societies to assist the freedmen, inspired the Christian Commission, sent leaders (rather unsuccessfully) to occupy pulpits in conquered areas, and furnished spokesmen to plead the Northern cause abroad. Yet the central purpose of the churches debarred them from intensely practical activity. Their primary concern was with the other world, not with this. After an immemorial concentration upon extramundane activities one day out of seven, they could not give full weekly labor to mundane concerns.

Nor had the concept of social Christianity, as preached in England by Kingsley and Maurice, in France by Lamennais and Buchez, yet reached America. In 1857 the Y. M. C. A. in New York had been torn apart by a secession of nearly 200 members, including prominent clergymen, who asserted that political and social topics, including slavery, were too much discussed, and that the society had wandered from its original objects.[34] This small but significant event emphasized the doctrine that the central business of the church was to save souls and quicken the spiritual life of the people. Any wide departure from that path—beyond, say, raising the $2,500,000 collected by the Christian Commission—would have aroused condemnation.

As for education, it had a far more uneven and precarious organization than religion. When Henry Barnard established his *American Journal of Education* at Hartford in 1855, the principle of a unified system of public schools under State control was fairly well rooted in the North. To implant it had required a long battle against penny-pinching enemies of public expenditures, religious bodies which wished to fractionize the educational system, and fossil obstructionists of "book learning." Associations of teachers and friends of education, fighting this battle, had founded numerous societies all over the East and Middle West.

Yet the results were so uneven and new that no powerful educational bodies useful for war work yet existed. New York and Illinois had not gained separate State superintendents on a permanent basis until 1854, and Pennsyl-

34 *National Intelligencer*, April 30, 1857.

vania until 1857. In 1861 a belt of States reaching from Maine and New Jersey to the far borders of Kansas had permanent State school officers, but only nine, including California and Alabama, possessed regularly organized combinations of State and county administrators.[35] Teachers' organizations had narrow scope and slight vigor. The one important national agency, the American Association for the Advancement of Education, was ten years old; but however commendable, it was unable to rally the nation's teachers in united effort.

Significantly, no educator made an effort to form classes in army camps, convalescent hospitals, or prison camps. The Northern volunteer regiments were full of youths torn from academy or college, of semi-illiterates, and of half-Americanized aliens, apt material for teaching. But no body capable of implementing an educational plan, had one been broached, existed.

The medical profession, like the ministers and teachers, had the aid of schools, journals, and societies in fostering its special aims. But standards of training were so low, quacks and charlatans were so abundant, and public interest in medical advancement was so slight, that the profession lacked organized power.[36] In Great Britain and Europe, S. Weir Mitchell later wrote, medicine by 1861 held places of trust in the government, but in America it was neglected. "Our great struggle found it, as a calling, with little of the national regard. It found it more or less humble, with reason enough to be so." [37] General medical societies had a history running back into colonial days, and before 1861 State-wide societies overspread the whole map east of the Mississippi, save in Louisiana, which left the field to a New Orleans association.

Most early medical societies, however, both State and local, were primarily social organizations of scant authority or prestige. For a time some State governments clothed specified societies with power to license physicians, regulate fees, and punish malpractice. Such authority was in general ill exercised, and the State tended to turn instead to special medical boards. Several close-knit, well-led urban societies gained more repute and influence than the loose State associations. In Philadelphia the College of Physicians, dating from 1789, in Boston the Society for Medical Improvement, from 1838, and in New York the Academy of Medicine, from 1846, all had a distinguished membership, listened to papers of merit, and commanded public respect. Societies in Cincinnati, St. Louis, and one or two Southern cities had dignity. The membership, however, was always smaller than it should have been. Their interest in medical education did not lead in the best direction, and when much later university medical schools of adequate standards came into existence, it

35 Cubberley, *Public Education in the U. S.*, 122 ff., 246 ff.; Cubberley and Elliott, *State and County School Administration Source Book*, 283 ff.
36 H. B. Shafer, *The American Medical Profession, 1783–1850*, pp. 169–173.
37 *In War Time*, Ch. IV.

was from other impulses and indeed against the opposition of some leading medical organizations.[38]

On the initiative of New York physicians, the American Medical Association was founded in 1846. Its committee on education did effective work to improve medical training within the old pattern, urging lengthened terms of study, the use of hospitals for clinical teaching, higher admission requirements, and stricter examinations. It labored also to improve American drugs, inculcate higher ethical principles, and stimulate original research and writing. Holding annual conventions in different cities, it enlisted adherents in each, until by 1856 it had more than 3,000 members.[39]

But on the whole, medical organization when the war broke was in its groping initial stages. Most societies were social or amateurish, and not one had produced a great administrator or initiator. They held banquets, combated quacks, and passed resolutions, but they did much more to promote *esprit de corps* than to increase medical knowledge or influence public opinion. Hampered by financial difficulties, languid interest, factional squabbles, and lack of professional dignity, many of them kept up but an intermittently active existence. The American Medical Association was as yet so narrowly professional, deficient in broad social interests, and fluctuating in strength, that it was of slender general value. Medical education would have to be revitalized before medical associations could grow powerful.[40] No society was able to give the government important aid during the conflict. The chief wartime organizers of medicine, surgery, and nursing were to be a clergyman, a landscape architect, a frontier army doctor, an attorney, and a woman clerk in the Patent Office.[41]

Of all the great professions, that most glaringly deficient in organization was the bar. When the nation sprang to arms, no legal society worth mentioning existed North or South. Although Philadelphia laid claim to a city association founded in 1802, it was nothing more than a lawyers' social club. Even New York City had no bar association until Samuel J. Tilden, under stress of a dire civic emergency in Tweed days, led the way in founding one, and the American Bar Association did not arise till some years later. The earliest State association seems to have been one which led a precarious life in Iowa for some years after 1874. Lawyers with an instinct for leadership or a cause to

38 W. F. Norwood, *Early History of American Medical Societies*, CIBA Symposia, 1947, No. 9.
39 Shafer, 232 ff.; John Shaw Billings, "Literature and Institutions," in E. H. Clarke, *et al.*
40 F. R. Packard, *History of Medicine in the U. S.*; W. D. Postell, *The American Medical Association*, CIBA Symposia, 1947, No. 9; F. C. Stewart, *On the Medical Schools and the Conditions of the Medical Profession in the USA* (1856), 116.
41 Bellows, Olmsted, Hammond, George T. Strong, and Clara Barton; but mention might also be made of three physicians, Drs. Tripler, Van Buren, and Agnew, and a scientist, Wolcott Gibbs.

promote turned naturally to political parties. For improvements in the efficiency and ethics of the bar they looked to legislatures, the State attorneys-general, and the courts.[42] If any officer of the national government wished legal advice—in making appointments to the bench, in drafting legislation, in searching for precedents, in dealing with questions of constitutionality—he could apply to individuals; but help from associations he could not get.

One of the greatest indirect contributions to the war strength of the nation was made by the press, both daily and periodical. It kept the people informed, it more than any other agency molded public sentiment, and despite shrill dissident voices and conflicting policies, it crystallized a spirit of national unity. Daily journalism was competitive in the extreme. In New York City the coarse, fickle *Herald*, the enterprising, solidly informative, and socially radical *Tribune*, the eloquent and cultivated *Evening Post*, and the moderate, judicious *Times* contended for leadership. While their daily circulation was almost wholly metropolitan, by weekly and semi-weekly editions they reached the entire North. Every city had its daily, almost every county seat its weekly.

The country was full of newspapers, read more voraciously, perhaps, than in any other land. New York State had more dailies than all Great Britain. A current story told of a minister who preached hell-fire without effect; but his announcement that the godless went to a land without newspapers made his congregation turn pale and profess conversion.[43]

While outwardly newspapers seemed to illustrate the essence of individualism, actually they possessed a remarkable solidarity. The practice of exchanging subscriptions was universal. A country editor might get twenty or fifty exchanges from all parts of America; he produced a better journal by swift use of the scissors than by laborious employment of the pen, with the result that the content of many newspapers was much the same. The government subsidized this system of exchanges by special postal concessions. A remarkably telling editorial by Greeley, Bryant, or Raymond, by Samuel Bowles or John W. Forney, was certain in the end to appear in many journals. A striking piece of special correspondence in the Chicago *Tribune* or Springfield *Republican* would be widely clipped. The Associated Press, originally a combination of New York dailies to collect news, had by 1860 taken almost complete control of news-gathering in the United States and Canada. Though bitterly assailed as a ruthless monopoly after it defeated the effort of the telegraph companies to establish separate news services, it did its work efficiently and cheaply.[44]

42 Charles Warren, *History of the American Bar;* M. Louise Rutherford, *Influence of the American Bar Assn.*
43 D. Macrae, *The Americans at Home,* Ch. 31.
44 Victor Rosewater, *History of Cooperative News-gathering in the U. S.;* Oliver Gramling, *The A. P.*

Indeed, the diffusion of intelligence was one of the best-organized branches of national endeavor. The New York *Tribune* or *Herald* published every night 55,000 copies, with each department—European correspondence, Washington, Albany, and metropolitan news, editorials, Wall Street article, agricultural column, produce and shipping news, letters to the editor—copiously filled; it dealt systematically with advertisements, legal printing, and birth, marriage, and death notices; it provided for paper supply, street sales, local deliveries, and subscriptions—all through carefully coordinated activity. This was possible because each journal had a body of trained employees, an eye to system, and an instinct for the latest inventions. Stereotyping, for example, developed by Charles Craske of New York, came into use just in time for the large war editions. The *Tribune* boasted that in the spring of 1862 its weekly edition circulated more than 150,000 copies, and its semi-weekly 18,000; its consolidated circulation of more than 220,000 copies was, it declared, much the largest in the world.[45] Altogether, it reached fully one-twentieth of the whole newspaper-reading public of the North. Such a feat was impossible without careful organization.[46]

The publication of books and magazines was likewise a vigorous department of American life, for mass education meant mass reading. The Scottish publisher William Chambers, looking primarily at New England, wrote that every American bought and read books—a gross exaggeration; Anthony Trollope declared that Americans were the greatest consumers of literature on earth, taking 10,000 copies of a book where Englishmen took one.[47] Although the invention of electrotyping ten years before the war had reduced costs, during the 1850's the annual dollar value of books trebled. Harper Brothers just before the panic of 1857 turned out 3,000,000 volumes in a single year. To be sure, the purchase of books hardly averaged a dollar a year for adults, but the market well repaid the largest firms. The houses of Appleton, Lippincott, Harper, Ticknor & Fields, Putnam's, and Scribner's flourished while they honorably allied their names with the best literature. *Harper's Monthly Magazine* before the war attained a circulation of more than 100,000; farm journals, religious journals, and women's magazines like *Godey's Lady's Book* were widely read; Robert Bonner's New York *Ledger* was reputed to sell 400,000 copies a week; and the two important illustrated journals, *Harper's Weekly* and *Frank Leslie's*, overcoming their initial crudities, were reaching and instructing great bodies of readers.[48]

45 N. Y. *Tribune*, April 10, 1862.
46 The census reported that in 1860 the nation had 383 daily newspapers, and more than 3250 weekly or semi-weekly newspapers. The totals were steadily growing.
47 Chambers, 219; Trollope, *North America* (1862), I, 271.
48 Martin, *Standard of Living in 1860*, 324, 325.

The largest book-and-magazine houses, like Harper's and Ticknor & Fields, were organized on a sturdy scale. But book-publishing in general was as much decentralized as most manufacturing, for prosperous firms were found all the way from Albany and Richmond to St. Louis and Nashville. Equally noteworthy was the wide diffusion of bookshops; just before the panic at least three thousand shops dealt exclusively in books and periodicals, while nearly seven thousand more sold them in connection with other wares. The book trade was not efficiently managed or systematized, for it perhaps never can be. The American Publishers' Association had recently been founded to bring publishers and booksellers into better relations, and its weekly organ, the *Publishers' Circular*, carried full information on the trade. But as of newspapers, it could be said that the seemingly chaotic book business had more internal solidarity and coordination than men supposed. It was well arranged to stimulate literature, and to keep the nation fairly informed upon events and forces.

While in a narrow view the manysided publishing activities of the North were of limited value to the war effort, in any broad view they were of priceless utility. The press kept the country informed of every phase of government activity, offered a free forum of discussion which was indispensable to the healthy workings of democracy, and through its best journals gave the nation encouragement and inspiration. "We cannot too often repeat that the first duty of the citizen at this juncture is to give the President a generous, confiding, and cordial support," said *Harper's Weekly* just after Bull Run,[49] and most publishers took a similar view in dark hours. One influential pamphlet on the nation's resources, scattered broadcast late in the conflict, was worth a small army.[50] It was unfortunate that in some other areas the national energies were not equally well organized.

[V]

The lack of associative elements, the plastic state of society, and the prevalent individualism, had their compensation. They fostered self-reliance, enterprise, and ingenuity. Blessed with great natural wealth, and aided by capital accumulations, energetic Americans wrought great achievements. "The period following California gold," writes one historian of technology, "developed an apex of individualism perhaps never before and certainly never since attained in the world's history." [51] The ingenuity was as striking as the energy.

49 August 3, 1861 (V, 482).
50 "Our Burden and our Strength," by David A. Wells (1864).
51 Roger Burlingame, *March of the Iron Men*, 312, 313.

Repeatedly a lonely experimenter who knew little of the general state of the arts would devise some memorable improvement. John Deere thus produced his self-scouring plough, Robert L. Stevens his T-rail, Linus Yale, Jr., his famous pin-tumbler cylinder hook, and Crawford W. Long, in an isolated Georgia village, his anaesthetic. Elias Howe thus solved the problem of devising a needle which, working from the top plane only of a piece of cloth, would stitch both its top and bottom.

Herman Haupt, a young Pennsylvania West Pointer, who went into railway construction, was suddenly faced twenty years before the war with the necessity of finding the laws by which the transmission of strains in a trussed bridge was governed. He sat down in a country town in Pennsylvania without books of reference or scientific apparatus, and by experiments on the resistance of timbers, and his own methods of obtaining mathematical formulae, met the exigent requirements of the York & Wrightsville Railroad. He did more; he arrived at some valuable new principles of bridge building. Just before the war, helping direct the boring of the Hoosac Tunnel, and confronted with the task of piercing strange rock strata, he devised drilling machinery comparable with that used in piercing Mont Cenis. In short, without supporting organizations, he repeatedly displayed a triumphant inventiveness. Brought into the army in 1862, Haupt showed his ingenuity in building bridges of novel materials (beanpoles and cornstalks, said Lincoln), making implements for twisting and straightening rails, devising torpedoes, and so on; while his skill in helping several generals move troops and meet fast-changing strategic situations was equally notable.[52]

But were these empiric methods good enough? A significant contrast might be drawn between Charles Goodyear in America and Charles Mackintosh in Scotland. While the Connecticut experimenter, without scientific training or advice, hit on the vulcanization of rubber by stubborn plodding and luck, the systematic Glasgow manufacturer arrived at great results by well-considered steps. He obtained the guidance of the brilliant chemist-surgeon James Syme of Edinburgh, dissolved raw rubber in coal-tar naphtha, and applied the solution as a varnish to cloth. While Goodyear sank into debt, Mackintosh became rich. It was only when well-organized groups placed themselves behind Goodyear's discovery that American rubber products far outstripped the British goods. There could be no question in 1860 that the inexorable process of business consolidation, the steady growth of industrial undertakings in size, and the new scientific knowledge, demanded group activity in place of individual enterprise; but individualism still reigned supreme.

52 See Haupt's pamphlet, "Hints of Bridge Construction," 1841; Frank A. Flower's useful preface to Haupt's *Reminiscences*.

Very different was the situation in England. John Stuart Mill, commenting on the intellectual progress of the working classes, remarked that their advance in the habit of cooperation was equally surprising. "At what period were the operations of productive industry carried on upon anything like their present scale? Were so many hands ever before employed at the same time, upon the same work, as now in all the principal departments of manufactures and commerce? To how enormous an extent is business carried on by joint stock companies. . . . The country is covered by associations." [53]

America was now ready to take wide and rapid strides on the same road. The transportation revolution was creating national markets; they in turn would help create the industrial revolution, with large national agencies of manufacture. Business giants governing huge combinations would soon arise. But as matters stood in 1861, Lincoln never thought of summoning a group of business leaders to assist him in wartime administration; the businessmen had no faculty of cooperation. Except for the Sanitary Commission, the government made practically no use of professional groups in war work; it picked men here and there, but in haphazard fashion. In short, it used little organized machinery, for the machines had never been created. Lincoln might well have found valuable assistance, for example, in a board of transportation. But how was such a board possible in a country where the first through train of freight cars did not pass from the State of New York into the State of Ohio until January 11, 1863? [54]

53 Mill, *Dissertations and Discussions*, I, 196, 197 (Boston, 1864).
54 Edwin A. Pratt, *The Rise of Rail Power in War and Conquest*, 22, 23.

14

McClellan and the Tasks
of Organization

LINCOLN was quick to ask McClellan for a memorandum on his proposed mode of using the new volunteer forces. He replied on August 4 that he would need for his main army of operations about 273,000 men, with 20,000 more for defending Washington and smaller forces to protect Baltimore, Fort Monroe, and the Baltimore & Ohio. His army would require 600 guns, twenty-five regiments of cavalry, proper engineering and pontoon trains, and adequate means of transport, while effective naval cooperation would have to be arranged. Still other troops would be needed to occupy West Virginia, Kentucky, and Missouri, while the size of the army to go down the Mississippi would have to be determined by its commander and the President. Admitting that the total force seemed large and its cost would be heavy, McClellan urged that it would be cheaper to crush the rebellion at one blow, and terminate the war in a single campaign, than to leave the conflict a legacy to the next generation.

Thus something of the optimism of the first months survived even Bull Run. One campaign, one blow!—and McClellan spoke not merely of driving the enemy from Virginia, but of occupying Charleston, Savannah, Montgomery, and New Orleans; in short, moving this great army into the heart of the Confederacy and stamping out resistance at its center. He was soon to tell a group of Philadelphians: "The war cannot be long, though it may be desperate." His memorandum said nothing about the time required for preparing the blow, but it was evident that he wanted plenty of it. He and Scott immediately disagreed as to the first army formations, McClellan insisting that brigades be rapidly united into divisions, while Scott declared this unnecessary, for in Mexico he had used brigades alone. McClellan cut through the dispute by obtaining a War Department order August 20 constituting the Army of the Potomac under his full and direct command.

"I at once designated an efficient staff, afterwards adding to it," McClellan later wrote. His chief of staff, a position new in America, was his father-in-law Colonel Randolph B. Marcy, a West Pointer now nearly fifty who had served on the northern frontier, fought in Mexico, and taken part in the so-called Mormon War; a big, soldierly man of moderate abilities. His adjutant-general was Seth Williams, a brigadier, assisted by Lieutenant Colonel James A. Hardie, both good officers, and the latter especially capable and industrious. As head of engineers McClellan kept the exceptionally clearheaded and experienced Major John G. Barnard, who later completed the Washington defenses and in time wrote a caustic analysis of his chief's generalship. The topographical engineers soon passed under Brigadier-General A. A. Humphreys, remembered as a military historian. As quartermaster-general McClellan appointed Captain (later Brigadier-General) S. Vliet, who loved his wine, but to whose efficiency he paid high tribute.[1]

Army health offered an appalling problem. Typhoid and other fevers raged in the camps. The sick took refuge in improvised general hospitals in and about Washington, some, like the deadly hospital at Cumberland, Maryland, so bad that they became a public scandal. Incoming regiments brought volunteer surgeons ignorant of army methods—and sometimes of everything else. To replace chaos by order McClellan appointed Charles S. Tripler as medical director, an officer who with the general's support did good work, but whose preparations for active campaigning proved inadequate.

As the staff steadily grew to sixty-five in the spring of 1862, it enlisted other notable men. The provost-marshal-general, Andrew Porter, soon halted the straggling, disorder, and criminality which made the Washington camps a byword. Major Albert J. Myer, who had been made head of the signal corps before McClellan assumed control, devised a good system of torch-and-flag signaling, and introduced an insulated telegraph wire which could quickly be strung; indeed, he was the father of the signal service. McClellan's telegrapher, Major Thomas T. Eckert, also organized a service of notable efficiency. This Ohioan, long an expert in telegraphy, was to rise rapidly to the position of general superintendent of military telegraphs in Washington, where he saw

1 O. R. I, v, 5 ff.; *McClellan's Own Story*, 113; McClellan, *Report on the Org. and Campaigns of the Army of the Potomac*, 39 ff., 51 ff.; Swinton, *Army of the Potomac*, 62 ff.; Kenneth Williams, *Lincoln Finds a General*, I, 103 ff. When McClellan took command July 27 the forces around Washington numbered perhaps 53,000. He insisted that his command be termed and organized as an army, while Scott clung to the idea that McClellan ought to head a geographical department. McDowell had already organized brigades south of the Potomac. Under McClellan, a division consisted (ideally) of three infantry brigades of four regiments each, four batteries, and one cavalry brigade. For McClellan to the Philadelphians see Philadelphia *Evening Journal*, Nov. 5, 1861. Gen. Peter S. Michie, an expert, speaks slightingly of Marcy's capacities, but Marcy's books indicate a likely intelligence.

much of Lincoln. The work of his men in the field was as dangerous as it was arduous. The balloonist T. S. Lowe was another young man who had impressed the government before McClellan took charge in Washington. Cameron, after Lowe had made some spectacular ascents, and had sent Lincoln the first telegram ever transmitted from the upper air, made him head of the new aeronautics section of the army. McClellan was glad to encourage him, and although the heavily wooded nature of the country and the difficulty of transporting and flying balloons limited his usefulness, he sometimes obtained information of value.[2]

The general's aides included several striking figures. John Jacob Astor was ultimately to inherit one of the great American fortunes. Richard B. Irwin in time became adjutant-general and historian of the nineteenth army corps. Louis Philippe d'Orleans, the Comte de Paris, saw hard fighting at first hand, which later aided him in the production of a masterly four-volume history of the war. His brother the Duc de Chartres also served on the staff through a long, hard campaign. Altogether, McClellan listed a personal entourage of nineteen, or, if he added the Prince de Joinville, who accompanied his two nephews of the Orleans family to headquarters and stayed for a time, twenty.

The young general stood almost alone in his early recognition of the vital importance of apportioning precise duties among a large body of staff officers, and in this respect showed a more modern understanding of command procedures than Robert E. Lee. His comprehensive grasp of administrative work in general made a startling contrast with the confused, nerveless methods of Cameron's War Department and Scott's headquarters. Although he often played favorites and unjustly criticized subordinates whom he disliked, he cultivated a real esprit de corps in his staff family. His faith in the special equipment and all-sufficing capacity of professional military men to win the war was accompanied by an unhappy contempt for politicians, and, since he was very much a Democrat, a strong dislike of Republican politicians. Indeed, he believed and openly declared that a military elite, to the great benefit of the nation, would thereafter play a larger part in public affairs. He was much more like a French or German general than those of the traditional American variety.[3]

2 Myer, who later established the U. S. Weather Bureau, is commemorated by Fort Myer. Eckert wrote a valuable book, *Recollections of the U. S. Military Telegraph Corps During the Civil War.* Mt. Lowe near Pasadena is named for T. S. Lowe, who built an observatory on it.

3 As we shall see, he had a Colonel Blimp attitude toward slavery. Irwin was another staff member later to pen a scathing review of McClellan's command; see his article on the Peninsular Campaign in *Battles and Leaders,* II, 435 ff. Dahlgren reported McClellan's views on the military in the nation's future; *John A. Dahlgren,* by his daughter, 344, 345.

[I]

McClellan struck everyone by his air of energy, confidence, and address. W. H. Russell, hard to please, liked the serenity of his dark blue eye, the firmness of his mouth, and the animation of his features; he liked the general's compact, powerful frame, massive throat, and well-shaped head. Dr. Henry W. Bellows of the Sanitary Commission wrote a more observant description. He too noted the muscular figure, well-knit and perfectly balanced, the handsome regular features, topped by dark, short hair, the calm, direct, and powerful eye. What seemed to him more remarkable was McClellan's leopard suppleness, as graceful as if his movements were controlled by some inner rhythm. "His manner," added Bellows, "is self-possessed, unaffected, though remarkably self-complacent, with natural dignity and frankness. His talk, to the point, earnest, honest, and intelligent. He is not afraid of responsibility; he knows his place, assumes its rights and an interest in meeting its requirements. While I should say that balance, availability of every talent, promptness, superiority to routine, and willingness to stand in the gap were more conspicuous in him than ingenuity, brilliancy, or originality, yet there is an indefinable *air of success* about him and something of the 'man of destiny.'"

It was this aura of destined greatness, this assurance radiated by a man not yet thirty-five, which made Napoleonic comparisons inevitable. "He looked like one who always had succeeded and always will succeed." Already men talked of him as the next President.[4]

A man of resolution, force, and belief in his star, but of more self-esteem than of absolute self-confidence; a soldier of long training, keen observation, and settled convictions, but not of imagination, depth, or subtle analysis—this was McClellan. His early environment had not been altogether fortunate. He had been all too carefully reared in Philadelphia, his father an active, prosperous, disputatious physician; the city was conservative, and the rather aristocratic circles in which he received his education and formed his social tastes were distinctly so. He was contemptuous in early years of "these wretched Dutch and Irish immigrants." The Mexican War and his regular army experience had confirmed his natural distrust of volunteers, an attitude unfortunate in the head of the greatest volunteer army in history. There was something decidedly spoiled in the temper of this proud, ambitious, inwardly haughty leader. As A. K. McClure, who knew him well, remarked, he would have taken the rough buffets of war better had he once been a ragged alley

4 H. W. Bellows to his wife Sept. 12, 1861, Bellows Papers, MHS; when the Prince Napoleon in August, 1861, repeated to McClellan Lord Lyons' remark that he would be the next President, the general "answered with a fine, modest, and silent smile"; "The Tour of the Prince Napoleon," *American Heritage*, August, 1957.

urchin, used to playing and fighting with other boys of tough material. From the time he was admitted to West Point by special permission at the age of fifteen and a half, until he was made vice-president of the Illinois Central at thirty-one, he had too easily won success after success. His lucky appointment in 1855 as an army observer in the Crimean War enabled him not only to study military affairs in Europe, but to talk with dignitaries of the highest rank, including the French and Austrian emperors.[5]

Being spoiled, he could be arrogant when given full rein, and petulant when crossed. Already his treatment of Jacob D. Cox in the West Virginia campaign had been unfair, and that of W. S. Rosecrans, whom he termed a silly, fussy goose, ungenerous. To cooperative subordinates and to admirers he showed a natural affability and kindliness. As Dr. Bellows put it: "His voice is sweet, his address affectionate, his manner winning." Because of this, of his leaderlike qualities, of his real mastery of the minor arts of war, and of his solicitous care of his troops, officers and men came to adore him. "How those brave fellows love me," one officer reports his saying, "and what a power their love places in my hands." A better man would have emphasized obligation rather than power.[6]

Behind the mask of seeming serenity and self-confidence, however, lay a great deal of self-distrust; behind the apparent energy, dynamism, and boldness lay caution and timidity. His services in Mexico had been those of an engineer. At Sevastopol he had stayed only two weeks (October 16–November 2, 1855), all in the British camp, and at the beginning of a siege that was destined to endure almost a year; he spent most of his time inspecting the Russian defensive works and measuring the Allied difficulties, and departed full of admiration for the fortifications erected by Todleben and the valor of the Russian defenders. It was the belief of the best authorities (Marshal Niel, General Wolseley, and Todleben himself) that a fierce, determined attack on Sevastopol late in September, 1855, would have carried that fortress, and that by declining to attempt it and cautiously sitting down to a prolonged siege, the Allies played into the Russian hands; but if McClellan knew this fact, he does not mention it in his reports.[7]

During his European tour he carefully inspected various military works in Austria, Prussia, and other countries; but it seems significant that he lingered over defensive positions, evincing no interest in the study of offensive strategy or tactics. In the West Virginia campaign his dispositions had been excellent,

5 W. S. Myers, *McClellan*, 16; McClure, *Recollections of Half a Century*, 316.
6 Myers, 190–194; Donn Piatt, *Memories of Men Who Saved the Union*, 295.
7 McClellan, *Reports* (35th Cong., Special Session, Senate Exec. Doc. No. 1). The British in the Crimea gave McClellan every possible facility, but the Russians and French refused him any; *Own Story*, 2.

but all the boldness in executing them was displayed by his subordinates. Short as the campaign was, it showed that he united a hard-headed, practical sagacity about some matters with an astonishing capacity for self-deception in others. He probably really believed, after Morris and Rosecrans had won Corrick's Ford and Rich Mountain respectively, two minor encounters involving minor losses, that he was justified in boasting that he had "annihilated two armies."

McClellan's intensity of purpose was as creditable as his integrity, industry, ability, and constancy to duty. Combined with his singular charm of manner, it diffused an impression of pleased, and even exalted, consecration to his great task, and recalled Wordsworth's portrait of the happy warrior. He could labor with tremendous fixity to reach the objects he had set himself, and at the same time show a warmhearted cheeriness to all associates. He had a sense of mission, a clear understanding of the means to be employed in reaching his goal, and a determination not to be swerved from his direct line. These commendable traits come out clearly in a letter he shortly wrote his wife:

> I shall take my own time to make an army that will be sure of success. . . . I do not expect to fight a battle near Washington; probably none will be fought until I advance, and that I will not do until I am fully ready. My plans depend on circumstances. So soon as I feel my army is well-organized and well-disciplined, and strong enough, I will advance and force the rebels to a battle in a field of my own selection.[8]

Unfortunately, this resolution of temper was lamed by several defects. One was his inveterate perfectionism; all preparations must be complete to the last detail, and all controllable conditions must be just right, before he would make a decisive move. As one Senatorial critic said, he would hesitate to order an advance if he learned that a part of his wagons lacked the extra linchpin required by army rules for each wheel.

Another crippling trait was stated by an observant subordinate in terms of pre-Freudian simplicity—his readiness to seek scapegoats for the inevitable mischances of war: "There are men so peculiarly constituted that when they have once set their hearts on any project, they cannot bear to consider the facts that militate against their carrying it out; they are impatient and intolerant of them; . . . inasmuch as it is impossible for any man to get angry with facts, such men instinctively fix upon certain individuals whom . . . they always accuse . . . of hostility or deception." McClellan, when his plans began to go wrong, wrote his wife: "History will present a sad record of those traitors who are willing to sacrifice the country and its army for personal spite and personal airs." When they had gone further wrong he was writing her: "I am tired of

8 *Own Story;* letter of Oct. 6, 1861.

serving fools." [9] But then his whole attitude toward his superiors was peculiar. He did not regard himself as the servant of the American people, or the subordinate of Lincoln or of Scott. He thought of himself as a man entrusted with a colossal task, under which he staggered; so that any criticism, any interference, even any advice, was an absolutely unforgivable wrong.

Finally, the worst evidence of his self-distrust was his inveterate disposition to exaggerate the magnitude of his difficulties. No matter how large his army, that of the enemy was always greater; no matter how formidable his guns, the opposing fortifications were always stronger. Of these traits we shall find abundant illustrations. The Polish diarist Gurowski, the Thersites of Washington, wrote that his imagination so overrode his sense of fact that he had a faculty for "realizing hallucinations." Charles Russell Lowell, who was on his staff, declared that he was like the Duke of Wellington in that he got everything completely ready, and then unlike the Iron Duke in that, once ready, he did not strike hard. Still another close observer, the war correspondent George W. Smalley, remarked that when the pinch came, McClellan was not a general but a council of war, and it was an axiom that a council of war never fights. [10]

McClellan's intensity of purpose, frequent arrogance in hours of prosperity, tendency to propound a devil-theory for failure, resentment of interference, and egotistic vein, are characteristics not understood in isolation. They are bound together and measurably explained by his conviction that he was under the finger of God. The war produced a number of generals, including Lee, Stonewall Jackson, Rosecrans, and O. O. Howard, of as profound religious fervor as McClellan, but he alone had a Cromwellian sense of selection for God's purposes. Dr. Bellows showed keen insight when he spoke of the general's natural faith in divine protection. This faith supplied a foundation for his loftiness of outlook, personal purity, integrity, and sincerity, qualities which kept for him to the end of his life the esteem of the country. It also gave him, once he had been made the foremost general, a delusion that God had chosen him to be the shield of the Republic; him alone. His Messiah complex was half piety and half disdainful pride.

"I feel sure that God will give me the strength and wisdom to preserve this great nation," he wrote his wife August 9, 1861, adding: "I feel that God has placed a great work in my hands." A little later he writes her of the tremendous responsibility God has laid upon him. "I was called to it; my previous life seems to have been unwittingly directed to this great end; and I know that God can accomplish the greatest results with the weakest instruments—therein

9 James B. Fry, "McClellan and his Mission," *Century*, vol. 48 (Oct., 1894), 931–946; McClellan, *Own Story*, 310, 453.

10 Gurowski, *Diary*, I, 99; Bliss Perry, *Life of T. W. Higginson*, 169; Smalley, *Anglo-American Memories*, 123, 124.

lies my hope." In November, busy drilling his army, he repeats: "I still trust that God will support me and bear me out. He could not have placed me here for nothing."

Those other exalted military organizers, the Emperor Constantine and the Caliph Omar, could not have been more certain of the *instinctu divinitatis*. It was as the instrument of God that he felt he had a right to be loftily contemptuous of older associates, so that the daughter of General James M. Wadsworth, long eminent in New York affairs, indignantly resented his haughtiness to her father. It was this sense of divine selection which enabled him to write his wife so scornfully of Lincoln as a "browsing President," of the Cabinet as "geese," and of the Administration as one which in general made him "perfectly sick." It enabled him to write (August 14) that "General Scott is the most dangerous antagonist I have." As a divine appointee, he had a right to expect his every demand to be met without demur.

Men of such intense religious justification commonly possess a martyr complex, and when hard trials came McClellan was quick to adopt the martyr pose: "I feel that the fate of the nation depends on me, and I feel that I have not a single friend at the seat of government." In all his trials he nevertheless remained confident of his destiny: "I believe in my heart and conscience . . . that all I have to do is to try to keep the path of honor and truth, and that God will bring me safely through." This piety, kept within limits, should have been an added source of strength; but when he carried it to the extreme point of regarding himself as God's lieutenant rather than servant, it became a grave defect. Unlike Cromwell, unlike Stonewall Jackson, who did their best and let Providence do the rest, he alternated between a sense of infallibility when God-inspired, and total fallibility when the inspiration failed. As William H. Russell was quick to perceive, moments of cocky self-certainty were followed by periods of hesitation, timidity, and irresolution.[11]

All in all, splendid gifts were mated with terrible handicaps. And the worst of the handicaps was revealed in the before-quoted letter to his wife in which he spoke of forcing the Confederates to a battle on a field of his own selection. "A long time must elapse before I can do this," he wrote (it was already October 6), "and I expect all the newspapers to abuse me for delay, but I will not mind that." A natural patrician, with little knowledge of or feeling for the plain people, he did not understand that this was a people's war, and that the people's will had constantly to be consulted to ensure popular support.

11 *Own Story*, 168, 175, 176, 316, 317 (see also the biographical introduction by W. C. Prime); Russell, *Diary North and South*, Chs. 55–57. "I like the man," wrote Russell Oct. 10, 1861, "but I do not think he is equal to his occasion or his place." The fact of McClellan's sense of mission under God that astute soldier James B. Fry (*op. cit.*) specially emphasizes.

[II]

All summer and fall new levies of infantry poured into Washington. Mc-
Clellan dealt with them systematically. As each regiment arrived it was carefully equipped, drilled, and disciplined as part of a provisional brigade, this
work being assigned first to Fitz-John Porter, then to Ambrose E. Burnside,
and later still to Silas Casey. Artillery and cavalry units were assigned to other
officers for equipment and training. As the troops were made ready, they were
transferred to permanent brigades on the south side of the Potomac, consisting
of four regiments apiece. Then as the drill and field maneuvers progressed, the
brigades were formed into divisions—three brigades, meaning twelve regiments,
to each division. McClellan had in view a larger unit still, familiar to military
men since Napoleon's time, the corps, but he postponed its creation until experience had given the division commanders familiarity in handling large bodies
of troops, and until he could determine by actual trial the best generals. Two
divisions would theoretically contain 24,000 men, an adequate number for an
army corps, and McClellan knew that not many officers are capable of commanding so large a body.[12]

It was part of McClellan's plan that he should command a large force of
artillery. Inheriting from McDowell a pitiable 9 batteries, totaling 30 guns, he
raised the total to 92 batteries of 520 guns; and he gave each division 4 field
batteries, one of them taken from the regular army. McClellan also decided to
create a reserve force of 100 guns, and a siege-train of 500. By the time his
army was ready to move the amount of ordnance and ordnance stores, far superior to that possessed by the South, sufficed to satisfy even him.[13]

Cavalry presented both a special problem, arising from the fact that army
officers had always regarded three years' training as a minimum; it also presented a special opportunity in that it could have been the best intelligence
arm of the service as well as a a unique striking force.[14] McClellan put Brigadier-General George W. Stoneman in charge, telling him to whip the volunteers into shape within six months. Stoneman, a West Pointer from upper New
York who had been captain in command of Fort Brown, Texas, and had

12 McClellan's *Report*, 53, 57. The corps by McClellan's plan was to have 3 infantry
brigades of 4 regiments each, 4 batteries of artillery, and 1 regiment of cavalry, giving it a
nominal strength of 12,000 infantry, 1000 cavalry, and 24 guns; an effective strength of
10,000 infantry, 700 cavalry, and 24 guns. *Own Story*, 114. The Confederate army formed
no corps in the Army of Northern Virginia until it had received eighteen months of
service.

13 Swinton, *Army of the Potomac*, 65. A shrewd Confederate officer, D. H. Hill, later
wrote that the Federal artillery was always the most effective arm of the service; *Battles and
Leaders*, II, 355.

14 W. W. Averell, in *Battles and Leaders*, II, 429.

escaped with part of his men when Twiggs joined the Confederacy, had gained McClellan's confidence in the West Virginia campaign. He was destined to write his name large in the history of the war. With great rapidity, all obstacles considered, he organized and trained a division of fourteen regiments, with two independent squadrons. To take raw recruits, often unused to arms or horses, and turn them into a disciplined, effective cavalry force was a task of complex difficulty; while they had also to be schooled in meeting problems of the Virginia terrain, with its forest, thickets, rivers, swamps, and hills, its deep mud after rains, and its burning midsummer sun.

Generally speaking, it was impossible to use cavalry as full regiments in Virginia; squadrons were the most efficient unit. When Stoneman got his division into shape it was distributed among the army, with a small body at headquarters, and a special reserve force under Philip St. George Cooke, a former colonel of dragoons who had commanded the Mormon Battalion in Kearny's historic march to California. Stoneman had been quartermaster of the battalion. Cooke, who had later fought the Sioux and Apaches, and had devised an improved system of cavalry tactics, was a stiff disciplinarian. He had the poignant task of fighting a Southern army which contained both his son John and son-in-law J. E. B. Stuart. Beyond hard drill this year Stoneman and Cooke did not go. McClellan by fall might have used the cavalry constantly in reconnaissance raids, but he showed no interest in risking them to gain information.[15]

"Squads right!" "Right oblique, march!" "Hep, hep, hep!" The immemorial bark of sergeants, the rattle of arms, the swirl of dust from red-clay fields trampled to powder, the clamor of fife and drum, encircled Washington north, west, and south. On some clear afternoons the breeze, bringing the fitful strains of massed bands, reported a grand parade in the distance. Visitors glimpsed McClellan galloping hard from post to post, a very Kléber in his hard-bitten, keen-eyed aspect, his staff following breathless and jaded behind. Seldom indeed now did a dirty, drunken soldier stain the Washington streets, for military police snapped such ragamuffins under stringent arrest. Colonel Andrew Porter, whom McClellan had appointed provost-marshal-general, used squads of regulars to close disorderly saloons, clear streets and hotel lobbies of loiterers, arrest every man absent without written leave, and put deserters in fear of their lives. He prohibited civilians from visiting camps or crossing the Potomac without permits. McClellan credited Porter with making Washington one of the quietest cities in the Union. Troop morale rose as men felt that they had both a master and friend at the head of the army.[16]

15 *Battles and Leaders*, II, 429 ff. Cooke was raised from the rank of colonel to that of brigadier-general in the regular army, Nov. 12, 1861.
16 O. R. I, ii, 769; *McClellan's Report*, 55; *Own Story*, 69; Shannon, I, 183; Ropes, I, 163.

The most difficult problems of discipline were presented by several mutinous regiments. Although they had considerable reason for discontent, McClellan properly made an example of them by prompt and severe action. He sent sixty-three men of the Second Maine to the Dry Tortugas for the remainder of the war. Their grievances were probably not unlike those of the Fourth Connecticut at Frederick, Maryland (outside McClellan's purview), who rebelled because of bad officers, bad fare, and such total lack of uniforms that none had coats, few had matching hats, and many appeared even on dress parade in underclothing. Fomenters of revolt in the Connecticut regiment were imprisoned. When the New York Seventy-ninth Highlanders rebelled, McClellan dealt summarily with them. He sent out a force of infantry, cavalry, and artillery to quell them. "The gentlemen at once laid down their arms," he wrote his wife, "and I have the ringleaders in irons. They will be tried and probably shot tomorrow." [17]

Such sternness was indispensable, even though the Highlanders had been badly treated. They had fought bravely at Bull Run, where their colonel, Secretary Cameron's brother, lost his life. After the battle they had been refused permission to return briefly to New York to recruit their ranks, although Secretary Cameron, the commander of the New York militia, and the engineering department of the army had all supported their petition. Later they had been outraged by news that they would be placed in the division of Dan Sickles, whose disreputable record decent men despised. Finally, while preparing to hold elections for a new colonel and other officers, they had suddenly been put under the command of a stranger, Colonel I. I. Stevens of the regular army; whereupon the major, senior captain, and four lieutenants summarily resigned. To cap their discontent, McClellan told them he would not inquire into their "frivolous and unfounded" complaints, and that their behavior laid them open to a charge of "the basest cowardice."

Nobody was shot. Ringleaders were sent briefly to the Dry Tortugas, and the regimental colors still more briefly taken away. Stevens won the devotion of all the men, who served with distinction. The happy subsequent history of the regiment indicated that mismanagement, at a higher level than that of its own officers, had been responsible for the trouble. Nevertheless, McClellan's peremptory course taught the whole army a salutary lesson.[18] He deserves the greatest credit for his insistence on discipline and order.

17 *Own Story*, 86, 99, 100; the Comte de Paris, I, 270, attributes the trouble in the 79th largely to grievances about pay and terms of enlistment. W. H. Russell says "the President was greatly alarmed" by the mutiny.
18 William Todd, *The 79th Highlanders, N. Y. Vols.* (1866), is a superior regimental history; see pp. 56–88.

[III]

The principal impediment McClellan met in bringing his army into efficient discipline arose from the poor quality of many officers, high and low. At a later date it was fashionable to say that no civilian should have been given an important command.[19] This was folly. The regular army simply did not have enough officers to go around. Of its small list, many lacked zeal, some shrank from responsibility, sticking to petty regular army posts when they might have had high volunteer rank, and many were needed in staff rather than field commands. It was out of the question to officer 500,000 men from the army register of 1860, and had it been possible, it would have been unwise.

Anglo-American history gave weighty arguments for using civilians in high posts. Cromwell and Hampden had left Parliament to fight. In colonial days Pepperell of the New England militia had captured Louisbourg from French professional soldiers. During the Revolution, Washington, Greene, and Knox, all with little or no military experience, had bested veteran British soldiers. In the War of 1812, Andrew Jackson, Jacob Brown, and Winfield Scott had all been appointed from civil life, and the two former were militia generals. During and after the French Revolution officers sprang from every walk of life to become generals and marshals.

Moreover, in so vast a people's war as this now beginning, with the armies on both sides representing almost a *levée en masse*, much was to be said for using popular leaders. The idea was to give talent a chance to rise to the top, as it did. Nobody could say in after years that John A. Logan, Jacob D. Cox, Carl Schurz, Benjamin Harrison, Lew Wallace, Joshua Chamberlain and James A. Garfield were not capable generals. On the Confederate side Nathaniel Bedford Forrest showed real distinction. After all, West Point did not differ materially from other good colleges except in a greater study of mathematics, engineering, and drill; the drill there and at army posts never went beyond company and regimental tactics; and Grant, Sherman, and others learned much more outside the army than in.

Yet the process of letting talent rise and incompetence fall took time, and was both painful and debilitating while it lasted. Too often the State authorities evinced an imbecile carelessness in putting the lives of their young men in the hands of stupid, ignorant, and irresponsible leaders. Much depended on the State system, the State adjutant-general, and the fiber of the governor. Ohio had allowed its regiments to choose their higher officers with some appalling results, for competition among aspirants produced neglect of discipline,

19 Ropes takes this view, and naturally some West Point officers always held it.

cheap electioneering, and occasional bribery. A few lucky regiments like the Twenty-third Ohio, with Rosecrans for colonel and Rutherford B. Hayes for lieutenant-colonel, obtained admirable officers. But repeatedly some local politician, an aspiring lawyer or slick talker, took the lead and held it until resignation or removal furnished relief. It was soon noted that cities and large towns monopolized the Ohio commissions at the expense of rural areas.[20] In other States the governors, acting hurriedly under heavy pressures, chose men sometimes well, sometimes ill.

Morgan in New York shrewdly called on local leaders for advice, and appointed committees to investigate candidates and counsel him. In the three counties of Chenango, Cortland, and Madison, for example, a committee of forty-five unanimously designated Elisha B. Smith, who admirably led the local regiment until he was mortally wounded at Port Hudson in 1863. Andrew in Massachusetts showed equal sagacity, scouring the State for men of West Point education, and next them giving preference to seasoned militia officers. He refused, despite pertinacious demands, to grant a commission to sly Caleb Cushing. Under still fiercer assaults, he stubbornly declined to make a colonel of a Democratic politician who had a large following among the Boston Irish. "I would not commission him," thundered Andrew, "if he was as good a soldier as Julius Caesar, and you should bring an angel from heaven to endorse him."

But even Andrew blundered in making a colonel out of a militia strutter who promptly led his men through Boston under the summer sun in a long-famous "overcoat march." This appointment, he confessed to Sumner, was inexcusable; but he made others nearly as bad—one hapless regiment getting a superannuated head who was both dishonest and cowardly, and a lieutenant-colonel who was an excitable Italian adventurer. The best governors could not avoid error.[21]

Cameron in a circular letter tried to inculcate greater care. After wisely urging the governors to commission nobody of doubtful health, morals, or patriotism, he unwisely suggested that they fix age limits for officers: nobody over twenty-two to be a lieutenant, nobody over thirty a captain, nobody

20 This was true of other States; see Wm. Croffut and John Morris, *Mil. and Civil History of Connecticut*, 75. Urban leadership was accelerated on a wide front by the war. We may repeat that officers were everything to morale. The Second Michigan, for example, did admirably until its colonel was made a brigadier-general, and its lieutenant-colonel took a post in the regular army. The new lieutenant-colonel and the major being poor heads, it went to pieces. "The regiment," wrote a Michigan veteran, Wm. W. Duffield, to Governor Austin Blair, "is very much disorganized, and it would be a work of great labor to bring it up." Aug. 23, 1861; Austin Blair Papers, Burton Hist. Coll.

21 Pearson, *Andrew*, I, 233–235. The colonel who marched his men on a hot day through the Hub wearing their overcoats, and soon repeated the performance in hotter Washington, declared that their shoddy uniforms had to be covered up.

over thirty-five a major, and nobody over forty-five a colonel, except when special circumstances dictated a qualification of the rule. Governor Andrew contemptuously declared that he would appoint a good man anywhere short of Methuselah's age. As a matter of fact, an excellent officer might be as old as Wadsworth, who was approaching sixty when slain, or as youthful as Nelson A. Miles, who formed a company but was deemed too immature by his superiors to command men in battle. Beginning with a minor staff position at twenty-two, Miles was major-general four years later. George A. Custer, a graduate of West Point in 1861, earned his spurs as lieutenant at twenty-one and was a general before the war closed. Arthur MacArthur, carrying the flag of his Wisconsin volunteers up Missionary Ridge at eighteen, commanded a regiment before he was twenty. And Thomas W. Hyde of Maine, making a report in Virginia to Major-General Sumner, startled that officer by his juvenile look. "You a major!" exclaimed Sumner, then in his mid-sixties. "My God, sir! You will command the armies of the United States at my age." [22]

Gradually the quality of the officers was bettered, though the work of providing an efficient body of regimental commanders was to take a long time. As one factor, Scott's objections to assigning regular army officers to volunteer units, supported by Cameron, were broken down. As another, the soldiers themselves forced many unfit men to quit. As a third, the examining boards authorized by Congress wielded an effective broom.[23]

Scott gave way slowly. He stood out against a plea by Governor Dennison that he provide five regular army officers, if possible West Pointers, to head five Ohio regiments. Olden of New Jersey met better fortune, however, when he sent an agent to Lincoln with a letter arguing that as he could not find men competent to lead his new regiments, the general government ought to provide at least the colonels. The President asked Scott to see what could be done, and in due course New Jersey got two regular officers as heads of her two newest regiments.[24]

Apparently Cameron did not bestir himself in such matters. Governor Andrew tried in vain to obtain an answer to his plea that Captain T. J. C.

22 *DAB*; Hyde, *Following the Greek Cross*, 45, 46.

23 Scott believed the integrity of the little regular army must be protected against all hazards and got Cameron to agree. Under the pleas of Governor Andrew, both Massachusetts Senators—and Henry Wilson and Charles Sumner were powerful men—tried earnestly but in vain to let the Bay State select a few regular army officers for colonels. Adjutant-General Lorenzo Thomas, a narrow bureaucrat, said that more than a hundred such applications had been made, that if they yielded in one instance they must do so in all, and that this would sorely damage the army, already hurt by the resignation of so many Southerners. "Your only hope is to obtain if you can the services of some experienced officers now out of the Army. . . ." wrote Wilson sadly to Andrew. June 27, 1861; Andrew Papers, MHS.

24 O. R. III, i, 380, 387; 451, 452. Olden's letter was dated Aug. 24, 1861.

Amory of the regular army should take charge of the Seventeenth Massachusetts. Finally, late in August, he appealed to McClellan. The general thereupon gave Cameron some common-sense advice. "I do not think it possible to employ our Army officers to more advantage than in commanding divisions, brigades and regiments of new troops," he wrote, "particularly when it is remembered that we have almost none of the old troops at our disposal." Amory was appointed.

Similarly, Frémont in the West made a test case of a regular-army lieutenant who had been sent to St. Louis by Governor Morton of Indiana in command of a regiment, but had been told by the War Department that he could not keep that position. Wishing to retain him and other regular officers, Frémont appealed to Montgomery Blair. The postmaster-general prevailed upon Cameron to agree that as many as a hundred regular-army officers of the grade of captain or lieutenant might be allotted to the volunteers, their places to be partially filled by commissioning the two upper classes at West Point as lieutenants, and Lincoln endorsed this plan. It went a long way toward making effective the stipulation in the new army law that the commanding general might detail any regular army officer to field service with volunteer regiments. From this time forward an increasing number of veterans of the Western posts began to appear in colonelcies of the new army.[25] The total, however, could not be large among the five hundred and more regiments.

The troops themselves had to take a hand in weeding out misfits and promoting able subordinates, and a half-thousand regimental histories prove that they were merciless in exerting pressure. An efficient officer had to have much more than some fair knowledge of tactics, strategy, and camp management; he had above all to be apt in commanding men. This aptitude could neither be acquired by study nor imparted by older officers—it was mainly inborn. One military chronicler speaks of "that rare faculty of enforcing rigid discipline without severity, and of exerting the most absolute command without harshness or arrogance." In unit after unit, the volunteers by giving evidence to examining boards, by letters to Congressmen, or by sharp indications of disapproval brought a bad major or captain down; and good sergeants and lieutenants moved up. Some troop choices were bad, but more were sound.

Thus Edward S. Bragg of Wisconsin wrote his wife from Arlington, October 26, 1861: "Our regiment has taken a purge this week. We have *forced ten resignations* from officers, and put better men in their place." He added: "The men who resigned, did not have our confidence, and we placed the dose to their lips, and made them swallow it." If an officer could not handle his men expertly on the drill ground, their contempt became patent. If he

25 *Ibid.*, 427, 444; F. B. Heitman, ed., *Hist. Register and Dictionary of U. S. Army.*

treated subordinates arbitrarily, flinched in battle, idled, or drank to excess, the contempt became intolerance.[26]

When Cameron appointed the examining boards authorized by Congress, incompetent officers fled like rabbits escaping a meadow before a pack of hounds. In one division two colonels and twenty-five other officers, summoned to appear, incontinently resigned. By the end of the first week in November, 1861, nearly 150 had thus severed their connections. To get rid of such men for good, the War Department lost no time in decreeing that resigned officers would not again receive commissions.[27] Probably more colonels would have gone but for the fact that many were so important politically that they felt well protected. McClellan speeded the work not only of examining boards but of courts-martial, which were specially useful because they were immune from the political pressures which the boards often felt. Having a deep West Point contempt for "scrub" officers, McClellan handled them without gloves. His discharge of one junior commander brought him into conflict with Lincoln himself. Altogether, within eight months after the establishment of the boards, 310 officers were dismissed or resigned to avoid dismissal.[28]

The indirect effect of the board examinations in deterring governors from rash appointments and in stimulating officers to hard study and vigilant effort was doubtless even greater than the direct results. McClellan notes how many of his junior officers taught themselves while teaching their men. They read Hardee, Mahan, Napier, Kinglake, Jomini, and other texts, keeping a few jumps ahead of their subordinates. The Comte de Paris also describes the laborious effort of unschooled officers to educate themselves. Often after a hard day of drill the colonel would first give his juniors a careful lecture on strategy, tactics, and camp management, and then, long after most men were asleep, he, his lieutenant-colonel, and his major would burn their desk lamps far into the night. L. A. Grant of the Fifth Vermont was typical of scores of officers who, entering with no military training whatever, by hard application to details, books, and operations, made themselves into generals. The striking fact is not that failures appeared, but that the citizen army produced so many admirable leaders, brave, conscientious, and resourceful.[29]

Public opinion after Bull Run also had a marked effect on the efficiency of

26 On forced resignations, see Burt, *Memoirs*, 56; Augustus Buell, *"The Cannoneer:" Recollections of Service in the Army of the Potomac*, 24; *History of the Fifty-Fifth Illinois*, 170, 465; Bragg Papers, Wis. State Hist. Soc. Charges against an officer were often tried before a regimental court of other officers; see Henry Lee Papers, MHS, for instances.

27 O. R. III, i, 411; General Order No. 57, Aug. 15, 1861.

28 Shannon, I, 186, 187; Eckenrode and Conrad, *McClellan*, 28; Swinton, *Army of the Potomac*.

29 *Own Story*, 97; Comte de Paris, I, 272, 273; G. G. Benedict, *Vermont in the Civil War*, I, 352, 353.

officers. New York newspapers on August 1 published a telling memorandum by some of the most influential men of the city. It complained of the government's failure to supervise the selection of officers closely; of the wretched intrusion of political, local, and personal considerations into the appointments by various governors; of the bad consequences of company elections of lower officers, and officer elections of colonels; of the lax discipline throughout the volunteer organization, generals hesitating to jerk up weak colonels and colonels to castigate inept captains; and of the reluctance of the government to remove incompetent generals. In dealing with officer efficiency, the people were plainly in advance of Washington. Indeed, they would have supported Lincoln and Cameron in much more vigorous measures than the Administration took. Public sentiment was strongly behind all McClellan's energetic steps in organizing and disciplining the army.[30]

[IV]

In still other ways the steadily increasing army about Washington was made ready for combat. McClellan gave careful attention to provisions, clothing, and health. In this he had willing assistance from that conscientious administrator, Quartermaster-General Montgomery C. Meigs, whose zeal and skill were invaluable. The Secretary of the Sanitary Commission very justly wrote the editors of the *National Intelligencer* August 12 commending "the prompt and generous action of the enlightened head of the Quartermaster's Department, to whose energetic and comprehensive views of duty the nation has yet to be informed in what innumerable ways it is indebted."

Down to Bull Run the diet of the Union troops had been ill balanced, ill prepared, and ill served. After the first confusions of the spring, abundant supplies of bread, pork, and beef were available in most camps, but army regulations permitted no green vegetables, and except by gift or foraging the soldiers got none. Even when food of proper variety was at hand, bad cooking often ruined it. The army that marched to Manassas was on the verge of severe losses by scurvy and dysentery. But after McClellan took charge, the subsistence department under Colonel H. F. Clarke and the quartermaster's department under Van Vliet acted with energy. They brought in ample stores, established depots, and trained distributing officers. Both had to attend in person to innumerable details, and the reports they soon submitted were not only a story of heavy labors well performed, but a shrewd guide for other officers bearing similar responsibilities. Not once during his command of the army,

30 S. S. Cox, *Three Decades*, 159–162.

McClellan later declared, did troops go without rations from any fault of the commissary officers.[31]

Though the sanitary and medical system of all American forces remained weak, Surgeon Charles S. Tripler, who in August became medical director of the Army of the Potomac, was able, with the aid of the Sanitary Commission, to effect many improvements. One of his first acts was to move the men camping on Arlington flats, a third of whom were sick with typhoid, malaria, or dysentery. The eagle-eyed Frederick Law Olmsted, famous for his volumes of Southern travel, was secretary of the Commission. Making an inspection just before Bull Run, he had found the captains specially indifferent to foul latrines, garbage-littered camp streets, crowded tents shut tight against "night air," and unbathed men. They tolerated such filthy violations of the most elementary health rules that he called the whole system pestilential.[32] Now they, and colonels and generals above them, were made to understand that discipline included minute attention to cleanliness, fresh air, good water, and recreation.

In September, Olmsted reported that sanitary regulations were being enforced with ten times the old rigor, that even the regiments most demoralized two months earlier were now hardy and cheerful, and that the best-disciplined units were the most contented units. Improvement continued steadily. During the fall and winter (September–February), the number of sick fell to 6.18 per cent, more than half the cases being slight illnesses under treatment in quarters. Meanwhile the Sanitary Commission had launched a determined drive to reform the medical department of the army and oust its feeble head, the aged Surgeon-General C. A. Finley.

Measles, which many regiments brought with them when they left home, was prevalent throughout the camps. Tripler knew of no way to prevent its ravages. Other causes of illness, which Tripler was powerless to remedy, were shoddy blankets, poor tents, and inadequate clothing. On November 8 the surgeon of the Eighth Illinois Cavalry reported that 200 of his men had received no overcoats from the government, and that many of them were reduced to their drawers. The historian of the First Massachusetts Infantry recorded much sickness in their Washington camp because the men's clothing did not protect them from variations of temperature; "when darkness came, instead of sleep, there was a perpetual shiver." Medical men knew how to prevent smallpox, and Tripler recorded with pride that though it was prevalent in many regions

31 See the Olmsted-Harris *Report* on Washington camps, 14 ff.; Sanitary Commission, *Document No. 28;* McClellan, *Report,* 69.

32 Adams, *Doctors in Blue,* 18, correctly attributes much of the bad sanitation to the "incorrigible individualism" of American recruits. Men whose position in society would have demanded cleanliness and decorum washed neither their persons nor their clothes in camp.

from which the army drew its men, vaccination and other precautions kept it from gaining a foothold in the army. They did not know how to prevent typhoid, and in October and November, with an army averaging 130,000 men, there were 7,932 cases of fever of all sorts, about 1,000 of them with a typhoid listing.[33]

The sicklists of regiments from different parts of the country varied greatly. For example, in November, with a mean ratio of 6.5% sick in the whole army, 12 Massachusetts regiments had an average of 50 sick each; 5 Vermont regiments, an average of 144 each; 35 Pennsylvania regiments, an average of 61 each. In January, 1862, the Twelfth Massachusetts, 1005 strong, had only 4 sick; the Thirteenth Massachusetts, 1008 strong, 11 sick; the Fifteenth Massachusetts, 809 strong, had 68; the Fifth Vermont, 1000 strong, had 271 sick; and the Fourth Vermont, 1047 strong, 244. Mortality rates for enlisted men ran twice as high as for officers.

The diseases from which the men suffered most were fevers, measles, various catarrhal complaints, and chronic diarrhea and dysentery. The two last maladies had always been the greatest plagues of armies. In November the Army of the Potomac reported only 280 cases of chronic diarrhea and 69 of chronic dysentery—the best record of any army in the world, Tripler believed. Of the 1331 cases of measles that month, nearly all were of a mild form, and the ailment soon ran its course.

Each regiment had its surgeons who had to be carefully instructed, often in the very rudiments of camp requirements, and kept in hand. Tripler assigned the responsibility for this to the brigade surgeons, competent medical men who had in large part seen the battlefield of Bull Run. Each was required to inspect brigade camps, maintain adequate medical supplies, send Tripler a weekly health report from regimental surgeons, and furnish casualty lists after battle. The improvised base hospitals first used about Washington were a disgrace to the country. Occupying old houses, shops, barns, and schools, with poor plumbing or none and poor ventilation, they literally murdered many a soldier. Their attendants, nurses, and general staff were as green, slipshod, and ignorant as if they had stepped from the pages of Tobias Smollett. When the Sanitary Commission insisted that well-designed new hospitals must be built and competently equipped, Tripler gladly endorsed the demand.[34]

33 Though an English doctor had announced in 1854 the theory that intestinal discharges, carried by flies or other agencies, cause typhoid, and the theory had been proved valid, most Americans still attributed it to "miasmas," fatigue, poor food, and whatnot. Troops refused to believe that it was a filth disease. Adams, *Doctors in Blue*, 203.

34 Stillé, *Hist. of the Sanitary Commission*, 95; McClellan, *Report*, 65–68. The general hospitals in Maryland and about Washington by September had 2700 beds; William Q. Maxwell, *Lincoln's Fifth Wheel*, 53.

Two able officers of the Sanitary Commission, after due investigation, brought forward a plan for building new base hospitals on the pavilion system, each ward to be a self-sufficient structure for forty or fifty patients. The first proposals were modest, providing merely for fifteen thousand sick and wounded. Tripler, Quartermaster-General Meigs, Van Vliet, and others worked out the details. In October Cameron approved them, and asked the Commission to help select five sites. Thus was inaugurated a great hospital system which became one of the noblest triumphs of the war—even though the five buildings were temporarily reduced to two, partly because Tripler did not have enough medical officers for more, partly because McClellan feared graft in hasty construction.[35]

McClellan had laid a sound foundation for future activity. The army was far better organized, officered, equipped, and trained than when he had taken charge, and its morale was infinitely improved. A new sense of confidence spread in early autumn from Washington throughout the North. Men waited eagerly for the young general to deliver an overwhelming blow; for the kind of battle that ends a war—a Ramillies, an Austerlitz.

[V]

As Northerners plucked up confidence in their armies, a piece of happy news from the navy burst upon the nation. On September 2 the press blazed with headlines that sent everybody looking for maps. "Brilliant Naval Victory," ran the captions. "Hatteras Inlet Forts Captured: 730 Prisoners, 35 Cannon Taken." Gideon Welles's department had for the first time seized national attention.

This surprise blow was delivered at a strategic spot. A long thin shield of outlying sea-banks, a prolonged wall flung eastward in bluntly triangular form, protects the Southern coast from Cape Henry, opposite Newport News, Va., down to Cape Lookout, opposite Beaufort, N. C. This sea-wall is composed of pebbly beaches, dunes that shift except where pinned down by wire-grass, and some clay stretches bearing loblolly pine, live oak, and holly. At the apex of the triangle lies Cape Hatteras, the boss of the shield fronting the stormy Atlantic. Here the treacherous Diamond Shoals extend twenty-five miles out to sea, a graveyard strewn with the skeletons of ships. Outside the sea-wall the roaring Atlantic is hag-ridden with fog, winter sleet, autumn hurricane, and year-long tempests; eagles and ospreys soar above the flashing waves. Inside are the calm waters of Albemarle and Pamlico Sounds, where

---

35 Maxwell, 54, 55. Regimental hospitals, usually made of three hospital tents, offered temporary accommodation for small numbers of men.

sailboats glide safely, and ducks, geese, and gulls feed in peace. Hatteras Inlet, ten miles below the cape, opens into these inland seas. Noted in peace-time for its tarpon, dolphin, marlin, and swordfish, it was now the exit from a hornet's nest. Raiders sped out it to harass Union merchantmen; blockade-runners moved in and out. Fort Hatteras and its flank defense, Fort Clark, protected the inlet.

The Union expedition seized these forts in a foray so sudden and easy that it seemed an adventurous lark. General Ben Butler and Commodore Silas Stringham commanded the amphibious force. Their flotilla of some fifteen craft left Hampton Roads August 25, and at sundown next day anchored at the rendezvous. Butler landed a small force of troops at the inlet; Stringham turned the Dahlgren guns of his larger ships—the *Minnesota, Wabash, Susquehanna*— on the defenses, easily outranging their smooth-bores. As shells burst inside Fort Hatteras, its commander saw that the place would soon be a shambles. He surrendered to save needless bloodshed, and the Union commanders decided to hold and garrison the position. On August 30 Ben Butler sent a jubilant official report to his superior: [36]

The importance of this point cannot be overrated. When the channel is buoyed out any vessel can carry 15 feet of water over it with ease. Once inside there is a safe anchorage in all weathers. From thence the whole coast of Virginia and North Carolina from Norfolk to Cape Lookout is within our reach by light-draft vessels which cannot possibly live at sea during the winter months. . . . In my judgment it is a station second in importance only to Fortress Monroe on this coast. As a depot for coaling and supplies for the blockading squadron it is invaluable.

No immediate steps, however, were taken to utilize the advantages which the Union had so swiftly gained. The stroke galvanized the Confederates into hurried action to strengthen their coastal defenses. While they did this, the North, it would seem, might have found it easy to land troops on Roanoke Island, forty miles north of Cape Hatteras, a gateway to all southeastern Virginia. But in fact nothing was done in this direction for three months. Why? One reason lay in diversionary action by McClellan. Just after the capture of Fort Hatteras, he obtained permission from the War Department to organize an amphibious force of ten regiments with a fleet of light vessels, of which Ambrose E. Burnside was appointed head. This force, under Mc-Clellan's direct command as part of the Army of the Potomac, was to operate in Chesapeake and Virginia waters as might best assist his main array. Before 1861 ended, Burnside had assembled 20,000 men and a hundred small craft— but McClellan made no use of this potentially quick-striking body.

36 To Gen. John E. Wool; Private and Official Corr. of Butler, I, 229–235.

COAST AND SOUNDS

OF

NORTH CAROLINA.

Scale of Miles

0   10   20   30   40   50

Ben Butler and Commodore Silas Stringham, Driving Through Hatteras
Inlet, Seemed to Confederates to Menace Richmond's Southeastern
Connections.

If the list of naval achievements was still short, it was clear that the government had capable administrators in the vigilant, hot-tempered Gideon Welles and his chief assistant, the cheerful, robust, self-confident Gustavus Vasa Fox, whose long naval experience gave him sureness of touch.[37] They had to deal with a tremendous complex of problems. When the war began only twenty-four steam-driven vessels were in active service; they were scattered all over the globe; only the newest ships were equipped with powerful guns; although France and Britain had experimented with armored vessels, and such warships had proved their effectiveness in the attack on the Russian works at Kinburn in the Crimea in 1855, the United States had no ironclads; and the supply of trained seamen was inadequate for a sudden expansion of the fleet. But though Welles became a target for acrid criticism, the two men grappled doughtily with their difficulties.

They augmented the naval force at hand by four obvious measures. That is, they recalled all the ships on foreign stations but three; they refitted all the usable vessels laid up in docks or harbors; they began constructing new warships in the navy yards; and they purchased or chartered good vessels wherever they could be found. They gradually put a construction program of fast steamers and ironclads under way. They resisted all efforts to institute State navies, and insisted on the strict equality of the naval establishment with the military establishment. It soon became plain that naval fighting would take place not on the high seas, but in coastal and river waters. It also became evident that the principal contribution the navy could make toward victory would lie in a steady constriction of the blockade. In the end this blockade, colossal and unremitting, was to be one of the greatest naval undertakings of all history.

An impossible task it at first seemed. The Confederate coast line came to 3000 or 3500 miles; it was pierced by innumerable bays, inlets, and rivers; and a considerable part of it, like that bordering the Virginia-Carolina sounds, was really a double line of coast. When Lincoln proclaimed the blockade (April 19, 27, 1861) few ships were available to enforce it. But Welles and Fox persevered. By July in 1861 they had sent 21 purchased or chartered steamers to join the blockade service; and these, with regular naval vessels, made forty-two steamships for the cordon. The list by the closing days of the year rose to about 150 ships. And though Confederates derided the blockade, it was already showing some results; it cut off much of the expected European aid in rearming and refitting the Southern forces after Bull Run.[38]

37 Fox, chief clerk of the Navy Department, May 9, Assistant Secretary, Aug. 1, 1861.
38 Owsley, *King Cotton Diplomacy*, 250–253; J. R. Soley, *The Blockade and the Cruisers*, 11 ff.

When the Confederate envoy Slidell held his first interview with high French officials they asked why it was that, if so many vessels had broken the blockade, very little cotton had reached neutral ports. The Foreign Minister was especially inquisitive. "I told him," writes Slidell, "that they were generally of small burden and that spirits of turpentine offered greater profits than an equal volume of cotton. That, although a very large proportion of the vessels that attempted to run the blockade, either to or from our ports, had succeeded in passing, the risk of capture was sufficiently great to deter those who had not a very adventurous spirit from attempting it." [39] A few excerpts from the diary kept by Jacob F. Schirmer in Charleston show how the pinch began to be felt: [40]

May 31 (1861).—News. The war steamers have again appeared for a blockade, and today they stopped a British schooner going out and ordered her back, the British consul has required an explanation.

June 1.—Schooner *Mary Clinton:* news today that she has been captured by a U. S. man of war and sent to New York, she sailed from here on the 10th from New Orleans with 814 casks of rice 285 of which was shipped by H. Corbin & Co.

June 23.—The men of war are still on the blockade, no arrivals of vessels, no more privateers have gone out from here, it is feared that Capt. Welsman's ship *Amelia* has been captured.

July 31.—Our privateers appear to be doing something on the wide ocean and in several cases are successful. Our blockade is still carried on and every article of consumption particularly in the way of groceries are getting very high.

September 9.—Our privateeers appear to have made a close of their business as all of the ports are closed against us.

September 17.—Arrival. The secession gun was fired this morning as a salute to the news of the arrival of a large English steamship owned by John Fraser & Co. into Savannah from Liverpool with a large cargo for our city.

September 25.—The blockade is still an eyesore. Every arrangements were made to send the *Nashville* to Europe, but there is no doubt the news have reached the blockade and they have been reinforced, and the experiment is partly abandoned.

October 16.—Ship *Thomas Watson* from Liverpool for this port went ashore on Folly Island. The blockaders raced her, the crew left the ship in boats and reached the shore, the ship was eventually burnt by the Lincoln rascals.

November 30.—Business perfectly prostrated everything enormously high salt selling at 15 and 20 cents a quart hardly any shoes to be had dry goods of every kind running out.

39 Undated MS entitled "Notes of Interview with Messrs. Thouvenel, Persigny, Baroche, and Fould" in George Eustis Papers, LC.
40 Joseph F. Schirmer Diary, Charleston Hist. Soc. The punctuation has been mended for clarity.

The blockade would have been stronger had it not been necessary to detach war ships at times to pursue Confederate cruisers. Thus when Captain Raphael Semmes with the armed steamer *Sumter* escaped from New Orleans to the high seas late in June, 1861, half a dozen blockading vessels were sent off in a vain effort to seize her. No form of service was more disagreeably monotonous and confined than that on a blockading squadron; its boredoms seemed endless. But no service was more important than this strangling hold on the economy of the South.

The General Who Would Not Dare

AN EXPERT German officer who acted as observer with General Kuropatkin in the Russo-Japanese War was inspired by his irresolution to write that no worse commander can be found than "the leader who does not dare."[1] By late fall of 1861 many Washington observers feared that the North had such a commander. McClellan had properly insisted that thorough preparation must precede his stroke; but how did he define thoroughness?

The first great requisite was to make sure of Washington's defenses. McDowell had begun to build fortifications, and McClellan with General J. G. Barnard as chief engineer rapidly pressed the work until about fifty posts, mounting three hundred guns, surrounded the capital. The initial redoubts and forts were thrown up to protect particular points. Then, as the engineers found time, additional works were built here and there. The main forts, placed about a half-mile apart, had parapets eleven or twelve feet thick, surrounded by an abattis, but without a glacis; the guns were fired through embrasures, or from barbettes. No continuous entrenchments connected the posts.

South of the Potomac the first line of forts reached from Georgetown to Alexandria in an arc about fourteen miles long and ten miles in radius. Here, before offensive operations opened, the line included eighteen strong posts, extending from the Virginia end of the chain bridge opposite Georgetown (Fort Mary) past Arlington Heights, past the Virginia end of the Long Bridge, and on to Forts Ellsworth and Lyon in front of Alexandria. A similar chain of forts also extended around Washington on the north side of the Potomac, at distances of four to eight miles from the city. Farther south in Virginia the government commenced a second line by building forts at Munson's and Upton's Hills, but when the Confederates retreated from Manassas it decided not to extend this outer arc. British officers who inspected the fortifications were impressed by their strength and by the fact that it would require a large

[1] Colonel Gaedke quoted in N. Y. *Nation*, vol. 80 (March 16, 1905), 205.

number of troops to man them efficiently. It was plain that unless kept well garrisoned, they might be quickly penetrated and overrun.[2]

With these fortifications at his back, McClellan intended to make his army complete in all respects, perfecting its arrangements with a thoroughness that von Moltke later taught the world to call Prussian. Everywhere improvisation must give way to plan. Each item of equipment—arms, munitions, tents, blankets, clothing, food, medicines, ambulances, entrenching tools, pontoon bridges, depots of supplies, transport—was given meticulous attention. Washington marveled at the endless trains of wagons, mountainous stores, and ever finer *tenue* of the soldiers. It was McClellan's ambition to put into the field the best-organized, best-trained, best-armed, best-fed, and best-uniformed army the hemisphere—perhaps the world—had ever seen.

By fall he was well on the way to his goal. With two glaring exceptions, the surgical and hospital arrangements, and the information system, his foresight covered every prime requirement. Part of the drill he instituted was highly specialized. The engineers, for example, were taught to make trustworthy reconnaissances of the roads in front, to fix the best lines for entrenchments, to choose the most advantageous positions for battle, and to build defensive works and siege lines in the most efficient fashion. The topographical corps, starting without reliable maps of any part of Virginia, became so expert that when heavy fighting took place before Richmond, they knew as much about some of the terrain—though not about the way in which weather affected it—as the Confederates.[3] The nation was to pay heavily, however, for lack of good intelligence agencies to collect data on enemy numbers and movements, for ignorance of streams and floods, and for lack of facilities to deal with an avalanche of battle casualties.

The army reviews, held primarily to inspire confidence among the men, became more and more imposing. They impressed Americans, who traveled even from New York to see them, more than experienced European observers. Régis de Trobriand, for example, son of one of Napoleon's generals and a cosmopolite, thought that the 3000 cavalry who were reviewed September 24 were indifferently mounted, and amateurish in the formation columns and other evolutions; W. H. Russell, looking at several parades, judged the men superior to the three-month militia, but still far from being soldiers. The Washington correspondent of the New York *Times*, describing an artillery-

2 See the confidential report of Captains T. Mahon and R. Grant, and Lieutenant T. C. Price, Aug. 1, 1862, to the British Commander in Chief, Canada; War Office Files, London. These officers visited the United States May 12 to July 7, 1862, spending much time with McClellan. A map of the fortifications is in *Battles and Leaders*, I, 172.

3 General J. G. Barnard not only took able charge of the Washington fortifications, but looked after the training of volunteer engineer forces. Brigadier-General A. A. Humphreys, succeeding J. W. Macomb, was chief of topographical engineers.

cavalry review October 8 on the plain east of the Capitol, praised the troops but criticized the "dull, heavy" way McClellan managed them: "It is a stupid performance generally, and today's was an aggravation of all previous defects." Most observers, however, were delighted, and some journalists, the New York *Herald* heading the McClellan claque, were ecstatic. Bayard Taylor gives us a spirited picture of the general and troops at a late September review:

There were McDowell, Porter, Keyes, Blenker, Smith, and Marcy, all manly, gallant faces and figures of true military bearing: Cols. De Trobriand and Salm-Salm, with their dashing, chivalresque air; the Prince de Joinville, twisted and stooping, lounging on his horse; the Orleans princes with their mild, amiable faces and aspect of languid interest—in all, a most remarkable group of figures. A horse's length in advance sat the smallest man of the party, broadshouldered, strong-chested, strong-necked, and strong-jawed, one hand upon his hip, while the other, by an occasional rapid motion, flung some communication to the passing squadrons of cavalry. The visor of his cap was well pulled down over his eyes, yet not a man in the lines escaped his observation. His glance seemed to take in at once the whole spectacle, yet without losing any of its smallest details. . . . Something in his figure, his attitude, and the square, tenacious set of his jaws reminded me strikingly of Field Marshal Radetzsky. I scanned the lines of his face. . . . All was cool, prompt, determined, and self-reliant.[4]

On November 20, McClellan staged his grandest exhibition. On a broad plain eight miles from Washington in the direction of Fairfax Court House, he gathered the entire Army of the Potomac. The long columns and solid squares, a hundred thousand men marching and countermarching under waving banners as bands played, made the brightest military pageant ever seen in America. Lincoln, the Cabinet, the diplomatic corps, and thousands of spectators watched. McClellan, escorted by a staff glittering with gold lace, a bodyguard, and two regiments of regular cavalry, radiated confidence. Countless recruits that autumn day, anticipating early victory, had not the slightest premonition of the terrible years of alternate defeat and victory that were to turn the glittering volunteer force into a tougher body of veterans than Hannibal's at Cannae or Frederick's at Leuthen. Yet had they been able to look ahead, few would have quailed, and not many would have repined. Word had run through the army that the review heralded an early advance, and if they were ready to give blows, they were also ready to receive them.[5]

4 Russell, *My Diary North and South*; De Trobriand, *Four Years with the Army of the Potomac*, 89–92; N. Y. *Herald*, Oct. 9; Taylor's letter Sept. 24, 1861, in N. Y. *Weekly Tribune*, Oct. 5, 1862. W. H. Beach, *The First New York (Lincoln) Cavalry*, 50, 51, says the reviews "excited the greatest enthusiasm" among troops.
5 Theodore B. Gates, *The War of the Rebellion*, 165; N. Y. *Herald*, *Times*, Nov. 21, 22.

[I]

While McClellan was thus imparting vigor and firmness to the army, he was making two blunders, one in his treatment of Scott, and one in his mishandling of Congressional and public opinion.

No real evidence supports McClellan's subsequent complaint that Scott regarded him jealously. It is true that the old general would have preferred the appointment of Henry W. Halleck, disapproved of McClellan's large staff, and thought an army organization by brigades sufficient. But these were the legitimate views of an old-fashioned commander, whose jealousy was for his opinions and dignity only, and whose conservative nature opposed innovation. It is also true that he doubted McClellan's scares about rebel attack. By birth and training a Southerner, he was usually more courteous to men of his own section than to Northerners. But if sensitive and irascible, he was always large-hearted; he felt a high regard for McClellan's abilities, and gave him an honest welcome to his high post.[6]

Had McClellan remembered this fall that he was technically subordinate to Scott, that with all his fussy pomposity the old general had performed unforgettable services, and that courtesy evokes courtesy, friction might have been avoided. He needed but to keep the deferential spirit of his message to Scott during the West Virginia campaign: "All that I know of war I have learned from you. . . . It is my ambition to merit your praise and never to merit your censure." He had arrived in the capital convinced that he would soon supplant Scott. Had he waited patiently, the old general's infirmities would soon have removed him—but, too impatient to wait, he first began lecturing his superior, then openly ignored him, and finally affronted him.

Spoiled by years of quick success, McClellan was made more cockily self-assertive by the adulation Washington gave him. "I find myself in a new and strange position," he wrote his wife: "President, Cabinet, General Scott, and all deferring to me. By some strange operation of magic I have become the power of the land." Not *a* power, but *the* power! Visiting the Senate to press his staff bill, he was "quite overwhelmed by the congratulations I received and the respect with which I was treated." While beseeching God for wisdom, he evinced a self-confidence more than superb. "I . . . am confident that I can lead these armies to victory once more," he wrote the day after reaching Washington. A week later he was more boastful: "I shall carry this thing *en grand* and crush the rebels in one campaign." [7]

6 Elliott, *Scott*, 733. For the West Virginia campaign, Scott even wanted McClellan given a gold medal; *McClellan's Own Story*, 82. E. B. Keyes, *Fifty Years Observation*, 407, calls Scott haughty to Yankees.

7 *McClellan's Own Story*, Ch. 5, with similar statements. Students of history must

THE GENERAL WHO WOULD NOT DARE

As scores of important men spoke to him as the leader who could save the country, suggesting the Presidency or even a dictatorship, his complacency mounted to arrogance. When Scott offered his own choice for inspector-general of the army, McClellan petulantly wrote that the old general was trying "to work a traverse." A few days later, on August 8, he pushed their differences to an open breach. Mistakenly convinced that Beauregard's forces at Manassas could and would try to overwhelm the capital, he sent Scott a description of the danger and a domineering lecture on what to do about it. McClellan in fact thought that Beauregard might attack that very night, though Beauregard was completely immobilized by insufficient subsistence and want of transport.[8] Scott resentfully called McClellan in and rebuked his impertinence. From this "row" the young general strode away angrily. Scott "is always in the way," he wrote his wife; "he understands nothing, appreciates nothing." At once seeking an interview with Seward, who offered sympathy and support, McClellan followed this by visits to other Cabinet officers. Lincoln, whom he held in low esteem, he ignored.[9]

Repeating that Scott was the great obstacle, McClellan wrote his wife on August 9 (only a fortnight, be it remembered, after he reached Washington): "Tomorrow the question will probably be decided by giving me absolute control independently of him." But if he expected his Cabinet friends to produce so abrupt a dismissal of Scott, he counted without the President of the United States.

Lincoln, dismayed by this sudden quarrel, intervened. He induced McClellan to withdraw his pert letter and write Scott a conciliatory note; he induced Scott to withdraw in part a very hurt letter of August 9 to Secretary Cameron complaining bitterly of McClellan's insubordination and proffering his resignation. Had the quarrel broken into the open with publication of the two letters, it would have done Northern morale grievous damage. Scott, withdrawing his offer to resign, refused, however, to abandon his charges of insubordination and in fact added to them. The young commander, he declared, had made arrangements with some members of the Cabinet (he meant Seward, Chase, and Blair) "by whom all the greater war questions are to be settled, without report to or consultation with me, the nominal General-in-

---

always be grateful that McClellan so frankly exposed his own weaknesses in this posthumous book.

8 Beauregard, with Johnston's approval, early in August moved some brigades to the Fairfax Court House area, some advance guards even reaching the heights south of Washington. But Johnston disapproved of his idea of harassing the Union forces in order to provoke them into an attack on ground chosen by the Confederates. Roman, Beauregard, I, 131-134. It was doubtless these movements which frightened McClellan.

9 McClellan's Own Story, 84 ff.

Chief of the Army." McClellan, he added, had failed to keep him informed of troop arrivals and movements, and had frequently talked with Cabinet members on matters pertaining to Scott himself. This was true. Because McClellan had received his appointment direct from Cameron, without Scott's official endorsement, he felt that he could by-pass the usual army channels of correspondence.[10]

For weeks the bickering continued. When in mid-September the irate Scott issued a general order restricting army correspondence with the President or Secretary of War to proper channels,[11] McClellan ignored it, continuing to write directly to Cameron. He also ignored a direct order from Scott calling for returns of troops with a specification of their stations. At a later date an anonymous friend explained that he did this because he had discovered that Scott's son-in-law, Colonel Henry Lee Scott of North Carolina, serving as the general's aide, had conveyed information to the enemy; but of this grave allegation no proof was ever presented.[12] The old commander, after waiting eighteen days for a response to his order for troop returns, sent Cameron a pathetic protest. McClellan had furnished returns to the President and some cabinet officers, he wrote, but withheld them from his military superior; he deserved court-martialling.

It is not difficult to comprehend why Scott placed so high a valuation on the abilities of Halleck, which had more than a superficial glitter. While this fifty-one-year-old officer, with degrees from Union College and West Point, had never enjoyed an opportunity to show what he could do in field command, he had distinguished himself as a military theorist, an attorney, and a business administrator. Scott knew that he had talked with two of Napoleon's marshals, had studied military arrangements in France, and had written authoritatively on defense and the art of war. He knew that Halleck, quitting the army because years of effort had brought only the starvation salary of a captain of engineers, had risen so high at the California bar that he might have become judge of the State supreme court. He knew also that Halleck had dexterously seized his

---

10 Scott's letters of Aug. 9, 12, are in O. R. I, xi, pt. 3, pp. 4–6.

11 O. R. III, i, 382.

12 The text of Scott's letter is in Townsend, *Anecdotes*. The accusation against Henry L. Scott, signed "Smith" and published in the N. Y. *Tribune* of March 12, 1862, declares that the young general learned of the colonel's misconduct. "General McClellan went to the President about the extraordinary denouement, and Col. Scott and Adjt.-General Thomas, who was also suspected of treachery, were summoned to the White House to be confronted on the charge. Colonel Scott confessed his guilt! What was done? Why, Colonel Scott, instead of being shot for his treason, was allowed to be placed on the retired list for life, and to receive the pay and emoluments of a lieutenant-colonel of cavalry! He immediately went to Europe, where he is doing all he can for secession!" An anonymous charge has no weight. C. W. Elliott, *Winfield Scott*, 716, asserts the patriotic constancy of the son-in-law. McClellan, *Own Story*, does not mention him.

business opportunities, becoming head of the New Almaden quicksilver mine, and of a railroad from San Francisco to San José. When the war began he was appointed major-general of the California militia, a position from which Scott lifted him to the same rank in the regular army (August 19, 1861). Of course the old general knew nothing about his personal traits. He did not know that Halleck was essentially a manager and not a leader, a bureaucrat and not a general, whose nerve in any crisis had the strength of a frayed cobweb.[13] He devoutly hoped that Halleck would succeed him, leaving McClellan the Eastern field command.

The controversy was finally ended by Scott's continued decline in health. As his dropsy, vertigo, and paralysis increased, he became unable to attend to business for more than two hours without sleep, and was hardly able to totter from his home.[14] To the approving Cabinet on October 18 Lincoln read a delicately-phrased letter notifying Scott that although he had thus far opposed any request for retirement, he would no longer object; adding that he would sometimes apply to the general for advice, and would deal generously with his official family. It is clear that some Cabinet member told McClellan of this, for next day the young general wrote his wife that although Scott was proposing to retire in favor of Halleck, the Administration had decided to accept his resignation without that condition. McClellan had been talking about forcing the issue, and was jubilant. He, of course, as the seemingly indispensable field general, had held all the trump cards.[15]

The final scene had poignant qualities. The cabinet at an early morning meeting on November 1st agreed to a formal request from Scott to be placed on the retired list. In the afternoon it accompanied Lincoln to Scott's lodgings, where, as the general lay on his couch, the President read the formal order that was required. Helped to his feet, Scott responded, and all shook hands with emotion. That night Lincoln called on McClellan to notify him of his promotion to the post of General-in-Chief. When the President expressed the hope that the vast increase of responsibility would not be embarrassing, McClellan buoyantly assured him that it would not.

A private car was provided by the Philadelphia, Wilmington, & Baltimore for Scott, who wished to go to Europe to consult medical specialists. Next morning at four, in pitch darkness amid a drenching downpour, a distinguished group headed by Cameron and Chase came to the station to see Scott off. Among them was McClellan, to whom Scott gave polite messages for his wife and baby. In a set piece of verbal pyrotechnics, McClellan showered

13 See the estimate of Halleck in J. D. Cox, *Military Reminiscences*, I, 248–262.
14 W. H. Russell had found Scott visibly weakening before Bull Run.
15 *Own Story*, 170; see the N. Y. *Times* October 24, N. Y. *Herald* Oct. 30, 1861, as reflecting the general sentiment for McClellan.

his departing commander with eulogy, which the simple-hearted old soldier received with genuine gratitude. At the same time McClellan characteristically revealed his insincerity by writing his wife: "The [general] order *was* a little rhetorical—but I wrote it *at* him—for a particular market! It seems to have accomplished the object." [16]

One wonders what were the emotions of the old hero of Lundy's Lane and Cerro Gordo as his train rolled north, and whether his classical lore gave him any sense that McClellan might yet pay the penalty of *hubris*. The new leader's impatient tactlessness not only blotted his personal record, but carried more immediate and positive disadvantages. By angering his superior, he caused Scott to diffuse the impression in important circles that Halleck—who had never seen a real battle, who had been in business since 1854, and whose reputation rested on a book, *Elements of Military Art and Science*, published at the outbreak of the Mexican War—was a martial leader of great power. The result was that Lincoln on August 19 appointed Halleck major-general, and expected important work from him. Moreover, by colloguing with Chase, Blair, and certain Congressional leaders, McClellan gave them the idea that he was determined on prompt, forcible, and decisive fighting, from which Scott's fumbling interferences withheld him. He thus aroused anticipations the disappointment of which was to cost him dear.

[II]

"How weary I am of all this business! Care after care, blunder after blunder, trick upon trick," wrote McClellan to his wife October 25. *He* was always the victim of others' acts. After long inaction, his forces did try to strike a blow—and the result was the new disaster of Ball's Bluff, October 21, 1861, only some forty miles from Washington. It illustrated both looseness of command and tactical stupidity. Brigadier-General Charles P. Stone, a West Pointer and Mexican War veteran, had been ordered to make a "slight demonstration." He undertook neither a reconnaissance nor an advance in force, both of which would have been safe, but a risky median venture. The gallant E. D. Baker, moving with somewhat excessive impetuosity, managed to become beleaguered on the Potomac bluff that Sunday afternoon with the right wing of Stone's forces.[17]

16 Nicolay and Hay, IV, 465, 466; O. R. III, i, 613, 614; Myers, *McClellan*, 226. A. K. McClure wrote in 1892 that the inside story of Scott's retirement had never been written, and it was best that it should not be. Gideon Welles gives a vivid account of a truly terrible scene between Scott and McClellan in Lincoln's presence about Oct. 1; *Diary*, I, 240–242.
17 For Ball's Bluff, see *Battles and Leaders*, II, 123–134; Committee on Conduct of the War, 1863, Pt. II, 252–510; Swinton, *Army of the Potomac*, 75–78; J. D. Patch, *The Battle of Ball's Bluff* (1958). McClellan was moving two units, one under McCall and one under Stone, and they coordinated their activities badly. A comrade who knew Baker intimately

Ball's Bluff, with its sickening scene of Union troops falling back under relentless fire in the dusk, half-scrambling, half-tumbling down the steep clay hillside to the water, shot, bayonetted, and clubbed as they searched vainly for the few boats, fell on Northern hearts like a knell of woe. Those who saw Lincoln emerge from the War Department after learning that the beloved "Ned" Baker, one of his staunchest friends, his happy, openhearted Springfield neighbor, his firm Senate ally, was dead, never forgot the moment. The President, his face streaming with tears, groped his way through the door, stricken with griefs both private and public. Stone paid a fearful penalty as scapegoat; while criticism also fell heavily upon McClellan for the vagueness of his orders, which some thought a factor in the defeat.

The army steadily gathered strength. By late November the Union volunteer forces as a whole, east and west, all along the great front from Norfolk to Leavenworth, were surpassing the authorized level of 500,000. On the 27th of that month the War Department, which had so recently been prodding the governors to lift their enlistment levels, began sending out word that all was well. You should make no plans for more regiments, it telegraphed Morgan of New York. "When those that have been authorized are filled we will be fully supplied." Cameron in a report of December 1 to Lincoln placed the total volunteer and regular strength at 660,971; and by General Order No. 135 on December 3 he made the slowing of recruitment official throughout the North. The great feat undertaken in July seemed achieved. This new national army of half a million, moreover, was no product of thoughtless enthusiasm, of heady emotion, but a force of remarkable toughness and determination. Every volunteer of common sense now knew that he was committed to a grueling, exhausting, nerve-racking conflict of uncertain duration, in which he must run a terrible gauntlet of bullets, disease, military folly, poor food, ignorant surgeons, and traitorous equipment. But to countless young men, gladly baring their breasts to the storm of war, the perils were a challenge of which patriotic devotion made light.[18]

Actually, nobody in the War Department knew the precise number of men enlisted, and it was presently found that Cameron had seriously overestimated the total. The stoppage of enlistments was a mistake for which the country would pay dearly. But the forces in hand seemed at the moment all that could be easily raised or effectively managed.

---

wrote: "As gentle and pure and unselfish and generous and eloquent and valiant a man as ever cheerfully gave his life for a noble cause." Elijah R. Kennedy, *The Contest for California in 1861*, pp. viii, 274–275.

18 O. R. III, i, 553–616, covers Cameron's efforts to stimulate recruiting, and later to slow it down. At the beginning of October he wanted New York to bring its force up to 200,000, and later to 125,000. His report of Dec. 1 is in O. R. III, i, 699.

Of the formidable national army, McClellan held by far the greatest single part. On October 15, his rolls listed 152,051 men. Of these, the men absent, sick, and under arrest totalled 18,850, while about 12,000 more were awaiting arms and equipment. This left 121,201 present for duty; but as about 20,000 were on "extra duty" only a little more than 100,000 were ready for use in active campaigning. Even so, this was a formidable force. Moreover, the totals rose during December, so that by Christmas Day the whole number of officers and men in the Army of the Potomac was not far from 220,000. This was within hailing distance of the figure of 273,000 which McClellan had stipulated as desirable in his midsummer memorandum to Lincoln.[19]

Even in early fall—a fall of warm, dry, pleasant weather prolonged till Christmas—the Northern public began to expect McClellan to use his army, and radical politicians, journalists, and businessmen, growing restive, spoke out bluntly. Montgomery Blair became suspicious of the general. He wrote his father October 1 that the cabinet were perplexed by enemy movements, that he and his friends suspected the Confederates had little force in Virginia but made the utmost show of what they had, and that "Lincoln himself begins to think he smells a rat." Zack Chandler, his irritation rising until he concluded that McClellan was utterly incompetent, descended on Washington late in October to try either to spur the general into action, or to induce Lincoln to replace him. "Trumbull, Wade, and myself have been busy night and day since my arrival," he wrote his wife October 27, "but whether our labor has been in vain or not, time alone must disclose. . . . If Wade and I fail in our mission, the end is at hand." And in mid-December a friend of Wade's wrote him from Indianapolis: " 'Young Napoleon' is going down as fast as he went up." [20]

McClellan, however, still working like a man possessed to bring his army to a higher pitch of efficiency, now regretted his earlier intimations that he might end the war in the autumn by a single blow. Though it would seem that by the shrewd use of spies, Virginia Unionists, and Negroes he could have collected trustworthy information, he possessed no accurate intelligence service. Instead, letting himself be deceived by the reports of his friend Allan Pinkerton, an energetic Scot who had established one of the nation's first private detective agencies in Chicago eleven years earlier, and whose services the general had transplanted from business to war, he grossly exaggerated the strength of Johnston's army at Manassas. The alarmist exaggerations of Pinkerton in handling the so-called Baltimore plot against Lincoln the

19 See Ropes, I, 258, 259, with references.
20 Blair Oct. 1, 1861, Blair-Lee Papers; Chandler Oct. 27, Chandler Papers, LC; A. Denny, Indianapolis, Dec. 16 1861, to Wade, Wade Papers, LC.

previous February showed that the reports of his operatives required much closer analysis than they received. In public and private affairs alike they tended to earn their pay by exaggerated statements of peril.[21] General James M. Wadsworth, whose force lay at Centreville, had a much better intelligence system, for he interviewed Confederate fugitives, and cultivated Negro spies. All fall and early winter he begged McClellan to strike and crush the rebels before him. They numbered only about 50,000, he correctly declared, and could be swept back like chaff. General Daniel Sickles, stationed after October on the lower Potomac, also obtained "valuable and reliable" information on the enemy from Negroes, whom he found faithful and sometimes remarkably intelligent as scouts; but McClellan distrusted Negroes and refused to meddle with slaves.

McClellan now believed, too, that he would have to leave at least 30,000 men to guard Washington, with another 30,000 on the upper and lower Potomac and at Baltimore. He believed that troops who have not been given fully three months of vigorous camp drill could not be trusted to behave with discipline in offensive operations, and knew that a large part of his army was too new to possess any such preparation. Altogether, he was positive that he must wait!

In actual fact, Johnston's army even by the end of the year amounted only to 57,337 men, of whom some 10,200 were kept in the Valley, and 6250 in the Aquia district. Thus only about 41,000 were posted at Manassas. His army was subject to the same deductions of men sick, absent, confined, and on extra-duty as McClellan's.[22] It was far more poorly equipped. We find D. H. Hill writing the Confederate War Department on Christmas Day that poor shells and an entire lack of ammunition for his best gun, a captured piece, made the artillery of his little force at Leesburg "very deficient." The Confederate troops captured at Fort Hatteras late in August had been armed with old pattern muskets, many of them roughly altered from flintlock to percussion, and had used home-made caps and ammunition of poor quality.[23]

Down to the end of December, hard ground and fair skies made military movements quite practicable. With real wonderment, Johnston later wrote that although McClellan had a much superior force near at hand, he never

21 See on Pinkerton the matter in McClellan's *Report;* R. W. Rowan, *The Pinkertons;* and Allan Pinkerton, *The Spy of the Rebellion.* For Wadsworth see Pearson, *Wadsworth,* 90–103; for Sickles, *Committee on the Conduct of the War,* 1863, Pt. 3, pp. 632–643.

22 On October 23, Confederate General Order No. 15 established the Department of Northern Virginia in three districts, the Valley (Jackson), Potomac (Beauregard), and Acquia (Holmes), with Joseph E. Johnston as head of the Department. He remained with the army based on Manassas.

23 D. H. Hill, Leesburg, Dec. 25, 1861, to Adjutant-Gen. Thomas Jordan, extra-illustrated edition *Battles and Leaders,* HL; Hatteras correspondence N. Y. *Tribune* dated Aug. 31, 1861.

interrupted the Confederate military exercises; and as the Southern cavalry was bolder than the Northern, the ground between the two armies was much more open to the Confederates. Johnston was always uneasy over his comparative weakness.[24] Had McClellan advanced with energetic celerity from Arlington against Manassas, or had he made a thrust, as Lincoln proposed, from the mouth of the Occoquan against Johnston's communications, he might have forced the main Confederate army to retreat behind the Rappahannock. In doing so, the Southerners would probably have lost guns and stores which they could ill spare, and would have had to abandon the batteries they had erected on the lower Potomac—positions from which the navy had been anxious to dislodge them. These batteries were in various ways a thorn in the Union flesh. They blockaded an important river channel, raised fears of an incursion into Maryland, threw an additional strain upon the railways reaching Washington, and flaunted Confederate energy in the face of Washington.

It would have been impossible for McClellan to advance farther than the Rappahannock. But even this limited success would have quieted the rising criticism of his inaction, and put heart into the Northern people. The clearing of the Potomac could have been followed, too, by an autumn expedition to capture Norfolk, and thus to put an end to the Confederate refitting of the Merrimac. But still McClellan did nothing but drill. Even the New York Herald, his special champion, demanded that the Potomac—"the grand highway for stores and reinforcements for the Federal army in front of Washington"—be opened, but the demand was coldly ignored.[25]

The degree to which McClellan was culpable for excessive hesitancy must not be exaggerated. A grave impediment to movement was the shortage of

24 Johnston, *Narrative*, 84 ff.; Ropes, I, 260 ff.
25 N. Y. *Herald*, October 23, 1861. The Navy Department, as Gustavus V. Fox later testified, had proposed to the War Department in June that joint measures be taken to seize the key position of Matthias Point and so assure the navigation of the Potomac. Nothing was done. In August the Navy Department renewed its proposals, but again nothing was done. In October Welles and Fox once more urged the matter, for the Port Royal expedition was soon to start, and the navy wished to send the greater part of the Potomac flotilla with it. If anything was to be done to secure the free navigation of the Potomac, it must be before the flotilla left. The navy assured Lincoln and McClellan that its gunboats would take and destroy the rebel batteries then beginning to appear on the river. This effected, a sufficient number of troops should be landed at Matthias Point to fortify and hold it.
McClellan at first promised to cooperate with 4,000 men, and the navy provided the transports, and assembled its Potomac flotilla at Matthias Point. But twice after agreeing on a date McClellan disappointed the navy. The first time his excuse was that his engineers believed so large a body of men could not be landed—so he did not send them. The navy promised *it* would get them landed. The second time he gave Fox to understand that he feared the landing might bring on a general battle. Fox Papers, N. Y. Hist. Soc.; Committee on the Conduct of the War, 1863, Pt. I, pp. 5–9.

good officers. Many regimental and some division heads were feeble reeds, and most of the men he was considering as corps commanders had never handled a thousand troops before the war. Another impediment was the rawness of numbers of the volunteers, who as W. H. Russell flatly put it, were not yet soldiers. Finally, the question of arms was paramount. Many muskets and part of the ammunition were more dangerous to the holder than to the enemy, while down to December the quantities of both were insufficient. McClellan might well decline any large-scale movement, especially as winter mud and snow could arrive any day. Nevertheless, he should have marched to Manassas, should have cleared the Potomac, and should have forced the enemy out of Norfolk. John G. Barnard, chief of engineers, was as emphatic on this as General James M. Wadsworth. General John E. Wool at Fort Monroe was equally realistic.[26]

As the opening of Congress approached in December the grumbling deepened. Senators Chandler, Wade, and Trumbull, whom John Hay already termed the heads of a Jacobin Club, had been badgering Lincoln to insist on a battle. They felt betrayed, for when they had assailed Scott as feeble, they had promised their friends that McClellan would move promptly. National morale, they told Lincoln, required a show of energy; delay would be as bad as defeat. Greeley was thundering in the *Tribune* that McClellan's inaction had allowed the rebels to close the Potomac east of Washington, and disrupt the Baltimore & Ohio west of the city. Already these Republicans had a suspicion that McClellan was letting politics color his military policy. They perhaps heard reports of such letters as that which he wrote his Democratic friend S. L. M. Barlow on November 8—a missive of the first importance in the light it throws on his thinking. After expatiating on Confederate strength and Union weakness, and declaring that he would "pay no attention to popular clamor," he went on:

I expect to fight a terrible battle. I know full well the capacity of the generals opposed to me, for by a singular chance they were once my most intimate friends.—tho' we can never meet except as mortal foes hereafter. I appreciate too the courage and discipline of the rebel troops. . . . When I am ready I shall move without regard to season or weather—I can overcome *these* difficulties. . . . But of one thing you may rest assured—when the blow *is* struck it will be heavy, rapid, and decisive.

26 Barnard wrote in his report at the close of the Peninsular campaign: "In the winter of 1861 and 1862, Norfolk could and should have been taken. The navy demanded it, the country demanded it, and the means were ample." Wool wrote Stanton February 27, 1862, that Fort Monroe was the proper base from which to assail Richmond. "The rebel army at Manassas ought not to escape capture. It does not amount to more than 30,000 men—at most 35,000 at both Manassas and Centreville." Copy in Hay Papers, Illinois State Hist. Library.

Help me to dodge the nigger—we want nothing to do with him. *I* am fighting to preserve the integrity of the Union and the power of the Govt—on no other issue. To gain that end we cannot afford to mix up the negro question—it must be incidental and subsidiary. The President is perfectly honest and is really sound on the nigger question. I will answer for it now that things go right with him.

As far as you can, keep the papers and the politicians from running over me—that speech that some rascal made the other day that I did *not dare* to advance, and had said so, was a lie. I have always said, when it was necessary to say anything, that I was not yet strong enough, but did the public service require it, I would *dare* to advance with 10,000 men and throw my life in the balance.[27]

Already Zack Chandler and Ben Wade were urging the enlistment of Negroes as soldiers; already they and others were hoping to make the extirpation of slavery a primary result of the war. The press was beginning to debate these demands. Bryant, Greeley, and Medill were urging emancipation; on the other side, the Philadelphia *Evening Journal*, a moderate Democratic sheet, was indicting the Abolitionists as men whose views would lengthen and embitter the conflict. The real struggle in the South, it declared, would be between aristocracy and democracy, not between slavery and freedom. "As affairs have now turned, the disenthralment of the poor white people of the slaveholding States has thrown entirely into the shade the worn-out question of Negro emancipation. . . . It is now becoming apparent that the population of Haiti by the colored people of the country will prove the ultimate and practical solution of the question." [28]

To the Chandlers and Wades such talk was unreal. They meant by hard blows military and political to revolutionize the South. Their violence of language was outrageous and inexcusable.[29] Much saner men, however, were convinced that the high financial costs, the danger of foreign intervention, and the importance of removing the sting of recent defeats, made bold aggressive action imperative. "Let us end the war!" cried the New York *Tribune* on December 18, declaring that winter was the best fighting season in the South. "The offensive," later wrote General Fry, "was demanded from all quarters, and in all ways." [30]

27 Barlow Papers.
28 October 21, 1861.
29 Chandler's letters this fall approached hysteria. "If we fail in getting a battle here now all is lost," he wrote his wife October 27, "and up to this time a fight is scarcely contemplated. Washington is safe. . . . therefore let the country go to the devil. If the South had one-tenth our resources Jeff Davis would today be in Philadelphia." In another letter he remarked that it might be better if the rebels really took Washington, President, Cabinet, and all, for then the true men would make proper use of the nation's powers. Chandler Papers, LC.
30 *Century Magazine*, vol. 48 (Oct., 1894), 931–946.

It was not only McClellan's caution, his perfectionism, and his readiness to exaggerate enemy strength while underrating his own, that was responsible for his immobility, for an even more important factor was involved. Already he was displaying a myopic indifference to those great forces of politics and public opinion which no democratic commander can neglect save at his peril. In a letter the day before he replaced Scott he lashed out at "the impatience of the people, the venality and bad faith of the politicians, the gross neglect that has occurred in obtaining arms, clothing, etc." But in a people's war, the people and their political delegates must be regarded. As they must not make excessively severe demands on military leadership, so military leaders must not make excessively severe demands on them.

In a public speech soon after reaching Washington, McClellan had promised a war short, sharp, and decisive. During his early rides south of the Potomac, he used to point toward the flank of Manassas and say to General McDowell: "We shall strike them there." [31] It was his duty to take account of the morale of the country as well as of the army. By Thanksgiving and still more by Christmas, the nation which had put such implicit faith in him felt it had a right to ask some justification for their faith. For the people were not content, any more than their British cousins in the Crimean conflict had been, to leave all decisions blindly to their military captains; as the historian of the Crimea had written, they "thronged in, and made their voice heard, and became partakers of the councils of state."

But while the East waited, in the Western theater a yet more remarkable series of events had been taking place; events both dramatic and momentous.

31 Swinton, *Army of the Potomac*, 69; McClellan's *Own Story*, 166–177.

16

Frémont and the Impossible Task

THE NORTH by the summer of 1861, as we have seen, had done more than enter upon a grim war effort. It and indeed the whole country had entered upon a revolution. Never before had the American people dreamed of such a mighty effort of organization as that required by the mustering of a volunteer army of half a million, and the commissioning of a tremendous fleet. No government, after such an effort, could ever sink back to the old level of small enterprises pettily pursued. Behind the drilling troops and scurrying ships new industries were taking form, new factories were belching smoke, banks, stores, and warehouses were being enlarged to seize new opportunities, and the wheels of transport were turning with new speed. Novel sources of credit, novel government contracts, and novel concepts of large-scale effort were transforming business and society.

Had some miracle of compromise ended the war in the summer of 1861, the country would have emerged with but minor changes in non-political fields. Bull Run had made it certain that a considerable socio-economic revolution would occur. If the mighty military effort planned for 1862 succeeded, it would be merely considerable. But if it failed, and the conflict continued, the country would face a major revolution, altering many of the organic functions of society. How deep such a revolution might reach, and what social agonies it might involve, first became evident to observers of events in the Western theatre, and especially in Missouri.

The Western situation differed completely from the Eastern in a half-dozen respects. Fighting raged in States—Missouri, Kentucky, Tennessee—whose people were implacably divided; in areas, therefore, where searing hatreds soon generated a vicious guerrilla warfare. In this region long Union lines had to be held: the Missouri River from Kansas City to its mouth, the Mississippi from Quincy to Cairo, the railroad from St. Louis to Rolla, and the Ohio River. The theatre was distant from Washington, the major arsenals, and the centers of greatest population and wealth. Here was the area where commanders first had to come to real grips with slavery. Here, military

306

jealousies showed their worst early forms, and here politics most seriously complicated the military effort. A rougher, harsher temper, derived partly from frontier individualism, pervaded the struggle.

The West required a commander who possessed great political skill as well as military ability. In Missouri he would have to rally loyal elements while repressing the disloyal men intermingled with them; in Kentucky he would have to evince a scrupulous respect for those who supported State neutrality. He would have to deal with difficult political leaders—one in particular. Frank P. Blair, who had thus far led the Union movement in Missouri with more drive than discretion, cherished high political ambitions. Valuing greatly his seat in Congress and chairmanship of the military affairs committee, he did not yet aim at a military command, for which he had no experience whatever. He expected, however, to be the main power in Missouri; and as the first freesoil man elected to Congress from a slave State, co-leader with Edward Bates of the Republican Party there in 1860, and the most brilliant orator of the area, he already possessed national renown and influence. The commander would have to defer to him, or risk the consequences—and he had a most imperious temper. The commander would also have to get along with governors of complex psychology, like Yates of Illinois and Kirkland of Iowa, keeping their confidence, meeting their wants, and enlisting their aid. Nathaniel Lyon had made so many enemies both in Washington and Missouri that he was impossible.

McClellan despised politicians, but the Western commander could afford no such attitude.

[I]

For this post of double danger Lincoln, pressed by the Blair family, selected a man of few military and no political qualifications—John C. Frémont. That Frémont had never commanded more than the few hundred men of his California Battalion, and they briefly and controversially, might not be a crippling disability; very few American officers had led a larger body. That as Senator from California and first Republican Presidential candidate he had shown no political flair was not important; he had been a novice. What did matter was that Lincoln should ignore Frémont's erratic career.

Frémont had indubitably proved himself an explorer of high distinction. Brilliantly intelligent, energetic, daring, and able to inspire expeditions with his own enthusiasm, he had united scientific skill with the ability to endure prolonged hardship. A pathmarker, not pathfinder, he had traversed, mapped, and described great areas of the West in a way that did the nation important service. His knowledge of mathematics, zoology, botany, astronomy, and geology outran that of other famous Western explorers; he wrote with a color and narrative interest that his best rivals hardly approached. The man who had climbed the Wind River Range, discovered Lake Tahoe, scaled the Sierras in midwinter, given the Golden Gate its name, and penned a book which guided the Mormons into Salt Lake Valley, deserved his first fame. The role he had played in the conquest and early government of California, while often indiscreet and at times calculating, contained some heroic pages; and his Presidential candidacy emphasized his rigid freesoil principles.[1]

Close scrutiny of his career, however, disclosed an impetuosity that had repeatedly brought him to the verge of disaster, a want of judgment that disturbed his friends, and a willingness to invade dubious ground for personal advantage. Although cultured, sensitive, and quietly attractive, he had made an equivocal impression. Because he grasped at prizes, such as the civil governorship of California, which he had not honestly earned, he appeared a little the charlatan; because he tempted fortune in so many fields, sometimes failing tragically, as in the fifth expedition, and sometimes succeeding magnificently, as when he emerged from his famous court-martial to find the California senatorship and rich Mariposa estate in his hands, he seemed a little the adventurer. Though he did useful work in helping open the West, all his other labors had an illusory value. While some intimates of great discernment and honesty, like Jessie Benton, Horace Greeley, and Kit Carson, felt a lifelong devotion to him, other people thought that his character was *au fond* questionable. In 1860 he was still a hero to millions of Americans, the recent titular leader of the Republican Party, and a figure of international renown. The Lincoln Administration had to employ him; but why in a post of such multifarious difficulties?

Frémont would have preferred the ministership to France, where his knowledge of the country, fluency in its tongue, and social brilliancy, with the charm of his wife Jessie, would have made him far more successful than the political hack whom Lincoln appointed. The Blairs, after failing to get Lyon the chief command, could have found a West Point man for Missouri. But Frémont and Jessie were old favorites whom they expected to control in Frank's interest and therefore pushed forward. Eager to serve, and convinced that his Western marches qualified him for command, he accepted. When war began he had been in Europe on business, and had shown creditable energy by contracting for $75,000 worth of ordnance and shells and 10,000

[1] See the author's volumes on Frémont, and especially the third edition of the biography, with the new material on the Civil War in the terminal chapter.

rifles at his personal charge if necessary. He reached Boston June 27 and reported forthwith to Lincoln.

Within less than a week after he landed, on July 3, the government created the Western Department, including not only Illinois and all the States and Territories between the Mississippi and Rockies, but Kentucky as soon as it was safe.[2] It should have taken this action at an earlier date. The fact was that Washington showed a censurable myopia concerning the West, and persisted in it. Once Frémont was appointed he might well have hurried West more promptly. He had his reasons for tarrying—he could learn more about the huge department, covering a third of the nation, in Washington than in St. Louis; when he was about to leave on July 16th or 17th he was told that Scott had further instructions for him; he talked with Governor Yates in Washington, learning that 7000 Illinois infantry were totally unarmed, the cavalry without mounts, and the artillery with few guns; he labored to assemble a staff, and obtain firearms and stores for his destitute forces. But Lincoln became disturbed by the delay. In the end he went West with vague orders and inadequate resources.

The President, Scott, and he agreed that the grand objective, once Missouri was cleared, would be a movement down the Mississippi to Memphis. Lincoln, after consulting with him in the kindliest way, escorted him down the White House steps, saying: "I have given you carte blanche; you must use your own judgment and do the best you can." Thus blithely did the overburdened government entrust the heaviest responsibilities to an untried man, and speak of seizing a river which it was to take two years of heavy fighting to clear![3]

When Frémont reached Missouri on July 25 he found the Western Department boiling with confusion, shortages, dissension, and perils. The State had far more white manpower of military age than Virginia, and as much as Kentucky and Arkansas combined. It was more fiercely divided among

2 From July 3 to Nov. 9, 1861, the Western Department comprised Illinois, Missouri, Iowa, Kansas, Minnesota, Arkansas, Nebraska Territory, Colorado Territory, Dakota Territory and for a time a portion of Kentucky. Indiana and Ohio were in the Department of Ohio; Wisconsin temporarily in no department. Frederick Phisterer, *Statistical Record*, 24-49.

3 Frémont, MS Memoirs, Bancroft Library. Frémont told the Committee on the Conduct of the War that his instructions were vaguely broad, embracing "full discretionary powers of the amplest kind," and that "when I was ready to descend the river I was to let the President know." Montgomery and Frank Blair, though suspect witnesses, doubtless testified correctly to the Committee on Lincoln's uneasiness over Frémont's delay; *Report*, 1863, Pt. 3, pp. 154-186. Rutherford B. Hayes's impressions of Frémont, who reviewed Ohio troops at Camp Chase on his way west, suggest why a high appointment for the explorer was a political necessity. "All his words and acts inspire enthusiasm and confidence," wrote Hayes after a chat, adding: "He is loyal, brave, and persevering beyond compare"; *Diary and Letters*, II, 43.

Southern-born, Northern-born, and foreign-born than any other in the country. Largely ignored by the War Department, it was slipping into a dangerous set of complications.

We have seen that full war had begun in Missouri before mid-June, when General Nathaniel Lyon had arrogantly told Sterling Price that before he made a single concession to the rebels, he would see every man, woman, and child in the State buried. Lyon immediately sent Colonel Franz Sigel to occupy southwestern Missouri, while he himself marched to Jefferson City, the capital, on June 15, and two days later took Boonville in an almost bloodless skirmish. But the Confederates showed equal energy. Governor Claiborne Jackson, resolute and resourceful, issued a call for fifty thousand volunteers to resist the Union "invasion." At Carthage on July 5 his gathering volunteers repulsed Sigel and forced him to retreat. Price, who had been a brigadier-general in the Mexican War, was ready to take the field with the State troops, reinforced by several thousand Confederate soldiers from Arkansas, Louisiana, and Texas under Ben McCulloch, a hard-riding, quick-shooting Texas ranger who had also served in Mexico. Encouraged by the smart victory at Carthage and the news of Bull Run, the Confederate and State forces by the time of Frémont's arrival raised their main army to 10,000 or 11,000 men.

Meanwhile irregular warfare covered half the State. The precipitate actions of Frank Blair and Lyon exposed the loyal population to guerrilla bands and marauders. Some 300 home guard men, driven from Knox and Lewis Counties into Hudson City at the beginning of July, reported that a force of 2700 rebels, chiefly mounted, were seizing food, arms, livestock, and clothing. In other areas Union men were being expelled from their homes. Small, undisciplined, badly-led bands of secessionists, animated by implacable hatred of the North, roved the countrysides. When Union forces appeared, they would separate; little groups would shoot stray soldiers, burn bridges, or waylay loyal farmers; then they would reunite. Particularly in the proslavery counties belting the Missouri River all the way across the State, the most ferocious feeling reigned. Neighbor armed against neighbor in an atmosphere of spreading terror.

The tension laid an iron grip on St. Louis, a Southern city which had recently become a metropolis of freedom for the State. Of its 160,000 people, more than one in four had been born in Germany, more than 30,000 in Ireland, and more than 21,000 in the free States; most of the forces of industry, commerce, and finance were inimical to slavery. Nevertheless, the old aristocratic families, Southern-born men of social position, and some wealthy business leaders, were Confederate in sentiment. Either openly or secretly secessionist, they gave their tone to clubs, restaurants, and drawing-rooms, lent business support to their kind, and influenced their employees. Since the breakup of Camp Jackson and the clashes between German recruits and the people, the malignity of some Southern sympathizers broke all bounds. Women were more rancorous than the men, and even ministers of the gospel spread hatred. After the victory at Carthage one secessionist jubilantly told a free-soil leader: "There is a bullet moulded for every Yankee sympathizer in St. Louis." [4]

Over the Berthold mansion in late July, conspicuous in the heart of the city, flew a Confederate flag, beneath whose folds recruits openly enlisted for the Confederate cause. The streets were bare of Union banners; city authorities were afraid to intervene against rebel activities; danger that the roughest of the unemployed Irish, aided by Southerners, would mount an insurrection, impressed all observers. The German and Yankee volunteers, a determined but undisciplined body of men, would have met such a rising implacably. "Arouse their enthusiasm," Gustave Koerner had written Lyman Trumbull, "and they are uncontrollable." [5] As Lyon had kindled their fervor, so later would Frémont. But bloody civil commotions in St. Louis, the principal Union base for the whole region, were at all costs to be avoided.

[II]

To this angrily divided city and State, humming like a hornet's nest, Frémont was ferried across the Mississippi at nine A.M. on July 25, to convoke a staff meeting at noon. It gave him alarming intelligence. The enemy had their troubles: their State and Confederate troops were separate and often discordant forces, they were ill-armed, and they suffered from Richmond's neglect as the Unionists suffered from Washington's. But Price and Mc-Culloch could concentrate their growing forces in a way that kept the Union commands, necessarily scattered, on the defensive. Lyon was at Springfield with about 7800 men, including Sigel's defeated troops; Brigadier-General John Pope commanded most of the troops north of the Missouri River; and Brigadier-General Benjamin M. Prentiss, a Mexican War veteran, had a weak contingent at Cairo. All three badly wanted reinforcements and supplies. On Frémont's desk lay a telegram from Prentiss, for example, reciting that he had only eight regiments, six of them three-months' men whose term was then

4 The MS Autobiography of Charles D. Drake, later Senator from Missouri, is indispensable (Mo. Hist. Soc.). W. L. Broaddus, Hudson City, July 5, describes the situation there; Broaddus Papers, Duke Univ. See also Snead, *The Fight for Missouri*, 99 ff. (anti-Blair); W. G. Eliot in Nevins, *Frémont*, 542 ff.; R. J. Rombauer, *The Union Cause in St. Louis, 1861, passim;* Galusha Anderson, *The Story of a Border City.*
5 Koerner, May 31, Trumbull Papers, LC.

expiring, and desperately needed more to hold his vital point. Lyon's force, rapidly diminishing, also threatened to disappear if the three-months' men left; he was naturally anxious to fight before they quit. Many were without shoes. Food, wagons, medicines, uniforms, but above all arms were wanting. "Our troops have not been paid," Frémont wrote Lincoln July 30, "and some regiments are in a state of mutiny, and the men whose term of service is expired generally refuse to enlist."

Had Washington created its Western Department as soon as hostilities opened, by June 20; had it brought Frémont home earlier, or put someone else in St. Louis betimes; had it paid closer attention to the West, the lowering storm might have been met. Yates, Morton, and other governors had been quite as strenuous as their Eastern compeers in getting men enlisted and brought into State camps; but up to the belated hour of Frémont's arrival too little had been done to assemble, arm, and drill them.

It may seem anomalous that the Confederates in Missouri were able to concentrate more efficiently than the Union forces. The explanation lies partly in the geographical situation of Missouri as an exposed salient, partly in the fierce secessionist passions that Blair and Lyon had aroused, and partly in confused Northern leadership. From southern Kansas, Arkansas, Tennessee, and Kentucky, all contiguous, the Confederates could bring what troops they had—which were few—to aid the Missouri volunteers. Meanwhile, the Union command had, as we have noted, to hold the Missouri River and its hostile belt, the Mississippi to Cairo, the Ohio to Louisville, and three railways, one running to Sedalia three-fourths of the way across the State, one southwest to Rolla, almost halfway across, and a third south to Ironton, also halfway across. It had to hold three vital centers, Jefferson City, St. Louis, and Cairo. All this meant overextended lines. And between Frank Blair's departure for Congress about July 1 and Frémont's arrival three weeks later, Lyon had done nothing to pull the situation together, for he was preoccupied with his own little army. Washington looked on aloof.[6]

Rather, Washington looked the other way! Frémont, rebuffed July 29 when he asked the Treasury office in St. Louis to allot his paymaster some funds, sent urgent telegrams to Montgomery Blair. Reaching Washington just after Bull Run, they fell on deaf ears. "I . . . find it impossible now to get any attention to Missouri or western matters from the authorities here," wired Blair. Jessie Frémont begged permission to hurry to the capital and tell Lincoln of the defenseless condition of the West, but her husband refused. Coming through Ohio, they had met Western troops on their way to the Potomac.

6 *Battles and Leaders*, I, 278 ff.; Nicolay and Hay, IV, Ch. 23; Smith, *Blair Family*, II, 59 ff.; O. R. I, iii, 617 ff.; Nevins, *Frémont*, Ch. 29; Drake, MS Autobiography.

THE FIELD
OF OPERATIONS
IN MISSOURI

In St. Louis she found troops only on paper, an arsenal without arms or ammunition, the enemy thick and unremitting as mosquitoes. If only she could get to the President!—"a Western man and not grown in red tape." But her letters to Washington accomplished nothing. She wrote Montgomery Blair four days after reaching St. Louis that her husband was overwhelmed:

He is doing the best he can without money without arms without moral aid. This city needs a force to repress it. All the arms and well equipped men of Ohio and Indiana we met moving *to the East.* Mr. Frémont says send anything in the shape of arms—but arms we must have. Send money, and both arms and money by the most rapid conveyance.

Frémont sounded the same desperate note in a letter to Blair July 31:

I begin to move today but am distressed by singular inadequacy and scarcity of equipment and great want of arms. At this moment I learn from the Adjutant that two regiments are refusing to move—refusing pay unless they get the whole. My boats have fires up and my movements are checked by this most inopportune lack of money. . . . One regiment had to be compelled to go to Ironton today by arresting officers—it had been in a state of mutiny all day.[7]

7 Jessie Frémont, July 28, Frémont July 31, to Montgomery Blair, Blair Papers, LC.

Frémont had not only to make bricks without straw, but to throw these bricks into hastily improvised walls. Into his first ten days he crowded a series of urgent measures. He policed St. Louis thoroughly, stopping Confederate enlistments at the Berthold mansion, clearing the saloons of soldiers, giving Union residents security, and enforcing rigid drill. Booksellers reported a rising demand for Hardee's *Tactics* and like books. He reorganized the home guard in St. Louis, enlisting men for the war in infantry, cavalry, and artillery divisions. He seized possession of the railroads to Rolla and Ironton, and sent small detachments to protect them. He garrisoned Ironton with a force under Colonel B. Gratz Brown, secured Cape Girardeau, and ordered Pope to organize local committees of safety north of the Missouri to stop guerrilla activities. He *took* from the paralyzed Treasury office in St. Louis $100,000 needed to pay troops. "I have infused energy and activity into the department," he wrote Lincoln, praising the spirit of his forces.[8]

At the outset he had to make a momentous decision. Imminent danger threatened both Lyon at Springfield in southwestern Missouri, and Prentiss at Cairo; he could not adequately reinforce both; and he chose to help Prentiss. Beyond question Cairo was the more important position. Real danger existed that the rebels would sweep all lower Missouri, seize Cairo by a sudden stroke, carry Kentucky into the Confederacy, and rally their sympathizers in southern Illinois and Indiana. If they succeeded in this, they might virtually win the war. Major-General Leonidas Polk, commanding the Confederates at Memphis, had prepared early in July to invade Missouri for a broad-fronted campaign. While McCulloch proceeded against Lyon at Springfield, columns under General Gideon Pillow and W. J. Hardee were to march up the Mississippi, cut off Lyon's retreat, take St. Louis if possible, and on their return to enter Illinois and capture Cairo. This was too grandiose a plan to be practicable. Nevertheless, at the very time Frémont arrived in St. Louis, Polk moved 6000 troops up to New Madrid, Missouri, full of enthusiasm and eager to attack. On July 29, the frightened Prentiss informed Frémont that more than 12,000 Confederates lay within fifty miles of his puny force. On August 1 he telegraphed that Pillow had 11,000 men at New Madrid and was about to be reinforced by 9000 more.

Even if these figures were cut in half, or in three, Cairo was in peril. Lyon was also telegraphing that he wanted "soldiers-soldiers-soldiers." But Lyon could retreat, and Prentiss with his little force could not.

Sending word to Lyon that he had best fall back to his railhead at Rolla, Frémont correctly decided to hurry reinforcements to the vital confluence of the Ohio and Mississippi. Amid the other labors of this first week, he char-

8 O. R. I, iii, 416 ff.; Frémont wrote Lincoln July 30.

tered eight steamboats, loaded them with soldiers, artillery, and stores, and set off down the river. He had hardly slept. Five P.M. on August 2 found his 4000 men landing amid wild cheers at the Cairo wharves. They had come in the nick of time, for Prentiss's force was fast disintegrating. Poorly fed, badly clothed, and only partially supplied with tents, it was suffering from the malarial fever and dysentery that ran rife in its swampy position. Now they could be paid, properly armed (for Frémont was able to bring west some of the equipment he had bought in Europe) and reënlisted. From that hour Cairo was never again in danger.[9]

But Lyon had been left unaided. Frémont was able to order two regiments from Rolla and Boonville, with James Montgomery's small force in Leavenworth, to join him, but their arrival would take time. The consequence was that little over a fortnight after Frémont took up his duties, Lyon came to disaster—and Lyon was a favorite of Frank Blair.

That this disaster was wholly needless there can be little question. Though the Confederate army which marched on Lyon numbered only 13,000 ill-trained, poorly armed men, it was far stronger than his own force of about 5000. It included a large mounted force which fetched it fresh horses and provisions without interference. Lyon's duty, as Ben McCulloch approached Springfield, was to retreat and save his army. His second in command, John M. Schofield, argued this with almost insubordinate vehemence. As he pointed out, while a victory was possible, it was not probable; defeat would sacrifice many lives and much valuable material; and the road back to Rolla was open and safe as late as the night of August 9th. Once Lyon joined the Union troops at Rolla, he could soon build up a strength sufficient to drive McCulloch out of the State. "This, I doubt not," wrote Schofield years later, "must be the judgment of history." Frémont for his part expected Lyon to fall back to meet his reinforcements. On August 6 he sent him instructions that if he were not strong enough to maintain his position, he should retreat until met by fresh detachments; and to a messenger from Lyon he said bluntly, "If he fights, it will be upon his own responsibility."

But Lyon was proud, pugnacious, and headstrong. He exaggerated both the perils of the retreat, and the disaster to loyal citizens if he abandoned them to Confederate wrath; and, stung by being passed over for the chief command,

9 O. R. I, iii, 416–437, cover the main Missouri events; *Comm. on the Conduct of the War*, 1863, pp. 3, 35 ff.; Frémont, MS Memoirs, Bancroft Library; Nevins, *Frémont*; Blair Papers, LC. News of Confederate movements toward Cairo reached the North through the New Albany (Indiana) *Ledger*, which had correspondents in Tennessee, Arkansas, and Southern Missouri. It reported in late July that 12,000 troops had crossed the Mississippi to New Madrid, where they would be joined by others from the three States named, with artillery, to make a swift attack on Cairo. The *National Intelligencer* of August 6 congratulated Frémont on opportunely rescuing Cairo.

he indulged an unworthy jealousy of his superior—his failure to get reinforcements seemed to him, says Schofield, "due to a plan to sacrifice him to another." Of course Frémont might have sent him a peremptory order. But the newly-arrived general deferred to Lyon's West Point education, knowledge of the local situation, and superior information on the enemy's capacities. On the 10th Lyon attacked at Wilson's Creek.

It was a characteristically confused, disorganized battle, the encounter of two badly armed mobs. McCulloch and Price had barely completed the distribution of their men into companies and regiments. Their troops were in great part armed only with the hunting rifles and shotguns they had brought from home. "We have an average of only twenty-five rounds of ammunition to the man," later wrote McCulloch, "and no more to be had short of Fort Smith and Baton Rouge." Not one Confederate in four had anything better than a cotton bag for his ammunition, so that a good shower would almost have disarmed the troops. They had to live on the country. Lyon, deciding to move upon the Confederates in their positions at dawn, lost the advantage of his long-range rifled muskets, and of the fact that later in the day thousands of Confederates would have been absent from the camp foraging. He used a bad battle plan devised by Sigel. Even so, the Union troops seemed winning until a Confederate battery opened on Sigel with heavy effect. Long lines of men battled at close range amid clouds of billowing smoke. In the mêlée a Confederate ball pierced Lyon's breast, and a few minutes later the surviving Union officers, after a hasty council, ordered a retreat.[10] Colonel John M. Palmer delivered his verdict in a letter to his wife: "The truth is that the battle of Wilson's Creek was a folly which the gallant death of Gen. Lyon does not atone for." [11]

The immediate result was an intensification of guerrilla warfare in central and northern Missouri, and an augmentation of Confederate strength. Frémont at once telegraphed Yates, Morton, and Dennison, with the adjutant-general of Iowa, to send him all their disposable forces. He pushed forward plans to fortify St. Louis so that smaller forces might hold it. From New York he ordered arms by fast freight "without further bargaining." He planned that while the remnants of Lyon's army rested and recruited at Rolla, he would occupy all the principal Missouri River towns by the new volunteer army, fortify Ironton, and garrison Warsaw on the Osage River. As soon as he could collect a strong army, he meant to march on Springfield again, and drive the Confederates out of southwestern Missouri into Arkansas. Lincoln,

10 Scofield, *Forty-Six Years*, 40 ff.; Frémont, MS Memoirs; McCulloch, Report dated Dec. 22, 1861, *Mo. Hist. Review*, Vol. XXVI, 354 ff.; Snead, 253.
11 Palmer August 15, 17, 1861, to his wife, describes the battle, Palmer Papers III. State Hist. Lib.

the War Department, and Montgomery Blair, shocked by Lyon's defeat, promised to do everything possible in his behalf.[12]

[III]

It is clear that Frémont found rough work in his first twenty days in Missouri—and his road got rougher and stonier at every step. His initial hardships grew out of the fact that Blair and Lyon had pushed Missouri into full war prematurely, that Washington had made practically no preparations in the West, that the War Department continued to think primarily of the East, and that in Lyon he had a rash subordinate. Thus far the story was simple, but now it grew fearfully, weirdly, calamitously complicated. To comprehend it we must understand the greenness of the troops, the lack of supplies, the difficulties of the contract problem, the bad officer morale, and the political aims of the Blairs. All these difficulties were heightened by his own blunders and miscalculations.

When appointed, Frémont was allowed only three aides from the army line, but the law of August 5 permitted him as major-general to nominate as large a staff as he needed. Lacking McClellan's advantages in choosing old regular-army friends, he gradually assembled a competent group of men, largely of foreign experience.[13] His chief of staff was Brigadier-General A. Asboth, a veteran of Kossuth's revolt, whom John A. Dix pronounced "a very able man as an engineer," and a good planner, "very intelligent on general subjects." He was hardworking and systematic. Asboth chose as personal aid Colonel Anselm Albert, an officer of fourteen years' experience in the Austrian army, of sound executive ability. The duties of adjutant were entrusted to Chauncey McKeever, and those of quartermaster-general to Major Justus McKinstry. The chief topographical engineer was Colonel John T. Fiala, capable in his field. The military secretary was a young chaplain, John H. Eaton, who would later make a creditable record in care of the freedmen and in education. A Cincinnati attorney of note, R. M. Corwine, joined Frémont as judge-advocate, to pass on the many arrests in Missouri, high and low, for disloyalty; and Lincoln himself later assured Stanton that he had done valuable service.

Competent as it was, the staff had in its foreign coloration one pronounced defect: It could give Frémont, himself unfamiliar with many sides of Ameri-

12 Comm. on Conduct of the War, *Report*, 1863, Pt. 3, pp. 110–114. One regiment Frémont wanted was stopped at Louisville as needed there, and another sent to Virginia; *Ibid.*, 117.

13 General Orders No. 15 announced to the staff, St. Louis, September 20; copy in McClernand Papers, Ill. State Library.

can life, little practical counsel in a situation full of political problems. Nor were the civilian aides who nominated themselves to his staff much more helpful. One was Owen Lovejoy, an abolitionist clergyman who had been a Republican member of Congress from northern Illinois since 1857; able, idealistic, and full of learning, humor, and eloquence, but fanatical on slavery. Another was Gustave Koerner, who had fled from the Frankfurt revolt of 1833 to become one of the founders of the "Latin settlement" (he held a Heidelberg doctorate) at Belleville, Illinois, and who after a term on the State supreme court had been elected lieutenant-governor. Still another was William Dorsheimer of Buffalo, a bright young German-American lawyer. Most important of all was Jessie, indefatigably busy, full of ideas, and as impetuous as her husband. This group had an earnest, radical, and impractical stamp.

The new commander toiled day and night, shutting himself all too rigidly away from time-wasting callers. While McClellan spent whole days in the saddle, Frémont stuck closely to his desk, for he had no War Department at hand to assist him, and no such experienced officer as Montgomery C. Meigs to lift part of his burden. For five weeks, according to one of his best aides, he never went farther from the door of his combined residence and headquarters than the sidewalk.[14]

Volunteer regiments swept into St. Louis by train, by steamboat, and afoot, as they swept into Washington. Their greenness was incredible. "The new levies," lamented Frémont, "are literally the rawest ever got together." Officers reported them "entirely unacquainted with the rudiments of military exercises." How could he drill the mob? When he asked permission to scour the nation for veteran officers, Cameron gave it. Not only did he collect a considerable number of drillmasters, but he created a special infantry unit, the Benton Cadets, which he expected to make a school for infantry officers just as his so-called Frémont bodyguard was a school for cavalry officers. Asboth was highly efficient in seeing that the new regiments drilled hard, steadily, and with growing precision. One of Frémont's plans was to form in each regiment a company of sharpshooters which would include the best marksmen, and a company of pioneers to include the most skilled mechanics.

Yet as the flood of volunteers rolled in from all parts of the Northwest, the difficulties grew. Confusion, wrote John Pope from St. Louis August 22, "is worse confounded every moment by the arrival without previous notice of regiments from every Western State in a condition of ignorance and

14 Comm. on the Conduct of the War, *ut supra*, 20 ff. See the *National Intelligencer*, August 20, 1861, for some of Frémont's organizational plans.

greenness altogether appalling. They are sent out to camp on the outskirts of the city without knowledge of their duties and with no one to instruct them in even the most ordinary details of service." [15] Other regiments went to interior railheads. These termini, Pope continued, "have become the seat of a struggling, disorganized mass of men who are swarming among and over each other like ants, and who are organized with the title of a 'military force.' What will be the result when it is attempted to move these disorderly bands forward for action will be hard to say." The Northwestern States had less of a militia tradition than the East, and no such venerable regiments as New York and New England had cherished. Its sons were rougher and more individualistic. Frémont, like McClellan, was determined not to move until his men were partly trained and fairly armed.

Shortages, shortages, shortages! When B. Gratz Brown was first sent to Rolla he had found no provisions, no water, no tents, no cartridge boxes— nothing. He telegraphed that supplies were "absolutely necessary." Lyon's troops had reached Springfield unpaid, ill-fed, in dilapidated clothing, and in part shoeless. S. A. Hurlbut, the drunken brigadier ordered to hold the Hannibal & St. Joe Railroad, had telegraphed July 17 that one of his regiments was wholly unarmed, and he could get weapons neither in St. Louis nor Springfield. And these shortages stubbornly persisted. Frémont had expected to draw arms from the St. Louis arsenal, but found that it afforded no more than 1300 pieces, good and bad.

Of his initial Western strength of perhaps 25,000 men before the three months' militia departed, as we have seen, 7000 Illinoisans had no weapons at all. When Frémont's messages to Montgomery Blair and Major P. V. Hagner gained him nothing, he made an emergency purchase of 25,000 Austrian muskets, 13,000 new and 12,000 old, for whose quality Asboth vouched. While in New York he had ordered 23,000 guns, but Hagner explained that after Bull Run the Administration directed all arms diverted to the Potomac, and the 23,000 went thither! The Hungarian muskets at least gave the incoming volunteers something with which to drill. For a time Frémont in desperation sought weapons wherever he could find them. Naturally, when an Eastern arms dealer telegraphed August 5 that he had 5000 Hall's rifled carbines—new cast-steel breechloaders—Frémont replied that he would take them all at the $22 rate demanded, and wished them shipped by express. This order, later vindicated by a government inquiry, was filled by mid-September, and gave real aid to the West.[16]

15 To Lyman Trumbull; Illinois State Hist. Library.
16 See *Comm. on the Conduct of the War*, III, 78–88, for a full record of the shortages. Hagner, a conscientious officer, had been given charge of War Department purchases from

Nevertheless, Western troops had to continue using whatever arms, if any, they possessed. Three officers who examined John A. McClernand's brigade at Cairo shortly reported that the queer mélange of weapons included Prussian muskets, English Tower muskets, French Minié rifles, three patterns of American muskets, and English muskets by Lacy & Company; of which all the Prussian and English muskets, and part of the American arms, were so defective that the men had no confidence whatever in them. McClernand told Frémont that little over half his force was armed at all, and they with dangerous and insufficient weapons, lacking a supply of available ammunition. One colonel said he would regard himself as a murderer if he took his defenseless men into battle. As late as October 6, McClernand, who had sent a purchaser of his own to Washington for supplies, was frantically writing this agent that he *must* get his requisition filled:

Master its contents and urge upon the Quartermaster-General the necessity of prompt and favorable action. Urge that justice, if not gratitude to Illinois, who has led the way in making pecuniary advances, requires such action. Urge that the faith of the Federal Government requires it. Urge that the public service requires it. If my brigade had been equipped with the expedition contemplated by the letter of the Secretary of War to Governor Yates, I would have routed or captured Jeff Thompson's force at Belmont last week. I would have done it with my own brigade. If necessary, show the accompanying communication to President Lincoln, who I am convinced will favor the most speedy outfit of my brigade.

Persevere! Persevere! Persevere! [17]

Horses, wagons, ambulances, and medical supplies were in equally short supply. Frémont made the error of suggesting that his former attorney Frederick Billings, of the California law firm once headed by Halleck, be empowered to buy horses in Canada. The War Department, holding that they could be obtained more cheaply in the Middle West, peremptorily stopped Billings, and this caused delay. Many of the medical wants went unfilled. At the beginning of July the head of the Sanitary Commission, after making a round of camps in Missouri, Illinois, and Ohio, reported: "We saw no ambulances in any Western camp, and no stretchers." Lyon went into the bloody action at Wilson's Creek with just two ambulances in service, so that it took nearly a week to transport some 700 wounded, suffering in the August heat, to hospitals. Even in November the troops gathering in great masses at Cairo

---

private sources in New York. For light on purchases in general and War Department confusion as well as a justification of Frémont's course see Gordon Wasson, *The Hall Carbine Affair, passim;* the pamphlet, "Vindication of Quartermaster-General McKinstry"; and the inquiry report in House Exec. Doc. No. 94, 37th Cong., 2d Sess.

17 Report of John A. Logan, *et al.*, Camp Cairo, Sept. 30, 1861; McClernand to Frémont, Sept. 17, 30, and to Colonel P. B. Fouke, Oct. 6, McClernand Papers.

possessed only two ambulances, and had done nothing to drill ambulance details for the battlefield. St. Louis organized its own Western Sanitary Commission under W. G. Eliot, and it rather than the Federal Government furnished the western troops their first real facilities for the sick and wounded.[18]

[IV]

The officer problem, as grave in the West as the East, was aggravated by two facts: Western officers, remote from Washington, less closely watched by newspaper correspondents, and working in a freer, bolder atmosphere than Eastern men, showed more carelessness and more aggressiveness; while Frémont's lack of West Point training, and memories of his oldtime troubles in the regular army—his quarrel with S. W. Kearny, court-martial, and popular vindication—fostered a strong antagonism among West Point graduates.

The new volunteer regiments about St. Louis and Cairo had as many wretched colonels, majors, and lieutenants as those about Washington. One reason why many ninety-day men refused to reënlist, West as well as East, was that they could not endure their regimental heads and demanded a complete new reshuffle. Gustave Koerner told Senator Trumbull that more than half the six regiments at Cairo would continue in the army, but never under their old colonels. He predicted that the thirteen new regiments which Yates was offering would be "officered in the usual way by incompetents." [19] More serious, however, was the exceptional degree of insubordination among the higher officers in the West.

John Pope, for example, talked and wrote in the most reckless fashion. An August letter to an Ohio friend foully abused Secretary Cameron: "Everybody in this wide land knows him to be corrupt and dishonest, a public plunderer and an unprincipled politician . . . a man notoriously plundering the Govt betraying his trust and neglecting every vital interest under his charge, cannot be gotten rid of except by public clamor." We have noted his favorite idea that Illinois troops should be formed into an Illinois army under an Illinois general; and he encouraged his men to display their resentment because Illinois units were mingled with Iowa, Missouri, Indiana, Ohio, and Michigan units, heaped confusedly together. In the same letter, pouring out venom upon Lincoln, he actually threatened a mutiny of troops:

18 Adams, *Doctors in Blue;* Nevins, *Frémont,* 491. Frederick Billings, a Vermonter and a graduate of the State university, had been attorney-general of California, and an influential Union leader there. He was destined in time to be the principal builder of the Northern Pacific, and a notable philanthropist; Billings, Montana, is named for him.

19 Koerner, Belleville, Ill., July 29, 1861, to Trumbull; Trumbull Papers, 10. Koerner's chief complaint was that some officers treated German-American recruits "like dogs."

They find themselves neglected, abandoned, and humiliated by the President they have themselves put into the White House, and they have resolved to endure it no longer. A deputation reached Washington yesterday [August 21] representing the State authorities and the military which will force upon Mr. Lincoln either an open rupture or a redress of their wrongs. They warn him that neither Banks nor Hunter will be suffered to take command of Illinois troops, and that if it is attempted the whole of the Illinois forces will march back into the State and have no more to do with the war.

We are certainly cursed with rulers in this country and especially at such a time. This Administration will do in a different manner what Jeff Davis is doing directly. I mean that by neglect, corruption, and outrage, the States of the West will be driven to group together and act without reference to the authority of the General Government. You would be surprised to find how prevalent this idea is today. . . .[20]

These vaporings ill befitted an officer whose father, once territorial secretary of Illinois, had been a friend of Lincoln; and the same irresponsible temper characterized his relations with Frémont. Vain, boastful, ambitious, Pope resented the fact that Lincoln had not made him brigadier-general in the regular army. "The injustice of overslaughing me in this way," he wrote Senator Trumbull, "needs no comment." [21] Brigadier-General Hurlbut was arrested early in September, along with an Iowa colonel, for drunkenness. "I hope it

20   Pope to V. B. Horton, Aug. 22, 1861; Civil War MSS, N. Y. Hist. Soc.
21   Pope to Trumbull June 16, 1861; Trumbull Papers LC. Pope's later epistle to Trumbull, July 6, 1861, deserves quotation at length. He wrote: "Illinois, if properly cared for, occupies today a most peculiar and commanding position in this country. On the one side Missouri has as much as she can do to take care of herself, while Iowa, Minnesota, and Wisconsin have had their troops drawn off for service eastward. On the other hand, Ohio and Indiana have been depleted of their volunteers for service in Western Virginia. Illinois so far stands nearly intact with a powerful force of nearly 20,000 men in the field.

"If this force can be kept together and properly officered and commanded, upon Illinois will devolve largely the reconquest of the Valley of the Mississippi. Where she moves, with such a force, she will of necessity stand first—and hers will be the voice which controls the warlike operations in this valley.

"If we can be kept together we shall constitute two-thirds of any army sent south from this region and our position and influence will cominate in any settlement of affairs west of the Alleghenys. To secure this vital object to our State I have been working from the beginning for some *head* to our troops, even if it be a wooden one—some commander who shall be a citizen and native of this State, and who shall move to the execution of any great military operation, with the concentrated forces of Illinois.

"For this reason I have also objected, whenever I could exercise any influence, to the separation of any isolated regiments from our troops. I deem this object vital to our military efficiency and reputation, and I appeal to you to interfere against this system which is now demoralizing us—frittering away our strength—subjecting our volunteers to the most obscure and odious service—and absolutely destroying the identity of the State. We want a military commander of our own troops, who shall have full authority in this State.

". . . Give us a Major-General and one of our own people to whom the welfare and reputation of our State are dear, and who can enable us to move with the whole military force of Illinois. I feel deeply on the subject and perhaps write too strongly." Trumbull Papers, LC.

will not be long until some of the rest of our drunken officers will have to walk the plank," a private wrote home. Still another brigadier, S. D. Sturgis, was infected by the prevalent West Point animosity toward Frémont as a major-general appointed for political reasons. His temper approached insubordination, so that he was as ready as Pope to impede Frémont's plans; and as the new commander of Lyon's army he occupied a position of critical importance.

Several volunteer officers destined to play striking roles were making their Western debuts. Franz Sigel, after organizing a Missouri regiment, became a brigadier-general in May. A sincere devotee of liberty, this romantic hero of the Baden revolt, still in his late thirties, had led 4000 troops and gained an international name before landing in America to become a humble teacher. The Germans of St. Louis greatly exaggerated his military proficiency. Another striking figure was John M. Palmer. Once a Jacksonian Democrat, he had broken with Douglas in 1854 on the Kansas-Nebraska bill, taken a prominent part in organizing the Republican Party, and supported Lincoln in the Chicago Convention. He was among the first to leap to arms. If the Middle West had a man of Hampden's principle, it was he. He shrewdly remarked of Frémont that he had lived much on the plains without becoming broad, but he was entirely loyal to the major-general.[22]

More important was the before-mentioned John A. McClernand, whose career had touched Lincoln's at many points. A Kentuckian by birth; a fighter in the Black Hawk War; in Congress 1843–51, covering Lincoln's years in the House; a Jacksonian who had turned against Douglas in 1854 as violently as Palmer did; an ardent war Democrat, anxious to mobilize men and money in overwhelming strength—here was an intrepid man who offered much that Lincoln could use. And right ready the President was to employ his services. Leaving Congress, McClernand had raised a brigade in central and southern Illinois. Inasmuch as he and the State authorities were anxious that it should not be sent off until prepared to take the field as an entirety, he lingered in Springfield and Jacksonville till the end of August. Then, as Frémont wished him to go into camp at Cairo for the moral effect his brigade would produce, he got his 2500 men thither at the beginning of September.

In short, McClernand really had a separate command, with its own commissary and quartermaster service and its own objectives. He wished a separate department established with headquarters in Cairo under his charge, coequal in authority with Frémont at St. Louis. Before long he and John A. Logan were

22 Palmer, *Personal Recollections* (1901), *passim*. His letters to his wife in Palmer Papers, Ill. State Lib., reveal fine traits. He read all Scott once a year!

pressing this idea on the semi-acquiescent Lincoln. Frémont could expect no aid from this independent brigadier, a man with a beak of a nose and a headlong, testy, irascible manner.[23]

[V]

While the Western theater was still ill organized, badly equipped, and poorly officered, Frank Blair immediately after the adjournment of the House on August 6 complicated matters by returning to Missouri. Just forty this year, and midway in his second term in Congress, he was anything but radical on the slavery question, for he was one of the chief advocates of gradual emancipation by colonization abroad, but flamingly violent in his demands for a rapid prosecution of the war. He proposed that the government accept all volunteers, take over railroads and telegraphs, and build a ship canal from Lake Michigan to the Illinois River to serve both military and commercial purposes. Seeing everything in black and white, he used language that never lacked heat or pungency. He reached St. Louis expecting to resume the reins of power he had held in June, and from that moment difficulties increased.

A clash between Blair and Frémont—between the attorney-politician who with Nathaniel Lyon had practically ruled St. Louis that spring, and the general who was now winning the warm loyalty of the German population—was almost inevitable. Blair's self-confidence brooked no opposition to his demands. He had broken General Harney, and was ready to break another commander. By his impetuous strokes, forcing premature warfare in Missouri, he had created many of the emergencies against which Frémont contended; and blinded by his affection for Lyon, he blamed Frémont for the recent disaster which was Lyon's own fault. Like Wade and Chandler in their attacks on McClellan, he could not understand military delay.

Seventy-year-old Francis P. Blair of Jacksonian fame and Montgomery Blair, both able to gain Lincoln's ear at a moment's notice, were certain to take Frank's side in any dispute. They hoped to see Frank, who in Lincoln's words was their joy and pride, reach the Presidency; and for that reason they wished him to hold Missouri as a political enclave which he could use as Andrew Jackson had used Tennessee. Montgomery termed his brother the greatest man in the country. Seeing Frémont's energetic acts win over the German population as the potential nucleus of a powerful State party, the Blairs took alarm, while they resented Frémont's apparent disregard of Frank's political henchmen in the letting of war contracts.

Frank Blair asked Major Justus McKinstry, Frémont's quartermaster-

23 See the full letters in McClernand Papers, Ill. State Hist. Lib., Aug.–Dec. 1861.

general, to "give Jim Neal a chance" at supplying horses—Neal being later termed a swindler by a Congressional committee. He urged a firm of wagon-makers on the quartermaster-general, unjustly attacking a rival firm as secessionists. He even sent a would-be contractor to McKinstry with the dictatorial command: "See that he is attended to." He was specially aggrieved when his friend ex-mayor John How, a leather dealer who had allied himself with Walter S. Burnee of Chicago in offering the Western Department clothing, shoes, and other equipment for forty thousand men, was turned away by McKinstry on the ground the order was too large and should be thrown open to competition. Blair naturally distrusted the men who got contracts from McKinstry, some of whom he later described as "obscene birds of prey." [24]

When Frank expressed his irritation to his father, the old Jacksonian decided to take the situation in hand. He wrote Frémont bluntly suggesting "a co-partnership in the West." He and his sons would do everything possible to aid the commander, he said, if Frémont would "exert your utmost influence to carry my points." To begin with, "I want to have Frank made a militia major-general for the State of Missouri." Frémont should induce the new provisional governor, Hamilton R. Gamble, to arrange the appointment for Frémont. The elder Blair had lived in an atmosphere of intrigue and bargain so long that he saw no impropriety in this proposal. Frémont on August 18 duly asked Gamble, as a special favor, to make Frank a brigadier-general at once. When Gamble replied that the State Constitution required the election of brigadiers by subordinate officers, Frémont accepted his statement, but he tried to cushion the blow to the Blairs by explaining that the colonelcy which Frank held, a place which he had gained by election of the regiment, would amount to a brigadiership. This was unsatisfactory to Frank and to his father. [25]

By late August the dispute was serious. Among its origins was of course a fundamental incompatibility of temper, for Frank was shrewd, practical, aggressive, and domineering, while Frémont was erratic, impulsive, and visionary. Both men were proud and hot-tempered. Frank, pluming himself on his repu-

24 For treatment of contracts, see McKinstry's "Vindication"; Frémont's defense in Committee on the Conduct of the War, *Report*, 1863, Pt. 3, 44 ff.; Nevins, *Frémont*, Chs. 29, 30; 37th Cong., 2d Sess., House Report No. 2 on "Government Contracts"; House Exec. Doc. No. 94 on "War Claims in St. Louis." The St. Louis correspondent of the N. Y. *Tribune* wrote in that paper of July 30, 1868: "It was freely asserted, and is believed to this day by thousands, that if the How-Gurnee contract had not failed, then Blair and Frémont would have remained friends." McKinstry wrote How in scathing terms on August 25: "The acceptance of your proposition would involve the expenditure of at least three-fourths of a million dollars—an enormous amount of money to be expended for a public object without throwing open the door to public competition." N. Y. *Herald*, September 23, 1861.

25 The letter of F. P. Blair is in the Frémont Papers, Bancroft Library, Univ. of California; see Nevins, *Frémont*, 310. See also Gamble Papers, Mo. State Hist. Soc., for Frémont-Gamble letters, August–September.

tation as savior of the Union in Missouri, believed that he had a right to control the State; Frémont, as departmental chief, was determined not to let his own authority be weakened.

Frank honestly convinced himself that Frémont lacked the high military talents his position required. Regarding St. Louis as overwhelmingly loyal, he objected to the measures which Frémont and McKinstry took to police it under martial law. Favoring the offensive against the defensive, he condemned Frémont's employment of large bodies of laborers to fortify the city. Later, he declared that Frémont's acts were "the offspring of timidity," an attempt to parry "imaginary dangers." Frémont, on the other hand, knew that his force of effective troops was much smaller than it appeared, and that he might have to denude the city of most of them to meet some urgent demand from the East or the West. He prosecuted his defensive works, including ten forts, until the War Department ordered them stopped in the middle of October. A year later he had the satisfaction of seeing the government order them put in complete readiness for service against attack.[26]

Conferences between the two officers led to no understanding. The tone of Frank's letters to his father and brother changed, as Lincoln recalled later, from doubt to condemnation. Late in August he and Colonel John T. Schofield, a West Pointer recently Lyon's chief of staff, went to Frémont's headquarters. The general, at a map-strewn table, devoted more than an hour to his plan for leading a well-equipped army through southwestern Missouri into Arkansas, and thence descending the Arkansas River to the Mississippi. On their departure, Blair inquired, "Well, what do you think of him?"; and Schofield replied in terms too strong to print. Said Blair, "I have been suspecting that for some time." It is difficult to follow Schofield's condemnation of Frémont's strategic plan. Before many months passed a Union army was to march through southwestern Missouri, defeat the Confederates at Pea Ridge, traverse Arkansas without material opposition, and emerge at Helena on the Mississippi. But it is not difficult to comprehend Blair's ready acceptance and perhaps partial inspiration of Schofield's opinion.[27]

The quarrel rapidly widened into a complete breach. Two political factions, destined to affect deeply the progress of the war, were crystallizing among Missouri Unionists: a conservative, moderate party, the Claybanks, who believed in gradual action against slavery; and a radical, uncompromising body, the Charcoals, ready for vigorous and implacable attacks on it. The Claybanks looked to Blair, Attorney-General Bates, and Provisional-Governor Gamble for leadership, while the Charcoals looked to Frémont and to Benton's

26 See Frémont's St. Louis speech in N. Y. *Weekly Tribune*, November 1, 1862.
27 Schofield, *Forty-six Years*, 48 ff.

old-time political lieutenant B. Gratz Brown. Thus began an alignment which would shortly divide Missouri into two implacable camps, open a battle running into Reconstruction years, and seriously affect national history.

The North as August ended could find even less comfort in the Western than in the Eastern military situation. The army on the Mississippi, as a result of many circumstances, but especially of Washington's neglect, was much less well prepared than that on the Potomac; the quarrel between Frémont and Frank Blair was much more ominous than that between McClellan and Scott; the first offensive would have to move from angrily divided Missouri into angrily divided Kentucky. Then just as the Blair-Frémont quarrel was breaking into the open, the Western commander took a step which electrified the country.

17

New Star, New Issue

LOW ON the horizon, late this summer, a small dim star began slowly to arise. It was the star of an Ohioan of Puritan ancestry, thirty-nine years of age, who had followed a variety of humble occupations and till lately had been regarded as a rather seedy failure, at times addicted to drink. Indeed, the use of liquor to alleviate homesickness and despondency had caused his resignation of a captaincy in the regular army nearly ten years earlier. He was Ulysses Simpson Grant, of West Point 1839–43, the Mexican War 1845–48, a Missouri farm 1854, and a Galena leather store 1860–61.

The adjutant-general of Illinois when the crisis came was so totally devoid of military experience and organizing capacity that the rush of troops to Springfield threw his office into chaos. The confusion became intolerable. One day Governor Yates exploded with chagrin. "In this bedlam," he said, "we *must* find somebody who can organize regiments." When a friend suggested Captain Sam Grant, who had just arrived in Springfield with the Jo Daviess Guards from Galena, Yates made him mustering officer at $4.20 a day to handle the incoming three-months men. Instantly a change overtook the adjutant-general's office. "In a corner," writes a State functionary, "at a small writing table, might have been seen a man of moderate stature, of exceeding gravity; modest, shy; speaking only when addressed; working busily all day long, making out muster rolls, writing orders, filing papers, bringing order out of confusion, with so little friction and noise that it required a second look to be sure he was doing anything at all." [1]

Grant's clerical duties ended May 22. He vainly wrote to Lorenzo Thomas, an old acquaintance who had become adjutant-general in Washington when Joseph E. Johnston left, and vainly visited McClellan's headquarters in Cincinnati. On the way back from this futile visit he stopped in Lafayette, Indiana, for dinner with several officers. One of them remarked that if he were about

---

[1] MS Reminiscences of Mason Brayman, Chicago Hist. Soc.; see also Lloyd Lewis, *Captain Sam Grant;* Cole, *The Era of the Civil War;* James Grant Wilson, *Life of Grant,* 20 ff.

to give battle to a Southern force, and heard that the Negroes were in insurrection, he would join the Confederates in putting down the slaves. Grant's ire flared. "Colonel W——," he said, "I don't wish to hurt your feelings, but I *must* say that any officer who can make such a declaration is not far from being a traitor!" Their friends had trouble averting an encounter. Then suddenly the grateful Yates offered Grant a regiment—and on June 15 he accepted.

Though soldiers called him "the quiet man," within a few days he had reduced a semi-mutinous camp to order. He marched his command from Springfield much of the way to Quincy on the Mississippi. Before Frémont arrived he reported to Pope, who stationed him at the town of Mexico, about fifty miles north of the Missouri River.[2]

It was on a hot day at Mexico that Grant received an unexpected telegram notifying him that he had been appointed brigadier-general. He knew that this was the work of his Galena Congressman, Elihu B. Washburne, although since Washburne was a Republican and Grant a man of no particular party allegiance they had only a nodding acquaintance. He rose, related his chaplain, pulled his black felt hat nearer his eyes, gave a few extra strokes to his whiskers, and walked off as unconcernedly as if he had been called to supper. One of Frémont's early acts was to order him to Ironton, which he reached August 8. As he totally lacked artillery and cavalry, and did not have enough force to drive away the guerrillas in the area, Frémont suggested that he fortify the town. But Grant objected that he had no engineer officer, while anyway, "drill and discipline are more necessary to the men than fortifications." A collision over rank and authority shortly developed between Grant and General Prentiss, in which Grant was clearly right. Frémont resolved the quarrel by giving him command (August 28) of southeastern Missouri and southern Illinois, with headquarters at Cairo, while sending the irate Prentiss to northern Missouri, which the guerrilla fighting made an uncomfortable place.[3] On September 3 Grant was able to write Washburne a grateful letter from Cairo, announcing that he had decided on John A. Rawlins, a Galena attorney who had helped raise the Forty-fifth Illinois, as chief of staff, and adding:

2 Brayman, MS Reminiscences, tells the traitor story. A clear indication of Grant's quality as an officer is given in his letter to his father from Mexico, Mo., August 3: "My services with the regiment I am now with have been highly satisfactory to me. I took it in a very disorganized, demoralized, and insubordinate condition and have worked it up to a reputation equal to the best, and, I believe, with the good will of all the officers and all the men. Hearing that I was likely to be promoted, the officers, with great unanimity, have requested to be attached to my Command." John H. Gundlach Collection, sold January 5, 6, 1927, Amer. Art Assn.
3 This violent quarrel of Prentiss and Grant, which almost came to fisticuffs, is vigorously described by General B. H. Grierson in his MS autobiography, "The Lights and Shadows of Life," Ill. State Hist. Lib.

I have been kept actively moving from one command to another, more so perhaps than any other officer. So long as I am of service to the cause of our country I do not object, however. . . .

Gen. Frémont has seen fit to entrust me with an important command here, my command embracing all the troops in South East Missouri and at this place. . . .

I can assure you my whole heart is in the cause which we are fighting for and I pledge myself that if equal to the task before me you shall never have cause to regret the part you have taken (in my behalf).

When Grant discovered great abuses in the quartermaster's department at Cairo, he exerted himself so resolutely to correct them that he made enemies both open and secret. One of the bitterest, he thought, was Leonard Swett, Lincoln's old intimate. Swett was hostile, Grant informed Washburne, because of "the course I pursued whilst at Cairo towards certain contractors and speculators who wished to make fortunes off of the soldiers and Government and in which he took much interest whether a partner or not." [4]

Beyond doubt, Grant was the type of officer willing to run risks. Frémont, some of whose associates wished him to send John Pope to Cairo, named Grant instead because he saw in him a man of iron will, dogged determination, great activity, and "promptness in obeying orders without question." Of his power of decision he soon gave a memorable illustration. All summer Kentucky was still "neutral." Neither the national government nor Frémont was anxious to make any movement against the State. It was the Confederacy which first violated its neutrality, General Leonidas Polk on September 3 sending General Gideon J. Pillow to seize Columbus, Kentucky, which was regarded as the key to the Mississippi. Late on the 5th, Grant, without permission, made the appropriate counter-move, capturing Paducah without firing a shot. Intestinal war at once began in the State, the legislature declaring for the Union while Confederate sympathizers summoned a secessionist convention. Had he been permitted, Grant would have tried to take Columbus, for by the end of September he had nearly 20,000 men. [5]

In the preference he showed for Grant, Frémont confirmed Pope's enmity, and made Prentiss violently hostile. But for once his judgment had guided him aright, and he did the country great service by his choice. More even than Washburne or Yates, he saw the qualities of the "quiet man." In his Missouri area of operations, with Hurlbut, Pope, Prentiss, and S. O. Sturgis, the West

4 See Grant to Washburne Sept. 3, 1861, and later letters in 1862, Grant-Washburne Papers, Ill. State Hist. Lib.
5 See Frémont, MS Memoirs, Bancroft Library, for comment on Grant. The first slight technical violation of Kentucky's "neutrality" was John M. Palmer's seizure of a steamer; but Pillow moved in force.

Pointer who had taken over Lyon's force, all holding important commands.[6] he was far more unfortunate in his subordinates than McClellan; and unlike Mc-Clellan, he had to fight at once, for the situation would not wait. He had invading armies and guerrilla bands in his midst.

[I]

Unlike McClellan, moreover, Frémont had to face complex political problems. Against military difficulties he might have made headway, but in the political field he was crippled by his comparative inexperience (for this former Senator and Presidential candidate had done no sustained political work), impetuosity, and excessive readiness to listen to radical advisers. His ripening quarrel with Blair demanded a discretion which he did not possess.

Just as this quarrel, as we have said, was about to become public property, Frémont took his rashest step. Frank Blair wrote Montgomery September 1 that affairs were growing worse in north Missouri; that an army of 10,000 rebels might soon be collecting there; that he had warned Frémont and got no satisfaction; and that the discipline of troops in St. Louis was bad. "He talks of the vigor he is going to use," wrote Blair, "but I can see none of it, and I fear it will turn out to be some rash and inconsiderate move—adopted in haste to make head against a formidable force which could not have been accumulated except through gross and inexcusable negligence." It was Blair's and Lyon's springtime violence which had done most to galvanize this force into action. "My decided opinion," he went on, "is that he should be relieved of his command and a man of ability put in his place." [7]

At that moment Frémont *had* determined on an ill-considered move. He felt driven to desperation by the guerrilla warfare—a warfare by which, wrote James O. Broadhead, "the Union sentiment was being crushed out and the Union men overwhelmed by the tide of rebellion, rapine, and plunder which has literally swept over the State." One loyal man in a loyal district wrote: "All we can hope to do is to escape with our lives." [8]

Frémont's rash step was the first resounding Northern attack upon slavery. The two radical advisers at his elbow, Representative Owen Lovejoy and Jessie,

6 The N. Y. *Tribune* later said editorially that Sturgis was accustomed to declare that the only gentlemen in the country were those of the South. In 1862 he denounced the radical Senator Zack Chandler of Michigan as "liar, scoundrel, and coward." N. Y. *Tribune*, June 30, 1862.
7 Blair-Lee Papers, Princeton University. Blair had been in the State a little over a fortnight when he made these charges.
8 The Carthage, Ill., *Republican*, Aug. 29, 1861, describes the exodus from Missouri into Illinois as astonishing. "Long trains of wagons pass our office almost daily, conveying families who have hastily gathered up a few of their household goods." The Broadhead Papers, Mo. Hist. Soc., contain vivid accounts of the terror by J. O. Broadhead and others.

had been reinforced by John A. Gurley, Representative from the Cincinnati district, a minister, journalist, and politician of strong antislavery views, who had arrived as aide August 6. He was persuasive and earnest. John P. Shanks, an Indiana Congressman of like opinions, had just come or announced his coming. These counselors urged him to fight fire with fire.[9] Slavery nourished the guerrillas; he should strike at slavery.

No doubt Frémont regarded the startling proclamation which he issued under date of August 30 as primarily a military measure. He had placed St. Louis under martial law on August 14; now he extended the regime over the whole State, assuming the administrative powers theretofore exercised by the flabby Gamble. He drew a diagonal line from Leavenworth through Jefferson City, Rolla, and Ironton to Cape Girardeau as separating the areas of Unionist and secessionist control; declared that all civilians caught in arms north of that line should be tried by court-martial and if found guilty, shot; and prescribed the extreme penalty for all persons found guilty of destroying railway tracks, bridges, or telegraph lines. He further announced that the real and personal property of Missourians who actively aided the enemies of the United States was confiscated to public use, and that their slaves would be freed. The geographical distribution of slaveowners in Missouri was peculiar. Of the total of 115,000 slaves listed in the 1860 census, the 31 counties contiguous to the Mississippi and Missouri Rivers north and west of St. Louis held almost 77,000. It was in these counties, and especially in the belt stretching along the Missouri across the State, that guerrilla warfare had its deepest roots. This belt, lying largely along Frémont's line, was subjected to his severe punitive order.[10]

Frémont might well feel desperate. He faced enemies in the field, covert treason within his lines, and insubordination behind his back. The warfare, as the St. Louis *Republican* said, was becoming atrociously savage; both sides killed without quarter, and looted with greedy eagerness. Grant had just written his father from Jefferson City that the country west of that point would be in a starving condition the next winter, for all Unionists were fleeing penniless, leaving farms, crops, and stock to be ravaged by the enemy. Secessionist guerrillas, after firing into many passenger trains, on September 6 weakened a 160-foot bridge over the Little Platte so that at midnight it collapsed under a train loaded with 80 or 90 men, women, and children. Martial law had become a necessity, and to that point Frémont was justified; it was when he went beyond that he invaded a sphere of policy belonging to Lincoln.

9 Shanks's official service as aide began Sept. 20, but he may have arrived in St. Louis earlier. Gurley sat in Congress 1859–63, Shanks 1861–63.
10 Frank Moore, *Rebellion Record*, III, 10, 26, Documents, pp. 33–71, gives the proclamation with some press opinion. Frémont's reasons, as stated in his MS Memoirs, are quoted in Nevins, *Frémont*, 500.

A wiser man would have telegraphed Lincoln in advance concerning the proclamation. Frémont instead followed it with a letter which, however placatory, gave the President no real explanation. He wrote of the enemy (September 3):

He has been fortifying new places, and creeping covertly forward into Kentucky lately, and I have been very anxious to anticipate him, but not quite able yet. Still, I am moving, and we are beginning to roll the war backward. I think the preparation in the South much greater than we had thought, and I believe that you will soon be compelled to exert the whole power of the nation and use every means of aggressive war. Here, I have been compelled to move fast and act with my best judgment as the occasion rose. I trust that the proclamation which I judged it right to issue on the 30th will meet with your approval and support. . . .

Gov. Gamble visits you at Washington. He has been professedly friendly but has shown no real disposition to cooperate. His inefficiency is quite remarkable, and in my judgment he had neither courage nor capacity for his position. . . . You notice that we are driving Pillow back, and you will in a short time see some changes for the better. . . .[11]

Union leaders believed at the time that the Confederacy had 60,000 or 70,000 armed men in Missouri, of whom 40,000 were Missourians.[12] Leonidas Polk had laid plans to hold a great part of the State while attempting to seize control of Kentucky. Nobody knew when Sterling Price and Ben McCulloch would make another attack from the southwest, or Pillow a move from the southeast.

[II]

Even as a military measure, Frémont's proclamation was open to sharp objection. To put Confederate guerrillas to death would simply invite reprisals. To begin the sweeping confiscation of secessionist property would create embittered resistance, not quiet it. And it was far more than a military measure; it was a sharp intrusion into the political field. Already Abolitionists and radical freesoilers of the North were loudly demanding that the war be expanded into a conflict for emancipation as well as Union. Joshua Giddings had published a flaming letter dated June 6 in the New York *Tribune* demanding just such action as Frémont now took; Gerrit Smith, in a letter of July 12 to Owen Lovejoy, had asked why the government took a costly, weary way to suppress

11 Grant's letter on the guerrillas, dated Aug. 27, was in the Gundlach Collection before its sale. Frémont's letter to Lincoln is in the Seward Collection, Rochester University. Lincoln must have referred it to Seward, who kept it.

12 An over-estimate, as subsequent events demonstrated. Military and political conditions are discussed in S. B. Laughlin, "Missouri Politics During the Civil War," *Missouri Historical Review*, v. 23 (April, 1929), 400–26.

the rebellion when a cheap, direct one was at hand. Liberation of slaves had obviously become a necessity, wrote Smith. "Let the President, in his capacity as commander of the army, proclaim such liberation and the war would end in thirty days." Moncure D. Conway was putting through the press a book, *The Great Method of Peace*, which urged emancipation as the key to victory. Charles Sumner was demanding an end to halfway measures. Greeley's *Tribune* declared it was time to stop handling traitors with kid gloves.[13] Frémont's proclamation, followed as it was by his creation of a commission to take evidence and issue deeds of manumission, reverberated on the sounding board these radicals furnished.

If Frémont was rash in issuing this proclamation without prior consultation of the War Department and President, he was to commit a worse folly. Lincoln could never countenance his step, and on September 3rd the President sent him a kindly letter, pointing out his objections. He ordered Frémont to shoot no Confederate without Presidential approbation or consent, for if he did "the Southerners would very certainly shoot our best men in their hands in retaliation"; and he instructed the general to modify his paragraph on the confiscation of property and liberation of slaves so as to conform to the recent Confiscation Act, which sanctioned the seizure of property only when actually used for insurrectionary purposes. It would have hurt Frémont's pride and sense of conviction to yield, and he refused. In a stiff-necked letter he requested Lincoln to *direct* the modification by open order—which Lincoln in a courteous letter of September 11 did.

Frémont was doubtless influenced in this not only by his radical advisers but by the enthusiastic reception of the proclamation in certain quarters. Approval came from a long list of the nation's most important newspapers; not merely radical journals like the Chicago *Tribune*, New York *Evening Post*, and Springfield *Republican*, but moderate papers like the Washington *National Intelligencer* and New York *Times*. In Lincoln's own State it was vigorously applauded. From New England to Kansas most of the clergy, all belligerent haters of slavery, and all citizens who thought Lincoln slow and Seward an evil influence, greeted it jubilantly. Representative George W. Julian of Indiana wrote later that it stirred and united the people of the North during the ten days of life allowed it by the Government far more than any other event of the war. Two Cabinet members approved of it. Secretary Cameron, at home ill, telegraphed his congratulations to Frémont before he found that Lincoln was hostile, and Montgomery Blair thought the emancipation provision justified. In Missouri the effect on loyal and disloyal was all that Frémont had

13   Gerrit Smith Papers, Syracuse University; Clarke, *Julian*, 217-20; N. Y. *Tribune*, Sept. 1, 1861.

hoped—or so at least he believed. "The Union people rejoiced openly," he states in his unpublished memoirs. "To the rebels everywhere it was a blow. It affected not only their principles but their property." [14]

Doubtless Frémont believed that a seemingly voluntary retraction would draw upon his head the censure of all the groups now applauding him, and would send a wave of disappointment and anger—directed against *him*—through much of the North. Though ready to let Lincoln overrule him, he was unwilling to overrule himself. In this he was stubbornly wrongheaded, for it was his duty to obey the Commander-in-Chief without demur, and he could have made it clear that he was yielding to higher authority.

Lincoln, who had to think of the whole country, was fearful of the effect of the proclamation on Kentucky, just now brought to the very crisis of decision as Leonidas Polk invaded her from the South, and Grant followed his example by occupying Paducah. Long poised on the knife edge of neutrality, most Kentuckians were at last coming down on the Northern side. The Frankfort *Kentucky Statesman* termed Frémont's proclamation "infamous"; the Louisville *Courier* thought it "abominable." These journals leaned to secession, but even the loyal Louisville *Journal* thought the general's action deplorable. Joseph Holt wrote Lincoln that while sound Kentuckians accepted the Confiscation Act as a necessary measure, the proclamation transcended and violated it. "You may well judge," he went on, "of the alarm and condemnation with which the Union-loving citizens have read this proclamation." They could not believe that Lincoln would let it be enforced; and anxious that nothing should chill the fervor of loyal citizens at this crucial moment, he asked for Presidential intervention. Condemnatory resolutions were introduced in the legislature. Frémont had some defenders even in Kentucky, but they were few.

Unquestionably, Lincoln was right as to the paramount importance of nurturing loyal sentiment in Kentucky. On the very day that he set aside the objectionable features of the proclamation, the legislature by overwhelming

14 Among the newspapers endorsing the proclamation were Bennett's New York *Herald*, the Chicago *Times*, a violently Democratic organ, and the Chicago *Morning Post*, a Douglasite journal. The measured praise of the *National Intelligencer*, always conservative, was especially notable (Sept. 7). So was the approval given by the St. Louis *Republican*, a Democratic paper highly critical of the Administration and of most of its Missouri measures. The Chase, Wade, Chandler, and Sumner papers contain much enthusiastic comment from a variety of correspondents. Orville H. Browning, Lincoln's old friend of Quincy, Illinois, a highly conservative man, wrote the President on Sept. 30: "His proclamation in my opinion embodies a true and important principle which the government cannot afford to abandon. . . ." Browning Papers, Ill. State Hist. Lib. He added that it rested "upon the well ascertained and universally acknowledged principles of international law," and would greatly weaken the enemy. For Montgomery Blair's approval see Dennett, *Diaries and Letters of John Hay*, 219.

majorities called on Governor Magoffin to demand the immediate withdrawal of the Confederates from the Commonwealth, and when Magoffin vetoed this resolution, the legislature repassed it over his veto.[15] "The mountains are alive with zeal for the Union," declared the Frankfort *Commonwealth.* "Come, then, let us gird up the whole strength of our bodies and souls!" exhorted young John M. Harlan as he began raising a Union regiment. Emancipationist activity would have paralyzed this enthusiasm.

And at this critical moment the Frémont-Blair quarrel burst dramatically into public view. While the press discussed it, Frank had every advantage in laying his side of the dispute before Lincoln. He was effectively abetted by Missourians of the Claybank faction. The impression they made in the White House is reflected by some notes of John G. Nicolay dated September 17:

It is now about in the third week since the Blair family . . . who were mainly instrumental in urging his [Frémont's] appointment upon the Prest., came to him and with many professions of humility and disappointment said they were compelled by the indisputable evidence of experience to confess that in regard to his capabilities for the very important duties to which he had been assigned, he had to their perfect satisfaction proved himself a complete failure, and that they now urged his immediate removal, as strenuously as they had formerly urged his appointment. Their testimony was supported by Governor Gamble of Mo. who came on purpose to Washington to inform the President that he had gone to St. L. to confer with the genl. about the defence of the State, and that after waiting patiently for two days, he was utterly unable to obtain an interview with or admittance to him, and that his necessity had compelled him to come here. A Mr. Broadhead, State Senator of Mo., also travelled all the way here with a similar complaint. Letters were also received from other parties making similar statements, and particularly one from L.I.G., Esq., an eminent lawyer and citizen of St. Louis. The substance of the various statements seemed to be that the Genl. had placed on his staff and surrounded himself with a set of men who had been with him in California and elsewhere and who made it entirely impossible for anyone except his pets to gain access to him etc.[16]

Edward Bates, a Claybank sympathizer, and a rooted conservative on the slavery issue, joined the Blairs in pronouncing Frémont a disaster.

15 For the situation in broad outline see E. M. Coulter, *The Civil War in Kentucky,* 111, 112. The Frankfort *Commonwealth* said editorially: "However objectionable the course of Frémont is in relation to slaves, one fact stands out conspicuously worthy of attention, and it is that rebellion is attended with eminent peril, while loyalty deserves and will receive all the security and protection of life, liberty, and property which the Government can give. Each day—nay, each hour—of the revolution now going on, and which threatens Kentucky, shows the utter recklessness and ruin which must inevitably follow the destruction of our Government. . . ." Sept. 11. The Louisville *Journal,* while regretting Frémont's willingness to give freedom to slaves, compared his proclamation with the far harsher confiscation law of the Confederacy; Sept. 3.

16 Nicolay Papers, LC.

Frémont's view of the quarrel was that Frank's passion had broken all bounds when he found that the general could not be made a tool, that he had laid unjust and unsupported charges before Lincoln through Montgomery Blair, and that the three Blairs were now engaged in a conspiracy to displace him. Gamble had been censured by Frémont for refusing active cooperation in certain measures; Broadhead had been a member of Blair's Committee of Safety. Both the Missouri *Democrat* (Republican) and Missouri *Republican* (Democrat) took Frémont's side, and the German press was strongly with him.[17] But these voices were not heard in Washington.

What could Frémont do to reach the White House? "I began to feel the withdrawal of the confidence and support of the Administration," he wrote later. In his anxiety he allowed Jessie Benton Frémont, gifted, high-strung, and impulsive, to carry a letter to Lincoln. He could have found no worse emissary, for it was in a mood of fierce resentment, steeled by the iron Benton determination, that Mrs. Frémont descended on Washington.

Of the ensuing interview we have two strikingly different accounts, the more authentic her own undated memorandum, and the less trustworthy John Hay's record of a discursive evening talk by Lincoln some two years after the event. Immediately on her arrival in the capital on the evening of September 10 Mrs. Frémont sent a note to the White House explaining that she had come with a letter from the general, and inquiring when she might deliver it. The messenger brought back a card with the reply, "Now, at once, A. Lincoln." She was disconcerted by this, for she had travelled two days and two nights in a hot, dirty day coach and was exhausted. But with Judge Edward Coles of New York accompanying her, she went to the mansion, where she had often played as a little girl in Jackson's day. She was shown into the red room, and after a short wait, Lincoln entered. It was soon plain that the overwrought woman and the anxious, harried President were at cross purposes. Lincoln later said that she taxed him violently with many things, and this is no doubt true. On her way east she had passed a train carrying Montgomery Blair and Montgomery C. Meigs going west to inquire into Missouri affairs; and she doubtless said just what she thought about the Blairs and about the government's neglect of the West. Both she and Coles thought Lincoln's voice hard, his manner repellant, and his anxiety to get rid of her plain. She writes:

It was clear to Judge Coles as to myself that the President's mind was made up against General Frémont—and decidedly against me. . . . Briefly, in answer to his "Well?" I explained that the general wished so much to have his

17 Bates to Chase, Sept. 11, 1861; Chase Papers, Pa. Hist. Soc. Broadhead in a letter of Sept. 17 to the editors of the St. Louis *Democrat* protested against their espousal of Frémont against Blair; Broadhead Papers. On the visit of Meigs see Russell F. Weigley, *Quartermaster General of the Union Army, A Biography of Montgomery C. Meigs.*

attention to the letter sent, that I had brought it to make sure it would reach him. He answered, not to that, but to the subject his own mind was upon, that *"It was a war for a great national idea, the Union, and that General Frémont should not have dragged the negro into it—that he never would if he had consulted with Frank Blair. I sent Frank there to advise him."* The words italicized are exactly those of the President.

He first mentioned the Blairs, in this astonishing connection.

It was a *parti pris*, and as we walked back Judge Coles, who heard everything, said to me, "This ends Frémont's part in the war. Seward and Montgomery Blair will see to reports against him made by a man authorized to do so, and as everyone knows, with his mind often clouded by drink and always governed by personal motives." [18]

A later statement by Mrs. Frémont [19] discloses that she lectured Lincoln on the difficulty of conquering the South by arms alone, and the importance of appealing to British and world sentiment by a blow against slavery; expressing ideas that Owen Lovejoy and Gurley cherished, but that Frémont never alleged as a reason for his proclamation. The irritated President remarked, "You are quite a female politician." It was at this point that he emphasized Frémont's error in converting a war for the Union into a war against slavery. She also spoke of Frémont's special position as former head of the Republican Party, apparently in terms that heightened Lincoln's irritation.

When old Francis P. Blair saw her next day he was irate. "Look what you have done for Frémont; you have made the President his enemy!" He could not forgive her opposition to Frank. Montgomery would talk with Frémont, he scolded, and bring him to his senses. One account quotes him as saying: "Madam, *I* made your husband what he is, and *I* will unmake him; *I* nominated him for the Presidency in '56, and *I* will defeat him in the future." [20] She sent her husband a cipher message warning him against any advice from Montgomery. Then, having done the general irreparable harm, she returned to St. Louis headquarters.

Frémont, hoping to remain head of the Western Department and soon move forward with his army, took the one step which he believed might appeal to public sentiment. On September 18 he arrested Frank Blair for insubordination, and notified Secretary Cameron that he would submit charges for his trial. Frank had used his family position, he later declared, "to lay private

18 Jessie Benton Frémont MSS, Bancroft Library. She referred to Frank Blair. See Appendix III for details of this interview.

19 In an unpublished biographical section on the explorer written by Mrs. Frémont and her son; Bancroft Library. Her undated memorandum was apparently written just after the interview. Hay's record of Lincoln's talk was made Dec. 9 or 10, 1863, after Lincoln had joined Norman Judd, J. P. Usher, Nicolay, and Hay as they sat "talking politics and blackguarding our friends." Such a record has dubious historical value.

20 So states W. M. Davis of St. Louis in a letter Sept. 17, 1861, to his wife, doubtless quoting Jessie; Davis Papers, Penna. Hist. Soc.

letters with unsustained accusations before the President, disturbing the President's confidence in the Commanding General and seriously impairing the efficiency of this Department." Mrs. Frémont, Montgomery decided, had prompted him—"it was General Jessie's doing." The Postmaster-General telegraphed him asking Frank's release, sensibly adding: "This is no time for strife except with the enemies of the country." When Frémont complied, Frank at first refused to accept a release, for he would have preferred a trial, and he was more implacably hostile than ever.[21]

Western affairs had thus been thrown into a crisis which damaged army morale, and aroused mixed feelings throughout the North. Would Frank Blair break Frémont as he had broken Harney? Or would Frémont redeem himself by a brilliant fall campaign? For the confusion, the resentments, and the embarrassment to military movements it is perhaps less profitable to seek out personal culprits than to analyze general causes. Although Frémont and Frank Blair divide a large culpability, the greater explanation of the sad situation of Missouri affairs lies in the factors already noted—the deep social divisions of the State, half slave and half free; its refractory geography, tying Union defenses to long lines of river and rail; Washington's inexcusable neglect of the trans-Mississippi region; and the readiness of men reared on the frontier to fly to violent measures.

[III]

One development, however, overshadowed all others—the new issue of emancipation. The vigor with which Lincoln rejected the concept of a war fought not only to save the Union but to destroy slavery reflected his concern over a growing public radicalism. He believed in evolution, not revolution; he wished to shorten the conflict, not lengthen it. He knew that to win the war he must keep Democrats and Republicans, conservatives and radicals, reasonably united, and that he must hold the Borderland behind the government. He wished to maintain conditions favorable to a fraternal reunion of North and South after the war. Throughout life Lincoln followed the precepts of the Epistle to the Philippians: "Let your moderation be known to all men." He was pondering his own plan of gradual compensated emancipation in the border area, and Frémont's action threatened to destroy its chances.

But while he rightly insisted that this was a war for a grand national idea, powerful elements now regarded it also as a war for a grand humanitarian ideal.

As a host of liberal citizens had risen to applaud Frémont's proclamation, so

---

[21] Smith, *The Blair Family*, II, 77; Nevins, *Frémont*, 520; see Blair-Lee Papers, Princeton, for the order of release.

a host received Lincoln's modification with anger and disappointment, denouncing it as a fearful blunder. Since Frémont issued his paper, they declared, public credit had improved, recruiting had increased, and patriots had felt greater elation and confidence. The nation could believe, for the first time, that it was fighting for not only a great patriotic object, but a splendid moral goal. Lincoln's action takes away the penalty for rebellion, declared the Chicago *Tribune* of September 16. "How many times," asked James Russell Lowell, "are we to save Kentucky and lose our self-respect?" Judge George Hoadly of Cincinnati reported that indignation in that city had risen to fury, and Moncure D. Conway asserted that if a cheer for Lincoln were proposed to a crowd there, the response would be a groan.[22] A new Philadelphia monthly, the *Continental*, with Charles Godfrey Leland for editor, raised the cry: "Emancipation for the Sake of the White Man." Senator Ben Wade wrote from his northern Ohio home in bitter execration:

What do you think of Old Abe's overruling Frémont's proclamation? So far as I can see, it is universally condemned and execrated in the North, and I have no doubt that by it he has done more injury to the cause of the Union by receding from the ground taken by Frémont than McDowell did by retreating from Bull Run. I shall expect to find in his first annual message a recommendation to Congress to give each rebel who shall serve during the war a hundred and sixty acres of land. Unless the President shall divest himself of such squeamishness, all the mighty exertions of the North to subdue this rebellion will be paralyzed. . . . The President don't object to Genl Frémont's taking the life of the owners of slaves, when found in rebellion, but to confiscate their property and emancipate their slaves he thinks monstrous. . . . Such ethics could come only of one born of "poor white trash" and educated in a slave State.[23]

Beyond question, the war, whatever happened to Frémont, had taken a new turn. His impulsive stroke had crystallized a mass of latent sentiment, and for the first time the idea that the conflict might result in a socio-economic revolution began to grip men's minds.

Meanwhile, Grant was having an interesting time at Cairo headquarters, and showing remarkable decision. He put a popular Illinois colonel, Richard J. Oglesby, in command at Bird Point just across the Mississippi in Missouri.

---

22 Chase Papers, LC, for Hoadly's letter; Lowell to Sibyl Norton, Sept. 28, 1861 in *Letters*, I, 314; Leland, *Memoirs*, 242–244; Conway to Greeley, Sept. 18, 1861, Greeley Papers, NYPL. Much rejoicing was aroused in radical Northern quarters by news that Frémont had by public advertisement freed two male slaves of Thomas L. Snead, who had taken an active part against the Union. William Pitt Fessenden wrote James S. Pike on Sept. 8 that Frémont's proclamation had had an electrifying effect on the country, and proved him a statesman; he believed that Frémont rather than McClellan might be the coming man. Pike Papers.

23 Wade, Jefferson, Ohio, Sept. 23, 1861, to Zack Chandler; Chandler Papers, LC.

He sent General C. F. Smith, one of the ablest regular army officers, to command at Paducah. A detachment occupied the mouth of the Cumberland hard by. Once he had a narrow escape from capture; while some Confederate prisoners under exchange were in his office for credentials to pass through the lines, somebody mentioned that he was going to Cape Girardeau next day—and though chance prevented his trip, a Union boat in the area was halted by Confederate artillery, and searched by a major confident he had bagged Grant. The general heard that an old acquaintance, the forty-one-year-old brigadier William Tecumseh Sherman, first-year man at West Point in Grant's last year, had arrived in Louisville to assist General Robert Anderson of Sumter fame. He knew that a blue-water naval captain, Andrew H. Foote, had reached St. Louis to take charge of naval operations on the western rivers under Frémont and the War Department. Foote's first task was to hasten the building of gunboats and mortarboats. "Spare no effort to accomplish the object in view with the least possible delay," ordered Frémont.[24]

Plainly, the western theater would soon see action. Whether Frémont realized his plans for clearing Missouri and swinging through Arkansas to the Mississippi, or Grant his plans for moving down that river, large movements impended. They would inevitably have a large influence on wartime policy respecting the slaves.

24 Grant, *Memoirs*, I, 164–168; Lewis, *Sherman*, 181, 182; Hoppin, *Foote*, 158 ff.

18

The Firepower of the North

THE FIRST battle autumn saw fully three-quarters of a million men ranked and accoutered on the American continent. Never in history had such a host been raised so quickly; but east and west on both sides, under McClellan and Johnston, Frémont and Price, troops complained of inadequate and defective arms. The Confederate need was desperate. Governor Isham G. Harris of Tennessee on November 2 earnestly entreated citizens of every county to deliver to his agents "every effective double-barrel shotgun and sporting rifle which they may have." Union troops in the West continued to suffer from crippling shortages, while even in the Washington camps some regiments were kept chafing for weapons. A decent uniformity of pieces and ammunition was beyond the dreams of the most ambitious commander. The world was in the midst of a small-arms revolution, and many problems would have to be solved before men could agree on standard requirements and learn to meet them.[1]

Nothing did more to expose the gangling, adolescent state of American

---

1 The arms revolution now slowly under way had two main parts: Acceptance of rifling (the Enfield standard was three grooves with a spiral twist of one inch in seventy-two to rotate a heavy conical bullet) in place of the old smoothbore; and the gradual acceptance of breechloaders in place of muzzle-loaders. Rifles (that is, guns spirally grooved to give the projectile a rotation which increases the accuracy of its flight) had been invented soon after Columbus discovered America; breechloaders had appeared in the first half of the sixteenth century. During the Revolution Major Patrick Ferguson invented a breechloading rifle used by some British troops. But in 1861 the infantry of practically all nations was still familiar with smoothbore muzzle-loading muskets; direct descendants of the "smoky muskets" of Shakespeare's *All's Well*. Rifles, and muskets converted by rifling, were steadily displacing the inaccurate smoothbores. The United States had adopted a muzzle-loading Springfield rifle for its tiny force of regular infantry in 1855. In various countries limited bodies of troops had been given superior equipment; the French chasseurs, for example, rifles which threw the bullet invented by Captain Minié, an elongated projectile with an iron cup fitting into a hollow cone at the base— this cup, when driven forward by the explosion, expanding the bullet into the grooves. Cavalry, who could not manage ramrods, had to have breechloading carbines or short guns. The Prussians early in the 1840's adopted the needle gun, a breechloader using a cartridge detonated by a spring-driven needle, and slowly improved it. The triumph of this rifle in the war with Austria in 1866 caused all civilized powers to rearm with similar weapons.

society than the effort to arm the swiftly gathered hosts. Both sections confronted an urgent industrial problem without the technological skills, manufacturing resources, and organizational experience required to master it. In no field were both the faults and virtues of large-scale improvisation more strikingly exhibited.

[I]

When Sumter fell the American stock of arms was at the ebb-tide level to be expected in a nation which had never put 50,000 men in the field and never expected to do so. The United States at the beginning of 1861 had in all its forts, arsenals, and armories, North and South, about 600,000 small arms, antique and new, wretched and passable. Of these 35,335 were rifles or rifled muskets, the latest improved arms; 42,000 were older percussion rifles; and about 500,000 were percussion smoothbore muskets.[2] These figures, however, are deceptive, for a great part of the muskets were unserviceable. Not untypical was the Thirtieth Illinois Infantry, which took the field this year armed with 90 "good" Enfield rifles, 183 serviceable American and English muskets, and 357 unserviceable muskets; a total of 357 bad as against 273 good pieces. As this regiment numbered 773 men, 121 possessed no arms at all.[3] Probably half of the 500,000 smoothbore muskets owned by the government were not worth carrying into battle. The other half would be useful, and some Union soldiers carried smoothbores without complaint to the end of the war. They fired an ounce ball at low velocity to a distance of some 600 feet, and could be lethal at nearly that distance; whereas a rifled musket fired a bullet at a velocity of 960 feet a second with a range of 3300 feet. The rifled Springfields and Enfields were usually sighted at 900 feet, and at any distance much above that figure the "drift" of the projectile made accurate sighting impossible.

Just what part of this stock was held in the seceding States it is difficult to say. Lincoln's message to Congress July 4, 1861, stated that a disproportionately large number had been sent to the South, and both Cameron and Scott lent their authority to the charge that Buchanan's Secretary of War, Floyd, had thus denuded Northern repositories. Floyd himself, on returning to Virginia, boasted that he had done so, and absurd assertions on this head crept into the Southern press. The Richmond *Enquirer* declared that by a single order in 1860 Floyd had sent 115,000 improved rifles and muskets from Northern to Southern arsenals; while the Memphis *Appeal* improved on this

2 H. K. Craig to Joseph Holt, Jan. 22, 1861; O. R. III, i, 42.
3 Acting adjutant Dec. 6, 1861, to McClernand; McClernand Papers, Ill. State Library.

by asserting that his transfers, with seizures from Federal posts and purchases abroad, had given the Confederacy more than 700,000 small arms and 200,000 revolvers. The fact is that Floyd had made no exceptional transfers of weapons to the South.[4]

Our best figures on arms allocation indicate that early in 1861 about 336,500 government muskets and rifles were deposited in the free area as against 273,500 in the slave States. Many in the second category, however, were in forts which the Union continued to hold, or in Missouri, Maryland, and the District of Columbia. Another official statement places the number of small arms in Union repositories at the beginning of 1861 at 422,500, a figure which includes deductions for weapons in arsenals already seized or soon to be taken. It did not, however, allow for losses shortly sustained in the capture of Harpers Ferry and the secession of Virginia and Tennessee.[5] Altogether, we are safe in saying that the small arms on hand for Union troops did not exceed 350,000 pieces, of which not more than 250,000 were fit for battle use; while the Confederates could hardly have had more than 200,000 government arms.

Thus the statement of one historian that the United States possessed in its arsenals and posts in April, 1861, enough muskets and rifles for an army of half a million,[6] is simply nonsense. It would, however, have had more than enough for the first armies called up had they been distributed fairly, and cared for efficiently. Unfortunately, systematic allocation was impossible during the first frenzied months, many arms were ruined by misuse, and some were captured at Bull Run, Wilson's Creek, and Ball's Bluff. Viewed broadly, 1861 was a year of distress, search, and complaint among Northern as among Southern officers.

And the armories? When fighting began, the United States had but two, at Harpers Ferry and Springfield, Massachusetts, and the first was immediately lost, with the destruction of all its manufacturing facilities. The nation's fabrication of small arms was therefore confined to one establishment. This armory, planted by Congress on the Connecticut in 1791, had never really emerged from infancy. Consisting of some small buildings on a hilltop, and "water-shops" for heavier operations on a branch of the river, its most imposing structure was the arsenal celebrated by Longfellow, where "from floor to ceiling, like a huge organ" rose the tiers of burnished arms.

4 Meneely, *War Department, 1861*, 41; T. B. Gates, *The War of the Rebellion*, 14; O. R. III, i, 311.

5 O. R. III, i, 321, 322; see the figures also of Craig to Holt, Jan. 21, 1861, O. R. III, *ibid*. The deduction is for weapons seized in arsenals in South Carolina, Louisiana, and Alabama, already gone, and in Augusta, Ga., and Fayetteville, N. C., soon to go.

6 Shannon, *Organization and Administration of the Union Army*, I, 110.

When Sumter was taken, only a thousand muskets a month were being made at Springfield. Indeed, in recent years production had fallen to a lower point than that reached in 1815. The government tried to speed up the work, but such bottlenecks developed that even in July only 3000 arms were made. Skilled workmen were hard to find, and the use of machine tools was still rudimentary. Of the 49 parts in the standard Springfield musket many had to be subjected to elaborate processing. The hammer alone, for example, had to be forged, dropped, trimmed, punched, drifted, milled, turned, filed, and finally case-hardened.[7]

Enough guns for only one regiment a month! This April rate meant that both State and Federal authorities had to turn elsewhere in frenzied haste.

[II]

First, let us look at the States.

From the Kennebec to the Sangamon, they sprang forward in a confused mêlée, characterized by inefficiency, duplication, and waste. They and the Washington authorities hurriedly placed contracts with the score of plants capable of producing arms, all concentrated in New England and the Middle Atlantic States, for the West had none. Arms could be made in quantity at Providence, R. I., Worcester, Mass., and Manchester, N. H.; at Hartford, Meriden, Norwich, Norfolk, Windsor Locks, Middletown, and Whitneyville, Conn.; at Watertown, Ilion, and in New York, N. Y.; at Trenton, N. J., at Bridesburg, Pa., and some other places.[8] Contracts were given foreign brokers and manufacturers, but we may first analyze the activities of Federal and State agents in the home markets.

The three principal mistakes made in home arms procurement, broadly considered, were the initial want of system, so that many agencies bid frantically against each other; the excessive orders, for down to July 1, 1862, these agencies contracted for 1,164,000 rifles or rifled muskets of Springfield pattern; and the exorbitant prices paid, averaging fully $20 a gun with appendages.[9] The first error was a product of haste, the second of panic, and the third of a general uncertainty as to costs. In quite a different category stood a more crippling mistake, the failure of the Federal Government to make the most of recent advances in arms design.

7 See description of Springfield armory, *Atlantic Monthly*, Vol. 12 (October, 1863), 436-451, and in Springfield *Republican*, April 22, 1861.

8 Felicia Deyrup, *Arms Makers of the Connecticut Valley*; W. W. Greener, *The Gun and its Development* (6th ed., 1897).

9 Meneely, *War Department, 1861*, 253-254, 262-263; 37th Cong., Sen. Exec. Doc. 72, pp. 15-20 ff.

In the initial scramble for arms on hand, Connecticut and Massachusetts fared especially well, partly because their governors had foreseen the emergency, partly because of their proximity to sources of supply. As early as January, 1861, Buckingham at Hartford had taken personal responsibility for purchasing knapsacks, bayonets, and other equipment for 5000 men. The State owned more than 1000 regular army rifled muskets, and more than 2000 smoothbores good for temporary service, while its factories could quickly turn out supplementary weapons. On Lincoln's first call, Buckingham decided to equip Connecticut forces only with good rifles. State banks furnished money. The first regiment received excellent Sharps rifles, the second Sharps and Enfields, and the third rifled Springfields. Thus a month after Sumter fell the State had sent three well-armed regiments into service. When the first reached Washington May 13, with shining barrels, ample ammunition, tents, and a baggage train, General Scott exclaimed: "Thank God, we have one regiment ready to take the field!" [10]

Before Sumter, William Schouler, the Massachusetts adjutant-general, had begun to press Cameron for arms. The Bay State already had 3000 rifled muskets, and he wished the national government to give it 2000 more. Governor Andrew made still more urgent pleas, demanding arms first from Springfield, and later from the Watertown arsenal. He obtained a supply that gave Massachusetts' early contingents a superior equipment, many of her troops boasting excellent rifles.[11]

In the West, Illinois alone, by dint of luck and enterprise in getting hold of so large a part of the contents of the St. Louis arsenal, was able to equip her early regiments fairly well. We have seen how, late in April, Captain James H. Stokes of Chicago, cooperating with Nathaniel Lyon, seized 21,000 muskets, 500 rifled carbines, 110,000 cartridges, and several cannon, which were promptly moved to Springfield.[12] While Illinois troops were benefited, those of neighboring states suffered. Only 7,000 muskets were left in St. Louis to equip the Union volunteers there. When Governor Dennison of Ohio complained and sent an emissary to Springfield with a requisition which the departmental commander supported by a telegram, Yates with bad grace allowed Ohio 5000 arms. He had good reason to hold on to all the equipment possible, for the State repositories had contained only 362 altered muskets, 105 rifles,

---

10   Croffut and Morris, *Military and Civil Hist. Conn.*, 67, 83–85.
11   O. R. III, i, 66, 71, 85, 93; Wm. Schouler, *Massachusetts in the Civil War*, I, 219, 220 ff. But some later Bay State regiments were badly armed. At Ball's Bluff the Fifteenth Massachusetts, carrying smoothbores useful only at short range, suffered heavily from Confederates armed with long-range rifles; C. F. Walcott, *Hist. of the 21st Massachusetts*, 14 ff.
12   Report Adjutant-General of Ill., I, 241.

133 musketoons (short, large-bore muskets used by artillery and cavalry), and 297 horse-pistols! Of course his St. Louis spoils did not carry Illinois very far, and the later regiments were as poorly provided as the others of the Northwest. Some got no arms at all until Christmas.[13]

The story of other States may be summed up in the experience of Pennsylvania and her eager, efficient executive Andrew Curtin. At the outbreak of war the authorities found that they had just about 4200 efficient small arms. The totals were much larger, to be sure, coming to 14,700 pieces on paper, but many were antique smoothbores with broken locks or rust-eaten barrels, and some were actually flintlocks that veterans of Valley Forge would have recognized as old friends. As unarmed volunteers fell into line in every town, Curtin sent a wild appeal to Secretary Cameron. Major-General Patterson, just made head of the department embracing Pennsylvania, made similar appeals. They sent demands not only to the War Department but to General Wool in New York.

In response, the War Department ordered Federal arsenals to supply weapons, for as General Scott wrote Patterson, Washington wished no troops sent away unarmed. General Wool also did his best, ordering some 26,000 muskets and more than a million cartridges sent to Pennsylvania. Replying to a special request for 10,000 guns for the 15 reserve regiments which the State was organizing on her own account, Cameron on June 13 announced that the Ordnance Bureau had been told to send them enough smoothbores.[14] Arms did trickle in, but they were never adequate in quantity. The Pennsylvania colonels and General Patterson also protested that many were worthless, and that much of the ammunition was of the wrong caliber. Like other States, Pennsylvania had to make efforts to obtain arms abroad.

The most hot-tempered of all the governors, Oliver P. Morton in Indianapolis, naturally raised the loudest uproar. He had scented approaching danger as soon as the Confederacy was formed. No governor hated slavery more than this explosive man who had walked angrily out of the Indiana Democratic convention the moment it endorsed the Kansas-Nebraska Act, and none stood up more sturdily for his State. "What does this mean? Why this discrimination against Indiana?" he blazed in a telegram to Washington when he thought it slighted. Before Sumter, he had demanded that the War De-

---

13 *Ibid.*, 6 ff. Illinois made vain attempts to buy arms in the East this summer, finding prices too high. When the Fifty-fifth Illinois, recruited during the summer, went to Missouri to fight, it did not draw arms until late December; and they were so wretched that a sergeant wrote Governor Yates that the regiment might better use alder popguns. A Committee of the Regiment, *The Story of the 55th Illinois*.
14 Egle, *Curtin*, 208 ff.; F. H. Taylor, *Philadelphia in the Civil War*, 17 ff.; O. R. III, i, 179–181, 256, 270.

partment store 5,000 small arms and other materials in Indiana in anticipation of trouble. He got approval of the idea, but no shipments. Just after Sumter, while hurrying two agents East and one to Canada to buy arms, he telegraphed Washington that of his 2,400 volunteers in camps, less than half had weapons: "Not a pound of powder or a single ball sent to us, or any sort of equipment." He hastened to Washington, obtained promises, returned home, and then posted to Washington again because the promises were broken. Ten thousand men, he rumbled, were awaiting equipment.[15]

When Cameron explained that a part of the arms ordered to Indiana had been destroyed at Harpers Ferry, Morton refused to be mollified. Nor did Cameron placate him by authorizing Indiana to draw 1500 pieces from the St. Louis arsenal, that arsenal which the Illinoisans had just emptied. Some rifled muskets did arrive from the Pittsburgh arsenal and other points. A peppery debate ensued between Morton and Cameron. Indiana, wrote the Secretary, was unjustified in her bitter scolding, for she had received 3000 new percussion smoothbores, 5000 flintlock muskets altered to percussion, and 1000 Maynard rifled muskets, along with some minor driblets. Altogether, the government had given Indiana 9500 arms for the 5000 men for which it had asked the State. Why, then, the Hoosier ululations? But this was not at all Morton's view. He pointed out that a great part of the arms were abominable, and that he had actually quelled something like a mutiny in the Twelfth Indiana because the men wished to reject unusable old smoothbores. Other troops grumbled that they were given muskets a century old.

The irritated Morton on May 30 appointed Robert Dale Owen the State agent to procure implements of war, and Owen left to join a clamorous group of similar agents in New York. Finally the governor established his own State ammunition manufactory in Indianapolis, which throve so well that in time it sold its surplus to the nation.

So the story went all over the map. New York made appeal after appeal, search after search. Her defeat in getting immediate supplies was writ large in newspaper advertisements on June 1 asking for bids to supply 10,000 Minié rifled muskets and 2000 Minié rifles, with ammunition to equip a force of 12 to 15 regiments of infantry, cavalry and artillery.[16] Iowa, after rebuffs from Cameron and Yates—the latter unwilling to spare any of the St. Louis

15 W. D. Foulke, *O. P. Morton*, I, 38, 39, 82, 113–117, 129; O. R. III, i, 64, 65, 89, 93, 116, 122, 149; Anon., *The Soldier of Indiana, passim.* Morton appointed Lewis Wallace the State adjutant-general. He and the quartermaster-general reported many of the Federal arms to be very inferior.

16 Rawley, *E. D. Morgan*; N. Y. *Tribune*, June 1; Burt, Memoirs; Capt. C. E. Minié of Vincennes had gained fame by his elongated bullet, widely used throughout the world. On Robert Dale Owen see the biography by Richard Leopold.

booty—appealed to the governor of Connecticut, to Simeon Draper of the New York Defense Committee, and to arms manufacturers, all without result. The first four Iowa regiments stayed in camp waiting for arms, which finally came as a mixture of antiquated and rubbishy pieces.[17]

To each worried governor, the War Department in the spring and summer of 1861 appeared obtuse and indifferent. Arms were lying at Watertown, Springfield, Pittsburgh: "Why don't they send the arms?" Harassed men in the little War Department took a different view. "It is not possible," James W. Ripley of the Ordnance Bureau wrote the Ohio governor in May, "to meet demands for arms to be distributed among the people without very soon exhausting our entire supplies, and making disproportionate distributions to different parts of the country. There are no Harper's Ferry rifles on hand, and the small supply of rifles should be reserved for the troops of the longer period of service."[18] As national forces grew, the States had to be kept rigorously stinted. As late as the autumn of 1862 Ripley was writing Yates:[19]

I regret very much that it is not within the power of the Ordnance Department to supply to all new troops, such arms as it would afford me pleasure to furnish, if we had or could by any means obtain them; but your Excellency is well aware of the utter impossibility of procuring a sufficient supply of first-class arms to supply to our large armies, and we are therefore compelled to issue the best to be had. In doing this the just rights of the different States are considered. The available arms are arranged in classes and distributed pro rata to the troops called for from each State.

The more energetic States quickly sent arms-buyers abroad. Massachusetts acted with special promptness. On legislative authority given April 20, Andrew appointed F. B. Crowninshield as State agent to procure muskets, rifles, and pistols overseas, and four days later, with a credit of £50,000 and an expert assistant from Springfield, he sailed from New York. His instructions were to buy 25,000 stand of the best quality, as nearly as possible like the guns used in the regular army. Maine and New Hampshire, hearing of his errand, commissioned him to buy for them 3000 and 2000 rifles respectively, and a little later credits came from Connecticut and Ohio. On arriving in London May 6 Crowninshield found that, early as he was, he had to compete with Southern emissaries and buyers from other Northern States, and that speculators were forcing up prices. His assistant, hurrying to Birmingham, where 25,000 first-class Enfield rifles were reported available at £3, found a Southern agent ready to pay £5 apiece for the whole lot, and thought himself lucky to buy

17 Upham, "Arms and Equipment for the Iowa Troops." *Ia. Journal of Hist.*, XVI, 3 ff.
18 Endorsement on letter of Gov. Dennison May 9, 1861; Ordnance Letters, War Dept.
19 Oct. 24, 1862; Ordnance Bureau, Misc. Letterbooks, No. 56, pp. 396, 397.

2000.[20] It was clear to Crowninshield that he should not haggle over prices; and before he sailed back, he obtained 19,380 good Enfield rifles for Massachusetts and shipped part of them, while he also bought 10,000 sets of knapsacks and cartridge boxes, with other equipment.

Leaders in New York meanwhile urged Governor Morgan to buy arms in Europe, and at their suggestion he sent over George L. Schuyler of Schuyler, Hartley & Graham, with authority to obtain about a million dollars' worth of small arms and ordnance. The anxious governor equipped him with a letter to Prime Minister Palmerston which obviously should have gone through the American legation.[21] Howland and Aspinwall also bought arms abroad.

[III]

All this work, however, was swiftly taken over by larger authority; and now we must turn to the national government. We may first summarize its action 1861–62 in two paragraphs.

Clearly, Washington alone could introduce order in place of the confusion and frustration produced by the competing States. As the great new volunteer army came into being, Federal authorities had to accept full responsibility for equipping the men. As fast as possible, they had to take over contract-letting at home and abroad, provide for rigid arms inspection, and accelerate manufacturing at Springfield. Step by step, they gained mastery of the chaotic field, making the Ordnance Bureau one of the nation's most powerful agencies.

Before the end of 1861, War Department contracts had been standardized and a good inspection service created. State purchasing for the national government was permitted only by specific War Department authorization. In many instances the Department refused to compensate States for high-cost purchases in the first months of the conflict, alleging loose methods and disregard of government price specification; in many other instances it reduced the valuation on purchases. Naturally the States were angry, and it was a relief all around when State buying on national account ceased.[22] Federal purchasing

20 Schouler, *Mass. in Civil War*, I, 219, 220; Pearson, *Andrew*, I, 192; Reports of the Master of Ordnance in Mass. Adjutant-General's *Reports*, 1861, 1862. The Master states that Crowninshield bought in all 20,380 rifled Enfield muskets for £73,900.

21 Schuyler bought for New York troops 25,080 rifled Enfields at $16.70 delivered in New York city. He was an able agent, and though his authority to act for the State was suspended in July, on the 29th of that month Cameron authorized him to purchase large consignments for the United States. Rawley, *Morgan;* Burt, *Memoirs;* N. Y. Bureau of Mil. Statistics, *1st Ann. Report* (1863); O. R. III, i, 355. The reports of the New York adjutant-general are singularly unenlightening, and that State lacks a sound history of its war effort. Morgan's 72-page message of January, 1862, contains valuable information.

22 Ripley endorsement on letter of J. N. Ray, March 13, 1862, Ordnance Letters to War Dept.; Cameron to Ripley, War Office Military Bk., No. 47, Jan. 10, 1862; Ripley to Curtin, Oct. 2, 1861, Ordnance Misc. Letterbook No. 55, p. 160.

of arms abroad slackened in the spring of 1862, when everyone hoped for the capture of Richmond, and began again on an improved basis. Government manufacture meanwhile rose until by the spring of 1863 the national armories were producing 30,000 first-class Springfield rifles a month.[23]

But this systematization of arms delivery was not achieved without blunders, delays, and failures of the most disheartening kind. What were they?

War Department confusion at the outset was staggering. Cameron, not allowed before Sumter to prepare for war lest he anger the South, remained ill-prepared because he lacked foresight and energy. When the aging Colonel H. K. Craig had to be dropped as head of the Ordnance Bureau, the Secretary appointed another infirm, incompetent veteran, Lieut.-Colonel James W. Ripley, whom the press soon dubbed Ripley Van Winkle. The bureau staff was so inadequate that extra clerks had to be employed on daily wages.[24] It was a signal misfortune to the North that its supply of arms and munitions was not controlled by a man as able, clearheaded, and progressive as the quarter-master chief, Montgomery C. Meigs.

Ripley was slow, unenterprising, and loath to accept responsibilities. As late as June 3, 1861, possessing no information about the size of the anticipated military force, he asked whether Cameron would approve of provision for 250,000 men in all branches. This was less than half the number envisaged by Congressional leaders, and little over half of what was in Lincoln's mind. Five days later he reported that the government had as yet purchased no muskets, that the Springfield armory was making only 2500 arms a month, and that the service lacked rifled muskets, accoutrements, artillery, and ammunition. But he optimistically declared that supplies on hand would meet all exigencies save the want of rifled muskets, that serviceable smoothbores could be used in their place, and that the Springfield armory and private establishments would maintain the supply and gather a reserve. No need to worry!—no reason even to hurry! Smoothbores would do! [25] A Pennsylvania regiment which compared its Harpers Ferry muskets with Enfield rifles found that the Enfields hit targets at 1000 yards which the muskets missed at 400, and that a mark at 500 yards was riddled by the Enfields while the "buck and ball" of the Harpers Ferry pieces (a ball topped by three buckshot) all fell ignominiously short.

Had the War Department moved with celerity in April–May, 1861, to buy the whole European supply of sound arms and contracted for the whole

23 For a time in the spring of 1862 the Ordnance Bureau refused even the best offers of new contracts like that by Lubback & Co., London, of 100,000 Enfields; Ripley to C. A. Field, April 30, 1862, Ordnance Misc. Letterbook No. 55, p. 160.
24 Meneely, *War Department, 1861*, 112–113.
25 O. R. III, i, 245, 260.

available output that year, it would not only have acquired an ample store, but would have severely crippled the unindustrialized Confederacy. Such action would have made State buying abroad unnecessary. A few shrewd men urged this. But the whole government, and indeed the American people, underrating the effort ahead and unused to large-scale Federal action, shared the blame. Ripley did not press his early suggestion that a Federal agent be sent abroad to obtain from 50,000 to 100,000 small arms and eight batteries of rifled cannon. He was unduly worried about uniformity of ammunition supply and red-tape standards of quality and cheapness. Cameron also was slow, partly because, like Seward and others, he hoped the war could be quickly ended, and partly because his protectionism made him insist on favoring home industry. Rebuffing Ripley's proposal, as late as July 1 he wrote Lincoln that it was important to encourage domestic manufactures by placing orders in America rather than abroad—especially as war with some European power was a possibility. General Scott and several Cabinet members supported this view.[26]

Two men saw the need of the hour more plainly. One was Henry S. Sanford, minister to Belgium, who tossed on his bed at night worrying about arms. "It distresses me," he wrote Seward a month after Sumter, "to think while we are in want of them, Southern money is to take them away to be used against us." The other was Frémont, who as we have noted had the courage to make provisional contracts. Sanford could merely exhort action; merely urge that because all Europe was arming, because every progressive nation was discarding smoothbores for rifles, because of the machinery shortage, and because supplies were low and prices rising, the United States should move instantly. He begged Seward to send agents to search England and France, to ransack Belgium, and to see if Sweden and Prussia would not sell arms.[27] He himself had no power to act. But Frémont, dropping his European business, did buy. The explorer overcame the Yankee caution of Charles Francis Adams, who reluctantly drew on Treasury funds for $75,000 worth of cannon and shells and $125,000 worth of rifles Frémont had ordered. Frémont, who had been willing to pledge his private means, never forgave Adams for refusing to do the same. A cold, selfish, heartless man, he wrote, who would see the republic sink before he would risk a penny of the Adams fortune!

Adams assured Seward that only his sense of the terrible emergency led him to approve of Frémont's purchases. Lincoln at once ordered the War De-

---

26 *Ibid.*, 263; Meneely, War Department, 1861, 285.
27 See Report of Committee on Ordnance and Ordnance Stories," July 1, 1862, 37th Cong., 2d. Sess., Senate Exec. Doc. 72; Sanford's warning letter of May 12, 1861, is in O. R. III, i, 277, 278.

partment to honor the drafts, and all the arms were later shipped to the front. But the State Department, agreeing with Cameron, wrote Adams in June that the government would authorize no more foreign contracts. Indeed, except for allowing Sanford to buy 10,000 pieces, Washington temporarily shut down on all purchases abroad, while Cameron and Ripley sat on their hands.[28]

Until Bull Run!—for that thunderclap awakened everybody. It was while its first echoes resounded that Cameron wrote the New York agent, Schuyler, to buy with all speed 100,000 foreign rifled muskets, 10,000 carbines, 20,000 cavalry sabres, and 10,000 revolvers; on July 29 his formal appointment came; and by mid-August, with a $2,000,000-credit at Baring Brothers, he was rummaging the British warehouses. No more home-market coddling!

Unfortunately, Schuyler came too tardily on the scene. He at once found that the Northern States and the Confederacy had almost completely cleared the market of the best rifles, and tied up the best arms factories by their contracts. Prices had risen to double their usual level. Of course antiquated arms, the refuse of decades, in all types, patterns, and calibres, could be had in unlimited quantities, but his instructions and good sense forbade his taking them. When he turned to government arsenals, he found that the British authorities interdicted any sales, but that he might get 45,000 to 48,000 French rifles of an 1853 model. At about the same time he persuaded the Birmingham manufacturers, who were united in a powerful association and had been busily engaged in filling Southern and State contracts, to agree to deliver 35,000 Enfields in New York within six months. Then he was suddenly tripped up by bad luck. He met trouble in getting his money sent from New York to Baring Brothers; the French transaction became public knowledge and Napoleon III forbade it; and Confederate agents snapped up the Birmingham contract at a high price per gun.

In the end, Schuyler did buy a large quantity of arms: 15,000 Enfield rifles in Birmingham at an average price of $18.45 apiece, 4000 French rifles at $17.60, and more than 97,000 good rifles from the government arsenals in Dresden and Vienna at slightly lower prices. These, with 10,000 cavalry carbines and a quantity of revolvers and sabres, cost slightly more than his two millions. His principal purchases were made possible by the friendly attitude of the Austrian Government. Throughout his mission Schuyler, working for only $10 a day and expenses, conducted his affairs with exemplary care, system, and dispatch. He and the expert armorer with him, who meticulously in-

---

28 Nevins, *Frémont*, 3rd ed., 474, 475; O. R. III, i, 293. Frémont bought cannon and shells in England, rifles in France. The Belgian muskets mentioned by Sanford were poor, and Prince Napoleon told D. D. Field they were not worth buying. Cf. T. F. Upson, *With Sherman to the Sea*, 27.

spected all purchases, were repeatedly insulted by men who offered them heavy bribes if they would take inferior equipment.[29]

In his letters home, Schuyler vainly tried to awaken the Ordnance Bureau to the realities of the foreign situation. He emphasized the fact that really excellent arms could not be obtained at any price, even $100 apiece, except from government arsenals, or from private manufacturers already busy with American orders. But Cameron and Ripley, never quite grasping this, contracted with dealers—often mere speculators—for extensive deliveries of foreign arms. They did not comprehend that the government was merely bidding against itself or the States.

The heavy War Department buying of foreign arms through dealers began just after Bull Run with such orders as that to C. K. Garrison, an American, for 10,000 rifled Liége muskets at $27. Ripley agreed in August to accept 4000 foreign rifles from John Pender of Philadelphia at $18.50. The same month J. P. Fitch of New York agreed to deliver 50,000 Enfield rifles at $20, a total later raised to 75,000, while another dealer contracted to bring over 26,000 Enfields at $20. The department bought some Vincennes rifles, a superior arm, at $23.50 delivered in the fall of 1861. This list might be much extended. Such emergency purchases, it will be seen, were at levels materially above those paid by Schuyler in his careful bargaining. He obtained 4000 rifles of Vincennes pattern at almost $6 less than the War Department, and Enfields at $1.55 less, though he gave them a much more rigorous inspection. The alert New Yorker was the keenest businessman abroad.[30]

Altogether, foreign purchases of the Federal Government mounted until by June 30, 1862, they totaled nearly 727,000. Of these Schuyler procured 116,000. Probably if the whole effort had been put in the hands of a purchasing commission directed by Schuyler, he could have obtained much greater firepower at less cost; that is, as many arms, of better quality, at lower rates. At that, the Federal acquisitions were in general better than those of the States. Schuyler kept pointing out how wretched were the weapons shipped to fill State orders, and pleading that State agents be called home and kept there.[31]

Alongside Schuyler labored Minister Sanford, the principal agent in pre-

29 For Schuyler's operations see O. R. III, i, 355, 418, 484–486, 581, 640, etc. See also Schuyler's Report, April 8, 1862, published as a pamphlet. The Chase Papers contain an interesting letter by John J. Cisco, Sept. 24, 1861, on possibilities of buying from Napoleon III; Pa. Hist. Soc.

30 For typical contracts see Ripley to Garrison, July 26, 1861, Ordnance Misc. Letterbook No. 53, p. 280; to Mitchell & Jones, Ibid., 286, 287; to N. V. Barkalow, Letterbook No. 54, p. 42; and see T. A. Scott to Ripley Aug. 5, 1861, War Dept. Military Book No. 45.

31 O. R. III, ii, 855. Asst.-Secretary Peter H. Watson wrote early in 1862 that many arms had been obtained by State agents against the advice of the War Department; to Henry Wilson, Feb. 20, 1862, War Dept. Military Book No. 47.

clusive buying. This bustling, indefatigable, resourceful Connecticut Yankee, not yet forty, with a degree from Heidelberg, found Belgium all too tiny a sphere, and loved to keep an eye on all Western Europe, popping in and out of half the capitals. With insatiable zest, he applied himself to running down Confederate contracts and obstructing or destroying them.

In a single month, with generous credits from the War Department, Sanford obtained 40,000 stand of arms about to go off in a blockade runner, and gobbled up a Confederate contract for 72,000 other arms of low price and quality. He chartered special vessels, in one instance paying a Hamburg company $40,000 for a single voyage, to get his war materials to the United States. After the Trent affair ended, he hurried forward some cargoes which the British had prudently embargoed.[32] All this was in addition to his unwearied prosecution of secret service work and propagandist activities in Europe—activities which, extending to England, gave Charles Francis Adams, jealously sensitive to meddling, acute pain.

As the foreign arms sent across the Atlantic by State agents, reputable dealers, shady speculators, and others were distributed, a roar of indignation and recrimination went up. The best Enfield, Vincennes, and Austrian Government rifles were dependable, but many other pieces were more horrendous to user than to foe. American orders had been a boom to European arsenals anxious to sweep away a clutter of antique and damaged pieces, some of them older than Austerlitz. Newspapers told of regiments taking foreign pieces out to practice, blazing away at the woods, and falling back in disorder with burst barrels and wounded men. Then, too, the conglomeration of arms made replacement of parts difficult, and use of uniform ammunition impossible. A letter which Ripley presently wrote a Pennsylvania officer tells the whole story:

The parts of foreign arms do not interchange. They cannot, therefore, be repaired in the way usual with American arms. It is the practise with some regiments, and should be the case with all regiments armed with foreign arms, to have a mechanic detailed to keep the arms of the regiment in good order. This Dept. will furnish the necesary tools and materials on requisition. If the bayonets do not fit, it is probable that they have been allowed to be mixed up in unpacking the boxes which contained them. In arming the new troops it has been necessary to issue supplies from different points, and in great haste.[33]

[IV]

The War Department's early purchasing of arms from home factories was as blundering and wasteful as the foreign buying. These contracts were chiefly

32 Sanford's papers are not yet available. See Meneely, *op. cit.*, 297 ff.; Moran Diary.
33 Ripley to Casey Aug. 25, 1862, Ordnance Misc. Letterbook No. 56, p. 50.

for Springfield pattern rifles, of a quality, if specifications were met, beyond question. Theoretically, they were regulated by laws requiring government advertising for bids, open competition, and systematic inspection. But the emergency was so severe and industrial facilities so weak that at the outset the laws counted for little. The government was no more able to wait than Britain was when Hitler invaded the Low Countries.

Buying had to be done by hurried emergency action outside the law. We have seen how Lincoln had three members of the Union Defense Committee of New York allowed $2,000,000 for immediate war expenditures. As part of this frenzied initial effort Cameron gave his old political supporter Alexander Cummings, now briefly editor of the New York *World*, free rein to make some preposterous purchases. Among other items, Cummings spent $21,000 on straw hats and linen trousers for troops, and bought large quantities of ale, porter, pickles, and tongue. He might have been planning a picnic!

The War Department was at once besieged by contractors and politicians. Its rule was that the Secretary must not directly concern himself with contracts, and Cameron strictly obeyed it. "I had really hoped," he wrote Horace Greeley at the beginning of 1862, "that you had long ago become convinced, from what you have often heard me say, that I have never made any contracts in connection with this Department." But Congressmen were besieged by manufacturers, and wirepulling unquestionably affected contract policy. Even Lincoln was teased into writing a letter for a good Western friend who desired some contracts for building river gunboats.[34] Some of the lesser contract irregularities concerned arms.

As no manufacturer was able to furnish a huge quantity of weapons, and as even the most efficient works often had to erect buildings and install machinery, the contracts had to be scattered in small orders among a variety of suppliers. The Starr Arms Company at Binghamton, New York, got a contract for 80,000 Springfield-pattern muskets, rifled; the Providence Tool Company for 50,000; Eli Whitney of Whitneyville, Connecticut, a son of the inventor, for 40,000; C. B. Hoard of New York for 50,000; and so on. By the spring of 1862 fully a score of orders for small arms had been let. Ripley was scrupulous in insisting that the rifles must conform strictly in design, materials, and workmanship to those made in the Springfield armory, and be subjected to the same inspection. He was rigid about delivery dates. Some manufacturers signed rashly on the dotted line.

Too rashly—for again and again they encountered unforeseen difficulties. Hardworking Eli Whitney, for example, had to build a new factory, and install a new outfit of machinery. He had to prepare four kilns to dry his gun-stocks,

34 Cameron to Greeley, Jan. 15, 1862, Cameron Papers; Lincoln to Commissioner Smith and others, March 28, 1862, *Collected Works*, V, 174.

and order his gun-barrels from another maker. He found it necessary to employ 200 new hands, and might need 325. Even then he was uncertain whether accidents might not prevent his making the first delivery when promised. "I do not think the price, $20, too high, considering the expedition required and the conditions of payment. I do not think the government will obtain more than one quarter of the guns ordered, taking all together, and enforcing stipulations as to time." [35] Whitney's contract, when delays actually occurred, was cut back to 25,000 rifles with a resultant loss.

Similar difficulties were encountered by Lamson, Goodnow & Yale of Windsor, Vermont. They received a government contract in July, 1861, for 25,000 rifled muskets and appendages, which was doubled within three months. At Windsor they had a large plant which had manufactured some 35,000 muskets of the model of 1842, and had furnished a good deal of machinery to the Enfield plant in England. Here they set two hundred men to work making gun machinery and finishing gun parts. They ordered barrels, bayonets, and ramrods from the Bay State works at Northampton, Massachusetts, and a Worcester factory; they forged locks, mountings, and other parts at their own cutlery works in Shelburn Falls, they bought gunstocks. But they, too, met unavoidable delays. After they had invested from $100,000 to $150,000, they plaintively wrote the War Department that they hoped to deliver guns soon, though the contract date had expired; "and now if, for any reason, the government will not receive the fifty thousand, we desire to be informed immediately." They were accepted. [36]

Even so efficient an establishment as Colt's Arms Company, with a factory in Hartford that contained some of the most ingenious machinery in the world, was unable to meet its contract dates. Samuel Colt agreed in July, 1861, to furnish 25,000 rifled muskets of Springfield pattern at $20, the first thousand to be ready in six months. He erected new buildings, installed machinery, and let sub-contracts for barrels, locks, and other parts. Troubles, however, soon thickened about his head—a shortage of skilled labor, the sudden demand of the War Department for special attention to holster pistols, and the tardiness of parts suppliers. The situation was complicated by his long illness, ending in death January 10, 1862. The government recognized that the Colt Company not only had a just claim to some modification, but was too useful to be treated harshly. With a two-million-dollar factory, 1500 employees working day and night shifts, and appliances for making 1000 guns a week, it stood in advance of every other private arms establishment in the land. [37]

35   37th Cong., 2d Sess., Senate Exec. Doc. 72, p. 386; testimony April 11, 1862.
36   *Ibid.*, p. 160.
37   *Ibid.*, 59–61. The destruction of the Colt factory by fire February 10, 1864, was felt as a national blow and caused arms prices to rise. See N. Y. *Tribune*, Feb. 10, 1864, and picture in *London Illustrated News*, April 16. It was at once rebuilt.

In general, however, Ripley pursued a severe policy in enforcing contract provisions. The department refused price readjustments, declined to make any allowance to Remington when new Federal taxes imposed a totally unforeseen expense, would not compensate arms importers for fluctuations in international exchange, and brusquely rejected Whitney's anguished appeals for a little more time.[38] Yet these severe policies were coupled, as we have noted, with the two prime errors of ordering too many arms, and paying excessive prices for many of them.

A cost plus system, had Congress been willing to authorize it and the Ordnance Bureau able to police it, would have been better than the allocation of so many hit or miss contracts at hit or miss prices. The before-noted total of 1,164,000 Springfield-type rifled muskets for which the War Department contracted by the summer of 1862 was about twice the amount of home deliveries required; the average price of $20 a gun, with appendages, was about twenty per cent above the proper level. It took time for both government and manufacturers to learn that on bargains for 25,000 rifled muskets or more, $16 would afford a fair profit to efficient makers. Remington & Sons, contracting for a large quantity at that price, gave the Ordnance Bureau its first trustworthy data on costs.[39] The War Department could then regret its numerous $20 contracts, and such orders as that to the Burnside Carbine Company for 7500 carbines at $35 each.[40]

By the summer of 1862 the errors mentioned were cured. The Congressional committee on ordnance reported that it had reduced the domestic orders for Springfields to 473,000, had revised prices, and by other steps had saved the government about $17,000,000. Ripley, in view of the urgent need for arms after the failure of McClellan's advance on Richmond, relaxed the more senseless inspection requirements. The main point, he wrote the Secretary of War, was to secure arms "of the prescribed calibre, of good strong barrels, stocks, and locks, and in all respects serviceable as military weapons." Blemishes could be overlooked.[41]

Disregard of the advertising requirement had not only permitted exorbitant prices, but offered contract jobbers an opportunity to peddle their influence. When the Savage Arms Company failed to get an order, it hired Thomas Dyer, who said he could manage it, and who collected $10,000 for obtaining a pistol contract. Later the same firm employed the adventurer Henry Wikoff, who

38 Ripley's Endorsement Sept. 1, 1863, Ordnance Letters to War Dept., No. 14, pp. 321-323.
39 Report, 37th Cong., 2d Sess., Senate Exec. Doc. 72, pp. 15-18.
40 These were, however, a special weapon weighing 7 pounds, of .54 caliber. Ripley to L. Hartshorne, August 27, 1861; Ordnance Misc. Letterbook No. 53, pp. 307, 308. Senate Exec. Doc. 72, *ut sup.*
41 Ripley to Stanton August 8, 1862. Ordnance Letters to War Dept. Bk. 13, pp. 464, 465.

actually urged the Savage Company to charge $22.50 for a $19 pistol just because he had filed an application for a contract on which he asked that amount! A specially scandalous offense was proved against Senator James F. Simmons of Rhode Island, a yarn-manufacturer and politician approaching seventy, who introduced a Providence manufacturer to the War Department, helped him get an order for 50,000 rifled muskets, and charged $10,000. As the Congressional committee on ordnance scorchingly put it, he sold his supposed influence; and public opinion forced him to resign in humiliation.[42]

By the end of 1862, but not until that time, the Northern need for proper quantities of weapons as good as the rifled Springfield or Enfield was being met. The helplessness of Frémont's command in Missouri the first war summer, or Sherman's at Louisville that fall, now seemed but a bad dream.[43] Yet it must be remembered that at all times the North had been far better provided with arms and ammunition than the South. When the war began the South, scouring all sources, found that the total number of usable guns for infantry in the Confederacy did not exceed 150,000, and only 20,000 of these were rifles. Several Southern States contracted for Northern arms before Sumter, but shipments were cut off by that event. European purchases brought in but small supplies. General Josiah Gorgas as head of the Ordnance Bureau revealed something like genius in establishing powder mills, arsenals, and arms factories. Weapons were made, altered, repaired, and stored at Richmond, Selma, Macon, Atlanta, Montgomery, Jackson, Little Rock, and other places. The ingenuity and persistence of Southern arms-makers must command the highest admiration. Yet receipts during the first year were negligible, and some Southern boys had to bear shotguns into the battle of Shiloh. Only the tremendous captures of Northern arms during 1862, placed at fully 100,000 pieces, kept the South weaponed.

Southern leaders, in fact, wrung their hands over the situation. When Gorgas on June 29, 1861, reported on all the arms in the Confederacy not in the hands of troops, he found but 15,000 available. The Richmond armory,

42 Report, 37th Cong., 2d Session, Senate Exec. Doc. 72, pp. 515 ff.
43 In fact, from this time surplus stocks began to accumulate. Ripley wrote September 1, 1863, that the government had on hand a very large supply of first-class arms, that monthly receipts from manufacturers constantly increased that stock, and that the Springfield armory alone was now supplying 20,000 arms monthly. Now and then a shortage of special parts appeared, as of gunstocks at the Springfield armory late in 1863, but this was transient. At the beginning of 1864 Assistant-Secretary Watson wrote that in view of the stored surplus and the unfilled contracts, the Springfield Armory could supply every musket needed even if the war continued for years. In the last year of the war the Ordnance Bureau was buying only revolvers and carbines, and it had contracted with the Remington Company, the best private supplier, for quantities of both. Ripley, endorsement on Whitney letter September 1, 1863, Ordnance Letters to War Dept. Book No. 14, pp. 321–323; Watson to Wheelock, Jan. 28, 1864, War Dept. Military Book No. 54b, p. 174; Ramsay to Stanton, Sept. 23, 1864, Ordnance Letters to War Dept., Book No. 15, pp. 180 ff.

beginning late that summer, could supply only a thousand small arms a month; the Fayetteville armory, beginning in March, 1862, could produce only about five hundred. That was the whole domestic picture for the South in the early part of the war! Down to August 16, 1862, the Confederate agent abroad, Caleb Huse, was able to land fewer than 50,000 arms in Southern ports. The Union by comparison held a position of growing wealth; and as the months passed the North also had an advantage in the rising superiority of much of its arms.

The obstacles met by the Confederates in getting arms from abroad were especially frustrating in the first year of the war, for after the foothill difficulties of purchasing came the high cliff of making shipments. Blockade running did not mean much to the arms trade until special steamers of great speed and low visibility were built for the purpose. Huse sent President Davis a gloomy letter from London just after Christmas in 1861, saying that he was miserable in having to look at the immense pile of packages on St. Andrew's Wharf without the power of sending anything: 25,000 rifles, 2,000 barrels of powder, 500,000 cartridges, and 13,000 accoutrements, besides great heaps of miscellaneous supplies. It took time, endless ingenuity, and worry to make inroads on this accumulation. Northern armies met no such frustrations.

The quality of the rifled muskets had steadily improved. Better machine tools counted for a great deal in this advance. Thus the Lamson, Goodnow & Yale Company of Connecticut used the Ball precision lathe machine, previously employed in making sewing-machine needles, the Robbins & Lawrence Company produced an efficient new rifling machine, and Brown & Sharpe of Providence brought on the market a universal milling machine that could be adapted to many purposes other than gun-making. Another important contribution, attributable to the Trenton ironmaster Abram S. Hewitt, was an ample supply of good American gun-metal, of the same quality as the famous Marshall iron imported from England. Hewitt, tremendously aroused by the war peril, did not hesitate to smuggle a spy into the Marshall plant to learn its secret. For this and other services, the Cooper, Hewitt works at Trenton received a glowing War Department citation. Finally, workers in the arms plants everywhere were gaining skill from experience.[44]

With stocks rising, with the Springfield armory getting under such headway that it alone would soon be able to meet national needs, and with prices falling, no more imported arms were needed after 1862. The firepower of the

44 *Mechanics Magazine*, VII, 105 (Feb. 14, 1862), 105. Guy Hubbard, series on "Development of Machine Tools in New England," *American Machinist*, vol. 60 (1924); Nevins, *Abram S. Hewitt*.

North had at all times been greater than that of the South, and the disproportion inexorably increased. Even when due weight is given the facts that the
South fought mainly on the defensive, initially possessed better marksmen, and
captured great quantities of Northern arms, this disparity was an important
element in deciding the outcome of the war. It might have been made greater.

[V]

The principal indictment against the Ordnance Bureau remains to be stated,
and can be summed up in the current press reproach of "old-fogyism." Critical
newspapers delighted to picture Ripley Van Winkle asleep in the Ordnance
Bureau guarded by two giants, Red Tape and Routine. When disturbed his
face would assume a disgusted frown, he would turn uneasily, and his lips
would mutter: "Keep him out!—inventor!—new idea!—can't come in here!—
Routine! Red Tape!" By the summer of 1862 an ambitious, hard-driving
junior, George T. Balch, was laboring to displace him. But he held power
until September 15, 1863, and continued to offer an unbreachable wall to
progress. In especial, his policy fatally impeded the large-scale adoption of
breechloading rifles.[45]

For the first two years of the war the use of muzzle-loading Springfields
and Enfield rifled muskets as standard patterns was absolutely unavoidable.
Thereafter, however, breechloaders might steadily have been introduced, and
larger and larger bodies of troops might have been equipped with repeating
breechloaders. Their use would have shortened the conflict.

The Springfield and Enfield rifles were effective weapons which used inter-
changeable ammunition, and thus simplified the problem of cartridge supply.
They were made in much the same way, for the Springfield plant had imported
sets of English rolling machines to make gun barrels, with English mechanics,
while the Enfield plant had bought much larger quantities of American machinery. The Springfield caliber was .58, the Enfield .57 plus; as the Springfields tended to foul after twenty-five rounds and become hard to reload,
many soldiers liked then to turn to the slightly smaller Enfield cartridge.
American factories could readily be tooled and manned to make Springfields
in quantity.

Breechloaders, however, posed a far more difficult problem. A number of
usable American models had been devised before 1861, notably the Colt, the
Hall, the Burnside, and the Sharps. Specific offers of the Spencer, Henry, and

45 N. Y. *Tribune*, Feb. 21, editorial "Rip Van Winkle in the Army Ordnance Bureau";
Bruce, *Lincoln and the Tools of War*, 260 ff.

Schenck breechloaders were made the War Department in that year. But as patterns varied greatly and the parts were difficult, breechloaders could at first be made only in small quantities and with excruciating delays.[46]

No two breechloaders, in fact, were constructed alike in 1861, so that the replacement of parts would soon have become a Chinese puzzle. Once the armies had been equipped with Springfields, Enfields, Vincennes, and other muzzle-loaders, as they had to be in 1861, it was impossible to arrange for any wholesale replacements before 1863. It can be argued that some buildings of the Springfield Armory might have been set aside to fix standard breechloading designs, to which private manufacturers could have been made to conform. But considering the crushing early demands, paucity of skilled workmen, and undeveloped character of machine tools, the equipment of such a branch would have been a slow task, carried out at the expense of more urgent requirements. When we say that the Colt, Hall, and other existing breechloaders were usable, we do not mean that they did not need great improvement. Army officers objected that they allowed an escape of gas at the junction of barrel sections where they were loaded, that the percussion powder needed for their cartridges was dangerous in jolting wagons, that they were not staunch enough for rough field service, and that troops in the excitement of battle would jam the delicate breech mechanism.[47]

This does not signify, however, that the Ordnance Bureau could not have provided great quantities of good breechloaders in 1863, for by energetic action it could. Not only had the cavalry used breechloading carbines for years, but American seamen and marines had employed them since 1858. The British navy was experimenting with them. Late in 1861 the government placed an order for 10,000 (later 16,000) Gibbs breechloading carbines at $28 each, with appendages.[48]

But this small order, with a delivery schedule of only 500 a month, was not followed up. At the end of 1862 the Ordnance Bureau was still experimenting cautiously with small orders let in a wide variety of quarters. When one contractor asked to have his new type of breechloader tested, Ripley objected on the ground that ten patterns of such arms were already being made, for eight of which tiny government contracts were in course of execution. This multiplicity of designs had caused so much confusion that he could not bear the thought of another.[49] From the ruck two superior arms decisively

46 S. B. Smith, "Military Small Arms," *Papers,* Ohio Commandery Loyal Legion, I, 174 ff. When the British had established their arms factory at Enfield in 1855 they were advised by officers who had carefully inspected American arms factories, and especially Springfield.

47 Ripley endorsement on Schenck's letter, Ordnance Letters to War Dept. Book No. 13, p. 170.

48 Ripley to W. F. Brooks, Dec. 13, 1861; Ordnance Misc. Letterbook No. 54, p. 215.

49 Ripley to Stanton, Jan. 9, 1863, Ordnance Letters to War Dept., Book 14, p. 55, National

emerged· one the Sharps carbine, a familiar single-shot breechloader specially adapted to cavalry, and the other the Spencer repeating rifle, a highly lethal weapon in the hands of infantry. With boldness and vigor, Ripley could have made both of them standard army equipment during the year of Gettysburg and Vicksburg. Had he done so, that might have been the war's last year.

The famous Sharps plant at Hartford was ready for a rapid expansion. Its single-shot breechloader, the most popular such rifle in the war, was especially liked by those who prided themselves on marksmanship. Hiram Berdan, a New York engineer of repute who had Lincoln's encouragement in organizing a famous sharpshooter regiment, did much to advertise it by his warm praise. The Ordnance Bureau placed contracts, especially late in the war, which eventually aggregated more than 100,000 pieces, so that in the last year the Sharps plant, greatly expanded, was employing 500 men day and night. It made more than 30,000 rifles that year. R. S. Lawrence, the master armorer, who under Sharps's direction had full charge of the factory, improved the arm in various ways during the conflict. Perhaps the first highly paid plant manager in the country, he wrote afterward with naïve satisfaction: "With my salary, speculations on machinery, etc., I found myself worth over $100,000." [50]

A good many telescope rifles for sharpshooters like Berdan, it may be interjected, were made by village blacksmiths and gunsmiths in the North. Indeed, telescope rifles had been frequently ordered before the war for the traditional Thanksgiving Day turkey-shoots and other matches. Weighing up to twenty pounds, they were necessarily fired from rests. In New England and the Middle States a village would sometimes not only denude itself of young men, but energetically forge weapons for the best marksmen. One Massachusetts company, going to war in 1861 with telescopic rifles, met first ridicule and then admiration. A member wrote back that the results were

---

Archives, explains his objection to the multiplicity of designs. Christian Sharps had patented his single-shot breechloading rifle in the 1840's. Christopher Spencer, who had worked in Colt's Hartford factory, patented his seven-shot repeating breechloader early in 1860.

50 *American Machinist*, vol. 60 (Jan. 31, 1924), 172. The Sharps Rifle Manufacturing Company made a variety of patent breechloading and self-priming arms—rifle, carbine, shotgun, and pistol. The superiority of the rifle had been established as early as 1850, when a board of ordnance officers under Major R. L. Baker made a report (Nov. 27), stating that of five makes of rifle and one of carbine presented, the Sharps was much the best. It was loaded with Mr. Sharps' special cartridge, and could be fired several hundred times without cleaning. The Sharps Company, using cast steel, boasted that their arms combined simplicity of design, rapidity of firing, extraordinary range, and perfect accuracy. See advertising circulars, NYPL.

Berdan asked the men he recruited to bring their own rifle with telescopic glass-sight or plain open sights. He wrote one of his enlistment agents, A. B. Stuart, Aug. 22, 1861, "You will see that no man is enlisted who cannot when firing at rest at a distance of 200 yards with a patent sighted rifle put ten consecutive shots in a target the average not to exceed five inches center to center, or with the plain open sight a distance of 300 feet same average." Austin Blair Papers, Burton Hist. Coll.

devastating. "They do good service at a mile, and are certain death at half a mile." At Edwards' Ferry, October 22, 1861, 70 men of this company repelled an advance of 1500 Confederates and drove them from the field with a loss of more than 100 killed, the Yankees suffering not a scratch: "The whistle of every bullet was the death knell of one." Tiffany's in New York offered some very fine and very costly telescopic rifles, among them the imported Whitworth target rifle, which soon sold out at $1250.[51]

Single-shot rifles were all very well, but a good repeating breechloader was something about which soldiers really dreamed. When Rosecrans took over Buell's army in the fall of 1862, he found his cavalry force low, and to compensate for this applied for 5000 Colt's repeating rifles. Raw recruits, he believed, if armed with repeaters that shot five times as fast as Springfields, would be superior to the toughest veterans using the old arms.[52] But while both Colt's and Henry's repeaters had merit, the Spencer carbines and rifles emerged as the cheapest, most durable, and most efficient of such weapons. They could sweep the ground with a deadly hail, and pick out men far beyond Confederate range. All the troops who saw the Spencer repeating rifle became clamorous for it.

That the armies preferred breechloaders, and that officers would have been glad to see at least picked companies in every regiment armed with repeating rifles, there can be no question. Had the soldiers determined Ordnance Bureau policy, they would soon have been adopted. The muzzle-loading smoothbores, which all too closely resembled the Brown Bess of Queen Anne's day, did execution only against masses of men, for they had to be aimed in barn-door fashion. Though troops who had rifled Springfields could pick out distant marks, they found it no fun to stand under fire loading them with ramrod and wad. Ripley's more energetic successor, Brigadier-General George D. Ramsay, grasped the rising demand for quick-firing weapons. He reported to Assistant-Secretary Watson early in 1864 that "repeating arms are the greatest favorite with the army, and could they be supplied in quantities to meet all requisitions, I am sure that no other arm would be used." He wrote again that summer in praise of the Spencer repeater: "It is, to a great extent, the only arm now asked for." [53]

The deadly effect of the repeating rifles used by some Union troops at the

51 *American Machinist*, vol. 59 (Oct. 18, 1923) 580, 581; "The Use of the Rifle," *Atlantic*, vol. 9 (March, 1862), 300–306.
52 W. D. Bickham, *Rosecrans' Campaign*, 25; Bruce, *Lincoln and the Tools of War*, 114, 115.
53 Endorsement on Applications of Sharps Co. and Burnside Co., Ordnance letters to War Dept. Book No. 14, p. 46; Brigadier-General George D. Ramsay to Stanton, July 14, 1864, *Ibid.*, Book 15, p. 98.

battle of Franklin this year appalled the Confederates who faced them; they were absolutely irresistible in repelling assaults.

After considering all excuses, we must pronounce the Ordnance Bureau under Ripley egregiously slow and cautious in providing both single-shot and repeating breechloaders. In 1861 it had to concentrate on muzzle-loading Springfields, Enfields, and the like. But in 1862 it could have encouraged capable arms manufacturers like the Remington, Colt, Sharps, and Whitney companies—like Merwin & Bray in New York, who made Ballard's very successful breechloading rifles and carbine, and like the New Haven Arms Company, which under Oliver F. Winchester made a variety of arms, including B. Tyler Henry's steadily improved repeater—to press their experiments. They could have agreed upon a standard breechloader design, and soon thereafter have commenced quantity production. By 1864, if not in 1863, it should have been possible to furnish the Northern armies wholesale as good an arm as the famous Prussian needle-gun which played so devastating a part in the Austrian War of 1866. This supply, and even a limited number of repeating rifles, would have transformed the military scene.[54]

What was needed was foresight, energy, and a planned effort to stimulate the great inventive capacity of Americans; what Ripley gave was stubborn caution. It was in spite of his objections that the army in 1863–64 finally contracted for some 41,000 Spencer repeaters—too late. When American makers exhibited arms at the Paris Exhibition of 1867 they gave breechloaders a dominant place, and among them were two magazine guns, the Spencer firing seven shots in twelve seconds, and a rifle made by the Windsor Manufacturing Company (Vermont) firing nine shots in eleven seconds. Of fourteen guns selected for the British breechloading competition in 1867, six were American and two more were made on American principles.[55]

The day of rapid-fire machine guns had not yet arrived. British officers inspecting McClellan's army in the Peninsular campaign found that he had fifty small "repeating guns," each drawn by a horse, but they were unsatisfactory. They were mounted on light wooden carriages. Two dozen cartridges at a time were placed in a hopper, they fell through its bottom into a

54 Cf. N. Y. *Tribune*, Jan. 30, 1864, "Improvements in Fire-Arms"; H. F. Williamson, *Winchester, The Gun That Won the West, passim.*

55 Ripley objected that magazine guns were too heavy, required special cartridges that might explode in transit, and were too costly; see his letter of Dec. 9, 1861, quoted in Williamson, *ut sup.* His attitude remained apparently unchanged until June, 1863, when he put in a trifling order for some 250 Henry repeaters. A British officer who saw seven-shot repeating rifles being made at the Parrott Works at Cold Spring, N. Y., late in 1864, thought them astonishing. He was told that although in action raw troops wasted much ammunition with them, cool marksmen made them very destructive, and a few men armed with them could hold a host at bay on a narrow front. Letter in London *Star*, Dec. 20, 1864, quoted in *Scientific American*, XII, Jan. 21, 1865.

revolving chamber, the gunner turned this chamber by a handle which also worked a percussion hammer, and as fast as he turned, the gun fired. The British observers were told that a hundred shots could be fired a minute; but in some practice at two hundred and fifty yards they observed that most of the ammunition was too small to take the rifling, the gun made few hits, and it soon got out of order. A mechanic, they thought, was needed to keep it in trim, and even then it might prove of little field utility.[56]

Here again, Ripley's disinclination to encourage experiment was unfortunate. Benjamin B. Hotchkiss, who filled war orders for projectiles and other munitions at his New York city factory, and who a decade later designed a five-barrelled weapon which quickly won worldwide adoption, might have been stimulated to devise an efficient rapid-fire piece. McClellan's hopper-and-handle contraption was at best defensive, useful only to hold a narrow bridge; Hotchkiss's gun was suited to offense. Richard J. Gatling, an inventive manufacturer of farm implements in the Middle West, patented a crude rapid-fire gun late in 1862. His first model, with ten revolving barrels, each with its own loading and ejecting mechanism, delivered 200–250 shots a minute. The Ordnance Bureau regarded the weapon with such chilliness that Gatling had to hire his own men to give several battlefield demonstrations during the war. Not until he made important improvements, took out a second patent in May, 1865, and got a Philadelphia arms company to manufacture twelve guns, did the War Department become keenly interested. Had he been given early aid, he might have had the Gatling gun, which the army adopted in 1866, ready for the campaigns of 1864.

[VI]

Ammunition was at first a perplexing problem, since the issuance of a weird variety of arms gave the officers who were responsible for providing it a maddening task. Powder was supplied by a number of firms, but by far the largest shipments came from the E. I. DuPont Company of Wilmington and the Hazard Company at Hazardville, Conn. The brilliant Lammot Du Pont shortly before the war had gone to Europe, inspected foreign powder mills, taken note of improvements resulting from Crimean experience, and returned home to begin a fruitful collaboration with Captain Thomas J. Rodman, ballistics engineer of the Ordnance Bureau. But British observers in 1862 thought the Du Pont method of manufacture inferior to their own.[57]

56 Report of Captains Thomas Mahon and R. Grant and Lieut. T. C. Price, August 1862, to Commander-in-Chief in Canada; Confidential Documents, British War Office.
57 See McClellan's *Report*, pp. 71, 72; William S. Dutton, *Du Pont: One Hundred and Forty Years, passim*; Report of Mahon, Grant, and Price, *ut sup.* Dutton estimates that Du

For muzzle-loaders the standard cartridge was a paper cylinder holding a soft-lead bullet and a charge of powder. Soldiers bit open the cartridge, poured the powder down the barrel, rammed home the ball (with a wad and some extra buckshot in smoothbores), and placed a percussion cap on the nipple to explode the charge. In the fever and noise of battle recruits often failed to notice that a weak hammer had failed to ignite the powder, and rammed down charge after charge until the gun was more dangerous to its holder than to the foe.

Breechloaders of course required a special cartridge. When the war began a number of metallic cartridges for them were available. They included the Burnside, invented by the versatile Ambrose E. Burnside, a percussion-cap cartridge for the Burnside carbine; the Maynard, a reloadable brass percussion cartridge invented by a dentist; and the Smith, with a brass foil or (experimentally) a rubber case. The most popular cartridge for cavalry was the Sharps, originally made of linen with a paper base nitrated for quick ignition, but later of metal. Part of the range, accuracy, and hitting power of the Sharps was attributable to its superior ammunition. The Spencer rifles, which were made in a distinctive bottleneck shape, used a rim-fire cartridge in which the priming charge was placed around the edge rather than in a central core. For all cartridges in all countries, the most troublesome problem was that of checking the escape of gas and fire at the breech, and Britons, Frenchmen, and Americans all toiled to solve it. Wesson of Smith & Wesson, revolver makers, had blazed a hopeful path by giving his rim-fire cartridge a projecting flange around the base.[58]

As the war continued and breechloaders became less rare, the brass or copper rim-fire cartridge became the universal favorite. It was manifestly

---

Pont furnished between 3.5 and 4 million pounds of powder to the Union army and navy, or probably 1 million pounds more than the plant which the Confederacy hurriedly built at Augusta supplied. The Du Pont business, struggling for a solid place, had been put firmly on its feet by the Crimean War, sending Britain and France huge shipments which wiped its books clear of debt. When war came in 1861 the Du Pont mills in Delaware constituted more than a third of the powdermaking capacity of the United States. Lammot Du Pont, the inventor of a new and excellent formula for blasting powder which had swept the markets, was at thirty the nation's leading expert in the chemistry of explosives. The North did not suffer from powder shortages. The South, on the other hand, dependent on its new Augusta mill and a small older establishment at Nashville, was soon paying an average of $3 a pound (more than ten times the normal price) for British powder shipped through the blockade; and seldom during the war was the Confederacy able to supply its infantry with more than 90 rounds a man, though the ordnance manual called for 200 rounds.

58 Leonard Davis, MS Paper on "Cartridges and the Civil War"; Williamson, *Winchester, the Gun That Won the West*. Leonard Davis states that the War Department bought 58,238,924 Spencer cartridges during the war. In spite of a growing uniformity of cartridges, the variety of missiles used remained preposterously wide. On Gettysburg battlefield one collector, J. M. Bush, picked up 125 different kinds of bullets, Union and Confederate, which may now be seen in the Gettysburg Museum.

superior to paper or linen types. As Ramsay wrote in the early summer of 1864, it was waterproof, a great consideration; holding its shape, it was easily inserted; it required no cap; the charge got the full force of the fulminate in the circular ring; and the flanged copper case, a perfect gas-check, gave the powder greater force. Manufacture was then in the hands of three firms, who charged what the Ordnance Department regarded as an excessive price, $28 a thousand. As the government would need 42,350,000 cartridges as a year's supply for the breechloading carbines on hand at the end of 1864, Ramsay proposed the erection of a special mill at the Frankfort Arsenal. So far as war needs went, this was a belated demand, for ere the mill could be put in running order, the war would be in its last stage.[59]

The South did not stand at such a disadvantage in ammunition as in small arms. Thanks to the energy of sleepless Confederate patriots, even in the summer of 1861, a stream of material for troops was coming from various sources: 50,000 to 100,000 rounds of ammunition a day from the Richmond ordnance laboratory, 20,000 to 30,000 rounds daily from the Augusta arsenal, 15,000 to 20,000 from the Charleston arsenal, and 30,000 to 40,000 from the Baton Rouge arsenal—with small amounts from other shops. But the quality of the ammunition fell below the Northern standard, battlefield shortages repeatedly tortured various commanders, and Gorgas and his able lieutenant in this field, G. W. Rains, worried constantly over the desperate need of the South for niter and other essentials. It was marvelous that the Confederacy did as well as it did.[60]

The Civil War was primarily an infantrymen's war, in which artillery played but a secondary part. Being a war of movement over great distances and rough terrain, so that the transport even of light fieldpieces like the popular Napoleon gun often involved great difficulty, it was best suited to mobile forces. Moreover, the rifled Springfields and Enfields had an effective range equal to that of field guns using canister, so that infantrymen could usually silence all but the best sheltered batteries and largest ordnance.

Artillery, like the small firearm, was undergoing a revolution. An English inventor of genius, William Armstrong, reading how the battle of Inkerman (November, 1854) was largely decided against the Russians by two eighteen-pounder guns which almost superhuman effort brought on the field at a late hour, asked himself whether lighter artillery might not be given equal range. When he prepared a design for rifled wrought-iron guns, the first in the world, obtained a contract from the War Office and set about improving his new

59 Ramsay to Stanton, June 25, 1864, Ordnance Letters to War Dept. Book No. 15, pp. 76, 77. Peter Peckham, an Illinois inventor, gained Lincoln's ear for a cartridge never adopted.
60 Frank E. Vandiver, *Ploughshares Into Swords*, 55–117, covers the subject admirably.

ordnance, the artillery revolution was under way. With the precise role played by artillery on American battlefields, however, we shall deal later.

It was a characteristic chapter of the times, this arms story. Initial bewilderment, hurry, confusion, improvisation, streaked with loss and disaster; a hectic meeting of immediate demands; the gradual emergence of a loose system—including termination of foreign orders, coordination of domestic contracts, and increased reliance on the Springfield armory; and finally a successful system. The arms story helps explain McClellan's delays, and Frémont's misfortunes. The steady improvement of arms supply underlay the partial successes of 1862. Only a long array of studies of individual effort, too numerous for general history, could do justice to the enterprise, resourcefulness and determination which dozens of able men, like Whitney, Colt, Winchester, Hewitt, Henry, and DuPont, brought to the service of the country; men far more anxious to save the Union than to promote their individual fortunes. The story of industrial mobilization has color and gallantry, and it touches the very heart of the developmental forces of the nation.

Yet, in the broad view, this chapter also records a very characteristic failure of vision and planning. Only halting, unimaginative use was made of the wide industrial superiority of the North, its fast-awakening energies in business and manufacture. Had the government looked ahead and taken suitable measures, had it by the end of 1863 given the armies a half-million good single-shot breechloaders and a quarter-million repeating rifles, the war might have ended far earlier, with a proportionate diminution of the misery and exhaustion that attended it.[61]

61 Kenneth P. Williams, *Lincoln Finds a General*, II, 782–785, explains the difficulties of introducing breech-loaders; but these difficulties could have been overcome.

19

December Gloom

IT WAS AN anxious autumn upon which the North entered in 1861. The weather in the Middle States and Virginia continued singularly bright, dry, and balmy; day after day throughout November and December the sun shone, mild breezes tossed the many-hued leaves, vehicles raised lines of dust, and men worked outdoors. But a leaden weight lay on the hearts of those who had hoped that the New York bells might ring peace. In the East, McClellan's army quivered and lay still like a basking crocodile. Although public sentiment could not easily forget the October whiplash of Ball's Bluff, McClellan made no response; and in the West, Frémont and Blair seemed more intent on fighting each other than on defeating Price and McCulloch.

Hope for quick action, inspired by McClellan's own words, had risen like a released fountain the moment he replaced Scott. Our young commander, confidentially wrote the Washington correspondent of the Chicago *Tribune*, will put a stop to all Sewardish schemes for paralyzing the war effort. "Look for an advance soon, for it will come, and we shall have some stiff fighting before winter sets in." [1] But still McClellan devoted himself to sedulous drill, admonishing Cameron that the Army of the Potomac should reach 300,000 to ensure decisive success; still the Confederates wondered why he did not move against their puny lines.

Under the delusion of heavy enemy superiority, McClellan believed concentration and caution the only safe policy. Any diversionary movement, any thrust, was too dangerous to be weighed. On August 25 he had written his wife that by the end of the week he would have 75,000 men and feel safer. "Last week he [Beauregard] certainly had double our force." On September 8 he had reported to Cameron that the Confederates meant to take Washington, but would probably move on Baltimore first. That is, they would engage Union pickets on the Potomac and make other demonstrations to draw off McClellan's forces, and then suddenly cross above Washington to

[1] Henry Smith, Nov. 4, 1861, to the *Tribune* editors; C. H. Ray Papers, Huntington Library.

pour their main army direct on Baltimore. "I see no reason to doubt the possibility of his attempting this with a column of at least 100,000 effective troops." [2]

In other words, the Confederates had the power to launch an attack, but McClellan's army was too weak for one! Actually, the Johnston-Beauregard forces in front of McClellan on October 31 comprised 44,131 men present for duty. These two commanders would have been glad to invade the North with 60,000 seasoned, well-armed, properly wagoned troops, but lacked the men, weapons, and transport. They and General W. H. Smith, at a pivotal field conference attended by President Davis, agreed that the only course was to take a defensive position. Yet weak as they were, the Confederates considered attacking Union forces along the north bank of the Potomac, and rejected the idea because Federal warships controlled the river. McClellan, who enjoyed this control, sabotaged the navy's plan for clearing the south bank. [3]

Allan Pinkerton as McClellan's "chief of the secret service" made army headquarters blench by reporting October 4 that the Confederates in Virginia had the fearful total of 184 regiments, numbering 126,600 men. Of this mythical array, 98,400 under Johnston and Beauregard lay at Fairfax Court House and vicinity, 11,000 under Lee, Floyd, and Wise in western Virginia, 10,400 at Norfolk and Portsmouth, and 6800 under Winder in the Richmond area. The Johnston-Beauregard troops retired to Centerville on October 19, when McClellan's growing army became capable of maneuvering. (Not that McClellan had any intention of maneuvering!) Pinkerton painted another Munchausen picture on November 15 in a memorandum placing Confederate strength (after a deduction of 5 per cent to be conservative) at 116,430. He had founded his first report on information from deserters, contrabands, and his own agents, and the second mainly on the observations of a detective who had visited Manassas, Centreville, and Warrington. This operative declared that the rebels were well armed, well fed, and well furnished with ammunition, but "dam'd badly off for winter clothing." Although McClellan should have realized that deserters would lie, that refugee Negroes could unconsciously exaggerate, and that one operative might be a fool or cheat, he made no real effort at verification. [4]

The pressure for an offensive in these autumn weeks, mistaken insofar as men like Ben Wade and Zack Chandler demanded a major battle, was justified

2 Swinton, *Army of the Potomac*, 72.

3 J. G. Barnard, *The Peninsular Campaign*, 12 ff.; Roman, *Beauregard*, I, 142–145; J. E. Johnston, *Narrative of Military Operations*; Davis Papers (President Davis called the Smith-Johnston-Beauregard council), Duke University; McClellan, *Own Story*, 196–197; Official Report (1864), 110–111.

4 Pinkerton Papers, courtesy of the late Howard Swiggett; J. E. Johnston, *Narrative*, 77.

insofar as it sought bold preparatory action. To clear the south bank of
the Potomac and capture Norfolk, we repeat, were objects of prime importance, feasible enough for the hero of West Virginia. Even the mild Senator Foster of Connecticut begged for "energy" along these lines. Union
forces held Fort Monroe, Newport News, and Hampton, the Union fleet
patrolled Hampton Roads, and the army in this area, well intrenched by contraband labor, was reinforced from time to time. An amphibious assault might
have driven the Confederates from Norfolk and compelled the destruction
of the *Merrimac*.

For the navy was a fast-growing power, and early in November it once
more gave the Union a transient gleam of sunshine. To maintain the blockade,
bases not too distant from the Southern ports were required; and the wide,
deep Port Royal Sound, lying squarely between Charleston and Savannah,
seemed ideal for an establishment. A fleet of seventy ships, carrying—soldiers,
sailors, marines—15,000 men, with heavy guns and six months' stores, put into
the Atlantic October 29, bands playing, banners flying, and Flag-Officer S. F.
Du Pont in the *Wabash* leading the way. Though it encountered a heavy storm,
November 4 found it anchored off its goal, "the water as smooth as a pan of
milk." Here two forts at Bay Point and Hilton Head, with a trio of weak
Confederate gunboats, guarded the entrance to the Sound. The works were
scientifically constructed and heavily armed; it was said that the Confederates
had hoped to disable their assailants in half an hour. But by fine management
of his ships on a semi-circular course and beautifully accurate fire, Du Pont in
less than five hours' bombardment forced an evacuation. The *Wabash* alone
fired 440 shells. General Thomas W. Sherman's troops took possession of the
posts and all the surrounding country.[5]

The Union thus gained a foothold near two of the chief Southern ports,
where it could plant a depot for coaling and supplying blockade vessels. The
sea islands, lying like peas in the pod of the Sound—Parris, Hilton Head, Port
Royal, St. Helena—were perfectly secure. Du Pont reported, "The negroes
are wild with joy and revenge," and the Union plainly faced a new problem
in administering freedmen. The President was delighted. He was pleased, too,
by simultaneous news that General William Nelson, formerly of the navy,
had won a fight at Pikesville, Kentucky, taking about a thousand prisoners.

Lincoln had talked frankly with McClellan about the impatience of the
radical leaders for action. While public sentiment had to be taken into account,
he said, "at the same time, general, you must not fight until you are ready."
He had assured McClellan his full support, remarking November 1: "Draw

5 For Port Royal, see H. A. Du Pont, *Samuel Francis Du Pont*, ch. VII; Daniel Ammen,
Battles and Leaders, I, 671–691; Dudley W. Knox, *Hist. of the U. S. Navy*, 202–205. Lincoln's
words to McClellan are given in Dennett, *Diary and Letters of John Hay*, Oct. 26, 1861, p. 31.

PART OF THE
Military Department
OF
THE SOUTH
AND OF
SOUTH ATLANTIC COAST

Scale of Miles

on me for all the sense I have, and all the information." Noting the flurry of alarm which Du Pont's expedition sent over the South, he called at McClellan's house the evening of November 11 to say that it seemed a good time to "feel" the Confederate forces. McClellan answered: "I have not been unmindful of that. We will feel them tomorrow." [6] General S. P. Heintzelman indeed made a reconnaissance on the 12th.

When the following day brought news of the capture of Beaufort, South Carolina, it was natural that Lincoln and Seward, attended by John Hay, should pay another evening call on McClellan. The sequel was a disturbing incident. They found the general out at a wedding. Hay records:

6 *Ibid.*, 33.

We went in, and after we had waited about an hour, McC. came in and without paying any particular attention to the porter, who told him the President was waiting to see him, went upstairs, passing the door of the room where the President and Secretary of State were seated. They waited about half an hour, and sent once more a servant to tell the General they were there, and the answer coolly came that the General had gone to bed. . . .

Coming home I spoke to the President about the matter but he seemed not to have noticed it, specially, saying it was better at this time not to be making points of etiquette and personal dignity.[7]

[I]

At this moment the Western drama reached its shabby, destructive climax.

The shortage of arms, equipment, and transportation in Missouri remained lamentable. "It becomes daily plainer that the Mississippi Valley is to be the greatest theatre of the war," wrote the St. Louis correspondent of Greeley's *Tribune* in mid-October; yet "the government fails to comprehend the magnitude of this department, and the extent of its absolute necessities." The Western people, who had poured out their sons generously, felt this bitterly, "and it is engendering a spirit which will prove disastrous if it is not removed."[8] General David Hunter, sent from the East to advise and aid Frémont, was given command of a division which Frémont ordered to move from Jefferson City to Tipton. He reported October 4 that for his forty wagons he had only forty mules; next day that his men had been without rations for twenty-four hours; the day afterward that two regiments had no transportation at all and two only sixteen teams between them, while another lacked side arms, cartridge boxes, gun slings, ammunition, and greatcoats. From Tipton he wrote October 18 that the division would soon be destitute. At Warsaw he found a hospital with 300 sick men who had gone without food for two days.[9] Even making some allowance for exaggeration, since Hunter, a harsh, morose, gloomy man, habitually saw the worst, it is clear that the situation remained painful.

It is unquestionably true that Washington, preoccupied with McClellan's front, still neglected the whole West. William Tecumseh Sherman, commanding in Louisville, raised precisely the same complaints as Frémont and Hunter in Missouri. Early in November he wrote Governor Dennison that the West-

---

7 *Ibid.*, 34, 35. Apparently something nearly as bad happened earlier. W. H. Russell recorded in his diary Oct. 9 that calling on McClellan a few nights earlier, he was told by the orderly: "The General's gone to bed tired, and can see no one. He sent the same message to the President, who came inquiring after him ten minutes ago."

8 Letter dated Oct. 17 in N. Y. *Weekly Tribune*, Oct. 26, 1861.

9 Committee on the Conduct of the War, III, 236–238.

ern State governments, except Ohio and Indiana, were slack, that inexperienced men were put in dangerous places, and that some officers were insubordinate, railing at him and each other. Worst of all was the Federal neglect: [10]

The requisitions made for ordnance and stores have yet been unfulfilled. Some Rifled Guns ordered last August are just received, boxed up and no soldiers to manage them. In like manner wagons came in pieces and time is necessary to set them up. Mules are wild and horses distempered, and worst of all no captains and lieutenants to teach the details—never before was such a body of men thrust headlong into such danger. I will not conceal from you that there is danger. I pointed it out in advance to the Sec'y of War, and wrote to Mr. Chase and the President who paid no attention to any of my warnings and appeals. The people of the country take advantage of our necessities and demand pay in good gold or Kentucky money for everything we want, besides the rails and damage sustained by their fields, and their claims would exhaust any Treasury. Now the Ohio Regiments just arriving come so late that I have no General to command them. These numbers unsupported and uncommanded will accomplish no result.

No one or a half dozen men can attend to all the wants of these new-raised levies, with all their tents and paraphernalia.

Competent observers believed that one main cause of the shortages, confusion, and excessive costs in the Western Department lay in the failure of Washington to provide adequate funds. When the terms of the ninety-day men expired Frémont had kept many of them only by a personal guarantee of their fourth month's pay. He had to buy large quantities of material on credit. Colonel I. C. Woods of his staff estimated that for every dollar lost through the collusion of suppliers, ten dollars were sacrificed for want of ready money. As soon as the department had to buy on credit, control over prices passed from the government into the hands of banks, brokers, moneyed merchants, and speculators, who made themselves intermediaries. In the purchase of mules and horses, waste resulted from want of funds to provide proper corrals, feed, shoeing, and care in St. Louis, and in the purchase of wagons, from want of funds for repairs. Treasury policy was responsible.[11]

"Chase," Montgomery Blair explained to Frémont on August 24, "has more horror of seeing Treasury notes below par than of seeing soldiers killed, and therefore, has held back too soon, I think. I don't believe at all in that style of managing the Treasury. It depends on the war, and it is better to get ready to beat the enemy by selling stocks at fifty percent discount than wait to negotiate and lose a battle." [12]

10 Sherman, Louisville, Nov. 6, 1861, to Dennison; Dennison Papers, Ohio Arch. and Hist. Soc.
11 See Woods' vigorous statement in Committee on the Conduct of the War, 1863, pt. 3, pp. 222, 223.
12 Quoted *Ibid.*, 115, 116.

Violent feeling was aroused in Missouri by a War Department order in mid-October that all claims for supplies sold to the army must be sent to Washington for scrutiny and approval. Both the St. Louis *Republican* and the *Democrat* denounced this action. The government, they declared, had been outrageously slow and parsimonious in doling out funds to the Western army. Since Frémont's arrival his quartermaster's department had received only $1,153,000, not enough to pay for even the army horses. Merchants, manufacturers, and contractors who had furnished supplies and taken vouchers would now have to drop all business, go to Washington, and hang around offices for days. "Our business men," said the *Democrat*, "came forward with great promptness, and have given their time and capital to the proper aiding and equipping of the army." The banks had been equally generous. What was the result? "The Government, after crippling the Department by keeping its officers destitute of funds," now issued this decree, "an outrage on our business community, and an insult to the Commanding General." [13]

The Frémont-Blair quarrel meanwhile had the most unhappy consequences. The two made formal charges against each other. Montgomery Blair took his brother's allegations to the White House, reading them to the President and then handing them to General Scott. He pressed Lincoln for Frémont's removal; "but," he wrote his father October 1, "I think the President does not think it quite fair to squander Frémont until he has another chance." [14]

One of the consequences, an impairment of troop morale, was heightened when the Administration early in October sent out Lorenzo Thomas, the adjutant-general, to review Frémont's activities. His record was that of a mediocre West Pointer who had risen by routine, and was himself under sharp criticism from some governors for delays in furnishing enlistment quotas; an obfuscated and garrulous man, Gideon Welles wrote later.[15] "Frémont ought to be let alone and have full confidence of the government or be removed," Colonel John M. Palmer told Senator Trumbull. "This halfway state is embarrassing. Even private soldiers can sniff trouble in the breeze if it exists." [16] This was the view of a prominent Missourian, J. S. Rollins, who from Columbia inquired of Frank Blair who *was* commander, and where were his

13 St. Louis *Republican, Democrat*, Oct. 17.
14 Both sets of charges are unimpressive. Frémont accused Frank Blair of using family position to lay unsustained accusations before the President; Blair accused Frémont of misfeasance in vague general terms. Montgomery Blair's letter to his father is in Blair-Lee Papers, Princeton.
15 C. Cadwalader, N. Y. *Herald* correspondent with Grant, termed Thomas an obstinate, intractable man, long a proslavery Democrat. His unsavory part in the events leading to Andrew Johnson's impeachment belongs to later history.
16 Palmer from Tipton, Mo., Oct. 13, 1861, to Trumbull; Trumbull Papers, LC.

headquarters. "Half of our people are ruined, and the rest will be, and all for the want of a single head." [17]

[II]

Hampered by deficiencies of means and equipment, acutely aware that Montgomery Blair and Bates in the Cabinet were hostile, and certain in advance that Lorenzo Thomas would write an adverse report, Frémont knew that his continued tenure hung by a thread. He later bitterly declared that he had enjoyed barely a month of real command—the month between his arrival in St. Louis and Frank Blair's advent on the scene. He was now blamed for another disaster which, as he protested, was not his fault. Colonel J. A. Mulligan's brigade from Chicago, with enough Illinois and Missouri troops to make a total of 3500 men, had taken an advanced position at Lexington, far up the Missouri River near the Kansas boundary. The indefatigable Price saw his opportunity and advanced. Frémont on September 13–14 ordered Generals Pope, Sturgis, and Jefferson C. Davis at Palmyra, Mexico, and Jefferson City respectively to march to Mulligan's assistance; but not one of them showed the requisite energy and determination. Pope was especially remiss. After promising that by the 18th he would have two infantry regiments, some cavalry, and four guns in Lexington, and that by the 19th he would have 4000 troops there, he completely failed to reach the point. So did the others. [18] Frémont himself on September 15 possessed in St. Louis only 6900 men, including home guards, and had just received imperative orders from Washington to detach 5000 infantry for the East. On September 21 Mulligan's whole force, with seven guns and large stores, was captured. [19]

A bright young New Yorker, George E. Waring, who had managed Greeley's farm at Chappaqua and been drainage engineer for Central Park, and who was soon to become colonel of cavalry in Missouri, gave Frederick Law Olmsted his frank opinion that the regular army generals, including Pope

---

17 Rollins to Blair, Oct. 18, Blair-Lee Papers.

18 For Frémont's orders to these generals see Frémont Order Book, Bancroft Library; also O. R. I, iii.

19 For Frémont's small numbers, and the Washington demand for 5000 troops, see O. R. I, iii, 493, 494; Schuyler Colfax in *Cong. Globe*, March 7, 1862, p. 1128. Jefferson C. Davis, who had 9700 troops, including home guards, at Jefferson City on the Missouri, might have sent a relieving force upstream. Frémont, however, chiefly blamed Pope, who was strategically placed; O. R. I, iii, 495. The Washington demand for 5000 men reflected McClellan's flurry of panic lest Beauregard attack. Cameron telegraphed for them "without a moment's delay," and Scott wired, "The President dictates." Frémont spared 2000 troops from St. Louis, 2000 from Kentucky, and 1000 from other sources. This order, Sept. 14, was later countermanded, but not before it had done its harm.

and Hunter, deliberately acted against Frémont, an outsider, through jealousy. Frémont himself was convinced of John Pope's treachery. That leader had a force of 5500 men, ample for Mulligan's relief, which could readily be moved westward by the Hannibal & St. Joe, which he himself had just reported open. He stood inert. Actually, incompetence and timidity offer a better explanation of Pope than treachery, though he certainly showed an insubordinate spirit.

Determined to vindicate himself, Frémont by strenuous efforts concentrated what he thought an adequate army to march through southwestern Missouri against Price and McCulloch. He and his staff reached Jefferson City on September 27. Although the breakdowns among a thousand rotten wagons sent him from the East impeded his march, by October 7 all his troops were on the road to Tipton. Herds of cattle were collected by foraging parties, and grain was fetched in and ground by portable mills, for while he had gathered three million rations in supply depots at Jefferson City and Tipton, he expected to subsist largely on the country, paying loyal citizens for impressed commodities and confiscating produce from the disloyal. The shortage of horses and wagons was partially cured by impressments. He hoped by rapid movement to bring Price and McCulloch to battle. "The army is in the best of spirits, and before we get through I will show you a little California practise," he wrote Jessie—"that is, if we are not interrupted." [20]

This march of some 30,000 men, including 5000 cavalry, with eighty-six guns, was the first formidable aggressive movement yet made by a Northern army. The army furnished evidence that Frémont and his staff had exercised greater organizing power in St. Louis than his critics admitted, and unquestionably its movement was well planned. The commander had divided his force into five divisions headed respectively by Generals Hunter, Pope, Sigel, McKinstry, and Asboth. [21] The proportions of infantry, cavalry, and

20 For Frémont's Missouri campaign see O. R. I, iii, *passim;* his MS Memoirs, Bancroft Library; Jessie B. Frémont, *The Story of the Guard;* Jacob Picard, MS Life of Franz Sigel, kindly lent to author; J. R. Howard, *Remembrance of Things Past,* Ch. 19; and files of the Missouri *Democrat,* leading Republican daily, stanchly on Frémont's side. See also Asa Mahan, *Critical History of the American War,* Ch. 3.

21 Pope revealed his spirit in a letter to his friend V. B. Horton, an Ohio Congressman, Oct. 1 (N. Y. Hist. Soc., Civil War Colls.), and one to General Hunter, Oct. 18 (Frémont MSS, Bancroft Library). The first, written from Boonville, declared that he was at the mercy of Price, with "fifteen or twenty thousand men," if Price advanced. Price, with barely thirteen thousand, was marching the other way. Pope added: "There is a state of dissatisfaction and discouragement among the troops which borders on mutiny." All good accounts agree that the morale of Frémont's troops was exceptionally high. After abusing Frémont roundly, Pope told Horton that since the surrender of Lexington, Price's army had swollen "to 40,000 men." This was more than three times its actual number. In the letter to Hunter, Pope renewed his abuse of Frémont, declared his conviction that half the army would be lost if they went south of the Osage (i.e., south of central Missouri), and asserted that although Frémont had ordered him to bring his whole command to assist

artillery were excellent. The cavalry demonstrated its sound training when a select troop of "prairie scouts" recaptured Lexington with some prisoners and stores, releasing a number of men taken with Mulligan, and when later another force under the Hungarian Charles Zagonyi routed some of the enemy at Springfield. The cardinal source of weakness was the spirit exhibited by Pope and Hunter; a spirit which they would have called distrust of Frémont's capacity, but which Frémont's friends termed one of rank betrayal.

From Tipton, Frémont's march took him south across the Osage, where his engineers laid an 800-foot pontoon bridge in thirty-six hours. His troops advanced rapidly on Springfield, the center of predominantly loyal southwestern Missouri and key to northwestern Arkansas. Here lay an Ozark region antipathetic to slavery. With characteristic exuberance, he spoke of joining Commodore Foote's gunboats on the Mississippi to advance southward. "I think it can be done gloriously, especially if secrecy be kept," he wrote his wife.[22] Late in October he reached Springfield, where by November 1 four of his divisions encamped. From information furnished by his scouts he concluded that a little beyond this town Price and McCulloch would face about and give battle.[23]

He was correct about the decision to fight but mistaken about the position. Price wrote Albert Sidney Johnston on November 7 that although Frémont's army far outnumbered his own, he and McCulloch had agreed to halt and give battle at Pineville, hoping the rugged country would favor them. In fact, they *had* to fight, for Price's Missouri State troops would not move across the boundary, and would shortly disintegrate. But Pineville was not just ahead; it lay deeper in southwest Missouri, seventy-odd miles away.

Frémont was also correct in believing that the chances favored Union victory. "Our combined forces," Price admitted, "cannot cope with them [the Unionists] in numbers." As he informed Jefferson Davis, his Missourians were half-fed, half-clothed, and half supplied. Ben McCulloch has recorded that they were also undisciplined, officered largely by incompetent politicians, and furnished with an incredible conglomeration of weapons; that five thousand of them, their time up, were anxious to go home; and that cooperation between the Missourians and Arkansans was feeble—"but little cordiality of feeling be-

in the movement, he would take only five regiments. Altogether, these utterances fortify Frank Blair's subsequent statement: "Pope is a braggart and liar, with some courage, perhaps, but not much capacity." Welles, *Diary*, I, 104. They should be remembered in their bearing on Pope's subsequent career as head of the Army of the Potomac. As for Hunter, that capable but grimly sour-tempered leader was well aware that the moment Frémont lost the command, he would succeed to it.

22 Jessie B. Frémont, *The Story of the Guard*, 72 ff., 85.

23 See O. R. I, iii, 731, for statements by both Price and McCulloch on their resolve to risk a battle. But Frémont would have had to advance fully four more days to fight it.

tween the two armies." It was with high hopes that Frémont's army, bands pounding, arms glittering, moved out of Springfield. On November 6 Price was near Cassville, fifty miles away. Frémont could get his much-wanted battle only with more time and more marching—and he would be allowed neither.[24]

For while he advanced his critics had been busy. Lorenzo Thomas and Secretary Cameron, visiting Missouri simultaneously, brought back unfavorable impressions. Cameron, talking with Frémont at Tipton on October 14, showed him an order for his removal that Lincoln had authorized him to use at discretion.[25] It is not astonishing that Frémont, as the Secretary wrote, was "very much mortified, pained, and, I thought, humiliated." The explorer made an earnest appeal. He had come to Missouri, he said, at the government's request; he had found his department without troops, preparations, or money; he had organized an efficient army, with which he was in pursuit of the foe; and to recall him at that moment would not only destroy him, but defeat his whole promising campaign. Cameron promised to withhold the order until after he returned to Washington, giving the general time to realize his hope, and Frémont for his part promised to resign if he failed. This was fair enough— but it left Frémont with a concentrating sense of what Damocles suffered.

Lorenzo Thomas made an incredibly hurried Western tour, devoting the single week of October 11–18 to Missouri and Kentucky, heard but one side, and wrote a highly critical report in which the press at once noted inaccuracies. In his loose way this veteran bureaucrat, who had been at West Point with David Hunter, let his supposedly secret statement reach the press.[26]

Raymond of the New York *Times* characterized Thomas' report as the most disastrous blow that the national cause had yet received. Its exposition of the confusion in the Missouri army, the lack of equipment, arms, and transport, and General Hunter's conviction that Frémont was incompetent, all in minute detail, was released "so as to reach Ben McCulloch, Sterling Price, and

24 *Ibid.*, 732 ff.; Ben McCulloch, "Memoirs," *Mo. Hist. Review*, 1932, pp. 354 ff.; Franz Sigel, "The Military Operations in Missouri in the Summer and Autumn of 1861," *Mo. Hist. Review*, 1932 (a view favorable to Frémont); John Hume, *The Abolitionists* (also favorable), 184, 185. At a later date Frémont erroneously claimed that he had been removed in the immediate front of the enemy, about to fight a battle; it was much less than immediate.
25 For Cameron's report see Nicolay & Hay, IV, 430; the N. Y. *Tribune* at once scored it. While Frémont marched, Montgomery Blair was laboring to mobilize opinion against him. "I am hurrying off," he wrote his father Oct. 4, "to see such men as Greeley, Sumner, Andrew, etc. to give them our views and to get them to sustain the Administration. I shall stop in New York and Boston for a day each en route for this purpose—probably shall stay longer in those cities. I saw the President this morning and told him what I intended and he approved. Seward also very cordial." Blair-Lee Papers, Princeton Univ.
26 O. R. I, iii, 540 ff.; N. Y. *Tribune*, Oct. 30, 1861; the two principal dailies, like the German papers, still stood firmly behind Frémont. The *Republican* declared that Lincoln had been deceived by statements wholly *ex parte*, and that the general had exhibited wonderful forbearance during his persecution. The *Democrat* severely condemned Thomas' report, both for its content and for the impropriety of its publication.

A. S. Johnston, and nerve them for the coming fight." Equally injudicious, said the *Times*, was Thomas' account of the situation in Kentucky. "The Southern Confederacy is distinctly told that General Sherman is not sustained by the people of Kentucky; that he has no hope of saving that State to the Union; and that he is preparing only for a hopeless fight before that State is given up." This would indeed be happy news to the rebels! As a matter of fact, Sherman, talking with Cameron and Thomas in a Louisville hotel, had told them in his vehement and excited manner that he would need 200,000 men to drive the Confederates from Kentucky, a statement which led them to conclude that he was insane![27]

Naturally, Lincoln was deeply impressed by the statements of Cameron and Thomas, concurring with what the Blairs and Bates had told him, and quoting Hunter and other Missouri officers. Brigadier-General S. R. Curtis in St. Louis, for example, gave it as his opinion that Frémont lacked the intelligence, experience, and sagacity necessary to his command. Elihu B. Washburne, visiting St. Louis as head of a Congressional subcommittee on government contracts, was shocked by stories of fraud and extravagance. The Cabinet was divided, for Cameron honestly believed that the government should await the outcome of Frémont's campaign, and the Cabinet meeting on October 22 found Seward and Chase earnestly for delay. The President was then still in painful doubt; but Montgomery Blair and Bates maintained their steady pressure for removal, which Lincoln had to give special weight because of their Missouri connections. On the 24th Lincoln yielded. He wrote an order relieving Frémont, whose command was to be given to Hunter, and sent it to General Curtis for delivery. However, he cautioned Curtis that the order must not be handed to Frémont, if, when the messenger reached him, "he shall then have, in personal command, fought and won a battle, or shall then be in the immediate presence of the enemy in expectation of a battle."[28]

Eight days after Lincoln wrote out the order in Washington it was given to Frémont just beyond Springfield. He believed himself then in the immediate presence of the enemy, for Sigel and Asboth had reported the Confederate

27 Thomas' report went to Cameron Oct. 21. Attorney-General Bates had made sure that the side unfavorable to Frémont should be presented to Thomas with emphasis. He wrote James O. Broadhead on Oct. 9: "Genl. Cameron is gone to St. Louis. Be sure to see him. Talk freely. You need not waste your delicacy nor be baulked by etiquette." Broadhead was Frank Blair's chief lieutenant. A complete text of the report was not made public until given to the Committee on the Conduct of the War (March, 1862), which controverted it. For Sherman's exchanges with Thomas and Cameron see Lloyd Lewis, *Sherman: Fighting Prophet*, 192 ff. Cameron on Nov. 9 appointed Buell to Sherman's place in Kentucky. Proceeding to Missouri, Sherman at once quarreled with Pope and Halleck. His wife took him home amid army reports that he was mad, and at home he frankly told friends: "Sometimes I felt crazy in Kentucky; I couldn't get one word from Washington." Lewis, *Sherman*, 200.

28 *Collected Works*, IV, 562.

advance guard nine miles distant; and he had made all dispositions for an immediate advance and battle. His conviction that Hunter, greedy for command, had hurried the messenger forward, did that high-minded officer injustice. But it was unfortunate that Lincoln had not waited. Sigel believed that if the Union army had pushed onward against McCulloch's position at Cassville, it would have separated him from Price, cut his natural line of retreat, and smashed his force.[29]

The Missouri chapter thus remained a dreary series of blunders and mischances to the end. The Administration was blameworthy for not doing far more to supply arms and money to the West; Frémont was to blame for political if not military ineptness; Frank Blair, who had needlessly accentuated the schism in the State, was blameworthy for his selfish, domineering attempt to exploit the situation; and the Blairs in Washington could be blamed for impetuously taking up the quarrel. It was no real loss that Frémont, like Harney, had been broken. In fact, it was a gain, for the way lay open to abler men. Nor was it any real loss that Frank Blair, whose course decisively lost him the support of the German-Americans, could no longer hope for political control of the State. But the needless deepening of animosities in Missouri, which lay henceforth in a feverish, disordered condition, full of hatreds and violence, was much to be deplored. And had the country peered closely into events, it would have seen displayed in Missouri the frightening fact which Gideon Welles shortly enunciated with reference to the Virginia theater: "Personal jealousies and professional rivalries, the bane and curse of all armies, have entered deeply into ours." [30]

[III]

The immediate results of the Missouri fiasco were bad; the larger and remoter results were worse.

Lincoln, in assigning the command to Hunter, had left him free to determine future operations, but had expressed his own opinion that the best plan would be to give up the pursuit, divide the main army into a corps at Sedalia and another at Rolla (the two rail terminals), and push on the work of drilling and equipping troops. Hunter consulted his subordinates. While Pope was

29 *Ibid.*, 562, 563. Frémont, anxious to fight his battle, fruitlessly tried to obstruct delivery of the order, which was sent into his lines by stratagem. He promptly relinquished the command to Hunter on Nov. 2, and forbade troop demonstrations; O. R. I, iii, 559. Montgomery Blair expressed great satisfaction. "If Rosecrantz [*sic*] could also be dropped," he wrote, "the people would have some idea we are in earnest, care for the Public not for men." Oct. 4; Blair-Lee Papers, Princeton.
30 *Diary*, I, 104.

noncommittal, McKinstry, Asboth, and Sigel were for advancing. Hunter decided to turn back. A pursuit and victory would of course vindicate Frémont's planning.

Sigel later stigmatized this decision as "an outrage without parallel in history," and it did result in terrible human suffering.[31] No sooner did the retreat of Hunter and Pope become known than the Unionists of southwest Missouri were struck with terror and despair. From a radius of more than fifty miles, abandoning their property, they flocked into Springfield and the Union lines. Then, as Sigel's and Asboth's troops reluctantly completed the evacuation of Springfield, the impoverished, woebegone mass of fugitives, including nearly every family in the city who had sympathized with the Union cause, took to the roads with the troops, condemned to the life of refugees and beggars.

After Hunter's superior army fell back, the Confederate forces which had been dispiritedly retreating to a point where they could make their last stand faced about and reoccupied all southwest Missouri. Lincoln had written that the enemy would probably not return to the State from Arkansas, and if they did could easily be repelled.[32] The fact was that they never left Missouri, occupied Springfield and the adjacent country throughout the winter, threatened even Rolla and Jefferson City, and were able to lay waste the country up to the Union encampments. Not until the new year did the Union forces advance again. This time they did not stop halfway, but completed their task—as Sigel believed they might have done under Frémont. Lincoln had been actuated, very reasonably, by a fear that Hunter's communications would become too attenuated, and by his conviction that the Western invasion of the South should be directed down the Mississippi. But after all, Washington was a poor vantage point from which to direct field strategy in Missouri.

Much more important than the Missouri results of Frémont's removal were its national repercussions. The anger in St. Louis spread through wide circles of the East. In New York the *Evening Post* declared that the government's action "smote the community like the loss of a battle." A mass meeting at Cooper Institute on November 27, addressed by Senator Sumner, eulogized Frémont and adopted resolutions defending him and his antislavery measures. Henry Ward Beecher spoke for his large Brooklyn congregation in incensed language. "The North is ripening every day for an abolition war," wrote Ethan Allen Hitchcock from New York on November 15. Whittier penned a poem hailing Frémont's trumpet peal for the emancipation of slaves as a Roland-blast "heard from the van of freedom's hope forlorn." And Thaddeus

31 "Military Operations in Mo. in the Summer and Autumn of 1861," *Mo. Hist. Review*, vol. 26 (July, 1932), 367.
32 O. R. I, iii, 241.

Stevens bade his fellow radicals in Congress rally to the cause: "Who are you that you let the hounds run down your friend Frémont?"

While public indignation was probably strongest in New England, it wa stormily evident in many Western centers. The editor of the Cincinnati *Gazette* believed that the region was threatened with a revolution. "Could you have been among the people yesterday, and witnessed the excitement," he wrote Chase just after Frémont's removal; "could you have seen sober citizens pulling from their walls and trampling underfoot the portrait of the President; and could you hear today the expressions of all classes of men, of all political parties, you would, I think, feel as I feel . . . alarmed." The Treasury agent in St. Louis declared that if the President had emptied the government arsenals into the rebel camps, he could not have better strengthened them. The Pittsburgh agent reported that enraged capitalists had stopped their subscriptions for government securities. Another Treasury correspondent, returning from a tour as far west as Iowa, reported: "I never have seen such excitement, such deep indignant feeling everywhere I have travelled."

Frémont had in a double sense made himself a symbol. Neither his effort to free the slaves of those whom Lincoln called "traitorous owners" nor his exhibition of martial energy could be forgotten. While McClellan sat still, he had organized an army of more than 30,000, marched it hundreds of miles, and tried to throw it into battle.[33]

For the Administration the skies were growing dark. Irritation with it ran high as members of Congress gathered in Washington in late November: irritation, anxiety, and discouragement. One disturbing piece of news after another contributed to this.

At Belmont on the Mississippi on November 7, Grant met a check which was accepted quietly only because it might have been much worse. On November 16 the country learned that Captain Charles Wilkes of the warship *San Jacinto* had seized two Confederate envoys to Europe, James M. Mason and John Slidell, aboard the British steamer *Trent*, and although the thoughtless rejoiced, judicious men knew that the stroke portended grave trouble. General

33 Zack Chandler expressed a widespread view when he wrote his wife: "Frémont has accomplished something with eight or ten millions, McL. has accomplished nothing with ten times that amount." Oct. 27, 1861; Chandler Papers, LC. General B. H. Grierson, serving in Missouri at the time, wrote long afterward of Frémont: "I considered him in the midst of his adventures as being, with all his failings, head and shoulders above many of his enemies and traducers. I believed then that he merited, and still think he deserves, a warm place in the hearts of all lovers of freedom, of which he was an earnest, constant, and fearless advocate." MS Autobiography, Ill. State Hist. Lib. Among contemporary defenders of Frémont were William T. Harris, later eminent as an educator, and John F. Hume. Hume believed that if Frémont had commanded a little longer, "he would have achieved a brilliant military success"; that he might have terminated hostilities in Missouri three years earlier than they actually ended. Hume, *The Abolitionists*, 184, 185; Leidecker, *Harris*, 202.

Halleck, who had just replaced Hunter in the chief Western command on November 20, issued an order from St. Louis that no fugitive slaves should thereafter be admitted within Union lines, alleging that Southerner sympathizers used them as spies. This so angered the radicals that when Congress met Lovejoy introduced a resolution of censure, which was defeated by only the close vote of only 78 to 64. The section of opinion for which Ben Wade spoke was bluntly expressing despair of quelling the rebellion under the Administration leaders. "They are blundering, cowardly, and inefficient," Wade confided to Zack Chandler. "I fear the evil is irremediable, having its seat in the very nature of the persons composing the Administration. You could not inspire Old Abe, Seward, Chase, or Bates with courage, decision, and enterprise with a galvanic battery." [34]

Democracy is unhappily prone to demand immediate results, or if unattainable, a dramatic show of action. Many Americans who hoped that they had elected a President of Jacksonian temper began to fear they had gotten a J. Q. Adams, his resolution sicklied o'er with the pale cast of thought. It was impossible as yet to measure the executive stature of Lincoln, for neither by dramatic act nor eloquent word had he illustrated his true qualities. To millions he seemed drifting. That was the precise term a citizen of Freeport, Illinois, writing Elihu Washburne, used: "We of this vicinity feel deeply interested for the welfare of our common country and the way affairs have been drifting our faith in the Administration begins to fail us." So felt C. H. Ray of the Chicago *Tribune*, declaring that although party harmony was important, "when the necessity for making progress is upon us we are ready to quarrel with Lincoln, the Cabinet, McClellan, and anybody else." Neither Lincoln nor McClellan had explained to the country why the troops on the Potomac attempted not even a minor blow. Lincoln did not know why, and in any event had not yet learned to reach the public by effective speech and letter; while McClellan was contemptuous of public opinion. Lost in a fog, the people wondered if they really had a pilot.[35]

Had McClellan dealt a blow to clear the Potomac, successful or unsuccessful, the country would have rejoiced in action. Had Lincoln let Frémont fight the battle which Price awaited at Pineville, win or lose, people would have felt refreshed. Chances of success in both instances were good, but even defeat would have been better than inaction. In war a nation must be ready to meet many defeats; what is important is that it should fight. Thus Americans dumbly, anxiously felt. While radical freesoil and abolitionist sentiment caught

34 Wade to Chandler, Jefferson, Ohio, Oct. 8, 1861; Chandler Papers, LC.
35 Wm. H. Wilson, Freeport, Jan. 11, 1861, to Washburne, Washburne Papers, LC. Ray, Chicago, Dec. 5, 1861, to Washburne Papers, *Ibid.*

up the fallen Frémont banner, it must not be supposed that many people of moderate views did not share the rising distrust. Inside Lincoln's Cabinet both Chase and Bates deemed the President unequal to his duties, Bates writing that he lacked firmness, decision, and grasp. Meanwhile, one of the harshest indictments of Lincoln ever penned came from Frank Blair. The nation in December waited for a sign: either martial action, or an aggressive change of policy.[36]

If the people had pinned high expectations to Lincoln's first annual message, they were disappointed. That long, dull document, dated December 3, holds a place among the more commonplace Presidential papers.[37] It was ill organized, for it unnecessarily summarized materials in the reports of the Cabinet officers. It warily said nothing of the burning question of the moment, the Mason-Slidell affair, nor of the situation in Mexico or Santo Domingo. In dealing with Negroes liberated under the Confiscation Act it took pains not to use the word "slaves," substituting the locution "certain persons." Paying tribute to Scott, Lincoln wrote that the general had repeatedly expressed himself in favor of McClellan as his successor, but did not mention that at the end Scott had earnestly preferred Halleck. The President expressed just satisfaction that Maryland, Kentucky, and Missouri had already furnished 40,000 soldiers to the Union, but he was much too optimistic in pronouncing Missouri comparatively quiet. To the factions of radical and conservative Republicans which were now fast taking shape, by far the most significant passages were his vague proposals for colonizing freedmen abroad, and the statements which followed:

In considering the policy to be adopted for suppressing the insurrection, I have been anxious and careful that the inevitable conflict for this purpose shall not degenerate into a violent and remorseless revolutionary struggle. I have, therefore, in every case, thought it proper to keep the integrity of the Union prominent as the primary object of the contest on our part, leaving all questions which are not of vital military importance to the more deliberate action of the legislature. . . .

We should not be in haste to determine that radical and extreme measures, which may reach the loyal as well as the disloyal, are indispensable.

36 Frank Blair's letter to Montgomery, Oct. 7, 1861, was a characteristic eruption. He wrote that the only way to save the nation was "to kick that pack of old women who compose the Cabinet into the sea"; that he had never dreamed "that such a lot of poltroons and apes could be gathered together from the four quarters of the globe as Old Abe has succeeded in bringing together in his Cabinet"; that the first duty of every patriot "is to stop fighting Jeff Davis and turn in on our own Government and make something out of it"; and that Davis and his whole crew had not done half the harm inflicted "by the cowardice, ignorance, and stupidity of Lincoln's Administration." Smith, *Blair Family*, II, 83, 85. Bates' acrid comments on Lincoln are in his *Diary*, 218-220, 223-226, etc.

37 Text in *Collected Works*, V, 35-53. Only at the close, though failing of eloquence, did Lincoln strike a high note. The nation relied on Providence, he wrote, and "the struggle of today, is not altogether for today—it is for a vast future also."

Before Congress met, Chandler, Wade, and Trumbull, the three Senators who had been badgering Lincoln to insist on a battle, had adumbrated a plan. They would create a Congressional committee which would both carry on a continuous investigation of the war effort and apply frequent pricks of the goad. The session no sooner began than Chandler proposed a Senate committee of three to inquire into Bull Run and Ball's Bluff. Grimes of Iowa substituted a broader resolution for a House-Senate committee of five to explore the causes of the disasters that had attended the public arms, with power to send for person and papers. Further amendments enlarged the committee to three Senators and four Representatives, and stated the mandate in a single comprehensive phrase: "To inquire into the conduct of the present war."

Thus, with nearly unanimous approval, originated the most powerful parliamentary engine of the time, the Committee on the Conduct of the War. This body was not tardy in proceeding to work. Under Wade as chairman, with Zack Chandler, Senator Andrew Johnson, and Representatives Daniel W. Gooch, John Covode, George W. Julian, and Moses F. Odell as members, it began sitting before Christmas. Within a few days this able group ascertained that McClellan's Army of the Potomac had present for duty on December 10 approximately 134,000 equipped infantry, 10,000 equipped cavalry, 10,350 equipped artillery, and 6850 officers.

The establishment of the committee served explicit notice that if the President had war powers, Congress possessed them too, and would jealously assert them. But a majority did not share the Wade-Chandler animosity toward Lincoln. The committee later asserted that it took care to aid and cooperate with the overburdened Chief Executive. Summoning in their first fortnight a series of generals, they made it plain that their inquisitorial gaze would be bent on laggard and incompetent field commanders. This was wise; while interference with President or Cabinet would have been a disaster, the military needed a searching scrutiny.[38]

[IV]

With reason, Lincoln felt much more worry over the Mason-Slidell affair than over the Congressional committee. When the appointment of Captain Charles Wilkes to command an American cruiser with a commission to search for privateers was first announced, a shrewd officer of the Treasury, George

38 See introductory matter, 37th Cong., 3rd Sess., *Report of the Joint Committee*, Vol. I (1863). The committee has been treated with undue severity by historians biased in favor of Executive or army. Actually it brought to light much that it was healthful for the public to know, and kept the military arm well reminded of civilian supremacy. In all, it was to issue eight volumes. W. W. Pierson, *American Historical Review*, v. 23 (April, 1918), 550–576, takes a fairer view of it.

Harrington, had urged Seward to get the mandate revoked. "He will give us trouble," said Harrington. "He has a superabundance of self-esteem and a deficiency of judgment. When he commanded his great exploring expedition he court-martialled nearly all his officers; he alone was right, everybody else was wrong." [39] The captain was grandnephew of the fiery John Wilkes famous in the days of Burke, Fox, and Dr. Johnson.

A scene in the Bahama Channel on November 8 verified Harrington's prophecy. Gray sea and gray skies; black smoke from the little warship *San Jacinto* and white smoke from one of her guns trailing across the waves; the jaunty mail-steamer *Trent* lying hove to, her British ensign flapping; a boat filled with armed marines rowing across—this scene heralded trouble. From the *Trent*'s deck the protesting James M. Mason of Virginia and John Slidell of Louisiana, Confederate special commissioners to London and Paris respectively, were haled by Union officers, to be clapped into prison at Fort Warren near Boston.

Fervent Northern jubilation at first greeted this capture of two arch-rebels and this challenge to British insolence. Most newspapers published exultant editorials, Boston tendered Wilkes a banquet, and Secretary Welles rumbled an approval which he was later anxious to forget. The House of Representatives voted Wilkes a gold medal. While the applause still echoed, arrival of the news in Britain on November 28 set off an explosion of resentment. The press blazed with denunciation, influential men expressed indignation over the affront, and talk of possible war at once sprang up. Prime Minister Palmerston blazed to the Cabinet, "You may stand for this but damned if I will!"; and the Ministry, which shared the popular anger, inevitably took steps to meet any eventuality. It ordered a steam squadron made ready, gathered 8000 troops with a supply of munitions for immediate transfer to Canada, and prohibited the export of war materials. That the British Government could easily have used the incident to open hostilities if it wished, there can be no doubt; and Confederates of course ardently hoped it would.

Happily, members of the British Cabinet wished to avoid war with the United States. Palmerston's rapid steps to strengthen Britain's military position were prompted partly by a wish to prepare for the worst, but also partly (as he told Parliament later) by his conviction that the demand for a peaceable restoration of the two prisoners would have to be supported by military strength. Six weeks earlier, he had written the Foreign Minister, Lord John Russell, reaffirming a policy of strict neutrality; British policy must be "to keep quite clear of the conflict between North and South," he declared, interfering only if the American conflagration threatened danger to Europe. Hap-

39 Undated memorandum, Harrington Papers, Mo. Hist. Society.

pily also, the American minister was a man of rare experience, sagacity, and restraint. Charles Francis Adams knew very well that the United States was in the wrong. This son of John Quincy Adams had an inherited animus against Great Britain. He was naturally combative—he had run for the Vice-Presidency on the Freesoil ticket in 1848, and had lately been one of the most active Republican leaders in the House; but he was also naturally cautious, and he possessed shrewd self-control. Realizing the gravity of the crisis, he now waited gloomily and taciturnly. Before news was received of Wilkes's act, Palmerston had spoken at a Lord Mayor's dinner, with Adams present, saying flatly that he was against intervention for the sake of cotton, and treating the American conflict with marked delicacy. Both men could be trusted to show discretion and moderation; and although Palmerston was determined to stand up for British rights, the gouty veteran had too keen a suspicion of Napoleon III—his mind "as full of schemes as a warren is of rabbits"—to care to embroil himself in the New World.

Indeed, Palmerston had foreseen the possibility of just such an incident as this, and had given Adams a hint that it should be avoided. In a friendly private conversation with the American minister on November 15 he had referred to the reckless utterances of Captain John B. Marchand of the U. S. S. *James Adger*, lying at Southampton, who while tipsy had said that he was going to watch for Mason and Slidell and capture them even in sight of the British shore if he could. Palmerston's remark that two additional Southern agents could scarcely make any difference in the course of the British Government once it had made up its mind gave Adams a clear hint (which he failed to take) that it *had* made up its mind adversely to any arguments the Southerners might present.[40]

The Prime Minister had in fact been so disturbed by the possibility of an incident that he had consulted the Crown's law officers on the legality of a possible American seizure of the Confederate envoys. This opinion, dated November 12, 1861, stated that an American warship would have the right to stop and search an English ship, and to take her into port for adjudication of the charge that she carried contraband goods or improper personnel, but would not have any right to remove the diplomatic agents and then allow the ship to proceed. Provision for adjudication was the crux of the matter. When news of the actual happening reached London, the law officers reaffirmed their view of the illegality of Captain Wilkes's step. It was unfortunate for the American position that Wilkes failed to bring the *Trent* into a North-

---

40 *Cambridge History of Br. Foreign Policy*, II, *passim*; E. D. Adams, *Great Britain and the Amer. Civil War*, I, Ch. VII; S. F. Bemis, ed., *Amer. Secretaries of State*, VII, 61–70; *Diplomatic Correspondence*, 1861, pp. 105 ff.

ern port, for if he had done so, the British Government would have been legally disabled from protesting. Palmerston deserved great credit for arming himself with a statement of the law, and for giving Adams an amicable admonition. Seward across the Atlantic had failed to look up any precedents or rulings in advance! [41]

That Wilkes had committed a grave infraction of international law there could be no question. He had a perfect right to search any suspected ship for goods contraband of war, and to take a vessel carrying contraband into port to await the verdict of a prize court. But he had no right to decide the question of a violation of neutrality by personal fiat on the spot, without judicial process. Moreover, it was extremely doubtful whether persons, as distinguished from goods, could ever be deemed contraband. In impressing men from the deck of a neutral ship, Wilkes had committed precisely the kind of act that did so much to provoke the United States to fight the War of 1812. Lord John Russell did not overstate the case when he called it a violent affront to the British flag and a violation of international law. No wonder that the frigid Charles Francis Adams, learning of the exultation of Americans, fell into indescribable sadness, or that the more emotional Henry Adams wrote home that the applauders were "a bloody set of fools." [42]

The situation was rendered more difficult by the fact that British ministers regarded the State Department with a mordant suspicion. They were well aware of Seward's devious ways, remembered some of his recent irresponsible statements, and suspected that just before Sumter he had played with the idea of provoking a conflict with England as a means of gaining Canada. C. F. Adams, Jr., understates the fact when he writes that in 1861 Seward commanded the confidence of no European foreign secretary; Seward in fact had the active distrust of most foreign offices. Dealing with him, the Liberal Cabinet naturally made their note stiff. They avoided an ultimatum, but they did

41 C. F. Adams, Jr., *C. F. Adams*, Ch. XII; J. P. Baxter, "The British Government and Neutral Rights," *Amer. Hist. Review*, v. 34 (October, 1929), 9–29. Palmerston did, however, believe that a division of the American republic would make Britain safer, for he disliked Yankee aggressiveness. He wrote Russell on Jan. 19, 1862, that he liked the scheme of a monarchy in Mexico. "It would also stop the North Americans whether of the Federal or Confederate states in their proposed absorption of Mexico. If the North and South are definitely disunited, and if at the same time Mexico could be turned into a prosperous monarchy, I do not know any arrangement that would be more advantageous for us." Harold Temperley and Lillian M. Fenson, *Foundations of Br. Foreign Policy, 1792–1902*, pp. 219, 220.

42 Russell's statement is quoted in John Bassett Moore, *Principles of Amer. Diplomacy*, 114–118; for the views of the Adamses, see W. C. Ford, ed., *A Cycle of Adams Letters*, I, 70 ff. The *Journal of Benjamin Moran*, II, 904 ff., is useful. Seward had sent Thurlow Weed abroad, and shortly after the Trent affair broke, Weed lunched with Russell at Pembroke Lodge. He found the foreign secretary as chilly as Adams himself always was, but he learned that Queen Victoria was anxious for a friendly settlement.

demand the surrender of the envoys, and an apology. Lord John Russell regarded Wilkes's seizure as a continuation of the old unfriendly American policy, now carried to the point of a direct slap in the face.

However, the language of the ministerial instructions to Lord Lyons was kept within moderate bounds. It was agreed at the Cabinet meeting of November 29 that Russell should draft these instructions, while Palmerston reported all the facts to the Queen. Next day the Cabinet met again, and both shortened and softened Russell's severe language. The revised draft was then sent to Windsor, where Queen Victoria (who had been touched by the cordial American reception of her eldest son the previous year) and Prince Albert were much distressed by the evident danger of war. They realized that the crisis needed emollients, not excitants.

Prince Albert, then in his final illness, could hardly hold a pen. Nevertheless, he wrote for the Queen an earnest memorandum to be laid before Lord Russell—his last political paper. In this document the Queen declared that she would like to have the Government take the position that while it could not allow its flag to be insulted or its mails endangered, it did not believe that the United States intended any insult, or wished to add to the American troubles by a dispute with the British nation; and that London hoped to learn that the American captain had acted without any instructions, or had misunderstood them. Palmerston and Russell immediately made the desired changes. The official biographer of Albert credits him with trying to remove from the dispatch to Lyons everything that could irritate the American people, and to offer them a full opportunity of receding honorably from the position in which Wilkes's indiscretion had placed them.[43]

The fact is that the Palmerston Ministry was so composed as to find a conciliatory policy natural. Such members as Gladstone, Newcastle, and Granville had an ingrained love of peace. The principal ministers, each representing his own group in the Liberal Party, carried on their special work much as they pleased. Palmerston, who had the deciding word in council, was chiefly concerned with keeping the governmental machine running smoothly, avoiding factional rows, and giving the Conservative Opposition few opportunities for attack. He and Russell, who represented different wings of the Liberal Party, curbed each other. Both well remembered the recent Russian war which Britain had entered so insouciantly, and in which victory proved so costly. It is true that the Prime Minister enjoyed living dangerously, or as Cobden put it: "Palmerston likes to drive the wheel close to the edge, and show how

43 Theodore Martin, *Life of His Royal Highness the Prince Consort.* V. A. W. Tilby, *Russell,* 208, 209, credits Gladstone with influencing the Queen and Prince in favor of peace.

dexterously he can avoid falling over the precipice. Meanwhile, he keeps people's attention employed, which suits him politically." Adams, nervous over this precipice-walking, feared that some sudden misstep might send him over the edge, but the old curmudgeon's foot was sure.

Not only was the dispatch to Lyons watered down, but it was accompanied by two private communications from Russell to the British Minister in Washington which lessened the tension. One of them instructed Lyons to see Seward informally before taking him the official paper, prepare him for the demands, and ask him to thresh out the matter with the President and Cabinet before the dispatch was formally read. The other authorized Lyons to give Seward seven days to formulate a reply. If the Secretary rejected the British demands, Lyons was to leave Washington, but from the outset he was to make it plain that he desired to abstain from anything like a menace. No minister could have been happier to pursue a conciliatory line than Lord Lyons. The previous spring, in delivering a Foreign Office dispatch to Seward, he had changed certain expressions to avoid offending the American Government—striking out "measures either by the Northern or Southern Confederacies of North America," for example, and substituting "measures by America." He understood and liked Seward, while he was learning to admire Lincoln.[44]

An unfriendly analyst of the British attitude might describe it as an effort to browbeat the United States by military preparations while privately paving the way for a termination of the quarrel without resort to arms. A truer estimate would credit the British with wishing to uphold their national dignity while giving Americans every opportunity for a graceful retreat. Russell wrote the pacific Gladstone on December 13 that if Washington would liberate the Confederate envoys, he would be glad to make a treaty giving up the British pretensions of 1812 and securing immunity from seizure to unarmed persons aboard neutral vessels. "This would be a triumph for the U. S. in principle, while the particular case would be decided in our favor." Soon afterward he informed Palmerston that if the United States wished to argue the matter, he would allow Washington more time for compliance, adding: "I do not think the country would approve an immediate declaration of war."

The United States, meanwhile, proved very reluctant to back down. The public and official praise of Wilkes was hard to disclaim. Seward, more regardful of public opinion than learned in international law, or skilled in diplomacy, had lost a golden opportunity in not promptly restoring Mason and Slidell on the ground of historic American belief in the illegality of such seizures. Lincoln, however, though at first pleased by the capture, was soon overcome by doubts,—"I fear the traitors will prove to be white elephants," he said—and

44 Lyons, June 17, 1861, to Russell; FO 84/1137.

again impressed on Seward the fact that one war at a time was enough. Charles Sumner, exchanging anxious letters with his friends Richard Cobden and John Bright, told Washington leaders that the government should recede. Edward Everett, former Secretary of State, Thurlow Weed, and numerous business leaders, swung to the same view. The assertion of the French advocate of the Union cause, Count Gasparin, that the Confederate envoys were a hundred times more dangerous in Fort Warren than they would be walking the streets of London and Paris, was echoed by August Belmont, staying in Nice: "Neither the violent and clumsy representations of the demagogue Mason nor all the energy and astuteness of your fierce Slidell could have changed the settled policy of England and France in this controversy."

At the end of November, Seward sent word to Adams that Wilkes had acted without orders, that he hoped the Ministry would consider the question in a friendly temper, and that the United States would show a conciliatory disposition. When Lincoln sent his annual message to Congress at the beginning of December, he wisely ignored the subject. From the moment that Adams on December 19 imparted the contents of Seward's letter to Russell, the situation brightened. Popular feeling on both sides had grown calmer, and the psychological reasons for American sensitivity to British antagonism made also, as Whittier wrote, for a rapid restoration of friendly feeling:

> O Englishmen! in hope and creed,
> In blood and tongue our brothers!
> We too are heirs of Runnymede;
> And Shakespeare's fame and Cromwell's deed
> Are not alone our mother's.

Lincoln thought for a time that the question might be arbitrated, and his Cabinet remained divided. But at a meeting on Christmas day, with Sumner present to read letters from Bright and Cobden, they agreed to admit that Wilkes had committed a wrong, and to restore the two envoys. As Attorney-General Bates put it, all yielded to the logic of the situation. Seward composed a note in his smartest Auburn-attorney vein, castigating British policy past and present even while he apologized for the violation of British rights; and his impudent irrelevances lent comfort to many Yankee jingoes. The peaceful outcome of the dispute gave general gratification on both sides of the water. In America, Everett wrote that a strong feeling of relief pervaded the community; in England, Adams recorded a striking revulsion—"The current which ran against us with such extreme violence six weeks ago now seems to be going with equal fury in our favor."

Dr. Whewell, master of Trinity College, Cambridge, made the right ironic comment: "According to American principles Mason and Slidell ought not to have been seized, but according to English principles their surrender ought not to have been asked." [45] What was perhaps the most perilous moment of the Civil War had been passed. It was already clear that when Mason reached London, he would accomplish—unless some new squall blew up—precious little. W. L. Yancey, Pierre A. Rost, and A. Dudley Mann, whom the Confederate government had sent to Europe as special commissioners just after Sumter, had been received very coldly by the British Foreign Office. In fact, they had hardly been received at all. After a first frigid interview, Lord John Russell had refused to see them again, requesting them to put in writing any communications they wished to make to him. And when they wrote, they got no reply to their letters until early in December the Foreign Minister crushed their hopes with two curt sentences: "Lord Russell presents his compliments to Mr. Yancey, Mr. Rost, and Mr. Mann. He has had the honour of receiving their letters of the 27th and 30th of November, but in the present state of affairs he must decline to enter into any official communication with them." It seemed certain Mason would fare no better.

While the excitement of the *Trent* affair hung over the country, much more stubborn problems were claiming attention. Lincoln's annual message had hardly reached Congress when an irreparable breach between him and the Secretary of War, touching the most sensitive point of national policy, came to light.

45 See MS Diary of Edward Everett, Nov. 1, 1861–Feb. 2, 1862, for comments on the affair. Gasparin wrote in the *Journal des Débats.* The fullest general treatment, T. L. Harris's *The Trent Affair,* is marked by bias. See also the able essay "The Trent Affair, 1861," by Charles Francis Adams, Jr., in *Mass. Hist. Soc. Proceedings,* v. 45 (1911), 35–148. Not only Edward Everett but Sumner at first held the seizure justified, Sumner sending the State Department some citations of favorable precedents; but both changed their minds.

20

"The Bottom Out of the Tub"

THE MOOD of the nation as it came to the end of a year barren of signal victory or real advance was expressed by the long speech of J. A. Gurley of Ohio in the House on the conduct of the war. Men generally felt, he said, that an active policy must be adopted or the conflict would drag on for years and acquire international scope. The army was ready, the troops were eager for action, the country was looking for a commander with the will, enterprise, and skill to gain victories; but where was the leader? More men had been lost by sickness in the past five months than a half-dozen battles would have claimed. The expense had been enormous. An occasional reverse would be better than this inaction, this waste of opportunity, this dreary disappointment.

Gurley had the clerk read an excerpt from the Richmond *Dispatch* which bit deeper than his own acid words. It declared that from the beginning of December the Yankees had possessed on the Potomac the best army on the continent, 200,000 strong, with formidable forces elsewhere. The weather had been favorable; they could have struck at numerous points; their blows could have done the Confederacy serious injury. Instead, they had given the South time to make itself safe at every point where it had been vulnerable. Why? Because, declared the writer, the Yankees enlist not to fight, but only to draw pay. Their factories being closed for want of Southern trade, the men had gone into the army to live, well fed, well clothed, and safe. The war was practically closed.

W. D. Kelley of Pennsylvania was soon making the House echo to a sterner indictment. The public mind and heart were sick, he said, that after all the sacrifices for war, no progress had been made: "Washington is beleaguered and Richmond is not." Even a leader less sensitive to the national mood than Lincoln was would have felt the importance of action to revitalize the War Department, spur McClellan into movement, and place a constructive solution for the problem of slavery among the objects of the war. Within the space of a few weeks the President, awakening to his authority and his capacities, had dealt with all three subjects.

395

[I]

Lincoln's distrust of Cameron's capacity, irritation with his methods, and hostility to his ideas, had steadily grown. From the first, the two had disliked each other. Lincoln had resented the apparent necessity, under half-promises which his friends had given at the Chicago Convention, of putting Cameron in his Cabinet.[1] He had been warned by various people that Cameron had a corrupt record. As early as May, 1861, one politician judged from separate conversations with both President and Secretary that "much feeling" existed between them. The President heard tales that some of the Pennsylvania contracts of the War Department were dishonest, and told callers that he meant to have them examined. By October, convinced that the Secretary was at least incompetent, he spoke of the man to young Nicolay with unwonted asperity. Cameron, he declared, was "utterly ignorant" of his proper affairs; "selfish and openly discourteous to the President"; "obnoxious to the country"; and "incapable of either organizing details or conceiving and advising general plans."[2]

Incompetent Cameron was; corrupt he was not, save in the sense that he kept a keen eye out for political profit. He made bad appointments, as other executives did. One man was privately denounced by Gideon Welles as infamous; another, placed in an investigative capacity, was assailed by the writer Epes Sargent as unfit save on the theory that one might set a thief to catch a thief. In the unavoidable hurry and confusion of equipping the troops, Cameron often signed bad contracts. But Lincoln himself defended him in the employment of Alexander Cummings to buy military supplies, and William Pitt Fessenden was quite right, as inquiry proved, in saying that much of the clamor against the Secretary was baseless. Rascals who offered regiments and demanded funds when they had no men, contractors disappointed in their hope of plundering the government, and rival politicians with old scores to pay, were prominent among the assailants. Chase defended Cameron's integrity earnestly. Charles A. Dana, who knew him well and was impressed by his personal force, warmth of heart, and literary cultivation, did the same.[3]

His abysmal lack of business capacity and incredible laxity, however, cost the country more than petty dishonesties might have done. Dozens of men

---

1 Ben P. Thomas, *Lincoln*, 234. Cameron equally resented Lincoln's post-election efforts (as he saw it) to wriggle out of a fair political bargain.

2 W. W. Orme, Washington, May 14, 1861, to Leonard Swett, David Davis Papers, Ill. State Hist. Lib.; Helen Nicolay, *Lincoln's Secretary*, 125.

3 Lincoln declared that Cameron's emergency steps in war purchasing "were not moved nor suggested by himself, and that not only the President but all the other heads of departments were at least equally responsible"; *Collected Works*, VII, 193, 194. Fessenden wrote his defense of Cameron Aug. 27, 1861; Fessenden Papers. See Dana's comment to Ida M. Tarbell, Tarbell Papers, Allegheny College.

who did business in the War Department have left us pictures of its bumbling clutter. Cameron refused to protect his time, saw everybody, forgot everything, established no routines, and deputed little to subordinates. "What was the last action I took on your case?" he asked an importunate caller. "You borrowed my pencil, took a note, put my pencil in your pocket, and lost the paper," replied the suitor. In July Trumbull had the Senate call on Cameron for information as to war contracts, but with little result. That same month the House appointed a committee under C. H. Van Wyck of New York to investigate the subject, and most of the evidence it collected of irregularities naturally pertained to the War Department. In August a group of bankers urged Lincoln to get rid of the Secretary. This deputation did not impress the President, who realized that if he yielded to them, they would shift the attack to some other Cabinet member; but even Cameron's best friends grew impatient with his slack, haphazard methods.[4]

Chase, for example, informed John Sherman in the fall that some remedy must be found for the absence of system and economy in war expenditures, and suggested various reforms. When in November he decided that the War Department bills were exorbitant, he refused to accept Cameron's estimates for the next year to lay before Congress. Returning them, he declared in a stinging letter, aimed at the whole executive branch, that both the failures of the armies and the financial difficulties of the nation had been traceable neither to want or an excess of men, but to the lack of systematic administration.[5]

Even more irritating to Lincoln than Cameron's woolly-minded lack of system was his meddling with the sensitive issue of slavery. Although initially Cameron had been under the influence of his conservative friend Seward, early in the war he shifted ground and became more intimate with Chase, who assisted him in military affairs. Already, what Montgomery Blair called a hard underground war had begun between Chase and Seward, and before long, Seward was quite willing to get rid of Cameron as a punishment for his defection. Chase was of course fundamentally hostile to slavery; and two of Cameron's old personal friends, Colonel John Cochrane, a New York Congressman who became colonel of chasseurs, and Samuel Wilkeson, of Greeley's *Tribune,* also used their influence to give the Secretary a growing anti-slavery tendency. The War Department, like the Navy Department, had to deal with innumerable pitiful cases of slaves who escaped into the Union lines, and both Cameron and Welles took the position that they should not be returned to their masters. Cameron sent Ben Butler a letter, written in part by Chase, approving

---

4 A. G. Riddle, *Recollections of War Times,* is the basis of the pencil anecdote; see also *Cong. Globe,* July 21, 1861; Meneely, *War Department in 1861.*
5 To Cameron Nov. 27, 1861; Schuckers, *Chase,* 279–281.

of that general's "contraband" policy.[6] This was unexceptionable. But the Secretary, who now honestly believed that slavery was the tap-root of rebellion, soon went further.

When General Thomas W. Sherman was preparing for his part in the Du Pont expedition against Port Royal, Cameron had drafted a comprehensive letter of instructions to govern him in the treatment of slaves. Laying down the principle that those who entered the Union lines might be used in government service, it was so worded that the general could have armed them; and it gave assurances that slaves employed by the army would never be sent back to bondage. Cameron had entrusted this letter, just before he left for his Missouri trip on October 9, to Assistant Secretary Thomas A. Scott for issuance. Lincoln saw it, struck out the pledge that slaves would never be returned to their masters, and limited the passage respecting government service by a dozen pregnant words: "This, however, not to mean a general arming of them for military service." As Thomas A. Scott pointed out in reply to an inquiry, this still left the door open, in great emergencies, to the arming of colored men by irregular enrollment; and the New York *Tribune* commented that it went beyond Frémont's proclamation in that it permitted the use of arms, in such emergencies, by slaves who had fled from loyal as well as disloyal masters. But Cameron's effort to commit the army to a radical position on slavery, probably abetted by Chase, had been defeated.[7]

Unquestionably he was sincere in his repeated assertions that to strike at slavery was to strike at the root of insurrection. The theory that he was taking an abolitionist stand in order to gain Radical protection against dismissal is unjust. For one reason, he was aware by October that his fate was determined. "I knew I was doomed when I consented to go to St. Louis," he shortly assured old F. P. Blair, "and was not altogether clear of suspicion that it was intended I should be by one of my associates [Seward], but having determined to shrink from no duty I went cheerfully, only taking care to let the President know my belief, and to get his promise that I should be allowed to go abroad when I left the Department." He knew Lincoln well enough to understand that no Radical intervention could help him. Moreover, this vigorous Jacksonian (now sixty-two, he was destined to live to ninety) had long detested slavery, and believed that blows at it would shorten the war. "I can safely say," he told Blair, "that I have not done an official act that I would not do again, under the same circumstances. But there are many things I would have

6 Welles, *Diary*, I, 127; see also Welles, "Narrative of Events," *Amer. Hist. Review*, XXXI, 486 ff.; Benjamin F. Butler, *Autobiography (Butler's Book)*, 259–261.
7 Meneely, 341–343; Nicolay and Hay, V, 123, 124; N. Y. *Tribune*, Nov. 25, 1861.

done, which were omitted only because my associates were not as advanced as I was in hostility to the rebellion." [8]

In mid-November, when the issue was sharply joined between those who would accept restoration of the Union with slavery and those who demanded the Union with emancipation, Cameron took a further step. He visited Springfield, Massachusetts, with Colonel John Cochrane. There he told numerous citizens privately that in outfitting T. W. Sherman's expedition he had included extra guns to be placed in the hands of any men who could use them. At a parade of Cochrane's regiment in Washington a few days later the colonel declared in the Secretary's presence that arming the slaves did not differ from utilizing other captured enemy resources: "We should take the slave by the hand, place a musket in it, and bid him in God's name strike for the liberty of the human race." Cameron, amid cheers by the regiment, stated his hearty approval of every sentiment uttered by Cochrane. This episode provoked a hot discussion in high military and political circles. McClellan, tender toward slavery, and already irritated because Cameron held a strong belief in the immediate striking-power of the volunteer army while the general distrusted the volunteers, became hostile. The conservative Caleb B. Smith lashed out at Cameron in Cabinet meeting, and Lincoln himself was much displeased.[9]

Yet Cameron, applauded by many Radical voices, stuck to his guns. At a reception which John W. Forney gave at his Washington home for George D. Prentice of the Louisville *Journal*, he bluntly reiterated his views. Speaking informally, and belligerently facing Caleb B. Smith, he again declared that he would arm any able-bodied men in the South who offered their services. Smith, who followed him, vehemently condemned any such policy. Reports of this clash appeared in the newspapers, and the New York *Times* advised Cabinet members to push on with the war instead of quarreling in public over controversial issues. Meanwhile, Montgomery Blair, always sensitive to Border State opinion, took sides with Bates and Smith. He found opportunity to twit Cameron upon a newspaper remark that the Secretary had now elbowed Frémont out of the abolitionist boat, and taken the tiller in the stern-sheets.[10]

Something of the temper of the Highland Scot, of the Cameronians who

8 From his home, "Lochiel," Feb. 8, 1862; Blair-Lee Papers, Princeton. A. K. McClure, who differed radically from Cameron in politics, gives a fair estimate of him in *Lincoln and Men of War Times*, 147–168; correctly stating that the most upright and sagacious statesman of the nation could not have administered the War Department in 1861 without flagrant abuses and errors.

9 N. Y. *Herald*, Nov. 14, N. Y. *Tribune*, Nov. 14, 15, 1861; Flower, *Stanton*, 115; *Amer. An. Cyc.*, 1861, p. 645; Bates, *Diary*, Nov. 20, 1861.

10 N. Y. *Times*, Nov. 20, 22, Dec. 2, 1861; Bates, *Diary*, Nov. 20, 27; Smith to Barlow, Nov. 22, 23, Barlow Papers. Prentice at once published a long attack on Cameron.

had battled to the hopeless end at Aird Moss, crying, "Lord, spare the green and take the ripe," had been aroused in Cameron. He defiantly told at least one Cabinet meeting how firmly he believed in arming and organizing Negro soldiers.[11] He also let friends know that his annual report would deal emphatically with the subject. This announcement startled conservative Pennsylvanians, and the editor Forney headed a delegation which late in November bearded Cameron at his house to remonstrate. He read them what he intended to say. "It will never do!" exploded Forney. "I beg of you not to press so certain a firebrand." Wilmot defended the passage. All night the angry debate raged. Then, as early daylight struggled through the curtained windows, Cameron rose, went to the sideboard, filled a glass with whiskey and water, and holding it aloft, declared: "Gentlemen, the paragraph stands." [12]

[II]

Seldom had patriotic Americans passed more anxious days. As December drew in the whole North knew that financial difficulties were thickening and the suspension of specie payments was at hand, that the Mason-Slidell affair held dire potentialities, and that radicals and conservatives would be at each others' throats throughout the session of Congress. No state paper would arouse more interest than the report of the Secretary of War. On November 25th Washington correspondents began announcing that Cameron would advocate the arming of slaves. The Secretary had not only shown his paragraph to intimates, but laid it before the new special counsel for the War Department, Edwin McMasters Stanton, who made changes to strengthen it from a legal standpoint, and gave it full approval. The key sentences ran: [13]

"Those who make war against the Government justly forfeit all rights of property. . . . It is as clearly a right of the government to arm slaves, when it may become necessary, as it is to use gunpowder taken from the enemy. Whether it is expedient to do so is purely a military question. . . . If it shall be found that the men who have been held by the rebels as slaves are capable of bearing arms and performing efficient military service, it is the right, and may become the duty, of the Government to arm and equip them, and employ their service against the rebels, under proper military regulations, discipline, and command."

This was a threat, not a statement of immediate intent, and within a year

11 Hugh O'Reilly, "Arming the Slaves for the Union," pamphlet published 1875; O'Reilly was secretary of the Association for Promoting the Organization of Colored Troops, one of various abolitionist bodies already demanding such action.
12 *Idem.* The MS Reminiscences of X. X. Cobb, NYPL, give a slightly different version.
13 Nicolay and Hay, V, 125, 126; *Cong. Globe,* Dec. 12, 1861. The N. Y. *Tribune's* Washington correspondent sent out word of Cameron's intention Nov. 25.

events were to make the threat good. But the expediency of arming the Negroes was not a purely military question—it was equally a political question; and the nervous condition of the Borderland made such an utterance highly indiscreet.

Why did Lincoln so lose touch with Cameron that the Secretary could pen this paragraph? For one reason, he always drove his Cabinet with slack rein, and often with no rein at all, a matter of frequent complaint by businesslike members. For another, he was engrossed with a multiplicity of urgent affairs, including the *Trent* dispute, Mexico, a memorandum on the military offensive which he sent McClellan about December 1, a plan for compensated emancipation in the Border States, and final touches on his own message. For a third reason, he had asked Cabinet members for an abstract of essential parts of their reports, and Cameron's had apparently given him no uneasiness. Yet all these reasons are unsatisfactory; Lincoln did find time in these days for comparative trifles, and he betrayed a lack of proper vigilance. Perhaps he would not have been so supremely great a man had he been a highly circumspect and efficient administrator. But we cannot excuse his secretaries for not reading the newspapers, listening to Washington talk, and seeing that he was warned betimes.[14]

The sequel was an unfortunate exposure of Administration differences. On Saturday, November 30, Cameron presented his report to Lincoln, who was too busy to read it that day. Next morning the Secretary mailed copies to postmasters in leading cities, to be delivered to newspapers as soon as Lincoln had sent his message to Congress. He also gave confidential copies to Washington correspondents. Sometime on Sunday Lincoln read the report. Astonished and dismayed, he at once called Cameron to the White House. Here two conferences took place in rapid succession, other Cabinet members participating in the second. The President insisted that Cameron suppress the paragraph on arming slaves. As Lincoln was presenting in his message some vague ideas on colonizing freedmen abroad, and was about to attempt to persuade Border State Congressmen to support a plan for compensated emancipation, he could permit no such untimely declaration. Cameron expostulated. His statement contained nothing especially novel, he argued, and it ran parallel with equally explicit and radical, though briefer, statements in Welles's reports.

It appears that Chase outspokenly and Welles at least tacitly supported him.[15] But Bates, Seward, Smith, and Montgomery Blair stood on the other

14 Mrs. Stephen A. Douglas, one of the many visitors, called Nov. 27 for advice on the property of her minor children in the South; *Collected Works*, V, 32.
15 Welles, "Narrative of Events," *Amer. Hist. Rev.*, XXXI, 486 ff.; Flower, *Stanton*, 116; N. Y. *Times, Herald*, Dec. 3–6; N. Y. *Tribune*, Dec. 4, a very full account probably inspired by Cameron or Chase; Nicolay and Hay, V, 126, 127.

side, and of course Lincoln's word was final. Cameron either gave way, or was overruled despite continued protestations; at any rate, he had to submit.[16]

But the mischief had been done. On Monday, December 2, Montgomery Blair telegraphed postmasters to return the packages containing Cameron's report. Congress met at noon buzzing with rumors about the dispute between Lincoln and Cameron, for Cabinet officers on both sides had talked excitedly to friends. The legislative branch had expected to receive the President's message, but this was withheld. The House at once showed its temper by passing a resolution for the emancipation of slaves of rebels within all military jurisdictions; that is, endorsing Frémont's policy. Many predicted an early breakup of the Cabinet and general confusion. On the 3rd Lincoln's message went to Congress unaccompanied by any departmental reports. Though moderate members liked it, radicals greeted it with little bursts of derisive laughter.[17] The press meanwhile took positions on Cameron according to its predilections. Greeley's *Tribune* of course doggedly supported him, while Raymond's *Times* stood doggedly with Lincoln. And to the amazement of millions of citizens who had not heard of the dispute, the newspapers began publishing Cameron's report in two versions!

The inevitable had happened. In some cities postmasters did not receive Montgomery Blair's order for withdrawal, and in others it was not heeded. The Cincinnati *Gazette*, for example, got Cameron's report unaltered. The editors immediately printed it on the front page of the next morning's paper; then, late that night, they got the version as modified under Lincoln's orders, and printed the changes on the inside pages. The New York *Times* and *Herald* on December 4 carried the report as amended, while the *Tribune* that day published it in the Secretary's original form. The *Congressional Globe* of December 12 printed the suppressed portion. Naturally all radicals were enraged. "What a fiasko!" C. H. Ray of the Chicago *Tribune* wrote Elihu Washburne. "Old Abe is now unmasked, and we are sold out." For the moment Cameron was the toast of all men who hoped for hard blows at slavery.[18]

16 Nicolay and Hay, and Flower, say Cameron declined to yield and was overruled; A. K. McClure, in *Lincoln and Men of War Times*, 162, 163, states he "submitted as gracefully as possible," the view taken by Meneely. That he did submit is indicated by the fact that he wrote a substitute passage.

17 Washington corr. in N. Y. *Tribune*, Dec. 5, 1861.

18 Washburne Papers, LC. The Cincinnati *Gazette* published an explanatory editorial Dec. 6, with a long news article from Washington narrating the whole dispute. This article declared that Cameron had refused to budge, but that Lincoln had compelled the change. The revision struck out Cameron's matter on the treatment of Negroes, and substituted a single paragraph. This, after stating that many slaves were in military hands and constituted a military resource which should not be turned over to the Confederacy, went on: "The disposition to be made of the slaves of rebels after the close of the war can be safely left to the wisdom and patriotism of Congress. The representatives of the people will, unquestionably, secure to the loyal slaveholders every right to which they are entitled under the Constitution of the country."

A deputation of Congressional leaders which included Vice-President Hamlin, Owen Lovejoy, John A. Bingham, and other antislavery men descended enthusiastically on the Secretary's house as he entertained W. H. Russell of the London *Times* at dinner, and acclaimed him in fervent speeches. At the next caucus of Republican Representatives others earnestly upheld him. Thaddeus Stevens, long a bitter political antagonist, wholeheartedly endorsed his course. And Stevens had a sensational bit of news. McClellan, he said, had come to Lincoln and threatened to resign if the offensive passages were not struck out. For this assertion he gave no proof.[19]

[III]

Lincoln hesitated to dismiss Cameron summarily because abrupt action would anger the Radical war party. Cameron, for his part, wished to make his now inevitable exit with dignity, taking a foreign post, and hoped to have a voice in selecting his successor. As he knew, he had few friends in Washington. Sumner stood firmly by him in the Senate, and Chase in the Cabinet, but many even of the extreme antislavery group had been alienated by his bad administration and his adroit haste in getting his report before the country. Much of the press comment on his recommendations was scathing; for example, Raymond's *Times* remarked that it was odd to talk of arming the slaves when the War Department had not yet succeeded in properly arming white men.[20] His position was worsened when late in December the House investigative committee under C. H. Van Wyck of New York submitted a report which, published in full by the press, dealt unsparingly with frauds practiced upon the War Department.

A new Secretary had to be chosen, but in a way that would spare Cameron's feelings, respect the growing war party which demanded advanced measures, and persuade the country that a truly constructive step was being taken. He must be acceptable to the editors, governors, Congressmen, and plain citizens who thought aggressiveness the cardinal need. By Christmas Lincoln realized that he and the country were in serious straits. One piece of news after another dampened Northern spirits: General Albin Schoepf's deplorable retreat from the neighborhood of Cumberland Gap, exposing the brave Unionists of east Tennessee; the loss of ground in Missouri, and Halleck's hostility there to Negro refugees; the sudden, one-sided communication of the French foreign minister, E. Thouvenel, taking part with the British in the *Trent* affair; Greeley's declaration that the country could not go on spending its

19 See N. Y. *Tribune*, Dec. 5, and Russell's diary Dec. 4 for the Congressional call; N. Y. *Weekly Tribune*, Dec. 14, 1861, for caucus.
20 Dec. 6, 1861.

colossal sums for another six months; and the unescapable humiliation of surrendering Mason and Slidell.

Union fortunes were in fact at a desperate point. The Treasury was almost empty, high new taxes were a necessity, and on December 28 the principal New York banks decided to stop specie payments. Many were asking
with Chase how it was that when the War Department reported 660,000 men
under arms, the armies of the Potomac, West Virginia, Kentucky, and Missouri did not contain more than half that many. Congress, President, and a
great majority of thoughtful citizens had a fast-ebbing faith in McClellan.
The Western army was essentially leaderless. "Our only hope now," General
James Wadsworth wrote Sumner, "is in the legislative branch. If you are
competent to the crisis you may save the country; but you must do it soon or
be too late!" [21] And to cap other misfortunes McClellan fell ill of typhoid. On
December 20 he failed to appear at headquarters, next day it was learned he
was very sick, and by Christmas staff intimates (but not the President!) knew
that his life was in danger.[22]

His illness was disastrous because it paralyzed all military planning. Mc-
Clellan had never delegated his principal powers, so that Marcy, head of his
staff—himself recently ill—dared make no decisions whatever. The general,
confined to his bed during some three weeks, saw nobody and kept his condition largely secret from the press. Lincoln lost practically all communication
with him. Calling sometimes when McClellan was asleep, the President was
denied entrance and given no trustworthy news. As the general later wrote,
Lincoln's anxiety induced him to fear that the disease was so acute that it
would terminate fatally. Not until January 10, 1862, was McClellan really
alert again.

All the while, with a formidable groundswell of opinion demanding action,
the leaderless armies stood immobile, giving the country only a few slight successes in Missouri and Kentucky. Perforce, the anguished Lincoln had to step
into the breach. In St. Louis Halleck did little beyond oversee Pope, Schofield,
and Prentiss in trying to halt marauding and bridge-burning; in Louisville
Don Carlos Buell, who had taken command of the Department of the Ohio
November 15, was concentrating his troops and eying Nashville as an objective. Hoping some large result could be achieved in the West, Lincoln tele-

21   Jan. 10, 1862; Pearson, *Wadsworth*, 102, 103.
22   The Comte de Paris, of McClellan's staff, in *Battles and Leaders*, II, 120, says his life
was in danger. McClellan in *My Own Story*, 155, asserts that "although very weak and ill,
my strong constitution enabled me to retain a clear intellect" and make decisions. A man
very weak and ill of typhoid is not a good judge of his own clarity of intellect, and Mc-
Clellan had reason to gloss over his disability. The N. Y. *Herald* on Friday, Dec. 27, said he
was better, was transacting business, and would be in the saddle again on Monday; he was
not in the saddle for at least two weeks more

graphed Halleck on New Year's eve asking whether he and Buell were acting in concert. He followed this with a message to both generals: "Delay is ruining us, and it is indispensable for me to have something definite." The generals responded that they were *not* coöperating with each other, that some of their regiments were unarmed, and that Halleck opposed any immediate movement. On a letter from that tactician the President wrote despairingly: "It is exceedingly discouraging. As everywhere else, nothing can be done."

And Lincoln had reason for depression! He had just presided over a joint meeting of the Cabinet and the Committee on the Conduct of the War, at which the radicals—Zach Chandler, Ben Wade, and John Covode—bitterly denounced McClellan, and clamored for giving McDowell charge of the Army of the Potomac.[23]

On January 10 Lincoln, in gloom and perplexity, sought out one of the few administrators who was demonstrating high capacity, Quartermaster-General Meigs. He seated himself before the blazing office grate. "What shall I do?" he demanded. "The people are impatient; Chase has no money and he tells me he can raise no more; the general of the Army has typhoid fever. The bottom is out of the tub."[24]

Meigs had a ready suggestion: As it was evident that McClellan would be incapacitated for some weeks, Lincoln should call a conference of the higher officers to talk over plans. The same night, January 10, what amounted to an Emergency War Cabinet—Lincoln, Chase, Seward, T. A. Scott, and Generals McDowell and Franklin—met in the first of four sessions. The President was in such a mood of desperation that he even spoke of taking the field himself. He voiced his anxiety over the exhausted finances, the impatient temper of Congress, the want of liaison between Halleck and Buell, and above all, McClellan's illness. He must talk to somebody, he said. "If General McClellan does not want to use the army, I would like to *borrow* it, provided I could see how it could be made to do something." While the civilians listened eagerly, he asked Generals McDowell and Franklin what military plans they would advise. McDowell proposed that the Army of the Potomac make a frontal advance in Virginia, moving against Aquia, Centreville, and Manassas; Franklin, who knew something of McClellan's ideas, proposed a lateral movement on Richmond from the head of the York River.

Next evening, the 11th, the group met again, augmented by Montgomery Blair. They debated the two plans, Chase arguing for the frontal movement, and Blair for an attack from the upper York. Lincoln wished that Meigs be

23 *Collected Works*, V, 86, 87; O. R. I, vii, 532–535; Meneely, 359; McClellan, *My Own Story*, 155 ff.
24 See Meigs's narrative in *American Hist. Review*, XXVI, 292, 293, and MS Diary, Meigs Papers, LC; Swinton, *Army of the Potomac*, 79–85.

consulted and that officers gather information on the transportation needed to carry troops down the Potomac and up the York. Much perplexed, he made no decision between the two plans, but arranged for a third meeting. To some observers in the group, a struggle for power between McDowell as backed by Chase, and McClellan as supported by Blair and Meigs, seemed emerging; but the President was thinking of the war, not of rival generals.[25] On Sunday afternoon, the 12th, they met again with Meigs present, and after some discussion agreed that as McClellan was better, they would consult with him next day.

Of course McClellan soon learned what was afoot, and to Lincoln's jubilant relief, he was on hand at a fourth White House meeting Monday afternoon. Apparently he was galvanized into action by a warning from the subtle Edwin M. Stanton, who had reasons of his own for wishing to curry favor with the general, and who warned him: "They are counting on your death and are already dividing among themselves your military goods and chattels." If Stanton could ally himself with McClellan, he would stand in a more powerful position.[26] McClellan at once leaped at the conclusion that a plot had been formed to get rid of him and put McDowell in his stead, and that Chase and McDowell were at the bottom of it. He appeared at the White House in a truculent mood. The President opened the meeting by explaining why he had called the Cabinet members and generals together, and then innocently asked McDowell to explain the plan for a direct forward movement. While McClellan glared angrily, McDowell argued that this march could be started in three weeks, whereas a transfer of the army to the peninsula between the York and James Rivers could not be begun, for lack of transports, for a month or six weeks.

Disconcerted by McClellan's haughty stare, McDowell added an excusing sentence about the urgent situation in which the government stood. To this the general replied coldly if not sharply, "You are entitled to have any opinion you please!"—and said no more. He regarded the whole affair—the conferences, the inquiries, the plans—as a treacherous effort to supersede him while ill. He was not advising the President of the United States, but foiling a group of conspirators![27]

Finally the anxious Lincoln asked, in effect: "What and when can any-

25　Meigs, *loc. cit.*; McDowell's memorandum on the meeting, Swinton, 79, 80; McClellan, *Own Story*, 155 ff.; T. H. Williams, *Lincoln and the Radicals*, 84–86.

26　Chase had told Stanton, who told McClellan. But we must not do Stanton the injustice of attributing to him a purely selfish motive. He was already sure of the Secretaryship of War; he and McClellan, as fellow Pennsylvanians, were warm friends. Others, including perhaps Meigs, must have told McClellan as soon as he began to get up, which was Jan. 11th.

27　McClellan had the impression that Lincoln had directed McDowell, Franklin, and Meigs to make a "secret examination" into the state of the army, which he says was unthing be done?" The surly general at last spoke up. "The case is so clear a blind man could see it," he snapped. Without explaining, he said he did not know what force he could count on: how many men Burnside would take for a projected attack on Roanoke Island, and Ben Butler for the proposed descent on New Orleans. Finally Secretary Chase, out of patience with him, brought the talk back to the main point by repeating Lincoln's question: "What do you intend doing with your army, and when do you intend doing it?"

A sullen silence ensued. McClellan, who regarded Chase as his principal enemy, ignored him. Finally he unbent enough to offer some remarks about Western operations. An advance in Kentucky was to precede that in Virginia, he remarked, and he had directed General Buell to *take* wagons if he could not hire them. Another pause followed. All were plainly waiting for an answer to Lincoln's and Chase's queries. At last the commander made the evasive statement that he was most unwilling to divulge his plans, always believing that in military matters the fewer people who knew his secrets the better. "I will tell them if I am *ordered* to do so." Lincoln then inquired whether the general had fixed any particular time, which he need not state. "Yes," responded McClellan. "Then," said the President, "I will adjourn this meeting." Already Seward had commented in his amiable way that they had better break up: "I don't see that we are likely to make much out of General McClellan." Chase, previously distrustful, thereafter detested the general.

A wiser leader would at once have gone privately to Lincoln, and given him his full plans and time-schedule, but McClellan remained sullen. During another fortnight he did nothing, keeping Lincoln still in the dark. The worried President thereupon felt himself provoked to a decisive and unhappy step. On January 27, yielding to pleas by the War and Navy departments, but consulting nobody and reading it to the Cabinet for information only, he issued General War Order No. 1. It directed a general movement of land and naval forces against the enemy February 22. The Secretaries of War and the Navy, all officers in national service, and their subordinates, would be held strictly responsible for executing the order. Four days later the President's Special War Order No. 1, addressed to McClellan, bade him use the Army of the Potomac, after safeguarding Washington, in a flanking movement to the southwest of the Confederate position at Manassas—to begin not later than February 22.[28]

---

necessary, for his staff could have informed the President of the "exact condition" of every branch. *My Own Story*, 156. Why the staff never did so is a puzzle. Nothing is more discreditable to McClellan than his willingness to believe that the transparently honest Lincoln, so patient and long-suffering, could be capable of double-dealing.

28 See text in O. R. I, v, 41 ff., and with previously unpublished passages, in Lincoln, *Collected Works*, V, 119 ff. Welles says in his Diary, I, 61, that he and Stanton had pressed for such an order. Both were preparing for the New Orleans expedition. Both wished the

It was obvious that General War Order No. 1 was intended primarily for popular effect. Political rather than military, it was expected to protect the Administration from accusations of inaction rather than to inaugurate a series of battles. Even so, it was unwise. Lincoln would have to learn to handle Congress and public opinion more adroitly. His order seemed impatient, his idea of a "general movement" was amateurish, and his choice of Washington's birthday was undignified. The Special Order to McClellan, however, evinced real sagacity, for it was well devised to make him show his hand. Lincoln waited to see how soon his reply would come and how much of his plans it would reveal.

[IV]

Meanwhile, Cameron's exit had been managed, his successor installed, and an initial effort made to fit a bottom into the tub. We must reëmphasize the fact that the central reason for Cameron's dismissal was not his antislavery position, which counted for little, but his lack of grasp, foresight, administrative energy, and organizing power. However numerous, fierce, and well-founded the charges brought against his successor, Stanton clearly possessed these particular qualities.

Lincoln knew that Cassius M. Clay was anxious to drop his place as minister to Russia and accept an army command. He ascertained through Thurlow Weed that Cameron would be glad to take the post. As the new Secretary, Lincoln thought of naming Joseph Holt, the stanch Kentucky Unionist who had done so much to put courage into the last acts of the Buchanan Administration. But Cameron believed that Stanton, who also had given iron resolution to Buchanan's last months, and who had assiduously curried favor at the War Department, was an abler man. Cameron had urged him on the radicals, introducing him to Zack Chandler at a breakfast party as the best choice, and making the same recommendation to Ben Wade.[29]

"I called on Mr. Lincoln," Cameron later wrote, "and suggested Edwin

---

Confederates driven from the south bank of the Potomac, their batteries demolished, and the river fully opened. Welles writes that "we united in requesting President Lincoln to issue his celebrated order of the 27th of January."

29 Years after, when Cameron was Senator, Charles F. Benjamin saw the ex-Secretary, Cameron told him "that soon after he became Secretary of War he received a call one evening from Stanton, who was cordial and effusive, and fervidly eloquent on the subject of depriving the Confederacy of its slave property and putting it to the use of the Union. Thenceforward, as he told me, Stanton was his confidant and adviser, and when he saw that his days in the Cabinet were numbered he set every agency at work that he could command to make sure of Stanton as his successor, and when he knew he had succeeded he was glad to get out." Charles F. Benjamin, Washington, June 1, 1914, to Horace White; White Papers, Ill. State Hist. Lib.

M. Stanton to him as my successor. He hesitated; but after listening to me for a time, he yielded, and sent me to offer the place of Secretary of War to him, and added: 'Tell him, Cameron, if he accepts, I will send his nomination as Secretary, and yours as minister to Russia, to the Senate together.'" This may be accurate as to Cameron's action, but the story is more complicated. Seward, as Gideon Welles, Montgomery Blair, and others assert, was the prime mover in bringing Stanton forward. He knew the man's strength and was impressed by Assistant-Secretary Peter H. Watson's warm endorsement. It is said that while Lincoln hesitated over Holt, who might have struck some radicals as being too much a Border State man, Winfield Scott, Ben Wade, and Sumner also urged the claims of Stanton. Lincoln of course consulted numerous men.[30] He did not know, and Cameron did not tell him, that Stanton had helped write the antislavery passage in Cameron's report.

The final stroke was not without drama. Lincoln on January 10, by Chase's hand—for Lincoln in his politic way wished Chase to think *he* had a prime part in the matter—sent a note to Cameron. It reached the Secretary late in the evening, and he was staggered to see that it was so worded as to give the public the impression of a curt discharge. At midnight he sought Thomas A. Scott's house in high emotion. Showing Scott and McClure the note, he wept as he said that it meant his personal and political destruction. They assured him of what seems to have been the fact, that Lincoln—then distracted over McClellan's condition—had dashed off the note without perceiving its implications. All agreed that next day they should ask the President to withdraw it, allow Cameron to submit his resignation, and accept it graciously. Speaker after speaker in Congress this month, using the Van Wyck report as ammunition, was assailing the Secretary, and Lincoln must not seem to throw him to the wolves. The result was that the President sent Cameron two letters dated January 11. One was a notification that as Cameron had more than once expressed a wish for another office, he could now gratify him with St. Petersburg; the other was a generous personal communication, declaring his personal esteem and his confidence in the Secretary's ability, patriotism, and fidelity.

Cameron departed with pride in the work he had done to raise and train the great volunteer army. "No man ever served with more disinterested integrity than I did, and I am sure in the end all will say so." In actual fact, the next generation criticized him more harshly than he deserved. The greatest of war ministers, confronted with his staggering tasks, and given the meagre

---

30 Different views on Stanton's appointment are given in Welles, *Diary*, I, 57–59, 127, 128; Bates, *Diary;* Chase, *Diary*, Jan. 12, 1862; Henry Wilson, "Jeremiah S. Black and Edwin M. Stanton," *Atlantic*, XXVI, 474 ff.; Maunsell B. Field, *Memories*, 267–269; Flower, *Stanton*, 116, 117, and A. G. Riddle, *Benjamin F. Wade*.

resources the government could then muster, would have blundered. In this office he was honest, and he did his best. But he was a misfit, whom Lincoln appointed against his best judgment; clumsy, forgetful, unsystematic, he failed to adapt himself to his responsibilities as Chase and Seward did; and his executive feebleness soon made him a sore clog upon the administration. The War Department, enlarged by Congress in late summer and now shaken down, gave Stanton a far more efficient agency than Cameron had found. Contract letting had been systematized, trustworthy manufacturers had been separated from cheats, and half a thousand regiments had been put in fair order.

The first drivers of the military machine, the men who jerked it into gear, were penalized by circumstance. The nation had to regard them as expendable, and they were all broken.[31]

In choosing Stanton, Lincoln took a man of whose true capacities or character nobody was informed. But he knew well that Stanton had been a Jacksonian Democrat, had held the Attorney-Generalship under Buchanan as a Union Democrat, and had other Union Democrats as his chief friends. He understood his well-earned eminence at the bar. No other aspirant combined so much executive support, Meigs alone disliking the appointment, with so much Congressional approbation. His public reputation overtopped that of Holt. With characteristic magnanimity, Lincoln dismissed any recollection of the slights Stanton had put upon him when they were fellow-counsel in the reaper-patent case in Cincinnati in 1855. He could not know that in recent letters, Stanton had violently abused him and his Administration, and

31 Cameron delivered a long defense of his record at a public dinner in Harrisburg just before sailing for Europe (N. Y. *Herald*, May 8, 1862). As a young man, he said, he had often worked twenty hours out of the twenty-four, "but that labor was nothing in comparison with the overpowering toil which I underwent at Washington." He found the Ordnance Department without a head, the man in charge being too old to be competent, and he appointed Colonel Ripley, who was believed capable, "but who soon proved, in the opinion of my associates, to be unequal to the crisis." To safeguard the Department, he directed Thomas A. Scott, his assistant, to see that every contract had a thirty-day cancellation clause to be invoked in case of failure to meet requirements. Cameron revealed that Lincoln had specifically approved one large arms contract. When on Sept. 4 Herman Boker & Co. of New York had offered upwards of more than 100,000 rifled percussion muskets, subject to departmental inspection, at not more than $18 each, Lincoln had endorsed on the letter of offer: "I approve the carrying this through, carefully, cautiously, and expeditiously. Avoid conflicts and interference." The Secretary defended his railroad arrangements to carry Eastern soldiers to Washington in the April crisis when the bridges of the Wilmington & Baltimore were destroyed. Massachusetts capitalists, he asserted, controlled that road, and their resentment when he arranged with the rival Harrisburg, Reading, and New Jersey roads to reduce the New York–Baltimore fare from $6 to $4 inspired the attack by Dawes. Cameron also charged that some of his Congressional assailants, who had passed a vote of censure in the House, had asked him for improper contract favors. "Having my whole time occupied in preparing an army out of raw and undisciplined soldiers, of course I may have run counter to the desires of such gentlemen."

had even advised the violent overthrow of the government, to be replaced by a military dictatorship under McClellan. If he had, he would have ignored the fact. Lincoln was willing to pay any personal price to obtain a powerful organizer of victory.

The transfer of the War Department to Stanton was widely hailed as a great national victory.[32] Its moral effect was tremendous. Senators and Representatives who in the dark winter of 1860–61 had seen how Stanton nerved the weak Buchanan to duty, and had exposed the dark purposes of Floyd and Cobb, particularly rejoiced. They recalled how fiercely he had risen to meet the crisis, what iron resolution, industry, and vigilance he had brought to this task, and how carefully, using Howard of Michigan and Sumner of Massachusetts as intermediaries, he had kept the Republicans informed of every movement tending to endanger the nation. They remembered gratefully how he had decided that his fellow Cabinet-member, Isaac Toucey, ought to be arrested, and had inspired a House resolution on that subject. Henry Wilson, as member of a Republican committee of vigilance, had received almost daily warnings and suggestions from Stanton. Sometimes they had conferred at one in the morning on the secession crisis. The Congressional radicals were also aware that for months now, Stanton had chafed over the seeming inaction of the army, and in intimate talk had berated the Administration for not pursuing a more determined and aggressive policy.[33]

The fact that Stanton was no politician, but simply a leader of the bar noted for his prodigious industry and powerful argument, pleased the public. The press drew the portrait of a man of large brain, complete absorption in any task he undertook, and absolute fearlessness. Greeley's *Tribune* credited him with "the highest qualities of talent, courage, and uncompromising patriotism." He told Winfield Scott that he would give the public but one pledge, to throttle treason, and everybody knew that he brought to his work no commitments, attachments, or predilections that could embarrass it. Joseph Holt wrote a friend that he found everybody rejoicing; "but that rejoicing would be far greater did the people know, as I do, the courage, the loyalty, and the

32 The Washington correspondent of the N.Y. *Times* wrote (issue of Jan. 14) that the capital was stunned by the news, and the Washington correspondent of the *Tribune* called it a bombshell.

33 McClellan, a friend of Stanton, was astonished but delighted, writing S. L. M. Barlow, the Democratic leader in New York City, that the nomination was an unexpected bit of good fortune. Stanton had been on the point of going to New York to become law partner of Barlow. Jan. 18, 1862, Barlow Papers. The rejoicings of the radicals in Congress are described by Henry Wilson, "Edwin M. Stanton," *Atlantic*, Feb. 1870. The Cleveland *Plain Dealer* said: "We know Edwin M. Stanton well. He has more of the Bonaparte in his composition than any other man in America. The army will move on now, even if it goes to the devil."

genius of the new secretary. . . . He is a great man intellectually and morally —a patriot of the true Roman stamp, who will grapple with treason as the lion grapples with his prey." [34]

And the first steps of the Secretary showed that his earnestness had method. He asked the Senate to postpone further consideration of military nominations till he could scrutinize the list. He had a frank talk with the Committee on the Conduct of the War, getting their views and making suggestions for further legislation. He rearranged his office space. He laid down firm rules of business: [35]

1. He would receive nobody at his house and transact no business there (Cameron had been overrun at home with callers).
2. The Department would attend to letters and other written communications the first thing each morning, this taking precedence of other business.
3. Instead of giving six days a week to members of Congress, as Cameron had done, he would give them one day, Saturday.
4. He would give all other callers one day, Monday.
5. The other days, Tuesday to Friday inclusive, he would give to the war, and only to business pertaining to the armies in the field.

Finally, Stanton announced he would strike from the Army rolls all officers found in Washington except those ordered there by superiors on military business.

[V]

The bottom had indeed seemed nearly out of the tub in this midwinter crisis. But early in the year the North could feel a greater firmness and confidence; the tub was being strengthened.

Not Chase's financial measures, nor Seward's surrender of Mason and Slidell, nor the new War Department administration, did this. The central fact was that Lincoln, on whom all the fortunes of the Union depended, had begun to lead firmly. In his early months he had shown sagacity, moderation, poise —but not a strong captaincy. He had frequently fumbled. He had hesitated to call out the full strength of the North, so that Zack Chandler had some grounds for declaring the Administration timid, vacillating, and inefficient. Not a single public utterance, not one letter, not even a dramatic act, had been stamped with the qualities men later learned to term Lincolnian. But in the last weeks of the year he faced the bluster of Wade and Chandler, the

34 Flower, *Stanton,* quoting E. D. Townsend on Stanton's remark to Scott; Curtis, *Buchanan,* II, 480, for Holt's letter; N. Y. *Tribune,* Feb. 12, 1862, for Greeley's opinion. A full treatment of Stanton's character, resources, and limitations will appear later in this narrative, as will a study of Chase's financial policies.
35 N. Y. *Weekly Tribune,* Jan. 25, 1862.

suaver pressures of Sumner and Trumbull, without yielding an inch. Zack Chandler dared to tell him: "I am in favor of sending for Jeff Davis at once, if your Administration views are carried out!" But the Washington correspondent of the *Times* correctly reported just before Christmas that Lincoln was adamant. "All thought of overruling the policy of President Lincoln in regard to the war is now virtually abandoned. After full consideration of all the reasons that have been presented to induce him to modify his plans to please the radicals, the President has firmly resolved to stand by his original purpose to regard the Union as unbroken, to restore the national laws over the seceded States as rapidly as possible, and to protect the lives and property of all loyal men." He had his own proposals for slavery, his first great constructive plan, which he was now about to present to the Border States, and which fitted his fundamental policy of the restoration of a truly fraternal Union.

This was the firmness of a strong leader, a chieftain who grew with the demands laid upon him. And the appointment of Stanton was the first great decided step, showing real statesmanship, which Lincoln had taken in front of the embattled nation. The President was beginning to feel his strength, to ride in the tempest, and direct the storm.

THE FIRST and worst year of the war, 1861, was over; an unhappy year, that upon a casual review seemed to contain far more of Union failure than achievement. It had been a year of hysterical excitements and skin-deep patriotism, of contract grabbing, office mongering, and political jobbery, of shortages, shoddy, and corruption. In foreign affairs it had been a year of humiliation: of Seward's wayward hankerings for war, of Napoleon III's sly meddling in Mexico and Spain's greedy intervention in Santo Domingo, and of America's chagrined surrender of Mason and Slidell. In the military sphere it had been stained with the blood of Bull Run, Ball's Bluff, and Wilson Creek, with the failure of McDowell, Patterson, and Lyon, with the dramatic collapse of Frémont, and with a widespread loss of faith in McClellan.

It had been a year of improvisation, and of the errors inseparable from haste, amateurishness, and disorganization. The loose, irresponsible management of half the recruiting had been almost incredibly faulty; the selection of untested incompetents to hold the lives of hundreds in their hands and spend enormous sums had often been shocking. Some new functions of the national government had never gained efficiency. The paymaster service in the army, for example, continually broke down. It was shameful that soldiers who risked their lives for a paltry thirteen dollars a month should not receive that sum; disgraceful that their families should often suffer for want of part of it. Yet it was a fact, and army morale felt its effects. Some weakness in the national character seemed involved in the early deficiencies of camp sanitation, the ill-checked indulgence of officers and men in drink, the easy habit of going absent without leave, and the general antipathy to discipline.

Yet on careful view the Northern achievement seemed more impressive. When in history had a people of twenty-five millions, so unused to martial pursuits and completely devoted to tasks of peace, compressed so mighty a war effort into nine months? To enlist nearly 700,000 men, soldiers, sailors, and marines; to clothe, arm, and train them, however roughly; to collect powerful naval squadrons out of nothing, and institute a new era of armored steam warships—this was a prodigious feat. As 1861 ended, Northern hosts were poised on the Potomac, Ohio, and Mississippi to march southward. Already they had made West Virginia, Kentucky, and Missouri seemingly secure, if but half pacified, for the Union. The navy had seized two footholds on the South Atlantic coast, had begun a blockade whose effectiveness was evidenced by the price of Southern products on the world market, and was preparing to strike at New Orleans. The *Monitor* was building. For the whole effort money and materials had been found in sufficiency, if not in abundance.

The war had shown that the North was still under-developed industrially; but it had demonstrated that the Union had a wide advantage over the South —little Massachusetts alone manufactured sixty per cent more goods in 1860 than the entire Confederacy, and New York more than twice as much. The North was actually overbuilt in railroads, and events already proved that this would be the first great railway war of history, the Northern lines carrying armies and material to every invasion point. Economically and militarily, they knit the North into a compact whole. Already perceptive men saw that the four trunk lines which bridged the Allegheny barrier guaranteed a closer union of East and Northwest, and a steady growth of population and power while the battle raged.

Like a tocsin awakening a lethargic giant, the war had brought into play unsuspected powers of mobilization and administration. Against the ineptness of Cameron could be set the proved resourcefulness of the shrewd, untiring Connecticut Yankee, Gideon Welles, in making the most of scattered ships and neglected yards. If Chase at the Treasury as yet offered only promise, that was because the formidable difficulties would have baffled a Hamilton. A chaotic, ramshackle structure of State banks; a body of investors too small, too unused to Federal securities, and too cautious to give the government proper aid; House and Senate committees which even under strong men like Thaddeus Stevens and William Pitt Fessenden were clumsy in framing large-scale financial legislation; a steady march of inflation—these difficulties were compounded by the general belief in a short war. But Chase had grasp, earnestness, and courage. Among the men of lesser prominence who proved the nation's latent organizational capacities stood Montgomery C. Meigs as head of the all-important quartermaster services, Gustavus V. Fox as the efficient second leader at the Navy Department, and, now emerging, Thomas A. Scott as Stanton's invaluable aid. Of each, observers could say what one Congressman wrote of Scott: "What a relief to deal with him, with his electric brain and cool, quiet manner."

Amid the confusion, blundering, and selfishness patriots could also find cheer in the unanticipated resourcefulness of the State governments. Generally regarded as weak, shackling mechanisms corroded by politics, they had shown both zeal and power. Three war governors in especial, Andrew of Massachusetts, Curtin of Pennsylvania, and Oliver P. Morton of Indiana, had earned honorable places in the nation's history. When the War Department telegraphed its first call for troops Andrew made instant reply: "Dispatch received. By what route shall we send?" He proved his acumen by a following letter stuffed with shrewd suggestions. This trio of governors had a special capacity for enlisting business and financial talent, and for arousing popular determination. Curtin in his insistence on a body of trained reserve regiments saw further ahead than Washington. Morton helped kindle a fervor which brought out 150,000 volunteers in Indiana, making the draft practically a superfluity. Other governors—Yates, Kirkwood, Morgan, Buckingham—did well, but these three proved the resilient strength of a union of States.

All over the map, too, voluntary effort had exhibited a vision and strength which shamed inertia and self-seeking. It was already clear that women could write a lustrous page in public affairs. Partly from the foresight of one feminine organization—the Women's Central Association of Relief in New York—was born a body which finely typified the possibilities of expert private endeavor: the United States Sanitary Commission. Its two principal founders, Dr. Henry W. Bellows, a Unitarian minister, and Dr. Elisha Harris, a prominent New York physician, rallied a devoted group of men: A. D. Bache, Wolcott Gibbs, Cornelius R. Agnew, George Templeton Strong, and others. They made felicitous choice of an executive secretary in Frederick Law Olmsted. This body had a rough road just ahead. But nothing quite like it, in its combination of specialized skill, sturdy common sense, and consecrated devotion to a great aim, had previously been known in American annals; and its success was to show that a new era of national organization was opening.

As mid-January brought news of the victory of George H. Thomas, with 4000 effective troops, over an equal force of Confederates at Mill Spring, Kentucky, Northerners hoped for a turning of the tide. Most people ardently wished that McClellan, Buell, and Grant would make the war short; some hoped it would be prolonged sufficiently to ensure the downfall of slavery. Actually the year of improvised war was giving way to a year in which the war would become revolution; for the nation had been deeply aroused, and it would not stop.

Bibliography and Appendices

BIBLIOGRAPHY

Abel, Theodore, "The Element of Decision in The Pattern of War," in *American Sociology Review*, vol. 6 (December, 1941), 853-859; Adams, Charles F. Jr., *Charles Francis Adams*, by his son (Boston, 1900), "The Trent Affair, November, 1861," in Mass. Hist. Soc. *Proceedings*, vol. 45 (1911), 35-148; Adams, C. F. Jr., and Henry, *A Cycle of Adams Letters 1861-65*, ed. by Worthington C. Ford (2 vols., Boston, 1920); Adams, E. D., *Great Britain and the American Civil War* (2 vols., New York, 1925); Adams, George W., *Doctors in Blue: the Medical History of the Union Army in the Civil War* (New York, 1952); Alexander, De Alva S., *A Political History of the State of New York, 1774-1882* (3 vols., New York, 1906-09); Ambler, Charles H., *History of West Virginia* (New York, 1933); Anderson, Galusha, *The Story of a Border City during the Civil War* (Boston, 1908); Angell, James B., *The Reminiscences of James Burrill Angell* (New York, 1912); Angle, Paul M., ed., *The Lincoln Reader* (New Brunswick, N. J., 1947)

Bailey, Thomas A., *A Diplomatic History of the American People* (New York, 1940 and later eds.); Bancroft, Frederic, *The Life of W. H. Seward* (2 vols., New York, 1900); Barnard, John Gross, *C. S. A. and the Battle of Bull Run: a letter to an English Friend* (New York, 1862), *The Peninsular Campaign and Its Antecedents. . . .* (New York, 1864); Bates, Edward, *The Diary of Edward Bates, 1859-66*, ed. by Howard K. Beale (Washington, D. C., 1933); Baxter, James P., "The British Government and Neutral Rights 1861-65," *American Historical Review*, vol. 34 (October, 1928), 9-29; Beach, W. H., *The First N. Y. (Lincoln) Cavalry from April 19, 1861 to July 7, 1865* (New York, 1902); Belmont, August, *A Few Letters and Speeches of the Late Civil War* (New York, 1870); Bemis, Samuel F., ed., *American Secretaries of State and Their Diplomacy* (10 vols., New York, 1927-29), *A Diplomatic History of the United States* (New York and London, 1936 and later eds.); Benedict, G. G., *Vermont in the Civil War* (2 vols., Burlington, 1886-88); Benton, Thomas Hart, *Thirty Years' View: a History. . . .* (2 vols., New York, 1854-56); Bickham, W. D., *Rosecrans' Campaign with the Fourteenth Army Corps* (Cincinnati, 1863); Bicknell, George W., *History of the Fifth Maine Volunteers* (Portland, 1871); Bill, Alfred Hoyt, *The Beleaguered City, Richmond 1861-65* (New York, 1946); Bishop, James L., *History of American Manufactures from 1608 to 1860* (3 vols., Philadelphia, 1861-68); Black, Robert C. III, *The Railroads of the Confederacy* (Chapel Hill, 1952); Blaine, James G., *Twenty Years of Congress: From Lincoln to Garfield* (2 vols., Norwich, 1884-86); Botts, John Minor, *The Great Rebellion: Its Secret History, Rise, Progress and Disastrous Failure* (New York, 1866); Boykin, Samuel, *A Memorial Volume of the Hon. Howell Cobb* (Philadelphia, 1870); Boynton, E. C., *History of West Point and its Military Importance. . . .* (New York, 1864); Bradford, Gamaliel, *Confederate Portraits* (Boston, 1912), *Union Portraits* (Boston, 1914); Bragg, Jefferson Davis, *Louisiana in the Confederacy* (Baton Rouge, 1941); Brooks, Noah, *Washington in Lincoln's Time* (New York, 1895); Brown, G. W., *Baltimore and the Nineteenth of April, 1861: a Study of the War* (Baltimore, 1887); Browning, Orville H., *The Diary of Orville H. Browning*, ed. by T. C. Pease and J. G. Randall (2 vols., Springfield, Ill., 1925-31); Bruce, Robert V., *Lincoln and the Tools of War* (Indianapolis, 1957); Buckingham, Samuel Giles, *The Life of William A. Buckingham, the War Governor of Connecticut.* . . . (Springfield, Mass., 1894); Buell, Augustus C., *"The Cannoneer": Recollections of Service in the Army of the Potomac.* . . . (Washington, D. C., 1890); Burlingame, Roger, *March of the Iron Men: a Social History of Union through Invention* (New York, 1938); Burt, Silas W., *My Memoirs of Military History of . . . New York During the War for the Union* (Albany, 1902); Butler, Benjamin, *Autobiography and Personal Reminiscences of Major General Benjamin F. Butler; Butler's Book* (Boston, 1892); Butler, William Allen, *A Retrospect of Forty Years 1825-65* (New York, 1911)

Callahan, James Morton, *History of West Virginia, Old and New* (2 vols., Chicago, 1923); *Cambridge History of British Foreign Policy 1783-1919*, ed. by Sir A. W. Ward (3 vols., Cambridge, 1922-33); Carman, Harry J., and Luthin, Reinhard H., *Lincoln and the Patronage* (New York, 1943); Carr, Lucien, *Missouri: a Bone of Contention* (Boston, 1888); Catton, Bruce, *This Hallowed Ground* (Garden City, N. Y., 1936); Charnwood, Lord, *Abraham Lincoln* (London, 1916); Chase, F. H., *Lemuel Shaw: Chief Justice of the Supreme Judicial Court of Massachusetts 1830-60* (Boston, 1918); Chase, Salmon P., *Inside Lincoln's Cabinet: The Civil War Diaries*, ed. by David Donald (New York, 1954), *Diary* (Annual Report Amer. Hist. Assoc., vol. II, Washington, D. C., 1902); Chesnut, Mrs. Mary Boykin, *A Diary from Dixie*, ed. by I. D. Martin and M. L. Avary (New York, 1905), new edition ed. by Ben Ames Williams (Boston, 1949); Churchill, Winston, *The Crisis* (New York, 1901); Clark, George L., *History of Connecticut; Its People and Institutions* (New York, 1914); Clarke, Mrs. Grace Giddings, *George W. Julian* (Indianapolis, 1923); Cleland, R. G., *A History of Phelps-Dodge, 1834-1950* (New York, 1952); Cole, Arthur Charles, *The Era of the Civil War 1848-70* (Springfield, Mass., 1919); Coleman, Mrs. Ann Butler, *The Life of John J. Crittenden with selections from his correspondence.* . . . (2 vols., Philadelphia, 1871); Commager, Henry Steele, ed., *The Blue and the Gray* (2 vols., Indianapolis, 1951); Commons, John Rogers, et al., *History of Labor in the United States* (4 vols., New York, 1918-35); Conger, A. L., *The Rise of U. S. Grant* (New York, 1931); Connor, Henry G., *John Archibald Campbell* (Boston, 1920); Cooper, James Fenimore, *The Correspondence of James Fenimore Cooper*, ed. by his grandson (2 vols., New Haven, 1922); Corbin, Diana F. M., *A Life of Matthew Fontaine Maury* (London, 1888); Corliss, C. J., *Main Line of Mid-America: the Story of the Illinois Central* (New York, 1950); Coulter, Ellis M., *The Civil War and Readjustment in Kentucky* (Chapel Hill, 1933), *The Confederate States of America 1861-65* (Baton Rouge, 1950); Cowley, Charles, *A History of Lowell* (Boston, 1868); Cox, Jacob D., *Military Reminiscences of the Civil War* (2 vols., New York, 1900); Cox, Samuel S., *Union—Disunion—Reunion, Three Decades of Federal Legislation 1855-85* (Providence, 1885); Crawford, Col. Samuel W., *The Genesis of the Civil War; the Story of Sumter, 1860-61* (New York, 1887); Croffut, William and Morris, John, *The Military and Civil History of Connecticut During the War of 1861-65* (New York, 1868); Cubberley, E. P., *Public Education in the United States.* . . . (Boston, 1934), *State and County School Administration.* . . . (New York, 1915); Cudworth, W. H., *History of the First Regiment of Massachusetts Infantry 1861-64* (Boston, 1866); Curtis, George Ticknor, *The Life of James Buchanan* (2 vols., New York, 1883)

Dahlgren, M. V., ed., *Memoirs of John A. Dahlgren* (Philadelphia, 1872); Daniel, Fred S., *The* Richmond Examiner *During the War* (New York, 1868); Davis, Jefferson, *Jefferson Davis, Constitutionalist: His Letters, Papers and Speeches*, ed. by Dunbar Rowland (10 vols., Jackson, 1923), *The Rise and Fall of the Confederate Government* (2 vols., New York, 1881), "Lord Wolseley's Mistakes," *North American Review*, vol. 149 (October, 1889), 472-482; Dawes, Henry L., "Two Vice Presidents, John C. Breckinridge and Hannibal Hamlin," *Century Magazine*, vol. 50 (o.s.) (July, 1895), 463-467; De Leon, T. C., *Four Years in Rebel Capitals: an Inside View of Life in the Southern Confederacy* (Mobile, 1890); Detroit Post and Tribune, *Life of Zachariah Chandler* (Detroit, 1879); Deyrup, Felicia, *Arms Makers of the Connecticut Valley* (Northampton, 1948); Dix, Morgan,

Memoirs of John Adams Dix (2 vols., New York, 1883); Donald, David, *Lincoln's Herndon* (New York, 1948), *Lincoln Reconsidered: Essays on the Civil War Era* (New York, 1956); Douglas, Stephen, "Reminiscences of Stephen Douglas," *Atlantic Monthly*, vol. 8 (August, 1861), 205–213; Dowdey, Clifford, *The Land They Fought For: the Story of the South as the Confederacy: 1832-65* (New York, 1955); Dupuy, R. E., *Where They Have Trod: the West Point Tradition in American Life* (New York, 1940); Dutton, William S., *Du Pont: One Hundred and Forty Years* (New York, 1942); Dwight, Theodore F., *Campaigns in Virginia, 1861-62* (Military Hist. Soc. of Mass., Boston, 1895)

Early, Jubal, *Autobiography, Sketch and Narrative of the War Between the States* (Philadelphia, 1912); Eaton, Clement, *A History of the Southern Confederacy* (New York, 1954); Eckenrode, Hamilton and Conrad, Bryan, *George B. McClellan, the Man who Saved the Union* (Chapel Hill, 1941); Eckert, Thomas T., *Recollections of the U. S. Military Telegraph Corps during the Civil War* (New York, 1907); Eggleston, George C., *A Rebel's Recollections* (New York, 1875); Egle, William H., *Life and Times of Andrew Gregg Curtin* (Philadelphia, 1896); Elliott, C. W., *Winfield Scott, the Soldier and the Man* (New York, 1937); Evans, Clement A., *Confederate Military History: a Library of Confederate States History* (12 vols., Atlanta, 1899)

Fairchild, C. B., *History of 27th Regiment New York Volunteers 1861-63* (Binghamton, 1888); Fertig, James W., *The Secession and Reconstruction of Tennessee* (Chicago, 1898); Fessenden, Francis, *Life and Public Services of William Pitt Fessenden* (2 vols., Boston, 1907); Field, Maunsell B., *Memories of Many Men and Some Women. . . .* (New York, 1874); Fish, Carl Russell, *The American Civil War, An Interpretation*, ed. by William Ernest Smith (New York, 1937); Fiske, John, *The Mississippi Valley in the Civil War* (Boston, 1900); Flower, Frank A., *Edward McMasters Stanton, the Autocrat of Rebellion, Emancipation and Reconstruction* (Akron, 1905); Forbes, John Murray, *Letters and Recollections*, ed. by Sarah Forbes Hughes (2 vols., Boston, 1899); Forney, John W., *Anecdotes of Public Men* (2 vols., New York, 1873-81); Foulke, William D., *Life of Oliver P. Morton, including his important speeches* (2 vols., Indianapolis, 1899); Fox, Gustavus V., *Confidential Correspondence of G. V. Fox 1861-65* (2 vols., New York, 1918-19); Freeman, Douglas S., *R. E. Lee, a Biography* (4 vols., New York, 1934-35); Frémont, Jessie B., *The Story of the Guard: A Chronicle of the War* (Boston, 1863), Fry, James B., "McClellan and his 'Mission,' a Study," *Century Magazine*, vol. 48 (October, 1894), 931–946; Fulton, John, *Memoirs of Frederick A. P. Barnard* (New York, 1896)

Gates, Theodore B., *The War of the Rebellion, with a Full and Critical History of the First Battle of Bull Run. . . .* (New York, 1884); Gordon, John B., *Reminiscences of the Civil War* (New York, 1904); Gosnell, H. Allen, *Guns on the Western Waters: The Story of River Gunboats in the Civil War* (Baton Rouge, 1949); Grant, Ulysses S., *Personal Memoirs of U. S. Grant* (2 vols., New York, 1885-86); Gray, Wood, *The Hidden Civil War: the Story of the Copperheads* (New York, 1942); Grinnell, Josiah B., *Men and Events of Forty Years. . . .* (Boston, 1891); Gurowski, Adam, *Diary 1861-62* (3 vols., Boston, 1862-66)

Hale, Edward Everett, *Memories of a Hundred Years* (2 vols., New York, 1904); Hamilton, Joseph De Roulhac, ed., *The Correspondence of Jonathan Worth* (2 vols., Raleigh, N. C., 1909); Hamlin, C. E., *Life and Times of Hannibal Hamlin 1809-1891* (Cambridge, Mass., 1899); Harlow, Alvin Fay, *Old Waybills: The Romance of the Express Companies* (New York, 1934); Harrington, Fred H., *Fighting Politician: Major-General N. P. Banks* (Philadelphia, 1948); Harris, Thomas Le Grand, *The Trent Affair. . . .* (Indianapolis, 1896); Harwell, Richard B., *The Union Reader* (New York, 1958); Hassler, Warren W., Jr., *General George B. McClellan, Shield of the Union* (Baton Rouge, 1957); Hawthorne, Nathaniel, "Chiefly About War Matters," *Atlantic Monthly*, vol. 10 (July, 1862), 43–61; Hay, John, *Lincoln and the Civil War, in the Diaries and Letters of John Hay*, ed. by Tyler Dennett (New York, 1939), "Life in the White House in the Time of Lincoln," *Century*

Magazine, vol. 41 (November, 1890), 33–37; Hayes, Rutherford B., *Diary and Letters*, ed. by Charles Richard Williams (5 vols., Columbus, O., 1922–26); Hazard, Blanche E., *Organization of the Boot and Shoe Industry in Massachusetts* (Cambridge, Mass., 1921); Heitman, F. B., ed., *Historical Register and Dictionary of the U. S. Army from 1789 to 1903* (Washington, D. C., 1903); Hendrick, Burton J., *Statesmen of the Lost Cause* (Boston, 1939), *Lincoln's War Cabinet* (Boston, 1946); Hesseltine, William B., *A History of the South 1607–1936* (New York, 1936), *Lincoln and the War Governors* (New York, 1948); Hill, Louise Byles, *Joseph E. Brown and the Confederacy* (Chapel Hill, 1939); Hitchcock, Ethan Allen, *Fifty Years in Camp and Field, A Diary of Major-General E. A. Hitchcock*, ed. by William Croffut (New York, 1909); Hoar, George Frisbie, *Autobiography of Seventy Years* (2 vols., New York, 1903); Hooper, Oscar C., *The Crisis and the Man* (Columbus, O., 1929); Hoppin, James M., *Life of Andrew Hull Foote, Rear Admiral* (New York, 1874); Horn, Stanley F., ed., *The Robert E. Lee Reader* (Indianapolis, 1949); Howard, John R., *Remembrance of Times Past* (New York, 1925); Howe, George F., *Chester A. Arthur, A Quarter Century of Machine Politics* (New York, 1934); Howe, Mark A. De Wolfe, *The Life and Letters of George Bancroft* (2 vols., New York, 1908); Hume, John, *The Abolitionists, Together with Personal Memories of the Struggle for Human Rights 1830–64* (New York, 1905); Hungerford, Edward, *The Story of the Baltimore and Ohio Railroad 1827–1927* (New York, 1928); Hurlburt, William H., *General McClellan and the Conduct of the War* (New York, 1864); Hyde, Thomas, *Following the Greek Cross; or Memories of the Sixth Army Corps* (New York, 1895)

Ingersoll, L. D., *History of the War Department of the U. S.* (Philadelphia, 1879)

Johnson, Rossiter, *A Short History of the War of Secession 1861–65* (New York, 1910); Johnson, R. V. and Buell, C. C., *Battles and Leaders of the Civil War* (4 vols., New York, 1887); Johnston, Joseph E., *Narrative of Military Operations Directed during the late War between the States* (New York, 1874); Johnston, R. M., and Browne, W. H., *Alexander H. Stephens* (Philadelphia, 1878); Jones, John B., *A Rebel War Clerk's Diary at the Confederate States Capitol* (2 vols., Philadelphia, 1866); Jones, John W., *Life and Letters of Robert Edward Lee, Soldier and Man* (New York, 1906)

Kennedy, Elijah R., *The Contest for California in 1861. . . .* (Boston, 1912); Keyes, Erasmus D., *Fifty Years' Observation of Men and Events, Civil and Military* (New York, 1884); Kinglake, Alexander W., *Invasion of the Crimea, Its Origin and Progress* (8 vols., New York and London, 1863–87); Kirkland, Edward Chase, *Men Cities and Transportation, a Study in New England History 1820–1900* (2 vols., Cambridge, 1948); Koren, John, *The History of Statistics; Their Development and Progress in Many Countries* (New York, 1918); Körner, Gustave, *Memoirs 1809–1896* (2 vols., Cedar Rapids, Ia., 1909)

Lamon, Ward Hill, *Recollections of Abraham Lincoln 1847–65* (Washington, D. C., 1911); Laugel, Auguste, *The United States During the War: 1861–65* (New York, 1866); Laughlin, Sceva B., "Missouri Politics during the Civil War," *Missouri Historical Review*, vol. 23 (April, 1929), 400–426; Leech, Margaret, *Reveille in Washington, 1860–65* (New York, 1941); Leidecker, Kurt F., *Yankee Teacher, the Life of William Torrey Harris* (New York, 1946); Leland, Charles G., *Memoirs* (New York, 1893); Lewis, Charles Lee, *Admiral Franklin Buchanan, Fearless Man of Action* (Baltimore, 1929); Lewis, Lloyd, *Sherman, Fighting Prophet* (New York, 1932), *Captain Sam Grant* (Boston, 1950); Lewis, Virgil A., *How West Virginia Was Made. . . .* (Charleston, 1909); Lincoln, A., *Collected Works of Abraham Lincoln*, ed. by Roy Basler (8 vols., New Brunswick, 1953); Livermore, Thomas L., *Days and Events, 1860–1866* (Boston, 1920); Lossing, Benson, J., *A History of the Civil War 1861–65* (3 vols., Hartford, Conn., 1868); Lowell, James Russell, *Letters of James Russell Lowell*, ed. by Charles Eliot Norton (2 vols., New York, 1894)

McClellan, George B., *McClellan's Own Story: the War for the Union. . . .* (New York, 1887), *Report of the Organization and Campaigns of the Army of the Potomac* (New York, 1864), McClure, A. K., *Abraham Lincoln and Men of War Times. . . .* (Philadelphia, 1892), *Col. A. K. McClure's Recollections of Half a Century* (Salem, 1902); McElroy, John, *The Struggle for Missouri* (Washington, D. C., 1909); McGregor, James C., *The Disruption of Virginia* (New York, 1922); McPherson, Edward, *Political History of the United States . . . During the Great Rebellion* (Washington, D. C., 1864)

Macrae, D., *The Americans at Home. . . .* (Edinburgh, 1870); Magruder, Allan B., "A Piece of Secret History—President Lincoln and the Virginia Convention of 1861," *Atlantic Monthly*, vol. 35 (April, 1875), 438-445; Mahan, Asa, *A Critical History of the Late American War* (New York, 1877); Martin, E. W., *The Standard of Living in 1860* (Chicago, 1942); Martin, Theodore, *Life of His Royal Highness, the Prince Consort* (London, 1875-80); Maurice, Sir Frederick, "A System for the Conduct of the War," *Atlantic Monthly*, vol. 137 (June, 1926), 772 ff.; Maxwell, William Q., *Lincoln's Fifth Wheel: the Political History of the U. S. Sanitary Commission* (New York, 1956); Meigs, Montgomery, "General M. C. Meigs on the Conduct of the Civil War," *American Historical Review*, vol. 26 (January, 1921), 285-303; Meneely, Alexander H., *The War Department, 1861, a Study in Mobilization and Administration* (New York, 1928); Merrill, Samuel, *The 70th Indiana Volunteer Infantry in the War of the Rebellion* (Indianapolis, 1900); Mill, John Stuart, *Dissertations and Discussions: Political, Philosophical, Historical* (5 vols., Boston, 1864); Milton, George F., *The Eve of Conflict* (New York, 1934); Mitchell, Silas Weir, *In War Time* (Boston, 1886); Moore, Frank, ed., *The Rebellion Record* (12 vols., New York, 1861-63); Moran, Benjamin, *Journal of Benjamin Moran 1857-65*, ed. by Sarah A. Wallace et al. (2 vols., Chicago, 1948-49); Munford, Beverley, *Virginia's Attitude Toward Slavery and Secession* (New York, 1909); Myers, William Starr, *A Study in Personality: George B. McClellan* (New York, 1934)

Nevins, Allan, *Ordeal of the Union* (2 vols., New York, 1947), *The Emergence of Lincoln* (2 vols., New York, 1950), *Abram S. Hewitt: and some account of Peter Cooper* (New York, 1935), *Frémont: Pathmarker of the West* (New York, new ed., 1955); Newell, J. K., *"Ours," Annals of Tenth Regiment Massachusetts Volunteers. . . .* (Springfield, 1875); Newman, Ralph, with E. B. Long and Otto Eisenschiml, *The Civil War* (Vol. I, *The American Iliad*, Vol. II, *The Picture Chronicle*, New York, 1956); Newton, Thomas W. L., *Lord Lyons: a Record of British Diplomacy* (2 vols., London, 1913); Nicolay, Helen, *Lincoln's Secretary: a Biography of John G. Nicolay* (New York, 1949), "Characteristic Anecdotes of Lincoln," *Century Magazine*, vol. 84 (August, 1912), 697-703; Nicolay, John G., and Hay, John, *Abraham Lincoln: a History* (10 vols., New York, 1890); Norton, Charles E., *Letters of Charles Eliot Norton* (2 vols., Boston, 1913); Norton, Clarence C., *The Democratic Party in Ante-Bellum North Carolina 1835-61* (Chapel Hill, 1930); Norwood, William F., *Medical Education in the United States Before the Civil War* (London, 1944)

O'Reilly, Hugh, "Arming the Slaves for the Union," pamphlet, 1875; Owsley, Frank L., *King Cotton Diplomacy; Foreign Relations of the Confederate States of America* (Chicago, 1931)

Packard, F. R., *History of Medicine in the United States* (2 vols., New York, 1931); Palmer, John M., *Personal Recollections* (Cincinnati, 1901); Paris, Comte de (L. P. A. d'Orleans), *History of the Civil War* (4 vols., Philadelphia, 1875-88); Parks, Joseph H., *General Edmund Kirby Smith, C. S. A.* (Baton Rouge, 1954); Parton, James, *General Butler in New Orleans. . . .* (New York, 1864); Patterson, Robert, *A Narrative of the Campaign in the Valley of the Shenandoah in 1861* (Philadelphia, 1865); Patton, James W., *Unionism and Reconstruction in Tennessee 1860-69* (Chapel Hill, 1934); Pearson, Henry G., *The Life of John A. Andrew, Governor of Massachusetts* (2 vols., New York, 1904), *General James S. Wadsworth* (New York, 1913); Peckham, James, *General Nathaniel Lyon and Missouri in 1861: A Monograph of the Great Rebellion* (New York, 1866); Perry, A. F., "A Chapter in Interstate Diplomacy," *Loyal Legion Papers, Ohio Commandery*, vol. 3, 333-363; Perry, Bliss, *Life and Letters of Henry Lee Higginson* (Boston,

1921); Peto, Sir S. Morton, *Resources and Prospects of America*. . . . (London and New York, 1866); Phillips, Ulrich B., *The Life of Robert Toombs* (New York, 1913); Phisterer, Frederick, *New York in the War of the Rebellion, 1861–65* (5 vols., Albany, 1912), *Statistical Record of the Armies of the United States* (New York, 1883); Piatt, Donn, *Memories of the Men Who Saved the Union* (New York, 1887); Pierce, Edward L., *Memoir and Letters of Charles Sumner* (4 vols., Boston, 1877–94); Pierson, William W., "The Committee on the Conduct of the Civil War," *American Historical Review*, vol. 23 (April, 1918), 550–576; Pinkerton, Allan, *The Spy of the Rebellion; Being A True History of the Spy System of the U. S. Army during the late Rebellion* (New York, 1883); Poor, Henry V., *History of the Railroads and Canals of the U.S.* (New York, 1860); Potter, David M., *Lincoln and his Party in the Secession Crisis* (New Haven, 1942); Pratt, Edwin A., *The Rise of Rail Power in War and Conquest, 1833–1914* (London, 1915); Pratt, Fletcher, *Civil War on Western Waters* (New York, 1956)

Quint, Alonzo, *The Record of the Second Massachusetts Infantry 1861–65* (Boston, 1867)

Radcliffe, G. L., *Governor Thomas H. Hicks of Maryland and the Civil War* (Baltimore, 1901); Ramsdell, C. W., "Lincoln and Fort Sumter," *Journal of Southern History*, vol. 3 (August, 1937), 259–288; Randall, James G., *The Civil War and Reconstruction* (New York, 1937), *Lincoln the President* (4 vols., New York, 1945); Rawley, James A., *Edwin D. Morgan, 1811–1883: Merchant in Politics* (New York, 1955); Reagan, John H., *Memoirs: With Special Reference to Secession and Civil War* (New York, 1906); Reavis, Logan U., *The Life and Military Services of General William Selby Harney* (St. Louis, 1878); Reid, Whitelaw, *Ohio in the War: Her Statesmen, Her Generals and Soldiers* (2 vols., Cincinnati, 1868); Rhodes, James F., *History of the United States from the Compromise of 1850.* . . . (9 vols., New York and London, 1893–1929); Rice, Allen Thorndike, *Reminiscences of Abraham Lincoln by Distinguished Men of his Time* (New York, 1909); Riddle, A. G., *Recollections of War Times: Reminiscences of Men and Events in Washington, 1860–65* (New York, 1895); Robinson, W. M., *The Confederate Privateers* (New Haven, 1928); Roman, Alfred, *Military Operations of General Beauregard in the War Between the States 1861–65* (2 vols., New York, 1884); Rombauer, R. J., *The Union Cause in St. Louis in 1861.* . . . (St. Louis, 1909); Ropes, John Codman and Livermore, W. R., *The Story of the Civil War . . . 1861–1865* (4 vols., New York, 1893–1913); Rosewater, Victor, *History of Cooperative Newsgathering in the U. S.* (New York, 1930); Rowan, Richard W., *The Pinkertons: A Detectvie Dynasty* (Boston, 1931); Russell, William H., *My Diary North and South* (2 vols., London and New York, 1863); Rutherford, Mary L., *The Influence of the American Bar Association on Public Opinion and Legislation* (Philadelphia, 1937)

Sandburg, Carl, *Abraham Lincoln* (6 vols., New York, 1926–39); Schaff, Morris, *The Spirit of Old West Point, 1858–1862* (New York, 1907); Schofield, John M., *Forty-Six Years in the Army* (New York, 1897); Schotter, H. W., *The Growth and Development of the Pennsylvania Railroad Company . . . 1846–1926* (Philadelphia, 1927); Schouler, William, *A History of Massachusetts in the Civil War* (2 vols., Boston, 1868–71); Schuckers, Jacob W., *Life and Public Services of Salmon Portland Chase.* . . . (New York, 1874); Schurz, Carl, *The Reminiscences of Carl Schurz 1852–63* (2 vols., New York, 1907–08); Schwab, John C., *The Confederate States of America 1861–1865.* . . . (New York, 1901); Seward, Frederick W., *Seward at Washington as Senator and Secretary of State 1846–61* (2 vols., New York, 1891), *Reminiscences 1830–1915* (New York, 1916); Seward, William H., *Works*, ed. by George E. Baker (5 vols., New York, 1883–84); Shafer, Henry B., *The American Medical Profession: 1783–1850* (New York, 1936); Shanks, Henry T., *The Secession Movement in Virginia, 1847–1861* (Richmond, 1934); Shannon, Fred A., *The Organization and Administration of the Union Army 1861–65* (2 vols., Cleveland, 1928); Sheldon, George W., "Old Shipping Merchants of New York," *Harpers' Magazine*, vol.

84 (February, 1892), 457-471; Sherman, William Tecumseh, *Memoirs, Written by Himself* (2 vols., New York, 1890); Sigel, Franz, "Military Operations in Missouri in . . . 1861," *Missouri Historical Review*, vol. 26 (July, 1932), 354-366; Smalley, George W., *Anglo-American Memories* (New York, 1911); Smith, Edward C., *The Borderland in the Civil War* (New York, 1927); Smith, William E., *The Francis Preston Blair Family in Politics* (2 vols., New York, 1933); Snead, T. L., *The Fight for Missouri.* . . . (New York, 1886); Soley, J. R., *The Blockade and the Cruisers*, Vol. I of *The Navy in the Civil War* (New York, 1883); Stampp, Kenneth, *And the War Came* (Baton Rouge, 1950); Stevens, W. B., *Centennial History of Missouri . . . One Hundred Years in the Union, 1820-1920* (2 vols., St. Louis, 1921); Stoddard, William O., *Inside the White House in War Times* (New York, 1890); Stovall, Pleasants, *Robert Toombs, statesman, speaker, soldier, sage; his career in Congress and on the hustings—his work in the courts—his record with the army—his life at home* (New York, 1892); Strode, Hudson, *Jefferson Davis, American Patriot 1808-1861* (New York, 1955); Strong, George T., *Diary*, ed. by Allan Nevins and Milton H. Thomas (4 vols., New York, 1952); Summers, Festus P., *The Baltimore and Ohio in the Civil War* (New York, 1939); Swinton, William, *Campaigns of the Army of the Potomac.* . . . (New York, 1882); Switzler, W. F., *Switzler's Illustrated History of Missouri from 1541 to 1877* (St. Louis, 1879)

Tasher, Lucy L., "The *Missouri Democrat* and the Civil War," *Missouri Historical Review*, vol. 31 (July, 1937), 402-419; Taylor, Frank H., *Philadelphia in the Civil War, 1861-65* (Philadelphia, 1913); Temperley, Harold, and Fenson, Lillian, *Foundations of British Foreign Policy from Pitt (1792) to Salisbury (1902).* . . . (Cambridge, 1938); Thomas, Benjamin P., *Abraham Lincoln. a Biography* (New York, 1952); Thomas, David Y., *Arkansas in War and Reconstruction 1861-74* (Little Rock, 1926); Thomas, Joseph W., "Campaigns of McClellan and Rosecrans in West Virginia," *West Virginia Magazine of History*, vol. 5 (July, 1944), 245-308; Thompson, Robert L., *Wiring a Continent, the History of the Telegraph Industry in the United States 1832-66* (Princeton, 1947); Tilley, John Shipley, *Lincoln Takes Command* (Chapel Hill, 1941); Townsend, E. D., *Anecdotes of the Civil War in the U. S.* (New York, 1884); Trobriand, R. de, *Army Life in Dakota; selections from the Journal of Philippe Regis . . . de Trobriand* (Chicago, 1941); Trollope, Anthony, *North America* (2 vols., London, 1862)

Upham, Cyril B., "Arms and Equipment for the Iowa Troops in the Civil War," *Iowa Journal of History*, vol. 16 (January, 1918), 3-52; Upson, Theodore F., *With Sherman to the Sea.* . . . (Baton Rouge, 1943); Upton, Emory, *Military Policy of the United States* (Washington, 1917)

Van Deusen, Glyndon G., *Thurlow Weed: Wizard of the Lobby* (Boston, 1947), *Horace Greeley, Nineteenth Century Crusader* (Philadelphia, 1953); Van Oss, S. F., *American Railroads as Investments* (New York, 1893); Vandiver, Frank, *Ploughshares into Swords: Josiah Gorgas and Confederate Ordnance* (Austin, 1952); Villard, Henry, *Memoirs 1835-1900* (2 vols., Boston, 1904); Violette, Eugene and Forest, Wolverton, *A History of Missouri* (St. Louis, 1955)

Wolcott, C. F., *History of the Twenty-First Regiment Massachusetts Volunteers.* . . . (Boston, 1882); Wallace, Lew, *An Autobiography* (2 vols., New York, 1906); Warren, Charles, *A History of the American Bar* (Boston, 1911); Wasson, Robert Gordon, *The Hall Carbine Affair.* . . . (New York, 1948); Watson, William, *Life in the Confederate Army.* . . . (New York, 1888); Wayland, Francis, *Thoughts on the Present Collegiate System in the U. S.* (Boston, 1842); Webb, Elizabeth, "Cotton Manufacturing and State Regulation in North Carolina 1861-65," *North Carolina Historical Review*, vol. 9 (April, 1932), 117-137; Weber, Thomas, *The Northern Railroads in the Civil War, 1861-1865* (New York, 1952); Weed, Thurlow, *Autobiography of Thurlow Weed*, and Weed, Harriet A., *Life of Thurlow Weed* (2 vols., Boston, 1884); Weeden, William B., *War Government, Federal and State, 1861-1865* (Boston, 1906); Welles, Gideon, *The Diary of*

Gideon Welles, Secretary of the Navy under Lincoln and Johnson, ed. by John T. Morse (3 vols., Boston, 1911), "Narrative of Events," American Historical Review, vol. 31 (April, 1926), 486–494, Lincoln and Seward: Remarks upon the Memorial Address of Charles F. Adams on the late Wm. H. Seward. . . . (New York, 1874); West, Richard S., Gideon Welles: Lincoln's Navy Department (Indianapolis, 1943); White, Andrew D., Autobiography (2 vols., New York, 1922); White, Horace, The Life of Lyman Trumbull (Boston, 1913); White, Leonard D., The Jacksonians: A Study in Administrative History, 1829–1861 (New York, 1954); Wiley, Bell I., The Life of Johnny Reb, The Common Soldier of the Confederacy (New York, 1943), The Life of Billy Yank, The Common Soldier of the Union (Indianapolis, 1951); Wilkinson, Spenser, War and Policy: Essays (New York, 1900); Willey, W. P., An Inside View of the Formation of West Virginia (Wheeling, 1901); Williams, Kenneth, Lincoln Finds a General: A Military Study of the Civil War (4 vols., New York, 1949–56); Williams, T. Harry, P. G. T. Beauregard: Napoleon in Gray (Baton Rouge, 1954), Lincoln and His Generals (New York, 1952), Lincoln and the Radicals (Madison, 1941); Williamson, Harold F., Winchester, the Gun that Won the West (Washington, D. C., 1952); Wilson, Henry, "Jeremiah S. Black and Edwin M. Stanton," Atlantic Monthly, vol. 26 (February, 1870), 463–475; Wilson, James Grant, The Life and Campaigns of Ulysses Simpson Grant. . . . (New York, 1868); Wilson, James H., Under the Old Flag: Recollections of Military Operations. . . . (2 vols., New York, 1912); Wilson, W. B., A Few Acts and Actors in the Tragedy of the Civil War in the U. S. (Philadelphia, 1892); Winthrop, Theodore, "Washington as a Camp," Atlantic Monthly, vol. 8 (July, 1861), 105–118; Wise, John S., The End of an Era (Boston, 1902); Woodward, Ashbel, The Life of General Nathaniel Lyon (Hartford, 1862); Wright, Marcus J., General Scott (New York, 1897)

A full list and description of manuscript sources will be published in the next volume of this work. It should be noted here that HL refers to Huntington Library, MHS to Massachusetts Historical Society, and NYPL to New York Public Library.

APPENDIX I

Northern and Southern Resources, 1860

I. WHITE POPULATION NORTH AND SOUTH

It is roughly correct to say that the Northern States had a white population of twenty millions, while the Southern white population was about five and a half millions. An accurate picture, however, requires a somewhat fuller statement.

The white population of New England by the census of 1860 was 3,110,000; that of New York, Pennsylvania, New Jersey, Maryland, and Delaware was 8,745,000; that of Ohio, Indiana, Illinois, Iowa, and Kansas was 6,126,000; and that of Michigan, Wisconsin, Minnesota, and Nebraska was 1,708,000. The total white population in this area, where strength could most effectively be mobilized and deployed by the Federal Government, was 19,689,500. In the Far Western area—California, Oregon, Washington, Dakota, New Mexico, Utah, Nevada, and Colorado—the white population was 587,500. This gave the North a total white population of approximately 20,275,000.

The border States of Missouri, Kentucky, and Tennessee, whose strength was divided between North and South, had a white population of 2,810,000. Of this the population of Tennessee, a member of the Confederacy, was 827,000.

The census of 1860 gave the white population of the ten Confederate States excluding Tennessee as 4,622,000. If the white population of Tennessee is added, the whole number of whites in the eleven Confederate States falls barely short of 5,500,000.

Looking at whites alone, the population odds against the Confederacy were thus almost four to one. The South, however, had an immense asset in its Negro population.

II. COLORED POPULATION NORTH AND SOUTH

Speaking in rough terms, the North had fewer than a half million colored people available for the war effort, while the South had not far from three and three-quarters millions. Again a fuller array of statistics is required for an accurate picture of the situation.

The colored population of New England, New York, Pennsylvania, and New Jersey by the census of 1860 was 153,983. That of the eight Middle Western States from Ohio and Michigan to Kansas, together with Nebraska Territory, came to 65,642. The total for these seventeen Northern States and one Territory was 221,625. If we add the Negro population of Delaware, Maryland, and the District of Columbia, the aggregate is almost 430,000. The Far Western States and Territories would add fewer than 5,000, nearly all of whom lived in California.

The colored population of the ten Confederate States excluding Tennessee, which was invaded and partly occupied in 1862, came to 3,371,000. If we add the 289,000 colored people of Tennessee, the eleven Confederate States had in all 3,654,000 Negroes and mulattoes.

III. POPULATION TOTALS

Missouri and Kentucky were so divided between North and South that an accurate brief comparison of strength is furthered by their omission. Leaving them out, the North had a combined white and colored population of approximately 20,700,000—just over that total. The eleven States of the Confederacy had a combined white and colored population of approximately 9,105,000. The North therefore had an advantage of more than two to one, even reckoning the colored population on a parity with the white. The Union, moreover, had the assistance of unrestricted immigration from Europe.

IV. POPULATION OF MILITARY AGE

The census of 1860 lists white males in two age categories, one 15 to 20, and the other 20 to 30, but does not break them down by years. The total white male population 15 to 30 in the seventeen Northern States of New England, the Middle Atlantic area, and the Middle West, with Nebraska, the main reservoir of manpower, was 2,582,678. But the whole number of white males 15 to 30 in the Confederate States came only to 791,000. This omits from computation on either side Missouri, which had 166,000 white males of 15 to 30 years, and Kentucky, which had 134,000. The whole number of white males in this age group available to the North was certainly a good deal more than three times the number in the South.

V. MANUFACTURES IN 1860

The census credited New York with 22,624 establishments holding a capital, in round numbers, of $172,896,000. It gave Pennsylvania 22,363 establishments, with a capital of $190,056,000. Ohio had 11,123 establishments of $57,295,000 capital, while Massachusetts was listed as possessing 8,176, with a capital of $132,792,000. In round numbers the North had 110,000 manufacturing establishments, with 1,300,000 industrial workers.

The South fell far behind. Virginia had 5,385 manufacturing establishments with a capital of $30,840,500; Alabama had 1,459, with a capital of less than $9,100,000; Louisiana had 1,744 with a capital of only $7,151,000; and Mississippi had 976, with a capital of but $4,384,500. The total number of manufacturing establishments in the Confederacy was about 18,000, with 110,000 industrial workers.

The value of the product of manufacturing in the four Southern States named in 1860 did not reach $85,000,000. But that of New York was placed at $379,000,000, and that of Massachusetts at $255,500,000.

VI. IRON MANUFACTURES

In 1860 the United States had 286 iron furnaces scattered through 18 States. Pennsylvania led with 125. Tennessee was the largest Southern producer of pig iron, with 17 furnaces, and Virginia came next with 16.

The number of forges and rolling mills in the country, producing bar, sheet, and railroad iron, was 256, in twenty States. Pennsylvania was by far the largest manufacturer, with 87 forges or rolling mills, employing more than half the whole capital investment of the country in this line. The value of its product amounted to between $15,000,000 and $16,000,000 a year. New York was the second largest producer. Virginia had 20 establishments with a product valued at $1,667,000, and Tennessee was proud of 35, with a product, however, of only a little over a half-million dollars.

Of 470 locomotives built in the United States in the year ending June 1, 1860, Virginia made 19, and no other Southern State any. In the manufacture of agricultural implements in 1860, the aggregate Southern production was worth a little over $1,000,000. But during the previous decade the Western States had raised their production from $1,900,000 to $8,700,000.

Firearms in 1860 were manufactured in 239 establishments, New England being far in the lead. Of the whole product, worth $2,342,700, the Southern States made less than $73,000 worth. One county in Connecticut—Hartford—valued its product at well over a million dollars.

VII. DRAFT ANIMALS

The dependence upon horses and mules in transporting troops and supplies makes statistics upon them important. The Middle and Western States in 1860 had more than 4,000,000 horses. The Southern States had less than one and three-quarters millions, of which more than one-sixth were in remote Texas, and nearly one-sixth in vulnerable Tennessee. But in the number of asses and mules the South had a distinct advantage. Its total for the eleven States of the Confederacy was 822,047; the total of the Middle and Western States was only a little over 310,000, while New England had practically none.

The eleven Confederate States had approximately 2,566,000 horses, asses, and mules combined, while the Northern States, excluding the Far West, had almost 4,600,000. The South had about one horse to every five inhabitants; the Middle Western States, about two horses to every seven inhabitants.

VIII. RAILROADS

Of the total railroad mileage in the United States in 1861, which by Poor's *Manual* was 31,256, the South contained 9,283, or less than 30 per cent. Federal inroads soon reduced this to something over 6,000 miles (J. C. Schwab, *Confederate States*, 273).

APPENDIX II

Documents on Mrs. Frémont's Interview With Lincoln

The Frémont Papers in the Bancroft Library of the University of California contain a copy, undated, of a letter which Montgomery Blair sent the general in St. Louis soon after his arrival, when Blair was still supporting him. This is the letter in which he criticized Secretary Chase for his parsimony, writing: "Chase has more horror of seeing Treasury notes below par than of seeing soldiers killed." (Nevins, *Fremont*, third edition, 509). He also criticized Lincoln in a passage worth quoting in full:

"I showed the President, Billings' letter, and read him yours about Adams. He says that you were right in saying that Adams was devoted to his money-bags.

"Schuyler had already gone to Europe about arms when I wrote and telegraphed you, and your letter in reply was handed to Mr. Seward, to be forwarded to him. . . . The main difficulty is, however, with Lincoln himself. He is of the Whig school, and that brings him naturally not only to incline to the feeble policy of Whigs, but to give his confidence to such advisers. It costs me a great deal of labor to get anything done, because of this inclination of mind on the part of the President or leading members of the Cabinet, including Chase, who never voted a Democratic ticket in his life. But you have the people at your back, and I am doing all I can to cut red tape and get things done. I will be more civil and patient than heretofore, and see if that won't work."

The MS continuation of Frémont's published volume of *Memoirs* (1887) which Mrs. Frémont and her son Frank wrote, partially from his dictation, contains a full account of the circumstances in which he prepared his proclamation of military emancipation. This is given almost in full in Nevins, *Frémont*, 500. It emphasizes the fact that, with an insufficient number of troops, ill-armed and unpaid, to repress guerrilla warfare, he felt that sharp measures were necessary to deal with the great numbers of secessionist sympathizers who would flock almost overnight to the Confederate camps, assist in some sudden stroke, and then return to their farms and villages. "He determined to force the rebel sympathizers, who did not join the rebel armies as soldiers, to remain at home, and to make them feel that there was a penalty for rebellion, and for aiding those who were in rebellion." When Judge Edward Davis warned him that "Mr. Seward will never allow this," for he wished to wear down the South not by blows but by steady pressure, Frémont persisted. "The time has come for decisive action; this is a war measure, and as such I make it." (Op. cit., 503.) Then as relations between Frémont and Frank Blair worsened, and he felt that Lincoln did not understand his position, he agreed to Mrs. Frémont's taking a letter to the White House. She was not only the wife of the departmental commander; she was daughter of a great American Senator.

Jessie Benton Frémont left St. Louis the evening of September 8 with the letter, dated that day. It dealt exclusively with strategic movements. The most significant passage concerned advances which Frémont wrote that he contemplated ordering in Kentucky and if possible Tennessee. On August 28 he had placed Grant in command in southeast Missouri, and had declared his intention of occupying Columbus, Ky. On September 2d Union forces had occupied Belmont just across the river from this place; and immediately thereafter Polk's Confederates had seized Columbus, while Grant had occupied Paducah. Frémont's letter to Lincoln looked to the future, not the past, and to the taking of strong Kentucky positions. He wrote:

"I have reinforced, yesterday, Paducah with two regiments, and will continue to strengthen the position with men and artillery. As soon as General [C. F.] Smith, who commands there, is reinforced sufficiently to enable him to spread his forces, he will have to take and hold Mayfield and Lovelaceville, to be in the rear and flank of Columbus, and to occupy Smithland, controlling in this way the mouths of both the Tennessee and Cumberland Rivers. At the same time, Colonel Rousseau should bring his force, increased, if possible, by two Ohio regiments, in boats to Henderson, and, taking the Henderson & Nashville Railroad, occupy Hopkinsville, while General Nelson should go with a force of 5,000 by railroad to Louisville and from there to Bowling Green."

Already Frémont had sent a spy, Captain Charles D'Arnaud, recommended to him by Colonel Lovell Rousseau and Judge Corwine of Cincinnati, to map the principal highways, bridges, and forts of Kentucky and western Tennessee, a mission from which D'Arnaud returned with maps showing the construction work the Confederates were doing on Forts Henry and Donelson. In this, and in his emphasis on securing the mouths of the Cumberland and Tennessee, Frémont showed foresight.

He wrote Lincoln that the movements he outlined were readily feasible, for the population in the area was predominantly loyal. If all went well, subsequent movements could be made against Columbus, Hickman, and eventually Nashville. He wished to have the bounds of the Western Department enlarged to cover Indiana, and, contemplating their partial occupation, Kentucky and Tennessee.

But while this letter carried by Mrs. Frémont treated military matters alone, Frémont had sent a separate letter by mail dated September 8 to Lincoln explaining his proclamation at some length, and asking Lincoln to send him an open order for its modification. It may have arrived on the afternoon of the 10th. When Lincoln answered it on the 11th he wrote that it was "just received." If it did arrive just before Mrs. Frémont descended upon the White House, that fact might account for the curtness of the reception he gave her, his failure to ask her to sit down, and his evident desire to cut the visit short. He did not wish to argue with her about the stubborn position of the general. If he had read the New York *Herald's* Washington correspondence published the previous day (September 9) it would not have soothed his feelings. For it asserted that the Cabinet had been taken aback by the proclamation; that for twenty-four hours they discussed it fully; and that then "it was finally unanimously determined that the proclamation was just the right thing made at precisely the right time, in exactly the right manner, and by the right man." The *Herald* was criticizing the Administration savagely for its dilatoriness in reinforcing the Western army.

But if Lincoln was abrupt in receiving Mrs. Frémont, a partial explanation might be found in physical fatigue. He had spent the greater part of the day with the troops. Early in the morning he had gone with Cameron and McClellan to attend a tedious ceremony at a camp beyond Georgetown where Governor and Mrs. Curtin presented Pennsylvania flags to the regiments of the reserve corps of that State, and had reviewed the ten thousand troops. Then he, Cameron, McClellan, the Curtins, and others had crossed the Chain Bridge to Virginia, where he saw McClellan restore the colors to the Seventy-ninth New York, heard Cameron make a speech, reviewed more troops, and inspected some of the new fortifications. He did not regain the White House until dusk.

It is certain that in this interview Mrs. Frémont exceeded her commission. Frémont, as he insisted in his letter to Lincoln and later said in his MS memoirs, had been inspired by military motives alone in writing his proclamation. But Mrs. Frémont, after referring to the opposition of the Blair family, began to talk about the political value of the proclamation, speaking of the difficulty of conquering by arms alone, and of the importance of appealing to public sentiment in Britain and France by a stroke against slavery. This justified Lincoln's remark: "You are quite a female politician." Some of the ideas that were in her head are disclosed by an undated letter which she wrote later, apparently just before Frémont's removal, to Dorothea Dix, an old friend. It is not certain she sent it, for the letter is in the Frémont papers, but it is revealing. It reads:

"I can but think that if the President had had an interview with Mr. Frémont there never would have grown up this state of injury to the public service—two honest men can quickly understand each other but the same good brain and bad heart that made the President so unjust and deaf to me has influenced not only the President but the newspapers of the kind that daren't offend Govt patronage. The truth has to come out victorious finally. Mr. Frémont can well afford to wait, but this lost time can never be regained for the country. Soon the river will be filling with ice and land work will be harder than the Valley Forge records. While it is yet day the work should be done.

"All we knew in the early summer, of the intrigue with France is becoming more and more sorrowfully apparent. If the South can bring themselves to play that last card—and you know as I do that Mr. Slidell is a gambler every way—politically as well as with money—then recognition by both England and France is very near. The worst would be that with all their enormities they would have the moral triumph too. You know from long experience abroad that America was neither loved nor hated, but very much feared and very much resented.

"Their chance has come to push us back and they will not lose it. The double bait of free trade and gradual emancipation (*very gradual* it will be) but enough to make a pretext for England, will not be repulsed by them, and Slidell has the backing of the Rothschilds. Their feelings have been sufficiently shewn by the *Times*. This is our last chance—it is a very hard pull—but a strong pull, above all a *pull altogether*, will bring us through. My dear chief is doing his duty . . . . but it is a shame and a crime to hamper and as far as they can disable him."

APPENDIX III

The Newspaper Press and the Impact of War

The country in 1860 had slightly more than 3,000 newspapers, and a decade of stormy political agitation had raised their influence to an unprecedented height. Their editors displayed a considerable amount of independence and courage. In August, 1861, the New York *Herald* was at pains to collect the names of "secession papers" in the North, and "Union papers" in the South, with some information on what had happened to them.

The phrase "secession paper" did not necessarily mean a newspaper giving outright and disloyal support in the North to the Confederacy, though a few of them ventured beyond that line. It meant rather a newspaper which, like the *Daily News* in New York or the *Times* in Chicago, had wished to see the erring sisters depart in peace; objected vehemently to any enlargement of war objectives beyond the restoration of the Union; and criticized Administration measures in terms so harshly as to lower the morale of their readers. The New York *Tribune* at this very time was denouncing the *Courrier des Etats Unis*, which stood for peaceable separation, as traitorous, and calling for its suppression. Most of the journals here listed did not go so far as this French-language paper. It will be noted that surviving "Union papers" in the South were all actually in the border States, and with few exceptions, like the Knoxville *Whig*, were safe under the protection of the Union flag.

SECESSION PAPERS YET IN EXISTENCE IN THE NORTH.

NEW YORK.

Argus, Albany.	Republican, Saratoga.
News, New York.	Democrat, Ithica.
Journal of Commerce, N. Y.	Gazette, Hudson.
Day Book, New York.	Union, Watertown.
Freeman's Journal, N. York.	Gazette, Geneva.
Prattsville News, Prattsv'le.	American Union, Ellicotville.
Budget, Troy.	Herald, Yonkers.
Observer, Utica.	Franklin Gazette.
Watchman, Greenport, L. I.	Democrat, Niagara.
Courier, Syracuse.	Democrat, Schenectady.
Advertiser, Lockport.	Gazette, Malone.
Union, Troy.	Sentinel, Mayville.
Herald, Sandy Hill	

NEW JERSEY.

Register, Paterson.	Democrat, Hunterdon.
Journal, Newark.	Herald, Newton.
Republican Farmer.	Gazette, Plainfield.
Journal, Belvidere.	

PENNSYLVANIA.

Valley Spirit, Chambersb'g.	Democrat, Coshocton.
Patriot, Harrisburg.	Republican, Pittsburg.
Catholic Herald, Phila.	Union, Wilkesbarre.
Examiner, Washington.	Herald, Honesdale.
Star, Easton.	Republikaner (German),
Democrat, Allentown.	Allentown.
Christian Observer, Phila.	

CONNECTICUT.

Times, Hartford.	Register, New Haven.
Mercury, Middletown.	Sentinel, Middletown.
Advertiser, Bridgeport.	

IOWA.

Bugle, Council Bluffs.	State Journal, Iowa City.
Herald, Dubuque.	Citizen.

Patriot, Concord.	**NEW HAMPSHIRE.** Gazette.
Democrat, Kenosha.	**WISCONSIN.** See Bote (Ger.), Milwaukee.
Argus, Portland.	**MAINE.** Watchman.
Enquirer, Cincinnati.	**OHIO.** Democrat, Galien.
Crisis, Columbus.	Empire, Dayton.
State, Winona.	**MINNESOTA.**
Post, Providence.	**RHODE ISLAND.**
Union, Cass county.	**ILLINOIS.** Times, Bloomington.
Democrat, Alton.	Signal, Joliet.
Gazette, Evansville.	**INDIANA.** Sentinel, Indianapolis.
Journal, Terre Haute.	
Spirit of the Age, Woodstock.	**VERMONT.**
Express, Marysville.	**CALIFORNIA.**
Bulletin, Atchison.	**KANSAS.** —

SECESSION PAPERS IN THE LOYAL SOUTHERN SECTIONS.

Sun, Baltimore.	Yeoman, Frankfort, Ky.
Exchange, Baltimore.	Statesman, Lexington, Ky.
South, Baltimore.	Gazette, Wilmington, Del.
Courier, Louisville.	Mail, Hagerstown, Md.
Argus, Weston, Mo.	News, Cynthiana, Ky.

UNION PAPERS IN THE SOUTH.

American, Baltimore.
Commonwealth, Frankf't, Ky.
Clipper, Baltimore.
Citizen, Centreville, Md.
Democrat, St. Louis.
Democrat, Louisville.
Examiner, Frederick, Md.
Eagle, Maysville, Ky.
Herald, Wellsburg, Va.
Herald, Hagerstown, Md.
Intelligencer, Wheeling, Va.
Journal, Louisville, Ky.
Journal, St. Joseph, Mo.
Journal, Wilmington, Del.
News, Milford, Del.
NationalUnion, Winc'ter, Ky.
Observer, Lexington, Ky.
Patriot, Baltimore.
Press, Wheeling, Va.
Republican, St. Joseph, Mo.
Star, Morgantown, Va.
Union, Frederick, Md.
Whig, Knoxville, Tenn.

EFFECT OF THE WAR ON SECESSION JOURNALS.

NORTHERN SECESSION PAPERS DESTROYED BY MOBS.

Jeffersonian, Westchester, Pa.
Sentinel, Easton, Pa.
Farmer, Bridgeport, Conn.
Democrat, Canton, Ohio.
Standard, Concord, N. H.
Democrat, Bangor, Me.
Clinton Journal, Kansas.

NORTHERN SECESSION PAPERS SUPPRESSED BY CIVIL AUTHORITY.

Catholic Herald, Phil'a.
Christian Observer, Phil'a.

NORTHERN SECESSION PAPERS DIED.

Herald, Leavenworth.
American, Trenton.

NORTHERN SECESSION PAPERS DENIED TRANSPORTATION IN THE MAILS.

Journal of Commerce, New York.
News, New York.
Day Book, New York.
Freeman's Journal, New York.

SECESSION PAPERS CHANGED TO UNION.

Eagle, Brooklyn, N. Y.
Republican, St. Louis.
*Democrat, Haverhill, Mass.
*Editor tarred and feathered and rode on a rail.

SOUTHERN SECESSION PAPERS DIED.

News, Charleston, S. C.
Tribune, Mobile.
Register, Mobile.
News, Mobile.
Courier, New Orleans.
Union, Wheeling, Va.
Herald, Paducah, Ky.
Herald, Norfolk.
Crescent, Columbus, Ky.
Courier, Hickman, Ky.
Telegraph, Rutherford, Tenn.
Courier, Gallatin, Tenn.
Confederation, Montgomery, Ala.

SOUTHERN SECESSION PAPERS SUSPENDED BY MILITARY AUTHORITY.

State Journal, St. Louis.
Observer, Booneville, Mo.
Bulletin, St. Louis.
Missourian, St. Louis.
Sentinel, Alexandria, Va.
Democrat, Savannah, Mo.
Gazette, Alexandria, Va.
Register, Macon, Mo.
Paper in Weston, Va.

SOUTHERN SECESSION JOURNAL CLEANED OUT BY A MOB.

Alleghanian, Cumberland, Md.

RECAPITULATION.

Northern secession papers........................... 73
Union papers South.................................. 23
Secession papers in loyal Southern sections........... 10
Northern secession papers mobbed.................... 7
Northern secession papers stopped by civil authority. 2
Northern secession papers died...................... 2
Northern secession papers denied mail facilities..... 4
Northern secession papers changed to Union.......... 3
Southern secession papers died...................... 13
Southern secession papers suspended by military authority.. 9
Southern secession papers mobbed................... 1

FROM N. Y. *Herald*, AUGUST 29, 1861

Index

Abolition (see slavery)

Adams, Charles Francis, on southern grievances, 20; on Douglas' plan, 29; ambassador to London, 33; on diehards, 45; and Lincoln, 72, 200; Seward to, 223–4; on army officers, 230; arms purchases, 352–5; Trent affair, 389–93

Adams, Charles Francis, Jr., 251, 390

Adams, Henry, 390

Albert, Prince Consort of England, 391

Alcorn, Julian, 115

Anderson, Robert, 4, 30–1, 41–4, 48, 65, 69, 74, 76, 134–5, 166

Andrew, John A., 77–80, 150–1, 170, 173–4, 177, 278–80, 346–9, 416

Arkansas, secession in, 106–7

Arms and munitions, Confederates seize arsenals, 18, 114–7; distribution of, 89–91; in Missouri, 122–4; in Norfolk, 155–6; at Harper's Ferry, 156–8, 171–4, 214, 221; McClellan and, 166, 274; in West, 308–9, 316–20; in Union army, 61–6, 342–59; in Confederate army, 359–61; ammunition supply, 366–9, 373–4

Army (of Confederacy), organization of, 17–18; recruitment of, 67–70, 92–5, 98–101; morale and equipment of, 113–8, 211–4; at Manassas, 179, 207, Bull Run, 214–22; numbers, 301; in Missouri, 312–5; arms, 359–61

Army (of Union), numbers, 70, 75–8, 86–90, 108, 111–2, 138, 148, 167–79, 191–5, 229–39, 299–303; at Washington, 144–6; morale in, 158–60, 187, 404–6, 412–4; organization of, 160–2; equipment, 171–3, 189, 211–7, 312–9; at Bull Run, 214–22; in Washington, 226–7; Military Act, 226–8; recruitment of, 229–39; under McClellan, 266–85, 291–9; firepower of, 342–69

Arthur, Chester A., 89

Asboth, A., 317, 378, 381

Bache, A. D., 41, 416

Badger, George, 105

Baker, Edward D., 61, 184–6, 298, 299

Baldwin, John B., 64, 103

Ball's Bluff, battle of, 298–9

Baltimore, secession in, 80–3, 87

Bancroft, George, 23, 75–6

Banks, Nathaniel P., 12, 198, 226, 322

Barlow, Francis, 210

Barlow, S. L. M., 24, 30, 49, 240, 303–4

Barnard, John Gross, 211, 267, 291, 303

Barney, Hiram, 33

Bates, Edward, 32, 37, 42, 45–6, 55–6, 128, 143–4, 154, 203, 229, 307, 326, 336, 377, 381, 386, 393

Bayard, James A., 143, 184

Beauregard, Pierre G. T., 17, 30–2, 41, 59, 68–9, 73, 95, 113, 117, 158, 179, 207–9, 211–21, 295, 370–1

Bee, B. E., 217–8

Bell, John, 23, 105–6, 120, 129–30

Bellows, Henry W., 269–70, 272, 416

Benjamin, Judah P., 2, 30, 40, 49, 68, 115

Benton, Thomas Hart, 26, 120

Biglow Papers, 75

Blair, Austin, 170–1, 177, 233

Blair, Francis P., Sr., and son's plan to resign, 47–8; and Lincoln, 229; and Missouri affair, 324–5; and Frémont, 338, 370, 375–6; and Cameron, 398

Blair, Frank P., Jr., and secession in Missouri, 88, 121–9, 157, 180–1; resolution of, 191; and Lincoln, 199–203, 386; and Butler, 213; and Curtis, 229, 295–8, 307–12; and Lyon, 315; returns to Missouri, 324–7; and Frémont, 331–9, 375–7, 382

Blair, Montgomery, in cabinet, 32, 42–58; and Lincoln, 72–3; Missouri conflict, 128; proposal on strategy, 150–4; on union, 173–7; and Butler, 211; and army, 226; and Frémonts, 280, 313–9, 334–8, 375–7; and McClellan, 300; and Frank Blair, 324, 331; and Cameron, 399–402; in Emergency war cabinet, 405–6; on Stanton, 409

Blockade, 151, 178–9, 209–10, 226, 288–90, 372, 415

Bocock, Thomas, 98

Border states, secession in, 52, 59, 77, 80–3, 93, 101–7, 119–44

Botts, John Minor, 27

Bragg, Braxton, 166

Breckinridge, John C., 106, 130–1, 184–6

431

PART II

The War for the Union

WAR BECOMES REVOLUTION
1862–1863

GRANT in 1863. This photograph, presented to Grenville M. Dodge during the Vicksburg Campaign, brings out the quiet determination and stern fighting power written in Grant's eyes and jaw. Here is the Grant of whom General David Hunter wrote to Stanton: "He is a hard worker, writes his own dispatches and orders, and does his own thinking. He is modest, quiet, never swears, and seldom drinks, as he took only two drinks during the three weeks I was with him. He listens quietly to the opinions of others and then judges promptly for himself; and he is very prompt to avail himself in the field of all the errors of his enemy." Courtesy of Mr. Fleming Fraker, Jr., and Mr. Claude R. Cook, Curator, Iowa State Department of History and Archives; reproduction by Des Moines *Register and Tribune*.

CONTENTS

ILLUSTRATIONS

NO VOLUME, no series of volumes, can do justice to the tremendous story of effort, devotion, and valor North and South, in the war which finally vindicated national unity. A writer can hope but to present a few truthful interpretations of the vast complexity of events and forces. In the first volume of *The War for the Union* I dealt with affairs from the inauguration of Lincoln to his order for a grand Northern advance on February 22, 1862. This was the phase, as the subtitle stated, of "the improvised war." My second volume takes up the narrative as four leaders step forward in powerful roles: Lincoln disclosing his plan for slavery, Stanton taking over the War Office, Grant delivering the first heavy blow in the West, and McClellan preparing to launch his army against Richmond. The book carries the story to the eve of the climactic events at Vicksburg and Gettysburg. Again the subtitle indicates one of the central themes: "war becomes revolution." And again the emphasis falls on the political, administrative, social, and economic developments of the time, though campaigns and battles cannot be neglected.

Far and wide in America, when Chancellorsville was fought in 1863, extended the ice-sheet of the war, seeming to congeal most of the normal activities of men, and still offering no sign of break or thaw; but underneath it the currents of change ran with accelerated force. War partly retards, partly stimulates, the factors of growth in a nation. In the South, with its scanty population and weak economy, the record was of retardation. In the North observers were struck by the ability of twenty-odd millions of energetic people to make use, while lustily fighting, of the new opportunities created by war contracts, tariffs, the great release of capital, and westward expansion. Anthony Trollope, touring the land from Boston to Dubuque, saw that although Illinois had sent one man out of eight to the armies, she choked under the volume of grain and meats she was producing. He saw in New England that the industrialists and traders were neither more covetous nor more generous than those of Britain. "But that which they do, they are more anxious to do thoroughly and quickly. They desire that every turn taken shall be a great turn."

Years of revolution these were on many fronts. Darwin's *Origin of Species* in 1859 had opened a revolution in thought, and given science a far stronger place in the roster of human activities. When Colonel E. L. Drake the same year struck oil in Pennsylvania, he ushered in an energy-revolution. Within a century all but one per cent of the labor performed in the United States, some experts have estimated, was to be done by machines, not muscle, and seventy per cent of the machine power was to flow from petroleum; facts which cast an ironic light upon the South's dependence on the muscle-power of four million slaves. If the North was deeply concerned with the idea of national unity, other lands were finding that the same principle loosed revolutionary currents that no man could check. Garibaldi invaded Sicily in the spring of 1860, entered Naples that fall, and soon afterward saw Victor Emmanuel on the throne of an Italy united save for the papal states. Bismarck became prime minister of Prussia in 1862, and with new power moved toward German unification.

The most farreaching change in the United States was organizational. Improvisation of troops, naval forces, munitions, quartermasters' services, chains of command, and modes of attack necessarily gave way to plan and system; the old individualism yielded in a hundred ways to disciplined association. The army with which McClellan began the peninsular campaign represented not only the largest but the best organized deployment of power ever seen in the New World; and behind the carefully planned array of corps, divisions, brigades, regiments, and batteries was a more and more elaborate network of agencies to provide everything the armed forces required, from tent-pins to siege-guns. Factories, machine shops, mercantile offices, and banks operated on a new scale, and in closer relationship with each other and government. The force of a revolutionary shift of commerce from old north-south channels to new east-west highways was illustrated by the prosperity of the trunk-line railways between the Lakes and the Ohio, and the building of a wholly new road, the Atlantic & Great Western. As a country which in Buchanan's time had made Federal expenditures of less than four hundred millions a year began making them in billions, the scale of all enterprises, public and private, was magnified.

In short, pressures of war were compelling the amorphous nation of 1860 to acquire form and structure. The necessity of rallying and concentrating its forces was converting the limp, sprawling North into a coordinated and directed society which set a new value on efficiency. A modern America was being born.

As the war was prolonged, it inevitably accomplished a revolutionary change in the status and outlook of the colored folk who comprised about an eighth of the population. When John Brown was hanged in 1859 slavery had seemed as strongly intrenched as ever. Had fighting ended in the spring of 1862 it might have survived for years. But it suffered shock after shock—the effort of many slaveholders to carry their property into interior fastnesses of the South; the thrusts of Northern columns into Alabama, Mississippi, and Louisiana; the thunder of Northern warships on the rivers and seacoasts; the pervasive propaganda of the grapevine telegraph. By the spring of 1863, with a systematic enlistment of colored troops, the future of the Negro was assured. Much else of the oldtime America died with slavery. E. L. Godkin visited the South just before and just after the war. On the second visit he was conscious of a changed atmosphere, as if the windows of a closed room had been suddenly opened; and when he mentioned the fact, a Southern friend replied, "Yes, sir, we have been brought into intellectual and moral relations with the rest of the world."

As the current of the war flows more strongly its interest deepens. This volume necessarily pays much more attention to the heroic endurance of the South, and the genius of Lee and Jackson. It attempts to do justice to three chief architects of Northern victory, Stanton, Farragut, and Grant; but the one great commanding figure is Lincoln, who grows in stature from crisis to crisis. Some chapters of the war have had to be postponed to later treatment: the blockade, for example, the financial measures, and the intellectual currents of the time. Throughout the book it will be plain that the primary heroes of the struggle are those whom Lincoln called the "plain people," whose belief in national destiny never faltered, and whose capacity for sacrifice knew no limits.

The author is under more obligations to friends than he can fully acknowledge. But he must express special thanks to Bruce Catton, E. B. Long, Henry Steele Commager, Harold Hyman, David Donald, Frank E. Hill, Joseph Rappaport, Ralph Newman, Carl Haverlin, Miss Marian McKenna, and Mrs. Jean Conti. Among librarians he owes a large debt to Dr. John Pomfret and the staff of the Huntington, Drs. Carl White, Richard Logsdon, and Roland Baughman of Columbia University, Stanley Pargellis of the Newberry, Paul M. Angle of the Chicago Historical Society, Clyde C. Walton and Miss Margaret Flint of the Illinois State Historical Library, and Dr. David Mearns and the staff of the Congressional Library. He must thank Mr. S. L. M. Barlow for allowing him to see a portion of the Barlow Papers before their transfer to the Huntington. The patience of Charles Scribner and Dr. Wayne Andrews in helping the book through the press has been invaluable. For constant encouragement he owes much to the late Dr. Abraham Flexner, and for material aid he is under obligation to Mr. Lessing Rosenwald, the late Mrs. David Levy, the Carnegie Corporation, and its able head, John W. Gardner.

A final word should be said about the spelling of proper names. I have followed the form used in the Dictionary of American Biography in identifying E. Kirby-Smith, who himself did not use the hyphen. I have also followed DAB usage with the name Fitz-John Porter, who sometimes used the hyphen and sometimes did not. I have preferred Savanna to Savannah for the Tennessee River town to avoid any possible confusion, among foreign readers, with the Atlantic port. In naming battles I have taken what seems the most familiar usage, and hope in a later volume to insert a table giving variant appellations.

Allan Nevins
The Huntington Library

1

Lincoln and Grant Launch
Two Thrusts

AS THE chill dawn of New Year's Day in 1862 broke over Provincetown on Cape Cod, townspeople flocked to the shore to see a British sloop of war, the *Rinaldo*, drop anchor in the harbor immortalized by the *Mayflower*. Curious Yankees in small boats, hailing her, got no information from the officers. But when the New York pilot who had brought her in came ashore with a cipher message to Lord Lyons in Washington, he divulged the news that James M. Mason and John Slidell were to be put aboard and taken to Halifax. Excitement mounted in the little town when word came by telegraph that the two Confederates had left Fort Warren in Boston harbor at eleven. About four the smoke of another steamer rose over Long Point, and a few minutes later the tug *Starlight* rounded it. Soon Mason, portly, bald, and pompous, and Slidell, a dapper man with a sulky air, clambered up the side of the British ship; their luggage followed; and the *Rinaldo* steamed smartly to sea. The American surrender of the envoys, managed tactfully in this quiet port, gave anguish to Southerners who had hoped for a collision between the North and Britain. Their chagrin would have been greater had they known of the talk at an evening dinner party at Secretary Cameron's two days earlier, when Lincoln had unceremoniously joined a group comprising Seward, Chase, and Sumner. After Seward had remarked that he gave up Mason and Slidell without the least rancor, the President made some statements which Sumner summarized in a sentence: "He covets kindly relations with all the world, especially England."

The termination of this anxious crisis was a gleam of sunshine. So, as the new year began, was the Senate's confirmation of Edwin M. Stanton as the new Secretary of War with but two dissenting votes, for faith in Stanton was prodigious. So was the intelligence that George H. Thomas had taken some prisoners, twelve guns, and large stores in what Stanton hailed as a brilliant victory at Mill Springs in Kentucky. A few such gleams had been badly needed.

For in most respects the year 1862 opened grimly. Both East and West, the war that had been so full of ardor seven months earlier seemed chilled into torpidity. McClellan in his Washington headquarters merely extended his inaction into a new phase when he fell ill of typhoid. Halleck in St. Louis was awkwardly clutching the reins in a scene of angry confusion left by Frémont's removal, and Buell in Louisville appeared unwilling to move forward. The North had seized the advantage in the Border States, planted outposts on the Southern coast, and begun a blockade, but the real work of reducing the Confederacy had scarcely begun. Behind lay a year of frustration; ahead clearly stretched another year of upheaval, effort, and perhaps graver reverses. The gaunt President, pacing between White House and War Office, could not escape an agonizing question. Was the Union really the land of the heroic old-time warriors, explorers, and state builders, of John Smith and William Bradford, of Washington, Hamilton, and Madison, of Jackson and Webster? Or was it the irresolute land of Pierce and Buchanan, of doughface Whigs and proslavery Democrats, of compromisers, time-servers, and outright traitors?

He never lost faith. And if the first ardent passion of war was gone, a better spirit was taking its place, and calling for fiercer resolution and sterner measures. A new year, a new War Department head, new troops and new generals—these, men hoped, would bring victory within grasp. This changed temper dictated a set of harsh orders by Halleck in Missouri. All secessionists who loitered near camps to gain information or who conveyed it to the enemy would be arrested, tried, and shot. The St. Louis authorities were empowered to aid the host of destitute refugees from the southwestern counties by quartering them in the houses of Southern sympathizers, while a commission in the city levied upon rich disloyalists for contributions running up to $10,000 apiece—resistance to this levy being punishable by death. In Kentucky, meanwhile, arrests of alleged traitors were filling the military prisons.

Congress had no sooner met in December than Senator Lyman Trumbull offered a radical measure for the confiscation of rebel property. The House by a party vote refused to reaffirm the moderate Crittenden resolution that the war was being waged for the Union alone; plainly, the Republican majority expected to cripple or extinguish slavery. Some members were declaring that all war costs should be paid out of Southern wealth. The Senate expelled John C. Breckinridge, the former Vice-President now in the Confederate army, and Jesse D. Bright of Indiana, who had written an improper letter to Jefferson Davis. Before Christmas the Committee on the Conduct of the War met in threatening mood and prepared to question a list of generals.

But it fell to a woman, a figure in letters and not war, to catch most memorably the spirit of the hour. The nation already had some stirring war songs, and George F. Root's "Battle Cry of Freedom" would soon resound on the Chickahominy. But it had no song of moral passion until Julia Ward Howe, a forty-two-year-old descendant of Cromwellian and Revolutionary fighters, appeared this winter in Washington. As her train entered the city at nightfall she had thrilled to the watchfires of a hundred circling camps; her hotel was bathed by the distant low thunder of cannon and the notes of drum, fife, and bugle. One evening as she returned from a review her carriage was blocked by columns of troops, and her party and the soldiers joined in "John Brown's Body." What a pity, she said, that the air had no better words. Before dawn next morning she was sitting in her nightdress scribbling the lines of "The Battle Hymn of the Republic." They soon appeared in the *Atlantic*. Wedded to the thudding folk tune, for the John Brown song was essentially a popular creation, her majestic stanzas caught the nation's ear and strengthened its heart.

Some manifestations of the growing Northern rigor were unfortunate. Halleck's orders could be so regarded.[1] William H. Russell, the London *Times* correspondent, had given offense by his graphically truthful description of the Bull Run panic. In vain did honest officers endorse his account, Sherman declaring every word of it true, and Keyes commenting, "I don't think you made it half bad enough." James Gordon Bennett of the *Herald* denounced him, a drunken Senator insulted him, and a German recruit leveled a cocked rifle at his head. Early in the new year he had prepared, with McClellan's full approval, to cover the advance into Virginia. But Secretary Stanton interposed with an order excluding him from the army, and no plea could modify it. The episode had larger consequences than appeared on its face. Not merely was Russell fair and expert, the ablest reporter the war had found, but he leaned to the Union side. His successor took the opposite attitude and abetted the *Times* in its unfriendly policy. Returning to London, Russell published *My Diary North and South*, so illuminating a record that all students of the war must regret that he could not continue it to the end.[2]

1 O. R., I, viii, 405-529, covers Halleck's decrees. His order barring fugitives from his lines aroused Northern wrath over its cruelty to helpless Negroes; his property levy on St. Louis sympathizers with the South was denounced throughout the border region and termed inhuman by the Unionist leader Senator John B. Henderson of Missouri. See *Cong. Globe*, 37th Cong., 2d Sess., 3348-3350, July 15, 1862. Coulter, *Ky. in the Civil War*, 147-150, treats arrests of disloyalists there.

2 Sam Ward saw Russell off in the *China* and set down some tart words on Stanton's tendency to "tomahawk" anybody he disliked; to Seward, April 9, 1862, Barlow Papers.

[I]

"For months past (and lately more pressingly)," wrote Attorney-General Bates on New Year's Eve, "I have urged upon the President to have some military organization about his own person. . . . I insisted that, being 'commander in chief' by law, he *must* command—especially in such a war as this." Other advisers thought that the President should organize a staff, require regular reports from each army, and direct large movements; and Lincoln did not wholly reject the suggestion. He continued to study manuals of war. To Buell on January 13, 1862, he sent a memorandum embodying shrewd thought. He wished Halleck to advance from St. Louis along the Mississippi line while Buell from Louisville pushed into East Tennessee. His general idea of the war, he continued, was that as the North had the greater numbers and the South the greater facility of concentration on points of collision, the proper strategy was to menace the enemy with superior forces at different points; so that if he weakened one to strengthen another, the Union could strike against the more defenseless front.

The President fixed a critical eye on the Western as well as Eastern theater, as he revealed in telegrams to Buell and Halleck inquiring whether they were acting in liaison. These generals were in fact not merely uncooperative but mutually jealous, each hoping to get the chief command in the West. Lincoln bluntly rebuked another jealous brigadier, who grumbled that he was being kept at Leavenworth with three thousand men while Buell had a hundred thousand. "He who does *something* at the head of one regiment will eclipse him who does *nothing* at the head of a hundred," commented the President.[3]

While watching the fronts, urging army ordnance to make proper use of mortars, and helping Seward draft some foreign dispatches, Lincoln showed his resourcefulness by a special approach to his principal problem: slavery. He had pondered the subject for years. With great uncertainty, with protestations that he would not know what to do with the institution if given absolute power, he had long before concluded that some system of gradual emancipation at national expense, coupled with an effort to colonize the freed people abroad, would offer the best solution. Now public and Congressional pressure compelled him to act, and before New Year's he had hammered into rough form a project which represented as bold a step as Jefferson had made in the purchase of Louisiana. Although the war was but nine months old, it was high time he grappled with the issue. A hundred Northern communities

3 *Works*, V, 84, 85 (to Hunter), 98, 99 (to Buell).

were circulating petitions for emancipation; anger over the annulment of Frémont's proclamation lingered, for Frémont, said *Harper's Weekly*, "undoubtedly touched the mainspring of the rebellion." [4]

"The nigger's in the Congressional woodpile," grumbled W. H. Wadsworth, a conservative Kentucky Congressman. "Abolition in the District—abolition in the insurrectionary States or districts—and general emancipation —this is their purpose, and it will blow them up." He meant that the radicals would be hoisted by their own petard. [5]

When in the previous summer John J. Crittenden had asserted in the House that the government possessed no power to meddle with slavery in the States, Thaddeus Stevens, recalling J. Q. Adams' prediction that a Southern rebellion would sweep away all barriers to emancipation, had scornfully replied: "Mr. Speaker, I thought the time had come when the laws of war were to govern our action; when constitutions, if they stood in the way of the laws of war in dealing with the enemy, had no right to intervene." Joshua Giddings held that *all* slaves might be freed under the war power, for even those who worked at home grew bread for Southern troops. [6] Sumner, Wendell Phillips, Owen Lovejoy, and Beecher with their voices, and Bryant, Whittier, George William Curtis, and Lowell with their pens, pleaded for lifting the war to a higher, bolder plane.

Lincoln was quite ready to elevate the objects of the war. Like nearly everyone, he cherished a hope that powerful advances in Virginia and down the Mississippi would end the fighting in 1862. During these advances, he expected to see slavery shaken and eroded. At the same time, however, he shrunk from antagonizing loyal Kentuckians, Marylanders, and Missourians by abrupt measures. A scheme of compensated emancipation in the Border States, he decided, could arrest heedless Congressional action, facilitate the surrender of the Confederacy, and give notice that slavery everywhere must be regarded as a temporary and not a permanent institution.

"Well, Mr. Sumner," Lincoln told the Massachusetts Senator early in December, "the only difference between you and me on this subject of emancipation is a difference of a month or six weeks in time." He asked for patience until he could disclose his plan of action, and Sumner promised to say nothing more for at least six weeks. [7]

Lincoln detested slavery for moral, economic, and democratic reasons alike; he had hated it ever since he told the Illinois legislature in 1837 that it

4 Lincoln to Hunter, *Works*, V, 84, 85, to Buell, 98, 99, *Harper's Weekly*, November 30, 1861.
5 To S. L. M. Barlow, Dec. 6, 1861, Barlow Papers.
6 Joshua Giddings, Washington, Dec. 19, 1861, Giddings Papers, Ohio Hist. Society.
7 E. E. Hale, memorandum of April, 1862, in *Memories*, II, 189–196.

represented both social injustice and bad policy. He regarded it as the principal root of the war. It had divided the national house. While at home it
had negated and crippled the American ideals of freedom and equality, abroad
it had sullied the principles which, as he said in his Independence Hall speech,
gave hope to the world for all future time. The South *must* be made to join
in laying plans for its extirpation. But his hostility to the institution never
carried him beyond a deep-seated belief that so disruptive a change should be
effected gradually in order to minimize its hardships, and that the results of
extirpation would be more wholesome if it were coupled with at least a
partial removal of the colored people to another land. Like most other
white men of the time in Europe and America, he at first believed that
inherent racial differences made it undesirable for Negro and Caucasian to
dwell together. The stronger race would oppress the weaker group, and thus
retarded, the colored man would pull down the white competitor to his
own level. Some system for colonizing the freedmen abroad should therefore
be attempted. But Lincoln had no fixed prejudices. As the war progressed,
and as Negroes proved themselves brave fighters, industrious workers, and
people of character, he began to discard the idea of inherent racial inequalities [8]; while he simultaneously realized that large-scale colonization was impracticable. At the beginning of 1862, however, he still clung to his old
preconceptions.

[II]

When Lincoln talked with Sumner, he had already taken secret action.
Early in November he had called Representative George P. Fisher of Delaware
to the White House to discuss compensated emancipation in that little State,
where the last census had enumerated only 587 slaveholders, holding fewer
than 1,800 slaves. An open-minded slave owner, at Lincoln's instance, was soon
brought into the talks. The President asked the two men to ascertain whether
the legislature could be persuaded to free the slaves if the government paid for
them at local and individual appraisals. "I am satisfied," he said, "that this is
the cheapest and most humane way of ending the war." The cost, after all,
would be trifling; the bill for a single half-day of hostilities would pay for all
Delaware's slaves, with enough left over to colonize them abroad. Once the
plan was proved feasible in Delaware, he hoped he might persuade the other
Border States to adopt it. Delaware would be bellwether of the flock.

When Fisher, who had been elected on a Constitutional Union platform,
broached the proposal to friends, he met with some encouragement. The op-

8 See his tribute to the Negro in his letter to J. C. Conkling, Aug. 26, 1863.

position came chiefly from Southern sympathizers—though a few antislavery Republicans thought that the State should emancipate without compensation, and some conservatives feared that the freedmen would become a burden. With advice from Lincoln, Fisher helped draw up a bill to be presented to the legislature when it met late in December. It provided that when the national government had appropriated money to pay an average of $500 each for the slaves, emancipation should go into effect. As soon as it was made public, this measure provoked an acrimonious debate, the Wilmington *Journal* supporting it while the Wilmington *Gazette* led the attack.[9]

Meanwhile, Lincoln clung to the idea that, as he had said years before in a tribute to Henry Clay, there was "a moral fitness in returning to Africa her children, whose ancestors have been torn away from her by the ruthless hand of fraud and violence"; or, if Africa offered no refuge, in sending them to another tropical land. He talked with Ambrose W. Thompson, a Philadelphian who had grown rich in coastal shipping. With some associates, Thompson had obtained control of several hundred thousand acres in Panama, and had devised a plan for opening coal mines in the Chiriqui district there and bringing in liberated Negroes as labor. He proposed to sell his coal to the Navy Department at half the price the government had been paying, and to use the revenue in sustaining his colored colony while it developed plantations of cotton, sugar, and coffee. Lincoln had the matter investigated. His brother-in-law, Ninian W. Edwards, a special commission, and Francis P. Blair, Sr., all in time made enthusiastic reports. At the very time that the President was secretly talking with the Delawareans, Thompson was pressing his proposal eagerly. "I am very anxious to have this contract closed immediately," he wrote the elder Blair in mid-November.[10]

For a time Lincoln felt hopeful of progress with his broad plan, which he still kept confidential. He thought that border slaveholders must see the inevitability of emancipation, for the grapevine telegraph rapidly diffused the idea of

9 H. C. Reed, "Lincoln's Compensated Emancipation Plan," *Del. Notes*, 1931, pp. 27 ff.; *Cong. Globe*, 37th Cong., 2d Sess., 1175, 1176 (Fisher's speech, March 11, 1862). There should have been no prejudice in Delaware against free Negroes, who were as sober, industrious, and thrifty as the poorer whites. When Senator Saulsbury talked about their laziness and vice, informed observers indignantly contradicted him. W. M. Connolly, Wilmington, July 5, 1862, to Fessenden; Palmer Coll., Western Reserve Hist. Soc. J. T. Scharf, *Delaware*, I, 345, 346, gives a dubious report of Lincoln's first talk with Fisher.

Lincoln's plan was of course not original, but could be traced back for years. Before he was inaugurated the New York *Tribune* had discussed the gradual compensated emancipation of 600,000 slaves in the Borderland, Texas, Arkansas, and Louisiana, saying that at $400 apiece the costs would approximately equal those of Buchanan's proposed purchase of Cuba; Jan. 30, 1861.

10 See letters of Thompson, Nov.-Dec., 1861, in Blair-Lee Papers, Princeton; and W. A. Beck, "Lincoln and Negro Colonization," *Abraham Lincoln Quarterly*, VI (September, 1950), 162–168.

freedom among the slaves, and they flocked eagerly to every Union standard in secession territory.[11] He found another favoring circumstance in Confederate efforts to stop cotton production, a blow at one of the principal economic foundations of slavery. To George Bancroft, calling at the White House in December, the President declared that the leviathan had already been harpooned near the heart, and that he was pondering what course he should take if slave insurrections broke out. At the same time he told Sumner how fervently he hoped he could soon announce a broad program of recompensed emancipation. Meanwhile, he directed Henry T. Blow, the capitalist and former protector of Dred Scott who was now minister to Venezuela, to investigate all the possibilities of the Chiriqui area: the lands, harbors, potential railway routes, and facilities for defense.[12]

But Delaware, alas! failed to come up to the mark. Party rancor conspired with proslavery sentiment and other motives to defeat the proposal. Our main work is to save the Union and not to meddle with slavery, declared the Democrats. Defiantly, they drew up resolutions that Congress had no right to buy slaves, that the State could not guarantee any debt depending on a mere pledge of Federal faith, and that when Delawareans wished to abolish slavery, they would do it in their own way. Early in 1862 the friends of Fisher's bill abandoned it as hopeless. They could have obtained a narrow majority in the Senate, but would have met defeat in the House. A quixotic opposition thus blocked Lincoln's plan; fundamentally, no doubt, because many Delaware voters could imagine no feasible mode of controlling race relations without slavery.[13]

Still, Lincoln had to do something, and do it immediately. The radical demand for drastic measures of emancipation mounted ever higher. The legislation which Lyman Trumbull had so promptly introduced provided for the forfeiture of every species of property belonging to those who in any way aided or abetted the rebellion. Lincoln just after New Year's paid Horace Greeley the compliment of attending a lyceum lecture given at the Smithsonian as part of an antislavery series arranged by the Washington Lecture Association. As the band played "Hail to the Chief," the President, Secretary Chase, Senators Preston King and Henry Wilson, and Speaker Galusha Grow

11   The governor of Kansas estimated that during 1861, 5,000 fugitive slaves came in from various areas; and a great efflux of Missouri slaves also took place to Illinois and Iowa. Washington *National Republican*, Jan. 22, 1862.

12   Some free Negroes in parts of the North early in 1862 were circulating a petition asking Congress to buy a tract in Central America for colonization, and Anna Ella Carroll, who favored the project, was writing letters to the press to support it; Washington *National Republican*, April 23, 1862. For Lincoln's statement to Bancroft see M. A. DeWolfe Howe, *Bancroft*, II, 147.

13   The one Lincoln Republican in the House was opposed; Conrad, *Delaware*, I, 205.

filed upon the platform. They heard Greeley's squeaky voice deliver sentiments as unflinching as Cato's. It was time to look the archenemy in the eye,
he said; slavery had been the aggressor, and had earned a traitor's doom. Conservatives had at first stood aghast at Butler's contraband order, he continued,
but soon endorsed it; they had condemned Frémont's order of liberation, but
had learned to accept the idea; and every Union man would yet agree with
Andrew Johnson that "no traitor has any right to own anything." [14] Explosive
applause followed Greeley's denunciation of compromise: "My motto is, the
Union forever as our fathers made it; but Liberty forever, with or without the
Union!"

Though Lincoln could not have joined in that applause, the occasion must
have impressed him with the force of emancipationist feeling. He knew that a
great part of the Northern press was as extreme on the subject as Medill's
Chicago *Tribune*, or Bryant's *Evening Post*.[15] The Harrisburg *Telegraph* was
asserting that the people called for general abolition; the Portsmouth (N. H.)
Journal pronounced any lasting peace impossible until Congress used the war
power, so far as it could, to exterminate slavery from the land. The principal
governors, from Andrew to Yates, were as emphatic as Wade, Bingham, Thaddeus Stevens, and other Congressional radicals. And Sumner, despite his promised
patience, continued to press Lincoln. At various periods, and this was one, his
influence in the White House was great. During the crisis of the *Trent* affair
he had told Lincoln that it would have caused much less trouble had he done
his duty against slavery, for he would have possessed stancher friends in Britain.[16] When the dispute was settled on December 26, he pressed Lincoln
again: "I want you to make Congress a New Year's present of your plan"—
the nature of which he did not know.

Lincoln, however, discouraged by Delaware's rebuff, absorbed by military
problems, and wrung by the mortal illness of his son Willie, put the subject
aside in February—to wait.

Yet he had adumbrated the boldest movement in the history of the

14 George Weston, editor of the Washington *National Republican*, declared that anything short of unconditional emancipation of all slaves of rebels was useless; Jan. 8, 13, 16,
1862. Later lecturers in the series mentioned, all strongly antislavery, included Emerson,
George William Curtis, and John Jay.

15 Medill was privately more radical than his paper. He wrote Elihu Washburne, January
13, 1862: "I guess between the doctors—i.e., West Point proslavery generals, a rotten Cabinet,
and a blind cowardly Congress, the public patient is done for and will soon require the
services of the undertaker." Washburne Papers, LC.

16 T. C. Grattan, recently British consul in Boston, thought this was true. In a
pamphlet published in England late in 1861 he wrote: "Terrible as would be the results of
a servile war, there is great likelihood that the inconsiderate shout for immediate abolition
would ring in the ears of all England like an alarm bell, and stir the depths of popular
feeling with the fervor of the Reformation, or the fanaticism of the Crusades."

Presidency. His conception ran beyond the mere liberation of four million colored folk; it implied a far-reaching alteration of American society, industry, and government. A gradual planned emancipation, a concomitant transportation of hundreds of thousands and perhaps even millions of people overseas, a careful governmental nursing of the new colonies, and a payment of unprecedented sums to the section thus deprived of its old labor supply—this scheme carried unprecedented implications. To put it into effect would immensely increase the power of the national government and widen its activities. If even partially practicable, it would mean a long step toward rendering the American people homogeneous in color and race, a rapid stimulation of immigration to replace the workers thus exported, a greater world position for the republic, and a pervasive change in popular outlook and ideas. The attempt would do more to convert the unorganized country into an organized nation than anything yet planned. Impossible, and undesirable even if possible?—probably; but Lincoln continued to hold his vision.

Such bold action would lie open, however, only to a government which won victories and became able to impose its will on its enemies. From Lincoln's West now came the first substantial augury of success in the war.

[III]

The Administration, hoping that the impending thrust in Virginia and the march down the Mississippi would quickly succeed, and that together with the blockade they would bring the Confederacy to its knees, had hardly paused to consider whether the Eastern or Western theater was the more important. Because of the sense of peril to Washington, it had given precedence to the East. This was a grave error. The severest single stroke that could be dealt the Confederacy would be the seizure of the Mississippi Valley, separating Louisiana, Texas, and Arkansas from the rest of the South, and giving the Union the important railroad ganglia of Corinth, Jackson, and Nashville. By comparison, a victory of McClellan in Virginia was unlikely to accomplish decisive results.

During most of 1861 the West had thus been given stepchild treatment. Weak officers were made brigadiers; Frémont was stinted in troops, arms, and intelligent support; and any man who complained of shortages as vehemently as W. T. Sherman did ran the risk of being pronounced insane —as Sherman was. Scott, McClellan, and Cameron all had difficulty in seeing over the Alleghenies. But Westerners had felt high hopes of a more dynamic attention to their needs when on November 9 Henry W. Halleck was appointed head of the new Department of Missouri, which included Arkansas and western Kentucky, and on the 15th Don Carlos Buell took command of the Department of the Ohio. The situation inevitably made the two men rivals. While Halleck was to direct the southward advance along the Mississippi, Lincoln expected Buell to liberate eastern Tennessee, rescue its Unionist population, and cut the vital railway linking Virginia with Chattanooga and the Southwestern Confederacy. Which would evince the greater capacity and achieve the larger results?

Buell's assignment was particularly promising at a distance, and particularly difficult at near view. Lincoln in his "Plan of Campaign" written about October first had declared that he wished troops sent to seize a point on the Virginia & Tennessee Railroad near Cumberland Gap, then guarded by F. K. Zollicoffer with 6,000 to 8,000 Confederates. McClellan all winter was equally anxious, for the sake of his Richmond campaign, that Western troops occupy East Tennessee and cut its railway lines north, so that the Confederates in Virginia would be isolated. "My own advance," he wrote Buell on January 6, 1861, "cannot, according to my present view, be made until your troops are soundly established in the eastern portion of Tennessee." That is, *he* could not move forward, but Buell could and must [17] Lincoln was eager to aid the sorely harried Unionists who might make northern Georgia, eastern Tennessee, and western North Carolina a free mountain domain, a cancer in the Confederate vitals. This area, which could be regarded as the back door of Virginia, held a situation which looked with menacing adaptability on other Atlantic and Gulf States. If only a strong Union army could be planted and supported there! With Andrew Johnson pressing for action, Lincoln fretted over lost opportunities. Of 45,000 adult males in East Tennessee, it was later said that 35,000 enlisted in the Union service; but just now they were cut off.

But Buell knew that the crow-flight distance from Lexington to Cumberland Gap is 110 miles, and that only crows can fly over mountains. In eastern Kentucky lie four ranges, the Pine Mountain, Little and Big Black, and Cumberland; one peak rises well over 4,000 feet. The few dirt roads wound through tortuous creek or river valleys, lined much of the way by steep mountainsides to which clung cabins where a hardy folk tilled patches of corn. This forested country produced little surplus food or forage. In winter rains even the road from Frankfort to Shelbyville in the rich center of the State was sometimes impassable. Rebel bushwhackers were active in the area. The general feared that problems of communication and supply would prove insurmountable. He went so far as to promise to send 12,000 men and three batteries toward East Tennessee as soon as possible, but that was all. His

17 O. R., I, vii, 531.

stubborn impassivity in maintaining that the true route of advance was up the Cumberland to Nashville gave Lincoln an accurate impression that he was slow, and he certainly exaggerated enemy numbers in informing Washington just before Christmas that while he could muster only 50,000 effectives, the Confederates had fully that number at Columbus and at least 30,000 more at Bowling Green, on his flank. But he had a clearer grasp of the situation than far-off Washington. Thomas, even after defeating G. B. Crittenden at Mill Springs on January 19, 1862, also thought that the terrible roads and lack of subsistence barred any extended advance.[18]

Halleck meanwhile remained in St. Louis, trying to cope with the murder, arson, and pillage committed by guerrillas, answering querulous letters from his subordinate John Pope, and complaining to Washington of the lack of proper men, officers, and arms. But his strength grew rapidly. General Samuel R. Curtis was soon to lead part of his forces into northwestern Arkansas, while Pope was to march other troops against New Madrid and Island No. 10.[19]

Neither of the two generals in top Western command was as yet well known to the country. Halleck, with bulbous brow, large staring eyes, pursed lips, and short dimpled chin, had a schoolmasterish face. He looked like a college professor about to open chapel with a learned discourse. His heavy cheeks, sagging into the short gray sideburns that clothed them, and his heavy-set, dumpish figure gave him an ineffectual aspect. His career—he was not yet fifty—seemed, however, to offer an earnest of ability. A Phi Beta Kappa student at Union College, third in his class at West Point, author of the best American treatise on the art of war, which he had revised to include data on the Mexican and Crimean conflicts, translator of Jomini, a sufficiently good engineer to be offered the chair in that subject at the Lawrence Scientific School of Harvard, the head of a prominent law firm in San Francisco—so the record ran. He had impressed Scott so much that he was made major-general in 1861. Numerous officers shared the opinion which Grant expressed: "He is a man of gigantic intellect and well studied in the profession of arms." But this awkward pedant, slow of speech and gait, who dressed shabbily, picked his teeth as he strolled after dinner, and scratched his elbows as he talked prosily in his office, had weaknesses of irresolution, confusion, and timidity which events shortly proved serious.[20]

The stiffly erect Buell, full-bearded and stern-eyed, looked more the

18 On Kentucky conditions see the WPA *Guide* to the State; Thomas D. Clark, *Hist. of Kentucky*, 261 ff.; F. Winston Coleman, *Stage Coach Days in the Blue Grass;* and F. G. Davenport, *Ante-Bellum Kentucky*. The Seward Papers for January, 1862, show how Senator Andrew Johnson and Representative Horace Maynard pressed Lincoln. W. R. Carter, *Hist. 1st Tenn. Cavalry*, pictures the tremendous war effort of Tennessee.
19 O. R., I, viii, 33 ff., 189 ff., 367-577.
20 See the characterization in Fuller, *Generalship of U. S. Grant*, 79.

military man. While this short, slight, hawk-nosed professional soldier, a graduate of West Point in 1841 and a veteran of the Seminole and Mexican Wars, was so chill and taciturn that he repelled casual observers, intimates thought well of him.[21] He was a firm disciplinarian, nearly the equal of McClellan in the organization and drill of troops, and despite his besetting fault of slowness, an officer of some imagination. Possibly he could have done more to help the harassed Unionists in the mountains southeast of him. But he saw how risky a large movement toward East Tennessee would be without well-coordinated operations in western Kentucky; as early as November 27, 1861, he recommended that two flotilla columns should move up the Tennessee and Cumberland, and that an advance should be launched against Nashville. In one respect Buell was Halleck's exact opposite, for he was happiest when fighting in the field. Both, but especially Buell, were blind to the political factors in the war, and both were deeply hostile to "political generals," meaning men who never saw West Point.

Buell took vigilant care of his command, selecting camps cautiously, insisting on proper sanitary measures, providing decent commissary service, and punishing desertion and drunkenness. One of his shortcomings was that in his emphasis on discipline, he did not sufficiently distinguish between the plodding regular soldier of the old army, and the high-spirited volunteer of the new, so that his harshness made him generally disliked. A graver fault was his lack of initiative. He hesitated when action was called for, and when committed to action he still hesitated. "I don't believe the general is capable of a decision!" wrote one incensed subordinate. In the end his want of aggressive vigor was to ruin him. But before this happened his clear-sighted activities did the Union great service.[22]

Grant, who was Halleck's principal advanced commander at Cairo as Thomas was Buell's advanced commander at Lebanon, Kentucky, was steadily growing into his responsibilities. At Belmont he had mismanaged his two brigades so that part of his troops became a rabble of looters and then a panicky mob, and he had almost lost the 27th Illinois. After Belmont he failed to organize an adequate staff, or give his officers and men really tough training. The fact was that like everybody else he knew little about large-scale war and had to learn step by step. This short, black-haired man with close-cut black-and-gray beard and small, keen gray eyes wore a look at once determined and thoughtful. Those about him were still uncertain

21 T. C. Smith, *James A. Garfield*, I, 181. Grant declared after the war: "Buell had genius enough for the highest commands"; *Memoirs*, I, 318, 319, 344 ff. See also the Comte de Paris, *Civil War*, I, 522 ff.; Freeman Cleaves, *Rock of Chickamauga*, 92 ff.

22 T. A. Mitchel, January 25, 1889, Hay Papers, Ill. State Hist. Lib., gives Ormsby Mitchel's opinion of Buell; Foulke, *Morton*, I, 197, 198.

whether he had sufficient foresight to plan a campaign or enough intellectual agility to handle complicated troop movements. But intimates knew he did possess invaluable qualities: integrity, singleness of purpose, hard common sense, industry, and above all an instinct for the enemy's jugular. He never lost his self-command or his cool combativeness. His taciturn inscrutability and his mixture of simplicity and strength threw an aura of mystery about him. He was a strange character, declared W. T. Sherman long after the war; stranger than any in Plutarch. "I knew him as a cadet at West Point, as a lieutenant of the Fourth Infantry, as a citizen of St. Louis, and as a growing general all through a bloody civil war. Yet to me he is a mystery, and I believe he is a mystery to himself." [23]

The vital word in Sherman's characterization is "growing," for as much as Lincoln did, Grant *grew*. And though he lacked the intellectual power of a Moltke, Foch, or Bradley, he possessed the faculty of sorting out from many facts the few that were critically significant. He was growing also in that asset which the Anglo-Saxon world has always esteemed most, strength of character. That is, he was growing in promptness, for once he made up his mind, he moved; in nerve, for in tight squeezes he kept his head, and in stubborn grit, for he never knew when he was beaten, and so could lose every battle till the last one. Modesty and magnanimity were inborn traits; the modesty that saved him from a single touch of brag, the magnanimity that was later to infuse his letter explaining why he treated his Vicksburg prisoners generously. From Alfred and Cromwell to Washington, Grant, and Lee, elemental strength of character has been held the prime requisite of leadership. Quick, clever men may supply the ideas, but it is the rarer man of character whose integrity, resolution, and clarity of view make them count.

[IV]

It was one of the weaknesses of the Confederacy in the West that two rivers, the Tennessee and Cumberland, reached inland from the North toward its center. The Cumberland, the less important, did not penetrate far. Nashville marked its southernmost navigable point. But the Tennessee bent a great arc deep into Confederate territory, giving a short northeastern boundary to Mississippi and traversing all northern Alabama before it drained the Great Smokies of North Carolina. Troops ascending it could thrust between Memphis and Nashville, outflanking both, could gain the railway centers of Corinth, Mississippi, and Decatur, Alabama, and farther upstream, if they had

23 Sherman, Nov. 18, 1879, in *Century Magazine*, LIII (April, 1897), 821. "Not a brilliant man," Sherman wrote his wife in 1862, "but brave, sober, hardworking, and kind; *Home Letters*, 228.

high water at Muscle Shoals, could reach the vital railroad junction of Chattanooga, Tennessee.

The Tennessee River, moreover, intersected the most important communication line between the Eastern and Western Confederacy, the Memphis & Charleston Railroad. This primary artery for traffic between the Mississippi and South Atlantic coast, running from Memphis east through southern Tennessee and northern Alabama, was cut or touched by the meandering river at several points. Gunboats with a few troops could disrupt it. They could also seal off Nashville, which lay on the Cumberland and was connected with the Memphis & Charleston by two railroads and a macadamized highway. A sufficiently large force on the Cumberland, in fact, could seize Nashville —a rich provision depot for the Confederacy, now rapidly being made into a busy manufactory of arms, munitions, and general stores.

A mere glance at the map would seem to reveal that the Tennessee-Cumberland river system offered the North a heaven-sent opportunity to thrust a harpoon into the very bowels of the Confederacy; but it did not. We have no more telling indication of the planless improvisation of this war than the fact that not until late in 1861 did Union commanders think of attacking along this line.

One retired naval officer did grasp the idea as early as June, 1861. We do not know his name; we know only that he approached a Unionist in Nashville, and proposed that the North should invade central Tennessee by the two rivers, capture Nashville, and at a single bound carry the war into northern Georgia. The rivers were then unfortified, and the rebel troops assembling in the region were unorganized, ill armed, and badly officered. The naval officer believed that a swift force could take Nashville, draw volunteers from that area and East Tennessee, and push on into northern Alabama, where several counties teemed with Federal sympathizers. But obviously he took no account of Kentucky's neutrality or of Northern military weakness, and his suggestion was not even considered.[24]

Not until autumn did others show equal prescience. Then various people saw the possibilities of the situation almost simultaneously. One was an experienced steamboatman of St. Louis, Charles M. Scott; one a strong-minded young woman, Anna Ella Carroll, daughter of a former governor of Maryland, who visited the Western theater and talked with Scott. Still another was Charles Whittlesey, chief engineer on the staff of General Ormsby M. Mitchel, who wrote Halleck on November 20, 1861, proposing the movement. Frémont during the summer and fall had a spy, Captain Charles D'Arnaud, make two trips within Confederate lines to map highways, bridges, and forts in

24 See letters signed "Tennesseean" in N. Y. *Times*, Nov. 17, Dec. 21, 1861.

THE MISSISSIPPI–TENNESSEE–CUMBERLAND CAMPAIGNS

Kentucky and western Tennessee, and report on enemy movements. Among the materials he brought back were maps showing the positions of Forts Henry and Donelson. It is certain, however, that nobody in Washington caught the early inspiration. McClellan thought of using gunboats and troops either on the Mississippi or the Cumberland-Tennessee system simply as a diversionary action to aid Buell in descending upon East Tennessee, just as Buell's first idea seems to have been to coordinate a flotilla movement on the two rivers with land operations against Nashville.[25]

25 For Colonel Whittlesey's plan see O. R., I, vii, 440; M. F. Force, *From Fort Henry to Corinth*, 25. Senator B. F. Wade in 1872 credited the conception to Miss Carroll, saying that Lincoln and Stanton had done so. No evidence exists that she submitted a matured plan to the War Department, or that Lincoln and the Department suggested her idea to any general in the field. She did, however, place a paper on the possibilities of a Tennessee River campaign, with a map, in the hands of the Assistant Secretary of War, Thomas A. Scott, on Nov. 30, 1861. Charles M. Scott drafted a plan which he sent Miss Carroll in Washington; and he says he gave a copy of it, with other information, to Grant, apparently on or about Dec. 15, 1861. Both Grant and Adam Badeau deny that Grant received any prompting from either Captain Scott or Miss Carroll. Grant wrote Washburne March 22, 1862, that no general could claim credit for so obvious a move, for gunboats had been running up the rivers all fall and winter, looking at Forts Henry and Donelson, **and it is true**

But as the year closed, light dawned on so many people that experts could hardly believe, later, that the idea had ever been ignored. Thus Lew Wallace, with perfect hindsight, declared that the true strategy had been too plain to miss; that the trend of the two rivers, their navigability by steamboats, their secure road to the rear of the Confederate forces in Kentucky and Tennessee, and their large advantages as a supply line, were visible to all. Late in December, Halleck conferred with W. T. Sherman in St. Louis. Sherman explained that the enemy's main line of defense ran from Columbus east to Bowling Green. Thereupon Halleck took a ruler, drew a line on the map well north of these two points, and drew another line perpendicular to the center. This second line roughly coincided with the Tennessee River, and he announced that it was to be the main route of attack.[26] Buell's ideas also had been maturing. On December 29 he wrote McClellan that all possible force should be brought to bear on the Columbus-Bowling Green front, for "the center, that is the Cumberland and Tennessee where the railroad crosses them, is now the most vulnerable point"; to penetrate it would unseat the enemy, "and give access through the two rivers to the very center of their power." He also wrote Halleck on January 3, 1862, urging that a Tennessee-Cumberland expedition be launched with all possible speed. Meanwhile Lincoln continued to reiterate that he wished Halleck to push down the Mississippi while Buell threatened East Tennessee, and said nothing of the two lesser rivers.[27]

Prime responsibility for deciding the direction of the great initial thrust in the West lay with Halleck, who on January 20, 1861, made up his mind. "This line of the Cumberland or Tennessee is the great central line of the Western theatre of war," he wrote McClellan.

Grant's shrewd view of strategy buttressed this decision, for thinking quite independently, he had decided that he should attack one of the river forts. He sent Brigadier-General C. F. Smith, whom he had placed in charge of Paducah, on a reconnaissance up the Tennessee, and Smith returned with word that the river defenses could be captured. Thus encouraged, Grant

that the *Conestoga* ran upstream and inspected Fort Henry on Oct. 18. Confederate defensive preparations alone would have indicated the plan. See Badeau, *Mil. Hist. of U. S. Grant*, I, 22 ff.; Lew Wallace, *Autobiography*, I, 333 ff.; Sydney and Marjorie Greenbie, *Anna Ella Carroll and Abraham Lincoln*, Ch. XXIII; Sarah Ellen Blackwell, *A Military Genius, Anna Ella Carroll*, Ch. IV, and Kenneth Williams, "The Tennessee River Campaign and Anna Ella Carroll," *Indiana Magazine of History*, XLVI, No. 3 (Sept., 1950), 221–248.
26 Sherman, *Memoirs*, I, 248.
27 Lincoln's exchanges with Halleck and Buell, Jan. 1–15, 1862, are illuminating. Lincoln wanted action; he was "deeply distressed that our friends in East Tennessee are being hanged and driven to despair"; but he did not see the true strategy of the hour. Halleck wrote Jan. 5 arguing against operations on an exterior as opposed to an interior line. Lincoln, *Works*, V, 87–100; O. R., I, vii, 533.

went to St. Louis January 23 to explain his ambition to Halleck. He met a frigid reception, for Halleck shared the regular-army prejudice against Grant as a drinker, and the resentment of many regular officers that he outranked C. F. Smith, an older, more experienced, and widely beloved officer. Embarrassed, Grant stumbled in his speech. "I had not uttered many sentences," he wrote later, "before I was cut short as if my plan was preposterous." He returned to Cairo crestfallen, and talked over his plans with Flag-Officer Andrew H. Foote, commanding the gunboats. Always stubborn in his purposes, he waited only a few days; then on January 28 he and Foote together telegraphed Halleck of their urgent wish to attack. This time he met better fortune. Halleck had changed his mind, and without authorization from Washington, wired Grant to prepare for his expedition.[28] That telegram loosed a wild scene of jubilation at Grant's headquarters.

Of course no amphibious assault was possible until gunboats and transports were ready. All fall, against legions of difficulties, Foote had been struggling in St. Louis, Cairo, and other river towns to complete a flotilla. Not until mid-January were his vessels finished. On the 15th he gave a trial trip to the *Benton*, a powerful iron-plated boat, carrying a large battery. He simultaneously put into commission the seven gunboats which had been built to fill James B. Eads's contract. Even yet, the gunboat fleet was hampered by want of gunners and deck hands, and the army had to press volunteers into the service.[29] But Foote, a shrewd Connecticut Yankee who had helped suppress the slave trade on the African coast, was indomitable. At one point he was shrewder than Grant, whose original idea had been to ascend the Cumberland against Fort Donelson. Foote convinced him that the initial blow should be leveled against Fort Henry on the Tennessee.[30]

The impatient general got his orders from Halleck on February 1, and the very next day he and Foote set out—three weeks before the date set by Lincoln for a general advance.

[V]

While the Union leaders in the West stumbled toward their proper strategy with little help from Lincoln and none from McClellan or the War

28 Grant, *Memoirs*, I, 286; O. R., I, vii, 120, 121, 930. Perhaps Halleck swung about because his slow mind took several days to grasp Grant's plan. Perhaps he did so because, jealous over the triumph which Buell shared with Thomas in the victory of Mill Springs, he saw that the Tennessee-Cumberland move would give him a counter victory; J. F. C. Fuller, *Generalship of U. S. Grant*, 82.
29 James M. Hoppin, *Life of Admiral Foote*, 154–190; Grant, *Memoirs*, Ch. VIII; Naval O. R., I, xxii, 502–506.
30 Secretary of the Navy, *Annual Report*, 1862; Hoppin, *Foote*, 194, 195.

Department, Confederate leaders had stumbled toward an inadequate defense with even less help from Richmond. Albert Sidney Johnston, to many the knightliest of Southern officers, to some the brightest hope of the Confederacy, had been put in command. A Kentuckian by birth, a graduate of Transylvania and West Point, the leader of the national troops in Buchanan's ill-conceived and bungled Mormon expedition,[31] he was now fifty-eight. Tall, handsome, magnetic, he had great prestige—but in resources little else. At the outset he possessed about 23,000 men to hold a line 430 miles long, running from Columbus on the west to Cumberland Gap on the east, against nearly 40,000 Union troops.

The day he took command he implored the governor of Georgia to furnish every possible assistance, for he desperately needed arms and supplies, and sent a copy of this letter to Jefferson Davis. Simultaneously, ex-Governor Neill S. Brown of Tennessee laid before Davis a piteous plea for the protection of the whole central section of the State. This district, Brown wrote, needed a gunboat each on the Tennessee and the Cumberland, a brigadier-general to attend to a thousand details which Johnston could not oversee, and a heavy enlistment of troops based on the fact that family men were willing to serve for one year, but not three. He pointed out that on the undefended Cumberland stood the largest iron mill of the Southwest, indispensable to gunshops and cannon foundries, and near it was a large powder mill, State owned but about to be transferred to the Confederacy.[32]

"Ill armed"—"ill armed"—that plaint rings a doleful refrain through the letters of all the Confederate commanders in the West: Leonidas Polk, Gideon J. Pillow, F. K. Zollicoffer, and the others who were attempting to thrust sandbags into a leaky dike. Ill trained, ill officered, ill clothed, ill fed might well be added. "The Army of Missouri," wrote Secretary of War Benjamin to Braxton Bragg as 1861 ended, "is represented to be a mere gathering of brave but undisciplined partisan troops, coming and going at pleasure, and needing a master mind to control and reduce it into order and to convert it into a *real* army." Other forces were not in much better condition. Polk had his headquarters at Columbus; Pillow, intently watching Grant, was at New Madrid with about 10,000 men; Zollicoffer, a former newspaper editor and politician, had a wretchedly inadequate array to protect the Cumberland Gap and Knoxville area. Pillow informed Richmond that to get his forces even partially equipped he had to make stupendous exertions, and that nearly all

31 The bungling was mainly by the War Department under Floyd, and by other officers in Washington, and none of it reflected on Johnston.
32 Johnston, Sept. 15, 1861, to J. E. Brown, in Davis Papers, Duke Univ.; N. S. Brown, Nashville, Sept. 22, 1861, to Davis, *ibid*.

the arms and munitions held by the State had been gathered by himself at an expense of $200,000.[33]

It seems almost incredible that in the West, as in Virginia, Union commanders quaked for fear of attack by these new, ill-conditioned levies. When A. S. Johnston sent the capable Simon Buckner with 5,000 men to occupy Bowling Green, panic seized Louisville. Its home guard hurriedly mobilized, Governor Morton of Indiana rushed several regiments to the city, and other forces were mustered. Under W. T. Sherman, they took a defensive position at the Lebanon railroad southeast of the city. Here it was that Sherman's evidences of nervous strain—his appearance in uniform with a stovepipe hat, his borrowing from a sergeant a fresh cigar to light his own cheroot, after which he threw the cigar into the mud—first gave rise to rumors that he was insane; and his apprehensions of rebel attack helped inspire his demand for 200,000 men. It was a mystery to Sherman then and later why Johnston did not advance on ill-defended Louisville. The mystery was not very deep. In mid-October Johnston, talking with his aide, said crisply: "There will be this winter, on this line, no military operations that I can prevent. We have no powder." [34]

As his son later wrote, Johnston lacked everything that winter: men, munitions, supplies, and the means of obtaining them. He had the right to ask for anything, and the governors had an equal right to refuse. The onset of the winter found fewer than 22,000 men at Bowling Green, not half of them really furnished with weapons. Even then public opinion had not awakened to the imminent crisis. On Christmas Day, Johnston beseeched Governor Harris to arouse the people to the danger, or the whole Mississippi Valley would be lost: "Ten or fifteen thousand additional troops would make me feel assured of victory. With this additional force I could avail myself of every fault of their movements. Without them, I must be a spectator without power to seize the opportunities." [35] All fall he had masked the weakness of his forces by a series of pinprick raids along his entire front, especially on the east, while he strove to create a real army behind this screen. By this con-

33 Benjamin, Richmond, Dec. 27, 1861, to Bragg, in Civil War Coll., Mo. Hist. Soc.; Pillow, New Madrid, n.d., to L. P. Walker, extra-illustrated Battles and Leaders, HL; Pettus Corr., Alabama State Archives. Polk, immediately after invading Kentucky and seizing Columbus, had been succeeded by Johnston, who assigned him to the defense of the Mississippi. Pillow, a quarrelsome, shallow strutter, who had been the senior major-general of Tennessee's provisional army, became a brigadier-general in the Confederate forces, repining because his Napoleonic genius was so ill recognized. Simon Buckner, a leader of fine spirit, whom Lincoln had personally offered a commission as brigadier-general, was sent with that Confederate rank to Bowling Green, Ky.
34 Col. R. M. Kelly, Battles and Leaders, I, 379–385; memorandum by Thos. C. Reynolds, Johnston's aide, Reynolds Papers, Mo. Hist. Soc.; Col. Wm. Preston Johnston, "Albert Sidney Johnston at Shiloh," Battles and Leaders, I, 542; Peter F. Walker, "Building a Tennessee Army, 1861," Tenn. Hist. Quarterly, XVI, 99–116 (June, 1957).
35 Johnston, Bowling Green, Dec. 25, 1861, to Isham G. Harris, Brock Coll., HL.

tinuous activity he did succeed in bluffing some of the Union commanders.

Johnston did something—perhaps as much as he could—to fortify the rivers. Fort Henry was the Achilles' heel of his defenses. The first gun had been installed there in July, and by fall a considerable work had been erected; but a young captain who arrived in September to command the artillery concluded that the men who had selected the site were guilty either of preposterous folly or outright treachery. The engineers had placed it on the east bank of the Tennessee, on low land commanded within rifle range by high hills. It was so low, indeed, that the ordinary February rise would put the highest interior point under two feet of water. The armament was with difficulty increased to seventeen effective guns, all but one smoothbores, and the ammunition was so poor that some quick-burning powder had to be added to each charge, a dangerous expedient. Reiterated complaints about the position caused Johnston to dispatch a competent engineer, who made an unavailing effort to improve matters by fortifying some heights on the opposite bank. General Lloyd Tilghman collected a garrison of about 4,000 men, armed chiefly with shotguns and hunting rifles—one of his best-equipped contingents carrying flintlock Tower muskets used in the War of 1812! [36]

Fort Donelson on the west bank of the Cumberland, ten miles away, was a far stronger post, which some Federal officers thought really formidable. Built on a bluff nearly a hundred feet above the water, it was covered on the north by Hickman's Creek, deep and wide in the high water of winter, and on the south by Indian Creek. In a half circle around the fort ran a crescent line of rifle pits, largely following a ridge and protected by felled trees which formed an abattis. Two water batteries sunk in the northern face of the bluff, thirty feet above the river, held twelve guns and a ten-inch Columbiad. The fort seemed well adapted to the height which it crowned. Attacking infantry would find Hickman's Creek almost impassable, and to reach the rifle pits they would have to struggle at most points up hillsides some seventy feet high. [37]

Yet actually Donelson was full of weaknesses. The yellow-clay rifle pits were shallow, and where they reached Indian Creek could be penetrated without scaling any slope. The garrison, some 18,000 ill-trained, ill-armed, ill-provisioned recruits, lacked spirit. These and other defects were summed up in a colonel's roughly eloquent letter to Governor Harris:

We have no preparations for defense comparatively speaking. The guns command the river tolerably well, though we have no practised companies to serve them. The line of fortifications is not complete, or closed, and our

36 Jesse Taylor, "The Defense of Fort Henry," *Battles and Leaders*, I, 368 ff. The engineers were hampered in choosing the sites for defense by Kentucky's neutrality.
37 Grant, *Memoirs*, Ch. VIII; Lew Wallace, *Battles and Leaders*, I, 398 ff.

force can be attacked in the rear coming up the river, from below us. There
are three hills, which, if the enemy gets possession of, will command our fortifications. There is a high hill in the rear that entirely commands our camp,
and if the enemy gets possession of it we will be unable to hold our position. . . .

All our provisions are in Dover—we have no well-drilled troops here and
very inferior arms—and badly supplied with ammunition—our caps are defective—the cartridges are made of coarse powder and will not suit our sporting guns—we have none of the sporting caps. The men generally have but
little confidence in their guns. . . .[38]

Could the Confederates, thus holding almost untenable forts, save the
situation? The boldest course would have been the best: Johnston should
have marched in person to reinforce the garrisons and take command against
the Union assailants. His will, courage, and reputation would have been
invaluable. It is true that he had never commanded troops on the battlefield.
But his keen intellect, sustained by his imposing presence, made him a force
on any scene. The troops which he kept with him at Bowling Green could
better have been employed at the critical point. They would have been
invaluable at Fort Donelson. He knew how much the loss of the forts would
cost the Confederacy. Later his aide wrote that a few weeks before Grant
moved, Johnston had remarked that he expected to see Union armies ascend
the river and break the line there, and realized that Buell would never attack
him in his strong fortifications at Bowling Green; he only wished he would! [39]

This, in fact, was the first of Johnston's two great lost opportunities. The
generals he had sent to Donelson were, with one exception, mediocre or
worse. John B. Floyd, the ranking officer, was the same muddleheaded incompetent who had been Secretary of War under Buchanan; the vain, hot-
tempered Pillow fancied that his reputation as lawyer, planter, and politician,
with two Mexican War wounds, made him a general; and Buckner alone, a
West Point graduate of ability, could be taken seriously. Grant later remarked
caustically that he had known Pillow in Mexico, and judged that with any
force, however small, he could move unmolested within gunshot range of any
position Pillow was holding. Johnston knew how weak his subordinates were.
Particularly when he was so ill served, it was his duty to be at the critical point
of the contest.[40]

[VI]

Landing his 17,000 troops just below Fort Henry on February 5–6, 1862,
Grant ordered an advance at 11 A.M. on the 6th. But Foote was before him.

38 Col. J. M. Head, Jan. 26, 1862; Palmer Coll., Western Reserve.
39 Statement by Col. Mumford of Johnston's staff in W. P. Johnston, *Life of A. S. Johnston,* 491. Fuller thinks that Johnston was bewildered.
40 *Memoirs,* Ch. VIII.

He had seven gunboats, including the *Essex* under Commodore William D. Porter. Tilghman had wisely sent practically all the garrison of 2,800 overland to Donelson. By a severe fire of an hour and a quarter the boats took the almost unmanned fort, which could train only eleven of its twenty pieces on the river. Seven of these eleven guns were knocked out by about four hundred gunboat shots. When Tilghman rowed out to Foote's flagship to ask for terms, the commodore made curt reply: "No, sir! Your surrender will be unconditional!" But hardly a hundred officers and men laid down their arms.

On February 12–13, Grant slowly moved his army across the frozen fields to throw a three-mile line around the outworks of Donelson. Here the gunboat attack failed, nearly all of Foote's vessels being crippled in a hot action lasting little more than an hour. Some infantry fighting began the first day. It grew more intense on the 13th, as Grant tightened his hold, and fiercer still on the 15th as the Confederates tried to cut their way out. The weather enhanced the cruelty of the struggle. Thursday the 13th grew very cold, the thermometer dropping to ten above zero; Thursday night it sleeted and snowed; Friday it froze all day, and Friday night more snow fell. The lines were so close neither side could build fires, and the troops lacked shelter tents. Wet uniforms quickly became as stiff as boards, and many of the wounded froze to death. The neighboring village of Dover was choked by dead and maimed, surgeons operating in nearly every house. Men could not open a door without hearing groans. On both sides the volunteers fought as fiercely as veterans, and officers distinguished themselves by heroism. Lincoln's friend Richard Oglesby, a Decatur lawyer who had been defeated for the House the year that Lincoln met defeat for the Senate, led his regiment with great gallantry. The South had to mourn Dabney Carr Harrison, a young man of fine talent who died shouting, "Rally to the charge!" [41]

In the end, the battle at Donelson was decided by three factors. One was Grant's quick grasp of the situation when he returned from a conference with Foote on his flagship to find that Pillow had tried to force his way through the Union lines, and had scattered John A. McClernand's division; a second was the spirited counterassault on the Confederate works which Grant ordered C. F. Smith to launch immediately with Iowa and Indiana troops; and the third was the elan with which Illinois and Ohio infantry recovered their positions. Though sixty, Smith spent the bitter ensuing night without shelter on a captured ridge—the greatest night in the career of that rough-mannered, warmhearted, and thoroughly dedicated soldier.

On both sides the brightest laurels of Donelson belonged to the rank-and-file, for the generalship had distinct flaws. Had the garrison launched its

41 Description by Cairo corr., N. Y. *Tribune*, Feb. 27, 1861. A Confederate Tract Society Pamphlet No. 57, "The Confederate Hero and His Heroic Father," eulogizes Harrison.

FORT DONELSON

attack at the moment when Grant moved with inescapable confusion from
Henry to Donelson, it might have smashed his column. Later, Pillow's at-
tempted escape from the fort was tardy, and he halted it just short of success.
As for Grant, he had distributed his forces defectively. He should have
anticipated a sortie by arranging for deployment in depth, with skirmishers,
a strong firing line, and adequate reserves to reinforce any attacked sector.
C. F. Smith, a master of tactics, did try to maintain a reserve brigade, but
McClernand's division was strung out in a long thin line, all too vulnerable.

However, Grant's decision to counterattack was a master stroke. Hearing that the Confederates had swarmed out with haversacks and knapsacks, he eagerly demanded, "Are the knapsacks filled?" Opening the captured knapsacks to find several days' rations, he saw how desperate was the Southern movement, and his order magnificiently seized the opportunity. Smith, too, realized that swift counterattack would bring victory, and his division poured over the rifle pits with such impetuosity that another half-hour of daylight would have put him inside the fort.[42]

Saturday night the 15th, while Smith's men huddled in the cold, a remarkable scene was enacted inside the fort. Buckner spurned a proposal by Pillow for another sortie, saying that it would cost three-fourths of their men, and Floyd assented: "We shall have to capitulate." Though it was Floyd's duty to share the fate of his troops, he knew that capture would mean trial in Washington for the theft of public funds when he was Secretary of War, if not for treason. Pillow declared that he and his men would die before surrendering. Buckner therefore assumed command, saying: "Give me pen, ink, and paper, and send for a bugler." To his note asking for a parley Grant sent one of the famous replies of military history: "No terms except unconditional and immediate surrender can be accepted. I propose to move immediately upon your works."

With Donelson, Grant took more than 14,000 prisoners, 40-odd pieces of artillery, and some stores. Though Pillow estimated the Confederate casualties at 2,000, Union officers put the total much higher. While on paper the captures of material seemed impressive, men who looked about the fort were struck by Confederate destitution. Most of the firearms were pitiable, the ammunition was wretched, and the two-wheeled ambulances were mere rough carts covered with white cloth. When the people of Chicago saw thousands of Confederate prisoners marching through muddy streets to Camp Douglas, they were struck by the gauntness of the privates, dressed in coarse butternut, with no trace of a uniform except perhaps a stripe on the trousers; carrying tattered blankets and a spoon, tin cup, or frying pan. They went to a new destitution, for the Federal ration cost eleven cents a day.[43]

The results of these river conquests were far-reaching. Albert Sidney Johnston, who knew that the chief blame for the Southern defeat ought to fall on public inertia, pronounced Donelson a disaster almost without remedy.

42 On Donelson, see Grant, *Memoirs*, Ch. VIII; Badeau, *Grant*, I, Ch. II; Lew Wallace, *Battles and Leaders*, I, 398–428, a stirring account but not wholly dependable; A. L. Conger, "The Military Education of Grant as a General," *Wis. Mag. of Hist.*, IV (March, 1921), 239–262, an indictment of Grant's tactics, but with credit for his crucial decision to assault; and Kenneth P. Williams, *Lincoln Finds a General*, III, 229–259, the best study, and one very favorable to Grant.

43 Chicago corr., N. Y. *Tribune*, Feb. 27, 1862.

Aware that silence would best serve his cause, he wrote a report which offered no explanations and delivered no judgments. Floyd and Pillow he reassigned to duty, while he stoically accepted the storm of censure which rained upon him. "The test of merit, in my profession, with the people, is success," he wrote President Davis. "It is a hard rule, but I think it right." [44]

The seizure of the forts at once smashed the Confederate line from Columbus to Bowling Green, compelled the evacuation of these posts, and made Nashville, a city of about 18,000, indefensible. Alarm bells called people into the streets. A special train was hurriedly made up to carry citizens southward. Buggies, carriages, and wagons, crammed with movables, blackened every road leading out of town. Officers hurriedly removed about 800 wagon-loads of pork, clothing, and fixed ammunition. On February 17–18 Johnston marched his main force out of Nashville to Murfreesboro, thirty-one miles away, and on the 23rd his rear guard left the city, which Buell's forces entered next day. In the forward swing of Northern forces, Foote felt chagrined that the naval elements were shouldered aside. "An army major told me," he shortly wrote in his report on operations, "that we were purposely held back from Nashville that General Buell might take it, although that officer sent for a gunboat, which went to Nashville before he entered the city."

All Kentucky now seemed safe in Union hands, the Mississippi was open as far as Island No. 10 on the Kentucky-Tennessee border, and strong Union forces stood in central Tennessee. They held not only the rich manufacturing center of Nashville, with its flour mills, foundries, leather tannery, powder mill, and field-gun shop, but most of the Memphis branch of the Louisville & Nashville Railroad—a line which ran from Bowling Green southwest through Clarksville, Tennessee, to Memphis. Washington's Birthday found C. F. Smith's troops busy listing the commissary stores, ammunition, and artillery which they had taken in Clarksville, and Grant joined them there on February 25. [45]

No wonder that Washington was elated, and Richmond correspondingly depressed! At the White House as late as the morning of February 17 Lincoln still felt great anxiety, for the previous day had brought news of the repulse

44 Johnston, Decatur, Ala., March 18, 1862; *Battles and Leaders*, I, 399. Peter F. Walker, "Failure in Command: Forts Henry and Donelson," *Tenn. Hist. Quarterly*, XVI, December, 1957, accepts the double condemnation of Johnston, first for not choosing abler commanders at the forts, and second for not taking charge there himself when the critical hour struck.

45 Foote's complaint, April 23, 1862, is in Naval O. R., I, xxiii, 10, 11. Nashville was making about 3,000 pounds of powder daily for the Confederacy, 6 good field guns a week, and large quantities of caps and fixed ammunition, while it had a plant for the conversion of flintlock muskets to percussion. James D. Porter, *Confederate Military History*, Vol. VIII (Tennessee), p. 8; Henry McRaven, *Nashville*, 93; Nashville Directory, 1860-61.

of Foote's gunboats, and the evening only some vague accounts of the land fighting, with a dispatch that Union forces had taken the "upper fort." Not knowing what the upper fort was, he could make no estimate of the situation. He feared that the Confederate forces at Bowling Green might suddenly be thrown upon Grant! The whole East lay in the same depressed fog. Then suddenly came Grant's announcement of the capture of the forts, throwing Lincoln's secretaries into transports of joy, and filling the streets of New York and Philadelphia with jubilant men.

"The effect was electrical," states Charles A. Dana. "It was the first significant victory over the rebellion, and filled the country as well as the army which gained it with confidence and enthusiasm; yet the Government and its military chiefs were amazed. They could hardly understand that this unknown man and undisciplined army had gained such an advantage over the public enemy, while the Army of the Potomac, with its perfect equipment and organization, its large number of trained officers and its enormous preponderance of force, had not yet begun its forward movement." [46]

And immediately afterward came another Western victory. The Missouri army under Major-General Samuel R. Curtis, 11,000 strong, pressing into northwest Arkansas, met the troops of Ben McCulloch and Sterling Price at Pea Ridge or Elkhorn Tavern. The supreme Confederate command lay with a dashing harum-scarum West Pointer, Major-General Earl Van Dorn, whose 14,000 men included 3,500 Indian warriors. The Missouri and Arkansas troops, both ill armed, failed to coordinate their movements, while the Indians broke in panic under artillery fire. Van Dorn reorganized the Confederate remnants at Van Buren, for Halleck ordered Curtis not to push far into Arkansas. [47]

Grant found the Donelson campaign a personal triumph, for his energy and judgment were primary elements in its success; and he sent an unwontedly jubilant letter to Congressman Washburne. Our volunteers, he wrote, "fought a battle that would figure well with many of those fought in Europe where large standing armies are maintained. I feel very greatful [*sic*] to you for having placed me in the position to have had the honor of commanding such an army and at such a time. I only trust that I have not nor will not disappoint you." [48] His unconditional-surrender dispatch to Buckner caught the imagination of the North. Millions applauded a man who could write: "I propose to move immediately on your works." The foundation stone was laid for the fame of a national hero. For the moment, Grant found but one bitter drop in his cup, the jealous pique of Halleck. He resented

46 Nicolay, February 17, 1862, to his wife, *Nicolay Papers*, LC; Dana in N. Y. *Sun*, July 24, 1885.
47 For Pea Ridge, see *Battles and Leaders*, I, 289–334; it was fought March 7–8.
48 To Elihu Washburne, February 21, 1862, Grant-Washburne Papers, Ill. State Lib.

to the end of his life the telegram Halleck sent Washington on the 19th awarding the victory to another, and by implication censuring Grant's leadership: "Smith, by his coolness and bravery at Fort Donelson, when the battle was against us, turned the tide and carried the enemy's outworks. Make him a major-general. You cannot get a better one. Honor him for his victory, and the whole country will applaud." [49] This was the old-army prejudice against Grant and admiration of Smith, along with a vein of petty jealousy that was Halleck's own.

For Halleck lost no time in arrogating the chief glory of the victory to himself and seizing precedence of Buell. The day after Buckner's surrender he telegraphed McClellan: "Make Buell, Grant, and Pope major-generals of volunteers, and give me the command in the West. I ask this in return for Donelson and Henry." Three days later he added: "I must have command of the armies in the West. Hesitation and delay are losing us the golden opportunities. Lay this before the President and Secretary of War. May I assume the command? Answer quickly." [50]

Golden opportunities! Halleck was the last man in the army with a right to talk of them. A fumbling leader before battle, he was always at his worst after one. He could exhibit sheer genius in making a victory less profitable than a sharp defeat. Beyond question, had he now vigorously pressed a Union advance all along the line, the richest fruits might have been garnered. Grant's army had been reinforced at Donelson to 27,000. Buell in Nashville had 15,000 to 20,000. Additional troops could be brought in from Ohio, Indiana, Illinois, and Iowa. For the time being the Confederate armies were disorganized, demoralized, and separated. The Union thrust into central Tennessee had cut squarely between Johnston's force, which fell back to Murfreesboro, and Beauregard's army at Jackson, Tennessee.[51] Grant, drawing on Pope in Missouri for troops, might march westward at once against the Confederates at Hickman on the Mississippi; or might join Buell at Nashville and enable that general to push Johnston back into northern Alabama.

If Grant did march west to the Mississippi, he might cut off the retreat of the Confederates who were evacuating Columbus, for Leonidas Polk, commanding there, had fewer than 15,000 badly armed, badly officered men. Even greater possibilities existed. While Buell immobilized Johnston at Murfreesboro, Grant might rapidly push on up the Tennessee River to northern Mississippi, seize the Memphis & Charleston Railroad there, and march west along the line to take Memphis itself. All the points on the

49 O. R., I, vii, 637; M. F. Force, *From Fort Henry to Corinth*, 64, 65. Halleck, graduating at West Point in 1839, with Smith a favorite instructor, had taught several years under Smith as head of the Academy.
50 O. R., I, vii, 628, 641.
51 Roman, *Beauregard*, I, 233.

Mississippi north of Memphis—Fort Pillow, Hickman, Island No. 10, Columbus, New Madrid—would at once fall. Polk's 15,000 troops would join their Donelson comrades in Northern prison camps. As Vicksburg was still hardly fortified, even that city might lie open to capture.[52]

Indeed, Grant declared later that by swift steps the whole West might have been subjugated. In his opinion, a determined leader, using all the troops west of the Alleghenies, could have captured Memphis, Corinth, and Chattanooga, and have taken Vicksburg. Volunteers were coming forward steadily in the Northwest. These wide seizures of Confederate territory would have stimulated enlistment, and prevented the recruiting of tens of thousands of able-bodied young men into the Southern ranks. "Providence ruled differently," wrote Grant long afterward. "Time was given the enemy to collect armies and fortify his new positions; and twice afterwards he came near forcing the northwestern front up to the Ohio River."[53] But for a brief hour Northerners who saw what *might* be done believed the end near. "After this, it certainly cannot be materially postponed," declared the New York *Times* of February 14, 1862. "The monster is already clutched and in his death struggle." Alas, that hope faded.

Why did it fade? For one reason, because for three critical weeks the high Western command remained divided between Halleck in St. Louis and Buell in his new post at Nashville, making unitary action practically impossible. For another reason, because Buell showed excessive caution. He no sooner arrived in Nashville than he indulged in McClellanesque exaggerations of enemy strength. He sent C. F. Smith a panicky telegram on February 25: "If the enemy should assume the offensive . . . my force at present is altogether inadequate." Smith justly termed this nonsense. Grant, who immediately visited Nashville, found it impossible to persuade Buell that he was in no danger. The enemy, Grant said, is retreating as fast as his legs can carry him. When Buell denied this, asserting that the enemy were fighting only ten or twelve miles southeast of Nashville, as if they meant to return, Grant rejoined sharply: "Quite probably; Nashville contained valuable stores of arms, ammunition, and provisions, and the enemy is probably trying to carry away all he can. The fighting is doubtless with the rear guard who are trying to protect the trains they are getting away with."[54]

The principal reason why the chance of overrunning the whole Western

52   So says Beauregard, who knew the situation; Roman, I, 234. The head of the Vicksburg police, M. Emmanuel, wrote the governor Nov. 27, 1861, that the city was "defenceless" against an invasion; Pettus Corr., Alabama State Archives. Grenville M. Dodge wrote Horace White, Aug. 5, 1909: "There is no question but if Grant's advice had been followed right after Donelson and Buell's army had joined him and without halting marched to Vicksburg, they would have taken it"; White Papers, Ill. State Lib.

53   Grant, *Memoirs*, Ch. II.

54   Grant, *Memoirs*, Ch. IX.

theater slipped away, however, was that Halleck never perceived it. The day before Donelson capitulated he had written McClellan: "I have no definite plan beyond the taking of Fort Donelson and Clarksville." [55] Before March ended, Grant, Buell, Pope, C. F. Smith, and Lew Wallace all received major-generalcies. On March 11, meanwhile, Halleck obtained command of the Department of the Mississippi. The whole valley was his; he could move the generals like knights on a board stretching from Arkansas to Chattanooga and Atlanta. But he had no program whatever for moving them and never held a serious consultation with any of them. Though it was his business to look far ahead, neither to the War Department nor to his subordinates did he specify what steps were to be taken. With the gates to the heart of the South thrown ajar, he paused outside.

"Transports will be sent you as soon as possible," he telegraphed Grant on March 1, "to move your column up the Tennessee River." But for what? Grant was merely to destroy by swift dashes a railroad bridge near Eastport, Mississippi, and rail connections at Corinth, Mississippi, and Jackson, Tennessee, and then fall back. "Avoid any general engagements with strong forces," enjoined Halleck. "It will be better to retreat than to risk a general battle. This should be strongly impressed upon the officers sent with expedition from the river."

And Halleck and McClellan between them came near dismissing the general with ignominy. "I have had no communication with General Grant for more than a week," Halleck informed McClellan March 3. "He left his command without my authority and went to Nashville." He added that Grant's army seemed demoralized. "I can get no returns, no reports, no information of any kind from him. Satisfied with his victory, he sits down and enjoys it without any regard to the future. I am worn out and tired with this neglect and inefficiency." McClellan telegraphed in reply: "Do not hesitate to arrest Grant at once if the good of the service requires it, and place C. F. Smith in command." On the 4th Halleck told McClellan he had heard "a rumor" that since Donelson, Grant had resumed drinking. He simultaneously placed C. F. Smith in command of the Tennessee River expedition, ordered Grant to remain at Fort Henry, where he was kept almost a week under virtual arrest, and sharply rebuked him. The difficulty actually lay with communications. Grant had written the chief of staff every day, reported every move, and gone to Nashville solely for the good of the service. "If my course is not satisfactory," he telegraphed Halleck, "remove me at once." [56]

---

55 O. R., I, vii, 616.
56 For this exchange of messages see O. R., I, vii, 679–682; Badeau, I, 59–69; Records U. S. Military Telegraph, National Archives; Grant-Washburne Coll., Ill. State Hist. Lib.

Halleck continued to nag Grant and to caution him and Smith against any general battle. The expedition up the Tennessee, crippled by his orders, accomplished nothing. It is difficult to avoid the suspicion that Halleck was jealous of Grant's achievements. Well might he be! Long afterward, one of the wisest Confederate soldiers was to write: "To my mind the Southern Confederacy died at Donelson." [57]

[VII]

During the four weeks in which his eleven-year-old son Willie sickened and died Lincoln was increasingly distraught and unnerved. The bright, gentle boy had been a ray of sunshine in the White House. When the ordeal ended on February 20, the President, who for some days had been almost incommunicado, resumed sorrowfully his postponed undertakings, of which the compensated emancipation scheme was chief.

In a message on March 6 he asked Congress to adopt a joint resolution: "Resolved, that the United States ought to cooperate with any State which may adopt gradual abolishment of slavery, giving to such State pecuniary aid, to be used by such State in its discretion, to compensate for the inconveniences, public and private, produced by such change of system." [58] He argued that the mere initiation of a gradual scheme in some or all of the Border States would do much to shorten the struggle, for it would cut off from Confederate leaders the hope that they could ever win that area. Other considerations played a part in his stroke. It enabled him to test the sentiment of slaveholders from the Chesapeake to the Missouri; it would temporarily quiet the radicals; and it advertised to the country two of his basic principles—that while the eventual extinction of slavery must be accepted, the work should be gradual, and the whole nation should bear the cost.

Lincoln sent his secretaries to fetch Charles Sumner to the White House early on March 6. "I want to read you my message," he told the Senator. "I want to know how you like it." As he finished, Sumner seized the paper to con it closely. He did not like the word "abolishment"—which is good English—and objected to one sentence bearing on reconstruction, which Lincoln struck out. When he asked what the Cabinet thought, Lincoln told him that they had all heard it read the previous evening, and all, including Seward, Bates, and even Caleb Smith, liked it. Sumner related later: "Well, I sat with it in my hands, reading it over and not bearing to give it up, but

57 John A. Wyeth, N. Y., Nov. 14, 1905, to J. W. DuBose, DuBose Papers, Ala. State Archives.
58 *Cong. Globe,* 37th Cong., 2d Sess., 1102, 1103.

he said, 'There, now, you've read it enough, run away. I must send it in today.' " [59] His secretaries took it at once to the Capitol.

The message pleased all but the most indurated conservatives and fanatic radicals.[60] Most of the press and pulpit gave it hearty praise. If Congress approved the resolution, said the New York *Times*, it would loom up as a landmark in American history, for the government would have declared in favor of freedom and of the use of national funds to promote it; Lincoln had hit "the happy mean." The *Evening Post* was delighted; so was the *Tribune;* and so, measurably, was the eccentric *Herald.* Greeley in an article in the *Independent* declared that the step placed Lincoln at the head of the nation, and would deter foreign powers from intervention. The *World* published a long editorial commending Lincoln's moderation and foresight. The Washington *National Republican* gave him full support. It is evidence of Lincoln's earnestness that he placed copies of these comments in these papers; and he furnished additional evidence when, replying to some doubts by Henry J. Raymond over the cost, he pointed out that charges for eighty-seven days of war would pay for all the slaves in Maryland, Delaware, Kentucky, Missouri, and the District at $400 each.[61]

Thaddeus Stevens summed up the bitter condemnation of the plan by abolitionists: "the most diluted, milk-and-water gruel proposition that was ever given to the American nation." [62] On the other side, reactionaries were hoarse with denunciation. They opposed it as vehemently as the confiscation bill. Democratic opponents quickly adopted the argument of the Cincinnati *Enquirer*, which asserted that after the President spent a billion dollars to buy freedom for the slaves, a great part of the freed Negroes would then come North, to be supported as paupers at public expense, or to compete with white laborers and thus take the bread from white children's mouths. Frank P. Blair, Jr., made a speech in the House April 11 which, aimed at border sentiment, angered great elements in the North. He denied that the war was a slaveholders' rebellion, and declared that emancipation would be a terrible mistake until arrangements could be made to colonize the Negroes abroad; they could not be sent back to Africa, but they could be shipped to areas south of the Rio Grande and settled under Federal protection. His indiscreet action did

59 E. E. Hale, *Memories of a Hundred Years*, II, 189–196.
60 T. D. Woolsey, president of Yale, wrote that Lincoln had acted gloriously in bringing slavery before the country in a way to allay agitation by both extremes; April 12, 1862, Lieber Papers, HL.
61 The N. Y. *Evening Post* published a full compendium of opinion in an article, "The Emancipation Movement: Its Progress in the Border Slave States," May 16, 1862. The Phila. *Evening Journal*, a moderate Democratic sheet, and the Wash. *National Intelligencer* were warm in praise.
62 *Cong. Globe*, 37th Cong., 2d Sess., 1154.

the Administration real harm in all circles friendly to the Negro and his early liberation. Both at home and abroad, many people agreed with the London *Times* of May 7, 1862, that the idea of forcible colonization was immoral.

The real test of the plan, it was evident, would come in the Border States, where its fate was doubtful. A Republican Congress could not fail to toe the mark; on March 11 the House passed Lincoln's resolution 97 to 36, and on April 2 the Senate followed, 32 to 10. The contest was on party lines, all but two Democratic Senators and four Democratic Representatives voting no. But while it was easy for Congress to act, in the Border States a battle royal lay ahead. While that struggle began, all eyes were turned to the battlefront in Virginia.

2

Stanton, McClellan, and the Virginia Front

VICTORY in the Virginia theater depended on three men: Lincoln, Stanton, and McClellan. The first two were eager to see the third give battle. "Now, gentlemen," said Stanton at his first reception to officers, "we will, if you please, have some fighting. It is my business to furnish the means, it is yours to use them. I leave the fighting to you, but the fighting we must have." [1]

Stanton's accession had been almost as unexpected by him as it was sudden. He had not spoken to Lincoln between the inauguration and the day the President handed him his commission. That the labors of his office would crush him he well understood. "I knew that everything I cherish and hold dear would be sacrificed," he wrote a friend four months later. "But I thought I might help to save the country, and for that I was willing to perish." [2]

Visitors at the War Department saw a short, sturdily built man whose broad shoulders bore a massive head, looking bigger still because of his heavy black beard and flowing dark hair. His full face, large, brilliant eyes, and flattish nose gave him a Socratic aspect. His forehead was broad though not high, his mouth firm and tightly compressed, and his general expression intensely serious. He exhaled an air of vigor, earnestness, and sternness. No other member of the Cabinet was so severely impressive. From his deep chest came a voice not only resonant but surprisingly musical. Though on occasion his gray eyes twinkled behind his large round spectacles, and his lips softened into an engaging smile, he was usually so intensely absorbed in his work that he bore a fiercely imperious aspect. When angered, his eyes blazed as he jerked out a harsh retort or a rebuke that made subordinates quail. He antagonized most of the people who did business with him. Don't

1 Donn Piatt, *Men Who Saved the Union*, 61.
2 To the Rev. Heman Dyer, May 18, 1862, Stanton Papers; N. Y. *Sun*, Dec. 25, 1869. McClellan, soon to change his mind, was delighted by the event, writing S. L. M. Barlow, "Stanton's appointment was a most unexpected piece of good fortune, and I hope it will produce a good effect in the North"; Barlow Papers, Jan. 18, 1862.

send me to Stanton to ask favors, John Hay once begged Nicolay: "I would rather make a tour of a smallpox hospital." [3] But he could inspire as well as terrify associates, and the affluent beauty of his language when he was moved would delight all hearers. It was no accident that perhaps the two most memorable sentences ever uttered upon Lincoln came from Stanton's lips.[4]

A dictatorial, arbitrary quality so consistently ruled Stanton that most men thought him a tyrant. He loved power, seldom brooked opposition, and showed an enjoyment of authority that struck—and offended—all who came in his path. The result was that Grant, Sherman, Gideon Welles, Seward, Lincoln's secretaries, and others have etched the lines of a caustic portrait. His arbitrary temper was accentuated by his tendency to jump to conclusions. He would impetuously take a stand just to prove his authority, as he did early in the war in trying to destroy the invaluable Sanitary Commission. It was accentuated also by his intolerant, vindictive nursing of prejudices and grudges. He almost never admitted himself wrong, tried to see a situation from an antagonist's eye, or showed generosity to a foe either victorious or defeated.

Few acts of the war were more outrageous than his treatment of General Charles P. Stone after Ball's Bluff, ordering the arrest, prejudging the case, delaying justice, and offering no regrets. He sometimes showed the capricious malignity of other despotic-tempered autocrats: Frederick the Great, Napoleon III, Stalin. His harsh treatment of unprotected men was the more glaring because he cautiously gauged the strength of those whose power and prestige surpassed his own. He took good care not to assail Congressional leaders like Wade, Stevens, and Sumner, treated powerful governors like Morton or Andrew respectfully, and was scrupulous not to press the patient Lincoln too far. Once he refused to obey an order of Lincoln's. "Mr. Secretary, I reckon you'll have to obey it," said Lincoln—and he did.[5]

At times an apparent duplicity seemed to actuate this fierce, ill-governed, dynamic executive. He burned with envy of his peers, for his thirst for authority, as James G. Blaine writes, was subject to its counterpart of jealousy. Gideon Welles never regarded him as trustworthy. Not merely did Welles shrink from a man who could be rude and domineering toward subordinates,

3 Helen Nicolay, "Lincoln's Cabinet," *Abraham Lincoln Quarterly*, V (March, 1949), 282; sketch in Fanny Seward's MS Diary, April 5, 1862; A. E. H. Johnson, "Rems. of Stanton," *Columbia Hist. Soc. Records*, XIII, 69–97 (1910).

4 Late in the Administration, "There goes the greatest ruler of men who ever lived"; at the deathbed, "Now he belongs to the ages." But while still uninformed, Stanton wrote Buchanan of Lincoln's "painful imbecility."

5 Provost-Marshal Fry has preserved the whole colloquy about this order, which related to prisoners of war; A. K. McClure, *Lincoln and Men of War-Times*, 185. McClure describes Stanton's brutally senseless imprisonment of a Pittsburgher; 177–181 (edition pages vary).

while a sycophantic dissembler with those he feared; the Secretary of the
Navy thought him a two-faced intriguer. That view was shortly taken also
by McClellan, who became convinced that Stanton was worse than Judas
Iscariot. It was taken by many more, down to the time when President
Andrew Johnson dismissed him for what he held to be barefaced treachery.
General Ethan Allen Hitchcock, however, a close observer inside the War
Department, and a man who detested his brutality and violence, declared
that Stanton was not a man of reason.[6] "He decides a point one day in one
way; and a week after (forgetting his decision and having no principle) he
will decide the same point in another way. [Then] he flies into a passion with
someone for having followed his first decision; and his fits of passion almost always break out upon a few individuals, against whom, without any
cause, he has conceived some prejudice."

A. K. McClure of Pennsylvania, who admired him greatly, declared that
he was capable of the grandest and basest actions alike. In this he was almost another Bacon, "the wisest, noblest, meanest of mankind." Only a
psychoanalyst possessing the fullest data could really explain his combination
of glaring weaknesses and brilliant virtues. A vein of hysteria amounting
to partial insanity had repeatedly appeared in his early career. After his
brother's suicide he had to be guarded against the same act; the loss of his
baby daughter had thrown him into a frenzy; and the death of his first wife
so prostrated him that for a month he could hardly be dragged from her
grave. Even in 1862 he was still easily overwrought. Numerous military men,
including Grant, believed that he was both morally and physically timid
in the hour of danger. Grant bluntly declares that, conscious of Union
weakness but ignoring that of the Confederates, he wished to keep protective
armies much nearer Washington than was proper. It is not strange that observers, seeing him in one of his sudden rages, hearing him sputter insults
or launch unfounded accusations, or watching him in a brief access of panic,
concluded that he was partially demented.[7]

One almost lifelong intimate, Donn Piatt, writes of him as rendered fiercely
aggressive by "disease that overwhelmed his nervous system," and this same

6 Blaine, *Twenty Years*, I, 563; Welles, *Diary*, I, 129; McClellan, *Own Story*, 137; Diary
of E. A. Hitchcock, W. A. Croffut Papers, LC. Hitchcock wrote Henry H. Hitchcock,
April 25, 1862: "He is coarse in the use of language and insulting in the mode of address
towards those he dislikes, and his dislikes are mere prejudices. . . ."; Hitchcock Papers,
Mo. Hist. Soc. But Horace White, who served in the War Department, states in an undated memorandum: "During all the time I was in Mr. Stanton's office I was never subjected to any ill treatment, roughness, or even impatience at his hands, although I witnessed
such treatment visited by him upon others more than once."

7 See Burton J. Hendrick, *Lincoln's War Cabinet*, 241 ff., for material on Stanton's private
life; Welles, *Diary*, I, 64–66, for Stanton's behavior during the *Merrimac* scare; Grant,
Memoirs, II, 537, for his timidity.

observer speaks of Stanton as "furious almost to insanity over the failures of his generals." [8] Two heads of the Sanitary Commission, Henry W. Bellows and George Templeton Strong, concluded that he suffered from cerebral disease. Admiral D. D. Porter received the same impression when, after the capture of Fort Fisher, Stanton kissed him! Generals, Cabinet members, newspapermen, disliked or detested him. Why, then, must he be called one of the chief architects of victory?

His abilities were great and they were combative abilities. Whether because of his timidity, his ambition, or his fierce nervous ardor, he battled savagely. In his career at the bar he had played the part not of an interpreter of legal principles but of a courtroom fighter, using every weapon within reach. He had achieved his widest popular fame when he got Daniel Sickles acquitted of the murder of Philip Barton Key on the ground of temporary insanity. Becoming Attorney-General just before Christmas in 1860, he had done the country unforgettable service in his adamant stand against the disunionist plotters in Buchanan's cabinet; he had written the resolution authorizing a House committee that winter to investigate clandestine plots against the government; and he had kept Seward informed of everything that went on in Buchanan's circle. In short, he had been a stubborn champion of the Union in the darkest months of its history. He had dealt with treason and stratagem without mercy. His patriotism was of the most unflinching kind. Now in 1862 he found joy in fighting both the Confederates and the sinister men who stalked in the shadowy byways of Washington. The battle he was waging was demanded, he felt, by every interest of the nation, of civilization, and of God. "I believe that God Almighty founded the government, and for my acts in the effort to maintain it I expect to stand before Him in judgment."

This was no pretense, for he was fervently religious. An associate, entering his office unexpectedly, found him with head bowed on his desk, in a passion of tears, muttering over and over: "God help me to do my duty! God help me to do my duty!" Nevertheless, he loved battle for its own sake. He liked to deal blows and see their effect. And he never lost courage, for he never doubted the end. [9]

This faith steeled him, while suffering paroxysms of asthma, to endure more grueling labor than perhaps any other leader, North or South, put into the conflict. As an attorney he had become famous for his tremendous industry in mastering the law and facts, and in marshaling his arguments.

8 Piatt, *Men Who Saved the Union*, 88 ff.; Strong, *Diary*, III, 226, May 15, 1862; Porter, *Incidents and Anecdotes*, 279.

9 Dana, *Recs. of the Civil War*, 161 ff.; Henry Wilson, "E. M. Stanton," *Atlantic*, xxv (February, 1870), 234–246.

Investigating California land titles for the government, he had carried his search of Mexican archives and other sources to the deepest level. In the War Department he now toiled day and night mastering the details of business. His carriage would come in the small hours, but he still kept it waiting. Often he stayed the entire night at his post; "receiving reports, requests, information, and suggestions by telegraph and mail," writes Henry Wilson, "holding personal consultations with military and civil officers of the government, and others having business, and issuing orders." As he expected bureau heads to keep pace, his department became a center of such unceasing, anxious labor that those who did not possess his physical endurance, powers of concentration, and iron will sank under the strain. Peter H. Watson, his best Assistant Secretary, a strong man, soon quit office quite worn out; his successor Walcott shortly went home to die; and Charles A. Dana, who followed, held on only because his eyes would not let him work at night, while the appointment of a solicitor to the department reduced his labors.

Like Lincoln, he never took a vacation, and unlike the President, never relaxed in informal talk or over a humorous book.

Stanton's industry was matched by executive genius. His decisions were rapid, his purposes inflexible, and his readiness to take the largest responsibilities unhesitating. When Morton of Indiana required more than $250,000 for war purposes which the legislature failed to appropriate, Stanton grasped the situation instantly and drew his warrant on the Treasury for the sum. If the cause fails, warned Morton, we shall land in jail. "If the cause fails," responded Stanton, "I do not wish to live." His instinct for system, method, and orderliness amounted to a passion. Finding the basic military arrangements of the nation in a clutter, he gave them pattern and harmony. His consolidation of regiments irritated State and local pride; no matter, it was sternly directed. His sweeping military censorship stung the press to violent protest; with scathing words on editors who would ruin an army to print a good news story, he maintained it. He gave the War Department practical control over the whole telegraph system of the country, Thomas T. Eckert, David Homer Bates, and other able young men manning the instruments in a room adjoining his own day and night. In that nerve center of the North, Lincoln spent much time. Stanton's rule that every military or political telegram on all the various wires, even a message from Lincoln, even a general's communication to his wife, must be read there, angered many leaders. Grant, deeming the delay intolerable, ultimately circumvented the rule. On the whole, however, it promoted efficiency.[10]

10 Dana, *Wilson, ut sup.;* W. D. Foulke, *Morton,* I, 260–261; A. E. H. Johnson, Stanton's confidential clerk, Wash. *Post,* July 14, 1891, in McClure, *op. cit.,* 176; D. H. Bates, *Lincoln in the Telegraph Office,* Chs. VIII–XVII.

His courage, which did much to earn him his reputation for cantankerous ill temper, was unflinching. He met politicians, generals, and businessmen in the open, rapping out his answers for all to hear. One reporter saw him dispatch man after man, more than two hundred in a five-hour period. More than once he literally shoved a rascal out of his office. His stern sudden judgments were sometimes wrong; his rule that his desk must be cleared every night meant rough surgery on complex problems; he could be outrageously unjust to other strong men who rasped him, like Surgeon-General Hammond. But, meeting slovenliness, stupidity, and dishonesty on every hand, he was like a powerful swimmer tangled in marsh grass; he had to lash out or be drowned. His blazes of anger were particularly fierce when he suspected selfishness or crookedness. In a nation of improvisation, of rule-of-thumb, Stanton thought of himself as conducting a one-man war for plan and foresight. With the country's life in the balance, slackness and clumsiness became crimes. He rapidly developed a scathing contempt for the cautious McClellan, the dilatory Buell, and the hesitant Rosecrans.[11] The arrogant ways of Little Mac grated upon his sense that the cause was everything, the individual nothing. Soon after he took office he called unexpectedly at McClellan's headquarters, and the general kept him waiting. His secretary, A. E. H. Johnson, reports his furious comment: "That will be the last time General McClellan will give either myself or the President the waiting snub."

All his virtues of industry, system, and courage would have availed nothing without sound judgment; and unquestionably he stood pre-eminent in Lincoln's cabinet for his sturdy common-sense sagacity. He quickly divined the weaknesses of generals who had been his personal friends. He just as quickly grasped the strength of two of the indispensable generals, Grant and Thomas, and gave them support in hours bright and dark. From Donelson to the end of the war his faith in Grant, bolstered by Dana's shrewd report of the man, never wavered; and he pushed the general steadily up the ladder, keeping him in charge of Vicksburg operations when the clamor for removal ran high, giving him Rosecrans' place at Chattanooga with enlarged authority, and urging through Congress the measure which made him head of the armies with the rank of lieutenant-general. His admiration for Thomas was unbounded. He stood by the calm Virginian when, just before the battle of Nashville, many wished to displace him, and he exulted when Thomas vindicated this confidence by one of the most crushing victories of the war.

---

11 Stanton was capable of fine generosity. Piatt, 90, 91, saw him brush aside high military officers to speak to a ragged private, obviously ill, who came to his office. The lad gave him a letter from Ormsby M. Mitchel stating that he was the sole survivor of a heroic band sent south to burn railway bridges. Stanton read it aloud, held it aloft, and exclaimed with emotion: "I would rather be worthy of this letter than have the highest commission in the army of the United States." He promised to make the boy an officer.

But the greatest proof of Stanton's judgment was his perception of the importance of the Western theater, which Cameron had slighted. As quickly as Lincoln, he saw that there the war was destined to be won.[12]

It should be added that Stanton always commanded the confidence of those men whose confidence was indispensable. Watson, Dana, and other office intimates were staunch adherents and admirers. The Congressional military committees always met his wishes and gave his measures firm support. Senator Henry Wilson later counted among his most cherished recollections the fact that no misunderstanding or unkindness ever marred his relations with the Secretary. Grant, while resenting Stanton's interferences with his generals, acknowledged his great powers; the sensitive Thomas, while conscious of some buffets, pronounced him a just man. Above all, the Secretary gained and held the faith of Lincoln, who, late in his Administration, said with feeling: "You have been our main reliance." [13] Indeed, the President spent more time with him than with any other Cabinet member, often stepping from the telegraph room at the War Department to Stanton's adjacent office, and sometimes driving with him to or from their neighboring cottages at the Soldiers' Home near Washington.

The popular supposition at the time that Stanton complemented Lincoln, supplying a firmness and decision which the President lacked, was untrue, for Lincoln needed no complement. But it is true that Lincoln's strength did not lie in careful planning and systematic administration—and Stanton's did. The two sometimes clashed. Stanton not only said cutting things of Lincoln but indulged in contemptuous gestures, as when he tore up a memorandum and tossed it into the wastebasket. But Lincoln was always the master. When he restored McClellan to command after Second Manassas, Stanton made his resentment as plain as did Chase. "No order came from the War Department," he said. "No," replied Lincoln, "I gave the order." That Lincoln soon learned to deem the Secretary indispensable we have ample testimony. He firmly repelled all proposals that Stanton should give way to N. P. Banks, Ben Butler, or some other favorite of the radicals. The two stood firmly together on critical issues. Once a talebearer reported that Stanton had said the President was a fool. "Indeed!" Lincoln replied, "then it must be true, for Stanton is usually right." [14] In general, however, Stanton was wise enough to deal with

12 For Stanton's unfailing support of Grant see Badeau, *Military Hist.*, II, 13 ff. The Secretary did not approve of Sherman's march to the sea, which was open to grave strategic objections, nor did he like Sherman.

13 Flower, *Stanton*, 311. Once when a friend protested against Stanton's brutality of speech, Lincoln replied that they might have to deal with him as some Westerners once dealt with a too-fervent Methodist exhorter, putting bricks in his pockets. "But I guess we'll let him jump awhile first." Mrs. H. B. Stowe, *Men of Our Times*, 370.

14 Julian, *Political Recs.*, 212.

Lincoln tactfully. He thought the President too slow in proclaiming emancipation and arming the Negroes.[15] But his method was to express his opinion forcibly, and leave the rest to time.

"Nor was it his practice," recalled Dana, "pertinaciously to urge upon the President the removal of a general in whom he had confidence no longer. Having fully expressed his opinion to Mr. Lincoln, he would wait until the President had himself come to the same conclusion."

[I]

We have said that Lincoln's Special Order No. 1, directing McClellan to lead his army by February 22 in a flanking movement southwest of Manassas, was meant to force the general to disclose his plans. That was precisely its result. Immediately on receiving it, McClellan wrote Stanton a twenty-two-page letter which for the first time revealed his hand.

Lincoln's proposal was essentially for a movement upon Joseph E. Johnston's army through Manassas, with Washington as base; it was for a direct overland attack. McClellan preferred to move the Union army down the Potomac and up the Rappahannock to a point opposite Richmond, a hamlet called Urbana. His base would be served from Chesapeake Bay. He argued that this course would place the army on the shortest feasible land route to Richmond, and would possess other advantages. The roads on the Urbana-Richmond line were passable at all seasons; the country, being sandy with sparse woods, and enjoying an early spring, was specially favorable to offensive operations; while a march in force southwest from Urbana would cut off Magruder's troops on the Peninsula, compel a quick evacuation of Manassas, and enable him to reach Richmond before it was reinforced. Failing that, he could, with the aid of the Navy, cross the James and attack Richmond from the rear. "Worst coming to worst," he could take Fort Monroe as base, and "operate with complete security," though with less brilliancy of result, up the Peninsula. He specially stressed the superior celerity of his plan. If the army used Washington as a base to advance through Manassas, it would have to wait until the roads, as yet sloughs of mud, dried, but if it moved by the roads of the lower Chesapeake area, it could calculate its march "almost to a day, and with but little regard to the season." [16]

This letter possibly still lay on Stanton's desk, but had more probably been shown to Lincoln, when the President on February 3 sent McClellan

---

15 Cf. Eaton, *Grant, Lincoln, and the Freedmen*, 179.
16 McClellan's long letter bears date Feb. 3, 1862; text in O. R., I, v, 41 ff.; with previously unpublished passages, Lincoln, *Works*, V, 119 ff.

some piercing inquiries. In a few lines he went to the heart of the issue between them. He would gladly yield his plan for an advance based on Washington and accept McClellan's if he could get five questions satisfactorily answered:

1st. Does not your plan involve a greatly larger expenditure of *time*, and *money*, than mine?
2nd. Wherein is a victory *more certain* by your plan than mine?
3rd. Wherein is a victory *more valuable* by your plan than mine?
4th. In fact, would it not be *less* valuable, in this, that it would break no great line of the enemy's communications, while mine would?
5th. In case of disaster, would not a safe retreat be more difficult by your plan than mine?

The point as to breaking the enemy's communications deserves emphasis. Johnston's army had two main railroad lines connecting it with the body of the Confederacy: one from Richmond southeast to Wilmington, one southwest to Lynchburg; the first of limited use for military operations, the second almost indispensable. The mere capture of Richmond would effect little except the seizure of some valuable works, notably the Tredegar iron mills, and a blow to Confederate morale at home and prestige abroad. Lincoln proposed a movement from the northwest on Richmond which would cut the lifeline to Lynchburg; McClellan, a campaign from the east which would leave the western escape route open.

The reasons why Lincoln demurred to McClellan's plan actually ran beyond the queries here stated. He and Stanton naturally accepted the general's estimates of formidable enemy strength. Pinkerton, chief of McClellan's intelligence service, placed the Confederate force in northern Virginia at 115,500 men, with 300 field guns and 26 to 30 siege guns.[17] They were reluctant to leave Washington unprotected by the departure of the main Union army while Johnston lay near with such great numbers. Lincoln had the support of McDowell for his plan. McClellan made no written response to his queries, and it is possible that he replied orally in a personal conference with the President; it is also possible that he did not, for Lincoln remained anxiously perplexed.

Unfortunately, Lincoln's three possible courses really boiled down to one. He could force McClellan to adopt a plan which the general believed might prove disastrous; he could remove McClellan while as yet he had no successor available; or he could yield. In deep distress, he gave way. On February 14 the War Department called for proposals to furnish transports,

17 Pinkerton's report of March 8, 1862; Greeley, *Amer. Conflict*, II, 129. Actually Confederate reports for the Potomac district Jan. 22 show the aggregate present as 24,882—though other forces lay in the Shenandoah and at Aquia; O. R. I, v, 1040.

and on the 27th ordered its agents to begin buying steamers and sailing ships. Lincoln told McClellan that his plan had been accepted, with its details still to be fixed.[18]

Stanton and other Cabinet members, in talking with Lincoln, saw how apprehensive he was over the removal of the great army which shielded Washington. The President suggested minor movements which would make the capital safer, such as the sending of N. P. Banks's division in Maryland across the Potomac against Winchester to open the Baltimore & Ohio. Mc-Clellan went up to Harpers Ferry to superintend Banks's stroke. His plan was to bring canal boats through the Chesapeake & Ohio Canal locks to that point, and use them for a pontoon bridge. But on the night of February 27 Stanton came to Lincoln's office with a dispatch from the general. The canal boats had been found six inches too wide to pass the locks! McClellan sent word that he could not build the bridge before Winchester was reinforced.

"What does this mean?" demanded Lincoln.

"It means," said Stanton, "that it is a damned fizzle. It means that he doesn't intend to do anything."

Lincoln was deeply dejected. Seward arrived, and the three held a long conference. They sent for Marcy, McClellan's chief of staff. The President addressed him with manifest anger.

"Why in the nation, General Marcy," he demanded, "couldn't the general have known whether a boat would go through that lock before spending a million dollars getting them there? I am no engineer, but it seems to me that if I wished to know whether a boat would go through a hole or lock, common sense would teach me to go and measure it. I am almost despairing at these results. Everything seems to fail. The impression is daily gaining ground that the general does not intend to do anything." As Marcy expostulated, Lincoln abruptly ended the interview. Marcy telegraphed McClellan that the President "was in a hell of a rage."[19] Perhaps Chase's thrust, "The expedition died of lockjaw," best summarized the episode.

It is plain that early in March, Lincoln and Stanton actually feared that some ulterior motive might lie behind McClellan's delays. Radical editors and Congressmen were intimating a sinister purpose. The general did not wish the South severely defeated, they said; he wanted the Union restored without emancipation, and without centralization of national power. When As-

18 Ropes, *Civil War*, I, 233; Nicolay, *Lincoln's Secretary*, Ch. XII. McClellan says in *My Own Story*, 237, that he held many conferences with Lincoln at this time. But since the evening when he went to bed leaving the President waiting downstairs, Lincoln required him to come to the White House.

19 Nicolay, *Lincoln's Secretary*, 142–144, for the Lincoln-Stanton-Marcy meeting; Horace White to Medill, March 3, 1862, on Marcy's telegram, C. H. Ray Papers, HL. The WPA *Washington Guide*, 486, gives a photograph of Lock No. 5.

sistant Secretary Watson had told him the previous November that unrestricted war was a necessity and the South must be subjugated, McClellan dissented, declaring that the North must avoid harshness and give the South as little offense as possible. "If I felt as you do," he informed Watson, "I would lay down my arms!"

Greeley was now accusing the McClellanites of seeking a compromise solution. By a war all expense and little fighting, they would make the exhausted, discouraged North "ready to buy a peace of Jeff Davis by almost any possible surrender." Congressman Gurley told Washington dinner parties that McClellan was a traitor, and Ben Wade went almost as far. Count Gurowski was writing Governor Andrew that if McClellan won a victory he would "throw off the mask and become champion of the preservation of slavery and of general amnesty to the traitors." Radical wrath rose when McClellan barred the Hutchinson Family singers from the army camps because their repertoire included such material as Whittier's "Hymn of Liberty," declaring that slavery whetted the knife for the nation's life. It was heightened when on Washington's Birthday the general appeared before the House to receive strong Democratic applause. Even the mild Seward was so disgusted with McClellan that after the canal boat episode he thought Lincoln generous in keeping him in command.[20]

As for Stanton, he had rapidly lost all confidence in McClellan. In a letter to Dana he spoke resentfully of the recent "ridiculous and impertinent effort" of S. L. M. Barlow at a railroad convention in the capital "to puff the General by a false publication of words I never uttered." He was irritated because a coterie of newspapermen representing the Associated Press, the *Herald*, and other agencies were magnifying McClellan. Still more was he outraged by the general's efforts to claim Grant's Western laurels. "Was it not a funny sight to see a certain military hero in the telegraph office at Washington last Sunday organizing victory, and by sublime military combinations capturing Fort Donelson *six hours after* Grant and Smith had taken it sword in hand and had victorious possession!" He, too, thought Lincoln generous in allowing McClellan to keep his command. As a matter of fact, Lincoln called the general to the White House on March 8 to rebuke his negligence and explain some new orders. During their talk he referred to McClellan's Chesapeake

20 N. Y. *Tribune*, Jan. 18, 1862, for Greeley's comment; Bates's *Diary*, 253, on Gurley and Wade; *Battles and Leaders*, II, 122, for McClellan before the House; Chase, *Diary and Corr.*, 50, 51, for McClellan's statement to Watson; Gurowski, March 1, 1862, Andrew Papers.

Seward never accepted McClellan's estimates of enemy strength. He told Sam Ward on March 26 that he did not believe the South had as many men in Virginia and thereabouts as New York had, or that there had been more than 30,000 at any time during the past three months. Ward, March 27, 1862, to S. L. M. Barlow, Barlow Papers.

plan as suggesting a "traitorous" intention of leaving Washington open to the foe. When McClellan quite properly resented the word, Lincoln explained that he did not use it himself, but that the circumstances wore a dark look, and others placed an ugly interpretation on them.[21]

This meeting, of which McClellan gives us all too brief a record, was a curious—and an ominous—episode. We may be sure that Lincoln measured his words carefully. Knowing how often McClellan had expressed the characteristic contempt of the military mind for politicians, he doubtless meant to remind him of the paramount rights of the civil authority, and of the fact that politicians also have their prejudices and suspicions. It is also probable that, suspecting that McClellan might really intend to strike cushioned blows, he wished to clear the air between them and make sure of his purposes. But his candor evoked no response. The two men parted without any enlargement of mutual confidence.

While acceding to McClellan's Chesapeake plan, Lincoln felt a lingering mistrust, and was determined to keep vigilant watch over the general's actions. Stanton, who made a similar resolve, told the Cabinet that McClellan as general-in-chief had required all army reports to be made to him, and then had kept the War Department in the dark, giving it neither information nor plans. It was partly for this reason that the Secretary insisted on the transmission of all telegrams through the War Department.[22] Still tormented by doubt, Lincoln directed McClellan to hold a conference of division commanders on the Chesapeake plan. Four generals, McDowell, Heintzelman, Sumner, and Barnard, voted against it, and eight supported it, though Keyes did so on condition that the Potomac batteries be first reduced. This was decisive, and Lincoln tacitly admitted as much.

But the President nevertheless restricted McClellan's execution of his plan by three orders of March 8. The first directed that the Army of the Potomac be divided into four corps, and nominated to their command Generals McDowell, Heintzelman, Sumner, and Keyes. Three of these men had

---

21 Memorandum by McClellan, W. S. Myers, *McClellan*, 245, 246.
22 The able Gen. James S. Wadsworth wrote Bryant that it was outrageous that McClellan with 135,000 men and 43 batteries had not advanced against the far weaker enemy; that the dreary inaction had dispirited the army; that the general never consulted any division commanders south of the Potomac save Fitz-John Porter; and that it was as impossible to move the army without dividing it into corps as it was impossible to move divisions without dividing them into regiments. McClellan seemed to think they were facing an army of British or French veterans instead of a hastily trained, inadequately equipped enemy. "Is it possible to account for all these errors on the theory of incompetence alone? Is there not in some high quarters a plan for putting down this Rebellion by some other means than by whipping the Rebels?" Upton Hill, Va., Feb. 3, 1862, Bryant-Godwin Coll., NYPL. Wadsworth probably found means of getting these views before Stanton and Lincoln. The conference of division commanders met March 8.

opposed McClellan's strategy, and the fourth had approved it only conditionally! The second order directed that the army should not move from the Washington base without leaving such a force as McClellan and the corps commanders deemed entirely adequate to its protection, that no more than two corps should be moved until the Potomac was cleared of enemy batteries, and that the movement must begin not later than March 18.

Most important of all was Lincoln's third order, which divested McClellan of the command of other departments than that of the Potomac. No longer was he general-in-chief. All the principal Cabinet officers approved this step, and Stanton urged it strongly. Seward spoke of the "imbecility" of McClellan's recent operations, and Bates said the general was "fumbling and plunging in confusion." Despite the wisdom of the decision, for not even a Napoleon could command the Army of the Potomac in an active campaign and oversee all other military operations, McClellan resented it. He always believed that it tied his hands so that he would have to fight in eastern Virginia without being sure of cooperative action elsewhere, while he found affront in the fact that it first reached him by a newspaper. It is not recorded that he came to the White House before leaving for the Chesapeake, and Lincoln certainly never revisited his headquarters before he went.

[II]

The campaign could now begin—and it began with an anticlimax. McClellan had predicted that by placing his base on the Rappahannock he would compel the evacuation of Centreville; on March 9, before he ordered a platoon to march, the Confederates left the place. Jefferson Davis, the Cabinet, and Joseph E. Johnston had agreed on this step in February.

So effective were Johnston's preparations and so weak was the Northern intelligence service that the Confederates were able to remove most of their stores without exciting any suspicion. Not until the torch was applied to huts and stores was the movement discovered. It was easily made, because the Southern forces actually numbered only 50,000 or 55,000 effectives. McClellan said later that the enemy retreated safely because information leaked out to them while he was discussing his plans with the Administration. This excuse is contradicted by two facts: the Confederates began preparations before his plans were settled, and their general gives an entirely different explanation. Johnston regarded one avenue of Union attack as so much more dangerous than any other that he was sure McClellan would adopt it. The Northern army could make a concealed march along the Maryland shore of the Potomac, swiftly cross near Aquia Creek, and occupy Fredericksburg.

Unless anticipated, they would then be two days nearer Richmond than his own army; and Johnston fell back to forestall this possible movement.[23]

McClellan at once broke camp and advanced toward Centreville. He hoped to strike a blow at the rear guard. He also wished to shake his troops free of camp habits, and get rid of useless baggage.[24] His cavalry shortly discovered the Confederates in force at Warrenton Junction, where he left them severely alone; but he did remain long enough in the area to stage a revealing performance.

Leaving the main force at Centreville, he, McDowell, and their staffs, with 2,000 cavalry, rode to the old Bull Run battlefield. It was a beautiful day. They inspected the Confederate debris—skeletons of burned machine shops, wrecked locomotives and cars, and broken weapons. McClellan then halted the cavalcade where the hardest fighting of 1861 had taken place, and the two generals, with the cavalry a blue wall behind them, took places in front of their staffs. All eyes were fixed on the handsome young leaders, seated on magnificent steeds. McClellan insisted that McDowell rehearse the story of Bull Run, pointing out troop positions, battle corners, and the scenes of flight. Telling the whole tale with no attempt at self-vindication, the humiliated McDowell could not restrain his tears over the whitened bones that illustrated the terrible reverse. When he had finished, McClellan wheeled with the curt words: "Gentlemen, we will now return to quarters." All observers noted the deep humiliation of McDowell, intensified by McClellan's frigid demeanor, without a single consoling word.[25]

The Confederates having dislocated his initial scheme, McClellan turned to his alternative plan for an advance up the peninsula between the York and James Rivers. This decision was confirmed at a council of high officers at Fairfax Court House March 13. In his long letter to Stanton he had written that if the Urbana plan were frustrated, he could make Fort Monroe his base and operate along the Yorktown-Williamsburg road to Richmond, "although with less celerity and brilliancy of results." It was unquestionably a

---

23 Johnston in his *Narrative*, 98–106, dilates on the unnecessary destruction of many stores at Manassas, against which he protested, and the loss of a large meat-curing plant there. He thought that, moving behind the Potomac shield, McClellan would cross slightly downstream from Aquia Creek. Comte de Paris, *Battles and Leaders*, II, 121, rejects McClellan's idea of a leak. Almost incredibly, McClellan had the effrontery to claim the unexpected evacuation as his own great victory. He wrote S. L. M. Barlow: "My movements gave us Manassas with the loss of one life—a gallant cavalry officer—history will, when I am in my grave, record it as the brightest passage of my life that I accomplished so much at so small a cost." Barlow Papers.

24 T. Jefferson Coolidge, *Autobiography*, 40, reports McClellan saying this in 1863.

25 Prince de Joinville, *Campagne de l'Armée du Potomac*, 1862, p. 14; T. B. Gates, *Ulster Guard*, 172–178. McDowell and McClellan had clashed on the wisdom of the Chesapeake plan.

sound plan. The council of war unanimously approved it on two fundamental conditions: that the safety of transports and communications be assured, and that the force left to cover Washington "shall be such as to give an entire feeling of security for its safety from menace." Lincoln also gave his approval, emphasizing that Manassas be held and Washington left safe.[26]

Off for the Peninsula! The movement of 130,000 men, with horses, wagons, and artillery, was a great adventure in logistics. Since late February the Assistant Secretary of War, John Tucker, had been busy chartering a fleet of nearly 300 steamers, schooners, and barges, including river, lake, and ocean vessels of almost every size.

A singularly impressive movement it was.[27] The flotilla, scurrying to and fro in the waters about Washington, filled the air with smoke, fluttering flags, and deep bass whistles. For three weeks the dingy streets of Alexandria were clangorous with military bands and the tread of marching boots. Lines of bayonets gleamed alongside rivulets of white-topped wagons, ambulances, and artillery caissons, all moving to the waterfront. With endless profanity, straining, and whipcracking, nearly 15,000 horses and mules, more than 1,100 wagons, and 44 batteries were loaded aboard. With them went rolls of telegraph wire, timbers for pontoons, forges for repairs, boxes of medicine for field hospitals, and an endless variety of stores. Throughout fickle March the transfer went on—in bright sunlight and driving rain, under star-bespangled skies and in murky nights of storm. Down the Potomac fell the craft, down the Chesapeake, past the mouths of the Rappahannock and York, and on to Fort Monroe and Hampton Roads. Richmond no longer lay to the south. Suddenly it was west—even a little northwest. On the map it seemed astonishingly close.[28]

A picturesque movement this was, but time-consuming. Though Tucker boasted that for speed it was without parallel in history, and a European observer termed it the stride of a giant, some officers thought it was badly handled. As troops passed through Alexandria many bought liquor from the crowds, and got drunk; the command failed to put enough vehicles ashore at the Hampton–Newport News landing places; shelter and rations there were scarce. It was on February 14 that Stanton advertised for vessels, and on the 28th that Tucker was told the movement was fixed. Yet not until April 2 did McClellan himself reach Fort Monroe, and not until the 5th was the transfer fully effected.

26 Webb, *The Peninsula*, 28, 29.
27 The N. Y. *Weekly Tribune* gives a good description, April 12, 1862.
28 Swinton, *Army of the Potomac*, 100; MS diary of David F. Ritchie, of the 14th N. Y. Vols., in private hands. This regiment, beset by mud, drunkenness, and other delays, took ten hours to cover six and a half miles from its camp to Alexandria.

While it was being completed, the atmosphere in Washington improved. A measure of confidence was restored between Lincoln and McClellan, for the fact that the army was at last moving heartened the President. Moreover, he saw that, the die once cast, he must give the general proper support. McClellan wrote Barlow on March 18 that the attack of the abolitionists did not bother him: *"The President is all right—he is my friend."* And Benjamin Stark assured Barlow that Lincoln was facing the radical pack courageously: "He has declared so emphatically that he will not back down on Mac that the hounds in and out of Congress have ceased their yelpings; but it is only for a time." [29]

At no point had Lincoln let the public or the Congressional leaders know about his doubts respecting McClellan. Instead, he told a group that probably the only man in the country more anxious for a battle than himself was McClellan. "He repudiated in words of withering rebuke," wrote Representative A. S. Diven, "those who make the charge that he or Mr. Seward or General McClellan were temporizing or delaying out of any consideration for rebels or rebel institutions." Lincoln knew the vital importance of an appearance of unity even when the reality was imperfect. And he certainly had much more faith in the general than Stanton had. He told his close friend Senator O. H. Browning that he was sure of the man's fidelity; but Stanton on the same day expressed a deep distrust to the Senator.

By the first days of April, troops of Heintzelman's, Sumner's, and Keyes's corps had occupied the plateau behind Hampton and moved inland. Union forces were pushing toward Big Bethel of unhappy memory. The low, flat, partly marshy, and well-wooded tongue between the York and James, ten to fifteen miles wide, lay before them. Here Captain John Smith had landed, and here Cornwallis had surrendered. Here Confederate forces had now gathered. Only seventy-five miles from Fort Monroe lay Richmond. On the road thither the army expected to inscribe a resplendent new chapter of history. [30]

29 Stark to S. L. M. Barlow, March 20, 1862, Barlow Papers.

30 For Diven, see Columbia, Mo., *Statesman*, Feb. 14, 1862. Representative P. B. Fouke of Illinois wrote Feb. 15 that he had talked with McClellan and learned "the President has justly unlimited confidence in his capacity to manage the greatest army ever known"; Gillespie Papers, Chicago Hist. Soc. Joseph E. Johnston, fearing the Union numbers, had wished to defer Confederate resistance until McClellan approached Richmond, but Davis, on the advice of Robert E. Lee and Secretary of War Randolph, decided to make a stand on the Peninsula; Johnston, *Narrative*, 114, 115.

[III]

Already, in fact, a memorable page had been written in Hampton Roads. The day Lincoln signed the three orders to McClellan, Saturday, March 8, the Confederate *Merrimac* made its dramatic appearance; the day Johnston's troops evacuated Manassas, March 9, the *Monitor* grappled with the Southern giant. Had McClellan made a determined attack on Norfolk the previous winter, this encounter would never have been necessary.

The *Merrimac*, a 40-gun frigate of 3,200 tons, left a ruined hulk at Norfolk, was now a formidable monument to Confederate industry and ingenuity. Her scuttled hull had been cut down almost to the water line, pumped clean, floated, and repaired. Lieutenant John M. Brooke and J. L. Porter had shielded the top and sides with heavy timbers, plated with rail-road iron; had installed 10 guns, 4 of them rifled and 6 of them 9-inch smooth-bores; and had fixed a powerful iron beak to the prow. The cost was trifling, the result astounding. When the ship suddenly lumbered out of Norfolk into Hampton Roads to meet the Union frigates, it looked like a huge float-ing fort, its black iron sides sloping up from the water, its guns protruding from small square portholes, and its flat deck topped by a flagstaff and one great funnel spouting smoke and cinders. With a length of 262 feet 9 inches, and a breadth of just over 51 feet, the *Merrimac* (which the Confederates called the *Virginia*) bore a complete cuirass of three inches of armor.

No naval encounter of the war, perhaps of all history, was more pic-turesque than this. Hampton Roads, a calm sheet about seven miles long and four wide, opening into the Chesapeake by a narrow channel past Old Point Comfort, is like a large inland lake, fed by three rivers: the Elizabeth, the Nansemond, and the wide James. On the northwestern side of the Roads, at the entrance from the Chesapeake, loomed the Union stronghold Fort Monroe; on the eastern and southern sides, protecting Norfolk, stood Con-federate ramparts and batteries. As the sinister *Merrimac* moved into open waters, the battlements of Fort Monroe and the island post called the Rip-Raps were crowded with men in blue, leveling their glasses on the ship. The opposite shores were full of Southerners brought to the scene by rumors of the attack. Before the majestic progress of the ironclad, dozens of small vessels —transports, sloops, schooners, tugs—began to scatter and scurry like chickens before a swooping hawk. Beneath a bright sun, with a crisp breeze whiten-ing the sea, these craft, from double-decked steamers to sailboats, hurried to shelter, while their protectors, the *Minnesota, Congress, Cumberland, Roanoke*, and others, moved in to engage. The combatants came steadily closer, till spectators on the distant strands thought them almost touching. Then a fierce puff of smoke shot out from the *Merrimac;* an instant later, jets of flame and rolls of smoke burst from the Northern warships.

The daylong battle which followed was a complete victory for the *Merrimac.* Her first task was to dispose of the old twenty-four gun sailing sloop *Cumberland;* putting on all steam, she twice sent her double beak into the very entrails of the ship, and left her sinking. Then she turned her cannon on the fifty-gun frigate *Congress,* covered her decks with dead and dying, and was ready to ram her when she surrendered. The *Roanoke, Minnesota,* and *St. Lawrence,* helpless to aid their comrades, would all have been destroyed had they not taken refuge in shoal water where the *Merrimac* dared not follow. As night approached Confederates on shore could see the debris marking the grave of the *Cumberland.* They could see the western sky reddened by the flaming *Congress,* hopelessly aground, her guns going off as they became heated, until at midnight the five tons of powder in her magazines blew up with a sullen roar. Not far away the *Minnesota,* badly crippled, quivered fast on the shoals.[31]

Captain Franklin Buchanan of the *Merrimac* had been wounded, and was succeeded by Lieutenant Catesby Ap. R. Jones. This officer expected to make the next morning one of the darkest in Union records. He did not know that at ten that night the ironclad *Monitor,* an experimental turreted two-gun ship just completed, had reached Fort Monroe, and immediately taken her station by the wounded *Minnesota.* Not until daybreak did the general body of Confederates espy this reinforcement, and then they took it for an odd floating battery.

Brilliant Confederate improvisation had been met by shrewd Union planning—last-minute planning. "We ask," Senator Ten Eyck of New Jersey had declaimed in the Senate as the summer session of 1861 drew near an end, "that we shall have an engine that we need for the protection of our coasts hundreds of miles in length, and our harbors, and the great harbor of New York." He was speaking for a bill authorizing a naval board to examine the so-called Stevens Battery and similar devices, and appropriating $1,500,000 for one or more armored craft. The debate showed that French and British experiments with ironclads had attracted world-wide attention,

31 J. L. Porter in the Charleston *Courier,* March 19, 1862, describes the rebuilding of the *Merrimac;* John S. Wise, *End of an Era,* 196–200, offers a superior eyewitness account of the battle. See also Church's *Ericsson,* I, 280 ff., and C. L. Lewis, *Admiral Franklin Buchanan,* Ch. XIII. Hawthorne, seeing the *Monitor* later, wrote that it was not a ship, but a machine, and that the wooden walls of Old England were no more. He rightly declared that nothing finer had been said in the war than the words of Commodore Smith, father of the commander of the *Congress,* when he heard that his son's ship had capitulated. He knew that his boy would never haul down the flag. "Then Joe's dead!" said he. And he was.

and that the French ship *La Gloire* and the British *Warrior*, both armored, were regarded as potential threats to American ports. It showed that while naval experts were uncertain of the value of such ships as cruisers—the *La Gloire* had never been tested outside the Mediterranean, and carried only five days' supply of coal—they agreed on their importance for harbor defense.

Out of that debate, and out of the able planning and indomitable energy of the Swedish-American engineer John Ericsson, had sprung the *Monitor*. Various members of Congress talked of "jobs," and some naval men expressed horror. There are experts, said Senator McDougall, who oppose everything that is more destructive than the ancient galley. But Welles had appointed a board immediately after the passage of the appropriation; Ericsson presented his plan, and spent two hours before the board explaining it; and that body, encouraged by Lincoln himself, made a swift decision. On October 25 the *Monitor* was begun in Brooklyn, and on January 30, 1862, was launched. Ericsson's basic ideas were that she should be of light draught for coastal work, with a hull submerged for protection, so that seen from below she looked like a ship-bottom fixed to a raft. On this deck stood a single small revolving turret, only 20 feet in diameter and 9 feet high, with two 11-inch smoothbore guns; well forward was a tiny square pilothouse, hardly big enough for three men. The craft was 179 feet long and 41.5 feet wide; her deck was just awash, and she drew only 10.5 feet. The sides of the turret were protected by eight layers of one-inch iron plate. Built in 118 days, she was ready in the very nick of time. Lieutenant John L. Worden took command, and she set out southward. On her way to Hampton Roads March 6–8, she was twice almost swamped in high seas.[32]

The battle of the second day was gripping, for the closely matched antagonists struggled for hours without result. Running slowly down on the *Minnesota*, the *Merrimac* resumed her shattering fire, when suddenly the iron battery swung out from behind the Union warship, and advanced like some cocky champion entering feudal lists. At first sight she seemed hopelessly outmatched. From the shore she looked a little shoe-polish tin on a shingle. A single shell from the bulky dark *Merrimac*, a single square blow by the iron beak, would apparently shatter her.

32 For the debate on armored ships see *Cong. Globe*, 37th Cong., 1st Sess., 345, July 30, 1861. The ironclad vessel called the Stevens Battery lay incomplete at Hoboken, N. J., with $12,000 needed to finish her. R. L. Stevens had built it. For a review of the building of the *Monitor* see speech by Rep. C. B. Sedgwick of New York, April 28, 1862, *Cong. Globe*, 37th Cong., 2d Sess., Appendix 124 ff. Material of value may also be found in *Century Magazine*, XXXIX (March, 1890), 798 ff. The fullest books are a standard British work, H. W. Wilson, *Ironclads in Action*, I, 1–36, and Robert S. McCordock, *The Yankee Cheese Box, passim*. For years the expert engineer Charles Ellet had been vainly urging the government to build rams; had he succeeded, his boats might have stopped the *Merrimac*.

But bold Worden ran alongside his enemy like a skillful boxer attacking a heavy lout. The *Merrimac's* first shot missed, and other shots glanced off the smooth armor of the tin can. Meanwhile, an eleven-inch missile from the *Monitor*, whanging against the *Merrimac* casemates with a tremendous blow, flung her crew to the floor with bleeding noses and ringing ears, and showed that the little craft bore stout guns. Two hours of grim tussle followed, amply proving that neither vessel could penetrate the other's armor. A shell bursting just outside the *Monitor's* pilothouse filled Worden's eyes with powder and dust, temporarily blinding him and forcing him to relinquish the command, but that was all. Their efforts at ramming each other were equally futile. The light-draft *Monitor* easily escaped into shoal water, while the *Merrimac* was too massive to be hurt by her frail enemy. Later the *Merrimac*, suddenly plunging at the *Monitor*, strained her machinery and broke her huge iron beak as it grated over the enemy's shallow deck.

"Thousands have this day blessed you," the engineer of the *Monitor* wrote Ericsson that night. "I have heard whole crews cheer you." The North boasted a new war hero. As the *Merrimac* retired to Norfolk, David had the better of Goliath. The loss of Union sailors stood at about 400; two Union warships were gone; Worden was wounded; the *Monitor* had been hit twenty-two times, and its pilothouse had proved vulnerable. But the Confederates had failed of their main goal, and acknowledged a final checkmate.[33]

The officers who had rebuilt the *Merrimac* had done well, but not well enough. As they designed the ship, it drew too much water. Then after she was launched, the base of the sloping armor-clad roof was found to be several feet above waterline, and she had to be ballasted so heavily that the draught was increased to eighteen feet. The beak was crudely attached, and the engines were weak. Worse still, the ironclad proved too cumbersome, slow, and ill fueled to cover long distances, leave deep waters, or maneuver smartly. She was useful only for defensive operations. The popular view that if unchecked she might have brought Washington, New York, and Boston under her guns was wide of the mark, for she could never have tubbed her way very far from Norfolk. The *Monitor*, on the other hand, proved the value of the most important innovation in the duel, the revolving armored turret. As her engineers wrote, this was "a splendid structure," destined to a great future in naval development.[34]

---

33 Alban C. Stimers, Hampton Roads, March 9, 1862, to Ericsson, *National Intelligencer*, March 15. "I consider that both ships were well fought," he wrote. The Confederacy thrilled to the exploits of what it called "the iron diadem of the South," the North to the feat of "the little bumblebee."
34 Ericsson's turret revolved on a central spindle; the British engineer Stines devised a safer system of roller bearings.

When the news reached Washington on Sunday, March 9, of the destruction the previous day, Cabinet members hastened to the White House—Stanton overwrought, Seward despondent, Welles worried but self-possessed. The President got neither comfort nor counsel from them. In a quick visit he found Dahlgren at the Navy Yard equally unable to suggest expedients, and even the resourceful Meigs offered no help. The frantic Stanton paced up and down the President's office painting frightful visions of the *Merrimac* shelling the capital, laying New York in ashes, and levying on the whole seaboard for money to continue the war. He even rushed off panicky telegrams to Northern governors and mayors. Alternately sneering at Welles and denouncing him, he showed a bitter malevolence. When Welles explained that the *Merrimac* could never leave the Chesapeake and that the *Monitor* was at hand, Stanton's scorn became volcanic. "You rely on that craft with *two guns?*" he thundered incredulously.

Indeed, the battle between the Secretaries of War and the Navy that day rivaled the battle of the *Merrimac* and *Monitor*. Welles met his assailant with icy contempt. At one point Stanton wildly besought Lincoln and Dahlgren to order a half hundred canal boats laden with stone sunk in the Potomac channel. Welles protested. "For six months," he told Stanton, "the Navy Department has argued and implored to get McClellan and the War Department to help us open the Potomac. And now that the rebels are leaving it, the War Department wants to block it with stone!" Lincoln forbade any closing of the channel unless it became certain the *Merrimac* was coming up the river. Gradually the mood of alarm, with Stanton pacing to the window to look for the smoke of the Confederate giant downstream, subsided. And when that evening news of the *Monitor's* successful resistance and the victory at Pea Ridge reached the White House almost simultaneously, the President indulged in some happy jubilation. A few weeks later, descending the Potomac and passing the unused canal boats, he jested about "Stanton's navy." [35] Lincoln showed the depth of his feelings when Henry A. Wise brought the wounded Lieutenant Worden up to Washington, put him to bed in Wise's own room, and went to the White House. Worden relates:

Wise found the President in counsel with his Cabinet, to whom he recounted the fight as he saw it, and when he finished President Lincoln got up and said, Well gentlemen, I am going to see that *feller*, he accordingly came to Wise's house where I was in bed and as Wise opened the door of my room he said, Jack, here is the President who has come to see you. I raised up and the President took my hand and I said, You do me great honor, Mr. President, by this visit, and for a moment he did not reply (and Wise said tears were in his

35 Welles' *Diary*, I, 63–67; G. T. Strong's *Diary*, III, 210, March 16, 1862; Worden's undated narrative, Lincoln Memorial Univ. Lib.; Ruth White, *Yankee From Sweden: John Ericsson*, 210–227.

eyes) and then he said, No, sir, you have done me and your country honor and I shall promote you. My eyes were filled with powder and much swollen, face lacerated, and hair burned and was a sad looking object which seemed to touch his feelings greatly. . . .

The battle marked a revolution in naval warfare, but its exact character and extent are often misstated. The fate of the *Congress* and *Cumberland* showed decisively that the day of wooden frigates was ended. The London *Times* declared that whereas before Hampton Roads the British navy had possessed 149 first-class warships, after that battle only two were available, the ironclads *Warrior* and *Ironside*. The naval revolution had actually begun during the Crimean War. While during that conflict the Russian guns at Fort Constantine, before Sebastopol, had badly damaged a wooden fleet of the Allies, at Kinburn some hastily built armored warships had smashed the Russian batteries with trifling loss. The French admiral had written afterward that "everything may be expected from these formidable engines of war," and France and Britain had undertaken ironclad ships. Ericsson was quick to boast that his *Monitor* outmatched anything in the European navies. But the *Warrior*, a seagoing ship of fourteen knots with 4.5-inch solid rolled plates, would have been a far more doughty antagonist than the *Merrimac*. The American navy could be content to emphasize coast-defense vessels, but British warships had to be able to keep the high seas.

The most significant feature of the *Monitor*, as we have said, was her turret system of mounting guns. The armor could thus be concentrated, instead of being distributed, as on the *Merrimac*, along a great casemate; and a revolving turret enabled the guns to reach every point of the compass. The success of the *Monitor* immediately inspired the United States to begin building other ironclads, some for ocean service and some for harbor defense, so that when the year ended about thirty were under way. "They are a vast improvement over the *Monitor*," Worden wrote Fox. Those which approximated the original Ericsson lines became unpopular with naval officers, who called them floating prisons, or after the *Monitor* foundered off Cape Hatteras during a storm, airtight coffins. Sailors complained that they were slow, that they carried only a small quantity of ammunition, that although the turret itself might be invulnerable, repeated concussions would disable the pivot, and that the rivet heads flew about like bullets. But Ericsson had done the country an unforgettable service.[36]

The sudden threat to Washington from an unexpected quarter, mean-

36 See report of Vice-Admiral Alex Milne, British Naval Command-in-Chief in North America, Bermuda, May 22, 1863, Admiralty Papers, Public Record Office; reports of Capt. S. Kennedy, H. M. S. *Challenger*, July 13, 1863, and Capt. R. V. Hamilton, H. M. S. *Vesuvius*, Dec. 3, 1863, *ibid.*; Church, *Ericsson*, II, 23 ff.; N. Y. *Tribune*, Jan. 27, 1863; Worden Papers, LMU.

while, enhanced Lincoln's conviction that the capital must not be left uncovered for an hour. And the *Merrimac* remained an embarrassment to Mc-
Clellan's campaign, for Lincoln ordered the *Monitor* to take no risks in attacking her, and she could not be enticed into a disadvantageous position. Lying
at Norfolk, she made it impossible for Northern ships to enter the James.
When the fleet area commander was asked to aid McClellan in his attack
on Yorktown, he refused on the ground that his first duty was to watch the
Merrimac. So skittish were the Union warships that on April 11 they let
her capture three Union steamers without molestation, and on May 8 broke
off an attack on Sewell's Point as soon as she approached. Thus she played
her part in the defense of Richmond.

[IV]

McClellan, who had represented that the movement by the Chesapeake
and the York River would be quick and certain, soon discovered that he
had miscalculated. At Fort Monroe he possessed 58,000 men and 100 guns
ready to move. Somewhere before him lay J. B. Magruder's small Army of
the Peninsula. His plan, simple and sound, was to march a right column
directly on Yorktown while a left column thrust toward Williamsburg. If
Confederate fortifications at either place offered stubborn resistance, Mc-
Dowell's corps should be brought from Washington to Gloucester Point
opposite Yorktown, so as to turn the two strongholds—"to take in reverse
whatever force the enemy might have on the Peninsula," as McClellan later
put it. A price would have to be paid. Soldiers about Fort Monroe noted
the many signs of undertakers: corpses embalmed and boxed, $50.

The march began on April 4. Yankees unfamiliar with the Southern landscape gazed wonderingly at snake fences, deserted houses, Negro huts, and
tangled pine woods. Occasional orchards were bright with apple and peach
blossoms. But as blue squads scrambled over the broken breastworks of Big
Bethel in triumph, the weather changed. Cold rain turned McClellan's assurances of dry sandy roads into mockery. The long lines of wagons, guns,
and ambulances constantly mired down; men in mud to their knees lashed
at mules and pushed at wheels; a thousand axes rang to cut logs for corduroy-
ing the quagmire; progress became snail-slow. In the marshy fields alongside, soldiers leaped from one hill of rotting cornstalks to another. Many
slept that night in puddles.[37]

On the 5th the march was resumed with more cold rain, and more splash-

37 Ritchie, MS Reminiscences; Webb, *The Peninsula*, 43, 44; O. O. Howard's letters to
his wife, Howard Papers, Bowdoin.

THE PENINSULAR CAMPAIGN

ing, swearing, and hauling. Colonel H. Berdan's sharpshooters deployed in front of the right wing, where fighting was sure to begin. Before long, as Confederate shots whizzed overhead, they saw looming through the mist and rain high earthworks, with barbettes protecting thirty-two-pounders. The first Union field guns came into play, while behind them began massing dense bodies of Northern troops. Southern engineers had utilized swamps and boggy streams to protect their positions, and around Yorktown had deepened some of the old British trenches. The twelve-mile front was soon ablaze; but when dusk shut down, the stars and bars floated over undented lines, and Southern bands gaily played "Dixie" and the "Marseillaise." The siege of Yorktown had begun.

McClellan had not expected to find Confederate fortifications extending wholly across the Peninsula, from the York to the James. His maps, like his intelligence services, were inaccurate. The one he trusted, made by an engineer aide to General Wool at Fort Monroe, failed to show that the Warwick River, in places very wide, barred most of his path; instead, it pictured the stream as running parallel with the James! [38] "We did not know of the line of works along the Warwick," McClellan later admitted. Expecting to surround Yorktown with little impediment, he had instructed Keyes to march to the Half-way House, six miles behind and above Yorktown, and encamp; but now Keyes and Sumner were brought up short by well-manned works on the Warwick River line. The army that McClellan had expected to swing around Yorktown was at a standstill. [39]

And now McClellan's temperament betrayed him. After being too sanguine, he reverted to a more characteristic mood of excessive apprehension. Finding his troops checked on a broad front, he jumped to the conclusion that Joseph E. Johnston had arrived with most of the army evacuated from Centreville. This was a delusion, for Johnston's advance division did not reach the line until April 10, and other divisions did not come up until several days later. For six or seven days McClellan's strength was fully four times that of the enemy.

During this week a determined thrust would have broken the defenses. Magruder on April 5 had only 11,000 men, of whom more than half garrisoned Yorktown, Gloucester Point, and Mulberry Island, leaving only about 5,000 to defend the remaining ten miles. The Confederates were so certain of an imminent assault that they slept in the trenches beside their muskets. But to Magruder's astonshiment, day after day passed without any test of his strength. The explanation was soon evident: in every direction picks flashed as Union troops dug trenches across fields, woodland, and swamp. While they dug, Richmond poured reinforcements forward, until, Magruder writes, "anxiety passed from my mind as to the result of an attack upon us." [40]

Why did McClellan not attack? Partly because he exaggerated the enemy strength. Partly because before leaving Washington he had fixed his mind on a siege of Yorktown, where the enemy was to be shut up in his fortifications, and captured by the most deliberate operations. Constructing batteries and parallels opposite the Yorktown redoubts, McClellan installed nearly a hundred heavy pieces—mortars, howitzers, Parrott guns—to bombard the defenses. This *idée fixe* of a siege indisposed him to rapid field maneuvering.

38 N. Y. *Weekly Tribune*, April 12, 1862.
39 Webb, 53, 54.
40 Magruder's *Official Report*, O. R., I, xi, pt. 1, pp. 405–411; *Battles and Leaders*, II, 160 ff. O. O. Howard thought it would have been far better to attack Yorktown the day after arrival there, and wrote his wife that McClellan "inclines too much to *engineering*"; May 7, 1862, O. O. Howard Papers. Three British officers who made a report to London declared that Yorktown might easily have been taken the first few days; War Office, Confidential File, Aug. 1, 1862.

Finally, he believed that Lincoln had unduly weakened his force by holding McDowell's corps in the Washington area, for the very day that his army reached Magruder's lines, he learned that Lincoln had ordered that it or Sumner's command must stay to protect the capital.

He immediately protested against this order, telegraphing Lincoln that he would now have to fight the whole Confederate forces at or near York-town, and needed his army intact. Though Lincoln did not know that Mc-Clellan had greatly outnumbered Magruder, he suspected some such state of affairs and sent a crisp reply:

You now have over one hundred thousand troops with you independent of General Wool's command. I think you better break the enemies' line from Yorktown to Warwick River, at once. They will probably use time, as advantageously as you can. A. LINCOLN.[41]

[V]

Behind Lincoln's order lay some simple logic. He had stipulated, in approving of the Peninsula strategy, that Manassas should be held in force and Washington kept entirely safe. On April 2 General James S. Wadsworth reported to Stanton that his force of 19,022 ill-disciplined men was entirely inadequate for the defense of Washington. Stanton immediately asked Adjutant-General Lorenzo Thomas and Major-General Ethan Allen Hitchcock to inquire, and they at once declared that Lincoln's order on the safety of the capital had not been obeyed. The President knew that the council of corps commanders had asserted that 55,000 men were necessary. He knew that the capture of Washington might be fatal, for foreign recognition of the Confederacy would doubtless follow, while half of the North would deem the war lost. As he could afford no risks, and as public feeling was very sensitive about Washington, it *seemed* essential to keep McDowell's corps at hand. Actually, as McClellan's defenders contend, it was not; the best defense was the offense. Under political pressure, Lincoln had already (March 31) detached Louis Blenker's division from McClellan to go to Frémont's new Mountain Department. Whether these steps were errors is a debatable matter —and it has been endlessly debated.[42]

41 R. T. Lincoln Papers for McClellan's dispatch, May 5; Lincoln, *Works*, V, 182.
42 O. R., I, xi, pt. 3, pp. 60–62. Wadsworth's veracity was later impeached by the N. Y. *World*, and he replied in a letter to the N. Y. *Times* (in *Tribune*, May 21, 1863). He stated that on March 31, 1862, the troops he commanded in and about Washington numbered 19,591 present for duty; on April 3, they were 19,045; on April 30, they were 19,475. But the low numerical strength was not the chief element of weakness. Many of the regiments were new; some had just received their arms; they were crippled by incompetent and drunken officers; they had poor liaison. McClellan ordered him to detail from this force four good regiments to Richardson's, Heintzelman's, and Hooker's divisions.

The amazing fact is that the President and the general had reached no clear understanding on this subject before McClellan left Washington. It seems almost incredible that room should have been left for a misunderstanding. McClellan, before going to Fort Monroe, should have obtained clear directions from the President; Lincoln, for his part, should have demanded a full statement, and made still plainer his intention of safeguarding Washington beyond mischance. This want of liaison was a terrible misfortune. Had McClellan and Lincoln discussed face to face the proper division of troops to defend Washington and troops to move against Richmond, and come to an explicit agreement, the expedition would have begun under a far brighter star.

It was McClellan who was chiefly in the wrong. Lincoln had been frank about his fears, even mentioning the talk of "traitorous" action, but McClellan had never been equally frank about his plans. McClellan knew that the corps commanders had declared on March 13 that Washington must have such force "as to give an entire feeling of security for its safety from menace." Yet he had made no such provision. "After you left here," Lincoln now wrote him, "I ascertained that less than 20,000 unorganized men, with a single field battery, were all you designed to be left for the defense of Washington and Manassas; and part of this even was to go to General Hooker's old position." While Lincoln was aware that public sentiment demanded above all else the security of the seat of government, McClellan was ignorant of and indifferent to public sentiment. The President had to think daily of the Committee on the Conduct of the War, of Congress, and of the great uneasy masses. If he allowed Washington to fall into perils like those of April, 1861, an angry Congress might impeach and remove him. It is true that in desperate emergencies a national chieftain may denude home defenses to strengthen some vital outer point, as Churchill in 1940 stripped England of essential materials to save North Africa and Suez, the backbone of Empire. But this situation was entirely different. Washington was the vital point, McClellan had an army far exceeding his foe's, and he could much better afford to take risks than the Union government could.

The spirit in which McClellan received Lincoln's order did him no credit. Regarding Washington as a "sink of iniquity," he now felt himself the victim of a conspiracy. His staff agreed that McDowell had taken advantage of his absence to play a "scurvy trick" in getting his corps withheld from the critical field of operations, and talked of foul play. General T. F. Meagher reported to Democratic leaders in New York that according to regular-army officers, although McClellan was as cool, determined, and active as ever, "it was his determination after the siege and battle of Yorktown to resign his command."[43]

Actually, McClellan's operations were not impeded by the retention of one corps in the Washington area. When he asked Stanton to spare two of McDowell's divisions for attacking Gloucester Point from the rear, the War Department cheerfully released them under a general specially congenial to him, Franklin. But preposterous delays occurred. Franklin's troops did not reach the Gloucester area until April 20, and then the mere preparations to disembark them consumed two weeks! In the end they were not used against Gloucester at all, for it was too strong to be taken from the rear. At no time, moreover, did McClellan lack enough men; what he lacked was promptness in using them.

For the Yorktown siege was doggedly prosecuted on classic lines. "I do believe that I am avoiding the faults of the Allies at Sebastopol, and quietly preparing the way for great success," wrote McClellan on April 23. Yorktown a Sebastopol! He installed his heavy guns and mortar batteries, built redoubts to protect his parallels, and exulted over successful reconnaissances. As he sat still and poured rockets, bombs, and solid shot at the Confederate lines, the impatience of Washington grew. Stanton even thought of handing the command over to Ethan Allen Hitchcock.[44] Lincoln sent an exasperated dispatch to the general: "Your call for Parrott guns alarms me—chiefly because it argues indefinite procrastination. Is anything to be done?" This was somewhat unjust, for McClellan, as he courteously explained, had been expecting the guns for two weeks, and was trying to hurry, not procrastinate; but he never properly explained his delays or his objects to the President or the War Department. He put his main dependence, as his opponent Johnston wrote Richmond, upon artillery and engineering. But he was now perfecting plans for a grand final assault which would probably have involved heavy bloodshed.[45]

Then, as all was ready for this climax, the Confederates at dawn on May

43 Meagher to S. L. M. Barlow, Yorktown headquarters, April 24, 1862, Barlow Papers. McClellan wrote privately, April 18: "No general ever labored under greater disadvantages," *Own Story*, 311. Franklin's letter of explanation is in *Own Story*, 335, 336; cf. Webb, 61, 62.
44 Hitchcock, grandson of Ethan Allen and veteran of the Mexican War, could hardly be seriously considered, for he was sixty-four this year. But he states in his Diary, April 13, 1865, that Stanton, who used him in an advisory capacity, became so irritated by the slow siege that he asked Hitchcock to accept an order giving him immediate command of McClellan's army. Stanton added that the President wished it, and that if Hitchcock said the word, he could have the order in two minutes. "I at once refused," writes Hitchcock. Hitchcock Papers, LC.
45 Lincoln, *Works*, V, 203. For an able defense of McClellan see W. W. Hassler, Jr., *McClellan, Shield of the Union*. We should remember that McClellan never had the time to grow that Grant had; both needed it.

4 deserted their works. They left behind some seventy cannon, with small quantities of ammunition and stores, but Union efforts at pursuit were futile, and not until nightfall did Northern troops regain contact with the Confederates at Williamsburg.

Here next day partial Union forces fought a pitched battle. This savage, confused combat, waged in heavy rain driven by an icy wind, and ending inconclusively, offered several points of interest. The soldiers, plastered with Virginia clay, struggled among trees, stumps, and interlaced bushes. The principal hero was a Pennsylvania brigadier, a West Point graduate named Winfield Scott Hancock, who showed true generalship in the most responsible movements of the day. He won the praise of his superior, William F. Smith, for "the brilliancy of the plan of battle, the coolness of its execution, the seizing of the proper instant for changing from the defensive to the offensive, the steadiness of the troops engaged, and the completeness of the victory." If he was the best figure of the day, General Sumner was the sorriest. This *vieux sabreur,* whose fire and dash were never matched by his judgment, proved unequal to the strategic demands of battle. As for McClellan, he was so busy at Yorktown helping Franklin embark his men to ascend the York River that he did not reach the field until late afternoon. Though when darkness fell the Confederates still held their key position, Fort Magruder, during the night they retired.[46]

McClellan made the most of his capture of Yorktown and Williamsburg. Of the former he telegraphed Stanton: "The success is brilliant, and you may rest assured that its effects will be of the greatest importance." He reported the Confederate works "most formidable," and British officers with him agree that they were. After Williamsburg he was similarly exultant—"a brilliant victory." But even in the hour of triumph he was certain he needed far more troops. Joe Johnston stood before him with an army "probably greater a good deal than my own," he telegraphed Stanton, adding: "My entire force is undoubtedly inferior to that of the Rebels. . . . but I will do all I can. . . ."

The national outlook at the moment seemed hopeful. McClellan by his own statement had 85,000 effective men, and by the adjutant-general's returns 105,000; Johnston in February had given his own force as 60,062 men, of whom 42,860 were effectives.[47] McClellan had now brought his army to a position where he could thrust directly at Richmond, upon which Johnston rapidly retreated. In the West the military and naval commanders had scored

46 Swinton, 115–118; Webb, 73–81. Heintzelman's MS Diary, LC, is explicit on Sumner's bad showing.
47 O. R., I, v, 1086; K. P. Williams, *Lincoln Finds a General,* I, 154–165.

success after success. The eastern navy had not merely stopped the South's greatest warship, but had broken through old rules of design to a wide new future. Foreign intervention, as C. F. Adams and John Bigelow labored astutely in Europe, seemed less likely than ever. The acutest problems of finance and supply had been met. All waited to see McClellen deliver his final blow.

[VI]

While they waited, Stanton took an unfortunate step. He had capably organized his department and stopped the incessant drain of politicians and officers on his time. As he put it, he had his machinery working, the rats cleared out, the ratholes stopped, and the champagne roisters on the Potomac ended. "God helping me I shall prevail," he wrote Charles A. Dana of the *Tribune*. "I feel a deep *earnest* feeling growing up around us." [48] Then on April 3, 1862, he suddenly closed the recruiting service throughout the North. Bryant's newspaper declared next day· "The Secretary of War cries out 'enough.' The Union armies are full."

With the war at its crisis, why this step? Though it was one of the principal blunders of the conflict, no satisfactory explanation has ever been offered. We can only say that it reflected the general mismanagement of recruiting, which in turn reflected the basic want of organization in the nation. McClellan by General Order No. 105, effective January 1, had given the War Department practical control of the field, decreeing that no more regiments or other units should be raised by the government except on its authority. The Department appointed superintendents for each State, under whom recruiting for all regiments old and new was to be conducted by specially detailed officers. Cameron had interpreted McClellan's order as meaning that enough troops had been raised to quell the rebellion, and that the only further need was for machinery to maintain the existing regiments. A steady flow of replacements was wanted—that was all. Congressional penny-pinching also played an unfortunate role in the situation. Economy-minded Senators declared early in the year that the government had more men than the law allowed, and that the costs of maintenance and recruiting were excessive.

Pressed by Congress, Stanton reported that he could not ascertain the exact size of the volunteer army raised by the States, but estimated it between 700,000 and 800,000 men. On March 28 Henry Wilson, head of the Senate Military Affairs Committee, declared that the government ought im-

48 Feb. 1, 1862, Dana Papers, LC.

mediately to stop enlistments. Stanton's discontinuance of the volunteer recruiting service followed within the week. He told Halleck that he had
stopped it for the purpose of forcing the governors to make accurate returns.
Henry Wilson said later that the step was taken to compel fragmentary
regiments to coalesce, and to clear the way for a better enlistment service.
The one fact certain is that it cut off the flow of replacements at the very
time the spring campaigns made them most needed, and threw recruiting
into a confusion from which it did not recover for months. It is also certain
that just as disease and battle losses began to reduce regiments at an alarming rate, full reports showed that the government had fewer troops by
150,000 or 200,000 than had been represented. Within a month the Administration and public began to realize what a fearful error had been made. A large
section of the press became clamorous for more troops, and May 19 found
Stanton frantically telegraphing the governors for as many regiments as
they could raise.[49]

But the war happily had its brighter pages. Suspense in the East was
coupled with achievement in the West, and to that theater we may now
return.

49 See Wilson's long review, *Cong. Globe*, 38th Cong., 1st Sess., 58 ff., Dec. 21, 1863;
Stanton, May 1, 1862. O. R., III, ii, 29; Phila. *North American*, April 22, *et seq.*; N. Y.
World, Times, May 23, *et seq.*; L. L. Lerwell, *The Personnel Replacement System in the
U. S. Army*, 86–88.

Shiloh

THE FACT that half of the Confederacy lay in the wide Mississippi Valley was always in men's minds. The same newspaper issues which described the occupation of Manassas detailed the grapple at Pea Ridge. McClellan's march on Yorktown had to share headlines with the jubilant return of Andrew Johnson and other Unionists to Nashville, the siege of Island No. 10 on the Mississippi, and Grant's push southward along the Tennessee. After all, Louisiana and Texas had a combined population exceeding that of Confederate Virginia, and greater wealth; Mississippi was richer and more populous than South Carolina. By far the largest port of the Confederacy was New Orleans.

After Donelson and Pea Ridge, March witnessed an extension of Union control over most of Arkansas and Tennessee, raising hopes for a rapid conquest of that area. On an April morning Island No. 10 surrendered to John Pope with artillery, small arms, 6,000 prisoners, and 3 generals. As Grant reached Savanna, Tennessee, people scanning their maps saw that this was close to the southern boundary of the State, close even to Florence, Alabama. Buell's troops were marching south from Nashville to join Grant.

[I]

These rapid advances were possible because American organizing talent, concentrated upon the transportation revolution, had achieved a substantial mastery of water commerce. The fact leaped from the newspapers as men read how Grant had put 15,000 men on transports at Cairo, and then within three days he and the gunboats had taken Fort Henry. As an example of engineering ingenuity the river steamboat was remarkable; as illustrations of business enterprise, the river packet lines were equally striking. These facts robbed the problems of Western logistics of half their difficulty. No British engineer, wrote Norman S. Russell, could visit America without perceiving "that a vast system, combining great engineering talent with dexterous naval architecture, is exhibited on the noble rivers of America." [1] Wherever navigable streams ran, armies could be carried swiftly and easily. While McClellan's host, under dripping skies, dragged a few weary miles through viscid Virginia clay, Western forces moved over the waters faster than any legion ever traversed a Roman road. And the Mississippi, Tennessee, and Cumberland led into the heart of Western rebeldom.

How was it done? A typical story is told by the historian of a Western regiment. His command had hardly averaged fifteen miles daily through the winter mud of Kentucky, leaving some wagons completely bemired. Then one night they reached the banks of the Ohio, and dawn revealed sixteen steamboats waiting in the stream. The sight of their comfortable decks intoxicated the tired soldiers. The brigadier in charge quickly issued his orders. The Thirty-sixth Indiana would board the *Woodford;* the Michigan Engineers the *Golden State;* the Sixth Kentucky, the *Switzerland* and *City of Madison;* the Forty-first Ohio, the *Silver Moon* and *Lady Jackson;* and so on. Embarkation proved a lark. Dense smoke rolled from the tall stacks of the sixteen craft, whistles boomed deep bass roars, steam exhausts contributed treble notes, and paddle wheels splashed musically. Down the river they went in two columns. The *Diana*, crammed with the general, his staff, a thousand Ohio and Indiana troops, a cavalry detachment, and mules, horses and wagons, led one line, the *Autocrat* the other. Playing cards, chatting, joking, singing, the troops watched the wooded shores drop effortlessly behind. Cannelton hove in sight. Then suddenly the general was on the hurricane deck reading the news of Donelson, and bands were striking up "The Star-Spangled Banner." [2]

Five decades of hard planning—of continuous steamboat development, engine improvement, river harnessing, and mastery of the techniques of operation—lay behind such smooth voyages. These decades had brought the art of steam navigation to a high level. In the years 1851–60 no fewer than 1,346 steamboats, of well over 300,000 tonnage, had been built in the West. During the period 1811–70, a total of 4,688 had been launched—a tremendous fleet.[3] It was on the thousand available vessels that Union armies rode into the Western Confederacy.

Steamboat design was governed by certain principles of which Henry M. Shreve was traditionally the discoverer, but which grew naturally out of basic river conditions.[4] A shallow, lightly built hull, one step above a raft,

---

1 Russell, "On American River Steamers," *Trans. Institution of Naval Architects*, II (1861), 105, quoted by Louis C. Hunter, *Steamboats on the Western River*, 61.
2 E. Hannaford, *The Story of a Regiment*, 195–198.
3 Louis C. Hunter, 105 ff.
4 A. B. Hulbert, *Paths of Inland Commerce*, 175; but see Hunter, 75, 76, 89, 90. Shreve,

was needed to run in low water. A wide, low main deck was required for cargo room and ease in handling freight, and this deck also accommodated the boilers and machinery. An upper cabin, which might be as plain as that of a canalboat or as palatial with crystal, polished woodwork, rugs, and snowy paint as that of the *Grand Republic,* gave passengers ample room. Above it rose the hurricane deck, which bore the pilothouse, and after the mid-forties perhaps also offered a row of luxurious staterooms on the texas. With their three decks and superstructure the big steamboats of the fifties, even after their length reached 200 or 250 feet, looked bulky and topheavy. Running without cargo, a fine Cincinnati packet might be submerged only four feet while its pilothouse towered forty-five feet above the water. But the broad low main deck, made wider still by the guards or extensions beyond the hull line at the sides, rendered them admirable freight carriers, rapidly filled or emptied by gangplanks. They had great stability, for most of the machinery and cargo was on or below this lower deck. Two ingenious devices, bow frames or longitudinal trusses arching through the superdecks on each side of the vessel, and hog chains or heavy iron rods rising from the hull timbers into these decks, helped to brace the construction.

Mark Twain, in his pages on the antebellum St. Louis–New Orleans boat which gave him a berth as a cub pilot, has drawn the portrait of the Mississippi packet at its shining best. The long gilded cabin, glittering with prism-fringed chandeliers and dainty as a drawing room; the boiler deck spacious as a church; the fires glaring fiercely from a wide row of furnaces under eight boilers; the big glass-enclosed pilothouse with red window curtains, sofa, leather cushions, and a costly inlaid wheel; the regiment of servants; the lordly pilot, master of commerce on the four-thousand-mile water system—all this was imposing, convenient, and sumptuous. American steamboat architecture, wrote a traveler, "is not only original . . . but it is sometimes splendid in appearance."[5] Such a boat could be quickly jammed with troops, guns, horses, and stores. So could a dingy old river tub, or any of the countless craft of intervening quality. And they could be handled as dashingly, as recklessly as men handled old wagons and muskets, for the steamboat tradition stood for a short life and cheap replacement.

The engine used on Western waters was a high-pressure, noncondensing device which conservative critics abused as wasteful, inefficient, and dangerous,

son of a New Jersey Quaker, had helped Jackson at New Orleans, built a new type of river boat, the *Washington,* and as superintendent of Federal river improvements designed the steam snagboats called "Uncle Sam's Toothpullers."

5 *Life on the Mississippi,* Ch. VI. Mark Twain noted the rapidity of loading: "You should be on board when they take a couple of those wood-boats in tow and turn a swarm of men into each; by the time you have wiped your glasses and put them on, you will be wondering what has become of that wood."

but which for good reason held its place. Why was it not replaced by the low-pressure engines of the East? Ocean seamen declared that ignorance, stubbornness, and crazy recklessness supplied the answer. But engineers who were really familiar with the demands of midland river navigation knew that the time-honored steamboat engine admirably met them. Shallow Western waters compelled steamboatmen to reduce the weight to the lowest feasible point. A high-pressure engine, using what the pioneer engine builder George Evans called "strong steam," was substantially lighter than its low-pressure counterpart.[6] It cost far less money; in 1861 a 180-ton low-pressure engine required an outlay of $50,000, but the smaller high-pressure engine of equal power only $20,000. The Western type of motive power, less ponderous and bulky, and more cheaply repaired, provided speed. By the later 1850's the typical time for a trip from Cincinnati to St. Louis was two days, twenty-two hours, and from Cincinnati to New Orleans eight days. In 1853 the *Eclipse* ran upstream from New Orleans to Cairo in three days and just over three hours.[7]

It needs spunk to run a river boat, said one fireman. A lake steamer doesn't burst her boiler once in five years. "But I tell you, stranger, it takes a man to ride one of these boats, head on a snag, high pressure, valve soldered down, six hundred souls on board and all in danger of going to the devil." In wartime, men had to make the most of high pressure and face the perils imperturbably.

As steamboat design was improved, so were the rivers. A canal was built around the rock ledges which created twenty-two-foot falls at Louisville. Army engineers, initially under Robert E. Lee, widened and deepened the channel at the Des Moines rapids. The Federal government year by year from 1824 expended large sums in bettering navigation not only on the Ohio and Mississippi, but on their major tributaries: the Wabash, Missouri, Cumberland, Arkansas, and Red. Competent engineers, using special boats, removed snags, boulders, logs, hidden wrecks, and other menaces from the channels. They dug away sand and gravel bars, and blew up rock reefs.[8] Thus was the river system tidied in preparation for the day when continuous improvement, patrolling, and beacon placement would make the Mississippi, in Mark Twain's words, a sort of 2,000-mile torchlight procession [9]—improved, also, for the day of war. At the height of the antebellum work, in thirty-one months in 1842–45, the government took from the lower Ohio, Mississippi, Missouri, and Arkansas 21,681 snags, 36,840 roots, logs,

6 Hunter, Ch. III, deals fully with mechanical development.
7 See tables of speed in Hunter, 490; *Life on the Mississippi*, Ch. XVI.
8 Hunter ably covers this subject in Ch. IV, pp. 181–215.
9 *Life on the Mississippi*, Ch. XXVIII.

and stumps, and 74,810 trees likely to topple into the water. The 700-mile Cumberland became a busy artery as far as Nashville, 200 miles, and in high water took steamboats on to Burnside, 200 miles farther. The Tennessee, meandering through three States, carried large boats 260 miles to Florence, Alabama, and small ones 650 miles to Knoxville.

Commercially, the railroads when the war opened were strangling the river trade. Their network served a far larger territory; they moved freight with greater celerity; they could send it by spurs and sidings to the factory door; they ran their carriers on frequent and regular schedules. But from the military standpoint, in enemy or disputed territory a river offered a far safer invasion road than a railway. Union commanders found that it was impossible to guard rail facilities over wide distances; guerrilla bands, organized cavalry detachments, or even single fearless men could spring from the woods to saw trestles, fire bridges, or tear up iron. Grant learned this lesson at heavy cost. Of course river vessels were also molested. But they could scatter the guerrillas by charges of grape, fight off larger forces, and sweep with little hurt past strong fortifications. The river lines could not be cut.[10]

Command of the Western rivers was held from the outset by the Union for the simple reason that the North owned most of the steamboats, produced a great majority of the trained rivermen, and had nearly all the facilities for building, fortifying, and repairing vessels. Pittsburgh, Cincinnati, Louisville, and St. Louis were in that order the important centers for steamboat construction in the 1850's. Conceivably New Orleans might have developed shipyards despite its lack of rolling mills and good machine shops, but it never did. The brave little start it made in the times of Madison and Monroe withered away. A search for steamboat builders along the whole lower Mississippi in 1861 would have turned up only a few craftsmen who made tiny boats for the bayous and lesser rivers. The small number of bottoms available at Memphis, Vicksburg, Port Hudson, and other places were soon crippled, sunk, or captured, so that Foote and Porter lorded it over the river world.[11]

One long-forgotten hero of the war, Colonel Lewis B. Parsons, took charge of Western army transport in St. Louis, where his foresight, vigilance, and energy made the most of water facilities in Western logistics. A single fact illustrates the thesis that in this theater of advance, as distinguished from the Eastern scene, rivers held a place more significant than rails: in the fiscal

10 Sherman wrote in the fall of 1863 that a railroad took a whole army to guard, "each foot of rail being essential to the whole; whereas they can't stop the Tennessee, and each boat can make its own game." Oct. 2, 1863, Naval O. R., I, xxv, 474.
11 Hunter, 106, 107; Hoppin, *Foote*, 154–168.

year 1862–63, almost 338,000,000 pounds of military stores were hauled by river as against 153,100,000 by cars.

Combined operations by land and water gave the conflict, especially in the West, what a European critic termed "an entirely distinctive character among all modern wars." A House committee later made a boast which was little exaggerated. "It is now practicable," it declared, "on twenty-four hours' notice, to embark at Boston or Baltimore a larger army than those with which Napoleon won some of his most decisive victories, and landing within three days at Cairo, twelve hundred miles distant, there embark it on transports, and within four days' more time disembark it at New Orleans, a thousand miles further, or two thousand two hundred miles from the point of departure." [12] The most strategic points of the war included those at which lines of rail touched a navigable river, for there huge supply depots were most useful.

[II]

The gunboat and mortar fleets embodied very special skills and enterprise.

When the war began James B. Eads, who as a poor boy had peddled apples on the streets of St. Louis, was at forty-one independently rich. By salvaging wrecked steamboats with a specially invented diving bell, he had become more expertly familiar with the Mississippi and its tributaries than any other man. When Lincoln called him to Washington to give advice, he proposed to the War Department a fleet of armored river gunboats. [13] As soon as the government asked for bids, he submitted plans for building 7 of 600 tons each, mobilized 4,000 men within a fortnight to speed the task, launched his first vessel in forty-five days, and had the others under way soon after. He proved a dynamo of well-directed energy.

Meanwhile the mariner Andrew H. Foote, whose short beard, tousled hair, mastiff jaw, and resolute look made him the image of an old sea dog, had arrived August 26, 1861, to take charge of Upper Mississippi operations with the rank of flag officer. He loved blue waves and a cloud of sail over his head. The "hybrid service" of the West, partly water, partly swamp, partly land, was utterly strange to him. But the officer who had led a stubborn crusade to abolish grog in the Navy was not daunted by his many difficulties. He found that his force consisted of three Ohio freight-and-passenger steamers recently altered and armed at Cincinnati and brought downstream,

---

12   Comte de Paris, *Civil War*, I, 215, 216; 39th Cong., 1st Sess., House Exec. Doc., I, 216, 217.
13   Nicolay and Hay, V, 118.

the *Conestoga, Tyler,* and *Lexington,* protected only by oak bulwarks; two vessels converted into gunboats by Frémont; the seven gunboats being built by Eads; and thirty-eight mortar boats constructed under Frémont's orders. Foote also found that because Washington had denied the Western Department money, credit, and materials, neither the gunboats nor mortar boats could be finished at the time stated by contract. If they *had* been finished only two months earlier, one of Foote's officers later wrote, no fighting at Columbus, Island No. 10, Memphis, and Vicksburg would have been necessary, and the Western forces might have been sent East.

"Our difficulties have been legion," Foote wrote Meigs October 29. He was still not certain of a successful result; "that is, of having guns and mortar-boats in efficient condition for going down the river in December." Like others, he complained of the Western propensity to grab contracts and then cheat in fulfilling them.[14] But by frenzied effort Eads and Foote met the demands thrown upon them. No chapter of hasty improvisation in the war is more striking than that which they wrote. They made and remade designs, solving many fresh problems—that of adequate clearance for the paddle wheel of an armor-weighted vessel in shallow water, for example. They built new yards and docks, invented new machinery, spurred rolling mills, machine shops, sawmills, and foundries to make the parts they needed, and kept the telegraph wires hot with demands for ordinance. When Eads and Foote began, "the timber to form the hulls of the vessels was as yet uncut in the forest, and the engines to drive them were unbuilt." They toiled incredible hours, seven days a week. The launch of Eads's earliest ship—the first armored river boat in American history—took place on October 12, at Carondelet, Missouri. The vessel, which had her boilers and engines in place, was named first the *St. Louis,* later the *De Kalb.* Then came the others, bearing the names of river places: *Pittsburgh, Cincinnati, Cairo, Mound City, Carondelet,* and *Louisville.*

Eads's gunboats, 175 feet long and 55.5 wide, had wooden hulls plated with iron two-and-a-half inches thick, and mounted thirteen guns, three in the bow, four on each side, and two at the stern. The largest of the early vessels added to this fleet was the *Benton,* of about 1,000 tons, a well-armored snagboat; but some boats of 1,200 tons soon came into service. Before the end of 1862 the Western Flotilla numbered 55 warships in all, of a great variety of sizes and types. Some were stern-wheelers. These had exceptional power and speed, but were difficult to manage in currents and headwinds. The

14 O. R., I, viii, 77–674, contains much about naval work on Western waters; so does Naval O. R., I, xxiii, *passim;* and see Gideon Welles, *Annual Report,* December 1, 1862. Foote was a captain until November 13, when his rank as flag-officer became effective; Hoppin, 184.

side-wheelers were more easily directed, better protected, and fast enough for most purposes. The counter-wheel boats, converted from ferries, were found too slow. For several reasons it was impossible to use propellers: the water was often too shoal to give them purchase, and they were easily broken by snags and floating timber. Eads's boats could make nine miles an hour under perfect conditions, but the others were slower. The most vulnerable elements were the boilers—a single penetrating shot might explode them, parboiling the crew—and the paddle wheels. In default of better plating, railroad irons and chains were used.[15]

The flotilla, manned largely by volunteer drafts, and subject to over-all army command, offered an arduous service. In summer, night and day, the cabins, wardrooms, and gun rooms were hot and stifling. Sharpshooters lurking on shore were ready to pick off any unwary man on deck. Hostile boats, batteries, and fire ships were a peril. But the fleet was endlessly useful. It carried troops, stores, wounded, mules—everything. Its fifty-pounder rifled guns, able to reach targets nearly five miles away, could disperse enemy columns, frighten guerrillas, and protect landing parties. From the low chimneys dense smoke advertised the imminence of the boats long before they rounded a distant bend, and the mere sight of this smoke and the hollow thud of the guns inspired terror. Even Eads's well-armored boats drew only six feet, while lighter craft among "Uncle Sam's web feet" carried deadly cannon up shallow creeks and bayous. No command gave better service for the money. "Our gunboat flotilla has not cost, including the building of the gunboats, $3,000,000 to date," wrote the fleet quartermaster to Foote late in May, 1862. Yet, he added, see what it has done.

The mortar boats which Frémont had commissioned were both a special asset and a difficult problem. The design was bad. Flat-bottomed, rectangular, with pointed bows and sterns, and vertical sides, a sort of scow, they offered great resistance to the water when towed—for they had no motive power of their own. In the center a structure of logs laid at right angles to each other supported the mortar beds and mortars, the whole weighing about thirteen tons. The recoil whenever a mortar was fired added about twenty tons to this vertical weight; and this soon sprung the seams, so that the boats had to be pumped. They had no conveniences to enable crews to live aboard. The novelty of the fittings made it hard to equip them. By herculean effort Abram S. Hewitt, stepping into the breach, got a number of mortar beds completed in his Trenton ironworks and sped them westward, earning the special thanks

15 Boynton, *Navy During the Rebellion*, I, 501; Hoppin, *Foote*, Ch. XIII; Report of Commander W. D. Porter, St. Louis, May 6, 1862, Naval O. R., I, xxiii, 82, 83; description of flotilla life in N. Y. *Weekly Tribune*, April 19, 1862.

of the War Department. The much-distrusted mortars soon proved useful against a variety of fortified strongholds.[16]

Another example of effective improvised effort was furnished by Charles Ellet, Jr., and his rams. A leading civil engineer, Ellet had long before the war conceived the idea of destroying enemy warships by ramming them with heavy steamers. He wrote the government. Stanton, in late March, 1862, when the *Merrimac* had demonstrated the power of a ram, ordered him west to buy and refit the boats immediately. He took old steamers, stiffened them by bulkheads of heavy timbers running through the hulls from head to stern, properly braced, strengthened the structure with tiebolts, and filled the bow with solid timbers. Within about forty days after quitting Washington, he had thus made seven rams and two consorts. The entire fleet, with its equipment and with coal and provisions for eighty days, cost less than $300,000. Ably commanded by Ellet himself, who was responsible to Secretary Stanton alone, it was destined to perform a spectacular feat at Memphis.[17]

Altogether, the building and mobilization of the river navy, first advertised to the world by the capture of Henry and Donelson, was one of the great initial achievements of the North. Along with the making of the new volunteer army of half a million men, it may be called the first impressive demonstration of the nation's war power. In a sense it was improvisation: the hurried, scrambling utilization of whatever came to hand in old boats, old ideas, and old methods, along with new machines, new conceptions, and new designs. But out of the improvisation came planned organization. Here at least, applied to war, was the peculiar American genius that had vanquished the greatest enemy of the pioneer—distance—by the Concord coach and Conestoga wagon, Fulton's steamboat, Baldwin's light basket locomotives, and Ellet's daring railway curves. Here was the quick energetic use of the trained expert, for Eads, Foote, and Ellet had three different varieties of proficiency.

Historians have written of the capture of Donelson as a turning point in the Western war effort. Not so; it was this capture together with the forging of the river fleets which was the turning point. The Confederates, who had a keen appreciation of the importance of the Mississippi and its tributaries, but who were poor in boats, yards, and pilots, were staggered by the sudden emergence of Foote's and Ellet's flotillas. General Pillow in August had dropped his projected attack on Cairo when he learned that Frémont had

16 Quartermaster George D. Wise, St. Louis, May 25, 1862, Naval O. R., I, xxiii, 105–107; Hoppin, 193, 194; Nevins, *Frémont*, 484, 492; *Rebellion Record*, III, 434, 435; Fox Corr., NYHS; Nevins, *Hewitt*, 199–204.

17 Ellet got his orders to build March 27, 1862. He reconstructed three of his boats at Pittsburgh, three at Cincinnati, and one at New Albany, Ind. Each had three heavy, solid bulkheads of timber 12–18 inches thick stretching fore and aft. Naval O. R., I, xxiii, 65–66, 274–277.

brought nearly 4,000 troops down from St. Louis by boat in 26 hours, and that the three steamers armed at Cincinnati had passed the New Albany bar downstream. From that hour the amphibious Union advance was sometimes delayed, but never stopped.

[III]

Organization and mechanization could solve the problems of logistics. But inexperience, rashness, and improvisation could bring any army to the brink of ruin once it was placed and supplied.

At Donelson the first Confederate line of defense in the West had been not merely pierced but shattered. The troops holding it sagged back toward the southern boundary of Tennessee, leaving Memphis on the west and Knoxville on the east in a precarious situation. Albert Sidney Johnston was temporarily stunned. A clamor for his dismissal arose; but Jefferson Davis told a complaining Tennessee delegation, "If Sidney Johnston is not a general, the South has none to give you." [18]

We have seen that one of the vital communication lines of the Confederacy connected Memphis and Chattanooga along the southern boundary of Tennessee: the Memphis & Charleston, which ran from the Mississippi River almost due east through Corinth and Huntsville to Chattanooga, whence it sent one fork northeast into Virginia and another southeast into South Carolina. Just after Donelson, Judah P. Benjamin wrote Lee that this lifeline "must be defended at all hazards." [19] It was so important that the Confederate Cabinet even discussed the possibility of abandoning the Virginia capital to defend it. Obviously, as much Tennessee territory as possible ought to be saved to the South, for every new Union advance sheared away more of the Confederacy's iron resources. The State, with 17 furnaces smelting some 22,000 tons in 1860, was the largest Southern producer of pig iron. Yet the Tennessee River, now that the forts had fallen, opened a broad avenue of invasion. [20]

When Albert Sidney Johnston left Nashville with about 10,000 discouraged, disorderly, ill-armed troops, he realized that he must retreat into Northern Mississippi, concentrate, and augment his forces. A powerful Confederate army must be assembled at some single point to block the pursuing Union cohorts. This principle of concentration was strongly espoused by Beauregard, who had succeeded to the command at Columbus, and by Bragg at Pensacola. The week after Donelson saw messengers scurrying about and detachments march-

18 Fiske, *Miss. Valley*, 70.
19 O. R., I, vi, 398, 828.
20 Eaton, *Confederacy*, 175, 176.

ing forward in a frenzied attempt to create a strong force while there was yet time. Although Johnston was chief in command, Beauregard was probably the prime mover.

Strenuous effort gave the undertaking success. Bragg brought up about 10,000 men from the Pensacola-Mobile area; Leonidas Polk helped gather together all the effectives scattered along the river at New Madrid, Columbus, and Fort Pillow; and Johnston besought the governors of Tennessee, Louisiana, and Alabama for at least 5,000 men apiece. West of the river Earl Van Dorn had a small force in Arkansas. Beauregard called on him to assist in forming a joint command of fully 40,000: "We must do something or die in the attempt, otherwise all will shortly be lost." The exuberant Creole spoke of launching a northward sweep, aided by twelve gunboats from New Orleans, to retake all the ground surrendered. To Corinth, a junction on the Memphis & Charleston, designated as the central rendezvous, Johnston on March 25 marched his own army. Unit after unit then came in, until 40,000 men were really assembled. The high officers, including not only Johnston, Beauregard, Polk, and Bragg, but Hardee, Breckinridge, and shoals of brigadiers, overawed ordinary soldiers who had never dreamed of seeing so much top brass.[21]

Considering the recent defeats and the poverty of the area, this force had been gathered with astonishing promptness. The sight of strong new levies and detachments from the Gulf filled veterans of Donelson with angry regret. "Why couldn't this help have come in January?" they demanded. "We begged for it; we foretold the disasters which lack of it entailed; and now that so much has been lost, the help arrives!"[22]

Before the concentration at Corinth was completed, Beauregard sent two regiments and some field guns to hold a bluff on the west bank of the Tennessee called Pittsburg Landing, where peacetime steamboats had unloaded cargoes for the neighboring countryside. Behind the abrupt red clay bluff lay a wide, roughly seamed plateau, stretching along the river about four miles, and at the highest point a hundred feet above the water. A small Methodist meetinghouse called Shiloh Chapel, log-built, was the principal landmark. On the south, northwest, and north, this tableland was bounded

21 Johnston's report on the loss of Nashville, O. R., I, vii, 426, 427; Roman, *Beauregard*, I, 367 ff.; A. P. James, "Strategy of Concentration of the Confd. Forces," Am. Hist. Assn. *Annual Report* (1919), 365–374; Beauregard to Van Dorn, Feb. 1, 1862, Brock Coll., HL. The State of Mississippi called for 10,000 men. But James Burnet of West Point, Miss., wrote that many were sneaking into the ranks of companies whose terms were soon to expire, while some who anticipated a draft were writing favorite commanders to find places. Feb. 18, 1862, to John J. Pettus, Miss. State Archives.

22 Polk, *Polk*, II, 87 ff. Beauregard wrote Van Dorn that by rapid marches of a large army they might "take Cairo, Paducah, the mouths of the Tennessee and Cumberland and most probably be able to take St. Louis by the river. What say you to this brilliant program?"

by deep creeks, while it was cut with minor ravines and hollows, and in part covered by a thick growth of oak, hickory, locust, sycamore, and other trees, interlaced with bushes and briars. The main road from Corinth, twenty miles away, entered it from the southwest, well masked by woods. But the Southern regiments did not long hold the place, for Foote's gunboats on the Tennessee soon made it untenable. Then General C. F. Smith, bringing up troops at the suggestion of Sherman, chose the Landing as the spot where Grant and Buell should unite their armies. Grant, on reaching Savanna farther down the river, at once ratified the choice without even inspecting it.

It was imperative for the Confederates to strike before Grant and Buell joined forces. From the moment he reached Corinth, Johnston was impatient to finish organizing his four corps and advance; but he labored under a great impediment in the woebegone state of his army. Bragg wrote on March 18 that he felt deep concern over their "disorganized and demoralized condition," and one soldier thought that May might approach before they could be whipped into shape.[23] The first days of April, however, found the men fairly ready, and the situation favorable for dealing a blow. Johnston knew that while Grant's main force had spread its camps over Pittsburg Landing, Buell's men had not arrived. He heard that Lew Wallace's division had appeared at Bethel Station, about twenty-odd miles north of Corinth and that far west of the Tennessee; if this were true, Wallace could give no aid to Grant. Johnston and Beauregard gave orders to the corps commanders to be ready to march at six the next morning, April 3.

The curtain was about to rise on Shiloh.

[IV]

While the Confederates were concentrating, the Northerners should have been doing the same, and planning their own swift offensive. But overconfidence, imperfect training for battle, the obtuseness of Halleck, and the carelessness of Grant placed the recent victors in a position of the utmost peril.

The overconfidence had some excuse, for Union leaders knew that the Confederate retreat southward from Nashville had been almost a rout. They were told that the ragged, hungry columns covered a line of twenty miles, that stragglers numbered thousands, and that at every crossroads soldiers deserted by squads. Military men concluded that the Army of the West was helpless to check Grant and Buell. The imperfect Union training was also a fact. All the Western forces had a dismaying proportion of inefficient, untrustworthy junior officers. Resignations and dismissals were getting rid of

23   O. R., I, x, pt. 2, p. 340; C. J. Johnson, March 23, 1862, to family, C. J. J. Papers, LSU.

many, but more remained. The troops, especially in Buell's Army of the Tennessee, included dozens of raw and undisciplined regiments who needed stern drill like that given in the Potomac camps. The quartermaster and commissary departments also required drastic reform. Rations, for example, were to a great extent dealt out to be miscooked by the soldiers individually or in squads, although in camp it would have been easy to establish company kitchens.

As for Halleck, he had hesitated in a complete muddle, and finally had directed Grant, as we have noted, to execute what was hardly more than a raid southward, for Halleck wished to be on hand when a great engagement was fought.[24] He had therefore ordered Grant to steam up the Tennessee and cut the Memphis & Charleston by penetrating into northern Mississippi, destroying a key bridge, and tearing up parts of the line. But he was to avoid a general battle, retreating rather than fight one; and it was under these limitations that his army on March 17 had reached Savanna. Here Grant had established his headquarters.[25] He had five divisions present or not far distant, commanded by Sherman, McClernand, Hurlbut, Lew Wallace, and C. F. Smith; reinforcements were arriving daily, and as they came in were organized first into brigades and then into a sixth division under Benjamin M. Prentiss. On the very day that Grant set up headquarters, Buell with 35,000 men began his overland march to join him. Grant, who despised Halleck's order against battle, later wrote: "When all reinforcements should have arrived, I expected to take the initiative by marching on Corinth." [26] He thought that might be soon, for on March 19 Buell was only 90 miles from Savanna.

It was thus to prepare for striking a blow that Grant accepted Pittsburg Landing as the spot for gathering the Union forces. Sherman had fallen in love with the place. "The ground itself admits of easy defense by a small command," he wrote Grant, "and yet affords admirable camping-ground for a hundred thousand men." [27] C. F. Smith was equally enthusiastic. The last ten days of March saw the plateau whitened by tents as unit after unit took station there. Sixty-nine puffing transports unloaded men and materials. Though the elderly Smith had nominal charge of dispositions, he was so ailing that Sherman took field control, pointing out to each division the ground it was to occupy. McClernand came in on the 27th, and Lew Wallace brought his division ashore at Crump's Landing, about halfway between Savanna

24 O. R., I, vii, 674; Fuller, *Grant*, 95 ff.
25 See Mil. Hist. Soc. Mass., *Campaigns in Ky. and Tenn.*, 104–109; O. R., I, x, pt. 2, pp. 32–43.
26 *Memoirs*, I, 332.
27 O. R., I, x, pt. 1, p. 27; cf. Greeley, *Amer. Conflict*, II, 58. Sherman comments in his *Memoirs*, I, 228, that "at a later period of the war, we could have rendered this position impregnable in a night."

THE LOWER MISSISSIPPI

and Pittsburg Landing; not so far away from the main force as the false report heard by Johnston had placed him, but too far for a rapid junction.

By April 1 a great army was comfortably settling at Pittsburg Landing. All too comfortably settled, all too negligently ensconced! The very choice of campsite had been characteristically casual, for Grant had accepted the recommendations of Smith and other officers without making any personal investigation. As the army settled in, Johnston was marching. At dawn on the 6th he attacked.

The most arresting aspects of Shiloh are not its charges, panics, and rallies, but its evidences that both sides were still waging war with impromptu confusion, inexperience, and planlessness. No battle of the war does more to justify Moltke's sneer at the American fighting as a struggle of two armed mobs. Everyone knows the outlines of the conflict: how the Confederate attack completely surprised the Union camp, how Grant's troops were forced back far toward the river, where 10,000 fugitives soon huddled under the bluff, how when utter defeat stared the Northerners in the face Albert Sidney Johnston was mortally wounded and the first detachments of Buell's army arrived on the field, how that night more of Buell's forces came into position, and how on the second day the Confederates were driven back and forced to retreat to Corinth. The battle abounds in controversial questions. Was Grant completely overwhelmed the first day, so that only Buell's arrival retrieved the field, or had he stopped the Confederates before Buell's first detachment appeared? Was the transfer of the Confederate command from Johnston to Beauregard, followed as it was by Beauregard's immediate order to halt, the fatal blow to the Confederates?

What is far more important is the fact that the battle illustrates as do few others the want of organization, plan, vigilance, and discipline which crippled both sections in waging war; defects connected, of course, with the whole character of American society.[28]

Grant was still learning his trade as soldier; his staff was still but partly filled and imperfectly trained. With him was John A. Rawlins, his assistant adjutant-general since the previous August, a grim, hard-jawed young attorney in his early thirties, with stiff black hair, a dark complexion, a gruff low voice, and brusque manners. Some said he was Grant's brains, and no question existed about his quick, razor-edged intellect; but he was more than that—he was Grant's conscience. From his lawyer days in Galena he knew that one of his responsibilities was to keep Grant away from drink. He stood no nonsense from anybody, his chief least of all. "Insubordination twenty times a day," commented one officer. Theodore S. Bowers, another Illinoisan, born in poverty, a printer who had become country editor, not yet thirty, was a faithful, efficient secretarial aide; "gallant little Bowers," an officer called him for his loyal courage. But the strong responsible figures of Grant's subsequent staff—the engineers, C. B. Comstock and W. F. Smith, the Mexican War veteran F. T. Dent, the Indian Ely S. Parker, the quick Adam Badeau, the skillful young West Pointer Orville E. Babcock—were still to be added. He had few capable helpers and lacked what he needed most, an intelligence officer.[29]

Overwork may explain why Grant paid no personal visit to Pittsburg Landing until April 1, but proofs that he had much to learn abound. Still insensitive to the need for an efficient intelligence service—spies, scouts, patrols —he knew practically nothing of Johnston's position, strength, and intentions. Sherman on April 1 made a mere steamboat reconnaissance from the Landing,

28 Good accounts of the battle are available in Military Hist. Soc. Mass., *Campaigns in Ky. and Tenn.;* 101–254; *Battles and Leaders,* I, 465–610; M. F. Force, *From Fort Henry to Corinth,* 91–182; A. L. Conger, *Rise of U. S. Grant,* 238–275; and Kenneth P. Williams, *Lincoln finds a General,* III, Ch. XIV.
29 On Grant's staff see Williams, III, 181 ff. Captain A. S. Baxter was quartermaster-general, and W. R. Rowley, W. S. Hillyer, and Clark B. Lagow were aides. Sherman wrote in 1885 that "his staff at Shiloh was very inferior, Rawlins, Lagow, Hillyer, etc."; to W. J. Eliot, Sept. 12, 1885, Sherman Papers, LC.

thirty miles up the river, and on April 3 sent the Fifth Ohio Cavalry on a nine-mile push west which discovered nothing; that was all. It was negligent of Grant to let Lew Wallace's Second Division be posted near Crump's, six or seven miles above Pittsburg Landing, and cut off from it by Snake Creek, a stream out of its banks with two dismantled bridges to mock at the troops. It was negligent of him not to hurry Buell along in his snail-slow advance from Nashville.[30]

These lapses intermeshed, obviously, with those of other Union commanders. Why did Buell take more than a fortnight to march his 30,000 men 90 miles from Columbia to Pittsburg Landing? Partly because this able soldier was deficient in stern energy. Lincoln's secretaries have endorsed General Ormsby Mitchel's verdict: "He lacked decision." Partly because nobody told him to hurry; Halleck, indeed, advised him on April 3 to concentrate his troops at Waynesboro, where they would have been useless, while Grant on the 4th suggested that he take his time, since it would be impossible to give him water transportation from Savanna to Pittsburg Landing before the 7th! He allowed a burned bridge at Duck River on his line of advance to delay him ten days, while he languidly built another. The imperious General William Nelson finally lost patience, obtained permission to lead the way, and found that with care a ford was feasible; and thus on the 29th McCook's division got across. Had it not been for Nelson's tremendous will and energy, Buell might never have arrived at Shiloh until too late.[31] An entry in Colonel Jacob Ammen's diary is illuminating:

March 27—Late in the evening General Nelson, in returning from General Buell's headquarters, informed me that he had General Buell's permission to take the advance, and gave me a verbal order to cross Duck River at daylight the 29th. I inquired if the bridge would be done. He answered, "No." "Are there any boats?" He said, "No; but the river is falling; and damn you, get over, for we must have the advance and get the glory." He enjoined secrecy, lest we should be prevented from taking the advance. March 28—Went to Duck River to examine the fords; sent some of my cavalry in; river 200 yards or more wide; fords crooked. Fortunately, some army wagons return with forage and ford the river; the water just touches the beds of the wagons; current strong; water above and below, deep; no boats. . . . March 29—Reveille at 3 A.M., breakfast, wagons loaded, column formed. . . . The Tenth Brigade, infantry and artillery and train, crossed Duck River this cold and disagreeable day without accident.

Worst of all was the failure of Sherman, despite ample warning of the enemy advance, to take precautions to meet it. Halleck had emphasized the

30 Conger, *op. cit.*, Chs. XVII, XVIII.
31 O. R., I, x, pt. 1, pp. 329–330.

importance of entrenching in the vicinity of the enemy, and Grant and Sherman knew well that Johnston at Corinth was but twenty miles away. But the West Point, regular-army theory was that field works made the troops cowardly, for they should be made to "stand up and fight man-fashion." Sherman later wrote that they did not fortify "because we had no orders to do so, and because such a course would have made men timid." [32] This was absurd; an obvious precaution can be taken without orders—and Halleck did instruct Grant to entrench. Moreover, far from dispiriting the troops, entrenchments with openings at intervals give special confidence to raw soldiers. One of the great lessons of the war was to be the power of the bullet as delivered by rifled breechloaders; but a still greater lesson was to be the power of the defensive once infantrymen learned to dig trenches and erect breastworks.

The Confederate army from Corinth, approaching Pittsburg Landing along two roads on April 5, was not in a position for attack until midafternoon. The previous day an advance force had come into collision with some Union troops who were busy drilling, and after a little fighting had retired; then that night some Confederate buglers had recklessly sounded calls. It seemed to Beauregard that all opportunity of surprise and hence success had been lost, and he advised a retreat; but Johnston insisted that they go ahead. "I would fight them if they were a million," he told a staff officer. The Southern army was then deployed in three parallel lines along the Union front, Hardee commanding the first, Bragg the second, and Polk and Breckinridge the third; and they were put in readiness to make their onslaught at dawn. [33]

Seldom in war has a surprise been more complete. It is true that Sherman sent out daily reconnaissances, but he made little use of the data gained. On the 5th, with Johnston two miles distant, he wrote Grant: "I have no doubt that nothing will occur today more than some picket firing. The enemy is saucy, but got the worst of it yesterday, and will not press our pickets far. I will not be drawn out far unless with certainty of advantage, and I do not apprehend anything like an attack on our position." In another note to Grant he wrote: "All is quiet along my lines now." He knew that some cavalry was on his front, and he thought that probably two infantry regiments and a battery were a couple of miles away. "I will send you 10 prisoners of war and a report of last night's affair in a few minutes." Several of the prisoners

32 Cortissoz, *Whitelaw Reid*, II, 336, 337.
33 *Battles and Leaders*, I, 495; T. Harry Williams, *Beauregard*, 133 ff.; Johnston, *A. S. Johnston*, 484–522; Jordan and Pryor, *Forrest*, 117 ff. Beauregard had hoped to attack on the morning of the 5th of April and was horrified by the delays. Johnston showed much greater firmness and courage. But Beauregard recovered his spirits when Hardee asked him to ride down the front of his men to encourage them.

boasted they were the advance guard of an army which within twenty-four hours would throw the whole Union army into the Tennessee. This talk might have been taken for loose vaporing, but one mortally wounded Confederate, when told he could not live, sent for a colonel whose relatives he knew, and warned him that a Confederate host of 50,000 was about to smash against the Northern lines. When the colonel sent word to Sherman, the general refused to believe the story.[34]

It is clear that Sherman had the *idée fixe* that no danger of attack existed. A man of nervous, excitable temperament, he was never lethargic, for his perceptions were acute and his mind incessantly active. But he sometimes lacked balance and judgment. As an admiring friend once said, his intellect was a beautifully intricate piece of machinery, with all the screws a little loose.[35] When on the afternoon of the 5th a sergeant brought word that Ohio pickets had noted rabbits and other small animals scurrying out of the woods, and had seen enemy cavalry, while one outlying soldier had descried infantry in line, Sherman actually ordered the sergeant put in confinement for circulating a false report. Additional reports he waved aside. "Oh, it is only a reconnoitering party," he said complacently.[36]

A few Union officers were alert for the Southern onset. Under orders from General Prentiss the advance guard on the Corinth road had been strengthened, and at 3 A.M. on April 6 five companies of Colonel David Moore's Twenty-first Missouri were nearly two miles out from the Union camp. Here at daybreak fighting began. But elsewhere the surprise was general. Many troops at the point of impact were first alarmed when soldiers of the advance guard stumbled out of the woods, shouting: "The rebels are coming! Get into line." Men just beginning to cook breakfast were startled by pealing orders and the long roll of drums. As they caught up their muskets messengers galloped off to notify brigade and division headquarters, and neighboring regiments sprang confusedly to arms. Firing all along the picket lines redoubled, and companies hurried forward to reinforce them. Everywhere coffee pots were being kicked over, sleepy officers were jerking on their trousers, and soldiers were loading their guns. "The searching bullet," wrote Major George Mason later, "found many an unfortunate in his bed." As one company which had rushed to reinforce the pickets fled back through

34 O. R., I, x, pt. 2, pp. 93–94; Grant, *Memoirs*, I, 334 ff.; Mil. Hist. Soc. Mass., *op. cit.*, 115 ff., 134 ff. Grant had shown uneasiness over the danger of attack by a considerable enemy force, but the blow he feared was one on Wallace's force at Crump's Landing, not an assault by the whole Confederate array on his own army.

35 See the perceptive article on Sherman's *Memoirs* in *Galaxy*, XX (1875), 325 ff., 450 ff.

36 T. Harry Williams, *Beauregard*, 132; Mil. Hist. Soc. Mass., *op. cit.*, 115–117; Fuller, *Grant*, 106 ff.

the brush in hot retreat, its captain yelled to the camp: "The rebels up there are thicker than fleas on a dog's back."[37]

A brilliant sun was beginning to mount in a cloudless sky. The bright green foliage, flecked by dogwood and redbud blossoms, half hid the advancing Southerners, but the barrels of new Enfield muskets carried by the Confederate battle line gleamed through the leaves, and puffs of smoke curled over the trees. The Southern battlefront suddenly emerged on J. J. Appler's flank within easy musket shot, and the colonel began to shift front to meet the attack. He hurried his sick, nearly a third of his whole command, out of their tents to the rear. Some cowards joined the fleeing invalids, and most of the remainder, who had never held a battalion drill, milled about in utter confusion. Sherman rode up with an orderly. At first he turned his field glasses to the empty woods in front, ignoring the advancing lines on the flank. "Look out, General!" cried Union soldiers. "You'll be shot! Look to the right!" As the Confederates loosed a new volley, the orderly fell dead. "My God, we're attacked!" cried Sherman. "Appler, hold your position— I'll support you!" He rode off for reinforcements. And Appler, seeing the Confederates advance amid the smoke and flame of their discharges, took to his heels with a shout to his men: "Retreat! Save yourselves!"[38]

Johnston and Beauregard had achieved their object of taking Grant's army unaware. The attack had begun at five. Johnston, mounting, told his aides: "Tonight we will water our horses in the Tennessee River."[39]

The surprise was not merely tactical, but represented strategic blindness of an unforgivable kind. The New York *Tribune*, reading the weather signs (including Southern journals), had concluded that an important movement was afoot. An editorial of April 2, "The Expected Blow," declared that no Eastern stroke seemed likely. "On the other hand, we see much that indicates a determination on the part of the Secession chiefs to strike a sudden and heavy blow in the Southwest. They are evidently concentrating their forces at Corinth or some other point near the south line of Tennessee, with intent to hurl the great mass of them suddenly on an exposed detachment of ours, thus repeating the lesson of Bull Run, Wilson's Creek, and Lexington. We trust they are to be baffled in this game by the cautious energy of General Halleck." If newspapermen on Park Row saw this, why did not

37 *Ibid.*, 117. The surprise and recovery are described in detail by Albert Dillahunty, *Shiloh*; Otto Eisenschiml, *The Story of Shiloh*; and *Battles and Leaders*, I, 558 ff. A mass of letters and reports may be found in O. R., I, x, pt. 2, pp. 93–627.

38 Lloyd Lewis, *Sherman*, 220, 221; Williams, *Lincoln Finds a General*, III, 356, 357. Useful papers may be found in Illinois Commandery Loyal Legion, *Essays and Recs.*, I, 9–124. Col. Jesse J. Appler commanded the Fifty-third Ohio.

39 Whitelaw Reid's comprehensive account of Shiloh in the Cincinnati *Gazette* of April 14, twelve close columns of more than 19,000 words, was exaggerated in some details, but in general surprisingly accurate; Cortissoz, *Reid*, I, 86, 87.

Grant see it? Or since he was harassed by a thousand details, why did not Halleck in St. Louis and Stanton at the War Department see it?

The failure of the Union commanders to raise any field works stupefied Beauregard, who had said after the clash on April 4, "Now they will be intrenched to the eyes."[40] A decent intelligence system and a service of advanced sentries would have been equally valuable. Colonel G. F. R. Henderson points out in a classic military text that throughout the war the armies never made laborious use of outposts and pickets. Surprises were frequent. More than one great battle opened with a sudden attack on sleeping men, and sometimes when two armies were in close proximity, one withdrew in the night leaving the other unaware. He contrasts this with the vigilance of the German armies in 1870–71, when surprises were unknown. "After a forced march or a hard day's fighting, no relaxation was allowed. Before the fires of the bivouac were lighted, scouts were moving far to the front. Through the night watches every road and path was traversed at short intervals by patrols; and the earliest light saw stronger parties pushing toward the enemy's lines."[41] American individualism had bred an ungirt lack of method.

Grant, Sherman, and others were learning their trade. Many a brave Illinois and Ohio youth died in agony that spring Sunday because generals learn by trial and error. Later Sherman would blush to remember he had written that "I think" two enemy regiments and a battery are "about two miles out," and Grant would blush to recall the letter he had sent Halleck just before the storm: "I have scarcely the faintest idea of an attack (general one) being made upon us. . . ."[42]

The generals erred because they underestimated not only the speed with which the Confederates recovered from their disasters, but the whole power and determination of the Confederacy. They lay under McClellan's illusion in the East, that one strong thrust would win the war. "Up to the battle of Shiloh," writes Grant, "I . . . believed that the rebellion against the Government would collapse suddenly, and soon, if a decisive victory could be gained over any of its armies." The fall of Donelson, Bowling Green, and Nash-

40   T. Harry Williams, *Beauregard*, 132.
41   *Science of War*, 208.
42   O. R., I, x, pt. 1, p. 89. Many Union officers criticized Grant and Sherman angrily. The saddest day of Illinois history, wrote John M. Palmer, was that melancholy Sunday when the flower of her troops were slaughtered at Shiloh; unless the day Grant was made a general might be regarded as sadder still. To Trumbull, April 24, 1862, Trumbull Papers, LC. After Washburne delivered a flamboyant defense of Grant in Congress, where Sherman of Ohio and Harlan of Iowa attacked him, Joseph Medill of the Chicago *Tribune* wrote it was no use—Grant "is played out. The soldiers are down on him."; May 24, 1862, Washburne Papers, LC.

ville had buttressed the view that the Confederacy was fast staggering to its doom. Both Grant and McClellan thought that the Confederates would retreat until cornered like Cornwallis; then, the capitulation. "I had no expectation of needing fortifications," Grant writes.[43]

By their courage and sacrifice the 80,000 men who struggled at Shiloh, in the bloodiest contest thus far fought on the continent, consecrated one of the greatest battlefields of the war. Here visitors may see the bluff below which the terrorized fugitives of Grant's most demoralized regiments took shelter, a mob which horrified Buell when he saw it. They may see the ground on Grant's left flank called the Hornet's Nest, where the Confederate losses were particularly staggering. They may find the spot where Albert Sidney Johnston, trying to put fresh nerve into a shaken Tennessee regiment, received his mortal wound. On one part of the battlefield is the Bloody Pond where many fell dying, and to which men of both armies crawled for their last taste of water. On another runs the sunken road where some of Prentiss' men, taking shelter, fought with indomitable devotion until the remnants of his surrounded division were forced to surrender. The Union losses were officially reported as 13,047 men; the Confederate, 10,699. "We can never forget what they did here"—but it is not a field on which qualities of generalship earned laurels for either section.

At the end, the lack of bold Union generalship made the battle far less decisive than it might have been. The Confederates, decimated, wearied, and in part almost famished, had become badly shattered by the end of the second day. "The fire and animation had left our troops," wrote one Southern leader of the last hours of fighting. Grant at nightfall intended to follow up his success with fresh troops and cavalry; and his failure to execute this intention, when the combined strength of his and Buell's armies so heavily overweighed the foe, excites wonderment. Confederate commanders expressed surprise over the lack of pursuit. Could Grant not have scattered Beauregard's forces to the wind, taken multitudes of prisoners, seized Corinth at once, and all but put an end to the war in the West? The best military historians think so.[44]

Some psychological deterrent, some half-hearted unwillingness to risk freshly won laurels, to push tired troops into desperate new exertions, and to stake all on a final cast, seems involved in the frequent Union failure during the war to follow a success by grasping complete victory. Grant makes three excuses: the Confederate retreat churned the muddy roads into morasses; he had not the heart to order wornout men to pursue; and his sen-

---

43 *Memoirs*, I, 332, 368.

44 Reports of Jacob Thompson and others, O. R., I, x, pt. 1, pp. 400 ff., treat Confederate demoralization. John Codman Ropes, *Civil War*, II, 90–92, and Fuller, *Grant*, 114, 115, emphatically condemn Grant's failure to pursue.

iority in rank over Buell was so recent that he hesitated to give him positive orders.[45] These excuses are fragile. If the Confederates could drag wagons, artillery, and wounded back over the roads, he could march over them; Buell's troops and Lew Wallace's division were comparatively fresh; and he had every right as chief commander to give Buell peremptory instructions. Sherman's explanation is still flimsier. Questioned by John Fiske, he jauntily remarked of the Confederates: "I assure you, my dear fellow, that we had quite enough of their society for two whole days, and were only too glad to be rid of them on any terms." Buell, who was anxious to pursue, is frankest of all. Everybody in Grant's army, he writes, "appeared to have thought that the object of the battle was sufficiently accomplished when they were reinstated in their camps." [46]

Once more Grant's lack of a good intelligence service crippled him, for he believed that the Confederate army, far from defeated, remained near his front ready for stubborn renewal of the battle. For a time he thought he could not safely remain west of the Tennessee much longer without large reinforcements. Yet in actual fact, the Confederates were broken.

Bragg wrote April 8, halfway back to Corinth: "Our condition is horrible. Troops utterly disorganized and demoralized. Road almost impassable. No provision and no forage. . . ." Breckinridge, whose force was to furnish a covering rear guard, declared: "My troops are worn out and I don't think can be relied on after the first volley." [47] The starved horses were dropping by the roadside; guns had to be abandoned. The sufferings of the wounded were indescribable. An observer who rode alongside the retreating columns the first night wrote that he saw more human agony and despair than he had dreamed possible. The army wound along a narrow, bottomless road in cold, drizzling rain which fell ever harder till it turned into hail. In the long lines of wagons the moaning casualties were piled like bags of grain, most of them without even a blanket. As hundreds died, they were thrown out to make room for the men who walked alongside with broken arms or fearful wounds. Several thousand men deserted on the retreat, while more arrived at Corinth sick of the war. They had lost irreplaceable arms, ammunition, blankets, and knapsacks. [48]

But in spite of their hopeless inferiority, their griefs and despairs, the

---

45 See Grant's report, O. R., I, x, pt. 1, pp. 108–111; *Memoirs*, I, 354, 355.
46 Fiske, *Miss. Valley in Civil War*, 99; *Battles and Leaders*, I, 534; and see Grant's letter to Buell, April 7, 1862, *ibid.*, I, 532, 533.
47 Bragg to Beauregard O. R., I, x, pt. 2, pp. 398, 399. Reports of Union officers on the battle (Sherman, Buell, Nelson, Wallace, and others) are in O. R., I, x, pt. 1, pp. 93–381; of Hardee, Breckinridge, and other Confederate officers in O. R., I, x, pt. 1, pp. 382–627.
48 An Impressed New Yorker, *Thirteen Months in the Confederate Army*.

heroic Confederates did return safe to camp. The Union troops were not in a much happier frame of mind. Burying the dead, picking up the battle-field debris, discussing the blunders of their officers, they were surly victors. Grant's and Buell's men exchanged recriminations which created a morose animosity outlasting the war. Meanwhile, the advent of the bumbling Halleck to take charge aroused general discontent among intelligent officers.

4

Springtide of Northern Hope

FOR THE three months from February to June, 1862, after their winter of discouragement, the Northern people plucked up hope. Stanton's vigor gave heart to everybody. After all his delays, McClellan did besiege Yorktown, and did fight a successful battle at Williamsburg. Meanwhile, the thrusts by Grant and Buell cheered the West, the blockade began to take a real grip, and those who kept an eye on the navy rubbed their hands over its energetic operations in the Gulf. People began to remember the twittering voices of autumn, when McClellan had told a Philadelphia committee that the war could not endure long, Robert J. Walker had predicted that the conflict would not outlast the spring campaigns, and Cameron had closed a description of the government's martial preparations with the words: "Therefore I say to you, our day of trouble has gone by." [1]

The gloom of the South matched the cheerfulness of the North. As the installation of the permanent Confederate Government in Richmond had been fixed for Washington's Birthday, it took place under the unhappiest circumstances. Donelson was less than a week old, Roanoke Island had just been lost to an amphibious Union expedition, and McClellan was imminently expected to deliver a series of sledgehammer blows. Under black skies, in cascades of rain, a dense crowd gathered before the Virginia capitol to hear Davis' inaugural. It departed chilled, for his speech was as limp as the wet flags. An appeal to the people to accept their meed of blood, sweat, and tears, a robust call to battle, might have set the South ablaze with new ardor. The Virginia press, much of it always critical of the cotton-kingdom leaders, loosed an avalanche of criticism on the despondent President. He is fainthearted, men said, he is trying to do too much and doing it badly, and he plays favorites in both civil and military affairs; he should summon abler lieutenants to his side. Davis was in fact one of those romantics who stand up to the realism of adversity badly.

1 Phila. *Evening Journal*, Nov. 5, 1861. "The backbone of the rebellion is already broken," said the Lexington, Ky., *Observer and Reporter*, Feb. 19, 1861, "and its utter annihilation cannot but follow."

"I have understood (from Judge Campbell)," wrote Kean of the War Department later,[2] "that in February 1862 just after his inauguration the President talked seriously of resigning, in consequence of the opposition in the Congress and his unpopularity in the country."

Yet the Davis Administration, grappling with crises that never ended and trying to surmount difficulties that were often insuperable, had gained in strength, and showed commendable ability, courage, and devotion. With all his faults and shortcomings—his physical frailty, his hypersensitive temperament, his tactlessness, his want of eloquence and magnetism—the President himself showed an energy, determination, and administrative dispatch that proved him the best leader the South could have found. He gave his principal attention to military affairs, and dealt with them capably. His problem here was very different from Lincoln's. The South did magnificently with its Eastern commanders and badly with its Western; the North did splendidly with Grant, Sherman, and Thomas in the West, but poorly in the East. This fact should be remembered in appraising the familiar criticism of Davis as neglectful of the Western theatre. A more valid charge was that he sometimes failed to protect his Cabinet members properly from attacks in Congress—but so did Lincoln; neither could do the impossible. The State Department had passed in the summer of 1861 from the sulky, intractable Robert Toombs to the sane, coolheaded R. M. T. Hunter, who in March, 1862, gave way to the brilliant Judah P. Benjamin— each change being for the better. In the War Department the highminded but feeble Leroy P. Walker, who lacked administrative capacity, had been ousted by Davis in September, 1861. After a brief interim service by Benjamin, his place was taken by George Wythe Randolph, grandson of Jefferson, who deserves credit for his stern attempts to enforce conscription in the face of State Rights opposition. Randolph was to hold office until the fall of 1862, when in November James A. Seddon would succeed. Stephen R. Mallory in the Navy Department, and Christopher G. Memminger in the Treasury, wrestled heroically with impossibilities.

The new Confederate Congress, an abler body than the old, showed less resolution than the critical situation demanded, but it did pass a series of stern acts. The most important was the draft law of April 16, 1862, a more Spartan measure than any other English-speaking land had ever enacted. Though Congress immediately weakened it by allowing many exemptions, it was a bolder law than the North dared make for nearly another year, or than Britain was able to put on her statute books until deep in the First World War. It withdrew every white male between 18 and 35 from State jurisdiction, placing him at the disposal of the President as commander-in-

2 Kean, MS Diary, July 27, 1863, Univ. of Va. Lib.; Pollard, *Lost Cause,* 215 ff.

chief, and extended all short-term enlistments by two years or, if less, the duration. It established in every State a training camp with a national commandant to take charge of organizing and instructing the new levies. All this awakened the wrath of State Rights men, so that Governor Joseph E. Brown was soon serving notice on Davis that the Georgians "will refuse to yield their sovereignty to usurpation." [3] Another drastic measure passed by Congress required the destruction of all cotton and tobacco likely to fall into Union hands.

The loss of Roanoke Island and subsequent capture of New Bern and Fort Macon, all on the North Carolina coast, were staggering blows to the South. Late in 1861 the Rhode Island brigadier Ambrose E. Burnside, a West Point graduate who had gone into arms manufacture, and was best known for the breech-loading rifled carbine he had devised, proposed to McClellan a plan for seizing historic Roanoke, the site of Raleigh's lost colony. It was accepted, and he was made head of the expedition early in the new year.

The South should have been ready to meet him, for the island, as its defender Henry A. Wise declared, was the key to the rear defenses of Norfolk, and unlocked Albermarle and Currituck Sounds with their half dozen rivers reaching into coastal Virginia and Carolina. But with McClellan about to launch his thunderbolt, Judah P. Benjamin in the War Department protested that he could furnish neither troops nor cannon powder. He refused even to order Benjamin Huger, who had 13,000 men at or near Norfolk, to reinforce Wise's little garrison of 2,500 on Roanoke. The consequence was that when Burnside's expedition steamed inside Hatteras Inlet and reached the southern tip of Roanoke Island on February 7, it went through Confederate defenses like a battering ram through pasteboard. The 20 Union gunboats with their 64 guns brushed away the 7 rickety Confederate vessels of only one gun each; the 13,000 Federal troops jamming the transports smashed the shore defenses, and took all Wise's force prisoners. That general made his escape, declaring that Roanoke had fallen because Benjamin had provided "Nothing! Nothing! Nothing!" [4]

Burnside at once directed his expedition against the useful little port of New Bern. Undergoing more fatigue from bottomless roads than peril from Confederate troops, he quickly took the town with guns, stores, and prisoners. Control of the entire North Carolina coast was now within grasp of the Yankees, and they achieved it when a Union attack on April 25 reduced Fort Macon at the entrance of Beaufort Harbor. This opened one of the best anchorages of the South to Union vessels. The occupation of the coast

3 O. R., IV, ii, 131.
4 Wise, *End of an Era*, Ch. XII; Shelby Foote, *Civil War*, 227–235.

brought large numbers of slaves flocking into the national lines. While these losses, coinciding with Donelson, shook the whole Confederacy, naturally Virginia showed special bitterness. As a public funeral was held in Richmond for Wise's brilliant young son Jennings, killed on Roanoke,[5] spokesmen for the State accused the Confederacy of sacrificing its interests, and demanded an investigation of Secretary Benjamin. He had blundered in underrating the Union peril, and although he had shown an industry and organizing capacity from which his successors profited, Davis had to transfer him, as we have seen, to the State Department. Actually the largest responsibility for the Confederate disaster rested upon the inert Huger.[6]

The North rejoiced over these spectacular gains, which by outflanking Norfolk helped force its evacuation on May 10. Stanton devised a quick plan for an amphibious attack on that city; he, Lincoln, Chase, and Egbert L. Viele descended the Potomac to put it into effect; and after running the perils of seasickness and sharpshooters, the President had the satisfaction of seeing the force they landed make an almost bloodless conquest of the port. "Every blow tells fearfully against the rebellion," exulted Greeley, adding: "It now requires no very far-reaching prophet to predict the end of the struggle."[7] The capture of Norfolk had the effect of gaining full and free entry for the Union forces into the James River, which they could ascend to the defences of Richmond. It was an exciting little operation—the only one in our history personally supervised by the President of the United States as commander-in-chief.

[I]

In Washington, meanwhile, Lincoln urged the borderland to agree to his project for compensated emancipation. From Delaware to Missouri the outlook for acceptance was dubious. Much of the inarticulate laboring population was hostile; white workers felt a deep antipathy toward Negro competitors, and the entry of colored hands into Baltimore shipyards as

5 A Norfolk correspondent of the Richmond *Dispatch* gives us a pathetic glimpse of Wise's grief: "Last night, when the steamer arrived at Currituck, Gen. Wise directed that the coffin containing the remains of his son should be opened. Then, I learn from those who were present, the old hero bent over the body of his son, on whose pale face the full moon threw its light, kissed the pale brow many times, and exclaimed in an agony of emotion, 'Oh, my brave boy, you have died for me, you have died for me.'" Quoted in Phila. *Evening Journal*, March 4, 1862.

6 R. W. Patrick, *President Davis and His Cabinet*, 162–183; R. D. Meade, *Benjamin*, 219–230; Jones, *Rebel War Clerk*, I, 118.

7 N. Y. *Tribune*, May 23, 1862; Viele, "A Trip With Lincoln. . . . ," Scribner's, XVI (Oct., 1878), 813–822, writes that Stanton felt such bitter prejudice against McClellan he could not bear to hear his name mentioned.

caulkers had recently caused a bitter strike. Most conservatives also remained adamant, asserting that discussion of emancipation would arouse public resentment, impair property values, and hinder the Union cause. The best policy, said Senator Saulsbury of Delaware, would be to assure citizens of all loyal States that property and business would be protected; the worst policy would be to nourish the incendiarism of abolitionists in slaveholding areas.[8]

Yet as Lincoln was not the man to bring forward his scheme without solid prior assurances of support, no little approbation also came from the border zone. First and last, he had talked with a good many slaveholders, some of whom had gladly endorsed the plan. When the first flurry of dismay died away, it was evident that many plain citizens stood with him. In Kentucky the eastern mountain folk were reinforced by bluegrass moderates who had been critical of slavery since the days of Henry Clay. The yeomanry of western Maryland took the same stand. In Delaware half of the citizens were on Lincoln's side. As for Missouri, all sensible men knew that emancipation in some form would soon be adopted in that State.

Indeed, a hasty observer might have wondered that Lincoln's plan was not immediately victorious. What had the borderland to lose? The novelist Trollope, after visiting Missouri, pronounced slavery so unpopular there that it would soon die out. As he wrote, even conservative slaveowners recognized that their property was of dubious value, prone to run away at the first opportunity, for Negroes dribbled into Kansas, Iowa, and Illinois by thousands. Missouri stood in a happy position, with a problem much simpler than that in the cotton kingdom, for she had only to get rid of slavery; she did not need to worry about a substitute labor system, nor would her 115,000 slaves, which were only about a tenth of the population, offer any complex problem of race adjustment. This spring some Missourians formed a powerful Emancipation Society.[9]

To Marylanders, who seemed about equally divided, antislavery editors appealed with pragmatic arguments. "We advise the people to take the money if they can get it," declared the Cecil County *Whig*, "for their negroes are running away as fast as they can. All of the slaveholders we have heard speak of the project are in favor of it." In Baltimore the *American* crisply declared: "The revolution has commenced, and must go on." [10]

While discussion thus raged in the borderland, Congress was abolishing

8 N. Y. *Evening Post*, April 2, 1862, for Maryland; *Cong. Globe*, 37th Cong., 2d Sess., 1357, 1358.
9 Trollope, *Travels*, II, 24 (1862 edition). See the excellent summary of border opinion in N. Y. *Evg. Post*, May 16, 1862.
10 All quotations are from the N. Y. *Evg. Post* article.

slavery in the Territories and the District of Columbia. Inasmuch as Republicans held that the natural condition of the Territories was one of freedom, the first measure had only a limited significance. The more important District bill, introduced by Henry Wilson early in the session, appropriated a million dollars to compensate slaveholders, the total sum paid not to exceed an average of $300. Slavery was a dying institution in the District, where in 1860 only 2 per cent of the white residents owned the 3,185 slaves (a drop of 500 in the decade), with a total value of two millions at most. A brisk antislavery agitation had enlisted many of the new politicians, contractors, lobbyists, and reformers who had swarmed into the capital. Within Washington most citizens realized that slavery was doomed and did not regret its passing.

In the acrid debate on the District bill Congressional radicals treated emancipation as a matter of fundamental right and Christian duty. "What God and Nature decree," blazed Sumner, "Rebellion cannot arrest." Other advocates declared that emancipation was an experiment, and the District was a good place to test it. Certain border members, however, took the stubborn stand expected. The venerable Crittenden stigmatized emancipation as inexpedient, unconstitutional, a threat to border institutions, and potentially a major impediment to restoration of the Union. Senator Garrett Davis tried to hamstring the bill by an amendment making foreign colonization of freedmen mandatory. After much oratory, moderate Republicans finally effected a compromise agreement that the released slaves might be colonized in Liberia, Haiti, or other places with their own consent. In the House, Thaddeus Stevens forced emancipation to a vote by ruthless tactics. The majority was more than two-thirds in each chamber, and it was significant of changing public sentiment that among 38 Democrats from free States, only 21 voted No.

When the measure reached Lincoln's desk April 14, some doubt existed whether he would sign it. His stand on the principle was of course clear, for as a Congressman in 1849 he had offered his own plan of District emancipation. He knew, however, of the feeling in the Border States that $300 was too low, that the price should be fixed by the courts and not by Congress, and that Maryland's consent should have been obtained; and he was above all anxious that the measure should not jeopardize his larger plan. For two days he kept the bill on his desk, while Sumner told him reproachfully that he was "the largest slaveholder in the country." Then on the 16th he signed it, assuring Congress that he had never doubted its constitutionality nor wavered in his wish to see Washington cleansed of the blot; but he retained his doubts about some details, and by recommendations for supplementary legislation showed that he was determined to assert his leadership in this field.[11]

"I am gratified," he noted, "that the two principles of compensation, and colonization, are both recognized, and practically applied in the act." Full civil rights, except that of jury service, were almost immediately granted all Negroes.[12]

The formal abolition of slavery in the Territories by the Lovejoy bill carried no compensation, for it was Republican doctrine that no valid title to slave property had ever existed there. This measure passed the House 85 to 50 by nearly a straight party vote, Republicans for it, Democrats and border men against it.[13] Conservative members of Congress, much alarmed by the rising tide of emancipationist feeling, held the first of two meetings in the House on May 10, with Crittenden presiding, S. S. Cox as secretary, and Garrett Davis a prominent speaker, in a hopeless effort to stem the swift-running current. Here, too, was a front on which most Northerners could feel that progress was being made.

[II]

As Lincoln was trying to move the Border States, as Grant was recovering from Shiloh, and McClellan was looking beyond Williamsburg toward Richmond, the navy was dealing the Confederacy the heaviest blow of all. When the previous November S. F. DuPont drove the Confederate garrisons out of the two forts protecting Port Royal on the South Carolina coast, Union leaders had realized that greater prizes might be taken in the same way. On November 15 a conference under Lincoln had decided to make the effort to seize New Orleans.

With this decision, the last of the half dozen greatest fighters of the war stepped upon the stage—David Glasgow Farragut.[14] Gideon Welles, Gustavus V. Fox, and Montgomery Blair were primarily responsible for selecting him to take command. During the Mexican War, Welles as head of a Navy

11 For summaries of the debate on the bill see Blaine, *Twenty Years*, I, 369, 370, and *Ann. Cyc.*, 1862, pp. 333-344. The N. Y. *Tribune*, April 16, 1862, carried an illuminating article, "Slavery in the District."

12 *Works*, V, 192; W. B. Bryan, *Hist. Nat. Capital*, 513, 516, 521-523; *National Intelligencer*, April 5, 12, 1862.

13 N. Y. *Tribune*, May 13, 1862.

14 The other five were Lee, Stonewall Jackson, Grant, Sherman, and Thomas. Farragut alone in this group was not of pure British ancestry. His father was a Spaniard, born under the British flag in Minorca in 1755; his mother a North Carolinian, Elizabeth Shine. He had passed his early boyhood in New Orleans and both his marriages were to Virginians, but he never hesitated in choosing the Northern side.

Department bureau had been present when an officer laid before Secretary Bancroft a plan for seizing the castle St. Juan d'Ulloa at Veracruz. Struck by its system and daring, he took pains to learn that the author was named Farragut. Indeed, boldness, decision, and ability to plan were among Farragut's primary traits. This Tennessee-born officer was now sixty, and since entering the navy in 1810 as midshipman had found scant opportunity to show his talents. While peace reigned he was a dignified gentleman, thoroughly alert but conspicuous for his serenity and cheerful talkativeness; once the bugle sounded he was an aroused lion. His spare, erect figure, his intent, determined bearing, at all times revealed the underlying force of his strong personality and dynamic temperament, and in action he could be overwhelming.

Like Grant, Farragut was made eminent by force of character rather than of intellect. Without brilliance, eloquence, or marked originality, he had three other qualities which rendered him a leader of power. He was intensely combative, always eager to attack; he was a stern disciplinarian, who made his subordinates see that every weapon was ready for action, every precaution taken, every sailor vigilant; and true to his motto of "Audacity, still more audacity, always audacity," he was fearless in seizing any opening. He kept constantly busy, made decisions quickly, and enforced them with a natural port of command. All the old tars recognized his fighting qualities. A veteran quartermaster urged that the government pick him for the Gulf Squadron: "If Davy Farragut came down thar, it wouldn't be long till the fur was flying."

Yet with all his driving power, his natural tact and courtesy enabled him to inspire his fleet as well as control it. It was his rule to familiarize himself with the duties of all his officers so that he could understand their special problems. His large brow, covered with curling black hair, his long face, keen hazel eyes, and tremendous jaw made him look the leader he was— "Old Heart of Oak"; but his face usually bore a genial smile. A man of great sensitiveness, himself easily hurt, he was considerate of the feelings of others; a simple-hearted Christian, who liked to hear his wife or flag-lieutenant read the Bible, he had a keen sense of justice. His pride in the service made him emphasize prolonged training: "You can no more make a sailor out of a land-lubber by dressing him up in sea-toggery and putting a commission in his pocket than you could make a shoemaker of him by filling him up with sherry cobblers." He was as devoid of mannerisms, guile, or vanity as Grant, and like Grant he had but one passion in war—to find the enemy, attack him, and hold on until victory was won.[15]

15 See C. L. Lewis, *Farragut, passim;* W. T. Meredith in *Battles and Leaders,* II, 70 ff.; W. S. Schley, *Forty-five Years Under the Old Flag,* 50 ff.; Stolzman, *Stormy Ben Butler,*

Though the strategic move against New Orleans was as obvious as that against Donelson, it was almost as tardily grasped. At first, the whole hope of seizing the city had rested on a combined army and gunboat expedition from Cairo. But in June, 1861, Commander D. D. Porter of the *Powhatan*, blockading the mouth of the Mississippi, had conceived the idea of a thrust *up* the river. Late that summer the Navy Department hammered out a definite scheme. Gustavus V. Fox, familiar with the lower Mississippi, believed that warships could pass the two forts below New Orleans, Jackson and St. Philip, without military assistance, and after Port Royal he converted the dubious Lincoln. McClellan agreed to the effort once he was assured that only about 10,000 troops would be needed—that the fleet would *take* the city and the troops simply hold it. Work then started in November on a tripartite expedition embracing a naval squadron, a mortar-boat flotilla under Commander Porter, and a small infantry force. Near the end of the year troops under Ben Butler were designated to go to Ship Island in the Gulf. Stanton sped the effort as soon as he took office.

When informed of his appointment, Farragut had flushed with elation. With even two-thirds of the forces proposed, he assured Fox, he would take New Orleans and the whole Confederate navy to boot! From that moment he acted with characteristic energy. The prevailing belief was that well-armed shore works could defeat wooden ships, as at Sebastopol; but he was confident that if the navy moved speedily, he could push his squadron past the forts below New Orleans and any other defenses the Confederates could make ready. Though Welles had ordered the expedition to *reduce* the defenses, Farragut determined upon the sounder plan of pushing past them, capturing New Orleans while it was still practically undefended, and leaving the forts below to wither upon the vine. Porter, who had personally explained to Gideon Welles and Lincoln his plans for taking the city, was equally elated. This black-bearded sea-dog, now nearly fifty, who had made his first cruise with his famous naval father, David Porter of War of 1812 renown, at the age of ten, and who had fought at Veracruz, was as combative as his chief. With high approval, he had heard Lincoln tell Welles a characteristic anecdote about an Illinois farmer and his shotgun—a story with a point: "Now, Mr. Secretary, the navy has been hunting pet rabbits long enough; suppose you send them after skunks." Behind Porter's heavy beard and weatherbeaten countenance lurked a spirit fiery, determined, optimistic, and erratic. Farragut would

---

57 ff. Few Civil War leaders had Farragut's breadth of interests, embracing art, literature, science, religion, and natural history; see the dedication in H. H. Brownell's *War Lyrics and Other Poems*. His letters in the *Correspondence of G. V. Fox*, I, 297–353, well express his personality.

gladly have left the mortar-boats behind, but the energy with which Porter had pushed his plans made their inclusion necessary.

Once more the naval forces demonstrated the value of that careful planning and preparation which the military arm too often neglected. Sailing from Hampton Roads in his trim flagship *Hartford* on February 2, 1862, Farragut reached Ship Island on the 20th, and took command of the blockading squadron on the Gulf Coast. Other vessels rapidly arrived until his force included 17 ships of 154 guns, 4 of them splendid new additions to the navy. Porter commanded a supplementary force of 20 schooners carrying one 13-inch mortar apiece, and 6 gunboats. Late in March the heavy ships were gotten across the bar at Southwest Pass into the Mississippi, where they joined Porter's command, which had entered from Pass à l'Outre.[16]

Farragut made certain of ample ammunition, drilled his crews interminably, and perfected their marksmanship. He neglected no detail in readying the fleet for battle. All spars and rigging that could be spared were stripped down, hulls were smeared with river mud to reduce their visibility, and decks were painted white to facilitate night work. All seagoing gear was sent ashore, even chronometers being temporarily discarded. Every aperture that could show light was darkened. When Porter brought his mortar boats into position near the riverbanks just below the two forts he carried camouflage a step further by dressing the masts with bushes to imitate trees.

[III]

Coast Survey officers piloted the fleet up its winding reaches to Forts Jackson and St. Philip, where on April 16 it anchored just below the point chosen for Porter's bombardment. At ten on the morning of the 18th the mortar boats opened a fire that continued until nightfall on the 23rd. They were not much more than platforms for their big black kettlelike pieces, one to each boat. The mortars let go with a terrific blast of flame and smoke, through which the bomb could be seen rising in a graceful parabola. Altogether, 7,500 bombs and shells were fired at the forts in these six days, some bursting in air with a flash and roar, some raising a heavy splash of brown water in the marshes, and some exploding in the rebel works amid flying debris. But beyond burning the wooden casemates, dismounting four guns, and injuring eleven carriages, the bombardment accomplished so little that

16 The beginnings of the New Orleans expedition are discussed by Montgomery Blair in the *United Service Magazine*, IV (Jan., 1881), 33–41; by Gideon Welles in the *Galaxy*, XII (Nov.-Dec., 1871), 669–683, 817–832, and in his *Diary*, I, 60, 61; and by Lewis, *Farragut*, II, 5 ff. See also Mahan, *The Gulf and Inland Waters*, 54–59. Porter's garrulous *Incidents and Anecdotes of the Civil War*, 63–81, is interesting but sometimes undependable.

THE DEFENSES OF THE MISSISSIPPI

Ben Butler termed it superbly useless. Gustavus V. Fox suspected later that Porter's squadron had actually been advantageous to the enemy in giving them time to augment their defenses.[17]

Fortunately for the expedition, victory did not depend on smashing the forts. As Farragut was intent on passing them, the greatest potential danger lay in the naval vessels which Confederate leaders had made a tardy, ill-coordinated effort to muster at the river barrier. Fortunately for the Union, both the naval and military auxiliaries were weak. In all their work of defense the Southerners had been hampered by poverty, disorganization, lack of skilled engineers and craftsmen, friction between State authorities and Richmond, and want of foresight.[18] Most of the perhaps 150 guns which the forts mounted were too small to be effective, many being mere twenty-four-pounders. The heavy boom stretched across the river was easily broken. Men of the *Itasca* on the night of the 20th made fast to the mooring hulk directly under Fort Jackson, and with sledgehammers and chisels intrepidly cut the chain, so that the hulk was swept down against the bank. The current rapidly enlarged the breach until the river was partially free.

On the evening of April 23 the Union ships took position for their effort, "What do you estimate our casualties will be?" Farragut asked his clerk. "We shall lose one hundred," was the answer. Startled by the low estimate, Farragut rejoined sadly: "I wish I could think so."

The risks might well have daunted him. To breast the current of three and a half miles an hour, run the gantlet of fire rafts, forts, and ships, and then encounter batteries of unknown strength above, seemed a foolhardy venture to some of his men. But the commander was serenely confident. At one o'clock on the morning of the 24th, officers quietly awoke the crews, an hour later two red lanterns on the flagship signaled anchors aweigh, and before three the advance division was moving upstream. Farragut clambered into the rigging of the *Hartford* to watch the action. At 3:40 St. Philip opened fire, and soon the guns of both forts enveloped the vessels with bursting shells and low-hanging smoke, but he leaned against the shrouds as calmly as if watching a beautiful sunrise.[19]

---

17 Porter in *Battles and Leaders*, II, 22–54, describes the bombardment as highly effective; Butler in his *Book*, 358, and C. L. Lewis in *Farragut*, II, 44–54, support Fox's view.

18 General Bragg had written Governor Moore from Pensacola when Lovell was appointed: "The command at New Orleans was rightly mine. I feel myself degraded by the action of the government and shall take care that they know my sentiments. I am not surprised at the President, who, in his feeble condition, is entirely under the control of a miserable *petticoat* government as tyrannical as Lincoln's despotism. But from Benjamin I expected better things." Later he could thank his stars that he had not been placed in so precarious a situation. Oct 31, 1861, Moore Papers, LSU Archives.

19 Later, yielding to his officers, Farragut returned to the poop deck.

For an hour and a half, as the Union ships forged upstream, the most exciting panorama of the war unrolled itself. The great turgid river, black and swollen, stretching in places so far inland that Fort St. Philip looked as if it had gone to sea; the two lines of Farragut's divisions, lighted up by fire rafts, shells bursting over ships and forts, and the lightning of their own guns; the *Richmond* blazing, heavily hit, in midstream; the forts bellowing in cross fire at each other, the flame of their guns reddening the smoke clouds of their previous discharges; the hissing round shot plunging into the water; far beyond the bend in the rear the red shimmer of the mortar boats, and high in the velvet sky the blazing crisscross of their bombs—it was a superb spectacle. A square mile of water seemed in conflagration.

One Confederate ship placed at the forts, the *Governor Moore*, fought valiantly until she sank the Union vessel *Varuna*. A well-aimed shot from Fort Jackson hit the boiler of the *Itasca* and disabled her. When the *Hartford* grounded, the Confederates immediately pushed a fire raft against her side, and flames leaped halfway to the mizzen tops. For a second Farragut thought his flagship doomed. "My God, is it to end this way?" he exclaimed. As some sailors flinched, he shouted: "There's a hotter fire than that for those who don't do their duty!" Then his quick-witted clerk uncapped three thirteen-inch shells, rolled them over the side upon the burning raft, and blew it apart. The *Hartford* backed off and continued on her way. Meanwhile the side-wheeler *Mississippi*, piloted by young George Dewey, sustained a hard blow from a Confederate ram, but went on. So did the *Cayuga*, hit forty-two times.[20]

The issue was quickly decided. The battle had but fairly opened, later wrote a Confederate naval officer, before the Union ships were standing upstream—"and the Uncle Sam of my earlier days had the key to the valley of the Mississippi again safely in his pocket." With casualties of only 37 slain and 149 wounded, Farragut's main fleet swept up the river and anchored at quarantine, seven miles above the forts, for breakfast. Before ten that morning New Orleans learned that the warships had run the gantlet. Business houses clapped their doors shut, steamboats puffed northward to safety, churchbells rang a summons to all military organizations, and dejected troops prepared to evacuate the city with their supplies. Before noon the cloudy skies were lighted by blazing stores of cotton and tobacco. The people, still heartsick over the long daily lists of men dying from their wounds at Shiloh, were in despair, and under a dismal rain, some joined in a stampede to the country.

20 The Confederates had a half dozen so-called rams, wooden tugboats with reinforced stems, at the first bend above the forts; they displaced only 900 tons and were so weak that some sensibly ran away.

That morning seventeen-year-old George W. Cable, standing in the doorway of the Canal Street store which his employers had abandoned to his charge, saw the masts of a Confederate vessel in the river tipping, sinking, and finally disappearing. He ran to the levee. About him the riffraff of the city were staving in boxes of sugar and rice, and barrels of molasses. "Are the Yankee ships in sight?" he asked a bystander. A gesture was the reply, and Cable saw their mast tops across the wide riverbend where they were silencing the Chalmette batteries. The firing soon ended, and then

Ah, me! I see them now as they come slowly round Slaughterhouse Point into full view, silent, grim, and terrible; black with men, heavy with deadly portent; the long-banished Stars and Stripes flying against the frowning sky. Oh, for the *Mississippi!* the *Mississippi!* Just then she came down upon them. But how? Drifting helplessly, a mass of flames.

And presently two officers, walking abreast, unguarded, impassive, never frowning nor flinching while a yelling mob cursed them and threatened them with knives and pistols, strode along Common Street to City Hall to demand the surrender. The mayor and council, advised by that fiery Southern leader Pierre Soulé, refused to lower the State flag over the city hall; whereupon a naval detachment, protected from the angry crowd by shotted cannon, did it. A young man named William B. Mumford who recklessly assisted in hauling down a United States flag raised over the mint was in due course executed for the offense. Farragut immediately handed the custody of the city over to Ben Butler and his 15,000 troops; and that general, making his headquarters at the St. Charles Hotel, agreed with the municipal authorities that they should retain power in all matters unconnected with military affairs. The transfer of the city to the Union, though a source of intense chagrin and resentment to most of the high-spirited population, was therefore accompanied with less friction than might have been anticipated.[21]

The Confederacy had lost its greatest city with scarcely a real battle. The main reasons, apart from confusion, myopia, and tardiness in high Southern circles—"too little and too late"—lay in better Northern power and leadership. Superior Northern engineering, constructive skill, and well-mobilized resources made the Union naval forces irresistible. The disparity of power was symbolized by the contrast between the best Confederate ship, the hastily converted *Manassas*, and Farragut's *Hartford*. The one excited derision; the other

[21] *Battles and Leaders*, II, 20. The builders of the ironclad *Mississippi*, in which the Louisianians had placed such faith, Nelson and Asa F. Tift of Florida, failed to complete it in time because they were ignorant of the foundries, machine shops, lumber yards, and labor sources of the area. H. A. Trexler, "The Confed. Navy Dept. and the Fall of New Orleans," *Southwest Review*, XIX (Autumn, 1933), 88–102. When the Tifts went to Vicksburg they were almost lynched by a mob.

was an almost new, finely finished Boston-built vessel of 2,900 tons, 225 feet in length, 44 feet in beam, and 16 to 17 feet in draft. The *Manassas*, proudly called a ram, was actually a tiny tugboat roofed over with a half-inch of iron, and armed with a 32-pound carronade of antique vintage pointing straight ahead. She looked like a hump of a black whale with a smokestack in its center, and shot went through her thin sides as through paper. The *Hartford*, armed with twenty-five guns, including 9-inch Dahlgren shell pieces and three rifled 30-pounders, had been built to match the best British warships in her wooden category. Her engines made eight knots, while sails brought her speed to a maximum of thirteen or more. All the Confederate ships were badly officered and manned, for Southerners had shown little taste for the sea. The *Hartford*, on the other hand, had a superb crew and experienced officers, led by one of the great admirals of history.[22]

For Farragut's leadership was the other primary element in the victory. His care in preparations, skill in fleet management, and courage in battle served his decision that the best strategy was to run past the forts. He knew that the city would be helpless under his guns. On the Confederate side Commodore George N. Hollins, who knew the New Orleans situation thoroughly and wished to launch a naval attack on Farragut's fleet below the forts, was transferred just as his plans neared maturity, and his place given to Captain John K. Mitchell, who had never commanded on the Mississippi before. Hollins might have done much better. After the city was lost, Louisianians complained bitterly that two strangers, Lovell and Mitchell, had held its fate in their untried hands. The remark of one Southern historian that "as a military leader Lovell was a fine horseman" is hardly too scornful. And while Farragut gripped the reins of his force tightly, the Confederate command had been hopelessly divided. Lovell's 8,000 or 9,000 troops, who would have been far more useful with Johnston at Shiloh, were disconnected from the river forces; each fort had its own commander; and each ship fought without reference to the other ships or the forts. Unified plans under an energetic unified leadership might well have saved the city to the South.[23]

News of the victory had to reach the North through the Confederacy. People had passed a quiet Sunday on April 27, 1862, for little of note seemed to be occurring. Union blockaders had captured some Confederate correspondence from the ship *Calhoun*, but even an impudent letter from T. Butler King of Georgia to Lord John Russell, suggesting a man to be the first British minister to the Confederacy, aroused no great interest. Next morning, how-

22 Lewis, *Farragut*, II, 15, 16; Naval O. R., II, i, 99.
23 *Corr. Between the War Dept., and Gen. Lovell; Corr. Between the President, War Dept., and Gov. T. O. Moore*, Richmond, 1863; Harold Sinclair, *Port of New Orleans*, 227–241; Alcée Fortier, *Hist. La.*, IV, 13–20.

ever, the sudden shouts of newsboys in Northern streets brought citizens to their doors. They read flaring headlines: "Fall of New Orleans." Flags began fluttering from every staff, steeple, and window. Crowds gathered in every square. Mobile had telegraphed Richmond that on the afternoon of April 25 all communication with New Orleans had ceased, and the news had rapidly percolated from Confederate picket lines into Northern camps.

With New Orleans the South lost a great deal of wealth, manpower, and manufacturing capacity, for its energetic people were already making an impressive amount of war material. It had opened machine shops and iron foundries, and had pressed its shipbuilding plans. Still more important was the fact that the lower segment of the Mississippi was gone. Because the river was the greatest single communication line tying the republic together—a bond which had kept alive, if latent, a strong Union feeling in New Orleans itself—a special moral value attached to its mastery. Thomas Hart Benton had called the Mississippi–Missouri–Ohio river system *Mare Nostrum*, our sea; to change the image, it had been the backbone of the nation. Men reared on its Northern waters now felt a new confidence. The capture of its lower extremity gave the Western armies both heart and help in the stubborn struggle for the remaining river strongholds, Port Hudson and Vicksburg, while it lessened the disloyal sentiment that smoldered under the surface in parts of Illinois, Indiana, and Ohio.

And the 145,000 proud people of New Orleans, conscious of their rich history and cultural heritage, now entered upon their most tragic years. A swarm of profiteers flocked in, with Ben Butler's approval and perhaps in some instances his secret and indirect partnership, to seize the many opportunities for making a fortune. Turpentine was $3 a barrel in New Orleans and $38 in New York; flour was $6 a barrel in New York and $25 in New Orleans; many other commodities showed a comparable spread in prices. The greedy activities of some Yankee traders, vividly pictured later by the Northern soldier-novelist J. W. DeForest in *Miss Ravenel's Conversion*, became in time one of the most poignant Southern legends. Butler stole no silver spoons, but he protected an unhappy amount of legal plundering of needy people—as well as much quite healthful trade.[24]

One additional river triumph remained to be scored, this time by forces coming down from the north. "Memphis may be taken," a Southern newspaper had said, "for even Saragossa was taken." It fell at the first stroke. A smart action, to be sure, was fought, but the Union won it with astonishingly

---

24 Butler's autobiography, *Butler's Book*, and James Parton's graphic *General Butler in New Orleans*, defend the general; Robert S. Holzman, *Stormy Ben Butler*, and Thomas E. Dabney, "The Butler Regime in La.," *La. Hist. Quarterly*, XXVII, 487–526 (April, 1944), present a more critical view. Butler's *Private and Official Correspondence*, arranged by Jessie Ames Marshall in five volumes (1917), amply proves his energy and decision.

little loss. On June 6 a flotilla of gunboats under Flag-Officer C. H. Davis came into collision, off the city, with the river fleet of the Confederates, the Southerners having the larger number of ships but weaker array of guns. When the engagement had raged for a half hour in full view of thousands of spectators on the Memphis shore, two of the rams which Charles Ellet had persuaded Secretary Welles to let him prepare and which lay upstream heard the rumble of the fray. Ellet on the *Queen of the West* waved his hat to his son on the *Monarch* and shouted: "The guns of the enemy! Round out and follow me! Now is our chance!" Churning through the line of Union gunboats, the two rams delivered an effective assault, instantly putting two enemy ships out of action. The running encounter lasted another hour, and carried the contending vessels ten miles below the city; when it ended, seven of the eight Confederate ships were sunk, aground, or captured—"totally destroyed," said the Southern commander Jeff Thompson.[25]

The battle was a memorable triumph for the river navy, a deep humiliation to the Tennesseeans, and a stroke pregnant with large economic results. Memphis had been a busy center of the sugar and cotton trade, and the metropolis of a wealthy slaveholding section. Under the Confederate regime it was as dead as Herculaneum. But immediately after the Union occupation an influx of merchants from Chicago, St. Louis, and Cincinnati crammed the hotels, the sound of saw and hammer filled the air, and packet boats lined the wharves to discharge goods and pick up Southern products. Cotton buyers, licensed and unlicensed, scattered into the interior as far as Forrest's cavalry would let them, and a brisk contraband traffic in medicines, percussion caps, shoes, and clothing began to nourish the Southern army. The gambling dens, saloons, and bawdy houses for which Memphis had been famous once more sprang to life.[26]

"On Tuesday of this week," the correspondent of the London *Daily News* wrote in mid-June, "3,000 bales of cotton, 5,000 full barrels and 3,000 half-barrels of molasses, and 6,000 barrels of sugar, were shipped to the North, and more, it was reported, would follow next day." The first day the post

---

25 Herbert P. Gambrell, "Rams Vs. Gunboats," *Southwest Review*, XXIII (Oct., 1937), 46–78; A. W. Ellet, "Ellet and his Steam-Rams at Memphis," *Battles and Leaders*, I, 453–459; Henry Walke, "The Western Flotilla," *Ibid.*, 449–452; Naval O. R., I, xxiii, 118–140. Ellet's papers are at the Univ. of Michigan. The only Union man injured in the action, this inventor, constructor, and independent commander of the rams died as his boat reached Cairo June 21.

26 N. Y. *Tribune*, Chicago *Morning Post*, June 11, 1862, *et seq.*; Knox, *Camp-Fire and Cotton-Field*, 179–196; Lew Wallace, *Autobiography*, II, 581–588; Capers, *Biog. of a River Town*, 146–155; Shields McIlwaine, *Memphis*, 124. Zack Chandler estimated the trade at 20 to 30 millions; *Cong. Globe*, 38th Cong., 1st Sess., 3324. One Northern cavalryman records that the colored women "felt loving towards us because they thought we were bringing them freedom, and they wouldn't charge us a cent."

office reopened, a thousand letters were mailed, mostly on business to Northern cities. Memphis swiftly became the chief depot for contraband trade between North and South, within two years sending an estimated $20,000,000 worth of supplies, or more, into the Confederacy. It also became a great and troublesome rallying point for Negro refugees. All in all, for the rest of the war it was probably the most picturesque city on the continent.

[IV]

As Yorktown fell, as the Union won at Williamsburg, and as McClellan on May 8 set his army moving toward Richmond, hopes ran high. It was in this context that Stanton issued the unhappy order to discontinue recruiting. Public sentiment greatly influenced him. Henry Wilson, in a letter in the N. Y. *Herald*, Aug. 8, 1862, explained the discontinuance on the ground that Cameron, Meigs, and the paymaster-general had reported that the Union possessed between 700 and 800 regiments, with at least 700,000 under arms; that hundreds of recruiting stations, supported at great cost, were doing little to fill the hundred or more partially organized regiments scattered over the land; *and that the recent victories had created an excessive optimism.* Congress had authorized the raising of 500,000 men for the new army, but it was supposed that the States might have enlisted altogether as many as 750,000, half again the number proposed. Unhappily, as we have seen, Stanton's order to stop recruiting was based on misinformation. When the War Department obtained exact figures on the forces, it learned that they aggregated not more than 500,000 to 550,000. But this was not known in May, when people supposed the armed forces ample for their task.

If now McClellan would but strike the decisive blow! It was a bold plan which he had made for placing a great army at the gates of Richmond, but success depended upon three vital elements: rapidity, strategic skill, and complete mutual confidence between the government and the general. Already, taking a month to seize Yorktown, he had sacrificed valuable time, and opened a door to strategic complications. Would he now show enough skill and energy to win the full trust of Lincoln and Stanton?

The troops who marched from Williamsburg up the peninsula, although it was only forty miles to the battle lines before Richmond, never forgot the experience. McClellan's promise of easy sandy roads and open country stood exposed in all its hollowness.

The weather had a New England fickleness, now lovely May brilliance, now broiling heat, now streaming rain. Two days of hot sun would make the dust intolerable; then downpours would leave the roads bottomless. On narrow ways under lashing sheets some columns took a day to traverse two or three miles. Wagons, ambulances, caissons, and guns filled the road, at times laboring forward, at times bogged down. Drivers lashed and swore, horses and mules plunged, and details of privates with arms slung pushed at the miry wheels, or in lines of thirty or forty tugged at ropes attached to fieldpieces. As the day closed in misty gloom, troops would crawl exhausted into dog-tents and brush shelters. Toiling in this world of mud and water, they thought of their former existence of dry clothes, warm houses, and good food as a Sybaris of luxury. "Yet would not swop!" exclaimed one soldier.

Till they reached the Pamunkey the country they traversed was almost deserted. Many farmers had razed their houses and filled their wells, or let Southern troops do it for them. Hardly a cow, horse, or cart was to be seen. At the few occupied dwellings only women, children, and old men were in evidence. Most of the slaves had been taken inland. Here and there patches of woods had caught fire and burned to piles of smoldering ashes.

But when finally the rear units emerged at the cluster of huts called Cumberland, on the crooked little Pamunkey River five miles from McClellan's base at the old mansion called the White House, they saw a magnificent sight. Covering the plain before them was an army of 80,000 men. By day columns drilled; by night innumerable campfires glowed and twinkled. When on May 15 McClellan held a review, the panoply of marching regiments, glistening cannon, and waving flags impressed every beholder. By May 21 the whole army was fairly in line seven to twelve miles from Richmond, and full of confidence.

For at last the antagonists seemed at close grips, with every prospect favoring the Union. When all of McClellan's force had come up he possessed about 115,000 men, much the largest and best-equipped army ever assembled in the New World. Facing him, Joseph E. Johnston had about 70,000 Confederates, far worse provided. In any battle in the open field McClellan should have a decided advantage. He would lose it only if he mismanaged his forces, or assaulted the enemy within their works, for as Union troops learned later, well-entrenched lines could repel twice their numbers. McClellan's strategy was entirely sound; he had taken a good road to Richmond. Yet he could now see the wisdom of Lincoln's warning that going down the bay instead of advancing through Manassas was only shifting a difficulty, for he would find the same enemy and equal entrenchments at either place. He was confident, however, that he could tempt or compel the enemy to fight outside their works.

Actually, on three battle grounds in the next three weeks McClellan was to have a full opportunity of defeating Johnston or Lee in the open field. He had looked forward to delivering *one* crushing blow. On March 19 he had written Stanton that it was important to make his base on the upper reaches of the York–Pamunkey River as soon as possible, and then "we shall fight a decisive battle between West Point and Richmond." He assured his wife on May 18 that he would close up on the Chickahominy to find out what Secesh was doing: "I think he will fight us there, or between there and Richmond." He kept protesting to Washington, however, that he needed reinforcements— more reinforcements. Under pressure of his entreaties, Lincoln on May 17 ordered McDowell to march down the Fredericksburg–Richmond railway to furnish the needed cooperation, with the vital condition that he should not uncover Washington. McDowell was to begin moving as soon as Shields's division joined him, about May 26. If and when he thus stood at McClellan's side, the Union array would reach 150,000 men, a more than satisfactory strength.

Lincoln by this time comprehended that he had in McClellan a complex psychological problem. He must prod the general into energetic action, yet treat him with sufficient tact not to arouse his latent insubordination. We have noted the crisp rebuke he had sent the general May 1 at Yorktown: "Your call for Parrott guns from Washington alarms me—chiefly because it argues indefinite procrastination. Is anything to be done?" Some days later he got a dispatch from McClellan complaining again of the organization of the army into corps. Already this had cost a thousand lives and a near rout, whined the commander. Lincoln replied bluntly but mildly:

> I wish to say a few words privately to you on this subject. I ordered the Army Corps organization not only on the unanimous opinion of the twelve Generals whom you had selected and assigned as Generals of Division, but also on the unanimous opinion of every military man I could get an opinion from, and every modern military book, yourself only excepted. Of course I did not, on my own judgment, pretend to understand the subject. I now think it indispensable for you to know how your struggle against it is received in quarters which we cannot entirely disregard. It is looked upon as merely an effort to pamper one or two pets, and to persecute and degrade their supposed rivals. I have had no word from Sumner, Heintzelman, or Keyes. . . . but I am constantly told that . . . you consult and communicate with nobody but General FitzJohn Porter, and perhaps General Franklin. I do not say these complaints are true or just; but at all events it is proper you should know of their existence.

The corps organization was kept, but Fitz-John Porter and Franklin were advanced on May 18 to the grade of provisional corps commanders. However, in mid-May McClellan was irascibly telegraphing Lincoln again. He could get no replies from Stanton, he grumbled. He had only 80,000 effectives to fight a much larger force, perhaps double his own. He must be reinforced without delay, and to get help he would waive some personal objections he had stated against McDowell. Lincoln could not gainsay McClellan's guess of an enemy force of perhaps 160,000, for McClellan was supposed to know. He could only move McDowell forward to add 41,000 men to the 115,000 men whom, on paper, McClellan already had.

On the Southern side, the necessity of facing this powerful concentration daunted the Confederate leaders. The prospect of a hurried evacuation of Richmond seemed so imminent that preparations were made to ship the military papers and government archives to Columbia, South Carolina. Members of Congress had gone home in late April amid the jeers of the Richmond *Whig* and the laments of the *Examiner*. Now Mrs. Davis, after seeing her husband privately baptized in the Episcopal Church, left with her children for Raleigh. The Treasury gold was packed ready to be loaded aboard a special train. Virginia legislators voted to put the city to the torch rather than surrender it to the Yankees. While rockets by night and the growl of guns by day warned of the near approach of the enemy, officers on leave from the Confederate lines told of seeing Union tents, artillery parks, and wagon trains cover the whole landscape in front of them. The *Merrimac* had been scuttled on May 11, and after that date nobody was sure that gunboats would not suddenly steam up the James, leveling their cannon on the city. The fortifications on Drewry's Bluff might or might not hold.

To make the Confederate position more desperate, many Southern troops were badly disciplined and despondent. In the trenches on the Yorktown line they had suffered from cold, rain, poor food, and bad water. Some had been stricken by malaria. After Williamsburg, clumps of wounded saddened the Richmond streets, and a host of stragglers, mud-bedaubed and exhausted, slept in doorways and sheds. "The men are full of spirits when near the enemy," Johnston wrote Lee on May 9, "but at other times, to avoid restraint, leave their regiments in crowds. To enable us to gather the whole army for battle would require a notice of several days."

The war seemed at its climax. The advances for which Lincoln longed had taken place, and those anaconda pressures on all the fronts which might yet crush every bone of rebellion were growing tighter and more powerful. But people who looked with high hope to the future little realized how swiftly incompetent generalship and ill fortune could change the scene.

5

McClellan Comes a Cropper

HIGH AS the hopes of Lincoln and the North had risen, the crucial tests still lay ahead. With well over half a million men under arms, with New Orleans, Roanoke Island, and Port Royal in Union hands, with powerful armies far up the Tennessee and on the outskirts of Richmond, could Northern leadership use its great opportunities?

The battle of Shiloh, and the immediate sequels in that quarter, seemed for a time to disappear into a dense cloud. For days all kinds of reports about the encounter circulated in New York and other cities; newspaper accounts conflicted, and the War Department was silent as the grave. All that people knew was that the Confederates had been repulsed, but had retired unmolested to their positions at Corinth, and that some Ohio regiments were uttering loud criminations. One Senator complained on April 13 that not a syllable had been communicated officially.[1] Four weeks after the battle Greeley pointed out that no official report had been given the North except the totally inadequate one which Grant had written while the guns were still warm. This omitted the fact of the surprise, understated the losses as merely 1,500 killed and 3,500 wounded, and left the panic, the captures of Union cannon, and other important facts in a fog.[2]

As we have said, the leaders of neither side had much to boast about in Shiloh. No great encounter of the war showed less prevision, science, or imagination. For both armies it had been simply a slugging match, marred by the bad discipline of two large elements, the Union troops who fled and the Confederates who stopped to plunder, and redeemed by splendid heroism. Northern troops blurted out a good deal of truth in their letters home. We were "more than surprised," one officer of the Forty-fifth Illinois wrote; "we

1 Benjamin Shanks of Oregon, April 13, 1862, Barlow Papers.
2 N. Y. *Tribune*, May 6, 1862. According to Phisterer, 213, the Union loss was 13,573, of whom 9,617 were killed or wounded, and 3,956 missing—mainly prisoners; the Confederate loss was 10,699. Greeley correctly declared that nearly all that people knew about the battle they gained from press correspondents, whom Stanton barely tolerated and Sherman treated like vermin. It was time for a reform. "The millions of anxious, aching hearts are not to be lightly trifled with."

were astonished." It is not strange that stories of Grant's intemperance again circulated freely. When Elihu Washburne defended him in the House, Medill of the Chicago *Tribune* wrote that such loyalty was admirable, but that his star seemed sinking, for the Western soldiers condemned him.[3] Grant did himself no credit when he sent Washburne a letter which misrepresented the battle, the subsequent criticism, and the motives of his assailants.[4]

Generals who were so painfully learning their job could not be expected to exhibit signal skill in garnering the fruits of victory. The main lesson of Shiloh, wrote Bragg later, was speed: "never on a battlefield to lose a moment's time, but leaving the killed, wounded, and spoils to those whose special business it was to care for them, to press on with every available man, giving a panic-stricken and defeated foe no time to rally." In saying this he was criticizing Beauregard's action just after Johnston's death in halting the Confederate onslaught; but his words were still more applicable to Grant's failure to pursue. The failure is only slightly palliated by the fact that when Northern troops recovered the battlefield, they had to treat thousands of casualties, reunite regiments and brigades, and restore morale, under conditions still highly chaotic.

The 8,000 wounded were a particularly grave problem. Theoretically, Grant's army had brigade field hospitals and ambulance trains; actually, only regimental medical units were available. Volunteer women nurses labored on the field as fighting raged, tearing up their petticoats or using leaves and grass for bandages. On Tuesday nine-tenths of the wounded still lay where they had fallen, some of them untouched since Sunday. Ambulances brought many to the shelter of tents, but others were dumped in rows outside. The scene about the rough surgical centers was sickening: mangled bodies of dead and dying, amputated limbs in piles, gouts of flesh, and puddles of blood, with a horrible stench. Grant telegraphed for hospital boats, most of which were furnished him by the United States and Western Sanitary Commissions; and a large

---

3 J. E. Smith, May 16, 1862, to Elihu Washburne, Washburne Papers, LC; Joseph Medill to Washburne, May 24, *Ibid.* W. R. Rowley wrote Washburne from Grant's headquarters April 19 denying the charge of intemperance as an unmitigated slander. Union authorities were sensitive about drunkenness in the army. "At this moment," wrote the N. Y. correspondent of the London *Times* on April 29, "common rumour and the newspapers accuse no less than six of the most prominent men of the country of habitual intoxication." The cheapness of whisky and prevalence of frontier manners had made drink a terrible evil in mid-century America.

4 In this letter of May 14 Grant covered up. He wrote that his critics expected the battlefield "to be maintained, for a whole day, with about 30,000 troops, most of them entirely raw, against 70,000"; actually his army had the advantage of numbers, arms, and natural position. He wrote that "looking back at the past I cannot see for the life of me any important point that could be corrected"; he had not taken obvious and cardinal precautions. He wrote that his critics "may have felt disappointed that they were not permitted to carry off horses, firearms, and other valuable trophies"; his important critics were honest men.

squadron soon evacuated many sufferers to the North. One striking innovation was born of the chaos. Military thinking of the period was antagonistic to large hospitals, for it was supposed that they favored mysterious concentrations of poisonous "effluvia," and all authorities distrusted open-air treatment. But under pressure of necessity Dr. B. J. D. Irwin of Buell's army commandeered enough infantry tents for a roomy field hospital, where casualties could be segregated according to needs, the medical staff could be given specialized functions, and a central administration of drugs, diet, laundry, and other functions would be possible. This, accommodating 2,500 patients, was the first hospital of the war entirely under canvas, and the fresh air made it both comfortable and salubrious.[5]

As the armies sent out their casualty lists, the shock of the battle spread up and down the Mississippi Valley in pulsations of anguish. Tens of thousands of families in the Northwest waited in dread; then as the names of dead, wounded, and missing were published, thousands of homes were prostrated with grief. For the first time the meaning of war struck home. Sorrow struggled with anger when war correspondents reported that on the fifth day after the battle began, untended casualties were still being brought in, and that hundreds had perished needlessly. In the South the shock was still greater. Throughout all the lower Valley the death lists, the return of the blind or limbless, and worst of all, the harrowing silences of those never again seen, knelled the end of the period when war had seemed a romantic experience.

The conflict was becoming implacable. But each side showed a chastened temper, for it had learned at last how dangerous the other could be. An exaggerated sense of this power of the enemy to sting and crush explained the bizarre performance now staged by Halleck. He had arrived at Shiloh with his dislike and distrust of Grant unabated. Taking command of the joint forces of Grant, Buell, and Pope—the armies of the Tennessee, the Ohio, and the Mississippi—he set out three weeks after the battle to march on Corinth. He had only twenty miles to traverse, without high ridges or deep streams, and his well-equipped army outnumbered the wretchedly armed Confederates more than two to one. The question whether Beauregard would venture a battle might have been resolved by a quick thrust or intelligent use of scouts. But Halleck, whose sobriquet should have been Old Pedantry instead of Old Brains, took no chances. He divided his army into a right corps under Thomas, a left corps under Pope, and a center corps under Buell, with McClernand commanding the reserve, and began an elaborate crawl forward. The humiliated Grant,

5 Adams, *Doctors in Blue*, 81, 82; Hannaford, *Story of a Regiment*, 286; N. Y. *Weekly Tribune*, May 10, 1862. The British in the Crimea had seen the death rate in the hospitals drop spectacularly as soon as they were opened to free ventilation, while the French losses in tightly closed wards were appalling.

nominally second in command, he ignored, sending orders directly to the four other subordinates without showing them to him.

Halleck marched his overwhelming force forward at an average rate of a mile a day, entrenching every night. When he had crept within five miles of Corinth he paused to erect double breastworks, put siege guns in position, and take additional precautions. For a week thereafter the ground gained daily was measured in hundreds of yards. He shelled every patch of woods before an advance. On May 30 he prepared for battle—and next day found that Beauregard had completely evacuated Corinth by rail. Halleck had ordered press correspondents ("unauthorized hangers-on") to quit his camps. But one man managed to inform the North from Corinth that the roads had been hard and unobstructed, the town's fortifications worthless, and the noise of the evacuating railroad trains unmistakable. It was clear that the foe had never for a moment intended any resistance.[6] Grant and Sherman agreed that the proper course was to march rapidly on Corinth and storm any works there. "Corinth was conquered at Shiloh," said Grant. But Halleck made Logan entrench to the end, so that his men were actually using shovels while Union cavalry were scouring the deserted Corinth streets. "My men'll never dig another ditch for Halleck except to bury him," exclaimed the wrathful Logan.

Generalship indeed! Halleck had thrown away a month, until the heat of summer shut down on operations. Once in Corinth, instead of using his irresistible concentrated force to seize a key position of the enemy, like Vicksburg, he dissipated it, sending Buell on a slow march toward Chattanooga, Pope in another direction, and Grant to Memphis, while he himself kept a large force inert.[7]

[I]

Equally unhappy was the anticlimax which followed Farragut's victory. Northern elation over the seizure of New Orleans gave birth to clamor for a victorious advance up the Mississippi, and Lincoln, Stanton, and Welles unwisely bowed to it. The river could be partly used, but not held, by naval forces alone. At most points along it, to be sure, warships could drive Confederate troops out of range; but the moment the ships steamed away, the troops would come back. Nothing but a powerful amphibious expedition,

6 Dispatch, April 23, in N. Y. *Weekly Tribune*, May 10, 1862. See also the scornful letters of C. C. Washburne and A. L. Chetlain on Halleck's march in Washburne Papers, LC.

7 William Wood, *Captains of the Civil War*, 105 ff., analyzes this well. For the expulsion of the correspondents and Halleck's combination of arbitrariness and shiftiness in the matter, see J. Cutler Andrews, *The North Reports the Civil War*, 182–188. Reporters for the Chicago *Tribune* and Cincinnati *Commercial* ridiculed the march into Corinth, and the Associated Press told the truth about it.

with enough infantry to capture and hold the principal strategic points on the banks, could accomplish effective results. So long as no Union army was available to co-operate with Farragut in an attack on Vicksburg, any naval attack would prove abortive.

It would have been wiser for the government to send Farragut eastward against Mobile, then still weakly fortified. From the beginning, however, its orders had been that he push upstream: "If the Mississippi expedition from Cairo shall not have descended the river, you will take advantage of the panic to push a strong force up the river to take all their defenses in the rear." This was a relic of Scott's idea that a joint army-navy expedition could rapidly traverse the whole artery. Farragut had hardly taken New Orleans when he was prodded again: "The only anxiety we feel is to know if you have followed up your instructions and pushed a strong force up the river to meet the Western flotilla." With but 1500 troops as a landing force, he had to undertake this preposterous campaign. After capturing Baton Rouge, he steamed on up to Vicksburg, 500 miles from the Gulf, fighting the current, dodging snags, bars, and shore snipers, and running a constant danger of going aground.

The result was inevitably disappointment and loss. When he and the able troop commander with him, General Thomas Williams, reached Vicksburg, they found 30,000 Confederate troops in that fortified town or within a day's march. To throw the small land force ashore would have been to court disaster. With stores running short, for his communications were precarious, Farragut had to return downstream. He arrived in New Orleans with less than a week's provisions, much loss of equipment, and a bad temper. "They will keep us in this river," he grumbled in a private letter home, "till the vessels break down and all the little reputation we have made had evaporated. The Government appears to think that we can do anything. They expect me to navigate the Mississippi nine hundred miles in the face of batteries, ironclad rams, etc.; and yet with all the ironclad vessels they have North they could not get to Norfolk or Richmond." [8]

Once more he was ordered up the river, on the ground that it was imperative to join hands with the upper Mississippi flotilla which Flag-Officer Charles H. Davis was bringing down to Vicksburg. Again he reached that city. With the aid of Porter's mortar boats, he ran past the fortifications on June 28th and joined Davis three days later. There he stayed uselessly waiting until mid-July, while the slow Northern military campaign against Vicksburg was beginning to take shape. When a dangerous ironclad Confederate ram, the *Arkansas*, appeared, he remained still longer in the hope of destroying her. Lying under the Vicksburg bluffs, she survived his forays, only to become

8 Lewis, *Farragut, Our First Admiral*, Chs. IX–XI; Naval O. R., I, xviii, 473 ff.

helpless when her engines failed and to be blown up by her crew. Finally, as the Confederates threatened an attack on Baton Rouge, he returned to the New Orleans area. Three of his gunboats helped to beat off this attack when it took place at the beginning of August. Then, his duty done, Farragut joined the blockading forces in the Gulf; two months of arduous labor had accomplished nothing, for Baton Rouge had immediately to be evacuated.

[II]

If the sequels of Shiloh and New Orleans were a disappointment, so on the political front were the results of Lincoln's effort to deal in a large-minded way with slavery. His appeal to the borderland met in the end a chilly response. We have seen that although Congress passed his resolution for compensated emancipation combined with an effort at colonization, the border members offered an almost solid phalanx of opposition.

Throughout May, throughout June, the months when Lincoln deemed action urgent, most border leaders continued to oppose his plan. The influential Crittenden hung back, while others denounced the measure. One adverse argument was that Congress lacked constitutional authority to spend national funds to compensate slaveholders within selected States. Lincoln's supporters of course replied that such expenditures were justifiable under the war-making power. Opponents also argued that even if Congress did possess the power, it would never exercise it, but after cajoling the States into emancipation, would leave them in the lurch. Was the government about to become a huge Negro-trader? demanded Saulsbury of Delaware incredulously. Above all, border members repudiated the President's proffer as a gross invasion of State sovereignty, and an interference with their domestic institutions. This interpretation did wrong to Lincoln, who intended his plan not as an interference in State affairs, but as a system of cooperation between State and nation, with the States holding the decisive voice. But it appealed to a deep sense of pride.

Behind these superficial arguments lurked the main obstacle, the perplexity of borderland leaders over the problem of post-emancipation adjustment. Like other Southerners, they knew how to manage Negroes as slaves; they did not know how to manage them as freedmen. Certain emotional factors also counted heavily. Abolitionism was detested all along the border, where even moderate men placed it among the virulent causes of the war, and it was easy to give Lincoln's plan a Garrisonian coloration. The President's suggestion that border emancipation was needed to deprive the Confederacy of all hope of gaining the border slave States offended Crittenden, who called it an insult;

Kentucky would never leave the Union, and the South knew it. Crisfield of Maryland believed that unless colonization abroad was total in scope, emancipation would prove inhuman: "We must either keep them as they are, or turn them off to be brutalized, and after a season of degradation and suffering to become extinct." [9] Altogether, a majority of leaders disliked the plan, even if they did not accept Powell's characterization of it as "a pill of arsenic, sugarcoated."

Kentucky first wavered, and then turned back. Its people were attached to the traditions of Virginia and North Carolina; they feared that since one-fifth of the population were slaves the problem of race adjustment would prove fearfully difficult, and they believed that in abandoning State neutrality for the North they had received a moral guarantee of their property. The legislature had declared the previous November that slavery was untouchable save by the States themselves, had demanded Cameron's dismissal for proposing to arm the Negro, and had forbidden the military liberation of any slave. Thus State pride was deeply involved in a firm stand. Lincoln's proposals received no real consideration from half the Kentuckians, who had already made up their minds.[10] Even stout Leslie Combs, the general and legislative leader who had fought secession, was certain that the plan would hinder Federal enlistments and endanger the Union party in elections.

In Missouri the situation was better, for hardly one citizen in fifty had any direct interest in slaves, while the emancipationist trend was clear. Late in the summer the people were to elect a governor, legislature, and Congressmen; emancipation was certain to be the central issue, and unless the legislature adopted a counter plan, the emancipationists would strive to write a liberating clause into the State constitution, without any Federal compensation. Bates, the Blairs, and J. B. Henderson exercised real influence, and all three called for a tender of support to Lincoln on his efforts to protect the border States.

---

9 When Seward, at Lincoln's instigation, explored the idea of an extensive colonization of freedmen abroad, he met a chill reception. The chief European nations wanted no concern with the matter. The minister of Guatemala and Salvador, A. J. de Yrisarri, called attention to the fact that those two republics allowed no colonization of foreigners without special permission. The American envoy to Nicaragua reported that the people there had a deep-rooted and strong opposition to the scheme, and the minister to Costa Rica called attention to "the excitement prevailing over Nicaragua and Honduras on account of a dreaded deluge" of American Negroes. See 37th Cong., 3rd Sess., House Exec. Doc. No. 1, pp. 881–910; Nicolay and Hay, *Lincoln*, VI, 357 ff.; L. C. Hill, *Dip. Rels. Between the U. S. and Brazil*, 158–162; N. A. N. Cleven, *Journal of Negro Hist.*, XI (Jan., 1926), 41–49.

10 Adoption of the plan, many Kentuckians believed, would increase a disorganization and unrest among the slave population which threatened to deprive agriculture of its labor. Already many slaves had become boisterous and disorderly, and some were escaping to the North. This was natural, but it was equally natural that many Kentuckians should want no talk of emancipation whatever. Coulter, *Kentucky*, 247.

"He should . . . in his oft-manifested determination to see that they shall not be wronged," wrote Henderson, "be met with a word of approbation." [11] The question in Missouri would soon be one not of slavery vs. abolition, but of gradual vs. immediate emancipation.

Even in Missouri, however, inertia, Democratic rancor, jealousy for State rights, and suspicion of the radicals in Congress all counted and all helped the opposition to magnify the practical obstacles. Nobody knew just how many slaves were left, for many had fled to freedom, and many had been dragged south into the Confederacy. Estimates of the remainder ranged from 70,000 to 100,000. Even at a low valuation, the cost of purchasing them would run from $28,000,000 to $40,000,000, and valuation was a sore point, for as soon as Missourians began discussing it their estimates of what they should be paid rose. An additional difficulty was the question of dealing with the slaves of Confederates and Southern sympathizers. As the State had no power to discriminate between loyal and disloyal owners, Congress would have to solve that problem. On all such points opponents found it easy to raise objections and throw up clouds of dust.

With the border leaders so largely recalcitrant, Lincoln doubtless felt great discouragement, but was too shrewd to show it. In March, General David Hunter had taken charge of the Department of the South, embracing coastal parts of South Carolina, Georgia, and Florida; and on April 11 troops under his command captured the old national post near the mouth of the Savannah River, Fort Pulaski. His abrupt issuance of two orders, the first on April 12 liberating the slaves in Union hands and the second on May 9 freeing all slaves in the department, gave the President opportunity for a fresh appeal, embodying the first full burst of Lincolnian eloquence the country had yet heard.

Hunter, who though morose and ambitious was devoted to Lincoln, had acted to meet what he thought a plain necessity. He had found the coast and sea islands in social chaos, the slaves abandoned by their masters to destitution and fear. Neither the Treasury Department nor philanthropic agencies could give adequate help. Believing that Negro recruits would be useful in garrisoning posts in malarial districts, he forthwith sanctioned the enlistment of a Negro regiment, the First South Carolina. He also held that since slavery existed only under civil law, it died whenever the slaveowner placed himself beyond the pale of such law. His assertion that slavery and martial law were "incompatible" exposed him to much ridicule, for Lincoln had insisted that

11 June 16, 1862, Gamble Papers, Mo. Hist. Soc. But Henderson hedged his support of Lincoln's plan about with conditions, such as a firm guarantee of the colonization of the freedmen, and an immediate appropriation of money by Congress to be deposited to Missouri's account. See the pamphlet version of his Hannibal speech, no date, NYPL.

generals had no right to free slaves under martial law, but this was only a soldier's verbal maladroitness. Hunter had meant well in a difficult situation —nearly as difficult as Frémont's.

The fact remained that in freeing *all* slaves he had gone much further than Frémont, and that he had meddled with a subject which the President was determined to keep in his own hands. While Bryant's *Evening Post* praised the general, such moderate organs as the Philadelphia *North American*, New York *Times*, and Boston *Morning Journal* condemned his action. Not only had he usurped improper powers; his hasty liberation without preparatory steps was a cruelty to colored people, and if it encouraged servile revolts it might lead to the slaughter of thousands. Though Lincoln was not angry with Hunter, he had to annul the order, and a Cabinet meeting on May 17 found all in agreement with him. Afterwards, the President tactfully met with leading members of Congress to tell them of his decision, and describe the pressure placed on him by border men. On May 20 he issued his revoking proclamation, a brief, emphatic document.

As men read it, against a background of news of heavy fighting in Virginia, they saw how skillfully the President had converted his annulment into a platform from which to exhort the Borderland once more. Asserting that emancipation under the war power was a responsibility which he reserved to himself, he pointed out that the offer of gradual compensated emancipation still held open a door. With heartfelt fervor, touching the high chord which was to make some later utterances immortal, he urged the border to pass through it. "I do not argue. I beseech you to make the arguments for yourselves. You can not if you would be blind to the signs of the times. I beg of you a calm and enlarged consideration of them, ranging, it may be, far above personal and partisan politics. This proposal makes common cause for a common object, casting no reproaches upon any. It acts not the pharisee. The change it contemplates would come gently as the dews of heaven, not rending or wrecking anything. Will you not embrace it? So much good has not been done, by one effort, in all past time, as in the providence of God, it is now your high privilege to do. May the vast future not have to lament that you have neglected it." [12]

12 The Washington correspondent of the N. Y. *Evening Post* suggests that Chase demurred; May 18-21, 1862. Lincoln's paper was dated May 19; *Collected Works*, V, 222, 223. Stanton helped Lincoln draft the proclamation of annulment, the two working in complete harmony. Chase doubtless assented to the revocation, but at heart he approved of Hunter's orders. "I think like orders should be promulgated in all the Gulf States at least," he wrote Murat Halstead; May 24, Chase Collection, Pa. Hist. Soc. At most points on the slavery issue Chase disagreed with Lincoln. He objected to compensated emancipation on the general abolitionist ground that slaves and slave labor were stolen property, to be released without payment. He thought colonization wrong.

This was Lincoln's first but not last reminder to the nation that man's "vast future" waited upon its decisions. But no answering voice came from the border. The giants Partisanship, Inertia, and Racial Intolerance still barred the way—or perhaps, rather, these were seneschals of the real fortress: "A castle, called Doubting-Castle, the owner whereof was Giant Despair." Slavery, by the year A.D. 1862, was synonymous with Despair.

Lincoln was resolved to make yet another effort to win the Borderland. He knew that appreciation of his high intentions was widespread. To be sure, few men believed in either the wisdom or practicability of colonizing the colored folk abroad; even Seward was against it, saying that he wished to bring men into the Union, not send them out. But gradual compensated emancipation did seem to offer a hopeful new path. Lincoln also knew that every obstacle only damned back forces that before long would become irresistible. Perspicacious men now saw that the problem of racial readjustment was impossible of quick solution, and that every step would be painful.[13] As with so much else in this horrible war, one exhausting effort but led to another. And how much would depend on the fate of McClellan's great stroke in Virginia!

[III]

On that campaign the North, as May passed into June, pinned its fairest hopes. The Virginia thrust was its supreme bid for a short war. In mid-May numerous observers thought that the great army just outside Richmond would prove irresistible. Then two unexpected elements altered the outlines of the situation: the Chickahominy River, and the strategy of Stonewall Jackson.

Few Northerners, unless they had read Captain John Smith's travels, had ever heard of the swamp-bordered Chickahominy. The first mentions by war correspondents described it as a narrow, shallow stream, said to be partly dry in summer. Yet it was potentially formidable. Rising in the hills northwest of Richmond, it flows east and south, describing the quadrant of a circle around the city, and emptying into the James about fifty miles below it. Although the main channel was easily passable, all the timbered bottom lands were low, and it was belted in places by actual bogs. Even in dry weather the swampy margins and the bottom lands, varying from three quarters of a mile to a mile in width, were too spongy for cavalry and artillery. If rain raised the river two feet above normal level, it would spread in channels through the

13 Bancroft, *Seward*, II, 346. The London *Daily News* and the Church of England daily, the *Record*, strong adherents of the Union, joined many Northern papers and the great body of Negroes in condemning the "deportation" of freedmen. It looks too absurd a plan in European eyes, said the *Daily News*, to be treated as real; Sept. 24, 1862.

bogs, while if continued storms lifted it three or four feet, it would overflow the whole low area. Even light infantry would then find the Chickahominy impracticable.

To add to its dangers, the woods made examination of the terrain difficult. Tall trees rose to a height level with the bluffs rimming the valley, so that unwary troops might think themselves safe until they found the ground abruptly dropping away and their advance files floundering in a morass. A Union private told a tearful woman who had a son in the Confederate army that he expected to get into Richmond without much fighting. "No!" she stormed, forgetting her fears, "you-all will drink hot blood before you git thar." [14] It was certain that the river would run red.

That the army command was astonished by the suddenly disclosed perils of the Chickahominy was not its fault. Scientific mapmaking in the United States was yet in its swaddling clothes, and those who wanted detailed knowledge of any district usually groped in vain; they were lucky if they could get anything better than a page from a school geography! Here and there a sharp ray of light fell upon a special area. The Army engineers had mapped some points of defense, while the topographical corps had prepared maps of rivers and harbors, of certain roads, and of routes of exploration. But as late as 1872, Captain M. Wheeler of the topographical engineers could declare: "The United States has thus far organized no systematic topographical survey of any portion of its territory." Not until four years later was the Geological Survey authorized. Virginia fell behind most of her sisters in the preparation of maps, and the counties of Hanover, King William, and Henrico, which the Chickahominy drains, fell behind sister counties with mining interests. Neither the Union nor Confederate forces had adequate maps of the country environing Richmond; nothing better than some old railroad surveys.[15]

McClellan's first dispatches exhibited a blithe contempt of the river. He examined the bridge which carried the Williamsburg–Richmond road over the stream, and on May 21 telegraphed Stanton that he would have it repaired by the morrow and would at once construct others. He was pleased by his base at the White House landing on the Pamunkey. The handsome two-story mansion of this name, recently held by W. H. F. ("Rooney") Lee, second son of the general and a colonel in Stuart's cavalry, was busy with officers coming and going. Along the Pamunkey stretched offices and warehouses of the quartermaster's department, and the roadways littered by boxes, barrels, hay bales, wandering Negroes, and mules; the stream was crammed with

14 W. L. Goss, *Battles and Leaders*, II, 130, 131.
15 L. A. Brown, *The Story of Maps*, 276; P. L. Phillips, *Virginia Cartography, A Bibliographical Description*. The Atlas volume of O. R. and the Coast Survey map of the Potomac (1862) indicate that real Virginia mapmaking began with the war, not before.

RICHMOND AND ITS DEFENSES

rows of vessels of every description, unloading at floating wharves their supplies of salt meat, biscuit, clothing, and ammunition. Moored apart were huge floating hospitals bearing the flag of the Sanitary Commission, their decks piled with boxes. Some large stores sold general goods, the biggest offering a miscellany from potted lobster and shoeblacking to toothbrushes and straw hats. From this base the Richmond & York River Railroad was swiftly put in running order up to the banks of the Chickahominy.[16]

16 See description in the London *Times*, July 10, 1862. Soldiers had trampled down the shrubbery and made the banks of the streamlets quagmires. The correspondent found the

As long as the army used this base it was able to maintain close liaison with Washington by telegraph. A curiously roundabout single-wire line had been carried from Washington by way of Wilmington and the eastern shore of Maryland and Virginia to Fort Monroe, about two hundred miles in length. The telegraphers worked under fire in the trenches before Yorktown, keeping McClellan in touch with his generals and the War Department. After the battle of Williamsburg the courageous construction party kept the main line up with the advance of the troops, and at every halt strung branches to corps headquarters. The Comte de Paris describes the surprise and delight of the generals at finding the telegraph always at hand. All the urgent orders for supplies and reinforcements, all the critical instructions, all the news of battle and lists of killed, passed over the one throbbing wire. Sometimes the telegraph was of vital importance; at Gaines's Mill, Fitz-John Porter was to obtain reinforcements at a critical moment through the prompt service of his operator. For important messages a simple cipher, frequently changed, was used.

Yet in reality the White House was a defective base for operations. The Pamunkey was too small to afford proper naval protection. Much more importantly, any army advancing on Richmond from the White House would have to push part of its force across the Chickahominy while keeping another part on the near side. That is, one section would have to remain on the north bank to hold the communications with White House Landing while the other crossed to the south bank to attack the Southern capital. Such a division of the army would be safe if the weather proved dry or the engineers erected numerous good bridges. It would be highly unsafe if storms raised the river, flooded the lowlands, and swept away jerry-built crossings. McClellan had not advanced far before his staff realized that the Chickahominy was no trifle. Prisoners dropped references to the great swamp, and a deserter told how apprehensive Magruder's forces retreating from Williamsburg had been lest the Union army should catch them before they crossed the stream.[17] But McClellan, following the plan he had made before he learned that McDowell would advance overland upon Richmond rather than by the Potomac and York Rivers, quickly put his army astride the Chickahominy.

That is, during May 20–25, the two corps of Keyes and Heintzelman were thrown across to the south bank to maneuver against Richmond, while the three corps of Sumner, Fitz-John Porter, and Franklin were kept on the north bank. This offered Joseph E. Johnston an opportunity he was quick to seize. He saw that if he could mass superior strength against McClellan's exposed

---

camps covering the countryside filthy, disorderly places, made worse by whole Negro families that had established themselves in tents and huts among the troops.

17 N. Y. *Tribune*, May 23, 1862.

wing under Heintzelman and Keyes, he might crush them before other troops could cross to their aid. On the morning of May 27 he received news that McDowell was advancing from Fredericksburg with his 41,000 men; and although a scouting movement by J. E. B. Stuart's cavalry quickly proved the report false, he concluded he must act before these reinforcements reached McClellan. "We could not afford to wait," writes General Gustavus W. Smith.[18]

The Confederate blow, ably conceived, was aided by good fortune. Johnston was able to attack at a time when the river had just flooded. On Sunday, May 25, the Keyes-Heintzelman forces, well across the stream, had strolled about the area of Fair Oaks or Seven Pines under a warm sun, listening to the church bells of Richmond seven miles away. Three bridges crossed the Chickahominy at their rear, two of them rough new structures. But Monday evening brought a drenching rain, which continued for much of the 27th. Troops gathered in dripping, gloomy groups about the smoking fires, on short rations. "The army is morose and savage this morning," wrote a correspondent, "and worse than all, the begging and borrowing of bread has begun." The river rose, and the narrow, tortuous roads became execrable. By the 30th Johnston's dispositions were completed. Late that afternoon nature renewed her alliance with the Confederacy, for a heavy thunderstorm began and continued all night.

"The face of the country was literally flooded," writes a Confederate general. "At daybreak on the 31st the Chickahominy was booming, passable only at the bridges, and it continued to rise during the day, although it had ceased to rain."

At daybreak Johnston expected his troops to attack like wolves; and indeed, only a combination of Confederate delays and Northern gallantry saved McClellan's forward wing from being torn to pieces at Fair Oaks. "My attempt," Johnston later wrote, "would have been a *full* success but for the sloth of a new division, which delayed Longstreet's attack six hours, which did not leave us time to complete the destruction of Keyes' corps." He himself was partly to blame. His plan required careful timing, for columns separated by forest and swamp had to be brought together; the commanders were novices in such co-ordinated movements; and Johnston erred in not giving his generals written orders defining their authority and tasks. Even so, his troops struck with crushing force before noon of the 31st. Silas Casey's division of Keyes's corps recoiled in hopeless disarray. By five in the afternoon it seemed that the Union forces would be cut into ribbons. But at that hour brave old Sumner, who had

18 Johnston had been so anxious to strike before the junction of McClellan and McDowell that he had contemplated delivering a blow from the still intact bridges downstream; letter to Wigfall, Nov. 12, 1863, Wigfall Papers, Univ. of Texas; cf. G. W. Smith, *Battles and Leaders*, II, 223.

put his corps in readiness, began moving across the river, and came on the field with almost the impact of Blücher at Waterloo.

No episode of McClellan's campaign was more creditable to Northern arms than this emergency crossing of swamp and swollen river by the Massachusetts veteran. Only one half-wrecked bridge was available. The log approaches were afloat, held by their fastenings to tree stumps, and the bridge itself was precariously kept in place by ropes. Many officers had doubted the feasibility of passage. As the solid infantry column came forward the structure swayed to and fro in the angry flood, settling down safely only when filled with men; and after they had crossed it quickly became worthless. Although Sumner expected to be wiped out along with Keyes and Heintzelman, he meant to exact a price. He told a division commander, John Sedgwick: "The enemy may win a victory, but we must make it a victory that will ruin him." [19]

In the end the Union lines held. The Confederate loss, about 6,150, materially exceeded the Northern loss of 5,000, while Johnston was severely wounded. Both sides, however, were so severely shaken that they were immobilized; and worst shaken of all was McClellan's reputation as a strategist. He had committed a terrible error in throwing his army astraddle a dangerous river and in leaving Keyes's corps standing isolated for several days within reach of a crushing blow from Johnston. Indeed, he was lucky to escape so easily. Johnston always believed that a vigorous renewal of the battle on June 1 would have destroyed Keyes and totally crippled McClellan. [20]

In a single week, the situation of the Union army had totally changed.

[IV]

Meanwhile, the second unexpected obstacle made itself felt: Stonewall Jackson's bold Shenandoah campaign, and its effect in exciting the deepest apprehension in Washington. To the campaign itself, a classic feat of modern warfare, we need yield little space. Lincoln and Stanton should have given the command of all Virginia operations, apart from McClellan's, to a single able general, and should have kept the forces west of the Blue Ridge well concentrated. Instead, they had offered the enemy a rich opportunity by dividing the leadership and troops among three generals; Banks with 19,000 men in the heart of the Shenandoah Valley, Frémont with 15,000 partly in the Alleghenies

19 A. S. Webb, *The Peninsula*, Ch. VI; Smith, *Battles and Leaders*, II, 225 ff.; N. Y. *Tribune, Times*, May 31, June 2, 3. Much ink was spent on the poor behavior of Casey's division in Keyes's corps. Sumner brought over 20,000 fresh men.
20 Johnston, *Narrative*, 141.

and partly in the Valley, and McDowell with 41,000 far to the east of Fredericksburg. Supreme command was retained by Lincoln and Stanton, who knew just enough about maneuvering to be dangerous practitioners.

For a fast-moving, hard-hitting leader like Jackson this presented an ideal situation. Lee in a historic dispatch of April 21 had submitted to Jackson three plans of action against Banks and his associates, writing: "I have hoped in the present divided condition of the enemy's forces that a successful blow may be dealt them by a rapid combination of our troops before they can be strengthened themselves either in position or by reinforcements." And never did a general use his opportunities more brilliantly. On May 21 Jackson suddenly smashed a small Union force at Front Royal. During the next five days —the days in which McClellan put two corps across the Chickahominy and that river rose in flood—Stonewall with 16,000 men drove Banks's troops up the Valley. By swift blows he pushed the Union forces out of Strasburg, out of Middleton, and out of Winchester, sending them flying on north to Martinsburg. Banks's shattered command, throwing away arms and covering more than thirty miles in one day, did not pause until it was safe behind the Potomac.

When he did stop, while Jackson's troops gleefully packed up the huge quantity of munitions and supplies taken at Winchester, Washington was in a state of wild alarm. The War Department in particular gave way on Sunday the 25th to what some Northerners later termed "the great scare." When Cabinet and Congressmen learned that day that Banks was fleeing helter-skelter, they leaped at the conclusion that Jackson might suddenly invade Maryland, or by a march through Harpers Ferry hurl himself on Washington. Senators Fessenden and Grimes jocularly assured Sumner that he would be among the first men executed. Stanton was as much alarmed as when the *Merrimac* had emerged; so frightened, in fact, that with the full concurrence of Lincoln, the Cabinet, and various generals he telegraphed the Northern governors for troops. John A. Andrew and others hastily began assembling militia. From the White House, Nicolay wrote his wife: "We have been 'stampeded' all day with news from Gen. Banks's army." The whole city was convulsed, he added, and a frightened woman had just rushed in to ask if she should leave immediately. To Sumner, Seward, and some military men that evening Lincoln gave a vivid description of the rout.[21]

Great excitement seized the North. Governors Curtin in Pennsylvania and Sprague in Rhode Island took steps to hurry off troops that they possessed ready for service. In Boston Governor Andrew, his adjutant-general, and their

21 Nicolay Papers; Sumner to R. H. Dana, Jr., May 31, 1862, Dana Papers. The Valley campaign is covered in O. R., I., xii, pt. 1, pp. 3–818; Freeman, *Lee*, Ch. IV; *Lee's Lieutenants*, Chs. XXIV–XXVI; Henderson, *Jackson*, Chs. IX–XII. See also the vivid record in Henry Kyd Douglas, *I Rode With Stonewall*, 68–94.

aides toiled all Sunday night, and at dawn on Monday, May 26, the newspapers were carrying his alarmed proclamation to the people. A barbarous horde of traitors, he wrote, had routed Banks and were marching on Washington. To arms! Let Massachusetts rise! By nightfall 2,000 militia had gathered on Boston Common and started to the capital. "Our people are rushing in as in April, 1861," Andrew telegraphed Stanton.

This sudden change in the situation disrupted the machinery in motion for taking Richmond. As Banks fled on the 24th, Lincoln and Stanton ordered McDowell to drop the march on that city fixed for the 26th, and put 20,000 men in motion toward the Shenandoah. They hoped to stop Stonewall and trap him in the Valley. McDowell telegraphed back that the order was a "crushing blow," and Lincoln replied: "The change was as painful to me as it can possibly be to you or anyone." His denial of aid to McClellan was a momentous decision, but it was not taken without careful thought of the consequences. The possible gains seemed to justify the risk. The President and Secretary were motivated partly by apprehension over the safety of Washington, and partly by a desire to use converging columns to cut off Jackson when he turned back toward Richmond. That they made a mistake time soon proved.

Actually, the Administration had no reason for its alarm over Washington. Troops could be and were rapidly brought in from Baltimore and other neighboring points for its defense. The march of Frémont alone into the Valley would compel Jackson's rapid withdrawal from his exposed position near the Potomac. No consideration of safety required a change in McDowell's destination. And when the President and Secretary planned to outwit Jackson and "bag" his force by using the telegraph office to move the separate armies in the Valley, they based their impromptu strategy on very dubious chances. The distances Frémont and McDowell had to cover in order to close the gate behind Jackson were excessive; the muddy, rocky roads were atrocious; and while McDowell's troops were well equipped, Frémont's had been shockingly neglected by the government. As Carl Schurz certified to Lincoln, they were largely destitute of clothing, tents, and even shoes, many marching barefoot. Their pioneer companies in this mountain country had no axes, picks, or saws; their horses were barely able to drag the artillery. Banks's troops were disheartened by defeat, Frémont's by repeated slights, and McDowell's by the unwelcome change in orders. Nor could these separated armies be maneuvered properly by telegraph.[22]

The three commanders did their best, and for a brief hour it seemed that they might actually cut off bold Jackson. McDowell's vanguard under

22 Schurz, *Reminiscences*, II, 344–347; Nevins, *Frémont*, II, 636–639.

THE VIRGINIA CAMPAIGNS

Shields on May 30 reached a point twelve miles from Strasburg on the east, and Frémont a village twenty miles on the west, while Jackson was still eighteen miles to the north. Woe to the Confederacy if they closed the pincers! [23]

23 Ropes, *Civil War*, II, 129, 130; Freeman, *Lee's Lieutenants*, II, Chs. XXVII, XXVIII. Kenneth P. Williams, *Lincoln Finds A General*, I, 187–213, strains the evidence to defend

But the trap remained unsprung. Shields, though a natural fighter, took a defensive attitude just when he should have moved forward. Frémont, after first misunderstanding his orders, was impeded by storms, the worsening of the mountain roads, and the fatigue of men and steeds. The upshot was that Jackson, taking the splendid Valley turnpike and exhibiting characteristic skill, slipped between the Union armies and escaped. When pursued, he used Turner Ashby's cavalry to check his assailants, and fought two effective rear-guard actions, one with Frémont at Cross Keys June 8, and one next day with Shields at Port Republic. He paused for a time to rest his army, and then quietly rejoined the main Confederate force. The detachment of McDowell had thus accomplished nothing in the Valley, while it gravely weakened the campaign against Richmond. Indeed, this detachment had been precisely what the Confederate leaders wished to effect!

Both McDowell and McClellan regarded the Administration's recall of McDowell's troops as a horrible mistake, and McClellan's bitterness intensified all his sullenness of attitude thereafter. He had reached the Richmond front deeply distrustful of the Administration. "Those hounds in Washington are after me again," he had written his wife on May 18. "Stanton is without exception the vilest man I ever knew or heard of!" He received Lincoln's telegram of May 24 announcing the suspension of McDowell's junction with his army just as he was putting his two corps in peril across the river. Next day brought a much more alarmed message from the President, declaring that the enemy seemed to be making a general movement northward: "I think the time is near when you must either attack Richmond or give up the job and come to the defense of Washington." [24] This expressed Lincoln's apprehensions over Banks's retreat and also his irritation over McClellan's long delays on the Peninsula. But, reaching the general at a moment of deep anxiety, it exploded all his pent-up anger. "Heaven save a country governed by such counsels!" he wrote his wife, and after reassuring Lincoln that the mass of Southern troops were still in Richmond, he burst out: "It is perfectly sickening to deal with such people and you may rest assured that I will lose as little time as possible in breaking off all connection with them." [25] McClellan believed that the best defense of Washington was an all-out attack on Richmond, and he was entirely right—though he himself failed to make it.

Once more he suspected McDowell of treachery—of conniving at the detachment of his force. The fact was that McDowell had protested sharply, writing Lincoln that he could not possibly rescue Banks, and that the change

Lincoln's leadership in the Valley campaign, quoting with approval Shields's statement, "The plan for Jackson's destruction was perfect."

24 *Works*, V, 235, 236.
25 Myers, *McClellan*, 291–293; Hassler, *McClellan*, 114 ff., a careful account.

of plan would paralyze the main Union activities north of Richmond.[26] He shortly sent a New York friend a letter of angry frustration:

It is now the middle of the third week since I was at Fredericksburg with a splendid little army of 41,000 men, 100 pieces of artillery, and 14,000 horse —fully equipped, admirably organized, and as a general thing well disciplined and well officered! We were all in high spirits. For this army which had been assembled quietly, was the *next morning* to march down and join the army before Richmond under McClellan. I had been held back by peremptory written orders from the President not to cross the Rappahannock. And not even for a while, to make the bridges over the River!! But he had given his consent, had issued his orders that I might go as soon as Shields' division should join. It had joined. The wagons were all loaded, the orders given, and we were to march the next day! When came the orders breaking us up and sending us over to the valley after Jackson!

I telegraphed the President that the order was a crushing blow to us all. That I could not get to the valley in time to affect Banks' position. His case would be disposed of one way or the other before I could arrive! . . .

But they were alarmed over the safety of Washington! Then came this extraordinary forced march over the Piedmont and Blue Ridge mountains to Front Royal, in which I estimate that we had 4,000 men broken down.[27]

When this letter was sent, Lincoln had just ruefully informed McClellan that Shields's division was so terribly out at elbows and toes that it would take a long time to get it in shape again. Except for McCall's division, McDowell's army never did join the resentful McClellan before Richmond.[28]

From the Valley campaign suddenly emerged one momentous fact: a military genius had appeared on the Southern side. The gifts of a surpassing commander were united in Stonewall Jackson: imagination, boldness, determination, vigilance, and rapidity. The least eloquent of men, he had no superior in holding the devotion of his troops. Of all Confederate officers the most careful in his precautions, he could be the most adventurous.

He had three cardinal rules. One was always to mystify the enemy; one

26 May 24; O. R., I, xii, pt. 3, pp. 220, 221.
27 To C. A. Hecksher, June 17, 1862, Barlow Papers.
28 McClellan still cherished the idea of a conspiracy. He said in Boston in February, 1863, that the cabal against him had gained great strength when he lay ill of fever. He thought that the fears of the President for Washington had been adroitly excited by men who knew the city was really safe, and who did not wish the Peninsular campaign to succeed, for that would mean the end of the influence of ultra-radical Republicans. McClellan said he knew the war had given a deathblow to slavery, but he did not want the property of innocent men a thousand miles away to be confiscated. T. Jefferson Coolidge, *Autobiography*, 41. On the other hand, McClellan should have realized that some radicals honestly doubted that his heart was in defeating the South, while his needless delays had discouraged Lincoln; and he should have seen that the supreme risk which the President could not afford to take was that of the capture of Washington.

was to maneuver his troops until he could throw his main force upon a weak part of his antagonist's army and crush it; and the third was to be utterly relentless in pursuit of a stricken foe. "Such tactics will win every time," he told a subordinate. The Spartan characteristics of this gentle-voiced, imperturbable, alert man stamped him as a soldier born, and he subordinated all his thought and activity to war. To start at dawn, to pray, to fight, to suck lemons, to live on hardtack and water, to look after his troops' welfare, to ponder long and hard—this was all his creed. He could be harsh, for he hated weakness. He was always ready to exact the last ounce of effort from his columns. His supply trains might be left behind, but his ammunition wagons had to get through. After this spring campaign the legend of his ways—his insistence on action, movement, quick-step, "bay'nets and grape" always characteristic, but so too his rocklike firmness in defense—possessed the South, and helped animate her soldiers:

> We see him now—the queer slouched hat
> Cocked o'er his eye askew;
> The shrewd dry smile; the speech so pat
> So calm, so blunt, so true.

The bloody, indecisive battle of Fair Oaks was followed by more than three weeks of waiting which sorely tried the patience of watchers North and South. Both sides in the interval had an opportunity to weigh the sad costs of battle. "Our loss is heavy," McClellan had telegraphed Stanton, "but that of the enemy must be enormous." In fact, all the carriages of Richmond were impressed to bring dead and wounded into the city, hotels were turned into hospitals, and the need for additional shelters evoked a bitter outcry against the churches for keeping their doors closed. A German-born officer in Confederate ranks who had seen the battlefields of Hungary and Italy wrote in the *Kölnische Zeitung* that he had never beheld such a butchery as that at Fair Oaks. He helped organize a midnight convoy of sixty wagons bearing two hundred gravely wounded. Reaching the first hospital in the city, he met a refusal. "All full!" was the reply to his inquiry. "Forward to the next hospital," he commanded, only to receive the same response: "All full!" At last a tobacco warehouse was thrown open and men with ghastly wounds were laid on hard planks in a stifling loft, without windows, in the June heat.[29] On the Union side, meanwhile, the casualties were in an even worse situation. Wrote one correspondent:

The wounded! It is now fifty-six hours since they received their injuries. Those away from water—oh, how they suffer! those in the wet—how they

---

29 Translated in N. Y. *Herald*, Dec. 25, 1862. This officer writes that after Johnston fell, Lee made preparations for 10,000 wounded in the hospitals.

contract new diseases, and how they undergo wintry torments from the night cold! I dread to go upon that battleground. For forty-eight hours I have worked, and slept, and ate, and served among a thousand wounded soldiers—wounded in every possible degree of severity. The screaming of stout men under surgeons' knives—the groaning everywhere over three acres of lawn—the piteous cries for drink, for help, for shade—the delirium of the dying—the blood and dis-coloration and disfigurement and dirt and wretchedness of the unfortunates who are brought in an uninterrupted stream of tardy discovery and lie under foot everywhere, waiting surgical help—the ceaseless labors on the operating table in the great hospital tent—the use of knife and probe by lantern light all around this country-seat, and the dressing of ghastly wounds all night and all day, and all day and all night—'tis a memory that shall make the Seven Pines painful till I die.[30]

Throughout the three weeks following the battle McClellan's inaction, re-flecting his chronic indecision and the atrocious weather, was complete. He beguiled the North by day-to-day promises. On June 2, sending news that Hooker had led a reconnaissance within four miles of Richmond, he added: "I only wait for the river to fall to cross with the rest of the force and make a general attack." The army was still dangerously astraddle the Chickahominy, but the larger part of it was now south of that stream. The 75,000 men who had entrenched beyond the river reached the Mechanicsville Bridge, bearing a signpost reading "To Richmond, 4½ miles," and on still nights the city clocks chiming the hours could be heard within the Union camps. But the weather again interposed, for on June 4 it poured for hours, until the river reached its highest level in twenty years and its current swept men off their feet. And McClellan was writing confidentially: "I dare not risk this army. . . . I must make a sure thing of it"—as if anything were sure in war! [31]

Lincoln sent him troops from Washington and from Fort Monroe, which with McCall's division from McDowell's army made 20,000 in all. McClellan announced June 7: "I shall be in perfect readiness to move forward and take Richmond the moment McCall reaches here, and the ground will admit the

30 Letter by N. Y. *Tribune* reporter dated Monday morning, June 2, in issue June 6. The first day's fighting was usually called Fair Oaks, and the second day's Seven Pines.
31 The London *Times* correspondent admired the patience of the volunteers under hard-ships which they did not realize were avoidable. They were often paid only after long delays. They had filthy water to drink. Whole divisions for days on end got no food but poor biscuits and wretched coffee, and when they did receive meat it was salt beef as hard as sole leather. "Nowhere is to be seen more military stupidity and more dishonesty than in this brave American army. You must not wonder if I get warm and bitter." Amid general muddle, the troops were exhausted by needless marches through swamp and mud. McClellan would not risk a battle, "and therefore he lets the volunteers die in the swamps." Embalmers did a large business in fever-killed soldiers, charging $25 for privates, $50 for officers, and shipping the corpses home in zinc-lined pine boxes by Adams's Express. One embalmer said that 2,000 corpses had thus been shipped since the war began. London *Times,* July 10, 1862. For the weather see O. R., I, xi, pt. 1, p. 31; pt. 3, p. 193.

passage of artillery." Five days later McCall's division was paraded at the White House. The North eagerly awaited word of the taking of Richmond. It knew that Jackson had not yet rejoined Lee, and saw no reason why the Union army should not advance. But McClellan had telegraphed on the 10th: "I am completely checked by the weather. The Chickahominy is in a dreadful state: we have another rainstorm on our hands." He was nervously asking Stanton to consider the propriety of bringing east a large section of Halleck's Western army to reinforce him. When Stanton assured him on the 12th that McDowell's full independent force would soon arrive to cooperate, he flared up angrily: "If I cannot control all the troops I want none of them, and would prefer to fight the battle with what I have, and let others be responsible for the result." Yet he certainly did not lack for men, for on June 20 his returns showed an army of 156,838, of whom 115,102 were present for duty.[32]

While McClellan waited, the enemy resolved to strike, for the Southern army was now headed by a man of lionhearted qualities. If the emergence of Jackson was one of the memorable developments of the war, the replacement of Johnston by Robert E. Lee signalized a quite new phase of the conflict. Since April 23, 1861, by State appointment, Lee had been major-general and commander of the Virginia forces, and since May 10, 1861, he had also held supreme control of all the Confederate forces in Virginia. Primarily concerned with organizing State forces, fortifying Virginia rivers, and (during the winter) improving the defenses of the South Atlantic coast, he had also been Jefferson Davis' military adviser. He kept aloof from the dispute between Davis and Johnston over the latter's rank. By common consent he was easily the ablest man to take Johnston's place, although he had never directed a battle. In the prime of life—fifty-five years old, powerfully built, in superb health—he was glad to exchange his empty if honorable desk eminence for a field command. On June 1 he took charge of the force he named The Army of Northern Virginia, and promptly began planning an offensive.[33]

Lee saw that he could not wait. If McClellan marshaled his hosts and brought his powerful siege guns to bear, Richmond would be lost. Nothing but fierce lunging blows could extricate the Confederacy from its disadvantages of inferior strength. Like Jackson, he was a thinker. Although his symmetry of character was so noble, and his reticence so complete, that many have credited him with greatness of personality rather than intellect, the fact was that he possessed both. In quickness of perception, subtlety of thought, and power of devising complicated operations, he equaled Marlborough or Frederick, as

---

32 Ropes, *Civil War*, II, 159, gives the figure 105,445 men on June 20; Webb, *The Peninsula*, 120, estimates the effective force at 92,500.

33 See the clear statement on Lee's official status 1861–62 in the *Nation*, Dec. 23, 1897, and in Freeman's *Lee*, II, Ch. VIII.

in coolness he surpassed them. He knew that a general must always take chances, that the leader with inferior forces must move swiftly and shrewdly to make his chances better than even, and that he must realistically equate the power to act with the power to imagine.[34]

If in many ways Lee seemed limited, it was intensity of purpose that limited him. All his thoughts, apart from religion and family, were centered on the profession of arms. He did almost no general reading; he never accumulated a library, never gave a leisure hour to literature, and never once in his letters refers to Shakespeare or Milton, to Dickens or Thackeray. The great scientific advance of the age of Darwin, Huxley, and Spencer made no appeal to him. Even in religion he paid no attention to austere theological thought; the Bible was enough for him. But in strategy and tactics, in engineering, and in what we now call logistics, he made himself proficient by hard study. Nobody in America knew military science so well.

War was in fact a passion with him, and as befitted a son of "Light-Horse Harry" Lee, he delighted in martial problems and exercises. A merciful man, he was sensitively aware of the suffering which war imposes. "You have no idea what a horrible sight a battlefield is," he wrote his family from Mexico. The knightliest of commanders, he set his face sternly, in his invasion of the North, against any retaliation for the devastation and plundering of which many Union forces had been guilty. But his energetic nature, which comprehended a taste for excitement and a delight in seeing intricate mental combinations translated into army evolutions, made conflict a congenial element. Remembering well what his father's unresting activity had accomplished at Stony Point, Paulus Hook, and in the long Southern campaign, he drew a special pleasure from swift movement and battles against odds.[35] When told after the war that such daring decisions as the splitting of his army at Second Manassas had risked the utter ruin of the Confederacy, he replied that this was obvious, "but the disparity of force between the contending forces rendered the risks unavoidable."

Yet he did his best to minimize the risks to be taken. While still in the Lower South, he had appealed to the governor of Virginia for more men, with the result that the legislature in February had provided for enrolling all citizens between eighteen and forty-five, and that Letcher the following month had called 40,000 men to the colors. It was Lee who had inspired the Confederate conscription law of April, Major Charles Marshall of his staff drawing up the main features of the bill, and Lee himself taking it to Jefferson Davis for introduction in Congress. Thus the peril of a disorganization of Con-

34 Cf. Henderson, *Jackson*, II, 4–7; Hendrick, *Lees of Va.*, 412 ff.; Freeman, *Lee, passim.*
35 See his edition of his father's *Memoirs*, with biographical essay (1869).

federate defense by the expiration of the terms of nearly 150 regiments was averted. Laboring in May to hurry troops up from the Carolinas and other points, he was hopeful that the arrival of Huger, Holmes, and Ripley would give the Confederate defenders of Richmond 80,000 or even 85,000 men.[36]

As yet untried, he did not command enthusiasm when appointed; the troops cheered tepidly, and the newspapers expressed little more than a belief that he would prove competent. But his qualities quickly impressed his army. He had a deep faith in his troops, and would have echoed Stonewall Jackson's exclamation as his lines swung past: "Who could fail to win battles with such men as these?" Such a faith was sure to be repaid. Another element of strength lay in his remarkable capacity for judging his antagonists. Whether they were formidable like Grant or contemptible like Pope, he keenly appraised their traits. He was wont to refer scornfully to Hooker as "Mr. F. J. Hooker," the initials being his abbreviation for "Fighting Joe," and he remarked that he could forgive his nephew for fighting on the Union side, but never for joining John Pope's staff. He deemed Ben Butler beneath contempt. Liking Burnside as a man, he was quick to take his short measure. "We always understood each other," he said regretfully when McClellan was displaced. "I fear they may contrive to make these changes until they find someone I don't understand." For all his modesty, he knew that the fighting power of his army was doubled by his and Jackson's talents.[37]

McClellan he now understood particularly well, for they had served on the same staff in the Mexican War. He had hardly been astonished by McClellan's strange winter inaction, his month-long pause before Yorktown, and his slow creep to White House Landing, for he knew that McClellan's taste was for a war of position. Invariably, in McClellan's strategy, boldness in conception was fettered by an appalling slowness in execution. Though Lee respected McClellan's abilities, he knew that his operations were always half defensive; that he never caught at a military opportunity without saying to himself, "Suppose the enemy has hidden reserves?" And Lee realized that the timidities of his opponent opened the way for operations impossible in the face of a more resolute foe.

[V]

McClellan's golden opportunity, unperceived and unused, came between the 18th and 25th of June. Jackson in the Valley was still distant from Lee. The Confederate works around Richmond remained weak. Although Lee had

36 Freeman, *Lee*, II, Chs. III, IV, V.
37 Allen, *The Army of Northern Va.*, 200; Swinton, *Army of the Potomac*, Ch. IV; Freeman, *Lee*, Chs. VII, VIII.

frantically called for troops from every quarter, his forces were still much
under the Union strength. But while McClellan waited, Lee matured a daring
plan. A magnificent cavalry raid by Jeb Stuart all the way around McClellan's
army gave him full information on the Union dispositions. He decided to
bring Jackson stealthily down from the Valley, so that the two commands could suddenly strike McClellan's right wing, one in the rear and one
in front, crushing it as in a vise. He gave the proper orders. On June 25
Jackson reached Ashland, seventeen miles north of Richmond. A council of
generals that day decided to begin the pincers attack at three the next morning.[38]

Would this new operation succeed? The attacker had become the attacked;
would McClellan, who so recently had expected to seize Richmond, himself
be destroyed? The answer was given in the Seven Days' Battles that followed;
an answer that comforted neither side.

Lee's first heavy stroke at Mechanicsville on June 26 failed partly because
a reconnaissance in force by McClellan the previous day had altered his plans,
and partly because of poor staff work and poor coordination of forces; but it
resulted in a Union retreat to Gaines's Mill. Here a renewed attack next day
smashed the Union right wing under FitzJohn Porter with heavy losses. Mc-
Clellan, now in real peril, concluded that the only way to foil Lee was to shift
his base from the shallow Pamunkey to the deep James, where he might find
full naval protection. On the night of the 27th he began the agonizing march.
His retreat across country was a masterly operation, executed despite heat,
thirst, hunger, and fatigue. When Lee discovered it he delivered sharp intercepting strokes in White Oak Swamp and at Frayser's Farm. The fighting at
the second point was so fierce that Union soldiers thrust their ramrods against
trees to force the charges into the hot barrels.[39] Then the retreat went on:

> The spires of Richmond, late beheld
> Through rifts in musket haze,
> Were closed from view in clouds of dust
> On leaf-walled ways.

Exhaustion and discouragement dogged the Union troops to the last. Finally
the movement ended at Malvern Hill on July 1 in a memorably spectacular
battle.

McClellan had gained refuge on a high, broad plateau, reaching to the
James on one side, and protected at the back by creek and ravine. On this
plateau he posted a major part of his army, with massed artillery in front,
cavalry in the rear, and gunboats protecting his flank. The Confederate host,

THE SEVEN DAYS

issuing from the forest in pursuit, faced tier on tier of grim batteries rising, as D. H. Hill wrote, in a huge amphitheater. It seemed almost suicidal to attack such a position. But Lee's army had passed over ground strewn with Union rifles, cartridge boxes, and knapsacks, amid a roadside litter of abandoned wagons and caissons; they had picked up scores of groaning wounded. Mistakenly concluding that Northern morale had sunk to a low ebb, Lee hoped that by one frenzied blow he might yet annihilate the Union forces. His decision to use his artillery to silence the Union batteries and storm Malvern Hill by mass assault was in some respects a rehearsal of the attack on Cemetery Ridge. When he found that only a small number of his guns could be forced up through swamps and brush, he tried to cancel the attack—but it was too late. At half past five in the afternoon, 10,500 unsupported men swept forward against the Union panoply, marching up the slope with the orderliness of columns in review; and a storm of grape and canister laid them in writhing swaths.[40]

Participants never forgot the magnificence or the horror of the scene. In the bright summer evening not a breath of wind stirred the air. From the artillery rose black columns of smoke, towering in stately columns to the sky. The crash of musketry and the deeper roar and thud of cannon were deafening and continuous. As one Southern brigade recoiled, another pushed forward with desperate courage. By seven o'clock the battle had reached its climax, with a mass of fresh troops under Stonewall Jackson fiercely pressing Fitz-John Porter and Couch, while Sickles' and Meagher's brigades hurried forward to help hold the Northern line. By eight, as the sun cast its last rays on the smoky crest of Malvern and on the green treetops below, the Confederate columns were breaking back to the shelter of ravine and swamp. As the artillery poured its last shells after them, from the river came the flash and thunder of the gunboat mortars, their bombs curving through the dusk in fiery golden lines. This closing scene, wrote a Pennsylvania captain, was indescribably picturesque:

The cavalry on either flank, galloping in haste to harass the retreating foe; the foaming, panting horses flying from point to point with aides or orderlies carrying dispatches; the stretcher bearers tenderly carrying the wounded to the rear; the less disabled limping in with gun for crutch or supported by a comrade, and, as the darkness gathered, the various colored signal lights advancing and waving and flashing back their messages, all served to impress the beholder with the pride, pomp, and circumstance of glorious war.[41]

40 Descriptions of the battle in Lossing, *Civil War*, II, 431–435; Comte de Paris, *Civil War*, II, 900; and *Battles and Leaders*, II, 406–427, have not been bettered by subsequent accounts.
41 MS Diary of Captain Robert Taggard, Pa. State Hist. Society.

But it was not all glory. While the troops on both sides sank exhausted on their arms, the moans, cries, and shrieks of the wounded on the field were heartrending, and little could be done to succor them. The sky grew overcast and inky darkness shut down. Toward dawn came a heavy downpour. "Such rain, and such howling set up by the wounded," wrote a Confederate soldier; "such ugly wounds, sickening to the sight even of the most hardened as the rain beat upon them, washing them to a pale purple; such long-fingered corpses, and in piles, too, like cordwood—may I never see the like again." [42]

The Confederate loss exceeded five thousand, nearly thrice that of the North, and the fourteen of Lee's brigades that had been repulsed were sadly demoralized. Many Union officers, elated by victory, felt that it was not yet too late to turn on the foe and attempt a new advance upon Richmond. But McClellan had the *idée fixe* that the army must establish a safe base of supplies, and early in the morning ordered the retreat to continue to Harrison's Landing. The angriest grumbling ensued. Fitz-John Porter, devoted as he was to his commander, urged him to turn about and attack. Hooker took the same view; they should be pursuing the enemy, not flying from him. Phil Kearny asserted that they could easily take the Confederate capital. "And I say to you all," he told a knot of fuming officers, "such an order can only be prompted by cowardice or treason." A bolder general would have renewed the struggle. [43] To McClellan, however, the first necessity was safety. Independence Day found the army occupying a broad level tract on the James, shielded by streams flowing through swamp and woodland, and protected by guns of the navy.

[VI]

It also found the nation facing the fact that every one of the luminous hopes of spring had been quenched. Halleck had thrown away the happy possibilities after Shiloh; worse still, he had frittered away the powerful army which had won it, scattering the forces in every direction. Farragut's campaign up the river had resulted in total frustration. Lincoln's effort to make the Borderland a constructive demonstration ground for the gradual elimination of slavery had broken down. Worst of all, the second invasion of Virginia had ended in

42 MS Autobiography of James Hewes, Palmer Coll., Western Reserve Hist. Soc.
43 Ropes, *Civil War*, II, 204–207, and *Battles and Leaders*, II, 423 ff., discuss McClellan's refusal to counterattack with a fair estimate of pros and cons. Some Southern officers expected McClellan to take the offensive, and declared later that their troops could not have stopped him. Ropes believed that he could at the very least have held the Malvern lines, nearer Richmond than Harrison's Landing.

failure; a failure that was one long tale of delays and defeats, that had called into play Southern generalship of the most formidable kind, and that ended in the deepest distrust between the chief field commander and the Washington Administration.

Before the North stretched the prospect of a prolonged war, with all its implications: dismaying financial problems, the necessity of conscription, a harsher scrutiny of Administration shortcomings, a deeper schism on war aims between moderates and radicals, rising discontent and disloyalty, a starker danger of foreign intervention. Until thus suddenly ringed by failure, most Northerners had hoped to see the insurrection suppressed without a profound national upheaval. Now revolution faced them on every hand: a party revolution as factional strife boiled up, an economic revolution as war contracts, tariffs, and inflation spurred industry forward, a social revolution, even an intellectual revolution as millions began to think more responsibly and more nationally. From the beginning it had seemed likely that the war would mean the extirpation of slavery, the subordination of the South to the North and West, and a business domination of government; now this was certainty. Transcending all other changes was the fact that every new day of war demanded a larger mobilization of national energies, and that under this demand an organized nation was taking shape, as different from the old as Hector from a babe.

6

After the Seven Days: Lincoln's Decisions

THE COLLAPSE of McClellan's thrust from the Peninsula made trying demands on Lincoln's patient resolution and resourcefulness. Haunting the War Department and often holding consultations far into the night, he passed some of the most anxious days of his life. When the combined onslaught of Lee and Jackson on McClellan cut off his communications with White House Landing, he sent a series of frantic messages to Burnside at New Bern, John A. Dix at Fort Monroe, and Hunter at Port Royal, urging them to hurry any reinforcements they could spare to the general. He telegraphed Flag-Officer Goldsborough to do what he could with the gunboats. He attempted to borrow some troops, even 10,000, from Halleck in the West. Finding that he could muster not more than 25,000 in all, he telegraphed McClellan on July 4: "Under these circumstances the defensive, for the present, must be your only care. Save the army—first, where you *are*, if you can; and secondly, by removal, if you must." [1]

The great fear, once McClellan was safe, was that Lee might turn northward and attack Washington before a large defensive army could be assembled. McClellan feared it; the enemy, he informed Lincoln on July 4, might prefer an advance upon the capital over an attack on his own force. Seward feared it; the Confederates, he wrote Thurlow Weed, might hold McClellan with a small force and immediately strike northward. General Keyes of McClellan's army feared it; shortly questioned by Lincoln, he said he thought that Lee had withdrawn and was preparing "to go to Washington." Most Northern editors, as the public mourned the hosts of slain and mutilated at Fair Oaks, Gaines's Mill, and Malvern Hill, thought the situation extremely grave. Greeley reproached the government for not telling the nation candidly that the army had been decimated and threatened with extinction, and calling every regiment of militia to Washington. "Men in authority!" he exclaimed. "We entreat you to lean upon the great heart of the people!" [2]

1 Lincoln, *Works*, V, 288, 289.
2 O. R., I, xi, pt. 3, 294; Seward, *Seward in Washington*, 114; Lincoln, *Works*, V, 311; N. Y. *Tribune*, July 5, 1862.

The nation had indeed been ill informed, but not by Lincoln's fault. On June 25, as the Seven Days began, McClellan had ordered all reporters excluded from the front lines. Nothing but rumors and overoptimistic reports got through in the next week. Not until July 3, when the New York *Times* scooped the other papers by a full account of the recent battles, did the North learn that the army had met severe reverses and was in a position of great peril. Next day the *Herald* partially relieved the country's anxiety by dispatches which included the Malvern Hill victory. But still gloom persisted, deepened by reports like that of the Chicago *Tribune* on a "stunning disaster."

The press was soon full of stories that aroused the most poignant emotion. Northerners read of the wounded lying untended for days, while every wagon shed, barn, and Negro cabin was turned into a hospital.[3] They read of the steam coffin factory working night and day on the Chickahominy to make thousands of pine boxes; the vulturelike embalmers with their engines, tubes, and chemicals; the burial parties who shoveled gashed corpses into trenches three feet deep. Battles were inevitable in war. But was it necessary to let pestilence slay more than rifle or cannon, and permit the "Chickahominy fever" to take the army by the throat? People read how the soldiers sickened by platoons: how their eyes brightened, their cheeks flushed, and then they shriveled as their vitality drained away, until their faces grew mummified in death. Southerners, meanwhile, read of a Virginia countryside as wasted as if Tamerlane had passed over it.

Northern feeling was deepened by the steady arrival, train after train, boat after boat, of the human wreckage of the battlefield. The press printed long columns of names with a single word: "J. Eaton, F, Ist N. Y., thigh; F. E. Gass, C, 5th N. H., kdy; T. Scott, G, 18th Ill., dead." Every large city had its tale of young wives searching for wounded husbands, themselves ill, destitute, and half crazed with anxiety. Convalescents were hurried forward as rapidly as possible to their home towns and villages, where their faded uniforms, thin sunburnt faces, and empty sleeves brought home to multitudes the brutality of war. Grief was edged by hatred as atrocity stories studded the press: the bayoneting of wounded, the murder of prisoners. Though mainly baseless, they were believed, and were repeated in the first report of the Committee on the Conduct of the War. Parson Brownlow was doing his utmost to stir up anger over the "fiendish outrages" reported from East Tennessee. Some Southern newspapers meanwhile shrieked for vengeance on despoilers and assassins. It was becoming an ugly-tempered war.

3 Lee wrote D. H. Hill on July 4 to continue the work of burying the dead and picking up the wounded. "I understand that many of the enemy's wounded on Monday's fight are still on the field, they must have suffered greatly, every effort should be made to remove all of them where they will be comfortable." D. H. Hill Papers, Va. State Library.

The two armies before Richmond settled down to recuperate. Lee wrote his wife on July 9: "Our success has not been as great or complete as we could have desired, but God knows what is best for us." Yet the victory was so signal that the spirits of his troops and of the Southern people rose to new heights. His losses totaled more than 19,000, as against 15,250 on the Union side, and in future campaigns he would sadly miss the brave men forever gone. This, however, seemed a small price to pay for the salvation of Richmond and the defeat of the enemy, and Jefferson Davis proclaimed a general thanksgiving. From abandoned Union stores the Confederates took a rich profit, for all along the roads the litter of materials enabled the troops to replenish their arms and supplies. Shoes were stripped from the Union dead. Rifles and cartridges were substituted for wornout powder-and-ball muskets. At Savage Station, Jackson captured not only the huge field hospital of the North, with 2,500 wounded, but ammunition, wagons, pontoon trains, mules, a war balloon, camp utensils, barrels of beef and pork, and what one rebel called a very Eden of other foods. For the first time in months many Southerners tasted butter and coffee, and slept under woolen blankets.

The morale of McClellan's army was now difficult to assess. Fighting magnificently, it had won victories at Glendale and Malvern Hill in the last days of the change of base; and though it had lost much of the pride and confidence with which it had entered on the campaign, to an astonishing degree the troops kept their faith in their leader and themselves. For this faith the army could offer two main reasons. First, it shared McClellan's conviction that it had been beset by superior forces, and that selfish politicians had denied it proper reinforcements. Frederick Law Olmsted of the Sanitary Commission wrote of the overpowering enemy array, which Union men thought more than double their own, and told how anxiously the Northern army had looked over its shoulders in every battle to see if reinforcements were coming. The rank and file at Malvern Hill believed, just as much as McClellan, that they had 200,000 Confederates facing them. And in the second place, the troops appreciated the care McClellan had taken to spare life and limb. Privates appalled by wholesale death and amputation were content that he had besieged, not assaulted, Yorktown, and that after Fair Oaks he had entrenched for a gradual advance instead of making frontal assults. During the perilous retreat to the James they were thankful for McClellan's cautious movements and foresight in providing so large an artillery park.[4]

4 See Olmsted Papers, July 8-20. Against excessive amputations a thousand voices were raised. "A cry comes up from our hospitals, and its echo is heard all over the land," said the N. Y. *Tribune*, July 30, 1862, "against the free use of the surgeon's knife and saw on the legs and arms of our wounded soldiers. That there is just cause for complaint we have the assurance of medical men. . . . Young aspirants for distinction in the profession of

Most soldiers blamed Northern radicals for not giving them sufficient force; few blamed their leader.

McClellan's own attitude united his faith in a providential mission with his conviction that treacherous men and stupid policies had ruined all his labors. At the beginning of the Seven Days he telegraphed his wife: "I am confident that God will smile upon my efforts and give our arms success." Just after the struggle he assured her that the power of the Almighty "has saved me and my army." [5] Positive that, outnumbered almost two to one, betrayed by the jealous McDowell, and stabbed in the back by Stanton, he had brought the nation through the storm, on June 28 he sent Stanton a hysterical dispatch that did him no credit. He had just fought the most desperate battle of the war, he wrote (though Gaines's Mill did not compare with Shiloh). He had lost it because his force was too small (though he had 20,000 more men than the Confederates, much better armed). With even 10,000 fresh troops next day, he would take Richmond, but he had no reserves whatever (though two of his corps commanders could have sent in more than that number of fresh men). He was not at fault—it was Washington!

"I have seen too many dead and wounded comrades," he concluded, "to feel otherwise than that the Government has not sustained this army. If you do not do so now the game is lost. If I save this army now, I tell you plainly that I owe no thanks to you or to any other person in Washington. You have done your best to sacrifice this army." The supervisor of telegraphs struck the two last sentences from the copy given Stanton, so that neither he nor Lincoln saw it. Happily for the national morale, no part of the dispatch was published till seven eventful months had elapsed. Stanton carried the telegram to Lincoln in the deepest agitation, saying, "You know, Mr. President, that all I have done was by your authority"; and Lincoln shared his resentment.[6]

Most of the Northern public took a realistic view of McClellan's record, for with few exceptions, the press gave an accurate report of the disasters to the army. Interpretation was naturally colored by party feeling. The Chicago *Tribune*, like other radical organs, began calling for his dismissal on June 20; the Cincinnati *Commercial*, with most conservative Democratic journals, placed the blame for his failure squarely on Stanton. While Bryant's *Evening Post* regarded the general's leadership as imbecile throughout, the *National Intelli-*

surgery easily persuade themselves that the wounded or shattered limb of a soldier is a proper subject on which to practise the science of amputation."

5 Quotations from *My Own Story*, 441, 445; on July 17, McClellan wrote of the Seven Days that "I stood alone without any one to help me." See also Browning, *Diary*, I, 559.

6 The dispatch without the two last sentences appeared in the *Report, Committee on Conduct of War*, I, 339, 340, published in the press April 6, 1863. The two offensive sentences were included by McClellan in his *Report*, published in book form in 1864; pp. 257, 258.

gencer pronounced the march to the James a masterly movement. However, although the *World* assailed Lincoln in a way which grieved its correspondent Edmund Clarence Stedman, and the *Herald* attacked the War Department, it was McClellan who suffered most. Great numbers of intelligent observers agreed that no faith could now be placed in this "hero of a hundred ungained victories." [7]

[I]

Lincoln was indeed ready to lean on the great heart of the nation, but not to issue appeals that would provoke a panic, to yield an iota of his due powers to Congress, or to foment sectional hatreds. On the date Lee began the Seven Days, June 26, Lincoln had consolidated the scattered forces of Banks, Frémont, and McDowell into one new command, the Army of Virginia, under Major-General John Pope. He had made a flying visit to New York for a five-hour consultation with Winfield Scott, who apparently recommended calling Halleck to the East. Stanton had just previously telegraphed the governors, on June 18: "We are in pressing need of troops. How many can you send on immediately?" Their replies had been most discouraging. Illinois alone could send troops at once, a regiment of infantry and cavalry apiece; Ohio could forward a regiment of ninety-day men within a fortnight; New Hampshire and Vermont could each supply a regiment in July—but the others pleaded helplessness. The fact was that at that date, as a news dispatch in the Springfield *Republican* asserted, most Northerners still believed the Union had troops enough if only they were properly distributed. It had taken a thunderclap of defeat to awaken the nation. Now that the blow had fallen, Seward proposed to hurry North to arouse popular determination, and arrange for raising new armies. Lincoln and Stanton approved the step, giving the Secretary their fullest encouragement.

Seward at once departed (June 28) to confer with Governors Morgan and Curtin, bearing a letter in which Lincoln declared that 100,000 new troops were imperatively needed. "I expect to maintain this contest," wrote the President, "until successful or till I die, or am conquered, or my term expires, or Congress or the country forsakes me; and I would publicly appeal to the country for this new force, were it not that I fear a general panic and stampede would follow. . . ." The situation clearly required a larger body than the number named, and the press was demanding it. "We have foolishly under-

---

7 The Chicago *Morning Post*, July 6, 10, and the N. Y. *Times*, July 7, published surveys of press opinion. Stanton was deeply hurt by the abuse showered upon him, and wrote a long letter to a friend defending himself, but made no public reply; Gorham, *Stanton*, II, 426–432. He refused to risk injury to the cause by an open quarrel.

rated the strength and pluck of the rebels," said the *World;* "we foolishly stopped recruiting." Out of Seward's New York conferences came a proposal that the governors should unite in asking Lincoln for a great new levy, and that the President should respond. Some of the governors thought that half a million men were needed, and Lincoln, after considering 200,000, telegraphed John A. Andrew that it seemed safest to set the figure high: "It is 300,000." On July 11 he called on the States for that number of additional men, chiefly infantry, who should serve for three years.[8]

The President's last hope that the war would be short expired in these bitter days. He wrote Governor Morgan on July 3 that time was everything, and that if he had 50,000 additional troops "here *now,* I believe I could substantially close the war in two weeks." But at this very moment the arrival in Washington of Marcy, McClellan's father-in-law and chief of staff, with a gloomy report of the army's situation, gave the President a bad shock. Furnishing Stanton his own and McClellan's views, Marcy said he would not be astonished if the army were obliged to capitulate. In angry consternation, Stanton flew to the White House with this statement, and Lincoln, equally incensed, at once summoned Marcy. "General," he said sternly, "I understand you have used the word 'capitulate'; that is a word not to be used in connection with our army." Capitulation would be precisely the treason of which many radicals suspected McClellan! As Lincoln proceeded with his reprimand, Marcy blundered out a lame apology, while later he returned to the War Department to make peace with Stanton. But it had been an ugly moment, and never after digesting the news of McClellan's failure did Lincoln make another statement like that to Morgan. He saw that two years was a likelier measure of the continuance of the war. He was now ready for a pragmatic experimentalism with commanders; he would take the best he could get, East and West, try them thoroughly, discard the unfit, and promote the able. This gaunt Illinois frontiersman, still mild, still patient, had developed a greater sternness than Andrew Jackson ever showed.

Lincoln needed steel traits to deal not only with the South, but with Congress. Some Republican leaders inevitably seized upon the opportunity for striking at McClellan, at Seward, and indirectly at the President; for emphasizing their own powers and setting a chisel to Lincoln's. They were abetted by the Democrats, who commenced a pitiless assault on Stanton as the real culprit in McClellan's reverses. But this Democratic attack, while irritating,

---

8 Frémont promptly resigned because he believed that Pope had deliberately frustrated him in the Missouri campaign, and could not bear to serve under Pope's orders. For Lincoln's call, see *Works,* V, 296, 297. The *World* followed its demand for more troops (June 21) with repeated editorials asking Stanton's dismissal. Seward, *Seward in Washington,* 100–124, presents full detail on the Northern trip of the Secretary.

was not really important. It scored just one heavy blow against Lincoln—the revelation that he and nobody else had been responsible for the order stopping the march of McDowell to reinforce McClellan; for in the light of subsequent events, this order appeared most unfortunate.[9] But Lincoln had no desire to conceal it, and no great fear of Democrats. The Republicans controlled Congress, and their maneuvers gave Lincoln his principal anxiety.

The chorus in denunciation of McClellan was led by Zach Chandler, who defended Stanton, and pointed out that the Democratic diatribes against the Secretary of War were really aimed at Lincoln. The President's hold upon public esteem was such that few had the hardihood to indict him, and Democrats therefore invented the fiction that Stanton really ruled the government in military matters. This fable the Republicans easily exploded. Chandler's indictment of McClellan's campaign was echoed by the Chicago and New York *Tribunes*. Congress meanwhile set up a renewed outcry for making the South feel the full edge of the sword; for waging war at rebel expense, on rebel property, and with rebel slaves and supplies. Numerous voices took up the exhortation. Lew Wallace told a crowd of serenaders in Washington that he favored putting a black regiment into every white brigade for digging trenches and driving teams, and that he would never again lead a column through a Southern countryside without seizing all that it offered. "Oh, if I could get a little backbone into those who are governing us!" The lieutenant-governor of Ohio proclaimed that he would enlist Negroes, confiscate property, and if necessary lay the South as waste as the Mojave desert.[10] Even Thurlow Weed, just back from a useful propagandist sojourn in England which had taught him a good deal, believed the military should accept and employ every slave it could get.

But nowhere did the cry for stopping "kid-glove warfare" ring louder than in the Senate. Henry Wilson of Massachusetts and Henry M. Rice of Minnesota solemnly avowed that the choice lay between harsher measures and a recognition of Southern independence. Wilson knew that Stanton was with them. A bill amending the Militia Act was before Congress, and many members favored enrolling large numbers of Negroes "for any war service for which they may be found competent," as a clause read. We need less tenderness toward traitors and murderers, asserted Fessenden of Maine, and John Sherman agreed.

As part of this Spartan severity, members swiftly resuscitated the confiscation bill lying in conference committee. Reported to the House with stiffened terms, it passed that body 82 to 42. Its direct provisions on confiscation were

9 Browning, *Diary*, I, 559, for the Marcy incident.
10 The N. Y. *Tribune*, July 11, 1862, gives these speeches in full.

much less important than its frontal attack upon slavery. To be sure, the bill declared it the duty of the President to cause the seizure of all property of long categories of Southerners, and made all other persons who abetted the rebellion, sixty days after he gave public warning, equally liable to loss of their estates; Federal courts being empowered to dispose of forfeited property for the benefit of the Treasury. Obviously, the effectiveness of these clauses depended on Presidential cooperation. But much more important were the provisions that the slaves of all who supported the rebellion should be deemed legitimate war seizures, "forever free"; that the President might employ as many Negroes as he saw fit, and in such tasks as he deemed best; and that he might also colonize freedmen abroad.[11] The Senate, passing the bill July 12 by a vote of 28 to 13, sent it to the uneasy President—for Lincoln saw how frontally it challenged his intention to keep the slavery question in his own hands.

During the debate Lincoln had tried to modify this legislation, talking with Fessenden and other callers at the White House, and even threatening a veto. Wade of Ohio angrily characterized his activities as illegitimate and unconstitutional, "the most unfortunate thing during the whole war," and Lane of Indiana was equally wrathful against what he called legislation under duress.[12] The President had his way, for Congress at the last moment averted the veto message he had prepared by passing an explanatory resolution which removed most of his objections. At heart, radical members and editors were apprehensive that he would not enforce the law with drastic vigor—and hence their outcries. They were quite right. He signed the Second Confiscation Act, for he saw that public sentiment demanded something of the kind; but he never wavered in his belief that such vindictive measures should be avoided, for the nation must in time be restored as a truly fraternal union, a union of hearts, and he never abated his determination to keep the handling of slavery, which would lie at the core of national reconstruction, under his own control.[13]

[II]

Yet the President could not stand still. Time, as July advanced, pressed him hard in the management of opinion no less than of the armies. He read snatches from the more extreme newspapers, in which Bryant, Greeley, and Medill were

11   *Cong. Globe*, 37th Cong., 2d Sess., 3197–3207; 3266–3268.
12   *Cong. Globe*, 37th Cong., 2d Sess., 3376 ff. for this debate. Chandler of Michigan continued pressing a motion to obtain the correspondence between the executive department and McClellan, obviously for the purpose of making trouble for both. Moderate opinion deplored both the motion and his speeches; N. Y. *Times*, July 10, 1862.
13   For Lincoln's views on the importance of a truly fraternal reunion, see Nevins, *Papers of the Abraham Lincoln Association* (1930), 51–92. The explanatory resolution of Congress, relieving the bill of all taint of ex post facto or attainder implications, is in *Works*, V, 328–331, along with Lincoln's draft of a veto message.

ever more clamorous against slavery; watched the closing Congressional debates, in which Sumner, Thaddeus Stevens, Trumbull, and other men he respected were nearly as outspoken as Wade and Chandler; heard echoes of the utterances of Owen Lovejoy, Parson Brownlow, and Henry Ward Beecher; talked with Congressional leaders; and in short, felt the quickening of the national pulse. Meanwhile, he devoted his own anxious thought to the Negro. Hating slavery, he was more intent on its ultimate eradication than ever.

Sumner had called at the White House twice on July 4 to plead that the President reconsecrate the day by a decree of emancipation. The first time Lincoln protested that while he might take such a step for eastern Virginia, a proclamation for the entire South was "too big a lick now." Sumner replied that the nation needed big licks. The second time Lincoln offered a detailed argument for delay, as if he might be weakening.[14] On July 11 Governor Yates exploded in a fierce dispatch to the White House. He telegraphed that "the time has come for the adoption of more decisive measures," that "blows must be struck at the vital parts of the rebellion," that loyal Negroes who offered to serve the Union should be accepted, and that Union armies should forage on the enemy. Lincoln knew that the governor spoke for general Republican sentiment in Illinois. On the 12th, the day the confiscation bill passed, he telegraphed his old Illinois friend: "Dick, hold still and see the salvation of God."[15]

It was plain to him that if he did not keep his leadership of the movement against slavery, Congress would wrest it from him. The true title of the confiscation act, as his secretaries later wrote, should have been: "An act to destroy slavery under the powers of war." The new law proposed freeing all slaves of all rebels wherever reached. It did not touch the slaves of loyal persons. But how many citizens in Missouri or South Carolina could prove their loyalty? Lincoln acknowledged that the Act was constitutional, and that Congress could free a slave if that slave had been forfeited to the government by a traitor. But he believed that as commander-in-chief he possessed larger powers than Congress over slavery. He also believed that, as President of the whole people, he possessed broader views and a more moderate temper than the extremists in Congress.

As the crowded first fortnight of July drew to a close, he therefore made a final plea for cooperation by the Border States. Calling their members in Con-

14 Sumner had taken steps to see that other men reinforced his arguments. "Won't you come here to help?" he wrote Carl Schurz July 5. "By voice and presence you can do much—very, very much. God bless you!" Schurz Papers, LC. What Lincoln and Sumner said to each other was reported by A. S. Hill, July 9, 1862, to S. H. Gay; Gay Papers. Sumner records that Lincoln told him July 4: "I would do it if I were not afraid that half the officers would fling down their arms and three more States would rise." *Works*, VII, 215.

15 Lincoln's reply to Yates is not in the *Works*. Yates later quoted it in a speech to a New York meeting; N. Y. *Tribune*, October 30, 1863.

gress to the White House on the 12th, he read a careful argument. He assured them of his conviction that if they had supported his gradual emancipation plan in March, the war by summer would have been substantially ended. He again promised an effort toward colonization, and spoke of ample room in Latin America. He described the tremendous outcry which had followed his annulment of Hunter's liberation order: "I gave dissatisfaction, if not offense, to many whose support the country cannot afford to lose. And this is not the end of it. The pressure is still upon me and is increasing." He appealed to self-interest, saying that if the war continued long slavery would be extinguished by mere friction and abrasion. "It will be gone and you will have nothing in lieu of it. Much of its value is gone already! How much better for you, and for your people, to take the step which, at once, shortens the war, and secures substantial compensation for that which is sure to be wholly lost in any other event." They could save the nation "the money which else we sink forever."

When next day two Illinois Representatives, Isaac N. Arnold and Owen Lovejoy, called on him at the Soldiers' Home, he showed an unwonted intensity of emotion. "Oh," he said, "how I wish the border States would accept my proposition. Then you, Lovejoy, and you, Arnold, and all of us, would not have lived in vain!" So Arnold later recalled his words, though we know that his thoughts were already turning in an alternative direction.[16]

While utterly sincere in this appeal, Lincoln was sadly aware that it would meet no response. Without delay a majority reply signed by Crittenden, Garrett Davis, and eighteen other border members reiterated the old objections. They protested that the original Northern policy was simply to restore the Union, that State Rights and a sacred domestic institution were at stake, that Congress had paid an average of only $300 for District slaves and would haggle over the costs, and that the step would not reduce but augment Confederate defiance. George P. Fisher and six others signed a statement, drafted by Neill of Missouri, promising to entreat the people to consider the proposal, while Henderson of Missouri and Maynard of Tennessee made the same declaration separately. The

16 Nicolay and Hay, *Lincoln*, VI, 111, 112; *Works*, V, 317-319; Arnold, *Lincoln*, 251; N. Y. *Times, Tribune*, July 19, 1862. Secretary Caleb Smith had informed the President that District of Columbia freedmen were unwilling to go to Liberia and that Haiti was objectionable, but that New Granada (Colombia) offered favorable conditions. J. Watson Webb, minister to Brazil, believed that the Brazilian plethora of land and shortage of labor would make colonization feasible there. For Smith's letter of May 9, 1862, to Lincoln, see Department of the Interior, Division of Slave Trade Suppression, National Archives. Panama and Chiriqui were part of New Granada. Webb suggested that the United States ship its freed Negroes to Brazil at its own expense, and that Brazil provide wild lands free of cost and guarantee eventual citizenship. When he asked for power to negotiate a treaty with Brazil covering this scheme, Seward, who had encountered such violent objections from Costa Rica, Nicaragua, and Honduras to any colonization there, replied that the whole subject was under discussion and until the public mind evolved some decision, the question must remain in abeyance. Webb's plan thus died. *Dip. Corr. U. S., 1862*, pp. 712-715.

response thus stood 20 to 9 against Lincoln.[17] His earnestly-pressed plan received its deathblow.

Did it ever really have a chance of success? Despite all appearances to the contrary, we may believe that the President's sagacity had not failed him. If Delaware had promptly accepted his proposal, selling her slaves for the $500,000 that Congress would have gladly distributed in bonds, the movement might have swept Missouri and Maryland along with it. Delaware refused by a close margin. Missouri sentiment was steadily ripening. Though a special convention which the governor had called for various purposes was unwilling to take action on Lincoln's proposal, antislavery feeling was crystallizing with such energy that abolitionists were forming local societies at many points, and met in convention on June 16 to call for gradual emancipation. The radical leader B. Gratz Brown elatedly proclaimed: "This is Transition, This is Progress, This is Revolution." [18] Certainly three-fourths of the people of West Virginia, as of western Maryland, were anxious to rid themselves of slavery. With more vision and nerve among border leaders, with less stiffnecked pride, these States might have trodden Lincoln's path.

Anticipating rejection, the President had now almost taken a great resolve. He knew that the nation, after its military humiliation, needed a fresh inspiration. He knew that liberal opinion overseas could not understand his delay in striking at slavery. It was difficult to give up his plan. Sumner was impressed by his earnestness. "His whole soul was occupied. . . . In familiar intercourse with him, I remember nothing more touching than the earnestness and completeness with which he embraced this idea." But as he had to give it up, one alternative alone was feasible.

Part of the morrow of the futile conference, Sunday, the 13th, Lincoln occupied in driving with Seward, Welles, and Mrs. Frederick Seward to the funeral of Stanton's infant child. His companions were struck by his gravity. The government had reached a crisis, he remarked; it must make new military arrangements to meet the astonishing strength of the Confederacy, find a fresh inspiration to stimulate volunteering, and tap the reservoir of slave power. For the first time in Welles's hearing he spoke of emancipation as a war weapon. It was a grave step, but he had "about come to the conclusion" that it was essential;

17 The division was actually closer than this figure indicates, for three out-of-town members, Whaley of Virginia, Leary of Maryland, and Blair of Missouri, would have signed the assenting paper. The N. Y. *Tribune*, July 16, 1862, believed that several who voted no were at heart in favor of Lincoln's plan.

18 F. A. Culmer, *A New History of Missouri*, 428 ff. Local emancipation societies were being formed in Missouri as branches of the General Emancipation Society in the State, and displayed enthusiasm in their call for gradual abolition. A bill to appropriate ten millions (amended to twenty) to pay for Missouri slaves was introduced in Congress. Trexler, *Slavery in Mo.*, 233 ff.

they must free the slaves or be subdued. When he asked Seward and Welles how the proposal struck them, Seward hesitated. "Emancipation involves consequences so momentous that I wish time for mature reflection before giving an answer," he said in effect. "But my present opinion inclines to the measure as justifiable, and I might say expedient and necessary." Welles agreed. After the funeral they reverted to the subject. Lincoln entreated them to give the question earnest thought, for "I am fixed in the conviction that something must be done." [19]

[III]

At this moment he was drastically reorganizing the structure of military command. On July 11 he appointed Henry Wager Halleck general-in-chief of the Union armies. The press reported on the 14th that Lincoln had the appointment in mind, and on the 16th that Halleck was about to reach Washington. On the 22nd he arrived, and next day Lincoln published the order giving him control of all the land forces of the nation. Obviously he would keep his headquarters in the capital and would not exercise a field command. This fact did not reconcile McClellan, who had no advance intimation of the step from either Lincoln or Stanton, for he found it grating to serve under the authority of a man "whom I know to be my inferior." He instantly wrote a friend that Halleck's appointment was intended as a slap in his face, and told his wife that he would be inexpressibly happy to resign: "I am weary, very weary, submitting to the whims of such 'things' as those now over me." [20]

Lincoln had made two new selections of the highest importance, and both Pope and Halleck were in different ways to prove weak appointments. It is natural to ask whether he had shown proper circumspection in his choices. Defective as the intelligence service of the Union armies was, that of the White House and War Department was worse. Had Lincoln possessed the means of gathering full, astute, and candid information, he would not have chosen such a swaggering, muddleheaded egotist as Pope to direct a critical army, and would have hesitated longer in designating such a myopic, indecisive pedant as Halleck to govern all the military forces. Here, as never before, he needed an industrious, tough-minded adviser on personnel.

The public knew John Pope as a West Pointer who had served capably in the Mexican War, accompanied Lincoln's party to the inauguration, and won a reverberant success at Island No. 10. Apart from his Illinois background, Lincoln

19 Welles, *Diary*, I, 70, 71, offers the only record of this drive. See also Browning, *Diary*, I, 553–559.
20 McClellan's *Own Story*, 450–453; McClellan to S. L. M. Barlow, July 23, 1862, Barlow Papers.

did not know much more. But a shrewd White House aide could have found out a good deal. Gustav Koerner could have told him that Pope was disliked by comrades in the regular army, and that as division commander in Missouri his tactlessness, aggressiveness, and braggadocio had made him unpopular with officers and men.[21] Frémont could have furnished clear evidence of insubordination. Journalists would have scored Pope for his false claim that he had taken 10,000 prisoners in the mopping-up operations after Corinth, when he had only a tenth of that number, while others would have assured Lincoln that he was an untruthful, undependable, and unintelligent Captain Bobadil. Dark, martial-looking, and handsome with his flowing hair, full beard, and flashing black eyes, he was too florid, too obese, and too loose in ideas and manners to be a good commander. Reporters were struck by his incessant smoking, garrulous story-telling, and shallow vanity.[22]

For Halleck much more could be said, and to many Lincoln's elevation of the man, recommended by Winfield Scott and accepted without enthusiasm by Stanton, appeared sound. We have rehearsed the impressive facts of his career, and army officers in general would have joined Joseph Hooker in pronouncing him a man of ability and expert military knowledge.

Nevertheless, he had received laurels which he had not earned. He had been credited with clearing up "abuses" in Missouri which were partly imaginary; with the movement against Donelson, which he did not conceive; and with the victories of Pea Ridge and Island No. 10, to which he had made but minor contributions. What was more significant, he had escaped blame for serious blunders. On the day of Grant's first great victory he had cautioned him not to be "too rash," while he was responsible for the costly delay after Donelson in moving on Nashville. His suspicions had almost robbed the army of Grant's talents. He had taken a month to get to Corinth when a week should have sufficed, and had given a misleading impression of the march that had deceived Stanton and half the country. Capping all this was the aplomb with which he flung away his opportunities after Corinth.

Before the war ended numerous men were to set down their judgment of Halleck in terms only less scathing than McClellan's. Actually he meant well, worked hard, had sound general views, and stood loyally by his superiors. But, fussy, pedantic, and plodding, he lacked grasp and imagination. General Ormsby

21 Koerner, *Memoirs*, II, 235.
22 He was temporarily a pet of Chase's, and Chase's diary is revealing. See also G. A. Townsend, *Campaigns of a Non-Combatant*, 218; Welles, *Diary*, I, 221; and Schofield's derisive statement in *Forty-Six Years*, 358, 359. For the false claim of 10,000 prisoners after Corinth see Villard, *Memoirs*, I, 279–281. Pope maintained that Halleck was responsible for this fabrication, and that he evaded admitting the fact. It involved both men in great ridicule, but when Pope later visited Congress he bragged that altogether he had taken 30,000 prisoners! Interesting Pope letters may be found in the Hay Papers, Ill. State Hist. Lib.

Mitchel, coming to discuss a critical problem, found him willing to talk only of his hay fever. "When the enemy are thundering at the gates," exclaimed Mitchel, "hay fever!" Sanitary Commission leaders, calling on him in Washington, retired in despair. "God help the country!" exclaimed one. W. T. Sherman came to detest him. He did not know the meaning of energy and foresight; new problems worried his legalistic mind, and new enterprises irritated him. "He sits and smokes and swears and scratches his arms," wrote Gideon Welles. Attorney-General Bates decided that he was "both knave and fool."

The harshest verdicts, however, were unfair. His letters in the *Official Records* prove his industry, understanding of general principles, and scholarly insight. He stood like an iron barricade against placing various unfit men in high commands, and bore the brunt of attacks for some unpopular acts that were really Lincoln's or Stanton's. Welles came closest to the truth when, making a valid distinction, he declared that Halleck was a good scholarly critic of other men's deeds and ideas, but was incapable of originating or directing military operations himself. Excellent in grasp of theory, he was inert, muddy-headed, and erratic in action. He had an unmilitary cast of mind, and recoiled from direct control of armies.[23]

It was unfortunate that the signal demonstration he had just given of his limitations as a field commander was not yet properly understood. At the beginning of June, as we have seen, he had possessed at or near Corinth an army of 128,315, of whom 108,538 were fit for duty. Their generals included Grant, Sherman, Thomas, Sheridan. After the capture of Memphis on June 6, this array, eager for action, was capable, as Grant later said, of rolling up half the Confederate map in the West. It might have taken the remaining river strongholds of Port Hudson and Vicksburg; it might then have marched to the mountain stronghold of Chattanooga, the gateway through which armies from the central Confederacy would have to advance if they ever tried to recover important parts of Tennessee and Kentucky. At the very least, one of these great Union objectives could have been secured before September browned cornfield and meadow.

---

23 A study of Halleck has been much needed. Badeau, *Mil. Hist. U. S. Grant*, is a treasury of information on his merits and defects; see index. Lincoln at first, with little real information, thought well of him, but in the summer of 1862 realized that he totally lacked nerve in critical situations, and let him become a colorless office general who deputed real authority to others. Hay, *Diaries*, (Dennett ed.), 176; J. D. Cox, *Rems.*, I, 254–262; G. T. Strong, *Diary*, III, 258 (Sept. 24, 1862). Ropes declared (*Civil War*, II, 234, 235, 285) that neither the Administration nor public can be criticized for calling Halleck to his high post, for his qualifications seemed great; and Ropes then concurs in Welles's balanced estimate. Grant's statement on Halleck's "gigantic intellect" is the more notable because made in a private letter; Grant to E. Washburne, July 22, 1862, Washburne Papers, LC. But then Grant was often overgenerous in estimates of other generals. For Sherman's views, see *The Sherman Letters*, 345.

But Halleck lost all the rich opportunities before him by dispersing his army in fragments of ineffective size. It is true that extenuating circumstances existed. He later told Sherman that he had been hampered by orders from Washington, and an abler general than he might have felt confused by the real difficulties before him. They included the great distances for offensive operations—some 200 miles from Corinth to Chattanooga, some 240 to Vicksburg; the problem of supplying more than 100,000 men at Corinth while the Tennessee River was steadily falling; the strength of the enemy, for Beauregard had nearly 60,000 effectives, and other commanders 30,000 in the Jackson-Vicksburg area, while considerable forces lay in Tennessee and Arkansas; and the possibility that McClellan's demands would force Stanton to withdraw troops from the West. But the sad fact was that he advanced against neither Vicksburg nor Chattanooga. To be sure, he moved Buell *toward* Chattanooga, but with inadequate strength and with unwise orders to repair and hold the railroad as he went.[24]

Official dispatches put the general in a dubious light. Lincoln on June 5 sent him a message from McClellan beseeching him to occupy Chattanooga and Dalton—"the importance of this move . . . cannot be exaggerated." Halleck was able to report that Buell's troops had already moved in that direction, but not that they were making any progress. He notified Stanton that Pope's force had met great impediments in its chase of Beauregard's army retreating from Corinth. "I do not propose pursuing him any farther, but to send all forces not required to hold the Memphis & Charleston to the relief of Curtis in Arkansas and to East Tennessee. . . ." Stanton approved of this, but added: "I suppose you contemplate the occupation of Vicksburg and clearing out the Mississippi to New Orleans." Halleck did *not* contemplate it, for he replied that he would send an expedition against Vicksburg only if Farragut and Davis could not take it, and only after reinforcing Curtis. When the heat and anxiety of the Seven Days came on, Lincoln had Stanton ask Halleck to spare 25,000 troops, unless their dispatch would endanger the Chattanooga movement. But as Halleck expostulated that the departure of this force *would* ruin it, Lincoln bade Stanton re-emphasize this insistence that the Chattanooga expedition must not be abandoned on any account.[25]

The upshot was that Bragg's Confederates got to Chattanooga first, and

24 The older treatments of Halleck's Western command range from the sweeping indictments by John Fiske, Ropes, and Adam Badeau to the more sober criticism of F. V. Greene; but practically all are condemnatory. Kenneth P. Williams, *Lincoln Finds a General*, III, 428–436, gives a moderate view, but on the whole is adverse.

25 O. R., I, x, pt. 1, pp. 668–671; I, xvi, pt. 2, pp. 8, 62–82. Halleck was disgusted by the call for 25,000 of his troops, happily at once revoked. He informed McClernand at Jackson, Tenn., on June 30: "The defeat of General McClellan near Richmond has produced another stampede at Washington," adding, "The entire campaign in the West is broken up by these orders and we shall very probably lose all we have gained."

Vicksburg remained unthreatened. Halleck had directed Grant, Buell, and Pope (later Rosecrans) to resume command of their armies of the Tennessee, Ohio, and Mississippi. He sent McClernand and Lew Wallace to Bolivar, Tennessee, northwest of Corinth; Pope to Rienzi, Mississippi, due south; Grant and Sherman to Memphis on the west; and Buell northeast. Ormsby Mitchel, who had a small force at Huntsville, Alabama, had shown what celerity could accomplish by a dash early in June to the very portals of Chattanooga, culminating in his erection of batteries on the north bank of the Tennessee opposite the town. Halleck, however, made no effort to hurry Buell to his assistance, and he had to fall back. At Vicksburg, meanwhile, the Confederates were toiling night and day to augment their fortifications, and were soon bringing in large reinforcements. Farragut in breaking off his river offensive made a statement on which Union leaders could soon reflect ruefully. "I am satisfied," he reported, "that it is not possible to take Vicksburg without an army of 12,000 to 15,000 men." Halleck could have spared twice that number without great difficulty; and in the end, five times as many would be needed.

One great gain from Halleck's transfer to Washington was that Grant obtained a fuller freedom of command and a larger field. From his Memphis headquarters he controlled all the troops in Tennessee west of the Cumberland, and in Mississippi so far as he could conquer that State. Halleck's first instructions to him from Washington began (July 31): "You must judge for yourself the best use to be made of your troops." Grant's advancement was to prove one of the momentous events of the war.

As for John Pope, on reaching the East he began working hard to put his troops in better condition. On July 14 he issued to his army a deplorable address. He saw fit, on the heels of McClellan's retreat to the James, to boast that Western troops had always seen the backs of *their* enemies. "I hear constantly of taking strong positions and holding them—of lines of retreat—and of bases of supplies. Let us discard such ideas." Foolish at any time, such an address at this moment rubbed salt in all McClellan's wounds, angered Fitz-John Porter and other corps commanders, and antagonized the troops on whom Pope must depend for cooperation. While his own men laughed at it, McClellan's men thought it outrageous. Its worst aspect was its suggestion that Pope expected to lead his army to separate and speedy victory, when if any need was paramount it was for unity of effort.[26]

However, Pope quickly did worse. On July 18 he issued a set of general orders which, inspired by Stanton, stained the whole Northern war effort. They were intended to show that Pope, unlike McClellan, had a mailed fist. Order No. 5 directed that his Army of the Potomac should subsist, as far as practicable,

26 For troop attitudes see N. Y. *Tribune*, Aug. 1, 1862.

on the country, giving vouchers for supplies taken; the vouchers to be payable at the end of the war, and then only if the owners proved they had been consistently loyal since the date of receipt. Order No. 6 declared that cavalry should dispense with supply trains and levy on the localities traversed for their needs. Order No. 7 notified the people of Northern Virginia that they would be held responsible for guerrilla outrages. If any railways, roads, or telegraphs were damaged, the inhabitants within a radius of five miles should be turned out to repair them, while any person detected in firing on Union soldiers from a house should be shot without civil process. Five days later Pope issued his still more Draconian General Order No. 11. This required officers to arrest immediately all disloyal citizens of Virginia within reach, to give them a choice of taking the oath of allegiance or accepting deportation to the South, to treat all who returned across the line as spies subject to the death penalty, and to shoot all who violated their oaths of allegiance.[27]

These orders had much better never been written. Those for subsistence on the country inspired an appetite for looting which responsible officers found it difficult to check. As for No. 7, President Davis immediately let it be known that the Confederacy would retaliate if anyone were put to death, and it remained empty bombast. Had it been enforced, it would merely have sent more men across the lines to strengthen Lee's army. But however ineffective, Pope's harsh edicts worsened the moral climate of the war, for troops East and West long remembered them and were influenced by their tone. They angered McClellan, and steeled Southerners to a more bitter resistance. Halleck, to his credit, pronounced them injudicious.[28]

It is true that Pope found much provocation in the fact that guerrillas had been picking off isolated soldiers. The marching troops, writes one regimental historian, occasionally saw a grizzled man hoeing vegetables near his cabin, oblivious to the passing column. But when the main body had passed and some footsore boy came limping along, the man had dropped his hoe. He was crouching with his rifle in the bushes—and at company roll call next morning another soldier was reported missing.[29] Some papers of Colonel John D. Imboden, which were captured in July, showed that members of his First Partisan Rangers were expected to stay home part of the time as noncombatants, and rove the countryside at others. "My purpose," wrote Imboden, "is to wage the most active war against our brutal invaders, and their domestic allies; to hang about their camps and shoot down every sentinel, picket, courier, and wagon driver we can find; to watch opportunities for attacking convoys and wagon

27 O. R., I, xii, pt. 2, pp. 50 ff.
28 O. R., I, xi, pt. 3, p. 359; I, xii, pt. 3, pp. 500, 501; Rhodes, IV, 101, 102.
29 Alfred Davenport, *Fifth New York*, 175, 176.

trains." [30] But such facts do not excuse Pope's orders to regularly organized troops.

It seems astonishing that Lincoln, who had so quickly annulled a milder order by Frémont, should have read all four edicts without objection. They contravened his characteristic spirit of magnanimity, and Order No. 11 violated the recognized rules of war. Doubtless he knew that Stanton was their real author; perhaps he did not wish to chastise Pope just as he took command; he had to consider the popular temper, and he was wrestling with many other problems. Still, he should have interfered. [31]

[IV]

The principal question before Lincoln, Halleck, and Stanton was what to do with McClellan. Should he be reinforced at Harrison's Landing, so close to Richmond, and encouraged to make a fresh movement against Lee, or should he be brought back to unite his army with Pope's in northern Virginia, or should he be dismissed? Montgomery C. Meigs thought he should be ousted, and his army combined with Pope's. Two members of the Cabinet favored an equally drastic course. Stanton and Chase urged the President to dismiss McClellan, send Pope to take his place on the James, and put Ormsby M. Mitchel in command of the forces covering Washington.

Lincoln's dejection as he considered this problem was plain to all. Throughout McClellan's campaign he had hoped as earnestly as the myriad anxious mothers of the North for an early end of the war. The Seven Days during which the army seemed battling frenziedly to extricate itself were a Gethsemane to him. He had felt the deepest relief when McClellan telegraphed that the withdrawal was completed, and had returned fervent thanks. "Be assured the heroism of yourself, officers, and men, are and will forever be appreciated. If you can hold your present position, we shall '*hive*' the enemy yet." [32] Anguish and frustration were still written upon his countenance when just after the Fourth he journeyed by the steamer *Ariel* to Harrison's Landing to talk with McClellan and review the troops. [33]

Lincoln arrived on July 8 accompanied by Assistant Secretary of War Peter H. Watson and Frank Blair. The terrible fatigue of the troops after three months of marching, entrenching, and fighting impressed every visitor;

---

30 W. H. Beach, *First New York Cavalry*, 182.
31 Cf. K. P. Williams, *Lincoln Finds a General*, II, 252–254.
32 *Works*, V, 307.
33 One soldier thought he resembled Don Quixote, The Knight of the Rueful Countenance, for he was "drooping, woeful, wan, like one forlorn, or crazed with care." Col. Wm. Kreutzer, *Four Years With the 98th New York Vols.*, 102.

fatigue was a disease, and a chronic disease, wrote one. But, bathing in the James, donning new uniforms, and parading to the bands, the men were recovering. Though the sick rate continued high, they shook off part of the malaria and diarrhea which had wasted thousands. The President, addressing the troops, said he knew they would never give up without going into Richmond. "He had been unable to sleep from anxiety, but after what he had seen and heard, he would go back to Washington, satisfied that it was all right with the army of the Potomac."

He indeed found the situation of the army better than he had dared hope. Its losses during the Seven Days, most stragglers having returned, were now officially put at only 10,400. The reports of desertion had been exaggerated, its spirit was good, and its position on the James was the best that it had held since the campaign began. In front, the wide river was busy with supply ships and transports. The camp was protected there by gunboats; on the west by a series of almost impassable ravines; on the northeast by the morasses of Herring Run Creek; and beyond the creek by the Heights of Eglington. This country of the lower James was reckoned the very garden of Virginia. Harrison's Landing, open, level, and dry, with abundant water and bathing facilities, and material to build arbors against the fierce sun where trees were lacking, gave the tired soldiers repose and security. "I feel as though I'd worked my passage through hell and come out in paradise," said one.

The troops lay amid historic surroundings. In the Harrison home, "Berkeley," a fine brick mansion, had dwelt Benjamin Harrison the Signer, and here William Henry Harrison had been born. Near at hand was the "Westover" of the Byrds, beautifully situated on the James. Not one Union soldier in a thousand had heard of William Byrd of *Dividing Line* fame, but the fine house and rich land were admired by all. A mile and a half back from the river lay the long, irregular house of ex-President Tyler, set in an 1,100-acre plantation somewhat more than half cleared of woods; and across the James was the plantation home of Edmund Ruffin, Jr., eighty feet above the water on a bluff. All these seats suffered heavily from the Union occupation. Fine mantelpieces that had cost £600 apiece in colonial days, furniture that was a triumph of British cabinetmakers, handsome rugs and old paintings, meant little to war-worn privates.[34]

34 The elder Ruffin has left a shocking picture of the destruction at his son's place. The yard was strewn with smashed chairs and other furniture, broken china and glassware, and feathers emptied from mattresses. Many windows were broken. Inside, every movable article had been broken or defaced. His papers, and some thousands of his and his son's books, had all been carried off. His harmonium had been ruined. The hand-molded plaster of the walls had been smeared with tobacco juice and covered with insulting charcoal inscriptions. Nearly all the livestock had been taken. Many trees had been cut down, and a large and

Lincoln had probing questions to ask of the outwardly polite, inwardly sulky McClellan, especially upon the evident wastage of manpower. On paper, the general had received 160,000 men. The President learned at Harrison's Landing that he had 86,500 remaining; where were the other 73,500? Assuming that 23,500 had been killed, wounded, or captured, and 5,000 had died of disease, 45,000 were absent—fully half of them, Lincoln believed, fit for duty. If McClellan regained these 22,500 troops, he could march into Richmond within three days. How could they be rounded up? McClellan's figures were different, but eloquent of bad army management. He counted 34,500 absent with leave, many of them sick or wounded, 3,800 absent without leave, and 16,600 present and sick; yet he himself believed that more than 20,000 absentees were probably fit for duty. If he could get these men and cure most of his sick, on his own statements he would have enough to take Richmond.[35] Still, of course, he demanded reinforcements—always reinforcements.

Other questions by Lincoln referred to the best use of McClellan's army. Certainly it would be worthless at Harrison's Landing unless it attacked soon and determinedly. McClellan was ready to attack—but only if he got additional troops. On the day of Malvern Hill he had telegraphed that he needed 50,000 more, and he still thought so. Altogether, Lincoln knew that only a miracle could make McClellan turn about promptly and fight; meanwhile, might not Washington be placed in real peril?

A fear that Lee's army of 200,000 (accepting McClellan's estimates) might use 50,000 men to hold McClellan immobile and the other 150,000 to execute a swift northward march on Washington, haunted many breasts. McClellan himself entertained the idea, for he had telegraphed Lincoln on July 4 that the enemy might prefer to advance on Washington instead of attacking his forces. Seward feared it, writing Thurlow Weed on July 7 that Lee might immediately organize a campaign against the national capital.[36] Quartermaster-General Meigs feared it; he had ridden out to the Soldier's Home just before Lincoln left to argue vehemently for bringing the army back, and had found Lincoln's noncommittal attitude disappointing. "How long," he wrote in his diary next day, "before he comes to my opinion to withdraw the army from a dangerous and useless position, and use it to defend the free states and as a nucleus for new armies?"[37] Stanton, naturally apprehensive and prone to sudden panic, feared it.

---

beautiful oak had been wantonly girdled. Ruffin noted that all but one of the thirty-one names he copied from the walls belonged to Pennsylvania regiments. MS Diary, LC.
  35 See Lincoln, *Works*, V, 322–323.
  36 For McClellan's views see O. R., I, xi, pt. 3, p. 294; for Seward's see his *Works*, III, 114.
  37 For opinions of corps commanders, see Lincoln, *Works*, V, 309–312. For Meigs's opinions see his pocket diaries, entries July 4, 5, 1862, Meigs Papers, LC.

On the other hand, the new base so near Richmond had manifest advantages if aggressively used. Three corps commanders were sharply averse to removal of the army. Sumner told Lincoln that it would be equivalent to giving up the cause, Heintzelman thought that it would be ruinous, and Fitz-John Porter used the same language—"move the army and ruin the country." Keyes, however, told Lincoln that the army could safely be shifted by rapid action, and Franklin declared that it ought to be moved, for the Rappahannock was the true line. The President may have learned that General J. C. Barnard, McClellan's chief of engineers, was also strongly for withdrawal, for he had always opposed using the Peninsula as a base.

In the back of everybody's mind lay the question whether McClellan should be retained. Confidence between him and the Administration was not eased by Lincoln's flying visit. The commander wrote disdainfully to his wife that His Excellency had come and gone, but had, he feared, profited little from his visit. As for Stanton, McClellan lacked vituperative talent to characterize this Judas; he hated to think that "humanity could sink so low." The general's anger as recently conveyed to Stanton in Washington by his chief-of-staff Marcy, and his apparent threat that he might surrender if he were not better supported had so shaken the Secretary, who was overwrought by the mortal illness of a child, that he wrote affirming his friendship and his readiness to offer any assistance within his power. McClellan replied with cool courtesy; but as the two men shook hands, each held a dirk behind his back. Writing S. L. M. Barlow on July 15, the general expressed sadness that so many brave men "have fallen victims to the stupidity and wickedness at Washington which have done their best to sacrifice as noble an army as ever marched," and made another veiled threat.[38]

"I do not care," he wrote, "if they remove me from this army—except on account of the army itself. I have lost all regard and respect for the majority of the Administration, and doubt the propriety of my brave men's blood being spilled to further the designs of such a set of heartless villains."

Lincoln was trying to remain patient with McClellan, though he knew how powerful a body of Northern opinion demanded the general's dismissal. At Harrison's Landing he was politely considerate. But McClellan put an intolerable tax on his forbearance when he handed the President a letter, dated July 7, expressing all his innate arrogance. It was time, he informed Lincoln, that the government determined on a civil and military policy which covered the whole ground of the national troubles; and he would kindly instruct the President of the United States on what it should and should not do. Lincoln silently read the paper. This was no longer rebellion, but war, McClellan wrote, and should

38 Barlow Papers.

be treated as such. But it should be waged mildly. Such orders as Pope's, such legislation as Trumbull's confiscation bill, such ideas upon reconstruction as Charles Sumner was enunciating, should—he implied—be repudiated: "It should not be a war looking to the subjugation of the people of any State in any event. It should not be at all a war upon population, but against armed forces and political organization. Neither confiscation of property, political executions of persons, territorial organizations of States, or forcible abolition of slavery, should be contemplated for a moment." [39]

We can well understand why Lincoln vouchsafed no comment to the waiting McClellan; why, as the general says in his memoirs, he coldly refrained from alluding to the letter during his visit, or at any time thereafter. No seizure of property for war uses, no subjugation of the enemy, no shooting even of red-handed assassins, no attack upon slavery! He even presumed to meddle with reconstruction; no territorial reorganization of the States! The grossness of this military intrusion into the political sphere matched the revelation that the commander believed in a limited, moderate, indecisive kind of fighting. All this was much worse for coming from a general whose chief of staff had just talked of capitulation. When Lincoln returned to Washington, he had not yet finally decided on the disposition of the army or of McClellan, but he must have moved close to a conclusion.

His next step, immediately after Halleck reached Washington, was to send that general to the James. As head of all the armies, Halleck's conclusions should be final.

And Halleck lost no time in deciding for a withdrawal. McClellan, in great agitation, pleaded for massing all available Eastern forces on the James for an attack. When Halleck told him that 20,000 men were all he could get, he said he would try an offensive with that number. His well-conceived plan was to cross the James, seize the still unfortified town of Petersburg, cut the railways to Lynchburg and Wilmington, and so take the rebel capital. But he and his officers showed so much hesitancy and such conviction of Lee's numerical superiority that Halleck emerged from his talks hostile and distrustful. Back in Washington he told Chase that he thought McClellan a poor general. His distrust was fortified when McClellan wrote him that fresh troops were pouring into Richmond, and that to meet them he wanted Burnside's men, Hunter's men, other units, and if possible 20,000 Western troops to boot. "The true defense of Washington consists in a rapid and heavy blow given by this army

39 McClellan, *Own Story*, 487–489. The letter, given in Nicolay and Hay, *Lincoln*, V, 447–449, contained one specially offensive sentence: "A declaration of radical views, especially upon slavery, will rapidly disintegrate our present armies." As Nicolay and Hay say, it had probably been prepared weeks before, and marked the beginning of McClellan's distinctively political career.

upon Richmond," he wrote. True enough; but if he got all these troops, would he not still demand more? Lincoln in profound discouragement told Attorney-General Bates that if he gave McClellan 200,000 men, the general would promise an instant forward movement, but would telegraph next day that he had proof of 400,000 in Lee's ranks, and could not possibly advance.[40]

By this time a decision had become urgent. Lincoln had two widely separated armies, not in communication, with a doughty foe lying between them ready to strike at either. They *must* be concentrated on the James, or on the Rappahannock. Had Lincoln known that Lee's forces did not reach 80,000 men, and had he possessed a firm faith in McClellan, he would have decided on the James. By straining every resource, he could have added 50,000 fresh troops to McClellan's 90,000; and this army of 140,000, moved into Petersburg, could have forced the evacuation of Richmond. But Lincoln had to give weight to McClellan's continued estimate of 200,000. One man alone, the astute Meigs, by careful study of Southern newspapers concluded that Lee possessed not more than 105,00 troops, and he was not credited. Lee, in fact, had encountered formidable obstacles in trying to bring his muster rolls back to the strength shown just before the Seven Days. After making the most of new conscripts, the return of the slightly wounded, and the elimination of unnecessary absences, and after receiving two new brigades from Charleston (July 28), he still had only 74,000 men.[41] So great was now Lee's prestige with the troops and public that he was an army in himself. The Richmond press lauded him deliriously, the *Enquirer* comparing his recent strategy with Austerlitz, and the *Dispatch* asserting that he must be enrolled with Hannibal, Caesar, Frederick, and Napoleon. Nevertheless, the vital fact was that his force remained what it had always been, much weaker in numbers and arms than McClellan's. Had Lincoln guessed this, his course would have been bolder.

Believing in the superior strength of the Confederate armies in the Richmond area, hopeful of Pope, and distrustful of McClellan, the President and Halleck determined to concentrate the two armies at a point where they could best cover Washington. Various engineer officers agreed with Barnard that this was the best strategy. Medical officers also predicted that the army, which had from 12,000 to 17,000 men sick, would suffer grave losses if kept on the malarial James in August and September. Already a plague of vicious horseflies made life a burden to men and animals.[42] On August 1 the die was cast: Halleck ordered

40 Welles, *Diary*, I, 221, 226; *Report, Committee on Conduct of War*, I, 437, 438; Shuckers, *Chase*, 448.
41 Meigs gave his figures to Halleck, O. R., I, xi, pt. 3, pp. 340, 341. Gen. Keyes controverted this; 200,000 was correct, he wrote. Meanwhile, Lee's army was troubled by internal divisions, revealed when Longstreet put A. P. Hill under arrest; Freeman, *Lee*, II, 256–258.
42 "The Peninsula is sickly here, as it was at the White House," wrote McClellan's aide

Burnside's force, balanced at Newport News halfway between the James and Washington, to join Pope on the Rappahannock. Two days later he telegraphed McClellan to take immediate measures to withdraw his army, of which he would keep command, from the Peninsula to Aquia Creek.

McClellan expostulated in great anguish, begging Halleck to rescind his order, which he characterized as ruinous. His army, now in splendid condition, could resume the offensive as soon as it was reinforced—the old condition! He pleaded eloquently. "Here, directly in front of this army, is the heart of the rebellion. It is here that all our resources should be collected to strike the blow which will determine the fate of the nation. All points of secondary importance elsewhere should be abandoned. . . . It is here on the banks of the James that the fate of the Union should be decided." [43] This was partly true. In the end the decision was to be reached in the James valley—but only when the Union army was commanded by an indomitable fighter in whom the Administration had perfect confidence.

Halleck, aided by Burnside, did his utmost to cushion the blow to McClellan and keep him in good heart for further service to the Union. They wrote arguing that he must forget his personal disappointments, suppress his irritation, and work valiantly for the cause. But would he? In a resentful letter to his wife McClellan actually intimated a hope that disasters to the army under its new leaders might prove him right. "Their game is to force me to resign; mine will be to force them to place me on leave of absence, so that when they begin to reap the whirlwind they have sown I may still be in a position to do something to save my country." Halleck had urged him to move his troops promptly; would a general animated by this spirit do so? [44]

Once the decision was made to move the army, speed was vital. Lee, taking the short chord of an arc, might reach the Rappahannock before McClellan's troops joined Pope. If McClellan, never a marvel of celerity, dragged his feet, the result would be disaster.

[V]

Meanwhile, ever since the carriage ride with Seward and Welles on July 13, Lincoln had stood by his determination to issue an emancipation proclamation. It

Rufus Ingalls, July 18; O. R., I, xi, pt. 3, pp. 326, 327. On the sick see O. R., I, xi, pt. 3, p. 341. Edmund Ruffin, who visited the Harrison's Landing vicinity just after McClellan left, pungently describes the unsanitary litter and the maddening clouds of flies; MS Diary, July–August, 1862, LC.
43   The full correspondence between Halleck and McClellan is in O. R., I, xi, pt. 1, pp. 75–105.
44   Olmsted, James River, July 13, 1862, to Bellows, Olmsted Papers, LC, reflects McClellan's hatred of Stanton as a "liar, hypocrite, and knave."

had become essential as a political measure, to keep the Republican Party behind him; a war measure, to cripple the South; a foreign policy measure, to align the humanitarian sentiment of the world, and especially Great Britain, with the North; and a measure to lift national morale.[45] Lincoln had begun to draft his proclamation. Going to the telegraph office at the War Department, where he could work with little interruption, he would seat himself in the cipher room and write deliberately on long foolscap sheets. The telegrapher Thomas T. Eckert records that he would set down a sentence or two, ruminate deeply as he stared out the window, and write again. When called away he would lock up the draft in the office. This continued for several weeks prior to July 22, when he had finished.[46]

The languor with which the army grew made it plain that a new inspiration was needed. Under Lincoln's call for 300,000 volunteers, the War Department fixed State quotas according to population, New York heading the list with 59,705 men. For a time a general bustle and enthusiasm presaged adequate results. The governors appointed field officers for the new regiments. Indiana and Illinois, competing to fill their quotas first, promised to put half their recruits in camp within a few days. The financial editor of Bryant's *Evening Post*, John S. Gibbons, published his stirring verses: "We are coming, Father Abraham, three hundred thousand more."

Vociferous war meetings were held all over the North, at which orators sounded a new note of anger, denouncing traitors and threatening condign punishment to the South. Towns, counties, and cities, aided by business firms and wealthy individuals, offered generous bounties to recruits. During July a group of New York businessmen subscribed $8,000 for the Produce Exchange Regiment. Northampton, Massachusetts, appropriated $30,000 for its volunteers, and many other towns and cities pledged payments of $100 to $300 a man. In a few places the total, added to the Federal bounty of $100, reached $500. Central squares in Chicago, Cleveland, Pittsburgh, and other cities once more took on the aspect of army camps. City Hall Park in New York was resonant with drums and bugles as twenty-five tents enlisted volunteers for the Halleck Guard, Stanton Legion, Pope Rifles, Doubleday Artillery, and other outfits.

The results, however, were disappointing. Government confusion once more interfered with systematic recruiting. For example, the War Department directed governors to organize *new* regiments, and they issued appropriate orders;

45 Much of the Northern press, led by Bryant and Greeley, was now stressing two contentions: that no foreign land but Dahomey would dare side with the South once the North made its antislavery position clear, and that public opinion was crystallizing that a permanent settlement with the South must include general emancipation. See N. Y. *Tribune*, August 13, 1862.
46 Bates, *Lincoln in the Telegraph Office*, 138–141.

but Lincoln told a New York deputation that 100,000 soldiers enlisted in depleted old regiments would be worth 300,000 in the new ones, and the press set up a clamor for sending volunteers only to units already in the field. Under War Department regulations, however, recruiting for the old regiments was controlled exclusively by Federal authorities, and State action was restricted to new formations. And recruits lagged anyway. Anxious citizens began writing to the newspapers urging universal conscription as the nation's only salvation.[47] Greeley's *Tribune* sent a correspondent on a wide tour to report on the situation. "The difficulty seems to be with the large cities," he wrote, "where most of the able-bodied young men enlisted and marched out with the first levies of the war." [48]

Finally, on August 4, Lincoln took a drastic step. He ordered that any State which had not raised its quota of the 300,000 new volunteers by August 15 should make up the deficiency at once by special draft; and at the same time, to lift the army to a round million, he called out 300,000 nine-months' men to be drafted from the militia. These approaches toward conscription electrified the North, which had dreaded it. Governor C. S. Olden of New Jersey, for example, had written that while the rebels filled their waning ranks by compulsory service, "let it be our boast that we defend the nation by the heroic volunteer." The Federal bounty and advance pay were limited to volunteers, and Lincoln's orders were intended primarily to stimulate volunteering. Unfortunately, drafted men were allowed to hire substitutes, and companies both private and public were immediately formed to obtain them; they sent out agents who scoured towns and countrysides, offering larger sums than the aggregate bounties in some places, and thus put a brake on volunteering. The effective way of meeting this evil, said Greeley, would be for the authorities to fix a sum of money which they would accept in place of a substitute, thus driving the companies out of business. Various modes of draft dodging appeared. The simplest was to sneak off to Canada; the most expensive was to bribe a doctor to give a certificate of physical disability; the most profitable and dangerous was to enlist, take the bounty, and desert.[49]

47 N. Y. *Tribune*, July 28, 1862, for Lincoln's statement. In the end, the call of July 1 brought in 421,465 men, but only after intensive prodding, and fewer than 50,000 of them were assigned to old regiments; L. L. Lerwill, *Personnel Replacement System in the U. S. Army*, 90.
48 See analyses in N. Y. *Tribune*, Aug. 13, 15, 1862.
49 Lerwill, *Personnel Replacement*, 90 ff.; N. Y. *Tribune*, Aug. 15, 1862; Croffut and Morris, *Connecticut*, 242–245. The London *Daily News*, Aug. 18, 1862, noted the results of the bounty system in stimulating mercenary impulses and numbing patriotism, and the London *Illustrated News*, Dec. 27, 1862, commented on the "large enrolment of Irishmen and Germans, to whom the bounty-money was the attraction rather than love of the cause." (Both papers strongly favored the Union.) The fluctuating price of substitutes gave rise to speculation; a Wesleyan College student sold himself for $300, found another man for $200,

In these weary weeks some dramatic step to lift men's hearts was needed. "You used to maul rails," Representative I. N. Arnold, preparing to return to Chicago at the end of the session, told Lincoln; "now you must maul rebels." "Tell the people of Illinois that I'll do it," responded the President.[50] Four days after Congress adjourned he told the Cabinet that commanders in all parts of the Confederacy had been ordered to subsist their troops in hostile territory, and to employ as paid laborers as many Negroes as were useful.

Then on August 22, in the most historic of Cabinet meetings, he made the momentous announcement that he had drafted an emancipation proclamation. Seward and Welles were of course prepared, but the others were taken aback. The apparent suddenness of the step bewildered one or two, and its boldness startled others. Even Stanton had never proposed going as far as a *general* emancipation in rebellious territory. He and Welles rallied to the defense of the proposal. Chase promised to give the measure cordial support; but as he was fearful of slave insurrections, he thought that emancipation could be accomplished more safely by directing the commanders of departments to proclaim it as soon as feasible, and allowing generals in the field to arm and organize slaves.[51] Montgomery Blair, coming in late, gave a response characteristic of his political-minded family: he apprehended that the proclamation would have a bad effect on the fall elections. No objection, however, moved Lincoln until Seward spoke up. The President later told the painter Carpenter just what Seward had said:

He said in substance, "Mr. President, I approve of the proclamation, but I question the expediency of its issue at this juncture. The depression of the public mind, consequent upon our repeated reverses, is so great that I fear the effect of so important a step. It may be viewed as the last measure of an exhausted Government, a cry for help; the Government stretching forth its hands to Ethiopia, instead of Ethiopia stretching forth her hands to the Government." His idea . . . was that it would be considered our last shriek on the retreat. . . . "Now," continued Mr. Seward, "while I approve the measure, I suggest, sir, that you postpone its issue until you can give it to the country supported by military success, instead of issuing it, as would be the case now, upon the greatest disasters of the war."[52]

and pocketed the difference; Middletown, Conn., *Sentinel*, Nov. 24, 1862. Harold Frederic's story *The Deserter* (1898) poignantly sets forth the situation of a New York State private who deserted to look after his dying father.

50 Wash. corr., N. Y. *Tribune*, July 31, 1862.

51 The treatment of the Cabinet meeting in Nicolay and Hay, VI, 125-130, is somewhat misleading. As Welles was previously committed, no emphatic statement from him was needed; he had a gift for self-effacement. Chase strongly favored both emancipating and arming the Negroes, but feared "depredation and massacre" if emancipation were not accompanied by military restraints. The intimation by Nicolay and Hay that these men refused support is unjustified. See Chase's not wholly candid statement of his views in Donald, ed., *Inside Lincoln's Cabinet*, 99, 100.

52 Carpenter, *Six Months in the White House*, 22. Obviously Carpenter is a secondhand authority, but we must take his record in default of a better.

It is curious that Lincoln did not himself think of Seward's demurrer, which was strongly stated by some newspapers when the proclamation later appeared. Seeing the wisdom of the view, and given pause by Chase's objections, he laid the paper aside for an hour of victory. "From time to time I added or changed a line," he tells us, "touching it up here and there, anxiously watching the progress of events."

Meanwhile, he dealt shrewdly with public opinion. As premature disclosure would have done great harm, he deliberately obscured his purpose, talking to different men in different veins. He often dissented from visitors anyway, just to excite them to a more vigorous statement of their reasons. To radicals, such as a deputation of ministers, he now argued reasons for delay; to conservatives like his old Maryland friend Reverdy Johnson he offered reasons for acting. He gave Chase the impression that he would let the field commanders arm Negroes for defensive action; Leonard Swett, however, departed with the impression that he was adamant against both emancipation and the use of freedmen as soldiers.[53] The last thing he could afford at the moment was to speak out. Nevertheless, he did drop some pregnant hints. He must save the government, he assured Reverdy Johnson, "and it may as well be understood, once for all, that I shall not surrender this game leaving any card unplayed." More caustically, he informed August Belmont that the nation would no longer play a game in which it staked everything and its opponents nothing. "These enemies must understand that they cannot experiment ten years trying to destroy the government, and if they fail still come back into the Union unhurt."

The general public guessed nothing. But the great decision had been taken; the most revolutionary stroke, in a war which had now become revolution in the broadest sense, hung poised for delivery.

53 Swett's curious record of his interview with Lincoln, sent to his wife Aug. 10, 1862, is in the David Davis Papers, Ill. State Hist. Library. As he was conservative, wishful thinking doubtless entered into his report that Lincoln would issue no emancipation proclamation; that Lincoln thought Union troops in Kentucky and Tennessee would go over to the enemy if he did; and that the President had no confidence in Negroes as fighting men. Like Hamlet with Polonius, Lincoln could fool some men to the top of their bent.

7

John Pope and Second Manassas

FOR HALF a dozen reasons, in these midsummer days of 1862, Lincoln and the Union needed a victory more urgently than ever before; reasons military, political, diplomatic, and financial. But victory depended on the generals, and some of the generals were aptly characterized by Attorney-General Bates: "The thing I complain of is a criminal tardiness, a fatuous apathy, a captious bickering rivalry, among our commanders—who . . . overlook the lives of their people and the necessities of their country." [1]

It was largely for lack of victory that recruiting for the new army of 300,000 men moved slowly. To be sure, high wages and abundant employment helped slow enlistment, but the London *Times* correspondent in New York had warrant for reporting that the people seemed to be losing faith in their generals.[2] In the end the State quotas were obtained; Illinois filled her ranks by mid-August, and New York eventually surpassed the levy made upon her. In many States the annual increase in the number of men reaching the age of enlistment more than met the new levy. But the spirit of the population, facing an obstinate war, was very different from that after Bull Run.[3]

The new recruits had to be armed; and where, asked the New York *Times*, were they to get their guns? Although part of the forces in the field were still equipped with smoothbores, the government could as yet make only 13,000 Springfields a month, and private contractors were hardly producing a thousand monthly.[4] The situation was rendered more difficult by the fact that great stocks of weapons had been worn out in the Virginia battles, captured by the Confederates, or destroyed during McClellan's retreat. To meet the emergency, the War Department had to turn to Europe. Stanton resolved to send a new agent abroad, and Governor E. D. Morgan and Robert Dale Owen,

1 Bates to Lieber, Sept. 3, 1862, Lieber Papers, HL.
2 London *Times*, July 26, 1862, with editorial comment.
3 The N. Y. quota was nearly 60,000, but under the call the State eventually supplied 86,097 men; *Annual Reports State Adjutant General*, 1862, 1863.
4 N. Y. *Times*, July 17, 1862; H. J. Raymond, like other editors, assailed Ripley, Chief of Ordnance.

deputed to make a choice, selected the sagacious New York merchant Marcellus Hartley. Before July ended he arrived in Birmingham with large credits on Baring Brothers, and instructions to buy all the good available firearms in Britain.

Hartley encountered a difficult situation. While McClellan threatened Richmond, rifles were a drug on the British market, and manufacturers were taking contracts at low prices to work up their materials. But immediately after the call for 300,000 fresh troops, speculators rushed out to buy all the ready-made guns. Large purchases were also being made for China, where the Tai-Ping rebellion was raging. The Birmingham combination of manufacturers called the Small Arms Company had given an option to a New York house which hoped to get a Federal contract at $17 a rifle, but Hartley was determined not to pay more than fifty shillings or $12, while he also insisted that the makers improve the quality of their weapons. Such was the dearth of available arms that he had to inform Stanton on August 30 that he would not be able to get more than 70,000 Enfields by November. He urged the bold step of taking the whole Enfield market.[5] Hartley's haunting fear in these weeks was that a sudden decision by the British government to recognize the Confederacy might cut off all further arms supplies. In the area of foreign relations the lack of Northern victory was as keenly felt as at home.

Financial circles, and above all the Treasury Department, also had reasons to long for victory. McClellan's reverses, combined with the steady expansion of the paper currency and the demands of European trade for exchange, precipitated an approach to panic in the New York money market. Early in July the premium on gold shot up in two days from 10 per cent to 17 per cent, and the premium on silver to 8 per cent, while demand notes commanded 8 or 9 per cent premium.[6]

Congress by this time had authorized the issuance of $300,000,000 in legal-tender notes or greenbacks, and Secretary Chase was trying hard to induce the public to use them and other media to buy a half-billion dollars worth of so-called five-twenties; that is, 6 per cent bonds redeemable in five years, and payable twenty years after the date of issue. Despite the government's dire need for ready cash, the average daily sale when the Peninsular campaign bogged down was a mere trifle, only about $150,000, and the reluctance of the public to take these attractive securities greatly distressed the Secretary.

5 Anon., *Marcellus Hartley; A Brief Memoir*, privately printed, 1903. In the end Hartley's mission was eminently successful, and he obtained 200,000 rifles before he returned home early in 1863; but for these critical months the stringency was acute.

6 N. Y. *Shipping and Commercial List*, July 13, 1862, describes the panic, which gave a pronounced impulse to inflation, particularly in costs of imported goods.

People were not merely unused to bonds; they needed reassurance as to the future of the republic. Another fact which had to be considered was that a comprehensive new tax law, including an income tax, had just been put on the statute books, and nothing would so much encourage the public to meet its burdens as a decisive victory.[7]

It was meanwhile clear that, in view of the approaching Congressional elections, the Administration would be assailed with equal venom by conservative Democrats and radical Republicans. On the evening of July 1, the day of Malvern Hill, a mass meeting of discontented New Yorkers gathered at Cooper Union to listen to ex-Mayor Fernando Wood, Representative James Brooks, and the jurist William A. Duer, son of a former president of Columbia, as they denounced the government in the most waspish Democratic style. Duer declared that if traitors were hanged in the order of their guilt, the next man who marched upon the scaffold after Jefferson Davis would be Charles Sumner.[8] At about the same time Byrant's *Evening Post*, voice of radical Republicanism, indicted the Administration for shameful inefficiency, asking why enlistments had been stopped that spring, why the militia had not been armed, drilled, and organized for instant service, why depots had not been filled with munitions.[9] Wendell Phillips assured an audience filling Boston Music Hall that Lincoln was a second-rate man, whose slackness was doing more than the malice of Conferates to break up the Union.

In vain did Lincoln look to the West, for the situation there had deteriorated with startling rapidity. Hardly had Halleck left for the East than Braxton Bragg executed the most masterly movement of his career. He saw that Buell, compelled by Halleck's fatuous orders to repair and garrison a long railroad as he marched against Chattanooga, was moving at snail's pace. Leaving 15,000 men as part of his army to guard Vicksburg, he marched his remaining 35,000 to Mobile, and as we have noted, hurried them by rail to Chattanooga. It was one of the most spectacular railway operations of a war in which rails for the first time played a critical part.

Safe in Chattanooga on July 29, Bragg held a vantage point from which he could seriously threaten Buell. At once Grant had to take steps to reinforce Buell's Army of the Ohio, weakening his own force until it was in danger from a sudden attack by Van Dorn. And when Bragg had saved Chattanooga, he could meditate bolder undertakings. By striking into the heart of Kentucky, even as far north as Louisville, might he not loosen the Union grip on that

7 The London *Economist*, Feb. 22, 1862, had published an editorial, "Will the State of the Federal Finances Bring the American Civil War to an End?"
8 Quoted in the *Atlantic*, "The New Opposition Party," X (Sept., 1862), 377.
9 Quoted in Chicago *Morning Post*, July 12, 1862.

commonwealth and on all middle Tennessee? Using their daring cavalrymen, Nathan Bedford Forrest and John Hunt Morgan, the Confederates began to harry Union detachments in two States.

[I]

As we have seen, Halleck's order to McClellan on August 3 to transfer his 88,000 men from the James to the Potomac emphasized speed. Lee, who had a good intelligence service, would infallibly hear of the movement as soon as it began and move to attack Pope before a concentration could be effected. When McClellan protested, Halleck wrote that this order must be obeyed "with all possible promptness." On August 7 he struck the note again: "I beg of you, general, to hurry along this movement; your reputation as well as mine may be involved in its rapid execution. I cannot regard Pope and Burnside as safe until you reinforce them. Moreover, I wish them under your immediate command, for reasons which it is not necessary to specify."

The irate McClellan, however, did not hurry. Three days after Halleck penned this anxious letter, he was still planning to redeem his badly smutched record by action on the James front. "I hope to be ready tomorrow afternoon," he wrote his wife August 10, "to move forward in the direction of Richmond. I will try to catch or thrash Longstreet, and then, if the chance offers, follow in to Richmond while they are lamming away at Pope." He did not care what happened to Pope! McClellan would never have dared to inform Halleck on the 10th that he proposed to move upon Richmond. He had received a dispatch from that general on the 9th that "you must send reinforcements instantly to Aquia Creek," and that "your delay is not satisfactory." But he unbosomed himself to his wife, adding that he was certain "the dolts in Washington" were bent on his destruction. Once more he was playing the spoiled child.[10] Ordered in one direction, he planned to move in another.

Pope's army, even when he had united the forces of McDowell, Sigel, and Banks, was small—only 43,000 men—compared with McClellan's, but on paper a fair match for any army Lee could bring against him without badly weakening Richmond. He took the field July 29, and under Halleck's orders moved forward swiftly to the Rapidan, so that he could occupy enough Confederate troops to enable McClellan to evacuate the Peninsula with safety. Unhappily, one of his three corps suffered a bloody defeat in this advance. Banks, attacking Stonewall Jackson's superior force at Cedar Mountain on August 9, was soundly trounced; after which the North had to watch a sorry

10 For these Halleck-McClellan exchanges see O. R., I, xii, pt. 2, pp. 4 ff.; McClellan Papers, LC; *Own Story,* 460 ff. (home letters), 490 ff. (official dispatches).

wrangle between him and Pope over the responsibility. By mid-August, Pope was at the Rapidan, Jackson was near Gordonsville—and Lee was on the move. For the Confederate commander, confident that McClellan was at last withdrawing, elated by Jackson's victory, and angered by Pope's harsh general orders, decided on the 14th to take advantage of his interior lines, and attack directly north. Leaving only three divisions to hold Richmond, he would join Jackson in an effort to crush Pope before material reinforcements from the James reached him.[11]

The Confederates held the trump cards. They could move across country, using the railroad much of the way, with a rapidity and secrecy impossible to Union forces moving down the Peninsula to Newport News, and ascending the Potomac to Aquia Creek. McClellan on the 12th was still arguing with Halleck. On the 15th, at 1:30 in the morning, Halleck was still imploring him to send up his troops "with all possible rapidity." [12] Meanwhile, from the 14th onward Lee was moving north with decision and vigor.

Out of the acrid exchanges then and later between Halleck and McClellan, out of the investigation presently made by a Congressional committee, out of a mass of collateral evidence, emerges one unquestionable fact. McClellan was inexcusably late and reluctant in his withdrawal. He pleaded a deficiency of transports and wharf space, and the necessity of providing for his sick. Nevertheless, energy and address could have mastered these shortages. He had complete control over a great flotilla of transports in the James, Hampton Roads, and Potomac. To shorten the journey, he could have begun just after August 1 marching his troops quietly by land to Yorktown, Newport News, and Fort Monroe instead of proceeding as if he expected to embark them all at Harrison's Landing. A capable observer, General Victor Le Duc, wrote that but for gross mismanagement, the whole army could have been transferred to Aquia within two weeks.[13] By August 10 at latest the movement should have been well under way. Actually, the evacuation did not really begin till four days afterward, only the sick, some batteries, and some cavalry being moved earlier. To hasten the movement of the force, Halleck had finally sent Burnside, a close friend of McClellan's stationed at Fredericksburg, to argue him into greater energy. And after talking with Burnside, the general belatedly promised his "full cooperation."

"On Thursday [14th August]," wrote a New York *Tribune* correspondent, "the army commenced evacuating in earnest. All the siege guns were removed from the front and safely embarked on Thursday and yesterday [Friday,

11 Freeman, *Lee*, II, 272–278. At Cedar Mountain, Banks had 2,353 losses; Jackson, 1,338.
12 *American Conflict*, II, 171. Williams, *Lincoln Finds a General*, II, 273–290.
13 General S. M. Quincy in *The Va. Campaign of 1862 under Pope* (Mil. Hist. Soc. Mass.), 24–26, condemns McClellan for making mountains out of molehills in the evacuation.

the 15th] on board barges and schooners. Porter's corps led the van of the overland portion of the army on Thursday night. On Friday morning every tent was struck, and then, for the first time, it was generally known that the *whole* army was about evacuating Harrison's Landing." [14] The last sick and wounded were carried into boats; Negroes, with much hilarity and shouting, struggled aboard a variety of craft; huge bonfires consumed tents, barrels, and all stores that might be of use to the Confederates. McClellan, taking pride in being the last to go, rode with his staff to Yorktown, whence on August 21 he embarked—ten days late.

He, his staff, and his favorite corps officers went in surly temper. They looked to the past with anger, and to the future with foreboding, The Administration, they reasoned, dared not remove McClellan for political reasons, but was determined that he should no longer be chief general. What could it do? It had brought Halleck east, but that was the smaller half of its plan.The larger scheme was that Pope should be helped to make so brilliant a record that all difficulty would disappear; parts of McClellan's army could be added to Pope's from time to time, until this force became the center of the war. As Pope rose, McClellan would be sidetracked. This was the opinion of Fitz-John Porter, who had been writing truculent letters criticizing the abolitionists, the government, and above all Stanton. It was the view taken by McClellan himself. The general's loyal lieutenants were as likely to abet this program as a proud church leader would be to abet heresy.

As McClellan's army tardily moved back toward Washington, the clouds began to lower blackly over Pope's forces. Lee's array, pushing toward the Rapidan fords some 54,000 strong, faced what was now a larger number, for Burnside had reinforced Pope; but the Southerners were full of confidence and the Union troops dispirited, the Confederate leadership superb and the Federal generalship mediocre.[15] Pope fell back to Culpeper, for he wished to get behind the Rappahannock. The general who never turned his back on the enemy was retreating. Could he get behind the river in time? Would he meet adequate reinforcements? By August 22 Pope's Army of Virginia had completed its retirement to the north bank of the Rappahannock and held every ford between Fredericksburg and Warrenton Springs. Falling back eighteen miles, they had gained positions of marked strength. But who could predict what Lee and Jackson, supposed to have such superior strength, would do?

14 Harrison's Landing corr., N. Y. *Tribune*, Aug. 19, 1862.
15 Longstreet later wrote D. H. Hill giving Lee's strength Aug. 29, 1862, as Longstreet 30,000; Jackson, 20,000; artillery for both, 4,000; total, 54,000. These figures were based on Col. Charles Marshall's testimony in the Fitz-John Porter Case. Hill adds that R. H. Anderson came up on Aug. 30 with 5,000 more. D. H. Hill Papers, Va. State Lib. Livermore in *Numbers and Losses*, 88, 89, gives Lee's strength at Second Manassas and Chantilly as 48,527; Pope's strength as 75,696.

At that critical moment McClellan's army hung suspended, like Mahomet's coffin, between heaven and earth. Though it had ceased to threaten Richmond, it had not begun to sustain Pope. A great part of it that day was afloat on the Potomac, and another great part trudging overland to ports of debarcation. Nor was the army in a mood for fighting. Thousands had broken away from their regiments and were wandering aimlessly without rations or shelter. Temporarily the Army of the Potomac, on which the order to return had fallen like a thunderbolt, was limp, grumbling, disheartened; it was shrunken, homesick, tired.[16] The decay of morale had begun among officers, whose desperation to get home, applications in shoals for furloughs, and readiness to invoke political pull had disgusted Frederick Law Olmsted. It had spread among soldiers who felt that after they had undergone an Iliad of woes which entitled them to return as heroes, they had been called back with the stigma of defeat.

Some high officers were in the worst possible frame of mind. McClellan in private letters wrote that he expected to see Pope "badly thrashed." He was sure the government would "throw upon me the blame of their own delays and blunders"; he was bitter over the failure of Washington to keep him informed—"they may go to the deuce in their own way"; and he expected to be traduced and shelved, unless Pope was defeated, "in which case they will want me to save Washington again." [17] Fitz-John Porter not only used scorching language about the Administration, but expressed the sharpest hostility toward abolitionist tendencies in the war. He wrote Manton Marble of the *World* that Stanton was an "ass"; that the President was "controlled" by this incompetent Secretary; and that the *World* ought to raise the question whether the Administration had a covert purpose in crippling McClellan— whether it wished "to cause defeat here for the purpose of prolonging the war." Such a prolongation would of course serve the interests of the abolitionists, whom Fitz-John Porter despised and hated as "our enemies in rear." But Stanton, "poor fool," wished to deprive McClellan of the credit of victory,

16 The N. Y. *Times, Tribune,* and *Herald,* and Phila. *Press,* Aug. 12–18, give full details.
17 McClellan could justly complain of want of information, for Lincoln and Halleck should have taken greater pains to inform him of their own and Pope's military plans. McClellan's spy, Allan Pinkerton, strolled into the White House August 22, first making sure that Lincoln was out, to pump Nicolay for information which he at once sent the general. Nicolay told him that the President believed McClellan an able and safe general, but like the country was impatient for action, and wanted vigorous compaigning. He added that McClellan's enemies constantly warned Lincoln that he would never fight unless sure he would win—he would take no risks. Even so, Nicolay felt sure that Lincoln would not supersede McClellan until the general had another chance. For one reason, sentiment favorable to Pope in his army had ebbed away, and apart from Halleck, Pope now had few friends. Pinkerton, August 23, 1862, to McClellan; Pinkerton Papers. McClellan wrote home August 21; "I do not know what they intend doing with me." Halleck should have told him.

and of the means of reconquering the South "in a manner that will develop Union feeling." [18]

Seldom has a stage been more elaborately set for a debacle. Lincoln, watching haggardly at the War Department from dawn to midnight, had dark forebodings of the tragedy to be played. As Lee moved forward, suddenly communications with Pope's menaced army were severed. "What news from the front?" the President telegraphed McClellan, who had just arrived at Alexandria, on the afternoon of August 27. "Any news from General Pope?" he telegraphed Burnside on the 28th. "What news from Manassas? What generally?" he telegraphed Herman Haupt on the 29th.

[II]

Throughout much of the North, men were aware on Thursday, Friday, and Saturday, August 28–30, that a terrible battle was raging in Virginia. For the first two days, because Halleck had barred reporters from the area,[19] the agonized public caught at a hundred rumors. On Friday came fragmentary intelligence that Jeb Stuart with 2,000 men had descended on Manassas Junction, taken trains, prisoners, and stores, and cut the only railroad between Pope's headquarters and Washington. Later that day the War Department released a dispatch from Pope which was boastful yet alarming. Stonewall Jackson and Stuart by a flanking march had gotten to his rear, he admitted, but he was moving to overwhelm them: "I do not see how the enemy is to escape without heavy loss." On Saturday morning the public read this dispatch in the press with a mixture of hope and apprehension. No more word came. Toward evening, in Washington, knots clustering atop public buildings distinctly heard the roar of cannon. Seeming to drag slowly nearer, its fury never slackened until nightfall. Still no authentic news came, and none next day. Not for nearly a week did the North realize that Saturday had witnessed one of the bloodiest defeats of the war.

What had happened? In a sentence, Lee had thrown a powerful force under Jackson around Pope's western flank to his rear; Pope had attempted to surround and crush this force, but his dispositions were blundering, while some of his generals were dilatory; Lee and Longstreet meanwhile broke through with the other part of the Confederate army to reinforce Jackson; and in the end a united, determined Southern host, rejoicing in unmatched

18 Porter, May 21, June 20, etc., Manton Marble Papers; Patrick, MS Diary, July 18, Aug. 4, 1862, LC.

19 Halleck gave his fatuous order Aug. 19 because intercepted Confederate letters spoke of information gained from Northern papers, because he mistakenly supposed that the Confederates had gotten word of McClellan's withdrawal from the James out of the N. Y. *Tribune*, and because he never understood the right of the public to full news. Starr, *Bohemian Brigade*, 130–132; A. S. Hill, Aug. 22, 1862, Gay Papers.

leaders and a proud record of victory, had crumpled up the disunited and dispirited Army of Virginia, forcing it back to the old field of Bull Run.

Lee had known from the beginning of the campaign that he would have to move rapidly if he hoped to crush Pope before McClellan's forces reached that general. He and President Davis showed great courage in stripping Richmond of all but two defensive brigades to permit of a northward thrust. It was the courage of desperation, for only by audacious strokes could the South snatch victory from the odds against it, but it nevertheless revealed leonine daring. Lee pushed the movement hard despite his grave lack of wagons and horses. When Pope in alarm retired behind the Rappahannock, and that stream and the Rapidan rose, the Confederate leader not only persisted, but resolved on a still more intrepid move. He detached Jackson with 20,000 men to make a long forced march, cross the upper Rappahannock, swing to Pope's rear, and sever the railroad to Alexandria. Thus to divide his inferior army of 54,000 men in the very face of his opponent's 65,000 troops defied all military maxims.[20] While Longstreet held the attention of Union commanders by some desultory fighting, Jackson would execute his march, strike at Pope's communications, and compel the Northern army to accept all the confusions and chagrins of retreat.

On the evening of August 24 Jackson's three divisions assembled. They put three days' rations in their haversacks; they caught a few hours' sleep. Under the morning stars, as the men struggled into line, they heard an unexpected order: "Unsling knapsacks!" With dubious faces, they laid them on the grass. "Left face! Forward, march!"—and they never saw the knapsacks again. A herd of cattle provided their only stock of food; a few frying pans, tin cans, and forks were their only impediments. As they turned northwest, away from Longstreet's guns thudding on the Rappahannock, their fast-moving columns caught a sense of exhilaration. The men could have echoed Stonewall's own exclamation: "Delicious excitement!" They guessed that their mysterious errand was taking them around Pope's army. With jest and hilarity, amid glad greetings from farm folk who brought out milk, water, biscuits, and ham, they swept across the river, marching twenty-six miles before the midnight halt. One later wrote:

Swiftly along the high country roads, day long and far into the night, through the fields to make short cuts, letting down the bars here, or pulling down a panel of fence there, along byways and farm roads, we pushed, unencumbered

---

20 See note 15 above. Col. Wm. Allen in Mil. Hist. Soc. Mass., *Va. Campaign of 1862,* 195 ff., puts Pope's army at 70,000, Lee's at 49,000; in *Battles and Leaders,* II, 500, Pope is credited with at least 63,000 and Lee with 54,000. But for three reasons Lee's army was much the stronger. He had in Jackson an incomparable lieutenant; the morale of his troops was superb; and he held them well in hand, while Pope's demoralized, badly led army lost men in large numbers by straggling.

by wagons—glad to rest and sleep when the night's halt was made—no rations issued, faring on green corn and apples from the fields, helped out by such bread and butter and milk as we had money to buy from the people, or they would give—so "Jackson's foot cavalry" went hurrying northward.

Or, as a Southern poet still more stirringly put it:

> Steady! the whole brigade!
> What matter if our shoes are worn?
> What matter if our feet are torn?
> "Quick-step! We're with him before morn!"
> That's "Stonewall Jackson's way." [21]

Pope's right wing extended to the Bull Run Mountains, a long ridge running from near Warrenton north to the Potomac. Moving under the western lee of this ridge, Jackson's swift columns swept upward until they reached Thoroughfare Gap, well northwest of Pope's lines. Through this winding gorge, the high forested hills about it all unguarded, the Confederates marched until at its eastern margin they could look down on the countryside from Fairfax Courthouse to the Rappahannock. Descrying the highway which ran southeast from the Gap, they could see it intersected at Gainesville by another road extending from Warrenton to the high-seated town of Centreville. Empty, unpatrolled, both roads stretched into the distance. No tower of dust, no glisten of bayonets heralded a Union movement to intercept Jackson's stroke. Instead, the way lay open to the Southerners to cut the principal highway between Pope's army and Washington. Then, pressing beyond it, they could seize the Alexandria line, his sole rail artery, at Bristoe Station or Manassas.[22]

Why Pope allowed himself to be thus outflanked he never explained.[23] The chief of railway transportation, Herman Haupt, declares that as early as the 22nd he had warned Pope of a possible flanking movement, and ascertained that he did not have his scouting parties well up on the headwaters of the Rappahannock. "Is that far enough?" inquired Haupt. "What is to prevent the enemy from going even as far as Thoroughfare Gap and getting behind you?" The general shrugged: "There is no danger."

Union headquarters were thus asleep to the situation when the gray columns poured into Bristoe Station as the sun sank on the 26th. They captured most of the garrison, smashed the bridge over Broad Run, tore up the tracks, and wrecked two trains. Other trains escaped, one north to Alexandria, one

---

21 MS Recollections of H. G. Benson, Southern Coll., Univ. of N. C.; John W. Palmer, "Stonewall Jackson's Way."
22 Henderson, II, 148.
23 He slips over the subject in *Battles and Leaders*, II, 460, 461, but made some excuses in *Supplemental Report, Committee on Conduct of the War*, Pt. II, 141, 142.

south to Warrenton, to give the alarm. With not a moment to lose, Jackson thrust two regiments of tired men up the railroad in utter darkness, and at midnight Manassas Junction was theirs. He himself followed with two full divisions, reaching that place the morning of the 27th.

Well might Halleck hide these events from public view! At Manassas, Jackson was only thirty miles from Washington, one long day's march; he was almost squarely behind Pope's main army; and he counted on Longstreet, with the other part of Lee's host, to follow and reinforce him! The Confederates in their midnight seizure of the Junction had captured 300 men, miles of freight cars, streets of bulging warehouses, and whole fields of barrels, boxes, and piled munitions. For a few brief hours Jackson's ragged, famished divisions held revelry amid the richest body of stores ever brought into the field, a prodigal variety of materials to feed, clothe, and arm the Union troops. After rations had been issued, and liquor locked up, officers threw open these treasures. Here men seized on toothbrushes, candles, coffee, and tea; here they choked down lobster salad, potted game, and jellies. From piles of new clothing the naked took blue uniforms, from heaps of shoes the barefoot carried off new boots, from stacks of rifled muskets the ill-armed drew burnished pieces. For sick comrades they pocketed delicacies and medicines. Then Jackson, aware that strong forces were moving up from Warrenton to attack him, put the torch to the remaining stores, and under cover of flame and smoke withdrew his rear guard before Pope's first units appeared.[24]

Jackson now had to join hands with the main body under Lee and Longstreet, which also had made for Thoroughfare Gap, before the aroused swarms of Northern troops could pounce on his 20,000 men and sting them to death. He knew that Pope might even block Thoroughfare Gap before the two Confederate armies could unite. He knew that some forward elements of McClellan's army were moving west from Aquia Creek. Indeed, on the afternoon of the 27th, Hooker's division, 5,500 strong, emerged near Bristoe Station and deployed for action, driving back small Confederate forces under Ewell. A cordon might yet be thrown around Stonewall's bold men. On the night of August 27–28, therefore, while burning stores lighted the skies above Manassas, Jackson hurried north and northwest by three roads, and by morning had his whole command hidden in the woods beyond Groveton, within reach of the Gap. Here he bivouacked to let his troops recover from their fatigues.[25]

The rest of the story presents a picture of Pope's complete miscalculation

24 Gordon, "Army of Virginia," in Henderson, II, 133, 134; A. C. Redwood in *Battles and Leaders*, II, 532, 533.
25 Ropes, *Civil War*, II, 266; O. R., I, xii, pt. 2, p. 644. Ropes remarks of Jackson that "no one could have displayed sounder judgment or acted with greater promptness." O. R., I, xii, pt. 2, contains a mass of relevant material.

POPE'S SECOND MANASSAS

projected against the screen of Lee's luminous mastery of the situation. Had Pope comprehended that as he had swung his main army back toward Gainesville, his forces stood between Jackson's and Longstreet's corps, and that by blocking Thoroughfare Gap, within easy reach, he could keep the two parts of the Confederate army divided, he might have won a tremendous victory. But erroneously thinking that Jackson was immobilized in the Manassas area and must entrench himself there, he decided to use all his forces to surround him. Instead of closing the Gap, he would move the army in three columns upon Manassas. "We shall bag the whole crowd, if they are prompt and expeditious," he crowed to Halleck.

When at noon on the 28th the first Union troops reached Manassas and halted amid the embers of the yet burning stores, they found it deserted. Whither had Stonewall fled? Pope was completely mystified. While he sought for intelligence, a report came that the Confederates were far north at Centreville, where they had cut the railroad to Alexandria. The army at once pushed on to Centreville, with Hooker and Heintzelman on the right, Sigel and Reynolds in the center, and McDowell on the left. Hooker reached the town late in the afternoon to find it deserted save for a few cavalry patrols. But suddenly the roar of cannon to the westward indicated that the left wing had found the Confederates. Around Groveton and toward Thoroughfare Gap, the flash and thud of artillery, rattle of musketry, and drift of smoke from distant woods indicated a fast-developing battle between McDowell and Jackson.

It was when he heard the news of this battle, shortly before 10 P.M., that Pope penned his last boastful dispatch. He thought that McDowell had intercepted the enemy retreat and that Jackson was at last trapped. Once more he miscalculated.[26] Jackson had no idea of retreating westward through the Gap; at that very moment Lee and Longstreet were moving through it eastward. As the bright sun of the 29th rose, the advance guard emerged well beyond the portal. Not only were all Pope's brilliant hopes dashed; he was put in the greatest danger, for while Longstreet thus broke through, fresh Union forces were slow in coming up, and were so ill coordinated that at the points of battle the Southern strength was superior.

Before noon on the 29th the whole Confederate panoply was on the field, with Lee, Jackson, and Longstreet now confident of victory. The Union army, on the other hand, was but half embattled, its brigades and divisions reaching the scene in hit or miss fashion, the generals in imperfect touch, most officers and men distrustful of Pope's capacity, and Fitz-John Porter's all-important corps not getting into action at all. As darkness fell, Pope had to confess that his efforts to crush Jackson had totally failed. Five successive assaults had broken down, with 8,000 Union soldiers killed or wounded. Not only had the Union army been worsted, but the stage had been set—though Pope did not realize it, for he did not even know that Lee had joined Jackson—for a greater defeat on the morrow.

At 2:30 that afternoon Lincoln had telegraphed McClellan another agonized appeal for news. From his safe coign at Alexandria, McClellan had returned the callous reply: "I am clear that one of two courses should be adopted. First to concentrate all our available forces to open communication with Pope. Second to leave Pope to get out of his scrape and at once use all our means to make the capital perfectly safe." [27] For himself, he favored the second course.

26 His staff and perhaps subordinate generals share the blame; K. P. Williams conjectures in *Lincoln Finds a General*, I, 320, 321, that inaccurate reports had reached him.
27 Lincoln, *Works*, V, 399.

Again on the 30th the fighting was terrible. Pope's half-shattered army badly needed rations, and his horses forage; he had both telegraphed and written urgently for them; but on this morning he got only a curt letter written by General Franklin at McClellan's order stating that goods would be loaded on wagons and cars at the Alexandria base if he sent back a cavalry escort to guard the train! [28] Still under the hallucination that he might crush a divided enemy, Pope ordered his hungry forces forward to the attack. Once more they made assault after assault until every division on the field had fought, and every division had been beaten back. The main reason for his failure was that his piecemeal deployment of his infantry never brought more than 20,000 into battle at once. As the last valiant charge broke down, Lee ordered his whole army to advance. Wave after wave of bayonets beat against the Northern positions, and as the Southerners came on like demons, the Union divisions stubbornly fell back.[29]

It was this Confederate advance amid the thundering guns which men standing on the Washington housetops divined; an advance which carried the surge of battle up to Henry Hill on the old Bull Run grounds. Here the Northern lines held, and as darkness fell Second Manassas ended in mutual exhaustion.

On Sunday, under a cold, drizzling rain, Pope's dejected troops filed into the old Confederate defenses about Centreville. Behind them they left more than mounds of slain and wounded; they left all the bright hopes with which the Union forces five months earlier had begun their advance on Richmond. All the fatigue, the sickness in malarial swamps, the toils under burning Virginia suns, the endless fighting, the mutilations, the deaths of hosts of comrades, were in vain. They were back just where they had started, discouraged, cynical, resentful. They knew that they had been betrayed; they looked to the future with dark foreboding. At the best a deep melancholy, at the worst a bitter hatred of their incompetent leaders, possessed them; but their determination to fight on never flagged.

[III]

Once more endless lists of the slain and wounded filled pages of the Northern dailies at a time. Some casualties had been brought off the field by

28 Pope said in his official report of the McClellan-Franklin message: "All hope of being able to maintain my position, whether victorious or not vanished with this letter. My cavalry was utterly broken down. . . . At the time this letter was written, Alexandria was swarming with troops, and my whole army was interposed between that place and the enemy." McClellan deliberately and brutally sacrificed him.
29 Henderson, II, 161-176, is supplemented by K. P. Williams, II, 320 ff.

the retreating Union forces. Long trains rolled into Alexandria and Washington with them, and meanwhile, trains of surgeons and nurses—one of them carried a thousand—crept south to Centreville. Pope's forces had of necessity left multitudes on the battleground, where Confederate surgeons were at first too busy with their own men to care for many Northern wounded. Later Lee had allowed Union ambulances on the field. Only sixty were sent, and they brought in but a small part of the stricken. The surgeons had neither time nor means to look after thousands who, with unstanched wounds, mortifying limbs, and severe shock, were dying by inches. Descriptions of that field offer as classic an indictment of the horrors of war as Henri Dunant's picture of Solferino. Over an extent five miles in length and three in width it was strewn with dead and wounded, lying sometimes in thick windrows. As late as Thursday, September 4, a week after the battle began, the *National Intelligencer* reported the estimate of one surgeon that 2,000 wounded had as yet received no succor.[30] One of the earliest workers on the scene was a devoted woman of Massachusetts birth, now resident in Washington, who had thrown all other activities aside to help organize the movement of supplies to wounded soldiers, and who later became first head of the American branch of the Red Cross which Dunant founded.

Clara Barton, heroically busy distributing supplies to the troops, went out the day after the battle ended to Fairfax, where the wounded were being brought down in ambulances and laid on the ground till they covered acres. Bales of hay for horses were broken apart to cover the wet earth. When night shut down with utter darkness Miss Barton's party had only one lantern. She obtained some candles, but the wind put them out every few minutes, and the wounded lay so thick—by midnight 3,000 of them, she thought—that she and her aides hardly dared take a step. "We had two water buckets, five dippers, the stores which we carried to eat, besides hard crackers, [and] my one stew pan which I remembered to take, and this made coffee for them. All night we made up compresses and slings, and bound up and wet wounds, when we could get water, fed what we could, travelled miles in the dark over those poor helpless creatures, in terror lest someone's candle fall into the hay and consume them all. Still the ambulances came down." They broke their bread into wine and water to help sinking wretches as the stretcher-bearers brought them in. "Oh," writes Miss Barton, "how I needed stores on that field." [31]

Louder than the cry of anguish in the North was the cry of anger; anger at the Administration for not uniting the armies in Virginia more swiftly;

30 This surgeon had left the battlefield Wednesday, Sept. 3. Confederates had done what they could to distribute hardtack and water.
31 Washington, Sept. 4, 1862, to John Shaver; extra-illustrated *Battles and Leaders,* HL.

anger at McClellan and his subordinates, especially Fitz-John Porter and Franklin, for not moving more promptly to Pope's aid; anger at Pope and Mc-Dowell for their incompetence. Ever since Cedar Mountain, Banks's men had cherished a fierce animosity toward Pope for pushing them into a trap. Other units were now equally angry. Reporters who talked with officers of all ranks in all corps found them unanimous in asserting that they must have a new commander. The army, they said—and so wrote home—demands a general. During the battle, McDowell at Groveton had ordered a brigade to advance to a position commanded on one side by woods swarming with the enemy. The incredulous brigadier made him repeat the order. A private blurted out in McDowell's face: "Don't the damned fool see that the Johnnies will flank us?" Inevitably, the brigade was flung back with heavy losses.[32] After the battle troops openly jeered McDowell. Whenever Pope appeared, a menacing rumble ran along the ranks. "I have lost a thousand men," said Carl Schurz, "and I dare not go into the hospital and look in the faces of those wounded, who, I know, have shed their blood bravely and in vain."

The troops, we repeat, wrote the facts home in letters which were passed from family to family, read aloud in country stores, and printed in local newspapers. Meanwhile, the press published home truths in scorching language. Ridiculing McClellan's idea that Lee had a magnificently equipped army of 200,000, the correspondents now had facts to show that all along he had really possessed fewer troops, with less artillery, arms, provisions, and transport, than the Union side. The unvarnished truth, wrote a *Tribune* reporter, is this: "We have been whipped by an inferior force of inferior men, better handled than ours." [33]

What particularly incensed Northern opinion, however, was not Pope's incompetence, but the willful limpness if not outright treachery of other officers. They would rather lose battles and sacrifice troops than abandon their jealousies. This was a portentous development, suggesting something rotten at the heart of American democracy, and raising question of a fatal flaw in the national character.

What was the evidence? Even after McClellan's late start, the earliest corps of the Army of the Potomac, under Fitz-John Porter, had reached Aquia in fairly good season. Burnside, who had come thither from Fort Monroe, ordered it forward to join Pope. Other troops in the Army of the Potomac, except for Keyes's corps, which was left to garrison Yorktown, came slowly up the

32 MS Diary, Capt. Robert Taggard, Ninth Pa. Reserve Infantry, Pa. State Hist. Lib.
33 Schurz to a war correspondent in camp near the Chain Bridge, N. Y. *Tribune*, Sept. 5, 1862; Bragg, Sept. 13, 1862, Bragg Papers, Wis. State Hist. Lib.; N. Y. *Tribune* reporter, Sept. 7; Ropes, *Civil War*, II, 276–338, and K. P. Williams, *op. cit.* I, Ch. XII, cover Pope's confusions in detail.

Potomac to Alexandria, and Halleck at first sent them to Pope's aid by direct orders to the corps commanders. But after McClellan arrived on August 26 at Alexandria, Halleck gave orders through him; and glass could not have stopped electricity more effectively than McClellan stopped some of Halleck's most pressing demands. A sequence of messages will demonstrate the fact:

Halleck by telegraph to McClellan 10 A.M. August 27: "Franklin's corps should march in that direction [Manassas] as soon as possible."

McClellan at 1:15 P.M. August 27 to Halleck: "Franklin's artillery has no horses, except for four guns without caissons. I can pick up no cavalry. . . . Can Franklin, without his artillery or cavalry, effect any useful purpose in front? Should not Burnside at once take steps to evacuate Falmouth and Aquia, at the same time covering the retreat of any of Pope's troops who may fall back in that direction? I do not see that we have force enough on hand to form a connection with Pope, whose exact position we do not know. Are we safe in the direction of the Valley?"

Halleck on the morning of August 28 to General Franklin: "On parting with Gen. McClellan, about two o'clock this morning, it was understood that you were to move with your corps today toward Manassas Junction, to drive the enemy from the railroad. I have just learned that the General has not returned to Alexandria. If you have not received his order, act on this."

McClellan at 1:05 on August 28 to Halleck: "Your dispatch to Franklin received. I have been doing all possible to hurry artillery and cavalry. The moment Franklin can be started with a reasonable amount of artillery he shall go."

Halleck at 3:30 P.M. August 28 to McClellan: "Not a moment must be lost in pushing as large a force as possible toward Manassas, so as to communicate with Pope before the enemy is reinforced."

McClellan at 4:45 P.M. on August 28 to Halleck: "Neither Franklin's nor Sumner's corps is now in condition to move out and fight a battle. It would be a sacrifice to send them out now. . . . I still think that a premature movement in small force will accomplish nothing but the destruction of the troops sent out." [34]

In the end Franklin and his corps got only as far as Annandale, a mere start toward Manassas. And Fitz-John Porter, if Pope's charges were to be believed, delayed shamefully the first day of battle, mishandled his men, and let one brigade at the crisis of the conflict avoid any fighting whatever. Later he offered a defence based largely on a conflict of opinion over orders; but was it valid? [35]

No wonder that Lincoln that black Saturday night, August 30, let his

[34] Dispatches from which these excerpts are taken were first printed, with others of the same purport, in *Report, Committee on Conduct of War*, I, 456–470.

[35] Jacob D. Cox, *Second Battle of Bull Run as Connected with the Porter Case*; Otto Eisenschiml, *The Celebrated Case of Fitz-John Porter*, take opposed views. Porter has left a MS defense in his papers.

wrath against McClellan blaze forth. No wonder that Pope next day, watching his exhausted ranks limp through the rain into the works at Bull Run, winced at sight of the spruce figure of General Samuel D. Sturgis, of Franklin's corps, his uniform unstained by battle. They were old Missouri rivals. "Too late, Sammy, too late!" called Pope in a voice of despair. And from Sturgis came an expression of McClellan's own malevolence: "I always told you that if they gave you rope enough you would hang yourself!" [36]

Why these attitudes? Fundamentally, because of that want of discipline, deeply felt patriotism, and selfless dedication to great causes which was an unmistakable canker in the overhasty, overmaterialistic growth of the country. Some of the jealousies had begun at West Point, but most of them had originated in the war. McClellan knew well that if Pope won a dramatic victory, then Pope might be given command of the combined armies in Virginia. The idea was intolerable to him. Just before the battle, on the 24th, he had written his wife: "I don't see how I can remain in the service if placed under Pope; it would be too great a disgrace. . . ." If he did not consciously wish Pope to fail so that he might emerge as the rescuer of the nation, subconsciously that was his desire, and he acted throughout on the callous principle of letting Pope, as he put it, get out of his scrape as best he could. Later that same day he sent his wife more of his wishful thinking: "They will suffer a terrible defeat if the present state of affairs continues. I *know* that with God's help I can save them. . . ." Porter shared his views, felt a passionate hatred of abolitionists, and longed for the humiliation of Stanton.[37]

[IV]

In this war, however, some of the greatest battles were fought not on hill or plain, but in cabinet chamber and government offices. While the dead of Second Manassas still lay unburied, and while Lee was swinging his victorious legions toward the invasion of Maryland, Lincoln won a moral victory so far-reaching that history should not fail to take due account of it. Against the somber stormclouds of vanity, selfishness, and malice raised by military leaders, the President gave the nation a lightning flash of magnanimity, patriotism, and courage so swift that the rush of events obscured it.

As the streets of Washington filled with ambulances bearing wounded, and as the press began publishing dispatches and editorials condemning the army

36　Jacob Piccard, MS Life of Sigel.
37　McClellan, *Own Story*, 472–521, covers this lamentable chapter. See also Peter S. Michie's indictment in *General McClellan*, 381–392, written by an officer and military expert who knew the general well. McDowell's condemnation of both McClellan and Porter may be found in Warden, *Chase*, 460.

leaders, Cabinet sentiment against McClellan boiled over. Stanton declared to his colleagues that he could no longer bear his intolerable burdens if he had to struggle against the general; that he could not and would not endure him; that Lincoln must dismiss him forthwith. He wrote a memorandum embodying these ideas which he showed to Chase, who was equally incensed, and who besought Gideon Welles to sign. "McClellan ought to be shot!" exclaimed Chase. Welles refused, primarily on the ground that the procedure seemed discourteous to the President. Thereupon Attorney-General Bates revised the protest against continuing McClellan in command, and in its softened form he, Stanton, Smith, and Chase all signed it. Though Welles still abstained he was sympathetic, and promised that when he conferred with Lincoln he would endorse the main sentiments of the paper.[38]

That Lincoln's anger burned deeply is unquestionable. He told the Cabinet just after the battle that McClellan's conduct had been "shocking" and "atrocious." The general, he remarked to John Hay, *wanted* Pope to fail: "This is unpardonable." He appreciated the desire of most Administration supporters, as of the Cabinet, to see McClellan sent home in disgrace.[39]

But Lincoln faced a crisis. The Union troops simply would not follow Pope or McDowell. Scattered, in part exhausted, bitterly discouraged, they could not be pulled together and reanimated by a Burnside or Franklin, a Sumner or Heintzelman. And the army must have a leader instantly, for the continuing emergency brooked no delay. Union generals might doze between battles, but Lee was an unsleeping tiger. While Second Manassas still reeked of blood and smoke, he launched his new stroke. Determined to keep the initiative, hopeful that Union disorganization would give him opportunity for another brilliant strategic stroke, cherishing the belief that large Maryland elements were ready to spring to his side, and realizing that he dared not attack Washington, he resolved to turn westward, open a new base in the Shenandoah Valley, and cross the Mason and Dixon Line. Ill prepared as he was, he lost not a single day.

To meet him, to strike back, to save the North, Lincoln put aside all animosities and resentments; his one thought was for the Union, and to save it he would make any sacrifice. "If McClellan will win victories," he had told Hay long before, "I will hold his stirrup." Only McClellan now could recall stragglers, reorganize the divided forces, and restore morale—for most of the men trusted him. The Army of the Potomac had never lost faith, and a majority of Pope's Army of Virginia were eager to turn to a commander who, whatever

38 Welles, *Diary*, I, 92–106.
39 Cabinet feeling is treated in Welles, *ut sup.*; Seward, *Seward at Washington*, 126–127; Hay, *Letters and Diaries*, 49; Chase, *Inside Lincoln's Cabinet*, 116–119; and Flower, *Stanton*, 178–181.

his lack of fighting edge, was always considerate of his troops. A passionate President, an Andrew Jackson, would have given way to his personal anger; a weak President, a James Buchanan, would have bent to Congressional and Cabinet pressure. Lincoln rose above such frailty to answer the nation's need.

When the first Cabinet meeting after Second Manassas took place September 2, with Seward absent, it was electric with tensions. As the members gathered before Lincoln came in, Stanton announced in a voice choked with emotion that the President had just notified McClellan to take command of all the forces about Washington. No formal reappointment as head of the Army of the Potomac was needed, for he had never lost this command. He had reestablished himself at his old quarters on Pennsylvania Avenue. General astonishment greeted the news. Amid dismayed murmurs, Lincoln seated himself, and began sadly to explain his action. He knew how culpable McClellan was, he said, but the general was needed: he was good at defense, he was an expert engineer, and he excelled in organizing capacity. Halleck had approved of the step.

Stanton's angry dismay was patent. Chase stormily declared that he was certain McClellan's retention would prove a national calamity. "Much was said," records Welles. "There was a more disturbed and desponding feeling than I have ever witnessed in council; the President was greatly distressed." No doubt Lincoln was distressed beyond measure. But in this decision he proved how completely he could rise above past resentments. He proved that he was determined to be commander-in-chief, and would not let Stanton usurp that position. He proved that he would not let Congressional radicals dictate war policy. Above all, he proved that in everything he would act with single-minded devotion to the best interests of the republic.

Pope was immediately informed that, his army having been consolidated with the Army of the Potomac, he should report to the War Department for orders; and he was soon bound for a routine post in the Northwest. He departed burning with hatred of the man who, he believed, had ruined him. "The greatest criminal," he wrote Halleck, "is McClellan." One of his staff published in the New York *Herald* of September 7 a defense of his commander combined with an attack on others unnamed. All Pope's movements, he wrote, had been dependent on support and reinforcements at fixed times and places—and again and again the support had failed. The country eagerly read the official report which Pope published four days later, reflecting severely on McClellan and most of his corps commanders. All these generals except Sumner, wrote Pope, had hung back, insisting that their commands were too dispirited since they left Harrison's Landing to fight; though events showed that the rank and file, when put to the test, fought with energy. Pope

The undersigned, who have been honored with your selection, as a part of your confidential advisers, deeply impressed with our great responsibility, in the present crisis, do but perform a painful duty in declaring to you our deliberate opinion that, at this time, it is not safe to entrust to Major General McClellan the command of any Army of the United States.

And, we hold ourselves ready, at any time, to explain to you in detail, the reasons upon which this opinion is founded.

To the President.

Edwin M Stanton
Secretary of War

S. P. Chase
Sec'y of the Treasury

Caleb B Smith
Secy. Interior.

Edw Bates.
Atty Genl.

UNDATED LETTER BY STANTON, CHASE, BATES, AND
CALEB B. SMITH, IN THE STANTON COLLECTION,
LIBRARY OF CONGRESS

leveled his gravest accusations against Fitz-John Porter. That leader, he stated, had been given written orders to attack the Confederates in flank; had he obeyed them the Union army would have destroyed Jackson; but after merely touching the enemy flank, he remained inert. Thus was launched a famous controversy that was to occupy public attention for decades. Much has been said in Porter's defence, and part of it is valid. Much of the evidence, however, strongly suggests that he felt at least a subconscious wish to serve McClellan before he served Pope or the country: McClellan of dark impulses and dark delays.

But Lincoln knew that he had done right. He summed up the situation in a single sentence to John Hay: "McClellan has acted badly in this matter, but we must use what tools we have." The country's great need remained just what it had been—a victory. But the underlying strategic situation had dramatically changed since May; instead of hoping for victory in a great offensive, men now had to hope for victory in a desperate defensive.

40 Pope had grounds for his hostility toward McClellan and Fitz-John Porter, but he had no basis for the rancorous feeling he later expressed toward Lincoln. The essential littleness of the man appears in the expressions of antagonism he sent his father-in-law V. B. Horton, a Representative in Congress; see especially a bitter letter of March 9, 1863, N. Y. Hist. Soc., accusing Lincoln of letting him be traduced and maligned while "the very men who betrayed their country and produced the disasters for which the country was denouncing me, were rewarded with the very object for which they perpetrated their treachery."

8

On Capitol Hill

THROUGHOUT spring and summer the news of battle had held every eye, so that people paid scant attention to civil affairs. Yet Congress was hard at work, and it ended one of the most constructive sessions of its history on July 17, 1862. The session had begun in angry gloom as the two chambers acted to expel disloyal members and inquire into the disaster at Ball's Bluff; it ended in gloomy anger as Zack Chandler made the Senate ring with his arguments laying the recent defeats at McClellan's tent door. Its own record, however, was brilliant, for it had opened a new chapter of national affairs by a dozen enactments of far-reaching social and economic import. It was the first Congress, as an Ohio Representative said, whose vision embraced the entire continent. Sumner, sending the Duchess of Argyll a list of the achievements, pronounced them sufficient to mark an epoch.[1]

The Republican majority, which had restricted itself to imperative war measures in the brief session of Bull Run days, now became a harvest force garnering the sheaves of party victory. Measure after measure that had been unattainable so long as Southerners held their seats went on the statute books. Land for the landless, higher tariffs, a national foundation for colleges of agriculture and the mechanic arts, the Pacific railroad, and an agricultural bureau or department were gains securely seized; and meanwhile blow after blow was leveled at slavery. The steps taken ranged from the establishment of a new arsenal at Rock Island to recognition of the black republics of Haiti and Liberia. The mood underlying Congressional action was sometimes sternly realistic, sometimes idealistic, sometimes both. It was realism to issue $300,000,-000 in greenbacks and make them legal tender;[2] it was idealism to create schools for colored children in Washington and Georgetown; while the Pacific railway was romance and realism combined.

Direct leadership in Congress was furnished not by the President in any such degree as Polk had exercised it in his littler war, but by the principal

---

1 A. G. Riddle, *Recs. of War Times*, 69 ff.; Sumner, Boston, Aug. 11, 1862, HL.
2 Congress did this in two steps, February and July; cf. Blaine, *Twenty Years*, I, Ch. XX.

committees and their chairmen—with whom he kept in rapport. The most powerful Senators remained Sumner, Fessenden, Trumbull, John P. Hale, and Henry Wilson, heads respectively of the committees on foreign relations, finance, judiciary, naval affairs, and military affairs; the most powerful Representatives were Speaker Galusha M. Grow, Thaddeus Stevens, John J. Crittenden, F. P. Blair, Jr., and Charles R. Sedgwick, the last four being heads of the ways and means, foreign affairs, military affairs, and naval affairs committees. With them should be named the men who gave a stern assessment to military operations—Senators Ben Wade and Zack Chandler, and Representatives John Covode and George W. Julian of the Committee on the Conduct of the War. Of the fourteen named, one was crooked, half were timeservers, and fully half were mediocrities; but four, Sumner, Trumbull, Crittenden, and Thaddeus Stevens were leaders of principle and of some statesmanlike vision, while Grow, Fessenden, and Henry Wilson, all earnest, capable, and honest-hearted, held highly creditable places. Wilson, in fact, was endlessly useful.[3]

Parties were in chaos when Congress met, and the session did little to fix firm lines. Radical Republicans, conservative Republicans, War Democrats, Peace Democrats, Lincoln-haters and Lincoln-defenders, made up an assemblage defying clear analysis. At the outset Joshua Speed, Lincoln's intimate friend, was fearful that a large party of Republican extremists was being organized to combat the President, and urged Joseph Holt to help form a coalition of conservative Republicans and War Democrats to resist them. This fear proved exaggerated, for the Congressional radicals never had enough public support to control the government, and they knew it. However abusive of Lincoln such men as Chandler and Thaddeus Stevens might be in private talk, they did not yet dare an open encounter with him. The caustic Stevens, in fact, served Lincoln well on many issues. His hardworking partnership with Chase in dealing with unprecedented financial problems was invaluable, and his rough treatment of Peace Democrats and Border obstructionists on the House floor sometimes gave the President satisfaction. Speed's suggested coalition was unworkable and unnecessary. On the main party program, apart from slavery issues, the conservative and radical Republicans labored well in harness. Lincoln never put either group into a position where it had to choose between fighting him or surrendering its vital principles, and hence neither was tempted to join hands with an undependable Democratic faction.

For "undependable" best characterized the Democratic membership of

3 E. H. Stiles, *Public Men of Early Iowa*, quotes Senator James W. Grimes of Iowa as saying that Fessenden was the greatest man in the Senate; he was certainly indispensable in financial affairs. Hale of New Hampshire took a large fee from a contractor who was later convicted of defrauding the government. He had sold his influence; but it should not be forgotten that he was the Senator who had flogging abolished in the navy.

Congress. Had Douglas survived, his skill, determination, and forensic power, his devotion to the Union, and his personal respect for Lincoln, would have given the minority party a constructive role it never played. Since his death no Democrat possessed sufficient foresight and ability to recall his fellows to Jacksonian principles. George H. Pendleton of Cincinnati, one of Douglas' best aides in the battle against Lecompton, a finely educated man now in his third term, rejected the opportunity; resenting the defeat of the Crittenden Compromise and the refusal to let the Southern sisters go in peace, he became a mere obstructionist. The witty S. S. Cox of Columbus in the same State followed a more positive path, steadily voting for supplies of men and money, but he lacked force, was anxious to end the war on any basis maintaining the Union, and kept on cordial personal terms with the egregious Clement L. Vallandigham of the Dayton district. Though able and useful in marshalling the War Democrats, and witty in debate, he could not be called a commanding leader. In the Senate, Crittenden was too old to be effective, James A. Bayard opposed every important war measure, and Garrett Davis of Kentucky showed a weathercock changeability which robbed him of all influence.[4]

The most irresponsible of the Democrats, Vallandigham, made personal capital of his party's confusion. A handsome, fluent exhibitionist, and a life-long dissenter on all kinds of questions, he was swayed more by Southern sympathies and love of notoriety than by any patriotic considerations. All his views were short-term views. He saw that by adoption of a firm support of Lincoln's war measures the party would suffer temporary eclipse. He did not realize that a strong body of War Democrats would be able by 1864 to compel Lincoln and his associates to accept a Union Party in place of the Republican Party—as Lincoln tried to do anyhow; he did not see that while War Democrats would have a good chance of recapturing the government soon after the inevitable Northern victory, the discredited Peace Democrats would wander in the wilderness for twenty years. In February he brought forward a scheme of reconstruction so absurdly unworkable and so patently designed to protect slavery that it met universal derision. He also arranged a House caucus in which thirty-one Democrats, by signing a compact to act together, bartered away their individual freedom for a worthless show of party unity. This group was thereafter an impediment, not an asset, to the nation.[5]

4 A vehement Unionist for a time, Davis was later the subject of a motion for expulsion because of alleged disloyalty; Coulter, *Kentucky*, 209.

5 Riddle, *Recs.*, Ch. XX. The wealthy, aristocratic Bayard would gladly have made peace on the basis of Confederate independence.

[I]

While Lincoln, endlessly occupied with the war, offered meager direct leadership on any subject but compensated emancipation, he did furnish general guidance, letting the influential men of Congress know by tactful pressure what he desired. He had been a Congressman himself, and knew their hopes and fears. In the control of government patronage he had a large source of strength. He took time month by month to study appointments in relation to the desires of members of the House and Senate; and by choosing a minister from one area, a postmaster elsewhere, a marshal or collector in another place, he bulwarked his own position as head of the party. It became more and more a national Lincoln party and less a federation of State organizations. However unsavory the work, he would not commit J. Q. Adams' error of neglecting it. He welcomed calls by men on the Hill, and if some came as seldom as Thad Stevens, others were as frequent visitors as Sumner. Contrary to a general view, he showed quite as much skilled leadership in cooperating with organization men as in direct addresses to Congress and people.[6]

He spoke consistently for moderate policies, following the principle which he stated to Zach Chandler: "I hope to 'stand firm' enough not to go backward, and yet not go forward fast enough to wreck the country's cause." He tried always to be reasonable. It is not strange that even amid recurrent disasters his prestige with other reasonable men steadily mounted; rather, it would have been marvelous had it not. Conservatives valued his moderation in proportion as they feared the incendiaries, while radicals valued it in proportion as they feared the diehards. He disliked flamboyant measures—and so did the country. When George W. Julian urged him to "stir" advanced groups by giving Frémont another command, he dryly remarked that this would irritate large conservative groups, and that his own emancipation proclamation had proved less "stirring" than many had hoped. In perilous times a democracy best trusts the cautious statesman.

Another element in Lincoln's popular strength was his manifest devotion to all his duties. He toiled nearly to exhaustion, giving an average of not less than fourteen hours a day, as Greeley recorded, to his public functions— not including state dinners. It was said that he entered the White House conservatory only once in his four years. His life, as John Hay testifies, was

6 Harry J. Carman and Reinhard H. Luthin, *Lincoln and the Patronage*, describe Lincoln's adroit use of patronage throughout the war; William B. Hesseltine, *Lincoln and the War Governors*, deals with his construction of a national party organization independent of State machines. David Donald in *Lincoln Reconsidered* calls him a politicians' politician, and this view is emphasized in Richard N. Current's *The Lincoln Nobody Knows*.

almost devoid of recreation, and most evenings he spent in his office, working or conferring with business callers. With difficulty his wife would sometimes carry him to Shakespeare or a concert. He felt keenly his responsibility as military commander-in-chief as well as head of the civil government, studying military treatises, scrutinizing every important dispatch from the field to the War Department, talking with generals, and making himself almost a one-man bureau for the examination of new weapons which offered some promise of shortening the contest. Endorsements on papers of the quartermaster bureau, some never published, show his interest in the flow of supplies. He was not a talented administrator, deputed labor poorly, and never organized the office of the President as it needed to be organized for war; but his vigilant attention to business was untiring.

His happiest moments were the rare occasions when a few intimates gathered after dinner in his office and he relaxed in political gossip and general talk, telling stories and giving his humor and surprisingly ready wit—for he spoke of himself as a slow thinker—free scope. In such a group he would talk of critical military and political affairs with complete candor, stating his opinion of men and events in plain prairie language, and it speaks well for his judgment of friends that his confidence was never abused. Sometimes he was glad to be repeated. When he told a correspondent of S. L. M. Barlow, "My idea of this war is that it should always have a peace in its belly," he knew that the statement would soon be circulated in the Barlow-Manton Marble-Samuel J. Tilden circle.[7] It amounted to a declaration that, once assured of maintenance of the Union, he would gladly consider a negotiated peace.

As he had faith in the people, so the people gathered faith in him. "This is essentially a people's war," he had told Congress when it first met after Sumter. It was a contest, he went on, for that form of government which would elevate the condition of all men—and he was "most happy to believe that the plain people understand and appreciate this."[8] He kept the White House doors excessively open to the people. At any time he could have lightened his burden by a simple refusal to see callers except at certain hours and upon business of public importance, but as fast as his secretaries tried to erect barriers he himself broke them down. Once when Henry Wilson remonstrated, he replied: "They don't want much; they get but little, and I must see them."

7 Julian in A. T. Rice, ed., *Rems. of Lincoln*, Ch. IX; Robert V. Bruce, *Lincoln and the Tools of War*; Greeley in N. Y. *Tribune*, Sept. 28, 1863; Hay in *Century Magazine*, XLI (Nov., 1890), 33-37. Carl Sandburg's *Lincoln: The War Years, passim*, is a rich treasury of material.

8 *Works*, VI, 320.

He even saw men who came to beg trifling positions as messengers, watchmen, and clerks, and devised his own plan for getting rid of them without illfeeling. Assistant Secretary Harrington in the Treasury Department found squads of them descending upon him with Presidential chits. One day at the White House he expostulated, saying that Lincoln ought not to spend time on such matters, and that he had no more places. "Why, bless you," said the President, with a twinkle. "Did you suppose I expected you to appoint everyone bringing you a note? Why, but for you and General Ramsey at the Arsenal I should die. One week I send all such applicants to you, and the next to General Ramsey."

Although Hay thought that the swarms of visitors wore upon him and aged him before his time, it seems perfectly clear that they more often refreshed him. He liked the chance of hearing about some old friend, as when one caller proved to be a daughter of Henry M. Luckett, who used to preach in Springfield; "a tall angular man like I am," said Lincoln, "and I used to be mistaken for him in the streets." He liked the opportunity for a merry quip. Once a solemn Buffalo citizen in the reception line ejaculated, "Up my way we believe in God and President Lincoln," to which Lincoln responded: "My friend, you are more than half right." On another occasion, at a time when the army complained of financial delays, a paymaster in major's regalia appeared in the reception line. "Being in Washington," he explained, "I have called to pay my respects." "From what I hear," rejoined Lincoln, "I guess that's all any of you do pay." He liked sometimes to cross his legs and have his talk out, as when he kept Governor Buckingham of Connecticut waiting more than a half hour so that he could enjoy his chat with that interesting Negro, Frederick Douglass. What aged him more than his burdens was such harsh talk as he heard from General Butler:

I said [writes Butler]: "Yes, Mr. President, the bounties which are now being paid to new recruits cause very large desertions. Men desert and go home, and get the bounties and enlist in other regiments." "That is too true," he replied, "but how can we prevent it?" "By vigorously shooting every man who is caught as a deserter until it is found to be a dangerous business." A saddened, weary look came over his face which I had never seen before, and he slowly replied, "You may be right—probably are so; but God help me, how can I have a butcher's day every Friday in the Army of the Potomac?" [9]

Above all, the clear logic and even temper of Lincoln's state papers and letters, his elevation, magnanimity, and kindliness, and his evident desire not

[9] Quotations from Daniel W. Voorhees, Frederick Douglass, and Butler in Rice, ed., *Rems. of Abraham Lincoln.* Hay, *ut sup.*, admits that Lincoln listened with the eagerness of a fascinated child to Garfield's graphic account of Chickamauga, and always delighted in the wise and witty talk of three tars, Dahlgren, Gustavus V. Fox, and Henry A. Wise. The papers of George Harrington, HL, contain his story.

to make smart points or win rhetorical triumphs, but to reason with fair-minded people and convince them, steadily won sensible men to his side. "If ever there could be a proper time for mere catch arguments, that time is surely not now," he wrote in his December message of 1862. "In times like the present, men should utter nothing for which they would not willingly be responsible through time and eternity." His letter to Greeley this summer assuring the editor that his overriding purpose was to save the Union, and that he would free none of the slaves, or part of them, or all of them, as his action might best serve that purpose, was memorable not only in its immediate logic, but in its demonstration of power to pierce to the heart of national perplexities, and resolution to cling to his purpose. He was always ready to admit his fallibility. In this same letter he told the editor: "I shall correct errors when shown to be errors, and I shall adopt new views so fast as they shall appear to be true views." His frequent references to God, or to the will of the Almighty, were coupled with an admission that no man could grasp the divine intent. "In the present war," he wrote in a scrap of religious meditation dated September 30, 1862, a prelude to the Second Inaugural, "it is quite possible that God's purpose is something different from the purpose of either party; and yet the human instrumentalities, working just as they do, are the best adaptation to effect his purpose." [10]

He occasionally expressed his profound sense of duty, avowing that he could never betray "so vast and so sacred a trust as these free people have confided to me." But he never thought that this gave him license to abuse honest opponents. He had only one political test: let men help carry the war for the Union to success, and they might quarrel with him on any other issue whatever. If they would only vote supplies of men and money, discourage desertions, and encourage enlistments, he would admit their right to support slavery, defend State rights, oppose tariff changes, and denounce the home-stead bill. Party differences were to him not merely permissible, but a necessity. "We cannot have free government without elections," he said; nor, he would have added, without Congressional battles. If dangerous men spoke up in debate, everyone would soon know their badness: "What kills the skunk is the publicity it gives itself." [11]

And the country chuckled over the sayings with which he spiced his large purposefulness. Men repeated appreciatively his remark that if McClellan was not going to use the army, he would like to borrow it a while. They relished his comment to a gentleman requesting a pass to Richmond: he had given McClellan more than 200,000 men with passes to the city, but

10 Lapsley, *Collected Works*, V, 535; Nicolay and Hay, *Complete Works*, VIII, 52.
11 Sandburg, *War Years*, II, 186.

not one had yet got there. They appreciated such fair hits as his statement to Montgomery Blair about his irascible brother Frank: "He has abundant talent —quite enough to occupy all his time without devoting any to temper." It was an equally fair hit to tell the unco-guid people who warned him about Grant's drinking: "If I knew what brand of whisky he drinks I would send a barrel or so to some other generals." This had the more force because it came from a rigid abstainer. "I am not a temperance man," he said, "but I am temperate to this extent: I don't drink." He remarked of the Congressional scolds and newspaper termagants who abused him only to a safe point: "Mrs. Grundy will talk, but she knows enough not to scald her bottom in her own pot." How apt, too, his little stories were! The one he told when, to his great relief, heavy firing was heard from Burnside's beleaguered army in Knoxville, had perhaps been related earlier of other imperiled forces. "A neighbor of mine in Menard Country," it ran, "named Sally Ward, had a very large family of children that she took very little care of. Whenever she heard one of them yelling in some out-of-the-way place she would say, 'Thank the Lord! there's one of my young ones not dead yet.' " [12]

While partisan haters of Lincoln abounded, and innumerable denunciatory or disparaging remarks might be quoted from editorials, speeches, and letters, two cardinal facts steadily added to his strength. The first was that close associates almost universally recognized his superiority. "He is the best of us all," Seward wrote, and the Secretary's biographer records: "The President was the only member of the administration whom Seward praised often." Welles could be critical, but was certain that the future would recognize his greatness: "The Cabinet, if a little discordant in some of its elements, has been united as regards him." Chase alone thought that *he* would make a better President. The other fact was that a tide of growing popular regard set in his favor. In general, to see him was to like him. Now and then a man took from his presence an unhappy impression. Henry Lee of Boston, for example, Governor Andrew's military aide, wrote his wife in the fall of 1861:

Then to the President's, where I waited in his room for one hour and a half while he slowly disposed of one caller after another.

He is enormously tall and bent and slab-sided and ungainly, his eyes are dead, his cheeks hollow, his skin gummy and sallow, his beard thin, and that and his hair dyed apparently.

His talk is shrewd and vulgar (not profane but uneducated) and as I sat there

12 For the comment on McClellan see Barton, *Lincoln*, II, 394; on Frank Blair, *Works*, VI, 555; on Grant, Nicolay and Hay, *History*, VII, 154; on temperance, B. A. Ulrich, *Abraham Lincoln*, 7; on Mrs. Grundy, Barlow Papers; on Sally Ward, Nicolay and Hay, *Lincoln*, VIII, 178.

I grew more and more cross to think that this Western mummy of a railsplitter should sit in Washington's chair. He seems like a perfectly honest and quite intelligent man.[13]

The highly perceptive attorney and diarist of New York, George Templeton Strong, saw the President far more clearly. He and other Sanitary Commission executives had an hour's relaxed talk in the White House at the end of January, 1862. Lincoln, manifestly enjoying it, stopped several movements of the group toward an exit by a little incident he recalled, or an anecdote he had "heered" in Illinois. He had little outward polish, spoke of "humans," and even used Sangamon Valley grammar. But Strong pronounced him "a most sensible, straightforward, honest old codger," "the best President we have had since Andrew Jackson at least," and a man whose evident integrity and simplicity of purpose would compensate for any amount of rusticity. He quoted the President: "I hain't been caught lying yet, and I don't mean to be." A bright young friend of Strong's who some months earlier had called Lincoln a "gorilla ape" had now learned enough to praise him as the most honest and patriotic man in the Administration.[14] Personal documents of the time, in fact, are studded with expressions of a growing faith. Josephine Shaw wrote in her diary May 22, 1862:

Yesterday we had a beautiful and touching proclamation from Lincoln, rendering Gen. Hunter's order freeing the slaves in North Carolina, South Carolina, and Georgia, null and void. One of the most extraordinary things that has happened for a long time was the calmness with which the order was received. We have certainly advanced in the year. The confidence in the President was shown by the entire acquiescence in everything he does. We feel that he is earnest and means to do right. A unique man. . . . As mother says, if his luck proves equal to his goodness, he's a paragon.

And John M. Palmer wrote a friend from Huntsville, Alabama, July 4, 1862:

I fully agree with you in regard to President Lincoln. I do not believe on the whole we could have a better man for the crisis. A brilliant man would have ruined the country long ago. On thinking over the list of Presidents our nation has had since its birthday, I cannot think of one with qualities better suited, all things considered, for the helm than Old Abe.[15]

"He never rubbed Congress the wrong way," Speaker Grow remarked of Lincoln. "He was masterful in diplomacy as in politics." Of course he repeatedly did rub Congress the wrong way, but never in such wise as to

13 Seward's opinion, Bancroft, *Seward*, II, 358; Welles's opinion, *Diary*, I, 500; Henry Lee, Washington, Nov. 2, 1861, to his wife, Henry Lee Papers, MHS.
14 Strong, *Diary*, III, 204, 218, 243.
15 Palmer Papers, Ill. State Hist. Lib.

leave any deep rancor. While in vital matters he had his way, he forced no humiliating capitulations; as he put it, he never planted a thorn in another man's pillow.

Yet his outward suavity was controlled by an iron resolution, and he was capable of bolder action than a Cromwell. Underneath half the debates of the session ran an implied discussion of the basic question: Where did the Constitution place the ultimate sovereignty in waging war and controlling reconstruction? On this subject Lincoln was granite. Final powers lay in the Presidency. Thad Stevens, applying to the suppression of rebellion the clause which authorized Congress to make all laws necessary and proper for carrying into execution its stated authority, declared that the two houses "possess all the powers now claimed under the Constitution, even the tremendous power of dictatorship." Sumner made the same sweeping assertion. "I claim for Congress all that belongs to any government in the exercise of the right of war," he said, adding, "it is by an act of Congress that the war powers are set in motion. When once in motion the President must execute them. But he is only the instrument of Congress under the Constitution of the United States." This went further than Henry Wilson's declaration that Congress was to make the laws defining policy, and the Executive was simply to administer them: "I had rather give a policy to the President of the United States than to take a policy from the President of the United States." But it was no more drastic than the statement by Lyman Trumbull that inasmuch as the President was a mere executor of Congressional law, "He is just as subject to our control as if we appointed him, except that we cannot remove him and appoint another in his place." [16]

These arrogant declarations in Congress presaged an opening of the conflict that was not to close until Cleveland successfully defied the Tenure of Office Act. Lincoln intended to resist such views to the bitter end. But he provoked no immediate collision. Instead, he at first merely inspired his warm friend Orville H. Browning, repeatedly his Senate spokesman, to make a speech defining his position. War, Browning said, vastly enlarged the powers of government.[17] "But is Congress the government?" It was not. "All the powers that Congress possess are those granted in the Constitution." He denied Fessenden's assertion that Congress held unlimited authority, for "it is invested with the absolute power of war." This, he commented, "is as broad and deep a foundation for absolute despotism as was ever laid." If the President ever abused the war powers, Browning pointed out, he was

16 *Cong. Globe*, 37th Cong., 2d Sess., 440 (Stevens); 2972 (Sumner); 2734 (Wilson); 2973 (Trumbull).
17 *Ibid.*, 1136.

answerable, when peace returned, to the civil authority for his excesses. But if Congress "usurps and prostitutes them the liberty of the citizen is overthrown, and he is helpless, without remedy for his grievances."

And soon afterward, Browning delivered an even more direct statement of Lincoln's views. He declared: "When the Constitution made the President commander-in-chief of the army and navy of the United States, it clothed him with the incidental powers necessary to a full, faithful, and forceful performance of the duties of that high office; and to decide what are military necessities, and to devise and to execute the requisite measures to meet them, is one of these incidents. It is not legislative, but an executive function, and Congress has nothing to do with it." [18]

In this conflict between Congress and the Executive, however, Lincoln was more interested in acts than in words. While Sumner and Stevens were dreaming of dictatorial powers, he was ready to checkmate them with the astuteness of a consummate master of the political chessboard. He was determined to keep the vital questions of slavery and reconstruction—questions affecting the whole future of the republic—in his hands and beyond the grip of the radicals. In March, 1862, he appointed Andrew Johnson military governor of Tennessee, instructing him to bring as much of the State as possible under Union authority; and at the same time he named similar governors for Louisiana, Arkansas, and North Carolina. In the Senate, Sumner offered a resolution demanding that the President revoke this action. [19] While Lincoln's friends blocked Sumner, the President was pressing his plan for ending slavery in the borderland; and when that failed, he took the breath of Congress away with his message of July 14 offering a draft bill for compensated emancipation in *all* slave States. Some Senators at once raised a question of the President's right to introduce a bill.

His boldest assertion of Presidential power against Congress, however, lay in his handling of the confiscation bill. By preparing a veto message and letting members know that he was ready to use it, he compelled a removal of the features that he found objectionable. This, said the radical Senators, was coercion. Then when he signed the bill, he advertised his leadership by giving Congress and the press the veto message he had prepared. Even Jackson would not have shown such audacity. The rage of Trumbull, Chandler, and other

---

18 *Ibid.*, 2922.
19 Sumner's resolution was offered June 6, 1862; see his *Works*, VII, 119. Lincoln also gave support to Francis H. Pierpont as provisional governor of Virginia. Pierpont converted the Unionist members of the old Virginia legislature, from the western counties, into a new legislature. This body adopted a constitution, and created the State of West Virginia, which chose a new governor. Pierpont meanwhile was given a four-year term as governor of the "restored" Virginia, a handful of counties under Union control.

Jacobins approached hysteria. "No one at a distance," states George W. Julian, "could form any conception of the hostility of the Republican members to Lincoln at the time of final adjournment, while it was the belief of many that our last session of Congress had been held in Washington. Senator Wade said that the country was going to hell, and that the scenes witnessed in the French Revolution were nothing in comparison with what we should see here." Their anger measured their chagrin in finding themselves over-mastered.[20]

The President, however affable, tactful, and gentle, was resolved to maintain his own supremacy in waging war and shaping the peace. This was what mattered to him most of all. On broad measures of mobilization and national development, meanwhile, he was a willing partner of Congress.

Did Lincoln comprehend, as he signed these successive measures, what a drastic economic and social revolution was transforming the nation? Did he grasp the fact that large-scale capitalism was taking control of the land, and that war contracts, tariffs, greenback issues, the expanded credit system, and railroad subsidies were helping defeat not only the South, but the old Jeffersonian ideals which he had shared? Did he see how portentously big business was looming on the horizon? No sure answer can be given, for he was too much engrossed in the conflict to discuss these matters.

We can only say that Lincoln was better equipped than most other leaders to understand both the good and bad aspects of the great changes accelerated by the war. By temperament he was a Jeffersonian. He disliked goals that represented a crass materialism; he did not wish to see America worshiping what William James later called the bitch-goddess success. His idea of social democracy was best represented by the contemplative, friendly life of the countryside or small city, and on one of his last drives with Mrs. Lincoln he spoke of returning to Springfield and its 12,000 people, and resuming his practice with Billy Herndon. But although in temper he belonged to the passing age, his political education had given him a clear appreciation of the new forces of the time. He had been a firm believer in Clay's American system, which derived partly from the politico-economic program of Alexander Hamilton. In the Illinois legislature he had contended for a rather reckless internal improvement system, and later had been attorney for the Illinois Central. As a matter of principle he supported all the measures fostering the new industrial order: tariff protection, a national banking system, railway subsidies, port improvements, and a strong national government. It is illuminating to find that after the Pacific railroad legislation passed, Lincoln called the engineer Grenville M. Dodge to Washington to discuss the point of

20 W. E. Binkley, *President and Congress*, 116–120; Julian, *Political Recs.*, 220.

commencement. Dodge found him much in earnest. "He took out the map and discussed with me for quite a long time the different lines and different views. I saw that he was very thoroughly posted in the demands of the different places." He leaned toward Omaha and Council Bluffs as the eastern terminus, and it was shortly so designated. He also believed that the promoters of the road could not raise capital unless their bonds were made the first mortgage, and the government's loan the second—a concession that was eventually granted.[21]

But Lincoln would have tried to reconcile the Hamiltonian transformation with the old Jeffersonian idealism and humanism of the early republic.

[II]

Congress deliberated in a city that had improved during the first year of conflict. It was less of a camp and more of a capital. The chief thoroughfares were better cleaned and policed, and street railways were being brought into operation. Of course the war atmosphere remained pervasive: endless lines of army wagons and ambulances, groups of spruce officers, knots of sick and wounded with white faces and weak steps or crutches, processions of dirty, ragged, yet unmistakably manly rebel prisoners, their heads held high even when they were shoeless and hatless, and galloping squads of cavalry. Throughout the year work was pressed on the Capitol dome so that the colossal figure of Liberty might be in place before Christmas, and presently the statue was there, with cape, shield, and sword, shining—as Walt Whitman noted on his visits to hospitals—like a star against the sky every bright morning and evening. The city grew in population, bustle, and affluence.[22] The chain of forts about the city had been strengthened until a complete line, connected by rifle pits, glowered down every road—about forty in all. Their clay sides were innocent of grass, and the fields around them showed by long vistas of tree stumps and sodden brush piles the sites of noble forests, now gone forever.

Nathaniel Hawthorne, visiting Washington in early spring, looked curiously at troops, generals, and legislators, at the tavern in Alexandria where Ellsworth had been killed, at Harpers Ferry, which reminded him of some Apennine village set beside a rushing stream, and at Fort Monroe, where old

21 J. R. Perkins, *Trails, Rails, and War*, Ch. IX, describes the meeting of Lincoln and Dodge. Every center from St. Louis (through Kansas City) to Sioux City asked to be made the terminus. Lincoln showed familiarity with railroad projectors in Illinois and sympathy with their struggles. See E. R. Richardson and A. W. Farley, *John P. Usher, passim*.
22 Noah Brooks, *Wash. in Lincoln's Time*, Chs. I and II; Bryan, *The National Capital*, II, *passim; Walt Whitman and the Civil War*, 163. Senator S. G. Arnold of Rhode Island ascribed the improvements to Yankee enterprise; to Manton Marble, Nov. 24, 1862, Marble Papers.

frigates like the *Minnesota* were now as obsolete as the Armada. He reflected that whether the war ended soon or late, the nation was in for a long domination by bullet-headed generals. A rainy day in Willard's Hotel gave him the impression that it could more justly be called the center of Washington and the Union than either the Capitol or White House. Among the crowd were office hunters, wire pullers, editors, army correspondents, inventors, artists, and railroad directors, mostly waiting for some favor, and meanwhile consuming whisky skins, gin cocktails, brandy smashes, and rum cobblers in an atmosphere of cigar smoke. [23] But the novelist was mistaken: the true centers of power remained the White House and Capitol, though the pressure of lobbyists was more fearful than ever before.

Pressures, indeed, accounted for much of what Congress did or refrained from doing. Members were not radicals or conservatives through innate wickedness, but rather because constituents made them so. George Pendleton represented the solid, conservative Ohio Valley citizens of Virginia or Carolina blood; Ben Wade and Elihu Washburne the Yankee stock of the Western Reserve and Chicago, with their economic interests.

"We are growing more radical every day," one citizen wrote Lyman Trumbull, who was well aware that many plain voters of Illinois were just as vehement in condemning McClellan as Medill's *Tribune*. "If things had not turned more favorable," one Rockford journalist assured Washburne just after Donelson, "I believe the people would have rebelled, they were becoming *desperate*." An Ohioan was warning Ben Wade that true men were distressed to find so many of those charged with the war more intent upon robbing the treasury than upon subduing the rebellion. "The people of the West are becoming disgusted by these delays, and beginning to inquire into the [real] cause. Our commerce is nearly prostrated by the closing of its natural channel, and the artificial ones Eastward are taxing our products beyond endurance. The Eastern capitalists may be suited with the delays of the war, but the yeomen of the *West* demand action, and they must soon be listened to." The audacious Zach Chandler, his temper alternating between jaundice and jocularity, but fierce as a panther for his opinions, precisely reflected the money-and-morality outlook of Detroiters.[24]

The ultraconservatives equally represented a great body of plain Americans. Some were men with Southern friends and relatives who would be ruined if Trumbull and Thad Stevens carried out their harsh measures; some were attached on principle to strict-construction ideas of the Constitution;

---

23 "Chiefly About War Matters, by a Peaceable Man," *Atlantic*, July, 1862, 43–61.
24 White, *Trumbull*, 171, 172; H. P. Sloan, Jan. 29, 1862, Washburne Papers, LC; Timothy C. Day, Cincinnati, Feb. 2, 1862, Wade Papers, LC.

some were agrarians who perceived that the new tariff and tax system would enrich industry at the expense of the farming interest. Less adept than the radicals in drawing a cloak of patriotism about their shoulders, these people had a case and needed spokesmen.

It was not Sumner or Wade, Chandler or Washburne who wrote and carried the truly important measures of the session. These men, indeed, were regarded as impracticable even by their own faction. "He originates no measures," Senator Grimes said of Sumner, "but simply makes two or three rather sophomorical set speeches." W. H. Russell had correctly remarked that Sumner was as ignorant of realities in the South as of the politics of Timbuctoo. Many thought that the Boston Senator had just one great aim beyond Union victory, an aim which Lincoln near the end summed up in a single sentence: "He hopes to succeed in beating the President, so as to change this government from its original form, and make it a strong centralized power." Charles Francis Adams, Jr., who knew Sumner intimately, enumerated the faults which disabled him from constructive action.[25] He was a theorist, agitator, and rhetorician, a doctrinaire who lacked insight into the men he attacked and the measures he discussed, and an egotist who let vanity override common sense. He was so intolerant that he regarded a difference of opinion on any subject as a moral delinquency. Once he let his emotions seize control of him, his voice vibrated in a tremulous rumble, he coined magniloquent phrases, he laid down the law, and he made opponents instead of friends. Of course he had great virtues, battling indefatigably for abolition, Negro rights, and honest government, but most Republican associates never really trusted him as a lawmaker.

Even in legislation touching race and slavery the real leaders were found elsewhere. It was Henry Wilson, hardworking, genial, shrewd, who did most to carry the bill for District emancipation, and Henry L. Dawes of the Berkshire district who stood foremost in the House for that measure. Wilson again, with Grimes in the Senate and Lovejoy in the House, provided for the schooling of the District freedmen. Arnold of Illinois, a close friend of Lincoln, introduced the bill which made freedom the rule in all Territories. While Trumbull was author of the confiscation measure, Collamer of Vermont gave it acceptable form. Early in the debate he expressed the opinion that private property could not be confiscated without judicial action, and offered an amendment to substitute due process for legislative seizure; and he with Fessenden and others hammered the legislation into such form that Lincoln could approve it.[26]

25 Stiles, *op. cit.*, 60, 61; Russell, *My Diary*, II, 121; C. F. Adams, Jr., *Autobiography*, 83-90.
26 *Cong. Globe*, 37th Cong., 2d Sess., *passim*; cf. Anna L. Dawes, *Sumner*, 171.

The debate on confiscation brought out the angriest exhibition of party feeling on both sides. "Sir, pass this bill," Saulsbury of Delaware told the Senate, "and if there ever was a hope of the reunion of these States, it is balanced upon this point." Thaddeus Stevens used still hotter language on the other side: "I am for inflicting all the consequences of defeat on a fallen foe in an unjust war. I am for confiscating the property of the rebels, and making it pay the cost of this rebellion." [27] When the bill finally became law, it seemed that the adverse arguments of reasonable men had been in vain. Radical members congratulated themselves upon the provisions for liberating all the slaves of those who aided the rebellion; for halting the return of fugitive slaves; and for the military employment of Africans in any manner the President might deem advantageous. They were delighted by the section which punished participation in or encouragement of rebellion by imprisonment up to ten years, or a fine not exceeding ten thousand dollars, or both, at the discretion of the courts. They rejoiced over other vindictive sections which made the property of designated categories of "rebels" subject to forfeiture.[28] Yet in the long run the views of moderates substantially prevailed. President Lincoln and Attorney-General Bates had such large powers to delay or restrict action, and most courts were so reluctant to press cases, that the Act remained almost a dead letter. Though hundreds were indicted for treason, not one was punished; though many confiscation actions were begun, little property was taken. The whole amount placed in the Treasury under the law was $129,680.67. Nobody was terrified, and almost nobody hurt.[29]

On the great constructive measures, meanwhile, party rancor was limited. Repeatedly members broke across old lines to unite in action for the nation's long-term growth.

[III]

Free homesteads—for whom, and how free? No man had earned a better right to answer these queries than Horace Greeley. When Speaker Grow on May 16, 1862, signed the engrossed copy of the Homestead Act, he congratulated the editor, recalling that the battle had been waged for more than ten years. "Its friends are more indebted for success to the unwavering support given it by the New York *Tribune* than to aught else." [30] Theretofore,

27   The hottest House debate occurred May 4 and 5, 1862.
28   See J. W. Grisfield's speech in *Cong. Globe*, 37th Cong., 2d Sess., 2129–2134; Greeley's editorial in N. Y. *Tribune*, June 19, 1862.
29   J. G. Randall's *Const. Problems under Lincoln* covers the subject in detail. See also A. C. Cole, "President Lincoln and the Illinois Radical Republicans," *Miss. Valley Hist. Rev.*, IV (March, 1918), 417–436.
30   N. Y. *Tribune*, May 22, 1862. It passed the House 82 to 42, and the Senate 27 to 12.

public lands had been open to private entry at a minimum price of $1.25 an acre, or, if they lay within a few miles of one of the land-grant railroads, $2.50 an acre. Advocates of the new law believed that it would offer the country two major benefits. It would drive from the field the pernicious speculators who, clutching large tracts, had compelled the actual settler to pay from $5 to $30 an acre for an unimproved quarter section, unless he took the risk of plunging into the wilderness long weary miles from churches, schools, mills, stores, and doctors. Now, since the nation's lands were thrown open to hardy colonizers without charge, dealers would see that it was a losing business to buy thousands of acres to hold for a rise. The second gain would be the laborer's; any workingman who felt cramped or maltreated could gather his possessions together and remove to the boundless frontier.[31]

The provisions of the law encouraged these hopes. After January 1, 1863, any citizen or intended citizen, male or female, over twenty-one, could file for title to any quarter section of the public lands. So could any citizen under twenty-one who was head of a family, or who had spent fourteen days or more in the military service of the government. For the land thus taken, the settler must pay $10, with some trifling legal fees. To perfect his title, he must then spend five years in actual residence and cultivation. Where would he find the fertile acres? Ten thousand railroad agents, editors, politicians, and emigrant outfitters pointed to the great Northwest, from Michigan to Dakota and from Missouri to Minnesota, as a region full of rich farming land subject to entry.

But the Americans were a nation of land-jobbers, and speculation did *not* stop; particularly as successive enactments opened wide gates to it. The new law was thrust into an older land system which clashed with and resisted it, so that it failed to operate as intended. Greeley himself was by no means unrealistic in his attitude toward homesteading. He urged people not to go West without careful thought. He pointed out that the law did not *give* people farms; on the contrary, those who paid for the land by $10 cash, legal fees, transportation costs, equipment costs, and years of rugged toil, commonly paid all it was worth. He recommended planned community settlement as far wiser than individual action. Let two or three hundred poor men contribute a dollar each to send an agent to find a promising township; then let each pre-empt his quarter section, and a well-rounded community, like those of Puritan New England, Mormon Utah, or New Zealand, would spring up, with its own grist-mill, sawmill, physician, clergyman, stores, and schools. Such a settlement would attract railroads. If people acted sensibly,

31 The homestead bill was impeded by efforts to combine with it a sentimental grant of a bounty to soldiers. Grow, who guided it in the House, struggled against this, and obtained the assistance of Wade in the Senate. Lincoln signed the Act May 20, 1862; *Cong. Globe*, 37th Cong., 2d Sess., 39 ff.; DuBois and Mathews, *Grow*, Ch. XIV.

Greeley saw great hope in the law: "Young men! Poor men! Widows! Resolve to have a home of your own! If you are able to buy and pay for one in the East, very well; if not, make one in the broad and fertile West!" [32]

A brief trial of the new Act, however, proved that few laborers indeed would benefit from it, and not many farmers. The average workingman, toiling for a meager wage, could not save money to buy railway tickets, horses, plows, and other tools, and if he went into debt for them, found that he must work several years before his farm became profitable. He lacked experience, and in most instances taste, for country life. It was farmers' sons, or other young farmers looking for a better chance, who filled the ranks of the homesteaders. Even they, however, found that land speculation and land monopoly remained lions in their path. Capitalists who were looking for 20 per cent on their money obtained a great part of the areas granted to railroads, canal companies, and builders of wagon roads. They alone were able to pay the high prices asked for the most desirable lands granted to certain States. Rich timber, cattle, and mining interests soon found means, by bribing local land officers, making false oaths, and using dummy entrymen, to lay their hands on broad areas. One of the few really vigilant heads of the General Land Office was presently reporting that the vast machinery of his department had been perverted to permit the alienation of the public domain by a bad construction of loose regulations.[33]

Nevertheless, the popular belief in 1862 and later that the Homestead Act was a landmark in the history of the farmer and the West had genuine validity. Driving home the fact that the government possessed nearly two billion acres of land, it helped advertise the nation's boundless trans-Mississippi resources. It gave multitudes who never used it a sense of potential freedom, of escape, of spaciousness. And it has been estimated that perhaps one acre in nine of the remaining public lands did go to true small pioneers!

Quite as important in the long run was the College Land Grant Act which, with Justin S. Morrill of Vermont—a largely self-schooled lover of books, travel, and art—in charge, offered the republic an endowment of higher education such as no other country could match. The bill gave the States of the Union, including those of the South once they returned, the right to select 30,000 acres for each Senator and Representative. This was 10,000 more than under the bill which Buchanan had vetoed. Men broke over party lines to support the measure. "To many Democratic leaders of Congress,

32   N. Y. *Tribune*, June 6, 1862.

33   See Paul W. Gates, "The Homestead Law in an Incongruous Land System," *Am. Hist. Review*, XLI (July, 1936), 652–681; J. B. Sanborn, "Some Political Aspects of Homestead Legislation," *ibid.*, VI (Oct., 1900), 19–37; and Ray Allen Billington, *Westward Expansion*, 698, 699.

and more outside, I am much indebted for kindly sympathy and cooperation," wrote Morrill later.[34] Some Western Republicans, led by Jim Lane of Kansas, fought the measure because they believed that the land properly belonged to their States, and saw no reason to make gifts to the Eastern sisters; while a few members feared that it would seriously diminish the national revenue. All Kansas, said Lane, will be lost to its people—nothing will remain!

Fortunately, believers in elevating agriculture and the mechanic arts had aroused an immense popular sentiment behind the bill, so that newspapers, pulpits, and farm organizations all battled for it. Their aims were more practical than intellectual, but that fact made success all the easier. Since 1850 Jonathan B. Turner, a high-minded Yankee settled in one of the little Athenses of the West, Jacksonville, Illinois, had campaigned for nationally endowed universities serving the "industrial classes." Greeley and others had meanwhile advocated a system of People's Colleges, and an institution of that name had reached puny infancy in upper New York. The primary strength of the movement was a farm strength, and the principal aim a greater dignity and larger success for agriculture. However, many well-informed men, including college presidents, shared the democratic sentiment which Ezra Cornell expressed to Andrew D. White: "I would found an institution where any person can find instruction in any study." Year by year the impulse had gained vigor. It borrowed part of its strength from a parallel British movement, and such passionate pleas for the education of ambitious artisans as Kingsley's *Alton Locke*. A number of legislatures instructed their senators to vote for the bill.[35]

When the measure came to final passage in June, the Senate approved it 32 to 7, the House 90 to 25; a rainbow of hope bent against the murky battlefields of Virginia. Lincoln signed it on July 2, 1862. Senator Timothy O. Howe of Wisconsin as debate closed painted a melancholy vision. He saw the States putting their land scrip up to raffle, greedy investors buying it as they might buy gaudy jewelry, and a national treasure frittered away without enough return to keep a professor alive for a year.[36] In actual fact, some States did dissipate their grants. New York, with the largest land endowment of all, would have done so but for the stout fight waged by Andrew D. White and especially by Ezra Cornell, who when urged to sell some of the acres at a sacrifice answered: "No, I will wear my old hat and

34 Parker, *Morrill*, 272. Morrill attended a Vermont academy.
35 *Cong. Globe*, 37th Cong., 2d Sess., 2275–2277, for a typical exchange of views; White, *Autobiography*, I, 300; W. E. Sawyer, "The Evolution of the Morrill Act of 1862," Ph. D. dissertation, Boston Univ., 1948; Paul W. Gates, "Western Opposition to the Agricultural College Act," *Indiana Mag. of Hist.*, XXXVII (March, 1941), 103–136.
36 *Cong. Globe, ut sup.*, 2634, 2770.

coat a little longer and let you have a little more money from my pocket." [87]
But others in Congress had a truer vision than Howe—a vision of crowded
lecture halls, rich libraries, and laboratories full of eager experimenters, a
vision of hundreds of thousands of lawyers, doctors, engineers, farm experts,
and other professional men scattering fruitfully over the land. Some of those
who gave the bill its overwhelming majority lived to see the new seats in
Ithaca, Urbana, Madison, Minneapolis, and Berkeley take places among the important universities of the world.

At long last, too, agriculture won a place in the national government.
Lincoln had pointed out in his annual message that the farming and stock-
growing interests possessed no department, bureau, or office—only a clerk-
ship; and he had suggested that Congress consider the matter. No Niagara
of support met this common-sense proposal, for this was precisely the area
in which American individualism was most rugged. Members expatiated upon
the sturdy independence of the yeoman, who wanted neither favors nor
interference, and wished to lean on his plow handles, not on Washington.
The National Agricultural Society, wary of politicians, favored the establishment not of a non-Cabinet department, but of a mere bureau. Fessenden
declared that not one farmer in a hundred wanted even a bureau. But after
much discussion Congress decided in May for a so-called department, headed
by a $3,000-a-year commissioner charged with diffusing useful information,
procuring and distributing new plants and seeds, keeping statistical records,
and making whatever special reports were requested by the President or
Congress. It was natural for Lincoln to promote to the new position the
Patent Office clerk who had looked after agricultural matters, Isaac Newton
—a Quaker with a farm of his own in Pennsylvania. Newton soon had a
chemist, an entomologist, a statistician, and most important of all, the
versatile Scottish-born botanist William Saunders, working beside him.[38]

One other great constructive measure, the Pacific railroad bill, passed
with little opposition. Since the Southerners had left Congress, almost everyone agreed on the central route for the road, a line equally fair to St. Louis
and Chicago, and to all trunk lines connecting the East with those cities.
Most people believed that within the lifetime of mature men the Pacific
slope would have at least ten million people, who must be tied by iron
strands to the Union. Great Britain had set an example of large-scale railroad-
building in India and Australia; Russia had employed the American engineer

37 White, *Autobiography*, 318.
38 See *Cong. Globe*, 37th Cong., 2d Sess., 2013–2017, for debate. Fessenden grumbled that
government was getting too big and too expensive; seed appropriations had risen in a decade
from $1,000 to $60,000. Newton's career is treated in *Lincoln Lore*, No. 1441, March, 1958,
pp. 1–3.

G. W. Whistler, father of the artist, in building the 420-mile double track railway from St. Petersburg to Moscow, and had undertaken still larger projects. Anyone with pad and pencil could compute the sums which might be saved by a pair of iron rails. Senator J. A. McDougall of California, for example, estimated that the cost of hauling men and goods between Eastern ports and San Francisco approached $76,000,000 a year, and that a railroad could furnish the same service for less than $23,000,000. Of course the inconvenience was worse than the annual loss of some fifty millions.

How long, Senators asked, would it take to construct the transcontinental line? On the basis of information furnished by Theodore D. Judah, the enthusiastic engineer whom Collis P. Huntington, Leland Stanford, Mark Hopkins, and Charles Crocker had sent to Washington to lobby for an endowment of the Central Pacific, McDougall declared that he expected to cross the continent by through train as early as the year 1870.

The debate showed a singular confusion in Congress about Western topography, about costs of railroad construction, about modes of railway operation, and about the best means of protecting the national investment. Some thought that $16,000 a mile would be a reasonable average cost, some much less. Some regarded a uniform gauge to the Pacific of the utmost importance; but McDougall declared that it did not matter, for merchandise and passengers should be shifted to new trains every thousand miles, or less —"Everybody knows that the engine, the locomotive, cannot run safely more than a thousand miles." Some believed that the government, in giving the Union Pacific and Central Pacific companies a specified land subsidy, was driving a rather hard bargain, but Howe of Wisconsin said that on the contrary Washington was supplying "a most ample, I was about to say a most profligate, bounty." Plainly, Congress was legislating in the dark; but amid many tokens of popular approval, the Senate passed the bill 35 to 5, and the House 104 to 21.[39]

Under this measure, the Union Pacific was authorized to build westward from the 100th meridian across the Rockies, and the Central Pacific eastward from San Francisco and Sacramento across the Sierra Nevada, meeting at the California-Nevada line. Five branch roads at the eastern end would connect the Union Pacific with Omaha, Sioux City, St. Joseph, Leavenworth, and Kansas City. Each of the lines received a 400-foot right of way, with necessary ground for stations, shops, and switches, and five alternate sections of land on each side of the railway as fast as it was built. The government agreed, moreover, to lend the companies $16,000 in United States 6 per cent

39 *Cong. Globe,* 37th Cong., 2d Sess., Appendix, 381 ff., offers the text of the bill; *ibid.,* 307 ff., McDougall's speech; 2804-2840, the best part of the debate.

bonds for every mile of track laid on the plains, $32,000 a mile in hilly country, and $48,000 a mile in the mountains, this loan to be a first mortgage on the roads. The President was to appoint two directors of the Union Pacific, and to fix a uniform width of track for all the lines. Telegraph lines were to accompany the railroads. If the roads did not finish building across the continent from the Missouri to the Sacramento by the middle of 1876, they and all their properties were to be forfeited to the government.

Without delay, the Central Pacific was off in the race. Judah, the son of an Episcopal clergyman of Connecticut, trained at Rensselaer Polytechnic, found his brightest dreams realized when on July 1 Lincoln signed the act. For years he had spoken and written on the necessity of a transcontinental line; he had done more than anybody else to agitate the subject in Washington during Buchanan's Administration, had discovered a practicable route across the Sierra, and had brought Huntington and Stanford into the organization of the company. While the Union Pacific marked time, for the government inducements did not at first call forth sufficient private capital, the Central Pacific obtained a loan of $1,660,000 from the State of California, and an opinion from Lincoln that the Sierra Nevada extended well down into the Sacramento Valley. The first rails were hammered fast in 1863. That same year John A. Dix was elected president of the freshly-organized Union Pacific. In due course Lincoln, after a premature decision in favor of a broad gauge, took the advice of experienced railroad executives, and set the width of the transcontinental at four feet, eight and one half inches, thus fixing a standard for the whole United States. During 1864 the Union Pacific, with enlarged aids from the government, also began construction.[40]

That is, to facilitate the raising of capital, Congress—with Lincoln approving—made the government loan a second and not a first lien on the railroad. The 100th meridian runs through the center of Nebraska, but the building of the road got under hesitant way at the then dismal hamlet of Omaha, fronting Council Bluffs across the muddy Missouri. It made scanty progress until the managers almost forcibly haled from the army General Grenville M. Dodge, who had learned some theoretical engineering at Norwich College in Vermont, and a great deal more of practical surveying and construction first with the Mississippi & Missouri in Iowa during the 1850s, and later in the rebuilding and equipping of wrecked lines for Grant's army. He knew Lincoln, and the President trusted him. The engineering work of the transcontinental road was to be as creditable as the financial record was to be dishonorable. Dramatic clashes

40 Stuart Daggett, *The Southern Pacific, passim;* Judah quarreled with Huntington and others the year of his death, 1863. Dix, *Dix,* II, 127, emphasizes the faith of the general in the Union Pacific.

had attended the controversy over the proper gauge. The Central Pacific had chosen a five-foot width, and Kansas railway projectors favored that type of line. But the Iowa-Nebraska branch, and most Easterners, insisted on four feet eight and a half inches, and after Senator Harlan of Iowa introduced a bill designating that gauge, Lincoln yielded.

The rattle of sledge hammers was drama to the world, as Jules Verne's *Eighty Days* attests, and music to the West. A terrible war had not numbed the constructive enterprise of the republic. Actually in many ways the time was propitious. The West was bulging with foodstuffs that had once gone down the Mississippi and could now be sent out to supply the construction gangs. The depressed iron industry was anxious to furnish rails, spikes, cars, and locomotives. While some of the Negro refugees from Missouri and Kentucky acted as navvies, paroled or discharged soldiers could fight off the Indians. Many people held an exaggerated idea of the trans-Mississippi region as a vast treasure house, which would yield everything from buffalo robes to gold bars; tap its wealth by railways, as Grant later said, and it might pay the costs of the war. At any rate, the North was showing its ability to wage a great conflict with one hand, and build up the West with the other.[41]

[IV]

The Confederates might fight without money, as various men said, for they had no national credit to protect; but the Union had to provide means for the war effort while avoiding a ruinous bankruptcy. Congress had failed, in its midsummer session of 1861, to use the taxing power energetically. When it met again in the winter of 1861–62, it found the country's financial needs instant and exigent; they would not wait for the slow institution of a machinery of taxes, assessment, and collection. A very limited stock of gold and silver was available. The Treasury notes which Chase had issued to help meet the emergency were not being paid in coin on demand, and had fallen into such disrepute that leading commercial banks refused to accept them as money of account, taking them only as a special deposit. They were therefore ceasing to circulate. The Eastern banks suspended specie payment as 1861 ended, and this left the country in a situation where its many reckless speculative bankers might fill the land with worthless paper.

41 It must be remembered that the country, despite some grumbling by agrarian elements, was still in a generous mood toward railways. And benefits were being reaped from earlier railway land grants. The Illinois Central hauled thousands of troops and huge quantities of supplies for the Union. Thomas A. Scott and Montgomery C. Meigs decided that the government was entitled under law to free use of the road, but should pay for use of locomotives and cars, and hence fixed freight rates one-third below the charges of other lines.

A dependable currency was desperately needed to pay the soldiers, buy supplies, and keep business active. It seemed to many that the only feasible course was to have the government take bold control, issue its own circulating medium, and give it credit by pronouncing it legal tender for debts. This step would be so unprecedented, so momentous, and so full of risks that many recoiled from it. Secretary Chase, who felt great aversion to making anything but coin a legal tender, was himself reluctant. But the House Ways and Means Committee, led by E. G. Spaulding, an experienced Buffalo banker, had the courage of desperation; and on January 22, 1862, it submitted a legal-tender bill which at once provoked a violent debate. It provided for the issue of $150,000,000 in legal-tender paper.

A powerful group of Republicans at once joined the Democrats in opposition. Justin S. Morrill, hopeful that the war could be ended by midsummer, assured the House that the measure would make the enemy grin with delight. V. B. Horton of Ohio declared it unnecessary, for an appeal to moneyed men would bring out an abundance of gold. Owen Lovejoy of Illinois proposed to tax the country at the rate of 200 millions a year, if necessary, to sell interest-bearing government bonds, and to compel the banks to return to a specie basis; thus the nation could avoid a bottomless abyss. Roscoe Conkling of New York also used the word "abyss." The bill was a legislative declaration of national bankruptcy, he said, for after the first issue of legal-tender bills another, and another, and another would follow. In the Senate, Collamer of Vermont and Preston King of New York threw their weight against the measure, the former arguing that it was unconstitutional. Opponents naturally made much of the fate of the American continentals and the French assignats. Even Sumner was deeply troubled by the apparent necessity of incurring all the evils of an inconvertible currency, forced into circulation by act of Congress.

But the argument of necessity could not be gainsaid. As members pointed out, the Ways and Means Committee estimated that the government must pay nearly $350,000,000 before July, and of this $100,000,000 was already due to soldiers, contractors, and other creditors. The aggregate capital of the banks of the three principal cities of the country hardly exceeded this latter sum. Secretary Chase, at first hesitant, came out for the bill in a letter which Spaulding read to the House on February 4, and which probably had decisive influence. The chambers of commerce in New York, Philadelphia, and Boston endorsed it. Particularly effective was the advocacy of Thad Stevens in the House, and of John Sherman in the Senate. In the end it passed the House by 93 yeas, all Republican, to 59 nays; and the Senate, after approving the legal tender clause by the close vote of 23 to 17, accepted the measure 30 to 7. The Rubicon was crossed! [42] The printing presses were put in operation, and greenbacks soon rustled in every hand.

This legal-tender legislation, passed in the nick of time, gave wide benefits to both the Administration and the nation. No doubt stringent taxation and the maintenance of a metallic currency, had they been practicable, would have reduced the costs of the war. But the nation's stock of hard money was quite inadequate to the needs of business, which the greenbacks helped revive; and heavier taxes would have excited grave popular discontent. Added to the gloom caused by military reverses, such discontent might have made Lincoln's prospects in the fall elections discouraging indeed. The nation was to pay a heavy penalty for its resort to paper money in the inflation, speculation, and widespread financial demoralization of the next ten years. But a different course might have cost it still worse disasters.

Along with its resort to greenbacks, the government of course had to raise large new revenues by taxation. The tariff had been increased in 1861 by placing tea and coffee on the dutiable list, and raising the average ad valorem rates from 18.8 per cent (under the very low tariff of 1857) to 36.2 per cent. Even so, the duties collected in the fiscal year 1862 fell short of fifty millions; they were obviously limited by the capacity of the people to consume foreign goods. The government therefore turned to excise taxes. It was a special felicity of Americans that for a long generation—since 1821 —they had been practically unknown. Now a comprehensive and heavy system of excise taxes was framed by Congress; a law so thorough that it took 30 royal octavo pages and more than 20,000 words to list its provisions.

Every manufacturing interest, every branch of commerce, and every profession save the ministry felt the weight of the new enactment. Liquor and tobacco were of course taxed; so were such luxuries as carriages, billiard tables, yachts, gold and silver plate, and confectionery. Manufacturers of textiles, iron, steel, and wood paid a tax of 3 per cent. Physicians, bankers, brokers, lawyers, livestock dealers, and even street jugglers paid their share. Butchers paid thirty cents for every beeve slaughtered, and ten cents for every hog. Men ruefully recalled Sydney Smith's lament over the British taxes entailed by the Napoleonic wars: "taxes on everything which it is pleasant to see, hear, feel, smell, or taste; taxes . . . on the sauce which pampers man's appetite and on the drug that restores him to health; on the ermine which decorates the judge and the rope which hangs the criminal; on the poor man's sauce and the rich man's spice; on the brass nails of the coffin and the ribbons of the bride."

42 Besides the *Cong. Globe*, 37th Cong., 2d Sess., Jan.-Feb., 1862, *passim*, see the interpretive narrative in Cox, *Three Decades*, 126-144, and Blaine, *Twenty Years*, 409-429.

In the summer session of 1861 Congress had provided for an income tax of 3 per cent on all incomes exceeding $800 a year, but had postponed the appointment of assessors and collectors to the following spring. Now the income tax was fixed at 3 per cent on incomes between $600 and 10,000 and 5 per cent (later 10) on incomes above $10,000. It was thought wonderful when A. T. Stewart of New York paid by one check $400,000 on an income of four millions.[43] The burdens which the excise and income taxes laid on manufacturers mainfestly handicapped them in competition with foreign exporters, and a general revision of the tariff was therefore carried through in June, 1862. This raised the rates on practically the whole range of imports, producing bitter complaints abroad, and much criticism in the West. But the effect of this second Morrill Tariff can best be considered when we turn to a study of wartime industrialism.

[V]

Congress in its seven and a half months of effort had written one of the most important parts of the Administration's record for 1862. The army and navy gained ground, but met defeat after defeat in the process; the departments managed their activities with increasing vigor and skill, but committed blunders like Stanton's interruption of recruiting; the President gained in strength, but failed to carry his great plan of compensated border emancipation. Congress marched steadily forward. In easy control of both Houses, the Republicans redeemed every important promise they had made to Northern voters. Such measures as the Homestead Act, the Pacific Railroad, the Morrill Tariff, and the expansion of the currency by legal-tender paper would shape the growth of the nation for decades to come. It was largely on the basis of this record that the party would face the electorate in the fall elections.

43 Sidney Ratner, *American Taxation*, 57–93.

9

Antietam and Emancipation

IN THE dark hours before dawn on September 4, Lee's veterans began splashing through the shallow fords of the Potomac midway between Harpers Ferry and Washington. He had chosen a point near the capital so that his invasion of Maryland might menace both Baltimore and Washington, and draw the Union army after him until he could fight it somewhere distant from its base. Thousands of his troops were barefoot, and nearly all tattered, darkly sunburnt, lean, and hungry-looking. Though a Union battery banged away with some effect near Edwards's Ferry, elsewhere they swarmed across with little opposition. D. H. Hill's fresh division had reinforced Lee, giving him in theory nearly 70,000 men, but he took only about 60,000 into Maryland and his ranks continued thinning.[1] On the morning of the 7th the Confederates marched into Frederick, where Lee issued a proclamation declaring that they had come to liberate Maryland, not harm it. As foraging groups scoured the country for livestock, paying partly in greenbacks, partly in Confederate paper, his major forces concentrated about the town. Here he could threaten even Philadelphia, and menace the communications of the capital with the North and West.

A tremor ran through the Union. Boston on the 9th gave a frantic ovation to the Sixth Massachusetts, leaving for the front once more. The New York

---

1 John Esten Cooke, himself in the army, writes: "All the roads of northern Virginia were lined with soldiers, comprehensively denominated 'stragglers'; but the great majority of these men had fallen out from the advancing column from physical inability to keep up with it; thousands were not with General Lee because they had no shoes, and their bleeding feet would carry them no farther, or the heavy march without rations had broken them down. This great crowd toiled on painfully in the wake of the army, dragging themselves five or six miles a day; and when they came to the Potomac, near Leesburg, it was only to find that General Lee had swept on, that General McClellan's column was between him and them, and that they could not rejoin their commands." He estimates that 20,000 or 30,000 thus failed to reach the Maryland battlefields. *Stonewall Jackson*, 341. Lee's numbers have been the subject of much dispute. O. R., I, xix, pt. 2, p. 639, gives a field return Sept. 30 of 62,713 present and 52,990 present for duty. Longstreet estimated after the war that the army should have numbered 63,000 at the passage of the Potomac; letter July 15, 1885, to D. H. Hill, Hill Papers, Va. State Library. A careful military critic in the N. Y. *Nation*, Dec. 20, 1894, computed that Lee had 60,000 in the campaign.

press declared that the hour of opportunity had at last struck, for Lee might be defeated so decisively as to crush the rebellion. Throughout New England and the Middle States enlistments, lagging again since Pope's defeat, showed tokens of a revival. In Philadelphia, as long troop trains of replacements began passing through the city, the armories were thrown open for volunteering, and green recruits were hastily drilled. In Scranton cannon and bells summoned the adult males for training; in Harrisburg, Governor Curtin conferred with Thomas A. Scott on emergency measures. Deepest of all was the alarm in Baltimore, where merchants, knowing what wholesale seizures of goods the Southern host would make, and Unionists, well aware that the "Secesh" element in the city was growing dangerous, looked to their defenses.

Lee's hazardous movement was not difficult to explain, for politically and militarily it was almost a necessity. His army was so ill equipped and so inferior in numbers to the growing Northern forces that he could not afford to stand still. As he had to move aggressively, he shared the view of most Southern officers and editors that it should fight on enemy soil, and there make the war support itself. Jackson was particularly anxious to invade. Some of the troops told Frederick citizens that to them the movement was a question of food or starvation—for three days they had lived on green corn, apples, and little else. The effort to buy out shops in Frederick and other towns disclosed other necessities. Lee wrote Davis that the army lacked shoes, lacked clothes, lacked transport animals, and lacked "much of the material of war." He knew with Napoleon that an army marches on both its shoe leather and its belly.[2]

The political motives were equally important. A victory beyond the Potomac not only offered the best hope of gaining Anglo-French intervention, but also presented the largest chance of raising Northern war weariness to the point of negotiations for peace. "There is but one method of putting an end to the war," declared the Richmond *Examiner*, "and that is by destroying the Federal credit"; in other words, financial pressures would compel a new attitude.[3] As soon as Southern legions made good their stand on Maryland soil, Colonel J. F. Marshall of South Carolina prophesied to Davis, the North would lose heart. "The tone of the Masses, the Press, and the Legislatures will all

2 Lee had information that Washington had already received 60,000 replacements who would soon be embodied in the army. Freeman, *Lee*, II, 350. McClellan actually had a mobile force of nearly 100,000 in addition to the troops about Washington and Harpers Ferry. The North continued to overestimate Southern force in the grossest manner; thus the N. Y. *Herald* on September 9 declared that Lee's army was "at least 150,000 strong."

The sad outward appearance of the Confederates led some observers to form hasty judgments. "They are the dirtiest, lousiest, filthiest, piratical-looking cut-throats white man ever saw," wrote Edward S. Bragg to his wife, Sept. 21, 1862, Bragg Papers; but they were gentlemen compared with some marauding troops under Pope and Grant.

3 July 21, 1862.

change from a thirst for our blood and property to that for peace." [4] And Lee no sooner reached Frederick than he wrote Davis that the time had come for the Confederacy to propose to the North a recognition of its independence, for it would obviously be negotiating from strength, not from weakness.[5]

Because Lee hoped to win both recruits and friends in Maryland, his army behaved with exemplary restraint. No citizen was maltreated, no goods were taken without payment, and no offensive display of Southern sentiment was permitted. General Bradley T. Johnson, the provost-marshal charged with enlisting as many men as possible, rode up to a soldier cheering in the Frederick streets for Davis, and smashed him over the head with his revolver. "There, you damned blankety-blank," he said, "see if you disobey orders again!" [6] The army brought with it a civil commissioner, E. Loring Lowe, a friend of Herschel V. Johnson, with authority from Jefferson Davis as well as General Lee to undertake any political mission for which victory might clear the way. Lee's proclamation in Frederick assured Marylanders that they would once more enjoy their ancient freedoms, and could freely decide their own destiny. One Union officer paid tribute to the conduct of the hungry, dysentery-weakened rebels as they marched through the Maryland towns. Though they looked haggard, their clothes were often mere bundles of rags, and many were so unkempt and unwashed that they stank, yet in discipline they surpassed the well-fed, well-clothed, Union forces.

"No one," wrote this officer, "can point to a single act of vandalism perpetrated by the rebel soldiery during their occupation of Frederick, while even now a countless host of stragglers are crawling after our army devouring, destroying, and wasting all that falls in their devious line of march." [7]

[I]

Lee had to open his campaign with a hazardous blow to maintain his communications. His hope that Marylanders would rally to his banner proved unfounded, for they remained timid or hostile. While Eastern Maryland, which held the great body of Southern sympathizers, was dominated by the Union forces, the invaded heart of the State stood mainly with the North.[8] Although

4 July 11, 1862, Davis Papers, Duke Univ.
5 See O. R., I, xix, pt. 2, p. 600, for evidence that he expected Maryland to rise.
6 Baltimore corr. dated Sept. 11 in N. Y. *Tribune,* Sept. 13, 1862.
7 MS letter of James Gillette, commissary officer, to mother, Sept. 13.
8 As the Barbara Frietchie legend, immortalized by Whittier, suggests. This legend has no basis in fact. Mrs. Frietchie, then ninety-six, waved a Union flag from her porch when Union troops passed through Frederick later, not when the Confederates passed, and she and Jackson never saw each other; *Battles and Leaders,* II, 618, 622. But it possesses poetic truth, for many Maryland women had the defiant valor imputed to Mrs. Frietchie, and Jackson had the chivalry. Cf. Lenoir Chambers, *Stonewall Jackson,* II, 192, 193.

some hundreds of young men did flock in, most of them soon flocked back, explaining that after "seeing and smelling" the rebel host, they had decided to stand aloof. It was a most heroic army, but its life was all too heroically arduous. Realizing that he could not rely for communications on the Leesburg-Manassas line close to Washington, Lee had to make sure of the Shenandoah Valley instead. He had supposed that his penetration of Maryland would compel the Union forces to evacuate Harpers Ferry and Martinsburg, and McClellan in fact urged their removal; but bad policy kept them there. He therefore determined to send Stonewall Jackson to take Harpers Ferry and open the Valley line while the rest of the army continued operating in Maryland.

This division of his tired, ill-equipped force was perilous, as Longstreet pointed out in a protest. But Lee knew McClellan well enough to be sure he would move slowly; he was aware how wretched a commander the North often put at places like Harpers Ferry, and he never forgot that the South had to take desperate chances. Before Little Mac rouses himself to active operations, he told one of his brigadiers, "I hope to be on the Susquehanna." He outlined the proposed operation with care in Special Order No. 191.

If Lee were to succeed—not only dividing his army in the presence of superior enemy forces, but placing a river between the two parts—he required complete secrecy, and he counted on the abysmal inefficiency of McClellan's intelligence service. Fortune, however, betrayed him. At this time his general orders were frequently transmitted by headquarters direct to each division commander; that is, the staff took Lee's instructions, wrote them down, entered one copy in the "confidential book" or held it to be copied later into the general order book, and sent another copy by orderly to the commander addressed. Sometimes the orderly was told to bring back a receipt, sometimes not.[9] This time Jackson, seeing the importance of a clear understanding of Special Order No. 191, wrote out a copy in his own hand and sent it to General D. H. Hill, of his command. It directed that part of the army was to march northwest on the morrow to Hagerstown and Boonesborough. The divisions of McLaws, Anderson, and Walker were to turn south, however, and seize Maryland Heights, Loudoun Heights, and Harpers Ferry, while Jackson by the longest march of all was to recross the Potomac, cut the Baltimore & Ohio, take Martinsburg, and pick up any fugitives from Harpers Ferry. All these detached forces, their mission accomplished, were to rejoin the main army at Hagerstown or Boonesborough.

This vital order some Union troops, entering Frederick on Lee's heels, found

9   Charles Marshall, Nov. 11, 1867, to D. H. Hill on procedure; Hill Papers, Va. State Lib. Lenoir Chambers, *Stonewall Jackson*, II, 188–191, 200–202, supplies details.

wrapped around three cigars in a field outside Frederick, and they sent it to Mc-Clellan on September 13! D. H. Hill has usually been held responsible for losing it, for though he later denied culpability, Charles Marshall, Lee's aide and military secretary, holds him to blame.[10] Whatever the circumstances, McClellan had early notice of the division of the Confederate army; the troops of Jackson and Walker had hardly recrossed the Potomac before he knew they were south of the river.

The forces which Lee sent on this daring mission moved with characteristic rapidity. By afternoon of the 13th they had taken Martinsburg and the two eminences overlooking Harpers Ferry, and held the Union garrison there at their mercy. The commander, D. H. Miles, should either have abandoned the trap in time or posted all his troops on one of the strong heights; he did nothing. The Confederate batteries were soon shelling him heavily, and at dawn on the 13th he surrendered his 11,500 men, with 73 guns, 13,000 small arms, 200 wagons, and much camp equipment.

Jackson as usual wasted not a moment. Astride his horse in the early sunlight, he received the Union officer sent to offer unconditional surrender, and penned a dispatch to Lee. Then he rode into Harpers Ferry past dejected Union troops, many of whom uncovered. "Boys," said one, "he's not much for looks, but if we had him we wouldn't have been caught in this trap." [11] Late that afternoon, the 15th, his forces were on their way to rejoin Lee. It was high time, for the main Confederate army by that hour was in a dangerous predicament. Stonewall and his fellow commanders in their brilliant two-day coup had taken a larger army than those of Burgoyne or Cornwallis, well armed, well provisioned, and established near highly defensible heights; as Northern newspapers said, Hull's surrender was nothing to that of Miles.[12] The guns, small arms, and wagons that the Confederates had seized were of inestimable value to them. Nevertheless, the South would have paid too high a price if Lee had been smashed before Jackson could get back to him.

10 Hill's denial is explicit. He declares no such order came to him from Lee, but that an identical one did arrive from Jackson, which he kept; "The Lost Dispatch," in *The Land We Love*, February, 1868. Colonel Marshall could not conjecture just what had happened, but admitted later that the loss of the order might have occurred in many ways. Randolph B. Marcy and S. W. Crawford, in affidavits written May 5 and Aug. 22, 1868, state reasons for believing that the order was found in the tracks of A. P. Hill, not D. H. Hill; D. H. Hill to Marshall, Nov. 11, 1867, Hill Papers. See also Hal Bridges, "A Lee Letter," *Va. Mag. of Hist. and Biog.*, LXVI (April, 1958), 161–166.

D. H. Hill had been accused of losing an important order during the Seven Days, which was recaptured on the person of a Union soldier before it got to headquarters; Fitzgerald Ross, *Cities and Camps*, 45, 46.

11 *Battles and Leaders*, II, 625–627.

12 Miles had been prominent in the Bull Run disaster, and critics demanded why he had been given such an important command; N. Y. *Tribune* editorial, Sept. 20, 1862. A chance shot as the white flag was raised mortally wounded him.

MARYLAND WITH HARPERS FERRY AND ANTIETAM CREEK

Indeed, Lee might have been crushed by the 16th but for McClellan's delays. The statement that he was warned in time that McClellan had obtained the lost order seems untrue. But McClellan had been displaying his characteristic defects and virtues. He had capably reorganized his forces, putting Banks in charge of the Washington fortifications, replacing McDowell (who now disappears from active duty) by Hooker as a corps commander, and keeping Burnside, Sumner, Franklin, and Fitz-John Porter in command of their old corps. But as Lee had anticipated, his movements were dilatory. In the six days from September 7, when he took the field in Maryland, to the 13th, he advanced barely thirty miles. Certain as usual that Lee outnumbered him, on the 11th he demanded reinforcements of 25,000. Halleck shared his nervousness.

Lee was thus able to bring his troops into good defensive position on the eastern slopes of South Mountain, the long irregular range of hills which continues the Blue Ridge into Maryland. Longstreet, Stuart, and D. H. Hill took their stand in the area of Crampton's and Turner's Gaps, passes from 400 to 600 feet high which pierce the thousand-foot ridge. Here on September 14, Confederate officers, peering through field glasses from the heights, descried an advance division of Jacob D. Cox's force on the turnpike to the southeast;

and soon they could see the blue uniforms and glittering bayonets of almost the whole Army of the Potomac swarming down from the far-off Catoctin Ridge near Frederick, and crossing the intervening valley. By noon that hot day the battle was raging violently. Along a wide stretch of South Mountain the Union troops performed astonishing feats in surmounting steep hills, penetrating dense woods, and scrambling over jagged rocks. The Northern artillery outranged the Confederate guns, while superior infantry strength permitted outflanking operations. By five in the afternoon Franklin had pushed his way through Crampton's Gap.

The day's fighting along South Mountain might be called a drawn battle. To be sure, it left the Confederates in a position of great peril. With one gap forced and the other rendered untenable, Longstreet and D. H. Hill at nightfall had to retreat. But the anxious Lee could take pride in the stubborn courage with which 18,000 Southerners had held the front against 30,000 Union troops. While the Northern volunteers displayed steady valor—"not a man fell back or straggled," wrote one reporter—the Confederates had fought with almost unmatchable devotion. And Lee had after all gained what was really important to him—time; time for Jackson to come up. He had in fact gained the whole twenty-four hours beginning at dawn of the 14th. His men fell back in exemplary order. At Keedysville, on the road to Sharpsburg, citizens later testified that the half-starved troops took nothing unless people were willing to sell. One miller, asked to dispose of grain and flour, refused, saying they could have nothing without breaking his lock. "We break no locks, sir," was the reply, and the hungry column marched on.[13] As Lee's forces crossed Antietam Creek he learned by a courier from Jackson that Harpers Ferry had surrendered, and he then disposed his troops on the hills about Sharpsburg.

McClellan next day indulged in exultant boasts. At 8 A.M. he telegraphed Halleck: "I have just learned from General Hooker, in the advance . . . that the enemy is making for Shepherdstown in a perfect panic, and that General Lee last night stated publicly that he must admit that they had been shockingly whipped." Two hours later he reported that the rout had been confirmed. "It is stated that Lee gives his losses as 15,000."[14] Actually Lee's losses had been only 3,400, and his retreat was effected without panic. Moreover, as he formed his lines in the new position near Sharpsburg, he had the comfort of knowing that Jackson was on the way. By a "severe" march after midnight, Stonewall reached Lee's lines early on the 16th.[15]

13 N. Y. *Tribune*, Sept. 19, 1862.
14 O. R., I, xix, pt. 2, pp. 294, 295.
15 Henderson, II, 226, 227; Freeman, *Lee*, II, 381, 382.

[II]

Although the Confederates had escaped a hammer blow while still divided, their position remained dangerous. At Sharpsburg, a hamlet only three miles from the Potomac, they lay behind the crooked Antietam Creek, which wriggles its way down to the river above Harpers Ferry. They had the advantage of holding a low crescent-shaped ridge, their right flank resting on the Antietam, and their left making some use of stone walls, limestone ledges, and thicketed woodlands. Perhaps because they lacked tools, they dug no entrenchments, though they could have strengthened their lines greatly at various points by hasty field works. With but 50,000 men at most, they faced McClellan's well-armed force half again as large. They were more tired, hungry, and ragged than ever, and their spirits had suffered by the retreat from South Mountain while those of the Federal army had risen. "The *morale* of our men is now restored," McClellan informed Halleck.

Lee's daring resolution was never better exhibited than in his decision to stand and fight. Longstreet, always cautious, advised retreat, and some military critics have regarded Lee's choice as a cardinal mistake. But Jackson, when he arrived, approved a decision that for several reasons was almost inevitable. The invasion of Maryland was a desperate effort to end the war at one stroke by laying a foundation for foreign intervention, and spreading discouragement throughout the North; luck, strategy, and heroism could yet win a victory, and if it were half as signal as Second Manassas it might achieve the object. McClellan exaggerated when he wrote later: "One victory lost almost all would have been lost. Lee's army might have marched as it pleased on Washington, Baltimore, Philadelphia, or New York . . . nowhere east of the Alleghenies was there another organized force to avert its march." This was McClellan's self-glorification as the savior of the Union. The Northern forces were now too numerous to be scattered by one blow, and each of the four cities would have remained well defended. Nevertheless, the effect of a Union defeat on foreign opinion and the autumn elections might have been disastrous. With so much to gain, Lee could only play his hand out to the end.

By retreating, Lee would put his army on the defensive for months to come. That no army fighting a defensive campaign with smaller numbers ever wins a decisive battle is a well-tested maxim of war; Hannibal, Marlborough, Frederick, Washington, Napoleon, Wellington, all won their victories when they took the offensive.[16] Moreover, if Lee fell back he could augment his forces but slowly while the Union army would grow rapidly in strength. Under

16 Sir Frederick Maurice, *Lee,* 151, 152.

recent calls, the North was putting 600,000 more men under arms; it was at last manufacturing artillery, small arms, ammunition, and camp supplies in almost adequate quantity; it was finding better brigadiers and colonels. As Herschel V. Johnson was writing A. H. Stephens, a protracted war must close in combatant exhaustion—and the South would be exhausted first.[17] If Lee waited, he would soon find that the North had trained its raw recruits and gained an overwhelming field superiority. McClellan could then enjoy just what he desired; a campaign of movement after full ranks, improved administration, and an overhauled supply system put his army in shape to prosecute the war without intermission to a successful end.

It was a remarkable battlefield that Lee had chosen, so compact that from some vantage points observers could witness the struggle in its entire length and breadth. The crescent-shaped ridge which furnished the main Confederate line was backed by a broad tableland of woods and ravines, offering cover for troops everywhere. Lee had two good highways, the Shepherdstown Road and the Williamsport Road, open at his rear for possible retreat to the Potomac. The sluggish Antietam flowed in front of the Confederate position, too deep for passage by artillery and well guarded at its three stone bridges. But in view of the heavy superiority of the national troops and of the guns which McClellan massed at the center, the Confederates needed every aid they could draw from the terrain.[18]

[III]

McClellan was as usual open to criticism. He had delayed in thrusting his columns forward on September 13 to reach South Mountain before the Confederates could establish themselves on its slopes, and he had then made a faulty use of his forces in attacking the Southern positions on that ridge.[19] He delayed again in pushing forward after the retreating Lee. He knew early on the morning of the 15th, when he telegraphed Halleck, that D. H. Hill and Longstreet had evacuated Turner's Gap, and he declared that "our troops are now advancing in pursuit of them." But they were not advancing.[20] A swift forward movement would have caught Lee off balance before he could con-

17 Johnson to Stephens, Sept. 28, 1862, Johnson Papers, Duke University. At the moment, the disparity in size between the two armies, while great, was not overwhelming. Livermore in *Numbers and Losses*, 92, 93, concludes that at Antietam, Lee had 51,844 men engaged, and McClellan 75,316 effectives.

18 The N. Y. *Tribune* of Sept. 20 has a graphic description sent from Sharpsburg.

19 Cf. Henderson, II, 226.

20 O. R., I, xix, pt. 2, pp. 294, 295. Some Union services were poorly organized, as usual. Lossing writes, II, 476: "There was found to be a lack of ammunition and rations, and these had to be supplied from tardily approaching supply trains."

centrate behind Antietam Creek. Instead, orders to move were inexcusably
delayed. Some units, like the Ninth Corps under Cox, did not receive them
until late afternoon. A correspondent posted near the Confederate lines wrote
the evening of the 15th that Union troops had been slowly coming up all day:

> Sumner arrived about three o'clock and took command, but his troops were
> mostly far back on the road. Very little artillery came, and altogether the
> whole movement was unaccountably slow. The road was good, and the ground
> on both sides favorable for parallel columns, but yet no considerable force
> arrived until nearly dark. Burnside emerged from the lower gap about five
> o'clock, but Hooker's own troops were not within a mile of the front at
> seven o'clock. . . .[21]

The Union army might, as many officers expected, have attacked on the
16th. McClellan, however, spent most of the day reconnoitering Lee's lines, and
fixing an exact position for not only every corps, but every division and
brigade. This annoyed subordinates. His battle plan, as he explained it, was
simple. His right wing under Hooker and Sumner, already partly across the
Antietam, would swing around to force the Confederate left back on the
center, while cutting off the roads to Hagerstown and Williamsport. His left
under Burnside would meanwhile force the Antietam at a stone bridge a mile
below the central turnpike, and crumple the Confederate right into Sharpsburg. This would pinch Lee in a vise, and bar his retreat towards the fords of
the Potomac. For any emergency, Fitz-John Porter's force at the center would
act as a reserve.[22]

At daybreak on the 17th desultory infantry firing began. As the sun rose
the musketry deepened to a roar, and before the mists lifted from wood and
field Hooker was hotly engaged with the veterans of Stonewall Jackson and
Hood. On the Confederate side the story was one of stubborn resistance, varied
by one magnificent charge—that of A. P. Hill's division, which, ordered up
from Harpers Ferry at dawn, after marching seventeen miles without rest, fell
with tigerish ferocity on the Union left. These roadworn troops flung an
advancing corps in confusion back down the ridge toward the Antietam. On
the Union side equal leadership was displayed by one corps commander,
Hooker, whose impetuous vigor fairly earned him his sobriquet of "Fighting
Joe"; but two others, Sumner and Burnside, failed to seize opportunities that
might have led to complete victory. Here McClellan's overall strategy was
chiefly at fault, for he had ordered piecemeal attacks instead of simultaneous
assaults along the whole front.[23]

21 N. Y. *Tribune*, Sept. 19, 1862; W. C. Cochran, "Political Experiences of Jacob D. Cox,"
MS, Western Reserve Hist. Soc., I, 669–671.
22 "Personal Recs. of the War," by a Virginian, *Harper's Magazine*, XXXVI (February,
1868), 281.
23 Ropes believes that if Burnside had attacked early and furiously, he might have gained
the victory before A. P. Hill's troops came up; Kenneth P. Williams indicts McClellan's

At Antietam the sun looked down on some of the bloodiest close-order fighting of the war. Where Hooker's men fought with Jackson's in a corn-field smitten by artillery on both sides, the losses were murderous. Thirty acres of grain, reported Hooker, were cut as close as by a scythe, and on the stubble Northern and Southern dead lay in heaps. Later, when two Union brigades struck Hood's Texan command, the blue and gray seemed like duelists who had lashed themselves together. They stood loading, firing, and reloading at fifty to eighty paces, determined to kill before being killed. In another area the slain lay in rows precisely as they had stood in their ranks a few moments before. Francis M. Palfrey commanded the Twentieth Massachusetts when Sumner marched a division into an ambush where ten Confederate brigades took three Union brigades in front, flank, and rear. "Change of front was impossible," wrote Palfrey later.[24] "In less time than it takes to tell it, the ground was strewn with the bodies of the dead and wounded. . . . Nearly two thousand were disabled in a moment."

The day closed on an undecided field. The Confederates had been forced back on their left by more than a mile, and on their right by half that distance. However, they still held a strong continuous line passing through Sharpsburg, and affording about as many natural advantages as that first chosen. On the field lay a multitude of dead and dying, for of the 130,000 men in the two armies, at least 21,000 or 16 per cent had been slain or wounded. "Who can tell, who can even imagine," wrote the colonel of the Twentieth Massachusetts long after, "the horrors of such a night, while the unconscious stars shone down, and the unconscious river went rippling by?" McClellan stated —or more probably understated—the Union loss as 2,010 killed, 9,416 wounded, and 1,043 missing. The Confederate casualties were fully as great; McClellan reported that, after the rebels themselves had buried many, 2,700 were counted and buried by the Northern forces.[25]

Lee and Jackson knew that although the army had fought magnificently, their gamble had failed. Nevertheless, Lee was unwilling to acknowledge defeat. Early that night the Confederate generals rode up, one by one, to report. They found Lee seated on his horse beside the highway. He asked each commander in turn, "What of your part of the line?" Each reported heavy losses, deadly

whole management of Burnside and others. Ropes, *Civil War*, II, 373–375; Williams, II, 450–458. A. D. Richardson wrote his managing editor Sept. 27: "The feeling with some of Burnside's staff officers (and I infer, with him also) is very bitter. They swear that Mc-Clellan tried to ruin him in the battle, by putting him where, with the force he had, he was sure to fail. They attribute it to jealousy of Burnside's reputation; Burnside *is* a great favorite with the troops." McClellan knew that Burnside earlier had been offered the command in his place, but we can agree with Richardson that he was above such an act. Gay Papers.
24 Palfrey, *Antietam and Fredericksburg*, 86, 87.
25 See map of the field, *American Conflict*, II, 205; Henderson, II, 261; Palfrey, *op. cit.*

fatigue, and a dismaying Federal superiority in numbers; the consensus favored retreat across the Potomac before daybreak. Even Jackson betrayed discouragement. He had never before met such odds, he said, and many of his best officers were dead. Hood was still more dejected, declaring that he had no men left. "Great God!" exclaimed Lee, "Where is the splendid division you had this morning?" "They are lying on the field where you sent them," responded Hood. "Few have straggled. My division has been almost wiped out."

Lee remained undaunted. He did not say, as a subsequent fable stated, that he was ready to give battle again in the morning; but he was confident that if McClellan delivered an attack, the Confederate lines would bloodily repulse it. At his back he had only one good ford over the Potomac, and in front a much stronger army, much of which McClellan had never used, for he had deliberately declined to throw in his reserves. No matter; with serene determination Lee posted artillery, distributed rations, and sent out guards to collect stragglers. He was ready for any eventuality except immediate retreat.[26]

Why did not McClellan hold a council of *his* lieutenants? Late in the afternoon he had met one of his division commanders, an old and trusted friend, who reported that his troops had done well but were somewhat scattered. "Collect them at once," said McClellan. "Fifteen thousand fresh troops have come up; more will arrive during the night. Tell your men that! We must fight tonight and tomorrow. If we cannot whip the enemy now, we may as well die upon the field. If we succeed we end the war." But he did not stick to this resolution.[27]

Lee counted on the cautious Union commander to lie still next morning— as he did. The long lines of troops faced each other, as the sun rose, with rifles and muskets loaded; the batteries stood unlimbered for instant action; pickets fingered their triggers nervously. While hour after hour ticked by, McClellan made no use of his overwhelming superiority in men and materials. Lee was encouraged by this quiescence to think of delivering an attack, but a brief inquiry showed it out of the question. He reluctantly admitted that it would be folly to attempt, as he momentarily thought of doing, to break the Northern right wing under Hooker. This was the unanimous judgment of his officers. When Jackson bade an able chief of artillery, Colonel Stephen D. Lee, to inspect the Union lines and ascertain positively whether with fifty guns and the available men he could smash the Union position, the report was unequivocal:

26 Henderson, II, 262, 263, Freeman, *Lee*, II, 403, 404. Longstreet wrote General E. A. Carman, Feb. 11, 1897, that the assemblage was not a council of war, but "the usual meeting of leading officers at night after battle to make their reports"; extra-illustrated *Battles and Leaders*, HL.

27 So reports A. D. Richardson, N. Y. *Tribune*, Sept. 29. McClellan also received large supplies of ammunition from Baltimore, while thousands of Pennsylvania militia had reached the Maryland boundary.

"General, it cannot be done." With evident dejection, Robert E. Lee accepted the verdict.[28]

All day September 18 the Confederate army waited in battle array. But its position grew more untenable every hour, for large national reinforcements were coming up. Late in the afternoon Lee decided upon retreat, and that night the Southern units, one by one, moved down to Boteler's Ford, two miles from Sharpsburg, and recrossed the Potomac. McClellan made no effort to molest them. Indeed, not until dawn of September 19 did reconnoitering Union detachments discover that Sharpsburg had been deserted, and by eight that morning the last Confederates were crossing the river.

[IV]

Of all McClellan's errors this failure to pursue was one of the most inexcusable. Had he pushed the national forces forward in a night attack, he might have thrown Lee's army into confusion. Rain fell throughout the night, roads and fields turned into pasty mire, and the single lane which led from the Shepherdstown highway to the ford was dangerously narrow. An enterprising commander would have inflicted heavy losses. As it was, the Union forces took not a single gun or wagon. "We were the conquerors," wrote one Northern reporter, "and yet our property—small arms and accoutrements by the hundred —was the only property thrown away to waste upon the field." [29] When McClellan on the 20th tardily ordered Fitz-John Porter to exploit the enemy retreat, he still had an opportunity to achieve a striking success. Union troops had now taken the ford, so that Porter easily crossed to the south bank:

The Confederates [writes Henderson] were in no condition to resist an attack in force. The army was not concentrated. The cavalry was absent. No reconnaissances had been made either of lines of march or of positions. The roads were still blocked by the trains. The men were exhausted by their late exertions, and depressed by their retreat, and the straggling was terrible. The only chance of safety lay in driving back the enemy's advanced-guard across the river before it could be reinforced; and the chance was seized without an instant's hesitation.[30]

So before Porter's force, inadequately sustained, could move a mile and a half beyond the Potomac, Jackson struck him and drove him back with a loss of 340 men. McClellan was so easily discouraged that he made no further effort to follow Lee, though he had received the quite fresh divisions of Humphrey

28 Henderson, II, 264-267, based on a letter by Gen. Stephen D. Lee; Freeman, *Lee*, II, 405.
29 N. Y. *Tribune*, Sept. 23, 1862.
30 Henderson, II, 269.

and Couch, and Washington made it plain that it expected pursuit and battle. Once more the Union intelligence service proved wretched. When a great cloud of dust had been espied in Virginia on September 18, one Union general demonstrated that it was Confederate reinforcements coming up. The morrow showed that the dust had been stirred by retreating rebel trains. It is very strange, commented one correspondent, that our generals, with their elaborate and expensive detective work, get such poor information. "The enemy outwit us under our very noses." [31] Lee's army, physically exhausted, disorganized by losses, and bereft of some of its ablest officers, was in sad estate. He informed President Davis that his force was too far diminished in numbers, and worse still, too much shaken in fighting spirit, to permit of a renewal of the offensive: "the hazard would be great and a reverse disastrous." [32] It was highly vulnerable to attack, but no attack came.

While Lincoln, Stanton, and the whole North waited for news of rapid movement and repeated blows, McClellan was writing Halleck: "This army is not now in condition to undertake another campaign nor to bring on another battle, unless great advantages are offered by some mistake of the enemy or pressing military exigencies render it necessary." He actually feared "a renewal of the attempt in Maryland"; he demanded every possible reinforcement.[33] The fact was that McClellan, as his letters to his wife show, had no thought of *destroying* Lee, for to check him seemed enough. "I feel some little pride," he wrote, "in having, with a beaten and demoralized army, defeated Lee so utterly and saved the North so completely." And again: "I feel that I have done all that can be asked in twice saving the country." [34] Not to conquer the South, but save the North—this was the object!

Lee's failure in his throw for high stakes was complete. The handful of recruits gained in Maryland did not equal his desertions; the captures of shoes, clothing, and other stores did not offset the loss of material by wear and tear; the gaps torn in Confederate ranks could never be repaired, for the men slain, disabled, and captured were among the best veterans of the army. But at any rate he had exerted himself to the utmost.

No such claim could be made for McClellan. Given a rare opportunity of overwhelming victory by his discovery, from the lost Confederate order, that Lee had divided his army, he had moved his troops at least twelve hours too late. Had he thrown the heavy bulk of his army through Crampton's Gap in South Mountain, he would probably have saved Harpers Ferry and would almost certainly have severed Jackson from Lee. Thereafter he moved so slowly

31   N. P. in N. Y. *Tribune*, Sept. 23, 1862.
32   O. R., I, xix, pt. 2, p. 627; Sept. 25, 1862.
33   *Ibid.*, pt. 1, pp. 70, 71.
34   *Own Story*, 613, 614.

that at Antietam, too, he fought his battle at least a day late—perhaps, says his subordinate Francis W. Palfrey, two days late.[35] Not only that, but his movements the evening before the battle advertised to the enemy his intention of using Hooker's right wing in the initial attack. His subsequent orders were of mediocre quality. He made practically no use at all of two corps, the Fifth and Sixth; permitted Burnside to delay his movement until six or seven hours after he had been ordered to seize a vital bridge and move forward; and failed properly to coordinate the action of the first, ninth, and twelfth corps, which should have moved forward in unison.

Lee, falling back to the area of Winchester and Bunker Hill, where the Shenandoah Valley afforded ample supplies, indulged his troops in much-needed rest while he made every effort to refill his ranks. The Richmond authorities so effectively assisted him that by October he had almost 68,000 officers and men. Though shoes and weapons were at first much needed, the government gradually supplied them. McClellan reoccupied Harpers Ferry as a safe bridgehead on the south side of the Potomac, placing Sumner with two corps in possession of it and the fortified heights. While he had just boasted that "our victory was complete," he was still not quite certain as to Sumner's safety, writing: "I think he will be able to hold his position until reinforcements arrive." His own strength was fully half again as large as Lee's. But believing that the Confederate army still outnumbered his own, he did not think it "safe" to go beyond Harpers Ferry, for it would not do to provoke this overwhelming Confederate host. Not until October 26th did the main national army, 110,665 strong (not counting the corps which was kept at Harpers Ferry under Henry W. Slocum and 4,500 troops guarding the upper Potomac) begin crossing the river.[36]

In the aftermath of the battle a telling illustration of the reliance Americans still placed upon improvisation was furnished by Oliver Wendell Holmes in his long-famous "hunt after the captain"—the captain being the future Justice Holmes. The night after Antietam the Autocrat of the Breakfast Table received from some unknown source a curt telegram: "Capt. Holmes wounded through the neck thought not mortal at Keedysville." He at once set off southward. After two days of travel he reached Frederick, where he heard a rumor that his boy was killed. Hiring a wagon, he began ransacking hospitals in all the towns about Sharpsburg—in Middletown, Boonsborough, Keedysville. It

---

35 Palfrey, who fought on the field, is explicit also in censuring McClellan for not doing more to inspire the troops by his active presence on the field once the battle was joined: "He passed the whole day, till toward the middle of the afternoon, when all the fighting was over, on the high ground near Fry's house, where he had some glasses strapped to a fence. . . ." *Antietam and Fredericksburg*, 119.

36 O. R., I, xix, pt. 1, p. 70; Ropes, *Civil War*, II, 440, 441.

would seem that colonels should have been able to report their dead and wounded; that hospitals could have made up central lists in each town; that nurses could have kept records to show when and where the wounded were forwarded to new destinations. But Holmes groped in the dark for his son. Finally he heard that the captain had set off north, not badly hurt, in a milk cart. Hotly pursuing this scent, at Harrisburg he learned that his son had taken the train to Philadelphia; but then came word that he had not appeared at the house of some Philadelphia friends whom he would naturally seek. Another frantic search of Harrisburg hospitals still disclosed no son. Finally, almost by accident, he lighted on the wounded captain in a train.

How many thousands of parents thus searched for their sons? How many wives waited weeks in anguish for news of a husband's fate? With no proper record of casualties by officers, no proper hospital lists, no burial records or graves registration, a darkness settled down on every great battlefield.

The dreary story of McClellan's complaints, delays, and excuses, which had so long irritated Lincoln and enraged the radicals who insisted on a vigorous war effort, was being resumed. Disappointment in the army itself over Mc-Clellan's failure to follow up Antietam was intense. Some soldiers read his excuse of "fatigue and exhaustion" with incredulity. "To us of the Thirteenth [Massachusetts]," wrote one "it seemed just possible that the enemy might be equally tired and a good deal more discomfited. . . . When men are stimulated by success in battle they forget everything but pushing their good fortune to a complete triumph." Many intelligent volunteers agreed with A. D. Richardson: "If McClellan had only attacked again early Thursday morning, we could have driven them into the river or captured them. . . . It was one of the supreme moments when by daring something, the destiny of the nation might have been changed." [37]

The anger of even moderate men in Washington when they saw that no effort was being made to press Lee's forces was emphatic. T. J. Barnett of the Interior Department talked at length on September 23 with both Lincoln and Caleb Smith. "I am convinced," he wrote S. L. M. Barlow, "that the government, if they dared, would supersede Mac." Why did they not dare? Because of apprehension that much of the army would be resentful, fear of a violent reaction in the North, and inability to find anyone to put in his place. But, records Barnett, Lincoln's praise for the victor of Antietam was very chilly: he felt "great confidence" in McClellan, he thought the general "well educated but very cautious," and altogether damned him with faint praise. In high circles, since Lee's escape, Barnett found men again whispering that McClellan was of a

37 C. E. Davis, Jr., *The Thirteenth Mass. Volunteers*, 142, 143; Richardson to S. H. Gay, Sharpsburg, Sept. 19, 1862, Gay Papers.

school and party which wished to exhaust the two sections, with a view to reconstructing the Union along conservative lines. This story had many variations and many believers.[38]

But if Northern discouragement after Antietam was keen, that of many Southern leaders was greater. The defeatism of Herschel V. Johnson and Alexander H. Stephens deepened. Jefferson Davis, subject to alternate waves of optimism and depression, was so hard hit that he again talked of resigning. "Our maximum strength has been mobilized," he told the Secretary of War, "while the enemy is just beginning to put forth his might." [39]

[V]

If McClellan could not use victory to convert the defensive into an offensive, Lincoln could. He had to deal with moral and political forces as powerful for harm as Lee's army, with Democrats hoping to use victory in the fall elections to save the South from utter revolution, selfish moneyed men whining about bankruptcy, and foreign haters of the United States who, encouraged by Confederate agents, hoped to use intervention to cripple the republic. But he knew how to strike promptly and effectively. As he said later, he did not wait for crushing victory; he waited only until Lee was driven from Maryland. That gave him sufficient vantage ground for the offensive he intended to launch.

Lincoln saw it was important, while waiting, to prepare the public mind for his decision to use emancipation as a war measure. Horace Greeley fortunately offered an opportunity. When readers opened the *Tribune* of August 20, 1862, they found the editorial page blazing with an open letter by Greeley headed "The Prayer of Twenty Millions," addressed to Lincoln. The editor

38 Barnett to Barlow, Sept. 23, 1862, Barlow Papers Judge Thomas M. Key of Cincinnati, an Ohio legislative leader who became aide and acting judge-advocate on McClellan's staff, gave Nathaniel Paige, a well-known Washington lawyer serving as war correspondent of the N. Y. *Tribune*, just three days before Antietam, a remarkable story. "He told me," later stated Paige, "that a plan to countermarch to Washington and intimidate the President had been seriously discussed the night before by the members of McClellan's staff, and his opposition to it [that is, Key's opposition] had, he thought, caused its abandonment." McClellan himself did not know about it. These staff officers wished to make Lincoln abandon his interferences with slavery, in the hope that thus the war could be stopped. Eighteen years later a writer for the Washington *Capitol*, who had known Paige, gave some corroboration. He declared that these staff officers used to call Lincoln, Halleck, and Stanton "the old women at Washington"; that they regarded Lincoln with contempt and Stanton with hatred; that it was their fixed belief that the war was folly, and bound to end in failure; and that they were really fighting for a boundary line, and not for the Union. Paige's statement, clipped from the *Tribune* without date, is in Hay Papers, Ill. State Hist. Library; Washington *Capitol*, March 21, 1880.

39 Edward Younger, *Inside the Confederate Govt.*, 28, 86; Strode, *Davis*, 307 ff.

stated at length what the twenty millions complained of, what they had a right to expect, and what they required.

They demanded, he wrote, that Lincoln execute the laws, and especially the provisions of the new Confiscation Act liberating the slaves of rebels. They insisted that he cease giving undue weight to the counsels of fossil politicians in the Border States, and recognize that whatever fortified slavery in this area also fortified treason. They wished the government to show more energy, opposing force to force in an undaunted spirit. They asked that he give up his mistaken deference to slavery in the South, and called on him to rebuke the army officers, including prominent generals, who showed greater regard for slavery than freedom. Finally, they demanded that he turn to the Negroes for aid. "We cannot conquer Ten Millions of People united in a solid phalanx against us, powerfully aided by Northern sympathizers and European allies. We must have scouts, guides, spies, cooks, teamsters, diggers and choppers. . . ."

This letter, with what Lincoln called its erroneous statements, false inferences, and impatient dictatorial tone, had to be answered. It gave him so perfect an opportunity for an explanation paving the way to his proclamation that Greeley three years later expressed the belief that the President had his statement ready written, and seized the occasion to promulgate it.[40] Lincoln saw that he must make his position entirely clear without prematurely betraying his decision on emancipation, and Greeley gave him a sounding board. He was President of the whole nation, Democrats and Republicans, conservatives, radicals, and moderates; he was not the tool of border reactionaries as Greeley intimated, or of Senate abolitionists as some Democrats said, but his own master, prosecuting the war with a single eye to maintenance of the Union. He sat down to produce one of his most memorable state papers—a paper that, published everywhere within the week, was worth a battle gained:

I would save the Union. I would save it the shortest way under the Constitution. The sooner the national authority can be restored, the nearer the Union will be to "the Union as it was." If there be those who would not save the Union, unless they could at the same time *save* slavery, I do not agree with them. If there be those who would not save the Union unless they could at the same time *destroy* slavery, I do not agree with them. My paramount object in this struggle *is* to save the Union, and is not either to save or to destroy slavery. If I could save the Union without freeing *any* slave I would do it, and if I could save the Union by freeing some and leaving others alone I would also do that. What I do about slavery, and the colored race, I do because I believe it helps to save the Union; and what I forbear, I forbear because I do *not* believe it would help to save the Union. I shall do *less* whenever I shall believe what I am doing hurts the cause, and I shall do *more* whenever I shall believe that doing more

40 Greeley's MS lecture on Lincoln, HL, published in *Century Magazine*, XX (July, 1891), 371 ff.; he was mistaken.

will help the cause. I shall try to correct errors when shown to be errors; and I shall adopt new views so soon as they shall appear to be true views.[41]

The applause given Lincoln's reply in moderate circles far outweighed the dissent from extremists on both sides. Greeley attempted a rebuttal; but Raymond's *Times*, the Douglasite *Morning Post* in Chicago, the Springfield *Republican*, the Cincinnati *Commercial*, and the influential Presbyterian *Observer* agreed on the President's cool sagacity. News was spreading around Washington (for the Cabinet had leaked it) that he had an emancipation proclamation ready, but that Seward and Blair wished it withheld.[42] Reports also spread of a colloquy between Lincoln and a Western delegation, including a couple of Senators, who had called to offer two Negro regiments—which under the new confiscation law he was empowered to accept. The President told them that he was ready to employ Negro teamsters, cooks, pioneers, and the like, but not soldiers. A warm discussion followed, which Lincoln was said to have closed with the words: "Gentlemen, you have my decision. It embodies my best judgment, and if the people are dissatisfied, I will resign and let Mr. Hamlin try it." Such heat had been generated that one caller exclaimed: "I hope, in God's name, Mr. President, you will!"[43]

Lee's retreat across the Potomac brought Lincoln the opening for which he had waited. At noon on Monday, September 21, occurred the famous Cabinet meeting at which he announced his final action. The members, summoned by messenger, were portentously solemn; and Lincoln, who did not like portentous solemnity, broke the spell by taking up a newly received copy of Artemus Ward's latest book, and reading aloud with happy enjoyment the chapter "Hihanded Outrage at Utica." Everybody except Stanton shared his laugh. Then the President also became solemn, and recalled their previous consultation on emancipation. Chase reports his speech:

"I think the time has come now. I wish it were a better time. I wish that we were in a better condition. The action of the army against the rebels has not been quite what I should have best liked. But they have been driven out of

41 Dated Aug. 22 and published in the *Tribune* Aug. 25, 1862; *Works*, V, 388, 389.

42 A few days before Greeley published "The Prayer of Twenty Millions," his reporter Adam S. Hill had written S. H. Gay, the managing editor, that Summer and Gurowski both possessed inside knowledge of the emancipation proclamation, and the fact that it had been temporarily suspended at the suggestion of Seward, Blair, and Thurlow Weed. Hill also wrote Gay that Senator S. C. Pomeroy gave him to understand that Lincoln would issue the proclamation as soon as he had assurance that his colonization project would succeed; Pomeroy being much interested in the Chiriqui plan. Greeley must therefore have known that the proclamation was impending when he brought out his letter of minatory tone. Perhaps he hoped to end all hesitations. See Hill's letters, Aug. 21, 25, 1862, Gay Papers.

43 The Chicago *Morning Post* and Chicago *Tribune*, Aug. 6, 1862, both carry accounts of this scene from their Washington correspondents.

Maryland, and Pennsylvania is no longer in danger of invasion." When they were at Frederick, he said, he had promised himself and God that he would issue his proclamation as soon as they were driven out. "I am going to fulfill that promise. I have got you together to hear what I have written down. I do not wish your advice about the main matter—for that I have determined for myself." But he would be glad to accept suggestions about phraseology or other minor points.

Lincoln added that he knew that various men in this and other transactions would do better than he, and if satisfied that another leader had a fuller measure of public confidence, he would—were it constitutionally possible— yield to him. "But though I believe that I have not so much of the confidence of the people as I had some time since, I do not know that, all things considered, any other person has more. . . . I must do the best I can, and bear the responsibility. . . ." [44]

All the Cabinet members acquiesced. Chase said he would have taken a somewhat different course, Blair reiterated his old fears as to the effect of the proclamation on the border and the army, and Seward suggested some verbal changes, but they were obviously pleased. Executed that day, the proclamation appeared in the morning newspapers September 23. Its essence lay in the third paragraph:

That on the first day of January in the year of our Lord, one thousand eight hundred and sixty-three, all persons held as slaves within any State, or designated part of a State, the people whereof shall then be in rebellion against the United States, shall be then, thenceforward, and forever free; and the executive government of the United States, including the military and naval authority thereof, will recognize and maintain the freedom of such persons, and will do no act or acts to repress such persons, or any of them, in any efforts they may make for their actual freedom.

Lincoln's sagacity did not fail him in the form of the document. It was an exercise of war powers; its main intent was not the liberation of a race (though he was fully conscious of this aspect) but the furtherance of the war effort and the preservation of the Union; and he did well to couch it in cold legal phraseology, direct and deadly as a bullet. Sumner and Greeley regretted the absence of rhetorical flourishes; "a poor document, but a mighty act," was John A. Andrew's verdict. But its moral import spoke for itself, and Lincoln, as Lowell remarked in the *Atlantic,* would have weakened it by an attempt at misplaced eloquence.[45]

44 Donald, ed., *Inside Lincoln's Cabinet,* 149, 150.
45 The proclamation did not embrace Tennessee, but in all of eight other States, and in the greater parts of Virginia and Louisiana, it did proclaim freedom. "We shall drive the conservatives of proslavery hunkerism into the very caves and holes of the earth," wrote Governor Andrew to Col. A. G. Brown, Sept. 23, 1862; Carnegie Bookshop Catalogue, N. Y.

That the proclamation was indeed "a mighty act" nobody could deny; but what were its precise results? To answer this question we must examine two entirely different subjects: first, its direct pragmatic effects in turning slaves into freedmen, and second, its impact upon public sentiment—the sentiment of the North, of the army, of the South, and by no means least, of Britain and the overseas world.

It is quite true that the popular picture of Lincoln using a stroke of the pen to lift the shackles from the limbs of four million slaves is ludicrously false. Since the proclamation was an exercise of the war powers, what its legal effect would be after the war ceased was uncertain. As the President could issue a proclamation, so he, or a successor, could revoke it. It did not apply to those districts which the Union armies held on the date Lincoln designated, January 1, 1863; could not be enforced in those districts which they did not hold; and had no application whatever to the four border slave States. To this extent it is a fact that, as Seward said, the proclamation emancipated slaves where it could not reach them, and left them in bondage where it could have set them free.[46] Lincoln himself continued to believe gradual emancipation better than summary liberation, and to cherish his plan for thus freeing the Negro in loyal areas. His friend David Davis, visiting him two months after the proclamation, found his ideas unchanged. Wrote Davis: "Mr. Lincoln's whole soul is absorbed in his plan of remunerative emancipation and he thinks if Congress don't fail him, that the problem is solved. He believes that if Congress will pass a law authorizing the issuance of bonds for the payment of emancipated negroes in the border States that Delaware, Maryland, Kentucky and Mo. will accept the terms. He takes great encouragement from the vote in Mo." [47]

But the proclamation had three immediate, positive, and visible effects. First, every forward step the Union armies took after January 1, 1863, now became a liberating step. Every county in Mississippi, Alabama, Virginia, and the Carolinas that passed under military control was thenceforth legally a free-soil county, the army bound to "recognize and maintain" emancipation.

In the second place, the percolating news of the proclamation encouraged slaves to escape, bringing them first in trickles and then rivulets within army

46 Greeley fiercely attacked Lincoln for not at once decreeing the liberation of all slaves in Louisiana and Tennessee; two States, he wrote, which "have more than One Hundred Thousand of their citizens in arms to destroy the Union." N. Y. *Tribune*, Jan. 3, 1863.

47 Davis found Lincoln weary, careworn, and heavily burdened with preparations for the imminent Congressional session. "It is a good thing he is fond of anecdotes and telling them," commented Davis, "for it relieves his spirits very much." To Leonard Swett, Nov. 26, 1862; David Davis Papers, Ill. State Hist. Lib. Missouri sentiment on slavery was changing fast, largely because of Lincoln's offer of reimbursement. Two months after Davis' letter the legislature was to pass a resolution declaring that $25,000,000 would be needed to carry out emancipation in the State, and asking Congress for that amount. H. A. Trexler, *Slavery in Missouri, 1804–1865*, p. 233 ff.

lines. How did it percolate? By grapevine telegraph, by the overheard discussions of masters, by glimpses of newspapers, by a new tension in the air. The idea that nearly all slaves wished to cling to their masters, a staple of Southern white folklore, did not fit the facts, for whenever escape became feasible, most of them were ready to embrace the opportunity. Edmund Ruffin, prominent among those who defended slavery as a positive good, must have been shocked when after McClellan's invasion nearly the whole work force decamped from his "Marlbourne" plantation in Princess Anne County. A few days later he wrote in his diary: "The fleeing of slaves from this neighborhood, which seemed to have ceased, has begun again. Mr. J. B. Bland lost 17 more a few nights ago, making his whole loss 27—though 5 were recaptured." [48]

The eminent cleric James Freeman Clarke, visiting a contraband camp in Washington early in 1863, asked one Negro just from Virginia whether the slaves down there had heard of the proclamation. "Oh yes, massa! We-all knows about it; only we darsen't let on. We pretends not to know. I said to my ole massa, 'What's this Marse Lincoln is going to do to the poor nigger? I hear he is going to cut 'em up awful bad. How is it, massa?' I just pretended foolish, sort of." [49] In the West the story was the same. The Cairo levees were black with fleeing slaves; Sherman wrote from Memphis that he had a thousand at work on the Memphis fortifications, and could send any number to St. Louis. Peter Cooper reported:

I learn direct from Mr. Dean, the provost-marshal of St. Louis, that the Proclamation of Freedom has done more to weaken the rebellion . . . than any other measure that could have been adopted. On his late visit to my house he informed me that he had brought on a large number of rebel officers and men to be exchanged at Fortress Monroe. During their passage he took the opportunity to ask the officers in a body what effect the President's Proclamation of Freedom had produced in the South. They reply was . . . that "it had played hell with them." Mr. Dean then asked them how that could be possible, since the negroes cannot read. To which one of them replied that one of his negroes had told him of the proclamation five days before he heard it in any other way. Others said their negroes gave them their first information of the proclamation. [50]

And in the third place, the proclamation irrevocably committed the United States, before the gaze of the whole world, to the early eradication of slavery

48 Ruffin MS Diary, July, 1862, LC.
49 *Autobiography*, 286.
50 Letter to Horatio Seymour, Sept. 28, 1863, Seymour Papers, LC. Sherman was using about 600 additional Negroes as stevedores, teamsters, cooks, and the like. More Negro men would have fled but for the fact they could not bring wives and children along. Sherman, Aug. 30, 1862, to Capt. Lewis B. Parsons, Parsons Papers. Herbert Aptheker in *Negro Slave Revolts* offers illuminating data on the readiness of slaves to escape.

from those wide regions where it was most deeply rooted; after which, all men knew, it could never survive on the borders. There could be no turning back! The government had dedicated itself to the termination of the inherited anachronism that had so long retarded the nation's progress, and crippled its pretensions to the leadership of the liberal forces of the globe. What was more, Lincoln had converted the war into a struggle for the rights of labor in the broadest sense.

[VI]

The reception given the proclamation ran the gamut from Greeley's paean of joy to Southern denunciations of it as a malignant effort to excite a servile revolt. The radical carping at Lincoln temporarily ceased. He had not merely pledged freedom to four million blacks, wrote Greeley; he was freeing twenty millions of whites from an ancient thralldom. For the moment Wade, Sumner, Chandler, Thad Stevens, Ashley, and their associates were transported. Charles Eliot Norton could scarcely see to pen a letter for his tears. "The President may be a fool," wrote George William Curtis to Frederick Law Olmsted, a stubborn critic. "But see what he has done. He may have no policy. But he has given us one." Among temperate free-soilers a great body undoubtedly took the view indicated by David Davis. "The people," he wrote an Illinois friend, "are fast getting into the belief that as quiet and moderate war measures have accomplished no good, severe measures are now necessary, and if the rebels will not lay down their arms, that is the duty of the Govt. to smite them hip and thigh." [51]

The highest note was struck by those who viewed the proclamation in the light of its liberating power: Whittier, Bryant, Lowell, all using pens tipped with flame. Most eloquently of all rose the voice of Emerson, declaring in the *Atlantic* that the force of the act was its commitment of the republic to justice. Doing this, it proved that the Northern soldiers had not died in vain; it made a victory of the sad defeats; it repaired the health of the nation. It was by no means necessary, he went on, that it should produce any sudden or signal results in the ranks of either the slaves or the slavemasters; indeed, the final redemption of the black race must lie with the blacks. Still, this ill-fated, much injured people would benefit at once. They will "lose somewhat of the dejection sculptured for ages in their bronzed countenances, and uttered in the wailing of their plaintive music"—a race naturally benevolent, joyous, and in-

51 Greeley in N. Y. *Tribune*, Sept. 23, 24, 1862; Curtis, Sept. 29, 1862, Olmsted Papers; Davis, Nov. 26, 1862, David Davis Papers.

dustrious, whose very miseries sprang from their talent for usefulness, "which in a more moral age, will not only defend their independence, but will give them a rank among nations." [52]

The jeers of the South were echoed by hisses and groans from the copperhead press of the North. The New York *Express* declared that this foolscap thunder would add 300,000 men to the rebel armies, and bring 30,000 Kentuckians to the side of Bragg. It was grand-scale bunkum, swaggering bravado, which, alas! converted a war for the Constitution into a war against Southern rights and liberties.[53] The Chicago *Times* took the same position. Two chords on which Northern objectors harped were that the proclamation altered the objects of the war, and that its direct result would be a heavy influx of Negroes into the free States. Indiana and Illinois already barred Negro immigrants. S. S. Cox of Ohio, a State which had no bar but repeatedly considered raising one, had already dwelt in his House speeches on Northern fears of a flood of freedmen. Could anyone be sure that Ohio troops would continue fighting if the fruit of their sacrifices was a northward flow of "millions of blacks?" [54] It saddened Lincoln to find his friend Orville H. Browning, his helper in revising the inaugural address, and an able exponent of his Borderland policy, taking the same Negrophobe stand.

In private utterances, few Northern critics were harsher than McClellan, who was aware that Democrats spoke of him as their next Presidential nominee. The ink was hardly dry on the newspaper headlines before he was sounding out the merchant William H. Aspinwall; "I am very anxious to learn how you and the men like you regard the recent Proclamation of the Presdt inaugurating servile war, emancipating the slaves, and at one stroke of the pen changing our free institutions into a despotism—for such I regard as the natural effect of the last Proclamation suspending the habeas corpus throughout the land." [55] His ideas were shared by Fitz-John Porter, who maliciously reported to Manton Marble of the *World:* "The Proclamation was ridiculed in the army—causing disgust, discontent, and expressions of disloyalty to the views of the administration, amounting I have heard, to insubordination, and for this reason—All such bulletins tend only to prolong the war by rousing the bitter feelings of the South—and causing unity of action among them—while the reverse with us. Those who fight the battles of the country are tired of the war and wish to see

52 *Atlantic Monthly,* X (Nov., 1862), 638–642; a forecast of free Ethiopia, Ghana, Liberia, Nigeria, and all the rest. Whittier's "Laus Deo" and Bryant's "The Death of Slavery" in due course fittingly commemorated the great step. "Great is the virtue of the Proclamation," wrote Emerson in his journals. "It works when men are sleeping, when the army goes into winter quarters, when generals are treacherous or imbecile."
53 Oct. 20, 22, 1862.
54 *Cong. Globe,* 37th Cong., 2d Sess., 2501–2503, June 3, 1862.
55 Sept. 26, 1862, extra-illustrated *Battles and Leaders,* HL.

it ended soon and honorably—by a restoration of the union—not merely a suppression of the rebellion." [56]

The question of the real attitude of the troops toward the document is too complex, and the evidence too conflicting, for easy summarization. The army was a reflection of the nation, possessing its radical and conservative wings. But certainly Fitz-John Porter misstated the attitude. The safest generalization is this: that most Northern soldiers approved of the proclamation, but did so not so much from humanitarian motives as because their blood was now up, they wanted to win a decisive victory, and Lincoln's edict seemed to herald a relentless prosecution of the war. The army, Colonel W. H. Blake of the Ninth Indiana wrote Schuyler Colfax, has one central idea, to whip the rebels and dictate peace. It contained little abolitionist sentiment; but "there is a desire to destroy everything that in *aught* gives the rebels strength," "there is a universal desire among the soldiery to take the negro from the secesh master," and so "this army will sustain the emancipation proclamation and enforce it with the bayonet." [57]

But though the plain soldier, like Lincoln, thought of emancipation primarily as a war measure, in countless instances he also rejoiced in its enlargement of human freedom. As the Union troops in marching South studied the worst aspects of slavery, they quickly learned to hate it. When they saw the auction block, the whipping post, the iron gyve, when they glimpsed the field hand cringing under his master's gaze, when the fleeing slave bared his scarred back, or told a tale of young children wrenched from the mother's arms, they resolved that slavery must die. [58]

One result of the proclamation was to turn a potentially harmful convention of Northern governors at Altoona, Pennsylvania, into an innocuous farce. Its prime mover was Andrew G. Curtin of Pennsylvania, who early in September had written Andrew of Massachusetts that the time was ripe to give the war a definite aim, and that the loyal executives should take prompt, united, decisive action. Correspondence among various Northern governors followed. Tod of Ohio, Blair of Michigan, Berry of New Hampshire, Pierrepont of Connecticut, and others were drawn into the movement. It inevitably aroused some pernicious newspaper speculation that it was hostile to Lincoln, that it aimed at the overthrow of McClellan, that it was a maneuver by Andrew and Curtin to get themselves re-elected, and so on. Happily, these two governors had enough sense to go to Lincoln beforehand. He told them of his impending proclamation, and with characteristic considerateness asked if they wished him to defer

56 Sept. 30, 1862, Manton Marble Papers, LC.
57 Glasgow, Ky., Nov. 7, 1862, Colfax Papers, Ind. State Lib.
58 See T. F. Dornblaser, *Sabre Strokes of the Pennsylvania Dragoons*, 120–121, for a vigorous statement.

its issuance until they had requested him to act. They replied that he should by all means bring it out first, and they would follow it with a strong address of commendation.[59] This was done; the conference met on the Allegheny crest September 24, and agreed to a paper written by Andrew. All appended their names but Bradford of Maryland, who, aware how deeply his State was torn, remarked: "Gentlemen, I am with you heart and soul, but I am a poor man, and if I sign that address I may be a ruined one." Misrepresentation of the conference nevertheless persisted, and it had better never been held.

The fact was that some of these governors had been as deeply pained as Stanton and Chase by the reassignment of McClellan to command. John A. Andrew, for one, detested the general. Like many other leaders in this terrible crisis, he became overwrought at times. Once this summer he fell on his knees in his office to pray for emancipation, and made a visitor pray with him! He had written Count Gurowski on September 6: "Besides doing my proper work, I am sadly but firmly trying to help organize some movement, if possible to save the Prest. from the infamy of ruining his country." Curtin, Yates, and Austin Blair felt much the same. But now they knew that Lincoln, after all, had not fallen into reactionary hands or taken a wrong step.

[VII]

Two facts were now abundantly clear: Lincoln was running the war, the reins of power held tightly in his muscular grip; and he was determined to run it so that the North would keep the initiative on all fronts—military, economic, and moral. If McClellan were not a useful implement in maintaining offensive operations, he would discard McClellan. But the Union would relax no pressure and neglect no effort. And no man better grasped the essence of statesmanship, which is the achievement of what is practicable within the limits of what is desirable.

That Lincoln regarded the proclamation not merely as opening a sterner war, but as announcing a revolution, is clear from the message he shortly sent Congress. It *was* revolution, though he hoped to keep it a controlled revolution. When at this very time he made his before-quoted remark to T. J. Barnett about so shaping the tragic conflict that it should always have a peace in its belly, he made it plain that if the South did not yield during the hundred days before the preliminary proclamation gave way to the final document, it must face a mighty socioeconomic upheaval. "What I write," Barnett warned S. L. M. Bar-

59 The Austin Blair and Andrew Papers have full correspondence; see also the statement Curtin gave Rufus Rockwell Wilson in 1881, *Lincoln Herald*. W. B. Hesseltine in *Lincoln and the War Governors, passim,* presents evidence that the governors were anxious to maintain State authority as against Lincoln's growing use of Federal power.

low for the benefit of New York Democrats, "was indicated plainly enough by the President—but I know more of his spirit than his publications imply. The idea is this—From the expiration of the 'days of grace' the character of the war will be changed. It will be one of subjugation and extermination if the North can be coerced and coaxed into it. The South [i.e., the old Southern system] is to be destroyed and replaced by new propositions and ideas." [60]

To those who had eyes, the lineaments of Lincoln's greatness were emerging. His great decision, premature to some, tardy to others, had been taken with his acute instinct for the ripening moment. No journal expressed this fact better than the Springfield *Republican:* "The President's action is timely—neither too soon nor too late. It is thorough—neither defeating itself by halfway measures nor by passionate excess. It is just and magnanimous— doing no wrong to any loyal man, and offering no exasperation to the disloyal. It is practical and effective—attempting neither too little nor too much. And it will be sustained by the great mass of the loyal people, North and South; and thus, by the courage and prudence of the President, the greatest social and political revolution of the age will be triumphantly carried through in the midst of a civil war." [61]

But the most remarkable aspect of Lincoln's stroke was its impact on world opinion—a subject of momentous consequence, requiring careful examination.

60 Dated "Friday" (Sept. 25, 1862), Barlow Papers.
61 Sept. 24, 1862. Congress had approved of Lincoln's general plan for colonizing freedmen on the Chiriqui coast of Panama in New Granada (Colombia), and in April and June, 1862, had appropriated $600,000 for the settlement there of Negroes liberated under the Confiscation Act and in the District of Columbia. Secretary Usher of the Interior Department was ready to push the undertaking. But Lincoln, seeing that some "political hacks"— Senator S. C. Pomeroy of Kansas was one—hoped to enrich themselves from the contemplated contract, drew back. His hesitancy was shared by Seward, who had become doubtful about the title to the Chiriqui lands and the existence of good coal there. In October, Lincoln bade Usher to tell Pomeroy that the enterprise would be abandoned indefinitely.

10

Britain, France, and the War Issues

AMERICANS hardly watched more closely than Britons the fighting at Second Manassas and Antietam, nor did New York newspapers report it with much more accurate detail than London journals. For Europe as well as the United States the war had critical meaning. Consequences of the greatest magnitude hung upon the deepening tension of European-American and especially Anglo-American relations in the late summer of 1862. It is hardly too much to say that the future of the world as we know it was at stake.

A conflict between Great Britain and America would have crushed all hope of the mutual understanding and growing collaboration which led up to the practical alliance of 1917–18, and the outright alliance which began in 1941. It would have made vastly more difficult if not impossible the coalition which defeated the Central Powers in the First World War, struck down Nazi tyranny in the Second World War, and established the unbreakable front of Western freedom against Communism. Anglo-French intervention in the American conflict would probably have confirmed the splitting and consequent weakening of the United States; might have given French power in Mexico a long lease, with the ruin of the Monroe Doctrine; and would perhaps have led to the Northern conquest of Canada. The forces of political liberalism in the modern world would have received a disastrous setback. No battle, not Gettysburg, not the Wilderness, was more important than the contest waged in the diplomatic arena and the forum of public opinion.

The popular conception of this contest is at some points erroneous, and at a few grossly fallacious. The framework of the received story is that the British aristocracy and "upper class" were bitterly hostile to the North; that by social pressure and the thunder of the London *Times* they controlled the Ministry, itself naturally unfriendly; that Lord John Russell, the Foreign Secretary, was ready to follow the eager Napoleon III in breaking the Union blockade and recognizing the Confederacy; that the heroic Lancashire cotton workers, starving but devoted to freedom, followed their champion John Bright in resisting intervention; and that Antietam and the emancipation proclamation came in the nick of time to prevent European interference and war. Thus stated, the story has all the fascination of melodrama—a melodrama that ends with the footlights blazing up, the orchestra playing "The Star-Spangled Banner," and liberal-minded Britons applauding the name of Abraham Lincoln as they prepare to pass the second Reform Bill.

This story has elements of truth, but equal elements of fiction. In reviewing it we must remember several corrective facts. It does injustice to the great intelligent middle class in Britain; it does some injustice to Earl Russell, and still more to the Prime Minister, Palmerston; it does injustice to other Ministers; it overstates the role of the Lancashire workers, and the immediate, though not ultimate, impact of emancipation; and it omits important elements. It attributes too much of British governmental policy to Machiavellianism. Palmerston and his Ministers were in fact actuated primarily by a desire to protect British interests in common-sense ways, keeping the realm out of trouble. While pursuing this policy they were acutely aware of the danger of some sudden embroilment in Europe, of the weaknesses of their navy, and of the flimsiness of their Canadian defenses. They were conscious, too, of the importance of respecting the right of blockade, for Britain had direly needed that right in Napoleonic times, and might direly need it again.

If the diplomatic scene had any key figure, it was Palmerston, experienced, wary, and doggedly devoted to those British interests which fared best in peace. He disclosed a fundamental attitude when he wrote October 16, 1861: "The love of quarrelling and fighting is inherent in man, and to prevent its indulgence is to impose restraints on natural liberty. A state may so shackle its own subjects, but it is an infringement on national independence to restrain other nations." [1] In brief, Great Britain did not like other nations to fight, but when they did, her true policy was not intervention but neutrality.

[I]

Americans were acutely sensitive to British opinion for various reasons. Great Britain was the one country which could heavily injure the United States. Old ties of kinship, two centuries of deference to British opinion, the universal influence of British literature, the economic and financial power of Britain, all counted strongly. "Why do Americans attack us and not France?" many Englishmen asked H. W. Beecher on his visit in 1863. "Because," he replied, "we in our deepest hearts care for England, and not much for France." [2]

---

1 Max Beloff, "Great Britain and the American Civil War," *History*, N. S., XXXVI (Feb., 1952), 47.
2 Brooklyn speech, Nov. 25, 1863, N. Y. *Tribune*, Nov. 26.

At the outset, when it was supposed the conflict might be short, British sympathy was primarily with the Federal government. "The English are really on our side," wrote Henry Adams from London, July 2, 1861, and his father the Minister said the same. But after Bull Run opinion became sharply divided.

The fact that after Bull Run most Tories and most of the aristocracy sympathized with the Confederate cause was patent. The London *Morning Star*, stanchly on the Union side, gibed at "that upper circle in which an aristocracy of blood acknowledges kinship with an aristocracy of color." [3] Charles Francis Adams wrote Seward that the chief desire of the aristocracy was to see the Confederacy victorious, and John Bright agreed. But it was by no means true that this attitude represented a deliberate calculation that a weaker United States would mean a stronger Great Britain. Rather, five principal reasons, all natural enough, might be assigned for the Tory predilection for the South.

One was a simple feeling of sympathy for the underdog. The Confederacy was so heavily outmatched, and her defeat after Donelson and New Orleans seemed so imminent, that the brilliant strokes of Lee and Stonewall Jackson aroused admiration. Another source lay in the belief, fostered by Thackeray's *The Virginians*, the fiction of John Esten Cooke, and much Southern oratory, that the South represented a Cavalier element, or at any rate, that Southerners were of good English stock, whereas the North was a motley conglomerate of British, Irish, Germans, Scandinavians, and whatnot. Much British journalism emphasized this view. Even William H. Russell, while giving accurate facts upon the "mean whites" in letters from the South, discovered gentlemen more easily there. And it was easy for English conservatives, perturbed by the growth of democratic and radical sentiment, to see that the collapse of American democracy would offer a good argument to check the movement. Lord Robert Cecil, later Lord Salisbury, who presently distinguished himself as an opponent of the Reform Bill, made the most of American troubles. Lord Derby had the same outlook.[4]

Another root of Tory unfriendliness to the North was the smoldering resentment over recent Yankee bluster and truculence. During the 1850's Lewis Cass, Douglas, and Ben Wade had continuously ranted against the British Government, even the reserved Jefferson Davis and cultivated Sumner had used harsh epithets in assailing British policy, and Seward had taken an occasional twist at the lion's tail. Britons remembered the hard American bargaining over the Maine boundary, the slogan "Fifty-four forty or fight," and the filibuster activities in Cuba and Central America. While Great Britain had her own record

---

3 May 12, 1862.
4 Herbert Paul, *Hist. Modern England*, II, 311. But Derby and other responsible Conservatives were consistently non-interventionist; W. D. Jones, "The British Conservatives and the Amer. Civil War," *Am. Hist. Rev.*, LVIII (April, 1953), 527-543.

of bullying, to Englishmen it did not seem so bad. So warm a friend of the North as John Stuart Mill wrote that the most operative cause of English feeling against the United States "is the general belief that Americans are hostile to England, and long to insult and humble her if they had but an opportunity; and the accumulated resentment left by a number of small diplomatic collisions, in which . . . through the reluctance of England to push matters to extremities, which do not vitally concern the national honor, bullying and blustering have been allowed to prevail." [5] Charles Francis Adams avowed to a close friend in 1861: "My feelings, as you know, have never been partial to the English. I suppose I owe the bias to those who have gone before me." [6] Why should he expect Earl Russell to be partial to the Americans?

The principal organ of upper-class anti-Northern opinion, the London *Times*, was the one British newspaper widely regarded throughout America. Its circulation of 60,000 did not compare with the *Telegraph*'s 200,000, but it had greater prestige than any other daily in the world. Lincoln, who knew that it represented old-time governing-class opinion, compared its power to that of the Mississippi.[7] Its manager at this time was Mowbray Morris, a Conservative whose West Indian birth gave him a sense of kinship with the South; its editor was J. T. Delane, who had visited the United States in 1856 without giving due attention to political and economic subjects. Before Sumter, Delane in a leader laid down the proposition that while the North was legally right on secession, it was impossible to keep so large and strong a portion of the nation as the Confederacy in the Union against its will, and that Lincoln was therefore wrong in condemning the land to the horrors of civil war in a hopeless undertaking.[8] The *Times* was not specially sensitive on slavery—it had published a review condemning *Uncle Tom's Cabin* as bad propaganda—and it had a high sense of British dignities and prerogatives.

In the early months of the war the *Times* showed editorial moderation, while its special American correspondent W. H. Russell was indefatigable, perceptive, and impartial. But after Russell returned home early in 1862 smarting under the castigation he had received for his accurate reports of Bull Run, of inefficiency in the volunteer army, and of the crudity of certain politicians, the United States, as we have said, paid a penalty for its ill treatment of this distinguished journalist.

Delane and Mowbray Morris chose as their new correspondent Charles Mackay, a popular versifier and former editor of the London *Illustrated News*

5 See his review of Cairnes's *Slave Power* in *Westminster Review*, (Oct., 1862).
6 To R. H. Dana, Jr., Aug. 28, 1861, MHS.
7 *Hist. of the Times*, II, 354–358, gives circulation; the *Telegraph* was a penny paper, the *Times* threepenny.
8 March 19, 1861.

who had lectured in the United States and written a shallow volume of impressions. They instructed him to mold his letters to the anti-Northern policy of the paper. Because he had presided at a secessionist lecture in London he met a frigid reception in Boston and New York, and found important Unionist sources of information closed. Fernando Wood, however, cultivated him and poured a special poison into his ear. From his residence on Staten Island, for he was less inclined than Russell to go into the field, Mackay sent home a series of prejudiced letters, making the most of military failures and evidences of popular discontent. His acrid reports, including one garbled by a proofreader to accuse both Northern and Southern soldiers of cowardice, gave so much offense that Bennett's *Herald* suggested tearing down his house. No single person did more during the war to create misunderstanding and animosity between Britain and America. At the end of the conflict Seward, a former friend, sent him a stinging letter: "I pray God to forgive you for the great crime you have committed." [9]

It should be added that the *Times* correspondent in the Confederacy meanwhile wrote well-informed, astute, and sympathetic articles.

Worse than Mackay's letters, however, were the malignant editorial articles of the *Times*. As the London *Daily News* put it,[10] the Thunderer dealt in "reckless misrepresentation, falsifying of facts, and tirades dipped in gall." The burden of the argument was that the North was spilling seas of blood and reducing large European populations to penury in a cruel effort to subjugate a section which asked only to be let alone. "Nine millions of people, inhabiting a territory of 900,000 square miles, and animated by one spirit of resistance, can never be subdued." [11] What of slavery? "Now, we are in Europe thoroughly convinced that the death of slavery must follow as certainly upon the success of the Confederates in the war as the dispersion of darkness occurs upon the rising of the sun." When the egregious John A. Roebuck, M. P., a Confederate supporter, called the Northern people "the scum and refuse of Europe," the *Times* applauded speaker and speech.[12] It assailed American taxation at a time when it

9 Mackay, (1814-1889), an irregularly educated Scot, was perhaps best known for his song "The Good Time Coming," which sold 400,000 copies. His *Life and Liberty in America* (2 vols., 1859) was not unfriendly, though he was much offended by politicians, Jefferson Brick journalists, and Irish agitators who continually insulted England. His autobiography, *Through the Long Day*, makes it clear that he wrote just what Delane and Mowbray Morris wanted. His garbled column on Oct. 14, 1862, declared that the recent heavy battles "proved anything but the courage of the combatants"; he had written "nothing but." Seward's letter, Nov. 3, 1865, replying to Mackay's note of sympathy after the attempt on the Secretary's life, is in *Through the Long Day*, II, 274. Marie Corelli was Mackay's illegitimate daughter. Cf. Cook, *Delane*, 165.
10 Aug. 8, 1862.
11 Feb. 7, 1862.
12 Oct. 7, 1862.

was only half the British rate, spoke of "drafting day by day the youth of their country" when conscription was still unknown, and referred to Northerners as "these degenerate and insensate people." [13] An outrageous financial article suggested that slavery was a lesser evil than the new American tariff, which must alienate every commercial nation.[14] These articles and editorials, reprinted entire in many Northern journals with angry comment, were all too generally accepted as the voice of the dominant element in British affairs.

Yet it was noteworthy that the *Times* never advised British intervention, and repeatedly rejected the idea. After the fall of New Orleans, Delane remarked that the North had a right to anticipate early victory, and to expect the South to re-enter the Union "on the easy and honorable terms which the North would be glad to offer." When McClellan failed and Pope was defeated, he argued that the hope of a voluntary change of Northern policy offered cogent reason for standing aloof. The late autumn of 1862 found the *Times* anguished by the suffering of Lancashire. "Yet we are still willing to bear and forbear," it declared, "if by any means we can keep out of this unnatural quarrel, and avoid giving the dominant faction in America the power of saying that England, out of jealousy or revenge, broke up the Republic." From that stand the Thunderer did not budge.[15]

[II]

Americans erred when they assumed that the aristocratic classes, with the *Times*, *Morning Post*, and *Saturday Review* as mouthpieces, controlled the nation. When Charles Francis Adams early in the war wrote that "the great body of the people and very much the largest portion of the press do sympathize with us," he meant that most of the middle as well as lower class stood by the North. And John Stuart Mill had correctly written in 1840 that the British government "is progressively changing from the government of a few to the . . . regime of the middle class." Richard Cobden expressed the fact a little differently when he wrote in 1864: "The House of Commons represents the wealth of the country though not its numbers, and I have no doubt the members hear from all the great seats of our commercial ship-owning and manufacturing industries that the busy prosperous people there want peace."

13 See London *Daily News*, Aug. 8, 15, 1862, for an indictment of the *Times*, with quotations from reckless leaders.

14 This *Times* article, July 21, 1862, aroused great anger. No Southern journal had gone further in upholding slavery.

15 That Tory organ the London *Morning Post*, which specially appealed to fashionable society and the landed gentry, also repudiated interventionism with vigor; see its leaders, November 11, 14, 1862. In *Punch*, Sir John Tenniel's cartoons repeatedly wounded Northern feeling without doing anything to please the South, but it too was stubbornly opposed to intervention.

William Michael Rossetti, poet-brother of Dante Gabriel and Christina Rossetti, penning a retrospective analysis just after the war, took the same view as Adams. Distinguishing at least seven important schools of thought, he concluded that the most significant party believed the North to be in the right, but for a time doubted both its reformative zeal in dealing with slavery, and its ability to win. When the North dispelled these doubts, the party took its side with tremendous power.

Indeed, wrote Rossetti, many Britons cared about nothing in the struggle but its antislavery impact. At first the cautious utterances of Washington leaders suggested that the North hardly threatened slavery, but most middle-class Britons watched eagerly for every act, every speech, which proved the vitality of abolitionist sentiment. They thrilled to the manifestoes of Frémont and Hunter, the liberation of "contrabands" by Northern legions, and the enlistment of Negro auxiliaries. After the emancipation proclamation, they felt "a genuine veneration and even enthusiasm for President Lincoln." Thus they gradually cast off hesitancies which chilled their sympathy. "This party was diffused over the length and breadth of the land." It numbered some of the aristocracy, and a multitude of the laboring millions, but its chief strength lay in the hard-working, religious, philanthropic sections of the well-to-do middle class; the groups which gravitated toward radicalism in politics, dissent in church affairs, and good works in social practice. The people who thus slowly made up their minds that the North *would* end slavery, and *could* win, strengthened and at last made irresistible the party which stood for Lincoln and freedom.[16]

Herbert Spencer, looking back in old age on the wartime tides of British sentiment, felt sure that the main body of thoughtful middle-class opinion had been with the Union. This was Henry Ward Beecher's impression in 1863. Three influences, he said on his return from England, had swayed most of the upper classes against the North: commercial interest and rivalry, class pride and fear of contagious radicalism, and a feeling that the United States was growing too powerful. "But if England is to be judged by her middle class . . . she is with us." While the plutocracy was hostile, "the brains that represent progress in Great Britain are in our favor." It was true, Beecher remarked, that a majority of the friends of the North were still without the ballot, but he had learned in England the surprising fact that the voteless men, when united and determined, could control the men who voted. Bishop McIlvaine,

16 Emerson, whose chapter on the *Times* in *English Traits* had contributed to its American prestige, noted that "the privileges of nobility are passing to the middle class"; Ch. XI. Rossetti's long paper appeared in the *Atlantic*, XVII (Feb., 1866), 129-149. A Londoner born and bred, a civil servant, and a Pre-Raphaelite leader, he had access to varied social circles.

the Episcopal leader whom Washington sent to Britain to use his influence, reported to the same effect.[17]

Though hostile British voices often had waspish vehemence, the adherents of the North showed greater conviction and moral fervor. They felt more deeply; Cobden wrote in 1861 that he and Bright regarded the war almost with the sorrow of a personal affliction. To them the outcome would be the victory or defeat of a mighty world cause. William E. Forster, agent of the Quakers in the Irish famine and champion of universal education; Milner Gibson, who had denounced the Crimean War and in Parliament and Cabinet had upheld the tenets of the Manchester Liberals; Wilfrid Lawson, a young radical from northern England; James Stansfeld, intimate friend of Mazzini; Monckton Milnes, poet, politician, and friend of Henry Adams—all exhibited burning earnestness. The principal liberal editors put passion into their utterances. Hutton, editor of the *Spectator*, for example, declared that the Americans were "the only people who . . . are still consciously toiling on to a higher future."

Despite notable exceptions, the best intellectual leaders of the kingdom were on the Northern side. No pro-Southern pamphleteers showed the energy of John Stuart Mill, greatest of English political thinkers; Goldwin Smith, professor of modern history at Oxford; J. E. Cairnes, professor of political economy at Galway; Thomas Hughes, whose *Tom Brown's Schooldays* had earned him a wide popular influence; and the young journalist Edward Dicey, who in his book *Six Months in the Federal States* praised the volunteer army and expressed wonder over the newborn strength of the American people. An impressive array of magazines, church organs, and provincial newspapers fought for the North.[18]

It hurt Northern admirers of Carlyle to find him indifferent to the great issues of the conflict. He abhorred the war, and thought it irrational for white

17 Beecher in N. Y. *Tribune*, Nov. 26, 1863. He said: "Men that are struggling for a better future for themselves and their children, that class is on our side. . . . Our allies have been the common people of England." The county franchise was restricted to those with a holding of £50 rental. McIlvaine wrote Bishop Bedell, Jan. 10, 1862, Seward Papers, Rochester Univ.

18 Among magazines *Macmillan's*, the *Westminster Review*, a radical organ, the *Dial*, the *Observer*, the *Reader* (literary), the *Beehive* (trades union organ), and *Lloyd's Weekly News*, edited by Douglas Gerrold, with a circulation of 400,000 weeky, chiefly among workers. Among church organs the *Freeman* (Baptist), the *British Ensign* (Congregationalist), and the *Nonconformist* (for dissenters generally). Among provincial newspapers the Manchester *Examiner*, widely circulated in Lancashire factory areas, the Liverpool *Daily Post*, the Birmingham *Daily Post*, the Newcastle *Chronicle*, the Bucks *Chronicle*, the Leeds *Mercury*, the Bradford *Advertiser*, the Preston *Guardian*, the Carlisle *Examiner*, the Dundee *Advertiser*, the Edinburgh *Caledonian Mercury*, and the Belfast *Northern Daily Whig*. The immense influence of these provincial dailies has never been properly assessed by students of the period.

men to butcher each other over the position of the blacks. His little *jeu d'esprit*, "Ilias Americana in Nuce," or the American Iliad in a nutshell, betrayed his dislike of democracy and his blindness to the moral evils of slavery. Mill, his old friend, broke with him, and administered a delicate thrust by replying to Carlyle's "The Nigger Question" in an essay called "The Negro Question." But Trollope, Kingsley, George Meredith, and George Eliot were in varying degrees for the North, while the two Brownings, Clough, and Landor made their sympathy clear. These writers knew the mind and heart of the middle class. Pamphlets like Dicey's "Labour and Slavery" and W. E. Baxter's "The Social Condition of the Southern States" were addressed to the plain people.[19] Beecher thought that pro-Northern newspapers circulated a million copies daily, a conservative estimate. Antislavery clergymen certainly addressed millions every Sunday. Cairnes's book *The Slave Power* was initially presented in the form of popular lectures, which, like Baxter's speeches, struck a deep chord.[20] Dicey contrasted the Southern and Northern meetings in England:

At the former you had upon the platform peers, members of Parliament, merchant princes, and many of the . . . leading men of England, but in the body of the hall you have never had a free, crowded audience. The head has always been there but the body has been wanting. At the latter class, you have had few men of note as leaders. . . . But, in return, you have had audiences crowded to the very roof.

The power of working-class and middle-class opinion became a powerful restraint upon British elements which wished to interfere in America. So long as the North seemed flabby on slavery and its chances of success dubious, this opinion was uncrystallized. Its strength grew until, once the Lincoln Administration struck at slavery and evinced a grim determination to win, it became one of the impressive phenomena of the war. "Do not forget," Cobden wrote Beecher, "that we have in this case, for the first time in our history, seen the masses of the British people taking the side of a foreign government against its rebellious citizens. In every other instance, whether in the case of the Poles, Italians, Hungarians, Corsicans, Greeks, or South Americans, the popular sympathy of this country has always leaped to the side of the insurgents."[21]

Unfortunately for subsequent Anglo-American relations, most expressions

19   Both issued 1862; Baxter, a Scottish M. P., expatiated on the moral, social, and economic evils of slavery, with interesting quotations from a journal he had kept while traveling in the South.

20   Marcellus Hartley heard Bright deliver his masterly presentation of the Northern cause in the Birmingham town hall just before Christmas, 1862, and at once obtained permission to print and distribute 10,000 copies in Britain; later 5,000 more. See his article in the N. Y. *Times*, Jan. 22, 1898.

21   Beecher read this letter in public, Nov. 25, 1863; N. Y. *Tribune*, Nov. 26.

of friendly middle-class opinion went unnoticed in the United States. People quivered with anger over the taunts of the *Times* and *Morning Post*, and were stung by Tenniel's cartoons of Brother Jonathan in *Punch*. But they did not read the eloquent defense of Northern principles in the *Daily News* and *Morning Star*, or learn that the mayors of Manchester, Birmingham, and many other towns were with them, or see what a phalanx of veteran reformers upheld the Union cause. Northern resentment rose to the pitch which Sumner described to the Duchess of Argyll in April, 1863. He had talked with Lincoln. "When the rebellion is crushed," he told the President, "a more difficult piece of statesmanship still will be to keep from instant war with England." Half a million Irish were said already to be enrolled for the conflict. "And now the worst is to be told," wrote Sumner. "Those who have heretofore most cordially stood by England with admiration and love—the best educated, the best principled, and the wealthiest of the land—are now embittered beyond Irish and Democrat." Friends whose English sympathies were once intense, he continued, "talk to me and write to me as strongly against England as against the rebellion." Sumner liked to exaggerate bad news and stir up trouble, but this time his statements had some warrant.[22]

[III]

Because the Ministry was divided, Parliament was confused, and the sufferings of Lancashire were increasing, real danger existed in the fall of 1862 of some rash British spasm. The general election of 1859 had given the House only a few more Liberals than Conservatives. When Palmerston became Prime Minister he bestowed the foreign office on Lord John Russell, and the chancellorship of the exchequer on Gladstone, who was nominally a Conservative. Three dukes went into this Liberal Cabinet, in which Cobden, disliking its head, stubbornly refused a place.[23]

Palmerston, a political veteran and an imposing figure, was a fascinating mixture of qualities good and bad. He was nonchalant, jaunty, and iron-willed. Lord Clarendon termed him "an artful old dodger," while Queen Victoria linked him with Earl Russell as "those two dreadful old men." A writer in the *Daily News*, angered by his swaggering insolence, remarked: "He has made

22 Sumner to Duchess of Argyll, April 26, 1863, HL. Some British papers criticized Sumner severely, and he never forgot criticism. The half-million Irishmen pledged to war were actually ten or twenty thousand Fenians whose movement Mackay exposed in the London *Times*.

23 Palmerston, writes Herbert Paul, had a superficial Liberalism, but the Conservatives could not cooperate with the Radicals to overthrow his composite government. *History of Modern England*, II, 320, 321.

himself the political incarnation of the English bully." [24] But it could fairly be said that he had perfect public integrity, and always stood to his word; that however flippant, he was a hard worker; and that he felt not only a strong sense of the dignity of Britain, but an earnest concern for the nation's welfare. He had been called to aid Spencer Percival's cabinet in 1809, as Jefferson was just leaving the Presidency; now, at seventy-six, he was capable of driving to Harrow in a rain, opening a library there with a speech, driving back, and sitting in the House until 2 A.M. [25]

He was in some respects farsighted, consistent, and logical, with a gift for connecting current policies with long-term principles. He understood the force of the great nationalist currents which were creating nations in Italy and Germany, and keeping patriotism alive in Poland, Bohemia, Hungary, and the Balkans. Like Russell, he comprehended and valued the liberalism that found eloquent voice in Mazzini, Tocqueville, and Gottfried Kinkel. He wished to see the aspirations of suppressed peoples and the hopes of patriot dreamers realized, at least in part, with as little disturbance to the peace of Europe as possible, and he had enough belief in the old diplomacy to hold that this could be done while maintaining the uneasy balance of power. He knew when to be daring, and when to be cautious. He tended toward arrogance, using too much of the *fortiter in re* with too little of the *suaviter in modo;* he had the instincts, as Metternich once said of him, of an autocrat; he was full of prejudices, and Victoria correctly noted that he was vindictive. [26] But if his realism could be hard, cold, and tactless, it could also be sagacious—and in the end his realism benefited the United States.

That frail intellectual aristocrat Lord John Russell stood in sharp contrast with the downright, overbearing Palmerston. With an ardent, restless temperament, and some of the brilliance that made his philosopher grandson famous, he was doctrinaire in politics, holding extreme stands with opinionated tenacity. [27] He liked to meddle in international affairs, preaching sermons the while. Since entering Parliament in 1820 he had played the part of a true liberal, supporting Catholic emancipation, the Reform Bill, the repeal of the Corn Laws, and the aspirations of small peoples. In 1860 he had defied the reactionary Powers of Europe by penning the celebrated dispatch which became one of the cornerstones of Italian unity: "Her Majesty's Government turn their eyes . . . to

24 July 12, 1862. This writer declared that Palmerston had "corrupted by social bribery a powerful portion of the London press."
25 Paul, II, 316.
26 Queen Victoria's *Letters, Second Series*, II, *passim;* Bell, *Palmerston*, II, 273–354; Temperley and Penson, *Foundations of British Foreign Policy, 1792–1902*, 88–304.
27 Russell was approaching seventy; a brother of the Duke of Bedford, in 1861 he succeeded to a small Irish estate and became earl. Bertrand Russell sketches his grandfather, "warm and affectionate and kindly," in *Portraits From Memory.*

the gratifying prospect of a people building up the edifice of their liberties, and consolidating the work of their independence, amid the sympathies and good wishes of Europe." Victoria had good reason for characterizing him as selfish, vain, "and often reckless and imprudent." [28] He was abysmally ignorant of the United States. He wrote indiscreet papers. But twenty million Italians never forgot his generous part in committing Britain to their liberation; and Palmerston, to whose domination he had become submissive, could curb his recklessness.

It must be admitted that Russell had some valid ground for feeling irritation over Northern foreign policy. He knew from Lord Lyons the essence of Seward's mad proposal for provoking hostilities with Spain and France to bring the South back into the Union. Lyons detailed to him Seward's conversations of April and May, 1861, adumbrating this plan.

On May 10, for example, Seward suggested to Lyons that Britain and the United States sign a convention for suppressing the slave trade at which Spanish officials in Cuba winked, and guaranteeing the independence of Santo Domingo, on which Spanish troops had already landed. "For my own part," Lyons reported Seward as saying, "I would have no objection to make an anti-African Slave Trade demonstration against Spain; if she were rash enough to provoke it." [29] Lyons and Russell knew that the United States was not strong enough to fight the Confederacy, France, and Spain all at once, and they resented a proposal that Britain should enter into a virtual alliance with the North which would estrange her from France and radically align her against the South. Russell unquestionably read with distaste Seward's threatening statement to the *Times's* correspondent that no foreign power could receive the Confederate commissioners, even if they called informally to hand in a document, without risking a breach of relations with the American Government.

Russell may also have been ruffled by Northern uproar over the British proclamation of neutrality, an act which was not merely justifiable under international law but indispensable under the political circumstances. Bryant's *Evening Post* exploded as wrathfully over "Britain's Blunder" as Greeley's *Tribune*, while *Harper's Weekly* and the *Atlantic* pronounced the British grant of belligerent rights to the Confederacy inexcusable.[30] By the summer of 1862 Leslie's *Illustrated Newspaper* was making the wild assertion on which Sumner later

28 *Letters, Second Series*, II, 625.
29 Lyons, May 11, 1861, to Russell, FO/4 1137.
30 *Evening Post, Tribune*, May 29, 1861; *Harper's Weekly*, June 8; *Atlantic*, VIII (December, 1861), 761–769. If Lincoln's blockade was a reality, Britain had to enjoin a strict neutrality on her subjects. The very newspapers which berated England were themselves ready to treat the army, navy, and government of the Confederacy as those of a belligerent. The South stood in a very different position from the Carlist and Hungarian rebels to whom Britain had refused belligerent status.

based a huge bill for damages: "The Rebellion would have been dead today . . . had not she [Britain] sided with the rebels and lent them moral encouragement and material aid." [31] These reproaches were as unreasonable as the counter-complaints of the South, which assailed Great Britain for not at once recognizing the independence of the Confederacy and breaking the blockade. In point of fact, the North had only itself to blame for so promptly giving the Confederacy the status of a belligerent. As Attorney-General Bates argued,[32] the government would have acted shrewdly if it had simply proclaimed a closing of the Southern ports instead of a formal blockade. The fact that Russell twice saw the Confederate mission to London unofficially and without the slightest commitment disturbed Northerners; the fact that he then refused to see the members again angered Southerners. He was hewing to a neutral line.

Fortunately Russell did not know the worst about Seward's peculiar diplomacy. He did not know that on May 21 Seward had written a dispatch, No. 10, which Adams' son and biographer justly characterizes as "so indecorous and threatening as to be tantamount to a declaration of war." It declared that if Britain gave shelter to Confederate privateers, the United States would once more, as twice before, become her enemy. A global war would ensue, in which Britain would have reason to lament her folly while the United States would emerge comparatively unscathed. This paper, had it been delivered as first written, would have made a collision with Britain almost certain. Happily, Lincoln took firm control, and not only expunged the offensive phrasing, but directed Adams to regard the dispatch as a mere confidential instruction, to be communicated to nobody.[33] But Lord Russell, if he read the *Times*, did know that Seward was indulging in the idea that a world-wide war would rescue the United States, for the Secretary told the *Times* correspondent on July 4: "If any European power provokes a war, we shall not shrink from it. A contest between Great Britain and the United States would wrap the world in fire, and at the end it would not be the United States which would have to lament the result of the conflict."

Nor, down to the late summer of 1862, could Lord Russell's displeasure have been mollified by any sense of the moral superiority of the North. Seward's early dispatches seemed almost to strike the slavery question out of the American contest. He expatiated on the Federal and State protection given to all the existing interests of slavery, and instructed Adams not to discuss "opposing moral principles." More than that, in a dispatch of July 5, 1862, to Adams, he

---

31 Aug. 9, 1862.

32 To Lieber, Aug. 23, 1861, Lieber Papers, HL. A majority of the Cabinet had wished simply to shut the ports; but when Seward argued in favor of a blockade because the rules governing it were clearly known, and it seemed less likely to create foreign difficulties, Lincoln and the others agreed. Welles, *Lincoln and Seward*, 123.

33 For the text before and after Lincoln revised it, see Randall, *Lincoln*, II, 35-37.

VULCAN ARMING NEPTUNE.
(INFLUENCE OF THE *MERRIMAC-MONITOR* BATTLE.)

From Punch, or The London Charivari, April 19, 1862

treated armed rebels and emancipationists as equally guilty of trying to precipitate a servile war, thus equating Jefferson Davis and Charles Sumner.[34]

As the North tightened the blockade and captured numerous blockade
runners, Earl Russell deprecated the rigor, "beyond the usual practise of nations," with which the United States treated British subjects engaged in the
traffic. He sent Washington a strong protest against this which arrived in the
gloomy hour after Pope's defeat. Meanwhile, divergent national policies on
two other matters, privateering and the slave trade, engendered temporary misunderstanding and friction.

As an outgrowth of the Crimean War, Great Britain and France had taken
the lead in 1856 in a movement to abolish privateering and secure fuller respect
for neutral commerce in time of war. The Declaration of Paris adopted that
year by six powers obtained the assent of nearly all European and South
American states. The United States, however, declined to give it the unconditional adherence required. When Seward in 1861 moved hastily to accede, it was
obvious that he did so in order to outlaw Confederate privateers. A civil conflict having begun, Britain was unwilling to change the rules of war in a way
favorable to either side. Russell declared that he would make no engagement
which had any bearing, direct or indirect, on the contest; whereupon Adams
testily remarked that he would rather a thousand times let the Declaration remain unsigned forever than accept such a proviso.[35] The British government
issued a decree June 1 that it would permit no privateer to bring prizes into
its ports—which meant, practically, that the Confederacy could have no privateers. But the Foreign Office continued to believe that Seward had attempted a
piece of sharp practice.

As for the African slave trade, as late as July, 1861, it was still to a considerable extent promoted from New York. The Federal marshal there sent Seward
in October affidavits of four crewmen of the American ship *Nightingale*, seized

34 For radical anger over this dispatch when it was finally published, see Pierce, *Sumner*,
IV, 110, 111.

35 For several reasons the treatment of this and other episodes by Charles Francis Adams,
Jr., in his life of his father (1900) must be taken with reserve. For dramatic effect, the
biographer unduly heightens British hostility, and improperly presents his story as a personal
contest between Adams on one side, Russell and Palmerston on the other. The Minister's
diary in the Massachusetts Historical Society shows that he was treated with much more
cordiality by high British circles than the biography suggests. The son also glosses over
weaknesses of temperament and policy in Adams which the diary of Benjamin Moran discloses. Finally, the life greatly overestimates the capacity and achievements of Seward, with
whom the Adamses had an old friendship, and underestimates Lincoln. (In 1873 Charles
Francis Adams, Sr., delivered a singularly ill-informed memorial address on Seward to the
New York legislature, portraying him as the real power in the Lincoln Administration. This
was deeply resented by the surviving Cabinet members, Chase, Blair, and Gideon Welles;
and Welles penned a small volume, *Lincoln and Seward* (1874), which completely crushed
Adams's statements.) The Minister's achievements were great enough to need no exaggeration.

in the port as a slaver. The enormous profits of the Africa-Cuba run tempted men to run any risk. "Until a few months ago," wrote the marshal, "a very large proportion of the vessels engaged in the African trade have been fitted out at this port." This was no news to the British consul, who had employed detectives and paid bribes to ferret out information. He knew all about the operations of Abranches, Almeida & Co., and other New York agents for slavers. In view of the long record of American laxity in dealing with this atrocious commerce, British leaders had some excuse for doubt concerning Northern intentions.[36]

One diplomatic difficulty after another was conquered. The British decree of June 1 stopped all possibility of a quarrel over privateering. The American execution of Nathaniel Gordon, captain of a slaver, early in 1862, with the drafting of a new Anglo-American treaty for cooperative action in stamping out the trade, banished English doubts in that field. Not only was the *Trent* affair peaceably settled; when Mason and Slidell finally reached England, the London *Times* itself expressed a hope that nothing like an ovation would be given them. But the vital facts are two: first, that Secretary Seward, with his ideas about provoking a war with Spain and France, had not impressed the British government as wise, moderate, or farsighted, and second, that neither Seward's notes nor Lincoln's major acts down to Antietam had given the Northern cause an aura of high nobility. Lord Russell did not have to be excessively hostile to ask whether the conflict was worth while.

That question pressed on humane Britons high and low after the Seven Days and Second Manassas. The war was fast becoming the bloodiest and costliest of modern times. The slaughter, the devastation of rich countrysides, the fierce mutual hatreds, were appalling. Decent families on the Dee and Mersey went in rags and hunger because of the blockade; the danger that some sudden incident would spread the conflagration abroad could not be underrated. And to what end, so long as no high moral object threw a gleam of sunshine over the scene of horror? Countless religious people felt with the London *Record* that the bloodshed affronted common sense, Christianity, and humanity.[37]

Fortunate it was for the United States that it had so able, firm, and high-minded a representative in London as Charles Francis Adams. He had gotten his earliest education in Russia, France, and England, and indeed, some knowledge of the English character had been beaten into him at an Ealing boarding school. He had studied law under Daniel Webster, served in legislature and Congress, and become one of the Free Soil leaders. He had all the cultivation,

36 The Federal marshal, Robert Murray, wrote Seward on Oct. 12, 1861; Seward Papers. The British consul, E. M. Archibald, sent Lord Lyons several letters on the trade; see especially that of Feb. 1, 1861, FO 84/1137.
37 London *Record* (Anglican weekly), July 14, 18, 1862.

probity, public spirit, and immovable courage characteristic of his family, with all their power of pungent expression. His very faults were those the British leaders could most easily overlook, for in pride, reserve, tactlessness, and rigidity he was one with many of them. He was totally unable to reach public opinion in England; he attempted few public appearances, showed no faculty for dealing with the press, and made no firm friendships even among those who freely offered friendship. Complaining of the chill manners of some Englishmen, he admitted that Westerners addressed the same reproach to Yankees: "It is irksome to me who have the same cold manners to attempt to make acquaintances, so that I hardly know how I shall get on." With frequent opportunities to talk cordially with Bright and Cobden, Grote and Milman, Sir Henry Holland and Monckton Milnes, and to open other doors, he made little use of them. At least once Palmerston made a frank after-dinner effort to improve Anglo-American intercourse, suggesting that Seward showed too much *brusquerie* (and Adams admitted this "awkward *brusquerie*") toward Lord Lyons. More geniality in the Minister, and less suspiciousness, would have served America well. But if his championship of America had an iceberg frigidity, it had also an iceberg massiveness.

[IV]

Had Britain and France been linked in a close entente, the chances of joint intervention would have been greater. But the two nations had an ancient enmity, while most Englishmen regarded Napoleon III as a dangerous adventurer. As lately as 1858 the island had suffered a scare over the possibility of a Gallic invasion. In 1860 the government had sternly disapproved of Napoleon's annexation of Nice and Savoy, Lord John Russell warning Parliament that the success of this stroke would lead the warlike French into other acts of aggression. Since the French resented the British condemnation, this disagreement was slow to heal.[38] The troubled European scene, moreover, was constantly in the minds of British and French leaders, and limited their freedom to act together.

August Belmont, the well-informed American agent of the Rothschilds, wrote Seward from Paris in the fall of 1861 that Napoleon wished to recognize the Confederacy at once. He was so assured both in London and Paris. Thus Napoleon would stop the derangement of industry and trade caused by the war, made doubly disastrous by the total failure of French grain crops. But British cooperation was essential, and the British hung back. "The fact is," Belmont

38 Hansard, Third Series, CLXVII, 1257, 1258; Temperley and Penson, *Foundations of Br. Foreign Policy*, 286.

noted, "the feeling between the English and French people is at the moment anything but friendly, whatever efforts their governments may make." [39]

Nor did the French adventure in Mexico improve British confidence in Napoleon's policies. When the Mexican Congress in July, 1861, suspended payments on the foreign debt for two years, the culminating act in a long series of outrages against Europeans, the governments most aggrieved decided to deal drastically with the republic. President Benito Juárez, a full-blooded Indian, was an honest, large-minded attorney who had reached his post by ability and hard work. But the state was racked by civil war, insurrectionary armies ravaged wide countrysides, property and even life had become insecure, and the British legation in Mexico City itself was despoiled of a large sum of money. France, Britain, and Spain agreed, by a joint convention in the fall of 1861, to protect the persons and possessions of their subjects, and compel the fulfillment of Mexican obligations. They also agreed, Britain and Spain sincerely but France dishonestly, not to exercise in Mexico's internal affairs any influence prejudicial to the right of the Mexican nation to chose freely the form of its government.

After the bloodless occupation of Veracruz by the three nations, Britain and Spain soon withdrew. For one reason, the shrewd Juárez made reasonable concessions to satisfy them. For another, it became plain that Napoleon III intended to capture Mexico City, overthrow the republic, and create a Mexican Empire, with a Catholic monarch of his own choice as head. His motives were mixed: to heighten the prestige of his dynasty, obtain a fresh outlet for French manufactures, restore to France some of the New World glories won by La Salle and Cadillac, and establish a Latin civilization south of the Rio Grande to counterbalance the Anglo-Saxon culture north of it. The economist Michel Chevalier expatiated in the *Revue des Deux Mondes* on the role that France, the eldest daughter of the Church, was to play as leader on both sides of the Atlantic. The one consideration which reconciled Englishmen to Napoleon's theatrical stroke was stated by the London *Times:* "The best guaranty of peace is the direction of French enterprise or restlessness to places beyond the pale of the finely-balanced community of Europe." [40]

Almost from the beginning of the American conflict the French emperor was ready to recognize the Confederacy and break the blockade—if the British would act with him. We wish, he wrote his chief agent in Mexico in 1862, to

---

39 London, Oct. 21, 1861, Seward Papers, Rochester Univ. Belmont thought that the appointment of the two Orleans princes to McClellan's staff had irritated Napoleon III, who was very sensitive to Bourbon prestige.

40 May 27, 1862. The same view was stated by the *London Illustrated News,* favorable to the North, May 24, 1862: Mexican occupation "will afford an outlet to those feverish energies of the French people which find themselves 'cribbed, cabined, and confined' within the narrow limits of their native land."

see the United States prosperous and powerful, but we do not wish her to dominate Latin America. If we can establish a government in Mexico supported by French power, we and Spain can maintain control of our colonies in the Antilles, can extend a beneficial influence over the whole area from the Rio Grande to Cape Horn, and can open fresh markets and obtain indispensable raw materials. If the Confederacy gained its independence, as he anticipated, he knew that the antagonisms of the North and South would give him free rein. Mercier, the French Minister in Washington, visited Richmond to canvass with the Confederate leaders the possibility of French mediation, and reported that they were prepared to fight to the last for their independence. Unlike Palmerston and his Ministry, Napoleon III did not have to take constant thought of public opinion; and the French elements which suffered economic damage from the war were almost unanimous in their sympathy with the South, for they felt little of the passion for democratic freedom which pulsed in Lancashire.[41]

In short, it became clear in the winter of 1861–62 that Napoleon would intervene if Great Britain ever agreed; but it was also clear that France was too weak to expose herself to European animosities by acting alone.

Chief among the friends of the North in France were six men; Edouard Laboulaye of the Sorbonne; Count Agénor de Gasparin, leader of the Protestant Liberal group in French affairs and a prominent publicist; Henri Martin, the historian; Auguste Cochin, journalist and member of Parliament; Count Charles F. de T. Montalembert, the famous Catholic Liberal; and August Laugel, mining engineer and prolific author. The American Minister, Dayton, knew no French, and displayed little enterprise, but happily the consul Lincoln sent to Paris, John Bigelow, was a young man of rare accomplishments. He had been Bryant's associate in editing the *Evening Post*, had traveled widely, read French fluently, and combined enterprise and insight with gracious manners. With Laboulaye in particular, he formed an alliance of great benefit to the North. Some ten years earlier the French scholar, loitering on the left bank to examine the bookstalls, had found a volume in English by William Ellery Channing, paid a few sous for it, read some pages, and becoming fascinated, sat down in the Champs-Elysées to finish it. In high excitement, he sought the office of the editor of the *Journal des Débats*. "Today I have discovered a great man!" he announced. That influential newspaper shortly published three articles, one on Channing's writings, one on the movement of religious ideas in New England, and one on "The Present Condition and Probable Future of the Great Republic." In the fall of

41 Cf. L. M. Case, ed., *French Opinion on the U. S. and Mexico, 1860–1867, passim;* Detroyat, *Intervention Française au Mexique,* 167 ff.

1849 Laboulaye began lecturing at the Sorbonne on the American Constitution, and gradually made himself an authority on the United States.

Gasparin had brought out his treatise on the free-soil movement, *The Uprising of a Great People*, in 1861, dating his preface two weeks after Lincoln's inauguration. Laboulaye was eager to use his pen in the same cause. Soon after Bigelow arrived in Paris, he noticed two careful papers in the *Journal des Débats*, highly sympathetic to the North, by Laboulaye. The consul asked permission to call; Laboulaye declared that he was only too happy to serve a cause identified with liberty and justice; and from that moment his literary talents were always at Bigelow's disposal, without thought of any material reward. The *Débats* articles were apparently evoked by Gasparin's second book, *L'Amérique devant L'Europe*, which had then recently appeared. Bigelow reprinted them in pamphlet form, sending copies to members of the Institute, most of the Paris bar, the diplomatic corps, and the more prominent statesmen and journals of Europe.

Unquestionably, Bigelow demonstrated great shrewdness in managing the French press. It was well that he did so, for in France as in England the economic impact of the conflict was heavy. "Our war," wrote Bigelow, "has deranged the financial calculations of the governments and bankers of Europe to a greater degree than any of the wars or revolutions that have preceded it in Europe." The textile factories of France suffered at first even more than those of Lancashire, because supplies of raw cotton in storage were small. Some members of the government were open propagandists for recognition of Confederate independence. On May 14, 1862, the foreign minister, Thouvenel, frankly told Slidell that in his opinion if it had not been for the capture of Fort Donelson and of New Orleans, France would quickly have recognized the Confederacy; and if the fortunes of war ran against the North, she might yet take the decisive step.[42] Bigelow, often fearing the worst, knew that only a great decisive Union victory would end the danger. Instead, the dispatches painted a dismal scene. "The advance of the [McClellan] army," commented Bigelow, "does not seem to be much more rapid than the original colonization of the country."

Strenuously as Bigelow labored, however, he could not affect the course of the journals under government patronage and control. All of these semiofficial sheets—the *Constitutionnel, Patrie, Pays*—were advocating recognition throughout the spring of 1862. They harped upon the rigors of the blockade. To Bigelow, the blockade was a mistake. He did not believe it would do much if anything to end the war, feared that it might force cotton-hungry nations to intervene, and believed that as a matter of world policy, all blockades ought in the long run to be abolished. Had his wishes been met, one of the greatest

42 Naval O. R., II, iii, 491; Clapp, *Bigelow, passim*; Bigelow, *Retrospections*, I, 371-587.

weapons of the United States in gaining its victory over the Confederacy, and of the Allies in defeating Germany in 1918, would have been struck out of their hands. His letters to Seward on this subject made no convert. Seward, indeed, knew how to drive home to the French Government the fact that the blockade was not the prime cause of the cotton famine; when Mercier suggested that it be lifted, he made a counter-suggestion that the North put an embargo on wheat to correspond with the Confederate embargo on cotton!

It was fortunate for the North, indeed, that wheat played so large a part in the French situation. While Europe reaped a short grain crop in 1860–62, the North had bumper yields. That fact, Bigelow wrote his old chief, Bryant, gave America the whip hand in France. While one Southern State after another forbade cotton shipments to Europe in 1861, a free flow of Northern breadstuffs left Northern ports for Liverpool and Bordeaux. But in France, as in England, many idealistic men could not understand Northern hesitations to attack slavery.[43]

At no time did the British Government respond to Napoleon's overtures. Though the London *Daily News* declared that Palmerston was like the Emperor in his arrogant irresponsibility, actually the Prime Minister was as wary as Napoleon was reckless. The difference in their attitudes was dramatically illustrated in April, 1862.

One of the principal British interventionists, the shipowner William S. Lindsay, M. P., crossed the Channel to confer with Slidell. On April 11 he saw Napoleon, who told him that he was prepared to recognize the Confederacy "if Great Britain set the example," but that he had twice proposed the step to the British only to be tacitly rebuffed, and would make no further offer. Two days later, however, if we may believe what Lindsay told the British ambassador in Paris, Napoleon did ask him to have private talks with Palmerston and Russell, and to try to bring about Anglo-French recognition of Confederate independence. As the British ambassador reported to Earl Russell, a "nasty intrigue" was being carried on, of which Thouvenel, the French foreign minister, said he had no knowledge. On April 18 Napoleon saw Lindsay again. But then came news of Shiloh and McClellan's impending peninsular campaign. We must

---

43 Thurlow Weed, who did really admirable work for the United States as an informal agent in Britain and France, impressing everybody by his geniality, tact, and statesmanlike vision, wrote Seward from Paris on Jan. 26, 1862; "There are two radical difficulties here. The Tariff is a stumbling block. It gave the Emperor decided offense. But that is not more, or perhaps not as serious, as the Slavery question. If ours was avowedly a War for Emancipation, this Government would sympathize with and aid us. My greatest difficulty with the Count de Morny, Prince Napoleon (the Emperor's brother), and other distinguished Frenchmen has been to explain our difficulty in this respect." Seward Papers, Rochester Univ.

cling to strict neutrality, Thouvenel wrote Mercier in Washington on May 18, until we see how the struggle develops.

When London learned in June, 1862, that the French army marching from Veracruz to Mexico City had received a bloody check at Pueblo the previous month, liberal British circles were pleased. Napoleon's organ, the *Moniteur*, edited by Prosper Mérimée, had predicted that the French troops would be received with roses and cheers, but instead they were met with bomb and bayonet. Mexico began to look like a dubious gamble.[44]

[V]

At the same time that McClellan's and Pope's failures taught Americans that the war would be long, European opinion awoke to the same fact. This realization coincided with a sharp increase in the British and French sufferings from the shortage of cotton.

For months after Sumter the prevailing British belief was that the conflict could not drag far into 1862. In the complicated story of the cotton famine, it is certain that British textile interests did not at first realize how critical was their position. Imports of cotton in 1860 had been excessively high, so that stocks had grown oppressive, and overproduction had glutted the textile market. The stoppage of cotton shipments by the Confederate embargo and Northern blockade was therefore temporarily welcomed by some manufacturers as enabling them to work off their heavy inventory. But the autumn of 1862 brought a tightening pinch. Lancashire and Lyons were shocked when they heard of the wholesale Confederate burnings of cotton at New Orleans and along the Mississippi; they were alarmed when they saw the war would go into 1863, and perhaps 1864 or 1865. The movement for intervention gained a new background.[45]

From one point of view British economic distress has been exaggerated. In the kingdom as a whole the number of persons on relief did not rise materially during the war, for heavy as was the unemployment in the textile areas, other industries enjoyed a compensating boom. Arms makers, ironmasters, and metal workers generally received large war orders. Linen and woolen manufacture

---

44 Clapp, *Bigelow*, 170–172; see Bigelow, *Restrospections*, I, 514–520, for Slidell's report of his own official audience with Napoleon on July 16, 1862, in which the Emperor said that "the difficulty was to find the way to give effect to his sympathies." For a rough characterization of Lindsay, see Moran, II, 963 ff., 1040 ff. This story is well covered in J. M. Callahan's *Diplomatic History of the Confederacy*, 147–149. As Napoleon himself took a hand in editing the *Moniteur*, it was rather more than semi-official. The French Government published many of the Thouvenel-Mercier dispatches in a *Yellow Book* late in 1862.
45 See the Manchester cotton trade circular republished in N. Y. *Tribune*, June 12, 1862; it warned manufacturers to be prepared to see cotton supplies "hermetically sealed."

expanded to take the place of cotton goods. British shipyards and sea carriers profited from the steady increase in the use of iron for ocean vessels, the depredations of Confederate cruisers on American commerce, and the high insurance rates on Yankee vessels, so that by the close of the war Britain was securely reinstated in her old maritime supremacy. Gladstone, a truly great finance minister, devised prudent fiscal measures and impressed the government with the need for economy.[46]

Nevertheless, the hardship concentrated in a relatively small area—in Lancashire, Cheshire, Derbyshire, and part of Yorkshire—became heartrending. The whole number of British cotton mills in the summer of 1862 was 2,877, and the total of workers in the cotton trade was 540,000. July found 80,000 people totally unemployed, and 370,000 working only two, three, or four days a week. This meant that two million people in Lancashire, and a quarter million in Cheshire and Derbyshire, were plunged into want.[47] During the summer and autumn the pressure of poverty increased. By the end of the year fewer than 125,000 operatives were working full time, while nearly 250,000 were completely out of work. "Distress in the North" was a standing headline in most journals. Public meetings were held all over the kingdom, relief committees organized, and subscriptions circulated. In the stricken region workrooms were opened, public improvements undertaken—Preston employed men on the moor, the marsh, and the stoneyard—and soup and bread distributed. In Manchester, by November, more than one-tenth of the people were on relief.[48]

The patient heroism of the workers was admirable. As long as possible they subsisted on their savings. At no time did they give way to the slightest disorder. Karl Marx was busily writing in the British Museum, but they offered no forcible illustration of the class conflict. Many pawned their belongings until they slept on the floor and ate without table or chairs from a cracked bowl and pitcher, shivering before fireless grates;[49] still they made the best of their situation, picking oakum if no better work was offered, and flocking to voluntary schools opened to occupy their time. Some asked alms in the streets or in railway carriages. Groups went through the large towns, singing such songs as they knew for pennies, and made London squares resound with hymns. When workers read the newspapers they found nothing but dark predictions. "The prospect is gloomy in the extreme," warned the London *Daily News* late in August. "Competent authorities estimate that during the next six months there

46   Max Beloff, *History*, N. S., XXXVII (Feb. 1952), 45.
47   Figures given by Edmund Potter, in House of Commons, July 24, 1862, Hansard, Third Series, CLXVIII, 739; see also W. O. Henderson, *The Lancashire Cotton Famine, 1861–1865*, 52–118 *passim*.
48   *Illustrated London News*, Nov. 29, 1862.
49   See sketches of four tenement interiors, *idem*, p. 585.

will be only sufficient cotton to admit of the operatives having two days' work a week, and this is upon the supposition that not a single bale will remain in stack at the end of that period." [50] Yet their overwhelming sentiment was for the North and against intervention.

This was true even before the emancipation proclamation. It was not for nothing that they had read *Uncle Tom's Cabin.* "There are signs," said the London *Morning Star,* "of a renewed attempt to extract from the sufferings of the Lancashire operatives some support for the Confederacy. Outdoor meetings have been got up, ostensibly to petition for a relaxation of the poor-law code, but really . . . against the blockade." As it commented, such expectations were futile. "The operatives are well enough read in contemporary history to understand that the people of the Free States are subjecting themselves to great sacrifices for what they believe to be a righteous cause." [51]

One striking event after another underlined this statement. At Blackburn in July, for example, an open-air meeting was called to petition Parliament to offer mediation. A great throng assembled. The large cotton manufacturer who presided accused the North of fighting for aggrandizement and plunder. Another speaker put the motion: the time had come for the British Government to use its influence to end the war. At this a stalwart worker, secretary to the Weavers' Association, was on his feet with blazing words and a countermotion: "That, in consequence of . . . the widespread destitution . . . this meeting is of opinion that it is the duty of the British Government to use every influence compatible with the maintenance of peace for the settlement of the American difficulty *by restoring the confidence of the Southern planters to the policy of President Lincoln, and the reorganization and preservation of the American Union.*" Amid cheers the throng passed this counter-motion, voted resolutions condemning the anti-Northern agitation, and carried a motion of censure on a prominent anti-Northern member of Parliament. [52]

Yet however stanch the general body of workers, danger existed, once the McClellan-Pope failures advertised the certainty of a long war, that irritations would grow, and that a divided Cabinet and confused House might take rash action. The second wartime tariff seemed to many Britons and Frenchmen a blow in the face. [53] Merchants, shipowners, and manufacturers exhibited alarm and anger. Cobden was deeply offended. Americans, wrote the *Times,* were rejoicing "because they hope they have shut out half the world, in-

50 Aug. 25, 1862.
51 May 6, 1862.
52 Manchester *Examiner,* quoted in N. Y. *Tribune,* July 15, 1862.
53 The *Daily News,* and indeed all Manchester Liberal groups and organs, were likewise distressed. The law showed, said the *Daily News,* July 15, 1862, that American control had passed from the slave power to the industrial power.

sulated themselves from Europe, brought famine to several millions of British, French, and German firesides, and made the Atlantic ten times as wide to all practical purposes." [54] While the blockade was temporary, the high tariff might be permanent. Meanwhile, of course, the Confederacy was promising Europe a low-tariff policy.

On the American side, at this anxious moment, great indignation was aroused by the negligence of Britain in the case of the *Alabama*. The British Government in general tried honestly to enforce its long-standing neutrality legislation, which among other provisions forbade the construction and equipment in British harbors of ships for belligerents in any war in which Britain remained neutral. But here was an instance of gross and culpable carelessness.

Minister Adams knew that the Confederates were having a ship built by Messrs. Laird at Birkenhead for use as a cruiser. On June 23, 1862, he warned Lord Russell, sending his evidence. Russell referred the matter to British officials in Liverpool, a port full of Confederate sentiment; and here, though the legal adviser to the Commissioners of Customs declared that "the evidence was almost conclusive" for the guilty character of the vessel, nobody interfered. The commissioners merely promised that the officers at Liverpool would keep a strict watch on the vessel. At the suggestion of Lord Russell, Adams then had the American consul in Liverpool gather a mass of new evidence to submit to the collector of the port. This evidence, though conclusive to any reasonable man, the collector practically ignored. Adams thereupon retained a distinguished legal figure, R. P. Collier, Q. C., to whom he showed not only the old evidence but some fresh depositions. Collier's verdict was emphatic. "I am of opinion," he wrote, "that the collector of customs would be justified in detaining the vessel. Indeed, I should think it his duty to detain her. . . . It appears difficult to make out a stronger case of infringement of the Foreign Enlistment Act, which if not enforced on this occasion, is little better than a dead letter." But still the collector delayed! [55]

The outraged American Minister at this point sent Collier's opinion, with a mass of relevant papers, to Lord Russell. "I ought to have been satisfied . . . ," admitted Russell afterwards, "and to have given orders to detain the *Alabama* at Birkenhead." [56] Instead, he forwarded the documents to the senior law officer of the crown, Sir John Harding. To cap this fresh delay, fate played the British and American Governments a sad trick. Had the senior law officer been the Attorney-General, Russell could have been sure of prompt action. But as he was not a member of the Ministry, the Foreign

54 July 11, 1862.
55 *Diplomatic Correspondence*, 1862, pts. i and ii, *passim*.
56 *Recollections and Suggestions*, 235.

Secretary did not know that he was becoming insane. For five days the papers lay unread at his house—days during which the final touches were put on the *Alabama*, and a possible cause of war between Britain and America received no remedy. At last, on July 28th, the Attorney-General and Solicitor-General got hold of the evidence. They at once decided that the *Alabama* must be halted, and on the 29th so reported. But that very day the ship put to sea, without papers, under pretense of making a trial trip.

Once the *Alabama* was gone, Lord Russell saw what a fearful blunder he had made. He proposed in the Cabinet that orders be telegraphed to seize her in any British port which she touched. At least three other members of the Ministry, Sir George Cornewall Lewis, Milner Gibson, and the Duke of Argyll, deplored the escape of the cruiser, and Argyll approved of Lord Russell's proposal. But the plan came to nothing. The *Alabama*, with a crew largely British, proceeded to the Azores, where she took on arms and ammunition, and Captain Raphael Semmes assumed command. For the next two years she was the scourge of the ocean.[57]

When the *Alabama* began burning the prizes which she could not take into neutral ports, Northern anger was passionately expressed. The Chamber of Commerce of the State of New York, condemning British negligence, passed a resolution declaring "that all who willingly aided and abetted this crusade of fire against the commerce of the United States, must be considered as participators in a crime against humanity." [58]

[VI]

It was thus in a situation of growing tension that the tremendous question of British or Franco-British mediation (which, involving recognition of Confederate independence, carried a threat of imminent war) came to a head late in 1862. Lord Russell suggested to Palmerston on August 6 that the government might make some move in October, and it was arranged that

57 The Confederacy converted two highly effective commerce raiders of its own, the *Chickamauga* and *Tallahassee;* Coulter, *Confederate States,* 304.

58 Adams in a long letter to Russell, Nov. 20, 1862, and subsequent communications, laid claim to compensation for the depredations of the *Alabama*, and Russell on Dec. 19, 1862, energetically denied liability. These interchanges (*Diplomatic Correspondence,* 1862 and 1863), were first published in the American press Jan. 22, 1864, attracting wide attention. Northern newspapers consistently referred to Confederate privateers as "pirates." The *Florida*, built at Liverpool for the Confederate service, had taken to the high seas in March, 1862, at once sailing to the Bahamas for arms. Court proceedings were begun to condemn her, but the judicial authorities, in what the British later admitted was a miscarriage of justice, released her. Governmental neglect in this instance was less flagrant, but the destruction of American shipping by the *Florida* aroused only less indignation than that by the *Alabama*. See the British Blue Books, *Papers Relating to Proceedings of the Tribunal of Arbitration at Geneva,* 1872, *passim.*

the Cabinet should meet October 23 to discuss the subject. In September Russell explored the intentions of the French Government and found that Thouvenel, always warier than Napoleon, was unexpectedly cool, for he feared that serious consequences might follow a breach with Washington. Palmerston declared that Russia also must be consulted, and this meant another delay. Then news came of Lee's invasion of the North and of Union hopes that he might be crushed. On September 23 Palmerston told Russell that he was in favor of an offer of mediation only "if the Federals sustain a great defeat." Thus far the Palmerstonian realism was sound.

The Prime Minister, in fact, had consistently declared against any immediate effort at mediation as both useless and dangerous. In a lively debate in Parliament on July 18 he had opposed W. S. Lindsay's motion on the subject, declaring that full freedom must be left to the ministry, and the London *Times* had endorsed his stand.

Then early in October, the influential Finance Minister went off at half cock. Gladstone, speaking at Newcastle on the 7th, let complex emotions carry him away. "We may have our own opinions about slavery," he said; "we may be for or against the South; but there is no doubt that Jefferson Davis and other leaders . . . have made an army; they are making, it appears, a navy; and what is more than either, they have made a nation." This unwarranted statement, coming from a powerful member of the Ministry, gave many Britons an impression that the government was about to act. Undoubtedly Gladstone's motives were good. He believed firmly in the principle of what men later termed self-determination. Always an admirer of the American Constitution, he particularly liked its nice balance between national authority and State autonomy. He did not see how the North, even if its armies subjugated the South, could in any way compatible with free institutions control so great and disaffected a minority. As a humanitarian, he was anguished by the red slaughter, for a cousin, Colonel Neville, who spent three months with McClellan's army in the futile peninsular combats, had just sent him a vivid account of the heavy mortality and the sufferings of the wounded. But the effect of his outburst, since he had a strong personal following, was bad.[59]

59 Gladstone was a hater of slavery, a well-wisher of democracy, a man of liberal vision. But he feared that Northern liberty itself might be endangered by the steps needed to pin down a conquered people. As for slavery, he believed that it had thus far been sheltered by the Union flag, that Lincoln's Administration had emphasized their unwillingness to interfere with it, and that the abolitionists had been a small and futile body. If the South separated and world opinion was concentrated on that section, slavery would sooner die; while the North might have a purer, stronger political and social life if relieved of the problem of race relations. Neville's letters made Gladstone feel that Europe could not much longer stand a silent witness of such horrors as Malvern Hill and Second Manassas; and he

And Lord Russell chose this moment for circulating a memorandum to the Cabinet (October 13) arguing that the combined European powers consider proposing an armistice in America. He gave the proposal no explicitly anti-Union cast. He merely asked whether, in view of America's terrible position ("military forces equally balanced, and battles equally sanguinary and indecisive, political animosities aggravated instead of being softened, social organization not improved by a large and benevolent scheme of freedom for the human race, but embittered by exciting the passions of the slave to aid the destructive progress of the armies") Europe ought not to ask both parties, in friendly terms, to halt the fighting in order to weigh calmly the relative advantages of peace or continued bloodshed. But in effect he was proposing Northern acknowledgment of defeat under foreign pressure.

In this crisis the antimediation forces of Britain rapidly mobilized. The *Spectator, Daily News, Morning Star,* and other journals denounced Gladstone's speech.[60] On October 14 Sir George Cornewall Lewis, the war minister, delivered a speech that crushed Gladstone's hasty plea. Lewis, an earnest, high-minded man who had made thorough studies of the lot of the laboring poor in Britain and Ireland, joined a liberal temper to complete sincerity; he was one of the best-trusted members of the House. Cool exactness was his forte. He pointed out that the South had not established a *de facto* independence, was not a nation, and was hence not entitled on moral or legal grounds to recognition. And on the 17th Lewis circulated to the Cabinet an able counter-memorandum to that of Russell, masterly in its handling of international law and the political situation. He pointed out that any mediation proposal would be made not to dispassionate men, but to heated and violent partisans; that an armistice could not be equal in effect on North and South, but must give the Confederacy an advantage; that determination on both sides was rock-like, and the North would be heatedly against compromise; that Washington would be sure to show its resentment in a fashion that might lead to hostilities; and that even if the North acceded, Britain and Europe would be utterly helpless in offering advice on boundaries, the slavery question, and other intricate matters. Implicit in Lewis' argument was his conviction that Great Britain could not afford to wage a costly and dangerous North American war.[61]

Palmerston's caution at once returned. Sounding out Lord Derby, he

---

thought it would be an act of charity to open American eyes to Old World condemnation. C. Collyer, "Gladstone and the Amer. Civil War," *Proceedings Leeds Philosophical Society,* VI, pt. 8 (May, 1951), 583–594. All this does not alter the fact that Gladstone, as he admitted later, made a deplorable *gaffe* by his speech.

60 E.g., *Morning Star,* Oct. 9, 1862.
61 Printed copy, seven pages, War Office 33/12 (1862).

found the leader of the Opposition opposed to any action. On October 22 the Prime Minister wrote Russell that he was "much inclined to agree with Lewis, that we must continue merely to be lookers-on till the war shall have taken a more decided turn." [62] This proved decisive. No formal Cabinet meeting took place on October 23. Instead, a number of ministers, not including Palmerston, held a general discussion which showed that a majority supported Lewis as against Russell. As events proved, the British nation and government had now taken a fixed position against intervention—though one additional crisis of special nature was to occur. Palmerston in a Guildhall speech, November 10, declared the time had not arrived for friendly mediation in America by any European power; and the *Morning Post* and *Times* applauded this stand. Palmerston also expressed hope that India might in some degree supply the nation's cotton needs. [63]

The British emphasized their decision when at the end of October Napoleon III, who had replaced Thouvenel with the more complaisant Drouyn de Lhuys, suddenly let Slidell's promptings and his own adventurous temperament carry him away and proposed that France, England, Prussia, Austria, and Russia suggest an armistice. Palmerston summoned the Cabinet for November 7. [64] But it was hardly necessary for Cornewall Lewis to prepare a second memorandum which, as the Duke of Argyll put it, smashed up the remaining interventionists. This paper contained some good epigrams: "A single intervening power may possibly contrive to satisfy both the adverse parties; but five intervening powers have first to satisfy each other." "What would an eminent diplomatist from Vienna, or Berlin, or St. Petersburg know of the Chicago platform or the Crittenden compromise?" [65] The Cabinet not only rebuffed Napoleon but immediately made its decision public.

By this time the news of emancipation was known throughout Europe. In England particularly the response of the middle classes was tremendous. The spirit with which they greeted Lincoln's proclamation was expressed by the *Morning Star;* "It is indisputably the great fact of the war—the turning point in the history of the American commonwealth—an act only second in courage and probable results to the Declaration of Independence. . . . Is not this a gigantic stride in the paths of Christian and civilized progress?" The *Star* reminded its readers that Granville Clark's inscription in the Abbey hailed him as one who had saved Britain from "employing the arm of freedom to rivet the fetters of bondage." [66]

---

62 G. P. Gooch, ed., *Later Corr. of Lord John Russell*, II, 327, 328; Ephraim Adams, II, 55–57.
63 Nov. 11, 1862.
64 Temperley and Penson, 298.
65 "Confidential," War Office 33/12, twenty-five printed pages.
66 Oct. 6, 1862.

Among conservative groups, to be sure, the response to the proclamation was hostile. The *Times* sneered at the Lincoln Administration: "Exactly when its military and political powers are most broken, it threatens." Delane predicted that the inevitable separation would now be accompanied by horrible scenes of servile rebellion, and that Lincoln might quit office amid the massacre of white women and children, and the extermination of the black race.[67] But nearly all liberal journals and leaders shared the feeling of John Bright, who wrote Sumner that the Union was great only when it was a Union of Freedom, and that any retreat from the proclamation would be the most deplorable event in history. The *Spectator* qualified its approval only by saying that the proclamation should have been national and complete.

And when the prophecies of slave revolt proved empty, British opinion veered heavily toward endorsement of the Union position. The middle class was rising, and the breeze of favor soon became a gale. Crowded public meetings, beginning in December, were held in all the large commercial towns: Sheffield, Bristol, Glasgow, Liverpool, Leeds, Edinburgh, Birmingham, Manchester, York, and by the end of March, 1863, fifty other places. Bright made the Birmingham meeting memorable by one of his finest bursts of oratory.[68] The veteran abolitionist George Thompson spoke twenty-one times in one month. Fervently worded resolutions were sent to the American Minister assailing slavery, and praying the North to press on until not a bondsman was left on American soil. Letters upholding Lincoln multiplied in the press. The London *Times* declared that the gatherings were made up of nobodies, but Adams reported to Seward that they were composed of just the people who had stopped the slave trade and compelled emancipation in the colonies.

One London meeting, that in Exeter Hall on January 29, 1863, the largest the city had seen since the Corn Law agitation, resounded like a clap of thunder. Long before it began the main hall was jammed; a lower room rapidly filled up; and thousands more organized a meeting in the street. Emancipation and Reunion were proclaimed the watchwords of the evening.

67 Oct. 6, 21, 1862.
68 Bright invoked the names of Cavour, Mazzini, and Victor Hugo as symbols, with Lincoln, of the movement of world liberalism. He expressed his faith that the Western republic would never be riven asunder. "I have another and a far brighter vision before my gaze. It may be but a vision, but I will cherish it. I see one vast confederation stretching from the frozen North in unbroken line to the glowing South, and from the wild billows of the Atlantic westward to the calmer waters of the Pacific main—and I see one people, and one language, and one law, and one faith, and, over all that wide continent, the home of freedom, and a refuge for the oppressed of every race and of every clime." He continued making effective speeches. It is not strange that Lincoln a year later (Dec. 17, 1863), pardoned a rash young man from Birmingham, caught in a privateering expedition, "especially as a public mark of the esteem held by the United States of America for the high character and steady friendship of . . . John Bright."

The enthusiasm of the triple assemblage exceeded all expectations. Speakers were interrupted by dispatches reporting similar demonstrations under way in Bradford and Stroud; the recent Union victory at Murfreesboro was hailed with cheers as loud as if it had been a British triumph; and at the first mention of Lincoln's name the whole gathering rose and applauded wildly for several minutes.

"In the Indian summer of 1859," said the London *Illustrated News*, "the genius of Emancipation was incarnated in the persons of John Brown and his motley score of followers; in the autmn of 1862 her instrument is the President of the United States, wielding the military and financial resources of one of the richest and most powerful nations of the earth." Henceforth, added the editor, the conflict became a revolution.[69]

[VII]

A great war—even a civil war—is a calamity to the whole world, and an international peril. By its destruction of wealth, dislocation of commerce, and impairment of order and security, it injures everybody on the globe. Americans, by a reprehensible failure of statesmanship, had involved themselves in the bloodiest and costliest war since Napoleon's day. They could not expect other countries to treat it as a purely American affair. When it brought great British and French populations to penury, it became a legitimate concern of the governments in London and Paris.

The danger of Anglo-French involvement did not arise from Machiavellianism in high places. It arose, fundamentally, from the fact that when the supposedly short war of 1861 was converted into the patently long war of 1862, without any grand moral purpose to justify it, without any prospect that either side could rationally impose its will on the other, and with steadily increasing hardship to other lands, impatience inevitably seized foreign peoples and leaders. They were certain to respond to the same impulse that led President Wilson in January, 1917, to appeal to the Allies and Central Powers for a negotiated peace without victory. British policy alone had decisive importance, for Napoleon, who *was* Machiavellian, was too weak to be important. When a man of the intellectual and moral stature of Gladstone took an impulsive stand on the wrong side, people of foggier vision might well turn against both warring sections and call for an armistice. Lord John Russell's proposal to discuss mediation was not prompted by the tariff, or a desire to reduce American power, or sheer bad temper. It was prompted

69 Oct. 18, 1862. The song "John Brown's Body" had become well known in Britain.

mainly by perplexity over a terrible transatlantic disaster that seemed becoming an endless international nuisance.

The threat of intervention was averted, in the first instance, by the realism of British leadership. It was not ended by the stubborn stand of Lancashire workers; courageous as they were, they had no great political power. It was not ended by Cobden or Bright. It was not ended by the Emancipation Proclamation, for the decision was taken when that edict was new and was regarded dubiously in wide British circles. What ended it was Palmerston's circumspect common sense, George Cornewall Lewis' brilliant analysis of what interference would mean, the blunt opposition of Milner Gibson and the Duke of Argyll, and the Ministry's wholesome fear of middle-class opinion.

Later, and in the long run, the British decision against intervention was taken by massive middle-class and working-class opinion, swayed by two forces, one moral and one material. So long as the war lacked a high moral object, and so long as it seemed uncertain that the North had the stamina and skill to fight to victory, a great body of British opinion was gelatinous. The Emancipation Proclamation dispelled the first ground of British doubt. The news of Antietam and the immense Northern preparations for the campaign of 1863 ended the second doubt. British opinion ran parallel to large sections of Northern opinion, for many Northerners had little heart in the war until the government adopted emancipation, and many in the summer of 1862 feared that with his weak and bickering generals Lincoln could never win. After the beginning of 1863 so massive a body of British opinion was with the North that no leader could have brooked its might.

The South might at any time have vastly improved its chances of foreign support and recognition had it been able to take a single mighty step: to promise that on obtaining its independence it would gradually liberate the slaves. But that step was out of the question. In the eyes of many Southerners the Confederacy was fighting to maintain slavery. The time was to come, late in the war, when desperate Confederate commanders would recommend the enlistment of Negroes in the army, with freedom as a reward. But even then the suggestion aroused the bitterest antagonism, and in 1862–63 any step toward liberation lay outside the realm of political possibility. The Confederacy could offer Europe, for breaking the blockade, free trade, abundant cotton, and long-term friendship. It could not proffer the one reform that would have silenced many enemies and won countless friends.

Examined in detail, the diplomatic record of Britain, France, and the United States alike offers much to censure. Seldom has a foreign minister committed a costlier blunder than Lord Russell's mishandling of the *Alabama*. Not often has a prime minister lost his temper in a more regrettable way than

Palmerston did over Ben Butler's order that New Orleans women who insulted Northern troops should be treated as women of the town. "Pam" wrote Charles Francis Adams that he could not adequately express his disgust, for it was absolutely infamous "to hand over the female inhabitants of a conquered city to the unbridled license of an unrestrained soldiery." Butler's order, deplorable as it was, did not reach such depths as that! Adams was quick to ask Palmerston whether this was an official or unofficial communication; obviously, it was indefensible in either light. The greedy machinations of Napoleon III respecting Mexico, and his shifty, timid suggestions of interference in the war, were contemptible. But it must be acknowledged that Seward's desire to provoke a collision with Spain and his wishful talk of a world conflagration present him in a worse light than any in which Lord Russell appears. And while Adams' conduct was always officially correct, his stiff, icy pride, touching the borders of rudeness, stood in unhappy contrast with the genial courtesy always exhibited by Lord Lyons in Washington.

The great redeeming feature of the record is the decisive part played by considerations of decency, justice, and humanity as felt by the plain people on both sides of the ocean. The liberal sentiment of America decreed emancipation; the liberal sentiment of Britain responded. Lincoln realized the significance of these facts. On December 30, 1862, six thousand workingmen and others of Manchester sent him an address declaring that the erasure of the foul blot of slavery would make his name honored and revered by posterity. Greatly touched, Lincoln replied that he knew well the sufferings of the Lancashire workers. "Under these circumstances, I cannot but regard your decisive utterance upon the question as an instance of sublime Christian heroism which has not been surpassed in any age or in any country. It is, indeed, an energetic and inspiring assurance of the inherent power of truth and of the ultimate and universal triumph of justice, humanity, and freedom."

11

The War-Torn West

WE HAVE seen how the West, a region bright with Union hopes, suddenly darkened when on July 24 the advance troops of Braxton Bragg's Army of the Mississippi marched into the vital railway center of Chattanooga. In this area, too, Southern generalship outstripped the Northern. Bragg, whose brilliant management of his artillery at Buena Vista had never been forgotten by Jefferson Davis, was making an impressive new record. He had capably assisted Albert Sidney Johnston to organize his army at Corinth, had led a corps at Shiloh with energy and dexterity, and had helped reconcentrate the shattered forces after the retreat. Davis, making him a full general in charge of the Western Department, naturally turned to him when he lost faith in Beauregard after the evacuation of Corinth, and when the Creole general made the mistake of leaving his command at this anxious moment, without permission, to recruit his health.[1]

It was obvious that the Confederates, since Halleck so obligingly dissipated the grand Union army, had three main objects: first, to fortify Vicksburg so strongly as to make its capture almost impossible; second, to hold Chattanooga as a base of operations against Nashville or Louisville; and third, to use the forces of Sterling Price and Van Dorn to keep Grant occupied at Corinth. Bragg, who had graduated at West Point seventh in his class with Hooker, John Sedgwick, and Jubal A. Early, was a close student of war but not a masterly strategist. In fact, his rapid movement upon Chattanooga had been prompted by Kirby-Smith, stationed at Knoxville, who possessed a more incisive mind. He had many faults and limitations, for he was brusque, narrow, and quarrelsome; his troops detested him as a martinet; and he showed a fatal hesitancy at critical moments. But he possessed cleverness, a firm grasp of fundamental principles of army management, and abundant energy directed by a meticulous sense of duty. He successfully achieved all three of his immediate objects. Clearly, he was a fair match for his principal antagonist, Buell.

1 Seitz, *Bragg*, 123–167; Roman, *Beauregard*, I, 400–420; T. Harry Williams, *Beauregard*, 161. Beauregard by the latter part of June had reconstituted an army of 47,000 men to face Halleck's forces of 120,000. His record was excellent.

This Southwestern theater was a region of grandiose distances, where armies seemed at times swallowed up in the landscape, and long cavalry raids found special scope. While in the East rival generals maneuvered in the relatively narrow space defined by the Potomac, Shenandoah, and James, in the West the fighting seesawed over a broad empire from the Appalachians to Texas. Bragg was fortunate in the service of two brilliant cavalry leaders, John Hunt Morgan and Nathan Bedford Forrest, who made distance an ally.

Nothing better illustrated Halleck's folly in scattering small armies over a huge territory than the successful forays of these cavalry leaders. Morgan, a Mexican War veteran, a successful Kentucky businessman, and the organizer in 1857 of the Lexington Rifles, had fought at Shiloh. Grasping the opportunity to seize supplies and derange enemy communications, on July 4 he set out from Knoxville on a thousand-mile dash into his own bluegrass region of Kentucky. Though nominally heading a brigade, he never had more than 1,500 well-drilled men, and almost any loyal county in his path could have turned out an equal force. Yet he took hundreds of prisoners, terrorized half the State, captured valuable stores, and while Indiana and Ohio were hurrying forces to the rescue, got back safely to Knoxville.[2] Louisville had been so panic-stricken that its banks moved their money to safety and hundreds of citizens prepared to flee across the Ohio. Morgan's blow was the more stinging because the Confederates accompanied and followed it by similar strokes. Raiding parties cut the Nashville & Chattanooga and Nashville & Decatur railroads, crippling the communications of Buell's army. Squadrons of cavalry made sudden descents upon Florence in Alabama, Chickasaw in Mississippi, and Savanna in Tennessee, and temporarily blockaded the Tennessee River.

Immediately after Morgan's raid, Nathan Bedford Forrest, the unlettered son of a blacksmith, a man of native genius who had risen from farm laborer and slave trader to become a rich planter and an alderman of Memphis, delivered an even more humiliating thrust. He had begun the war by equipping a mounted battalion at his own cost. After extricating his command at Donelson and fighting at Shiloh he had now become a brigadier. On July 13 he and 1,400 hard-riding troopers caught a larger Union garrison at Murfreesboro, Tennessee, and with a loss of only 25 killed, captured 1,200 men, four guns, and a half million dollars worth of material. This surrender outraged Buell, then at Huntsville, Alabama. "Few more disgraceful examples of neglect of duty," he wrote, "can be found in the history of wars."[3] The Union troops in

2 B. W. Duke, *History of Morgan's Cavalry*, 114 ff.; Louisville corr., N. Y. *Tribune*, Aug. 7, 1862; Columbus, Ky., corr., N. Y. *Tribune*, Aug. 6, 1862. Morgan's report is in O. R., I, xvi, pt. 1, pp. 767-770.

3 General Order 32, July 21, 1862; O. R., I, xvi, pt. 1, pp. 810, 811, pt. 2, pp. 131-157; Wyeth, *Forrest*, 83-103.

northern Alabama, reduced to half rations whenever their railways were cut, shared his anger.

While these raids checked and embarrassed the Union forces, so did a sudden blaze of guerrilla warfare. The wide distances, the scattering of Union forces, and the absence of any heavy campaigning fostered it, for when open war ends, irregular fighting begins. Forrest and Morgan could not be called guerrilla leaders, nor M. Jeff Thompson, who in August did some smart fighting with Union forces near Helena, Arkansas. Eastern Tennessee, however, was infested with vicious guerrilla bands, the endemic guerrilla activity in Missouri became epidemic during the summer, and the same fever infected Union-occupied parts of Mississippi, Alabama, and western Tennessee.

The Missouri situation became particularly serious. Notorious rebel bushwhackers took courage from McClellan's failure, the Western standstill, and the factional bitterness between "claybanks" and "charcoals." They found unexpected aid in General John M. Schofield's policy of ordering the militia, which he commanded, into the field along with national forces, for this aroused the apprehension of Southern sympathizers that they would be drafted into the army, and thousands flocked to the guerrilla standards where hundreds had been expected. An indiscreet order by Stanton directing the military authorities to enforce the new Confiscation Act, though soon annulled by Lincoln, also fanned the embers.[4] Early in August some observers estimated that 10,000 Confederate guerrillas were abroad in Missouri, their temper so ferocious that in certain districts all able-bodied men took to camps in the woods and left only women and children to occupy the houses.[5] Once more, men could well question the wisdom of the order which late in 1861 had annulled Frémont's agreement with Price, under which hostilities were to be restricted to armies in the field, and guerrilla groups on both sides suppressed. Meanwhile, in East Tennessee one guerrilla outrage aroused special indignation in the North. Brave General Robert L. McCook, one of eight brothers who gained fame as "the fighting McCooks," seized while ill and carried in an ambulance, was slain in cold blood by rebel partisans.[6]

The disorders in Missouri were in part the natural result of the deep social and political antagonisms that divided the people, in part the fruit of the rash precipitancy with which Frank Blair and Nathaniel Lyon had opened the war there, and in part the consequence of the growing harshness with which Union

4 Schofield, *Forty-six Years*, 56, 57; R. S. Brownlee, *Gray Ghosts of the Confederacy*, 53-179.
5 So dilatory did Schofield seem to the radical faction in Missouri in repressing guerrilla warfare that a St. Louis meeting early in August appointed a committee to visit Lincoln and ask for a new commander, but it met a cool reception. *Ibid.*, 58 ff.
6 Nashville corr., dated Aug. 14 in N. Y. *Tribune*, Aug. 23, 1862.

commanders—Halleck, Schofield, Curtis—enforced military government. Martial law, first exercised by Frémont and formally authorized by Lincoln on November 1, 1861, was a necessity. The rigor of its application, however, was not. Halleck's arbitrary fines and assessments, his many death sentences, Curtis's wholesale arrests, the suppression of all freedom of speech and publication, the banishment of citizens and restrictions on trade, did more harm than good. They fomented bitterness, rebellion, and bloodshed.

Elsewhere the upflare was fiercely spasmodic. In Louisiana, Alabama, and western Tennessee, as Union detachments spread over a large area, helpless people fell into a mood of desperation. Many communities had been almost completely drained of able-bodied men; the overseers fled as troops approached; and large numbers of Negroes flocked into the Union camps, while those who remained were often insubordinate. Raiding parties of Union troops searched the countryside. Most planters had chafed under the cotton-burning activities of Confederate detachments, but they resented far more the rough seizures by Yankee forces, which took all the cotton in sight even to the widow's single bale, offered a pitiful compensation of ten or twelve cents a pound, and if that was refused, paid nothing. They also often seized livestock, grain, vegetables, and household possessions.[7] Inevitably, citizens past military age organized bands to attack the scattered Federal units, cut supply lines, and inspire Negroes with their old deference to white Southerners. When ably led, such groups not only heartened the Southerners, but crippled Union operations, playing almost the part of Marion and Light-Horse Harry Lee in the Revolution.[8]

We have said that all three of the main objects of the Confederates were achieved in the summer of 1862. Vicksburg, high on its bluffs from 100 to 200 feet above the Mississippi, was fortified front and rear. When Farragut's fleet ran past on June 28 the Confederate batteries possessed only 29 guns, with 10,000 troops in or near the city. More guns were mounted, the new well-armored ram *Arkansas* anchored under them in mid-July, and the capable engineer S. H. Lockett began about September 1 an elaborate system of redoubts, redans, lunettes, and field works.[9] Meanwhile, Grant in the wide new command which the departure of Halleck left him was immobilized, for Bragg posted 35,000 men at Grand Junction between Corinth and Memphis to menace his communications, and he dared not stir. At the end of August he had fewer than 50,000 men in the whole area from Cairo to Corinth, including Sherman's

7 E. L. Acee, Coahama County, Ala., to Gov. J. J. Pettus, July 29, 1862, Pettus Papers.
8 Edward Delong, June 26, 1862 to Earl Van Dorn, Palmer Coll. Western Reserve Hist. Soc.
9 For Lockett's account see *Battles and Leaders*, III, 482–492.

force at Memphis.[10] As for the final Southern objective, Bragg collected enough troops at Chattanooga to ensure the safety of that key point.

Indeed, Bragg had an army strong enough to attempt more. After he seized the invaluable railroad junction, his logical next step was the invasion of Kentucky. By mid-August a new drama was about to unfold in the West. It held terrifying possibilities to the North. If Bragg marched through Kentucky unchecked, the Union armies would have to take their stand on the Ohio; Nashville, isolated, would have to be evacuated; and the nation's battlelines in the West, as in the East before Antietam, would be pushed farther back than when the conflict began.

Thus began one of the most picturesque campaigns of the war. It had pictorial beauty in its theater, the Kentucky country of bluegrass, rhododendron, and laurel, of deep narrow rivers, limestone caves, and hazy peaks. Some of its leaders were impressive figures, like the blithe Kirby-Smith, a large-spirited man who delighted in books, war, and hunting, and the fearless, swaggering Forrest. The campaign was above all picturesque in its crisscross of movements, and its plunge on both sides from high aims to impotent endings.

[I]

Bragg of course took pains to mystify his opponent. Buell knew that he was planning an aggressive movement—but on just what line? He might drive into eastern Kentucky, he might strike at Nashville and central Kentucky, or he might attempt to move around Buell's northern flank and into his rear, severing his communications. What was certain was that, having gained the initiative by his concentration of forces and the cavalry raids, he meant to keep it. Both generals knew that they were playing for the highest stakes. If Bragg could defeat Buell he might regain most of the valleys of the Tennessee and Cumberland; but if he were so defeated that he lost Chattanooga, all of Kentucky and Tennessee would pass forever under Union sway, and the vital railroad which linked Richmond with Georgia would be severed. The stakes also included men and supplies, for if Bragg repossessed central Tennessee and lower Kentucky he might obtain thousands of recruits and valuable stores.

Like a pugilist whirling to meet an adversary, Buell shifted his forces to a new line running from Stevenson, Alabama, through Winchester, Tennessee, to Murfreesboro, facing east toward Bragg.[11] He had barely completed the

10 *Memoirs*, I, 395.
11 This new line gave middle Tennessee and southern Kentucky a better protection from Confederate invasion, but it abandoned the Memphis & Charleston Railroad in northern Alabama.

movement when on August 28 Bragg began to move northward. The Confederate War Department had advised the timing of Bragg's thrust: as Lee's rebel army invaded Maryland, Bragg's would strike at Louisville and Cincinnati. "The country is in peril," declared Greeley. "Viewed from the standpoint of the public estimate of 'the situation,' it is in extreme peril." [12]

In the West excitement ran high. Governor David Tod of Ohio reached Cincinnati on September 2 to find martial law in force, large numbers of men fortifying the hills on the Kentucky shore, and citizens enrolling themselves for home defense. That same day the Kentucky legislature met in emergency session in Louisville, where martial law also reigned. Governor James F. Robinson three days earlier had issued a proclamation calling the people to arms, and the legislature passed measures to strengthen the forces. Everywhere in Bragg's path towns were being evacuated by Union forces. Lew Wallace abandoned Paris to fall back on Covington and Cincinnati, and General H. G. Wright, under a supposed threat from Forrest's and Morgan's cavalry, was preparing to quit Lexington and Frankfort.

Bragg had decided against an attack on Nashville, for he had in view a bolder plan which if successful would leave that city an easy prey to subsequent movements. It was to thrust his army all the way from Chattanooga across Kentucky to Louisville, taking steps as he went to cut Buell's supply line, the Louisville & Nashville Railroad, and thus impede his intercepting movement. Relying upon Van Dorn and Price to hold Grant, he had expected other lieutenants to aid him in defeating Buell and overrunning Kentucky. E. Kirby-Smith, who held a coordinate command, would move his army from Knoxville, isolate the Union troops at Cumberland Gap, and take Lexington; General Humphrey Marshall would simultaneously descend from western Virginia into eastern Kentucky. "We confidently hope," Bragg wrote Van Dorn just before starting, "to meet you upon the Ohio." [13]

Did he have enough men for so dangerous a movement? The answer was doubtful. After the campaign Confederates were wont to say that they had been outnumbered two to one, and though the army statistics are foggier than usual, odds were clearly against them. Bragg's returns on August 27 gave him 27,816 officers and men fit for duty, while Kirby-Smith, who had headquarters at Knoxville to guard East Tennessee, wrote him that he would bring to Lexington about 12,000 effectives.[14] Against this total of about 40,000, Buell in

12   N. Y. *Tribune*, Sept. 4, 1862. Bragg as early as July 21 had telegraphed Davis that he meant to advance from Chattanooga (Seitz, 149); later on direct evidence of coordination with Lee's invasion appears. See Appendix II.

13   Cincinnati *Enquirer*, Sept. 2, 1862; Eggleston, *Confederate War*, II, 62.

14   Union officers as always overestimated Confederate numbers. Gen. A. M. McCook, putting a spy into Chattanooga, reported to Buell Aug. 19 that Bragg had 80,000 men! O. R..

June reported 57,706 in his scattered units present for duty. Bragg made a cardinal error in leaving 10,000 men in Middle Tennessee just to watch Nashville, for if incorporated in his army of invasion they would have heavily augmented his striking power. He had no choice but to attack.[15] After the defeats and retreats earlier in the year, the Western Confederacy demanded a victory, the army lost health and morale whenever it stood idle, and he desperately needed supplies and new recruiting grounds.

At first all went well for the Confederates. Kirby-Smith, at thirty-nine a marvel of energy, marched his 12,000 men through the mountains into the bluegrass region of Kentucky, struck a smaller force at Richmond, and totally routed it, taking some 4,000 prisoners, 10,000 small arms, 9 guns, and quantities of wagons and provisions. Union leaders after the battle could collect only 1,500 survivors. The result was the abandonment of nearly all central Kentucky to the invaders. "From the eastern borders of the State almost to the line of the Louisville & Nashville Railroad," wrote a correspondent, "the rebels have it now their own way." While Union troops in and about Lexington, with those along the Lexington & Covington, fell back to the Ohio, Kirby-Smith's ragged, partly shoeless, and till now indifferently armed forces occupied the town. Some Southern sympathizers flocked to his colors. "Kentucky is rising *en masse*," joyously proclaimed his chief of staff.[16]

In Cincinnati the versatile Lew Wallace had taken command and begun energetic preparations for battle. He felt certain that Kirby-Smith would march on the city. "Here is the material of war," he told an aide, "goods, groceries, salt, supplies, machinery, and so on—enough to restock the whole bogus Confederacy." Summoning citizens to work on entrenchments or shoulder guns, he brought out artisans, storekeepers, and professional men, with a large Negro contingent, to toil with desperate energy. A pontoon bridge built in a single day carried them across the Ohio to dig a semicircle of trenches, ten miles long. The works were garrisoned in part by Cincinnatians, and in larger part by a motley array of minutemen who poured in from half of Ohio—"the squirrel hunters." Young, middle-aged, and old, they had left the plow, anvil, and desk bearing all types of arms. While field pieces were wheeled into place, seven steamboats rudely fitted out as warships began patrolling the river.[17]

But though Southern reconnaissance units under General Henry Heath came

---

I, xvi, pt. 2, pp. 367, 368. The question of numbers is discussed in *Battles and Leaders*, III, 4–8; Ropes, *Civil War*, II, 393–405; Cist, *Army of the Cumberland*, 68, 69, without any absolutely dependable result. Eaton, *Story of the Confederacy*, 193, 194, gives Bragg 40,000 men, and Buell (ultimately) 58,000.

15 See Buell's defense of his campaign in O. R., I, xvi, pt. 1, pp. 21–65.

16 Louisville corr., N. Y. *Tribune*, Sept. 12, 1862; Parks, *Kirby Smith*, 220. Kirby-Smith had started so early that he took Lexington on Aug. 30.

17 T. B. Read, "The Siege of Cincinnati," *Atlantic*, XI (Feb. 1863), 229 ff. Read was a

THE BRAGG-BUELL CAMPAIGNS

close enough to skirmish with Northern pickets, their main objective lay else-where. Wallace told Cincinnatians that they could boast to posterity of their impromptu fortifications: "The enemy came and looked at them and stole away in the night." The Confederate goal, however, was Louisville. By September 12 Buell, who had strengthened the forces at Nashville by three divisions under Thomas, realized the true direction of the Southern thrust, and called Thomas back. The two armies began a race for Louisville, using parallel roads—Bragg in front.

It was obviously Bragg's duty to intercept Buell's march, force a battle, and try to crush him. As Richard Taylor wrote later, Buell had so scattered his

---

staff associate of Wallace. The two men hold real if minor places in American literature. At first practically all work before Cincinnati was done gratuitously, but later laborers were hired. In St. Louis the fortifications which Frémont had built were hastily put in order for defense.

forces that the chance of besting him was good.[18] The crisis came just after mid-September, coinciding with that in Maryland. Bragg on September 16–17, in full drive for the Ohio, captured a strong Union fort at Munfordville, some sixty-five miles south of Louisville, taking 4,000 prisoners, 4,000 stand of arms and 10 cannon. His troops, greatly elated, expected to take a stand there, halt Buell's oncoming forces, and overthrow him. Their expectations rose high when Bragg placed his army in a strong position south of the Green River with the fort as part of his line. He was squarely across Buell's communications with Louisville, able to get ample supplies from middle Kentucky, and within easy reach of Marshall's and Kirby-Smith's reinforcements. All observers along Bragg's march were impressed by the destitute condition of many Confederate troops, and their poor physical condition. Neither in Lexington nor elsewhere had they found much. One weary barefoot soldier in Lexington was heard mournfully exclaiming: "Plenty of socks and drawers, but nary a shoe!"

On the 18th, writes Joseph Wheeler, the rebel cavalry leader, Bragg called him in and explained his plans for battle. "I never saw him more determined or more confident. The entire army was in the best of spirits. . . . It is true our back was to a river, but it was fordable at several places. . . ."[19] In fact, no better position could be wished from which to fight a battle.

And then, with one of the greatest opportunities of the war in his hands, Bragg fell a victim to his mortal weakness, lack of grit in a crisis. On the 20th Thomas united with Buell's army, while Kirby-Smith's independent force had not yet joined Bragg. Actually Kirby-Smith was waiting for Bragg's orders to march against Louisville. But Bragg would neither make that march nor fight Buell. He feared that the Union columns, which refused to attack his chosen line, were too strong to be met elsewhere. "With my effective force present reduced by sickness, exhaustion, and the recent affair before the intrenchments at Munfordville to half that of the enemy," he wrote later, "I could not prudently afford to attack him there in his selected position." He turned aside to Bardstown.[20] Bragg's statement cannot be reconciled with Buell's subsequent assertion that he was ready to give battle to Bragg at Munfordville if he remained there; that skirmishing took place, but the main body of Confederates withdrew that night; and that he drove Bragg's rear guard out of Munfordville next day, and pressed it "until he turned off the main road toward Bardstown." The fact was that neither general had stomach for a battle.

When he did so Buell pressed forward with determined speed, and easily

18 *Destruction and Reconstruction,* 101; cf. the exhaustive investigation of Buell's operations by a military commission, O. R., I, xvi, pt. 1, pp. 5–726.

19 *Battles and Leaders,* III, 10. Buell reached Bowling Green, Ky., more than a third of the distance from Nashville to Louisville, on Sept. 14.

20 Buell, *Battles and Leaders,* II, 42; cf. Bragg's report, O. R., I, xvi, pt. 1, pp. 1088 ff.

crossed the Green River, with a clear road ahead. On September 25th his advance guard was marching down the Louisville streets. All along the road his flank offered an inviting target for attack, but Bragg, Polk, and Hardee pleaded the exhaustion of their divisions as a reason for remaining inert. Once ensconced in Louisville, Buell displayed remarkable administrative power in reorganizing his troops, while he collected from Indiana and Ohio numerous fresh troops. The Western blow of the Confederacy had been parried at almost the same time that Lee's Eastern stroke was halted at Antietam.

It was now the turn of the Union forces to take the offensive. At the beginning of October, Buell's three corps moved southward from Louisville by forced marches over three roads to find and fight the enemy. By that time the Confederates had broken into numerous units scattered through seven or eight counties busily foraging and recruiting. They made few enlistments, for as Kirby-Smith wrote Bragg, although the hearts of many Kentuckians were with the South, their heads bade them cling to the bluegrass and their horses. And then, Bragg had won no great victory! The Union leaders expected that the approach of their army would force the Confederates to concentrate and retreat into Tennessee.

[II]

This Kentucky campaign, costly and inclusive, created deep dissatisfaction North and South. The North felt a sense of outrage when it heard that Buell had been compelled to leave northern Alabama and fall back across Tennessee, across Kentucky, in a frantic effort to save Louisville and Cincinnati. Andrew Johnson made an urgent demand for Buell's removal, which many Kentucky Unionists seconded; Governor Oliver P. Morton of Indiana led a still fiercer outcry in that State; Ohio throbbed with anger. Lincoln himself, to whom the borderland was especially dear, was perplexed and irritated. Buell, a cold, reserved, formal man, had never been popular with officers or men. "Now," wrote the Louisville corespondent of the New York *Tribune*, "the want of sympathy between him and his command has grown into utter hatred and contempt. . . ." Although an exaggeration, this expressed a widespread feeling.

As soon as Buell arrived in Louisville, Halleck had united all the troops of the region under his command so that three corps might be formed. General William Nelson, the former naval officer who had expedited Buell's march to Shiloh, had been working day and night to organize old troops, new regiments, and home guards to meet Bragg if he approached. He was a man of imperious temper, demoniac energy, and brutal manners. Nobody could come nearer doing the impossible in an emergency; nobody could earn the mortal enmity of more associates. His language to subordinate officers, soldiers, and citizens was often a mixture of forecastle profanity and Billingsgate obscenity, roared out in a way that earned him the name of "Old Bull Nelson." After his return from the defeat at Lexington he was said to have boasted that he cut down some Union men who fought badly. Indiana soldiers felt such hatred that many were thought determined to kill him in the first battle.[21] The day before Buell's army marched south against Bragg, an aggrieved Indiana officer, Jeff. C. Davis, had a hot altercation with Nelson in the Galt House and fatally shot him.[22]

At the same time, as a result of Western pressure, Washington ordered Buell to turn his command over to George H. Thomas. With characteristic modesty, Thomas, who knew how well Buell had met adverse circumstances, at once telegraphed Halleck requesting that Buell be reinstated. Capable division and brigade commanders also remonstrated, while some of Buell's old troops showed resentment. The outcome was his restoration, but his position remained precarious.

Northern anger at Buell, however, was nothing compared with Southern anger at Bragg. Why had he not required Kirby-Smith to unite with him? Why did he not fight Buell near Munfordville? If he did not mean to fight, why had he wasted precious days there instead of marching posthaste against ill-defended Louisville? He held all the aces, and then refused to play them.

It is true that certain excuses could be made for Bragg. His army was smaller than Buell's, and poorly armed; he had lost heavily by hard marches, sickness, and casualties; and he was fettered by the Confederate leaning toward independent commands, which gave Kirby-Smith an equal authority.[23] The result was that at the decisive moment the two Confederate armies were more than a hundred miles apart, neither was fully informed of the other's plans, and although Kirby-Smith was anxious to cooperate, he followed his own ideas about strategy. Nevertheless, a bolder general in Bragg's place would have occupied Louisville. Had he marched on the city just before or after the Munfordville fight, he could almost certainly have taken it. Buell on September 22 instructed Nelson that it would not be "advisable for you to attempt a defense of Louisville unless you are strongly intrenched." Once settled there, Bragg

21 Cincinnati *Enquirer*, Oct. 1, 1862.
22 *Papers*, Mil. Hist. Soc. of Mass., VII, 178-179. Davis's crime went unpunished, because of his good military record, the general feeling against Nelson, and the influence of Governor Morton, who had accompanied him to the Galt House; James B. Fry, *Military Miscellanies*. Chase (*Diary and Correspondence*, 98) commented on the contrast between Nelson's great talents and his "cruelty and passion and tyranny," especially when drunk.
23 Ropes remarks on "the folly, which both the Union and the Confederate Governments were so constantly committing, of having more than one commanding officer in one theatre of war." *Civil War*, II, 403.

could have refitted and rearmed his troops, left a small garrison, and marched out to meet Buell where he liked.[24]

While North and South thus hummed with indignant critics, Buell and Bragg commenced a short-lived game of hide and seek. The Confederate general still had it in his power, if he acted with decision and energy, to strike a heavy blow in a new direction. Since Nashville had been left with a weak garrison, he could turn thither, and by a rapid march seize the capital. This was precisely what Buell feared he would do. But Bragg's vacillation was matched by a dyspeptic pessimism. He decided against attempting a partial restoration of the Confederate lines held just after Donelson, for he was still much more interested in Kentucky than in regaining central Tennessee. Leaving his army at Bardstown under Leonides Polk, he wasted time in hurrying to Frankfort to assist in the futile inauguration of a provisional Confederate governor and to confer with Kirby-Smith. In the days that followed, Bragg and Buell, each with his forces scattered, each misconceiving the purposes of each other, fumbled nervously to bring on an encounter.[25]

When parts of the two armies stumbled on each other at Perryville, one of the most peculiar battles of the entire war in the West unexpectedly occurred. The date was October 8. A heavy drought had seared central Kentucky, with such severe hardship to men and beasts that the movement of troops was affected by desperate searches for water.[26] Bragg was on the field in person, though Leonidas Polk had selected the main position of the 16,000 rebels engaged. Buell, injured by a fall from his horse, was only a few miles distant, but conditions of terrain and atmosphere were such that the battle raged violently for hours without his knowledge. The most striking tactical feature of the combat was the assault of Cheatham's division upon the Union left, where two Northern generals fell and green troops gave way in panic. Savage fighting continued until dark, when the Southern troops held possession of the field. "At every point of battle," Joe Wheeler writes, "the Confederates had been victorious," [27] and Bragg later asserted that they had

24 "General Bragg is a good officer, a man of fair capacity," wrote Gen. Jones C. Withers this fall, adding that he was "self-willed, arrogant, and dictatorial"; Feb. 13, 1862, to C. C. Clay, Clay Papers, Duke. But his martinet qualities were of slight consequence compared with his hesitant defeatism. For a defense of him see K. P. Williams, IV, 108.

25 Bragg said he still hoped to give battle to Buell; O. R., I, xvi, pt. 2, p. 896; Polk, II, 147. But, when Buell's forces reached Bardstown they found Bragg gone.

26 Greeley, *American Conflict*, II, 217, 218. The examination of Buell by a court of inquiry, O. R., I, xvi, pt. 1, pp. 8–726, is a mine of information, and Lew Wallace, *Autobiography*, II, 641–653, furnishes a commentary.

27 *Battles and Leaders*, III, 17. One Union officer relates that as he reached the crest of a ridge, the whole sight and sound of the conflict burst upon him. "At one bound, my horse carried me from the stillness into the uproar of battle." Mil. Hist. Soc. of Mass., VII, 286. Perryville was heralded in the Northern press as a Union victory—"the rebels two to our one"; see N. Y. *Herald, Times*, Phila. *Press*, Oct. 15, 16, 1862.

driven their opponents back two miles. They had taken ten or fifteen cannon.

But if a Confederate victory, Perryville was also a Confederate blunder. It was folly on Bragg's part to let his army be drawn into battle before he had concentrated his troops with those of Kirby-Smith. Confronted now by immensely superior forces, he had no choice immediately after the fight but to retreat to Harrodsburg. There he did unite all the Confederate forces. But the preponderance of Union strength, the large number of sick and wounded, exceeding 4,500, and the difficulty of guarding supply lines, made the evacuation of all Kentucky imperative. So Bragg, Kirby-Smith, Polk, and Hardee decided, and on October 11 the army crossed Duck River southward.[28]

In their flight from Kentucky, screened by Wheeler's cavalry, the Confederates left behind hundreds of men too sick or badly wounded to move, and abandoned much of the spoils they had gathered. On his emergence into the Knoxville area Bragg was in as bad estate as when he had begun on his adventurous invasion; even worse. The general's defenders pointed out that he had ascertained Kentucky's real temper, obtained some clothing, and driven off large herds of beeves. What was more important, he had taken more than 5,000 prisoners with quantities of small arms and cannon. But in any large view his offensive had been a failure; he had not defeated Buell, had not inspired the Kentuckians to revolt, and had not captured any large city. The army was back in the Tullahoma-Chattanooga area where it had started, its cavalry resuming their old watch over the Union forces in Nashville.

On the Union side, the equally impotent conclusion of the campaign sealed Buell's fate. Neither people nor government could forgive his failure to defeat Bragg. The slaughter at Perryville sickened many, so that even the judicious General John M. Palmer lashed out at him in intemperate language.[29] Governor Morton could not contain himself. "Another three months like the last six," he wrote Lincoln October 7, "and we are lost—lost." Governors Yates, Tod, and Andrew Johnson also pressed for Buell's removal. Perspicacious soldiers in the field, like the future historian of the Sixth Ohio, believed that with his numerical superiority Buell early in October should have pinned Bragg down and wiped out his army.[30] Most Chicago, Indianapolis, and Cincinnati newspapers were sharply condemnatory.

A highly persuasive defense of Buell was published by a Confederate in a Lexington newspaper this fall. The author pointed out that when Bragg commenced his advance, Buell's forces were widely scattered. Gathering them together, he began his march, moving straight toward Louisville. Leaving Nash-

28 O. R., I, xvi, pt. 1, p. 1088, see *idem*, pp. 1088–1094, for Bragg's report.
29 Nashville, Nov. 8, Palmer Papers, Ill. State Hist. Lib.
30 Foulke, *Morton*, I, 196, 197; O. R., I, xvi, pt. 2, p. 634; Hannaford, *Story of a Regiment*, 374, 375.

ville to care for itself, avoiding any collision that would delay him, and yet braving the dangers inescapable if he were to accomplish his great purpose, he pressed on past Bragg and reached his goal. In Louisville he mobilized the large body of recruits there and started on the return march. Sending out three columns, he adopted the only plan that could promise success, probably hoping to fight at Bardstown, or to turn Bragg's flank and get in his rear. Morgan's troopers, said the author, knew well the difficulties of the route followed by Buell in his northward march, and how great was his feat.[31] But the West was in no mood to listen to such arguments. A court of inquiry, after hearing testimony by Generals Thomas, A. D. McCook, and T. L. Crittenden, presently declared that if Buell had concentrated his forces and attacked the rebel army before it crossed the Cumberland, he could have defeated it; and that if later, as Bragg was retreating, he had vigorously intercepted the Confederate columns from Perryville or Danville he could have crushed them before they got away.

Buell made matters worse by once more flatly disobeying orders in a matter close to Lincoln's heart: East Tennessee. After Perryville he followed the enemy to the upper waters of the Cumberland, but then halted and swung his columns toward Nashville. The Administration, directing him to press into East Tennessee, had not required him to follow the route which Bragg laid waste behind him. Halleck gave him two alternative roads, one eminently sagacious. He suggested that the Union army march directly across Tennessee to Chattanooga, for the road was nearly as short as that to Nashville, and led through a country whose autumn crops could subsist the troops. Had Buell taken this counsel while fine weather reigned, roads were firm, and Bragg was weak, he might not only have taken Chattanooga, but by repairing the railroad to Nashville could have laid a firm grasp on both cities. Halleck believed that it was possible to drive the rebels out of the whole area. "If we cannot do it now, we need never hope for it," he wrote.[32]

East Tennessee, harried by irregular warfare, had sent numerous regiments into the Union armies. Though Lincoln's attachment to it is sometimes dismissed as sentimental, most Northerners lamented that the loyal population had never been brought under Union protection. The President was distressed by Buell's rejection of Halleck's plan. He knew what strong political reasons existed for a vigorous campaign and the seizure of Chattanooga, for the elections were at hand, and the North needed positive victories. Buell, who should have realized that Lincoln could lose the war if he ignored politics and public opinion, apparently never gave the fact a thought. The conclusion of Lew Wallace, after careful study, that while Buell was a brave, industrious, and

31   "Morgan's Vidette" in Lexington *Observer and Reporter*, Nov. 22, 1862.
32   O. R., I, xvi, pt. 2, pp. 623, 626.

loyal general, capable in routine operations and brilliant in logistics, he was either too cautious or too rigidly methodical to meet a great crisis successfully, seems entirely justified.

On October 24, the Administration removed Buell, never to use him again, and put William S. Rosecrans in his place.[33] This West Point graduate and Mexican War veteran, still in his early forties, had a deserved reputation for hard application to military studies, and bore on his brow the laurels of his West Virginia campaign and his recent partial victory over Price at Iuka. He at once reorganized the Army of the Cumberland, as it was now called, with its base at Nashville. Bragg meanwhile revamped his Army of the Tennessee, and toiled hard to recruit its strength. But he too remained unforgiven; some Kentucky Confederates would gladly have burned him at the stake. President Davis, however, was unwilling to remove his old friend, and tried to soften the complaints of Kirby-Smith by writing him:

I have held long and free conversations with Gen. Bragg. . . . He has explained in a direct and frank manner the circumstances of his campaign and has evinced the most self-denying temper in relation to his future position. That another Genl. might excite more enthusiasm is probable, but as all have their defects I have not seen how to make a change with advantage to the public service. His administrative capacity has been felt by the Army of Misspi. his knowledge of the troops is intimate and a new man would not probably for a time with even greater ability be equally useful. Of the Generals, Cooper is at the head of the adjutant-general's Bureau, Lee is in command of the army in Va., Johnston still disabled by the wound received at Seven Pines, Beauregard was tried as Commander of the Army of the West and left it without leave when the troops were demoralized and the country he was sent to protect was threatened with conquest. Bragg succeeded to the command and organized the army and marched to your support with efficient troops.[34]

But it was not Kirby-Smith alone who had lost faith in Bragg; other generals, Breckinridge, Hardee, Cleburne, and Polk, were emphatically of the same mind.

[III]

In a real sense, the double invasion by Lee and Bragg represented the high tide of the Confederate cause. Never again would armies be as confident as those which almost simultaneously crossed the Maryland and Kentucky bound-

33 Buell, a man of character, showed an excellent spirit while kept waiting for orders, his record meanwhile the subject of investigation. Discharged from the volunteer service in the spring of 1864, he at once resigned his regular commission. See James B. Fry, *Operations of the Army Under Buell, passim.*
34 Kirby-Smith Papers, Southern Coll., Univ. of N. C.

aries; never again would they have so good a chance of victory. The fundamental causes of Confederate failure on both fronts were the same: lack of manpower, weakness in firepower, inadequacy of general equipment, and exhaustion after arduous marches and heavy fighting. The quartermaster and commissary departments of the Western forces, as J. L. M. Curry wrote President Davis this summer, had no system, no economic strength, and no efficiency whatever.[35] Lesser causes played a part: the divulgence of Lee's plan of campaign, the division of authority between Bragg and Kirby-Smith, Bragg's irresolution, and miscalculation as to popular support in both Maryland and Kentucky. But had Lee and Bragg possessed 10,000 more men apiece, well furnished with shoes, food, and firearms, possibly both would have won. The Confederacy failed in this supreme double effort partly because it was inferior in population and industrial resources, partly because the brains it put into mobilizing men and materials were inferior, and partly because States Rights sentiment crippled its efforts to get recruits and supplies.

These facts suggest that the Davis Administration would have been wiser to stand on the defensive in the West and summon all its available strength for the Eastern blow. It might have been able, without risking Chattanooga, to transfer 20,000 men from Alabama and Tennessee to the Virginia theater. Had it done this as soon as Halleck dispersed the great army at Corinth, these troops might have taken part in the Seven Days; had they arrived later, they might have shared Lee's invasion of Maryland. The practice of the South, like the North, was to let each department and section fend for itself; Davis and Seddon seldom tried a large-scale concentration of troops for a special campaign, and never until late in 1863 did they transfer a great body of men across the Alleghenies. A powerful reinforcement of Lee in the summer of 1862 might have produced incalculable consequences.[36]

Even as matters stood, the South was far from beaten. In the East fortune was soon to turn her wheel. In the West, Jefferson Davis placed his trust in new offensive operations. He told Kirby-Smith that he must stay in that area, and cooperate with Bragg. "To recover from the depression produced by the failure in Ky.," he wrote, "no move seems better than to advance into middle Tenn. If Buell comes he will be weaker than in Ky. and I hope will be beaten." [37] Davis hoped that if Bragg re-entered Tennessee he might obtain 30,000 new troops from Confederate sympathizers, soothe his almost mutinous officers, and reanimate the spirits of his drooping army.

35 Talladega, June 20, 1862, Davis Papers, Duke Univ.
36 Cf. Ropes, Civil War, II, 416–418; he believes Davis should have made the transfer.
37 Kirby-Smith Papers, ut sup.

[IV]

The great southwestern region, by the fall of 1862, was in a convulsed condition. An ill-defined line between Union and Confederate military control severed Tennessee, Alabama, Mississippi, and Arkansas into jagged, quivering halves, a broad zone in each State suffering from devastation, arbitrary martial law, and guerrilla warfare. Never before had large American populations lain in such terrible distress. To find any parallel men had to turn back to Thomas Sumter's horrifying account of the Carolinas late in the Revolution, when Whig and Tory bands turned the country into such a desert that the very buzzards went hungry.

Poverty, unemployment, disorganization, inflation, and shortage of necessities ruled from the Missouri and Ohio to the Gulf. In St. Louis early in 1862 a summons to wage earners filled Verandah Hall with ragged laborers and pinched seamstresses. After speakers expatiated on the prostration of industry, the meeting passed resolutions urging the national government to provide some remedy.[38] In Kentucky, Governor Magoffin's annual message to the legislature declared that trade was largely stopped, that wide regions had been desolated, that farm products lacked their old outlets, and that in much of the State property could not be sold for a third of its value. Universal gloom, said the governor, pervaded a once happy commonwealth, thousands of families had been broken up, and starvation stared many in the face. "You would shudder," one Union soldier wrote home from Kentucky, "to see how destitute some families are left." [39]

In the district around Corinth, Mississippi, General John M. Palmer was distressed by the abject poverty of small farmers. He had visited families with half a dozen children living in a roughly boarded log cabin almost empty of furniture. Their ignorance was pitiable. The women looked hungry and hopeless, the men sullen, the children frightened and wild. Yet they were being plunged into still deeper gulfs of want.[40] In Louisiana the tale was the same. When Union forces occupied Baton Rouge, many were so destitute that the authorities opened a center to which charitable people brought their surplus.[41] The French consul in New Orleans reported in the spring of 1862 that half the inhabitants of a city lately renowned for its opulence were on the verge of famine.[42]

38 St. Louis *Republican*, Feb. 6, 1862.
39 *National Intelligencer*, Feb. 22, 1862; S. F. Martin, Jan. 24, 1862, Palmer Coll., Western Reserve Hist. Coll.
40 May 6, 1862, to his wife, Palmer Papers, Ill. State Hist. Lib.
41 Gen. John McGrath, Baton Rouge *State-Times*, Dec. 3, 1915.
42 Gordon Wright, "Ec. Conditions in the Confederacy as Seen by the French Consuls," *Journal of So. Hist.* VII (May, 1941), 195 ff.

The guerrilla warfare which racked much of this great region afflicted the helpless civilian population even more than the troops. Many bushwhackers were just what the Memphis *Union Reveille* called them, "bands of heartless pirates," who preyed on Confederate and Union adherents alike.[43] In Kentucky, Tennessee, northern Mississippi, and northern Alabama the ghastly outrages inflicted on helpless people grew worse after the Bragg-Buell campaign. No man not bred in Central America, wrote a Confederate soldier from Arkansas, could form a conception of affairs in that state.[44] A press correspondent who journeyed to Holly Springs, Mississippi, in midwinter of 1862–63, found the roads as deserted and silent as the fields. Mile after mile he met nobody; on four plantations out of five he saw not a soul; sometimes gaping windows revealed a gutted shell, sometimes nothing remained but the tall chimneys whitened by the flames. Many men settled old scores, for family feuds had been frequent, by gun or torch. In a few Mississippi counties Unionists grew bold enough to raid Confederate stores, intimidate conscription officers, and seize and parole Southern soldiers; the authorities in retaliation then used bloodhounds to track them into the swamps, and shot or hanged them.[45]

One leader of Tennessee Unionist irregulars, Dave Beattie, was so ferocious that when Bragg caught sixteen of his men he promptly hanged them by the roadside. He was matched by the Confederate guerrilla Chamez Ferguson, who in the summer of 1862 boasted of dispatching thirty-two men, and when ordered by General Basil W. Duke never to murder prisoners, muttered that if he caught any hound who deserved killing he would slay him on the spot.[46] Late in the summer of 1862 bands in the mountainous tip of North Carolina, partly Unionists, partly draft evaders or deserters, captured the seat of Madison County and seized some stores. The colonel of the Sixty-fourth North Carolina retaliated with what Governor Zebulon B. Vance called shocking barbarity, shooting more than a dozen men and flogging women; and Vance protested hotly to Richmond.[47] Unionist Germans in western Texas meanwhile organized guerrilla groups which did severe fighting with rebels, whereupon the vengeful Confederates undertook to exterminate them. In one encounter only a dozen Union men out of eighty escaped shooting or hanging.[48]

Conditions in Missouri were the most appalling of all. The fanatic Indianian Jim Lane, recruiting a brigade of Kansas troops, led them into western Missouri

43 July 1, 1862.
44 Cyrus Franklin Nov. 30, 1863, Davis Papers, Duke Univ.
45 Letter Jan. 5, 1863, copied in Frankfort, Ky., *Commonwealth*, Jan. 29; J. K. Bettersworth, *Confd. Miss.*, 213–241.
46 Duke, *Reminiscences*, 123.
47 Vance, Feb. 28, 1863, to Secretary Seddon, Lieber Papers, HL.
48 Galveston *Union* article in N. Y. *Tribune*, Jan. 10, 1863.

to burn houses, shoot citizens, and loot shops. Charles R. Jennison with a body of Kansas cavalry was equally ruthless. When John M. Schofield took over the chief command, his militia retaliated against the outrages of Confederate irregulars by furious maraudings, hangings, and slayings. In the spring of 1862 a frightful guerrilla warfare burst into full flame. The murderous William C. Quantrill organized a band to combat Jennison and others, and was soon leading vicious raids into Kansas. In March, Halleck issued his General Order No. 2, declaring that any man who enlisted in an irregular band would, if captured, be hanged as a robber and murderer, thus going far beyond the order by Frémont which Lincoln had modified; and the natural result was that on both sides the fighters ceased to give quarter. The ferocity of the struggle increased so fast that by midsummer the richest and most populous counties were ablaze with warfare. On July 22, 1862, Schofield issued an order drafting every able-bodied man capable of bearing arms "for the purpose of exterminating the guerrillas that infest our state." [49] Great parts of Missouri and Arkansas by fall were verging on anarchy. Albert Pike exhorted the tribes of Indian Territory to defend themselves against Union attackers without rest, "for they are more merciless than wolves and more rapacious." In one Missouri county in six months rebel guerrillas killed nearly a hundred Unionists, while the militia in revenge dispatched thirty men, one eighty-six years old.[50]

Everywhere from the Great Smokies to the Nueces, groups of Confederate deserters, hiding in swamps and woods and preying on the countrysides, intensified the lawlessness of the region. Estimates of their number ran above 10,000 each for Arkansas and Mississippi, and companies of volunteer "rangers" took the field to hunt them down in what often became an implacable conflict.

One Union officer who distinguished himself by savagery was Ivan Turchin, a Russian who had come to the United States after serving in the Crimea, and had been made colonel of the Nineteenth Illinois. Insisting that war should be ruthless, he subsisted his men on the country so freely that Southerners called him the robber colonel. He gave notice that if his force was attacked after a town surrendered he would punish the community ruthlessly, and in Athens, Alabama, allegedly told his men: "I close my eyes for two hours." His troops looted stores and dwellings indiscriminately, destroyed civilian property in the most wanton manner, and insulted women. Buell ordered him court-martialed, and he was sentenced to dismissal. But the War Department made him a brigadier, his Chicago admirers presented him with a sword, and although

49 Jay Monaghan, *Civil War on the Western Border*, 251 ff.; Richard S. Brownlee, *Gray Ghosts of the Confederacy*, 53–109; O. R., I, xiii, *passim*, but esp. Schofield's report, 7–21.
50 Pike in O. R., I, xiii, 869–871; W. C. Reynolds to T. B. Garesche, June 23, 1862, Reynolds Papers, LC.

the South outlawed him and set a price on his head, many in the North regarded him as a hero.[51]

The Pope-Stanton general orders in Virginia for punishing civilians and levying on their property had a malign influence everywhere. From an early date, however, the most rigorous of the responsible Union leaders was W. T. Sherman, who became commander at Memphis July 21, 1862. Aware that most of the surrounding population was implacably hostile, and angered by Forrest's exploits, he jumped to a drastic conclusion. The government, he wrote Secretary Chase, should act on the principle that everybody in the South was an enemy of the North, and that all who could get arms would bear them either in proper regiments or guerrilla units.

From this generalization that the whole Southern population was in arms it was but a step to the conclusion that all should feel the wrath of the North. He assured his wife in the summer of 1862 that if the North could hold on, the war would soon take a turn toward the extermination not only of the rebel armies but of civilians. He quickly put his ideas in practice. Exasperated by the way in which Confederates fired on supply steamboats from the banks of the Mississippi, he ordered an Ohio colonel, September 24, 1862, to destroy every house in the town of Randolph, scene of such an attack, and this without inquiry into the guilt of the inhabitants. Three days later he ordered that for every instance of firing into a boat, ten families should be expelled from Memphis, and began placing rebel prisoners on boats exposed to attack. While we cannot convert the Southern people, he wrote Grant, we can make war so terrible that they will be ready to exhaust all peaceful remedies before taking up arms.[52] When further attacks on steamboats occurred, Sherman broke through all restraints. Insisting on condign penalties, he ordered his troops to lay waste all the houses, farm buildings, and fields in a strip for fifteen miles along the Arkansas bank of the Mississippi.

One exploit of Sherman's command, lying on the borderland between what was legitimate and what illegitimate in war, is related by General Benjamin H. Grierson in his unpublished autobiography. This brilliant cavalry commander in mid-November, 1862, overheard Sherman, then about to leave Memphis,

51 The New Orleans *Daily Picayune*, March 11, 1862, declared that 4,541 officers and men deserted from the Louisiana forces during the first year of the war and estimated Arkansas desertions at 10,029, Mississippi desertions at 11,604. See Edwin A. Leland, "Org. and Admin. of the La. Army During the Civil War," M. A. thesis, La. State Univ., 1938. For the story of Ivan (J. B.) Turchin, see *National Intelligencer*, July 22, 1862; MS Recs. of James Fenton, 19th Ill. Vols., Palmer Coll., Western Reserve; O. R., I, xvi, pt. 2, pp. 273–278.
52 O. R., I, xvii, pt. 2, pp. 259–262; John Bennett Walters, "Sherman and Total War," *Journal of So. Hist.*, XIV (Nov., 1948), 447 ff.

upbraiding his quartermaster for not supplying his transportation wants. The quartermaster protested that horses and mules were simply unobtainable. At this Grierson interposed. "There is no need for any trouble in the matter," he said, "for I can get you 2,000 mules and horses by tomorrow night, and more." Sherman turned toward him in amazement, exclaiming: "How? Where in the world can you get them?" "Take them from the rebels wherever they may be found," replied Grierson. Sherman smiled, and turning to the quartermaster, ejaculated: "We must have them. Do it, Grierson—do it!" "All right," the cavalryman responded, "I will do it by your order." During recent scouting expeditions he had kept his eyes open, and knew where the animals could be found. "I sent my men throughout the country," he relates, "and swept them in by tens, twenties, fifties, and hundreds. I stopped wagons and carriages and took the mules and horses from the traces, and scoured the plantations, and thus quickly obtained the animals from barns, corrals, and pastures." A hornet's nest soon raged about headquarters—but Sherman had his transportation.[53]

In Kentucky rebel forces at various times in 1862 burned hotels, railway stations, houses, and every other building that Union commands might use, while they consumed vast quantities of grain and fodder, and drove away all the horses and cattle worth having. Bragg early in the year, with great mortification, denounced acts of pillage, plunder, and destruction of Southern property by his own men; but when he retreated before Buell he felt constrained to lay waste a wide ribbon of country south of Green River, so that one inhabitant called it the Land of Sorrow. Stragglers became a great nuisance in both armies, living like locusts on the country. One of Greeley's correspondents wrote from Buell's army that hundreds of these loiterers occupied their time in stealing horses, wantonly shooting hogs and cattle, and insulting women.[54] The moment Union troops entered Louisiana they began to misbehave, and by the spring of 1863 were almost out of hand. Lieutenant John Merrilies of an Illinois artillery unit relates that as the troops advanced through the rich and beautiful country north of New Orleans a succession of blazing houses indicated the line of march.[55] When his company halted before some specially fine mansions he saw that every previous unit had taken a hand in destruction, smashing mahogany tables and damask-covered sofas, splintering china, breaking fine mirrors, and thrusting bayonets into oil paintings; but the soldiers of his own outfit completed the vandalism, till he was glad to seek quiet outdoors. The diarist of the Fifty-second Massachusetts, writing of the march through

53 MS "Lights and Shadows of Life," Ill. State Hist. Lib.
54 Lexington Observer and Reporter, Jan. 13, 1862, for typical devastation; "Junius," Frankfort, Ky., Oct. 12, 1862, in N. Y. Tribune, Oct. 17.
55 MS Diary, April–June, 1862, Chicago Hist. Soc.

the country about Opelousas, Louisiana, in April, 1863, was frank: "We have left an awful scene of desolation behind us." [56]

The climax was reached in Sherman's work of devastation in Mississippi in the spring and summer of 1863. Frank P. Blair, acting upon his instructions to lay waste the Yazoo Valley, destroyed half a million bushels of corn, immense stores of pork, and every grist mill in the area. While Grant repeatedly and peremptorily required the punishment of officers and soldiers caught in acts of violence or pillage, Sherman in general set such orders at defiance. In May his troops entered Jackson, Mississippi, primarily to destroy Confederate government property. This was effectively done and much sugar and tobacco was confiscated. "The town all day was a scene of the wildest confusion," writes Merrilies, "plundering going on universally among the stores, which the guards made very feeble efforts to prevent. . . . By night . . . private property was still being pillaged by the men." Later, in July, the sack of the capital was completed, the business section being burned and even churches and the State Library being looted.[57] One regiment alone, the Fourteenth New York, in the spring of 1863 seized 800 horses and 3,000 cattle in the neighborhood of Brashear City, Louisiana.[58]

To add to the distress of the white population, restlessness increasingly pervaded the slaves. Many remained loyal to their masters, so that Susan Dabney Smedes could later write that they were the greatest comfort of white women during the war, but many others became uncontrollable. Sometimes stragglers from the army persuaded slaves to quit work, and sometimes antislavery officers did so, but commonly they quit by their own impulse. While they usually fled to the nearest Union camp, in many parts of the South they formed gangs, hid in the brakes and woods, and raided plantations and farms to supplement the game and fish they caught. Often they stayed at home, but in a new status. Mrs. C. C. Clay of Alabama found that her Negroes would obey no orders: "They say they are free." If her husband left the place and the overseer tried to punish a hand, one slave told her, they would kill the overseer.[59] Her slaves would not even build fires or milk cows without grumbling and making threats.

A typical Mississippi planter of the better sort, John Huston Bills of the Holly Springs district, furnishes in his diaries a record of continuous anxiety over mounting evils. He suffered greatly from Union depredations in the late

56   J. F. Moors, *Hist. 52nd. Mass.*, 133, 134.
57   Merrilies, MS Diary, May 15, 16, 1863.
58   E. P. Pellet, *History of the 14th New York*, 45.
59   Mrs. Clay to her son, Sept. 5, 1863, Clay Papers, Duke University. "I have to work harder than I ever did," she writes, "but am patient, prayerful, and silent." On Sept. 19 she informed her son "I fear that if the cars run all the negroes that are capable will go. None work."

spring of 1862; his son-in-law was badly wounded at Shiloh; his debtors insisted on paying him in Confederate notes which, though they were "almost worthless" to him, he had to take under pressure of the law and public opinion; and he found that Confederate cavalrymen burned a hundred bales of his cotton in one swoop. The wanton, useless destruction of property by Northern soldiers, he wrote, would better suit an army of savages than of Christians. "The Negro girls cannot pick cotton in the field unless guarded by their husbands and brothers." But his principal concern was the growing insubordination of the slaves on his four fine plantations. On July 31, 1862, he wrote: "Gloom and despondency on the countenance of all property holders. We fear all the Negroes are demoralized and lost for further use." A few days later he made a trip: "Meet 40 to 50 Runaway Negroes Comeing in to join the Federals and be free." [60]

Now and then, moreover, the former slaves became violent. One planter near Selma watched them assist Northern troops in burning his dwelling and gin house. A friend to whom he told the story wrote: "The 'faithful slave' is about played out. They are the most treacherous, brutal, and ungrateful race on the earth." This, however, was a very unusual ebullition of feeling. Most masters knew quite accurately how much—or how little—reason their Negroes had for gratitude and attachment. [61]

Over all the conquered portions of the western Confederacy, meanwhile, brooded the spirit of exploitation and speculation. Despite Confederate efforts to carry out the law for the destruction of cotton and tobacco, large quantities of it escaped destruction. New Orleans, Memphis, Nashville, and other cities became centers of a feverish traffic in Southern staples, which drew into the region a cohort of buyers, some of them estimable men doing a legitimate business, but more of them a crew of adventurers and harpies. The significant fact is that the influx contributed to a social demoralization fast pervading the region. Grant denounced the cotton speculators whose love of gain surpassed their love of country, and he might have added that the greed for money made them contemptuous of all moral law. Corruption attended all their activities, and extravagance and vice followed in their footsteps. John M. Palmer wrote his wife in the autumn of 1862 that Nashville had become intolerable, for "the war has undermined and demoralized the whole foundation of society in Tennessee." Two years earlier the city had been prosperous, happy, and decent; now many families, with husbands and fathers away in the army, lived in utter poverty. The natural consequences of a choice between want and shame

60 MS Diary, Univ. of N. C. The Bills plantations were called Hickory Valley, Cornucopia, Bonnie Blue, and Home, and were evidently rich. Bills, while not enthusiastic about the Confederacy, supported it.
61 John F. Andrews to Mrs. C. C. Clay, July 10, 1863.

flaunted themselves everywhere, officers and soldiers spending all their pay on fallen women.[62]

Worst of all were the vindictive passions searing men's hearts. The human race, Lord Bryce wrote Charles W. Eliot just after the First World War, is subject to startling relapses. "That of our own time seems to me one of these; the saddest part of it being the virulence of hatred. . . ." In 1862 Parson Brownlow was touring the North, preaching grape for the rebel masses and hemp for their leaders; asserting that he would arm every bear, catamount, and crocodile, every devil in hell, to defeat the South, and would put down the rebellion if the task exterminated every man, woman, and child south of Mason and Dixon's Line. *Harper's Weekly* published unfounded atrocity stories of wounded men shot in ambulances, of poisoned wells, of decapitation and massacre. On the Southern side Howell Cobb, Robert Toombs, and other Georgia leaders preached unrelenting warfare, even to scorched earth, against an invader who came "with lust in his eye, poverty in his purse, and hell in his heart." No anger equals the anger of brother for brother, and none leaves a worse legacy of evil.[63]

Before the end of 1862 the upheaval of war had thus so racked and brutalized large areas from the Ohio to the Gulf that even if the conflict could then have been halted, the task of reconstruction and regeneration would have been staggering. Of numerous areas men might have said just what Charles D. Drake wrote later of Missouri: "Falsehood, treachery, and perjury pervaded the whole social fabric." The decent people of the republic were learning that sad as is the material destruction that accompanies war, the cultural, moral, and spiritual losses are far more fearful. And the struggle was not yet half finished!

62   Nov. 22, 1862, Palmer Papers, Ill. State Hist. Lib.
63   Fisher, *Bruce*, II, 274, 275; *Harper's Weekly*, June 14, 1862; Coulter, *Brownlow*, Ch. X.

12

The Voters and the Administration

WHEN McClellan fell back from Richmond to Harrison's Landing, the curtain had already risen on the nation's first wartime political campaign. In mid-June the Union men of Indiana, both Republicans and War Democrats, rallied by Oliver P. Morton, held a mass convention in Indianapolis; before the month ended the "regular" Democrats met there; and the next few weeks witnessed party conventions from the Kaw to the Kennebec. Everyone realized the gravity of the autumn elections. It was barely possible, though unlikely, that the Democrats would win control of the House. Certainly they might elect governors in New York and New Jersey who would hamper the Administration, and might choose legislatures elsewhere which would obstruct such earnest executives as Yates, Morton, and Curtin.

The Administration entered the political campaign under so many disadvantages that its supporters feared an ignominious defeat. It had staked its prestige on the Peninsular thrust and rapid opening of the Mississippi, and in both areas had failed. Prices and taxes were rising. Many farmers were caught between a glut of grain and high freight rates. Hatred of the draft was widespread. Arbitrary arrests and other invasions of fundamental civil liberties had created sharp resentment. Most disturbing of all in some States was the apprehension of an influx of liberated Negroes, which would take jobs away from white men, depress wages, and breed violence. The Democratic Party, naturally, was regarded as the strongest barrier against such a tide.

Seeing how desperate a fight they had to wage, Republican politicians took what hasty steps they could to strengthen themselves. They knew that they could make no direct use of Lincoln, who wisely chose to devote himself to the war, standing above the political melee. When Mark W. Delahay asked his advice on party strategy in Kansas, the President endorsed the letter: "Answered July 29 declining to suggest any course of action, preferring to rely upon intelligence and patriotism of friends." [1] The situation differed so widely from State to State that national leaders of the party left management

1 RTL Papers; this endorsement not in the *Works*.

and tactics in local hands. But they did try, wherever feasible, to effect a coalition of Republicans and War Democrats in a Union Party; they mobilized all their newspapers; and they assailed the Peace Democrats, who were talking of an armistice, a national convention, and the restoration of the old Union under the old Constitution.

This political campaign of 1862 was in various ways a confused battle. The North had no single date for polling: Connecticut, New Hampshire, and Rhode Island had held their elections in the spring, Pennsylvania, Ohio, and Indiana voted in October, and elsewhere the final decision waited until November. While Massachusetts, New York, and New Jersey would elect governors, the other principal States would choose only Congressmen and minor State officers. The most confusing fact, however, was the chaotic situation in the party system.

Parties, as everybody saw, were in a state of flux, with their ultimate character indeterminable. The War Democrats who invoked the name of Douglas and the Peace Democrats who shared the prejudices of Franklin Pierce heartily abominated each other. James Sheahan, the Douglasite editor of the Chicago *Morning Post*, assured Elihu Washburne in June that he was almost ready to join the Republican ranks, for he could never accept fellowship with Democrats of the appeasement school.[2] On the Republican side, everyone knew how bitterly the Wade-Chandler radicals detested the Seward-Blair conservatives. Many moderate Republicans hoped that a Union Party of national scope would soon emerge behind Lincoln—a party insisting on victory but disclaiming any desire for utter subjugation of the South and a complete social revolution there. Seward, Montgomery Blair, Bates, and conservative Senators like Preston King cherished some such dream. This new party might be brought into existence on a program embracing restoration of the Union, gradual compensated emancipation, and a mild reconstruction policy, but only if a large body of loyal Democrats lent their assistance.

Unfortunately for this dream, the campaign demonstrated that extremists in both parties were steadily gaining strength at the expense of moderates. As the strains of the war became more painful, tempers grew shorter. Throughout the summer and fall Lincoln's Administration was under a double fire, and if his Democratic opponents exhibited the more brutal manners, some Republican enemies were really more venomous and dangerous.

To be sure, the immediate tests applied to Administration policy by the opposed forces were entirely different. The radical Republicans had three principal demands: Would Lincoln dismiss McClellan? Would he confirm the emancipation of the slaves? And when he did this, would he arm them for

2 June 19, 1862, Washburne Papers, LC.

service in the Union armies? The "regular" Democrats hoped for the retention of McClellan, the deferment of emancipation, and the modification or non-enforcement of the confiscation laws. But the two camps agreed in their hostility to several Cabinet members, and particularly Stanton. The Secretary of War is distinguished only by cant, ignorance, and imbecility, said the New York *Express;* he has utterly lost the confidence of the people, grumbled the *World;* his attacks on slavery are merely a cover for his failures, asserted the Cincinnati *Commercial.*[3]

It is unquestionably true that, as F. L. Olmsted believed, confidence in Lincoln remained unshaken among the masses and slowly increased as people comprehended his firmness, patience, and sagacity. But from both sides, some leaders assailed him mercilessly. Sumner grumbled to intimates that he was honest but inexperienced, and had too much *vis inertiae.* Joseph Medill of the Chicago *Tribune* believed that Seward held him in a spell while "West Point pro-slavery generals, a rotten Cabinet, and a blind, cowardly Congress" were ruining the country. The Secretary "has been President *de facto* and has kept a sponge saturated with chloroform at Uncle Abe's nose all the while, except one or two brief spells." Henry Ward Beecher, temporarily editing the *Independent,* told its great body of churchgoing readers that neither Lincoln nor the Cabinet had furnished any kindling inspiration, for they had let Fear prove stronger than Faith. "Not a spark of genius has he [Lincoln]; not an element of leadership; not one particle of heroic enthusiasm." Senators Trumbull, Wade, and Chandler scolded as stridently. Thaddeus Stevens, denouncing McClellan on July 5 as a general who sympathized with slaveholders, extended his indictment to the President; Lincoln was the most honest of men, but altogether too amiable, and too much misled by malign Kentucky counselors.[4]

After every military defeat, it was natural for radical Republicans to call for more harshness, and for radical Democrats to protest that the nation's only salvation lay in conciliation. Voters tended to gravitate to one of two extremes.

3 All quoted in Chicago *Morning Post,* July 12, 1862. Its editor, Sheahan, early in the campaign remarked: "The few men who represent the extreme end of the Republican Party, men who were loudest in shouting for the election of Abraham Lincoln, are fast becoming his enemies. On the other hand, those who opposed his election from principle are fast becoming his friends." *Morning Post,* July 8, 1862.

4 Pierce, *Sumner,* IV, 83; Elmer Gertz, *Joe Medill's War,* 8; N. Y. *Independent,* July 17, 1861; *Cong. Globe,* 37th Cong., 2d Sess., 3125, July 5, 1862. Greeley was urging that the army accept at least a hundred thousand former slaves, giving them ax, spade, or rifle. "We do not fear that the right thing will not ultimately be done, but that it will be done too late." N. Y. *Tribune,* June 17, July 21, 1862.

[I]

By far the most important contest, that in New York, illustrated the movement toward violent attitudes. Governor E. D. Morgan had decided not to run for a third term. The Democratic strategist Dean Richmond, veteran of a hundred political battles, resolved to make the most of the war weariness. Refusing to listen to a proposal that the Democrats and Republicans unite on John A. Dix, he decided that the ideal candidate was Horatio Seymour, who though only fifty-two had been in public life for thirty years, and had made a creditable governor in 1853–54. This Utica attorney, immersed in his profession and conscious that his sensitive, subtle character hardly fitted him to be an opposition leader in a bitter civil war, was reluctant, but the boss refused to take no.

And Richmond, coldbloodedly intent on party victory, brought Seymour forward in the most effective way possible. A group of old-line Whigs opposed to emancipation and other radical policies held a Constitutional Union convention in Troy early in September. Here Richmond saw to it that a well-controlled body of delegates effected Seymour's nomination; and the very next day a Democratic convention in Albany ratified this choice.[5] Party heads could thus assure voters that the Democrats, renouncing partisanship, had accepted the nominee of the Constitutional Unionists, who included Millard Fillmore. The regular Democratic organization was actually in complete control—an organization which Richmond and Seymour would soon dominate more powerfully than any pair since Marcy and Van Buren.[6]

The platform on which Seymour stood gave comfort to all enemies of the Administration and most sympathizers with the South, for it re-emphasized the Crittenden Resolution, and while pledging a hearty effort to suppress the rebellion, declared that the Democrats would endeavor to "restore the Union as it was, and maintain the Constitution as it is." One plank denounced arbitrary arrests. Seymour, who was present, assailed emancipation as "a proposal for the butchery of women and children, for scenes of lust and rapine, and of arson and murder, which would invoke the interference of civilized Europe." [7]

While personally the man who used this intemperate rhetoric was an appealing figure, politically he was both puzzling and offensive. Even the abolitionist Gerrit Smith admitted that he was a gentleman of wide reading, winning manners, and pure life. Essentially a moderate, before the war he had opposed nativism and prohibition, and had denounced Northern and Southern firebrands

5   N. Y. Herald, Tribune, Sept. 10, 1862.
6   Stewart Mitchell, Seymour, 245; Blaine, Twenty Years, I, 437 ff.
7   Mitchell, 245; Alexander, Pol. Hist. N. Y., III, 18, 19.

with equal fervor. He was hard-working, conscientious, and talented. But he was fiercely hostile to the more advanced Administration measures: to attacks on slavery, the confiscation laws, the draft, and all restrictions upon civil rights. When nominated, he expected to meet defeat, but hoped to demonstrate the existence of a strong party which would oppose the forcible subversion of the white South and a reign of intolerance in the North. "I enjoy abuse at this time," he wrote his sister, "for I mean to indulge in it." [8] Certainly his acceptance speech was abusive of the Administration. His unique combination of cultivated manners and acrid partisanship, of candor and casuistry, was always to make his course hard to understand. [9]

So strong a nomination demanded an effective counterstroke. Of the two men most discussed for the Republican leadership, James S. Wadsworth and John A. Dix, both had originally been Democrats; but Wadsworth, heir to the greatest landed estate in western New York, had always been sternly antislavery, had helped organize the Free Soil Party, and had become a fullfledged Republican by 1856, while Dix had remained a Democrat, so recognized when Buchanan gave him a Cabinet post and Lincoln appointed him major-general. Wadsworth was fifty-five, Dix sixty-four. While Wadsworth had never occupied a political position and had never even practiced law, Dix had held high offices. Patriotic men might well hesitate between two leaders so able and earnest. But radical Republicans naturally favored Wadsworth, while conservatives preferred Dix. The Greeley-Bryant-Preston King half of the party was aligned against the Seward-Weed-James Gordon Bennett half. [10]

All the currents of the hour set in favor of the radical Republicans, for many believed that no successful fight could be made against Seymour if the party took Seymour's conservative stand. While Wadsworth wrote letters protesting that the military situation required him to keep his command of the Washington defenses and that he hoped he would not be nominated, actually he was receptive if he could get an aggressively radical platform. Thurlow Weed, seeing which way the Republican cat was going to jump, had a long talk with Chase, and tried to ingratiate himself with that leader; it was clear that he had concluded that Wadsworth would be nominated and elected, and did not wish to be left shivering in the cold. A few days later he sent word to Chase that he was

8 Sept. 18, 1862; Mitchell, 146, 147.
9 A State Rights conviction almost as impassioned as Calhoun's was one key to the man. In a speech nearly a year earlier, Oct. 26, 1861, Seymour had inveighed against Republican leaders "animated by a vindictive piety or a malignant philanthropy," and had declared against emancipation in stringent terms: "If it be true that slavery must be abolished to save this Union, then the people of the South should be allowed to withdraw themselves from the Government which cannot give them the protection guaranteed by its terms." N. Y. *Times*, Oct. 29, 1852; *Public Record of Horatio Seymour*, 32 ff.
10 Pearson, *Wadsworth*, 150–152; Martin Lichterman, MS Life of John A. Dix.

ready to make Wadsworth's nomination unanimous if it were "not to be considered a triumph over him"; that is, if he could have his share of loaves and fishes afterward. Wadsworth, however, could afford to refuse any pledges, for his selection was inevitable. On September 22 he dined with Chase, and when told of Weed's overtures, declined to budge an inch.[11]

The Republican convention, meeting two days later in Syracuse, was a complete triumph for the radical wing. In the atmosphere produced by Lincoln's proclamation, any other outcome would have been a repudiation of his policy. Raymond of the *Times*, chosen to preside, told the delegates that he favored Dix because his chats with politicians had convinced him that Wadsworth could never be elected,[12] and the War Democrats attending the convention shared this view. On the first ballot, however, Wadsworth received the nomination, and the convention tailored a platform to suit him, hailing emancipation and urging a relentless prosecution of the war. Bryant's son-in-law Parke Godwin was head of the resolutions committee, and Bryant and Greeley were exultant. Both had often said that slavery was the deadly foe of the nation, and Wadsworth typified the determination to crush it.

The campaign was inevitably tinged by bitterness. Seymour in his convention speech had thrown down a gage which the Republicans were quick to catch up. Greeley indulged in an orgy of villification, and even the mild Henry J. Raymond declared that a vote for Seymour was a vote to destroy the Union. According to the *Tribune*, Seymour was hand in glove with men openly hostile to the war. Actually, copperheadism at this time was weak except in New York City, and the great mass of voters demanded an earnest continuance of the struggle; but some excited upstate editors were almost as vitriolic as Greeley.

Seymour, after his first harsh speech, conducted his battle on a high plane. Fully aware of his responsibilities, he emphasized his loyalty to the Union, spoke of Lincoln respectfully (protesting, indeed, against abuse of him), and founded his appeal primarily on the failure of Republicans to save the country. The victorious Democrats, he promised, would give Lincoln fuller support than radicals like Chase and Wadsworth. Democratic victory, moreover, would bring the Administration back to the right track—the crushing of the rebellion, as distinguished from the overthrow of the Southern social system—and thus reduce the danger of foreign interference.[13] But some of Seymour's supporters were

11 Chase, *Diary* (Amer. Hist. Assoc. *Report*, 1902, II), 83, 90; cf. Van Densen, *Weed*, 295 ff.

12 Brown, *Raymond*, 237; N. Y. *Tribune*, Sept. 25, 1861.

13 Of Seymour's patriotism no doubt whatever exists. But it was also politically expedient for him to follow a dignified and moderate course, for thus he could best win War Democrats and conservative Republicans to his side. August Belmont, for example, a War Democrat, would have voted against Seymour had he hesitated. While in Europe in 1861–62, Belmont had tried to make himself useful to the country, and in all his talks with

wildly intemperate, declaring that Northern boys were being killed merely to satisfy antislavery fanatics. Bennett in the *Herald*, for example, predicted that if Wadsworth were elected, he would inaugurate a reign of terror worse than anything since the French Revolution—for his acts while commander in Washington proved it. On the Republican side, Weed and Seward remained chilly, and a letter Seward finally sent in behalf of Wadsworth disgusted Charles Sumner by its feebleness. We need a bugle note, he snorted, and Seward gives us a riddle!

So disruptive did the campaign become that some frightened men tried to get both Seymour and Wadsworth to retire in favor of a new coalition of moderates under Dix. Bennett's *Herald*, which had opposed Wadsworth, on October 13 vainly urged Seymour to use a great meeting that night in Cooper Union to surrender his place to Dix.[14] General Wadsworth did not appear in the State until October 30, when he arrived in the metropolis to address a mass meeting. Conservative Republicans were shivering in anticipation, for they knew, as Weed said later, that he would make an emancipationist speech which might throw away the State.[15] All efforts to persuade him to confine his remarks to Lincoln and the Union met a peremptory rejection. Whether his uncompromising deliverance lost votes it is impossible to say, but it was certain that Seymour's final speech, unflinching in its insistence on restoration of the Union, won him a host of friends. The Democratic majority, as we shall see, was to prove decisive.

[II]

In Massachusetts the extremists triumphed in a different fashion. A Republican victory was certain, and in that party Sumner and John A. Andrew, two thorough-going radicals, carried everything before them.

Nearly everybody had a high regard for Andrew's gifts. This aggressive, generous, choleric little man, the Miles Standish of the Bay State, had proved far-sighted, fearless, and unwearied. To be sure, his judgment was erratic, for he was emotional and impulsive; he was tactless, and his fierce bluntness made many enemies. He liked to write fiery letters about the sins of Ben Butler and other opponents, and declaim them aloud to everybody within earshot. His fits of

European statesmen had defended the Lincoln Administration. He thought that the people both South and North were "in the hands of reckless politicians, and are dragged willing victims, to ruin and desolation." But as a Union Democrat he wished to see Lincoln upheld, and scolded S. L. M. Barlow vigorously for carrying his opposition too far. See Belmont to Barlow, various letters, Aug., 1862, Barlow Papers.

14 Dix helped spike the movement by declaring that he could not leave his Maryland desk; N. Y. *Herald*, Oct. 20-25.

15 To S. H. Gay, Nov. 7, 1862, Gay Papers.

impatience, his violent language, his exaggerated loves and hates, however, were easy to forgive, for he put a manly honesty into all his acts. Working day and night, seeing far ahead, and planning astutely, he made Massachusetts a pillar of strength for the Union. In spite of his one occasional weakness, a Websterian taste for drink, he was unquestionably the ablest of the war governors. To Sumner much stronger objection could be made. His vanity, fanaticism, lack of humor, savage use of invective, and belief in his own infallibility had raised up a host of antagonists. But Massachusetts in general was proud of him—proud of his eloquence, learning, dignity, and elevation.[16]

When the Republican convention met in Worcester on September 9, a stubborn group of conservatives—R. H. Dana, Jr., Leverett Saltonstall, Joel Parker of the Harvard Law School, and others—were ready for battle. They were mainly old-time Whigs, resentful of the ascendency of former Free Soilers. They knew that nothing could prevent Andrew's renomination, or Sumner's re-election once the Republicans won the legislature, but they did hope to prevent any formal endorsement of emancipation and Sumner. Dana proposed that the platform should consist merely of a brief resolution supporting the government in the prosecution of the war.[17] The devoted antislavery men, with the Puritanical young George Frisbie Hoar a prominent figure, quickly overrode this move. With a roar of ayes, they carried resolutions calling for the destruction of slavery and re-election of Sumner, and then renominated Andrew.[18]

Chagrined and angry, a group of conservatives, chiefly former Whigs, left the hall prepared to create a new party—the People's Party, supporting Lincoln, the war, and the Constitution alone. But seldom has a schismatic movement been so quickly crushed. Dana, Saltonstall, and others, with the approval of the Springfield *Republican*, prepared a manifesto which, after assailing Sumner's incessant outcry for emancipation, declared: "We want no impotent proclamations now." The next morning Massachusetts men, opening their newspapers at the breakfast table, saw the headlines over the Emancipation Proclamation! We hope, wrote one journalist, that Parker had finished his coffee and muffins before he read this impotent paper! [19]

Andrew rejoiced that the enemy was delivered into his power. "*Go in for the war*," he exhorted his friends. "Hurry up the recruitments. Have grand *war*

16 H. G. Pearson, *John A. Andrew*, II, Ch. IX, offers a good portrait; see the *Nation*, XXXIII (July 28, 1881), 77–78, for another.
17 Dana's letter to C. F. Adams, Sr., Nov. 25, 1861, crisply states: "We cannot justify war on the domestic institutions of the Southern States as an end and object." Adams, *Dana*, II, 260. Joel Parker of Massachusetts and the Joel Parker elected governor of New Jersey this year had no relationship except their devotion to Democratic conservatism.
18 Pearson, *Andrew*, II, 54; Pierce, *Sumner*, IV, 100, 101.
19 W. S. Robinson (Springfield *Republican* corr.), *Warrington Pen Portraits*, 286.

meetings all over the State." He thought they could destroy the dissenting movement in ten days. The new party, composed of Democrats, Bell-Everett Whigs,
and conservative Republicans, did take shape at a convention in Faneuil Hall
on October 7, but it was pitifully weak. Brigadier-General Charles Devens, reluctantly accepting the nomination for governor, refused to leave his Virginia
command to take part in the campaign, and when Charles Francis Adams was
chosen to stand for the Senate, his son John Quincy instantly withdrew his
name.[20] The natural result was that the Democrats, who on October 8 endorsed
Devens, took charge of the opposition, and after that happened, the parties battled with increased ferocity. John Chipman Gray, an anxious young Bostonian,
compared America with France in 1793.[21] So alarming did the enhanced fanaticism of the hour seem to conservative men!

But Andrew and the whole slate of Administration Congressmen were certain of triumph by wide margins.

[III]

Since Pennsylvania, Ohio, Indiana, and Illinois elected no governor, their
campaigns lacked the drama of the battles in New York and Massachusetts. All
presented the familiar spectacle of radical Republicans berating the Administration from the rear while Democrats and ultraconservative Republicans abused
it from the front. The most distinctive feature of the struggle, however, was the
part played by public apprehension of a large Negro immigration. All four states
bordered upon slave territory, and their people realized that a rush of freedmen
across the Potomac and Ohio could create appalling problems. The Philadelphia *Inquirer*, a Republican paper, pointed out two days before Lincoln's proclamation that while New England and upper New York would receive few liberated slaves, States further south might get many. Their voices should therefore
be potential; "and they *have* spoken, every one of them"—for Ten Eyck of New
Jersey, Cowan of Pennsylvania, Sherman of Ohio, Wright of Indiana, and
Browning of Illinois had uttered warm remonstrances.[22]

Ohio had long felt distinct tremors on the subject. When the legislature met
at the beginning of 1862 petitions had been submitted against any further immigration of colored people, while one even demanded the removal of those
already in the State. The House laid this inhuman plea on the table by the close

20 Devens, a Worcester man, had been severely wounded at Fair Oaks; see memoir by
J. C. Ropes, *Mass. Hist. Soc. Proceedings*, Series II, Vol. VII (Nov., 1891), 104–117.
21 *Gray-Ropes War Letters*, 6–14, Oct. 15–20, 1862. Gray, of a wealthy family, was
commissioned lieutenant this fall. The Springfield *Republican* after the Democratic endorsement of Devens turned back to Andrew and Sumner.
22 Phila. *Inquirer*, Sept. 20, 1862.

vote of 53 to 51. Memorials for debarring Negroes continued to pour in from all parts of the State, to increase in number, and to receive wide press publicity.[23] S. S. Cox played heavily on the fear that Ohio would become the chief asylum for the slaves of Virginia and Kentucky.[24] A lively apprehension that Negro competition would take the bread from the mouths of poor laborers inspired midsummer race riots in Cincinnati and Toledo, where colored men were employed on boats and along the waterfront. Though the Cleveland *Leader* ascribed these outbreaks to the machinations of Democratic agitators among the ignorant Irish,[25] their source was plainly economic.

Indiana also took the Negro question with intense seriousness. The State in 1860 had about 11,000 colored people, and many thought that number quite enough. When the Emancipation Proclamation appeared, the New Albany *Sentinel* and other papers predicted that a deluge of lazy, helpless, and thriftless freedmen would roll across poor Hoosierdom. In Illinois, too, where the latest census had reported a colored population of 7,628, the subject had become painful as soon as the capture of Donelson and Nashville brought a host of refugee slaves into Cairo.[26] David Davis warned the President in mid-October that if they infiltrated into central Illinois, they would do the party grave injury in the election, and Governor Yates telegraphed Lincoln to the same effect. Since 1853 Illinois had on its statute books a law which imposed a heavy fine on every Negro, slave or free, who entered the State, and though many regarded it as unconstitutional, in certain localities it had been enforced. Now, shortly before election day, the Secretary of State prohibited any further entry.[27]

Everywhere, as the campaign rolled forward, the "regular" Democrats accepted the issue drawn by the Emancipation Proclamation, and made the most of it. But to *loyal* War Democrats the proclamation offered a more painful issue, for it posed two plain alternatives. The Administration intended to use every weapon to achieve victory, and it meant to reconstruct some Southern States, if not all, without slavery; should the party acquiesce, or should it demand that what Lincoln had done must be undone? For us, T. J. Barnett warned S. L. M. Barlow, "The issue is, shall we sustain the President, or is a revolution necessary?"[28] Either the country would witness a rigorous effort to carry out Lin-

---

23   See Cleveland *Leader*, Jan. 16, 1862, for petitions, with editorials April 18 and May 2 on public sentiment; John R. McLean's *Enquirer* verged toward copperheadism.
24   David Lindsey, *Cox*, 62–65.
25   Editorial, July 19, 1862.
26   See, for example, Chicago *Morning Post*, Aug. 30, 1862.
27   Davis to Lincoln, Oct. 14, 1862, RTL Papers; Cole, *Era of the Civil War*, 225, 226. The statements by Davis and Yates measured their fear of a disastrous change in Illinois. Lyman Trumbull warned Lincoln that Democrats there were led by men who, if they gained control, would paralyze the war effort of the State, and perhaps even turn it against the Union. Sept. 7, 1862, RTL Papers.
28   Sept. 25, 1862, Barlow Papers.

coln's policy, or it would see a general overthrow of his authority. Could the Democratic party risk demoralizing the army, inciting generals to mutiny, and creating political chaos throughout the North? War Democrats said no; and the effect of the proclamation was thus to deepen the schism between them and the Democrats who demanded reunion under the old Constitution, leaving slavery untouched.

[IV]

It was inevitable that the party battle should involve the issue of disloyalty. Democratic speakers made the air resound with their championship of civil liberties. "I am glad to see that you follow up the subject of illegal arrests," Horatio Seymour wrote Manton Marble of the *World*. "It must be made the issue." [29] No aspect of the campaign was more interesting than the widespread protest against suspension of the writ of habeas corpus, arbitrary arrests, and interferences with the press. On this issue of civil rights the Administration had laid itself open to an attack based upon principles which every true American revered.

Lincoln's primary anxiety, unescapably, was for the nation's safety. As he later wrote, a limb must often be amputated to save a life, but a life must never be given to save a limb. "I felt that measures, however unconstitutional, might become lawful by becoming indispensable to the preservation of the constitution, through the preservation of the nation." As a broad guiding rule this was unexceptionable. It implied Holmes's later test of clear and present danger.

The difficulty was that the unsystematic Administration, struggling with a thousand problems at once, devised no workable system to implement the rule. The whole problem was clumsily handled. Attorney-General Bates, approaching seventy, inclined to boggle over details, and erratic of judgment, was unequal to the task. Lincoln assigned the field to Seward, who seemed a good choice, but who had quite enough to do in supervising foreign affairs, and was sometimes too irresponsibly casual for the preservation of exact justice. It could be said for the Administration that it executed nobody, established no police state, and rather than institute a reign of terror, let many petty traitors escape its net. But it could also be said that it never created a machinery adequate to protect all innocent men from injustice, that to the end of the war it too often preferred the swift judgment of military tribunals to civil procedures, and that it indulged in too many arbitrary arrests and imprisonments.

Lincoln had solid grounds for authorizing General Scott in April, 1861, to suspend the habeas corpus along the vital communication lines between Phila-

29 Nov. 11, 1862, Manton Marble Papers.

d Washington, a power which Scott deputed to his subordinate com-
' The crisis was desperate; the Constitution provided for suspension
�in in cases of invasion or rebellion the public safety required it.[31] But the
military arrests in Maryland, where heads of the Baltimore police, certain secessionist members of the legislature, and others were clapped into prison, troubled many observers. Futile descents were made by officious Dogberries, sometimes a mere captain, and the grounds alleged for detention were often flimsy.
General Banks, in seizing the police officers, merely asserted that they entertained "some purpose not known to the government" which was believed inimical to safety!

During the latter half of 1861 arbitrary arrests had become more numerous,
and produced so much resentment that as soon as Congress met in December
Lyman Trumbull introduced a resolution calling on Seward to report the number of persons being held, and to state under what law they had been jailed.[32]
Various Senators expostulated with Trumbull. If Lincoln and Seward had not
seized the dangerous men undermining the government in the North, said Dixon
of Connecticut, they would have been guilty of moral treason themselves. Henry
Wilson recalled what dire perils had beset the government just after Bull Run,
with the army defeated, the ninety-day men leaving, and treason stalking the
very Capitol.[33] But Trumbull stood by his guns: "Sir," he said, referring to vital
civil liberties, "it is in just such times as these that the greatest danger arises."

While arbitrary arrests continued to excite dissension in the North, the
question of the President's right to suspend the habeas corpus reached the courts.
John Merryman, who had been drilling some secessionist volunteers near
Cockeysville, Maryland, and preaching rebel doctrines, had been arrested May
25, 1861, by General George Cadwalader, and thrown into Fort McHenry. He
petitioned Chief Justice Taney, sitting as Federal Circuit Judge, for a writ ordering the general to bring him into court for a hearing. Taney issued the writ, and
Cadwalader at once refused to obey it. Thereupon Taney sent a marshal to
serve the commander with a citation for contempt of court. The officer, who
expected this, ordered men with bayonets to prevent entrance to the fort. The
helpless Taney could only prepare a written statement denying the constitutional
right of the President to suspend the writ, file it in the Circuit Court, and send
a copy to Lincoln, calling upon him to perform his constitutional duty by see-

30 For Lincoln's rule, see *Works*, VII, 281, 282; for the suspension, O. R., II, i, 567, 568.
On Oct. 14, 1861, Seward notified Scott that the military line for suppressing the rebellion
having been extended as far as Bangor, Maine, "you and any officer acting under your
authority are hereby authorized to suspend the writ of habeas corpus in any place between
that place and the city of Washington"; Seward Papers, Rochester Univ.
31 Cf. speech by Andrew Johnson, *Cong. Globe*, 37th Cong., 1st Sess., 289, 290. During
the Revolution Pennsylvania authorities had suspended the writ.
32 *Cong. Globe*, 37th Cong., 2d Sess., 90 ff.
33 *Ibid.*, 97, 98.

ing that the civil process of the nation was enforced; whereupon Lincoln obtained the Attorney-General's opinion that his suspension order had been quite correct.[34]

By no means all objectionable seizures were made without legal formalities. In the second half of 1861 numerous citizens were arrested on sworn charges which were often of the most trifling character. This was notably true in Kentucky. During the spring of 1862, 34 citizens were indicted in Bourbon County, and after the invasion by Bragg and Kirby-Smith later that year, 205 persons were indicted in Fayette County.[35] Some arrests, however, were amply justified. A great pother, for example, was made over the detention of former Governor Charles S. Morehead, and his release from Fort Warren early in 1862 aroused wide rejoicing in Kentucky; but he was thoroughly disloyal, and soon appeared in England as an agent of the Confederacy—a "blatant traitor," said Senator Henry Wilson.[36]

While the total of arrests throughout the country continued to grow, not one case came into court for a real hearing. This neglect to bring a single person to trial out of the many seized diffused an unhappy impression of governmental inefficiency and fairness. The *National Intelligencer* and *Evening Post* agreed that the Administration's methods savored of the old *lettres de cachet*,[37] and this judgment was heightened by Seward's insouciant remark to W. H. Russell that whenever he wished to arrest any suspect, he had only to touch a little bell on his desk. Horace Greeley, deeply troubled, took steps to lay an eloquent protest before the Secretary. Of course fomenters of sedition must be locked up, he wrote, but Seward should understand that the essential question was whether men should act according to law, or according to Jack Cade's rule, "My mouth shall be Parliament." In Maryland the government, obstructed as it

34 Randall, *Const. Probs. Under Lincoln*, 152–163; O. R., II, i, 574 ff.; White, *Trumbull*, 194–196. The British consul in Baltimore, Frederick Bernard, was in the courtroom when Taney declared the validity of the habeas corpus. He congratulated the aged jurist. "He made a very feeling reply," Bernard wrote Lord John Russell, "that he had been brought up to study, and revere, the English common law, and that, pained as he was to be so obliged at such a moment, he would not shrink from asserting its glorious principles, which were likewise those of the Constitution of the United States." May 30, 1861, FO 5/784. During the Napoleonic Wars the British Government had gone to great lengths to preserve the validity of the writ of habeas corpus. Merryman was shortly released to the civil authorities, and indicted for treason, but the case—like practically all others of the sort—never came to trial. For Bates's opinion sustaining Lincoln see O. R., II, ii, 34.

35 J. T. Dorris, "President Lincoln's Treatment of Kentuckians," *Filson Club History Quarterly*, XXVIII (Jan., 1954), 3–20. Henry Clay's son John was arrested but released on bail, as were many others. A large business of oath-taking, bond-filing, and paroling sprang up in Kentucky, the amount of bond required ranging from $500 to $20,000. Five volumes of records in the Federal Circuit Court file in Louisville measure the extent of this business.

36 *Cong. Globe*, 37th Cong., 3rd Sess., 35.

37 *Nat. Intelligencer*, Feb. 12, 1862; Greeley, Oct. 3, 1861, to Samuel Wilkeson, Seward Papers, Rochester.

was by bad Federal judges, might have to move in a highhanded way. But in New York and Connecticut it had no occasion to use any law except such as was bound in sheep; "and when you grab such men as Col. Wall of New Jersey," wrote Greeley, "you tear the whole fabric of society."

Public irritation was increased by well-founded reports that prisoners were being treated inhumanely. Much disturbed, some influential New Yorkers went to Henry W. Bellows, head of the Sanitary Commission, asking that he investigate, and on October 5, 1861, he requested permission to visit some of the New York jails.[38] He found several scores of civilians confined in Fort Lafayette in New York bay. In one small casemate twenty-three prisoners, two-thirds of them in irons, were crammed together without beds, bedding, or the commonest necessaries; in other casements, fourteen feet by twenty-four, they were almost equally crowded. According to a remonstrance which some of the prisoners sent Lincoln, the misery of inmates approached that of slaves on the middle passage. Two battery rooms, dark and close, held sixty-nine men. Though many of the prisoners had become ill, they had no fresh water except for drinking, and little of that, while their food consisted of coarse soldiers' rations badly cooked.[39] Yet they included such distinguished men as Severn Teackle Wallis, a leader of the Maryland bar, reformer, and philanthropist, and Charles J. Faulkner, who after representing a Virginia district in Congress for eight years had been Minister to France.

Conditions at Forts Monroe and McHenry were similar.[40] But the most dismal of all prisons was one in Washington within an easy walk of Congress and the White House.

This was the Old Capitol, a decaying jail hastily refurbished for captured Confederates, refugee Negroes, blockade runners, and state prisoners. The verminous rooms stank of open drains, sweaty inmates, and the eternal fare of salt pork, beans, and rice. A military guard clattered its arms on the cobblestones outside while patrols thumped up and down the wooden hallways. The dark, ill-ventilated cells, kept full to bursting, became breeding places for all kinds of maladies. During 1862 a midsummer influx of captured Confederates raised the population to 600. The one redeeming feature of this ramshackle barn was its convivial jollity, for most prisoners were herded into five large second-story rooms partitioned out of the great chambers which had been occupied by Congress just after the burning of the Capitol in 1815. Here, by pooling their resources, the inmates could while away the hours with poker, dominoes, tobacco, whisky, and talk.

38 *Nat. Intelligencer*, Oct. 5, 1861.
39 Memorial of State prisoners in Port Lafayette to Lincoln, Oct. 8, 1861, Seward Papers, Rochester.
40 Dix to Seward, Sept. 18, Oct. 21, Seward Papers.

[V]

By 1862 the lengthening roll of prisoners, the irritation of the public and Congress, and the demands of military leaders, made it imperative for Attorney-General Bates to take some action. General Buell laid the problem squarely before him. Bates in reply tried to draw a line between judicial arrests on one side, and political or military arrests on the other, saying the judicial cases must go to the civil courts, but the others were subject to the "somewhat broad, and yet undefined, discretion of the President, as political chief of the nation" and commander in chief. The Attorney-General wisely decided that the Department of Justice had no powers in connection with prisoners held on political or military grounds, for it could deal only with offenses against clear Federal statutes.

Bates was also wise in making it clear that he was anxious to avoid indictments for treason, so strictly defined in the Constitution, except when the offense was flagrant and clear.[41] He knew how many difficulties the First Amendment threw in the way of prosecutions. Early in 1862 he instructed the Federal attorney in Missouri, J. O. Broadhead, that a few examples should be made, if only to prove that the Union was vigorously alert; but no cases should be pushed to trial except those in which conviction was certain. Not only was treason a crime hard to prove, but conviction often accomplished nothing except to create a political martyr. Federal officers had to beware of men who made charges and demanded trials out of personal malice or love of publicity, and should remember also how much harm a series of acquittals would do the government. It would be far more politic, Bates thought, to try to punish internal enemies for vulgar misdemeanors or felonies than to proceed against them for treason, which had an aura of dignity.[42]

Two conspicuous instances of arbitrary confinement were military, but they had a political coloration. Though a certain murkiness attaches to the case of Major Justus McKinstry, he was unquestionably handled tyranically. As acting

41 "Overheated zeal," he wrote, would produce a reaction; Randall, *Const. Probs.*, 87. Incidentally, the Attorney-General had but a tiny office force. In fact, when the war began, he had only an assistant, a clerk, and a messenger. This force was enlarged in August, 1861, to eight persons, the salaries of the nine totaling $20,500. Yet his duties, even at the outset, were considerable. An Act of Aug. 2, 1861, gave the Attorney-General supervision over Federal district attorneys and marshals, authorized him to employ counsel to assist them in their work, and required them to report to him. A. G. Langeluttig, *The Dept. of Justice*, 6-8.
42 Bates to Broadhead, April 10, 15, 16, etc., Dept. of Justice Records, Letters Sent, Nat. Archives. In the spring of 1862 Pierce Butler of Philadelphia brought suit against Simon Cameron for trespass, assault and battery, and false imprisonment, Cameron having supplied the troops who arrested Butler. A similar suit was brought against Gideon Welles. Lincoln instructed the Justice Department to defend such suits. Attorney-General Bates took appropriate action, and Congress passed protective legislation. See Bates to U. S. Dist. Attorney G. A. Coffey, May 5, 1862, Justice Dept., Letters Sent, Nat. Archives.

quartermaster in St. Louis with Harney, remaining on as quartermaster of the Western Department under Frémont, this Regular Army officer incurred the hostility of the Safety Committee which had broken Harney. He was arrested November 13, 1861, and confined in the arsenal. No basis for the arrest was stated, and seven months later he was still ignorant of the grounds. General S. R. Curtis, who gave the order, received it from somebody else. From whom? Horace Greeley, who became interested, made inquiries which showed that the President, Secretary of War, and Adjutant-General knew nothing about it. Reports were meanwhile circulated that McKinstry had handled contracts corruptly. But the Judge-Advocate in St. Louis found no facts to support such charges, the board of claims sitting in the city discovered nothing to impeach his integrity, and when the Van Wyck committee repeated the charges, he published a detailed refutation. He was seemingly a passable officer, but the affair had blasted his military career, and early in 1863 Lincoln confirmed his dismissal.[43]

Still worse was the arbitrary eight months' imprisonment of Brigadier-General Charles P. Stone, which in time became a *cause célèbre*. This graduate of West Point, veteran of the Mexican War, and friend of McClellan was held responsible by Congressional radicals for the Ball's Bluff disaster, and sharply questioned by the Committee on the Conduct of the War. Stanton then ordered his arrest, and on February 10, 1862, he was confined at Fort Lafayette, on charges vaguely reported as misconduct in the battle, correspondence with the enemy, treachery in letting the Confederates build a fort under his guns, and an intention of sacrificing his whole command. He was guiltier than people supposed, declared the New York *Tribune:* "The knell of traitors within already tolls." [44] Pleading in vain for trial, he lingered in prison more than six months. Lincoln had written: "Whether he be guilty or innocent, circumstances required, as appeared to me, such proceedings to be had against him for the public safety." McClellan, who might have insisted on an early trial, played an equivocal part. When on August 16 Stone was curtly released it was without acquittal, and—though he did serve later with Banks in Louisiana and with the Army of the Potomac—he was never restored to important command.[45] He

---

43 N. Y. *Tribune*, Jan. 18, 1862; see the documented pamphlet, "Vindication of General McKinstry." As provost-marshal in St. Louis, McKinstry had tried to restrain sedition by numerous arrests high and low. But Frémont had handled such arrests with judgment. He brought with him to St. Louis a Cincinnati attorney of distinction, Richard M. Corwine, whom he appointed judge-advocate; and Corwine (succeeded later by Gustav Koerner) sat on cases, took depositions, and recommended releases or courts-martial. Koerner, *Memoirs*, II, 170–173.
44 Editorial, Feb. 12, 1862.
45 Flower, *Stanton*, 136; T. Harry Williams, "Investigation, 1862," *American Heritage*, VI (Dec. 1954), 16–21; *Committee on Conduct of War, Report*, II, 252–510. Stone, though

thought that Stanton lied about the affair, and that McClellan treated him very shabbily. Certainly the episode must be regarded as one of the grossest breaches of civil liberty in our history. During his prison days Stone sent a friend a letter that might have come out of Russia.[46] "For one hundred and thirty days," he wrote, "I have been hoping what you have hoped—a trial and acquittal; but up to this time have not advanced so far as to receive a word of charges."

Lincoln was well aware early in 1862 that he must find some fairer solution of this problem, and the advent of Stanton to office offered an opportunity for turning a new page. An executive order of February 14, 1862, therefore decreed that all political prisoners in military custody should, after due inquiry, be released on parole, with an amnesty for past offenses; that all extraordinary arrests should be made in the future under the direction of the military authorities alone; and that spies, secret agents, and others whom the Secretary of War regarded as dangerous to the public safety, should be held in custody under his control. Much was to be said for thus handing the subject over to the War Department. After all, arrests usually had to be made, wherever military rule prevailed, by armed force, and the line between civil and military offenses was often thin. Yet some men who knew Secretary Stanton must have shuddered, for of all members of the Cabinet, he had the least judicial mind and most arbitrary temper.

Free as yet from the kind of odium that had gathered about Seward, Stanton began with a fairly clean slate. He adopted a sensible course for sifting the great mixed body of prisoners on hand, appointing John A. Dix and Edwards Pierrepont of New York commissioners to examine each case separately and render a verdict. These men held personal interviews, allowed friends of the accused to appear, and invited written statements, all with dispatch—in one day at Fort Lafayette they handled ten cases. Visiting one jail after another, they completed their work before May, 1862, releasing most of the prisoners. Meanwhile, with all eyes fastened on the advances of McClellan and Grant, and hope of victory running high, extraordinary arrests almost ceased. Public opinion warmly approved of the clearance of prisoners and the relaxation of tension.[47]

However, the liberalization of government policy during the first half of

---

not a knave, was a good deal of a fool. His second wife was a Louisiana woman, and he showed sympathy with slavery. Commanding on the Maryland shore in the early days of the war, he issued an order which his officers took as calling for active enforcement of the Fugitive Slave Act. When John A. Andrew censured an officer of the Twentieth Massachusetts for following the order, Stone wrote an insulting letter on the "usurpations" of the governor. Pearson, *Andrew*, I, 312-316.

46 To S. L. M. Barlow, June 26, 1862, Barlow Papers.

47 Exec. Order No. 1 Relating to War Prisoners, O. R., II, ii, 221-223; Pierrepont was a noted attorney of New York.

1862 proved only a prelude to new rigors in the second half. Military failure East and West bred pessimism and distrust, so that disloyalty grew bolder, while the Administration became less inclined to take risks. Moreover, the first limping draft act in July provoked evasion and resistance, to meet which the War Department had to exercise extraordinary powers. Hence on August 8, 1862, the War Department laid down a whole series of stringent rules. Draft eligibles were forbidden to quit the country or make uncontrolled journeys at home. Any man who left his community to evade enrollment might be instantly arrested and sentenced to nine months (the usual draft period) in the army. The habeas corpus was suspended for all persons guilty of "disloyal practices," which now specially meant the discouragement of enlistments. Many detentions, some of them highly controversial, followed.

Happily, within a short time Stanton introduced a certain regularity into his procedures. He had Major L. C. Turner, judge-advocate for the Washington district, take charge of political arrests, and decreed that none should be made except on Turner's warrant, or (within military districts) that of commanders, or of governors of States. Responsibility was thus concentrated in a small number of men. Turner might cite any arrested civilian for trial by a military commission, but this was not mandatory, and most prisoners were released without appearing before any tribunal. Late in September, 1862, Stanton by War Department order provided for the appointment of provost-marshals in the several States, responsible to a provost-marshal general; and to this last office he temporarily assigned Simeon Draper of New York, an intimate friend of Seward and Weed, and a genial, broad-minded merchant of shrewd judgment. The men named as state provost-marshals were in general civilians, and were well chosen.[48]

But the habeas corpus remained suspended with respect to persons held for disloyal practices, and during the summer and fall many men suffered. Two Iowa editors, Dennis A. Mahony of the Dubuque *Herald* and Dana Sheward of the Fairfield *Constitution and Union*, were arrested, carried to Washington, and thrown into the Old Capitol prison. At the same time a number of prominent Illinoisans were seized, including William J. Allen, who had been elected to Congress from Logan's district, and three judges, Andrew D. Duff, C. H. Constable, and John H. Mulkey. In Ohio the arrest of Dr. Edwin B. Olds of Lancaster aroused great indignation; in New Jersey, that of an able attorney and writer, James W. Wall. The country had applauded the apprehension of draft "skedaddlers" as they tried to escape into Canada, but the jailing of prominent Democrats for their denunciation of Lincoln's policies was a different matter. It was significant that Manton Marble, whose *World* had at first

48 Weed, *Memoir*, II, 483. Stanton allowed the travel restrictions to die.

treated the extraordinary arrests as largely an unfortunate necessity, now joined other editors in angrily indicting *lettres de cachet* and bastilles. The *World* was a real power, for it had a circulation of 40,000, and a brilliant editorial staff.

Moreover, Stanton's characteristic arrogance had made itself felt. A case in point was offered by two brokers in substitutes whom he had the New York police summarily arrest in the summer of 1862. They had advertised in the press that they would obtain substitutes for draft eligibles. Stanton decided that this was an interference with enlistments, and after keeping the men several days in a city jail, sent them to Fort Lafayette. He did not allow the story of the arrests to be published until one day after the report that he had decided that such brokerage was improper. Thus the public got the impression that a warning had preceded the offense; but when Judge-Advocate Turner visited Fort Lafayette he was horrified to learn that the prisoners had not been warned, and were being held on *ex post facto* proceedings. And though Stanton laid down rules, he allowed vast confusion to envelop the subject. Overzealousness by officers who made arrests was followed by carelessness in getting charges tried and endless buck-passing. Thus in the Mahony case the buck was passed from Marshal Hoxie to the provost marshal, then to the military governor of Washington, then to Assistant Secretary Watson, then to Judge-Advocate Turner, then to Halleck, and then to Stanton—and nothing was done until after the election! Mahony had powerful friends to follow the buck, but what of those who were friendless? [49]

Horatio Seymour and other Democratic leaders hence met a large response from independent voters when they made the arrests a major issue of the fall campaign. Some of the imprisoned men profited from their political martyrdom. Mahony was nominated for Congress; Allen was renominated and re-elected; a citizen who had been arrested in Galena was chosen mayor. Lincoln made matters worse by an ill-timed proclamation on September 24 announcing that the habeas corpus could not be invoked on behalf of persons who discouraged enlistments, resisted the draft, or engaged in "any disloyal practice." He was simply trying to clarify Administration policy, but as he gave no argument justifying his course or explaining his intentions, his statement seemed

---

49 Mahony wrote a crisp, vivid book, *Prisoner of State*. He and Sheward appealed to Stanton and Lincoln by letter, in vain; then Charles Mason, former chief justice of Iowa, took up their case. Assistant Secretary of War Watson actually told Mason: "Let them prove themselves innocent and they will be discharged!" In his diary Mason gives a fascinating account of the way in which Turner, Halleck, Stanton, and others all evaded his efforts to gain a hearing for the editors. He became convinced that partisan politics was behind their detention during the campaign. MS Diary, Columbia University. But Allen, unlike many others, would seem to have deserved his arrest. A Tennesseean by birth, he had openly proposed to Logan that Illinois be divided so that the southern half could join the Confederacy, and he advised young men to go south to fight; Cole, *Era of the Civil War*, 302. In the House he played a role considerably more clownish than sinister.

to many to offer a threat of overriding all opposition by punitive arrests. Senator Bayard and other Democrats declared that any man who protested against the draft, or expressed gloomy views about the war, or quarreled with any Administration activity, might be accused, thrown into jail, denied trial, and kept in some fort, arsenal, or other place of confinement until the close of the war.[50]

In the midst of the battle an Indiana grand jury issued a report (August 4) which estimated that the Knights of the Golden Circle had 15,000 disloyal members in that State, and handed down 60 indictments for treason, conspiracy against the government, and other crimes. Democrats were quick to declare that this document reflected a keener interest in the fall elections than in the safety of the nation, and its estimate was certainly a wild exaggeration. The Knights flourished especially in areas of Southern blood. Founded long before the Civil War to promote filibustering and expansion in the circle around the Caribbean, their secret order had been readily converted in 1861 to underground support of the Confederacy. Just how numerous, active, and dangerous it was nobody will ever know, for its activities were clandestine.[51] It was true that some Knights were trying to embarrass enlistments and encourage desertion. But it was also true that Governor Morton was a partisan who foresaw that a Democratic legislature would resist efforts to make the war (in his words) "instant and terrible," [52] and would try to keep it moderate. Probably the indictments did the Administration ticket more harm than good.

It was clear, as election day approached, that the civil-rights issue was strengthening the Democrats by stiffening their lines and converting uneasy citizens. Even the Springfield *Republican* asserted that the methods which the Administration employed did not befit a free government.[53]

[VI]

The October elections revealed a powerful wave of discontent—but not an overwhelming current. In Pennsylvania, Ohio, and Indiana the Democrats

50 *Cong. Globe*, 37th Cong., 3rd Sess., 72.

51 The founder, G. W. L. Bickley of Cincinnati, set energetically to work in 1861 in transforming the order. After planting lodges in Kentucky and Tennessee, he encouraged agents who established others in Southern Indiana and Illinois. Prentice of the Louisville *Journal* in 1861 charged that the Knights were the very brain and soul of secession in Kentucky. Governor Morton in Indiana used Colonel Henry B. Carrington in an excited, harsh, and vindictive warfare against their machinations which all too often presumed that nearly every Democrat was a potential traitor. See George Fort Milton, *Lincoln and the Fifth Column*, Ch. IV; Stampp, *Indiana Politics*, 151, 152.

52 Foulke, *Morton*, I, 118.

53 Editorials, Sept. 27, Nov. 1, 1862. The *Republican* thought Lincoln's proclamation of Sept. 26 badly timed, badly phrased, and unfortunate in omitting qualifications and restraints.

polled a majority of the popular vote and took a majority of the House seats. Their margins, however, were moderate. In Pennsylvania the vote stood 219,140 to 215,616; in Ohio, 184,332 to 178,755; and even in Indiana only 128,160 to 118,517. In Pennsylvania, the two major parties split the Congressional places almost evenly, but in Ohio the Democrats won fourteen seats and the Republicans only five, while in Indiana the Democrats took seven of the eleven seats. Vallandigham lost his place only because a Republican county had been added to his district. Although these three States definitely aligned themselves against the Administration, Republicans could find a good deal in the results to comfort them. In Pennsylvania, for example, part of the slender Democratic margin was provided by the sheer efficiency of the party organization, far surpassing that of the Republicans. In Ohio the small Democratic margin could be traced, at least in part, to the absence of many Union men in the army, and to the fact that, as the Cincinnati *Commercial* put it, "the prejudice of race has been inflamed, and used by the Democratic party with an energy and ingenuity perfectly infernal." [54]

All eyes now turned to New York, New Jersey, and Illinois—and particularly to the first. The real stake in the New York contest, it seemed to many, was national power. Behind the mask of Wadsworth, conservatives of both parties saw the sinister figure of Chase, archenemy of Seward and of moderate policies; already staggered by the Republican defeat in Ohio, the Secretary must not be allowed to triumph in the Empire State. Not only Seward, but Montgomery Blair and Bates, were believed to be at heart against Wadsworth, and it is certain that Thurlow Weed was lukewarm if not disloyal in the Republican cause. Bennett's *Herald*, professedly for Lincoln and the Union, exerted all its influence to help elect Seymour. On the Democratic side, efficient city machines for once worked in unison. The Mozart Hall Democracy and Tammany Democracy had made a bargain which ensured Fernando Wood, his brother Benjamin Wood of the *Daily News*, James Brooks of the *Express*, and Anson Herrick of the *Atlas* seats in Congress; these three newspapers gave stanch support to each other, while the halls united with the Albany Regency in forming a solid front behind Horatio Seymour. McClellan could hardly contain his hatred for Wadsworth. "I have so thorough a contempt for the man and regard him as such a vile traitorous miscreant that I do not wish the great State of New York disgraced by having such a thing at its head." [55]

54 *Tribune Almanac*, 1863, *passim; Annual Cyc.* 1862, *passim.* Of the Pennsylvania seats, according to the *Tribune Almanac*, 54, the Democrats took eleven, the People's Union Party (Republicans) ten, the War Democrats one, independent Union ticket one, and Independent Republican one. In Pennsylvania a Republican legislature had done some gerrymandering. See S. L. Davis, *Pennsylvania Politics, 1860–65*, 176 ff.

55 N. Y. *Tribune*, June 16, 1863, describes the bargain of the halls; McClellan Oct. 17, 1862, to Barlow, Barlow Papers.

The November elections gave the New York Democrats a decisive victory. Seymour had a majority of nearly 11,000, and the Democrats won 17 Congressional seats, the Administration only 14. Roscoe Conkling, Lincoln's brilliant young supporter in the House, lost his place. Though weariness, Republican disunity, and resentment over arbitrary arrests all counted in the result, here the major explanation lay simply in the military reverses. Bryant had written Lincoln just before the election that Seymour's election, "a public calamity," might be averted if the armies would only win a timely battle, but that continued military inactivity would lose New York and other States.[56] And John Cochrane later wrote Lincoln that the adverse vote expressed not hostility to him, but disappointment in the dragging war.[57]

If Bryant thought New York a disaster, he might well have called New Jersey a debacle. Joel Parker, a tall, dignified, well-educated Douglas Democrat, ran away with the governorship by a vote of 61,307 to 46,710, while Democrats took four of the five House seats, and gained full control of the legislature. In Illinois a similar dissatisfaction prevailed. "If we are beaten in this State two weeks hence," Horace White telegraphed Lincoln late in October, "it will be because McClellan and Buell won't fight." On election day the Democrats carried Illinois 136,662 to 120,116, taking nine of the fourteen House seats. The President's friend Leonard Swett was defeated in a district which had been Republican in the last two elections. Lyman Trumbull, anticipating a dark future, wrote Zach Chandler that the results might prove revolutionary. "Should not be surprised if the Democrats in the end became the war party. This is their true policy. I fear a humiliating compromise. . . ."[58] Unquestionably the reverse in his own prairie home cut Lincoln to the heart.

In peripheral States, where emancipation had been the chief issue, the outcome was somewhat equivocal. Kansas elected a Republican Congressman. Final Missouri returns gave Congressional seats to two Democrats, as against seven men who labeled themselves Republican, emancipationist, or independent Unionist—one of them Frank P. Blair; a result hailed as a notable victory for the Administration. Emancipation had won, said one editor, because the people had seen slavery and freedom in competition, and taken note of the superior prosperity of the free States.[59] The fact was, however, that an ordinance the previous June had disfranchised many Missourians, that the polls were guarded by troops who barred anyone who had not taken an oath of allegiance to the

56 Samuel J. Tilden wrote the peroration for one of Seymour's speeches, promising the South if it but re-entered the Union absolute local self-government and fresh guarantees of equal rights; *Letters and Memorials*, I, 167.
57 N. Y. *Times*, Nov. 5, 1862; Cochrane, Nov. 5, 1862, RTL Papers.
58 White, Oct. 22, 1862, RTL Papers; Trumbull, Nov. 9, 1862, Chandler Papers.
59 Providence *Journal*, Nov. 17, 1862. Andrew carried Massachusetts 70,000 to 50,000; Pearson, *Andrew*, II, 60.

Union and the provisional State government, and that numerous citizens were absent in the Confederate army. Delaware chose a Democratic Representative; Maryland and Kentucky held no elections.

Altogether, the oft-repeated statement that the Border States stood by Lincoln while almost the whole North outside New England went against him is inaccurate. After all, Michigan, Iowa, and California took their stand beside the Yankee Northeast, while a change of 2,000 votes in Pennsylvania and 3,000 in Ohio would have altered the whole outcome there. Considering the unfavorable circumstances, the Administration did fairly well in the North. As for the borderland, its voice was muffled by force. In Missouri even loyal Democrats felt an element of intimidation; that State was not, indeed, to know a full, free, and fair election until 1876. In Delaware also the use of troops to guard the polls aroused lasting resentment, for more than a thousand soldiers were brought into the State.[60]

That the election was a serious Administration reverse nobody ever doubted. It filled Democratic leaders with exultation, and encouraged disloyalists. It was a vote of want of confidence, and under a parliamentary system, the government headed by Lincoln might have been compelled to resign. Though under existing conditions, with the South gone, it was almost impossible for the Republicans to lose the House, their strength was sadly shaken. The best computation available, based on the vote for Speaker in the next Congress, gives 77 out-and-out anti-Administration members against 101 Administration men.[61] Had they taken fifteen additional seats, the Democrats would have gained control. As it was, the Administration on clear-cut party measures could carry the day. But measures were seldom clear-cut, and as we have said, the party situation was chaotic. Lincoln had as many foes in the Senate on the Republican side as on the Democratic, while in the House many members, from Thad Stevens down, were ready to show their independence. Time was to prove that, like Presidents before and since, he would have to rely on bipartisan support to carry some of his most cherished measures.

Lincoln's explanation of this reverse, set forth in a letter to Carl Schurz, was inadequate. He believed three main causes were responsible. The Democratic voters had been left in a majority by the departure of Administration supporters for the war; their leaders had taken advantage of this by making frenzied efforts to reinstate themselves in power, and part of the Republican press, by villifying the Administration, had given them the weapons. He added a fact of greater weight: "Certainly the ill success of the war had much to do with this." Secretary Chase expressed his feelings acridly: "But after all can

60 Lucien Carr, *Missouri*, 354–356; H. Clay Reed, *Delaware*, I, 163 ff.
61 Greeley, *American Conflict*, II, 254; *National Almanac*, 1864, pp. 78, 79.

we complain that the people are not satisfied with an unfruitful debt and a mismanaged war?"[62]

Unquestionably many elements, including high prices, high taxes, talk of corruption, the suspension of the habeas corpus, the arrests, the draft, and fear of Negro competition in the labor market, had played a part in the grand result. If the Emancipation Proclamation gained votes for the Administration in New England, northern Ohio, and Michigan, it lost votes in other areas. But looming above all other considerations was the failure of the government to bring a close of the horrible struggle within sight. "The people," said the Cincinnati *Gazette*, "are depressed by the interminable nature of this war, as so far conducted, and by the rapid exhaustion of the national resources without progress."[63] That was the gist of the matter.

62   To Hiram Barney, Oct. 15, 1862, Chase Coll., Pa. Hist. Soc.
63   Editorial, "The Moral of the Election," Oct. 17, 1862. The RTL Papers are full of letters to Lincoln on the subject. He wrote Schurz on Nov. 10, 1862, and Schurz replied that the people had some reason to administer their "severe reproof."

Administration interferences with freedom of the press also played a part in the election. But these became graver at a later date in the war, and full treatment is reserved to a subsequent chapter. Thomas F. Carroll offers a sound introduction in "Freedom of Speech During the Civil War," *Virginia Law Review*, IX (May, 1923), pp. 516-551.

13

Lincoln Dismisses McClellan and Faces Congress

IN THE weeks preceding and following the election, Lincoln was far less concerned with politics than with the progress of the war. Antietam was too indecisive to satisfy him, for McClellan had merely parried Lee's blow, striking none in return. In the West, Perryville and its sequels were equally disappointing. When Buell's sluggishness seemed to match McClellan's, young Nicolay dryly commented: "It is rather a good thing to be a major-general; one can take things so leisurely." To the President, as to Cabinet and Congress, one question was paramount: Would the Army of the Potomac try to crush Lee before the first wintry storms?

One of the many evidences of Lincoln's anxiety for action lies in the irritable telegraphic exchanges between Halleck and McClellan. The President's long strides carried him several times a day to the War Department, where he not only conferred with Stanton and Halleck but shaped many of their dispatches. Stanton hated McClellan, for he could never forgive the general's bitter reproaches after the Seven Days; Halleck was taciturnly antagonistic; Lincoln was grimly patient.[1] Why, Halleck demanded by wire, did McClellan not pursue the enemy instead of tarrying to bury the dead? How many had been slain and wounded on each side? What was the exact position of the two armies? When would he move? Lincoln's own sense of frustration breathed in these messages.

The President put the same queries to Allan Pinkerton when that confidential agent of McClellan brought his Scots accent into the White House on September 22. Knowing that Pinkerton would report everything to his chief, Lincoln took pains to mention the priceless value of the two recent victories. But—why had McClellan been so slow in reaching South Mountain? Why had

---

1 Stanton freely expressed regret that Burnside had not taken the army after Pope's failure; Butterworth, Sept. 23, 1862, to Barlow, Barlow Papers. For Halleck's antipathy see Comte de Paris, II, 540; for the Halleck-McClellan exchanges, O. R., I, xix, pt. 2, 339 ff.

he not renewed the battle the day after Antietam? Why had he allowed the rebels to recross the Potomac? Pinkerton expatiated upon the superior strength of the enemy (crediting Lee with 140,000 men at Antietam!), the exhaustion of the Union troops after the battle, and the facilities which the low stage of the Potomac gave for Lee's retreat. The agent thought he had made an impression upon Lincoln. "For myself, you know," he wrote McClellan, "I am rather prejudiced against him—but I must confess that he impressed me more at this interview with his honesty toward you and his desire to do you justice than he has ever done before." [2]

The dreary story of McClellan's delays and excuses, which had so long exasperated the radicals in Washington, was being resumed. Some of his soldiers read his pleas of fatigue and discouragement in the ranks with incredulity. "To us of the Thirteenth Massachusetts," wrote one, "it seemed just possible that the enemy might be equally tired and a good deal more discomfited." Many officers felt the same. Robert Gould Shaw records their disappointment when Lee withdrew. "When we heard that he had gone, the day after the battle, we said it would ruin McClellan." The general had not properly exploited his victory, Meade informed his wife: "I think myself he errs on the side of prudence and caution. . . ." As we have noted, Lee, falling back to the area of Winchester and Bunker Hill where the rich Shenandoah Valley afforded full supplies, indulged his veterans in a much-needed rest while he labored strenuously to refill his ranks; and Richmond aided him so effectively that by October he had about 70,000 fighting men. McClellan meanwhile satisfied himself with reoccupying Harpers Ferry as a bridgehead on the south side of the Potomac, and putting Sumner with two corps in possession of it and the fortified heights above. His own strength was not far from twice Lee's, but he did not think it safe to go beyond Harpers Ferry, lest he provoke the overwhelming enemy host! [3]

The chagrin of Administration leaders when they found that no effort was being made to press Lee was explosive. Barnett of the Interior Department talked at length on September 23 with Lincoln and Caleb Smith. "I am convinced," he wrote Barlow, "that the government, if they dared, would supersede Mac." [4] Why did they not dare? Because they feared the resentment of the army; because, too, they did not know whom to put in his place. "Oh, put anybody!" said Ben Wade, but Lincoln replied: "Wade, *anybody* will do for you, but I must have *somebody*."

2   Pinkerton, Sept. 22, 1862, to McClellan; Pinkerton Papers.
3   C. E. Davis, Jr., *Three Years in the Army*, 142; Nicolay, *Lincoln's Secretary*, 149; Shaw to his wife, Jan. 10, 1863, Shaw Papers; Meade, *Meade*, 319. On Oct. 20, 1862, McClellan reported an aggregate of 159,860 present, with 144,433 effectives; Lee at the same time had 79,595 present for duty, with 68,033 effectives.
4   Sept. 23, 1862, Barlow Papers.

The visit to the front was significant. In his uneasiness, Lincoln felt that he must carry his demands directly to McClellan. Cabinet members demurred, Stanton in particular declaring that McClellan would use the visit as an excuse for thereafter writing the President direct instead of going through channels. Lincoln however insisted, and taking a special train to Harpers Ferry on October 1, met the general at Sumner's headquarters. He reviewed Sumner's corps, riding along its ranks as unit after unit dipped colors, presented arms, and cheered. Everyone thought him thin and careworn; a future President, Hayes, noted that, mounted on a white horse with his trousers hitched nearly to the top of his boots, Lincoln was heedless of the ludicrous figure he cut.[5] One corps commander, Hooker, was not there, having been invalided to Washington. But Lincoln talked with other generals, viewed the two battlefields, looked at the John Brown engine house, and in particular conferred with McClellan.

The public impression that he wanted to hurry little Mac was correct. In fact, he told the general emphatically that he must now act with spirit, or he was lost. The President wished him to cross the Potomac east of the Blue Ridge, thus keeping his army between Lee and Washington, while McClellan wished to cross west and attack Lee in the Shenandoah. On his return, Lincoln issued an order, through Halleck, which any other officer would have regarded as peremptory (October 6):

The President directs that you cross the Potomac and give battle to the enemy or drive him south. Your army must move now while the roads are good. If you cross the river between the enemy and Washington, and cover the latter by your line of operations, you can be reinforced with 30,000 men. If you move up the valley of the Shenandoah, not more than 12,000 or 15,000 can be sent you. The President advises the interior line between Washington and the enemy, but he does not order it. He is very desirous that your army move as soon as possible.

Lincoln was peremptory because he had come back totally unable to understand why an immediate forward movement was not undertaken. The troops seemed rested and well equipped, and the officers eager for movement. Several of McClellan's generals had written strong complaints to Cabinet members. Hooker, holding a series of conferences in his Washington sickroom with Secretary Chase, assured him that it was not true that the troops or officers idolized the little Napoleon, that McClellan really had no dash or boldness, and that he was unfit to lead a great army.[6] Garfield, waiting for a new command, agreed. Pinkerton, learning all this at the War Department, hastened to warn

5 Fitz-John Porter hailed Lincoln's arrival in a note to Manton Marble: "The President is here. His visits have been always followed by injury. So look out—another proclamation or war order." Sept. 30, 1862, Manton Marble Papers, LC.

6 "Hooker is looking for promotion to be General-in-Chief," wrote Fitz-John Porter, "and will turn a somersault to get it. . . . Watch him. . . . He is ambitious and unscrupulous." Lincoln's order above is in O. R., I, xix, pt. 1, p. 72.

McClellan that he faced a clear alternative: If he attacked and won a reasonable success, he would be advanced to the highest command, but if he stood still, he would be dismissed.

For two main reasons McClellan elected to stand still. He must wait until the Potomac rose to be sure Lee would not recross it; and he must finish drilling new recruits, reorganizing his forces, and procuring sufficient blankets, shoes, uniforms, and camp equipment. A wrangling interchange between McClellan and Halleck continued through most of October and grew steadily more acrimonious. The War Department insisted that it had furnished adequate supplies, and certainly Meigs made every effort to do so. But Meade was telling his wife that hundreds of his men were shoeless, and nothing would satisfy McClellan. "The men cannot march without shoes," he wrote, at precisely the same time that Lee was confiding to Jefferson Davis what pain it gave him to watch 8,000 barefoot veterans "limping over the rocky roads." During October 95,000 pairs of footgear were sent to McClellan.[7]

As McClellan waited, Jeb Stuart made a daring raid into Pennsylvania with 1,800 hard-riding troopers at his back. At dawn on October 10 he drove through Mercersburg, occupied Chambersburg that night, and swept south again into Virginia, bringing out some prisoners, 1,200 fresh mounts, and valuable information. Three Union cavalry leaders, Averill, Pleasanton, and Stoneman, had ridden furiously to intercept him, and gotten nothing but hard knocks for their pains. Why did you not catch Stuart in your toils? demanded the War Department of McClellan. His explanation that the government had provided a wretched remount service angered Meigs, who hotly replied that he was furnishing 1,500 horses a week, meeting strict national specifications, but that McClellan's troops did not know how to take care of them.[8]

At this point Lincoln resumed the process which Nicolay termed poking sharp sticks under Little Mac's ribs. On October 13 he sat down to remind the general of a previous rebuke for overcautiousness. Was he not overcautious when he assumed that he could not do what the enemy was constantly doing? McClellan had telegraphed Halleck that he could not subsist his army at Winchester until the railroad from Harpers Ferry to that town was repaired. But Lee was now subsisting his army at Winchester without rail communications, wagoning stores a distance twice as great as that from Harpers Ferry, and with half the wagons that the Union army possessed. Time was essential to the

7 Pinkerton to McClellan, Oct. 6, 1862, Pinkerton Papers; O. R., I, xix, pt. 2, 422–424, 465, 466.

8 Thomason, *Stuart*, 291–319. The Confederate remount service is treated in Charles W. Ramsdell, "General Robert E. Lee's Horse Supply, 1863–1865," *Am. Hist. Review*, XXXV (July, 1930), 758–777. McClellan's army of 122,000 at this time required 34,000 draft horses, 6,850 artillery horses, and 5,000 cavalry horses, or about 46,000 in all; Report of General Rufus Ingalls, O. R., I, xix, pt. 1, 94–97.

Union, Lincoln declared. Why not attack Lee's communication lines, so badly exposed, forthwith?

Change positions with the enemy, and think you not he would break your communication with Richmond within the next twenty-four hours? You dread his going into Pennsylvania. But if he does so in full force, he gives up his communications to you absolutely, and you have nothing to do but follow, and ruin him; if he does so with less than full force, fall upon, and beat what is left behind all the easier.

Exclusive of the water line, you are now nearer Richmond than the enemy is by the route that you *can*, and he *must* take. Why can you not reach there before him, unless you admit that he is more than your equal on a march? His route is the arc of a circle, while yours is the chord. The roads are as good on yours as on his.[9]

The President recalled how he had suggested that McClellan move down east of the Blue Ridge, thus at once menacing Lee's communications with Richmond. If Lee should then advance into Pennsylvania, McClellan could follow him closely; if he should retire toward Richmond, McClellan could try to reach that city first, meanwhile giving battle on any good opportunity:

If he makes a stand at Winchester, moving neither North nor South, I would fight him there, on the idea that if we cannot beat him when he bears the wastage of coming to us, we never can when we bear the wastage of going to him. This proposition is a simple truth, and too important to be lost sight of for a moment. In coming to us, he tenders us an advantage which we should not waive. We should not so operate as merely to drive him away. As we must beat him somewhere, or fail finally, we can do it, if at all, easier near to us than far away. If we cannot beat the enemy where he now is, we never can, he again being within the entrenchments of Richmond. . . .

This letter is in no sense an order.

But McClellan continued to delay, putting Lincoln off with a vague reply. He would give the President's views the fullest consideration, and would advance "the moment my men are shod and my cavalry are sufficiently renovated." [10] Lincoln, beset by Bryant, Raymond, and a hundred other editors to give the country some progress, returned to the charge. On October 21, through Halleck, he repeated his order of the 6th, stating that while he did not expect impossibilities, he was very anxious that the continued good weather should not be wasted by inactivity. "Telegraph when you will move, and on what lines you propose to march." An epidemic had broken out among the

9 *Works*, V, 460–462.
10 Oct. 17, 1862; O. R., I, xix, pt. 1, 16. From Harpers Ferry to Washington was five hours by train. McClellan could have left the Ferry any day at noon, conferred with Lincoln, Stanton, Halleck, and Meigs for two hours, and gotten back soon after midnight. But his relations with all were such that he did **not** want a conference, nor would one have been fruitful.

army horses, giving them sore mouths and backs, and McClellan on the 24th made this an excuse for immobility. Lincoln returned one of the sharpest messages of his career. "I have just read your dispatch about sore tongues and fatigued horses," he telegraphed. "Will you pardon me for asking what the horses of your army have done since the battle of Antietam that fatigues anything?"

At last McClellan, on October 26, began throwing his army across the Potomac at Harpers Ferry and Berlin, an operation which took him six days. He followed this by a rapid march to the New Baltimore–Warrenton area. At the outset he was east of the Blue Ridge, Lee on the west; he had the inside line to Richmond; but his deliberate movements enabled Lee, leaving Jackson's force in the Shenandoah, to cross the Blue Ridge at leisure and place himself at Culpeper between McClellan and the Confederate capital. Lincoln had told John Hay that if McClellan sacrificed the advantage of inside lines, he would relieve the general. Would he now act? [11]

[I]

McClellan's last movement was strategically sound. By his forward swing to Warrenton he had put himself in position to strike between Lee at Culpeper and Stonewall Jackson west of the Blue Ridge, thus either fighting each army separately, or forcing them to concentrate as far south as Gordonsville. He should have told Lincoln of this plan. But he failed completely to keep Halleck, Stanton, or the President advised of his intentions, telling them only of his fears and demands. He sent long telegrams October 25–30 on measures to guard the Potomac against an attack on Maryland during his advance, but he did not inform Washington just what this advance contemplated.

And if Lee and Jackson concentrated at Gordonsville, what then? Would McClellan fight, or would he find more excuses for delay? On November 5–6 water froze and snow fell; winter was beginning.[12] McClellan's subsequent report of operations throws doubt on his determination to give battle. Once he faced Lee at Gordonsville, he writes, the army would be "in position either to adopt the Fredericksburg line of advance upon Richmond, or to be removed to the Peninsula if, as I apprehended, it were found impossible to supply it by the Orange & Alexandria Railroad beyond Culpeper."[13] The Peninsula again! How long would removal to the James take? And if Maryland was in danger

---

11 Lincoln, *Works*, V, 460–462.

12 N. M. Curtis, *From Bull Run to Chancellorsville*, 215. On the 7th Virginia had one of the heaviest snowfalls in years; Richmond *Examiner*, Nov. 8.

13 O. R., I, xix, pt. 1, 84–87. McClellan worried lest Bragg's faraway troops suddenly join Lee!

while McClellan lay at Warrenton, what about Washington after he moved down to the Peninsula? The President feared a resumption of the old postponements.

And Lincoln, who wished to keep politics out of military operations, was doubtless also uneasy about McClellan's political attitudes. The President had just dismissed Major John J. Key, brother of one of McClellan's staff, for saying that the "game" was to prolong the war until both sides were worn out, when the Union might be saved with slavery intact. He knew that, as Schurz tells us, such silly treasonable talk was rife among the staff, and hoped that an example might cut it short.[14] Everyone knew of McClellan's tenderness toward Southern institutions. In his order to the army publishing the Emancipation Proclamation, he had not only avoided any word of approbation, but had forbidden political discussion with a pregnant hint: "The remedy for political errors, if any are committed, is to be found only in the action of the people at the polls." [15] This, a few weeks before the November elections, was sure to be given a partisan interpretation. It was said that he even prepared a public protest, which his officers induced him to suppress. The President had no anxiety about the general's possible insubordination, and when John Hay spoke of the matter responded sadly: "McClellan is doing nothing to make himself either respected or feared." Nor was Lincoln in the least inclined to follow Madison and Polk in letting party considerations affect his own decisions. He wrote at this very time that "in considering military merit, the world has abundant evidence that I discard politics"—as the names of McClellan, Buell, and Halleck proved. But he had to give consideration to the fact that McClellan had around him men who wanted a compromise peace.[16]

Lincoln at this moment commands our deepest sympathy. Winter was coming with no prospect that the long record of Eastern defeat and stalemate would be broken; Congress, partly angry, partly sullen, was about to meet; though the elections showed that popular impatience was rising, still more men and more money would have to be demanded from the country. He was bitterly assailed by men who wanted sterner war, and men who wanted peace. The governors, as the Altoona Conference had shown, were restive. The Cabinet was filled with dissension to a degree which interfered with public business, and though Lincoln did not know it, early in October Chase and Stanton were talking together in harsh terms about the President's shortcomings, and trying to enlist Gideon Welles.

Lincoln was still reluctant to remove McClellan, for he thought the man

14 *Works*, VIII, 47–49; Schurz, *Rems.*, II, 382.
15 O. R., I, xix, pt. 2, 395, 396.
16 Nicolay and Hay, VI, 180; Lincoln, *Works*, V, 486.

might deserve another chance, and he told friends that he was not certain any-body else could effectively maneuver a great army. Sumner was too old, Mc-Dowell had lost the troops' respect, Buell wavered at critical moments, and Grant and Sherman were too inexperienced, or at least too little known in the East. There remained Hooker and Burnside, neither surely known to be quali-fied, and the former at sword's point with McClellan. From Halleck, mean-while, Lincoln got no useful advice. At a Cabinet meeting on November 4, Stanton sneeringly remarked that Halleck did not consider himself responsible for army movements or deficiencies east of the Alleghenies, for McClellan did not report to him but to the President direct. Lincoln cut in sharply to say that Halleck would and should be considered responsible; he had told Halleck that he would remove McClellan at any time he required it, and would bear the public brunt of the decision.[17] Clearly, nobody had an exact idea of just what Halleck's functions were. As the discussion continued, Lincoln said, with full Cabinet concurrence, that Halleck was quite unfitted for field command, and shirked the position he held; in Welles's words, he was a moral coward.

Had Lincoln decided to keep McClellan, he would have had to face the condemnation of almost all the really determined Union leaders.[18] The Presi-dent of course acted on his own reasoning. He knew that McClellan could organize a splendid army, hold its devotion, and save it from calamity; that he could protect Washington and the North. But the Union could never be re-stored in that way. What he needed was a general who would hit hard, boldly, and often. He had been all too patient.

On November 5, 1862, Lincoln relieved McClellan and appointed Ambrose E. Burnside in his stead. With McClellan went Fitz-John Porter. O. B. Willcot was assigned Burnside's corps, while Hooker took Porter's. The order carried by General C. P. Buckingham reached McClellan in his tent at night on the 7th, taking him by surprise. Reading it with a silent smile, quite alone, he ex-claimed: "Alas for my poor country!" Some of his officers advised him to refuse to obey. He might, he wrote later, have led his troops against Washing-ton to take possession of the government—an idea that should never even have occurred to him. But on November 10, in a painfully impressive scene, he parted from his great army of 120,000 men.[19]

17 Welles, *Diary*, I, 179 ff. At this meeting Lincoln reviewed his relations with McClellan, and belatedly read his long patient letter to McClellan dated Oct. 13. Halleck's moral cow-ardice is shown by the fact that although he was anxious to get rid of McClellan, he said nothing to Lincoln; see his letter to C. P. Buckingham, Dec. 22, 1862, Ill. State Hist. Lib.
18 Including Montgomery M. Meigs, whose letters refuting McClellan's charges of inadequate supply were withering invectives; O. R., I, xix, pt. 2, pp. 422 ff., 465.
19 Stanton asked Gen. Buckingham to carry the orders (1) because he might specially persuade Burnside to take the command—and Burnside indeed accepted only when told that Hooker would get it if he refused; and (2) because Stanton, doubting McClellan's loyalty,

[II]

If Lincoln's removal of the general was questionable, as many army officers believed at the time and many military analysts have written since, it was a decision rendered unavoidable by McClellan's faults. The Young Napoleon could waste weeks before Yorktown, fail before Richmond, drag his feet in bringing aid to Pope, fail once more in not attacking on the morrow of Antietam —and still be forgiven; but his whole course since Antietam seemed to presage continued failure. That battle had been fought September 17. But McClellan, despite Lincoln's orders, despite Halleck's reiterated demands, did not move his army forward until six and a half weeks later—forty days which saw precious autumn ebbing away. Had he taken but four weeks and explained his course thoroughly to his superiors, he might have kept his command, for he had good reasons to justify a limited wait. Many of the regiments he had taken from Pope were wasted by fighting and desertion to two or three companies apiece; Pope's loss of stores caused a grievous shortage of equipment, and many of Pope's troops were demoralized. Antietam had inflicted new losses of men and material and left some units exhausted. Many incoming regiments, too, were green and ill disciplined.[20]

But McClellan was stubbornly reticent. Instead of explaining his situation, he wrote ill-tempered letters about wagons, tents, and horses. To the end he gave Lincoln and the War Department no clear indication that he meant to fight before winter halted operations. The breakdown of confidence between him and the leaders of Congress and Cabinet was perhaps not adequate reason for dismissal—though McClellan's total indifference to popular opinion in a war of the people was inexcusable. But the breakdown of effective communication between his headquarters on one side, and the White House and War Department on the other, a breakdown for which he was primarily responsible, was a very broad ground for his ouster. His successor's first important step was to send Lincoln a detailed plan of campaign.[21]

McClellan returned to New Jersey, out of the war for good, a victim not of

feared that the general would refuse to give up the army. This was the same unworthy suspicion that some men had held of Frémont in 1861, and just as unfounded. Buckingham in Chicago *Tribune*, Sept. 4, 1875; Comte de Paris, II, 555, 556. If we may believe Montgomery C. Meigs's notes on Lincoln and Stanton in his papers, the President had been willing to put Burnside in command just before the Seven Days; if we may believe Orville H. Browning (*Diary*, I, 589, 590) he had been willing to do so when Lee invaded Maryland.

20 See G. W. Bicknell, *Hist. of the Fifth Maine*, 142 ff., on army needs.

21 O. R., I, xix, pt. 2, 552–554. Some critics of McClellan accused him of delaying action until after the election to further Democratic chances; critics of Lincoln accused him of delaying the removal lest he hurt Republican fortunes. Lincoln at least was far too high-minded to put party above national welfare.

incapacity or inexperience but of his character and temperament. Impatient of authority, querulous under criticism, religiously certain of divine guidance, deeply egotistical, he lacked the central quality of a great commander as defined by a famous modern soldier. "Most vital of all," writes General Archibald Wavell,[22] "he must have the fighting spirit, the will to win"; he must be "the man who plays his best when things are going badly, who has the power to come back at you when apparently beaten, and who refuses to acknowledge defeat." Napoleon remarked: "If the art of war consisted merely in not taking risks, glory would be at the mercy of very mediocre talent." McClellan excelled at not taking risks; a perfectionist, he was reluctant to move until the last linchpin and map case was ready, while he always feared that just over the hill the enemy had unseen reserves. This spirit would save the army and lose the nation.

Much was lost when McClellan departed. (1) The changeover of command entailed friction and fumbling. The staff work of the Army of the Potomac had reached immense volume, and all but one or two top staff members left with the general.[23] Subordinate staff officers, a numerous body, had to establish working relations with Burnside's entourage. (2) McClellan, unrivaled in organizing ability, had been brigading depleted veteran regiments with units recently raised and taking other steps to improve army arrangements; this work was now broken off. (3) Above all, the confidence and energy of many troops were impaired when the popular McClellan gave place to a little-known general who at Antietam had not done conspicuously well. Numerous regimental histories describe the grief which the troops manifested when McClellan rode through the camps on November 10 to take leave.[24] The ranks sent up wild cheers and cries of farewell; some men heaped sweeping denunciation on the government; the color bearers of Meagher's brigade cast their flags in the dust for the general to ride over. The army he so splendidly organized, declared Meagher, "has been grossly outraged." Edward S. Bragg wrote his wife: "Little Mac has gone, and my heart and hopes have gone with him." Meade commented on the general gloom, and Francis A. Walker, though far from uncritical of the general, wrote: "When the chief had passed out of sight, the romance of war was over for the Second Corps." [25]

---

22 "The Qualities of a General," N. Y. *Times*, March 16, 1941; see also Wavell's book, *Generals and Generalship* (1941).

23 Comte de Paris, II, 557 ff.

24 E. g., C. B. Fairchild, *Hist. of the 27th N. Y. Vols.*, 111.

25 Meagher, Nov. 10, 1862, Barlow Papers; Bragg, Nov. 16, 1862, Bragg Papers; Meade, *Meade*, I, 325; Monroe, *Walker*, 57. C. F. Walcott, *Twenty-first Massachusetts*, 217-219, states his opinion that the general sentiment of the army would have sustained McClellan if he had refused to recognize the order of removal "until after the probably impending battle had been fought." McClellan made Meagher's troops pick up the flags.

Press comment was what might have been anticipated, with the Republican newspapers approbatory, and the Democratic journals critical. Greeley, rejoicing over McClellan's severance from what courtesy called active service, genially added that all his friends were traitors. Raymond's *Times* expressed relief and hope, saying that the general's calamitous inactivity had given strength to the rebels and encouragement to foreign enemies.[26] But the Democratic press sharpened its knives for the Administration. The *World*, accusing Lincoln of removing McClellan for party reasons and under Cabinet pressure, placed squarely on his shoulders "the terrible responsibility" of displacing a tried soldier "from the command of a great army actually in the field and moving in the face of an enemy."

Southern comment on the removal was naturally restricted and acrid. In the past he had been treated favorably, partly through genuine admiration for his organizing talent, partly perhaps because Southern victories seemed sweeter if he were credited with genius, and partly because of his strict adherence to rules of civilized warfare. Now he was treated more caustically. The Richmond *Whig*, for example, savagely dissected his record. "The Yankees might have taken Richmond after the battle of Seven Pines, when our forces were in confusion," it said, had he seized his opportunities. "After the battle of Hanover Court-House he might have done the same thing. After the battle of Antietam the same." And the *Whig* concluded by saying he was the victim of his own pretensions. "How fortunate for us that he was chosen chief of the Yankee army!" Such comment must be taken with as much reserve as the now-familiar story that Lee later declared McClellan by all odds the best of the Union generals; a story from dubious second-hand sources reported long after the event. Lee had shown his real opinion of McClellan by dividing his forces before South Mountain, and staying in his positions after Antietam.[27]

The removal was a misfortune, but under the circumstances an unavoidable misfortune. McClellan had left the patient President no choice but to act as he did. The selection of Burnside as McClellan's successor, another misfortune,

26 Both the *Times* and *Tribune*, Nov. 10 ff., carried reports from field correspondents ridiculing the tales of excitement and dismay in the army. Two *Times* writers declared they heard only expressions of rejoicing from the soldiers, and a *Tribune* man quoted some officers as saying that McClellan's removal had saved the army from going to pieces. Certainly some soldiers took the removal philosophically. D. W. Judd, in *The Story of the Thirty-third N. Y.* (p. 217), for example, states that the whole Ninth Corps had begun to question McClellan's capacity when he failed to attack after Antietam. B. W. Crowninshield, *First Mass. Cavalry*, 38, 39, indicts him for his failure. One of his staff, Van Vliet, informed S. L. M. Barlow just before his removal that he might have been commander-in-chief if he had advanced in mid-October, adding: "We *should* have marched, perhaps, though it is not for me to decide." This is a significant admission. Oct. 22, 1862, Barlow Papers.
27 Richmond *Whig*, April 21, 1863; R. E. Lee, Jr., *Lee*, 415, 416; K. P. Williams, *Lincoln Finds a General*, II, 478, 479. Hassler offers an able defense in *McClellan*, 296–330.

seemed a logical act, for Lincoln could only take the most promising subordinate. The fact that Burnside had twice declined the command, and that he now wept, declaring himself unfit for the place, was a bad omen. In the Crimean War, when Raglan died amid general relief, General James Simpson had been named commander after he opposed his own appointment and bore testimony to his own incapacity; and after three months of failure he resigned. But—what better man was in view than this graduate of West Point, a veteran of Scott's march to Mexico City, inventor of a superior carbine, the victor of Roanoke Island and New Bern, and a corps commander known to have favored renewal of the battle the day after Antietam? He was a truly chivalric leader, as his recent order sternly forbidding indiscriminate plundering and the unauthorized seizure of private property had demonstrated.[28]

Happy were the Confederates who faced no problem of supreme command, but rested content with Lee, Stonewall, Longstreet, the two Hills, and Jeb Stuart. During this beautiful autumn of dry sunny weather half of Lee's sick recovered, and most of his stragglers, protected, fed, and often equipped by friendly Virginians, rejoined his ranks. "In the shelter of the dense woods about Culpeper," wrote the London *Times* correspondent from Confederate headquarters November 14, "in wonderful spirits, with physique ineffably improved since the bloody days of Sharpsburg, are clustered the tatterdemalion regiments of the South. It is a strange thing to look at these men, so ragged, slovenly, sleeveless, without a superfluous ounce of flesh upon their bones, with wild matted hair, in mendicants' rags, and to think when the battle flag goes to the front, how they can and do fight." Lee had told this correspondent, "There is only one attitude in which I should never be ashamed of seeing my men, and that is when they are fighting." With this heroic force, led by two of the greatest commanders of history, the much-tried Army of the Potomac was now required to grapple.

But hardly had Lincoln dealt with the exigent problem of army command before he had to turn the equally heavy responsibilities presented by the assembling of Congress. He had in fact to meet one of the most formidable crises in the governmental history of the nation, a crisis thick with difficulties.

28 At New Bern, on March 15, 1862, Burnside had faced a well-built Confederate breastwork and several redoubts protected on one side by the Neuse River and on the other by an impassable swamp. These works were defended by about 5,000 men, 3 field batteries, and 13 heavy guns; but Burnside moved his troops within short range, formed them in battle order, charged, and carried the entrenchments with a loss of only about 600 killed and wounded. He was to remember this victory when he faced entrenchments at Fredericksburg. For his General Order No. 8 against the Stanton-Pope scheme of looting see Poore, *Burnside*, 156, 157.

[III]

Difficulties of Congress—and his own official family. "The Cabinet are far from being a unit. Part of them really hate each other. Blair hates Chase and speaks openly on the street—and so it is with others. [Caleb B.] Smith says Lincoln don't treat a Cabinet as other Presidents—that he decides the most important questions without consulting his cabinet." So David Davis wrote late in November after four days of talk with Lincoln and his associates.[29]

His statements were true, and the transfer of the army to a new leader naturally stimulated a demand for changes in the Cabinet. Most of the radical editors, long hostile to Seward in particular, wished to see shifts made all along the line in the interests of greater unity and a more aggressive policy. If the armies were to hit hard and fast, so should the government. The Cleveland *Plain Dealer*, and Cincinnati *Commercial*, reiterating their familiar demands for more energy and less queasiness in attacking slavery, spoke for scores of other papers in asking for a drastic reorganization.[30]

The general utterances of the radical politicians indicated an apprehension that Lincoln would vacillate or even retreat, and must have a sterner set of advisers. Even Raymond's *Times* declared that any Administration "less timid than that which has now possession of power" would have ousted McClellan long before—as if timidity were dominant.[31] Nothing could be more certain than that when Congress met its extremists would bring pressure for the removal of several men. Fessenden, whom many wished to see in Seward's office, wrote the Boston capitalist John Murray Forbes that the prime need of the hour was to get the New Yorker out of the Cabinet. This would be difficult, for he would never willingly retire, and the President was so blind to the importance of a change that they would just let the ship of state drift. "For myself," protested Fessenden, "I can only say that there is no political calamity I should look upon with so much dread as being asked to share the responsibility of guiding it." What this meant was that he was aching to step into Seward's shoes.[32]

In the jangling Cabinet, Chase was the mainspring of opposition to the President. He not only talked with Stanton about Lincoln's faults, but discussed them with various Senators and Representatives. A story crept around Washington that just after the elections Lincoln had expressed grave doubts about pursuing the policy of emancipation; whereupon Chase had faced him defi-

29 To Leonard Swett, Nov. 26, David Davis Papers, Ill. State Hist. Lib.
30 Nov. 17, 1862.
31 Nov. 10, 1862.
32 J. M. Forbes, *Letters and Recs.*, I, 336–338.

antly, threatened to join forces with the radical leaders of Congress, and declared that sooner than carry on the war without destroying slavery they would stop it by cutting off all appropriations.[33] This was a fable, but Lincoln did tell Frank P. Blair about this time that Chase "runs the machine against me," and years afterward Montgomery Blair expressed the opinion that Chase was the one man whom Lincoln actually hated—that is, disliked, for Lincoln was incapable of hate. Chase's egotism made him sublimely condescending toward the President, whom he pronounced kindly, sensible, and honest, but "greatly wanting in will and decision, in comprehensiveness, in self-reliance, and clear, well-defined purpose." [34]

The mistrust of Lincoln, strongest in New England and some Yankee communities of the mid-West, was rooted in ignorance. Lincoln led, and Seward, so far as his innate selfishness permitted, gave him loyal support. If Lincoln's leadership was cautious, it was firm and increasingly masterful. Where the President really lay open to censure was in failing to consult his Cabinet adequately as a body, as Wilson later consulted his in the First World War, and to improve its unity and harmony. While Presidents have obeyed no rule in their use of the Cabinet, public interests suffer if it is rent by dissension, and Lincoln had read enough history to know of the experience of John Adams and Andrew Jackson with unruly heads of departments.

But the Chief Executive, watching Burnside move his army from Warrenton to Falmouth on the Rappahannock, and putting the final touches on his annual message, appeared unperturbed. His calm, sagacious outlook on affairs was reflected in a conversation with T. J. Barnet at the close of November. Barnet, calling informally at the White House, read the President a letter from the Democratic leader S. L. M. Barlow without divulging the name. Later he described to Barlow its reception.

The President gave me to understand that he should abate no jot of his emancipation policy; but that by imperceptible (comparatively) degrees, perhaps, military law might be made to relent. He says that he highly appreciates the loyal sensibilities of the Opposition—and he scouts the idea of impugning their motives—but he remarks that issues are swept away so fast by over-topping

33 This story was given in a cock-and-bull version in the N. Y. *Herald*, Nov. 10, 1862. T. J. Barnet reported it to S. L. M. Barlow on Nov. 18 in less sensational form: "Chase has got the inside track against the predisposition of the President to regard the late elections from a desirable standpoint, by threatening him with a conspiracy among the Radical members of Congress to stop the supplies, and end the war in that way, making him have the responsibility. This has been the course pursued by Mr. Chase—and for the moment, at all events, he has overslaughed the opinions of the President, of Seward, and Smith." Barlow Papers.
34 F. P. Blair, Jr., to father, n.d. but just after McClellan's dismissal, quotes Lincoln; Blair-Lee Papers. Welles, who like Seward deeply distrusted Chase, records Chase's estimate of Lincoln in his *Diary*, I, 413.

facts that no party will have time to mature until after the war. He thinks u. foundations of slavery have been cracked by the war, by the Rebels; and that the masonry of the machine is in their hands—that they have held its fate and can't complain. He believes that there will be no intervention and derides the notion that servile insurrection is stimulated by his proclamation. He feels that Emancipation will occur, if at all, as hitherto it has progressed, etc.

Lincoln, according to Barnet, thought that he could make it clear to the nation that he usurped no power by the Proclamation. Barnet went on:

What most troubles him is to provide for the blacks—he thinks still that many of them will colonize, and that the South will be compelled to resort to the Apprentice System.[35]

[IV]

As Congress assembled at the beginning of December, the two questions which most troubled members were whether Lincoln would carry the Emancipation Proclamation into effect January 1, and whether he would retain the existing Cabinet. They troubled the whole North. All doubt on the first issue, however, was quickly dispelled. Lincoln told responsible newspapermen that the proclamation stood and he would recommend legislation to carry it into effect. He had promised that he would once more urge Congress to adopt the policy of gradual compensated abolition, and this promise he had to keep. But as he assured Congress, neither the war nor proceedings under the proclamation would be stayed because of this recommendation.

Much of his annual message, published in the newspapers on December 2, was devoted to an enlarged version of his old Border State plan. He recommended that Congress should offer the several legislatures a constitutional amendment, to consist of three articles: first, providing compensation in Federal bonds for every State which should abolish slavery before 1900; second, guaranteeing freedom to all slaves who had gained it by the chances of war, but compensating loyal owners; and third, authorizing Congress to make some provision for colonizing freedmen abroad. In arguing for this plan, Lincoln—who felt that it offered the only means of recreating a fraternal Union—reached a new height of eloquence, and illustrated as never before his largeness of view.[36]

He looked forward not to the next year, but the next generation; he dealt not with slavery alone, but with the far graver problem of race adjustment. The Northern people, he argued, should unite behind a broad and permanent

35 Barnet, Nov. 30, 1862, "confidential," Barlow Papers. I have broken the letter into two paragraphs.
36 Nevins, "Lincoln's Plan for Reunion," *Abraham Lincoln Assn. Papers*, 1930, pp. 51–92.

policy. "By mutual concession we should harmonize and act together. This would be compromise; but it would be compromise among the friends, and not with the enemies of the Union." One editor spoke of the quaint simplicity, the rough-diamond quality, of Lincoln's style; and although it now seems incredible, it is actually true that the predilection of many Americans of that era for stump-speech rhetoric blunted their appreciation of Lincoln's lucidity, force, and grace.[37] He begged the people of the North to remember that they were as much responsible for the original introduction of slavery as the Southern people. He urged them not to give way to selfish fears that the freedmen would displace white workers. "If they stay in their old places, they jostle no white laborers; if they leave their old places, they leave them open to white laborers." He pleaded with them to abandon any mean prejudice against colored settlement in their communities. Equally distributed over the land, the Negroes would be but one colored to seven whites. "Could the one, in any way, greatly disturb the seven?" And in closing, he spoke with lofty eloquence of the necessity for rising to the height of the crisis:

Fellow-citizens, *we* cannot escape history. We of this Congress and this Administration will be remembered in spite of ourselves. No personal significance, or insignificance, can spare one or another of us. The fiery trial through which we pass will light us down, in honor or dishonor, to the latest generation. . . . In giving freedom to the *slave* we *assure* freedom to the *free*—honorable alike in what we give and in what we preserve. We shall nobly save, or meanly lose, the last, best hope of earth.

Lincoln really hoped that his plan, when adopted by five Border States and perhaps two Southern States (for seven slave States would have to join the North in ratifying the amendment before it became (effective) might halt the fighting.[38] The South could obtain peace, partial payment for its bondsmen, and a transitional period in which it could still keep vestiges of the former labor system; would this not be better than continued bloodshed and a probability of abrupt emancipation without a cent of recompense? Lincoln spoke of ratification of the amendment as a consummation which "would end the struggle now, and save the Union forever." He spoke hopefully also of colonization abroad, and of the emptiness of Northern fears of a wide Negro dispersion. "Their old masters will gladly give them wages at least until new laborers can be procured; and the freedmen, in turn, will gladly give their labor for the wages, till new homes can be found for them, in congenial climes, and with people of their own blood and race."

37 *Works,* V, 518–537.
38 Lincoln's emancipation proclamation of Sept. 23 had applied to the States and districts at war against the Union; his amendment, though not limited in application, would seem to be aimed primarily at the North, the border region, and the three States fast approaching reconstruction, Louisiana, Tennessee, and Arkansas.

This trust in reason was rather naïve; the Southerners after their many victories could not now be diverted from their struggle for independence, and colonization was always an impracticable will-of-the-wisp. In the North it was certain that radicals and extreme conservatives alike would reject Lincoln's plan. After he had read the draft of his message to the Cabinet, rather for their information than their criticism, Chase had warned him of this fact. The subtle Ohioan, while paying tribute to the noble sentiments and admirable language of the message, suggested that it would be wise to omit the plea for a constitutional amendment. No probability existed that a two-thirds vote could be mustered in Congress to support one, or that it could obtain approval by the States. Would it not weaken rather than strengthen the Administration thus to march forward to certain defeat? [39] The conservative Orville H. Browning termed Lincoln's scheme a hallucination; the radical Charles Sumner characterized it as mere "surplusage" in his message, to be ignored. Ben Wade and Horatio Seymour, for divergent reasons, were both scornful and both certain of its futility.

The newspaper press was similarly almost a unit in rejection. To free the slaves by instalments, observed the *Evening Post*, was like cutting off a dog's tail by inches to get him used to the pain. The New York *Herald* did its best to tear the plan to pieces. "We have always admired the President as a joker, but we never imagined that he could so aptly blend exquisite humor and practical common sense in an official document. He knows that the agitation about slavery hinders the war, and he is right in deciding to postpone this agitation. In fact, a truce on the negro question until 1900 is a military necessity. . . ." This was the *Herald's* usual heavy irony. Greeley's *Tribune*, while praising Lincoln's sincerity, condemned his ideas on colonization—"Our country has no laborers to export"—and declared that slavery should be ended at once, not gradually. The Cincinnati *Commercial* had a conviction that the fanatics in both parties would reject his plan, and disliked the colonization feature—there would be time later to decide what was best for the colored folk.[40] *Harper's Weekly* similarly scoffed at the colonization scheme. Thus far, it commented, persons with dark skins had shown the same predilection for staying in their own country as persons with white skins, this being patriotism in the whites but stupidity in the blacks.

In general, however, comment was moderate, and much Republican disapproval was veiled under silence. Even Greeley avoided any detailed discussion. Give us six months' fair trial of rigorous emancipation, he exclaimed, the Union forces pressing southward with freedom pinned to their bayonets, and if that

39 Nov. 24, 1862; RTL Papers.
40 See files of the journals named Dec. 2–6. Some papers, like the *Herald*, voiced somewhat varying opinions in successive editorials. The Phila. *Press* (Dec. 2) and Cincinnati *Commercial* (Dec. 4) gave Lincoln a sustained personal eulogy.

does not bring the traitors to their marrow bones, we shall be glad to talk of a compromise peace. In the same spirit other papers avoided criticism of the President by ignoring gradual compensated emancipation, and emphasizing Lincoln's assertions that slavery must be given a death sentence. A number of journals, echoing much popular comment, expressed regret that Lincoln had said so little about the progress of the war and the means of expediting it.[41]

[V]

The temper of Congress had been worsened by recent events. The Republican Jacobins, as John Hay called them, interpreted the military defeats and the election as requiring much more drastic and pugnacious action. Democrats and Border Republicans, on the other hand, interpreted them as requiring a return to strict interpretations of the Constitution and the single war-object of restoring the Union. More fighting, more confiscations of rebel property, more liberation of slaves, and full use of colored fighters—these were the demands vociferated by extreme Republicans. An instant stoppage of arbitrary arrests, a repudiation of emancipation as unconstitutional, or inexpedient, and a halt in the headlong progress toward despotism—these were the ultimatums of extreme Democrats.[42]

One powerful figure, in a speech long remembered, struck not only at the Congressional minority but at the Administration. When Thad Stevens rose to assail the contention of Representative A. B. Olin of New York that the rebellious States were still inside the Union, and that their loyal people were entitled to its full protection, he took issue with Lincoln as well. Stevens at least subconsciously cherished a resentful belief that he and not Cameron should have sat for Pennsylvania in the Cabinet. He never saw Lincoln when he could help it, and never spoke cordially of him. While close to Chase, whom he had known for full twenty years and with whom he worked closely in meeting the financial needs of the nation, he felt contempt for Seward, and dislike for Montgomery Blair. It would have been well had Stevens devoted himself exclusively to financial affairs; but this iron-willed man held deep con-

41 The message astonished Orville Browning by "its singular reticence in regard to the war"; *Diary*, I, 591, Dec. 1, 1862. On foreign affairs the President diplomatically made little comment. Touching on finances, he declared that on the whole the best mode of raising money for the war was by establishing a system of banks of issue, whose notes should be uniform in appearance and based on the deposit of United States bonds in the Treasury; but he left details to Chase.

42 Cf. Donnal V. Smith, *Chase and Civil War Politics*, 60 ff. Cox and Vallandigham in the House, and Bayard in the Senate, brought forward resolutions against the arbitrary arrests; G. H. Yeaman of Kentucky and John Crisfield of Maryland among others assailed the Emancipation Proclamation as unconstitutional. *Cong. Globe*, 37th Cong., 1st Sess., pt. 1, *passim*.

victions about the war, in which force must be used to the utmost, and about the peace, in which the North must show no softness, no spirit of compromise, no magnanimity. In brooding over what he regarded as Lincoln's delays and excessive generosity, Stevens sometimes exhibited a frenzy of anger.

So it was as 1862 closed. For the past fifteen years, asserted Stevens, he had always been a step ahead of the Republican Party, and always the party had caught up. Once more, he predicted, they would have to overtake him before this infamous and bloody revolt was ended. They would find that they could not execute the Constitution in the seceded States, and must forget that document in levying war. "They will come to the conclusion that the adoption of the measures I advocated at the outset of the war, the arming of the negroes, the slaves of the rebels, is the only way left on earth in which these rebels can be exterminated. They will find that they must treat these States now outside of the Union as conquered provinces and settle them with new men, and drive the present rebels as exiles from this country; for I tell you they have the pluck and endurance for which I gave them credit a year and a half ago in a speech which I made, but which was not relished on this side of the House, nor by the people in the free States. They have such determination, energy, and endurance, that nothing but actual extermination or exile or starvation will ever induce them to surrender to this Government." [43]

Stevens knew well that this talk of conquered provinces was so much shrapnel aimed directly at the White House. He had to be taken much more seriously than Martin F. Conway of Kansas, who on December 15 introduced resolutions calling for the conquest of the South, the extirpation of slavery, and the reorganization of the executive, the alternative to be a cessation of the war. [44] By a vote of 132 to 1, the House tabled these resolutions. But everyone knew that Sumner, Chandler, Wade, Henry Winter Davis and others took the same view (barring extermination) as Thad Stevens. Washington correspondents reported secret meetings of radical intriguers—Senators, Representatives, generals, and some Cabinet members—to plan a new leadership and a drastic new tendency in the war. An ominous sense of coming changes, of dramatic political events impending, filled the air of Washington. [45]

The Democrats meanwhile were eagerly discussing the best means of using their recent election victories. Daily, Bayard, Cox, Vallandigham, and others gathered to exult over the popular discontent and lay plans for fomenting it. The best of them, like Cox and Powell, regarded themselves as patriotic defenders of constitutional liberty; the worst, like Bayard and Vallandigham,

43 *Cong. Globe*, 37th Cong., 3rd Sess., pt. 1, pp. 242, 243; Jan. 8, 1863.
44 *Ibid.*, 91, 92.
45 For example, N. Y. *Herald*, Dec. 8–15, 1862.

were sympathizers with the South and with slavery. Bayard stood for peace at almost any price, frankly avowing that he would rather let the Confederacy go than continue a war ending in Southern subjugation and the establishment of a centralized despotism.[46]

A passing flurry of peace talk gave the closing weeks of 1862 a bizarre touch. It was started by a Marylander named Chase Barney, who came home from a sojourn in Richmond with what he pretended were Southern proffers of terms for returning to the Union. The mischievous Fernando Wood shortly made a New York speech outlining these supposed terms. They included, he said, the restoration of the old Constitution unchanged, adoption of the Crittenden Compromise, assumption of the Confederate debt, and ejection of the French from Mexico, to be followed by the annexation of that country to make nine slave States.[47] Having made this preposterous statement, Wood maneuvered to bring about an exchange of views with Lincoln. Through Mayor George Opdyke he sent the President an impudent letter stating that he had learned from an unnamed source that the South would send members to the next Congress provided they be given full amnesty; and he begged Lincoln to let him conduct negotiations with the Confederate leaders.

The President brushed Wood aside with a reply marked "confidential." If the South would cease all resistance and submit to the national authority, he stated, the war would stop, and he would be willing within a reasonable time to grant a general amnesty. But he did not think it proper to communicate this to the Confederates, who already knew it, and could at any time approach him directly.[48] Meanwhile, other men took part in the talk about peace: among them Horace Greeley, who wrote Lincoln December 12 that he was confident the rebels were sick of war, and an eccentric humbug named J. Wesley Greene, who stung the President into penning a short memorandum exposing his real character. But before Lincoln dismissed Greene's shallow deception, Greeley had published in the *Tribune* an editorial speculating hopefully on the peace feelers. Actually, of course, the South had no idea whatever of surrender, for while suffering terribly from the strain of the conflict, it rejoiced in the fact that Lee's army, checked but not defeated, still held Union forces at bay in the East, while Confederate armies still firmly gripped Vicksburg and Chattanooga in the West.

And suddenly, in the midst of this talk, occurred a series of events which elated the South, depressed the North, and brought the demand for Cabinet reorganization to a head.

46 "Occasional" in Phila. *Press*, Dec. 10, *et seq.; Cong. Globe, ut supra*, 67, 68; Dec. 11, 1862.
47 Barney to Lincoln, Nov. 23, RTL Papers; Wood's speech in N. Y. *Tribune*, Dec. 1.
48 *Works*, V, 517, 518; N. Y. *Tribune*, Dec. 11, 1862.

14

Fredericksburg and Government Crisis

IT WOULD be difficult to overstate the anxiety with which all patriotic Northerners during November awaited the movements of Burnside. Despite recent snows and rains, the authorities in mid-November still expected nearly a month of good weather for campaigning. Newspaper accounts emphasized the imposing strength of the army McClellan had just left, corps on corps advancing like mere regiments. It was unquestionably well clothed, well fed, well armed, and in excellent spirits. Lying about Warrenton, it was only some twenty miles from Lee's main force at Culpeper, the Rappahannock between them. As McClellan returned North to meet a warm demonstration in Trenton and hear "Prince" John Van Buren suggest him for the Presidency to a New York meeting, all eyes were turned on his successor. He bore the scrutiny well. Modest, dignified, of imposing presence, Burnside impressed Lincoln by his evident strength of character. In North Carolina and at Antietam he had shown high gallantry under fire; his management of troops combined firm discipline with a kindly, parental attitude; and he had a remarkable power of attaching people to himself. The vital question of his intellectual endowment, however, was unanswered.

McClellan had intended to advance against Lee by striking southward between Culpeper and the village northwest of it called Washington, but Burnside decided to swing east and establish a new base at Fredericksburg.[1] That McClellan's plan was much the better there can be no doubt. Without much fighting, he would doubtless have compelled Lee's retreat to Gordonsville, and might then by a march south of the Rappahannock have seized Fredericksburg, whence he would have a choice of two routes toward Richmond: the water path to Harrison's Landing on the James, or a land path along the railroad through Hanover. Burnside's plan was more difficult, because instead of leaping the Rappahannock at its easy headwaters, he would have to make a considerable march downstream to a point where crossing might be hard. The

---

[1] McClellan's *Report* (1864), 435, 436. Hassler, *McClellan*, 309, points out that Lee had fervently hoped that McClellan would advance up the Shenandoah Valley.

initial question was whether he could effect the transit at Fredericksburg by surprise. He would have to get his pontoon bridges, which had been in the vicinity of Harpers Ferry, sent down the Potomac and waggoned by Aquia Creek to Falmouth, opposite that town. If his army and the bridges arrived simultaneously by stealth, a surprise attack would be possible; if they failed to arrive together or the movement was detected, the Confederates would make Fredericksburg bristle with cannon and bayonet.

Halleck, conferring with Burnside on November 11, expressed a preference for McClellan's plan. The new leader, however, insisted on his own, and three days later, Halleck telegraphed Lincoln's authorization for the move: "he thinks that it will succeed if you move rapidly; otherwise not." Secrecy was important. Yet the Philadelphia *Press* on November 19 was blurting out its endorsement of the thrust against Richmond by way of Fredericksburg. As delays ensued, Northern editors grew pessimistic. Bennett's *Herald* on November 28 accused the radical press in Philadelphia and New York of disclosing the plan of campaign to the enemy, and then depressing the North by gloomy pictures of Burnside's prospects. On November 26–27 Lincoln visited the general on Aquia Creek, and soon after he returned to the capital Burnside followed for hurried news conferences. Why? The New York *Times* told its readers that he had gone to Washington to ascertain why his pontoon bridges were coming up so tardily.

Actually, Burnside, Lincoln, Stanton, and Halleck had discussed the whole miltary situation, which Lincoln termed "somewhat risky." The pontoons were but part of the picture. Lincoln had proposed that the crossing of the Rappahannock be accompanied by some diversionary action, the fleet assisting. When Burnside and Halleck rejected the idea, he gave the general full freedom in executing his movement.[2]

The story of the delayed pontoons, one of the worst pieces of blundering in the whole war, exhibited gross incapacity in Halleck and some of his subordinates. McClellan's chief engineer had ordered the bridges sent down the Potomac to Washington, and Halleck on November 12, from Burnside's Warrenton headquarters, had directed that they be forwarded to Aquia Creek. It was natural for Burnside, setting out on a march which made direct communication with Washington impossible for several days, to rely on Halleck to push the transfer through. As a matter of fact, Meigs, Haupt, and Halleck had all visited Burnside's headquarters,[3] and it would seem that one or all of the three could have arranged for rapid transport of the pontoons to the

2 Comte de Paris, II, 560, 561; Swinton, 234–240; Ropes, II, 448–450; K. P. Williams, II, 502–505; Shelby Foote, 766, 767.
3 Daniel Reed Larned, Nov. 13, 1862; Larned Papers, LC.

Fredericksburg area. But Halleck allowed indistinct orders, carelessness about details, and general confusion to entangle the operation and fatally impede the transfer.

Burnside and his army marched at top speed, covering forty miles from Warrenton to the Rappahannock opposite Fredericksburg in two and a half days, so that advance units reached Falmouth November 17. But the pontoons, after appalling delays, did not get to Aquia Creek until the 18th, and were not on the Falmouth shore until the 25th. Too late! [4]

The *Tribune* correspondent who suggested that this footless blundering might cost several thousand lives did not overestimate the penalty. Lee, to be sure, was not quick to grasp the new threat. He at first, on November 15, suspected the direction of Burnside's movement and started some small reinforcements toward Fredericksburg; he then hesitated, mistrusting even reports sent him by Stuart's cavalry; and not until November 18–19 did he move four of Longstreet's divisions toward the town. But he did not need to be quick. By the 25th, when the pontoons were ready, Longstreet's fifth division had arrived; by the 26th Stonewall Jackson, the two Hills, and Lee's main body were rapidly coming up. [5]

And once more the Virginia river gods turned against the Union army. The day that Sumner's troops marched into Falmouth, November 17, rain fell lightly, and on the 19th a heavy downpour began. While roads turned to sloughs, the Rappahannock swelled into a deep barrier in front of the massing Union forces. Burnside's communications with Washington were poor, for the landing piers at Aquia Creek were wretched, and the railroad for the dozen miles thence to Falmouth, using Haupt's new bridge over Potomac Creek, was inadequate; his long wagon trains of provisions crept at snail's pace across the countryside. The troops suffered from shortages. They suffered still more from seeing Longstreet's grim legions, while they fretted on the northern shore, settle into formidable positions opposite. Lincoln's emphasis on speed had been correct, for instead of taking the Confederates by surprise, the slow Union movement had simply enabled them to gain the shelter of a difficult river.

Rain and cold might at any time give way to freezing weather. In fact,

4 Kenneth P. Williams gives the best account of Halleck's tangled blundering, and convicts him of trying to cover it up afterward; II, 502–505. For a good description of pontoon bridgebuilding, see J. P. Bloodgood, *Personal Rems.*, 121, 122.

5 Freeman, *Lee*, II, 429–438, praises the Confederate leader for marvelous prescience; Williams, II, 509–514, by stricter analysis of evidence, shows his uncertainty and hesitation. But for the delayed pontoons, he would have had to face Burnside's superior army after it gained a strategically favorable position, holding Fredericksburg securely. Yet Lee's intelligence service was incomparably superior to Burnside's, as it had been to McClellan's; Freeman, II, 439, 440. Ropes gives a somewhat different view of Lee's strategy; II, 451–455.

Nicolay in Washington wrote his wife on December 7 that real winter had begun. "It snowed day before yesterday, and last night froze up tight and fast. I pity the poor soldiers who had to do guard and picket duty last night." [6] The roads would get worse, so that even if Burnside effected a crossing and drove Lee back, he could not follow far. Two sensible alternatives presented themselves; he could go into winter quarters where he lay, or transfer his army to the James. If he took the first course, however, Northern opinion would rage at his inaction, while if he took the second, he would merely adopt Mc-Clellan's plan while the public chafed under new delays. He had 145,500 officers and men, of whom nearly 120,000 with 312 pieces of artillery could be mustered for combat, while Lee had only 92,000 officers and men, of whom but 72,500 were ready for battle. Burnside knew that his superior strength might compensate for a disadvantageous position if he handled his troops well. The Administration and country had expected him to move forward, find Lee, and attack him. He therefore resolved to stake everything on a frontal attack, and on the night of December 10–11 laid two-thirds of his pontoon bridge.

Northern expectations were indeed maintained at a curiously high pitch. The field correspondent of the New York *Times* reported on December 3 that Burnside had come back from his visit to Washington well satisfied with his conferences. He "will now be let alone—allowed to follow out his own plans, in his own time and way, free from bureaucratic dictation at Washington, and confident that he will have from the government all the assistance he asks for." Editorially, Raymond was so fearful that the rebels would make use of delaying tactics that he urged Burnside on December 6 to attack at once.[7] The general was under heavy pressure to justify his appointment by an energetic offensive.[8]

[I]

The response came; on December 12, the press flamed with dramatic news. Columns of jubilant writing described how Burnside had crossed the Rappahannock under fire, seized the town, and begun preparations for assaulting the enemy on the heights beyond. Rejoicings over this initial success were fervent and universal.

It was a bright, gay, picture-book action, this river crossing. From the Confederate side the scene was one of the most magnificent of the war. As noon

6 Nicolay Papers, LC.
7 Dec. 3, 1862, and dates following.
8 The Wash. corr. of the N. Y. *Times*, reported that Lincoln had said, "The war is now virtually at an end." We may be sure he did not, but Seward did utter such a prophecy.

approached on the clear, sunny morning of the 11th, Burnside ordered all of the hundred or more guns within range of Fredericksburg to fire fifty rounds into it. Some women and children were still in the town. To Southern watchers on Marye's Heights the streets were half veiled in a dry haze, out of which rose only the steeples. Above and within this canopy incessantly bloomed the fire-hearted clouds of bursting shells. Soon high over the mist rose three or four columns of thick black smoke, lifting vertically in the still air hundreds of feet before they shredded apart. Beyond the town the river glistened dimly, and beyond that the Union bank for two miles was studded with batteries which incessantly jetted flame and smoke. Still farther back, their dark blue uniforms and glistening rifles set vividly against the brown landscape, lay the massed formations of more than a hundred thousand infantry, with endless orderly parks of white-topped wagons and ambulances, awaiting the hour of clear transit across the stream. High above the troops, a thousand feet or more, hung two large balloons. The scene, as a Confederate officer wrote, conveyed a memorable impression of the disciplined power of a great army, and of the vast resources of the nation which had sent it into the field.[9]

Completion of the bridge that day was a nightmare. Two-thirds of the pontoon structure had been laid in the previous hours of darkness, and the engineers, aided by Michigan and Massachusetts infantry, undertook to finish it under a hot fire of Mississippi sharpshooters. Ever and anon the builders would be driven back, and come rushing over the lip of the bank dragging their wounded and dying with them; then they would re-form, dash down again, push out another boat under a new hail of bullets, and lay a few more planks— frequently just in time to catch the bleeding bodies of the men who bore them. At last the fire grew so furious that the builders could no longer reach the bridge end; halfway across, timber and men would go down in a heap together or topple into the water.[10] Infantry had to be rowed across to dislodge the sharpshooters. Franklin on the 11th and 12th got two corps over the Rappahannock farther down and aligned them for battle where the ridges along the river ended and the country opened out. But Sumner's two corps did not cross till the 12th.

Meanwhile the Confederates finished their concentration. Jackson's outlying divisions under Early and D. H. Hill reached the scene of action on the morning of the 13th. Once more fate had denied Burnside an opportunity. Had he pushed his troops over in time to attack on the afternoon of the 12th,

9 Alexander, *Military Memoirs*, 290–292. It was perhaps with such pageantry in mind that Lee next day made his famous remark to Longstreet: "It is well that war is terrible, or we would grow too fond of it."

10 C. H. Weygant, *Hist. 124th N. Y.*, 62, 63, covers the bridgebuilding.

or (as Franklin urged) at daybreak next day, he might have taken advantage of the small remnant of Confederate dispersion. As it was, he faced an iron front; when the sun lifted on the 13th, the Confederates were ready for him.

At this point Burnside, realizing that his preparations had miscarried, lost his nerve. Had he massed all available forces on his left, in the open area downstream, he might have crumpled up the Confederate right flank, where Jackson had just arrived to take command and Hood had erected only weak defensive works. Instead, he decided on a bifurcated attack, Sumner to assault the Confederate left at Marye's Heights while downstream Franklin, with six divisions on a line more than three miles long, was to deal a blow at Jackson's intrenched troops. By thus rejecting a single powerful thrust at the weakest point of the Confederates in favor of two isolated advances, he threw away his last chance of achieving a success.[11] The movement against Marye's Heights was folly, for here the Confederate line, occupying the low ridge back of the town, embodied Telegraph Road, sunk three to five feet below the surrounding terrain, and affording a broad trench with parapet, invisible from the front.

In a short winter's day the Union army suffered the cruelest defeat in its history. At noon, under the bright cold sun, Sumner's troops began to swarm out from the smoldering town, where Union forces had been sheltering from the continuous Southern fire—and indulging in considerable looting.[12] They deployed in dense lines at the edge of the fields below the heights.

Instantly the carnage began. As the troops advanced into the great slaughter pen in front, they met so terrific a storm of shell, grape, and canister that even the bravest quailed. To one Pennsylvanian the air seemed so full of missiles that even a finger could not be pointed up at the Confederate lines without being hit; a New York soldier declared, "We might as well have tried to take Hell." [13] The infantry knew that they were in a death trap, even the simplest

11 Alexander, 294, 295. Burnside's reason for separating the two attacks, as stated in orders to Franklin, were "with a view of avoiding the possibility of a collision of our own forces, which might occur in a general movement during the fog." O. R., I, xxi, p. 71.

12 D. H. Larned of Burnside's staff wrote a friend Dec. 16: "While [we were] waiting for the means to cross the river, the enemy have fortified their position to make it impregnable. From this side of the river we can count 20 crests and hills, each mounting from two to five guns, and all can be brought to bear on any given spot. Each line of earthworks is covered by a second or third, which can be held independently of the first and second, and from the guns that opened on our infantry on Saturday from the high hills and woods in the distance there are batteries which we have not seen. These guns are so placed that they rake every street in the city running at right angles with the river, and their sharpshooters are concealed in every bush and behind every stone wall and rock, so that it was certain death for anyone to show himself beyond our pickets." Larned Papers.

13 T. H. Parker, *Hist. of the 51st Pa. Vols.*, 270; G. H. Washburne, *Hist. of the 108th N. Y. Vols.*, 26, 27.

realizing that assault was hopeless; but with steady step and even ranks they advanced as indomitably as if Columbia cheered them on. When their resolute march brought them within range of Cobb's and Kershaw's troops in the sunken road, a fierce hail of musket balls struck them down in companies. Within minutes the ground was carpeted with the dead and dying. As at every step men fell, some with clean bullet wounds, some with legs or arms torn off, some with brains oozing out, the ranks broke. They rolled back "like chaff before the wind," writes one Confederate, and as they retreated, the artillery fire swept through their ranks anew.[14]

The first attack had hardly ended before fresh troops began filing out of Fredericksburg to the assault. This time the tide swept nearer Cobb's defenders in the sunken road, but again the ranks were blown back like chaff. As a third assault ended and a fourth began, over ground so filled with bodies as to impede the marchers, Lee became alarmed lest such stubborn bravery might yet pierce his defenses. "General," he told Longstreet, "they are massing very heavily, and will break your line, I am afraid."[15] A fifth charge came and recoiled; a sixth fell back across a field heaped with bodies. But the Union forces did not retreat entirely. Regiment after regiment flung itself on the ground, until in some areas eight or ten lines of battle were thus extended, the troops frenziedly loading and firing until the hundred rounds they had brought were spent. At dark Sturgis reported by telegraph to Burnside's headquarters: "Our men only eighty paces from the crest and holding on like hell."[16]

Then night closed on the field. Under bright stars in freezing cold the sound of gunfire ceased, and from the windrows of wounded came a dolorous symphony of pain and despair: screams, groans, cries for help, for stretchers, for water. Rescue was impossible, for Union regiments held picket lines on the field, no truce was considered, and any movement drew a dozen balls. As the gray morning of the 14th broke, writes Longstreet, "the spectacle we saw upon the battlefield was one of the most distressing I ever witnessed." On the Confederate right, where Franklin by a determined attack might have won a success ("he would in all probability have given us trouble," concedes Long-

14 James Longstreet, *Battles and Leaders*, III, 79.
15 *Ibid.*, 81.
16 Larned, Dec. 16, 1862; Larned Papers. William McCarter, in his MS volume on life in the army, NYPL, says that the troops who returned that night to the town saw a scene of wild demoralization. Every house still standing was rapidly filled with wounded men; the principal streets were blocked by disabled horses, dismounted guns, and debris; and the sidewalks and alleys were choked with troops so full of excitement and anger that officers gave up trying to control them. Other survivors declare that the men execrated Burnside. "No epithet could be severe enough to express their sense of his folly and stupidity," says Augustus Buell, *The Cannoneer*, 60 (a dubious source, but here accurate).

street) he accomplished nothing. Because of unintelligible orders, he brought only about half his men into battle,[17] and Jubal Early's reserves, from superior positions, threw them back. In this area, too, the scene of butchery appalled even hardened Confederate officers.

In one day Burnside's splendid army had lost approximately 12,650 killed, wounded, and missing, and was as far from Richmond as ever. Why the general persisted in his futile assaults on Marye's Heights after the first two or three waves failed is incomprehensible. Midway in the action Hooker remarked: "There has been enough blood shed to satisfy any reasonable man, and it is time to quit." [18] William Swinton, who was with Burnside's staff, thought that a mood of desperation seized the unhappy general as he watched line after line recoil. Certainly such a mood must have dictated his preposterous notion of renewing the assault with the Ninth Corps, himself at its head, the next morning. When Sumner and others vehemently expostulated he gave it up, and with tears running down his cheeks ordered the evacuation of Fredericksburg. General William F. Smith, calling at headquarters December 14, found him alone in his tent, pacing up and down in anguish. "Oh, those men! Oh, those men!" he exclaimed, pointing across the river to the field of dead and dying. "Those men over there! I am thinking of them all the time!" [19]

He might well feel that central responsibility for the disaster rested on his head. At last men knew how much intellect he had. Too late in the war for either, an improvised general had fought an improvised battle.

[II]

The storm of sorrow and wrath which at once swept the North fell more heavily on Lincoln, Stanton, and Halleck than on Burnside, whose reluctance to command was well known. Privately if not publicly, people castigated Lincoln worst of all, for they did not know that he had warned Burnside that he would fail unless he moved promptly, and that he had given the general complete freedom. He had in fact sent Burnside no message, much less orders,

17 As Greeley says (*Amer. Conflict*, II, 346), a Blücher would have found in such orders as Franklin received a warrant for throwing his whole force against Hill; but the orders were certainly badly worded. See F. W. Palfrey, *The Antietam and Fredericksburg*, 174-180.

18 *Battles and Leaders*, III, 82. Larned writes of the afternoon of the battle, "Hooker expressed his mind very freely at headquarters—ungentlemanly and impatient"; undated memorandum, Larned Papers.

19 Burnside's anguish was sincere, but he was not the man to feel it long. At the end of the week he went to Washington to see Lincoln. The Sunday after this lament he was eating a splendid dinner at the table of the Assistant Secretary of War, John Tucker, with game, oyster patties, *mouton en papillote*, fruit, and wine, and sitting late to enjoy the brilliant talk of Robert J. Walker. Larned Papers.

since their meeting in late November. But many naturally held him responsible for what Joseph Medill called the Central Imbecility.[20] George Bancroft was extremely severe. "How can we reach the President with advice?" he demanded of a friend. "He is ignorant, self-willed, and is surrounded by men some of whom are as ignorant as himself." The Democratic press of course seized the occasion for lamenting anew the President's removal of McClellan, and correctly observed that he would not have committed Burnside's blunder. At the other political extreme Zach Chandler was writing his wife: "The fact is that the country is done for unless something is done at once. . . . The President is a weak man, too weak for the occasion and those fool or traitor generals are wasting time and yet more precious blood in indecisive battles and delays." [21]

Such defeatism seized many observers that even firm patriots were heard to talk of a war for boundaries. When the head of the Chicago *Tribune* did so we may be sure that frailer spirits succumbed. Medill assured his old friend Elihu Washburne that as the rebels could not be defeated by the existing machinery, and they must fight for a division of territory, the Northwest should see to the conquest of the whole Mississippi Valley and the Southwest before a partition took place. "An armistice is bound to come during the year '63." Before it came, they must take Vicksburg and Port Hudson, clear the Mississippi, and make sure that Missouri, Arkansas, Texas, Louisiana, and the Territories would stay in the Union. Once Grant had conquered the whole Mississippi River, they could offer an armistice, at the end of which the Confederacy might be established with only seven States. After that, the Northern republic could wait on events—a reconciliation or a reconquest; and meanwhile, added the highminded Medill, "we might grab Canada to indemnify us for loss of territory." [22]

This type of defeatism, joining surrender with sectional selfishness, was the worst possible. Of course most men remained resolute in holding that the war must be fought through to victory. But the demand for a reorganization of the Administration now swelled up more loudly and widely than ever. The New York *World* beseeched Lincoln to call the best men to his aid in a final effort for the salvation of the republic, and get rid of Stanton, Chase, and Halleck at

20 Lincoln's recent experience had made him wary of interfering with generals. Herman Haupt relates that he brought the first news of Fredericksburg to Lincoln before midnight of the day it was fought. They went together to see Halleck. Haupt heard the President direct Halleck to telegraph orders to Burnside to withdraw to the north bank; but when Halleck expostulated, Lincoln dropped the demand. *Century Magazine*, March, 1882, XXIII, 796, 797.
21 Bancroft to Lieber, Oct. 29, 1862, Lieber Papers, HL; Norton to G. W. Curtis, Nov. 12, *Letters*, I, 258; N. Y. *Herald*, Dec. 16; *World*, Dec. 17; Chicago *Times*, Dec. 17; Cincinnati *Enquirer*, Dec. 17–22, etc.
22 Medill, Jan. 14, 1863, Washburne Papers, LC.

once. Raymond of the *Times*, without suggesting names, wanted new personnel. American opinion had gone beyond the point reached in 1814, when it compelled Secretary of War Armstrong after the capture of Washington to resign. Ever since Congress met there had been talk of resignations; now many people wanted not a scapegoat, but a sweeping change.[23]

Lincoln had reeled in anguish under the news. What he first learned of the defeat from Burnside himself was fragmentary and misleading. He had no complete account of the extent of the disaster until the war correspondent Henry Villard supplied its details on the evening of the 14th. Next day brought confirmation, and the President told a friend: "If there is a worse place than Hell, I am in it." [24]

On Tuesday, December 16, immediately after the Senate's adjournment in early afternoon, Republican members met in secret caucus. When the doors were shut Anthony of Rhode Island asked someone to state the purpose of the gathering. Thereupon Lyman Trumbull, rising, set the stage by asking what the Senate could do to rescue the nation; and Wilkinson of Minnesota, taking the cue, launched into an invective against Seward, who had ruined the country by his halfhearted, compromising views. Other Senators followed in a vehement clamor against the Secretary. All were convinced that he was the nation's evil genius. He had obstructed a vigorous prosecution of the war, constantly advocated a patched-up peace, and overruled the demands of the earnest members of the Administration. Lincoln was criticized on various grounds, but the general view was that he was blameworthy for yielding too much to Seward's influence.[25]

It soon became clear that behind Wade and other critics loomed the figure of Salmon P. Chase, who had spread his poison into every channel he could reach. Fessenden, who spoke at length, held close relations with Chase and in indicting Seward made it plain that his information originated with him and Stanton.

23 Seaton of the *National Intelligencer* had written Seward on Dec. 12 asking if the Secretary had really resigned his office; Seward Papers. For the quoted opinions see N. Y. *World*, Dec. 17, 18, 1862; *Times*, Dec. 19. *Harper's Weekly* declared that the loyal North was rapidly becoming filled with sickness, disgust, and despair. The people had shown unexampled patience. "They have borne, silently and grimly, imbecility, treachery, failure, privation, loss of friends and means, almost every suffering which can afflict a brave people. But they cannot be expected to suffer that such massacres as this at Fredericksburg shall be repeated. Matters are rapidly ripening for a military dictatorship." Dec. 27, 1862.

24 H. Wadsworth reported this to S. L. M. Barlow, Dec. 18, Barlow Papers. Wilkeson also reported it, adding that Lincoln was "awfully shaken"; Dec. 19, Gay Papers.

25 Several members, like Chandler, had worked themselves into frenzy, for Zach's letters suggest a psychopathic state. He thought that McClellan and Franklin had approached treason. As for Seward, he was a traitor. "I believe sincerely," Zach wrote his wife Feb. 10, 1863, "that he is today plotting for the dismemberment of the government. I believe he would prefer to see England or France intervene rather than see the Rebellion crushed by force of arms." Chandler Papers.

Indeed, he used a phrase about Seward's "back-stairs influence" which came straight from Chase's lips.[26] Grimes, whose closest Washington friends were Chase and Fessenden and who had declared that the nation was going to destruction as fast as imbecility and corruption could carry it, spoke in the same vein; so did Collamer of Vermont. Everyone seemed agreed that in so terrible a crisis, the Senate could not rest upon its strict constitutional duties, and must intervene in executive affairs. But how? Ben Wade proposed that the Senators go in a body to Lincoln to demand Seward's removal. Grimes, knowing that this would offend the President and country, made a counter-suggestion that Anthony be instructed to present a resolution in the Senate expressing want of confidence in Seward.

For a few minutes it seemed that the Senate and President were about to be brought into direct collision. But Preston King of New York and others protested against Grimes's proposal, and several members agreed with Orville H. Browning that the best course would be to send a deputation to call on the President, learn the true state of affairs, and give him a frank statement of their opinions. The caucus broke up to sleep on the matter. When they met next day, feeling against the Administration had hardened. Several Senators even wished to propose a resolution calling on the President to resign. Trumbull, like Browning the first day, warmly defended Lincoln, extolling his high character, asserting that he wished to fight the war with all his might, and declaring that only a bad Cabinet and worse generals had thwarted his purpose. The conservative Harris of New York proposed a resolution for general reconstruction of the Cabinet. But to this John Sherman objected that it sounded as if the whole body were to go: "No one wishes Mr. Chase to leave the Treasury, which he has managed so ably." And, added Sherman, merely changing the Cabinet would not help, for the root-trouble was with Lincoln, who lacked proper dignity, orderliness, and firmness.

Finally the caucus decided to pass a resolution calling for "a change in and partial reconstruction of the Cabinet," and to send a deputation to call on the President. Of thirty-two Senators present, thirty-one voted for the resolution. The deputation included seven radicals, Wade, Trumbull, Howard, Fessenden, Sumner, Grimes, and Pomeroy, and two moderates, Collamer and Harris; Collamer by an astute stroke was named chairman. Its work done, the caucus

26 Chase had written Chandler on Sept. 20, 1862, that he knew nothing of affairs outside his own department. "There is no Cabinet except in name. The heads of departments come together now and then—nominally twice a week; but no reports are made; no regular discussions held; no ascertained conclusions reached. Sometimes weeks pass by and no full meeting is held." Chandler Papers. Chase had also written Rosecrans lamenting that his influence with the President and War Department in military affairs was weak. "Had it been greater some serious disasters would have been avoided. . . ." Rosecrans Papers, UCLA Library.

broke up in high spirits. The majority believed that they had sealed the political death warrant of Seward, and made certain of radical domination of the Cabinet.[27]

Some dissenters, however, were convinced they had gone too far. Preston King of New York, an old friend of Seward, took immediate steps to warn the Administration. Rushing from the caucus to Seward's house, he told the Secretary what was taking place on Capitol Hill. At once Seward declared that he would not allow the President to be put in a false position by his unpopularity, wrote out a curt resignation along with that of his son the Assistant-Secretary, and dispatched both to the White House. King followed on the messenger's heels.

Lincoln, astounded at his dinner hour by the sudden resignations, turned to the portly New York Senator to demand an explanation. When King told him about the caucus action, his perplexity increased. Later that evening the dismayed President went to Seward's house to get him to withdraw his resignation, but all arguments were in vain—Seward would not budge. If he remained obdurate, the radicals would have won a sweeping victory at one blow—and Lincoln roused himself to prevent that disaster.

He was not helped in this by some confused counsel from the elder Blair, who came to the White House that same evening—for he had doubtless heard what the Republicans were doing—and next day wrote Lincoln an emphatic letter.[28] Perhaps Lincoln told him that Seward had resigned; more probably he did not. But Father Blair, as Lincoln called him, at any rate knew that a strong movement to reconstruct the Cabinet was afoot, and offered his own ideas. He urged the President to recall McClellan, get rid of Stanton, and put Preston King into the War Department. This of course would make Seward stronger than ever. The reinstatement of McClellan, thought Blair, would rally the army, which was a great political as well as military machine, behind the Administration, while the choice of King would replace the unpopular Stanton by a man of admirable judgment, business talent, and nerve, who was also politically strong in the Empire State. It need hardly be said that this scheme for putting the ultraconservatives in control was politically preposterous.

Lincoln of course knew that the proposal was in part motivated by family

27 This whole account is based on the diaries or reminiscences of Welles, Chase, Bates, Fessenden, Browning, W. E. and F. H. Seward, and others, contradictory in detail, but in essentials generally agreeing. The MS Diary of Fanny Seward, in a long retrospective passage of unclear date, relates that during the crisis no Senator called on Seward. "Father and Fred went to dine at Baron Gerolt [the Prussian Minister], and there C. Sumner had been invited, accepted, and recalled his acceptance at the eleventh hour." T. Harry Williams, *Lincoln and the Radicals*, offers a thorough study of the political background.
28 Blair to Lincoln, Dec. 18, 1862, RTL Papers.

hatred of both Chase and Stanton. The Blairs had detested Stanton ever since the Buchanan Administration. But the Blairs also honestly thought that Preston King would make a much better head of the War Department than Stanton, an untenable opinion. "Pardon my zeal—it is love for the cause and you—no selfish promptings," concluded old Blair. Lincoln ignored his proposals.[29]

Collamer, after drawing up a statement of the sentiments of the caucus and getting members of his committee to approve it, asked for an appointment with Lincoln on the evening of Thursday the 18th. To this the President, deeply hurt and despondent, assented. He knew what injurious reports were flying around the city—reports summarized by Samuel Wilkeson of the *Tribune* in a private letter to his managing editor:

Fessenden has refused to go into the State Department unless the whole Cabinet rookery is cleaned out. He has said if that were done he would consider if he could serve the country by taking the place.

Lincoln said yesterday that if there were any worse Hell than he had been in for two days, he would like to know it. He is awfully shaken.

The feeling is everywhere of exultation at the prospect of getting rid of the *whole Cabinet*. There is no exception to this in Congress or anywhere else.

There is little doubt left that Burnside made his awful blunder on his own responsibility.

Just one fortnight ago Seward sent off the thousandth reiteration of his dispatch that the Rebellion was just going to be crushed. A foreign minister remarked today that Congress should long since have passed a law forbidding Seward to prophesy, for horrible disasters always followed his efforts in that line.[30]

One rumor announced that a delegation of the solid businessmen of New York was coming to Washington to demand from Lincoln a change of men and measures. The distressed Executive, talking to his old friend Orville H. Browning, asked what the caucus Senators really wanted. Browning replied that he hardly knew, but that they were exceedingly hostile to the Administration, and that the resolution adopted was the gentlest action acceptable to the majority: "We had to do that or worse." Lincoln dejectedly remarked that he believed the Senators wished to get rid of him, and was half disposed to let them. The country, he mournfully declared, stood on the brink of ruin: "It appears to me the Almighty is against us, and I can hardly see a ray of hope." Browning, who loathed the radicals, advised him to stand fast, for the main force of the onslaught was directed against Seward, and this statement simply

29 Smith, *Blair*, II, 194 ff., 228 ff.; Flower, *Stanton*, 255; Blair-Lee Papers.
30 Collamer's note, Dec. 18, is in RTL Papers; Wilkeson's letter, "Friday night" (Dec. 19), is in the Gay Papers. Wilkeson raged against the telegraph censorship, which forbade his sending direct news of the Cabinet crisis to the *Tribune*. Its only effect in the case of Seward's resignation, he wrote, was to enable the men Seward told of the affair to buy stocks for a fall in New York; " 'Tis said this was done."

added to Lincoln's sad perplexity. "I wonder," he said in effect, "why sane men can believe such an absurd lie as the charge of Seward's malign influence over me."

Everybody in Washington was now remaking the Cabinet. Father Blair was buttonholing men, urging them to call on Lincoln to oust Stanton and Halleck, and place Preston King and McClellan at the head of military affairs. Browning thought that Collamer would make a good head of the State Department, Banks of the War Office, and Thomas Ewing of the Treasury. Reverdy Johnson wanted Dix for the War Department. Ewing suggested the pompous cotton-Whig, Robert C. Winthrop, as Secretary of State. Meanwhile in the White House, Lincoln, aghast at the thought that the radicals under Chase might seize the helm, pondered means of keeping his quarrelsome family intact.[31]

[III]

On Saturday evening the President received the caucus committee with his usual urbanity. Collamer read the prepared statement, which demanded that Lincoln give the country a Cabinet composed exclusively of men determined upon vigorous prosecution of the war, and entrust military operations only to generals in hearty accord with the objects for which the war was being fought. Wade, Grimes, Howard, and Fessenden spoke, repeating the old charges against Seward. When Fessenden referred to the imperfect support the Administration had given to McClellan, Lincoln produced and read letters showing that he and Stanton had sustained that general to their utmost ability. Sumner then brought up Seward's recently published diplomatic correspondence, saying that he had subjected himself to ridicule at home and abroad, and had written some letters that were most objectionable. To this Lincoln replied simply that he had no memory of these offensive dispatches. As chairman of the Foreign Relations Committee, Sumner had a special right to criticize Seward's correspondence.[32]

In making its demands on Lincoln, the committee offered an amazing new interpretation of the Constitution. As phrased by Collamer, whose study of

31 Browning, *Diary*, 599–602; the press was also busy suggesting changes. For a good general summation of public attitudes toward the President see Herbert Mitgang, *Lincoln as They Saw Him.*

32 Sumner and others particularly objected to Seward's Dispatch No. 287 to Adams, July 5, 1862, reading: "It seems as if the extreme advocates of African Slavery and its most vehement opponents were acting in concert together to precipitate a servile war—the former by making the most desperate attempts to overthrow the Federal Union, the latter by demanding an edict of universal emancipation. . . ." But he had made other offensive statements. See the long letter signed Truth and Courage (perhaps Sumner?) in N. Y. *Tribune*, April 15, 1863.

history should have taught him better, it ran: "The theory of our government and the early and uniform construction thereof, is, that the President should be aided by a cabinet council, agreeing with him in political theory and general policy, and that all important public measures and appointments should be the result of their combined wisdom and deliberation." This was a thrust at the coalition character of Lincoln's Cabinet. As if Washington, balancing Jefferson against Hamilton, had not possessed a similar Cabinet! The committee asked for changes that would bring about unity at once, but it wanted unity on its own lines, and actually proposed that the President should make appointments only *after* submitting names to the Senate and getting its approval. No wonder that ex-Governor Dennison of Ohio wrote:

Is it not a dangerous innovation for Senators to interfere in Cabinet matters in caucus form? Will it not be a precedent that may in future completely subordinate the Executive to the Legislative branch of the govt., and thus virtually destroy the whole theory of our political system? Will not the next step be for Congress to vote its want of confidence in the President and so embarrass as to compel him to resign? Was not some such purpose in the Senatorial caucus? [33]

The committee obviously wanted a Cabinet congenial to Chase.[34] Throughout the three hours' discussion, indeed, the figure of Chase was always in the background. It was plain that he had been conferring with radical Senators, was the source of half the criticism of Seward and Stanton, and hoped to dominate the new Cabinet. Lincoln, as he allowed the Senators to do most of the talking, was studying them coldly, and at the end he ushered them out with the noncommittal statement that he would think the subject over. If they had expected him to yield, they were much disappointed.

Actually, he had determined to recede not an inch. His first step was to call the Cabinet together, with Seward of course absent. After asking them to keep his statements secret, he told them all he knew of the Republican caucus, of Seward's resignation, and of the committee's call on him. He described the Senators' attitude fairly, saying that they were "earnest and sad, not malicious nor passionate, not denouncing anyone, but all of them attributing to Mr. Seward a lukewarmness in the conduct of the war, and seeming to consider him the real cause of our failures." [35] They thought that whenever the President had any good purpose, Seward contrived to suck it out of him. Lincoln explained that he had defended his Cabinet loyally, and was most emphatic in repelling the idea of a general upset. He could not go on without his old friends,

33 Dec. 22, 1862, to Blair, Sr., Blair-Lee Papers. Dennison was conservative.
34 The committee knew that Seward had resigned; Fessenden says he heard rumors Wednesday evening, confirmed Thursday morning.
35 Bates, *Diary.* Lincoln plainly feared precipitate new resignations, discrediting the Administration and weakening morale.

and declared that this unjustifiable movement should never be allowed to break up the Cabinet.

Thus far the President had worn the air of a man who held a losing hand, but suddenly he placed an ace card on the table. He proposed that the Cabinet meet with him and the committee that night; thus he would have the support of his associates in facing Wade, Sumner, Fessenden, and the rest, and would put Chase in a spot where he would have to show whether he stood with the President or with the radicals. Though neither Chase nor Bates liked the idea, Welles and Blair spoke so heartily in favor of it that finally everyone acquiesced. Both were anxious to see Chase forced to show his true colors; for every perceptive person in Washington now believed the Ohioan was at the bottom of the whole movement.[36] Lincoln's intentions were becoming plain. He did not think that a Senatorial junta should be permitted, at the height of a terrible civil war, to dictate Cabinet membership and Administration policies to the President; and he did not think that anyone in his Cabinet should be allowed to play the traitor.[37] He did not object to one unimportant change in his official family, the long-contemplated resignation of the colorless Caleb B. Smith of Indiana, who had been given the Interior Department as a reward for helping deliver his State delegation in the Chicago convention. Smith left December 31 to accept a judicial post, and was at once replaced by John P. Usher. But Lincoln was resolved to permit no drastic alteration.

That night, from seven-thirty till almost midnight, the White House witnessed one of the most momentous meetings in the nation's history. Lincoln managed it with superb adroitness. He did not make the mistake of having the Cabinet with him when the committee arrived. Instead, the committee (without Wade) and Cabinet (without Seward) gathered in the same anteroom. The committee trooped into Lincoln's office first, and he asked their permission to admit the Cabinet for a free discussion; when they came in, fourteen in all were seated. The President opened the proceedings in a carefully matured speech. After reading the committee resolutions and recapitulating the previous night's conference, he launched into a defense of his Cabinet relations. He did not pretend, of course, that the Cabinet had decided all policies, for everyone knew that *he* made the critical decisions; he mentioned instances, including the appointment of Halleck, the restoration of McClellan before Antietam, and the new Banks expedition to Louisiana, when under emergency pressures he

36 Tom Ewing, who was an active Washington lawyer and heard all the gossip, so told Orville Browning; Browning, *Diary*, I, 602.

37 See Welles, I, 193, for Smith's attacks on Seward. He had made up his mind to leave because of failing health and interest. David Davis hit the nail on the head when he wrote Swett: "Smith has no faith and no hope and wants to retire on the District Judgeship. Smith repels me very much. There can be neither heart nor sincerity about him, and he cannot be a man of any conviction." Nov. 26, 1862; David Davis Papers.

had acted without Cabinet consultation or even the knowledge of several members. But all the members had acquiesced once a policy was determined.

"Did they not?" he demanded, turning to the Cabinet. Calling upon them to say whether there had been any lack of reasonable consideration or unity, he looked pointedly at Chase. Indeed, all eyes fell on Chase. The Secretary was horribly embarrassed, for he was trapped in an equivocal position; he had to make good his accusations to the radicals, or his loyalty to his chief. Blurting out that he would not have come had he known he would be arraigned before such a body, he looked about for a way of escape. According to Gideon Welles, he endorsed Lincoln's statement, but regretted the lack of a thorough discussion of every important measure in open Cabinet. According to Fessenden, he said that questions of importance had usually been weighed by the Cabinet, though not as completely as might have been desired, and that acquiescence had indeed been the rule, no member opposing a measure once it was adopted. By either account, he made a weaseling statement.[88]

Fessenden, one of the astutest lawyers of Maine, was irritated to the point of tart speech by Chase's dodging. He assured the Cabinet that the Senators had no idea of offering dictation to the President, only friendly advice. Then, turning to Chase, he answered the charge of arraignment by saying that it was the President who had unexpectedly brought the two bodies together. He went on to express his own views with deep feeling. Lincoln, he thought, had settled too many questions without Cabinet advice—he should have had all important questions discussed, though he was not bound to follow the majority —and had leaned too much on Seward. He spoke approvingly of an instance in J. Q. Adams' Administration in which the Cabinet, led by Clay, had overruled the President. Collamer expressed the same opinions, stressing the value of combined wisdom.[89]

The most radical members, Sumner, Grimes, and Trumbull, were emphatic in condemning Seward. "I have no confidence whatever in him," said Grimes. Sumner, agreeing that he should be ousted, once more brought up his alleged misconduct of foreign affairs, reading aloud his letter about emancipation and servile revolt, which shocked even stout Gideon Welles. "For one in his place," reflected Welles, "he is often wanting in careful discrimination, true wisdom, sound judgment, and discreet statesmanship." Trumbull, who had been angered by Seward's arbitrary arrests, was equally unrelenting in his condemnation. These three agreed that the main issue was no abstract question of Administration unity; it was Seward.

38 Fessenden, *Fessenden*, I, 244 (Fessenden wrote a long record of the whole affair, apparently soon after it occurred); Bates, *Diary*.
39 Welles notes the tartness for which Fessenden was famous; I, 196–198.

Bates and Montgomery Blair with rambling prolixity came to the defense of Lincoln, insisting that no President need consult his Cabinet unless he pleases; and Chase did Seward the justice of recalling that he had offered suggestions which strengthened the emancipation proclamation. But Lincoln, making several speeches and lightening the occasion by deft anecdotes, was his own best advocate. Near the end he brought the Senators up to the point of responsible action by asking them bluntly whether they still wished Seward to leave the Cabinet, and whether this step would please their constituents. Grimes, Trumbull, Sumner, and Pomeroy answered yes. But Fessenden, Collamer, and Howard declined to commit themselves, while Harris said that Seward's influence in New York was so great that his departure would hurt the party. Fessenden, still in irritable mood, declared that while he could not answer for his constituents, he believed that many who had formerly been zealous friends of Seward had lost their confidence in him. As for himself, he did not wish to discuss the subject until he learned whether the President meant to follow the wishes of the Republican Senators; if so, he would try to ascertain these wishes.

As the meeting broke up, Trumbull came to the President with angry mien: "Lincoln, somebody has lied like hell!" Lincoln coolly replied, "Not tonight." Fessenden among others remained to press Lincoln on the acceptance of Seward's resignation, and to repeat his offer to canvass the Republican Senators. Lincoln good-naturedly parried every attack, and to Fessenden's query about polling the Senators replied: "I think not." He made it plain that he desired to avoid any Cabinet changes whatever, for he feared that if Seward left, Chase and Stanton would also withdraw in "a general smashup." [40]

The unhappiest man that evening was Chase. Fessenden was angry at him for his double-dealing; Stanton commented that he was ashamed of the way Chase had lied about the manner of doing business in the Cabinet—*he* would not have done it, for the Senatorial charges were true; Caleb Smith said later that he had been strongly inclined to contradict Chase on the spot. Doubtless Chase passed a sleepless night. Conscious that his duplicity had been discovered, that the President was indignant, and that if the radicals forced Seward out the conservatives would demand his own head, he saw that he must write his resignation. Yet no more than Seward did he wish to leave; no more than Seward did he think he could safely be spared; and much more than Seward, he thought he would make a good Presidential replacement in 1864.

Gideon Welles also had passed a sleepless night, for it seemed to him a

40 Helen Nicolay had the "lied like hell" story from Robert Todd Lincoln; *Abraham Lincoln Quarterly*, V (March, 1949), 287. Nicolay and Hay, VI, 267, write simply that Trumbull turned back after leaving the room to tell Lincoln vehemently that Chase "had held a very different tone the last time he had spoken with him."

national calamity to let a Senatorial cabal dictate to the President the make-up of his Administration. Fessenden, too, fearful that Stanton and Chase would go, was racked with anxiety. Calling on Stanton, Fessenden to his relief found that pugnacious man determined to stay. "Seward shall not drive *me* out," he blazed. Posting over to the Treasury, however, Fessenden was startled to learn that Chase had already decided to resign. If he stayed, he explained, he would be accused of having maneuvered to get Seward out (hardly a false accusation!), while conservative attacks would make his Treasury burden, already crushing, quite intolerable. In vain did Fessenden expostulate; Chase insisted he would leave.[41]

Welles, meanwhile, went at an early hour to the White House. His white beard tremulous with agitation, his stern eyes blazing, he bade Lincoln stand firm, for it was his duty to maintain the rights and independence of the Executive. He remarked that while Seward obviously had grave faults, his self-exalting ways and invasions of the sphere of his associates, from which Welles had suffered much, did not call for Senatorial interference. Lincoln fully agreed, observing that if he yielded, the whole government must "cave in." At the President's request, Welles then hurried to see Seward and repeat Lincoln's words. He found the Secretary much excited, deeply wounded and chagrined, and voluble on the subject of his own sagacity and invaluable services to the nation—for his vanity never failed. That he—*he* in his own eyes practically the architect of the Republican Party, the founder of its success, and the sheet-anchor of the Administration—should be thus assailed by men who had once professed the greatest deference, was an outrage without parallel.

And this New Yorker whose whole career had been founded on shifts and compromises had the effrontery to criticize Lincoln for not taking an adamant stand. The President, said he, should have rejected his resignation without hesitation, and defied the Senate majority by refusing to talk with its committee. Delighted by Welles's attitude, Seward told him he might inform the President that the resignation could quickly be withdrawn. As if Lincoln did not know this! Welles, elated, hurried back to the White House.[42]

Here occurred the culminating scene of the crisis. When Welles entered the President's office Chase and Stanton were there, the President out. Welles spoke to them of his strong opposition to Seward's resignation, and thought them evasively acquiescent. The President entered, his eye on Welles. "Have you seen the man?" he demanded. "I have, and he assents to our views," replied Welles. Thereupon the President turned to Chase and said that he had sent for

41 Fessenden, *Fessenden*, I, 249, 250.
42 Welles, I, 200, 201. Seward's own diary is silent, but his son writes that he had begun to pack for his return to Auburn; *Seward in Washington*, 146–148.

him because he was deeply troubled by the situation—an obvious hint. The Secretary, expressing pain over the previous night's conference, replied that he had prepared his resignation.

"Where is it?" demanded Lincoln, his eyes lighting up. Chase hesitantly took it from his pocket. "Let me have it," ejaculated the President, stretching out his long arm. The Secretary wished to say something, but Lincoln ripped open the seal and hastily scanned the letter. "This," he said with a triumphant laugh, "cuts the Gordian knot." An expression of deep satisfaction overspread his face. "I can dispose of this subject now without difficulty," he went on, turning in his chair. "I see my way clear." Stanton interposed with a pompous offer of his own resignation, which Lincoln waved aside. "The trouble is ended," he said, and dismissed all three.[43]

[VI]

The crisis was indeed over. Lincoln, holding both resignations, could let the radicals understand that if Seward went Chase must go too. In his delight he fell back upon frontier imagery. "Now I can ride," he told Senator Harris. "I have got a pumpkin in each end of my bag." He told another man: "Now I have the biggest half of the hog. I shall accept neither resignation." Later he remarked to John Hay that he was sure he had managed the affair correctly. "If I had yielded to that storm and dismissed Seward the thing would all have slumped over one way, and we should have been left with a scanty handful of supporters." The radicals were actually too few and weak to govern the country, and when Lincoln formally announced December 22 that he had requested both Seward and Chase to withdraw their resignations, public comment admonished them of the fact.[44]

The storm not only cleared the air, but taught a needed lesson to all concerned, not excluding the President.

Chase, so abruptly exposed, had most to learn. His standing with his old friends sank; Fessenden accused him of betraying them, and Wade, Chandler, and Sumner saw that their movements would no longer find a secret ally inside the Cabinet.[45] When Collamer reported to the Senatorial caucus on the com-

43 Welles describes the scene in detail, I, 200 ff., and says that Chase left "moody and taciturn."

44 Nicolay and Hay, VI, 271; Dennett, ed., *Hay Diary*, 111. William H. Schouler, head of the Massachusetts Military Administration, wrote Seward that all Boston was cheering. When it heard the Secretary was out, the city was plunged in gloom; one man had offered to bet that within sixty days the nation would have a military dictator; and if it had appeared that Sumner was responsible for the breaking of the Cabinet, the Legislature would probably have refused to re-elect him to the Senate. Winfield Scott sent Seward his fervent congratulations. Seward Papers.

45 "You have no right to abandon your friends in this way," said Fessenden when he

mittee meeting with Lincoln and the Cabinet, Orville H. Browning asked how Chase, after telling Senators about Seward's backstairs work, could have made his statement on Cabinet unity. Collamer answered: "He lied." After this lesson, Chase restrained his tongue, and somewhat modified his attitude toward the President. Lincoln's secretaries tell us that it had varied between active hostility and benevolent contempt, and it had certainly lacked due respect; but now he had a new insight into both Lincoln's masterful qualities and his magnanimity—for the President repeatedly thanked him for remaining in the Administration. He continued to criticize and to intrigue, but less offensively.

Seward, too, learned a sharp lesson. Egotistical, erratic, meddlesome, he had long helped diffuse a totally false impression that he managed the Administration. By devious methods, unsleeping vigilance, use of his great experience, and skillful exploitation of Lincoln's friendliness, he had indeed done more to affect public policy than his colleagues; and boasting of his activities to friends, he flaunted them in the face of foes. To Chase, Smith, Welles, and Stanton he had behaved with exasperating insolence. Now he suddenly learned that half his own party not only bitterly hated him but thirsted for his blood. He saw that his ideas, methods, and loose use of words had raised a storm from which only Lincoln's consummate skill had saved him. He was henceforth content to confine himself to State Department business.

The President was triumphant. His expedient of bringing the Cabinet and Senate committee together was a perfect illustration of his grasp and shrewdness, combining frankness, honesty, dexterity, and insight into human nature. He alone emerged from the crisis with enhanced prestige. Yet he also had a lesson to learn, and knew it.

Lincoln's conception of his functions as wartime administrator and organizer was defective. He had no taste for administration, not the slightest experience in it, and little aptitude; he did not organize even his own office very well. Had he been more imaginative about governmental machinery, he might have enlarged his Cabinet for war purposes, for somebody of Cabinet rank was needed to deal with arms, munitions, supplies, and transport, leaving Stanton and Welles to direct the recruitment and general management of the army and navy. With no chief of staff yet dreamed of, the vagueness of Halleck's role was painful. And Halleck was undependable. Lincoln, long conscious of this, fairly lost patience with him after Fredericksburg, as a stern letter of rebuke on New Year's Day showed. Halleck had known that Burnside's strategy was wrong, yet let him go ahead; he had helped pave the way to defeat by his blundering with pontoons; and when later Burnside wished to recross the

learned of Chase's resignation; and he speaks pungently in his memorandum about Chase's change of tone on Seward and Cabinet unity; Fessenden, *Fessenden*, I, 250 ff.

Rappahannock and his best generals disapproved, Halleck failed to visit the spot, find out the true state of affairs, and deliver a decided judgment. As Lincoln wrote, all Halleck's "military skill" was useless unless he used it firmly. Yet Lincoln did not dismiss Halleck.[46]

It was wonderful how well Lincoln managed matters on which he thought deeply; it was also wonderful how completely he refused to think about some matters at all. Administration was one of them. The lack of liaison between McClellan and Halleck had remained painful till the day McClellan left; McClellan and Stanton, hating each other, had hardly been on terms of communication; and a painful failure of rapport between Halleck and Stanton had developed. To say that the public interest suffered is an understatement. It was defective administration which permitted the decision to send Banks's expedition to Louisiana without consulting Welles in advance, though Welles had to make the naval preparations. Welles wrote December 14, when he had not yet heard of the defeat at Fredericksburg: "It has struck me as strange that Banks was not sent up James River with a gunboat force. Such a movement would have caused a diversion on the part of the Rebels and have thrown them into some confusion, by compelling them to draw off from their strong position at Fredericksburg." [47] It was indeed strange, and much of the informal public agreed with the Secretary.

That Lincoln did not use his Cabinet efficiently is clear. While he was right in holding that he alone should make the great decisions, and that its consultative value was limited, he could have used it more largely for mutual exchange of information. He went to the War Office daily, and saw Seward frequently, for Seward was a "comfort" to him; the others he neglected. Chase, though a leader of one of the two great wings of the party, fell into the role of mere financial specialist, and resented the fact. Stanton complained that in important military matters the President took counsel of none but army officers, though he ought to be consulted, or at least be kept informed. Yet Stanton himself in Cabinet meetings imparted little information, and had a way of drawing Lincoln into a corner and talking with him in a low voice. Seward meanwhile aroused ill feeling by sending his son Frederick, the Assistant Secretary, to some Cabinet meetings, which provoked Stanton to declare that he would discuss no important business while an outsider was present, a feeling shared by others.

Fessenden, Sumner, Lyman Trumbull, and Grimes were highminded, patriotic men, sincerely anxious to promote the national welfare. The movement

46 Welles wondered that Lincoln gave such weight to the judgment of "the dull, stolid, inefficient, and incompetent" general; *Diary*, I, 320.
47 *Ibid.*, I, 192.

which they helped to lead had four capital objects: (1) to insist on a vigorous prosecution of the war; (2) to drive home the principle that no important military enterprises should be entrusted to lukewarm generals; (3) to ask the President to get rid of any Cabinet members who were not "cordial, resolute, unwavering supporters" of a determined war—meaning Seward; and (4) to induce Lincoln to give his Cabinet more, and take more from it. On the first two objects all were agreed; the third was improper; but the fourth was sound, and needed pressing home.

Lincoln learned from the crisis that, unsystematic, often abstracted, so intent on great aims that he thought little of minutiae, he had neglected details which, each trifling, amounted in the aggregate to something important. He realized that his principal associates were entitled, as Chase put it, to full systematic accounts of the progress of the struggle, the purposes entertained, and the means to be used. Full of natural good will to everyone, he had forgotten that some might resent his apparent favoritism toward Seward. At the next Cabinet meeting, December 23, the proposed creation of West Virginia received exhaustive discussion; and at the two following sessions the President, inviting careful discussion of his draft of the final Emancipation Proclamation, heard criticism from Chase, Welles, Blair, and Seward, and adopted some of their changes, including apparently a felicitous closing sentence by Chase invoking the considerate judgment of mankind and the gracious favor of Almighty God.

This proclamation enabled Lincoln to end a year full of frustration and failure with a document breathing hope and inspiration. On New Year's Day Seward and his son took the sheet to the White House for signature. Lincoln, dipping his pen, held it suspended as he observed: "I never, in my life, felt more certain that I was doing right than I do in signing this paper. But I have been receiving calls and shaking hands since nine o'clock this morning, till my arm is stiff and numb. Now, this signature will be closely examined, and if they find my hand trembled, they will say 'he had some compunctions.' But anyway, it is going to be done." With firm hand, he signed the declaration that all slaves throughout the areas in rebellion were then and forever free.[48]

[VII]

With the crisis behind him, the President could deal firmly with the military situation in Virginia. He was willing to give Burnside another opportunity to show what he could do. That commander behaved in sportsmanlike fashion. When he learned that rumor placed responsibility for his march against Fred-

48 Seward, *Seward in Washington*, 151; Lincoln, *Works*, VI, 23-31.

ericksburg on Lincoln, he sent Halleck a letter (December 17) assuming complete blame: "The fact that I decided to move from Warrenton on this line, rather against the opinion of the President, Secretary of War, and yourself, and that you left the movement in my hands, without giving me orders, makes me responsible." [49] The army, however, was dejected and demoralized. Late in December, Burnside decided to march up the Rappahannock to the fords above Fredericksburg and make a sudden movement across the river there. His chief subordinates sharply disapproved, and two brigadiers, John Cochrane and John Newton, hurried to tell the President that any such stroke might be ruinous. Lincoln therefore curtly directed Burnside not to move the army without letting him know.

While officers continued to express opposition, Burnside determined to proceed with his plan. After talking with Lincoln, he notified him of his resolve, enclosing his resignation if the President rejected the plan. Dry weather had hardened the roads; he commanded nearly 200,000 men, of whom 120,000 stood before Lee's forces; and he thirsted to retrieve his fortunes. Lincoln was deeply perplexed. On New Year's Day he wrote Halleck, bidding him for once to do his plain duty: to go over the ground with Burnside, confer with his officers, ascertain their temper, and decide whether the movement was good or bad. Halleck cast his vote in favor of the movement, saying it would not do to keep the large army inactive, and Lincoln assented—though still with doubts, for he enjoined Burnside: "Be cautious, and do not understand that the government, or country, is driving you." [50]

Then General January interfered. As the troops began to move, a terrific rainstorm turned the countryside into a quagmire in which the army bogged down. Artillery, pontoon trains, and supply wagons stuck fast, pushed on a few feet when men with spades dug them out, and stuck fast again. Infantry sank to their knees. It was obviously impossible to keep on. As Burnside the second day admitted failure, his army dragged its wet, miserable way back to its old camps.

But it did not return to a continuance of Burnside's command. That general, angered by the resistance of his best officers to his ideas, and by an illtempered interview Joseph Hooker had given a newspaperman, had attempted a drastic housecleaning. He prepared orders dated January 23, 1863, dismissing Generals Hooker, Newton, Cochrane, and W. T. H. Brooks, and relieving Generals W. B. Franklin, W. F. Smith, Samuel D. Sturgis, and two others from duty. At the same time he telegraphed Lincoln for an appointment, and seeing him early on the 25th, declared that if the President did not endorse

49   Lincoln was pleased; Sandburg, *Lincoln*, 1-vol. ed., 356.
50   O. R., I, xxi, 998.

the dismissals, he would resign.[51] Just what Lincoln said to him we do not know. But the President summoned Stanton and Halleck at ten that morning, and announced that he had made up his mind to relieve Burnside and place Hooker in command. He knew that the army, which was so outraged by Burnside's incompetence that it treated him in public with icy silence, would receive the news with gratification.

The mud march, the new change of commanders, and a shower of reports showing that the Army of the Potomac was ill sheltered and ill fed, did nothing to relieve the gloom in the North. Soldiers fed on salt pork and hardtack were actually dying of scurvy. Frigid tent-hospitals were so poorly provided with nurses and orderlies that some patients froze to death for want of fires and blankets. Meanwhile soldiers savage after months of defeat sent letters home that lowered public morale. "I am sick and tired of disaster," declared one, "and the fools that bring disaster upon us." Charles Dudley Warner believed that many soldiers in the army had become "McClellanized," and by tens of thousands wrote home to express a conviction that "we can never whip the South." This was unfair to a devoted army, which had good reason to excoriate Pope and Burnside, but which never lost its dogged courage. Yet the Northern discouragement for the moment plumbed great depths. People said later that this was the Valley Forge winter of the war.[52]

One measure of the discontent and bad discipline East and West was the high desertion rate. More than 200,000 men deserted during the conflict; 25,000 from New York units alone, 24,000 from Pennsylvania. The monthly desertion rate during 1863 averaged 4,650 and was especially great after Fredericksburg and the mud march. It would have gone hard with the Union armies had not the Confederate desertions been equally heavy. The percentage of desertions, strangely enough, was much higher among the regulars than the volunteers.

But it was in the Northwest that the situation seemed most alarming. Here, too, the people heard sorry news from troops in the field. The health of Western soldiers was so bad that some regiments had more men sick than well; the commissary arrangements were no better than in the East; and medical work was so mishandled that invalids died on hospital steamers for sheer lack of nourishment. Many of the people were as downhearted as the volunteers. They wrote letters, as an Illinois captain put it, "which would discourage the most loyal of men." The Northwest gave the President some of his chief worries. It had hitherto achieved the most; if it now faltered, all would be lost. Sumner wrote Francis Lieber in January: "The President tells me he now fears

51 *Works*, VI, 77, 78; O. R., I, xxi, 1008, 1009. Burnside's march began January 20; it broke down on the 22d; he saw Lincoln, as here stated, early on the 25th.
52 Warner to J. R. Hawley, Jan. 18, 1863, Hawley Papers, LC; Catton, *This Hallowed Ground*, 206: N. Y. *Tribune*, Feb. 11, 1863, etc.; Dorsheimer to F. P. Blair, Sr., Dec. 3, 1862.

'the fire in the rear'—meaning the Democracy—especially the Northwest—more than our military chances." [53]

What was the real situation in this vast area of hill, prairie, and river valley? What were the forces and events which made Lincoln so uneasy in thinking of it?

[53] Ephraim A. Wilson, *Memoirs*, 151; Pierce, *Sumner*, IV, 144. On desertion see O. R., III, v, 109, 757 ff.; Ella Lonn, *Desertion During the Civil War, passim.*

15

The Darkest Hours of the Northwest

FOR SEVERAL reasons the difficulties and defeats of 1862 had an especially malign effect in the Old Northwest, and particularly in Indiana and Illinois. All the States bordering on the Ohio, but most notably the two named, had many citizens of slave-State extraction. Their southern counties were full of folk drawn from Virginia, Kentucky, and Tennessee. Many, of course, were as strong free-soilers as Moncure D. Conway, Benjamin Harrison, and John M. Palmer, three men of Virginia blood who made their mark in Ohio, Indiana, and Illinois respectively, but many had proslavery sympathies. These sympathizers felt but faint approval of the war, which they blamed equally on Southern fire-eaters and Northern abolitionists. When they perceived that it would be long and burdensome, they became restive.

At Xenia, Ohio, in the summer of 1861, Moncure D. Conway, trying to arouse the people, had emerged from his hall to hear an excited Democrat exclaim, "Every word was as false as hell!" In Dayton, Conway argued that the President could abolish slavery by martial law. Vallandigham rejoined in his Dayton newspaper: "It seems to us that about three months in Fort McHenry, in a straight uniform, with frequent introductions to the accommodating institution called the town pump . . . would have a tendency to improve the gentleman mentally." [1] After military reverses, such dissidents were sure to revolt.

In Ohio, Indiana, and Illinois the Democratic Party had a historic ascendancy. Of twenty-three governors from admission to 1860, Ohio counted fifteen Democrats. In Indiana all the governors but two were Democratic from admission until 1861, while every governor of Illinois was a Democrat until W. H. Bissell took office in 1857. The party simply regained its old position in Indiana and Illinois when it swept the elections of 1862. Ohio remained Republican. But the Hoosiers put Democrats in the lesser State offices by more than 9,000 majority; and Lincoln's own State gave the Democratic candidate for Congressman-at-large 53 per cent of the vote, placed the legislature firmly

---

1 Conway, *Autobiography*, I, 338, 339.

in Democratic hands, and strengthened the influence of such sharp critics of the Administration as William A. Richardson. Well it was for Lincoln that Governors Oliver P. Morton and Richard Yates held four-year terms, and that in Ohio the Union Party chose in David Tod an executive of the stanchest temper.

Another element in the rising discontent was the war losses. In all three States the Democrats, in true Jacksonian spirit, had done their full share in sending volunteers to fight. In Illinois, for example, the adjutant-general's report for 1862 showed that of about 270,000 men liable for duty, the State had sent nearly one-half, or 135,000, into service. Democratic counties like Massac, Union, and Williamson had actually led the way, and an exceptionally high proportion of those liable to duty had volunteered. Early in the war the legislature in Indianapolis created a voluntary militia organization called the Indiana Legion. As it was most active where border raids were feared, southern Indiana bore the chief burden of State defense, and thousands of men passed through it into the Union armies.[2] A natural consequence of exuberant volunteering from Democratic areas was heavy casualty lists in these counties. The four relatively indecisive battles of Iuka, Corinth, Perryville, and Murfreesboro late in 1862 cost the Northwest at least 3,000 slain and 12,000 wounded, totals which outran the cost of Antietam or Fredericksburg in the East.

The Democratic population meanwhile suspected that what had begun as a national war to save the Union had become a Republican war to destroy slavery, create a strong centralized government, and hold the South in permanent subjection. The partial draft after McClellan's failure angered much of the public; in Indiana, for example, men forcibly resisted it in various places.[3] Arbitrary arrests and other infractions of civil liberties simultaneously aroused widespread resentment. Early in 1863 General Burnside took command of the Department of the Ohio. He no sooner reached Cincinnati than he kicked over a hornet's nest by his General Order No. 38, proclaiming that he would not tolerate "the habit of declaring sympathy for the enemy" or allow any form of "expressed or implied" treason. This doctrine of implied treason, new to Anglo-Saxon law, evoked angry protests from the Democrats. A little later Burnside, if Governor Morton had not interfered, would have declared martial law in Indiana.[4]

Most of all were conservative Democrats offended by the emancipation proclamation. Many thousands of people who had sprung from slaveholding

2 *Report*, Illinois Adjutant-General, 1862; Stampp, *Indiana Politics*, 80. Frank L. Klement's *Copperheads in the Middle West* appeared too late for use in this volume.
3 Stampp, *op. cit.*, 155, 156.
4 O. R., I, xxiii, pt. 2, 147, 237; pt. 1, 398, 728.

areas, and who had relatives and friends in them, knew what bitter hardship any abrupt military emancipation would cause. They sympathized with the Southern feeling that the problem of race relations was too delicate to be surrendered to rough surgery. A New Englander who had never been near a slave State could afford to be callous, but not an Illinoisan who had scrutinized the relations of Negro and white in Kentucky. And as we have seen, countless people of Ohio, Indiana, and Illinois deeply feared an influx of freedmen. This fear was held without respect to party, though it was naturally keenest south of a line drawn from Quincy east through Springfield and Indianapolis to Columbus.

The Illinois constitution had long penalized the introduction of free Negroes. In 1862 the voters strengthened this constitutional barrier by a new provision authorizing the legislature to pass laws for discouraging, and if possible totally preventing, any such immigration. The winter session of 1863 had hardly begun when a member introduced a bill punishing any Negro attempting to enter by fine, imprisonment, and thirty-nine lashes. Harsh items blossomed in the Democratic press:

The Contrabands at Cairo.—There are now nearly 1500 "contrabands" at Cairo, 500 having been sent up from Columbus last week. They are a dirty, ragged, and filthy lot of human beings, most of them being the refuse of Southern plantations which the owners were very probably glad to get rid of. Only a small portion of the whole number are able or willing to work. The smallpox is among them, and there is an average of ten deaths a day.[5]

As still another cause of discontent, an apprehension was spreading that the war was being used to enrich Eastern industrial, mercantile, and banking groups, and injure Mississippi Valley farmers. Hundreds of articles, editorials, and speeches expressed this feeling. Just after Fredericksburg, $100 in gold would purchase $135 in greenbacks. A banker with $7,500 in gold could buy enough greenbacks to purchase $10,000 in United States gold bonds, paying 6 per cent and redeemable in five to twenty years. The interest, $600 in gold, would buy almost enough greenbacks every year for another $1,000 bond. Then in 1868 or later all the bonds would be redeemed in gold. While the poor bled, many said, the wealthy would grow richer.

The wartime tariffs, meanwhile, seemed as hurtful to agriculture as they were helpful to industry. They raised consumer prices while limiting foreign ability to buy foodstuffs. Daniel Voorhees of Indiana in 1862 made protection the target of bitter attacks in the House, and that summer the Democratic

5 Chicago *Morning Post*, Jan. 25, 28, 1863. The *Post* declared that about two-thirds of the Republicans of Illinois had voted for the new constitutional provision for excluding Negroes.

State Committee published an appeal against it in the Indianapolis *Sentinel* which was later reprinted as a campaign document.[6] In Illinois one of Douglas' Chicago friends, Samuel S. Hayes, made a number of speeches in the winter of 1862–63 denouncing the tariffs, and when the legislature met he argued that the North could best cajole the South back into the Union on a free-trade basis. As Democratic leaders pointed out, Eastern manufacturers got the great majority of war contracts. The trunk-line railroads, mainly owned by Eastern capitalists, were garnering a rich harvest from war traffic and the closing of the Mississippi. Agrarian groups complained of extortionate freight and elevator rates.

All the while, of course, the Northwest shared the ardent longing of the whole nation for victory. To Westerners victory meant above everything else the clearing of the Mississippi. The East-West railways had not yet taken the place in men's imaginations so long held by the central river system. The Northwest never forgot Douglas' asseveration that the men of Illinois would follow the Mississippi inch by inch with the bayonet to the Gulf. When defeat followed defeat in the East, some Westerners began to fear that Washington might fight for boundaries and let the cotton States go. If that happened, many said with Joseph Medill, the Northwest would secede, continue the war until it conquered the Valley and the Southwest, and erect its own republic.

[I]

In the West, in the winter of 1862–63, the armies were held in a deadlock which encouraged the widening discontent. The Union lines had pushed down to the long southern boundary of Tennessee, at some points slightly below it, as at Corinth, and at others above it, as northwest of Chattanooga; there they seemed almost immobile. Grant commanded in West Tennessee, with movable headquarters. His forces were much scattered, but the armies might be regarded as comprising a left wing at Corinth under Rosecrans, a center to the northwest of that town under Edward O. C. Ord, and a right wing based on Memphis under Sherman. Grant could readily manage all of them, except part of Sherman's, by telegraph, and did so with more expertness than good luck in the early autumn battles of Iuka and Corinth.

Grant's own account of Iuka is fair and lucid. This pretty village, a resort with mineral springs twenty miles east of Corinth on the Memphis & Charleston Railroad, and only seven miles from the Tennessee River, fell without resistance to Sterling Price in mid-September, 1862. "I was apprehensive," writes Grant, "lest the object of the rebels might be to get troops into Tennessee

6 *Cong. Globe*, 37th Cong., 2d Sess., 1150; Stampp, *op. cit.*, 139, 140.

to reinforce Bragg." The apprehension was well founded. Before Bragg began his northward march, he had informed Price and Van Dorn that he left the enemy in West Tennessee to them. Later, supposing that Rosecrans, then at Tuscumbia, was moving north to join Buell in pursuit, he had directed Price to follow; and Price with about 12,000 men had seen his chance to take the exposed post at Iuka, where large Union stores had been collected. Of course Grant, who kept well informed of Confederate movements by cavalry reconnaissances, saw that it was important to crush him. Rosecrans did not have enough men at Corinth to attack the enemy singlehanded. But Grant

MEMPHIS, IUKA AND CORINTH

believed that if he sent Rosecrans with 9,000 troops and Ord with 8,000 to fall simultaneously on Price, one from the west and the other from the northwest, their combined strength would carry the day. Unfortunately, faulty maneuvering by Rosecrans, and the tardy arrival of Ord on the battlefield, ruined the effort, so that Price escaped without crippling damage, and joined Van Dorn. This result gave Grant, who had been almost certain of annihilating his foe, the greatest chagrin. "I was disappointed," he writes in his memoirs, "but I had so high an opinion of General Rosecrans that I found no fault at the time." Word of the abortive fight (September 19) reached Northern hearths on the heels of news of Bragg's victory at Munfordville (September 17) and of Antietam.

7 For Iuka see *Battles and Leaders*, II, 701–736; O. R., I, iv, 175–565; Grant, *Memoirs*, I, 404–413.

As Bragg drove on north in Kentucky and joined Kirby-Smith at Frankfort, Van Dorn and Price prepared to make a determined onslaught on Rosecrans at Corinth—for the Union general returned to that town on the 26th. Grant and Rosecrans knew that it was vital to hold Corinth, with its immense stores. If they were defeated there, Bolivar and Jackson to the north might also fall, West Tennessee to the gates of Memphis would again come under Confederate sway, and the victorious Van Dorn–Price army would establish communication with Bragg's troops through Middle Tennessee.

On October 2 Van Dorn's army camped ten miles from Corinth, and early next morning the battle began. On the first day the Confederates seemed to carry everything before them. By fierce charges they hurled the Union forces from a key hill, capturing two guns, and forced them back to the outskirts. Van Dorn sent an exultant telegram to Richmond: "Our troops have driven the enemy from their positions. We are within three-fourths of a mile of Corinth. The enemy are huddled together about the town. So far all is glorious." All night Rosecrans stayed on the field, while Negroes threw up a fresh fort.[8] At first on the 4th the Confederate drive again seemed irresistible; but as the Union artillery asserted its superiority, the Southerners fell back. They knew that Northern reinforcements were at hand, and in fact, as the battle ended McPherson unloaded a body of fresh troops from the cars.

Once more Rosecrans failed to show promptness. Had he moved with dispatch in pursuit of Van Dorn the moment the Confederates began retreating, he might have annihilated their army. Grant had given him specific orders to follow without delay. But he did not begin his march till the morning of October 5th, took the wrong road, and let his troops be hampered by a wagon train. "Two or three hours of pursuit on the day of the battle," writes Grant disgustedly, "without anything except what the men carried on their persons, would have been worth more than any pursuit commenced the next day could have possibly been." Rosecrans' excuse was that his troops needed rest, while the thicketed country made progress difficult by day and impossible by night. Badly mauled, Van Dorn got clean away. After a brief futile chase, Rosecrans returned to Corinth to find the press full of his praises. In the aura of his imperfect victory he was ordered to Cincinnati, where he found that the government had given him Buell's place in command of the old Army of the Ohio.[9]

The Northwest was distressed to learn how sadly this force (now renamed the Army of the Cumberland) was weakened and demoralized. In nine months it had accomplished little beyond a hazardous retention of Ken-

8 Rosecrans himself describes Corinth in *Battle and Leaders*, II, 737–756. See also his testimony in *Report, Committee on Conduct of War*, Second Series, III, 1–109.

9 Lossing, *Civil War*, II, 538; John Fitch, *Annals of the Army of the Cumberland*, 367 ff.; Van Horne, *Army of the Cumberland*, Chs. XVI, XVII.

tucky and Nashville. Its effective numbers had fallen from about 100,000 to 65,000; the absentees, including about 10,000 in hospitals, were estimated at 33,000. The cavalry were far less efficient than Forrest's and Morgan's hard-riding commands. Recent events, in the words of its provost-judge, had left "its spirit broken, its confidence destroyed, its discipline relaxed." Many citizens believed this the fault not of Buell, a Democrat, but of neglect by the War Department; and the way in which Oliver P. Morton and other Republicans had accomplished Buell's dismissal angered Western Democrats just as McClellan's ejection angered their Eastern brethren.

Rosecrans, an excitable, temperamental man who possessed keen intelligence but only spasmodic energy, knew that he was expected to strike a blow. When he took command he found that Bragg had concentrated the rebel forces at Murfreesboro, where they covered northeastern Alabama, Georgia, and the vital rail line through Chattanooga to Richmond. Only thirty miles or so southeast of Nashville, Bragg menaced that city while himself feeling quite safe as he entertained Jefferson Davis at the handsome house he made his headquarters. Balls and parties enlivened Murfreesboro, for few expected a winter campaign. The Confederates, their ranks augmented by a rigid conscription, in fact felt so confident that they sent a large body of cavalry into western Tennessee to harass Grant, and another into Kentucky to try to cut the railroad north of Nashville.

But having amply supplied his forces, Rosecrans the day after Christmas pushed them southward in three columns under George H. Thomas, Alexander M. McCook, and T. L. Crittenden. Driving back outlying units, they reached the main Confederate position on Stones River before Murfreesboro on the 30th. Here, as 1863 ended and the new year began, they fought one of the stubbornest battles of the war. In chill, rainy weather, over rough and partially wooded terrain, some 75,000 effectives, in fairly equal numbers,[10] grappled in grim charges and hand-to-hand fighting. Though Rosecrans had expected to hold the offensive, Bragg by prompter movement on the 31st seized it from him. For a time that first day, as two divisions on the Union right buckled, Northern defeat seemed almost certain.

Fortunately, the Union officers had learned much about fighting since Shiloh;[11] fortunately also, Thomas and Sheridan held their positions against heroic Southern attacks. Soldiers called a particularly bloody segment of the

10 Livermore, p. 97, states that Rosecrans had 41,400, and Bragg about 35,000; but Cist, *Army of the Cumberland*, credits Bragg with 46,600 effectives, Rosecrans with 43,400.

11 "Our generals are now learning how to fight and save their men," wrote Lieut.-Col. James I. Davidson of the Seventy-third Illinois. "We fight a great deal lying flat on our breasts making breastworks of rocks, fallen trees, stumps, or anything we can get, and never allow the enemy to come upon us in full overwhelming force and take advantage of us. We place the batteries whenever practicable on high land or the edge of timber where our infantry can be concealed." Davidson Papers, Ala. State Archives.

field "Hell's Half Acre." One Northern colonel thought it wonderful anybody survived. "The shells, grape, balls, railroad iron and such like fired from the enemy's cannon was a constant storm. Their columns came on with yells as fierce as devils. . . ." William B. Hazen's brigade of 1,300 Ohio, Indiana, Illinois, and Kentucky volunteers beat back every wave, though one-third its men went down. At the end Sheridan greeted Rosecrans elatedly: "Here we are, all that are left of us." He might well say this, for his command alone had lost seventy-two officers. The struggle closed when at noon on January 3 Bragg, in council with his generals, decided to retreat behind Duck River. Both armies had been terribly mangled, each reporting more than 9,000 men killed or wounded, while the combined death roll alone came to about 3,000.[12] If Bragg had lost the field, Rosecrans had lost the larger number of prisoners, twenty-eight pieces of artillery, and much of his wagon-train.

In effect, Murfreesboro or Stones River was a drawn battle. Fierce dissensions broke out among the Confederate officers. Breckinridge, Hardee, Cleburne, and Polk agreed that Bragg had mismanaged his army and should be removed from its command, while he was so violently assailed by the press and general public that he appealed to President Davis for vindication or dismissal. On the Union side, Rosecrans' army was immobilized for the next six months, for the brilliant Confederate cavalry leaders constantly threatened its long single-track communication line with Louisville. Among the Northern officers special criticism fell upon the right wing commander, McCook. On both sides, the devotion of the common soldiers defied praise. Bragg spoke of their "glorious work," and Rosecrans paid them a more emphatic tribute: "the sturdy rank and file showed invincible fighting courage and stamina, worthy of a great and free nation, requiring only good officers, discipline, and instructions to make them equal, if not superior, to any troops in ancient or modern times." This devotion accounted for the heavy losses.

Altogether, in the indecisive battles of autumn and early winter, the Western armies of the Union suffered fully 25,000 casualties. Disease took larger toll in the Western forces than the Eastern. Thinking of so many fresh graves, of the cripples in the streets, and of the coffins stacked in railway stations, countless Northwesterners asked, "To what end?"

Everyone who knew the West realized that political as well as military reasons made early capture of Vicksburg and clearance of the Mississippi desirable. Yates and Morton knew it; editors like Medill and James Sheehan knew it; the

12 Livermore, 97, gives the Union losses as 1,677 killed, 7,543 wounded, and 3,686 missing, a total of 12,906; the Confederate losses as killed, 1,294, wounded, 7,945, and missing, about 2,500, a total of 11,739. But Confederate officers estimated the number of their missing as not over 1,000; Polk, *Polk*, II, 197. Full dispatches and reports are given in O. R., I, xx.

popular Democratic politician John McClernand knew it. The President had a clear grasp of the fact. Orville H. Browning, Senator until the end of January, 1863, was on terms of warm intimacy with the Lincolns. One day when he called, Lincoln picked up a map and pointed to the counties on each side of the river from Memphis downward, showing that Negroes averaged three-fourths or four-fifths of the population. Rapping the line of the Mississippi, he said: "I tell you, I am determined to open it, and if necessary will take all these Negroes to open it and keep it open." [13] His mind was receptive to men who had a plan, as Morton and McClernand did.

Morton's plan, unfortunately, was poor. He wrote Stanton just after the fall elections that the fate of the Northwest trembled in the balance, and that an immediate advance was imperative. Most Democratic leaders, he declared, believed that rebellion would triumph and the South gain its independence. The Democrats, asking what Ohio, Indiana, Illinois, and Iowa should then do, were replying that they should form a Northwestern Confederacy to save the Mississippi; and their arguments had wide appeal, for even ignorant men saw the value of the channel. "I give it here as my deliberate judgment," Morton told Stanton, "that should the misfortune of arms, or other causes, compel us to [grant] the independence of the Rebel States, Ohio, Indiana, and Illinois can be prevented, if at all, from a new act of secession and annexation to these States only by a bloody and desolating Civil War." But his program? He proposed that 100,000 men be immediately sent by sea to conquer and hold Louisiana, Texas, Arkansas, and the whole west bank of the Mississippi. This, he thought, could be done in ninety days. Thus even if the cotton States made good their new republic, the free navigation of the Mississippi could be secured. As a plan for putting 100,000 troops out of the war, this was superb. [14]

McClernand, the stout Jacksonian who had left Congress to become a brigadier, and since March, 1862, a major-general, perceived the military requirements of the hour much more accurately. He had been in Washington during the late summer drumming up support for an ambitious scheme. The 10,000-mile river system with its immense commerce was locked up, as he had written Lincoln, by a comparatively small garrison at Vicksburg. He would enlist a new force of his own—a special appeal to Democrats was implied. Then he would strike at that key city with not less than 60,000 men and a fleet of river gunboats. In this he would use what then seemed a shrewd plan of attack. That is, he would send transports laden with troops

13 The Brownings stayed in Washington till midsummer of 1863 and were much missed when they left; *Diary*, I, 512–568.
14 Morton's letter, Oct. 27, 1862, is in the Stanton Papers, LC.

down the Mississippi to the mouth of the Yazoo just above Vicksburg; have them ascend that river to the first eligible landing on the side toward Vicksburg; and thus throw his powerful force within about a dozen miles of the city. After capturing Vicksburg, the army should seize Jackson forty-five miles to the east, and march on to Meridian, from which railroad junction it could menace either Montgomery or Mobile.[15]

But the story of autumn and winter operations against Vicksburg was one destined to keep the Northwest in painful suspense.

Grant had been having a difficult time the whole summer and fall of 1862. As commander of the Army of the Mississippi, he had suffered from the haziness of his authority. Halleck had been uncommunicative. "Practically I became a department commander," Grant writes, "because no one was assigned to that position over me and I made my reports direct to the general-in-chief"; but he felt uncertain of his authority and tenure. The mediocre performance of Rosecrans and Ord distressed him. He was constantly worried by guerrilla warfare, and by the activities of cotton traders, which demoralized his troops. The public criticism he had received after Shiloh, the humiliations visited upon him by Halleck, exaggerated stories of his drinking, and the hawklike surveillance by Rawlins to see that these stories gained no substance, created a certain self-distrust. Since his dreary garrison duty at Humboldt Bay in 1853 Grant had been through harsh experiences, but none more galling than the anxieties of this dark national period.

While he, too, had a plan for taking Vicksburg, he did not offer it until in late October the government put him in command of the new Department of the Tennessee with clear powers. He had been waiting, he explained to Halleck, for guidance. "You have never suggested to me any plan of operations in this Department," he wrote October 26. Grant's troops were badly scattered on overextended lines.[16] He proposed concentrating them, and moving them down the Mississippi Central Railroad toward Jackson, Mississippi; an advance which he thought feasible because once his column reached Grenada it could be supplied from Memphis by way of the railroad connecting those two cities. When his army reached points east of Vicksburg, Grant believed it would force the evacuation of that place.

15 McClernand's important letter was written to Lincoln from Washington on Sept. 28, 1862; McClernand Papers, Ill. State Hist. Lib. We may repeat that as a veteran of the Black Hawk War, lawyer, Congressman, and opponent of the Kansas-Nebraska bill, he knew Lincoln well; and he talked with him in the White House.

16 The Army of the Tennessee under Grant supplanted the Army of the District of Western Tennessee and the Army of the Mississippi; Phisterer, 53, 54. Of Grant's forces in October, 4,800 were in Kentucky and Illinois, 7,000 in Memphis, 19,200 from Mound City south, and 17,500 at Corinth; reinforcements soon came in. *Memoirs*, I, 420, 421. Grant humbly assured Halleck that he was ready to do whatever that general might direct with all his might and without complaint; Oct. 26, 1862, Grant-Halleck Papers, Ill. State Hist. Lib.

Of the three plans advanced, the Administration chose McClernand's, which was soundest. Though his vanity, grasping ambition, and want of tact made him an unpleasant figure, the idea that his project represented either political intrigue or military insubordination, as some critics have stated, is absurd. On the contrary, it was a thoughtful effort to meet the political exigencies of the period by prompt action to clear the Mississippi under a Democratic leader who had wide influence with his Northwestern party.[17] It was strategically superior to Grant's plan because a river advance would be far safer from interruption by raids than an advance down a railroad. Moreover, McClernand's proposal for raising fresh forces for the expedition was sound, for he had already been prominent in recruiting men. The country needed more Jacksonian Democrats thinking as constructively as he did.[18]

At the end of October, McClernand, after long interviews with Lincoln, Stanton, and others, was back in Springfield. He had obtained confidential orders from Stanton to range through Indiana, Illinois, and Iowa, organize troops he found there or could freshly collect, and forward them immediately to Cairo, Memphis, or some other spot. This was "to the end that, when a sufficient force, not required by the operations of General Grant's command, shall be raised, an expedition may be organized under General McClernand's command against Vicksburg. . . ." He immediately established close relations with Morton, Yates, and Kirkwood. "I feel deep interest in the success of the expedition," Lincoln endorsed on the order, "and desire it to be pushed forward with all possible dispatch, consistently with the other parts of the military service." The newspapers laid hold of the news, which afforded good Western ammunition for the Administration just before election, and the popular response seemed enthusiastic.[19]

By November 10, McClernand had sent twenty regiments of Indiana, Illinois, and Iowa troops, with two batteries, to Columbus, Kentucky, and Memphis. He urged Stanton to continue supporting him, writing that the popular delight in the Mississippi expedition would curdle into anger and disillusionment if any neglect ruined it. Among the officers eager to join him was Frank P. Blair, Jr., who also had been raising troops.[20]

Grant watched all this with unhappy gaze. The newspaper praise and

17 John Fiske in *The Mississippi Valley in the Civil War*, 202, calls it political intrigue, and F. V. Greene in *The Mississippi*, 60, "a violation of all military discipline"; both statements ignore the Lincoln-Stanton endorsement and Northwestern unrest.

18 For McClernand's services see Cole, *ut sup.*, 262, and Force, *From Fort Henry to Corinth*, 21, 28, 38 ff.

19 Stanton's orders were dated Oct. 20–21; McClernand Papers. For newspaper publicity see John M. Thayer, St. Louis, Oct. 24, 1862, to McClernand, *ibid.*, and files of the Chicago *Morning Post*, *Illinois State Register*, and Indianapolis *Daily State Sentinel*.

20 McClernand to Stanton, Springfield, Nov. 10, McClernand Papers; Blair to McClernand, Nov. 12, *ibid.*

popular congratulations showered on McClernand worried him. He thought two commanders in the same field one too many, and was quick to express concern over McClernand's inexperience, the possibility that he would get his raw troops into trouble, and the chances of imperfect cooperation. He therefore on November 6 asked Halleck whether he was to lie inert while this expedition was fitted out from Memphis, or whether he could push as far ahead as possible. Halleck well realized that Grant outranked McClernand, and always favored professional soldiers. He knew that Stanton had authorized McClernand to move only when he had a sufficient force not required by Grant's operations, and that Lincoln wished to expedite him only in a way consistent with other parts of the service. He therefore assured Grant: "You have command of all troops sent to your Department, and have permission to fight the enemy where you please." [21]

At this point everything began to go wrong for Grant. The general, according to his plan, concentrated his forces at La Grange, Tennessee, marched south on November 20 along the line of the Mississippi Central, and had Sherman move from Memphis (November 24) to join him on that railroad. On December 5 they camped side by side at Oxford and College Hill in northern Mississippi. The Confederates under Pemberton retreated before them to Grenada, about 140 miles by road from Vicksburg. All looked roseate until the perils of dependence on a long line of railway appeared. Grant had established his main depot at Holly Springs, to which he had to bring supplies by 180 miles of track from Columbus, Kentucky, a precarious lifeline. If he pushed on south to capture Grenada he would reach the direct lateral line from Memphis, but it was in bad condition. Moreover, at Grenada he would still be 140 miles by road from Vicksburg, while the railway in advance had been torn up, the highways were poor, and Pemberton was sure to gather strength to meet the advance. Grant realized that he had made a false start.[22]

On December 8, therefore, he decided to divide his forces for *two* movements against Vicksburg. He ordered Sherman to return to Memphis with one division, collect enough troops thereabout to give him more than 20,000 men, and move down the river with Admiral Porter's gunboats in a strong amphibious expedition. Grant would meanwhile hold his army ready to advance against Vicksburg from the central Mississippi rear, immobilizing Pemberton. If the Confederate army opposed one force, the other could snatch the

21 Nov. 12, 1862, Grant-Halleck Papers. Grant states his objections in *Memoirs*, I, 426. Full military papers are given in O. R., I, xvii, pts. 1 and 2, *passim*.
22 Greene, 63, 64; Liddell Hart, *Sherman*, 160, 161. Much light is thrown on Grant's serious supply problem by the papers of Col. (later Gen.) Lewis B. Parsons, who had charge of river transport; Ill. State Hist. Lib. For his Mississippi Central expedition he wanted more locomotives, for that line had only eighteen in working order; Grant, Nov. 12, 1862, to Halleck, Grant-Halleck Papers.

prize. But two blows immediately befell Grant. The Sherman-Porter amphibious advance would be using what was essentially McClernand's plan. It is not strange that when Sherman reported his orders, Halleck warned him the President might insist on keeping the original projector in charge. After all, McClernand had a better claim than Sherman, his junior in years, rank, and influence. And Lincoln did just this. On December 20 Sherman steamed down the river with 20,500 troops, to be reinforced at Helena by 9,500 more; but meanwhile, on December 18 Halleck telegraphed Grant that, by the President's direction, McClernand was to lead the river expedition.

And then suddenly, just after mid-December, the Confederates completely smashed Grant's supply line and main base by two brilliant cavalry strokes. Forrest, with 2,500 horsemen based on Columbia, Tennessee, destroyed numerous stretches of track along sixty miles of Grant's supply railroad. And simultaneously Earl Van Dorn with 3,500 cavalry, striking from Grenada, fell upon Grant's supply base at Holly Springs, captured 1,500 of the Union troops guarding it, and burned $1,500,000 worth of supplies. Grant was outraged by the feebleness of the commander, who had 2,000 effective men able to shelter behind brick walls and cotton bales, and who had been given ample warning. "The surrender at Holly Springs was the most disgraceful affair that has occurred in this Dept.," he wrote.[23]

Yet Grant himself was censurable for not making sure that so vital a point had a heavy defense force under competent officers. His position was now sad indeed, for with his principal depot gone and his communications broken he was compelled to retreat. To stand still long was to starve, while to go forward, depending on the country for food, was too dangerous—though he seriously contemplated doing just this. For a time he sustained himself by collecting supplies from the district about Oxford. He sent out scores of wagon trains, heavily guarded, for twenty-five miles on every side. They stripped the country bare of livestock, grain, and forage, and when the inhabitants begged for enough to live on, Grant sternly bade them move further south. Then, putting his men on three-quarter rations, he turned back behind the Tallahatchie, and retreated to his starting point near La Grange. On January 10, 1863, he himself was in Memphis. He made the more haste to reach that city because he had been stung by the telegram giving Lincoln's order that McClernand, not Sherman, should lead the river expedition against Vicksburg.[24]

23   Grant, Jan. 14, 1863, to "Dear Cousin," Grant Letters, Colo. State Hist. Soc.
24   Grant, *Memoirs*, I, 422–436, gives a vigorous account of his movements. See Liddell Hart, 162, for his desire to get to Memphis to cut out McClernand. McPherson wrote Grant on Dec. 20 of the Vicksburg expedition: "I would, if in your place, proceed to Memphis and take command of it myself. It is the great feature of the campaign, and its execution

THE VICKSBURG CAMPAIGN

Grant had not covered himself with glory. He had marched from Grand Junction nearly a hundred miles to Oxford, and then marched back again. His two months of effort had merely lost valuable supplies and demonstrated that his route was badly chosen. If he and his staff had learned a good deal about handling a large body of troops, it was an expensive education. Meanwhile, Sherman continued to execute the plan of a rapid amphibious descent of the Mississippi, followed by a drive up the Yazoo just behind Vicksburg—in effect, McClernand's plan. For Lincoln's order that McClernand should take command had been received by Grant just as Forrest cut all communications, so that it was relayed neither to Sherman in Memphis nor to McClernand in Springfield. Sherman put all speed into the assignment Grant had given him because both men were anxious to forestall McClernand, and because he hoped to take the defenders of Vicksburg by surprise, perhaps capturing the city by a single blow.

In other respects this was not Grant's happiest hour. On December 17 his headquarters in Holly Springs published General Orders No. 11: "The Jews, as a class violating every regulation of trade established by the Treasury Department and also department orders, are hereby expelled from the department within twenty-four hours from the receipt of this order." Post commanders were to eject "all this class of people" and to arrest anyone who returned. Plenty of chicanery, thievery, and illegal dealing in connection with cotton shipments could be found in the department, but more Gentiles than Jews were concerned in it. Indignant Jewish delegations at once visited Washington to protest. One was headed by Rabbi Isaac M. Wise of Cincinnati. They had no trouble seeing Lincoln, who promptly revoked the order. The President, whose antagonism to Know-Nothingism was well known, told Rabbi Wise that he would never permit any citizen to be in any manner wronged on account of his place of birth or his religion.[25]

[III]

But Sherman fared as badly as Grant, for once more the Union leaders reckoned without Confederate enterprise. The Southerners had spies in Memphis to report the start of his expedition on December 20, and yet more spies

---

rightfully belongs to you." Liddell Hart thinks that Grant might well have remained in Pemberton's front to keep him from reinforcing Vicksburg. James Harrison Wilson in *Under the Old Flag*, I, 120–127, relates that he had seen much in Washington during October of McClernand, who offered him a place on his staff. McClernand thought poorly of Grant, but Wilson warned him that Halleck would assuredly favor Grant for chief command of the Vicksburg expedition.

25 For Grant's order see O. R., I, xvii, pt. 2, p. 424; for Halleck's statement on it, *idem*, p. 530; for Wise's report, *The Israelite*, Jan. 8, 1863. Bertram W. Korn's full analysis in *American Jewry and the Civil War*, 121–155, should be read.

to record its hourly progress. As this army descended the river, Forrest was capturing small posts behind Grant, while Van Dorn, leaving the Holly Springs base in ashes, was mopping up Union detachments in that area. Grant was estopped from furnishing Sherman any cooperation and his letter of December 23 announcing that he had been compelled to fall back did not reach Sherman until long after its intelligence was of any value. The result was disaster. When Sherman the day after Christmas landed three divisions on the bank of the Yazoo, Pemberton had 13,800 men facing them in entrenched positions on hills. The Union attacks during the next three days met a bloody repulse. Nearly 1,800 Union soldiers were lost in an action which one participant, Frank P. Blair, Jr., acridly described:

The Grand Mississippi Expedition has been a failure. Everybody in the West supposed it would contain at least 100,000 men, [but] it numbered 30,000. Grant, it seems, preferred to operate in two lines, one interior and the other by the river. His communications were cut off and he with 45,000 men compelled to fall back on Memphis. The enemy then concentrated against us at Vicksburg. Sherman instead of concentrating his force at some one point of the fortifications of Vicksburg scattered them along the whole line from Haines Bluff on the Yazoo to the city of Vicksburg.[26]

Meanwhile, the defenses of Vicksburg were being feverishly augmented. "The work here goes bravely on," reported the Vicksburg correspondent of the Yazoo *Banner*. "General Pemberton's energy and skill have accomplished wonders. He is a great worker. What he lacks in genius he makes up in industry. He has not established any headquarters yet. One day he is with the army of the north, the next at Jackson, the next at Vicksburg. . . . The whole place is being fortified. Forts, breastworks, and batteries outside the city, rifle-pits and intrenchments in the streets. The line of defense is twenty-odd miles in length. . . . The iron-clad is not feared." [27]

While Sherman was being repulsed, McClernand, who had at last discovered that he was entitled to command before Vicksburg, was hastening down the Mississippi. He reached the mouth of the Yazoo on January 2, 1863, to find the defeated Sherman glad to subside into the position of a corps commander.[28] As nobody knew how long it would be until Grant arrived—cer-

26 Blair-Lee Papers; casualty lists reached the Northwest along with those of Murfreesboro.
27 Dec. 17, 1862.
28 McClernand suspected that Lincoln's order putting him in command had been deliberately withheld. Certainly Grant was not to blame—he had tried to relay it promptly; but why had Halleck not sent a copy direct to Springfield? "Either accident or intention has conspired to thwart the authority of yourself and the Secretary of War and to betray me," McClernand wrote Lincoln from Memphis on Dec. 29, "but with your support I shall not despair of overcoming both." He complained he had to push down to his command at Vicksburg, running a gauntlet of guerrilla bands, in a common river steamer. His letter is in Rufus Rockwell Wilson, "President Lincoln and Emancipation," Lincoln *Herald*, LI (June, 1949), 43, 46.

tainly not within a fortnight—Sherman proposed that while awaiting him the army and gunboats should move against the so-called Post fifty miles up the Arkansas River, where a garrison of about 5,000 under T. J. Churchill presented a threat to Mississippi operations. McClernand, who had already thought of this, agreed. On January 11, 1863, gunboats silenced the fort's artillery, Union troops pushed to within a hundred yards of the intrenchments, and the white flag went up. With just over a thousand casualties, McClernand and Porter took 4,800 prisoners, killed or wounded 110 more, and captured 17 guns.

At this point Grant dealt with McClernand in an arbitrary spirit. His feeling against that officer suggests a jealous determination never to let him get the credit for capturing Vicksburg. Thus far, the "political general" had done better than Grant himself. But on the very day Arkansas Post was taken, Grant sent a letter of stern disapproval, ordering him back to the Mississippi unless he was acting under superior authority. He simultaneously telegraphed Halleck that "McClernand has gone on a wild goose chase to the Post of Arkansas," a most unjust statement. Halleck was glad to seize on this telegram as a basis for action. Without waiting to learn the facts he replied: "You are hereby authorized to relieve General McClernand from command of the expedition against Vicksburg, giving it to the next in rank or taking it yourself." When on the 13th Grant heard from McClernand of the capture of the fort he directed him to return to Milliken's Bend, clearly intending to reduce him to subordination as corps commander. But as soon as Grant learned that Sherman had advised the operation, he praised it as a wise step! [29] The best that can be said for the victor of Donelson is that he was acting on incomplete knowledge, and that at a time when both the situation and orders from Washington demanded an immediate strengthening of the Mississippi River column, he had been genuinely alarmed by a dispatch from McClernand implying that the general might go on from the Post to a rash foray through Arkansas.

Throughout the war it was all too often evident that when a professional soldier blundered his West Point associates helped gloss over the slip, and whenever a West Pointer scored a success his friends made the most of it; but any error on the part of an officer from civil life was unpardonable. Had McClernand marched a large army to Oxford and back again he would have been accused of something worse than a wild-goose chase; had he lost Holly Springs with 2,000 men and large stores he would have been assailed as mercilessly as Frémont after the loss of Lexington. The statement of reasons

29 Sherman deals with Arkansas Post in Ch. XII of his *Memoirs*, emphasizing McClernand's vanity as he boasted of his star "ever in the ascendant." It is unfortunate that McClernand left no personal record. Nearly all judgments of him have been based on *ex parte* evidence, without examination of his papers or his son's MS biography in the Illinois State Historical Library.

for attacking Arkansas Post which he now sent to Grant's adjutant-general was an honest and reasonable document. He pointed out that the necessity for reducing the Post was obvious—he had urged General W. A. Gorman at Helena, on his way down the river, to seize or invest it; that after Sherman's repulse at Chickasaw Bayou, the movement against Vicksburg could obviously not be renewed for some time; that Grant's retirement had left Price's army at Grenada free to reinforce Vicksburg; and that if he had not made this attack his forces would have rusted in idleness. He added two sentences which must have stung Halleck like a whiplash: "Vicksburg cannot be reduced by a front attack, unsupported by cooperation from the rear of the place, except by a very large land and naval force, and after great delay. *The golden moment for the reduction of Vicksburg was allowed to pass unimproved.*" [30] It was Halleck who, after his slow march on Corinth, had neglected that moment.

McClernand, with all his faults, understood the situation in mid-January more clearly than his superior. Grant scolded him because Grant entertained three glaring misapprehensions. He believed that N. P. Banks would lead his army up from the south into the Vicksburg area any day; that with this augmentation a fresh attack on Vicksburg could succeed; and that Arkansas Post was of little consequence. The truth was that Banks did not even reach Port Hudson until late in May, and then was disastrously repulsed; that even his 15,000 additional men would not have enabled the Union forces to make a successful attack on Pemberton from the Yazoo; and that Arkansas Post was too troublesome a threat on the Union flank to be tolerated. The Confederates, as Sherman assured Grant, believed they had made it impregnable. "Could we have followed up," added Sherman, "the capture of Little Rock would have been easy; but even as it is. . . . I assure you when next at Vicksburg I will feel much less uneasiness about our communications." [31]

McClernand no sooner got Grant's order to return to Milliken's Bend than, on January 14, he assured Grant that he would obey it immediately. He left Arkansas Post, however, with a feeling of pique. Why had he not been allowed to move against Vicksburg by the Yazoo route in early December with all the troops available? Why had Grant waited two months, let his communications be cut, and allowed his base to be destroyed? Why had Sherman, hurrying to forestall him, stumbled so clumsily into defeat? When

---

30 O. R., I, xvii, pt. 1, p. 709; my italics.
31 Napolcon, Ark., Jan. 17, 1863, to Grant; O. R., I, xvii, pt. 2, pp. 570, 571. Some of Grant's biographers have accused McClernand of being ready to commit his army to a hare-brained attempt to seize Little Rock; but the record plainly shows (1) that Sherman believed this possible if the Arkansas River remained high, and (2) that McClernand was closely watching the stage of water, fully aware that he must not let transports get stranded upstream. See McClernand to Sherman, Jan. 14, 1863, O. R., I, xvii, pt. 2, pp. 563, 564.

at last he, McClernand, had been permitted to appear on the scene he had gained a victory only to be loaded with reproaches. A core of truth lay in the foolish letter he sent Lincoln from Arkansas Post on January 16:

> I believe my success here is gall and wormwood to the clique of West Pointers who have been persecuting me for months. How can you expect success when men controlling the military destinies of the country are more chagrined at the success of your volunteer officers than the very enemy beaten by the latter in battle? Something must be done to take the hand of oppression off citizen soldiers whose zeal for their country has prompted them to take up arms, or all will be lost.[32]

McClernand still hoped that Grant, keeping his headquarters in Memphis to exercise over-all control, would give him a free hand in taking Vicksburg. This dream quickly vanished. On January 13, 1863, Grant had informed General J. B. McPherson in La Grange, Tennessee: "It is my present intention to command the expedition down the river in person." [33] For the good of the country, this was a wise decision. There is truth in Sherman's observation that McClernand excelled in short-range views of any situation, but was poor in long-range judgment; that he, Sherman, excelled in long-range plans, but went astray in short-range thinking; and that Grant was good in both. But February and March were to pass before any real progress was made, just as in the East an even longer period was to expire before the Army of the Potomac initiated any movement.

Western officers, it is true, were beginning to see the lines of future success. "Russ" Jones, a cotton-trader friend of Elihu Washburne, rode on the steamer *Magnolia* on January 27–28 with Grant, Rawlins, and other staff officers between Memphis and the mouth of the Yazoo. Writing Washburne, he made it plain that he had listened to the talk of officers lounging on deck. One fact was especially interesting:

> Grant has about 36,000 men down below. Will get 6,000 men from Helena and has about 16,000 at Memphis ready to come down making in round numbers about 60,000 and as many gunboats as can be used at one time. He has ammunition enough here for present use and enough on the way to give each man 700 rounds, with artillery ammunition in proportion. I was under the impression that Sherman failed for lack of men, but he tells Grant that he had as many men as he could use, that the result would have been the same if he had had 700,000 men. *As I understand it, the only hope of getting Vicksburg is in being able to get below it and in behind. If that can be done we are all right, if not it is doubtful.* On the 2nd water had entered the Butler Canal and that may

---

32 O. R., I, xvii, pt. 2, pp. 566, 567.
33 *Ibid.*, p. 557. Grant in a report to the War Department on Jan. 20, 1863, stated this intention—unless the government interfered, which of course it did not.

prove available. I told Grant I hoped he would not let the outside pressure influence him to be in too great a hurry.[34]

Yet as winter passed into early spring, doubts about the capacity of Grant persisted. Lincoln felt them; he told a New York *Tribune* man on March 20 that he was not sanguine about capturing Vicksburg. Radical leaders felt them: Grimes of Iowa went to the White House to demand the removal of Grant as an incompetent utterly callous about human life, and when Lincoln refused, flounced out of the office in a rage. Cadwallader C. Washburn, who as a commander of Wisconsin troops had full opportunities for observation, was completely skeptical. "Grant has no plans for taking Vicksburg," he wrote his brother Elihu on March 28, "and he is frittering away time and strength to no purpose. The truth must be told even if it hurts. You cannot make a silk purse out of a sow's ear." This to Grant's chief political sponsor! Like some others, "Cad" believed Rawlins infinitely Grant's superior.[35]

[IV]

While the winter thus passed in discouragement, the tide of Northwestern discontent rose. Every setback gave it strength. A number of editors and politicians trod the narrow zone between legitimate criticism of the government and treasonable obstruction of the war effort. The Chicago *Times*, which the city board of trade late in 1862 denounced for almost daily articles calculated to give aid and comfort to traitors, was one. Cyrus H. McCormick had financed its purchase by W. F. Storey, who after the emancipation proclamation bitterly attacked the Administration. Samuel Medary's Columbus *Crisis*, edited by a professional agitator who supported Vallandigham, was so objectionable to Unionists that angry soldiers wrecked its press in the spring of 1863. Such other organs of the Peace Democrats as the Cincinnati *Enquirer*, which declared the idea of a Union established by force ridiculous, the Detroit *Free Press*, and the Indianapolis *Sentinel*, were abetted by smaller newspapers like the Peoria *Demokrat*, which the government excluded from the mails, the Terre Haute *Journal and Herald*, which was mobbed, and the Ashland (Ohio) *Union*, which termed Lincoln a bloodstained tyrant.

34 Jan. 28, 1863, Washburne Papers, LC; italics mine. By the Butler Canal, Jones meant the canal that had been started by General Thomas Williams the previous summer, under directions from Farragut, across the peninsula opposite Vicksburg, in an effort to bypass and isolate that city.

35 A. D. Richardson, March 20, 1863, to Gay, Gay Papers; W. M. Thayer, *Grant*, 208, 209; Washburn, Helena, Ark., to Elihu Washburne, Washburne Papers, LC. The Chicago *Morning Post* strongly took McClernand's side. The troops had been greatly disheartened, wrote its army correspondent, by the repulse of Sherman's attack, "which was insane in conception, and inspired, it is affirmed, by jealousy"; but the victory at Arkansas Post had restored confidence. Letter from the front Jan. 10 in issue of Jan. 29, 1863.

The precise strength of disloyalty was for three reasons difficult to measure: a clear definition was impossible; its worst manifestations were kept secret; and its vigor fluctuated from place to place and day to day. Who was disloyal? Any patent conspirator for Confederate success, like Dr. William Bowles of French Lick Springs, Indiana, who organized the Knights of the Golden Circle along the border, was certainly a traitor. So was any Northerner who strove actively for peace at the price of disunion, or on the basis of a new nation to include the South and exclude New England. Any man who corresponded with Confederate leaders, tried to block recruiting, committed acts of sabotage, or disseminated false reports designed to cripple the government, could be termed disloyal. But a twilight penumbra surrounds such words. Seward himself had stood for peace at the price of temporary disunion; multitudes of good citizens asserted that they would support recruiting and heavy taxation to save the Union, but not to enforce emancipation. The Newark *Evening Journal* declared: "It will be seen that Mr. Lincoln has called for another half million of men. All who wish to be butchered will please step forward. All others will please stay at home and defy Old Abe. . . ." [36] Were such words treasonable?

The epithet "traitor" was assuredly used with reckless looseness. The wealthy Illinois landholder Isaac Funk, losing his temper this winter in the State Senate, burst into a violent philippic. "These villains and traitors and secessionists in this senate," he vociferated, "are killing my neighbors' boys, now fighting in the field." The galleries rang with applause as he went on: "Mr. Speaker, these traitors on this floor should be provided with hempen collars." He glared at some of his colleagues. "Hell itself could not spew out a more traitorous crew than some of the men who disgrace this legislature." Radical members of the assembly agreed that the legislature contained downright traitors. Morton of Indiana, certain that traitors abounded in the Northwest, described their conspiracy as Machiavellian:

The Democratic scheme may be briefly stated thus: End the war by any means whatever at the earliest possible moment. This, of course, lets the Rebel States go, and acknowledges the Southern Confederacy. They will then propose to the Rebels a reunion and a reconstruction upon the condition of leaving out the New England States; this they believe the Rebel States will accept, and so do I. It would withdraw twelve votes from the Senate, and leave the Slave States in a permanent majority. . . . Govr Seymour and the leading Democratic politicians of New York and Pennsylvania are in the scheme. . . . [37]

Yet a great deal of so-called treason was no worse than the utterances of the eminent S. F. B. Morse, who urged men to stop fighting as long as emancipation

36 Quoted in Robert S. Harper, *Lincoln and the Press*, 126.
37 E. M. Haines of the Illinois legislature described the situation on Jan. 10, 1863, to Elihu Washburne; Washburne Papers, LC. Morton's letter is in Stanton Papers, Feb., 1863.

bject of the war.The veteran Jacksonian Amos Kendall wrote
ould not fight the enemy unless the President first recalled his
ce chances were that he would soon have neither constitution
ballot box to fight for.[38] And who would apply the epithet of traitor to
Nathaniel Hawthorne? He assured a close friend in the fall of 1861 that he did
not wish to see the Union restored as it was. "Amputation seems to me much
the better plan; and all we ought to fight for is the liberty of selecting the point
where our diseased members shall be left off. I would fight to the death for the
Northern Slave States, and let the rest go." The next spring found him of the
same mind: "It would be too great an absurdity to spend all our Northern
strength for the next generation in holding on to people who insist on being let
loose." And even after Gettysburg, Hawthorne clung to his belief: "The best
thing possible, so far as I can see, is to effect the separation of the Union, giving
us the west bank of the Mississippi, and a boundary line affording us as much
Southern soil as we can hope to digest in another century." [39] But no more than
Morse would Hawthorne have performed an act of overt hostility to his country.

In Indiana and Illinois many people thought that a midwinter crisis offered
imminent peril to the nation. Governor Yates was impressed by letters making
accusations of disloyalty in various localities. Washburne and Trumbull in
Washington received word from town after town that the "secesh" were more
dangerous than ever before. Early in the new year disturbing news reached
Springfield. The 109th Infantry at Holly Springs became insubordinate, some
men deserting while others declared they would never fight for emancipation;
and though the colonel remained true, numerous officers and privates had to be
arrested, and Grant disbanded the regiment. It had been raised in Union
County, where most people were of Southern ancestry, and where the Knights
of the Golden Circle, with their mummery of oaths and passwords, had fostered
hostility to antislavery measures. News of the mutiny threw the "copperheads"
of the section into a fever of excitement. Democrats who had at first winced
under this epithet began wearing heads of Liberty punched from big copper
cents or polished cross-sections of a butternut, and holding angry meetings.
Yates wrote Secretary Chase in alarm that he was sitting on a powder keg, and
the Administration should recall John M. Palmer, with at least four regiments,
to Illinois ready for instant hostilities.[40]

38 Kendall, March 28, 1864, Morse Papers, LC.
39 See Hawthorne's correspondence with Horatio Bridge, *Century Magazine*, N. S., XIII
(Jan., 1888), 489, 490. He wrote President Chamberlain of Bowdoin May 26, 1861: "I rejoice
that the old Union is smashed. We never were one people and never really had a country
since the Constitution was adopted." N. Y. *Times*, Jan. 25, 1883.
40 See the Yates, Trumbull, and Washburne Papers, Dec.–April, 1862–63, for numerous
letters from citizens on "treasonable" activities. Yates's letter to Chase, Feb. 2, 1863, is in the
Stanton Papers, LC. The term "copperhead" was used at least as early as July 30, 1862,

In Indiana, Morton was equally frightened. He knew well that his autocratic regime had aroused deep resentment. The vast majority of Indiana folk were entirely loyal, but his vehement radicalism and acquiescence in arrests had aroused the detestation of Democrats. So had his enforcement of the draft of 6,000 men when, as it was later shown, Indiana had really met the full quota under Lincoln's calls.

When the new Democratic legislatures gathered in the snows of Spring-field and Indianapolis, they presented programs which indicated that copper-head leaders of the two States were working in unison. The extremists brought forward resolutions denouncing emancipation, the tariff, and the arming of Negroes. They proposed that a national convention of State commissioners be held in Louisville in the spring to arrange terms of peace, Congress mean-while agreeing to an early armistice. They also undertook to reorganize the administration of the militia, the plan being to establish new boards and transfer to them all the governors' powers over home troops, camps, and arms.

It is clear that the danger was by no means so great as the excited governors supposed. Organization of revolt was impossible. Local malcontents could not communicate with each other, could not drill without inviting the attentions of home guards and the military, and could find no real leaders. Under these circumstances sedition was like the ghost in Hamlet; it was here, it was there, it was nowhere.

When the Indiana houses met on January 8, 1863, rhetorical Democrats, attacking the usurpers ruling Hoosierdom, asserted they would not give another man or dollar to the war. At this the Republican members of the Senate refused to go into an election of United States Senators unless the Democrats would first pledge themselves to vote for appropriation bills, and for resolutions urg-ing a vigorous prosecution of the war. Their bolt aroused such sharp condemna-tion in some Republican as well as all Democratic quarters that they recon-sidered, and returned to their seats long enough to let their opponents send Thomas A. Hendricks and David Turpie to Washington. Then the Democrats brought forward a reapportionment bill, and a measure which placed primary control of the militia in the hands of a new board of Democratic State officers. At this Morton blew up with a loud bang. "I knew that, if passed," he wrote later, "it would involve the State in civil war in twenty-four hours." [41]

---

when it was employed to stigmatize Democrats of the Indiana State Democratic Convention; see Cincinnati *Gazette* of that date. For the "copperheads" see Paul S. Smith, *Amer. Hist. Rev.*, XXXII (July, 1927), 799, 800; Wood Gray, *The Hidden Civil War*, 140, 141; James F. Flower to Lucius Fairchild, March 26, 1863, Fairchild Papers, Wis. State Hist. Lib. For the early history of the Knights of the Golden Circle see Nevins, *Emergence of Lincoln*, II, 306, 328.

41 Foulke, *Morton*, I, 198–251; Stampp, *op. cit.*, 166 ff.; see Chicago *Morning Post*, Jan. 14, 1863, for Republican censure of the Senate bolt. We shall recur to Morton's feat in keeping spies within the Knights of the Golden Circle.

Actually it might never have passed. It went through the house, but the senate might have stopped it, and if he vetoed it both chambers would have to give it a majority once more. But he took no chances. "I knew there was but one way to prevent the passage of that bill, and that was to break up the legislature. The Republican members determined to withdraw from the House."

This extralegal step was in reality not so much a coup to frustrate a treasonable conspiracy as a party maneuver to make political capital, keep control of militia patronage, and block reapportionment. The struggle was selfish enough on both sides. For a time it seemed that the angry Democratic rump would itself take extralegal action. It proceeded with the forms of a legislative body, threatened to pass the military bill without a quorum, and debated resolutions denouncing the carnage and demanding a war for the restoration of the Union alone. But in the end the legislature died, not to meet again until early in 1865. As it failed to pass any appropriations, Morton had to resort to unconstitutional measures. By strenuous effort, he obtained loans for $135,000 from county officials and private sources, and $250,000 from a special fund held by the War Department. Placing these funds in an extralegal bureau of finance which he created, he carried Indiana through the two crowning years of the war with an energy for which he deserves enduring fame.

Thus the conflict between parties in Indiana temporarily destroyed constitutional government, and made Morton as much a dictator as Charles I. He long edified Union meetings with the tale of how his vigilance had saved a commonwealth on the brink of revolution. Democratic leaders for their part boasted how, if the legislature had been let alone, they would have taken weapons from the arsenal to arm 90,000 men and make sure that the radicals did the people justice. These were revolutionary times, in which dangerous precedents are set.[42]

Governor Yates had to intervene in Illinois with equal directness. At Springfield the Democrats held such control of the legislature that they could maintain a quorum. After electing William A. Richardson to Douglas' old Senate seat, they took up a measure to revamp militia controls, a habeas corpus bill aimed to stop extralegal arrests, and an inquiry into the public and private conduct of Yates. Finally their conduct became so exasperating that Yates decreed the first prorogation of the legislature in the history of the State. The House continued its sessions for a fortnight, but its position was so clearly illegal that the troublemakers gave up in defeat. Not one of their important bills passed.

Indeed, a reaction soon set in throughout the Northwest. Militantly loyal mass meetings were held in all the large cities to answer the anti-war gatherings.

42 Indiana affairs can be most closely followed in the Indianapolis *Daily Journal* and Cincinnati *Commercial*, Jan.–Feb., 1863.

At a tremendous gathering in Indianapolis on February 26, for example, Andrew Johnson read the original manuscript of a letter by Andrew Jackson assailing Calhoun's nullification movement. The sight of the rigid handwriting of Old Hickory moved veteran Jacksonians to tears.[43] Citizens of Chicago organized a boycott of the Chicago *Times*, which some smaller communities supported. "Things look better to me," a Chicago friend wrote Elihu Washburne on February 20, 1863, and a Galena neighbor was equally reassuring: "Everything looks much better than it did thirty days ago . . . these scoundrels are again hunting their holes and keeping quiet." [44] Albert D. Richardson, a shrewd correspondent of the New York *Tribune*, reported early in April, after a week of travel in the Northwest, that the tone of the people had never been better, and that the men of the Valley would sacrifice more for the country than the East. King Sedition would do no more for the Confederacy than King Cotton:

As Prentice has it, the Rebels went in for cotton, and got worsted. Their greatest delusion now is concerning the North-West. Their leading politicians and editors actually seem to believe that, while the great manufacturing and commercial interests of New-England, New-York, Pennsylvania, are fostered and fattened by the war, the farmers of the North-West are in a state of pecuniary ruin, if not of starvation. They would be astonished to see the evidence of prosperity everywhere visible in the great agricultural districts. Chicago, today, is the most flourishing city on the continent, and the vast grain-producing region tributary to it, the most flourishing section.[45]

Spirited war rallies were held in many smaller cities throughout the Northwest. More and more Western regiments in the field held meetings, passed resolutions, and sent them home with indignant letters. As spring approached and the Union girded itself for mighty new efforts, patriotic sentiment mounted.

[V]

This ebb in the opposition to the war revealed the essential weaknesses of Northern disloyalty. It suffered from the fact that while loyal support of the war effort was ever better organized and ever more united, dissent remained amorphous. Malcontents could gather in a single community or a State legislature, but found it impossible to adopt coherent plans on a regional basis. Sedition suffered also from the fact that many of its adherents, like Irish laborers in New York and the rural folk of southern Ohio, Indiana, and Illinois, were poor, ignorant, and illiterate. It suffered from the violent acts and language of hot-

43 "The largest and most enthusiastic meeting ever held in Indiana," ran the N. Y. *Tribune* report; March 3.
44 J. R. Jones, Chicago, and C. L. Stephenson, Galena; Washburne Papers.
45 N. Y. *Tribune*, April 10, 1863. Anthony Trollope's book of wartime travels presents a vivid impression of exuberant growth and prosperity in the Northwest.

heads, for the threats to assassinate Morton in Indiana repelled decent men. It was hampered by inability to gain complete control of any single State government. In the East the legislatures were Republican; in Iowa, Illinois, and Indiana the governors were a citadel of strength for the Union. Despite inflation, prosperity sucked the life out of much of the discontent. But above all, disloyalty was crippled by weak leadership.

The strongest Democrats whom the election of 1862 swept into office were fundamentally loyal. Horatio Seymour as governor of New York knew how searching would be the gaze turned upon him. One of his first acts was to offer Major John T. Sprague of the United States Army the post of adjutant-general as evidence that he desired a man able to work harmoniously with the War Department.[46] He took another judicious step in conferring with Chief Justice John D. Caton of Illinois. Caton, while emphatic that the West would never consent to Southern independence, agreed with him that prostration of the South would upset the proper balance of Union; and Seymour prompted the judge to publish a letter declaring that the North must fight not to crush the South, but to crush the rebellion. The President, thought Caton, might liberate himself from the wild men about him, whereupon the moderates of the South would respond. He and Seymour called themselves conservative Unionists.[47]

Seymour had discounted Lincoln's quasi promise of what he would do if the governor wheeled the Democratic party into line. "Tell him for me," Lincoln bade Weed, "that if he will render this service to his country, I shall cheerfully make way for him as my successor." [48] Weed had delivered this message to Seymour, only to be disappointed by the tone of his inaugural address. The fact was that impassable differences of principle lay between the governor and President—differences centering mainly in the issue of State rights and the future position of the South. Seymour hotly opposed centralization in government, and a "bloody, barbarous, revolutionary" emancipation policy that would disorganize a whole section. But his devotion to national unity and his anxiety to overthrow the Confederacy were indubitable. "For the preservation of this Union I am ready to make every sacrifice," he wrote Lincoln on April 14, 1863. In this he stood with two abler Democrats, Samuel J. Tilden and Abram S. Hewitt.

"Damn those New York men!" said one Cabinet member. "They bleed well, fight well, grumble like hell, and *submit like patriots*."

The strongest opposition editors, too, were entirely with the Union. The idea of its possible overthrow horrified nobody more than James Sheahan in

46 Mitchell, *Seymour*, 333, 157.
47 Caton, *Miscellanies*, 17–31; see Hesseltine, *Lincoln and the War Governors*, 282–284, for Seymour's emphasis on the importance of maintaining a balance among the sections.
48 Weed, *Memoirs*, 428.

Chicago and Manton Marble in New York. Marble was responsible for some bad policies, but when the *Tribune* characterized the *World* as a secessionist journal, he sent Greeley an indignant protest. The epithet was false, he declared. "You know it to be so. The *World* is not in any possible sense a 'secessionist' newspaper. You know that it is not. You know too that whatever means it may advocate or oppose for the suppression of the rebellion and the overthrow and utter discomfiture of the secessionists, its desire for that speedy consummation is as ardent and patriotic as that of any living being." He might have added that it was firmer for the national cause than were a good many nominal patriots who thought only of their wealth.[49]

No editor made louder protestations of patriotism than Medill of the Chicago *Tribune,* but none did more harm by his defeatism than this Republican. His newspaper columns reflected the statements he made in letters to friends: that the armies could not be filled even by drafts, that an armistice was bound to come during 1863, and that the proper goal was to fight for a boundary, confining the Confederacy to the seven coastal slave States. They reflected his belief that the Administration was a "central imbecility," in which Lincoln was but half awake.[50] Douglas' old lieutenant James Sheahan of the Chicago *Morning Post* compared well with Medill. Such Illinois critics as Sheahan, Caton, William A. Richardson, and Storey were often indiscreet, and consistently offensive to Northern radicals. But they had every right to differ from Lincoln and Congress on emancipation, on financial measures, on arbitrary arrests, and on Southern reconstruction. Their dissent was a token of democratic vitality. Lincoln was quite right in saying that those who were not for saving the Union were against it. But it could be saved with varying degrees of departure from the past, and the country needed men who would put brakes on the now sweeping revolution.

Vallandigham, the most theatrical fomenter of sedition, lacked the weight to command any large following. This handsome Ohioan, forty-one when the war began, a graduate of Jefferson College when that Pennsylvania institution had a Southern clientele, had been a friend in Congress of many Southerners and a devotee of State rights. He was essentially a dogmatist, who in any era of

49 Francis Lieber called them the rich fogies. "I was at Senator Fish's last evening," wrote Henry W. Bellows, Feb. 11, 1863, to Frederick Law Olmsted; "met half a dozen men, Aspinwall, Dodge, Beekman, Roosevelt, and so on. The talk *not* good and wholesome! I had to pitch in very extensively, and *put on my jacket*, as you do. I feel full of fight with these rich and lazy do-nothings who use their comfortable castles to make desperate raids with their tongues into the public confidence. Talk—idle, conceited, ignorant talk—is our most fatal enemy." Olmsted Papers, LC. For striking glimpses of the feeble-hearted, selfish, defeatist old-family millionaires of New York see the third volume of the diary of George Templeton Strong. T. J. Barnett, May 13, 1863, reports the Cabinet member's remark; Barlow Papers.
50 To Elihu Washburne, Jan. 16, 1862, Washburne Papers.

religious struggle would have been a Torquemada. Though intelligent, and in his humorless way attractive enough to become speaker of the Ohio house in his mid-twenties, he was unhappy unless he was immolating himself and others for a cause. At Jefferson College he had quarreled with the president on a constitutional question and refused to accept his diploma. Setting his face against the war from the outset, he refused to vote a man or penny toward its continuance. With noncoercion his original shibboleth, after the Emancipation Proclamation he made tolerance of slavery a new watchword.

Vallandigham would rather have seen the nation lost by strict interpretation of constitutional powers than saved by broad construction. The idea of a violent revolt against Washington was always a sweet morsel under his tongue; so was the idea of martyrdom—of course properly publicized. Early in 1863 he told Congress that rather than abet the war, "I had rather my right arm were plucked from its socket, and cast into eternal burnings." As Lincoln wrote, the whole tenor of his speeches had been to arouse men against the conflict, and justified the inference that he was obstructing the war effort. But this perverse mixture of exhibitionist, fanatic, rabble-rouser, and traitor, highly adept at rallying Ohio malcontents, never gained a substantial following outside his own State, and approached so close to the line of the ridiculous that a single adroit push by Lincoln was presently to send him tumbling across it.

The fact that, thus lacking any strong leader, sedition subsided in the late winter and early spring of 1863, justified a greater moderation in dealing with political offenders. The conscience of liberals, as we have seen, had long been sensitive. William Cullen Bryant, commenting on Seymour's inaugural, wrote that his arguments against arbitrary arrests and martial law had so much force and truth that they must appeal to a majority of all parties. The conviction of Samuel Bowles, Bryant, and George William Curtis was that while harsh measures had been a necessity when the war first began, the abatement of the crisis made leniency desirable. Without stern action, declared Bryant, we would have lost Maryland, Missouri, and Kentucky; now it was no longer needed.

Thanks to the growth of an improved organization for administering the war,[51] a workable system for policing troublemakers emerged by the spring of 1863. Control under Stanton had been concentrated in the offices of Joseph Holt as Judge-Advocate General, and James P. Fry as Provost-Marshal General. Both offices had been specially created by Congress. Lincoln personally had selected Holt, confident that this Kentucky Democrat, whom he appointed September 3, 1862, would deal justly with political prisoners. He brought to his duties courage, energy—and ruthlessness. While it was the intention of Congress that civilians suspected of disloyal acts should be arraigned before

51 See *National Almanac*, 1863, 1864, sections on War Department, for its steady growth; L. D. Ingersoll, *Hist. of the War Dept.*, 344-352.

civil courts, Lincoln believed that trial by military commissions was often preferable. Holt adopted a policy which enabled the military authorities to arrest, imprison, and try many supposed political offenders who were never properly subject to courts-martial.

As for Fry, an Illinois graduate of West Point, he was recommended for his post by Grant. Taking over his duties on March 17, 1863, he showed the traits of an efficient martinet. Much the greater part of his work concerned recruiting, conscription, and desertions, but he was expected also to deal with general enemies of the government. He did this by the appointment of provost-marshals for each Congressional district, who in turn named deputy provost-marshals for the counties. The machinery thus created soon became one of the most potent arms of the government, systematic, thorough, by no means free from corruption, and widely hated. By the time the war ended Fry was as hotly controversial a figure as Holt, which is saying a great deal.[52] But the treatment of political offenders had unquestionably been given system, and officers worked by rule, not whim.

Some of the worst injustices, meanwhile, had been partially rectified. Just before Congress met in December, 1862, the Administration directed the liberation of all persons confined on charges of discouraging enlistments or impeding the draft. At once a sweeping release began. Prisoners who had sighed in as many as four different "bastilles" heard the locks grate to release them. As we have seen, Marshal George V. Kane of Baltimore and nine fellow townsmen long in jail breathed free air again. Stanton had previously empowered Judge-Advocate Turner of the Washington district and others to release prisoners, after inquiry, pretty much at discretion. Colonel Lafayette C. Baker, appointed a special provost-marshal, had become head of an alert body of War Department spies, and enjoying use of the Department's secret fund, he came perhaps as near a Fouché as the United States could produce. His jurisdiction touched political offenders as well as deserters, bounty jumpers, shady speculators, and saboteurs, and his zeal outran his sense of propriety.[53] But if the government still had to observe the rule of safety first, the period of its worst offenses against civil liberties was now over.

[VI]

"Mammoth War Demonstration. Immense Meeting at the Cooper Institute. Unity and Victory the Battle Cry." These were the headlines which the New

52 The Univ. of Chicago has a doctoral dissertation by Mary B. Allen on Holt. Fry was highly praised by Nicolay and Hay; for a more critical estimate see Milton, *Lincoln and the Fifth Column*, 250, 251.
53 Baker's cloak-and-dagger thriller, *Hist. of the U. S. Secret Service*, must be used with reserve.

York *Herald* on March 7, 1863, placed over its account of a demonstration headed by War Democrats; the largest and most fervent gathering in the metropolis, it declared, since the Union Square mass meetings of 1861. William Cullen Bryant had presided. Similar meetings of War Democrats, as we have seen, took place in the Northwest.

Even more significant of the nation's purpose was the fact that the Congress which adjourned March 4, 1863, had carried through the first clearly national conscription law. The work primarily of Henry Wilson in the Senate and Thaddeus Stevens in the House, it made every able-bodied male citizen between twenty and forty-five liable to military service. An elaborate machinery for its enforcement was provided, and the War Department left no doubt that it would be employed with rigor. Lincoln had urged the legislation, writing that the country could no longer waste time in trying to revamp a volunteer system that was patently inadequate. The terms of the new draft act, as we shall see, were highly unfair; its application was to encounter heavy difficulties, and its history to reveal gross inefficiency and scandal. It in fact disgraced a nation which might easily have profited from Europe's long experience with conscription. But the determination which dictated it and the defiance of disloyal and half-hearted groups which inspired its passage were thoroughly creditable.

Five Union forces, as spring drew on, stood poised against five points in the long Confederate line; the armies of Hooker on the Rappahannock, Rosecrans in southern Tennessee, Grant before Vicksburg, and Banks near Port Hudson, with the squadron of Flag Officer S. F. DuPont before Charleston. The North waited prayerfully, hopefully, resolutely to see what they would accomplish.

In each previous spring of the war men had confidently hoped that the conflict would end by New Year's. Millions had believed this in 1861; millions again in 1862. Now Northerners were too disillusioned to indulge in prophecy. Here and there a voice was lifted in encouragement to the people, as when the New York *Tribune* in March asserted its faith that the next Fourth would be celebrated throughout a restored and peaceful Union, but such statements had a hollow ring. When men thought of the future, too, they now realized that peace would merely raise the curtain on a complex array of harassing new problems. Every day brought nearer the time when Johnny would come marching home. It also brought nearer the time when men must grapple with financial disorder, a new economic world, the reconstruction of conquered States, the care of the freedmen, and a dozen other situations so tremendous and so baffling that prewar America began to look like some far-off peaceful Arcadia.

16

Roads to Vicksburg

IT WAS clear to men in Washington that even amid reverses, Lincoln revealed a steady augmentation of self-confidence and decision. The Emancipation Proclamation had enhanced his prestige. He had fully established his personal and Presidential authority. As he had defeated Seward at the outset, so now he had defeated the Congressional radicals by compelling them to revise their Confiscation Act, and drop their intended reorganization of the Cabinet. He knew how far to trust Stanton, whose brutal temper seldom impaired a sound judgment and an unshakable devotion to the cause. He knew how to use Chase, whose Presidential ambitions, as he said, were like a horsefly on an ox, keeping him up to his work. A Lincoln legend was gaining currency: the legend, as John W. Forney put it, of a great, peculiar, mysterious man who with quaint sagacity did his work in his own honest way without regard to temporizers or hotheads.[1]

Though now emphatically commander-in-chief, his attitude toward the army had a certain ambivalence. He was ready to make and unmake commanders with decision. He had brusquely displaced, or approved the displacement, of generals who proved incompetent or put themselves in impossible situations: McDowell, Frémont, McClellan, Buell, Burnside. As in civil affairs he told Sumner and others, "My policy is to have no policy," so in military affairs he was ready to experiment pragmatically. To some extent the appointments of Halleck and Pope had been the result of radical machinations directed less toward the elevation of these men than the destruction of McClellan; but to a greater extent they sprang from Lincoln's despair over McClellan's delays and willingness to use trial, error, and retrial. He had been swift to discard Pope. Unfortunately, his field of choice was always limited. He knew when he turned to Hooker that the general had a bad record of drinking, gambling, and emotional instability; but who else was so available? Welles wagged his gray beard

---

1 Welles, *Diary*, I, 212, 219, 227, etc.; Forney's statement to a Gettysburg crowd in the fall of 1863 is in Hay, *Diary and Letters*, Dennett ed., 121.

dubiously and Montgomery Blair spoke of John Barleycorn, but they suggested no alternative.[2]

As a practical man, Lincoln knew that although West Point could teach engineering and old-style tactics based on Jomini, with a little strategy, it could do no more to guarantee character than Oxford or Harvard. While it prided itself on fostering standards befitting "an officer and a gentleman," its graduates in the slack atmosphere of the regular army all too often developed what were euphemistically termed habits. And certainly West Point singularly failed to armor its officers and gentleman against the sin of selfish jealousy. In political life personal jealousy is a much larger element in conduct than is usually supposed: the mutual jealousy of a Jackson and a Clay, a Blaine and a Conkling. In military affairs it may be far more dangerous, for it plays with human lives. On January 21, 1863, Lincoln approved the verdict of the court-martial which, under General David Hunter, had tried Fitz-John Porter on accusations growing out of Second Manassas.[3] Pronounced guilty of all the charges preferred, Porter was immediately dismissed from the service. The finding was dubious. After a long interval, a board of review was to report in Porter's favor (1879), and the President was to cancel his disqualification from holding office under the United States (1882). The verdict nevertheless underlined the fact that after the appointment of Pope, McClellan and his army partisans had failed of the zealous cooperation that was their duty, had chilled the spirit of their troops, and had contributed to the loss of a great battle and thousands of lives.

It is probably just to say that Porter deserved removal, but that dismissal in disgrace was too severe a penalty, and it was imposed for the wrong reasons. He had a strong defense for his conduct at Second Manassas. But that his spirit was viciously bad is proved by his many letters, some prudently left unsigned, in the papers of Manton Marble of the *World*. "Bah!" he burst out at one point. "You have fools at the head of our country, and our people are no better." On August 5 he predicted Pope's imminent failure, and the overthrow of Halleck if that general did not succeed in ousting Stanton—with a possible revolution. He was venomously suspicious of Lincoln, whom he accused of trying to cause McClellan's defeat to prolong the war, and violently hostile to all who wished to fight "an abolition war." He was better out of the army.

Lincoln had no patience with the harsher disciplinary ideas of professional soldiers. He knew that a great citizen army gathered from an undisciplined

2 Welles, *Diary*, I, 229, 230. Welles learned that Hooker "indulges in the free use of whisky, gets excited, and is fond of play." Everyone knew that he talked too much and too indiscreetly.

3 Besides Hunter, the judges were Generals Hitchcock, Rufus King, Garfield, Prentiss, Ricketts, Casey, Buford, and Morris. Lincoln acted on an able review by Judge Advocate-General Holt. For army ideas cf. David Donald, *Lincoln Reconsidered*, Ch. 5.

democracy could not be treated like the professional army of an Old World kingdom. If hard-jawed generals insisted on regular "butcher's days" for sleeping sentinels, men absent without leave, and other delinquents, the people would rebel. His repeated interference with military executions reassured the Northern public.[4] Lincoln believed also that the military mind often adhered to strategic preconceptions at the expense of common sense. He so concluded when Rosecrans insisted that the proper time to attack Bragg would be not while Grant was approaching Vicksburg, but after he had taken the city; and he told Rosecrans this in no uncertain terms.[5] While McClellan initially conceived of his campaign in terms of sieges of Yorktown and Richmond, Lincoln kept trying to make him comprehend that the real object was the destruction of Lee's army in open battle.

Yet Lincoln at the same time showed high respect for army organization and the leadership of professional soldiers. Halleck had a profound regard for both, and great as was the President's irritation over Halleck's limpness and total incapacity for any active command, he was influenced by his adviser's attitude. Halleck constantly exerted himself against what he called political generals. He helped frustrate the many radical friends of Frémont who pressed Lincoln to give him another army; he helped frustrate radical friends of Sigel, like Bryant; he stood in the way of Lew Wallace, who had once expressed contempt for him all too freely. He was undoubtedly pleased when another political figure, Ben Butler, was relieved on November 9, 1862, from command of the Department of the Gulf, closing next month his efficient but controversial administration in New Orleans. For Lincoln to keep Halleck as nominal head of the armies and confer with him steadily was to give partial assent to his strong professionalism, particularly as Stanton supported it.[6]

Lincoln showed his deference to professional soldiers when he acquiesced in Grant's assumption of the chief command of the Vicksburg expedition on February 2, 1863. Sometime in December, Blair in the Cabinet had alluded to the fact that McClernand was being crowded aside, saying that a combination existed to prevent his getting the command. Records Welles: "The President started from his chair when the remark was made and said it should not be so." Stanton reassured him. But now it *was* so. Grant, three weeks after McClernand's

4 For one of many examples see Lincoln's order May 21, 1863, stopping the execution of T. M. Campbell; *Works*, VI, 225.
5 Lincoln to Rosecrans, Aug. 10, 1863; *idem*, VI, 377, 378.
6 A strong New York committee, supported by Greeley, Bryant, and Daniel S. Dickinson, urged Lincoln on May 30, 1863, to give Frémont command of 10,000 colored troops; and Senator Sumner endorsed the project. Lincoln assented to the idea in principle, but practical obstacles were insuperable; *idem*, VI, 239, 242–244. For Lew Wallace, see *Autobiography*, II, 579, 580. The MS Diary of Fanny Seward, who liked Butler, reflects his ambitions.

capture of Arkansas Post, had taken full control. All McClernand's protests were in vain. The President assented because Grant outranked McClernand, had far better professional equipment, and possessed Halleck's firm support. He wrote McClernand that he must accept the situation, for he was doing better for himself and the country than he could if he provoked a controversy—and Lincoln already had enough Army squabbles on his hands.[7]

The Union, as spring in 1863 stole up from the South, possessed a new and untested commander in Virginia, Hooker. It possessed three commanders in the Mississippi Valley whom people regarded as still on trial: Grant, Rosecrans, and N. P. Banks. The first two had inconclusive records, and Banks no record at all. The general situation was not bright. During the fall the Army of the Potomac had been forced back into Maryland, and the Army of the Cumberland back to the Ohio; Grant's march down the Mississippi Central had been broken up with loss and confusion. Lincoln, in daily consultation with Stanton and Halleck, could find little encouragement in recent minor gains in ground.[8]

[I]

Banks was a clever, interesting, showy politician without much depth or purpose. But he was a favorite of Seward's, and a man of influence in the Bay State, where he had honestly earned his prominence. The son of a cotton mill superintendent, he was almost as much self-educated as Lincoln, for he had been taken out of school to become "the bobbin boy of Waltham." He trained himself in languages, public speaking, acting, and law. At thirty-seven, after service in the legislature, he was chosen president of the able State constitutional convention of 1853. Three years later, in 1856, a nominal Know-Nothing but actual Republican, he was elected speaker of the national House after a historic struggle; and in that office he displayed tact, fairness, and decision. Nobody did more that year to bring forward Frémont, with whom he formed a fast friendship. Elected governor of Massachusetts, he made a shrewd and progressive record, paying special attention to education. When Sumter fell he volunteered, and Lincoln lifted him from his new presidency of the Illinois Central to become a major-general. But he lacked high capacity, and his service in the Shenandoah suggested that he had little aptitude for war.[9]

The inception of the Banks expedition had been peculiarly maladroit. Ref-

7 Welles, *Diary*, I, 217; Lincoln, *Works*, VI, 70, 71.
8 Uncertainty in Washington as to Grant's capacities was reflected in Browning, *Diary*, I, 591, and Welles, *Diary*, I, 387. Welles states that as late as the fall of 1862 neither Stanton nor Halleck cared much for Grant. Cf. Cadwallader, *Campaigning With Grant*, 60–62.
9 For caustic estimates of Banks see Moncure D. Conway, *Autobiography*, I, 235; Welles, *Diary*, II, 18, 26.

ugees from Texas had assured Stanton that their State might easily be won back to the Union, while a Northern force could also cut off the large flow of European supplies overland from Matamoras. With Stanton's consent, they applied to Governors Curtin, Morgan, and Andrew for troops. With characteristic enthusiasm, Andrew assented on the understanding that the expedition would invade Texas, that Frémont would be put in command, and that the volunteers should be given facilities to settle there as a staunch Union community. Other Northerners shared his hopes. But the plan went completely awry. In the first place, the Administration sent the troops not to Texas, but to Louisiana, largely because it felt it had to displace Butler from New Orleans. (A small force that did go to Galveston was soon compelled to surrender.) In the second place, Stanton gave the command not to Frémont, but to Banks, and in the third, all idea of permanent settlement in the area soon went glimmering. Banks quickly found his energies fully occupied in fighting.

As Ben Butler's successor, he was expected to hold the conquered parts of Louisiana, seize the lower Red River as highway to an early conquest of Texas, and move up the Mississippi to help Grant take Vicksburg. It was a large assignment; too large for an army of about 30,000, half of which had to be used for garrison work. Banks reached New Orleans in mid-December, 1862. A third of his force immediately ascended to Baton Rouge, which Brigadier-General Cuvier Grover recaptured with little fighting.[10] This brought the Union troops within eighteen or twenty miles of Port Hudson, a natural stronghold which the Confederates had diligently fortified. Using abundant slave labor, they had mounted twenty heavy siege guns along the bluff eighty feet above the river, and built strong defenses on both the water and land sides of the town. The garrison numbering about 15,000 men, Grover's 10,000 could not assault the place. Yet to reach the Red River and then approach Vicksburg, Banks had somehow to get through. Both Port Hudson and Vicksburg drew most of their supplies from the Red River Valley.

His first plan, which he tried to carry into effect late in January, 1863, was to move a force up west of the Mississippi, through a country full of rivers, bayous, and swamps, past Port Hudson to the Red. This force was stopped by an accumulation of debris blocking a vital bayou. Meanwhile, the Confederate capture of two Union warships which had run past Vicksburg and entered the Red River alarmed Farragut, who decided he should take his fleet past Port Hudson at once.[11] It was important to Grant's movements that Northern ves-

---

10   Fred H. Harrington, *Fighting Politician: Major-General N. P. Banks*, 119.
11   One of the captured ships was the new ironclad *Indianola*, armed with nine- and eleven-inch Dahlgrens; the Confederates briefly hoped to use her to command this section of the Mississippi, but in a panic over an attack by an old ship disguised as a Union ram shortly blew her up. *Lossing*, II, 590.

sels command the 200-mile stretch of the Mississippi between Vicksburg and Port Hudson, and blockade the Red.

Farragut asked Banks to make a diversionary demonstration against Port Hudson while he steamed past the guns. He gathered his fleet of four frigates, five gunboats, and six mortar boats at a convenient island while Banks mustered 12,000 men for a simulated attack. But although the admiral managed the movement with skill and dash, he met only partial success. His squadron began moving before ten at night (March 13) under a plan that the big ships would do the fighting while the smaller ones added power. The Confederates, however, touched off bonfires which made the river light as day; the force of the current slowed the vessels; the enemy fire proved extremely hot and effective; and the troops gave no help. Receiving word that Banks was five miles away, Farragut growled: "He had as well be in New Orleans or Baton Rouge for all the good he is doing us." In the end the flagship *Hartford* and gunboat *Albatross* got by, but the others were forced back, and the frigate *Mississippi*, set on fire, blew up with sixty-five men missing.

Much pained, Farragut used the word "disaster" in his report to the Navy Department. Nevertheless, he had accomplished the greater part of his purpose. The two ships he had taken up could not patrol the 200 miles to Vicksburg, but they could blockade the Red and cut off its supplies. Their utility justified the risk he had taken. "The Mississippi is again cut off," Pemberton lamented to Richmond on March 19, adding that "neither subsistence nor ordnance can come or go." The next day he sent word to General Richard Taylor on the west bank: "Port Hudson depends almost entirely for supplies upon the other side of the river." One of Taylor's commissary officers, rejoicing on March 17 that four supply steamers had just arrived from the Red, wrote that the prospect for more was gloomy. "Five others are below with full cargoes designed for Port Hudson, but it is reported that the Federal gunboats are blockading the river." [12]

Banks would have done well to keep his army near Port Hudson, where the garrison was soon threatened by hunger. His best usefulness lay in aiding Grant's movement to clear the Mississippi. But he found the temptation of the wide Louisiana hinterland irresistible. April 20 found him marching into Opelousas, where he announced plans for a corps of Negro troops which would ultimately reach eighteen regiments. Early next month he reached Alexandria on the Red River only a few hours after Admiral Porter's gunboats had seized the place. This town is almost in the center of Louisiana, and Banks's operations had brought under control a region of fertile plantations, cattle ranches, and great forests, interlaced by waterways and swamps. His troops were delighted by

12 Mahan, *Farragut,* 200-225.

what they had accomplished. They had defeated enemy columns, taken mountains of cotton bales and a mass of booty, and captured twenty guns. Thousands of slaves had fled to their army camps. But all this contributed little to the main Union object.

In a sharp reprimand, Halleck pointed out to Banks that his real duty was to maintain a heavy pressure on the Mississippi. It was all too true that, as Halleck declared, the enemy rejoiced in Banks's relaxation of grip. Kirby-Smith termed it one of the most desirable events of the war. Not until May 14 did Banks, yielding to the War Department, begin to swing his army back to invest Port Hudson. He had just heard from Grant, by a letter dated May 10, that the Northern forces in the Vicksburg area had crossed to the east bank of the river below that city. On May 23–24 Banks's troops encircled Port Hudson as if for a siege. They were commanded by generals of ability, Grover, C. C. Augur, T. W. Sherman, and Godfrey Weitzel; and Farragut was at hand to shell the Confederate works.[13]

Then, on May 27, Banks committed a terrible blunder. Before his army was fully assembled, before his officers had finished reconnoitring the position, he made a furious but ill-coordinated assault. Two regiments of colored troops, the First and Second Louisiana, fought in this first important test with a valor matching that of the white soldiers. The defenders, with every advantage of entrenchments and artillery, held the Union forces at bay along the whole line. When the day closed Banks had lost nearly 300 dead and 1,550 wounded, while Confederates casualties fell short of 300. Under the hot June sun, Banks then began a close siege; the garrison suffering more and more from shortages of food, medicine, and general supplies.

[II]

More than 300 miles northeast of Vicksburg as the crow flies, Rosecrans in his hard-won occupation of Murfreesboro faced a question mark. If Bragg had retreated to Chattanooga, the Union army could have turned in that direction without anxiety. But Bragg had marched instead to Tullahoma, almost due south of Murfreesboro. Here he could move by rail or road to protect Chattanooga; he could equally send troops to the Vicksburg area. Nor was Rosecrans, at late as April 1, 1863, free from apprehension that reinforcements from both

13 Harrington, *Banks*, 119 ff. James K. Hosmer in *The Color Guard* describes the plantations, ranches, and bayous, the fighting, and the plundering. He saw mansions sacked with ruthless destruction of furniture and mirrors. This was war. "Great barbarities, however, I fear have been committed. They say ear-rings have been torn from the ears of women, and brooches from their bosoms, while they sat with children in their arms."

Vicksburg and Virginia might swiftly be sent to Bragg, who would then advance against the areas which Rosecrans was protecting; against Nashville, against Kentucky.

On the Confederate side Joseph E. Johnston, recovering from his wound at Seven Pines, had been assigned late in November, 1862, to chief command in the West, with the armies of Kirby-Smith, Pemberton, and Bragg under his supervision. He arrived at Chattanooga, his headquarters, on December 4, to learn that Pemberton was falling back before Grant's march down the Mississippi Central, and that Richmond had peremptorily ordered Lieutenant-General T. H. Holmes and his army near Little Rock to reinforce him. He also learned that Jefferson Davis, fearful that Holmes might not arrive in time, requested him to detach sufficient troops from Bragg's command to succor Pemberton. Johnston replied that the Little Rock forces could get to the Vicksburg area much more quickly than any of Bragg's, and that it would be unwise to weaken the army in Middle Tennessee. He contented himself with telegraphing Bragg to send a large cavalry force to raid in Grant's rear and cut his communications. The alert Bragg had already acted, and we have seen how effectively cavalry tore up the railroad behind Grant and destroyed his Holly Springs base.[14]

The Confederate government had in fact been highly alarmed in December for the safety of Vicksburg. Jefferson Davis hastened westward to examine the situation in Mississippi and Tennessee. "Private information from many sources," wrote R. G. H. Kean, third in rank in the War Department, on December 13, "represents the tone and temper of the people of the Mississippi Valley as very unsound. *They are submitting.*" [15] At Murfreesboro and Chattanooga the uneasy Davis, overruling Johnston, ordered 9,000 of Bragg's infantry and artillery transferred to Pemberton's command; a force that at the moment was useless to Pemberton, but would have been invaluable to Bragg at Murfreesboro. In mid-January Governor Pettus of Mississippi convoked the legislature to mobilize the whole military force of the State behind Pemberton. Although the retreat of Grant and repulse of Sherman gave Southerners momentary relief, they remained anxious in the extreme. Johnston, visiting Vicksburg with Davis on January 20, was disheartened by errors of fortification.[16]

Johnston had grounds for personal despondency in the vague and precarious nature of his command, in his uncertain health, in the dissensions between Bragg and his chief officers, and in the weak information services of the widely scattered Western forces. He was nominally in command of three Confederate

14 Johnston, *Narrative*, 147–150.
15 Edward Younger, ed., *Inside the Confederate Government*, 33.
16 Johnston, *Narrative*, 152.

armies. But how real could his command be? One army was on the Tennessee; another, hundreds of miles away, was on the Mississippi; still another, Kirby-Smith's, soon operated behind the river in Louisiana. Each had its special object and problems; each faced an adversary with a special goal. How could one general direct all three? When Johnston explained this to Davis, the President replied that since Richmond was so distant, it seemed necessary to have an officer in the West possessing authority to transfer troops in an emergency from one command to another. Johnston rejoined that such transfers were impracticable, for each army was weaker than its foe, and the forces were too far separated to help each other effectively. This exchange did not soften the mutual dislike long felt by the two men, and thereafter the testy Johnston made his lack of confidence in the President and Secretary Seddon plainly felt.[17]

Meanwhile, grave dissensions in Bragg's camp after Murfreesboro threatened not only his summary overthrow, but an impairment of public morale throughout that part of the South. A quarrel had long smoldered between him and Breckinridge. When Bragg retreated from Kentucky his volunteers from that State, realizing they were going into a long exile, grumbled that they were being marched south to protect the Mississippi and Alabama planters; Breckinridge expressed sympathy with them; and the two generals became deadly enemies. Soon afterward a Kentucky soldier was tried for a small offense, and Bragg ordered him shot. He was quoted as saying that Kentucky blood was too feverish for the health of the army, and that he intended to stop the corn-crackers' grumbling if he had to execute every man. Breckinridge, angrily declaring that Kentuckians would never be treated like slaves, asserted that the shooting would be military murder. Company after company of Kentucky troops, swept by angry excitement, rushed from their tents to stack arms. With difficulty the mutiny was composed—and the man was shot. Then, after Murfreesboro, some Kentucky soldiers charged that Bragg had ordered them to make an attack which he knew would end in useless slaughter.[18]

In fact, Kentuckians and Tennesseeans demanded Bragg's retirement as hotly as Ohioans and Indianians had demanded Buell's. He was a martinet whom men would have hated even without his failures. A Louisianan who traveled through the region in January found the people violently denouncing him. Intelligent citizens averred that he had never intended to hold Kentucky, and that from

17 *Ibid.*, 154, 155. Kean wrote April 12, 1863, of Johnston: "He treats the Department as an enemy with whom he holds no communication which he can avoid and against which he only complains and finds fault."

18 This is the account given in the Frankfort, Ky., *Commonwealth*, Feb. 11, 1863, in a long editorial purporting to be authentic; and in the Nashville *Union* quoted in the Chicago *Morning Post*, Feb. 23, 1863.

the time when, standing between Buell and Louisville, he failed to crush the first and take the second, they had lost all faith in him. Most of his own officers called his campaign indefensible.[19]

Bragg quarreled with Leonidas Polk, who condemned his mismanagement of the forces at Perryville. He quarreled with Buckner, who refused to answer his questions upon the extent to which he had sustained Polk in what Bragg called "acknowledged disobedience." One reason why he kept silence, Buckner explained, was that he did not wish to "aggravate the feeling which public rumor imputes as existing between you and your subordinate commanders." Bragg also quarreled with Hardee. When he sent a belated report of his Kentucky campaign to Davis late in May, he explained its tardiness on the ground that he had waited to gather evidence refuting the charges against him by Hardee and Polk; charges which, if unanswered, "would subject me to the severest criticism and injustice." All these officers, while disliking Bragg's frigid manner, morose temper, and harsh acts, were actuated primarily by a belief that he had proved utterly incompetent; that, as General Basil W. Duke later put it, his vacillation and timidity had thrown away one of the greatest Southern opportunities to win the war. They made it clear to Richmond that they wished him removed.[20] When Bragg himself queried Generals Breckinridge, Cleburne, and Hardee upon their attitude, they told him bluntly that they believed a change in the command of the army was imperative.

Davis, who never forgot his Mexican War debt to Bragg, went so far as to send Johnston in late January to make an investigation at Bragg's headquarters. But his faith in his old favorite remained unshaken, and when Johnston advised against removal—on the ground that the troops retained a strong fighting spirit —he kept Bragg in command. The general's army, however, was soon much weakened. On May 10 Johnston sent two of his brigades west to reinforce the Confederates struggling to save Vicksburg, and a fortnight later ordered Breckinridge's division to follow.[21]

The Union army in Middle Tennessee meanwhile fared better, but remained quite inert. Rosecrans was as popular with his officers and men as Bragg was unpopular. He was an excellent organizer and disciplinarian, and a tremendous worker. As he needed little sleep, he sometimes toiled at his desk from ten in the morning until one or two that night—to the anguish of his aides. He had a keen instinct for system, and when he took over the army from Buell immediately reorganized its staff work. He established courier lines connecting head-

19   J. G. Leach, Waterproof, La., Feb. 2, 1863, to R. M. McKee; McKee Papers, Ala. State Archives.

20   Polk, *Polk*, II, 198 ff.; Buckner, April 26, 1863, to Bragg, Palmer Coll., Western Reserve Hist. Soc.; Duke, *Reminiscences*, 308.

21   Johnston, *Narrative*, 161, 162.

quarters with all the camps, collected military maps from every source, called in Unionists from the surrounding area to give information, and kept a large body of clerks hard at work on papers. Slovenliness angered him, for he regarded war as an exact science. Any officer who brought in an incomplete report was sternly rebuked: "How did you know this? How did your informant know? Why didn't you get all the particulars? What are you an officer for? War means killing!" No officer was allowed to take a furlough or resign unless his health broke. He was swift to get rid of incompetents. "I care not for individuals," he would say. "Everything for the service, nothing for individuals."

Yet he spent much time among troops, riding out for reviews or inspection. Examining equipment with searching care, he would sharply rebuke a private for not getting a defective bayonet, canteen, or knapsack replaced. "Go to your captain and demand what you need," he would order. "Go to him every day for it. Bore him for it!" He liked young men, full of vigor and snap. "Young men without experience are better than experienced old men, for they will learn." And he did his best to lick young officers into shape. "Your knowledge of geography is bad," he would say raspingly. "You make a poor statement. You don't observe closely." One of his fixed ideas was that cavalry must be energetically employed as the eyes of the army, and he lost no time in forming a strong mounted force under General David S. Stanley. Using the cavalry, he strove to improve his maps, which were one of his passions.[22]

Yet the lively, temperamental Rosecrans was one of the many officers who displayed high capacity in routine tasks, but who in the hour of adversity became prey to irresolution and frustration. Grant's distrust grew after Iuka and Corinth. When Charles A. Dana found opportunity to study "Old Rosey" closely in the field he noted a curious mixture of weakness and strength. "He has invention, fertility, and knowledge," Dana reported to the War Department "but he has no strength of will and no concentration of purpose." This accurate judgment harmonized with the conclusions of the correspondent Cadwallader. Intensely ambitious, and fond of command, the general was feeble at just those times when decision was most needed. At critical junctures he became erratic in judgment and deficient in administrative grasp. One fault was his inability to depute work; he insisted on personal supervision of every department, so that subordinates could not act until he gave the word. Another fault was "his passion for universal applause," and his reluctance to hurt the feelings of high officers by censuring their blunders.[23]

22   W. D. Bickham (Cincinnati *Commercial* correspondent), *Rosecrans' Campaign, passim;* N. Y. *Tribune,* Jan. 8, 1863; *Diary and Letters of Rutherford B. Hayes,* II, 27 ff. For Grant's critical views see his *Memoirs,* Ch. 40.
23   Dana to Stanton, Chattanooga, ct. 14, 17, 1863, Dana Papers, LC, offer a thorough estimate; Cadwallader's MS Diary, Ill. State Hist. Lib., "Four Years with General Grant,

This winter and spring found him managing his army well, but also keeping it inert. With Vicksburg the central goal in the West, his refusal to contribute anything toward its capture gravely offended Grant and Sherman in the field, and Lincoln and Stanton in Washington.

Struggling to seize his prize, Grant sent repeated petitions for help. At first his desire was simply that Rosecrans should occupy Bragg sufficiently to prevent him from sending aid to Pemberton. He wrote repeatedly to Halleck urging that the army be moved energetically in one of two directions: to threaten Bragg at Tullahoma, or lay Chattanooga open to capture. Halleck, approving the proposal, repeatedly ordered Rosecrans to advance. But the general took a stubborn stand on the old military maxim which forbade commanders to fight two decisive battles at the same time. As Grant later dryly remarked, it would be bad to be defeated in two decisive battles fought the same day, but it would not be bad to win both! [24]

His inaction puzzled and offended the President. When Lincoln learned that part of Bragg's force had gone west, he felt keen anxiety lest Grant be overwhelmed by a concentration of enemy strength. As he wrote Rosecrans later, he thought this "the exactly proper time for you to attack Bragg with what force he had left." At one point he told Halleck that he should give explicit orders to this effect, and Halleck replied that he had already done so in substance. "Soon after," Lincoln recalled in reviewing the record with the general, "dispatches from Grant abated my anxiety for him, and in proportion abated my anxiety about any movement of yours. When afterwards, however, I saw a dispatch of yours arguing that the right time for you to attack Bragg was not before but would be after the fall of Vicksburg, it impressed me very strangely. . . . It seemed no other than the proposition that you could better fight Bragg *when* Johnston should be at liberty to return and assist him, than you could *before* he could so return to his assistance." [25]

The important fact was that as Grant before Vicksburg received no aid from Banks, so he got none from Rosecrans. That general could say much for his position. He not only gave the detachment of aid anxious thought, but on June 8 queried all his principal officers for their opinion. Without exception,

---

1862–66," contains passages on Rosecrans omitted from the printed version. Dana's criticism of the general was sharp: "His mind scatters, there is no system in his use of his busy days and restless nights, no courage against individuals in his composition. . . ." Cadwallader also summed him up harshly: "a military demagogue of the most pronounced type." But Rosecrans had important virtues; he was hard-working and conscientious, he looked after his troops' welfare, and he was more dynamic than Buell. Rosecrans Papers, UCLA.

24 Grant, *Memoirs*, Ch. 40. See Bruce Catton's admirable study, *Grant Moves South*, 304 ff.

25 Aug. 10, 1863, *Works*, VI, 377, 378.

all of them—Sheridan, Thomas, T. L. Crittenden, and others—advised against it, most of them in strong terms. "If Grant fails before Vicksburg," wrote John M. Palmer, "it would be unfortunate if this army is then found entangled in the interior of Tennessee." However, Rosecrans might well regret later that he had not taken a bolder course.

[III]

It was a mighty force which Grant commanded when at the end of January, 1863, he arrived at Young's Point before Vicksburg to take direct charge of the movement against the fortress; and mightily did he employ it. Jefferson Davis had said at Jackson on his Western tour that retention of the Mississippi was a question of life and death for the Confederacy. If Vicksburg and Port Hudson fell, all the men and supplies in the rich areas of Arkansas, Texas, western Louisiana, and the Yazoo district of Mississippi would be lost to the South. Hope ran high in Confederate circles that the Union troops, repulsed in their first effort at a breakthrough, could be baffled. Some Northern officers of the army were daunted by the obstacles, but with the dogged determination that always marked him, Grant was ready to take every risk to win.[26]

With determination, with faith in his Western fighters—and with the courage of desperation, for Grant knew that he was still on trial, and that a long delay or new retreat might send him home broken. His enemies and detractors were urging that he be removed, and some newspapers were insisting on it. Before long Lorenzo Thomas was sent from Washington on a double mission; one errand to examine conditions in the contraband camps along the river and encourage military use of the Negroes, the other to investigate military affairs with an eye to a possible reshuffle of high officers. On his heels would come Charles A. Dana, also with a double charge; ostensibly to straighten out delays in the paymaster service, actually to ascertain the true capacity of Grant and others. The commander knew that he had to do something, and do it soon. But it was part of his character to drive forward against all impediments, and he took heart from the mighty panoply under his orders. He had a hundred thousand volunteers, reported the press; and though this nearly doubled his real num-

26 Jesse Grant, paying a visit to his son's department early in 1863, paused at Covington on his return to write Elihu Washburne. Ulysses, he commented, had a big contract on his hands; he had a good many generals with him in whom he placed confidence; but "I have been thinking it might be good policy to send one of the able generals from Washington now out of command to advise with him. I mean Franklin or Burnside. Franklin was his classmate at West Point, and I know he has a high opinion of his skill and abilities." Jesse added that this idea was original with himself. Grant would not have thanked him for it!

bers, it was true that he possessed a massive superiority—if he could bring it to bear on the enemy.

Grant in fact had a quadruple ordeal to face, with enemy forces not the principal threat to his future. He had to meet all the obstacles of an impracticable country, the river, the bayous, the mud, the high water, and a sickly climate. He had to face resentment amounting almost to enmity in McClernand, now reduced to corps commander. Not least, he had to face weakness in himself, and a possible stumble of which his ill-wishers would take instant advantage. Finally, of course, he had to defeat Pemberton, possibly reinforced by Johnston. Never did he have to cope with greater dangers than this spring, and never did he act with more heroic resolution or greater skill.

After a talk with Sherman, McClernand, and Porter at Napoleon on January 17, Grant concluded that time and a large force would be required to take Vicksburg. The four men agreed that McClernand and his 13th corps should at once drop down the river to Young's Point on the Louisiana shore, nine miles above Vicksburg. The city lay near the top of a great loop of the stream; at Young's Point was the opening of the canal planned months before to cut across the bottom of the loop and thus bypass Vicksburg. McClernand landed his men on January 22, and they and Sherman's 15th corps began toiling in the watery clay, tortured by incessant rains, rising water, uncertain commissary arrangements, and malaria. Only a few days passed before churning paddle-wheels and resonant whistles heralded the arrival of Grant with more troops. Additional armored gunboats came in to augment Porter's fleet. The smoke of a hundred vessels at a time floated over the town on its high bluffs; batteries were planted on the west bank to cut off Confederate vessels from Port Hudson; the camps grew ever larger. Plainly, a supreme effort was under way.[27]

But the canal, badly placed and not greatly improved by a slight re-siting under Grant's orders, proved an abortive undertaking. The commander no sooner saw it than he lost all faith in it, for an eddy at its head thrust the current away from it. Father Mississippi was a giant who moved as he pleased. Grant kept on with the effort because the soldiers were better busy than idle, and because Washington pressed him. Gustavus V. Fox wrote Porter early in February that the canal should be opened farther upstream, and that the whole army should be set to work on this new line. "I dislike to see you all sit down for a long siege at Vicksburg. The country cannot stand it at home or abroad. The President is of my opinion that you had better cut through farther back and do it at once." [28] Grant, despite private pessimism, had the troops toil on.

27   Vicksburg observers Jan. 25 reported 93 transports and 14 gunboats; N. Y. *Tribune*, Feb. 16, 1863.
28   Feb. 6, 1863; Fox Corr., NYHS.

They toiled in a world of broken levees, rising water, dark skies, wet tents, viscid clay, and rain, rain, rain. Every day it seemed more likely that the swelling river would flood the camps, and with spade and dredge the troops threw up an embankment to protect them. Finally on March 8 came catastrophe. The river broke through the protecting dam at the head of the canal in an eight-foot rush which buried channel and implements, and forced men to run for their lives.

Already Grant had shrewdly turned to other efforts to flank Vicksburg, for though some men talked of a frontal attack, he knew it would end in appalling losses and defeat. An amphibious expedition of 7 gunboats and 18 transports bearing 5,000 troops was making an attempt to get to high ground northeast of the city by way of a chain of waters—Yazoo Pass, the Coldwater River, the Tallahatchie, and finally the Yazoo. But they were completely blocked in mid-March by Confederate obstructions and batteries at Fort Pemberton on the upper Yazoo, and on March 23 Grant ordered them to come back. Meanwhile, another attempt to flank Vicksburg on the east by getting into the Yazoo through Steele's Bayou and other waters met difficulties of navigation; the bayous and streams which Porter's boats had to thread were narrow, full of snags, and half blocked by overhanging trees. After heavy toil, the troops and vessels were glad to turn about. And on the west side of the Mississippi, a plan for moving troops and gunboats past the city through Lake Providence, a couple of bayous, some intervening streams, and the Tensas River—a long, tedious, untrustworthy route—also broke down, though not until Grant had invested heavy labor in digging channels and cutting stumps.[29]

The last week of March found the Union army seemingly defeated by the tough river country. It had explored every possible flanking line in the soggy bottoms. To many it seemed that Grant would have to give up, return north to Memphis, and try once more a march down the precarious Mississippi Central. The possibility that he would be removed was very real. As Francis Vinton Greene writes, his real qualities were as yet unknown; for a year he had apparently done little, and for three months his army had been seemingly lost in the swamps, with no news but of fruitless expeditions, fever, smallpox, and sinking morale; and many thought he was just another in the dreary line of failures that included McClellan, Frémont, Burnside, and Buell.[30] But at this crisis of his career Grant had no intention of turning back; he meant to go forward. He would march down the west side of the river, get the gunboats and empty transports to run the Vicksburg batteries, and establish a

29 Adequate accounts in Greene, *The Mississippi*, Ch. IV; *Battles and Leaders*, II, 441 ff.
30 See C. C. Washburn, March 24, 28, 1863; Washburne Papers, LC. "Cad" suggested using most of Grant's troops to reinforce Rosecrans and defeat Bragg.

base at Grand Gulf below. On March 29, two days after Sherman returned from his abortive Steele's Bayou expedition, Grant ordered McClernand to move down the river toward the villages of Richmond and New Carthage, with some point below the Warrenton defenses his objective. He simultaneously wrote Porter explaining this movement, and proposing that the gunboats run the Vicksburg gantlet to engage the enemy at Grand Gulf and protect a landing in that area.

How did the idea for this bold stroke originate? Grant tells us in his memoirs that all winter he had contemplated a movement by land to a point below Vicksburg, waiting only for the improbable success of some one of the expedients used to achieve a different base. Keeping the plan secret even from his staff, he believed that he had first mentioned it to Porter, whose cooperation he could request but not command.[31] Porter's story is slightly different. Grant, he states, had from the first the idea of turning Vicksburg, but *how* to do it he did not know. He knew he was dependent on transports for troop carriage and provisions, and feared that the shore batteries would quickly disable these frail vessels. But when the Yazoo enterprises failed, he made up his mind. "I will go below Vicksburg," he said, "and cross over if I can depend on you for a sufficient naval force. I will prepare some transports by packing them well with cotton bales, and we'll start as soon as you are ready." Porter replied that he would be ready by sunset next day.

Other men in time made claim for the origination of the bold concept. James Harrison Wilson, serving on Grant's staff, was one. He relates that just before he departed on a fruitless Yazoo expedition he talked with Rawlins. Arguing that such operations were dubious, and that a direct assault from the Vicksburg wharf would be suicidal, he declared there was only one alternative. It was to run the batteries with the ironclads, gunboats, transports, and barges and march the troops to such a point below as might be selected as the base of operations against the interior of the State and the defenses of the city.[32] And Farragut also made a claim. Late March found him and the *Hartford* patrolling the river between Port Hudson and Vicksburg. On the 20th, lying only a few miles below Vicksburg, he communicated with Grant, asking him and Porter to send down two rams and an ironclad from above. On the 26th he and Grant met on the flagship for a talk. The ship log merely states: "Major-General Grant came on board." But when Farragut dined later in the war at George Bancroft's house in New York he told of their conversation. "I made Grant's acquaintance off Grand Gulf on the Mississippi," he recalled, "and told him *that* was the direction for threatening Vicksburg.

31 *Memoirs,* I, 460, 461; Grant gives no dates.
32 *Under the Old Flag,* I, 156–158.

He reflected, studied the map carefully, and instantly changed the whole plan of campaign. He had caught my idea." [33]

All this is an oversimplification. Grant already knew the concept well; he has grasped it, others had grasped it. What Farragut doubtless did was to encourage him in the idea and assure him that a dash of the requisite naval forces past Vicksburg was quite practicable, for several ships had recently dashed past. All this the general and the admiral unquestionably discussed on the *Hartford*.[34] As Grant says in his memoirs, his campaign was developed by circumstances. He could not flank Vicksburg east or west by bayou and lake; he could not deliver a frontal assault from the river. If he took his army back to try marching down the Mississippi Central again, public anger would force his removal. Elihu Washburne had been so disturbed by one all-is-lost letter from his brother Cadwallader, saying that Grant was surrounded by a drunken staff, and predicting that when the weather turned hot, the men would die by regiments, that he sent it to Chase. That Secretary had so little faith in Grant that he favored using most of his army to reinforce Rosecrans in a push against Chattanooga. In dismay, he took the letter—this was about April 10—to the White House, and read it to Lincoln, who seemed much impressed.[35] Fortunately, the President remained patient, for he liked Grant's fighting temper. But if the general had not moved forward decisively on the one road open to him, his head—and he well knew this—might soon have rolled beside Buell's; and McClernand was second in rank.

[IV]

Actually the plan for an amphibian movement adopted by Grant, Porter, and Farragut had two components, one so spectacular that it has eclipsed the other and equally important feature. The army was to link together a line of bayous, roads, and bridges west of the Mississippi extending from Milliken's Bend and the Young's Point area to New Carthage about thirty miles below Vicksburg. This meant much canal digging, road repairing, and bridgebuilding. Advance detachments pushed slowly forward on this route, skirmishing as they went. The wagon trains on some stretches struggled through beds of bottomless black mud, and at other points took to clumsy barges. Sometimes the troops followed the levees; elsewhere they used the highway. "What we

33 A. Laugel, "A Frenchman's Diary in our Civil War Time," *Nation*, July 24, 1862.
34 Farragut to Porter, Naval O. R., XX, 12; Grant to Farragut, *ibid.*, 14. Cf. C. L. Lewis, *Farragut*, 189; Mahan, *Farragut*, 226, 227.
35 Grant, *Memoirs*, I, 574, 575. C. C. Washburn declared that he feared some catastrophe; that Grant was desperate, and might undertake a ruinous frontal assault. Chase would gladly have seen Grant ousted and blamed Lincoln for delay; to Elihu Washburne, April 11, 1863, Washburne Papers.

planters . . . had been anticipating," ruefully wrote a Southern lady of the district, "came to pass. Grant perceived that he could very easily march down the Richmond road, where we drove our carriages at nearly all seasons of the year except during an overflow of the river." [36] On April 6 advance troops occupied New Carthage; by the 14th McClernand's remaining divisions took the road; and the 20th found the whole corps assembled at the first goal.

Meanwhile, the river navy had done its part. On the night of April 16, Porter's veteran flagship the *Benton* led his flotilla of eight gunboats and three cotton-protected transports (of course without troops) past the waiting batteries of Vicksburg. As they approached the dark heights, bonfires of tar barrels, pine, and blazing buildings lighted up the levee, city, and forts as if the sun shone. Confederate guns spat shells and solid shot as fast as the men could serve them, and Porter's warships answered with all their broadsides. The transport *Henry Clay*, catching fire, belched flame like a volcano, her men leaping into the water to save themselves. Another transport was hulled and disabled by two direct hits. Shells bursting against the boats threw blazing cotton bales into the stream until the water was strewn with fragments of burning material, a thousand floating lamps. The fleet needed an hour and a half to pass the four miles of guns, and by the time it reached the last battery a dozen vessels seemed afire. The panorama of smoke and flame struck Porter like a picture of the infernal regions. Yet when the ships anchored off New Carthage he found that only one (with a few coal barges) had been lost, and but a single man killed.[37] He writes:

> When daylight broke . . . I was besieged by the commanding officers of the gunboats, who came to tell me of their mishaps; but when I intimated that I intended to leave at Carthage any vessel that could not stand the hammering they would be subject to at Grand Gulf, everybody suddenly discovered that no damage had been done their vessels, which, if anything, were better prepared for action than when they started out. Generals McClernand and Osterhaus came on board the *Benton*. . . . Osterhaus was beaming all over:
> "Now," said he, "does dampt fellers, dey'll catch it; give dem gunboat soup." [38]

Grant reached New Carthage by land on April 17, assured himself that the naval movement was completely successful, and returned to Milliken's Bend to hasten forward the remainder of the army. Because of high water about New Carthage, that town proved unsuited to the concentration of a

---

36   Sarah W. Dorsey, *Recs. of Henry W. Allen*, 158; Greene, *The Mississippi*, 110.

37   Porter, *Incidents and Anecdotes*, 178. Each ship was under fire about a half hour when off Vicksburg, and perhaps ten minutes at Warrenton. The unwieldy steam ram *Queen of the West* had passed the Vicksburg batteries at the beginning of February in a spectacular run described in the N. Y. *Tribune* of Feb. 12.

38   N. Y. *Tribune*, May 26, 1863.

large army. McClernand, however, by reconnaissance discovered two points farther downstream, Perkins's Plantation and Hard Times, where bodies of men could be camped, and Grant ordered the army moved there at once. On the 29th most of it was at Hard Times, nearly opposite Grand Gulf, and seventy miles from the Bend. It was ready for ferriage to the east bank of the river, and Porter's squadron struck hard at the Grand Gulf fortifications, with Grant midstream in a tugboat watching. The attack miscarried. Porter's vessels, throwing some 2,500 projectiles, many from nine-inch and eleven-inch guns, failed to silence the Southern batteries, and killed only three defenders, while two of his ships were badly damaged. It was clearly out of the question to throw the army across at Grand Gulf.

Undaunted, Grant simply decided to drop downstream to the vulnerable neighborhood of Port Gibson. McClernand took the van. Confederates who had expected an assault on their fortifications were left bewildered. "When McClernand gave Grand Gulf the go-by," wrote one correspondent, "and pushed his corps swiftly up the hillsides ten miles to the south, they were confounded. They had for once been fairly outwitted and out-generalled. They met us with a force wholly inadequate, and were routed before their reinforcements could save them." As Union troops marched into Port Gibson on May 2, the Confederates at Grand Gulf realized that they had been cut off in the rear. They blew up the magazines, dismounted the guns, and abandoned the place without substantial resistance. The river navy at once took possession.

Grant's main army, 41,000 strong, was now firmly ensconced on the east bank of the Mississippi, some twenty-five miles as the crow flies from the Vicksburg lines. His rapid movements, disconcerting the enemy, had at last turned the Confederate flank. On the other bank of the river, protecting his communications, he had about 10,000 men. The whole North—even men doubtful, like Lincoln, of the wisdom of going below Vicksburg—took heart at the spectacle of energetic action. His aggregate force of some 51,000, which was soon reinforced, faced Confederate armies which if united would have nearly equal strength, but which were divided. Could he maneuver to defeat them, and take a city so heavily fortified that Sherman called it a veritable Gibraltar?

For, giving up his initial thought of uniting with Banks against Port Hudson first and Vicksburg second, he had resolved to strike directly at the greater fortress. He received at Grand Gulf a letter from Banks saying that he could not be at Port Hudson in less than ten days, and then with only 15,000 men. "The time was worth more than the reinforcements," wrote Grant later; "I therefore determined to push into the interior of the enemy's country." [39] In this decision we see Grant at his best; his instinct for rapidity of action was marvelous. On May 3 he sent directions to Sherman for bringing the 15th corps to reinforce him. "It's unnecessary for me to remind you of the overwhelming importance of celerity in your movements," he wrote. And after speaking of the engagement at Port Gibson in which they had driven the Confederates back with large losses, he continued: "The enemy is badly beaten, greatly demoralized, and exhausted of ammunition. The road to Vicksburg is open; all we want now are men, ammunition, and hard bread. . . ." [40]

Charles A. Dana had been with Grant since April 6, when he arrived at the Milliken's Bend headquarters by way of Memphis. Some of Grant's staff, regarding him as a spy from Washington, had proposed giving him a cold shoulder, but Rawlins wisely overruled them, treating him with the utmost cordiality. Grant and he took to each other at once. He found the general elated by the opening of the road down the west shore to New Carthage, and confident that a combination of siege operations and starvation would shortly reduce Vicksburg. In the ensuing weeks Dana performed two memorable services. He encouraged Grant in the course chosen, and he sent Stanton a series of letters giving complete information on plans, shrewd estimates of all the officers, and hopeful views of the future. He made it plain to Washington that while Grant's staff was a queer mixture of good and bad, the general deserved the utmost confidence. Influenced by Grant's and Rawlins' dislike of McClernand, he praised Sherman and McPherson highly as corps commanders at the expense of the former Congressman. If anything happened to Grant, it would be McClernand who would automatically succeed; and Dana made it quite clear that while McClernand might be a passable corps commander, he could never direct a great army. [41]

---

39 It was a decision which, according to Dana, he had hesitated to take when on April 10 he received a letter from Halleck ordering him to Port Hudson. "It is now determined," wrote Dana on the 12th, "that after the occupation of Grand Gulf, instead of operating up the Big Black toward Jackson and the bridge in rear of Vicksburg, the main force shall proceed against Port Hudson. Dispatches will at once be sent to cooperate. There is still some uncertainty respecting the time of the movement." On April 24 Dana added: "It is now settled . . . that McClernand will not go farther than to Grand Gulf, but will remain there to command the post, while General Grant himself will go on to Port Hudson, taking McPherson and thirty thousand troops with him. Enemy still, however, have no idea of the movement, but look constantly for an assault on Haines' or Vicksburg." Grant however reached Grand Gulf on May 3, he heard there on May 10 that Banks did not expect to get to Port Hudson until the 25th at earliest, and he hence took his final decision; Greene, *The Mississippi*, 223, 224.
40 May 3, 1863; Grundlach Collection, Amer. Art. Assn. Catalogue, May 3, 1927.
41 Dana to Stanton, April 27, 1863; Stanton Papers.

[V]

When during the autumn of 1862 Richmond belatedly realized the gravity of the situation in the West, and sent Johnston to Chattanooga with military power over the area between the Alleghenies and the Mississippi, it acted without proper forethought. Johnston, wary, deliberate, and temperamentally pessimistic, was not the proper man for a position demanding lionhearted courage and dynamic action; the authority given him was not the proper authority. We have seen how quickly he pointed out to Jefferson Davis that with three armies separated by vast distances under his nominal control, he was in an impossible predicament. "I must either take the immediate direction of one of the armies, thus suspending its proper commander, or be idle except on rare occasions when it might be expedient to transfer troops from one department to another." In the first contingency he would deprive an officer of the command he had earned; in the second he would be an inactive and distant spectator. He earnestly begged to be appointed to a less equivocal position.

The request was denied. Johnston was inspecting fortifications at Mobile on February 12, 1863, when he learned that the War Department ordered him to take direct charge of the Army of Middle Tennessee, Bragg having been ordered to Richmond for conferences. Because Bragg's wife was believed lying at the point of death, Johnston withheld the orders from him, but he did assume command of the army at Tullahoma. While here he learned that Farragut with the *Hartford* and *Albatross* had passed Port Hudson into the stretch of river just below Vicksburg. This fact, he realized, greatly reduced the value of both Port Hudson and Vicksburg, for the South no longer held control of the stream between them. A few days later he fell seriously ill, and Bragg reverted to active control of his forces.[42] While he was still weak, Grant threw his troops across the river south of Vicksburg and seized Port Gibson and Grand Gulf. A crisis had arisen. Richmond at once, on May 9, ordered Johnston to try to meet it:

Proceed at once to Mississippi and take chief command of the forces there, giving to those in the field, so far as practicable, the encouragement and benefit of your personal direction. Arrange to take for temporary service with you, or to be forwarded without delay, three thousand good troops who will be substituted in General Bragg's army by a large number of prisoners returned from the Arkansas Post capture.[43]

Johnston set out for Mississippi on the first train from Tullahoma. We can well imagine the anxiety he felt as his train made its bumpy, uncertain

42 Johnston's *Narrative*, 163-174.
43 *Idem*, 172, 173.

crawl through lower Tennessee, upper Alabama, and on to Jackson, which he reached the evening of May 13. From that point he sent a despairing message to Secretary Seddon that the enemy was already between him and Pemberton, cutting off communication: *"I am too late."* He meant that Pemberton and Seddon had been too late, but in fact all three stood indicted by events.[44]

Pemberton, with the rank of lieutenant-general, had been in command of his department since October 13, 1862. A man now forty-eight, of Philadelphia Quaker stock, West Point education, and long military experience, for he had served in the Seminole hostilities, the Mexican War, and the Mormon expedition, he was a captain when the Civil War began, with a brevet as major for gallantry at Molino el Rey. Married to a Virginia girl, and holding strong State Rights views, he took the Southern side although every consideration of personal interest counseled him to remain with the Union. His rise since had been rapid. As major-general early in 1862, he had seen that Sumter was worthless for the defense of Charleston, and had built Fort Wagner and Battery B instead. When he took command at Vicksburg he had shown skill and energy in erecting forts and batteries. Time, however, disclosed two crippling weaknesses. Primarily an engineer, and vigorously capable in defensive operations, he was confused and uncertain in mobile field activities. His public relations were always bad. Though utterly loyal to the South, his Northern birth and education inspired distrust and even wild charges of treason; and his chill, stern demeanor, severity of speech, and disciplinary strictness augmented his unpopularity.[45]

Because Pemberton had long thought it impossible for Grant to approach Vicksburg from the south, he had taken inadequate precautions there. The batteries at Grand Gulf, though in a strong position, were small; a force of only 6,000 men held that place and Port Gibson; a small picket force lay at New Carthage, and a camp of instruction, a battery, and a cavalry company at Lake Bruin—that was all. On April 17, after Porter's flotilla sped past the Vicksburg batteries, he awoke to his peril; he notified Johnston in Tullahoma that Grant could now transfer his army to the east bank. Later he blamed

44 *Idem*, 506.
45 Pemberton, *Pemberton*, 1–48. "Pemberton seems confused and uncertain about everything," wrote Pickens June 12, 1862; Pickens Papers, Duke Univ. A New Orleans refugee in Pike County, Miss., reported to the governor on March 3, 1863, that recent events combined with Pemberton's antecedents had created a growing distrust of the general. "A Lovell's incompetency lost New Orleans—a Pemberton's treachery may bring worse evils." Pettus Papers, Miss. State Archives. On the other hand, the perceptive Thomas C. Reynolds wrote a friend from Camden, Ark., April 13, 1863: "Here, as at Charleston, the evidences of his capacity have overcome, in great measure, the prejudices engendered, on first acquaintance, by his martinet foppery"; Reynolds Letterbooks, LC.

Johnston for not acting to meet the fast-deteriorating situation. *"Then,"* he wrote a friend, "(if such an order was ever proper), was the time to have directed me to unite *all* my forces, if Grant should land, to beat him. Had he then said, 'it is my order, that if Grant lands on this side of the river, you will, if necessary, abandon Port Hudson and Vicksburg and its dependencies to beat him,' I could not have been in doubt as to his intentions." [46] Yet he knew that Johnston favored a concentration of the forces of Pemberton, T. H. Holmes, and Frank Gardner, commanding at Port Hudson, in the field.[47]

It was Pemberton's fate to suffer from the radically conflicting views of his two superiors, Johnston and Davis, and from his own indecision. President Davis believed it vital to hold Vicksburg even at the risk of losing a powerful army, and instructed Pemberton to defend the city at all costs. Johnston, knowing that Union warships ranged the river north and south of the city, believed it of secondary value compared with Pemberton's force of 32,000 well-armed men; the main object to him was to preserve this army intact, unite it with other troops, and seek an opportunity to strike Grant a decisive blow. Davis, as the situation of Vicksburg grew desperate, might have asked Lee to send several divisions—or at least one, Pickett's—west to help relieve the place; but Lee believed that this would be tantamount to a sacrifice of Virginia, and he and Davis hoped for a new invasion of the North, while considerations of time and geography stood in the way. The Confederate President did make strenuous efforts, by telegraph, to summon assistance from every quarter; from Charleston, from Arkansas, from the militia and home guards of Alabama. All these efforts failed. His insistence on the supreme importance of the stronghold, however, harmonized with Pemberton's natural taste for a defense of fortifications, so that the general determined to hold it.[48]

The hour of decision for Pemberton was May 14. Johnston the previous day, ill and exhausted, had sent from Jackson a message which he hoped would effect an immediate concentration of the Confederate forces. He had just come, he had incomplete and uncertain information on Grant's movements, he possessed only 6,000 infantry of his own, and he was prey to the defeatism exhibited in his telegram "too late"; but he broke through his palsy with his first peremptory orders. "I have lately arrived," he wrote, "and

46 To Sarah W. Dorsey; Dorsey, *Allen*, 182, 183.
47 Johnston did write Pemberton from Tullahoma on May 2: "If Grant crosses, unite all your troops to beat him. Success will give back what was abandoned to win it." This was equivocal. He did not order Pemberton to abandon Vicksburg and Port Hudson for field operations, yet he could later say (indeed, his partisans did say) that this was what he meant. Certainly Pemberton could have accepted it as an order. *Idem*, 194.
48 Figures on Confederate strength are in O. R., I, xxiv, pt. 1, p. 273. Davis's telegrams asking reinforcements are in Pemberton, *Pemberton*, 51-56.

learn that Major-General Sherman is between us, with four divisions, at Clinton. It is important to reestablish communications, that you may be reinforced. If practicable, come up in his rear at once; to beat such a detachment would be of immense value. The troops here could cooperate. All the troops you can quickly assemble should be brought. Time is all-important." [49]

Had Pemberton acted on this order, a junction of the small force in Jackson with Pemberton's army could possibly have been effected, and the joint command might have preserved mobility; but the chances were against this. In any event, Pemberton took a different course. He called a council of war and argued against Johnston's orders. A majority of the council voted for accepting them; a minority wished to try to cut the communications of the advancing Federal forces. Though Pemberton was adverse to this, he accepted the plan. He thus determined upon a measure of which he and a majority of his council disapproved, and which violated the orders of his superior. In so doing, Pemberton was actuated by a conviction that he must not abandon his base at Vicksburg, as he explained to Johnston in a note of May 17. His movement to cut the Federal supply line failed after involving him in some circuitous marching, and a stinging little defeat at Baker's Creek. The next certain news that Johnston obtained was that Pemberton, after a futile effort to hold a bridge over the Big Black River behind Vicksburg, had retreated to that city. [50]

One important factor in Confederate weakness and fumbling was the difficulty in filling the ranks of the army, and in supplying the men with shoes, uniforms, and blankets. The conscription law worked so badly that officers grew wrathful over its poor enforcement. Longstreet wished a provost-marshal placed in every town in the Confederacy, with deputies authorized to round up all stragglers; he wished evaders punished, and men who furnished substitutes held liable if the substitute deserted. Robert W. Barnwell was shocked by the reluctance to serve and the innumerable evasions in Georgia and South Carolina. [51] In Mississippi the situation was as bad as anywhere, and in Louisiana it was worse than in most States. "Desertions are numerous and frequent and the demoralization of the militia complete," one brigadier told Governor Pettus early in 1863. As Union forces marched through Louisiana many able-bodied men, concluding that the struggle was hopeless, refused to fight. In Arkansas, General Holmes reported the same situation to President Davis. Numerous State officers having taken the oath of allegiance to the

49 Johnston's *Narrative*, 523.
50 *Idem*, 181–188; Pemberton, *Pemberton; Battles and Leaders*, III, 478, 479.
51 Aug. 17, 1863, to Senator Wigfall; Wigfall Papers, Univ. of Texas. Barnwell, Nov. 2, 1862, *ibid*.

Union, the whole machinery of Confederate law was paralyzed. Bands of deserters openly resisted conscription, even murdering suspected informers. Holmes put his finger on the principal grievance of those Southerners everywhere who grumbled over the rich man's war and poor man's fight:

The greatest cause of complaint is the feature of the conscript law exempting the owner of 20 negroes, and the state law that requires a white man to remain on every plantation where there are negroes. This has effectually aroused the non-slaveholders, and as there is really in many places very great suffering among the poor, the disposition of disloyal persons to raise bands for marauding purposes is almost unopposed.[52]

Grant believed that Pemberton's troops were better armed than his own. But many of them, like many of Holmes's, Kirby-Smith's, and Johnston's troops, were in rags, with rough rawhide shoes or none. As the winter had set in, Major-General Hindman at Fort Smith had predicted that unless the nakedness of his troops was cured, half of them would die ere spring. Food shortages in the Arkansas-Mississippi region were growing, for although Grant's troops found the country south of Vicksburg full of grain and livestock, in other areas the wholesale removal of Negroes southward, and the ravages of armies and guerrillas, had stripped the country bare. The British officer Lieutenant-Colonel Fremantle of the Coldstream Guards, who reached Natchez from Matamoras this spring and pressed on to Jackson and Virginia, found Mississippi and Alabama in an extremity of anguish. He saw boys of fifteen and sixteen badly wounded, and sometimes vain over a missing limb. He visited farmhouses where the women had scarcely any clothes, nothing but the coarsest side meat and cornbread to eat, and sweet-potato coffee to drink; they were in miserable uncertainty as to the fate of their relatives and their own future. When he ate with Johnston and his staff the only cooking utensils were a battered coffee pot and frying pan, and they shared a one-pronged fork among them. He found the railroad to Meridian almost unusable, the cars had proceeded but five miles when the engine left the track.[53]

---

52 Gen. J. J. George, Grenada, Miss., Jan. 12, 1863, Pettus Papers; Holmes, Little Rock, Jan. 21, 1863. Desertion in the South, like the North, early became a tremendous problem. The New Orleans *Daily Picayune*, March 11, 1862, estimated that 8,024 officers and men deserted from the Louisiana forces during the first year of war; it put Arkansas desertions at some 10,000 men, and Mississippi desertions at 11,604. See Davis, *Rise and Fall*, II, 218, for the revolt en masse of the garrison at Fort Jackson. Late in 1863 Gen. W. H. Allen reported to the Confederate government of Louisiana that 8,000 deserters were skulking in his vicinity in that State. Edwin A. Leland in "Org. and Admin. of the La. Army During the Civil War," M. A. thesis, La. State Univ., 1938, concludes that the nonslaveholding farmers of the State, averse to authority under any circumstances, resisted conscription with desperate tenacity.
53 Fremantle, *Three Months in the Confederacy, passim.*

But the genuine rebel, as Fremantle observed, with his bare feet, ragged garb, and thin rations, would fight grimly on.

Difficulties of transport also beset Johnny Reb, and even on the defensive he had to envy the better Union fortune. Command of the Western waters was as important as that of the Atlantic and Gulf, for sea power wrought its triumphs there as elsewhere. Northern domination of the Ohio, Tennessee, and Mississippi was an extension of the Atlantic and Gulf blockade, shutting off supplies from the Confederacy. Amphibious fighting, supply boats, hospital boats, dispatch boats, all at Northern disposal, were totally out of Southern reach. Johnston repeatedly complained of the difficulties of movement. "The whole of the [Mississippi] valley is said to be impassable for large wagon trains," he declared early in March. Reinforcements between May 20 and June 4 brought his own force up from 6,000 to about 24,000 infantry and artillery. This small army, not one-third, he thought, that of the enemy, lacked ammunition, batteries, but above all transport, so that it could not be moved with any hope of success. The country had been so stripped of horses and mules that draught animals did not arrive from distant points until too late. Food could be found, but for want of wagons and horses could not be brought in. Had he wished to attempt the relief of Port Hudson, want of transport would have blocked him. The same deficiency put Vicksburg in its terrible predicament, for stores could not be collected to endure a long siege. The railroads, lacking proper fuel, rolling stock, and personnel, and crippled by bridge burning, were breaking down.[54]

In despair, Johnston on May 18 sent Pemberton a final appeal. If he were invested in Vicksburg, he must ultimately surrender. "Under such circumstances, instead of losing both troops and place, we must, if possible, save the troops. If it is not too late, evacuate Vicksburg and its dependencies, and march to the northeast." But Pemberton, who thought the march impracticable, made no effort to carry out the order—if such it could be called. With sixty days' rations, he decided to hold Vicksburg to the end in the hope that Richmond would relieve it. "I still conceive it to be the most important point in the Confederacy," he wrote.

[VI]

Grant, aware when he reached Grand Gulf that he must strike hard and fast, carried out in the next eighteen days a campaign as brilliant as any

54 See Johnston to Wigfall, March 4, 1863, Wigfall Papers; Johnston's final report to Adjutant-General S. Cooper, Nov. 1, 1863, on the campaign. The letters of President W. Goodman of the Mississippi Central R.R. and Supt. J. L. Fleming of the Mobile & Ohio to Gov. Pettus in the Alabama State Archives throw light on the endless railroad difficulties.

of Marlborough's or Napoleon's. If his numbers and equipment were not overwhelmingly greater than those of Pemberton, his confidence, mobility, and generalship were incomparably superior. His troops, tough men from the Western prairie who made hard-bitten, tenacious fighters, were in fine fettle. He pushed his army northeastward along the line of the Big Black between Vicksburg and Jackson, so as to separate Pemberton and Johnston; McClernand's corps at first leading the way, Sherman's following close behind, and McPherson's striking forward on the right flank to threaten the capital and cut the railway between the two cities. Sharp fighting occurred at Raymond and other points on the march. On May 14, after another action, Grant occupied Jackson, which the army systematically reduced to a shell; on the 16th he fought a heavy battle at Champion's Hill, completely routing Pemberton's forces; and on the 17th he flung Pemberton's disheartened troops back across the Big Black. The Southern general, his command so mauled and scattered that only about 21,000 effectives were left, retreated hastily toward Vicksburg.

This succession of victories, after the months of defeat and immobility, filled the North with delight. "Within the last three days," trumpeted "Xenophon" in the New York *Tribune*, "God has crowned our arms with two decisive victories; not simply repulses leaving our columns bleeding and crippled; not simply steady advances in the face of an enemy beaten, but still at bay and defiant; not victories on a small scale over a puny antagonist, and securing small results, but victories in the largest sense of the word, with all their laurels and trophies, rout, pursuit, disorganization of the enemy, capture of prisoners, ensigns, and cannon; victories on the grandest scale, over a vast and desperate enemy in the heart of his own territory and defending his great stronghold." [55] Lincoln and Stanton were now hopeful of the early liberation of the Mississippi. The country had at last the military hero for which it had longed, and Grant's name was on every lip.

Reporters wrote with enthusiasm of a rapidity of advance entirely novel in the war. The enemy had been taken by surprise, defeated, followed up before he had time to rally, and defeated again and again by a strategy that put two Union divisions at every point where Confederates posted one. Under the May sun the blue columns rolled swiftly through a singularly variegated country of hills, ravines, clumps of timber, and high open plateaus, the lines of bayonets flashing under the waving flags; skirmishers in advance, artillery close at hand, ammunition always ample. Impedimenta was reduced

55 Behind Vicksburg, May 20, in *Tribune* of June 1; the two battles referred to were Champion's Hill, much the bloodiest of the campaign, and Big Black River Bridge. In eighteen days Grant marched 200 miles, captured 88 cannon, took 4,500 prisoners, and inflicted heavy losses, while his own casualty list was only 3,500; Greene, *The Mississippi*, 170, 171.

to the lowest point; the men lived on the country. "I am afraid Grant will have to be reproved for want of style," Elihu Washburne, who had been West, wrote Lincoln. "On this whole march for five days he has had neither a horse, nor an orderly nor servant, a blanket, or overcoat, or clean shirt, or even a sword; that being carried by his boy 13 years old. His entire baggage consists of a toothbrush." Soldiers feasted on hams, cornmeal, dried apples and peaches, honey, butter, molasses, and preserves; they shot the cattle and roasted the fowls. From all quarters slaves flocked into the camps, some on foot, some in carts drawn by their masters' horses and bearing their masters' goods, and some driving pigs and sheep.[56]

Grant's victories rendered Haines's Bluff on the Yazoo untenable, and Union forces were eager to reach that river and re-establish direct communications with the North. "My first anxiety," writes Grant, "was to secure a base of supplies on the Yazoo River above Vicksburg." He and Sherman impatiently joined the advance, and amid whistling bullets climbed to the very point on Walnut Hills from which the Confederates had repulsed the Union troops in December. At the brow Sherman turned to Grant. "Up to this moment," he said, "I doubted your plan of campaign. Now I am absolutely certain of its success." The army was delighted by the reopening of direct transit with Memphis and Cairo. They had missed their bread and coffee, and as Grant came back to the main line, after watching pioneers building a road from the Yazoo, they greeted him with a chorus of "Hardtack! Hardtack!"

Southern soldiers and harsh terrain were not the only obstacles with which Grant contended; all spring he had been fighting a battle with his old enemy, drink. In this as in his military planning Rawlins was his sleepless aide. Gossip about the commander's old weakness was incessant. His onetime West Point associate, Brigadier-General Charles S. Hamilton, wrote a Wisconsin friend in February: "I will now say what I have never breathed. *Grant is a drunkard.* . . . When he came to Memphis he left his wife at La Grange and for several days after getting here was beastly drunk, utterly incapable of doing anything. Quinby and I took him in charge, watching him day and night and keeping liquor away from him and we telegraphed to his wife and brought her on to take care of him." As relations between Hamilton and Grant were strained, this statement might be rejected, but other evidence bears it out.[57]

56 Correspondence N. Y. *Herald, Times, Tribune,* and Chicago *Tribune* May 25–June 10; Washburne, Hay Papers, Ill. State Hist. Lib.; Fremantle, *Three Months,* Ch. 5. Details of men on the march slaughtered enough beeves and poultry each night to supply the army. "The chivalry through this region," wrote the Chicago *Tribune* correspondent, "are perfectly confounded and horrorstricken."

57 Hamilton, Feb. 11, 1863, to James R. Doolittle; Doolittle Papers, Wis. State Hist. Lib. Hamilton thought Grant an able commander, but Sherman still abler. See also "Unpublished War Letters of Grant and Halleck," *North American Review,* March, 1886.

The correspondent Cadwallader describes a spree on which Grant embarked while on the steamboat *Diligence* in the first week of June. "He made several trips to the barroom of the boat in a short time, and became stupid in speech and staggering in gait." Cadwallader locked him in his stateroom, threw his whisky out of the window, and fanned him to sleep. But later Grant obtained a new supply, and while intoxicated ordered the boat to proceed to Chickasaw Bayou. "If we had started then," writes Cadwallader, "we would have arrived at the Bayou about the middle of the afternoon, when the landing would have been alive with officers, men, and trains from all parts of the army. To be seen in his present condition would lead to utter disgrace and ruin." Measures were taken to delay the boat, which did not reach the Bayou until sundown. But Grant had been drinking again, and on leaving the gangplank put spurs to his unruly horse, which carried him through the dusk at breakneck speed over a tortuous road and dangerous bridges. The correspondent followed, hid him for a time, and about midnight got him back to camp in an ambulance. He had slept off his liquor, and climbing out, started to his tent as steadily as he had ever walked. Cadwallader concludes:

My surprise nearly amounted to stupefaction. I turned to Rawlins and said I was afraid that he would think I was the man who had been drunk.

But he replied in suppressed tones through his clinched teeth, "No, no. I know him. I know him. I want you to tell me the exact facts—and all of them, without any concealment. I have a right to know them, and I will know them." The whole appearance of the man indicated a fierceness that could have torn me into a thousand pieces had he considered me to blame.[58]

Even this circumstantial account might be discounted did not the Rawlins papers contain a letter to Grant, dated at one in the morning on June 6, which gives it color. "The great solicitude I feel for the safety of this army," wrote Rawlins, "leads me to mention, what I had hoped never again to do, the subject of your drinking." He had heard that one Dr. Mcmillan had induced Grant, at Sherman's headquarters, to take a glass of wine; and that day he found a box of wine in front of Grant's tent, and had learned that he forbade its removal. Then "tonight . . . I find you where the wine bottle has just been emptied, in company with those who drink and urge you to do likewise; and the lack of your usual promptness and decision, and clearness in expressing yourself in writing, conduces to confirm my suspicion." Rawlins went on:

You have the full control over your appetite, and can let drinking alone. Had you not pledged me the sincerity of your honor early last March, that you would drink no more during the war and kept that pledge during your

58 MS Diary, Ill. State Hist. Lib.; not in the printed selections.

recent campaign, you would not today have stood first in the world's history as a successful military leader. Your only salvation depends upon strict adherence to that pledge. You cannot succeed in any other way. . . .

As I have before stated, I may be wrong in my suspicions, but if one sees that which leads him to suppose a sentinel is falling asleep on his post, it is his duty to arouse him; and if one sees that which leads him to fear the General commanding a great army is being seduced to that step which if he fails to sound the proper note of warning, the friends, wives, and children of those brave men whose lives he permits to remain thus in peril, will accuse him while he lives, and stand strict witnesses of wrath against him in the day when all shall be tried.[59]

We hear of no more faltering. Possibly some of the harshness with which Grant treated McClernand, and the alacrity with which he soon found an excuse for sending him back to Springfield, derived from his knowledge that if he were ever discovered drunk, McClernand (to the dismay of the army) might succeed. But the important fact was that Grant almost completely overcame his one frailty.

[VII]

On May 18 the first worn division of Pemberton's army, under General M. L. Smith, filed into the fortifications on the northeastern outskirts of Vicksburg, throwing out skirmishers behind as it did so. Within a half hour the line of skirmishers was under rifle and artillery fire—so closely did the blue press on the heels of the gray. By nightfall half of Grant's army was within sight of the works about the city. Next day, after the two armies had spent the morning disposing their men, Grant delivered a preliminary attack which was thrown back with serious losses. At various points the Union troops planted their flags on the parapets, but could maintain no foothold. They had hoped to find the Southerners demoralized after their retreat, but as Pemberton telegraphed Jefferson Davis that day, sending his message out by courier, the Confederates had quickly recovered their morale.[60] Though Grant planned another early assault, it seemed clear the struggle would be prolonged and grim. One of the famous sieges of history was about to begin.

But while the flag made such stirring progress in the West, a darker story was being written in the East.

59 Dated "Before Vicksburg"; Rawlins' father had been ruined by drink. Captain John M. Shaw of the 25th Wisconsin, a Galena friend of Rawlins, made this letter public after the war, with an endorsement by Rawlins attesting its genuineness. Cadwallader's story may deal with a different incident, or may be a distorted and exaggerated remembrance of this one. Cf. Catton, *Grant Moves South*, 463-465.
60 O. R., I, xxiv, pt. 1, p. 274; pt. 3, p. 842; Pemberton, *Pemberton*, 180-184.

17

Hooker at Chancellorsville, and After

THE CENTRAL fact of the war situation by the spring of 1863 was that the South could win a great battle and emerge permanently weakened, while the North could lose again and again with an Antaeus-like growth in strength.

Though a Confederate soldier could with difficulty be replaced from a white population which conquest had now reduced to five or six millions, Union losses were easily restored from the natural increase of twenty-odd millions, and the stream of European immigration. A wrecked Confederate cannon imposed a fresh strain on the only two sources of heavy ordnance, the Tredegar works and the Selma foundry, but a wrecked Union cannon could be made good by a score of firms. Secretary Mallory of the Confederate Navy wrote President Davis in the summer of 1862 that iron shortages were "severely felt throughout the Confederacy," and the evacuation of much of Tennessee and North Alabama increased the pinch. But from Trenton to Pittsburgh, meanwhile, furnaces roared and rolling mills rumbled to meet every order. Want of textile machinery made Southern clothing scarce even while Confederate squads burned cotton, yet the North remained well clad. The strain on Southern railroads was becoming insupportable; the president of the Mississippi Central, for example, reported this spring that unless he got supplies from abroad, his dilapidated line must soon be abandoned.[1] Confederate resourcefulness and devotion were accomplishing wonders in the manufacture of powder, muskets, medicines, shoes, and harness. But the blows of attrition and the coils of the blockade nevertheless made the South a land of want, makeshift, and dread.

---

1   The South rolled no railroad iron during the war; C. W. Ramsdell, "The Confederate Govt. and the Railroads," *Amer. Hist. Review*, XXII, July, 1917, 794 ff.; Black, *Railroads of the Confederacy*, 22 ff., 85 ff. Goodman sent his complaint to Secretary of War Seddon, Jan. 23, 1863; O. R., IV, ii, pp. 381, 382. In a message to Congress, Nov. 18, 1861, Davis emphasized the importance of closing some bad gaps in the Confederate railroad system, but the sorely needed link between Danville, Va., and Greensboro, N. C., was not finished until late in May, 1864, and that from Augusta, Ga., to Columbia, S. C., was never built. Southern gauges ran from four feet, eight and one-half inches to five feet, six inches, and two different gauges were laid during the war. Black offers the best railroad map.

The North as the besieging power, prospering and growing, felt only two heavy pressures for victory in battle: it would sustain morale at home and bolster prestige abroad. But these pressures *were* heavy. Every such blow as Fredericksburg encouraged the copperheads and inclined Napoleon III to lend a readier ear to the wily John Slidell. Down to May Grant's success in the West was still dubious, and in the grim Eastern slugging match, the press, politicians, and plain citizens demanded a victory as overdue.

It is clear that Du Pont's attack on Charleston in April, 1863, was undertaken for reasons quite as much political as military. The government, to be sure, wished to release the blockading fleet off the city, partly to help hunt down Confederate cruisers on the high seas, partly for operations in the Gulf. But it was actuated mainly by other motives. The seizure of the cradle of the Confederacy, the proud capital of nullifiers and secessionists, would humiliate every follower of Calhoun and exalt every Northern heart. It would prove to Europe that the new American navy was a power to be dreaded. Since Roanoke Island, Port Royal, New Orleans, and Memphis, the armored ship seemed to many invincible.

Secretary Welles and Gustavus V. Fox were encouraged in aiming their blow against Charleston by the rapidity with which the navy was being strengthened. The first monitors under the extensive new building plan had been delivered late in 1862, and had proved their fair-weather seaworthiness in coastal voyages. The navy also received the *New Ironsides,* a casemated warship of more than 5,000 tons, whose 16 Dahlgren guns and 2 Parrott rifles on pivots were able to deliver a broadside of 1,100 pounds. Her four-inch iron plates covered the heaviest oak framing ever put on a ship, and extended four feet below the waterline. With this ironclad, and eight monitors each mounting an eight-inch and a fifteen-inch gun, Fox expected to deal the Carolinians a stunning blow. Du Pont was less sanguine. He had taken pains to make two tests of the single-turreted monitor *Montauk* against Fort McAllister in Georgia, and his report to Welles on January 28 was decidedly chilling, for he listed three grave objections. To begin with, while ironclads might be impenetrable, they were not sufficiently destructive against forts, their slowness of fire affording the garrison time, as some said, to smoke a cigar between shots. In the second place, success against strong coastal forts would always be uncertain without the help of troops. Finally, it was difficult if not impossible to remove sunken obstructions in shallow water under fire.[2]

2 Naval O. R., I, xiii, 503 ff.; Dudley W. Knox, *Hist. U. S. Navy,* 264, 265; *Battles and Leaders,* I, 671–691. The *Naval Register* for 1863 listed 530 vessels, of which nearly 140 had been constructed since Sumter as warships, and nearly 50 were ironclads. Immediately after the *Merrimac-Monitor* battle the Navy Department ordered 20 monitors built.

The Navy Department heads did not realize how energetically Beauregard had ringed Charleston with formidable guns and impediments. He had strengthened the walls and batteries of Forts Moultrie, Wagner, and Johnson, made Sumter more dangerous than ever before, and filled the channels with mines, pilings, and ropes to tangle propellers. The harbor batteries could concentrate a heavier volume of fire on an assailant, it was said, than the defenses of any other port in the world. Moreover, the area possessed ample troops. According to James Chestnut, Jr., who made an inspection trip through the State only a fortnight before Du Pont's assault, South Carolina had 21,300 effective soldiers, and the forces between Savannah and Charleston were capable of holding five times David Hunter's 10,000 men at Port Royal. The proud Carolinians could be trusted to fight to the last ounce of powder. Wade Hampton, home on furlough, assured Beauregard how happy he would be to give everything to the defense, and Judge A. S. Magrath declared complete destruction of the city preferable to its surrender.[3] Some Northerners had doubts of the issue. Lincoln let Fox know early in April that he believed the fleet would be repulsed, and made the same statement to Sumner.[4]

Reluctantly, Du Pont began his assault early on the afternoon of April 7. Four monitors moved in against the forts; he followed on the *New Ironsides;* then came four more monitors. Immediately the fleet found itself in trouble. Shallow water and strong tidal currents made steering difficult. Once the flagship had to drop anchor to avoid grounding; a little later it collided with two monitors and had to drop anchor again. John Rodgers of the *Weehawken,* leading the line, decided that he could not breach the channel obstructions, and turned aside, followed by other monitors. Thereupon Fort Sumter opened fire at point-blank range (700 yards), and Moultrie and Wagner quickly followed. For an hour and forty minutes ships and forts exchanged a tremendous fire in which the batteries had much the best of it. Then, discouraged by his steering difficulties, Du Pont signaled the fleet to withdraw. Though he intended to resume the attack next morning, a gloomy evening council of the captains dissuaded him. The ships had fired only 139 shots against some 2,200 from the batteries; the *Keokuk,* hit 90 times, was so badly hurt that she sank next day, and others were extensively damaged.

"I attempted to take the bull by the horns, but he was too much for us," wrote Du Pont on April 8. "These monitors are miserable failures where forts are concerned." Not only Welles but Lincoln was disappointed. Fearful

3 James Chestnut, Jr., March 22, and Magrath, June 14, 1863, to Davis in Jefferson Davis Papers, Duke Univ.; Hampton, Columbia, Feb. 26, 1863, to Beauregard in Beauregard-York Papers, CU.
4 Sumner to Lady Argyll, April 13, 1863, Sumner Papers, HL.

of public opinion, the Navy Department tried to throw a shroud of partial secrecy about the event, and to cast the blame on Du Pont, whom it accused of failing to push the attack with the imagination and pluck which Farragut had shown at New Orleans. Critics declared he had made no use, for example, of his wooden gunboats, keeping them out of range. The real blame, however, lay with the ships, not the admiral. The monitors could neither sustain the fire they met, which jammed the turret gear of some and closed the port stoppers of others, nor return it with effect. Moreover, their poor design made them purblind—the officers could not keep a clear outlook. Members of Congress were soon violently denouncing the whole investment in monitors.

The public thus had to digest still another defeat. It was discouraging, for plainly the fleet could never take Charleston, and it was the harder to accept because European naval experts found proof in the battle that the claims made for the monitors after the Hampton Roads affair were quite unfounded. American naval designers obviously had much to learn.[5]

But all Eastern eyes now turned to Virginia and Hooker's impending campaign.

[I]

When news of Hooker's appointment to head the Army of the Potomac had flashed to the country at the end of January, 1863, Northerners plucked up hope. Observers had been impressed by the dashing courage he had shown at Williamsburg, Fair Oaks, Malvern Hill, and Antietam. Taking the Fifth Corps when Fitz-John Porter was removed, he had handled it well. It was known that Lincoln liked him. The President, meeting him after Bull Run, had been impressed by his confident analysis of that battle; he had been pleased later on by Hooker's ardent desire to open the Potomac; and he rewarded the general's stubborn courage at Williamsburg by making his commission as major-general date from that action. Halleck, who possessed firsthand knowledge of Hooker's raffish life in old California days, was hostile to the appointment, and his dislike infected Stanton. Both had been irritated by the general's flagrant maneuvers to get the command when McClellan was removed, and by his indiscreet talk. But Secretary Chase and the radicals of

5 See London *Times*, Jan. 7, 1864, with long quotations from the N. Y. *Times;* Henry Winter Davis in *Cong. Globe*, 38th Cong., 2d Sess., App., 34–40; H. W. Wilson, *Ironclads in Action*, I, 86–97. Du Pont's report in Naval O. R., I, xiv, 5–8, declared that the outer defenses of Charleston should first have been taken by land forces. H. A. Du Pont, *Du Pont*, 213–270, spiritedly defends the admiral.

the Committee on the Conduct of the War favored this impetuous son of Massachusetts.[6]

Hooker took charge of an army which had clearly lost moral tone and unity in the three months since McClellan left. Two of its corps historians declare bluntly that it had been controlled by West Pointers who often made patriotism subservient to military ambition, and that other officers had placed political aims above country. Carl Schurz was alarmed by its mood of surly discouragement. "I have spent several days here," he wrote Lincoln from Stafford Court House the day before Hooker's appointment, "and feel compelled to say to you, that I have seen and heard a great many things which deeply distressed me." Several of the generals, he continued, had systematically undermined the spirits of the men and their confidence in Burnside. The mud march had worn out many regiments, they were badly fed and badly housed in rain-damaged tents and huts, and many had not been paid in six months. "I have heard generals, subordinate officers, and men say that they expect to be whipped anyhow, that 'all these fatigues and hardships are for nothing' and that they might as well go home."[7]

That the new commander had done his share in fomenting army discontent Lincoln well knew from Henry J. Raymond and Burnside. Hooker was moreover accused of chronic bad temper, immoral conduct, and weakness for drink, while his vindictiveness toward opponents was as notorious as his devotion to those who did him a service. Critical, cynical, and outspoken, he left enemies wherever he walked. A nervous man, working with rapid intensity and going at every task with a dash, he was always blowing off steam, as tactless as he was talkative. The worst trait in his volatile nature, however, was not his sharpness of tongue, but his tendency toward intrigue. His recent remark to William Swinton of the *Times* that Lincoln and his Administration were "played out" was harmless compared with his underhand activities first against McClellan and later Burnside.[8] Lincoln, aware of

6 For Lincoln's attitude see N. Y. *Herald*, Jan. 27, 1863, and W. F. G. Shanks, "Fighting Joe Hooker," in *Harper's Mag.*, XXXI (Oct., 1865), 640–642. For the attitude of radical leaders see *Report, Committee on Conduct of War*, 1865, I, 175; Warden, *Chase*, 488; Hebert, *Fighting Joe Hooker*, Chs. XI, XII. Chase was suspected of planning a tacit compact to promote Hooker's military fortunes in return for Hooker's support for the Presidency. Stanton and Halleck strongly favored Meade for control of the army.

7 A. C. Hamlin, *The Battle of Chancellorsville*, 33, 34, and J. H. Stine, *Army of the Potomac*, 310, are frank on the bad spirit of the officers. Hebert, *Hooker*, 174, quotes H. E. Tremain of Hooker's staff as saying that some regular officers were reluctant to end the war because they would lose their high rank in the volunteer service.

8 Hebert, *Hooker*, Chs. XI, XII. Gen. Charles P. Mattocks and others in the volume published by Massachusetts when the Commonwealth erected a statue in 1903 do justice to Hooker's heroism, tactical insight, and brilliant charm. But of his vindictiveness Judge W. M. Dickson of Ohio gives a harsh instance in *Century Mag.*, N. S., XIII (April, 1886), 961, 962.

his faults yet appreciative of his fighting temper, now wrote him a letter that was kind yet sharply admonitory.

"I think," declared the President, "that during Gen. Burnside's command of the Army, you have taken counsel of your ambition, and thwarted him as much as you could, in which you did a great wrong to the country, and to a most meritorious and honorable brother officer. I have heard, in such a way as to believe it, of your recently saying that both the Army and the Government needed a Dictator. Of course it was not *for* this, but in spite of it, that I have given you the command. Only those generals who gain successes, can set up dictators. What I now ask of you is military success, and I will risk the dictatorship. The government will support you to the utmost of its ability, which is neither more nor less than it has done and will do for all commanders. I much fear that the spirit which you have aided to infuse into the Army, of criticizing their Commander, and with-holding confidence from him, will now turn upon you. I shall assist you as far as I can. Neither you, nor Napoleon, were he alive again, could get any good out of an army, while such a spirit prevails in it."

Lincoln also understood Hooker's impetuosity. "And now, beware of rashness," he concluded. "Beware of rashness, but with energy and sleepless vigilance, go forward, and give us victories." To Raymond the President remarked that it was true Hooker talked badly, "but the trouble is, he is stronger with the country today than any other man." In a people's war, Lincoln had to give due weight to the fact that Hooker was more popular with press and Congress than Meade. He apparently handed the letter to the general at a White House interview of which little is known; only that Hooker felt rebuked, and that, apprehensive of Halleck's hostility, he arranged to communicate directly with the President.[9]

For two months Hooker devoted himself to reorganization and the restoration of Army morale. The rolls showed that absentees from their regiments had reached the shocking total of 81,964 soldiers and subalterns, and 2,922 officers, the great majority without valid excuse. Desertions had risen to 200 a day, some families sending their sons bundles of civilian clothing to aid their escape! With restless energy, Hooker improved training, discipline, and general confidence. He increased the quantity and raised the quality of the food, seeing that the men had an abundance of beef, bread—

9 *Works*, VI, 78, 79; H. W. Raymond, "Extracts From the Journal of Henry J. Raymond," *Scribner's Monthly*, XIX (1879–1880), p. 705. Much criticism of Hooker was irresponsible. Charles Francis Adams, Jr., for example, caustically writes (*Autobiography*, 160–163), that he was "little better than a drunken West Point military adventurer," showy but without character, and that he brought to his side two other totally unprincipled men, Sickles and Butterfield. This was the testy prejudice characteristic of aging Adamses.

fresh bread twice a week—soup, potatoes, and onions. He enforced rules of camp sanitation which reduced mortality to the level of a city of similar population. Although he punished deserters severely, he granted many furloughs to those who had earned them. Small festivities and the visits of officers' wives were allowed. Early in April, Lincoln, Mrs. Lincoln, Attorney-General Bates, and others visited the camp and took part in an imposing review of some 12,000 men. From the hills beyond Fredericksburg the Confederates, using glasses, could see the broad plain black with moving masses of infantry and horses.[10]

Abandoning Burnside's organization of the army in four grand divisions, which had worked badly, Hooker regrouped the troops in corps: the First Corps under John F. Reynolds, the Second under Darius N. Couch, the Third under Daniel E. Sickles, the Fifth under George G. Meade, the Sixth under John Sedgwick, the Eleventh under Franz Sigel, and the Twelfth under Henry W. Slocum, youngest of the number. Burnside and the Ninth Corps were remanded to Fort Monroe. General George Stoneman's body of 10,000 cavalry was concentrated into one corps, which was better than leaving it distributed by regiments throughout the army; and the artillery was henceforth to be considered still another corps in the general organization of forces, though Hooker neglected to regroup it and reofficer it properly. As Sigel was discontented with his place, he was relieved, and O. O. Howard, a West Pointer of thirty-two with the unique distinction of never drinking or swearing, was put in his stead; a change which displeased the Germans constituting nearly two-fifths of the unit, who thought that Howard had crowded their old chief aside. All the corps commanders except Sickles were worthy officers, and two, Reynolds and Meade, were men of high distinction.

Hooker's chief of staff was Daniel Butterfield, a graduate of Union College who had become an express-company executive in New York City, and had there distinguished himself in militia activities. The Twelfth New York under his colonelcy had been the first regiment to enter Virginia. Quick, industrious, and judicious, he had become major-general and head of the Fifth Corps before Fredericksburg. During the previous spring he had prepared a careful manual on camp and outpost duty for infantry, which appeared from Harper's early in 1863, quickly selling more than 10,000 copies. McClellan

10 E. K. Gould, *Major-General Hiram G. Berry*, 241-243, gives a lively account of a wedding in camp attended by ten bridesmaids and ten groomsmen, followed by banqueting, drinking, and a ball at Sickles' headquarters. He also describes a St. Patrick's Day hurdle race witnessed by all the ladies in camp, with drinking, gambling, and such reckless fence jumping that two horses and one man were killed. Such scenes gave Hooker's camp a bad name, but they no means justify C. F. Adams's statement that his headquarters were "a combination of barroom and brothel." Actually, his headquarters were under constant, close, and critical scrutiny by many men, and he worked like a slave day and night.

urged the War Department to distribute it wholesale and Sherman bought a large order. Butterfield also originated the shoulder patch as a corps insignia. Under McClellan he had unsuccessfully urged the marking of troops, artillery, ambulances, and baggage wagons with corps and division badges, and the flying of special headquarters flags. On the Peninsula, Philip Kearny had given his division troops a red patch with good effect. Now, with Hooker's support, Butterfield distributed to each corps its distinctive badge, two inches square, to be worn on cap or shoulder. This fostered *esprit de corps* in a literal sense, and served as a means of quickly indentifying wounded men, culprits, and stragglers.[11]

Altogether, by the latter part of April, Hooker's firm hand had brought into existence a new army of 125,000, happy, united, and vigorous. The troops were paid at last. Their rebuilt huts and repaired tents kept them comfortable; fresh vegetables banished scurvy; the new sanitary regulations cut the sickness rate from 10 per cent to 5; the rule that not more than one field officer or two staff officers could be absent from a regiment at once, and not more than two privates in a hundred could take a furlough simultaneously, kept the ranks filled. Picket lines had been made so tight that Confederate spying was almost impossible. The general kept the troops healthfully busy with drill and maneuvers.[12] Northern newspapers this month were full of Grant's spectacular advance, Banks's showy marches, and the sweeping Republican victories in Connecticut and Rhode Island. The Eastern troops must keep pace with the Western; Lincoln was eager for an early offensive, for the terms of at least 23,000 men would soon expire, and Lee must not be allowed to capture the initiative.

Hooker was eager too, promising that he would put every reserve unit into the next battle, for he was determined either to gain a complete victory or suffer overwhelming defeat. He had created a special agency to collect information on the foe, and felt utterly confident of success. "So are all who know anything of the situation here," wrote a friend from headquarters to Manton Marble. "We have a moral certainty of all that it is necessary to know in regard to the enemy, every regiment and brigade, division, etc., all their latest arrivals and departures, etc., all collated, compared from many sources, and fully confirmed. The secret service of Gen. Hooker is far superior to anything that has ever been here before." Whereas McClellan and Burn-

---

11 Julia L. Butterfield, *Butterfield*, 116–118, 119 ff.

12 Alden, *Harper's Hist. of the Great Rebellion*, 484; Survivors' Assn., *Corn Exchange Regt.*, 165, 166; Bates, *Diary*, 287 ff. Hooker's General Order No. 52 reduced to formal system the best sanitary practice in the army. Tents were to be pitched on fresh ground with drainage ditches eighteen inches deep; refuse and garbage were to be burned or buried daily; latrines were to be dug eight feet deep and covered with a half-foot of earth every night; personal cleanliness was to be enforced. Adams, *Doctors in Blue*, 198.

side had possessed the murkiest half-facts about Confederate affairs, Hooker could see the situation clearly: "nothing transpires in the enemy's camp which he is not speedily informed of." [13]

The Virginia spring this year was chill and wet, retarding operations. On April 23, after another soaking rain, the roads were such red quagmires that wags declared movement possible in only one direction—downward. Then, after a final storm on the 24th, the army on its muddy hills above the Rappahannock began to dry out. Sunday the 26th found the camps full of movement. At daybreak on Monday three corps, those of Meade, Howard, and Slocum, struck their tents and marched westward, aiming at fords twenty-five to thirty miles upstream. They found pontoon boats in readiness, and early Tuesday evening Howard's troops began crossing the river at Kelley's Ford, above the junction with the Rapidan. Lee's guards reached upstream only as far as the Rapidan, along which he had strung out some small detachments. He did not suppose that the Union forces would march higher over difficult roads into a country where they must depend on transported stores, or would cross the two rivers, both likely to flood under sudden rains, in order to attack his left flank. But this was just what Hooker with 45,000 men was attempting.

Hooker possessed nearly twice as many men as Lee had in his entrenched lines behind the Rappahannock, some 115,000 effectives against Lee's 61,800. His bureau of military information apprised him that Lee held only three days' rations at one time, so that if his lines were cut he must retreat. Hooker had therefore originally meant to send Stoneman's 10,000 cavalry up the Rappahannock and across it to describe a wide circle in Lee's rear, cutting off his supplies, compelling his retirement, and then harassing his columns. "Let your watchword be Fight! and let all your orders be Fight!" he instructed Stoneman. But when storms swelled the Rappahannock and delayed the march, he fixed on a larger enterprise. "I concluded," he said later, "to change my plan and strike for the whole rebel army, instead of forcing it back upon its line of retreat. . . ." His basic concept for his movement was masterly.[14]

In a sentence, the plan was to catch Lee between two powerful Union forces, each nearly equaling his whole army. He would send three corps far upstream to cross beyond the hostile lines, and with cavalry assistance turn

13 Frederick Law Olmsted to Mark Skinner, April 24, 1863, Olmsted Papers; J. E. Hammond to S. L. M. Barlow on Hooker's new military information bureau, April 22, Barlow Papers.
14 See Hooker's testimony in *Report, Committee on Conduct of War*, Second Series, I, 120 ff.; Hebert, *Hooker*, 180, 191; Bigelow, *Chancellorsville*, Chs. 1-3; N. Y. *Times, Herald, Tribune*, April 24-30. A useful table of official returns of the Army of Northern Virginia is in Alden, *Harper's History*, 383.

Lee's flank. Meanwhile the four other corps would make threatening movements at Fredericksburg and the fords nearer that town. Sedgwick was
ordered to march his own corps and those of Reynolds and Sickles a short
distance downstream, cross there, and open a demonstration against Lee's right
wing. The hope was that Lee, fancying the operations near Fredericksburg
the true threat, would concentrate his troops to resist them. Then, in Hooker's
words, the three corps which had crossed the upper Rappahannock and
Rapidan would sweep down the riverbank, "knock away the enemy's force
holding the United States and Banks's Fords by attacking them in their rear,"
open these fords, and join the men of Couch's corps in a grand assault. If
Lee tried to bring up reinforcements from his right, Sedgwick's blue host,
fully 55,000 men, would be upon him instantly, and his whole army would
be ground like wheat between two millstones.

At first all went magnificently. Meade's, Howard's, and Slocum's troops
made a swiftly efficient march up the Rappahannock. Wednesday, April 29,
saw the fields beyond Kelley's Ford covered with their dense moving masses.
In two columns they pushed on to the Rapidan fords, taking the Confederates
so unawares that they captured a small bridgebuilding party. That same day
Sedgwick's troops broke across the Rappahannock four miles below Fredericksburg, and deployed in fighting order.

News that the army was across the river electrified the North. "Lee,"
exulted Greeley's *Tribune*, "has beyond question been deceived, flanked, and
probably forced from his position—in other words, out-generaled." [15] Meade's
forces continued eastward along the south bank of the Rapidan and past its
junction with the Rappahannock, to the neighboring United States Ford,
eleven miles from Fredericksburg. As the two Confederate divisions guarding
the ford retreated, Couch's troops on the north bank greeted Meade's
column with a cheer and began laying pontoon bridges. They were soon
across, with Sickles's corps ready to follow. Altogether, four corps, with a
fifth at hand, were now massed on Lee's left, with Sedgwick's powerful force
on his right. Meade and Couch might have pushed on toward Fredericksburg
had not Hooker, at 2:15 on the afternoon of April 30, warned them not to go
beyond the crossroads and brick mansion called Chancellorsville. Here, about
a fifty-acre clearing where a plank road and macadam turnpike intersected,
he ordered them to concentrate.

[II]

The principal reason why Lee had only 62,000 men was that Longstreet's
corps had been detached early in the year for service south of the James.

15 Editorial, May 2, 1863.

Union forces under John J. Peck, advancing from the Norfolk area under gunboat protection, had seized Suffolk, an important railway junction on the line to Petersburg, and Longstreet with 24,000 men whom Lee could ill spare had been charged with holding him back. He readily accepted the task because he thought he would not be needed on the Rappahannock. In fact, he had informed D. H. Hill that he really believed Burnside's mud march would be the last against the Army of Northern Virginia, that they could hold their line with a reduced force, and that the war would be over in five or six months at most. "Our Army seems somewhat spoilt," he crowed. "The troops seem to think they can whip the Yankees with the greatest ease whenever they may choose to come, and wherever they come. I have more confidence myself than I ever had before, and I believe that I have always had more than any other man in the Confederacy." At the very crisis of Hooker's advance he kept his aplomb, and before he heard the final result wrote Hill again that he was certain "we had abundance of time to operate whenever we chose." Abundance of time! Yet it was essential to maintain Longstreet where he was, his department (which soon included Richmond and North Carolina) requiring its 44,000 effective troops, for Northern forces were as strong.[16]

The other main reasons for Lee's numerical weakness lay in the bad operation of the conscription laws, widespread evasions and desertions, and crippling shortages of transport, food, and clothing. The heavy toll of the Seven Days, Second Manassas, and Antietam, with the steady drain from disease and exhaustion, could not be made good. The draft act passed in the spring of 1862, applying to male whites between seventeen and thirty-five, was amended that fall to raise the age limit ten years higher. But the exemptions from the outset included a wide range of men: civil officials, railroad and river workers, miners, laborers in cotton, woolen, and metals establishments, ministers, college and academy teachers, and hospital personnel. Moreover, they were soon enlarged. Any master or overseer controlling twenty or more slaves was exempted, and any stockman with 500 head of sheep or cattle or 250 horses and mules.[17] Skulking, cheating, and malingering stained the splendid record of Southern heroism as badly as the Northern. Fraudulent exemption papers were as well known in the Confederacy as in the Union, diseases were as often feigned, and bombproof positions in the government were as anxiously sought. Conscripts could hire substitutes among men not subject to the draft, and a brisk brokerage business in supplying them arose. And as absence without leave more than decimated every Northern camp, so it played havoc with the Southern army. Some deserters were Union sympathizers conscripted against their will, some were men whose wives wrote that they were

16 Longstreet, Jan. 29, May 6, 1863, to Hill, D. H. Hill Papers; Freeman, *Lee*, II, 499 ff.
17 Coulter, *Confederate States*, 314-330.

barefoot and ragged and their children crying for proper food, and some, of course, were plain slackers.[18]

Confederate authorities had estimated that the conscription laws of 1862 would add 105,000 men to the armies, raising their totals to about 500,000; only those between 35 and 40 years of age being called out immediately. The problem of supply was so difficult that a larger number could not well be kept in the field. Uniforms, footgear, meat, grain, and above all transportation were painfully limited. Lee was especially troubled by shortages of horses and forage, while supply trains moved on the railways with increasing uncertainty.[19] Along the railway lines an immense congestion was becoming evident, and a city or army might be threatened by famine while the countryside bulged with food, and supplies piled up at a bottleneck fifty miles away. The shortage of labor for military work was approaching a crisis which would compel Davis to consider gathering tens of thousands of slaves by purchase or confiscation.

But however few and ill-supplied Lee's veterans might be, their heroism never wavered; and the smaller the army, the firmer the bonds which knit it togther. Seeing his men brave heat, thirst, ravines, thickets, and murderous artillery fire to attack at Malvern Hill, Lee had exclaimed: "No fighting on earth could surpass it." Yet again and again the Southern troops equaled that display of combined endurance and valor. They would advance unhesitatingly to certain death, as Hood's men did in the cornfield at Antietam. Their very hardships, patiently shared, gave them a sense of fast comradeship. Building "merrimacks," or improvised lean-tos, for night shelter; cooking dough by twisting it around a ramrod and holding it over the fire; eating calamus, green corn, bullfrogs, and anything else remotely edible; charging with the rebel yell—through it all they took pride in the sense that they were making history. Some youths suffered from homesickness, and then became so attached to comrades, the camp mess, and the company file that when on leave they longed to get back, a strange conflict between homesickness and campsickness raging in their breasts. The drafted men fought as bravely as anyone, though a certain stigma did attach to the name "conscript." Vigorous boys found delight in a leisurely march, twenty miles a day,

18 Conscription is fully treated in Coulter, *Confederate States*, Ch. XV; Moore, *Conscription and Conflict in the Confederacy*, 114–161; Wiley, *Life of Johnny Reb*, 123–150; and Wesley, *The Collapse of the Confederacy*, 74–104, as in numerous military biographies.

19 Freeman, *Lee*, II, 491–495, describes Confederate shortages, the cruel severity of the winter of 1862–63, the onset of scurvy, and the danger that lack of wagons, horses, and feed would paralyze artillery as well as needed supplies. Appendix I of Freeman, *Lee's Lieutenants*, I, 677 ff., offers an analysis of the weakness of Virginia railroads. They began the war with 136 good and 44 defective locomotives, and 2,220 passenger and freight cars. But sidings and turnouts were inadequate, the 432 wooden bridges could easily be destroyed, and even when lines served the same city managers often refused to connect their tracks.

through the Virginia landscape, ending with camp in the woods where fire after fire sprang up in the darkness, gleaming redly on stacked arms and dark forms moving about the blaze.[20]

The individualism of the Confederate soldier excelled that of the Eastern troops in the Union army. The men marched loosely, and though they might go into battle in good order, the first shots from enemy rifles scattered the ranks and set every man to fighting for himself. He might stand up, kneel, or lie down, he took shelter as he liked, and he spoke freely to his comrades: "How many cartridges you got?"; "Looky here, Butler, mind how you shoot, that ball didn't miss my head two inches"; "Cap'n, don't you think we'd better move up a little, just along that knoll?" [21] Sometimes a quick-eyed private in the line would see an opportunity that must be seized without delay. He would spring up, shouting "Charge, boys, charge!" and with a volley of shots and yells, the long, loose-jointed line would coil rapidly forward, while its slain and wounded dropped here and there. Many a Southern lad had a touch of poetry in his nature. One North Carolinian who became a Northern prisoner thus hymned the Confederate battleflag:

The colors drop, are seized again—again drop, and are again lifted, no man in reach daring to pass them by on the ground—colors, not bright and whole and clean as when they came first from the white embroidering fingers, but as clutched in the storm of battle with grimy, bloody hands, and torn into shreds by shot and shell. Oh, how it thrilled the heart of a soldier, when he had been long away from the army, to catch sight again of his red battle-flag, upheld on its white staff of pine, its tatters snapping in the wind!—that red rag, crossed with blue, with white stars sprinkling the cross within, tied to a slim, barked pine sapling with leather thongs cut from a soldier's shoe! This rough red rag my soul loved with a lover's love. How often in long prison days have I sat and dreamed over it, imagining friends come to release us, and my first meeting with its fairness! How I clasped it in my arms, and kissed it, and cried over it! [22]

How could such soldiers, magnificently led, be defeated?

[III]

"I have Lee's army in one hand and Richmond in the other," Hooker exultantly told his aides as he rode up to Chancellorsville. But did he? He had to reckon with Lee.

That general, recently ill and under medical attention at Guiney's Station,

20 Joseph Clay Stiles Papers, HL; Henry Kyd Douglas, *I Rode With Stonewall, passim.*
21 MS Recs. of Henry Greenwood Benson, Univ. of N. Carolina.
22 *Ibid., ut sup.*

and just returned to duty, was asleep when one of Jackson's staff captains awoke him with news that the enemy was crossing. "Well," he remarked genially, "I thought I heard firing, and was beginning to think it was time some of you young fellows were coming to tell me what it was all about. Tell your good general I am sure he knows what to do. I will meet him at the front very soon." He at once joined Stonewall in studying reports of Union movements in the fogbound territory as couriers came in. His first telegram to Richmond gave warning of a general advance, and asked that troops not needed south of the James be moved up. His second telegram the same day, April 29, was more urgent. Hooker was crossing downstream in large force while upstream at Kelley's Ford the 14,000 infantry of Howard's corps, with cavalry and artillery, had swarmed over. He wanted all available troops sent by rail or road as rapidly as possible.[23]

As Hooker's main forces concentrated by various lines at Chancellorsville crossroads, Lee saw that their primary object was to crush the Confederate left. The wide area covering the western approaches to the crossroads, filled with scrubby trees and brush, was called the Wilderness. Its unworkable clay soil, boggy in spring and brick-hard in summer, was useless for crops, and in places nearly as impassable as an Amazonian jungle. Union troops had swarmed into this tangled terrain by three roads, pushing through it to a point beyond, where a ridge and open field gave advantageous scope for maneuver; then Hooker had called them back to a really detestable position on low flat ground amid the trees and thickets. Lee saw that he must swing his northward-facing army around toward the west to confront them. This he did, leaving Early on the river at Fredericksburg. As the Confederate lines stiffened, their scouts and advanced parties felt out the whole line of the Northern forces. They made strong feints, drove in pickets, and used sharpshooters to kill officers and artillery horses. From their reports Lee gathered that the four corps which assembled at Chancellorsville, after their swift advance, had unaccountably paused, as if their leader had yielded to timidity. Hooker had obviously forgotten his injunction to Stoneman and the cavalry: "Celerity, audacity, and resolution are everything in battle."

Even so, to the Southern commanders the situation must have seemed desperate; for they were outnumbered two to one, taken in flank, and forced hurriedly to reshift their lines. Far into the night of May 1, Lee and Jackson debated their slender possibilities. What could be done? Lee had ascertained by a reconnaissance that the Union left was too powerful in numbers and too well protected by Mineral Springs Run to attack, and he now received

23 Greeley, *Amer. Conflict*, II, 354; cf. Freeman and McWhiney, *Lee's Dispatches to Jefferson Davis*, 84-86.

reports that the center was almost impregnable. There remained Hooker's right. As the generals talked, Jeb Stuart rode up with fateful news. Fitzhugh Lee with his cavalry had found the enemy there badly exposed, its lines resting on no stream or hill, and its entrenchments facing in only one direction, south. Lee might throw part of his army around it by rapid stealthy marches, and take it in flank or rear.[24]

The decision was swiftly taken, and just as swiftly Lee confided the movement to Jackson, whom he could trust to march without pause and fight with demoniac energy. "General Stuart will cover your movement with his cavalry," he promised. Jackson, glowing with pleasure, rose and saluted: "My troops will move at four o'clock." But just how would he move? That question was resolved before dawn. A chaplain whose family owned land in the district, and who therefore knew something of the roads, said that he had heard of a route across Hooker's front to his right, and the proprietor of an iron furnace deep in the woods furnished the clinching information: a twelve-mile woods road, fit even for artillery and largely concealed from Union view, led around to the desired point.

Before eight o'clock of a cloudless day, May 2, the head of Jackson's column took up its march along the Wilderness byway or "furnace road" thus pointed out, and a little later men standing by the highway saw Stonewall and his staff pass on horseback. He and Lee had parted with a few pregnant sentences. Asked how many men he proposed to take, Jackson replied, "My whole corps." This meant fifteen brigades, or 28,000 infantry, and would leave Lee dangerously weakened. In fact, he would have fewer than 20,000 effectives. But a dire crisis justified dire risks, and after a moment's reflection Lee calmly rejoined, "Well, go on." This was the last meeting of the two great captains.[26]

Jackson's flanking march was efficiently but not hurriedly executed. He took no provisions, admonishing his men that they must either capture the Union supplies or starve. He ordered that all stragglers who failed to rejoin their commands and fight must be shot. Every effort was made to avoid detection, a cloud of cavalry scattering out to the right, with a line of skirmishers behind them, to drive back any Union scouts. In passing over ascents the troops crouched half-bent, trailing their arms, behind bushes. At the outset some Northern artillery on a distant hill shelled them, and once or twice sharpshooters fired into the column. They saw Lowe's balloon in the sky, and felt sure it had espied them.[20] Noon came, and they marched

24 Thomason, *Jeb Stuart*, 375–377, offers a vivid record.
25 Henderson's account is excellent, *Jackson*, II, 432; Freeman's in *Lee's Lieutenants*, II, 540–551, still better.
26 See army corr. in N. Y. *Tribune* May 8, quoting prisoners.

steadily forward. Early afternoon found them deep in the tanglewild between the Culpeper plank road and the Rappahannock. They must attack and win before dark. Jackson was now separated from Lee by many miles of brake, ravine, and forest, and if he were repulsed, he might lose the war, for Hooker could then drive his powerful center between the two Confederate leaders and destroy them both.

It was past two when Stonewall halted his men along and south of the plank road until, with Fitzhugh Lee as guide, he could reconnoiter the Federal position. Slipping to the top of a cleared hill, the two officers saw below them the Union entrenchments facing south, with an abattis in front, arms stacked in the rear, and two cannon on the turnpike running east to Chancellorsville. The soldiers were congregated in small groups, cooking, eating, sleeping, or playing cards, with one knot butchering cattle. Jackson, who must have worried throughout the march lest he find the foe strongly fortified on the west and sternly alert, felt inexpressible relief. "I watched him closely when he gazed on Howard's troops," writes Fitzhugh Lee. "His expression was one of intense interest, his eyes burnt with a brilliant glow, and his face was slightly flushed, radiant at the success of his flank movement." His lips moved in prayer. Seeing at once that Fitzhugh Lee was right in recommending an attack along the turnpike, he ordered three divisions to form in line of battle. At that moment Hooker and nearly all other high Union officers were persuaded that Lee was retreating toward Richmond. Hooker at 4:10 P.M., in fact, ordered Sedgwick to capture Fredericksburg and vigorously pursue the Confederates: "We know that the enemy is fleeing, trying to save his trains." [27]

In the disposition of his troops Jackson took the greatest pains. He saw that every brigadier and colonel had his instructions, posted staff officers to maintain liaison among the divisions, and made sure that his guns were ready for action. At six o'clock his preparations were completed. "Are you ready, General Rodes?" asked Jackson. "Yes, sir," replied Rodes. "You can go forward, then," quietly instructed Jackson. The bugles rang out, their last notes drowned by the rebel yell. Confederacy artillery bellowed, and the musketry of the advancing line rattled.

The Union cannon planted on the road were instantly taken. The two outer regiments on the Northern flank, German troops under Leopold von Gilsa, were thrown into a helpless huddle before they fired three rounds. Regiments behind them, attacked on three sides, were routed and driven back in sheeplike confusion. The whole right brigade of Howard's corps was quickly churned to pieces, and when another brigade faced about it was

27   O. R., I, xxv, pt. 2, p. 363.

shattered by Jackson's canister and the overwhelming rush of the Confederate mass. Union officers died in scores trying to form their lines, their men strewed the field, and General Devens was carried back wounded. For a time it seemed that the whole Eleventh Corps would be captured before any of it could rally on the open ground about Hooker's headquarters at the Chancellor house, and if one of Rodes's brigades had not lost touch and halted, this might have happened.[28]

JACKSON'S ATTACK ON HOWARD

Within an hour, or before seven, the Confederates had completely defeated the 10,000 men of Howard's corps, and had scattered their remnants through the woods west of Chancellorsville, or sent them flying past that crossroads. Then the rebel advance slowed down. As twilight drew on, Confederate units became inextricably mixed in the broken fields and woodland, the men unable to find their leaders. Still Jackson, galloping along the lines on horseback, his hair streaming, his face alight with enthusiasm, urged his troops forward. The growing darkness, the thickening numbers of the enemy,

28 Howard's defensive story, *Autobiography*, I, 347-377, is less honest than might have been expected of "the Christian General."

the exhaustion of his men after sixteen hours of marching and fighting—some died of sheer fatigue—he disregarded. Before the action ended they must, if possible, seize the White House road half a mile ahead, the only road by which Hooker could retreat to the United States Ford. A full, brilliant moon shone down from the clear sky, and by its light the struggling Southerners fired, reloaded, and fired again, while Union and Confederate shells burst together in the thick, scrubby woods.

Meanwhile Lee had been attacking on his front. When he heard the boom of artillery and clatter of musketry in the distance, he passed word along the line: "Jackson at work; press them heavily everywhere." [29] Press them Mc-Laws did, attacking along the plank road and pike, and keeping the Second and Fifth corps so busy that Hooker sent in hot haste for Sickles and Pleasanton to hurry to his aid. For a bad half hour, half-ringed by the up-roar of battle, hearing the yells and drumfire of Jackson's men draw nearer, and seeing Howard's fugitives sweep past the house, Hooker must have felt that all was lost. But the broken remnants of Howard's Eleventh Corps finally formed a line. Other units hastened to their support, artillery raced up and opened with fifty guns on the Southerners, and as the troops of Rodes and Colston groped blindly in the gloom and Wilderness tangle, the rebel advance stopped. The firing died away, and officers of some Confederate units ordered their men to lie down on their arms.

[IV]

Hooker, after an able beginning, had made a cardinal error. He had gotten his army across the Rappahannock, had united the bulk of his troops there, and had pushed through the Wilderness and out into the open country beyond. He had compelled Lee to swing around to meet him. Had he then instantly used his superior force to crush Lee's main body, he would have been in a position to take in the rear the Confederates who under Early and Barksdale were holding the fortified ridge behind Fredericksburg. He had about 78,000 men as against Lee's 47,000, and by swift action might have carried everything before him. Who can explain why at the critical moment he lost his nerve, drew back from the open manueverable country, made his army fortify itself along the tangled Wilderness, and handed the initiative to Lee? While he entrenched, he left his right wing in the air, its flank un-protected. This particular blunder was not so much his own as Howard's, for when Hooker, aware that the flank was exposed, sent an extra brigade

29 London *Times,* June 16, 1863; corr. from Lee's headquarters dated May 6.

and battery to reinforce it, Howard rejected them as unnecessary. But the major error was all his own.

It arose from his irreparable delay at the critical moment. When he had concentrated four corps about Chancellorsville before 6 P.M. on April 30, with a fifth at hand, Lee's main force was still at Fredericksburg, for he had feared that Sedgwick would initiate the main attack there. Had Hooker pushed forward only four miles that evening, he could have seized favorable ground, gained perfect command of Banks's Ford, thus bringing Sedgwick's force much closer, and compelled Lee to fight under signal disadvantages. But as he failed to press on, the Confederates next morning gathered formidable forces in front of him and threw up entrenchments. When on May 1 he finally did move he got a hot reception from the enemy. He also found that his rear forces were impeded by the heavy thickets through which they had to move, the brush breaking up his regiments, sending aides wandering about aimlessly, and preventing concert of action as effectively as a heavy fog. Dismayed and confused, he ordered the army to draw back. Warren, Couch, and other officers protested bitterly, for they knew that only on open ground could large infantry forces and artillery be used freely. They knew, too, that Hooker's whole talent lay in the offensive, that the troops would be disheartened by a retrograde movement, and that while the absence of his cavalry—for Stoneman had started on his expedition was not of prime importance while he advanced, he would miss its scouting and screening activities as soon as he fell back to the defensive.[30]

But Hooker had insisted on his stand. He had notified his army that he was giving up the initiative by an order at 4:30 P.M. on May 1: "The major-general commanding trusts that a suspension in the attack today will embolden the enemy to attack him." [31]

The main Union line on Saturday morning, May 2, the day of Jackson's flanking march, ran from the Rappahannock southwestward along Mineral Springs Run to the Chancellorsville crossroads, thence turning westward to form an obtuse triangle. It was a well-connected, well-fortified line, strong everywhere except on the right extremity. In a single night Howard's troops could have felled trees for an abattis, built breastworks, and placed artillery in redoubts which could sweep the ground west as well as south, but they remained inert. Hooker, inspecting the line at dawn, saw the defenseless nature of Howard's position. When he returned to his headquarters he learned

---

30 Doubleday, *Chancellorsville and Gettysburg*, 9–16; Bigelow, *Chancellorsville, passim;* Walker, *Second Army Corps*, 202–234; De Trobriand, *Four Years*, 435–470; Howard, *Autobiography*, I, Ch. XXII.
31 O. R., I, xxv, pt. 2, pp. 360, 361.

that enemy forces had been seen moving northeastward across his front, and realized that this might presage a flank attack. At 9:30 A.M. he therefore sent Howard and his neighbor Sickles identical warnings to examine the ground for favorable positions in the event of such a blow, and to keep strong reserves in hand.[32] He was explicit and emphatic. "The right of your line does not appear strong enough. No artificial defenses worth naming have been thrown up, and there appears to be a scarcity of troops at that point, and not, in the general's opinion, as favorably posted as might be. . . . Please advance your pickets. . . ." This while Jackson's column was stealthily moving on!

Though Howard later denied receiving this order, it is clear that Carl Schurz at his headquarters both read it to him, and put it in his hands. A few minutes later Howard received another and shorter order of the same purport.[33] Tired, sleepy, and convinced that Lee was retreating, he may have listened inattentively. He certainly paid no heed to Schurz's energetic monitions, based on information of his own, that the Confederates might at that moment be coming to fall upon his flank. "General," Schurz argued, "do you not think it certain that the enemy, attacking from the west, will crush Gilsa's two regiments, which are to protect our right and rear, at the first onset? Is there the slightest possibility for him to resist?" Howard merely mumbled, "Well, he will have to fight." In desperate mood,[34] Schurz took two regiments from his line facing south, and placed them facing west. Here, as we have seen, they were shortly caught in one of the great "skedaddles" of the war; a flight so headlong that some of the participants, streaking toward Fredericksburg with cries of "*Alles ist verloren*," ran through the Union battle line and picket line on the east into the Confederate ranks.

Even after the collapse of the Eleventh Corps, a body on which Hooker had never counted heavily, the contest remained undecided. Sunday morning, May 3, found Hooker in a better position than the previous evening. His main forces were intact, and he still outnumbered his foe eight to five. The divided Southern army could apparently reunite only by the heaviest fighting, for two divisions of Sickles' corps held a position between Lee and Jackson. Had they been maintained on their high ground here at Hazel Grove, a junction of the separated Southern forces would in fact have been impossible. But Hooker threw this last golden chance away by ordering the troops to fall back at dawn of May 3 to specified positions; and the moment they left, one of A. P. Hill's brigades seized the elevation. Jeb Stuart, grasping its

32   O. R., I, xxv, pt. 2, pp. 360, 361; *Battles and Leaders*, III, 196.
33   Text in Bigelow, *Chancellorsville*, 276, 277.
34   Schurz, *Reminiscences*, II, 416.

vital importance, crowned it with artillery, and began a brisk bombardment of Chancellorsville and other Northern positions below. He was able to enfilade the Union lines from the position which Hooker had thus presented him, and his murderous fire contributed largely to the result of the battle. The Union forces were pushed back into the Wilderness north of Chancellorsville and the house was set on fire.[35]

At its height the carnage and horror of this second day's battle surpassed the first. The fighting was "mad and desperate," writes one participant.[36] Behind the Northern breastworks which Stuart's fire raked, the dead were piled in every attitude of agony; along the roads were heaps of slain, mutilated horses, cannon overturned, and men still contending fiercely. When the woods caught fire many of the wounded, shrieking with fear, tried to clear away the brush and leaves from their position, and some were burned alive. Hooker, leaning against a column of Chancellorsville House when a cannonball struck it, was incapacitated for several hours, unable to give commands. Not for this reason, but because he was obsessed with the idea that he must keep a strong reserve ready for emergency, he never brought anything like his full force into the battle. Some 37,000 men, near at hand, eager to fight, and able if properly handled to sweep back Stuart's tired 26,000, were never used.

All the while Lincoln was tormented by fear that Hooker was not using all his forces. Butterfield telegraphed him early on May 3 that a battle was in progress. Lincoln telegraphed back: "Where is Gen. Hooker? Where is Sedgwick? Where is Stoneman?" To this Butterfield replied later in the day that Hooker was at Chancellorsville, Sedgwick was three or four miles from Fredericksburg on the road to Chancellorsville, and headquarters did not know where Stoneman was. Immediately on receiving this message Lincoln wrote an anxious reply: "I assume that Howard, Meade, and Slocum were in the main fight with Hooker. Was Sickles in it? Was Couch in it? Was Reynolds in it? Where is Reynolds? Is Sedgwick fighting Lee's rear? Or fighting the intrenchments around Fredericksburg?" He had in mind the order he had given Hooker when he reviewed the troops: "In your next fight, put in all your men." [37]

Although Meade and Reynolds wished to fling their fresh corps against

35 Doubleday, *Chancellorsville*, 45, 46; Dodge, *Chancellorsville*, 182 ff.

36 De Trobriand, *Four Years*, 457.

37 O. R., I, xxv, pt. 2, p. 377, with Hooker's own telegram to Lincoln, p. 379; Lincoln, *Works*, VI, 196, 197; N. M. Curtis, *The Sixteenth New York*, 254. When it was too late to help, Stoneman's cavalry raid did reach the outskirts of Richmond. A. L. Holliday wrote from that city May 8: ". . . had the Yankees chosen, I am confident that last Sunday night they might have dashed into Richmond and remained long enough to burn the Tredegar Works and the depots and then have gotten away with trifling loss." Cabell Papers, Univ. of Va. Library.

the Confederates, Hooker refused to let them do so. Later, when he was prostrated with pain, the line in front sent an urgent request for reinforcements, and he directed General Meade, who was with him, to take what action he thought best. It was an opportunity which Meade should have seized, for he could have turned the tide and driven the Southerners back. But because he did not wish to act without a clear order by Hooker or the next in command, Couch, and because of the late stage of the battle, he declined the responsibility. Reynolds also waited for orders. Meanwhile, an attempt by Sedgwick, who had crossed the Rappahannock three or four miles below Fredericksburg, to crash through Lee's rear and unite with the main Union army at Chancellorsville, achieved only a limited success. He overran Fredericksburg, took Marye's Heights behind the town, and then, after an unfortunate delay, moved forward only to meet a check. When darkness ended the fighting, the Confederates still held their lines between him and Hooker, they had the night to strengthen their position, and they were in less peril than Sedgwick himself—for Hooker made it plain to a messenger that he could not aid the general.[38]

Next day, May 4, while Hooker's army lay inert, Lee, after elaborate preparations, attacked Sedgwick on three sides. He forced the Union troops back toward the river, so that when night came on with a heavy fog, Sedgwick was glad to recross the Rappahannock. He had lost almost 5,000 men and accomplished nothing.

That night Hooker called a council of his corps commanders, stated the situation, and invited them to decide whether to remain on the field or fall back behind the river. Howard wished to remain for the poor reason that he hoped his corps could retrieve its reputation. Meade also wished to stay for the equivocal reason that he thought a crossing unsafe. Reynolds, exhausted, had gone to sleep saying he would vote as Meade decided. Sickles and Couch were for retreat. Hooker had in fact already decided to fall back. The force thus returned to its original ground, leaving its killed and wounded on the field, and abandoning 14 guns, 20,000 stand of arms, and other spoils to the Confederates. The total Union casualties, 12,197 killed or wounded and 5,000 missing, materially exceeded the Confederate losses of 10,266 killed and wounded, and 2,753 missing.[39] But such figures are far from stating the full truth. The Union army had again suffered a bitter blow to its morale, and the North was once more sunk in discouragement; the Confederate dead or disabled were irreplaceable.

38 E. S. Welch, *Sedgwick, passim;* G. T. Stevens, *Sixth Corps,* 200 ff.
39 These are Doubleday's figures. Freeman, *Lee's Lieutenants,* II, 644, puts the Union casualties at 16,804; the Confederate at 13,156.

[V]

One gap torn in the Southern command, indeed, made the Confederacy reel. We have seen that on the night of his attack Jackson, as his battle lines paused in the Wilderness, had insisted on pressing his advance to the vital Union road ahead. Meeting one brigadier, he gave peremptory orders, "Push right ahead, Lane; right ahead." General A. P. Hill came up and got the same directions: "Press them; cut them off from the United States Ford, Hill; press them." He hoped that the Confederates could extricate themselves from their disorder, reform their lines, and sweep onward. He could guess, though he did not know, that in front of him Union regiments were frenziedly using bayonets and canteens to scoop up earth, and with bare hands piling it in improvised breast-works.[40]

While he was thus heroically occupied in the front lines, with late twilight deepening the gloom among the trees, an officer expostulated with him. "You should not expose yourself so much," he pleaded. Jackson cut him short. "The danger is all over—the enemy is routed," he said. But the officer was right. Skirmishers on both sides were firing wildly; the lines of battle were stiffening. As Jackson and some companions turned their horses toward the Eighteenth North Carolina, an officer, alarmed by the strange horsemen coming from the direction of the Union forces, gave the order to fire. The volley brought down men and steeds. Jackson received three bullets—one through the right hand, two mangling the left arm and cutting the artery. As his horse Sorrel bolted, he was struck by a low branch in the face. An aide caught the steed and helped him to the ground. To A. P. Hill, who arrived on the scene after himself being fired on by Confederates, he said that he was badly hurt. So intertwined were the advance forces of the two armies that even while Hill spoke to him, two Union skirmishers emerged from the thickets a few feet away. Under heavy Union shelling, he was taken toward the rear. As he went, a brigade leader, Pender, told him that he feared his men must retreat. Jackson roused himself. Writes an eyewitness:

At this moment the scene was a fearful one. The air seemed to be alive with the shriek of shells and the whistling of bullets; horses riderless and mad with fright dashed in every direction; hundreds left the ranks and hurried to the rear, and the groans of the wounded and dying mingled with the wild shouts of others to be led again to the assault. Almost fainting as he was from loss of blood, desperately wounded, and in the midst of this awful uproar, Jackson's heart was unshaken. The words of Pender seemed to rouse him to life. Pushing aside those who supported him, he raised himself to his full height,

40 Freeman, *Lee's Lieutenants*, II, Ch. XXXIII; Henderson, II, 450; De Trobriand, *Four Years*, 449 ff.

and answered feebly, but distinctly enough to be heard above the din, "You must hold your ground, General Pender; you must hold out to the last, sir." [41]

Before dawn, Jackson's surgeon, Dr. Hunter McGuire, amputated his arm. The general recovered to learn that Hill had been wounded and that the Confederate lines were in great disorder; then he sank into exhausted sleep. Stuart ably took his place. The battle came to an end short of that complete victory which Stonewall might have won had he lived to carry his troops forward to the road which commanded the United States Ford.

The general, transferred to Guiney's Station, fell ill of pneumonia, sank, and on May 10 died. His last delirious words were characteristic. From the beginning of the war three ideas had burned in his brain: battle, the welfare of his soldiers, the hope of ultimate peace. "Order A. P. Hill to prepare for action! Pass the infantry to the front!" he ejaculated. Then, "Tell Major Hawks to advance the commissary train." And after an interval, very distinctly: "Let us cross over the river, and rest under the shade of the trees." [42] The words rang across the South:

> Yet even in battle-dreams, he sends supplies
> To those he loved so well.
> His army stands in battle-line arrayed;
> His couriers fly: all's done: now God decide!
> And not till then he saw the Other Side
> Or would accept the shade.[43]

The Southern wounded, in their base hospitals about Richmond, heard the tolling bells and knew what they meant. "Such gloom therefor as fell upon all the people!" wrote one.[44] Not since the death of Washington had the South so mourned a son. People had come to look on him as a man made invulnerable by his mission—to believe that the Providence in which he so firmly trusted would armor him against mischance. Their gratitude for his services, admiration for his character, and faith in his genius were given warmth by a deep affection for his personal traits. He was one of the two men whom the South could not spare.

Both armies were exhausted. With the Rappahannock between them, both were glad to settle into their former lines and rest. To be sure, unused Federal troops could have been thrown into battle again at once—had they possessed any confidence in Hooker. But most of the Union army had been badly mauled;

41 Quoted in Henderson, II, 452; cf. Burke Davis, *Jeb Stuart*, 293, 294, quoting W. F. Randolph of Jackson's staff. Lenoir Chambers, *Jackson*, II, 411–423, gives all the facts.
42 Henderson, II, 471; Freeman, *Lee's Lieutenants*, II, 670–682; Hunter McGuire, *Jackson*, 227–229.
43 Sidney Lanier's poem, written in 1865.
44 H. G. Benson, MS Recs., Univ. of N. C.

the men were torn by briers, stung all over by mosquitoes and flies, chilled by sleeping on the wet ground at night, dirty, tired, and discouraged. The Confederates had marched and fought until they could hardly stand; their units were badly disorganized; the damage done their railroads by Federal cavalry had put them on short rations. In Richmond, moreover, many men in the government hoped that a pause might lead to peace negotiations on the part of the North. All winter and spring the South had taken false hope from the outcries of the copperheads. Ever since Fredericksburg multitudes had shared Longstreet's belief that peace might be only a few months away. The great new victory seemed to open the way for a surge of Northern sentiment which would compel the Lincoln Administration to put an end to the bloodshed and suffering; and a cessation of fighting might give that sentiment opportunity to register itself.

This was of course a miscalculation. As the North reviewed the battle, feeling was divided between confusion over its course, for even the higher officers did not understand its complications, and disgust with the blundering leadership. "Once more the gallant army of the Potomac," exclaimed the *World*, "controlled by an imbecile department and led by an incompetent general, has been marched to fruitless slaughter." [45] Soldiers wrote home that they were unable to understand why, when Hooker had victory in his hands, he so stupidly let that golden prize turn into apples of Sodom. Bragg of the Wisconsin Iron Brigade told his wife that the whole experience seemed a wild, baffling nightmare. "I heard guns, shells passed over me, bullets whizzed by me, but whether discharged by friend or foe I know not. We were in a dense wilderness and backed out in an immense storm. I am alive—can eat—ride horseback—swear and smoke—that's about all the humanity there is left in me." [46] As fuller information filtered in, men were able to assess Hooker's follies: the folly of sending away his cavalry, which could have scouted Jackson's march; the folly of stopping his triumphant advance, retiring into the Wilderness, and tossing the initiative to Lee; the folly of employing his best arm, the artillery, so feebly; the folly of leaving nearly 40,000 troops unused in the battle; the final folly of giving up the vital ground of Hazel's Grove. They could see that his staff work had been poor, his boasted intelligence bad, his communications weak. Of what avail the immense Northern strength if put in such hands?

Yet no true patriot thought of giving up, and the Union began girding itself for still more titanic efforts. Some expressions of its fighting temper were unfortunate. The day real fighting began at Chancellorsville, May 1, Clement L. Vallandigham addressed a Democratic meeting at Mount Vernon, Ohio. Among

45 May 8, 1863.
46 May 10, 1863; Bragg Papers, Univ. of Wis.

the audience were two captains in plain garb taking notes. Nearly a month earlier Burnside, now head of the Department of the Ohio, had issued General Order No. 38, declaring that assertions of sympathy with the enemy, or any other manifestations of treason, real or implied, would not be permitted. Learning that Vallandigham had said that the "wicked and cruel war" was an attempt to erect a Republican despotism on the ruins of slavery, the general decided that he had breached the order. He sent soldiers who broke into Vallandigham's house in Dayton, arrested the ex-Congressman, and amid a riotous demonstration by would-be rescuers, haled him to Cincinnati, where he refused to plead before a court-martial.[47]

Sober men at once saw that large constitutional questions were bound up in the case. It was debatable whether Burnside had any right to arrest the man. It was still more questionable whether Vallandigham's speech justified his detention, for S. S. Cox, appearing in his defense, maintained that he had merely appealed to the public forum and the ballot box. The civil courts were open. Southern Ohio, now that the threat of the previous fall to Cincinnati had rolled far away, was no longer properly under martial law. Vallandigham should have been cited to a judge and grand jury. Instead, in a two-day trial the court-martial found him guilty of attempting to cripple the government, and sentenced him to close confinement until the war ended. Being a shrewd politician, Vallandigham used the pedestal to which he had been elevated to make a ringing appeal to the Democrats of Ohio to rally to his side in defending the Constitution, the laws, the Union, and liberty.

It was indispensable that Lincoln should act, for he was commander-in-chief and Burnside merely his lieutenant, and he was also guardian of civil liberties and constitutional right. With his fine sense of justice and of the spirit of Anglo-American law, he was taken aback by the arrest. Yet he could not feel sure that Burnside did not have real provocation, and he feared the effect on the army and public sentiment of a flat annulment of what the general had done. "All the Cabinet," the President telegraphed Burnside,[48] "regretted the necessity of arresting . . . Vallandigham, some perhaps doubting there was a real necessity for it; but being done, all were for seeing you through with it." This was the voice of expediency, which ill suited Lincoln. How deeply the President was troubled was made manifest by his action in altering Vallandigham's sentence of imprisonment to one of transfer within the Confederate lines. Thus made a figure of mockery, "Val" was taken under military escort to rebel outposts, and was soon being greeted, none too enthusiastically, by Southern leaders.

47 J. L. Vallandigham, *Life of C. L. Vallandigham*, 277 ff.; N. Y. *Times*, *Tribune*, May 6–7, 1863.
48 May 29, 1863; Nicolay and Hay, *Lincoln*, VII, 329–339.

Lincoln's sensitiveness was further illustrated by the pains he took in composing a long justificatory document. Addressed to Erastus Corning and other protestants against military arrests, it was in the main a labored and unhappy document. Here and there, however, it was illumined by touches of the simple eloquence that was seldom far from his pen. He met the objection to Vallandigham's arrest on two grounds: that the man was damaging the army, on which the existence of the nation now depended, and that since the government was compelled to shoot deserters, it had an unquestionable right to deal severely with wily agitators whose words induced guileless soldiers to desert.[49] The first argument raised a question of fact; the second the dubious claim that men might be punished for the *tendency* of their words. It was true, however, that Lincoln's duty was to think first and foremost of the nation's safety, now desperately imperiled, and that he could well wonder, as he remarked, whether posterity would not censure him for arresting too few men rather than too many. The land in which Vallandigham now began wandering had far less liberty of speech and action than the North. Infringements on the right of free speech were not carried to such an unjustifiable extreme during the Civil War as later during and after the First World War, when the Espionage and Sedition Acts of 1917–18 lent authority to deplorable interferences.

But for the reasons why the nation took in its stride not only such episodes as this, but grave reverses in the field, we must turn to the progress it had made in organizing its energies.

49 June 12, 1863; *Works,* VI, 260–269. I shall later resume this subject. The best modern thought endorses Justice Jackson's statement of 1950 (in 339 U.S., 442, 443): "While the Governments, State and Federal, have expansive powers to curtail action, and some small powers to curtail speech or writing, I think neither has any power, on any pretext, directly or indirectly to attempt foreclosure of any line of thought." Cf. David Fellman, *The Limits of Freedom,* 87–123.

Business of War

"THE GOVERNMENT," wrote Seward as the news of Chancellorsville sank in, "is performing its painful duty with no abatement of energy, and no diminution of confidence." [1] Lincoln, visiting the Army of the Potomac once more, declaring that he would gladly take a hundred thousand colored troops into the service, trying to allay the chronic disorder in Missouri by appointing John M. Schofield to command, and studying the problem of reconstruction in Louisiana, was certainly doing his best, as he assured the Presbyterian General Assembly, to keep the ship of state afloat. Chase, toiling to organize the national banking system which Congress had authorized early in the year, and helping Jay Cooke sell the 5-20 bonds, was indefatigable. Stanton never paused in his labors. Had military leaders done as well as the Administration, the country would have been in happy estate.

Several commanders were particularly vexatious. Burnside followed his arrest of Vallandigham by a still more unjustifiable order June 1 forbidding circulation of the New York *World* in his department (Ohio, Indiana, Illinois), and suppressing the Chicago *Times*. A meeting of representatives of fifteen New York dailies and weeklies, with Greeley as chairman, delivered a spirited protest. Interferences with freedom of the press are particularly obnoxious, and Lincoln asked Stanton to revoke or suspend the *Times* order. Hooker, meanwhile, was demonstrating his lack of character in two ways, by garbling the news of his defeat, and encouraging friends to shift the blame to Howard and Sedgwick.

Making no report on the battle, Hooker issued instead a mendacious general order dated May 6, 1863. The army had added to its glory, he wrote; it had executed long marches, crossed rivers, surprised the enemy in his trenches, inflicted heavier blows than those received, taken 5,000 prisoners, and put *hors de combat* 18,000 troops. Only the subordinate generals, he made it plain, had failed! What was worse, Hooker and his intimates spread reports through the army and press that Halleck, ignorant and prejudiced, had hampered him on every hand and fatally botched his plans. He even intimated that he had been

1 May 19, 1863; *Seward at Washington*, III, 166.

given only two hours to attend to the battle, the other twenty-two being absorbed by the Washington authorities.[2] Another center of discontent was Carl Schurz, eager to see Howard displaced and Sigel restored to his corps command. Hooker, quite ready to have Howard made a partial scapegoat, encouraged the tactless Schurz to use all his influence with Lincoln, and promised that if Sigel came back he would strengthen his force and help him use it.[3]

Not unnaturally, the press demanded a general shake-up of officers. Chase, who continued to stand behind Hooker, was as usual slightly two-faced. Visiting Washington, Howard talked with Chase as "my friend and favorite"; yet Chase had written Hooker a few days earlier urging that Sigel be put in place of Howard.[4] Radical members of the Committee on the Conduct of the War of course rallied to Hooker as their old favorite, and in due time issued a report which whitewashed him and stained the scutcheons of other officers. Halleck wanted to oust the commander. For the time being, however, the patient Lincoln made no changes. He determined not to remove the young "Christian general" without another trial, telling critics: "Give him time, and he will bring things straight." [5] He also decided to give Hooker a longer tenure, though he remarked with unwonted acidity: "If he had been killed by the shot that stunned him, we should have been successful." Couch with equal acidity declared that the trouble with Hooker at the critical moment was not that he had too much liquor, as some men falsely asserted; it was that he did not have liquor enough.

2 *Works*, 234-254. Many soldiers believed such stories; see David Craft, *Hist. 141st Pa. Vols.*, iii; J. D. Bloodgood, *Personal Rems.*, Chs. VII, VIII. The fact was that between crossing the Rappahannock and retreating behind it Halleck had no communication with Hooker; neither did Stanton; and Lincoln merely telegraphed for information on the struggle and the use of troops. Halleck to Lieber, Oct. 13, 1863, Lieber Papers, HL. For Hooker's letter of Feb. 28, 1864, placing on Sedgwick the onus of the failure to win victory, see *Century Mag.*, N. S., XIII (April, 1888).

3 Schurz was horrified by press criticism of the German troops and particularly his own division for their confusion and panic. He wrote in his official report of May 12 that "we have been overwhelmed by the army and the press with abuse and insult beyond measure. We have borne as much as human nature can endure." It was not his division that was driven back, but Devens'. The angry general wrote Howard so bitter a letter that, said Howard, "I thought I should never survive it, but I have." See Schurz's letters in Sigel Papers, N. Y. Hist. Soc.; *Rems.*, II, 432-433; Gen. George N. Gordon, *A War Diary of Events*, 149.

Some German troops did fall into panic at Chancellorsville, just as Yankee troops ran elsewhere. Ella Lonn's *Foreigners in the Confederacy* and *Foreigners in the Union Army and Navy*, taken together, explode the myth that a polyglot Union army fought a completely Anglo-Saxon Confederate army. She proves on the one hand that tens of thousands of foreign-born helped fill the Southern ranks. On the other, she shows that nearly four-fifths of the Northern soldiers were native-born. These books, like those of Bell I. Wiley, make it clear that Yank and Reb were surprisingly alike. The Northerner was more literate, more intellectual, more political-minded, and more practical; the Southerner had more humor, more imagination, a warmer emotionalism, and a deeper concern for his cause.

4 Carpenter, MS Life of Howard; Schuckers, *Chase*, 467.

5 Howard, "Personal Recs. of Lincoln," *Century Mag.*, N. S., LXXV (April, 1908), 873-877

But Hooker's days as head of the army were numbered. The most dangerous of all generals is the general who loses his nerve in a supreme crisis. A. K. McClure said of "Fighting Joe": "He could play the best game of poker I ever saw until it came to the point when he should go a thousand better, and then he would flunk." And Lee was about to bet ten thousand!

The North quickly rallied from the news of Chancellorsville, for it saw that its main strength was untouched. The strain of war, felt with such increasing rigor in the South that May opened with an ominous bread riot of white-faced, emaciated people in Richmond,[6] was accepted by the North with elasticity. From early June people were hopeful of the capture of Vicksburg—"within a day or two," predicted the *Tribune*'s Wall Street column of June 8. News that the Negro outfit at Port Hudson, the Second Louisiana Native Guards, had lost 600 out of 900 men in its impetuous charge, dispelled some of the doubts about colored troops. "The repulse of Hooker and the disappointment attending it," Charles Eliot Norton assured Olmsted, "have strengthened and improved the public spirit. Our defeats are doing more to make us a nation, and to free the land from slavery, than our victories."[7]

[I]

By the standards of the time, the war administration in the middle of 1863 had become an enormous machine. The executive departments were no longer grossly understaffed, and their labors were increasingly complicated and proficient.

Visitors at the War Department, for example, which now hummed like a hive in several buildings, found Stanton working three chief assistants to death—quite literally in at least one instance: Peter H. Watson, who had taken over most of the duties once performed by Thomas A. Scott, John Tucker, who handled the large contracts and the shipping, and C. P. Wolcott, who supervised State relations and most other correspondence. Stanton and Watson had been law partners, and when Stanton was offered the Secretaryship at $8,000 he had told his associate: "Why, I cannot afford to give up a practice worth three or four times as much." Watson sternly reminded him of his patriotic duty. Later Stanton summoned Watson to Washington, and when he arrived, handed him his appointment as Assistant Secretary at $3,000. "Why, I cannot afford—" began Watson; and Stanton instantly turned the tables on him.[8] Elsewhere in the department nearly two score executives

6 For McClure, *Hebert*, 225; for the riot, Strode, *Davis*, 381–383.
7 May 20, 1863, Olmsted Papers, LC.
8 L. D. Ingersoll, *Hist. War Dept.*, 345, 346. Tom Scott left the War Dept. in June, 1862, and C. A. Dana became Asst. Secretary in December, 1863; Dana, *Recs.*, 156 ff. Wolcott sank under overwork.

pushed and tugged at the careening car of Mars; and two of them, Montgomery C. Meigs as Quartermaster-General and William A. Hammond as Surgeon-General, displayed superlative imagination and address.

The Navy Department similarly had not only Welles as head and Fox as Assistant Secretary, but a score of bureau chiefs and their aides supervising ever-crescent activities—equipment and recruiting, yards and docks, construction and repair, provisions and clothing, medicine and surgery. The Treasury Department, with George Harrington as Chase's able Assistant Secretary, again mustered a score of important functionaries, of whom Joseph J. Lewis as commissioner of internal revenue and John J. Cisco in charge of New York affairs were the chief. All the departments groaned under a load of paper work that old-time bureaucrats found stupendous. The mere enumeration of the excise taxes to be collected filled seventeen pages of fine print;[9] the list of Army rolls, returns, and reports to be sent continuously to the War Department made filing clerks and auditors shudder. And the undertakings of every department seemed to ramify endlessly.

An illustration of this fact is furnished by the government railroad and telegraph service. Railway transportation was indispensable to haulage of supplies and most active field operations alike. After the emergency activities of Scott and Carnegie in 1861, Congress early the next year authorized the President to take possession of all roads and telegraph lines in the nation, and if necessary operate them for the government's benefit. In February, 1862, Stanton appointed Daniel C. McCallum as military director and superintendent of railroads, with full power to seize and use all equipment necessary. This Scottish-born engineer, bridgebuilder, and poet, beginning with the seven-mile line from Washington to Alexandria, steadily expanded his corps of construction workers. Most of his activities in the first two years lay in Virginia, where he built and rebuilt roads, raised and re-raised bridges, as the battle lines swayed back and forth. He was indispensable in McClellan's Peninsular and Antietam campaigns, and in Pope's, Burnside's, and Hooker's operations. Near the close of 1863, his Eastern railroad corps being fully organized and trained, he went West to take up his headquarters at Nashville. Before the war ended he administered more than 2,000 miles of railway, bossed 11,000 construction workers at a time, built about 650 miles of lines, and spent nearly $40,000,000.[10]

"Not only were the men continually exposed to great danger from the regular forces of the enemy, guerrillas, scouting parties, etc.," wrote McCallum later, "but owing to the circumstances under which military railroads must

9 See text in *Natl. Almanac*, 1864, pp. 90–107.
10 McCallum's Report on Mil. Railroads of the US, 39th Cong. 1st Sess., House Exec. Doc. No. 1; Ingersoll, *War Dept.*, 353–360; Weber, *Northern Railroads in the Civil War*, 134–168.

be constructed and operated, what are considered the ordinary risks upon civil railroads are vastly increased on military lines. . . . It was by no means unusual for men to be out with their trains from five to ten days, without sleep, except what could be snatched upon their engines and cars while the same were standing to be loaded or unloaded, with but scanty food or perhaps no food at all for days together. . . ." The expertness of McCallum's men excited admiration. One story related that as the enemy was about to blow up an important tunnel, a Confederate exclaimed that it was no use; the Union army carried long duplicates of all tunnels! The total length of McCallum's wartime bridges was put at twenty-six miles.

Principles upon which McCallum and his friend and subordinate Herman Haupt could efficiently work were laid down by a War Department directive in the fall of 1862. Officers were ordered on pain of discharge to refrain from interference with the civilian superintendents of the roads, and to furnish them sufficient men to load and unload cars promptly.[11] McCallum worked in particularly close liaison with quartermasters. Over the lines going south went troops, arms, ammunition, forage, clothing, food; over the same lines coming north passed the wounded, sick, refugees, prisoners, freedmen, and captured war material. He had altogether 419 engines and 6,330 cars under his control. Both he and Haupt showed admirable leadership, and both faced up to military commanders with unflinching nerve. When the drunken Sturgis at the crisis of Second Bull Run held up four trains which were carrying wounded and were needed to bring back reinforcements—an act that kept 10,000 men out of the battle—Haupt threatened him with arrest. As Burnside began his inept command of the Army of the Potomac, Haupt told him bluntly what an idiot he was to think the Orange & Alexandria could be counted on to supply his troops.[12] Then Haupt went on to make the line almost accomplish the impossible.

Rates for government work on the privately owned lines were a matter of complex difficulty. The War Department by a circular of July 12, 1861, fixed a general tariff of two cents a mile per man for troops, and normal first-class rates for equipment, munitions, and supplies. But the government encountered so many instances of exorbitant charges that it called a convention of representatives of the principal railroads in Washington in February, 1862; and this body drew up an elaborate schedule which Quartermaster-General Meigs shortly approved.[13] It continued the general rate of two cents a mile for carrying troops, each man being allowed eighty pounds of baggage.

11 Weber, *Northern Railroads*, 158.
12 Haupt, *Rems.*, 74, 76, 79, 158, 159.
13 Meigs, Circular, May 1, 1862, QMG Letterbook No. 60, pp. 33-35, NA.

The general charge for supplies, munitions, and other freight was to be 10 per cent below the printed tariffs of the various companies. The department for its part gave the lines assurance that it would not deliberately encourage harsh competition for the purpose of bringing down rates.[14] Meigs also made every effort to divide freight equitably among the available roads, materials carried West, for example, being apportioned among the Erie, the New York Central, and the Pennsylvania lines. It appears that the government did its best to treat the railways generously. For example, Meigs early in 1863 recommended that the Louisville & Nashville be allowed prewar freight rates, exceeding those fixed by the convention, to compensate it for its repair of damages inflicted by military action.[15] The government instructed its agents always to negotiate with the proper company officers, and to allow them to direct all transport operations free from meddling interference.

The provision of sufficient cars, locomotives, and appurtenances was another thorny problem. Congress empowered the President to take possession of needed equipment, but did not specifically authorize purchase. McCallum therefore at first obtained cars and engines on loan, it being understood that he would get an impartial valuation made, pay a per diem allowance for ordinary use with an extra sum for any unusual depreciation, and make full compensation for any property not returned. The railroads proved reluctant to lend their stock, however, and once more the government bowed to their wishes, buying material in the regular markets and contracting for manufactures.[16] In the summer of 1862 McCallum placed his first contract for 20 locomotives and 250 cars, and April, 1864, found manufacturers delivering the government one locomotive a day. Outright purchases of rolling stock were meanwhile made from the Illinois Central and other roads.

"There was but one way," he later wrote,[17] "to secure the locomotives and deal fairly with the manufacturers. They were required to discontinue work in their then existing contracts, and use the materials in and upon engines to be built at once for the Government, for which they were to be paid such additional costs for material as they could satisfactorily show had arisen. . . . I was met by them in a spirit of hearty cooperation."

The railway administration made steady contributions to the unification of

14 Meigs to Trowbridge, March 4, 1862, QMG Letterbook No. 58, p. 325; NA.
15 Meigs to Stanton, March 19, 1863, QMG Letters to War Dept., Book No. 7, pp. 32, 33; NA. The railroads did not always show equal scruple in return. Rebates, pooling arrangements, the short-and-long-haul abuse, and other practices later indicted by the Grangers, were already common, as government officers found; so were overcharges. On this subject more will be said later.
16 McCallum to A. P. Robinson, March 21, to G. O. D. Lilly, March 29, 1862, Press Copybook Office of Supt. of Govt. Rrs., Series A; NA.
17 McCallum to Meigs, Aug. 26, 1862, *ibid.*

the rail system of the North. It forged links between separated lines, as in connecting the North Missouri with the St. Louis & Iron Mountain, and the Allegheny Valley with the Pittsburgh, Fort Wayne, & Chicago, in 1862. It built extensions to the roads converging in Pittsburgh so that they all reached the arsenal there.[18] It altered the gauges of some lines—for example, the 5-foot gauge of the Norfolk & Petersburg—to make them conform to the standard English gauge of 4 feet 8½ inches. It improved terminals, and gave efficiency to their freight handling. This mobilization of the railroads was one phase of Union operations which deeply interested a group of German observers, including Count Zeppelin, who visited the country, and they later applied its lessons in the wars of 1866 and 1870.[19]

[II]

The first task of the government, as it girded itself in 1863 for greater efforts, was to fill up the armies; the second was to improve their arms, equipment, and sustenance. Under the bludgeon of disaster, the unsystematic nation was learning system, the formless society was taking form, the adolescent economy was gaining maturity. Progress, however, was sometimes timid and blundering—and nowhere more so than in the management of recruiting.

If any fact was clear to the North early in 1863, it was that volunteering was inadequate and that the nation needed more system instantly to fill its ranks. Battle and disease had struck heavily in the previous year. The 88,000 militia who had enlisted under Lincoln's August call for nine-months' men would begin going home in May; and few now believed that victory could be won before the terms of the three-years' regiments of 1861 expired. These 300 regiments of veterans could ill be spared. Meanwhile, discharges for disability, an inevitable sequel of worthless physical examinations at the time of enlistment, continued numerous. The Sanitary Commission had reported to Lincoln, on the basis of a survey, that probably a quarter of the men accepted during 1861 were unfit for service; and it and C. S. Tripler, medical director of the Army of the Potomac, agreed that some examining doctors had been bribed to fill up regiments.[20] The horrifying total of desertions presented a problem so baffling that when Provost-Marshal General Simeon Draper made

18 Watson to J. Rollins, April 22. 1862, War Office Military Book 49b.
19 Cf. Edwin A. Pratt, *Rise of Rail Power*, 23, 24, on McCallum.
20 Halleck informed Banks June 27, 1863, that he could not send him more troops; the discharge of nine-months' and two-years' men "has so reduced our forces that we can hardly defend Washington and Baltimore." Early in August he wrote Gov. Austin Blair of Michigan that those discharged and to be discharged amounted to something over 70,000. Halleck Papers, HL.

an estimate late in 1862 that 100,000 men were absent without permission, he believed that not more than a third could be caught. Meanwhile, said Henry Wilson, "volunteers we cannot obtain." [21]

One reason why seven million white Southerners had been able to hold more than twenty million Northerners at bay, as Greeley's *Tribune* said, was that the South had a better recruitment system. It resorted to a general draft nearly a year before the North. When men were accepted, the South distributed them among the old regiments, keeping each as nearly as possible up to full strength; the North, on the contrary, kept raising new regiments and letting the old ones dwindle to weakness. "Our many memorable successes," wrote Davis, "are with justice ascribed in large measure to the reorganization and reinforcement of our armies under the operation of conscription." [22] Some of the Northern defeats could be ascribed to the failure to intermingle veterans and raw recruits. In theory, everybody applauded Napoleon's plan of dividing regiments into battalions, one of which, the depot battalion, stayed at home in a garrison town, training and forwarding troops. McClellan's dictum that 50,000 recruits in old regiments would be better than 100,000 in new ones was well remembered. But the government kept on letting the States raise new outfits.

Congress at last, by the law which Lincoln approved March 3, 1863, decreed a general conscription of male citizens between 20 and 45, for three years' service. It permitted few exemptions: none but the mentally or physically unfit, high government officers, and the only sons of dependent parents. Conscripts were to receive the same advances and Federal bounties as volunteers. Henry Wilson declared that it would be used to restore the strength of shattered units: "The nation needs not new regiments and more officers; it needs new bayonets in the war-wasted ranks of the veteran regiments." This seemed a momentous step. The measure passed the House 115 to 49, received wide editorial praise, and was hailed by commanders in the field. Rosecrans predicted that two months of the draft would increase the power of his army by half; Sherman wrote Grant that if the men were really used to fill the old regiments, a work which would require 600,000 men in all, the step would be more important than the capture of Vicksburg and Richmond together. Under the new law the Provost-Marshal General's office became a separate bureau in the War Department. Colonel James B. Fry correctly anticipated that

---

21 *Cong. Globe*, 37th Cong. 3rd Sess., 976 (Feb. 16, 1863). Of the nearly 200,000 men who deserted from the Northern armies during the war, not quite 76,000 were arrested and sent back; Lerwill, *Personnel Replacement System*, 76. Lincoln on March 10, 1863, proclaimed an amnesty to all absentees who reported for duty on or before April 1, 1863.
22 N. Y. *Tribune*, Feb. 6, 1863; *Messages and Papers of the Confederacy*, I, 294.

about 3,000,000 men would be enrolled, but he was all too optimistic in his calculation that some 425,000 would flow into the fighting forces.[23]

No measure of the war was a more stunning disappointment than this Draft Act of 1863. If the spirit had merits, the text was hopelessly blundering. To begin with, Congress, influenced by old militia practices, foreign examples, and bad arguments, provided that any drafted man might furnish a substitute or by payment of $300 obtain total exemption. It seemed to some members that citizens holding important civilian positions or with special family responsibilities should have the right to hire an alternate. It also seemed to them that with $300 for extra bounty, the government could hire as good men as most draftees. But Congress really opened a Pandora's box.[24] In the second place, Congress wrote into the law a provision that whenever a regiment fell below half the legal maximum, its companies were to be consolidated and its surplus officers discharged. Commanders in the field protested that this would deprive them of an indispensable array of the most experienced officers. They were able to resist execution of the foolish clause and minimize its effects, but it did harm nonetheless. And in the third place, the law was so loosely written that the government could easily forget about filling up depleted regiments. Just after Chancellorsville the War Department began permitting governors to enlist quite new units—forty regiments in all.

Amid sharp criticism, and in many places angry hostility, Fry's bureau organized a costly machinery, calculated the quotas of States and districts, and enrolled citizens. By July 1 it was actually drafting men in some areas. Grave difficulties instantly arose. The size of quotas was fixed according to the proportion of the population of a given district previously furnished to the armed services. Several States had already sent more than their share to the front, and were hence exempted. The computation of quotas proved an intricate matter. Figures of prior enlistments were often disputed; Fry's mode of reckoning, which made one enlistment for three years equal to four enlistments for nine months, was disputed; New England States which had long sent males West and kept females at home disputed the justice of balancing a million people in Massachusetts against a million in Illinois: and each State was ready to dispute about the number of its sons who had enlisted elsewhere. In New York, Governor Seymour expressed suspicion that Fry's office had assessed excessive quotas upon the Democratic districts of Man-

23 Sherman to Grant, June 2, 1863, O. R., I, xxiv, pt. 3, pp. 372, 373. Sherman wrote that the Western regiments did not average 300 men. Lerwill, *Personnel Replacement*, 93, 94, gives Fry's predictions.
24 Lieber to Halleck, March 16, 1863, Halleck Papers, HL; Morton to Stanton, March 6, Stanton Papers, LC. The money-commutation privilege was restricted in 1864 to conscientious objectors; Shannon, *Admin. and Org.*, II, 87. O. R., III, i, pp. 19–1198 covers recruiting and the draft fully, with illuminating letters by Fry.

hattan and Brooklyn to make sure that the Republicans would carry them in the next election, and he demanded an inquiry. Altogether, a running battle soon raged between governors and the War Department, with plenty of popular and official obstruction of the draft. The fierce local and State antagonism and the ebullitions of open violence we shall treat later.

It was soon plain that the draft would require a costly system of enforcement. It was also clear that it would breed swarms of cheats and cormorants, and that its directors would have to guard against the most ingenious evasions and frauds. Bounty jumpers, substitute brokers, and corrupt doctors appeared in noisome swarms. Their activities in all the large cities became one of the chief scandals of the war. Agents tried to palm off cripples, old men, escaped lunatics, and dipsomaniacs as substitutes. Emigrant-runners and sailor-kidnapers turned to the new source of revenue. In some districts a majority of the men drafted refused to come before the boards until compelled to do so. Substitutes by thousands pocketed their payments and bounties, deserted, and sold themselves over again. Fry, giving up hope of nearly a half-million new men, declared before the end of the year that the law was not really designed to raise and maintain an army, and that no sophistry could disguise its failure.[25]

A failure it was; yet not entirely so. The Draft Act did something, as its authors had expected, to stimulate volunteering. A young man reaching twenty was obviously wiser to offer his services, escape the stigma of conscription, get special State and local benefits, and join the regiment he liked, than be taken by the neck for service. For the War Department, as we have seen, authorized governors to recruit quite new regiments. This defeated the hope that the thin veteran units would be substantially strengthened. Altogether, they received only 21,331 men in the first ten months of 1863, with the result that one army corps which fought at Chickamauga this fall reported that its 33 regiments had an average strength of only 325 men.[26] Some regiments were kept alive only by the zealous exertions of their officers in canvassing farms, villages, and towns in occupied parts of the Borderland and South for recruits. In the end the drafts of 1863–64 gave all the armies a direct accretion of fewer than 170,000 men, and continued to offer a lesson in how *not* to manage recruiting.[27] But 170,000 men were worth a great deal, and the value of the Draft Act in its spur to volunteering, its proof of the

25 Fry to H. S. Lane, Dec. 20, 1863, O. R., III, iii, 1175–1177; Lerwill, *Personnel System*, 94, 95; "Examinations and Exemptions," N. Y. *Tribune*, Sept. 28, 1863; "The Recruiting Business in our City," N. Y. *Tribune*, Feb. 16, 1864; Gov. Austin Blair's message, Detroit *Free Press*, Jan. 20, 1864; Whitelaw Reid, *Ohio in the Civil War*, I, 204 ff.
26 Lerwill, *Replacement System*, 99.
27 O. R., III, iv, 927, 928; v, 486, 487. Of this number about 46,000 were conscripts and 118,000 substitutes. Nearly 87,000 men paid commutation money.

determination of the government, and its illustration of the possibilities of nation-wide organization, was by no means slight.

The national forces that had a total strength of 556,000 officers and enlisted men when 1862 ended had grown to a nominal 918,121 a year later. So many veterans had re-enlisted that the armies had gained in skill and toughness. Two Britons, Lieutenant-Colonel T. L. Galloway of the engineers and Captain H. J. Alderson of the artillery, who made an inspection tour early in 1864, pronounced the soldiers well behaved, brave, intelligent, and possessed of remarkable initiative.[28] The discipline of the artillery was good, of the infantry poor, and of the cavalry wretched; the visitors concluded that its defects arose from the scarcity of good officers and noncoms, but American individualism was probably a larger factor. Certainly the desertion rate alone proved bad discipline. But that the great volunteer armies were growing stronger, and that they showed splendid fighting qualities when led with even halfway talent, nobody could deny.

[III]

One prime source of increased army strength was the steady improvement in arms, equipment, commissary, and medical care. By Chancellorsville the infantry had enough good Springfield and Enfield rifled muskets (though not always well distributed), with an ever-larger sprinkling of Spencer repeating rifles. An equally great advance in firepower lay in the artillery, which in the East, as D. H. Hill on the Confederate side wrote, was "always the most effective arm." [29]

The artillery did a great deal, in the war of movement during the first three years, to overcome the general Confederate advantage of defensive positions. Throughout the century and the world, the defense was gaining in strength. Competent authority has estimated that in the Napoleonic Wars 20,000 fighting troops to the mile, including reserves—the number Wellington had at Waterloo—were normal to a defensive position. In the first three years of the Civil War 12,000 to the mile were regarded as standard, and later 5,000 were found sufficient, Lee holding the long Richmond-Petersburg line with even fewer.[30] If the Union superiority in artillery and general firepower could not atone for bad leadership, on such a field as Antietam it could make up for disadvantages of position.

We have noted the care which McClellan took before his Peninsular

28 *Report Upon the Mil. Affairs of the U. S. A.*, Br. War Office, 1864. The tour was made Feb.–June, 1864, and the report was expert.
29 D. H. Hill, *Battles and Leaders*, II, 355.
30 Liddell Hart, *Manchester Guardian Weekly*, June 25, 1959.

campaign to provide a powerful artillery arm under William F. Barry. He wished every division to have four batteries, consisting of at least four and if possible six light fieldpieces. He especially liked the 12-pounder smooth-bore Napoleon, a handy bronze muzzle-loader with an extreme range of 1,300 yards for solid shot and half as much for canister. He also insisted on an artillery reserve of a hundred guns, and a siege train of at least half that many—actually he took nearly a hundred to Yorktown. Altogether, when his forces set out in March, 1862, they had 92 batteries of 520 guns, with 12,500 men and 11,000 horses. In the broken, forested Virginia terrain, where canister and shrapnel were much more effective than long-range shells, McClellan correctly thought two-thirds of his guns should be Napoleons, but it was not until Antietam that he was able to approach the desired proportions. He could well pay tribute to the feat of the ordnance bureau in providing within seven months, by manufacture, purchase, or supply from arsenals, the splendid panoply he had for use.[31]

After the Peninsular campaign Barry's place was taken by H. J. Hunt, who had managed a hundred guns at Malvern Hill with memorable skill, and who remained the capable chief of artillery till the end of the war. Both men were West Pointers, Mexican War veterans, and members of the board which in 1856 had adopted a new set of artillery tactics. Hooker neglected his artillery, and paid a heavy price for it. At Murfreesboro, Rosecrans had 39 batteries, and put 27 of them into the contest under his able chief of ordnance, Horace Porter, who was later to become one of Grant's best aides. In the West Grant and Sherman made effective use of artillery. Just before the siege of Vicksburg the returns showed that Grant had 224 fieldpieces and 88 heavy guns, and was then ordering more from the North. Sherman always believed that ordnance was more important to raw troops than to veterans, but he employed it well.[32]

After the first two years Northern artillery supply never posed an acute problem. The ordnance bureau bought more than 2,000 cannon during 1862, and issued about 8,000 pieces altogether during the conflict; and the supplies of shot and shell were adequate. The weird early variety of calibers and patterns, which had compelled the government to carry 600 different kinds of ammunition, was rapidly reduced to manageable size.

But in artillery design the bureau showed the same conservatism as in its

31 *Own Story*, 115-118. State troops brought with them a conglomeration of cannon, causing ammunition difficulties. American facilities for making wrought-iron and cast-iron guns were at first much superior to those for making bronze pieces. Washington fortifications had to take large coastal cannon for lack of light artillery; O. R., I, xix, pt. 2, pp. 391-393. Just after Antietam, McClellan's army had 126 Napoleons and 64 light Parrotts as against 128 larger guns; *ibid.*, 407.

32 *Memoirs*, II, 396.

approach to small arms. Although it would have been easier to experiment with the breech-loading principle in designing ordnance than it was in buying the first sorely needed Springfields and Enfields, for the emergency was less desperate, the head, J. W. Ripley, set his face against innovation. He rebuffed a manufacturer who offered to make breech-loading cannon for him with the curt declaration that however perfect such a piece might be, it would not suit the service, for a muzzle-loader of equal weight must necessarily be stronger, cheaper, simpler, and less liable to derangement. He also declined to support experiments with steel fieldpieces in place of bronze. No single prototype of small-caliber artillery was ever adopted, though among larger cannon the 15-inch Rodman gun, made in Pittsburgh by the Fort Pitt Foundry, found special favor.[33]

The British officers who reported on Northern military affairs in the first months of 1864 found that the Army of the Potomac had an ample supply of artillery, both smoothbore and rifled. Two-thirds of its light artillery was smoothbore for the simple fact that in fighting over rough country small shot was the best ammunition; most artillerymen going into battle liked to carry one-third canister, one-third shrapnel, and one-third solid balls. Four different field guns were in common use: the Napoleon, the 10-pounder Parrotts, a 3-inch ordnance gun, and a 20-pounder as a gun of position.[34] The officers also saw the large Parrotts made at Cold Spring on the Hudson, great cast-iron guns strengthened at the breech by wrought-iron hoops. They thought the operation very rough, and reported a number of instances in which the guns had bulged their hoops, burst at the breach, or blown off their muzzles.

As for small arms, the North did better and better. By Chancellorsville the early deficiencies had been so well cured that, as we have seen, the government was refusing to make new foreign contracts and letting the old ones run out; though it still bought some first-class Enfields on a non-contract basis. Marcellus Hartley, who had been sent abroad to purchase for the government, had returned in the spring of 1862 after doing a memorable piece of work in buying good arms, breaking up a combination of British maunfacturers, and frustrating the activities of Confederate agents. He received Stanton's warm praise, and it was not considered necessary to send him back again.[35] During 1862 the ordnance bureau bought 734,500 rifles and

33 To H. F. Mann, May 28, 1862, Misc. Letterbook No. 55, p. 285; to McClellan, July 7, 1862, *ibid.*, 447; Watson to Normal Ward, April 22, 1863, War Office Mil. Book No. 52c, p. 242.
34 Report, Br. War Office, 1864; cf. O. R., III, iii, 108.
35 For Hartley's remarkable work see L. W. Hartley, *Marcellus Hartley*, 33–49; Alden Hatch, *Remington Arms*, 100–102; O. R., III, i, ii, iii, *passim*, cover munitions thoroughly.

muskets, 48,000 carbines, and 120,000 pistols. The spring campaigns of 1863 found it with 381,000 rifled muskets in storage, expecting the delivery of 80,000 Enfields under contract, and obtaining new Springfields from the national armory at the rate of 30,000 a month.

In short, good arms were so abundant that Grant's statement that the Confederates before Vicksburg carried better weapons than his own troops excites amazement. This may have been true of some units, but not of the armies as a whole. The government could now afford to be contemptuous of the vast quantity of inferior foreign muskets that had seeped into the country. It warned the States against them, bought 18,000 bad Prussian guns at $4 for free distribution to militia for drill, and before the summer ended, allowed merchants to send the rusting foreign hardware back to the place of original shipment.[36] Meanwhile, it encouraged the domestic manufacturers who strove to make the Union self-sufficient.[37]

Little by little, first in the cavalry and later the infantry, breechloaders were reaching select bodies of troops. Ripley remained the Great Obstructor. Fussily swathed in red tape, he was skeptical of their merits, irritated by the number of types placed before him, and disturbed by prices which averaged $28–$30.[38] In the early period of the war he had been quite right in concentrating on a full supply of good muzzle-loaders. Many Army officers, for that matter, shared his opinion that men firing breechloaders tended to waste ammunition, and that careful training would be needed. But by energetic and farsighted action in 1862, when shortages eased, he could have made sure that a large part of the troops at Gettysburg and Chattanooga had the efficient new weapon. Prussian officers ever since 1861 had been confidently asserting the superiority of the needle gun type of breechloader, declaring that it fired three times faster than the Minié muzzle-loader. The Swedish army had turned to breechloaders. The two British observers found officers of the Army of the Potomac in 1864 generally agreed that a number of the more intelligent men in each regiment, at least, should carry breechloaders.

Repeating rifles were particularly valued, and the troops fortunate enough to get seven-shot Spencers were positively enchanted by them. George D. Ramsay, who succeeded Ripley in September, 1863, and was far more progres-

36 Ripley to Casey, Aug. 25, 1862, Ord. Misc. Letterbook No. 56, p. 50; Watson to J. B. Hupey, Aug. 18, 1862, *ibid.*, Letterbook No. 50; Watson to Naylor, May 11, 1863, *ibid.*, No. 52c; Hardie to Joseph Foulke's Sons, Sept. 7, 1863, *ibid.*, No. 53a.

37 See G. D. Ramsay's endorsement, Nov. 2, 1863, Ord. Letters to War Dept., Book No. 14, pp. 375, 376, praising Abram S Hewitt's production of fine gun metal.

38 Ripley wrote Lincoln May 5, 1862, that he did not think it wise to increase the number of breechloader types on the market; Ord. Misc. Letterbook No. 55, p. 183. Later he wrote Stanton to the same effect; Jan. 9, 1863, Ord. Letters to War Dept., Book No. 14.

sive, was anxious to enlarge their use. Beyond doubt, he declared in the spring of 1864, "repeating rifles are the greatest favorite with the army, and could they be supplied in quantities to meet all the requisites, I am satisfied that no other arm would be used." Of the three types of repeaters available in limited numbers in 1863, he thought the Spencer alone really cheap, durable, and efficient.[39] When he wrote, only 9,502 Spencer rifles and 9,500 carbines were in service, and the demand for more was tremendous. "It seemed as if no soldier who had seen them could be satisfied with any other." Along with their other merits, they used a copper cartridge which could not be injured by water and obviated all need for caps.

Ramsay advised a policy which the bureau should have adopted much earlier: "These facts are significant and should teach us to offer every encouragement to the manufacturers of the repeating arm using the copper cartridge." The visiting Britons were much impressed by what they heard from General A. H. Terry of the performance of the Spencers at Olustee, Florida. Here, on February 20, 1864, a Connecticut regiment maintained a rapid continuous fire which kept the enemy completely "subdued" and their own losses trifling.

During 1863–64 owners of Spencers were writing home enthusiastically of the powers of that arm. It was "a most formidable piece," declared a Massachusetts lad; "equal to a small battery in itself," stated a Pennsylvania volunteer.[40] The only difficulty was that of supply. The Burnside Rifle Company, for example, was so tardy in its contract for making 30,500 Spencer-model repeaters that it did not get them in until the very end of the war. Too little and too late was the general story. When firing stopped probably a hundred thousand breechloaders were in the hands of Union troops; had twice that many repeaters been ready in the middle of 1863 the war might have been cut short by a year.[41]

Imagination sometimes seemed conspicuously lacking in the Northern war effort. The soldiers even in 1862 were asking for a portable regimental oven to bake fresh bread, which private firms could then supply but which the government never troubled to furnish in quantity. A British general, Hugh M. Rose, in a celebrated thousand-mile fighting march in burning heat during the Indian Mutiny, had demonstrated the value of khaki uniforms, and Britain shortly used them in her Abyssinian campaign (1868); but though

---

39 He pronounced Colt's and Henry's too expensive, Colt's dangerous to the user, and Henry's too delicate for service; see his endorsement on applications of Burnside Rifle Co. and Sharps Co. for new contracts. Ord. Letters to War Dept., Book No. 14, p. 46. But Rosecrans thought the five-shot Colt rifle first-rate and demanded 5,000 for his cavalry arm; Bickham, *Rosecrans*, 25. Cf. Holt-Owen Report, 37th Cong., 2d Sess., Sen. Exec. Doc. No. 72.
40 Survivors Assn., *Hist. 121st Pa. Vols.*, 45; J. L. Bowen, *Hist. 37th Mass.*, 354, 355.
41 Cf. *War for the Union*, I, 361–363.

its six-pound woolen uniform was much too hot in summer, the North never experimented with a cool, dust-repellent cloth. The Prussian army had developed an excellent nine-ounce cooking tin in two fitted parts, large enough that one man might cook meat and vegetables for several while another boiled coffee; but Americans stuck to kettle and pan. It was to the Army's credit, however, that it did widely adopt the small shelter tent, which if made of waterproof cloth had more uses than a blanket; or rather, this was to the credit of the great supply bureau under whose sheltering wings it fought the war.

[IV]

That the quartermaster bureau under Montgomery C. Meigs accomplished a herculean task with remarkable efficiency, honesty, and expedition no reasonable person could deny. It performed so great a work indeed that Meigs should be given a place near that of Seward and Stanton, Chase and Gideon Welles. He brought to his office a high reputation as supervisor of the principal prewar undertakings, both architectural and engineering, for the improvement of the capital. A man of dogged industry, marked reserve, and utter devotion to the nation, he sometimes seemed a mere machine for toil. Yet his papers actually reveal a kinetic spirit and a warmly emotional nature, sensitive to blame and responsive to praise. The terse diary which he kept discloses his intense pride in his son John, who graduated from West Point in 1863 with honors, and his still intenser grief when the next year this promising lieutenant of engineers, "a noble boy, gallant, generous, gifted, who had already made himself a name in the land," was slain by guerrillas near Sheridan's Virginia headquarters. One younger son, fortunately, survived.

The diary also reflects a singular streak of martial ardor in this quiet executive. Viewing the capture of Missionary Ridge, he was thrilled beyond words by the wonderful sight, and could only write: "I am rejoiced—I took part in it—a wonderful day." In the spring of 1864 he thirsted to join Grant at his Virginia headquarters, but Stanton wisely decided that for the time being he could not be spared from his Washington post.[42]

Unescapably, Meigs was often violently criticized, for every step he took involved friction. "He is a most arbitrary man," declared Senator John P. Hale. His acrimonious correspondence with McClellan's chief quartermaster, Rufus Ingalls, upon the supply services just after Antietam, gave him particular pain. But he triumphantly outrode every storm, even McClellan

42 Meigs Papers, LC; brevetted major-general July 5, 1864, Meigs commanded Grant's supply base at Belle Plain later that year, and refitted Sherman's army at Savannah early in 1865. Russell F. Weigley, *M. C. Meigs*, analyzes his work as administrator.

acknowledging his efficiency. Spending about one and a half billion dollars, or nearly half the direct cost of the war, and directing it into channels that largely remade the American economy, he was an ideal administrator.

The extent of his well-organized activities was impressive. The quartermaster bureau had to supply the army with horses, mules, wagons, carts, harness, fuel, and forage, while even after the government had a cavalry bureau Meigs purchased cavalry mounts. He had to build barracks, quarters, storehouses, and hospitals. His bureau gave the troops their uniforms, overcoats, underwear, blankets, shoes, and mess gear. It delivered them their ambulances. It provided stoves and office furniture. It erected portable sawmills. It paid the costs of army spies and interpreters, met the expense of courts-martial, and furnished many of the coffins for officers who died on duty. It shoed mules and hired veterinaries. To do all this required tremendous depots of supplies in appropriate cities—veritable department stores. A large staff of procurement officers and inspectors had to be maintained to buy everything from steamboats to pins; every regiment had its own quartermaster; and the commander of every company was accountable to the bureau for national property. It swam in a flood of paper work.[43]

As the first confusions of the war were conquered, the government gradually formalized its control over quartermaster contracts. By Federal law, bureau officers had to advertise for sealed bids, basing their advertisements on approved requisitions. While minor contracts might be let on the spot, all large orders had to be submitted to Meigs himself. Contractors were required to make an explicit statement of quantities, qualities, and terms of delivery, guaranteed by posted bonds. Though some regimental quartermasters were dishonest, the central activities of Meigs' bureau were never touched by scandal; his code of integrity was perfect.

As he was constantly under severe pressure from State politicians and regional business interests, Meigs saw that it would be wise to scatter his orders as widely as possible. He insisted that wagon contracts, for example, be distributed among different areas and as many capable firms as seemed practicable, for this would spread employment and assure at least minimal deliveries. But time soon proved that many small new firms were inexpert or unreliable, and in the end he was compelled to trim his sails to the wind of an increasingly concentrated economy. It was the big horse dealer, the big tentmaker, the big ambulance supplier, who increasingly got the orders, for in the emergent industrial America the big establishments usually showed more

43 For the organization of the bureau see O. R., III, iii, 894–897; for the Meigs-Ingalls corr. see O. R., I, xix, pt. 2, pp. 168–587. Ch. XXV, Laws of the 37th Cong., approved Feb. 9, 1863, outlines Meigs' main duties. His annual report for 1863–64 (O. R., III, iv, 874–902) is especially illuminating. He has been scandalously neglected by Civil War historians; Rhodes barely mentions him thrice, and Channing, Schouler, and McMaster not even once.

efficiency. We find him instructing an agent in clothing procurement to reject bids which appeared certain to plunge the contractor into loss, or force him to put his workers on a sweatshop basis, or require the cribbaging of materials. If several of the most respectable houses divided the order, "I am convinced that in the end the service, the soldier, and the government will be benefited." [44]

As the war went on stricter rules became necessary. Inflation and the ebb and flow of fortune on the battlefield caused violent fluctuations in the price of materials. The government therefore forbade long-term contracts, for if prices rose contractors failed with disastrous results, while if they dropped the bidders made fortunes. Congress asked for monthly estimates of needs, monthly advertisements, and monthly reports of contracts. Meigs always insisted, however, that a heavy burden of red tape would injure the war effort. For example, he attacked a Congressional proposal that every contract should carry affidavits sworn before a magistrate, pointing out that many purchases had to be made in the field amid all the confusion of advance or retreat, when nobody had time for affidavits, and that some army quartermasters signed so many contracts that they would have to hire a magistrate as full-time office clerk. He was hostile also to an excessive centralization of supply operations in Washington, arguing that responsible buyers and inspectors scattered all over the map should be allowed due discretion. [45]

Army consumption rapidly grew staggering. To outfit a single regiment with clothing even at the low prices of 1861 required $20,000, so that the 500 new regiments authorized that July meant an initial expenditure of ten millions; and an active soldier would wear out a good uniform in three months of camp, or a few rough marches. Shoes needed constant replacement. Meigs assumed that after Burnside's army marched from Harpers Ferry to Falmouth, it needed a complete new supply of shoes. And what a wild conglomerate of other demands had to be met! The records of a high quartermaster officer in the Army of the Potomac have been kept. They show him receipting within a short period for 39 barrels of coal, 7½ tons of oats, 23 boxes of bandages, 31 of soap, 4 of lanterns, 80 beef cattle and 450 sheep, 180 mules, a miscellany of ropes, nails, rags, forges, lumber, and wagons, rolls of canvas, shipments of stoves, parcels of wire, "sundries," and sacks—how the army needed sacks! He had to sign for everything, and keep accurate records of distribution.

At first the shortages had been appalling. Meigs had written just after Bull Run: "The nation is in extremity. Troops, thousands, wait for clothes to

44 To D. M. Vinton, Sept. 9, 1861, QMG Letterbook No. 18, p. 407.
45 To E. D. Morgan, Aug. 7, 1861, QMG Letterbook No. 56, p. 167. The States helped with supplies, but had to be reimbursed. For the liberal affidavit provisions actually enacted, see Acts of the 37th Cong., Ch. XXII, approved Feb. 7, 1863.

OFFICE OF ASSISTANT COMMISSARY GENERAL OF SUBSIST-
ENCE, No. 4 State-st., New-York, May 13, 1863.

PROPOSALS WILL BE RECEIVED BY the undersigned until 4 o'clock p. m., on WEDNESDAY, the 20th instant, for supplying for the use of the United States Army SUBSISTENCE STORES, to be delivered in New-York or Brooklyn, as follows, viz: For delivery on the 3d of June:

1,000 barrels first quality new MESS PORK, or PRIME MESS PORK, to be full salted, 200 ℔ meat, in full-hooped oak barrels, with two iron hoops; meat to be free from rust or stain.

1,000 barrels of first quality NEW EXTRA MESS BEEF. The meat to be packed in full-hooped oak barrels, with two iron hoops.

Five barrels to be examined as a sample before accepting the bids, and to be retained until all shall be delivered.

25,000 pounds first quality THOROUGHLY SMOKED NEW BACON SIDES.

12,500 pounds first quality THOROUGHLY SMOKED NEW BACON SHOULDERS.

62,500 pounds of first quality *thoroughly cured* SMOKED HAMS. Proposers will state whether their Hams are pickle-cured or dry-salted; also their average weight.

The bacon and hams to be delivered in bulk for inspection and packing, at such points in the cities of New-York or Brooklyn as may be designated.

750,000 pounds first quality PILOT BREAD, to be made of good sound Extra Ohio or other equally good flour; crackers to be thoroughly baked and perfectly dried before being packed, and in size, thickness, openness, &c., to conform to standard samples which can be examined at this office; to be packed in boxes of 50 pounds bread to each box; boxes to be made of fully seasoned wood, of such kinds as will impart no taste or odor to the bread; bottom and top of single pieces, or if two pieces, tongued and grooved together. Boxes to be strapped with light straps of suitable wood. The Flour and Bread will also be examined by the Inspector, who will reject all that in the quality of the flour or in any other respect is inferior to the standard Samples. Bidders to state the location of their bakeries.

50 barrels first quality kiln-dried CORN MEAL. The barrels to have two iron hoops and to be full head-lined.

500 bushels of first quality NEW WHITE BEANS, well seasoned and dry—to be packed in good, bright, well coopered flour barrels, to be full head-lined with green hickory.

50,000 pounds of prime RICE, in clean, good, stout oak barrels, like samples to be seen at this office.

7,500 pounds first quality white flint corn HOMINY, in well-coopered, head-lined flour barrels.

12,500 pounds prime RIO COFFEE, to be packed in barrels, like samples to be seen at this office.

50,000 pounds prime RIO COFFEE, to be roasted, ground, and packed in barrels, like samples to be seen at this office.

Parties offering to furnish Coffee, either green or to be roasted, are required to send in full-ch p-samples in the green state of all the coffee they propose to furnish.

12,500 pounds carefully selected TEA, in half chests, ⅓ Green, ⅓ Souchong, ⅓ Oolong; boxes to be well strapped and in perfect order. Cargo and Chop-marks to accompany the usual samples. Bidders are requested to offer not more than two samples of each kind of Tea.

45,000 pounds of good hard SOAP. Bidders to give the location of their manufactories.

POTATOES—Such quantity as may be required during the month of June; 60 pounds to the bushel, in good, ordinary, well-coopered barrels.

All the stores will be carefully inspected before their delivery, and compared with the retained samples. Returns of weights signed by a professional Public Weigher must be furnished whenever required.

Payment, as heretofore, to be made in such funds as may be furnished by the United States.

Contractors are expected to hold their goods, without expense to the United States, until required for shipment.

Proposers whose bids are not accepted, are requested to send for their samples on MONDAY, 25th instant.

Blanks for Proposals will be furnished at this office, which must be inclosed in an envelope addressed to the undersigned, and indorsed " Proposals for Subsistence Stores."

A. B. EATON, Colonel and A. C. G. S.

ADVERTISEMENT FOR PORK AND OTHER SUPPLIES

From The New York *Tribune* for May 18, 1863

take the field. Regiments have been ordered here [Washington] without clothes. Men go on guard in drawers." At the onset of winter he had to place large orders for blankets in England.[46]

But by the middle of 1862 surpluses were developing in many items, depots were becoming well stocked, the placing of foreign orders had been stopped, and even domestic contracts were being restricted. Meigs wrote in April, 1862: "The hurry is over. There can be little occasion now for purchases of clothing, tents, etc., under such urgency as would justify purchase without advertisement." In August he estimated that the supplies on hand would furnish 600,000 new recruits with clothing and general equipment.[47] Most of the shortages thereafter were traceable to distributive difficulties. Footgear, for example, had long been one of his worries, and like Kipling's warrior he must have been haunted by a vision of boots, boots, boots. When Second Manassas was fought, however, the armies had enough shoes; the Washington depot alone held 116,000 pairs, and issued an average of 25,000 weekly. Offers of foreign shipments were rejected. Carts, stationery, and blacksmith's outfits were all abundant.

The worst difficulties were connected with transportation, from steamboats to wagon trains and ambulances. Horses and mules were required in seemingly endless numbers. Even in September, 1861, the Army of the Potomac needed 20,000 cavalry horses and 20,000 artillery and transport animals, and this was but the beginning. Small contracts were at first made for lots of 200 to 1,000 at an average price per horse of $120. In the summer and fall of 1862 a weekly average of 1,500 horses were supplied to the Army of the Potomac, and McClellan still grumbled that he did not get enough. Because the government had political reasons for favoring the border States, rather high rates were allowed for Kentucky stock, this decision being taken, Meigs explained later to his aides, "after the parties representing Kentucky interests had seen the President, the Secretary of War, and other members of the Cabinet."[48]

The bills grew so high that Meigs earnestly exhorted officers to take better care of their animals. That outrageous cruelties and abuses were common there can be no doubt. Cavalry horses were sometimes ridden by heavy and unskillful men for twenty-four or thirty-six hours without rest, while artillery and wagon horses suffered just as badly. Battle losses were also high; at Murfreesboro alone men estimated that more than 1,500 horses of all branches

---

46 Meigs to Vinton, July 24, 1861, QMG Letterbook No. 16 (Clothing and Equipage), 185, 186; to Cameron, Oct. 14, 1861, QMG Letters to War Dept., Book No. 5, p. 487.

47 To Allen, April 12, 1862, QMG Letterbook No. 19, p. 393; to Vinton, Aug. 12, 1863, *ibid.*, 693.

48 Meigs to Swords, Dec. 7, 1861, QMG Letterbook No. 57, p. 383.

were killed. The national supply in 1863 ran so low that one agent who was sent out with a fund of $100,000 to replenish the Army stock reported that he would get nowhere against other buyers unless he could go above the allowed price of $110.[49] By July, Meigs was willing to pay $150 for a good cavalry or artillery horse delivered in Washington, and the next year the price went to $170. It is not strange that he burst out in a violent admonition to Rosecrans:

Compel your cavalry officers to see that their horses are properly groomed. Put them in some place where they can get forage near the railroad or send them to your rear for grass and ear corn. When in good order start them, 1,000 at a time, for the rebel communications, with orders never to move off a walk unless they see an enemy before or between them; to travel only so far in a day as not to fatigue their horses; never to camp in the place in which sunset finds them; and to rest in a good pasture during the heat of the day. [Also], to keep some of their eyes open night and day, and never to pass a bridge without burning it, a horse without stealing or shooting it, a guerrilla without capturing him, or a negro without explaining the President's proclamation.

Operate on their communications. Strike every detached post. Rely more upon infantry than upon cavalry, which in the whole war has not decided the fate of a single battle rising above a skirmish, which taxes the Treasury and exhausts the resources of the country, and of which we now have afoot a larger nominal strength than any nation on earth. We have over 125 regiments of cavalry, and they have killed ten times as many horses for us as for the enemy.[50]

Meigs felt severely the burden of feeding all the animals in camps, depots, and on the march. While both the Union and Confederate armies made use of meadows and pastures, the Union forces relied much the more heavily upon delivered hay, corn, and oats. Moreover, the Northern troops carried a far greater bulk of impedimenta than the Southern. Like Sherman in the West and Butterfield in the East, Meigs believed that the armies might usually cut in half the amount of freight they dragged over the countrysides. According to his estimates, 40,000 men ought to get their necessities into 500 wagons, instead of the 1,200 for which they asked. He thought that McClellan had carried egregiously large trains down to the outskirts of Richmond. "After all its losses," he grumbled to Halleck in the summer of 1862, "the Army of the Potomac had in camp on the James River nearly 2,800 wagons, which was at the rate of 28 wagons to a thousand men."[51] Every wagon meant four or six draft animals.

49 C. E. Fuller to Meigs, May 13, 1863, QMG Letterbook No. 68, pp. 504, 505.
50 Meigs to F. W. Kellogg, July 23, 1863, and to Rosecrans July 1, 1863; Letterbooks Nos. 69 and 70. Lincoln in the fall of 1863 forbade the export of horses. During the first nine months of 1864 cavalry horses were purchased at the rate of 500 a day, which was the rate of destruction; O. R., III, iii, 289.
51 Meigs to Halleck, Aug. 18, 1862, QMG Letterbook No. 62, pp. 79, 80.

In the following spring the Army of the Cumberland had about 3,000 wagons, most of them with six-mule teams, or enough, if formed in one line, to extend thirty miles; it had about 600 ambulances; and its horses and mules numbered about 50,000. At one time it had on hand 24,000 bales of hay and 200,000 bushels of grain, the hay costing at the base about 25 dollars a ton, and the corn 25 cents a bushel.[52] As armies grew, so did the trains. Grant in the spring of 1864 had about 4,000 wagons in Virginia; and in the middle of that year the forces East and West were using 300,000 horses and mules. Meigs continually urged Halleck in Washington and the generals in the field to make more summer use of grass, green fodder, and wheat or oats in the sheaf. He implored them to get rid of bulky Sibley tents, officers' camp beds, and all like luxuries. He wished a clearance made of many of the sutlers, who sold illicit liquor, traded slyly with the enemy, and above all choked the roads with their wagons; it was hard enough to get necessities to the troops without giving space to their candies, pies, soft drinks, and gewgaws. In all this he had the support of Herman Haupt, who was disgusted with the way in which baggage trains impeded army movements.[53]

The West fared better than the East in transportation because of its river arteries. We have already noted the efficient work of Lewis B. Parsons. Commissioned captain in the quartermaster service, and ordered to St. Louis, he took charge in the last days of 1861 of all water carriage in the department. Soon rising to the rank of colonel, he continued in control until late in 1864. All the important expeditionary forces were transported under his direction. Grant's army was taken to Pittsburgh Landing before Shiloh by a great fleet of 153 river transports; Sherman's army of 40,000 was lifted from Memphis to its point of attack above Vicksburg in eight days. "Since the commencement of the war," wrote the chief quartermaster officer at Louisville on August 14, 1864, "no western army has ever been thwarted for the want of transportation or the lack of supplies." An ordinary steamboat of 500 tons capacity could carry enough stores in one trip to subsist 40,000 men and 18,000 horses nearly two days. The quartermaster-general's bureau found an ample supply of boats of low tonnage which could be brought up to the bank almost anywhere to disembark troops, animals, wagons, cannon, and general supplies.

One of the sorest initial shortages, that of ambulances, also began to be filled in the latter part of 1862. By October a total of 3,500 had been bought by Meigs. Hundreds of them were of the two-wheel model, cheaper by $27

---

52 *Annals of the Army of the Cumberland*, by an Officer, 274–288.
53 Meigs to Clarey, Aug. 27, 1862, QMG Letterbook No. 62, p. 201; Haupt, *Rems.* In the summer of 1863 Stanton actually nursed the crazy idea that he might mount cavalry on large-size mules; to Meigs, Aug. 17, 1863, War Office Military Book No. 52b.

than the $170 four-wheel type, but productive of agony, grating bones, and loss of blood in their heavy jolting over uneven ground. After 1862, happily, the government bought no more. But still this was one of the areas in which the record was bad. Near the end of 1862 a trial was made of litters, fitted on the backs of mules, for carrying wounded. Poor Yankee lads!—maimed, hauled to the rear on balky, uncertain mules, and then perhaps turned over to a quack surgeon for unnecessary amputations. The wretched quality of many of the four-wheel ambulances excited frequent complaint. Their axles broke, their bolts slipped out, their bodies splintered, and their covers admitted the rain. Meigs, denying that the surgeon-general's office could have done better than he, laid the blame for shortcomings on the pressure of war emergencies.[54]

But in 1863 even ambulances were at long last fairly adequate in numbers and equipment.

[V]

The commissary bureau, too, was mastering most of its difficulties. The poor, ill-balanced, ill-prepared diet given the troops in the first months, nearly as serious a cause of sickness as camp filth, was less the fault of Joseph P. Taylor, the commissary-general, than of custom, haste, ignorance of nutrition, and bad distribution. The old army ration of salt pork or beef, hard bread or flour, coffee, and dried beans or peas, was so obviously inadequate that Congress in the summer of 1861 took steps to have potatoes and fresh meat, whenever possible, added to the menu. Vinegar and molasses were also put on the ration list. Initially the quality of food was often inferior: the "sowbelly" was fat and stringy, the beef tough, the hardtack so weevily that soldiers called it "worm castles." And despite official prescription, vegetables were so hard to get at some seasons and so difficult to transport great distances that for long intervals the men seldom had a taste of fresh food. But, with the press raising frequent complaints and the best officers and medical service cooperating, the commissary did increasingly well. Many members of Congress regarded Taylor as one of the most capable administrators in Washington. Surgeon-General Hammond thought that the troops had the best basic army diet in the world, and foreign observers were impressed, especially when they saw dried apples, pickles, and canned or pressed vegetables served to the messes. Sutlers and local peddlers helped to vary the fare.[55]

Voluntary initiative was especially valuable in meeting emergency short-

54   To Henry I. Bowditch, Oct. 20, 1862, QMG Letterbook No. 63, p. 400.
55   Adams, *Doctors in Blue*, 206 ff.; Wiley, *Billy Yank*, Ch. IX; Maxwell, *Lincoln's Fifth Wheel*, 34-36.

ages and supplying fresh food. The Sanitary and Christian Commissions were both active. On March 4, 1863, telegrams throughout the Northwest announced: "Rush forward anti-scorbutics for General Grant's army." The results were astounding. Newspapers scattered the appeal broadcast; committees sprang up in hundreds of localities; from every Northwestern State vegetables, jellies, and dried fruits poured into Chicago, down the Illinois Central, and down the Mississippi. Soon a traffic link of a thousand barrels a week connected Chicago with the Vicksburg area.[56] The previous summer soldiers with McClellan on the James had testified that they were well fed. Wrote one: "I must say that a very great change is being and has been brought about in the diet. Vegetables are now furnished by each commissary."[57] Some observers, like Frederick Law Olmsted with Grant in the summer of 1863, and the British officers in Virginia in 1864, believed that the rations could hardly be improved except by a diminution in quantity, for in camp especially, soldiers tended to overeat. Much always depended, of course, on the ability of the regimental commissaries.

National expenditures for army rations, culminating in an appropriation of $140,000,000 for the fiscal year 1863–64, were always adequate. The occasional shortages and hardships, amounting sometimes to brief semi-starvation, were an inescapable accompaniment of the fighting. But the improvement was fairly steady, and was attributable to four principal factors. One was the rising efficiency of Taylor's commissary bureau, strengthened by Congress in 1863. One was the heightened understanding of dietary principle: army surgeons knew from the beginning that the Russian defeat in the Crimea had been largely attributable to a wretched diet, and that vegetables were essential; they gradually learned that onions and apples were better than potatoes, and that berries and salads, even of weeds, were valuable. A third factor was the increasing reliance of troops upon foraging: they lived off the country when they could, and so got more milk, fresh meat, and garden produce. Finally, the army profited from the growth of the canning and meat-packing industries during the war. Experiments with desiccated potatoes and with a combined baked-wheat ration and sausage ration invented by E. N. Horsford of Harvard were failures, but tinned vegetables became more and more widely esteemed. Canneries of sea food, peas, and sweet corn had flourished along the Atlantic Coast before the war, the first recorded Western cannery had been established in Cincinnati in 1860, and a year later the Van Camp Company began its activities in Indianapolis.

56 Andreas, *Hist. of Chicago*, I, 319, 320, gives an account of this episode. The Cincinnati *Commercial*, July 1, 1862, describes the work of the Sanitary Commission of that city in improving Army fare.
57 Seth Paine, July 31, 1862, to E. Wilkeson, Gay Papers, Columbia Univ.

The business of Gail Borden, who opened his first large condensed-milk plant at Wassaic, New York, in 1861, was given immediate impetus by the war. His manufactory was issuing cans of sweetened condensed milk when Sumter was bombarded, and the troops and government made eager customers. In pork packing Philip Armour, who began business in Milwaukee in 1859, and Nelson Morris, who reached Chicago the same year, profited and expanded with the aid of war orders. Taylor's commissary bureau became an enterprise of a magnitude scarcely conceivable in prewar years; and its activities stimulated undertakings that were to seem tremendous before it went out of existence.[58]

United States Sanitary Commission. — The Treasurer acknowledges the receipt of the following contributions since Feb. 16:

Sunday-School Class in High-st. Church, Portland, Me., by B. Thurston (additional)	$1 10
M. J. L., N. Y.	3 00
John Taylor Johnston. (additional)	100 00
Citizens of Washington Territory, by W. W. Miller, Treasurer	4,520 77
Lieut. F. B. Crosby, U. S. A.	15 00
Citizens of Spanish Ranch, Plumas Co., California, by Thos. J. McCormick, Marysville	107 00
Premium on Gold from do	71 32
Chas. B. Hart, N. Y., (additional)	25 00
Sawyer, Wallace & Co., by John T. Agnew	500 00
Woodland Soldier's Aid Society, Woodland, Yolo Co. Cal. by Mrs. C. W. Lewis, President, Mrs. F. S. Freeman, Treas., Mrs. G. D. Fiske, Sec	1,222 60
Seven Gold and Silver Bars from Storey Co., Nevada Territory	19,366 37
Premium on do	10,554 67
One Silver Bar from Ladies' Social Benevolent Society, Gold Hill, Storey Co., Nevada Territory	860 16
Premium on do	468 78
Edmund H. Miller, New-York (additional)	250 00
Citizens of Oregon, by the Hon. A. Holbrook	377 34
Citizens of Walla Walla, Washington Territory, by the Hon. A. Holbrook	427 00
The Hon. Wm. H. Seward, being funds placed in his hands for the benefit of the Army by American residents of Santiago de Chili	8,688 84
George G. Briggs, Santa Barbara County, California, by Fowler & Wells	100 00
Thomas C. Smith	50 00
Anonymous, proceeds of a bet	25 00
N. R. Vail, St. John's, N. F., by J. M. Requa	150 00
Lathrop, Ludington & Co	250 00
Proceeds of Concert by Young Men's Association, West Troy, by S. H. Rogers, Secretary	152 50
Citizens of California, by James Otis, Treasurer, San Francisco	15,000 00
Premium on gold from do	8,006 50

GEO. T. STRONG, Treasurer, No. 68 Wall-st. New-York, March 18, 1863.

COLLECTING FUNDS FOR THE SANITARY COMMISSION

From The New York *Tribune* for March 19, 1863

The chariot of Mars was gaining momentum. On every side, by the date of Chancellorsville, observers could see evidence that improvised war was giving away to large-scale organized war, and that a new republic was emerging. The wagon trains of the armies were modeled on those of the Western plains, with practically the same vehicles, but were gigantic in comparison.

---

58 Much general material on activities of the commissary and quartermaster bureaus is scattered through O. R., III, iii and iv, Meigs's annual reports being specially valuable.

The four chief depots of quartermaster supplies, in New York, Philadelphia, Cincinnati, and St. Louis, closely resembled general stores, but were so much larger that even A. T. Stewart would have found them marvelous. The military telegraph system under Colonel Anson Stager and Major Thomas T. Eckert was growing toward the total of 6,500 miles which it would reach before the end of 1864.[59] One undertaking in social welfare, the rescue of the Negro refugees who had flocked to Washington, with the provision of housing, schools, police, and water, and the finding of employment, was unprecedented in government annals.

Northerners everywhere were learning entirely new lessons of resourcefulness, initiative, and organization. Herman Haupt's bridge over the Potomac Creek chasm was one of the marvels of 1862. In Napoleon's time trestle bridges of more than one story had been regarded as impossible, but this four-story structure lifted a railroad eighty feet above the stream bed. Built in nine working days in May, almost entirely of materials growing about the site, the 400-foot structure looked fragile—"corn stalks and beanpoles," said Lincoln—but it daily carried ten to twenty heavy trains in each direction and withstood severe storms. Yet other engineering feats were as remarkable, and some works, such as the model planning and construction done at Forts Richmond and Lafayette, defending New York harbor, were to be far more durable.[60] The nation's topographical engineers were giving a new vigor to mapmaking; in 1862–63 they made 8,841 military maps. Medicine was being regenerated by the war. As S. Weir Mitchell later recalled, the conflict found it with little professional status, self-confidence, or national regard; but the building and staffing of great base hospitals "left it with a pride justified by conduct which blazoned its scutcheon with endless sacrifice and great intellectual achievements." [61]

Most important of all were the lessons learned in organization. Frederick Law Olmsted pointed out that the meaning of the word was hardly known in prewar America. But young James A. Garfield, Rutherford B. Hayes, and Benjamin Harrison as brigade commanders necessarily learned organization. And how many others! Francis A. Walker was but twenty-two when, twice wounded at Chancellorsville, he became assistant adjutant-general in Couch's Second Corps of the Army of the Potomac. He had to collect and interpret every day the innumerable facts on the fighting strength of the corps; to digest the thousands of complaints, requests, and bits of information which welled up from 20,000 men; to conduct all correspondence and help frame

59 W. R. Plum, *The Military Telegraph During the Civil War*, tells an impressive story.
60 Haupt, *Rems.*, 45–50; Chanal, *The American Army*; Gilbert Thompson, "The Engineer Battalion in the Civil War," Occasional Paper 44, U. S. Army Engineer School.
61 Introduction, *In Wartime*.

all orders; to ride camp and battlefield alertly; and advise his commander. This training fitted Walker for directing two national censuses and building the Massachusetts Institute of Technology into the world's greatest engineering institution.

The inevitable outcome of the war was foreshadowed by the fact that while in defeat the North grew stronger, in victory the South became weaker. In the larger view, however, it was the steady growth not only of a more powerful Northern society, but a new type of society, which was significant. The old Pilgrim chronicler Nathaniel Morton, relating how the founders of Plymouth had taken leave of Europe, committed themselves to a fateful experiment, and by hard labor triumphed over their first trials, concluded that from their late estate they were forever parted: "If they looked behind them, there was a mighty ocean which they had passed, and was now as a main bar or gulph to separate them." When Americans in 1863 looked back a short three years, they saw that they were separated from their former world by a stormy ocean, and that an impassable chasm shut them off from their earlier history. To discern just how wide that main bar or gulph was, we must turn to the changes in private industry.

19

Shape of Revolution: Anvil, Loom, and Piston

UNSTEADILY, sometimes obscurely, but inexorably, forces of internal change by 1863 were transforming American life. The South stood face to face with a socioeconomic revolution from which not even victory could extricate it. In the North the multiform changes, the most powerful of them economic, were still more significant. Parallel with the waste and sorrows of war ran a stimulation of individual initiative, a challenge to large-scale planning, and an encouragement of cooperative effort, which in combination with new agencies for developing national resources amounted to a great release of creative energy. The principal Northern cities by the end of 1862 seemed electric with fresh ambitions, ideas, and methods. It was as if the shock of arms, with its tremendous affirmatives, had invigorated a people too long fettered by hesitancies. As a mighty human upheaval, the industrial resurgence outstripped the military effort.

Even in its worst months of defeat and discouragement, the period from the Seven Days through Chancellorsville, the country was steadied by a sense of economic well-being. Cheap and abundant food, ready employment at fair wages, heavy business profits in many lines, and a steady continuance of western settlement, sustained Northern courage. "Our people bear the burdens of the war without inconvenience," declared a circular of Samuel Hallett & Company in the summer of 1862, "because they have an abundance of everything that supports war—men, money, food, clothing, and munitions of all kinds. All these can be had in the greatest profusion upon such terms as the government offers. A similar strength, stability, and confidence displays itself in all the operations of society. Prices of property of all kinds are well maintained. There is no check to the progress of all useful enterprises that bid fair to be remunerative." [1]

---

[1] The writer of "Why the Country is Prosperous," an editorial in the Chicago *Tribune*, Oct. 31, 1861, found the explanation in increased exports, diminished imports of luxuries, and gold receipts from the Far West.

From the economic prostration just before and after Sumter, the North had made a sharp recovery in the first battle autumn. One of its sources lay in the abundant harvests gathered to meet an unprecedented world demand. Another root sprang from the war contracts which expanded so rapidly after Bull Run, and a third from the practical exclusion of many foreign commodities from the home market by the Morrill Tariffs, shipping difficulties, and incipient inflation with its resulting exchange difficulties. Not the least important source was the imagination displayed by industrial leaders in adapting themselves to changed demands. Finally, the use of new machinery and technological devices in field, factory, and foundry had its effects. This recovery had been continued into 1862 as a firmly rooted prosperity, which by 1863 was bearing gaudy flowers of wealth, speculation, and luxurious spending.

Nathaniel Hawthorne, studying the country, marveled at the rapidity with which it took on a military veneer. The demand just after Bull Run for a new army of half a million was translated into the sudden appearance of soldiers everywhere, parading on New England greens, clattering along Philadelphia streets, crowding prairie railway stations; privates buttoning their French-gray overcoats against the autumn chill, officers fingering their swords and gilt buttons. War contracts were translated into another language. They meant the hammering of countless carpenters on new buildings, the scream of saws hewing out gunstocks, the roar of forges making wagon tires. Bank presidents sat up late studying applications for credit. Newspaper editors, "free," said Grant, "to the point of open treason," toiled to distribute their swelling circulation by newsboys and post offices. Storekeepers wrung the hand of the departing clerk and asked the deacon if his bright daughter would like the place. In Washington, in State capitals, in city halls, administrators saw that the kind of regulation Andrew Jackson had established when he forbade the employment of women would have to be jettisoned. The manpower shortage meant higher wages, employment of young and old, and an eager search for labor-saving devices.

The United States, an underdeveloped nation in 1860, needed more capital, more entrepreneurial brains, more organization, more technology; in short, more of what a later generation called economic dynamism.[2] By mid-1863 the dynamism was a rushing flood.

2 The principles of capital formation and growth were not at this time understood anywhere. For these principles see the volume by the National Bureau Committee for Economic Research and various university scholars, *Capital Formation and Economic Growth* (Princeton Univ. Press, 1956), and Simon Kuznets, W. E. Moore, and J. J. Spengler, *Economic Growth: Brazil, Japan* (Duke Univ. Press, 1956).

[I]

The changes of these years were the more dramatic for being set against the brief paralysis which accompanied and followed secession. The failure of banks whose notes were based on Southern bonds, the collapse of firms to which Southern interests owed large debts, the embarrassment of businesses trading in Southern cotton, sugar, and naval stores, the suspension of commission houses acting for Southern shippers, all added heavy blows to the initial shock and uncertainty. The breakdown of Illinois banks, for example, which had based their note issues on Southern State bonds, was calamitous. In all Illinois only the fourteen or fifteen banks which had been wise enough to prefer Northern State securities survived. As for merchants, hundreds staggered and fell. Greeley's *Tribune* bitterly remarked that although some individuals had made money from the South, New York City and other centers had in general lost, for repudiation in the bad years 1827, 1837, 1841, 1854, 1857, and 1861 had wiped out all profits. Just how large the total debts of Southerners to the North were nobody knows, but $150,-000,000 would be a median estimate. This suspension of debt payments must not be discussed in moralistic terms, for Southerners found themselves without money to pay, but it created indignation as well as pain in the North.[3]

All businessmen, as the South seceded, turned nervous eyes to that great pillar of the Northern economy, the cotton business. Cotton textiles excelled any other branch of American manufacture in value of product, employment of capital, and importance to internal and foreign trade. With some reason, Southerners had believed that cotton was king in several Northern states as well as Britain and France. Nearly half of the nation's spindles were in Massachusetts and Rhode Island. New England employed about 200,000 operatives, or half as many as the mother country. Fortunately for the Yankee millowners, they had laid in a full annual supply of cotton during 1860, for they knew that the crop was heavy and that prospects for the future

3 For the breakdown of the Illinois banks, see *Annual Statement*, Chi. Bd. of Trade, 1861; Cole, *Era of Civil War*, Ch. XVI. One authority, J. C. Schwab, places the total of Southern obligations as low as $40,000,000; *Hist. Confederacy*, 111, 112. R. G. Dun & Company, after a close examination of their books, estimated it at about $300,000,000; they reported (N. Y. *Times*, Jan. 2, 1862) that the total owed to New York businessmen was $159,800,000; to Philadelphia businessmen, $24,600,000; and in Baltimore, $19,000,000. The Southern journalist E. A. Pollard puts the debt at not less than $200,000,000; *Jefferson Davis*, 183. Philip S. Foner, *New York Business and Slavery*, 218, sets the amount at $150,000,000. On May 21, 1861, the Confederate Provisional Congress made suspension legal by prohibiting debt payments to Northerners; those owing money were authorized to pay the amount due to the Confederate Treasury, which would give them a certificate payable after the war in specie or its equivalent.

suggested a diminished yield as well as political uncertainty. Even so, the outbreak of war instantly disrupted the cotton-textile trade, for it cost the North the large Southern market, and faced the businessman with fears both spectral and substantial.

Between Sumter and Bull Run, most large mills completed their orders and shut down either completely or in part. The venerable Merrimack Company in Lowell, Massachusetts, made what that city long remembered as a stupendous blunder, for believing that the war would end soon and suddenly, the managers closed its mills, dismissed its hands, and began to sell stocks of raw cotton which soon became almost priceless. Some other mills followed this unlucky example. After Bull Run the industry relapsed further into the depression, for cotton spinners perceived that the war might last long, business might get worse, and the market could not absorb their textiles if they hastily manufactured all their reserve cotton. The Pepperell Company on the Saco, for example, in August discharged all but 200 or 300 of the 1,400 hands in its three mills. For the first year of war American mills averaged about half-time. Meanwhile, machinery makers found orders for textile equipment dwindling to a trickle.

In the closing weeks of 1861 observers doubted whether half the cotton mills were operating on any considerable scale. The export trade for the year had fallen by a quarter, and many discouraged hands had enlisted or found other employment. Suffering among the mill workers would have been serious but for enlistments and the fact that many women simply scattered to rural homes. Only a few favorable circumstances had saved the cotton-textile business from being beaten prostrate. For one, prices of goods had slowly risen, so that even on reduced sales many maufacturers could show a profit. The mills closed the year with 75,000 bales still on hand, a stock augmented by meager shipments slipping through from the South, or returned from Europe by speculative holders anxious to take advantage of the high market; and this stock gave manufacturers hope they could hold on until McClellan overthrew the Confederacy. Even so, the outlook was gloomy, for raw cotton cost so much that many mills could not afford to buy new supplies and process them.[4]

Meanwhile, the Northern trade in many other commodities experienced an agonizing wrench. New York had special reason for feeling the national upheaval. The loss of credits to the South, of shipping business, of brokerage

4 *Annual Reports*, Boston Bd. of Trade, 1861 and 1862, cover textile manufactures in New England. The Commissioner of Agriculture stated the cotton crop of 1860 at 5,192,746 bales, of which 3,812,345 bales were exported in that year, leaving 1,384,599 bales for domestic consumption; Annual Report, 1862, p. 561. In England, writes John Watts, "mills began to run short time or to close in the month of October [1861], but no noise was made about it"; toward the end of the year in England, speculation in cotton became unusually active. *Lancashire and the Cotton Famine*, 113.

and banking fees, and of a large retail trade through Southern ports, hit the city hard. It had stood supreme in the sugar trade, and now Louisiana shipments and Southern orders went by the board. It had been the chief market for naval stores, and dealers groaned when the last parcels of crude turpentine were sold in October. Shoe manufacturers and jobbers, catering almost entirely to the South, were left with a dead weight of stock on their hands. Until late summer, the sale of all kinds of iron and ironware was so completely checked that furnaces in the Hudson Valley, which had specialized in expensive grades of charcoal iron, had to be blown out.[5]

Philadelphia, with an advantage over most centers in the variety of her manufacturing, fared better. The census had shown that the city had 1,523 clothing factories, 525 textile factories, and 649 iron and steel works, producing about $60,000,000 worth of goods a year. But in addition, Philadelphia had a remarkable range of establishments making wagons, farm implements, paper, leather, glass, wooden wares, pottery, soap, and chemicals, a situation which facilitated its adaptation to new conditions. When cotton supplies ran low, some factories quickly put in woolen machinery, and when luxury goods fell their producers turned to army supplies. "Business has, of course, been greatly disturbed and deranged," remarked the Board of Trade in its review of 1861, "and heavy losses have ensued to many parties"; but, it added, industry had shown such resourcefulness that the great majority of employers and workingmen were fully and usefully occupied.[6]

The trade of Baltimore, however, was nearly paralyzed well into the summer of 1861, and recovered but slowly. Providence, which had specialized in cotton textiles, found that instead of receiving 160,000 bales as in 1860, it obtained little over one-third of that amount during 1861.[7] Most iron furnaces on the Susquehanna and Schuylkill shut down. Pittsburgh suffered from the interruption to the iron trade. All the cities along the border—Wheeling, Cincinnati, Louisville, St. Louis—were for a time badly hurt, for they expected more fighting than they actually saw, and were rent by factional divisions.

Cincinnati in particular had a well-justified fear from the beginning that its trade would be largely shattered. When war became imminent most of the people of Yankee and German origin called for an interdict on all traffic with the Confederacy. Pork packers, manufacturers, and merchants protested angrily that they would be ruined, but majority sentiment prevailed. While competitors in Louisville, St. Louis, and other places continued sending mixed shipments south, for the government imposed no blockade until May, the

5 See *Fourth Annual Report*, Chamber of Commerce, State of N. Y. (1861).
6 See *29th Annual Report*, Phila. Bd. of Trade (1861).
7 Theodore Collier, "Providence in Civil War Days," *R. I. Hist. Soc. Colls.*, XXVII, Nos. 3 and 4 (October, 1934), 102.

patriotic Cincinnatians paid a heavy price. In the fiscal year 1860–61 the city had butchered nearly twice as many hogs as Chicago, but now its Southern trade collapsed, and when 1861 closed it held the only oppressive stocks of pork in the West. Its expanding manufacture of furniture, designed largely for the Southwest, almost went to pieces; in the five months beginning with April it shipped only 27,000 pieces as against 78,000 in the same months of 1860. Iron manufacturers had to suspend wholly or in part. Altogether, Cincinnati underwent severe hardships.[8]

The trade of Chicago with the South had been lucrative. Merchants shipped cereals, flour, hay, and meats—for the city excelled in packing beef as Cincinnati did pork—by the Illinois Central and Alton railroads to St. Louis and thence by packets down the Mississippi and up every large tributary. A return river-rail traffic in cotton and sugar was just becoming appreciable, and nourished a dream of Northwestern cotton mills. The link between the Illinois Central and Mississippi Central was so far advanced that men had hoped to run through trains between Chicago and New Orleans early in 1861. Lately, moreover, buyers from Richmond, Charleston, and other points in the South Atlantic area had appeared in Chicago markets. The sudden curtailment of business by the political upheaval in the winter of 1860–61 dismayed everyone. "The South was never so bare of provisions and breadstuffs as at the present moment," remarked the annual trade review as 1860 ended. Until midsummer the depression persisted.[9] St. Louis meanwhile, as we have seen, suffered a paralysis as severe as Baltimore's.

But for most interests the war quickly healed the first wounds it created. Shuttered stores, smokeless factory chimneys, and ragged clumps of unemployed faded like a bad dream. Throughout the summer of 1861 men commented on the plethora of money which made call loans easily obtainable at 4 to 6 per cent. Though in the panic of 1857 notes signed by the best names had sold as high as 5 per cent a month, during the troubled early weeks of the war good paper v as sought at legal interest rates. "One was a financial and the other a political panic," remarked the New York *Tribune*.[10] R. G. Dun & Co. reported more Northern failures in 1861 than in 1857, but for diminished totals; 4257 mercantile failures in 1857 for $265,800,000, as against

8 The Cincinnati Chamber of Commerce published annual reviews Sept. 1–Aug. 31, which are supplemented by annual reports of the Ohio State Commissioner of Statistics.

9 For Chicago's hardships see *Annual Statements*, Chi. Bd. of Trade, 1861–63; Chicago *Tribune*, 12th, 13th, and 14th annual reviews of trade and commerce, 1860–62; A. T. Andreas, *Hist. of Chicago*, II, 616 ff.; and Bessie L. Pierce, *A Hist. of Chicago, 1848–73*, pp. 127–129. The war shattered the dream of through Chicago-New Orleans rail traffic; direct trains did not run until the end of 1873.

10 N. Y. *Tribune*, June 29, 1861; as early as May 29 a *Tribune* editorial had predicted great war prosperity.

5935 failures in 1861 for $178,600,000. Jobbing houses had been the greatest losers.[11] And before the autumn began, a great change was under way. As early as July the Allegheny arsenal at Pittsburgh was employing 400 hands. In October the Cleveland *Leader* remarked that business was better than before the war, for machinists, manufacturers, shipbuilders, railroads, and clothing merchants were all filling war orders.[12]

[II]

Recovery came first in an unprecedented sale of grain, meats, and other farm staples to Great Britain and Continental Europe. During three years, 1860–62, British crops were a failure, and in one of these years the whole European crop was wretched.

Chicago, already the nation's chief rail center, boasted at the end of 1861 that it had carried on a richer commerce in cereals than ever before. "Our city may well be proud of her position." It forwarded much more than twice the flour shipped in the year Lincoln was elected, it was drawing ahead of Cincinnati in pork packing, and its receipts of lumber fell little short of the previous year's mark. Cold statistics tell little, but one may be cited: against shipments of just over thirty-one million bushels of grain and flour in 1860, Chicago in 1862 sent out more than fifty-six millions.[13] The city was a center of trade not only in cured meats, but in livestock on the hoof. In the summer of 1862 the New York *Tribune* noted that every channel to the Atlantic coast was teeming with agricultural products—"Illinois alone sends now to the great market at New York an average of 2000 head of cattle weekly." [14] Transportation facilities in the fall of 1861 were overtaxed, with every lake vessel fully employed and car shortages on all the railroads.

Other centers made the same report. The trade of St. Louis, which reflected army as well as civilian demands, curved upward during the fall. That city had shipped 443,000 barrels of flour in 1861; the figure rose to 484,000 in 1861, to 647,500 in 1862, and to 689,000 in 1863. Foodstuffs went down the Mississippi and up the Tennessee, Cumberland, and Arkansas rivers in the wake of the armies. Cincinnati also took courage from the avidity of the European market. Lard and meat exports to Britain broke all records in

11 N. Y. *Times*, Jan. 1, 1862.
12 Baldwin, *Pittsburgh*, 318; Cleveland *Leader*, Oct. 19, 1861.
13 Chicago had forwarded 698,000 barrels of flour in 1860; in 1861 it forwarded 1,604,000 barrels; and in 1862 it sent 1,828,000. *Annual Statement*, Chi. Bd. of Trade, 1865, p. 24; C. B. Kuhlmann, *Devt. of the Flour-Milling Industry in the U. S.*, 94 ff. For the decade before the war the United States had averaged wheat exports of about twenty millions a year, but in 1862 it sent overseas three times that much. *Statistical Abstract*.
14 July 29, 1862.

1861, for British consumers took the equivalent, from all America, of two million hogs. "Nothing like this ever happened before," wrote Cincinnati's trade annalist. "It shows . . . that there is now secured a market for our pork in Great Britain and on the Continent of such magnitude that . . . the amount consumed heretofore in the Southern States sinks into comparative insignificance." In Philadelphia the Pennsylvania Railroad erected large grain elevators for the export trade.[15]

The sizable military markets which appeared in the fall of 1861 rapidly widened to immensity. Providence noted the brisk new demand in September. Several firms held contracts for army cloth, a tool company had a contract for 25,000 rifles, Corliss and Nightingale were making breech-loading cannon, and other establishments were turning out bayonets and the Burnside rifle: "plenty of work, good prices, and general contentment." [16] By the end of August the New England shoe trade was busy on its first army contracts. Cincinnati clothing makers received batches of army orders early in the fall, and by September, 1862, had contracted for more than six million uniforms. The shoemakers found that they had cut back their facilities too sharply when Southern demand fell, for as the armies began engrossing the Eastern supply, a Midwestern shortage appeared which the revived factories could not meet. Pittsburgh, meanwhile, was busy making river steamboats, army wagons, and a variety of arms. New York found the consumption of sugar rising, for soldiers consumed more.[17]

Another stimulant to industry, the tariff, first became strongly felt in the summer of 1862. The original Morrill tariff, passed just before Sumter, had been moderate in temper, its most important changes being the enhanced duties on iron and wool. Its authors had asserted that they meant simply to restore rates to those of the Walker tariff of 1846. But the second Morrill tariff (July 14, 1862) went well beyond the avowed purpose of Thaddeus Stevens and Justin S. Morrill, the compensation of domestic producers for the sharp internal revenue taxes just laid. Western Democrats in Congress protested that the high duties, made still higher by the fact that they had to be paid in gold, laid an unjust burden on Western agriculture for the benefit of Eastern industry. "Let this process go on a few years, and the wealth of the West will be transferred to the pockets of New England monopolists and capitalists." And Francis Lieber wrote his friend Sumner declaring that such enactments fed the very real hatred which other sections felt for New

---

15 *Annual Reviews*, Cincinnati Ch. of Commerce, 1861, 1862; St. Louis Union Merchants Exchange, *Annual Report*, 1865; *29th Annual Report*, Phila. Bd. of Trade, 12.
16 Theodore Collier, "Providence in Civil War Days," *R. I. Hist. Soc. Colls.*, XXVII, Nos. 3 and 4 (July, 1934), 82.
17 *5th Annual Report*, Ch. Commerce, State of N. Y., 1862, p. 104.

England. The tariff actually shut out many articles so completely that it failed of its revenue-raising goal, and forced the growth of certain lines of industry as in a hothouse.[18]

In particular, it and a thousand war requirements revived the iron industry with galvanic effect, and with special benefit to Pennsylvania. Several other States, as prices soared, hastily refurbished old furnaces, rolling mills, and forges, and opened new ones. New York turned to disused shafts in the Adirondacks, and the Cooper-Hewitt works at Trenton increased their demands on New Jersey ores. But Pennsylvania drew ahead of all rivals—another step in that process of national disequilibrium which Horatio Seymour had deplored in his inaugural speech.[19]

During 1862 two extensive rolling mills were opened at Allentown and Bethlehem, with an annual capacity of 40,000 tons, another began operation at Sharon, and two steel works were established in Pittsburgh. The war never completely stopped railroad construction, while it accelerated the demand for rolled iron, merchant bars, forgings, and plates. The Phoenixville Iron Works soon made a specialty of the widely used three-inch rifled guns; the Fort Pitt Works at Pittsburgh, enlarged in 1862, turned out castings so huge that they were a wonder of the time. Meanwhile the heavy burden on existing railways created an urgent requirement for rails, cars, and locomotives which Pennsylvania did more than any other State to fill. Before the conflict ended the State doubled its output of iron rails, and its shops made most of the 3,000 freight cars and 50 locomotives put into service by the Pennsylvania Railroad alone.

By 1863 Philadelphians were rejoicing over a clear national primacy. Eastern Pennsylvania had turned out 381,000 tons of anthracite iron the previous year, and expected to make 580,000 tons in the current twelvemonth. "It is certain that the production of iron, which has been immensely stimulated during the last two years, has more than ever been concentrated in Eastern Pennsylvania, establishing our supremacy. . . ." The pig-iron production of the whole nation in 1860 had been roughly 920,000 tons. That of the North alone dropped in 1861 to 730,500 tons; reached 788,000 tons in 1862; and in 1863 broke the old records with a total of 947,600 tons.[20]

18 Taussig, *Tariff Hist.*, 162–170; S. S. Cox's speech in House, Jan. 22, 1863; Lieber, Jan. 14, 20, 1863, to Sumner, Lieber Papers, HL. New England for the good of the nation should "relax her protective acerbity," declared Lieber; but Pennsylvania was an equally greedy champion of protection, while Ohio sheep-growers benefited from the wool duties.

19 Nevins, *Hewitt*, 206 ff. Bernard Levin, "Penna. and the Civil War," *Pa. History*, X (January, 1943), 1–10.

20 Insofar as the United States had an infant Ruhr, it was in the Schuylkill and Lehigh Valleys. In 1862 the Lehigh Valley produced 178,000 tons of iron; the Schuylkill furnaces 80,000 tons. The Juniata and Cambria furnaces made 63,500 tons, the former specializing in

But the most interesting stimulant of industrial expansion in 1861–63 was the resourcefulness and ingenuity of Northerners, an asset worth an army. Of a thousand possible illustrations of quick adaptation to new circumstances that furnished by the Waltham Watch Company will suffice. Thrown on its beam ends in 1861, like other luxury craft, the corporation first reefed sail. Then, the managers, noting that the tariff, high exchange, and insurance rates had shut out foreign watches, while international complications made people favor a home product, began studying the market. They saw that soldiers, clerks, and workmen wanted cheap watches within the $12–$18 price range; and sales and profits climbed until in 1863 they were a third higher than in the last prewar year.[21]

[III]

Some industries were so altered and dilated by the war that men were tempted to call them new industries. The transformation was sometimes manifest in the rapid utilization of newly invented machines for quantity production or the replacement of lost manpower; sometimes in the adaptation of facilities which furnished one type of goods to the making of a substitute staple; and sometimes in the swift development of a quite novel resource. The use of the new shoe machinery offers a classic instance of the first kind of resiliency; the expansion of woolen manufactures to take the place of cotton goods an example of the second; and the rise of the petroleum industry an illustration of the third.

No chapter of our economic history has more drama than the wartime transformation of the boot and shoe industry. This was one of the largest industries of the nation, employing in 1860 some 123,000 persons in 12,500 establishments, and producing goods valued at $91,900,000—a sum not prodigiously below the $115,600,000 total for cotton textiles. But when the war began it was still mainly in the stage of domestic production, most so-called factories being mere assembly rooms for products fabricated at home. In New England, the consolidation of small shops into big factories had become pronounced in the 1850's, and had been accelerated by the panic of 1857,

---

charcoal and coke for fuel. Though steel production was trifling by subsequent standards, more was being made in the United States than most people realized. It was needed for files, saws, cutlery, and edged tools in general; and the N. Y. *Tribune* of Feb. 18, 1861, stated that twenty-one establishments were making at least 13,800 tons a year, some of it better than the Sheffield make. The N. Y. *Times* attacked the first Morrill tariff on steel as prohibitory, but the *Tribune* declared that it was time the British monopoly was ended. Files of the *Iron Age* contain much on iron manufacture, tariffs, the brisk wartime search for new iron deposits, and the shipments of Lake Superior ore, which dropped badly in 1861, recovered to the prewar level in 1862, and broke records (203,797 tons) in 1863.

21   C. W. Moore, *Timing a Century*, 42 ff.

for the factory system checked waste, speeded production, and insured a higher standard of work. The largest single establishment, that of the Batcheller family at Brookfield, Massachusetts, in 1860 produced goods valued at $750,000, and it and four other factories under the same proprietorship made more than a million pairs of boots and shoes. But uppers were as yet generally hand-bound to soles in homes, and often the whole shoe was made there.

Lyman R. Blake, who in 1858 patented a machine to sew the uppers to soles, and Gordon McKay, who promoted it, made it possible to abolish the principal bottleneck in shoe manufacturing; but their invention needed the war and the shortage of manpower to accomplish its rapid adoption. Blake's device consisted of a hollow arm tapering to a small rounded end with a hooked needle, and an accompanying mechanism for making a loop of thread, which the needle caught and drew through the sole. The early months of war found him, still only twenty-five, traveling about New England with McKay to introduce his machine, improve it, and instruct workers in its use. He began, he related later, by sewing shoes for the Massachusetts Light Artillery. "Next I sewed the shoes for one or two regiments, and afterwards many thousands of pairs of army shoes. This army work was very heavy, and was undertaken with a view to test the machines, that they might be rendered nearly perfect before they were sold to the public." In 1862 he patented an improved machine. That same year McKay organized a company with a capital of $250,000 to distribute it, and then leased it to manufacturers for a down payment of $500 and a royalty of 5¢ for each pair of shoes stitched.[22]

The new machine came in steadily. Seth Bryant, a Massachusetts manufacturer, helped break a path for it when he took samples of machine-sewed shoes to Washington to show Stanton. The War Department gave him a contract on condition that he would guarantee the sewing, to which he agreed with the stipulation, in return, that as he would stamp his name on every

---

22 The North could have made shoes for its armies by the old methods, for more shoes were produced just before the war, selling both North and South, than at any time during the conflict. But shoe workers enlisted heavily, and women could not fully close the labor gap; machine-sewn shoes were stronger and more flexible than handmade shoes; and the machines kept prices down. These factors rather than army exigencies brought in the new era. Blake had been unable to finance his invention himself, and in 1859 had sold his rights for $50,000 to men who, when they ran into difficulties, induced Gordon McKay to take an interest. Blake then joined McKay on a wage basis supplemented by a limited royalty payment. During a period of three years he experimented with improved models, and produced 150,000 pairs of shoes for the army, of which 30,000 were rejected. Army contracts stipulated oak leather, which was staple in the Pennsylvania area, whereas hemlock leather was common in the Massachusetts market, and this handicapped New England manufacturers. See B. E. Hazard, *Organization of the Boot and Shoe Industry in Massachusetts Before 1875,* 112 ff.; C. H. McDermott, *History of the Shoe and Leather Industries of the U. S.,* I, 58 ff.; and D. N. Johnson, *Sketches of Lynn or the Changes of Fifty Years, passim.*

pair, Stanton should compel all other makers to do the same. While this contract for 300,000 pairs gave Bryant little profit, it did afford the new machine an effective advertisement. At the end of 1863 about two hundred machines were in use, and had already stitched two and a half millions of shoes. Steam power could of course be applied to quantity manufacture. A typical newspaper article in the Lynn *Reporter*, describing the growth of factories at the expense of domestic output, related that little handicraft shops were being vacated all over town, while "operatives are pouring in as fast as room can be made for them; buildings for shoe factories are going up in every direction; the hum of machinery is heard on every hand." McKay's ingenious idea of leasing rather than selling the machines saved small factory owners from burdensome capital charges and thus encouraged the change. As the skill of the Yankee handworker was now less important, factories appeared in cities of the Middle West, where the cattle industry furnished a plentiful supply of leather.[23]

An equally remarkable transformation occurred in the woolen industry, the swift rise of which was partly a compensation for the crippling of cotton textiles, and partly a response to voracious military needs. Here was one of the most impressive economic shifts of the time. When fighting began, the army had clothing stocks for only 13,000 men. The inability of mills to meet the sudden demand for uniforms, leaving a gap that foreign importations and the use of wretched cloth did not fill, resulted in a frenzied effort to increase facilities and output, which the war spurred on without pause. Early autumn in 1861 found the wool market swept bare; the new clip had been taken voraciously, and California shipments were sold before arrival. Within six weeks prices rose by a full third. Demand for woolens continued to outstrip supply, and as the war continued many millowners reaped large fortunes. In 1862 the mills took nearly half again as much raw wool as the previous year, and in 1863 double the 1861 total. Philadelphia, Providence, Lawrence, and Lowell, in that order the largest makers of woolens, could hardly find enough hands.

"The woolen machinery of the country is now fully employed," re-

23 At the beginning of 1862 the Boston board assured Montgomery C. Meigs that as the State probably had more machinery in motion than any other, "and as our people adapt themselves to circumstances with wonderful facility, we think it entirely safe to remark that in a year's time our shoe towns could provide for an army of half a million, of as good materials and workmanship, and at a lower price, than elsewhere." *Eighth Annual Report* (for 1861). A typical conversion story was that of T. H. Nowell of Portsmouth, N. H. Early in the war he gave home workers their materials, each handmaking the whole shoe and averaging three pairs daily. Then he introduced machinery and filled a large room with employees. Each team of five men thereafter finished thirty-six pairs daily, and as wartime wages rose, this gain of 133 per cent in labor output was important. Portsmouth *Journal*, Aug. 27, 1864.

ported the Boston board of trade for 1863. New mills had sprung up like Jonah's gourd, while old ones were renovated into something (literally) rich and strange. The Pacific Mills at Lawrence, for example, a combined woolen, cotton, and textile-printing establishment, wrote under Abbott Lawrence a striking page indeed of business enterprise. When Sumter roused the nation it threw away the red ink used since the panic of 1857, increased its profits under the new tariffs, and was soon a dazzling success. The Riverdale Mill in Providence, managed by a sagacious Scot, Robert Blaikie, became equally noted. The Assabet Mill at Maynard, Massachusetts, grew rapidly into the largest woolen (as distinguished from worsted) establishment in the nation. With high prices as stimulants, such factories ran day and night and maintained an urgent pressure on machinery makers. Down to the war the industry had lagged far behind the English mills in mechanical equipment, but now their facilities became equal to any in the world.

The sudden new demand for raw wool was felt over half the globe. In every pastoral country sheep growers responded to it; Australia, Canada, South Africa, Argentina, New England, the Far West, and the Scottish border all saw flocks whitening their green pastures so that Yankee looms might be kept whirring. The sunshine of high prices brought out a May-fly dance of speculators. Half the foreign wool taken for American mills came from Buenos Aires and Montevideo, with Britain and Europe the next largest sources. Everyone made money from the staple: Ohio farmers, Victoria station-owners, jobbers, shippers—but above all, manufacturers. Stockholders in the Pacific Mills, after investing $2,500,000, drew out wartime dividends aggregating nearly $3,000,000. The James Steam Mills Corporation of Newburyport in twelve months beginning May 1, 1862, earned $240,000 on a capital of $250,000, paying dividends of 80 per cent while increasing its reserves. A student of company reports finds evidence that dividends rose from an average of 9 per cent during the eight years before the war to 25.2 per cent in 1865.[24]

Contrary to a widely accepted legend, the ready-made clothing business was well established in America before the war. The first systematic manufacture, with coarse materials and rough workmanship, had begun in the 1830's. Garments ready-made in large quantities were sold to seamen, miners,

24   In this quick growth of the woolen industry statistics take on a certain aura of romance. The wool clip of the twenty-three loyal States in 1860 was 47,901,000 pounds; by 1864 the increase of sheep and improvement of breeds had lifted it to 97,385,500 pounds—it had more than doubled. *Ann. Cyc.*, 1865, p. 4. W. C. Ford, *Wool and Manufactures of Wool*, 317, gives the imports of raw wool as 31,000,000 pounds in 1861, just over 43,000,000 in 1862, some 73,200,000 in 1863, and 90,200,000 in 1864. See also A. H. Cole, *The American Wool Manufacture*, I, 268 ff.; and "Report Upon Wool" in *Reports* of U. S. Commissioners, Paris Exposition of 1867. Cole, I, 380, gives figures on wartime profits.

farm hands, and above all, owners of slaves. The invention of the sewing machine accelerated the business, while by the later 1850's woolen mills were manufacturing materials on a large scale. Use of sewing machines, and, just as the war opened, power cloth-cutters, assisted in the supersedure of many small shops by large wholesale establishments. This change is forcibly indicated by the fact that during the fifties the capital invested in the business nearly doubled, yet the number of establishments fell by 11 per cent. Trousers, cloaks, and vests were more readily made on a factory basis than coats, which required some skill in craftsmanship.

The disappearence of the Southern slave market confronted the ready-made trade with a crisis which war orders helped to erase. A single manufacturer received an order for $1,250,000 worth of uniforms. At first uniforms were made largely on the old "inside" system of manufacture; that is, workers went to a wholesaler for materials already cut and marked for putting together, and on completing them returned the garments for payment. As demands for Army clothing became exigent, however, factories were erected for the making of complete uniforms and nothing else. The government furnished measurements better adapted to males of various sizes than those previously used in the trade. The subdivision of labor increased, standards of workmanship became better established, and efficient new factory methods were introduced. The second Morrill Tariff, placing a duty of 24 per cent *ad valorem* on ready-made garments, almost completely excluded foreign competition. By 1863 Boston, New York, Rochester, Philadelphia, and Cincinnati were thriving centers of the business.[25]

In the swift development of a novel resource, the oil business meanwhile astonished not only America but the world. "Colonel" Edwin L. Drake had rubbed his Aladdin's lamp at Titusville, in the forested Allegheny hills, only fourteen months before Lincoln's election. The rush to northwestern Pennsylvania had taken on dramatic proportions before Sumter. In dash, color, and the exuberant production of wealth the oil boom rivaled the California and Australia gold rushes.

In certain essential respects this was not so new a business as it looked.

---

25 See the *Report* on clothing and woven fabrics by the U. S. Commissioners, Paris Exposition of 1867; U. S. Dept. of Commerce, *The Men's Factory-Made Clothing Industry* (1916), p. 9 ff. The wagon industry enjoyed an expansion not unlike that of the woolen industry. Carriage making in New York, like other luxury trades, was hard hit in 1861. But harbingers of revival appeared when the Union Defence Committee in June, 1861, ordered 50 ambulances, and that month and the next the Quartermaster's Department took 906 baggage wagons and 380 ambulances. In November, 1861, the New York *Coach-Makers' Magazine* was able to report: "The number of wagons, ambulances, and gun-carriages manufactured in this city and other places, for the army, is immense." By December, 1861, some 2,500 men were employed in making army wagons in Cincinnati; *Scientific American*, Jan. 2, 1862.

The extraction of lubricants and illuminants from coal had become a lucrative industry in various Eastern states during the prewar decade. Processes of distillation, well-designed lamps, and methods of barreling and selling "coal oil" (which was precisely that) had become well accepted. Petroleum was able to build on this foundation. However, the novelty of oil pumped in huge quantities from the earth, the quick returns made in "black gold," and the wide ramifications of oil-refining astonished observers. Amid bulletins of battle, the North read of fortunes made by the click of a drill, of frantic, noisy, populous towns like Oil City rising magically from the mud, and of the narrow gorge of Oil Creek studded for fifteen miles with derricks. The business soon developed the widest extensions. It gave half a dozen railroads a new source of freight for which they competed savagely, it required the swift building of tanks, terminals, docks, and warehouses; it replaced teamsters by pipelines; and it impelled a resourceful Englishman to establish a line of direct oil-carrying steamers to Liverpool. Lake and river shipping profited.

Though some cautious souls feared that the Pennsylvania fields would soon run dry, by the end of 1863 the economic importance of the flow was unmistakable; with an estimated production of ten million barrels that year, it was feeding refineries from Portland to Baltimore and from New York to Toledo. The market was insatiable, for petroleum furnished much the cheapest illuminant yet known. It made candles a luxury. Though the price of kerosene rose from 28 cents a gallon in 1860 to 41 cents in 1864, even the latter charge was only a third of the old-time cost of coal oil. Lard-oil, camphene, and other "burning fluids" were able to keep the merest vestige of customers. The fleets of whalers seeking sperm oil would have vanished from the seas, even had Confederate cruisers not assisted in scattering them. To fill the gap left when turpentine shipments ceased, petroleum derivatives were used with partial success for paints and varnishes. By the time Fredericksburg was fought, Pittsburgh had perhaps sixty refineries, the "oil regions" forty, and Erie, Pennsylvania, twenty. Speculation led to the rise of disreputable stock-peddling concerns and the formation of an excessive number of both producing and refining companies, many of which soon withered under excessive competition and high Federal taxation. A mining-camp atmosphere, with plentiful violence, enveloped the oil fields. But shrewd or lucky men made large profits, and before the last shots of the war were fired it was estimated that $450,000,000 had been invested in the "regions" alone.[26]

26 A meeting of crude-oil dealers held in New York on June 10, 1862, to combat some hostile Brooklyn restrictions, heard interesting facts from its chairman, A. C. Ferris. He declared that the bulk of the export trade centered in New York; that more than a million dollars had been invested in and around the city in it; and that the business grew mar-

This new industry brought a rising flow of much-needed gold into the country. New York in 1863 exported nearly half a million barrels, and other ports lifted the total to more than 800,000. In fact, oil shouldered its way up beside grain as an earner of foreign gold. "During the latter part of the year 1863," commented the Philadelphia board of trade, "petroleum exports constituted the leading article relied upon by the commercial cities for the creation of exchange in Europe." While Liverpool, London, Havre, Antwerp, Bremen, and Amsterdam were the largest importers, literally every important land on the globe, from China to Peru, wanted its quota of oil.[27]

[IV]

A number of other industries, new or renovated, added to the tale of business enterprise. Ironmasters, shipbuilders, textile makers, and arms manufacturers almost universally took the view that it was *their* war and they should monopolize the task of supply. If the government would only confine its orders to home interests, and compensate for heavy taxes by high duties, they would meet all its needs. A roar of protest went up from New England woolen men when word got about in the fall of 1861 that Quartermaster-General Meigs was about to buy five, or ten, or according to some, sixty million dollars worth of foreign cloth. The Boston board of trade telegraphed that this was entirely unnecessary and injurious to government and people, for home manufacturers could meet any demand. Meigs replied with asperity. Many soldiers were half naked; the governors were daily complaining that enlistments must stop unless abundant clothing was instantly sent to the camps; a hundred thousand uniforms were desperately needed at once; and having tried vainly to buy them at home, he felt justified in spending $800,000 —for that was all—abroad. Yet he had to agree that if home supply sufficed, he would hold the imported cloth for reserve supplies only.[28]

Advances in technological skill were illustrated by the arms factories, farm-implement shops, locomotive works, printing establishments (especially newspapers), machine shops, food canneries, and a hundred other businesses.

velously although the government taxed petroleum half its value. "The oil belt," he explained, "reached from Canada to the Gulf. . . . Another oil belt extended from Texas through Kansas to the Mississippi River. . . . Also upon the Pacific Coast there was a belt beginning about San Diego and so on by Los Angeles to Upper California." One man at the meeting held interests in 187 oil wells in Pennsylvania. N. Y. *Tribune*, June 11. Arnold Daum's MS history of "The Revolution in Illuminants," treats the coal oil industry and the superimposed oil industry in its early years; S. J. M. Eaton, *A Hist. of the Oil Regions of Venango County, Pa.*, 211, 271 ff., offers graphic material on early production.

27 *Annual Cyc.*, 1865, p. 700; Giddens, *Birth of the Oil Industry, passim*. The annual reports of the Phila. Bd. of Trade cover the petroleum industry.

28 Boston Bd. of Trade, *Eighth Annual Report*, 40 ff.

In the second year of the war 490 patents were granted for improved agricultural devices. Better reapers, mowers, threshers, grain drills, gangplows, and cultivators were needed to save manpower and bring in the large wartime harvests. Every curious foreigner visited the large meat-packing plants, and August Laugel was equally impressed by the Chicago elevators. He wrote:

Imagine an immense building without windows, very high, and divided on the inside into several storys; the ground floor is cut in two by a long gallery, where two trains and their engines can come in. . . . The Chicago River flows on one side of the elevator, a canal on the other connected with the river, so that boats can lie alongside the building as easily as trains can go inside. When a car loaded with grain has gone inside, a door on the side is opened, and the corn pours out into a deep trench. . . . An iron axle turns at the top of the enormous building, put in motion by a 130-horsepower steam engine. This shaft supports a drum at intervals, on which runs a belt to which buckets are fastened. These come down and are filled with corn . . . and raise it to the upper story; a few turns of the wheel bring the corn to the roof, and there it is emptied into a square wooden box of great size. The river of nourishment flows, flows incessantly. . . .

Thirteen elevating wheels raise each one 4,000 bushels an hour, so that 52,-000 bushels can be stored in that space of time. The whole building can be filled in half a day.[29]

The engineer John Fritz gives us an illustration of the way in which war contracts, tariff protection, and general industrial activity facilitated the installation of superior equipment in iron mills. In 1861–62 he erected a stone building on the Lehigh River for the Bethlehem Iron Company and began installing furnaces and machinery. By the fall of 1862 the mill, with all its features, was completed. In every respect it met new standards. "The roll housings were of new design and were dressed out inside with hammer, chisel, and file; the fittings inside were fitted up in the same manner. The furnace plates, being corrugated, were strong and handsome . . . ; the train was of the largest diameter used in any rail mill in the country." Machine shop, foundry, blacksmith shop, and pattern shop were all of improved design. For some years the Bethlehem Works were a Mecca for iron men. We may

29 *The U. S. During the War*, 127, 128. As much as four and a third million bushels of grain were stored in Chicago in 1861 at one time; *American Agriculturist*, October, 1861, p. 292. The importance of the grain elevator in the growth of traffic centers has been overlooked. An English correspondent wrote his editor just after the war: "That the grain elevator has made the cities of Buffalo and Chicago is not saying too much; and Mr. Joseph Dart made the elevator. . . . Today Buffalo has 27 of these buildings, storing together 5,830,000 bushels, handling daily 2,808,800 bushels. . . . In fact, a vessel alongside may either receive or discharge in six hours a cargo of 150,000 bushels of wheat or corn by means of the elevator. What the elevator means may be understood from the trade of both last year (1865). Buffalo did 40,937,000 bushels, and Chicago came up behind with 40,836,000 bushels." *English Mechanic*, Vol. III, No. 66 (June 29, 1866), 275.

take with reserve Fritz's boast that they were the best ironworks in the world, for after the war American experts found British, French, and German iron and steel plants vastly superior; but they did mark an advance.[30]

Perhaps no changes were more remarkable than those in the shops which equipped the navy and mercantile marine. Depredations of Confederate cruisers, high insurance rates, and the shift from wooden to iron vessels made the war period disastrous for American ocean shipping. Its collapse was but the culmination of a process already well advanced by the time of Sumter. But the fleet employed in the coastal, lake, and river trade maintained its growth, reaching 2,600,000 tons in 1862. When the Navy Department added its special contracts, establishments making marine engines found themselves choked with orders.[31]

A deafening rumble arose by 1863 from a score of machine shops in the New York area: the Neptune, the Morgan, the Novelty, the Continental, the Allaire, the Delamater, the McLeod, and others. They were turning out engines both vertical and horizontal, boilers, furnaces, plates, anchors, and miscellaneous fittings. The Fulton Iron Works, for example, were using seven hundred men to supply engines for eight government vessels, boilers for two more, twenty-four heavy buoys, and equipment for some privately owned vessels. The Novelty Iron Works with twelve hundred men were rebuilding the *Roanoke* with more than a thousand tons of armor and three revolving turrets for fifteen-inch guns, and making a beam engine for a Pacific Mail steamship and machinery for three side-wheel steamers. As various ship-yards were building warships for Italy, Russia, and China, the machine shops furnished engines for them too. Although the decline of the merchant marine made the ultimate outlook gloomy, as long as the war crisis lasted the machine shops did well, and their precision, ingenuity, and scope grew as in no previous period.[32]

[V]

This industrial advance was accomplished by a far-reaching transforma-tion of commerce. As soon as the Mississippi was closed, it became evident that the shift of trade from north-south to east-west channels, begun years before, would be accelerated. When some 1,600 steamboats ceased moving up and down the Ohio-Mississippi system with freight and gave way to war

30 The Bethlehem Works added a second furnace of novel design before they began rolling rails in September, 1863; Fritz, *Autobiography*, 141.
31 J. G. B. Hutchins, *The American Maritime Industries and Public Policy, 1789–1914*, 304–306. The appearance of low-cost iron-hulled steamships, British built and owned, to carry immigrants, had been especially disastrous to American packets.
32 Able articles appear in the N. Y. *Tribune*, Jan. 31, 1861, Feb. 7, May 1, 1863, etc.

flotillas, a huge tonnage of grain, meats, hay, and merchandise that had floated down to the Gulf had to turn toward the Atlantic by rail, lake, and canal.

Though no adequate statistics of steamboat trade exist, a table of steamboat arrivals at Cincinnati, chief commercial center of the Ohio Valley, is eloquent of the change. In the five years ending 1860 the average annual arrivals of steamboats from New Orleans had been 157, and from St. Louis 265; in the five years ending 1865 the arrivals from New Orleans fell to 41, and from St. Louis to 99. And most of what traffic still followed the river during the war served martial and not peaceful purposes.

The transports black with troops, the rams and "tinclads" with protrusive cannon, the sluggish flat-bottomed hospital boats and supply boats, kept the stretch south from Cairo busy; but Midwestern freight to and from the seaboard and Europe depended more and more on rails. For a decade three separate branches of water commerce had been declining. The movement of Western crops and manufactures to the South and Europe by way of New Orleans had declined; transfers between the Ohio Valley and the seaboard by canals had declined; and the movement between the Ohio River and the upper Mississippi and Missouri had declined. The war accentuated this threefold drop. While nobody can cite dependable figures, Cincinnati, Louisville, and St. Louis all now witnessed the final passing of the scepter from river packet to railway train.

The principal railroads paid off their floating debts, resumed dividends suspended in the recent panic, extended their lines, and in some instances accumulated surpluses. "At no former period," declared Greeley's *Tribune* late in the war, "has the whole Northern railroad system been so prosperous."[33] This prosperity encouraged the consolidation of small lines into trunk systems, and the building of new railroads for districts poorly served.

The Pennsylvania system, under the presidency of the brilliant engineer J. Edgar Thomson, achieved a highly successful series of consolidations. During the secession winter, replacing a short-term lease of the Harrisburg-Lancaster railroad by a 999-year lease, it obtained absolute control of a through line from Philadelphia to Pittsburgh. Before Donelson was fought it took another 999-year lease on the uncompleted Philadelphia & Erie, which would connect the main line with the Great Lakes and the oil district. Work was briskly pressed to finish this 289-mile road. For its connection with the Middle West the Pennsylvania used the Pittsburgh, Fort Wayne & Chicago, itself a merger of several lines, and by interlocking directorates and ownership of stock, the Pennsylvania managers obtained perfect control of this 465-mile road through Ohio and Indiana to Chicago, with branches to Cleveland

33 Jan. 27, 1864.

and Toledo. During the war Thomson also effected a close alliance with several short roads from Pittsburgh southwestward to the Ohio, thus gaining connections with Cincinnati and St. Louis. Altogether, by 1863 his powerful combination of lines was able to collect in St. Louis and Chicago the Midwestern crops, in Cleveland the Lake Superior ores, and in Erie the Michigan lumber, while it would soon tap the oil fields.[34]

The closing of the lower Mississippi to grain traffic, and the plans for a Pacific railroad, encouraged other roads to wrap their iron tentacles around more territory between Lake Michigan and the Missouri. The Rock Island line was one. The Chicago, Burlington & Quincy, which grew from a small feeder of the Michigan Central into a powerful network—as John Murray Forbes wrote, "located, planned, and built by the right set of men"—was another.[35] When Congress passed the Pacific Railroad bill in 1862 the stock of the Rock Island rose twenty points in a few weeks. The Chicago & Northwestern, however, was first in the race to reach Omaha.

The most ambitious railway built during the war was the Atlantic & Great Western, an arresting example of the nation's power to expand while fighting a tremendous conflict. It had originated in the fertile brain of Marvin Kent of Ohio, an entrepreneur who had managed such diverse enterprises as a woolen factory, a flour mill, and glass works. About 1850 he decided that a line of six-foot gauge connecting the Erie Railroad with the embryo Ohio & Mississippi might greatly benefit the Middle West. Obtaining an Ohio charter in 1851, he cast about for means of building across Pennsylvania. To go to the legislature directly was beyond his means, that body, as Horace Greeley wrote, "being then one of the rottenest and the surrounding lobby the most rapacious and shameless on earth." But, learning that the Pittsburgh & Erie possessed charter powers which would furnish the required facilities, Kent induced several other capitalists to join him in buying that road for $400,000. Another half-defunct line, the Erie & New York City, he purchased as a basis for building into New York. Then, all his legal preparations complete, he began collecting subscriptions. Desperate efforts, however, availed to furnish only a million, and this being obviously insufficient, he sent an agent to Europe to procure additional capital.

34 H. W. Schotter, *Growth and Devt. of the Pa. R. R. Co.*, 52–60; *Amer. R. R. Manual*, 1873, pp. 227, 228. Late in 1860 the Pennsylvania had taken a car full of Philadelphians on a three weeks' visit to all the chief Midwestern cities; *Annual Report*, Phila. Bd. of Trade, 1860.

35 Van Oss, *Amer. Rrds as Investments, passim*, contains a wealth of accurate material on mid-century growth. See also A. T. Andreas, *Hist. of Chicago*, II, 133 ff.; Bessie L. Pierce, *Chicago, 1848–1871*, pp. 147, 148; and Cole, *Era of Civil War*, 359, 360. The career of Forbes, who turned from the China trade to use Yankee capital in promoting the Michigan Central and C. B. & Q., sums up much of the best enterprise of the period; *Letters and Recs.*, I, 163.

The tangled financial history of the road involved the well-known Anglo-American capitalist James McHenry and much British money, while the construction history involved the remarkable Sir Samuel Morton Peto, who had played a leading role in railway building in Australia, Canada, Denmark, and France. But the important facts are that construction began, that the war did not interrupt it until the seizure of the *Trent*, and that after this cloud blew over, it was energetically resumed in 1862. The English engineer prosecuted the work so tenaciously that a year later, despite labor scarcity and rising costs, he had trains running from Salamanca, New York, to Akron, Ohio, with branch lines into the oil regions; in all, about 200 miles of track. In the month of Gettysburg the managers leased the Mahoning Valley line, a coal and iron road, and at once laid an extra rail, giving them a broad-gauge track into Cleveland. At the same time, rails were being laid from Akron to Dayton, whence an existing line, when widened, would carry trains to Cincinnati—the Salamanca-Cincinnati stretch covering 438 miles. Machine shops and a hotel were erected at Meadville, Pennsylvania.[36]

Even during peace the construction of this line within two years would have been a notable feat. Amid the din of war, in districts which the oil-rush and iron-boom had helped to drain of hands, it was a spectacular exploit. By this enterprise, remarked Greeley's *Tribune*, Cincinnati and St. Louis gained closer communication with New York, "while Columbus, Dayton, Indianapolis, and nearly the whole of Indiana and Illinois have secured a new and in many respects superior outlet to the seaboard. The value of the Erie Railroad to its stockholders and to our city is nearly doubled by it."[37] Had as much planning, integrity, and respect for the public interest gone into subsequent management as into the building, the nation would have reaped large gains; a statement applicable to the Erie as well.

Richer, greater, and ever more firmly rooted became the east-west trade as the war went on. New Orleans had been taking from the Northwest about ten million bushels of grain and flour annually; Chicago in 1860 had shipped twice that much. Now that New Orleans was stricken from the list of exporters, while crops and foreign demand swelled, Chicago moved far to the front. During the war years it shipped an annual average of forty-five million bushels of corn, wheat, and flour.[38] This increase represented the expansion of agriculture and the railroads far more than a mere transfer from the Mississippi, but the transfer counted. The growth of east-west trade was assisted by the fact that transportation rates, instead of rising with the general

36 N. Y. *Tribune*, Jan. 19, 1864. See my *Rockefeller*, I, 177, 180 ff., and Mabee, *Railroads and the Oil Trade, passim,* for the importance of this railroad to the oil regions.
37 Jan. 19, 1864.
38 E. D. Fite, *Social and Ind. Conds.*, 47 ff.

inflation, actually fell during the war. The competition of the truck-line rail-roads with each other and with the Great Lakes-Erie Canal route kept them in check. The narrow and shallow canal greatly needed enlargement.[39] Nevertheless, it transported a great deal more wartime tonnage than the New York Central and Erie Railroads combined. The lake boats fixed their freight rates first, and for the greater part of the year the railroads had to adjust their charges accordingly.

As early as January, 1861, the superintendent of the Michigan Central was able to assert that "this secession movement is making the North rich"; that his line was carrying great quantities of fresh pork which would not other-wise have come to it; and that "the products of Kentucky, Tennessee, and so on are all coming this way on account of Southern troubles." The London *Economist* commented on the spectacle of Southwestern cotton and pork moving up the Mississippi instead of down. Ohio's commissioner of statistics reported at the close of 1863 that the revolution in channels of business was unquestionably permanent. "Producers, merchants, and carriers have all found that the markets of New York, Baltimore, and Boston are more stable and reliable than the Southwestern ports have been or can be. The great stream of western produce is running steadily and strongly to the North Atlantic cities—thence a large part of it is shipped to Europe." [40]

Agricultural products were by no means the only great component of the flow, for a rich body of copper, iron ore, and lumber also came by the Soo canal from the upper lakes, or by rail from Milwaukee and Chicago. Iron-ore shipments through the Soo rose from 45,000 tons in 1861 to 113,000 tons in 1862, and to 161,500 in 1863. Particularly remarkable were the figures for lumber. Ax and saw, long busy in the white pine and hardwood forests of Michigan, were now at work in Wisconsin, where the Chippewa River valley contained the most impressive stand of white pine in the world. Although much of this lumber went down the upper Mississippi for wide distribution over the Middle West to build towns, villages, and farmhouses, shipments eastward through the Soo rose from 384,000,000 feet in 1861 to 1,411,000,000 in 1863.[41] During the war, in fact, lumber was rebuilding America. Midway

39 Circular of Samuel Hallett & Co., June 9, 1862. This firm reported that even with the small canal boats, freight produce could be transported down the lakes and canal for $60 a ton. In winter, when cold closed the lakes and canal, railroads sharply advanced their rates. Moreover, carriers between the Missouri River and the lakes tended to overcharge. The Chicago Canal Convention of 1863 expressed irritation over high east-west freight charges.

40 N. Y. *Tribune*, Jan. 16, 1861; London *Economist*, Feb. 2, 1861; Ohio Bur. Statistics, *Seventh Annual Report* (for 1863), p. 21.

41 George G. Tunell, *Report on Lake Commerce* (Bur. Statistics, Treasury Dept., 1898), 24.

in the conflict the Chicago *Tribune* remarked that on every street and avenue new buildings were going up—immense stone, brick, and wooden business blocks, and new residences; and the next year, 1864, Chicago building surpassed all previous records, every street being choked by bricks, mortar, and lumber. While in New York building declined, in Brooklyn it reached remarkable levels. In Philadelphia the new factories erected rose from 9 in 1861 to 37 the next year, and 57 in 1863, while the new dwellings built in the same period rose from 1,535 to 2,462.[42]

Altogether, before the war was halfway through it was clear that the future of American transportation would belong to the east-west channels, and that on the economic landscape no giants could for years to come rival the trunk-line railroads; the Pennsylvania, New York Central, Baltimore & Ohio, and Erie, the longer lines west of Chicago, and the new Union Pacific. It was also clear that the railroad system would at last soon become standardized. Among the eight or more different gauges that of four feet eight and a half inches, the Stephenson gauge of England, was emerging as dominant. It already prevailed in the northeastern part of the country. When in 1862 the Pacific Railroad gauge had to be fixed, everyone realized that it would determine the future width of all roads. Of the eleven railroad presidents asked to suggest a gauge, seven recommended the Stephenson standard; and though Lincoln, as we have noted, favored five feet, this was under a misapprehension, and he promptly adopted the majority view. Other roads soon conformed.[43]

[VI]

The exuberant growth of Northern population, agriculture, and industry registered its force in the rise of a new security and finance capitalism, in the multiplication of corporations, and in the emergence of business captains of large vision and practical grasp. New York became unmistakably the nation's financial center. Investment and management demanded companies able to carry on transactions of unprecedented magnitude. Business leaders, and especially the younger leaders, brought a new imagination to affairs. The expansion of western and world trade alone would have begun to revolutionize the thinking of industrial chieftains; instead of dealing with a restricted region,

42   *Thirty-third Annual Report*, Phila. Bd. of Trade, p. 81; Fite, 213 ff. Receipts of lumber in Chicago doubled during the war, rising from 249,000,000 feet in 1861 to 501,000,000 in 1864–65.
43   Fite, 56, 57. The before-mentioned revolutionary occurrence of Jan. 11, 1863, when the first train of cars passed from New York into Ohio, was made possible by the fact that the new Atlantic & Great Western had the same six-foot gauge as the Erie.

they had to concern themselves with half a continent and lands overseas.

The chief money market, New York, was far from efficient prior to the change wrought by the national bank act of 1863. It has been well called an organization without a head, a witless monster, for no central bank exercised leadership in financial affairs. The reserve funds of the land flowed into a number of banks, not one; they were invested for the behoof and profit of separate banks, not of the banking system as a whole; and instead of being used according to rational plan by wise heads of a central reserve bank, they went in great part to the call loan market. When the cash reserves of New York banks fell by more than half in ten months, reaching a low point of $29,350,000 on December 7, 1861, the suspension of specie payments became inescapable. The nation's total bank circulation on New Year's Day, 1862, just after this event, was only $132,000,000, inadequate for the needs of government and industry alike. The Treasury called for an issue of legal tender notes, and by March 3, 1863, Congress had authorized the printing of $450,000,000 in greenbacks.[44]

These issues, augmented by fractional paper currency and large issue of short-term interest-bearing notes, made money abundant. The rapid expansion of local bank circulation during the first two years of the war added to the inflation, and helped furnish capital for new enterprises. By the second anniversary of Lincoln's inauguration, New York banks had deposits of $174,000,000, very nearly $40,000,000 in specie, and outstanding loans, with call money at 6 or 7 per cent, of $171,000,000; the total loans of New York, Boston, and Philadelphia banks came to $297,000,000.[45] The creation of money and credit on an enormous scale by the war had much to do with the nation's economic dynamism.

It also had much to do with less pleasant accompaniments of the conflict. "The current of speculation in the stock market sweeps on with undiminished volume," said the *Tribune*'s financial editorial for May 16, 1863; and gambling swept into every business area.

Speculation accompanied the secession movement. Sam Ward and others used inside knowledge to play the stock market. It accompanied every step of the war. When McClellan landed his army on the Peninsula, stocks rose; his first reverses brought them down; they went up again on news of the fall of Williamsburg and New Orleans, combined with a report of high earnings by the Hudson River Railroad; and they sank once more with the defeats on the Chickahominy. The speculative excitement was accelerated by in-

44 Margaret G. Myers, *The N. Y. Money Market*, I, Ch. X; John Crosby Brown, *A Hundred Years of Merchant Banking*, Chs. VII, XII, presents the Civil War atmosphere.
45 N. Y. *Tribune*, March 6, 1863, commercial column.

flation. A fluctuating currency, a constant rise in values, a sellers' market for most goods, a sense of virile national growth, all made business hum with speculators as a clover field hums with bees. Their activities sometimes reached frenzy:

The excitement in stock circles today we have never seen equalled in our very long experience of the street [wrote the *Tribune's* financial editor January 8, 1862]. The amount of transactions . . . is, we think, larger than ever before known in the history of stock speculations, and the intense desire to buy almost any kind of securities amounted almost to insanity. No better illustration of the excitement in the Board can be found than that the same stock on the same call was often selling at one and two per cent higher at one end of the room than at the other. The oldest members of the Board cannot remember such a day of rampant speculation. The greatest rise, and one which has no precedent in the history of the Board, was in Toledo & Wabash stock, which sold yesterday at 40, and today at 60.

Commodity speculation was equally violent. Many shrewd capitalists saw early in 1862, for example, that wool was bound to soar. Thus, as the New York Chamber of Commerce noted, arose an army of speculators of every nation under the sun in New York, and as the prices advanced, the army grew. A Cincinnati annalist the following year noted that participants in the drygoods trade had made almost incredible profits. Many dealers speculated, and all who had stocks on hand became rich by the advance, several firms showing net profits of more than $100,000. Petroleum was a paradise for speculators. The receipts from a single Pennsylvania well opened in March, 1862, eventually reached $1,700,000. Andrew Carnegie drew such tropical dividends from the Columbia Oil Company, organized in 1861, that the subsequent erection of his steel mill became much easier.[46] The iron trade had its share of eager gamesters, who complained bitterly in 1863 that the furnaces were so far behind their orders for pig iron and the contracts for more were so numerous that no stocks for speculation existed. A production half again as great would sell instantly without giving the speculator a chance at a gain.[47]

While speculation in cotton became almost a national disease, grain speculation was a widespread occupation. Many a businessman in the army would have echoed Major-General C. C. Washburn's letter to his brother Elihu in 1863: "If I could now be at home, I would rake down largely!"[48] As it was, this lumberman and lawyer, acting from the Sixteenth Corps head-

46 *Fifth Annual Report of the Chamber* (for 1862), pp. 156–161. *Annual Statement*, Cincinnati Bd. of Trade, year ending Aug. 31, 1863, pp. 25, 26. Giddens, *Birth of the Oil Industry*, 42, 43.
47 *Sixth Annual Report*, Ch. of Commerce N. Y. (for 1863), pp. 105–107.
48 July 12, 1863, Washburne Papers, LC.

quarters, sold logs and lumber on a broad scale at high prices. Even as a soldier, he raked down quite a bit.

The leap in transportation securities was especially sweet to speculators. From early in the conflict freights exceeded carrying capacity, and net earnings for many lines surpassed the most roseate calculations. Between the beginning of January, 1862, and the same date in 1863, New York Central stock rose from 87 to 130, Illinois Central from 57 to 125, and Pacific Mail Steamship from 111 to 236. Railway securities were specially vulnerable to "movements" managed by bulls and bears. Rock Island Railroad shares in the winter of 1863–64 rose swiftly from 106 to 147, and then slid down to 115, this particular maneuver giving manipulators a reputed profit of a million. The period witnessed the first heavy combats between Vanderbilt and the New York Central on one side, and Drew, Gould, Fisk, and the Erie on the other, the "street" supplying ammunition. Years before, Jacob Little, autocrat of speculators, had familiarized men familiar with dashing operations in which fortunes were made and lost in a day; now a new set of gamblers carried out raids which excited the indignation of law-abiding citizens.[49]

Particularly outrageous were the activities of gamblers in gold. When the New York Stock Exchange, conservatively managed, forbade its members to sell government bonds at a discount or speculate in gold a plain need dictated the formation of the Gold Exchange; but that need was abused. In late winter of 1862–63 "the Jeff Davis gold gamblers," as Greeley called them, forced prices to high levels. As twenty-year 6 per cent United States bonds were selling at 85 or better, and greenbacks were convertible at par into such bonds, the premium on gold ought to have been limited; yet at one time it was forced up to 73—that is, $173 in greenbacks was needed to buy $100 in gold. Union men insisted that the speculation was pushed by interests sympathetic with the Confederacy and hostile to Chase's efforts to maintain the national credit. Excitement rose to a peak on March 6, with transactions aggregating perhaps three millions; the gamblers sold desperately, "in the vain hope of repelling the rising tide of loyal faith in the nation's future"; and the press rejoiced that a drop of seventeen points ruined most of them.

"We do confidently believe," trumpeted the *Tribune*, "that the secesh gold gamblers have received their quietus"; but the worst was still ahead.[50]

Secretary Chase had a limited power to check gold speculations, but no

49   Table in *Hunt's Merchants' Magazine*, XLIX (Sept. 1883), 221; N. Y. *Tribune*, financial column, Feb. 13, 1864. Daniel Drew, chosen a director of the Erie in 1857, used his position for stock manipulation shamelessly. In the famous Harlem Railroad corner planned by Vanderbilt and others in 1864 he was badly worsted.

50   N. Y. *Tribune*, March 5, 6, 7, covers this flurry; gold sank from 173 to 148, then back to 158, then down again (March 20) to 153.

legal mechanism existed to discourage raids in the railroad stock market, corners of supplies, or the sale of worthless oil shares to servant girls. Instead, some government operations underwrote the business of making fortunes at public expense. Whisky speculation was promoted by three successive increases in the Federal excise, not one of which, as the law was administered, applied to existing whisky stocks. As the tax rose from twenty cents to two dollars a gallon, the profits from this Federal wand-waving amounted to perhaps a hundred millions. This gift to one group, without a parallel in the tax history of any modern nation,[51] would have made buyers of government securities in anticipation of Hamilton's funding law livid with envy. Many rates in the second wartime tariff, obtained by lobbying and logrolling, were written to enrich special localities, groups, or even individuals at the cost of the general public. The duty on spelter, for example, was inserted by Elihu Washburne for the benefit of zinc manufacturers at Galena, Illinois, and Bethlehem, Pennsylvania, and largely for one man, Joseph Wharton.[52]

A striking example of skill in gaining special privileges was offered by the Onondaga Salt Company. It had silently lobbied through the Albany legislature a law giving it a monopoly of the great salt deposits near Syracuse. Three successive tariff rises brought the duty to forty cents a bushel, after which almost no foreign salt entered. The company at once more than doubled the price of its salt, while it watered its stock to conceal the egregious size of its dividends. Within five years, on a capital of $160,000, it distributed profits of $5,858,000! One member of the company had been speaker in Albany, and another sat on the ways and means committee in Washington.

In the fall of 1861 the *Herald* carried an editorial on the Shoddy Aristocracy of profiteers. Though they had filched the nation's money without giving value in return, it remarked, so had similar gentry in all the great military nations from France to Russia. They wanted to ape the knickerbocker, the cotton, and the codfish aristocracies, and were not much more vulgar, but their reign, predicted the *Herald*, would be brief. Instead, it proved long. Even the New York Chamber of Commerce admitted at the close of the conflict that the city had sold the government great numbers of pasteboard and shingle-stiffened shoes, and recalled the manufacturer who apologized for a boot whose sole dropped off after a half-hour march by saying that it was designed for cavalry use. The war on one side produced countless magnificent examples of heroism and self-sacrifice; on the other, it made dishonesty common. Fat contracts, speculative gains, the sight everywhere of

51 So stated Revenue Commissioner David A. Wells, 39th Cong., 1st Sess., House. Exec. Doc. 62.
52 See Joseph Wharton's letter, July 1, 1862, to Washburne, Washburne Papers, LC.

men making easy fortunes, were demoralizing. People despised Jim Fisk; but what about the respectable Dean Richmond, who with his picked directors controlled the lucrative Buffalo & State Line Railroad, and sold insiders at par a large issue of 7 per cent bonds which at once shot to 117? [53]

When the merchant Abiel A. Low just after the war reviewed the recent changes in business life, he fastened upon two as pre-eminently significant: the rise of establishments which made and shipped goods on a great scale to every important European market, and the multiplication of large corporations. But Low should have included two other major developments. One was the rise, after the national bank act approved February 25, 1863, of a sturdy new banking system centered in New York. The clearance house totals in the metropolis in the year beginning October 1, 1860, had been $5,916 millions; in the year beginning October 1, 1864, they were more than $26,000 millions. [54] The other was the appearance on the American scene of a bold new type of business captain.

It was in these war years that the firm of Plankinton, Armour & Co. was formed in Chicago (1863). Philip D. Armour, just over thirty, was ready for enterprising coups which before Appomattox netted him some two millions. The Havemeyer family began to assert their paramount position in the sugar business, its young members—one of them destined to be mayor of New York—succeeding the founder when he died at the beginning of the war. Wartime operations gave new vigor to the enterprises of Frederick Weyerhaeuser in lumbering, of Collis P. Huntington, far out in Sacramento, in general merchandising, and of Clement Studebaker in the wagon business. All Americans are familiar with the impetus which these years lent to three future titans, Rockefeller, Carnegie, and Morgan. Marshall Field, a young man from Massachusetts who had reached Chicago in 1856 and four years later had borrowed his way into a promising drygoods firm, gained such profits from the overwhelming wartime demand for goods of all kinds that he was able to join Levi Leiter in taking control of Potter Palmer's great merchandise business. A thousand lesser men, like Philo Remington of the famous gun works, achieved note as planners and organizers. The whole national map, in retrospect, appears studded with young entrepreneurs whose imaginations were stirred by the new era opening before them. Each had a marshal's baton in his knapsack, and several were future Napoleons.

One of the most significant facts of the era was the sudden complete release of organizing energy in the nation. Many of the new business captains

53 See James Parton's pamphlet exposé of the nefarious stock-manipulating activities of Wm. B. Ogden in connection with the Chicago & North Western, *Manual for the Instruction of Rings, Railroad and Political* (1866).
54 *Annual Report*, Ch. Commerce N. Y., 1866–67, Pt. 1, p. 7.

who took charge of this release had learned lessons of command and organization as majors and colonels; others had learned as head of new firms furnishing the nation essential wartime supplies. They were intent on making fortunes, and sometimes did so unscrupulously. But the important fact was that they were planners and organizers, and knew that they enjoyed such opportunities for planning and organizing as no business groups on the planet had ever before seen. They could create a new economic world as the Revolutionary generation had created a new political world. Tremendous natural resources, new fountains of credit, steady technological advances, a high wall against world competition, and the sense of confidence born of the tremendous war effort—these combined to put the future into their hands. They would swiftly remake America.

20

Shape of Revolution: Chattels No More

"WHERE ARE ye marching, soldiers, with banner, gun, and sword?" As Union forces pulled themselves together for fresh efforts after Chancellorsville and the first Vicksburg repulse, a larger answer could be given the query. They were marching to the liberation of a race, and the advance guard of the race marched with them. T. J. Barnett, Lincoln's Indiana friend, had important news for the lawyer-politician Sam Barlow just after Chancellorsville. "At present," he wrote, "the President is busy arranging his program for a negro army as a Southern reserve; he is perfectly assured, from facts which he gets from cavalry raids, that the whole available force of Rebeldom is in front; that the negroes understand that they are free; that the interior of rebeldom is now helpless in view of our threatening lines everywhere—and hence he is in fine spirits for a summer and fall negro campaign." [1]

Within a fortnight after this letter three resounding events took place. On May 22 the War Department established a bureau for colored troops with Assistant Adjutant-General C. W. Foster as head. On the 27th the Negro troops of the First and Third Louisiana Native Guard sharply and conspicuously engaged the enemy at Port Hudson. Under a capable colonel, the 1,080 men struggled over broken ground and through a tangle of felled trees to make repeated attacks on a strongly entrenched force. One out of five fell, but they never flinched. White officers, including Generals Banks and Daniel Ullman, declared that they had behaved magnificently. [2] And the next day the Fifty-fourth Massachusetts, the first colored regiment organized by a Northern State, paraded through Boston and was reviewed on the Common by Governor Andrew and Senator Henry Wilson. The scene as it left for the front, its band playing "John Brown's Body," was unexampled; no other regiment had shown greater discipline and dignity, none had collected such vast crowds, and none had been cheered so fervently. A second Negro regiment, the Fifty-fifth, was ready to follow.

1 May 15, 1863, Barlow Papers.
2 Banks to Halleck, O. R., I, xxvi, pt. 1, p. 45; Cornish, *The Sable Arm*, 142, 143. A later chapter in this work will deal with the general position of the freed slaves.

A notable story of State effort the Fifty-fourth represented; a story of which the Commonwealth could be proud when the dusky soldiers marched to death at Fort Wagner this summer, and when years later St. Gaudens reared on the Common, in their honor, the nation's finest battle monument, adorned by one of Lowell's most eloquent stanzas. The country had expected Massachusetts to lead in this field, and under Andrew it did. His service lay not in originating a Negro command—that had been done before; it lay in giving the well-chosen troops the most careful officering and training, and the fullest support of the State. He had entrusted the recruiting of the Negroes to his rich merchant friend George L. Stearns, Sumner's intimate and the whilom protector of John Brown, and Stearns had put unwearying exertions into drawing the men from many States. For colonel, Andrew turned to Robert Gould Shaw, of a distinguished Boston and Staten Island family, an officer who had given exemplary field service to the North from the outset; for lieutenant-colonel he selected Norwood P. Hallowell, scion of a Philadelphia family noted for philanthropy and antislavery zeal.

"This," Andrew wrote Shaw's father, "I cannot but regard as perhaps the most important corps to be organized during the whole war." [3] He wished to lend it all the prestige possible. The junior officers represented other prominent families. The readiness with which young Shaw and Hallowell left their comrades of the Second Massachusetts and Twentieth Maine respectively, and the scorn with which they faced Confederate threats of execution for all officers leading Negro recruits, were as honorable as the statement Shaw's mother made when she heard he had been offered the command. "I shall be nearly as proud to hear that he has accepted," she said, "as I would be to hear that he had been shot."

The national record down to these events of May was much less stirring. Congress in two acts of the summer of 1862 had expressly authorized the employment of colored men for labor or for military service, at the discretion of the President. But months elapsed before Lincoln thought the time ripe for putting arms into black hands. Opposition along the border, particularly in Kentucky, the hope of getting much of the South to accept compensated emancipation, and the desirability of letting events educate Northern Democrats, all reinforced his natural dislike of precipitate steps. He accepted Negro service in principle, but was concerned over the timing of the step.

Of three widely separated attempts, in fact, to marshal colored commands, all had been hesitant and irregular, and two were in the end disappointing. When General David Hunter took command over the sea islands at Port Royal in the spring of 1862, he began recruiting Negroes for a proposed regiment.

3   Jan. 30, 1863, Andrew Papers, MHS.

He actually dragooned many of them. But he got no pay for his recruits, was denied authority to muster them in, and was kept on the defensive by Stanton, hostile Congressman, and Edward L. Pierce, the Treasury agent in charge of a grandiose cotton-growing project in the islands. He finally disbanded all his men but one company, which did irregular garrison duty on St. Simon's Island. Meanwhile, in Kansas the irrepressible Jim Lane, not only without authority but against Stanton's express warning, also recruited colored men for projected regiments. His First Kansas Colored Volunteers drilled, scouted, and did a little fighting with Confederate bushwhackers in Missouri, but was not accepted by the government until early in 1863. The troops impressed newspapermen by their energy, discipline, and neatness, but accomplished little of military value.[4]

Greater material results flowed from the efforts of Ben Butler, who at first had low expectations of the Negroes as fighters, but found apt materials at hand. Governor T. O. Moore of Louisiana had enlisted a body of some 1,400 free Negroes in the militia during 1861. When the Union took New Orleans, they gladly forsook the Southern cause, and Butler shortly called on them to enroll in the volunteer service of the United States. Asking only for free colored men, he assured Halleck that he was keeping clear of the vexatious question of arming the slaves—though Southerners would have called many of them just that. The darkest of his recruits, he wrote Stanton, "will be about the complexion of the late Mr. Webster." Although the War Department gave him no specific approval for his action, in rapid succession he took into his forces the First, Second, and Third Native Guards. The free Negroes of New Orleans were a superior group, and they supplied him with some able company officers. It was two of these regiments that fought so manfully at Port Hudson, and one captain who died heroically close under the Confederate ramparts was given a funeral in New Orleans that rivaled Albert Sidney Johnston's. These fighters proved the martial spirit of their race.[5]

But a large-scale enlistment of colored troops waited on decisions in Washington.

4 Hunter's intentions were good but his methods outrageous; see Pierce's report, O. R., III, ii, 50–60; Cornish, *Sable Arm*, Ch. II. Lane, now a brigadier, built his activities on the long-standing free-soil and abolitionist tradition in Kansas; see the early pages of W. H. Stephenson, *Pol. Career of Gen. James H. Lane;* Cornish, 69 ff.

5 D. E. Everett, "Ben Butler and the Native Guards," *Journal So. Hist.,* XXIV (19–58), 202–217; for Stanton's clandestine support see Flower, *Stanton,* 186.

[I]

The earliest clear evidence that the Administration was dropping its opposition to military use of the Negro appeared in Stanton's orders of August 25, 1862, to General Rufus Saxton, military governor at Beaufort, authorizing him to arm and equip not more than 5,000 colored men as part of the volunteer forces of the nation. For the first time the government, and not a general acting independently, would be responsible. Saxton found his task difficult. Many officers showed a prejudice against the blacks; he divided his authority with Hunter's successor, J. M. Brannan; and many colored men had gone into the navy or the quartermaster service. But he finally mustered enough men for a weak regiment, the First South Carolina, and early in November sent a company on a profitable raiding expedition along the coast of Georgia and upper Florida. It fought with bravery and coolness. Later that month Colonel Thomas Wentworth Higginson arrived to take command, a happy choice. This militant antislavery clergyman of Massachusetts, widely known in the East for his essays and lectures, his book on Kansas, and his share in the attempted liberation of Anthony Burns, made a superb drillmaster and leader. What was equally important, his pen soon gave the fighting spirit of his troops a record eagerly read throughout the North.[6]

But even after the orders to Saxton the Administration necessarily carried water on both shoulders. Stanton, who held advanced views on emancipation and the arming of blacks, appealed to radical sentiment by his bold step; Lincoln by his silence appealed to the conservatives and Border State men. As long as he hoped that the South might make some response to the offer in his preliminary emancipation proclamation, the President could do nothing to close the door.[7]

Meanwhile, pressure for affirmative measures increased. Negro enlistment seemed a great cause, to which old-time free-soil leaders, most churchmen, and many editors rallied with fervor. To some it served a military necessity, to still more an idealistic purpose. Once Lincoln issued his final emancipation

6 Higginson's glowing report on the Edisto expedition of his colored troops, N. Y. *Tribune*, Jan. 20, 1863, is a good illustration of his graphic writing.

7 In any list of first places for Negro soldiers, Hunter's troops would be the first under fire, Lane's the first to lose men in combat, Butler's the first to become members of regiments accepted by the nation and to fight in a heavy action, and Shaw's the first to immortalize themselves and their leader. But Hunter deserves great credit for his pioneer efforts, by virtue of which the First South Carolina, though officially the fifth Negro regiment, should really be accounted the earliest—for it was a reorganization of the force he had recruited. Cf. Benjamin Quarles, *The Negro in the Civil War*, 108 ff.; Cornish, *The Sable Arm*, 92, 93.

proclamation, the movement became overwhelming. As Chase and Stanton pointed out to the President, the best way to render that paper something more than a bull against the comet was to make full use of freedmen in waging war. Thaddeus Stevens fulminated in the House, Trumbull in the Senate, and radical governors outside. Wendell Phillips toured Northern cities delivering his oration on Toussaint l'Ouverture, the central thesis of which was that Toussaint had taken a people demoralized by two centuries of slavery and "forged a thunderbolt." Greeley in the *Tribune* asserted that the Union could arm 50,000 black soldiers in the Carolinas alone. John Murray Forbes spoke for conservative businessmen anxious to shorten the conflict. And Frederick Douglass pleaded with passion for his race: "Give them a chance. I don't say that they will fight better than other men. All I say is, Give them a chance!"

The inevitable opposition of most Borderland leaders and copperhead Democrats was not easily overcome. All informed men realized that any really important body of colored troops would have to come from the South, and from the recent slaves. The Fifty-fourth Massachusetts was not prophetic of a coming army, for the North lacked an adequate Negro population. Superintendent J. C. G. Kennedy of the Census estimated the total free colored men of arms-bearing age in the free States at about 45,000. The free Negro males between 18 and 45 in Vermont numbered 140; in Wisconsin 292; and even in Illinois only 1,622. New York and Pennsylvania could possibly raise three regiments apiece, but no other State but Ohio could enlist even one of full numbers within its own borders.[8] And the arming of recent slaves seemed to some a reckless step. Even after emancipation many Northerners doubted whether large numbers of Southern freedmen could or should be used for anything but military labor. Might Negro regiments not touch off bloody slave revolts? Might they not rekindle Southern anger and prolong the war? Troops of Southern antecedents, as from southern Indiana and Illinois, or of marked color prejudice, found the idea that Negro recruits would suddenly become their equals repugnant.

William Tecumseh Sherman was so deeply opposed to the use of black troops to fight white men, and even to the placing of Negro garrisons in Southern cities, that his critics accused him of an almost criminal dislike of the race. Frank P. Blair, Jr., took a similar attitude. The colored people, in his opinion, should be colonized abroad. When General H. R. Milroy took command of troops in Western Virginia he found some of them habitually beating and abusing Negro teamsters and laborers. Peremptorily ordering them to stop, he explained to Schuyler Colfax: "I have labored hard and had much

8 Kennedy's report to the Interior Dept. is in O. R., III, iii, 43–45; Feb. 11, 1863.

trouble in abolitionizing my Virginia regiments. . . . Ignorance and prejudice are the great barriers in the way." General Thomas G. Stevenson, assigned to the sea islands, said publicly early in 1863 that he would rather have the Union forces defeated than win with Negro troops; whereupon General Hunter clapped him under arrest. White Middle Westerners who saw officers employing some handsome young Negro as orderly, mounting him on a fine horse, and taking him on dashes through the camp, were resentful.[9]

Friends of the Negro had therefore to contend not merely for his right to fight, but for his right to be trusted by other men. General Hunter, replying to the sharp interrogatories of Congress, was the first high officer to enter a wholehearted defense of the fighting power of the blacks. They are sober, docile, attentive, and enthusiastic, he wrote; "eager above all things to take the field and be led into action"; and in the unanimous opinion of their officers certain to prove invaluable auxiliaries.[10] Ben Butler was soon converted to their side. He later testified of his first three regiments of infantry that better soldiers never shouldered a musket; that not only were they brave, intelligent, and obedient, but they had learned to handle arms and march more readily than Harvard or Yale men could have mastered these arts, for they were already drilled and were highly imitative. This was the opinion of John C. Palfrey, son of the Massachusetts Congressman and historian. They drill well, he wrote his father from Ship Island in the summer of 1863; for working, marching, and roughing it they are splendid; and with good officers they make good soldiers. In short, he wished a Negro command. Higginson diffused through the North a particularly discriminating but sympathetic verdict on Negro capabilities.[11]

It was the pressure to fill Union ranks after the failure of volunteering, however, which most effectively broke down the opposition. Representative John M. Broomall of Pennsylvania drove home the point crisply: "I have never found the most *shaky* constituent of mine who, when he was drafted, refused to let the blackest Negro in the district go as a substitute for him." And Charles G. Halpine helped to effect a broad change in public sentiment when he addressed to his fellow-Irishmen the song "Sambo's Right to be Kilt." This happy effusion of his invented character, Private Miles O'Reilly, asserted that some might think it a shame to let the Negro fight, but as for himself

9 Liddell Hart, *Sherman*, 352, 353; Milroy's General Order No. 28 and his letter are in the Colfax Papers, Ind. State Hist. Lib.; for Stevenson see N. Y. *Tribune*, Feb. 27, 1863; for Middle Western attitudes, see Chicago *Morning Post*, July 22, 1863. Robert K. Murray in "Sherman, The Negro, and Slavery," *Negro History Bulletin*, XXII (1959), 125-130, concludes that Sherman was a lifelong believer in Negro inferiority and white supremacy.
10 *Amer. Conflict*, I, 516; cf. O. R., l, xiv, 3-469.
11 Palfrey, Aug. 16, 1863, Palfrey Papers, Houghton Lib.; Higginson summed up his conclusions in the *Century Mag.*, N. S., XXXII (1897), 194 ff. See *Butler's Book*, 494, 495.

Don't think I'm tippin' you chaff,
The right to be killed we'll divide wid him,
And give him the largest half! [12]

Lincoln's change of front after the final Emancipation Proclamation, which declared that former slaves would be received into the armed forces, was complete. He unquestionably approved Stanton's order of January 26, 1863, authorizing Andrew to proceed with his regiments. When Higginson's First South Carolina took a gallant part in the reoccupation of Jacksonville, Florida, he warmly congratulated Hunter, noting the significance of the fierce Confederate counterattack. "It is important to the enemy that such a force shall *not* take shape, and grow, and thrive, in the South; and in precisely the same proportion, it is important to us that it *shall*." [13] He and Stanton agreed late in March to send Adjutant-General Lorenzo Thomas to the Mississippi Valley with plenary authority to enlist and officer Negro regiments. Thomas would start in at Cairo and move down the river to Grant's headquarters and beyond, creating Negro commands at such places as Helena, Columbus, Milliken's Bend, Corinth, Memphis, and Nashville. He was a narrow, plodding, dour-tempered man, whom Stanton was glad to get out of the War Department for a while, but he threw himself into this labor with enthusiasm—Washington supporting him to the best of its ability.

"I would like to raise on this river twenty regiments at least before I go back," Thomas presently told the troops at Lake Providence, Louisiana. Grant gladly collaborated with him. The record of the Western forces had not been good. Complaints had reached Stanton, as Halleck wrote the general, that many officers not only discouraged the Negroes from seeking Union protection, but by ill treatment forced them to return to their masters.[14] Quite without prejudice himself, Grant assured Halleck that he welcomed the new policy, and he saw that his subordinates supported it. At least three of his corps commanders, he reported on April 19, were zealously helping to recruit and arm the Negroes. "They at least are so much of soldiers as to feel themselves under obligation to carry out a policy (which they would not inaugurate) in the same good faith . . . as if it was one of their own choosing." And the Western troops had a new object lesson in the quality of colored soldiers at the end

12 R. B. Roosevelt, *Coll. Works of Charles G. Halpine.* The son of a talented Church of England minister in Ireland, for a time editor of the Dublin *Evening Mail*, Halpine remained a Protestant, but attached himself to the Young Ireland Party. His patriotic lyrics did much service to the colored folk as well as to the Union.

13 April 1, 1863; *Works*, VI, 158. Negroes of the Second South Carolina under James Montgomery fought alongside Higginson's men.

14 March 31, 1863, Lieber Papers, HL; Halleck added that he expected Grant to use his personal and official influence to remove prejudice.

of May. One of the naval officers in the Vicksburg area penned a spirited account of their heroism:

A boat came rushing down from Milliken's Bend (about 15 miles above here on the Mississippi) and said that about 5,000 rebels had attacked our troops there. The Union troops at the Bend consisted of about two negro regiments and part of a white regiment. The *Choctaw* and a Light Draft were immediately sent up there, and shortly after, the Flag Ship went up. The *Choctaw* arrived just in time—the negroes fought bravely (their white officers running away), but they were outnumbered, and were beginning to give up, when the *Choctaw* opened on the rebs with her big guns, and drove them away.

We went ashore and took a look at things. There were about 100 dead bodies on the field, about equally divided, half secesh and half negroes. The blacks fought like bloodhounds, and with equal numbers would have won the day. . . .

Grant later that summer expressed to Halleck his high opinion of colored volunteers. They stood the hot climate better than whites, they preserved discipline with less oversight, and "all that have been tried have fought bravely." [15]

Lincoln meanwhile gave orders to Banks paralleling those to Lorenzo Thomas; he and Stanton sent General Daniel Ullman to enlist freedmen in Baton Rouge, where a multitude of hungry, ignorant, and almost naked Negroes, 7,000 in two days, were pouring into the Union lines; and he wrote a singularly hopeful letter to Andrew Johnson, now military governor of Tennessee. Its tone bears out what T. J. Barnett had reported of his elation in planning a grand Negro campaign. The black population offered the Union its greatest untouched resource for victory, he told Johnson. "The mere sight of 50,000 armed and drilled black soldiers upon the banks of the Mississippi would end the rebellion at once." Why did he believe this? He did not say, but the plain implication is that he thought a formidable Negro army would arouse such fears of a general slave insurrection that Southern soldiers would break for home to protect their wives and children.

[II]

If Lincoln did believe this, he miscalculated; Southernors were not so much frightened by the early Negro regiments as angered. In Kentucky the Frankfort *Commonwealth*, a Union paper of copperhead tinge, had expressed the attitude of most slaveholders toward Negro enlistments: "The

15 Grant's letter of April 19, 1863, to Halleck, is in the Eldredge Papers, HL.; his letter of July 24 on the fine quality of the Negro troops is in the Grant-Halleck Papers, Ill. State Hist. Lib. For the description of Milliken's Bend see C. F. Guild, June 1, 1863, to G. V. Fox, Fox Corr., N. Y. Hist. Soc.

vile injustice and barbarity of the proposition overshadow its unconstitutionality." The official Confederate position was one of extreme harshness modified by a prudent fear of Northern retaliation. Jefferson Davis had lost no time after the emancipation proclamation in telling the Confederate Congress that unless it otherwise directed, he would order all Union officers captured at the head of colored troops to be delivered to the States to be dealt with under their laws for punishing those who excited servile insurrection. This implied a death penalty. Congress showed more restraint. By joint resolution it declared that such officers should be put to death or "otherwise punished" at the discretion of a military court. Mere privates were to be sent back to their States of origin.

Certain Southern leaders at first showed a reckless temper. When General H. W. Mercer captured a uniformed Negro soldier in South Carolina in the fall of 1862 he wrote Beauregard suggesting a "terrible punishment," and Beauregard referred the matter to Secretary Seddon. He in turn laid it before Davis with the Christian endorsement: "With his concurrence my decision is that the negro be executed as an example. J. A. S., Sec'y War." Late the next summer some Negro troops were captured on James Island. Beauregard was for summary and ignominious penalties: "Let the execution be with the garrote." Davis, when consulted by Governor Bonham, advised against execution. It is certain, however, that four Negroes taken in uniform on St. Catherine's Island *were* put to death.

As it was in the Mississippi Valley that most Negro recruiting was done, there the Confederates faced the most acute problem in dealing with colored soldiers. They knew that they were on precarious ground. The Tennessee legislature in the first autumn of the war had empowered Governor Harris to enlist free Negroes for military service, Moore of Louisiana had paraded 1,400 Negro militia, and various Southern officers had used slave labor for fortifications. Nevertheless, so cultivated a gentleman as E. Kirby-Smith, West Point 1845, issued brutal orders. When Richard Taylor's troops first captured Negroes in arms, Kirby-Smith rebuked him for not killing them on the field. Refusal to give quarter would offer the simplest (he did not need to add the cruelest) way out of a painful dilemma, for if the South executed Negro soldiers by formal order, the North would assuredly execute as many Southern soldiers with the same formality. Secret murder was the only safe method. Secretary Seddon was guilty of the same cowardly type of brutality. Recommending to Kirby-Smith that Negro soldiers be treated kindly and returned to their masters, he advised that their white officers be dealt with "red-handed" on the field or immediately afterward.

It was in the West, too, that executions and denials of quarter were most frequently reported: the murder of twenty Negro teamsters in Union service near Murfreesboro, the public hanging of three Negroes at Holly Springs, and so on. How much truth the atrocity stories contain it is impossible to say; Grant flatly contradicted one. At various times Southern troops humanely returned disarmed Negroes to their masters. On the other hand, the Confederates unquestionably killed some black prisoners summarily, and they may even have followed Seddon's counsel by slaying some white officers. The tale of Fort Pillow we shall tell later. After the Milliken's Bend engagement General Richard Taylor remarked in his official report that many Negroes had been killed, but "unfortunately, some fifty, with two of their white officers, were captured"; he meant it was unfortunate that they had not been dispatched on the spot. One encounter in Arkansas, according to a Confederate participant, left the battlefield a sickening sight, for defying all restraints, the Southerners fell on the surviving colored soldiers and butchered them in great heaps.[16]

The Northern use of colored troops directly affected the vexatious question of the exchange of prisoners. In fact, it was the basic obstacle which first interrupted the exchange, and kept tens of thousands in the misery and starvation of prison camps.

When Secretary Stanton learned that three colored soldiers captured in South Carolina had been confined at hard labor, he ordered the same treatment given three South Carolinians. Other incidents of the same sort soon occurred. Agreements for exchanging prisoners presently covered the South Carolina area, but no colored troops were returned. At this a storm broke in the North. John Murray Forbes called for putting a proper number of Southerners in irons; Frederick Douglass declared he could no longer urge Negroes to enlist. Lincoln was prompt to take action. In a General Order of July 30, 1863, he asserted that the law of nations permitted no distinction of color in the treatment of prisoners of war, and that the United States would give equal protection to all of its soldiers. He directed that for every Union soldier murdered a rebel soldier should be executed, and that for every man enslaved by the enemy a Confederate soldier should be put at hard labor on the public works. Since the Confederacy took the stand that it would not return Negro prisoners on the same basis as white men, exchanges stopped.

16 For Confederate legislation on captured Negroes, see *Journal Confed. Congress*, III, 386, 387; for the Davis-Seddon approval of the execution of four Negro soldiers, see O. R., II, iv, 945, 946, 954, the final order being dated Nov. 30, 1862; for the Davis-Seddon exchange of views with Governor Bonham, see Seddon's letter of Sept. 1, 1863, Pickens-Bonham Papers, LC; for Kirby-Smith's rebuke of Taylor for not murdering Negroes, see O. R., II, vi, 21, 22, June 13, 1863; for Seddon's advice on red-handed action, see O. R., I, xxii, 964, 965; for Beauregard's invocation of the garrote, see *Amer. Conflict*, II, 523; and for the Arkansas engagement of tragic aftermath, see Cornish, *Sable Arm*, 177.

As an assertion of moral principle, the Northern attitude was admirable. But unquestionably the War Department was actuated by practical as well as moral principles, for it wished to deprive the South of as much manpower as possible.

A calamitous deadlock resulted; calamitous at least to a host of poor fellows North and South who gave up their lives in Camp Douglas, Andersonville, and other lethal detention holes.[17] Each side was too stubborn to yield. Northern generals, including Grant, were as determined as Lincoln and Stanton; Lee was as determined as Davis. To Southern leaders the Negroes were property—the property of white Southerners; to Northern leaders they were freemen and equal soldiers. The fact that the Union had far more prisoners than the Confederacy, which desperately needed more men, accentuated Washington's unwillingnesss to reopen the exchange, and the impasse was destined to last out the war. Naturally Negroes who believed that they would be murdered, or kept in hopeless durance, fought all the more frenziedly.

It meanwhile became clear that the systematic arming of freedmen involved a thrust against not only slavery but caste lines. To this fact Greeley attributed much of the opposition in Congress, the press, and conservative Northern circles. Charles B. Sedgwick of New York, supporting a Negro-enlistment bill in Congress, avowed that it had a class character—it was aimed at the detestable Southern aristocracy. That caste, he said, was the foe of labor, free public education, commercial prosperity, and true democracy; it was proud, intolerant, and insolent, and it must be brought low.[18] Many Southerners were quick to perceive that a new era was opening for the colored race —and for themselves.

Thus Julian Alcorn, a North Carolinian, described to his wife a visit he paid to the camp of General N. B. Buford near Mound City, Mississippi, where he and the general reviewed the Negro troops—"truly a fine looking and well drilled body of men." In the neighborhood were a so-called contraband area where several thousand Negroes were fed at government expense and a freedmen's district where Negro farmers were tilling twenty-acre plots carved from abandoned plantations. White teachers conducted two schools with ninety pupils. At church on Sunday a Methodist minister presided over an Episcopal service, the Negro soldiers and their white officers filling the pews on one side, while Negro and white citizens, men and women, mingled at will on the other.

17 By the end of 1863 the Union held some 26,000 prisoners, the Confederacy some 13,000; Cornish, *Sable Arm,* 171. Greeley gives a contemporary view of the problem; *Amer. Conflict,* II, 525; Rhodes emphasizes the North's material reasons for wishing to hold its prisoners, V, 498. We shall later consider prison camps and exchanges more fully.

18 *Cong. Globe,* 37th Cong., 3d Sess., 629, Jan. 30, 1863. "The cornerstone of this aristocracy is slavery," said Sedgwick.

"My observations at headquarters," wrote Alcorn, "induced melancholy reflections. The poor miserable southerners that cringed at the feet of power presented a contrast with the saucy well dressed negroes with faces bright, head erect, and scornful look at the 'poor secesh trash' that graciously yielded the walk to their sable superiors in position." He added that the South used to scoff at the idea of Negro garrisons in her cities. "But here is an important post, near the heart of the southern confederacy, that is garrisoned by negroes, and I believe our people think the place very securely held." [19] At such places one phase of Reconstruction was beginning. The best of the Northern recruiting officers knew that their long-term object was to make not merely good soldiers but good citizens.

[III]

General Thomas' mission, concluded in May, was successful. Though the Negro troops were subjected to unfair discrimination, getting only $10 a month and one ration while white volunteers received $13, full rations, and free uniforms, they came forward with alacrity. Thomas earnestly exhorted the white troops to welcome all refugee blacks, to feed and clothe them, and to give the able-bodied men arms. He had power to dismiss anybody guilty of maltreating Negroes. He also had authority to give commissions to white soldiers, irrespective of rank, who showed enthusiasm for using colored volunteers. Creating a line of regiments down the valley, he laid a foundation for steady continuance of the work. It was after his return in May that the War Department opened its new bureau, and systematized the enlistment of freedmen by General Order No. 43.[20] That fall recruiting stations were established in Maryland, Missouri, and Tennessee, loyal slaveholders who manumitted their hands and offered them for enlistment receiving $300 each. By December, more than 50,000 men had been organized and were in actual service, while the total was swelling daily. Thomas could later boast that he had initiated the organization of about two-fifths of all the colored regiments in the war.

Northern believers in the Negro read with pride of the number who became good officers, about a hundred gaining commissions. The white officers were carefully selected, particularly after General Silas Casey, author of a famous manual of infantry tactics, became head in Washington of the busiest of the several examining boards. He and others set high standards. Governor Austin Blair of Michigan was much irritated when, trying to officer the First Michigan Colored Regiment, he found the board examining his initial nominee

19   J. Alcorn, Mound City, March 22, 1864; Alcorn Papers, Univ. of N. C.
20   Most accessible in *Ann. Cyc.*, 1863, p. 27.

in trigonometry and conic sections; subjects which, he sarcastically wrote Zach Chandler, even Lincoln did not know. There was no lack of applicants for places, and two out of five of them were rejected. Most Northerners were delighted by stories of the rapturous enthusiasm of the Negroes. A private who marched through Beaufort, for example, declared that he had looked neither right nor left: "Eb'ry step was worth a half-a-dollar." As the recruiting progressed, all observers could reach the wise conclusion which Grant stated this summer:

The people of the North need not quarrel over the institution of slavery. What Vice-President Stephens acknowledges the corner stone of the Confederacy is already knocked out. Slavery is already dead and cannot be resurrected. It would take a standing army to maintain slavery in the South if we were to make peace today guaranteeing to the South all their former constitutional privileges.

I never was an abolitionist, nor even what could be called Anti-Slavery, but I try to judge fairly and honestly and it became patent to my mind early in the rebellion that the North and South could never live at peace with each other except as one nation, and that without slavery. As anxious as I am to see peace reestablished I would not therefore be willing to see any settlement until this question is forever settled.[21]

The situation of the colored troops remained in some respects unpleasant. They were usually regarded as inferiors. The discrimination in pay, despite Stanton's protests, endured until the close of the war. Many officers were disposed to use Negro units only as labor outfits, a tendency against which William Cullen Bryant conducted a crusade in the *Evening Post*. Other slights were numerous; and Northern States were soon sending recruiting agents south to enlist colored men and thus make up their quotas, a discreditable type of exploitation.

Segregation was the general rule, though the summer of 1863 saw one mixed force of Negroes, Indians, and whites winning the battle of Elk Creek on the Southwestern frontier. It could not be considered a hardship, for the colored man preferred association with his own people. But it was noteworthy that no effort was made to break it down. When Robert Gould Shaw's father questioned him on the subject, he replied that any intermingling would have to be preceded by a long process of education. White orderlies, he had noted, made no objection to living in the same tent with black orderlies; but if white volunteers were asked to receive Negroes in their regiments, they would object fiercely.[22] The navy, with a specially creditable record of

21 To Elihu Washburne, Vicksburg, Aug. 20, 1863, Grant-Washburne Papers, Ill. State Hist. Lib.
22 Shaw's letter is in the R. G. S Papers, privately held; courtesy of Mrs. Pierre Jay.

colored recruiting, showed that more could have been done than was attempted. At the beginning of the war Secretary Welles had directed officers to accept the services of everyone, black or white, who promised to be useful. An order in the spring of 1863 instructed the flag officers of blockading squadrons that as the sickly season was about to begin, and contrabands were acclimated, Negroes should be enlisted without constraint.[23] Both free Northern Negroes and Southern freedmen thus served at sea alongside white sailors, though at generally lower pay; and Stringham at Hatteras and Du Pont at Port Royal praised the work of the colored gun crews. In the West, Commodore Porter enlisted hundreds of Negroes on his river gunboats. But the army kept the colored soldier with his own folk—where, to be sure, he was most content.

The year 1863 was definitely a year of apprenticeship for the colored soldier, in which he proved himself. General Saxton, when given a long list of questions about the Negro's qualities, ordered his secretary to draw a line through them, and write: "They are intensely human." This nearly covered the ground, and by 1864 the army was ready to accept them as invaluable fighting reinforcements.

All the more discreditable was the conduct of Northerners who, like Horatio Seymour, continued to oppose any military use of colored men. The full story of Seymour's obstructiveness is full of drama. New York was one of the two Northern States which could send a really strong contingent of its own free Negroes to the front. As fighting ended at Chancellorsville a meeting was held in the metropolis to take measures for enlisting large numbers of colored volunteers, and a deputation immediately afterward waited on Lincoln, who told them that the national government could not support the undertaking until it was assured of the governor's cooperation. Memorials were thereupon laid before Seymour, who ignored them. A pertinacious citizen of Albany, asking that a well-known colonel be empowered to raise one colored regiment, finally got a curt reply: "I do not deem it advisable to give such authorization, and I have therefore declined to do it." Prominent citizens of New York rallied to the battle. Peter Cooper, Bryant, Henry J. Raymond, William E. Dodge, and others formed an association, and applied themselves anew to Lincoln and Stanton. The newly formed Union League Club joined the fray. Still Governor Seymour, making fresh excuses, was a lion in the path. If he could help it, New York would never arm a Negro.[24]

23 See approbatory editorial, Wash. *National Republican*, May 13, 1862. Representative Sedgwick, reviewing naval use of Negroes (*Cong. Globe*, 37th Cong., 3d Sess., 630), stated that the navy at the beginning of 1863 had about 5,000 colored seamen.

24 Bellows, *Union League Club*, 83-87; Mitchell, *Seymour*, 300; Flower, *Stanton*, 241; Strong, *Diary*, III, see index for numerous favorable references to Negro troops; Alexander,

In the end the angry citizens persuaded the War Department to take the units they organized into the army under national, not State, authority. The Twentieth New York, departing for the front, was given an ovation which in heartfelt enthusiasm equaled that tendered the Seventh New York in the first days of war. Two more colored regiments followed. But Seymour had hopelessly delayed the effort of the Empire State, which should have outstripped that of Massachusetts.

The Massachusetts story came to its stirring climax in midsummer of 1863, when an amphibious force under General Quincy Adams Gillmore and Admiral John A. Dahlgren undertook to renew the assault on Sumter and Charleston in which Du Pont had failed that spring. The first point of attack was Fort Wagner on Morris Island, commanding the central channel into Charleston Harbor. If this were taken, Union guns could batter Sumter to pieces, and perhaps throw shells into Charleston, the spires of which were plainly visible. A force under General G. C. Strong landed on the island, took possession of three-fourths of it, and pushed their lines up to within musket range of the fort. It was a formidable position, fully garrisoned by Confederate veterans under that Congressional fire-eater of the fifties, Lawrence Keitt, and sure to be tenaciously held—for if it was lost, Charleston might be lost. The approach was by a narrow road of sand with the sea on one side and a creek and marshes on the other; a deep ditch had been dug in front of the fort; and strong bastions at the corners mounted howitzers. Strong's preliminary assault on July 11 was thrown back with loss.

Just a week later Gillmore's artillery and Dahlgren's monitors opened a heavy fire on Wagner, while a storming party of three brigades formed on the island. From noon until dusk the roar of Parrotts, mortars, and light artillery continued. The Confederates made little reply, their flag still waving over their works, and actually they lost only four men killed and fourteen wounded. As night fell the first assault column moved toward the fort— the Fifty-fourth Massachusetts in the van. When Strong offered the regiment this post of honor, Robert Gould Shaw might have declined, for his Negro troops had been marching for two days through sand and marsh, in pitiless heat, and were worn out; but he accepted with exultation. The knightly young officer knew that the eyes of the country were upon his men. He gave the order of quick-march, to become double-quick. The troops had almost reached the ditch when a sheet of musket fire flared from the parapet, and as they pressed on hand grenades and the howitzers caught them. An

---

Pol. Hist. N. Y., III, 77–80. But the story of Seymour's intransigence is best covered in the New York press, and in Henry O'Rielly's pamphlet "First Organization of Colored Troops in the State of New York."

CHARLESTON AND FORT WAGNER

intrepid group gained the interior of the fort, planted the colors there, and then had to fall back. Shaw fell dead among scores of his followers. Nearly half of the black troops were slain, wounded, or missing, and more than half of the officers.

The death of Shaw sent a wave of sorrow over the nation as heartfelt as that which had followed the loss of Elmer Ellsworth. Vindictive Southerners buried him under his Negroes. The immediate request of his father that the Union forces forgo all effort to recover the body, leaving him with the men he led, added a fitting touch to the battle; they mingled their dust in a common glory. Colonel Charles Russell Lowell, who later this year married Shaw's sister Josephine, and who himself was to perish in battle, sent her the most fitting words of comfort: "The manliness and patriotism and high courage of such a soldier never die with him; they live in his comrades." In reality, Shaw, who had died calling "Forward, my boys!" was to live in the memory of a State, a nation, and a race; all colored Americans stood on higher ground after Fort Wagner.

Heroism was not confined to the soldier; the colored refugees, the millions of humble freedmen and slaves, exhibited it abundantly. Soon after the Emancipation Proclamation an illiterate black woman of Franklin County, Virginia, found opportunity amid the war turmoil to move to Malden, near Charleston, West Virginia, her three children trudging most of the way. They had lived in a one-room cabin without wooden floor or glass windows; the littlest, a boy aged seven, had never slept in a bed, and had sometimes been so hungry that he ate the corn boiled for the livestock. He had heard his mother praying that she and her brood might be free—and in Malden they *were* free. His name was Booker T. Washington, and one of the first uses he made of freedom was to apply himself to a copy of Webster's blue-backed spelling book. His mother was neither less nor more heroic than thousands of other black women.

But the colored fighters, whose large final contributions to the war we shall treat with the later campaigns, were path-breakers in a special sense. Lincoln had said in his December message that the dogmas of the quiet past were inadequate to the stormy present, and that men must think anew and act anew. Late this summer, writing that peace seemed nearer, he paid the Negro soldier the tribute he had so well earned: "And then there will be some black men who can remember that, with silent tongue and clenched teeth, and steady eye, and well-poised bayonet, they have helped mankind on to this great consummation; while, I fear, there will be some white ones, unable to forget that, with malignant heart and deceitful speech, they have strove to hinder it." The neglected slave, clothed in the national uniform, and realizing that he was battling for his own freedom and dignity, was lifted to the height of the great national purpose, and showed that he too had in him the stuff for epic deeds.

[IV]

No change in the fortunes of war could now long halt the multiform revolution of the time: the emergence of the North to industrial strength, the replacement of improvisation by plan and organization, the shattering of the slave system. Reflections on the subject must have haunted the pillow of a Confederate senator who lay dying this summer in his Alabama farmhouse. Nobody had done more than William L. Yancey to blow the glowing coals of sectional alienation into the flame of war. Without him the Confederacy might never have been born. He had written the Alabama Platform of 1848 demanding positive national protection of slavery in all the Territories; he had led in splitting the Democratic Party asunder as a prelude to dividing the nation; he had penned the Alabama ordinance of secession. Although on his deathbed he clung passionately to the principles he had long upheld, he knew that all his hopes were dust and ashes. His mission to England had been a failure. He comprehended before he died on July 27, 1863, that the tread of Union armies already shook Alabama, and that the old slaveholding civilization was doomed.

But fresh Union defeats East and West could still have the gravest consequences, and with nerves on edge Northerners waited in June for the latest news from Mississippi and Virginia. Grant delivered his second assault against Vicksburg on the 22nd, and his 35,000 men were again flung back with serious loss. Plainly, he must begin a regular siege. In Virginia as June opened, Lee's elated veterans still held the Rappahannock at Fredericksburg, and their commander was bending his eye northward. Striving to ascertain his plans, Hooker sent Pleasonton's cavalry corps on a reconnaissance; and on the 8th these forces struck Jeb Stuart's command at Brandy Station in the heaviest cavalry battle of the war. The Southerners kept the battlefield and inflicted the greater loss, but Hooker learned that Lee was moving some of his men toward the Shenandoah, the natural avenue for invasion of the North.

The Confederate Government had just confronted the most fateful dilemma of the war. Should Lee's troops be used to strike once more at the heart of the North, or should they stand on the defensive while strong detachments were sent west by rail to assist Johnston and Pemberton? Secretary Seddon understood the strategic importance of the West better than any other man in the Richmond administration. As early as April 6 he had suggested to Lee that two or three of Pickett's brigades, with perhaps one other, would give an encouraging reinforcement to the Army of the West, and he later repeated the proposal.[25] But Lee, determined to invade the North, was against any such step. On May 26 one of the most important cabinet meetings of Confederate history discussed the question. John H. Reagan of Texas pleaded earnestly for sending immediate assistance to Pemberton, but the majority overbore him. We are already greatly outnumbered by the enemy in the East, declared Lee, and Jefferson Davis took his side. The troops would be held for a great Eastern Thrust.

Of this debate the North knew nothing, but with rising anxiety it saw storm signals mount in the sky. "Lee's Force Nearly Doubled," ran headlines in the New York *Tribune* of June 13, 1863. "East Virginia and All North and South Carolina Drained. The Rebels Preparing a General Movement."

---

25 After Hooker's defeat, Beauregard suggested that Longstreet's corps should be dispatched with all possible speed on the two railroad lines available to Chattanooga, and used to defeat Rosecrans. Thomas Jordan, Notes, extra-illustrated *Battles and Leaders*, HL.

Bibliography and Appendices

Bibliography and Appendices

BIBLIOGRAPHY

MANUSCRIPT SOURCES

In this list *LC* signifies Library of Congress; *NYPL*, New York Public Library; *MHS*, Massachusetts Historical Society; *IHS*, Illinois State Historical Society; *UNC*, University of North Carolina Library; *CU*, Columbia University Library; and *HL*, Huntington Library. The author specially thanks Mrs. Pierre Jay for access to the diary of Josephine Shaw and the papers of Robert Gould Shaw; Mrs. Laura Stryker for partial use of the Frederick Law Olmsted Papers in the Library of Congress; and S. L. M. Barlow for entry to the valuable archive of his distinguished grandfather of the same name. He thanks also Bruce Catton, E. B. Long, Freeman Cleaves, and many others whom he cannot name for transcripts of valuable documents.

MANUSCRIPT COLLECTIONS

Charles Francis Adams Papers and Diary, MHS; William Allen Papers, LC; John A. Andrew Papers, MHS, Mass. State Archives; Gen. Christopher C. Augur Collection, IHS.

S. L. M. Barlow Papers, HL; Samuel G. Barnes Diaries, LC; Edward Bates Papers, LC, Missouri Historical Society; John A. Bayard Papers, LC; Henry W. Bellows Papers, MHS; H. G. Benson MSS Recollections, UNC; John Huston Bills MS Diary, UNC; Jeremiah S. Black Papers, LC; Austin Blair Papers, (Burton Collection), Detroit Public Library; Blair Family Papers, LC, Mo. Hist. Soc.; Blair-Lee Papers, Princeton Univ.; Francis A. Boyle Diary, UNC; Edward S. Bragg Papers, Wisconsin State Hist. Soc.; Brock Collection, HL; Orville A. Browning Papers, IHS; Bryant-Godwin Collection, NYPL; Buchanan Papers, Dickinson College, Pennsylvania Hist. Soc.; Buchanan-Lane Papers, LC.

Sylvanus Cadwallader Papers, IHS; Cadwallader-Washburn Papers, Wis. State Hist. Soc.; Simon Cameron Papers, LC; John D. Caton Papers, LC; Zachariah Chandler Papers, LC, Salmon D. Chase Papers, Pa. Hist. Soc., LC, Ohio State Hist. Soc.—see preface to *Inside Lincoln's Cabinet: the Civil War Diaries of Salmon P. Chase*, edited by David Donald; Civil War Collection, Mo. Hist. Soc.; C. C. Clay Papers, Duke Univ.; Cornelius Cole Papers, Univ. of California (Los Angeles); John Coleman Papers, Mo. Hist. Soc.; F. P. Corbin Papers, NYPL, Duke Univ.; W. W. Corcoran Papers, LC; Samuel S. Cox Papers, LC, New York Hist. Soc., NYPL, Ohio State Hist. Soc.; S. W. Crawford Papers, LC, IHS; John J. Crittenden Papers, LC, Duke Univ.; William A. Croffut Papers, including E. A. Hitchcock material, LC; J. L. M. Curry Papers, LC; S. R. Curtis Papers, IHS; Caleb Cushing Papers, LC.

John A. Dahlgren Papers, including Ulric Dahlgren Diary, LC; Charles A. Dana Papers, LC; David Davis Papers, IHS; Jefferson Davis Papers, Confederate Museum, Richmond, Duke Univ., LC, HL, NYPL. See introduction on sources in Dunbar Rowland, *Jefferson Davis, Constitutionalist, His Letters, Papers and Speeches*, I, iii–xi; J. D. B. De Bow Papers (include three MS volumes on the Confederate Treasury), Duke Univ.; John A. Dix Papers, N.Y. State Hist. Library, and family possession; Stephen A. Douglas Papers, Univ. of Chicago; Dubose Papers, Alabama State Archives.

Eldredge Collection, HL; William G. Eliot Papers, Mo. Hist. Soc.; William H. English Papers, Indiana State Hist. Soc.; John Ericsson Papers, LC; Edward Everett Papers, MHS; Thomas Ewing Papers, LC.

Lucius Fairchild Papers, Wis. State Hist. Soc.; William Pitt Fessenden Papers, Palmer Collection, Western Reserve; William B. Franklin Papers, LC; John C. Frémont Papers, Univ. of California (Berkeley), LC, CU.

Hamilton R. Gamble Papers, Mo. Hist. Soc.; S. H. Gay Papers, CU; Joshua Giddings Papers, Ohio State Hist. Soc.; Gillespie Papers, Chicago Hist. Soc.; William A. Graham Papers, UNC; U.S. Grant Papers, LC, IHS, HL, MHS, NYPL; Grant-Lee Papers, IHS; Grant-Washburn Papers, IHS; Horace Greeley Papers, LC, NYPL, HL. Greeley Papers are scattered everywhere; see notes on sources in the lives by William A. Linn, Glyndon C. Van Deusen, William Harlan Hale, and R. R. Fahrney's *Horace Greeley and the Tribune in the Civil War;* Gen. Benjamin H. Grierson Papers, IHS.

Henry Wager Halleck Papers, IHS, LC, HL; William J. Hardee Correspondence, LC; George Harrington Papers, HL; John Hay Papers, IHS, LC; Heintzelman MS Diary, LC; William H. Herndon–Jesse Weik Papers, IHS; D. H. Hill Papers, Virginia State Library; Ethan Allen Hitchcock Papers, Mo. Hist. Soc.; Ethan Allen Hitchcock Diary in W. A. Croffut Papers, LC; Rev. Mr. Moses Hoge Diary, Mission to London, 1863, Univ. of Va. Library; Joseph Holt Papers, LC; Howard Papers, Bowdoin College.

Andrew Johnson Papers, LC; C. J. Johnson Papers, Louisiana State Univ.

Robert Garlick Hill Kean, MS Diary, Univ. of Va. Library, admirably edited by Edward Younger (1957), but the author had used the MS; Laurence M. Keitt Papers, Duke Univ.; Horatio King Papers, LC; Gustav Koerner Papers, IHS.

Robert E. Lee Papers, LC, Duke Univ., Confederate Museum—see notes on MS sources in Douglas S. Freeman, *R. E. Lee, A Biography*, IV, 543–8; Gen. Stephen D. Lee Papers, UNC; John Letcher Papers, Va. State Archives; Francis Lieber Papers, HL, CU; Abraham Lincoln Papers, LC, HL, MHS, Chic. Hist. Soc., NYPL, IHS, including Abraham Lincoln Assn. Photostats of Lincoln documents—see the foreword by Roy P. Basler to the *Works of Abraham Lincoln*, 9 volumes; Robert Todd Lincoln Papers, IC; Martin Lichterman, MS life of John A. Dix, private possession.

George Brinton McClellan Papers, LC, NYPL; Gen. John A. McClernand Papers with MS biography by his son, IHS; Hugh McCulloch Papers, LC; Edward McPherson Papers, a valuable collection made by a member of the 36th and 37th Congresses, who became clerk of the House in 1863, LC; Gabriel Edward Manigault, MS autobiography, UNC; Manton Marble Papers, LC; Charles Mason MS Diary, CU; Montgomery Meigs Papers, LC; William M. Meigs Papers, LC; John Merrilies MS Diary, Chic. Hist. Soc.; William Porcher Miles Papers, South Caroliniana Library, UNC; W. O. Moore Papers, La. State Univ.; E. D. Morgan Papers, N.Y. State Library; S. F. B. Morse Papers, LC.

John G. Nicolay Papers, LC; John G. Nicolay and John Hay, MS, proofs, and notes used in writing *Abraham Lincoln: A History*, IHS.

Richard J. Oglesby, letters and papers, IHS; Frederick Law Olmsted Papers, LC; J. A. Orr, Papers and Scrapbooks, UNC.

Palmer Collection (Civil War Papers), Western Reserve; Gen. John M. Palmer Papers, IHS; Lewis B. Parsons Papers, IHS, Mo. Hist. Soc.; Marsens Patrick MS Diary, LC; J. J. Pettus Correspondence, Alabama State Archives; Andrew Pickens Papers, Duke Univ.; Pickens-Bonham Papers, LC; Allan Pinkerton Papers, IHS.

Charles H. Ray Papers, HL; Whitelaw Reid Papers, LC; Thomas C. Reynolds Papers, Mo. Hist. Soc.; W. C. Reynolds Papers, LC; David F. Ritchie MS Diary, private possession; Edmund Ruffin MS Diary, LC.

Carl Schurz Papers, LC, NYPL, Wis. State Hist. Soc.; see prefatory note to Joseph Shafer, *Intimate Letters of Carl Schurz 1841–69;* James A. Seddon Papers, Duke Univ.; William H. Seward Papers and Fanny Seward Diary, Univ. of Rochester, N. Y.; Horatio Seymour Papers, N. Y. State Library and Barlow Collection in HL; John Sherman Papers, LC; W. T. Sherman Papers, HL, LC; Kirby-Smith Papers, UNC; Clara E. Solomon Diary, La. State Univ.; Edwin M. Stanton Papers, LC, and two letterbooks, Univ. of Va. Library; Alexander H. Stephens Papers, Manhattanville College of the Sacred Heart, Purchase, N. Y.; LC, Duke Univ.; see prefatory note to Rudolph Von Abele, *Alexander H. Stephens: A Biography;* Thaddeus Stevens Papers, LC; see information on other sources in Fawn M. Brodie, *Thaddeus Stevens, Scourge of the South,* pp. 13–4; William H. Stiles, UNC; George Templeton Strong MS Diary, photostat copy, CU (the author edited the Civil War volume, but material of value remains unprinted in the MS); Charles Sumner Papers, Harvard Univ., LC, HL.

Robert Taggard, MS Diary, Pa. State Hist. Soc.; Joseph Terry Papers, UNC; Samuel J. Tilden Papers, NYPL; J. H. Tomb MS Memoirs, So. Caroliniana Library; Lyman Trumbull Papers, IHS, LC; John Randolph Tucker Papers, UNC.

United States Sanitary Commission Records, NYPL.

Clement L. Vallandigham Papers, UNC, Ohio State Hist. Soc.

Ben Wade Papers, LC; Elihu Washburne Papers, LC; Thurlow Weed Papers, Univ. of Rochester; David A. Wells Papers, NYPL; Gideon Welles Papers, LC; Horace White Papers, IHS; Louis T. Wigfall Papers, Univ. of Texas; J. L. Worden Papers, Lincoln Memorial University.

Benjamin C. Yancey Papers, Duke Univ.

NEWSPAPERS

Baton Rouge *State-Times;* Boston *Journal;* Boston *Transcript;* Cincinnati *Commercial* quoted in Providence *Journal;* Cincinnati *Enquirer;* Columbia, Mo., *Statesman;* Charleston *Courier;* Chicago *Morning Post;* Cleveland *Leader;* Cleveland *Enquirer;* Frankfort, Ky., *Commonwealth;* Lexington, Ky., *Observer and Reporter;* Lexington, Ky., *Observer and Courier;* London *Times;* London *Daily News;* London *Morning Post;* London *Punch;* London *Record;* London *Illustrated News;* London *Morning Star;* Manchester *Examiner;* Middletown, Conn., *Sentinel;* New Orleans *Daily Picayune;* New York *Tribune;* New York *Times;* New York *Evening Post;* New York *World;* New York *Herald;* New York *Shipping and Commercial List;* [New York] *Harper's Weekly;* Philadelphia *Evening Journal;* Philadelphia *North American;* Philadelphia *Press;* Philadelphia *Inquirer;* St. Louis *Republican;* Sacramento *Bee;* Springfield *Republican;* Washington *Star;* Washington *National Intelligencer;* Washington *National Republican.*

BOOKS

Adams, Charles Francis, *Richard Henry Dana 1815–1882* (2 vols., Boston, 1890–1); Alexander, D. S., *Political History of New York, 1774–1822* (3 vols., New York, 1906–3; Allan, William, *The Army of Northern Virginia in 1862* (Boston, 1892); Andrew, J. Cutler, *The North Reports the Civil War* (Pittsburgh, 1955); Arnold, Isaac N., *Life of Abraham Lincoln* (Chicago, 1887).

Badeau, Adam, *Military History of U. S. Grant* (3 vols., 1868–81); Ballard, Colin R., *The Military Genius of Abraham Lincoln* (New York, 1952); Bates, David H., *Lincoln in the Telegraph Office* (New York, 1907); Beck, Warren A., "Lincoln and Negro Colonization in Central America," *Abraham Lincoln Quarterly,* VI (Sept., 1950), 162–83; Beldon, Thomas G. and Marva R., *So Fell the Angels* (Boston, 1956); Bell, Herbert C., *Lord Palmerston* (New York, 1936); Beloff, Max, "Great Britain and the American Civil War," *History,* N. S., XXXVII (Feb., 1952), 40–8; Bettersworth, John K., *Confederate Mississippi:*

People and Policies of a Cotton State in Wartime (Baton Rouge, 1943); Beymer, William
G., *On Hazardous Service* (New York, 1912); Bigelow, John, *France and the Confederate
Navy* (New York, 1888); *Retrospections of an Active Life* (5 vols., New York, 1909–13);
Blackford, Lieut. Col. W. W., *War Years with Jeb Stuart* (New York, 1945); Blackwell,
Sarah Ellen, *A Military Genius, Anna Ella Carroll of Maryland* (Washington, D. C., 1891);
von Borcke, Heros, *Memoirs of the Confederate War for Independence* (2 vols., New York,
1938); Boynton, C. B., *The Navy during the Rebellion* (1867); Brigham, Johnson, *James
Harlan* (Iowa City, 1913); Brinkerhoff, Gen. Roeliff, *Recollections of a Lifetime* (Cincinnati, 1900); Brodie, Fawn M., *Thaddeus Stevens, Scourge of the South* (New York, 1959);
Brown, E. F., *Raymond of the Times* (New York, 1951); Brown, L. A., *The Story of Maps*
(Boston, 1949); Brownell, Henry H., *War Lyrics and Other Poems* (Boston, 1866); Brownlee, Richard S., *Gray Ghosts of the Confederacy: Guerrilla Warfare in the West 1861–5*
(Baton Rouge, 1958); Bryan, T. Conn, *Confederate Georgia* (Athens, 1953); Bryan, Wilhelmus B., *A History of the National Capital* (2 vols., New York, 1914–16); Burton, Theodore
E., *John Sherman* (Boston, 1906); Butler, Benjamin F., *Autobiography* (*Butler's Book*),
(Boston, 1892); *Private and Official Correspondence* (5 vols., Norwood, Mass., 1917).

Cadwallader, Sylvanus, *Three Years with Grant*, ed. by Benjamin P. Thomas (New York,
1955); Callahan, J. M., *A Diplomatic History of the Southern Confederacy* (New York,
1901); Capers, Gerald M., *Biography of a River Town: Memphis, Its Heroic Age* (Chapel
Hill, 1939); Carpenter, Francis B., *Six Months at the White House with Abraham Lincoln*
(Boston, 1866); Carr, Lucien, *Missouri: A Bone of Contention* (Boston, 1894); Case, L. M.,
ed., *French Opinion in the United States and Mexico 1860–67* (New York, 1936); Catton,
Bruce, *Glory Road* (Garden City, 1952); *Grant Moves South* (Boston, 1960); *Mr. Lincoln's Army* (Garden City, 1951); Chandler, Peleg W., "Chandler's Memoir of Governor
Andrew," *Nation*, XXXIII (July 28, 1881), 77–8; Chase, Salmon P., *Diary and Correspondence of Salmon P. Chase*, Annual *Report* of A. H. A. (1902), (Washington, 1903):
Chetlain, Gen. A. L., *Recollections of Seventy Years* (Galena, Ill., 1899); Church, William
C., *The Life of John Ericsson* (2 vols., New York, 1890); Cist, Henry Martin, *Army of
the Cumberland* (New York, 1882); Clapp, Margaret A., *Forgotten First Citizen: John
Bigelow* (New York, 1947); Cleaves, Freeman, *Rock of Chickamauga: the Life of Gen.
George H. Thomas* (Norman, Okla., 1948); Clemens, Samuel, *Life on the Mississippi* (New
York, 1923); Cleven, N. Andrew, "Some Plans for Colonizing Liberated Negro Slaves in
Hispanic America," *Journal of Negro History*, XI (January, 1926), 35–49; Collyer, C.,
"Gladstone and the American Civil War," *Proceedings*, Leeds Philosophical Society, VI,
pt. 8 (May, 1951), 583–94; Commager, H. S., *The Blue and the Gray* (2 vols., 1950); [Confederate States of America] *Correspondence between the President, War Dept. and Gov.
T. O. Moore* (Richmond, 1863), *Correspondence between the War Department and Gen.
Lovell* (Richmond, 1862); Confederate Tract Society, "The Confederate Hero and his
Heroic Father," pamphlet No. 57; Conger, Col. Arthur L., "The Military Education of
Grant as a General," *Wisconsin Magazine of History*, IV (March, 1921), 239–62; *The
Rise of U. S. Grant* (New York, 1931); Connolly, James A., *Three Years in the Army of
the Cumberland* (Bloomington, Indiana, 1959); Conrad, H. C., *History of the State of
Delaware* (3 vols., Wilmington, 1908); Cook, Sir Edward T., *Delane of the Times* (New
York, 1916); *Autobiography of T. Jefferson Coolidge 1831–1920* (Boston, 1923); Cornish,
Dudley Taylor, *The Sable Arm: Negro Troops in the Union Army* (New York, 1956);
Cortissoz, Royal, *The Life of Whitelaw Reid* (2 vols., New York, 1921); Coulter, E. M.,
William G. Brownlow (Chapel Hill, 1937); *The Confederate States of America, 1861–1865*
(Baton Rouge, 1950); Cox, Jacob D., *Second Battle of Bull Run as Connected with the
Fitz-John Porter Case* (Cincinnati, 1882); Crane, Mary Powell, *Life of James R. Powell*
(New York, 1930), valuable for reprint of Caleb Huse's "The Supplies of the Confederate
Army," (1904); Crozier, Emmet, *Yankee Reporters 1861–5* (New York, 1956); Culmer, F.
A., *A New History of Missouri* (Mexico City, 1938); Current, Richard N., *The Lincoln*

Nobody Knows (New York, 1958); Curtis, Newton Martin, *From Bull Run to Chancellorsville* (New York, 1906).

Daly, Louise Haskell, *Alexander Cheves Haskell* (Norwood, Mass., 1924); Dana, Charles A., *Recollections of the Civil War* (New York, 1898); Davenport, Alfred, *Camp and Field Life of the Fifth New York Volunteer Infantry* (New York, 1879); Davis, Burke, *Gray Fox: Robert E. Lee and the Civil War* (New York, 1956); *Jeb Stuart: The Last Cavalier* (New York, 1957); Davis, Stanton L., *Pennsylvania Politics 1860-3* (Cleveland, 1935); Davis, Jefferson, *Rise and Fall of the Confederate Government* (2 vols., New York, 1881); *Letters, Papers, and Speeches*, Ed. by Dunbar Rowland (10 vols., Jackson, Miss., 1923); Dawes, Anna Laurens, *Charles Sumner* (New York, 1892); Detroyat, Léonce, *L'Intervention Francaise au Mexique . . .* (Paris, 1868); Dillahunty, Albert, *Shiloh National Military Park, Tennessee* (Washington, D.C., 1951); Dodd, Ira S., *The Song of the Rappahannock* (New York, 1898); Dodge, Grenville M., *Personal Recollections of President Abraham Lincoln, Gen. Ulysses S. Grant, Gen. William T. Sherman* (Glendale, California, 1914); Donald, Henderson H., *The Negro Freedman* (New York, 1952); Dorris, J. T., "President Lincoln's Treatment of Kentuckians," *Filson Club History Quarterly*, XXVIII (January, 1954), 3-20; Dorsey, Sarah A., *Recollections of Henry Watkins Allen* (New York, 1866); Douglas, Henry Kyd, *I Rode with Stonewall* (Chapel Hill, 1940); Dowdey, Clifford, *Experiment in Rebellion* (New York, 1946); Dubois, James T. and Gertrude Matthews, *Galusha A. Grow, Father of the Homestead Act* (Boston, 1917); Duer, William H., "The New Opposition Party," *Atlantic Monthly*, X (September, 1862), 377-80; Duke, Basil W., *Morgan's Cavalry* (New York, 1906); DuPont, H. A., *Rear Admiral Samuel Francis Du Pont* (New York, 1926); Durden, Robert Franklin, *James Shepherd Pike: Republicanism and the American Negro* (Durham, 1957); Dwight, Wilder, *Life and Letters* (Boston, 1868); Dyer, John P., *"Fightin Joe" Wheeler* (Baton Rouge, 1941).

Eaton, John, *Grant, Lincoln and the Freedmen* (New York, 1907); Eckenrode, H. J., and Conrad, Bryan, *George B. McClellan* (Chapel Hill, 1941); Eggleston, George Carey, *A Rebel's Recollections* (Indianapolis, 1958); Eisenschiml, Otto, *The Celebrated Case of Fitz-John Porter: An American Dreyfus Affair* (Indianapolis, 1950); *The Story of Shiloh* (Chicago, 1946); Elliott, Maud Howe, *Uncle Sam Ward and His Circle* (New York, 1938).

Fahrney, Ralph Ray, *Horace Greeley and the Tribune in the Civil War* (Cedar Rapids, Iowa, 1936); Fish, Carl Russell, *The American Civil War* (New York, 1937); Foote, Shelby, *The Civil War from Fort Sumter to Perryville* (New York, 1958); Force, Manning F., *From Fort Henry to Corinth* (New York, 1881); Franklin, John Hope, *From Slavery to Freedom: A History of the American Negro* (New York, 1950); Freeman, Douglas Southall, *R. E. Lee* (4 vols., New York, 1934); *Lee's Lieutenants: A Study in Command* (3 vols., New York, 1942-44); *A Calendar of Confederate Papers* (Richmond, 1908); *Lee's Dispatches . . . to Jefferson Davis, 1862-65* with Grady McWhinney (New York, 1957); Fremantle, Lieut. Col. A. J. L., *Three Months in the Southern States, April-June, 1863* (New York, 1864); Freidel, Frank, *Francis Lieber: Nineteenth Century Liberal* (Baton Rouge, 1947); Fritz, John, *Autobiography* (New York, 1912); Fry, James B., *Military Miscellanies* (New York, 1889); Fuess, Claude M., *The Life of Caleb Cushing* (2 vols., New York, 1923); Fuller, J. C. F., *The Generalship of Ulysses S. Grant* (London, 1929); *Grant and Lee: A Study in Personality and Generalship* (Bloomington, 1957).

Gambrell, Herbert P., "Rams and Gunboats," *Southwest Review*, XXIII (October, 1937), 46-78; Garland, Hamlin, *Grant, His Life and Character* (New York, 1920); Gates, Theodore B., *The "Ulster Guard" (20th N. Y. Militia) and the War of the Rebellion . . .* (New York, 1879); Gertz, Elmer, *Joe Medill's War* (Chicago, 1945); Gilmore, James R., *Personal Recollections of Abraham Lincoln and the Civil War* (Boston, 1898); Gooch, G. P., ed., *Later Correspondence of Lord John Russell, 1840-1878* (London, 1925); Gorgas, Gen. Josiah, *Civil War Diary*, ed. by Frank E. Vandiver (Tuscaloosa, 1947); Gorham, George C., *Edwin M. Stanton, Life and Public Services* (2 vols., Boston, 1899); Govan, G. E. and

Livingood, J. W., *A Different Valor: The Story of Joseph E. Johnston* (Indianapolis, 1956); Grant, U. S., *Personal Memoirs* (2 vols., New York, 1885); Grattan, Thomas C., "England and the Disrupted States of America," (a pamphlet, London, 1861); Greeley, Horace, *The American Conflict* (2 vols., Hartford, 1864); Greenbie, Sydney and Marjorie B., *Anna Ella Carroll and Abraham Lincoln: A Biography* (Tampa, 1952); Guedalla, Philip, *Palmerston, 1784-1865* (New York, 1927).

Hale, William Harlan, *Horace Greeley, Voice of the People* (New York, 1950); Hall, Clifton, *Andrew Johnson: Military Governor of Tennessee* (Princeton, 1916); Hart, B. H. Liddell, *Sherman: Soldier, Realist, American* (New York, 1929); Hartley, J. W., *Marcellus Hartley* (New York, 1903); Hartley, Marcellus, *A Brief Memoir*, privately printed (New York, 1903); Haupt, Herman, *Reminiscences* (Milwaukee, 1901); Hebert, Walter H., *Fighting Joe Hooker* (Indianapolis, 1944); Henderson, Lieut. Col. G. F. R., *Stonewall Jackson and the American Civil War* (2 vols., New York, 1898); Henderson, W. O., *The Lancashire Cotton Famine, 1861-5* (Manchester, England, 1934); Hendrick, Burton J., *The Lees of Virginia* (Boston, 1935); Henry, Robert Selph, *The Story of the Confederacy* (Indianapolis, 1931); Hesseltine, William B., *Lincoln and the War Governors* (New York, 1948); Higginson, Thomas Wentworth, *Army Life in a Black Regiment* (Boston, 1869); Hill, Lawrence F., *Diplomatic Relations between the United States and Brazil* (Durham, 1932); Hitchcock, Ethan Allen, *Fifty Years in Camp and Field* (New York, 1909); Hooker, Joseph, *Dedication of the Equestrian Statue to ...* (Boston, 1903); Howe, M. A. DeWolfe, ed., *Some Letters of Gen. Sherman* (New York, 1909); Hulbert, Archer Butler, *The Paths of Inland Commerce; A Chronicle of Trail, Road and Waterway* (New Haven, 1920); Hunt, Gaillard, *Israel, Elihu and Cadwallader Washburn* (New York, 1925); Hunter, Louis C., *Steamboats on Western Rivers* (Cambridge, Mass., 1949).

Irwin, Richard B., *History of the 19th Army Corps* (New York, 1892).

James, A. P., "Strategy of Concentration of the Confederate Forces," A.H.A. Annual *Report*, (1919); Johnston, William Preston, *Life of Albert Sydney Johnston* (New York, 1878); Joinville, Francois Ferdinand, le prince de, *Campagne de l'Armée du Potomac (mars-juillet, 1862)* (New York, 1862); Jones, Virgil Carrington, *Ranger Mosby* (Chapel Hill, 1944); Julian, George W., *The Life of Joshua R. Giddings* (Chicago, 1892); *Political Recollections 1840-72* (Chicago, 1884).

Kamm, Samuel R., *The Civil War Career of Thomas A. Scott* (Philadelphia, 1940); Kelley, William D., *Lincoln and Hamlin* (New York, 1885); Knox, Dudley, W., *A History of the United States Navy* (New York, 1948); Knox, Thomas W., *Camp-Fire and Cotton-Field: Southern Adventure in Time of War ...* (New York, 1865); Kreutzer, William, *Notes and Observations Made During Four Years of Service with the 98th N. Y. Volunteers in the War of 1861* (Philadelphia, 1878).

Langeluttig, Albert G., *The Department of Justice of the United States* (Wash., D. C., 1927); Lanman, Charles, *Haphazard Personalities* (Boston, 1885); Larson, Henrietta M., *Jay Cooke, Private Banker* (Cambridge, 1936); Lathers, Richard, *Reminiscences. ...* (New York, 1907); Lawrence, William, *Life of Amos A. Lawrence* (Boston, 1888); Lee, Capt. Robert E., *Recollections and Letters of General Lee* (Garden City, N. Y., 1904); Leland, Edwin A., "Origin and Administration of the Louisiana Army During the Civil War," M. A. Thesis, Louisiana State University, 1938; Lerwill, Leonard L., *The Personal Replacement System in the United States Army* (Washington, D. C., 1954); Lewis, Charles Lee, *David Glasgow Farragut: Our First Admiral* (2 vols., Annapolis, 1941-3); *Admiral Franklin Buchanan* (Baltimore, 1929); Lindsey, David, *"Sunset Cox," Irrepressible Democrat* (Detroit, 1959); Livermore, Mary A., *The Story of My Life* (Hartford, 1897); Livermore, Thomas L., *Numbers and Losses in the Civil War* (Boston, 1900); Logan, Mrs. John A., *Reminiscences of a Soldier's Wife* (New York, 1916); Lusk, William T., *War Letters 1861-3* (New York, 1911); Lytle, Andrew Nelson, *Bedford Forrest and his Critter Company* (New York, 1931).

Mackay, Charles, *Life and Liberty in America* . . . (New York, 1859); *Through the Long Day* (London, 1887); Mahan, Alfred Thayer, *The Gulf and Inland Waters* (New York, 1883); Mahony, Dennis A., *The Prisoner of State* (New York, 1863); Maurice, Sir Frederick, *An Aide-de-Camp of Lee: the Papers of Colonel Charles Marshall* (Boston, 1927); *Robert E. Lee, the Soldier* (Boston, 1925); *Statesmen and Soldiers of the Civil War* (Boston, 1926); Meade, R. O., *Judah P. Benjamin* (New York, 1943); Mearns, David C., *The Lincoln Papers* (2 vols., New York, 1948); Michie, Peter S., *General McClellan* (New York, 1901); Military History Society of Massachusetts, *Campaigns in Kentucky and Virginia; Campaigns in Virginia, 1861–2; Virginia Campaigns of 1862 under Pope* (Boston, 1895 ff.); Milton, George Fort, *Lincoln and the Fifth Column* (New York, 1942); Mitchell, Stewart, *Horatio Seymour of New York* (Cambridge, Mass., 1938); Monaghan, Jay, *Civil War on the Western Border 1855–65* (Boston, 1955); Moors, J. F., *History of the 52nd Regiment, Mass. Volunteers, by the Chaplain* (Boston, 1893); Morison, Stanley, *History of the [London] Times* (5 vols., London, 1935–   ); Mosby, John Singleton, *Memoirs* ed. by Charles Wells Russell (Bloomington, Indiana, 1959); Munroe, James Phinney, *A Life of Francis Amasa Walker* (New York, 1923).

McCordock, Robert S., *The Yankee Cheese Box* (Philadelphia, 1938); McIlwaine, Shields, *Memphis, Down in Dixie* (New York, 1948); McKinstry, Justin, "Vindication of General McKinstry," undated pamphlet in NYPL; McRaven, Henry, *Nashville, Athens of the South* (Chapel Hill, 1949).

Nevins, Allan, *Frémont* (New York, 1955); *Abram S. Hewitt* (New York, 1935); Nicolay, Helen, "Lincoln's Cabinet," *Abraham Lincoln Quarterly*, V (March, 1949), 255–92; Nicolay, John G., and Hay, John, *Abraham Lincoln: A History* (10 vols., New York, 1890).

Oberholtzer, Ellis P., *Jay Cooke, Financier of the Civil War* (2 vols., Philadelphia, 1907); Owsley, Frank L., *State Rights in the Confederacy* (Chicago, 1925).

Page, Charles A., *Letters of a War Correspondent* (Boston, 1899); Palfrey, Francis Winthrop, *Memoir of William F. Bartlett* (Boston, 1878); Palmer, George Thomas, *A Conscientious Turncoat: The Story of John M. Palmer 1817–1900* (New Haven, 1941); Palmer, John M., *Personal Recollections* (Cincinnati, 1901); Palmer, John Williamson, *Stonewall Jackson's Way* (Cedar Rapids, 1915); Palmer, Gen. William J., *Letters 1853–68* (Philadelphia, 1906); Parks, Joseph H., *General Kirby Smith, C.S.A.* (Baton Rouge, 1954); Patrick, Rembert W., *Jefferson Davis and His Cabinet* (Baton Rouge, 1944); Paul, Herbert, *A History of Modern England* (New York, 1904–06); Pellet, Elias P., *A History of the 114th Regiment, N. Y. State Volunteers* (Norwich, N. Y., 1866); Phelan, Sister Mary Cortona, *Manton Marble of the New York World* (Washington, D. C., 1957); Phillips, Philip Lee, *Virginia Cartography: A Bibliographical Description* (Washington, D. C., 1896); Piatt, Donn, *Memories of Men Who Saved the Union* (Chicago, 1887); Plum, W. R., *The Military Telegraph During the Civil War* (Chicago, 1881); Polk, W. M., *Leonidas Polk, Bishop and General* (2 vols., rev. ed., New York, 1915); Pollard, Edward A., *The Lost Cause* . . . (New York, 1867); Porter, David D., *Incidents and Anecdotes of the Civil War* (New York, 1885); Pratt, Fletcher, *Ordeal by Fire: An Informal History of the Civil War* (New York, 1948).

Randall, James G., *Constitutional Problems under Lincoln* (rev. ed., New York, 1951); *Lincoln and the South* (Baton Rouge, 1946); *Lincoln, the Liberal Statesman* (New York, 1947); Read, T. B., "The Siege of Cincinnati," *Atlantic Monthly*, XI (February, 1863), 229–34; Reed, H. Clay, ed., *Delaware; A History of the First State* (3 vols., New York, 1947); "Lincoln's Compensated Emancipation Plan," in *Delaware Notes* (1931); Rhodes, James Ford, *History of the U.S. From the Compromise of 1850* (vols. 1–5, 1892–1904); Richardson, Elmo R. and Farley, Allen W., *John Palmer Usher: Lincoln's Secretary of the Interior* (Lawrence, Kansas, 1960); Robinson, W. S., "*Warrington*" *Pen Portraits* (Boston, 1877); Ropes, John Codman, *The Army under Pope* (New York, 1882); *The Story of the*

Civil War (2 vols., New York, 1894–1898); Rossetti, William Michael, "English Opinion on the American War," *Atlantic Monthly*, XVII (February, 1866), 129–49; Rowland, Dunbar, ed., *Jefferson Davis, Constitutionalist: His Letters, Papers and Speeches* (10 vols., Jackson, 1923); Russell, Lord John, *Recollections and Suggestions 1813–1873* (Boston, 1875).

Sandburg, Carl, *Abraham Lincoln: The War Years* (4 vols., New York, 1939); *Lincoln Collector: The Story of Oliver R. Barrett's Great Private Collection* (New York, 1950); Scharf, J. T., *History of Delaware 1609–1888* (2 vols., Philadelphia, 1888); Schley, W. S., *Forty-Five Years under the Flag* (New York, 1904); Sherman, John, *Recollections* (2 vols., Chicago, 1895); Sherman, William T., "General Sherman's Opinion of General Grant," *Century Magazine*, N. S., XXXI (April, 1897), 821; *Memoirs* (2 vols., New York, 1891); *The Sherman Letters*, ed. by Rachel Thorndike (New York, 1894); Sievers, Harry, *Benjamin Harrison, Hoosier Warrior 1833–1865* (Chicago, 1952); Smith, Theodore C., *The Life and Letters of James Abram Garfield* (2 vols., New Haven, 1925); Stampp, Kenneth M., *Indiana Politics during the Civil War* (Indianapolis, 1949); Stanton, H. B., *Random Recollections* (New York, 1887); Starr, Louis, *Bohemian Brigade* (New York, 1954); Stephenson, W. H., *Political Career of Gen. James H. Lane*, Kansas State Historical Publications, III (Topeka, 1930); Stiles, Major Robert, *Four Years Under Marse Robert* (New York, 1904); Strode, Hudson, *Jefferson Davis, Confederate President* (New York, 1959); Sumner, Charles, *Works* (15 vols., Boston, 1870–83).

Taylor, Richard, *Destruction and Reconstruction: Personal Experiences of the Late War* (New York, 1900); Tharp, Louise Hall, *Three Saints and a Sinner* (Boston, 1956); Thorndike, Rachel S., ed., *The Sherman Letters* (New York, 1894); Tilden, Samuel J., *Letters and Literary Memorials* (New York, 1908); Townsend, George Alfred, *Campaign of a Non-Combatant* (New York, 1866); Trexler, Harrison A., "The Confederate Navy Department and the Fall of New Orleans," *Southwest Review*, XIX (Autumn, 1933), 88–102; *Slavery in Missouri, 1804–65* (Baltimore, 1914); Trobriand, Regis de, *Four Years with the Army of the Potomac* (Boston, 1889); *Life and Memoirs*, ed. by Marie Caroline Post (New York, 1910).

Walker, Francis A., *History of the Second Army Corps* (New York, 1891); Warden, Robert B., *Account of the Private Life and Public Services of Salmon Portland Chase* (Cincinnati, 1874); Watts, John, *The Facts of the Cotton Famine* (London, 1866); Webb, Alexander, *The Peninsula* (New York, 1882); Weeden, William B., *War Government, Federal and State, 1861–5* (Boston, 1906); White, Ruth, *Yankee from Sweden* (New York, 1960); Williams, Kenneth P., "The Tennessee River Campaign and Anna Ella Carroll," *Indiana Magazine of History*, XLVI, No. 3 (September, 1950), 221–48; *Lincoln Finds a General* (5 vols., New York, 1949–1959); Williams, Harry T., "Investigation—1862," *American Heritage*, VI (December, 1954), 16–21; *Lincoln and His Generals* (New York, 1952); *Lincoln and the Radicals* (Madison, Wis., 1941); Willson, Beckles, *John Slidell and the Confederates in Paris* (New York, 1932); Wilson, Henry, "Edwin M. Stanton," *Atlantic Monthly*, XXV (February, 1870), 234–46; Wilson, H. W., *Ironclads in Action: A Sketch of Naval Warfare from 1855 to 1895* (Boston, 1898); Wilson, James H., *Life of Charles A. Dana* (New York, 1907); Wood, William, *Captains of the Civil War: A Chronicle of the Blue and the Gray* (New Haven, 1921); Wright, Gordon, "Economic Conditions in the Confederacy as seen by the French Consuls," *Journal of Southern History*, VII (May, 1941), 195 ff.; Wyeth, John Allen, *With Sabre and Scalpel, the Autobiography of a Soldier and Surgeon* (New York, 1914); *Life of General Nathan Bedford Forrest* (New York, 1901).

Younger, Edward, *Inside the Confederate Government: the Diary of Robert Garlick Hill Kean, Head of the Bureau of War* (New York, 1957).

APPENDIX I
Reporters After Shiloh

One of the dubious distinctions of Shiloh is that of being a battle in which a few press reporters boldly invented eyewitness accounts, and others used their pens to serve favorite commanders rather than truth. The contemptuous phrase "Cairo war correspondent" arose when men found that some of the reporters who sent "vivid" descriptions of down-river combats had stirred no farther than the Illinois river port. However, several good observers who were on the field at Shiloh wrote accounts which deserve scrutiny, with special attention to the kind and degree of bias they exhibit.

The two first full records to reach Northern readers appeared respectively in the New York *Herald* on April 9 and the Cincinnati *Gazette* on April 14, and were in such serious conflict that they seemed to present different battles. The *Herald* reporter was long thought to be one Frank Chapman, for George Alfred Townsend, in a series of articles in the San Francisco *Chronicle* in 1882, stated (or guessed) he was the author. Actually the writer was W. C. Carroll of New York, who wrote a frank statement of his exploit to Elihu Washburne under date of December 24, 1862. The writer of the *Gazette* story was Whitelaw Reid.

Of Carroll we know almost nothing beyond his own assertion that he had briefly served Grant as volunteer aide in Cairo. But Reid, though not yet twenty-five, was recognized as a gifted and responsible journalist. He had graduated from Miami University in Ohio, had taken active part in Frémont's presidential campaign, had been legislative correspondent for several papers in Columbus, Ohio, and had become city editor of the *Gazette*. He left this post to follow the war, and in 1861 had been volunteer aide to General Thomas A. Morris in the West Virginia campaign. Later, of course, he was to succeed Horace Greeley as owner and principal editor of the New York *Tribune*, was to run for the Vice-Presidency with Harrison in 1892, and was to be minister to France and ambassador to Great Britain.

Carroll tells in his letter to Washburne exactly how he came to write his report. After the battle he kept his ears open. "I discovered the bitterness of feeling and jealousy of Gen. Buell and his officers towards Gen. Grant and the Illinois troops, it being evident to me that no effort would be spared on their part to bring them into disrepute by a series of false and slanderous reports." He determined to defeat the Buell partisans. Without disclosing his intentions, he got permission to catch one of the numerous boats descending the Tennessee. On board it he discovered reporters for Cincinnati papers who were friends of Buell and were profuse in their denunciation of Grant. They had their stories ready written, he asserts; and "to overcome this disadvantage I got off the steamer at Fort Henry, the first telegraph station, and there secured the line and sent my account to the New York *Herald*, which was received in advance of all the Government and other dispatches forwarded to the President, Senate and House, and then transmitted to all the leading newspapers of the United States."

This is a clear admission of bias; and though Carroll assured Washburne that his account was truthful and impartial, it was actually inaccurate, exaggerated, and partisan. He used sensational language: "The bloodiest battle of modern times just closed. . . . Slaughter on both sides immense. . . . [Federals] eighteen to twenty thousand; that of the enemy is estimated from thirty-five to forty thousand. . . ." He gave Grant unbounded praise, writing that on the afternoon of the 7th the general personally led an infantry assault, brandishing his sword and waving his men on to victory, "while cannon balls were falling like hail around him." His narrative produced a great effect. Later he went on to Washington, where Washburne took him to the White House, and he told Lincoln, as he put it, "all about the Illinois troops."

Reid's account of Shiloh had faults, but was a superior piece of work. His description of the combat was extraordinarily comprehensive in view of the chaotic nature of the fighting. He used moderate language, but wrote with color, and studded his narrative with episodes that gave it dramatic force. Some of the information he received from participants was incorrect; his tale of soldiers shot and bayoneted in the initial assault while trying to surrender is not supported. But by and large his report carried confidence. He ascribed blame to Grant and Sherman where blame seemed due. That is, he declared that the high command was responsible for lack of precautions, bad placing of picket lines, want of protection for the batteries, the location of Grant's headquarters some miles downstream, and once the battle began, the apparent confusion of orders to Lew Wallace. Reid believed that the army had been surprised, and was in danger of defeat when Buell's reinforcements began to arrive. But no personal antagonism to Grant marred his report. Instead, he wrote of seeing Grant calm and resolute in the worst of the fighting, and extolled his confidence in victory once reinforcements arrived.

Both Carroll's and Reid's reports were widely copied, compared, and commented upon. The Cincinnati *Commercial*, edited by Murat Halstead, condemned the New York *Herald* story as a piece of "enormous puffery." It declared that the battle had caused deep uneasiness in the West. "It is certain that at least for some days after the battle the troops under Gen. Grant's immediate command had lost faith in him. The surprise which so nearly proved fatal. . . . is a fact that cannot pass unnoticed." When the Chicago *Tribune* published Reid's story with sharp disapproval of Grant, Elihu Washburne gave the editors a lashing for using "the infamous and slanderous article," and failing to defend the home-State general "who has done the only fighting that has been done in this war." Joseph Medill rejected this criticism. Meanwhile, as hospital ships with wounded men reached Northern towns, and letters from soldiers pictured the horrors of the field, feeling against the commanders grew. A correspondent of the Cincinnati *Times* related how a multitude of wounded "lay, without a surgeon or attendant, without a mouthful to eat or drink, until Wednesday morning." The New York *World* correspondent called the field "the most awful spectacle of human suffering which even the horrors of a battlefield can exhibit." And the correspondent of the St. Louis *Republican* gave a still more horrifying picture of agony left unrelieved, ebbing lives left unsaved. He said the army had been "completely surprised."

The debate at once spread into Congress. John Sherman of Ohio vigorously defended the troops of his State, but admitted that Colonel J. J. Appler of the Fifty-third Ohio ran away, and quoted a letter of Colonel R. S. Buckland, commanding the Fourth Brigade of William Tecumseh Sherman's own division, who stated: "It is true that we were taken by surprise, and had hardly time to form into line of battle and advance about thirty rods when we met the enemy, and opened fire upon him." Senator James Harlan of Iowa was stingingly severe upon Grant, blaming him for horrible loss of life. He read a letter from a district judge of Iowa who spent several days on the battlefield just after it ended, and talked with officers and men. "There is no use," the judge wrote, "in trying to disguise or cover up the fact that our army was badly surprised on Sunday morning." The fieriest defense of Grant in Congress, as stated in the text, was by Elihu Washburne, who maintained that with 40,000 men he had withstood 80,000.

Controversy on the question of surprise was obviously idle until men agreed on a definition of the word. The two best summations by reporters were perhaps those of Henry Villard, a free-lance unconnected at the moment with any paper, and A. D. Richardson of the New York *Tribune*. Villard arrived on the field with Buell, was in the thick of the second day's fighting, and talked with many officers. He concluded that Grant and Sherman had not felt the remotest suspicion that the whole rebel army was within artillery range, that the disconnected position of Grant's six divisions was not such as a vigilant commander would have allowed, that Sherman's brigades were spread out over too much ground, that the approaches from Corinth were not properly guarded, that the failure to entrench was culpable, and that it was an error to place a number of wholly raw regiments in the very front divisions. He calls Grant's subsequent report "about as poor a production as the Rebellion brought forth in that line on the Northern side."

As for Richardson, he arrived after the battle on a boat crowded with Sanitary Commission workers, and scoured every part of the field with participating officers. On April 16 he wrote his managing editor, Sydney Howard Gay: "There is great feeling in Buell's army against Grant's, and a disposition to give Grant no credit whatever. The truth is, it was very bad that Grant had no heavier picket lines out, and so was partially surprised; but after the battle had fairly commenced, Grant and all his division commanders did admirably; and in spite of the skulkers, the tenacity and obstinacy with which his army contested every inch of the ground, and covered it with dead, during all that terrible Sunday before Buell came up, is deserving of all praise."

W. C. Carroll, Dec. 24, 1862, to Elihu Washburne, Washburne Papers, LC; Washington *National Republican*, April 24, July 22, 1862 (summaries of reports of Shiloh in other papers); St. Louis *Republican*, April 12, New York *Tribune*, April 12, Cincinnati *Commercial*, April 14, 15, 1862; W. R. Rowley, Grant's Headquarters, April 19, 1862, to Elihu Washburne, Washburne Papers, LC; Villard, Memoirs, I, 244-262; Richardson, *The Field, The Dungeon, and the Escape*, 236-242; Richardson, Pittsburgh Landing, April 16, 1862, Gay Papers, CU; Starr, *Bohemian Brigade*, 100-104; Crozier, *Yankee Reporters, 1861-1865*, pp. 208-225.

APPENDIX II

The Invasions by Lee and Bragg

One piece of evidence that Confederate leaders in the summer of 1862 planned the invasion of Maryland, the invasion of Kentucky, and a drive for British recognition as a grand coordinated piece of strategy is to be found in the London *Times*, September 5, 1862. It is a public statement by the audacious George N. Sanders, whilom leader of the "Young America" movement and President Pierce's unconfirmed consul in London, who had just arrived in England by way of Canada. He came as agent for the Confederacy, bearing information which he implied was officially entrusted to him by Jefferson Davis immediately on the discovery that McClellan would evacuate his army from the James.

Sanders announced that Lee in August had an army of 200,000 infantry, 400 guns, and 11,000 superior cavalry, ready to march on the North and confident of victory. In the West, meanwhile, Bragg, Hardee, Price, and Kirby-Smith were leading forces which aggregated 150,000 to the flanks and rear of Grant and Buell, equally confident of defeating them. In southeastern Kentucky General Humphrey Marshall was advancing to effect a junction with Kirby-Smith, while farther west Generals T. H. Holmes and T. C. Hindman were about to roll into Missouri with 30,000 men, and there enlist numerous recruits. Altogether, a grand sweep was under way, and Sanders expected British sympathizers to rally to the Southern cause.

From the moment of his arrival Sanders labored to produce an atmosphere favorable to a British offer of mediation. He came authorized to raise money on bonds secured by cotton, and to let contracts for ships to enter the Confederate navy (Owsley, *King Cotton Diplomacy*, 387). At once he saw William S. Lindsay, the largest British shipowner, member of Parliament, and Confederate sympathizer. Within a fortnight after the *Times* printed his statement, Russell and Palmerston exchanged letters asking whether the moment would not soon be auspicious for an offer of good services in ending the war (E. D. Adams, II, 38; Spencer Walpole, *Russell*, II, 349). These leaders were moved primarily by news of military events in America, but they had probably read Sanders's statement.

Index

Other Titles in Our Civil War Library

R. E. Lee
Four Volumes
by Douglas Southall Freeman

R. E. Lee
An Abridgment
by Douglas Southall Freeman

Lee's Lieutenants
A Study in Command
by Douglas Southall Freeman

Grant and Lee
The Virginia Campaigns
by William A. Frassanito

Antietam
The Photographic Legacy of America's Bloodiest Day
by William A. Frassanito

Gettysburg
A Journey in Time
by William A. Frassanito

The Gettysburg Campaign
A Study in Command
by Edwin B. Coddington

The Greatest Battles of the Civil War
by John Macdonald

Why the North Won the Civil War
by David Donald

Company Aytch
by Sam Watkins